SAFE FOR DEMOCRACY

W9-CHT-881

ALSO BY JOHN PRADOS

Hoodwinked: The Documents That Reveal How Bush Sold Us a War (ed.)

Inside the Pentagon Papers (ed., with Margaret Pratt Porter)

The White House Tapes: Eavesdropping on the President (ed.)

Lost Crusader: The Secret Wars of CIA Director William Colby

Operation Vulture

America Confronts Terrorism (ed.)

The Blood Road: The Ho Chi Minh Trail and the Vietnam War

President's Secret Wars: CIA and Pentagon Covert Operations from World War II Through the Persian Gulf

Combined Fleet Decoded: The Secret History of U.S. Intelligence and the Japanese Navy in World War II

The Hidden History of the Vietnam War

Valley of Decision: The Siege of Khe Sanh (with Ray W. Stubbe)

Keepers of the Keys: A History of the National Security Council from Truman to Bush

Pentagon Games

The Soviet Estimate: U.S. Intelligence and Soviet Strategic Forces

The Sky Would Fall: The Secret U.S. Bombing Mission to Vietnam, 1954

SAFE FOR DEMOCRACY

THE
SECRET WARS
OF THE CIA

JOHN PRADOS

Ivan R. Dee   Chicago

SAFE FOR DEMOCRACY. Copyright © 2006 by John Prados. All rights reserved, including
the right to reproduce this book or portions thereof in any form. For information, address:
Ivan R. Dee, Publisher, 1332 North Halsted Street, Chicago 60642, a member of the Rowman
and Littlefield Publishing Group. Manufactured in the United States of America and printed on
acid-free paper.

www.ivanrdee.com

The paperback edition of this book carries the ISBN 978-1-56663-823-4.

Library of Congress Cataloging-in-Publication Data:
Prados, John.
   Safe for democracy : the secret wars of the CIA / John Prados.
     p. cm.
   Includes bibliographical references and index.
   ISBN-13: 978-1-56663-574-5 (cloth : alk. paper)
   ISBN-10: 1-56663-574-8 (cloth : alk. paper)
     1. Intelligence service—United States. 2. United States. Central Intelligence Agency.
   3. United States—Foreign relations. I. Title.
JK468.I6P715 2006
327.1273—dc22
                                                                              2006006269

To a More Perfect Union

Contents

Acknowledgments

MANY PEOPLE AND INSTITUTIONS contributed to the making of this book. My work on it began as a fellowship project of the International Center for Advanced Studies of New York University. I thank NYU and ICAS for their belief in and support of this initiative. I am especially indebted to my colleagues and friends at the National Security Archive, where I am a senior fellow. A portion of the research was underwritten by a grant from the Gerald R. Ford Library Foundation. I am grateful to them as well. A special thanks goes to all those editors on assorted other projects on which I have worked who patiently endured delays at various points so that this manuscript could move to completion. Speaking of editors, Ivan R. Dee's vision, suggestions, and deft hand added immeasurably to this book, and I also thank Jason Proetorius and everyone who contributed to its production.

This work would not have the depth and scope that it does without the insights of those who spoke to me or exchanged correspondence, so I wish to express my appreciation to all those interviewees who helped educate me on these matters. Certain reviewers of my earlier biography of William E. Colby chose to select out some of the individuals whom I acknowledged as an excuse to damn the entire work. For this reason, as well as because some interviewees wished to remain anonymous, I do not mention anyone by name. But all should know how thankful I am to them.

For assistance with documentary research I extend great thanks to the staffs and archivists of the National Archives and Records Administration (NARA); and the Harry S Truman Library, Dwight D. Eisenhower Library, John F. Kennedy Library, Lyndon B. Johnson Library, Richard Nixon Library Project, Gerald R. Ford Library, and Ronald Reagan Library, all of NARA. My special appreciation goes to John Taylor, Herbert Pankratz, Moira Porter, Michele DeMartino, David Humphrey, Regina Greenwell, Nancy Smith, Linda Seelke, Ted Gittinger, Shannon Jarrett, Irene Lonedo, Karen Holzhausen, and Donna Lehman. Some of these excellent archivists have moved up, on, or retired during the long years I have been following these subjects, but I am proud to have worked with each of them. In addition I am grateful to the staff and archivists of the Library of Congress and to the staffs of Columbia University, New York University, George Washington University, and Wheaton Regional libraries. For specific help with particular documents or tips on materials, I thank Anna Kasten Nelson, Malcolm Byrne, Mario del Pero, Peter Kornbluh, and William Burr.

For a brief moment in the 1990s and until 9/11 the Central Intelligence Agency made an effort to open its files to the American people. Its Historical Review Program declassified a number of documents central to the story. The CIA's Center for the Study of Intelligence produced a number of documentary collections, some of which contained useful material. The Center sponsored more than a dozen conferences where the subjects of these collections were considered by (mostly former) intelligence officers and scholars together. I was asked to speak at several of these meetings. But since September 11 these initiatives have ground almost to a halt, as have most CIA document declassification efforts. This deplorable state of affairs bodes ill for the effort to build an American consensus on the need for intelligence and the future of the CIA.

Having said that, let me hasten to add my appreciation for the efforts of the Kennedy Assassination Records Commission. Due to Americans' intense interest in the events of the Kennedy assassination, for another brief moment in time the declassification shoe was on the other foot, and U.S. government agencies faced a board with the statutory responsibility to put information before the public. The results of its review have enabled us to move the discussion of U.S. covert operations against Cuba to a whole new level. I also wish to express my indebtedness to my own National Security Archive. The sustained efforts of the Archive to petition for the release of records through the Freedom of Information Act and other declassification avenues have opened up material relevant to almost every aspect of American foreign policy. The Archive's physical collection of documents, and its collaboration with other institutions in hosting conferences that brought together historians and participants within a document-rich context, are a great source of knowledge. The Archive's work in putting these materials before the public in the form of microfiche collections of primary source material, document readers, and electronic briefing books accessible on the internet, makes available a rich vein of research. Even this book can barely scratch the surface of that material.

Many acute analysts of American policy, intelligence, and national security have exchanged ideas and suggestions or helped me sharpen my thinking. Some of them are mentioned above, but I also wish to thank Kai Bird, J. Kenneth McDonald, Stephen Coll, Mary Nolan, Gregory Treverton, Jeffrey Richelson, Gerald K. Haines, Marilyn Young, Andrew Bacevich, Phillip Deery, Michael Warner, Timothy Naftali, Lloyd Gardner, Svetlana Savranskaya, James Bamford, Richard L. Aldrich, Maria Eleonora Guasconi, Loch Johnson, Walter LaFeber, Max Holland, Richard K. Betts, and Thomas Blanton. For reading and editing the manuscript I am deeply indebted to Ellen Pinzur. For putting up with me during this lengthy process I thank my daughters Danielle and Natasha. All these persons added value to the book. For its errors and omissions I alone am responsible.

J. P.

Washington, D.C.
July 2006

Foreword

PUBLIC OPINION POLLS in many countries today portray the United States as the greatest threat to world peace on the globe, worse than terrorism or any other nation. This is an unfamiliar role for a country that has consciously articulated—and advanced—over many decades the notion that democratic values are the solution for many of the world's ills. How strange it is that Americans, fond of the vision of the nation's exceptionalism as seen in the image of the City on a Hill, their democracy the admiration of the world, should find themselves an object of the world's fears. The City is supposed to be a place of wonder and delight, even a state of grace. Its values are worth emulating, its freedom an example of achievement for all.

The Founding Fathers articulated the vision well, and at some point American leaders translated that ideal into a mission to bring its values to the world. President Woodrow Wilson enshrined the mission into a policy to implant democracy and self-determination among peoples everywhere. His successors in the presidency, every one, have continued and enlarged that quest—which has led America into a variety of foreign adventures, with widely varying motives, accomplishments, and failures. Those who fear America worry that the adventures themselves have supplanted the quest for democracy as the real content of United States policy.

Critics of this policy argue that American presidents have pursued their proximate goals, defined in terms of U.S. power, while cloaking them in the language and trappings of universalist desire. This is not a new argument—and, one may hope, not a correct one. But at the moment millions of people in many lands believe it, or something very like it. Their fears, and the extent of them, bode ill for American purpose in the world as well as for the feelings of Americans about their country and their government.

One way to look at the world's fears of America is to review U.S. actions on the world stage, where a major policy tool has been the secret operations of the Central Intelligence Agency (CIA), created after World War II. The agency quickly became the locus of open and covert efforts that have engaged many nations across the globe. Because of the secrecy of most CIA activities, it has been exceedingly difficult for historians and observers to evaluate them. Even today information about the CIA remains scattered, shrouded in misinformation, is poorly understood, or has remained inaccessible to researchers. The "need to know" has been used by government bureaucrats to restrict knowledge to a few, even in the case of events long past. Nevertheless an appraisal has become possible and is long overdue.

In the sixty years since the formation of the Central Intelligence Agency, presidents have continually harnessed the agency in service of their foreign policy goals. Three decades ago the "problem" of the CIA appeared to be the agency's status as a "rogue elephant"—unsupervised, tearing about the globe, acting at whim. By now it is evident that the agency and its cohorts were in fact respond-ing to presidential orders. This seems to make it much more urgent to attempt to tell the story of exactly what the CIA has accomplished. What has the agency con-tributed toward the success of larger U.S. policy goals, and the global quest for de-mocracy?

Perhaps the problem is more one of the "rogue" president than it is about an out-of-control Central Intelligence Agency. The control and oversight of United States intelligence needs to be examined in specific contexts where the overseers concern themselves with covert operations. In the past the question of oversight has been viewed as one of congressional supervision of the intelligence commu-nity, but we can now see this is an inadequate approach. The truth is that White House mechanisms for control and supervision of intelligence activity predate those instituted by Congress. Each branch of government has had its own objec-tives and degree of success, or lack of it, in overseeing the CIA. Existing studies of presidential or congressional oversight ignore key facets of the problem and do not take into account the most recent developments. And CIA attempts to pursue operations beyond the limits of the oversight system highlight the need for fresh examination. The oversight question must not only be examined in much greater detail but must be reframed as a competitive process between two branches of government. *Safe for Democracy* does that. While it is impossible to say where oversight is headed, we can show where it has been and why it has generally not worked.

This book surveys Central Intelligence Agency covert actions on four conti-nents. In the most recent version of their dictionary of terms, the Joint Chiefs of Staff define a "covert operation" as one planned or conducted so as to conceal the identity of the sponsor or permit a denial of involvement. To that category the U.S. military adds the "clandestine operation," defined as one in which emphasis "is placed on concealment of the operation rather than on concealment of the identity of the sponsor." Special operations are covert or clandestine, are carried out by military forces, and may combine elements of both varieties. All these form part of our terrain of inquiry.

Aside from labels based on secrecy, covert actions may also be viewed along functional lines. The several types include political action, in which the objective is to influence opinion-makers or the politics of nations; psychological warfare and propaganda, which are tactical tools in many actions; support for military operations, an intermediate category between traditional covert action and military special operations—which consumes an increasing fraction of CIA effort; and paramilitary operations, which are covertly coercive. *Safe for Democracy* examines activities along this entire spectrum.

This book contributes important new detail to our understanding of many CIA operations, including those in Italy, Korea, Poland, Iran, Guatemala, Hungary, China, Tibet, the Philippines, Indonesia, Syria, Iraq, Cuba, Bolivia, the Congo, Ghana, Vietnam and Laos, Kurdistan, Chile, Angola, Afghanistan, and Nicaragua; and it provides a first-cut view of actions in Somalia, Bosnia, Iraq, and other most recent activities. Whenever possible I have related all these events to specific presidential decisions expressed through White House control mechanisms and moderated by congressional oversight procedures. To prevent the work from growing completely unmanageable, the secret wars in Vietnam and Laos have been treated in less detail than is possible—they could easily consume an entire book by themselves—and the war against terrorism has been placed to one side except where it impinges directly upon our main subjects.

The conclusions of this inquiry tend to bear out the critics. American undercover actions have resulted in upheavals and untold suffering in many nations while contributing little to Washington's quest for democracy. Despite considerable ingenuity, technological wizardry, operational flexibility, and an impressively competent cadre of secret warriors, the results of covert operations have been consistently disappointing. Yet the very drive to maintain and use these capabilities has had consequences—often unforeseen—both for America's image around the globe and for constitutional control of the United States government by its own people. Secret warriors are known to argue the unique reasons for failure in specific actions but—except in secret studies unknown to the public until now—to resist broad overall evaluation. This book, however, does not stop short. Its content is not speculation, idle rumination, mindless ideology, or uninformed criticism. The evidence gathered in these pages is broad and deep. Covert operations have been a negative factor in the American pursuit of democracy throughout the world.

I have written on these matters earlier in *Presidents' Secret Wars,* a book published in the mid-1980s, and in fact the present work began as a revision of that book. Time had passed, and an updating seemed appropriate. But preparations for the project quickly revealed that a mere revision would be inadequate—sources have multiplied, the understanding of what constitutes a covert action has widened, and the terrain has shifted in other ways as well. The 1980s public concern about the CIA as rogue elephant obscured a great deal about the impact of agency operations on American foreign policy goals. Much of what we knew then has been modified by fresh evidence. It seemed to me clear that the entire subject needed to be recast in terms of what matters today.

A steady stream of newly declassified secret documents and a parade of memoirs of former CIA officials has enriched the record. Many things that once had to be inferred or addressed on the basis of interview material can now be described from hard evidence. Further interviews have extended the envelope. Throughout this book pseudonyms for CIA officers have been replaced with real names where possible; actual code names of operations are supplied; project costs, assigned personnel, and other details are revealed. The mountain of new detail on CIA operations ranges widely, from the recollections of participants to the dates and contents of headquarters decisions, White House deliberations, and the proceedings of key meetings. Thus while some measure of text remains unchanged, most of *Safe for Democracy* is brand-new. It is the closest we can come at this juncture to a definitive history of U.S. covert operations.

I have also widened the scope of the inquiry to include a larger slice of CIA political and propaganda activity, which was deliberately excluded from the earlier work. Thus the agency's interventions in elections in a number of countries, its association with at least one major U.S. domestic controversy, and its active propaganda programs are explored in some detail. So are the initiatives of both presidents Bush (though with less detail on the younger) and those of the Clinton era. This treatment is coupled with another major theme already alluded to: a systematic examination of the functioning of White House control mechanisms for covert operations, and an attempt to contrast them with congressional oversight efforts. Finally, for the first time this book examines covert operations from a foreign policy perspective and places them solidly within the context of American diplomacy.

The story of the secret wars is an important component of the American experience in the years since World War II. It is also a feature of the histories of those many lands where the secret warriors plied their trade. Neither the Cold War years nor the present era can be properly understood without taking this story into account. The time has come for taking stock, and that evaluation may begin here.

Major Figures in the Book

(comprising primarily senior CIA officers, government officials, foreign individuals, and intelligence officers who appear at more than one point in the narrative)

JAMES L. ADKINS: Paramilitary specialist who served with the Hmong in Laos and rose to lead the Nicaraguan Operations Group during the *contra* war.

PRINCE TURKI AL-FAISAL: Chief of Saudi Arabian intelligence for two and a half decades, Prince Turki cooperated on several CIA projects, most notably Afghanistan and Nicaragua, before becoming Saudi ambassador to London and later to the United States.

RICHARD ALLEN: National security adviser to President Reagan.

ROBERT AMORY: Deputy director for intelligence at the CIA, 1953–1962.

MANUEL ARTIME: Cuban exile leader at the Bay of Pigs, and again in the mid-1960s after being released from a Cuban prison, when he took part in a CIA project to create a new exile force.

GEORGE AURELL: Far East Division chief for the CIA, supervising covert action projects in Burma and China; station chief in the Philippines during political action there in the late 1950s.

HOWARD T. BANE: CIA clandestine services officer who had roles in the Tibet project and, as station chief in Ghana, in CIA African operations.

TRACY L. BARNES: Among the original secret warriors, Barnes served with the OSS and joined the Psychological Strategy Board staff, then later the CIA, playing major roles in covert operations in Guatemala and against Cuba.

JOSE BASULTO: Cuban exile fighter who continued efforts against Castro for decades after the CIA gave up.

RICHARD M. BISSELL: Special assistant to Allen W. Dulles, Bissell developed the U-2 and SR-71 aircraft for CIA, managed development of reconnaissance satellites, and played an increasing role in covert actions from Guatemala through the Bay of Pigs, rising to head the Directorate of Operations.

GEN. WILLIAM BOYKIN: An operator for Special Forces Operational Detachment Delta during the Iran hostage rescue mission, Boykin's career with Special Forces continued through the second Bush administration.

THOMAS BRADEN: Special assistant to Director Allen Dulles and creator of CIA's International Organizations Division.

WILLIAM V. BROE: Latin American Division chief who supervised the effort to keep Salvador Allende from assuming the presidency of Chile, Broe's later actions helped create the legal case against Richard Helms for perjury before Congress on this same matter.

JOHN A. BROSS: Longtime CIA officer involved with European operations, managing the DO for Allen Dulles, and senior adviser to Bill Casey.

WINTHROP BROWN: American ambassador to India during the first part of the Tibetan operation, and to Laos at the inception of the secret war there.

DAVID K. BRUCE: After gaining an intelligence background by heading OSS operations in the European theater, Bruce became a professional diplomat and adviser to presidents. He served as ambassador to London during the CIA operation against Guyana, and worked with the PFIAB.

ZBIGNIEW BRZEZINSKI: National security adviser to President Jimmy Carter, 1977–1981.

WILLIAM BUCKLEY: Paramilitary specialist who worked on Eastern Europe, the Bay of Pigs, Laos, and Pakistan; station chief in postwar Laos; deputy chief of counterterrorism staff until sent to Beirut as station chief, where he was kidnapped in 1984 and died under interrogation a year later.

MCGEORGE BUNDY: National security adviser to Presidents Kennedy and Johnson, 1961–1966.

ADM. ARLEIGH BURKE: Naval officer who served as chief of naval operations and arranged cooperation for Indonesia and the Bay of Pigs; Burke also became a member of the Taylor Board that reviewed the conduct of the Cuban operation.

FORBES BURNHAM: Guyanese political leader who benefited from CIA covert operations carried out between 1962 and 1964, and continuing agency political action until 1968.

GEN. CHARLES P. CABELL: Seconded from the air force, Cabell served as deputy director of central intelligence under Allen Dulles, 1953–1961, and had important roles in covert operations in Indonesia and Cuba.

FRANK CARLUCCI: Exposed to covert action as a young diplomat in the Congo, Carlucci rose through work at many government agencies until being brought directly into intelligence work as deputy director of central intelligence in the Carter administration; he remained concerned with this activity in the Reagan-era Pentagon, and then as national security adviser to President Reagan.

HARRY L. CARR: British intelligence officer who directed covert operations against Russia in the Baltic and cooperated with CIA's efforts in these areas.

GEORGE CARROLL: Covert operations specialist who worked in the CIA project in Iran and later became baron heading the Far East Division.

PHILLIP CARVER: Clandestine services officer who transferred to the analytical side of the CIA after his cover was blown in an abortive coup in South Vietnam; Carver became the agency's senior officer on Vietnam affairs.

WILLIAM J. CASEY: A veteran of OSS operations, Casey made his fortune in business and served briefly on President Ford's PFIAB; he headed Reagan's 1980 political campaign organization and was rewarded with appointment as director of central intelligence.

FIDEL CASTRO: Revolutionary leader, then dictator of Cuba, who became the target of many CIA operations.

GEORGE W. CAVE: Clandestine services officer who opened the CIA station in Afghanistan in 1957, headed stations in Iran and Saudi Arabia, ran a unit to support the Iran hostage rescue mission, was deputy chief of NE, and headed a policy coordination staff. In retirement Cave became involved in the Iran-Contra affair.

HAROLD CHIPMAN: Covert operations specialist who worked on Cuban projects and Vietnam.

DUANE R. ("DEWEY") CLARRIDGE: Clandestine services officer from the Near East and South Asian tribe, Clarridge served in Nepal, India, and Turkey, led the CIA station in Rome, then the Latin America Division and the Counterterrorism Center.

CLARK M. CLIFFORD: Adviser to Presidents Truman, Kennedy, and Johnson, Clifford helped draft the law that created the CIA, served on the PFIAB for some years, and was secretary of defense in 1968.

RAY L. CLINE: Officer who held both operational and analytical posts at CIA, Cline served as chief of station on Taiwan during Chinese and Tibet operations, headed the Directorate of Intelligence during Mongoose and the Cuban Missile Crisis, and later led the State Department's INR.

THOMAS C. CLINES: Paramilitary specialist who worked on Cuba operations and in Laos; in retirement became involved with "private benefactors" covert operation with Nicaraguan *contras*.

CHARLES G. ("CHUCK") COGAN: Moving between African and Middle Eastern assignments, Cogan was station chief in Jordan and headed the NE division; he was involved in covert operations in the Congo, the Iran hostage crisis, and Afghanistan.

WILLIAM E. COLBY: Director of central intelligence during the critical congressional investigations of the 1970s, Colby had risen through CIA ranks, working on Soviet operations, the Italian political action, Vietnamese operations, and general Asian activities.

MILES COPELAND: Covert operations specialist for the CIA in the Middle East, especially in Egypt and Lebanon.

THOMAS G. CORCORAN: Washington lawyer who represented Civil Air Transport when it was acquired by the CIA, and United Fruit in preparations for the CIA action in Guatemala.

ALFRED T. COX: An experienced covert operator, Cox oversaw CIA's interests in Civil Air Transport, served as chief of base in Hong Kong and on the paramilitary staff at headquarters before and during the Bay of Pigs, and led the Miami station at the beginning of Project Mongoose.

JAMES M. CRITCHFIELD: CIA officer who had a major role in the creation of the German intelligence service, helped establish its connections with the CIA, and then moved into CIA Middle Eastern operations.

WILLIAM J. DAUGHERTY: An agency hostage taken in Iran during his first tour, with his cover blown Daugherty served in headquarters management positions on covert operations staffs.

ROBERT K. DAVIS: Clandestine services officer who arranged cooperation of Guatemalan authorities with the CIA's effort to train anti-Castro exiles to invade Cuba; he later served as chief of station in Peru.

PEER DE SILVA: Operations officer who managed CIA initiatives against Russia in the Far East, served in Austria, and headed CIA stations in South Korea, South Vietnam, and Thailand, then became the first CIA special assistant for Vietnam Affairs.

JOHN DEUTCH: Director of central intelligence in the mid-1990s.

JOHN J. ("JACK") DEVINE: An operations officer in Chile during the CIA covert action there, Devine rose steadily, leading the agency's Iran operations group, its Afghan task force, stations in three Latin countries, Rome and London, and the Latin America Division, and served as associate deputy director for operations.

LAWRENCE R. DEVLIN: Twice served as CIA's station chief in the Congo, also as chief of station in Laos and head of the Africa Division.

GEN. JAMES H. DOOLITTLE: Air force general who reviewed court activities for President Eisenhower, then served for many years on the advisory boards PBCFIA and PFIAB.

ALLEN W. DULLES: A key figure in CIA history, Dulles served with the OSS, advocated creation of a peacetime intelligence agency, became deputy director for operations, then deputy and director of central intelligence and led the CIA through the Eisenhower years and into the Kennedy administration.

JOHN FOSTER DULLES: Lawyer and diplomat, brother of Allen, Dulles served as secretary of state under President Eisenhower and played a larger part in covert operations than previously acknowledged.

RALPH A. DUNGAN: Political adviser to Presidents Kennedy and Johnson whose special interest in Latin America led to his posting as ambassador to Chile, where he became involved in CIA projects.

SHEFFIELD EDWARDS: Chief of the CIA's Office of Security, Edwards became involved in assassination plots against Fidel Castro.

RUDY ENDERS: Paramilitary specialist and boatman, Enders made his mark as a maritime officer with the Miami base on Cuban operations; later in the Vietnam War he rose to a senior field officer and by the 1980s headed CIA's Special Activities Division, where he played a major role in the mining of Nicaraguan ports during the *contra* war.

JACOB D. ESTERLINE: An important figure in CIA Latin American operations, Esterline was deputy chief of the task force that carried out the Guatemala covert operation, and led the task force that carried out the Bay of Pigs; he served as chief of station in Panama and deputy chief of the Western Hemisphere Division, and headed CIA's Miami base.

DESMOND FITZGERALD: A primary figure in covert activities from the early 1950s to the mid-1960s, FitzGerald rose to head the CIA Directorate of Operations.

JOHN KENNETH GALBRAITH: American ambassador to India who opposed the CIA project in Tibet and helped President Kennedy decide to restructure this endeavor.

ROBERT M. GATES: Officer from the analytical side of the CIA who rose through the ranks to become deputy director for intelligence, then DDCI under Bill Casey; he left to become deputy national security adviser during the first Bush administration but returned as director of central intelligence until retiring in January 1993.

LLOYD GEORGE: Far East Division chief for the CIA during the Korean War.

JUSTIN F. GLEICHAUF: A CIA analyst, Gleichauf ran the refugee reception center in Miami that interviewed Cuban exiles for intelligence purposes.

GEN. ANDREW GOODPASTER: Staff secretary to President Eisenhower, Goodpaster became a key figure, with Gordon Gray, in helping the president keep track of CIA activities.

GORDON L. GRAY: A key figure in U.S. intelligence history, Gray served as secretary of the army, helped establish the Special Forces, led the Psychological Strategy Board, consulted for President Eisenhower, became Eisenhower's national security adviser, and worked on the PFIAB for more than a decade.

ERNESTO ("CHE") GUEVARA: Argentinian doctor and early Castroite leader in Cuba, Guevara attempted to export revolution to Africa and Latin America and became a special target of the CIA.

ALBERT HAKIM: Iranian businessman who helped with the Hostage Rescue mission and later became involved in a series of ventures with Richard V. Secord that ensnared them in the Iran-Contra affair.

SAM HALPERN: Covert operations specialist with the CIA's Far East Division, later executive assistant to the deputy director for operations.

COL. ALBERT HANEY: Chief of station in Korea during the Korean War, Haney later headed the task force that carried out the Guatemala covert action project.

W. AVERELL HARRIMAN: Adviser to presidents and U.S. diplomat, Harriman assisted Truman, Kennedy, and Johnson, attempting to negotiate an end to the AIOC crisis in Iran in the early 1950s and the civil war in Laos in the early 1960s, both of which formed episodes in the secret war.

JOHN L. HART: A covert operator in the classic CIA mold, Hart worked on Soviet operations, headed the Tibet branch of the FE Division during that operation, and later served as station chief in South Vietnam at the height of the war there.

WILLIAM K. HARVEY: Covert operations specialist who led the CIA base in Berlin through much of the 1950s, returned to headquarters to run the agency's assassinations unit, then headed the task force that carried out Project Mongoose and later the agency's station in Rome.

JOHN HASEY: Operations specialist in Laos who built ties to Gen. Phoumi Nosavan, complicating U.S. policy, and then worked briefly in the Congo.

COL. JACK HAWKINS: Marine officer seconded to CIA as chief of the paramilitary branch of the task force that carried out the Bay of Pigs invasion; later deputy to the head of the Pentagon office responsible for cooperation with the CIA.

HENRY D. HECKSCHER: A major figure in CIA operations, Heckscher served in Berlin during the 1953 riots there, worked on the Guatemala covert operation, and headed CIA stations engaged in covert operations in Laos, Japan, and Chile.

RICHARD M. HELMS: A key figure in CIA history, Helms rose through the ranks of OSS and SSU to CIA, heading the German Division, the Operations Directorate, and the intelligence community as a whole for Presidents Johnson and Nixon.

PAUL B. HENZE: A psychological operations specialist, Henze worked as an analyst and deputy division chief for Radio Free Europe, a case officer and station chief in Turkey and Ethiopia, and on the Brzezinski NSC staff.

ADM. ROSCOE H. HILLENKOETTER: Director of central intelligence from the Berlin Blockade to the onset of the Korean war, Hillenkoetter presided over the creation of the OPC and its integration into the CIA sytem.

PAUL HOLDEN: Chief pilot for Civil Air Transport's detachment assisting the French in Indochina, Holden went on to fly for the CIA in its Indonesia project.

RICHARD HOLM: A paramilitary officer who served in Asia and Africa, notably in Hong Kong, Laos, and the Congo; later he led the Counterterrorism staff, stations in Brussels and Paris, and advised on the Directorate of Operations post–Cold War reorganization.

FRANK HOLOBER: A Far East Division officer, Holober worked on operations against mainland China and led the task force carrying out the CIA project in Tibet.

LAWRENCE HOUSTON: General counsel to the CIA from its inception through the early 1970s, his cautionary views on the legal authorities for covert operations were never adequately taken into account.

GEN. JOHN E. HULL: Army general who advised CIA analysts in the early 1950s; trusted by President Eisenhower and appointed second chairman of the PBCFIA.

E. HOWARD HUNT: Among the major figures in CIA political action, Hunt played roles in psychological warfare and covert operations in Albania, Guatemala, and Cuba, headed agency stations in Latin America, and became involved with the Nixon White House in the Watergate scandal.

FRED IKLE: Undersecretary of defense for policy in the Reagan-era Pentagon, Ikle's hard-line views contributed to the Casey covert action offensive.

ADM. BOBBY RAY INMAN: Officer with a long background in naval intelligence, Inman had been an attaché in Sweden, was involved with the *Pueblo* affair, headed naval intelligence, and had been deputy director of DIA before heading the NSA, from which he was appointed to become deputy director for central intelligence.

C. D. JACKSON: A propaganda and psychological warfare expert, adviser to President Eisenhower, and executive for the Time-Life Corporation; he conducted the review that led to the termination of the Psychological Strategy Board.

WILLIAM H. JACKSON: Participated with Allen Dulles in an important early review of U.S. intelligence operations, then served as deputy director of central intelligence under Walter B. Smith, helping with the creation of the Directorate of Operations.

CHEDDI JAGAN: Guyanese political leader who became the target of CIA covert operations, 1962–1964.

ROBERT J. ("RED") JANTZEN: Clandestine services officer who worked in India and Singapore; legendary as station chief in Thailand, Jantzen also led the CIA station in Canada and in retirement became associated with the Nugan Hand Bank.

GORDON L. JORGENSEN: Senior clandestine services officer who led stations in both Laos and South Vietnam, among others.

THOMAS H. KARAMESSINES: Among the first generation of CIA officers and an associate of Richard Helms, Karamessines led CIA stations in Vienna and Athens, then rose to deputy director for operations, the post he held during the National Student Association affair, at the high point of the Vietnam War, and during the Chilean covert action.

COL. JAMES KELLIS: Detached from the air force to CIA, Kellis worked in covert operations in Greece and Korea and other Far East Division activities.

GEORGE KENNAN: Professional diplomat whose work furnished the basis for the U.S. Cold War doctrine of "containment," and who made important contributions to the creation of the OPC.

JAMES R. KILLIAN: Scientist and adviser to President Eisenhower, Killian had a key role in the early development of the U-2 aircraft, on the basis of which he was appointed first chairman of the PBCFIA.

JOSEPH CALDWELL KING: Headed the CIA operations division for Latin America from its creation through the Kennedy administration.

LYMAN D. KIRKPATRICK: A mover in the creation of the Directorate of Operations, Kirkpatrick served as executive assistant to Walter B. Smith, chief of the Office of Special Operations; as CIA's inspector general his evaluation of the Bay of Pigs failure would be highly controversial.

HENRY A. KISSINGER: Though Kissinger would have a peripheral Cold War role as a consultant to the Eisenhower and Kennedy administrations, he had a quite direct role in intelligence activities as national security adviser, 1969–1975, and secretary of state, 1973–1977.

E. HENRY ("HANK") KNOCKE: An officer from the technical intelligence side of CIA, Knocke had been special assistant to McCone and Helms; he led analytical staffs and the Foreign Broadcast Information Service, was CIA liaison to the Rockefeller and congressional investigations, and finally became deputy director for central intelligence.

WILLIAM LAIR: Paramilitary specialist with long service in Thailand, Lair proved instrumental in enlisting Thai help for the CIA project in Laos, where he supervised Hmong operations until the late 1960s.

PAT LANDRY: An agency paramilitary specialist, Landry conducted field missions during the Indonesian operation and later played a vital role in Laos as deputy, then chief of the unit that ran the Hmong partisan army.

GEN. EDWARD G. LANSDALE: Air force officer detached to CIA and later in Pentagon assignments cooperating with the agency, Lansdale had primary roles in CIA covert operations in the Philippines, South Vietnam, and China.

BRIAN LATELL: Agency analyst on Latin American affairs whose reports on Haiti became controversial for the CIA.

JAMES R. LILLEY: Clandestine services officer who served in the Far East, in particular Hong Kong, was deputy chief of station in Laos, and became the first CIA station chief in Communist China, to which he returned as U.S. ambassador.

FRANKLIN A. LINDSAY: Agency officer who headed the European Division of OPC and the DO, left to become a corporate executive, and headed a consultant study on covert operations for the Nixon administration.

JAY LOVESTONE: A key CIA labor operative.

JOHN MACGAFFIN III: Among the CIA's Middle East specialists, MacGaffin worked against Soviet spies in Beirut and elsewhere, ran the agency's base in New York, became chief of a post–Cold War Central Eurasian Division and then associate deputy director for operations before moving to the FBI as an intelligence adviser to its director.

GEN. JOHN MAGRUDER: Led secret operations for the OSS and later was chief of the Strategic Services Unit; Magruder played a formative role in the creation of the CIA and later served as Pentagon representative on the board supervising the Office of Policy Coordination.

HUBER MATOS: A Cuban leader who later turned against Fidel Castro, believing he had betrayed the revolution; he was imprisoned for two decades and after his release made common cause with anti-Castro exiles, including involvement in the CIA *contra* war against Nicaragua.

ROGER MCCARTHY: Paramilitary officer who worked on many projects in the Far East, including China, Indonesia, and Tibet; worked as a trainer on Saipan and later headed the CIA's Tibet task force.

GEN. ROBERT A. MCCLURE: Founder of peacetime psychological warfare organizations within the U.S. Army.

JOHN A. ("ALEX") MCCONE: Senior official under Presidents Eisenhower—for whom he led the Atomic Energy Commission—then Kennedy and Johnson, whom McCone served as director of central intelligence; he returned to industry, joining the board of the ITT Corporation, and played a further covert action role when the CIA acted in Chile.

ROBERT C. ("BUD") MCFARLANE: A former Marine lieutenant colonel, McFarlane was detached to serve on the NSC staff under President Ford, returning later as deputy and then national security adviser to President Reagan. After leaving government he became involved in the Iran-Contra affair.

JOHN N. ("JACK") McMAHON: With a background in technical intelligence, McMahon early worked on U-2 operations, on reconnaissance satellites, and on electronic interception before becoming an administrative coordinator, serving on the Intelligence Community Staff, then as deputy director for operations; he rose to deputy director for central intelligence.

STEWART METHVEN: Covert operations specialist who first recruited Vang Pao in Laos, later worked on irregular warfare projects in South Vietnam and headed the CIA station in Zaire during the Angolan project.

CORD MEYER: An agency political action specialist, Meyer headed psychological operations staffs or CIA's International Organization Division from the mid-1950s to the early 1970s, paying special attention to activities of the "Radios," then served as station chief in London.

ROBERT MURPHY: American diplomat, PBCFIA member, and adviser to President Eisenhower.

ROBERT J. MYERS: A station chief for the Office of Special Operations on Taiwan during the Korean War years, Myers rose to deputy chief of the Far East Division early in the Vietnam War.

GAMAL ABDEL NASSER: Egyptian army officer who took power in a 1952 coup and cooperated with the CIA early on, only to become a target later as the U.S. opposed his efforts to create a multinational Arab movement and an alliance of nonaligned countries.

PAUL H. NITZE: American official who succeeded George Kennan as head of the State Department's Policy Planning Staff and remained at the center of national security decisions until the Reagan administration.

JAMES NOEL: Clandestine services officer who became the last CIA station chief in pre-Castro Cuba and later ran networks for the Bay of Pigs task force.

OLIVER L. NORTH: Marine officer detached for service on the Reagan NSC staff who became a prime mover in the Iran-Contra affair.

ROBERT OAKLEY: American diplomat whose political-military work repeatedly brought him into the arena of CIA operations in the Middle East, Afghanistan, and Somalia.

CARMEL OFFIE: Controversial character in early operations by the Office of Policy Coordination, CIA European activities, and later its labor operations.

THOMAS A. PARROTT: Officer detailed from the CIA to the NSC staff to handle staff work for the 5412 Group and its successors, the Special Group (Augmented) and the 303 Committee.

WILLIAM B. PAWLEY: Businessman and friend of President Eisenhower, Pawley used his Latin American networks to participate in CIA covert actions in Guatemala and Cuba.

JACK PFEIFFER: An agency historian, Pfeiffer later conducted extensive classified research to compile the CIA's four-volume official history of the Bay of Pigs.

DAVID A. PHILLIPS: An agency psychological warfare specialist, Phillips was important in radio propaganda during the Guatemala and Cuba operations, and headed CIA stations in Latin America and the task force that carried out the 1970 covert action in Chile.

ADM. JOHN POINDEXTER: Deputy, then national security adviser to President Reagan.

THOMAS POLGAR: A European operations specialist for CIA, Polgar worked in Germany in the early 1950s and on Hungarian operations, and headed stations in Latin America and South Vietnam, where he became the last CIA station chief.

ALLEN POPE: Air force pilot who joined Civil Air Transport for its airlift supporting the French in Indochina, Pope flew for the CIA project in Indonesia, where his shootdown essentially terminated the operation.

LUIS POSADA CARRILES: Cuban exile fighter initially with the Bay of Pigs; responsible for bombings in Mexico City and of a Venezuelan airliner, and a participant in the "private benefactor" airlift in Nicaragua.

ANTHONY ("TONY PO") POSHEPNY: CIA field officer who worked on covert operations in Indonesia and Tibet and became an agency base chief in Laos.

RAFAEL QUINTERO: Anti-Castro Cuban exile, active from before the Bay of Pigs through Project Mongoose and the Artime Brigade, right through to the 1980s *contra* war against Nicaragua.

MANUEL ("MANOLO") RAY: Cuban exile politician at the Bay of Pigs and in Project Mongoose.

JOHN REAGAN: Paramilitary officer who served in Korea, Japan, on the Tibet project, in Vietnam, and headed the station in Pakistan at the outset of the Afghan project.

ROBERT REYNOLDS: Miami base chief for the Bay of Pigs operation.

JOHN H. ("JOCKO") RICHARDSON: CIA covert operations specialist, Richardson headed agency stations in Austria, South Korea, and South Vietnam, and had a key role in the antecedents to the military coup in which Ngo Dinh Diem was killed.

STEPHEN W. RICHTER: Clandestine services officer who worked with Iranian agent networks and, as chief of the Near East Division, presided over covert operations in Iraq in the mid-1990s, later rising to head a DO technology management group.

WILLIAM A. ("RIP") ROBERTSON, JR.: CIA field operator or contract officer in Guatemala, the Bay of Pigs, Project Mongoose, and Vietnam.

FELIX I. RODRIGUEZ: Cuban exile fighter and CIA contract officer; starting from before the Bay of Pigs, Rodriguez worked for the agency on Project Mongoose, in Bolivia, in Vietnam, and on Nicaraguan "private benefactor" operations from El Salvador in the 1980s, where he also was a consultant to the Salvadoran air force.

KERMIT ("KIM") ROOSEVELT: An early covert operations expert, Roosevelt specialized in the Middle East and played key roles in Egypt and Iran, and as a DO official had some involvement in Guatemala. He retired to work for oil companies.

HARRY S. ROSITZKE: An important Cold War covert operations manager, Rositzke headed the CIA's Soviet Bloc Division during actions against Russia and later oversaw the Tibet operation as station chief in India.

WALT W. ROSTOW: Psychological warfare consultant to PSB, later deputy national security adviser and State Department Policy Planning chief 1961–1966, and national security adviser 1966–1969.

DEAN RUSK: Secretary of state for Presidents Kennedy and Johnson, 1961–1969.

JOSE ("PEPE") SAN ROMAN: Cuban exile brigade commander.

NESTOR SANCHEZ: A Latin America specialist, Sanchez served as deputy station chief in Guatemala during the CIA operation there and was with the Miami station during Mongoose, serving as case officer for a Cuban operative in one of the Castro assassination plots; he led CIA stations in Guatemala, Venezuela, and Madrid before heading the Latin America Division; in 1981 he moved to the Pentagon with Frank Carlucci, becoming deputy secretary of defense for Inter-American affairs, with a role in the Nicaraguan secret war.

ARTHUR M. SCHLESINGER, JR.: Historian and adviser to President Kennedy, especially on Latin American affairs, Schlesinger had roles in covert operations against Cuba and Guyana.

JAMES R. SCHLESINGER: An official whose background lay in defense analysis, Schlesinger served briefly as director of central intelligence in 1973 before being appointed secretary of defense.

GEN. RICHARD V. SECORD: Air force special operations expert with important roles in the Laotian paramilitary operation and the Iran hostage rescue, and later a "private benefactor" in the Nicaraguan *contra* operation and the sale of weapons to Iran.

TONY SFORZA: Clandestine services officer who served in Cuba before Castro, in Mongoose, with the CIA station in Mexico City, and undercover during the Chilean project that led to the assassination of Gen. René Schneider.

THEODORE ("TED") SHACKLEY: Clandestine services officer who rose through the agency to become associate deputy director for operations; Shackley ran Polish operations from Berlin base, went to Miami station to lead field operations for Project Mongoose, headed the CIA stations in Laos and South Vietnam, and the Chilean destabilization operation as chief of the Latin America Division.

GEN. WALTER BEDELL ("BEETLE") SMITH: Army general who led the CIA from 1950 to 1953, creating the Directorate of Operations by merging the OPC and OSO; supervised the OPC during its major covert actions.

ANASTASIO SOMOZA: Nicaraguan director who collaborated with the CIA on covert operations in Guatemala and against Cuba.

ADM. SIDNEY W. SOUERS: First director of central intelligence under President Truman, later his first staff chief for the National Security Council.

EDWARD A. STANULIS: Former army officer and CIA paramilitary expert, Stanulis planned initiatives to counter Fidel Castro, then became a senior officer on the task force that prepared the Bay of Pigs operation.

JOHN H. STEIN: An officer who served in Zaire at the end of the CIA operation there, became chief of station in Cambodia during the war, then in Libya, and later rose to become deputy director for operations.

ADLAI E. STEVENSON: U.S. ambassador to the United Nations during the Bay of Pigs invasion and the Cuban Missile Crisis.

GORDON STEWART: OSS and SSU veteran, longtime chief of CIA operations in Germany, leader of the DO's foreign intelligence staff, later a senior agency estimator and the CIA's inspector general.

GEN. RICHARD G. STILWELL: Headed CIA Far Eastern operations during the Korean War period and proved instrumental in the agency's acquisition of its first air proprietary; Stilwell also played an important role in the evolution of U.S. Special Forces.

JOHN STOCKWELL: Paramilitary specialist who served in Vietnam and Laos and later led the CIA task force for the Angolan project.

RICHARD F. STOLZ: A clandestine service officer who specialized in Russian operations, Stolz worked in Germany and Bulgaria, led stations in Moscow, Rome, Yugoslavia, and London, and headed the Soviet Division; he came out of retirement to lead the Directorate of Operations.

HOWARD STONE: A CIA covert operations specialist, Stone worked on the Iranian coup project, headed the agency's station in Syria attempting to mount a similar initiative, and later became station chief in Nepal during the final phase of the Tibet project.

ADM. WILLIAM O. STUDEMAN: An intelligence specialist who had headed that department for the navy, Studeman became deputy and briefly acting DCI during the interregnum between James Woolsey and John Deutch.

GEN. MAXWELL D. TAYLOR: Army general and chief of staff in the late 1950s, Taylor later became a key adviser to Presidents Kennedy and Johnson, heading the board that reviewed implementation of the Bay of Pigs operation, and chairing the Special Group (Augmented) until he left to become chairman of the Joint Chiefs of Staff.

ADM. RUFUS L. TAYLOR: Deputy director of central intelligence under Richard Helms, Taylor had headed naval intelligence and had a long background in communications intelligence.

GARFIELD THORSRUD: Air operations specialist for the CIA, Thorsrud played important roles in CIA projects in Indonesia and Tibet, and headed airfield operations for the Bay of Pigs.

HANS V. TOFTE: Covert operations specialist in China, Korea, Guatemala, and later deputy chief of CIA Domestic Contact Division.

B. HUGH TOVAR: Clandestine services officer who led the CIA station in Indonesia at the time of the 1965 coup there, and later the station in Laos at the height of the paramilitary effort there.

RAFAEL TRUJILLO: Dictator of the Dominican Republic, Trujillo became the object of CIA planning for a covert operation in 1960–1961.

GEN. LUCIEN K. TRUSCOTT: Deputized from the army as CIA Director Walter B. Smith's special representative in Germany, Truscott had a key role in European operations through the early and mid-1950s and served as troubleshooter for President Eisenhower.

BRONSON TWEEDY: Old-line CIA officer who supervised the Congo operation as Africa Division chief.

THOMAS A. TWETTEN: Clandestine services officer who served in Cairo, headed the station in Jordan, the Office of Technical Services, was deputy and then chief of the NE Division, and associate, then deputy director for operations, retiring as station chief in London.

AL ULMER: Operations officer with wide experience, Ulmer headed CIA stations in Vienna and Madrid, and the Far East Division, supervising covert operations in Indonesia, Japan, and the Philippines.

GEN. HOYT S. VANDENBERG: Air force general who directed the Central Intelligence Group and managed the creation of the CIA.

TONY VARONA: Cuban exile politician active during the Bay of Pigs project and later CIA anti-Cuban efforts; he involved his organization in plots to assassinate Castro.

JOHN WALLER: Covert operations specialist who worked in the Near East Division primarily, including in Turkey and on the coup project in Iran; deputy chief of the Africa Division during key operations of the 1960s and later the CIA's inspector general.

GEN. VERNON A. WALTERS: By virtue of his linguistic abilities, Walters long hovered at the edges of intelligence work, executing special missions for many presidents before Nixon made him deputy director of central intelligence; as President Reagan's ambassador to the United Nations, Walters again played a role in the Casey covert action offensive.

JUDGE WILLIAM WEBSTER: A career lawyer who was FBI chief when President Reagan selected him to be director of central intelligence.

EDWARD WELLES: Congo task force chief.

DAVID WHIPPLE: CIA field officer who served in Europe, Africa, and the Far East for almost three decades.

WHITING WILLAUER: An official of the CIA proprietary Civil Air Transport, Willauer was appointed ambassador to Honduras to help with the Guatemala operation and later served as State Department overseer of the CIA's Cuba task force.

EDWIN WILSON: Covert operations specialist whose commercial deals in retirement became a U.S. headache.

DONALD H. WINTERS: Deputy chief of station during the CIA operation in Chile, Winters rose through the ranks as a Latin American specialist; he had a role in the Nicaraguan secret war as station chief in Honduras, then Panama.

FRANK G. WISNER: Founder and head of the Office of Policy Coordination, he directed the transition to the Directorate of Operations, then led CIA covert operations through the late 1950s. Subsequently chief of station in London.

R. JAMES WOOLSEY: A lawyer with little intelligence background except as a congressional staffer or U.S. negotiator, Woolsey's appointment as DCI was politically opportune for President Clinton.

Acronyms Used in the Book

ABN	Anti-Bolshevik Bloc of Nations (organization of anti-Communist groups)
AF	CIA African Division
AFL	American Federation of Labor
AFL-CIO	American Federation of Labor–Congress of Industrial Organizations
AFSCME	American Federation of State, County, and Municipal Employees
AID	U.S. Agency for International Development
AIFLD	American Institute for Free Labor Development
AIOC	Anglo-Iranian Oil Company
AMCOMLIB	American Committee for Liberation from Bolshevism
AOG	CIA African Operations Group (Angola task force)
ARC	U.S. Air Force Air Resupply and Communications Wing
ARDE	Nicaraguan *contra* political/military group (*Alianza revolucionaria democrática*)
BBC	British Broadcasting Corporation
BDPS	Lithuanian partisan movement (*Bendrasis Demokratinio Pasipriesinimo Sajudis*)
BNE	CIA Board of National Estimates
BNL	Banca Nazionale del Lavoro (Italian bank)
BOSS	Bureau of State Security (South African intelligence service)
CAT	Civil Air Transport (CIA proprietary)
CATF	CIA Central America Task Force
CCRAK	Combined Command Reconnaissance Activities Korea
CDNI	Committee for the Defense of National Interests (Laotian political movement)
CDP	Christian Democratic Party (Chile)
CI	Counterinsurgency
CIA	U.S. Central Intelligence Agency
CIC	U.S. Counter Intelligence Corps

CIDG	Civilian Irregular Defense Group
CIG	U.S. Central Intelligence Group
CORDS	U.S. Civil Operations and Rural Development Support (pacification unit)
CPPG	NSC Crisis Pre-Planning Group
CPSU	Communist Party of the Soviet Union
CTC	CIA Counterterrorism Center
DCI	CIA Director of Central Intelligence
DDCI	CIA Deputy Director of Central Intelligence
DDI	CIA Deputy Director of Intelligence
DDO	CIA Deputy Director for Operations
DEA	U.S. Drug Enforcement Administration
DGI	Cuban government intelligence service (*Dirección general de inteligencia*)
DI	CIA Directorate for Intelligence
DIA	U.S. Defense Intelligence Agency
DNI	U.S. Director of National Intelligence
DO	CIA Directorate for Operations
DP	Displaced Person
DRA	Democratic Republic of Afghanistan
DRE	Cuban exile group (*Directorio revolucionario estudiantil*)
DRVN	Democratic Republic of Vietnam (North Vietnam)
EXCOM	Executive Committee of the National Security Council
EXCOMAIR	CIA Executive Committee for Air Proprietaries
EXIM	U.S. Export-Import Bank (international trade finance unit)
FAR	Cuban government armed forces (*Fuerzas armadas revolucionarias*)
FBI	U.S. Federal Bureau of Investigation
FDN	Nicaraguan *contra* armed force (*Fuerza democrática nicaraguense*)
FDR	Franklin Delano Roosevelt
FE	CIA Far East Division
FECOM	U.S. Far East Command
FLI	Front for the Liberation of Iran
FNLA	National Front for the Liberation of Angola (Portuguese acronym)
FOG	U.S. Foreign Operations Group (a military clandestine unit)
FRD	Cuban exile political front (*Frente revolucionario democrático*)
FSLN	Nicaraguan Marxist political party (*frente sandinista de liberación nacional*)
G-2	Military intelligence (U.S. Army, also Cuban government intelligence)
HMS	Her/His Majesty's Ship
HPSCI	House Permanent Select Committee on Intelligence
ICJ	International Court of Justice
IG	CIA Inspector General
INA	Iraqi National Accord (Allawi exile faction)

INC	Iraqi National Congress (Chalabi exile faction)
INR	Bureau of Intelligence and Research (State Department intelligence unit)
IOB	Intelligence Oversight Board
IOG	CIA Iraq Operations Group (also Iran Operations Group at a different time)
ISA	U.S. Intelligence Support Activity (a military clandestine unit)
ISI	Inter-Services Intelligence (Pakistani military intelligence agency)
ITT	International Telephone and Telegraph Corporation
IVAG	U.S. International Volunteer Air Group
JACK	Joint Activities Commission Korea
JCS	U.S. Joint Chiefs of Staff
JFK	John Fitzgerald Kennedy
KGB	Soviet intelligence and security service (Russian acronym)
KHAD	Afghan Government secret police agency (Afghan acronym)
LBJ	Lyndon Baines Johnson
LCI	Landing Craft Infantry (amphibious ship designator)
LS	Lima Site (Laotian Airstrip designator)
LSD	Landing Ship Dock (amphibious ship designator)
MACSOG	MACV Studies and Observation Group
MACV	U.S. Military Assistance Command Vietnam
MIT	Massachusetts Institute of Technology
MNR	Bolivian political party (*Movimiento nacional revolucionario*)
MON	CIA Memorandum of Notification (presidential finding)
MPLA	Popular Movement for the Liberation of Angola (Portuguese acronym)
MRR	Cuban exile group (*Movimiento de recuperación revolucionario*)
NATO	North American Treaty Organization
NE	CIA Near East Division (of the Directorate for Operations—Near East and Africa until 1959)
NESA	CIA Near East and South Asian Division (of the Directorate of Intelligence)
NHAO	U.S. Nicaraguan Humanitarian Assistance Office
NIA	U.S. National Intelligence Authority
NIC	CIA National Intelligence Council
NID	National Intelligence Daily (CIA publication)
NIE	CIA National Intelligence Estimate
NIO	CIA National Intelligence Officer
NIST	National Intelligence Support Team (community-wide)
NKVD	Soviet intelligence and security service (Russian acronym)
NLF	National Liberation Front (Vietnam)
NLHX	Lao Patriotic Front (*Neo Lao Hak Xat*)
NOG	CIA Nicaraguan Operations Group
NSA	National Student Association

NSA	U.S. National Security Agency
NSAM	National Security Action Memorandum
NSC	U.S. National Security Council
NSDD	National Security Decision Directive
NSDM	National Security Decision Memorandum
NSPG	NSC National Security Planning Group
NSSM	National Security Study Memorandum
NTS	Russian exile group (*Natsionalno Trudovoi Soyuz*)
NVDA	National Volunteer Defense Army (Tibetan rebel movement)
OAS	Organization of American States
OCB	NSC Operations Coordinating Board
OPC	CIA Office of Policy Coordination
ORIT	Latin American labor group (*Organización regional inter-Americano de trajabadores*)
OSO	CIA Office of Special Operations
OSO	U.S. Department of Defense Office of Special Operations
OSS	U.S. Organization for Strategic Services
OUN	Organization of Ukrainian Nationalists (Ukrainian acronym)
PARU	Police Aerial Resupply Unit (Thai Special Forces)
PBCFIA	President's Board of Consultants on Foreign Intelligence Activities
PDF	Panama Defense Forces
PDPA	People's Democratic Party of Afghanistan
PERMESTA	Indonesian rebel movement (*Piagam Perjuangan Semesta*)
PFIAB	President's Foreign Intelligence Advisory Board
PLA	People's Liberation Army (Chinese armed forces)
PLO	Palestine Liberation Organization
PNC	People's National Congress (Guyanese political party)
PP	CIA Political and Psychological Warfare Staff
PPP	People's Progressive Party (Guyana)
PRC	People's Republic of China
PSB	NSC Psychological Strategy Board
PSI	Public Services International
RFE	U.S. Radio Free Europe
RIAS	Radio in the American Sector (U.S. radio outlet in West Berlin)
RIG	NSC Restricted Interagency Group
RL	U.S. Radio Liberty
RLG	Royal Laotian Government
SACSA	U.S. Special Assistant (to the Secretary of Defense) for Counter-insurgency and Special Activities
SAD	CIA Special Activities Division
SADF	South African Defense Forces
SALT	Strategic Arms Limitation Talks
SAM	Surface to Air Missile
SAOG	CIA South Asia Operations Group (Afghanistan task force)

SCC	NSC Special Coordinating Committee
SDECE	French intelligence service (*Service de documentation extérieure et de contre-espionnage*)
SEAL	Sea-Air-Land soldiers (U.S. Navy special forces)
SEATO	Southeast Asia Treaty Organization
SGU	Special Guerrilla Unit (CIA combat unit of Hmong warriors in Laos)
SIS	Secret Intelligence Service (British intelligence service, aka MI-6)
SNIE	CIA Special National Intelligence Estimate
SOE	Special Operations Executive (British)
SOF	Special Operations Forces
SOG	Special Operations Group (Unconventional warfare command Korea)
SPG	CIA Special Procedures Group
SSCI	Senate Select Committee on Intelligence
SSU	U.S. Strategic Services Unit
STTGI	Stanford Technology Trading Group International (a Secord-Hakim company)
TUC	Trades Union Council
UCLA	University of California, Los Angeles
UF	United Front (Guyanese political party)
UN	United Nations
UNITA	National Union for the Total Independence of Angola (Portuguese acronym)
UNO	Nicaraguan *contra* political front (*Unión democrática nicaraguense*)
UNPFK	United Nations Partisan Forces Korea
UPA	Ukrainian Partisan Army
USAF	United States Air Force
USIA	United States Information Agency
USSR	Union of Soviet Socialist Republics
WEI	Western Enterprises Incorporated (CIA cover agency on Taiwan)
WH	CIA Western Hemisphere Division
WIGMO	Western International Ground Maintenance Organization
WIN	Polish partisan movement Freedom and Independent (*Wolnosc I Niepodleglosc*)

A standing force . . . is a dangerous, at the same time that it may be a necessary, provision. On the smallest scale it has its inconveniences. On an extensive scale, its consequences may be fatal. On any scale, it is an object of laudable circumspection and precaution. A wise nation will combine all these considerations; and whilst it does not rashly preclude itself from any resource which may become essential to its safety, will exert all its prudence in diminishing both the necessity and the danger of resorting to one which may be inauspicious to its liberties.

—James Madison, *The Federalist*, No. 41

SAFE FOR DEMOCRACY

1

The Gamut of Secret Operations

THREE DECADES LATER, Jack Kennedy's man apologized. What had happened at the time had been deadly serious, so serious that, in order to get an ally to go along, the United States had threatened an invasion of another enemy that would have led to nuclear war. The Central Intelligence Agency (CIA) did not quite kill Cheddi Jagan but did its best to put him out of business. Jagan, the prime minister of British Guiana, headed for independence as the nation of Guyana, had raised hackles in Washington. The CIA had orders to get rid of him.

In the early 1960s this attempt at regime change, filtered through America's Cold War struggle with the Soviet Union, was the latest in a long series of CIA covert operations. Jagan became both victim and exemplar. "We misunderstood the whole struggle down there," Arthur M. Schlesinger reminisced in 1994. President John F. Kennedy's court historian and private adviser had made Latin America one of his special interests. Guyana became Schlesinger's special mistake.

Of course Schlesinger had help. In fact he had initially held a relatively relaxed view of Jagan as Guyanese leader. The CIA seemed more pessimistic. In an intelligence estimate issued in March 1961, the agency, looking ahead to elections in the South American country, concluded that Jagan's political party "will probably succeed in winning the right to form the next government." The CIA further concluded: "Jagan himself is not an acknowledged Communist, but his statements and actions over the years bear the marks of the introduction and advice the Communists have given him." Further, "Jagan's US-born wife, who exercises very strong influence over him, is an acknowledged Communist." The only bright elements lay in the U.S. intelligence belief that Jagan, to preclude interference in Guyana's move toward full independence, would not immediately lead the country toward the left and would hesitate to do so later.

President Kennedy's National Security Council (NSC) assessed the Guyana situation a few weeks after the disastrous CIA failure in the April 1961 Bay of Pigs operation, a covert attempt to invade Cuba. They feared Guyana succumbing to the same dark forces as Fidel Castro. Significantly, the task of figuring out what to do about Guyana rested with the same officials responsible for U.S. policy on Cuba.

Guyana began as a British rather than an American problem. Unable to sustain its empire following World War II, Great Britain responded to rising nationalism by granting increasing self-government and then independence to many of its colonies, Guyana among them. Europeans had arrived there about 1620, settling on the coast and leaving indigenous peoples in the interior. The Dutch West India Company held on to the territory until 1796 when it fell to the English during the Napoleonic wars. In 1814 Guyana was ceded to England by treaty. The Dutch, Portuguese, and English brought in African slaves, and in the 1830s the British also introduced indentured workers from India. By the 1950s the "East Indians," as they were called, had become the dominant population at about 46 percent of the total, with Africans the next largest group at 36 percent. Cheddi Jagan came from East Indian stock.

Sugar and rice were Guyana's main products. The country had a classic plantation economy, with large British corporations controlling most of the production, and plantation workers poorly paid and restive. Their energy fueled Guyanese politics. Born in 1918, the eldest of eleven children of a cane cutter, then a driver, from a village outside the capital, Georgetown, Cheddi Jagan saw the depredations of Big Sugar through his father's eyes. Cheddi graduated from Northwestern University in the United States and became a dentist. He used his income to put other family members through college. Attracted even then to progressive causes, Cheddi met Janet Rosenberg at a political event in Chicago. In 1943 they married. Once a member of the Young Communist League, Janet Jagan had, if anything, stronger views than Cheddi's. When the Jagans returned to Guyana they thought themselves destined to organize the workers. In 1947 Cheddi Jagan won election to a consultative council advising the British governor. Three years later he and Janet were founders of the People's Progressive Party (PPP), the first mass political party in the country and for a time the multiracial exponent of Guyanese nationalism.

Cheddi Jagan campaigned constantly for better working conditions and wage increases from the Sugar Producers Association, representing the corporations that controlled the plantations. The corporations' efforts to keep Jagan off their plantations only increased his appeal to the workers.

Great Britain, committed to fostering self-government in Guyana, in 1953 permitted an election for an assembly and cabinet. British officials convinced themselves during this early period that Cheddi Jagan was a Communist. When he won, Jagan formed a government; Janet Jagan, also elected, became deputy speaker in the assembly. Cheddi argued that British measures were insufficient and pressed for full autonomy. After barely four months in office, the British dismissed Jagan's cabinet and in 1954 imprisoned both Cheddi and Janet for half a year. That merely increased their popularity.

British hopes of dampening Guyanese sympathy for Cheddi Jagan hinged on creating alternative political movements. One materialized in 1955 when Forbes Burnham, another founder of the People's Progressive Party and its former vice chairman, formed a new People's National Congress (PNC). The PNC drew mostly African Guyanese support and ended the former PPP monopoly. In new elections in 1957, however, Jagan's party won the most votes and returned him to the cabinet, though not as prime minister. Business interests formed another political party in 1960, the United Front (UF), but this stood primarily for minority Portuguese and had little chance for electoral success.

The next election occurred in August 1961. Washington wanted to employ the CIA to forestall a Jagan victory. By now the British were less convinced that Cheddi Jagan was a political extremist and acquiesced in his participation. In late May, U.S. officials met with the British to agree on a program of action, but London refused either a joint operation or unilateral American action. Kennedy's secretary of state, Dean Rusk, wrote to his British colleague Lord Hume, "We are not inclined to give people like Jagan the same benefit of doubt which was given two or three years ago to Castro." The British foreign secretary replied that any action would only make things worse, that London had no grounds to resume direct rule as it had done in 1953, and that Jagan had not been so difficult since his return to government in 1957. In the 1961 election the PPP won eighteen of the twenty-four seats in the assembly; there was now no alternative to Cheddi Jagan's becoming prime minister.

In writing about not giving the Guyanese leader any benefit of the doubt, Dean Rusk referred subtly to a CIA initiative. In August 1961, within days of the election, the State Department sent President Kennedy a proposal that involved two tracks: open cooperation with the Guyanese in hopes of inducing Prime Minister Jagan to align with the West, but a CIA covert political action against Jagan if he did not. Director of Central Intelligence Allen Dulles figured prominently in the group who hammered out this strategy. At this early stage, Arthur Schlesinger actually helped keep the CIA out of the act, objecting that the covert initiative could easily get in the way of the overt policy of assistance. President Kennedy sided with Schlesinger.

A second round of talks with the British took place in London in early September. Ambassador David Bruce led the American team, with CIA, technical assistance, and State Department officers to help. Among them sat William C. Burdett, Washington's point man on Guyana policy. The CIA's senior officer in London at the time, station chief Frank G. Wisner, the agency's former director of operations, also participated. Bruce received instructions to minimize the importance of the covert track if necessary, telling the British the project was only a plan, that any specific move would be subject to high-level U.S. consideration—but to get British approval. Secretary Rusk told Bruce, "We should keep in mind [the] possibility Jagan is [a] Communist-controlled 'sleeper' who will move to establish Castro or Communist regime upon independence." The British again rejected a secret operation.

Arthur Schlesinger saw Dean Rusk's cable to Ambassador Bruce and objected—the term "sleeper" had very specific meaning in the spy business, he told one of Rusk's top aides, and no one, Schlesinger noted, had suggested that Cheddi Jagan was a disciplined agent or pretending to be someone else.

Prime Minister Jagan, perfectly aware that American officials viewed him with suspicion, knew Guyana needed foreign aid. Jagan sought a meeting with Kennedy to plead his case directly. He traveled to Washington and saw JFK in the Oval Office on October 25, seeking to allay U.S. fears. Cheddi Jagan described himself as a socialist who believed in state planning but political freedom for all Guyanese. Then Jagan made his pitch for aid. Kennedy avoided talk of dollar numbers. The American record notes that Jagan "was evasive on all ideological and doctrinal issues." In his biography of Kennedy, Schlesinger adds that Jagan made a serious *faux pas*, saying he admired the Marxist journal *Monthly Review*, and further raised JFK's hackles with a television appearance in which he refused to criticize the Soviet Union, leaving "an impression of either wooliness or fellow-travelling."

In the wake of Cheddi's visit there would be no new help for his country. The policy of overt cooperation languished until January 1962, when President Kennedy ordered the State Department to send a survey mission to Guyana to prepare an expanded technical assistance effort, an extension of a program begun under President Dwight D. Eisenhower. But Kennedy took no action on another initiative, a road-building project that represented by far the largest element of contemplated U.S. aid.

A month later violent riots erupted in Georgetown. Starved of funds, Jagan's government had proposed tax increases plus tight spending controls. Protests ensued. A general strike began on February 12, degenerating into vandalism and looting. Four days later, when police fired on rioters, killing two, all hell broke loose. The situation assumed a racial character as rioters aimed at stores owned by East Indians in the center of Georgetown, while the opposition parties and those trade unions that catered to the African population maneuvered to take advantage. Jagan could have mobilized East Indian laborers from the plantations to fight the brawlers but instead asked the British governor for security assistance. London deployed a battalion of troops, some flown from Jamaica, about half direct from the United Kingdom, reinforcing the company normally on duty in Guyana.

From the prime minister's residence, Red House, a beautiful nineteenth-century structure in the colonial style, Jagan could see the devastation. Whole blocks of downtown Georgetown burned to the ground. Jagan later told a British diplomat, as relayed to the Americans, that he thought leaders of the United force and CIA officers had fomented the riots. Prime Minister Jagan asked for a United Nations inquiry but ultimately settled for an investigation by British Commonwealth officials.

Jagan's charges that the CIA fomented the 1962 riots have been widely repeated but on balance should be rejected. Over the succeeding weeks assurances were given—by the CIA to President Kennedy, by the State Department to other officials, and by the United States to Great Britain—that the spooks had had nothing to do with this tragedy. It is suggestive that Edward Lansdale, a political action expert monitoring CIA operations simultaneously under way against Cuba, asked agency officers a few months later why they figured they could provoke a general strike in Cuba when the CIA itself admitted its inability to carry off labor actions elsewhere in Latin America. The CIA had some influence over Guyanese trade unions as a result of its early work in this area (about which more in a moment) and had given a little money to anti-Jagan unions, but the covert action project for Guyana had yet to be approved and there is no other indication of U.S. activity at this time.

What *is* true is that U.S. officials used the Georgetown riots as an excuse to write off Cheddi Jagan. On February 19, with smoke still rising from the ruins in Georgetown, Dean Rusk sent a strong demarche to the British foreign secretary declaring it "mandatory" that "we concert on remedial steps." Rusk thundered, "I must tell you now that I have reached the conclusion that it is not possible for us to put up with an independent British Guiana under Jagan." Rusk saw the Guyanese leader as espousing a "Marxist-Leninist policy" paralleling Castro's. Ominously, Rusk ended, "It seems to me clear that new elections should now be scheduled, and I hope we can agree that Jagan should not be allowed to accede to power again."

There remained dissenting voices within the Kennedy administration, however. One was Adlai E. Stevenson, Washington's ambassador to the United Nations. When Stevenson learned of the Rusk letter to Lord Home he wrote the secretary—and sent a copy to JFK—that British stalling on Guyanese independence would simply strengthen Jagan. American involvement would be impossible to conceal over time, Stevenson argued, while disclosure would substantially damage the U.S. position in Latin America and its carefully nurtured reputation for anti-colonialism. What was more, "the damaging effect of such disclosure would be magnified if the U.S. involvement were of the character which might be inferred from the last sentence of your letter." Stevenson ended by asking to be briefed on CIA plans for Guyana.

Lord Alec Hume was no more persuaded. The foreign secretary's reply to Rusk declared that Great Britain would not go back upon its course of bringing the colonies to independence, and certainly could not gain from failing to pursue that course in the single case of Guyana. Hume met Rusk's declaration head on: "You say that it is not possible for you 'to put up with an independent British Guiana under Jagan' and that 'Jagan should not accede to power again.' How would you suggest that this can be done in a democracy?"

Even within the CIA there were sometimes less hysterical voices. Participants at the CIA director's morning staff meeting on February 26 listened as officials reported three Cuban merchant vessels en route to Guyana laden with weapons. Within a day CIA analysts were able to prove the report false. No evidence of Cuban arms shipments anywhere in Latin America would emerge for another year.

At the White House, Arthur Schlesinger warned JFK that both the CIA and the State Department had the notion that the president had made a firm decision to get rid of Jagan. On March 8, 1962, President Kennedy signed a directive, a National Security Action Memorandum (NSAM), explicitly stating that no final decision would be taken on Guyana policy until after a British survey mission, conversations with London, and answers to Kennedy's specific questions. The NSAM was unusual in that the White House addressed it directly to CIA Director John McCone, Rusk, and so on, not as a single document circulated to the entire top level of the U.S. bureaucracy. It was also striking in that where NSAMs typically ordered action, this one mandated inaction. Also, many Kennedy-era NSAMs were signed in his name by national security adviser McGeorge Bundy, but the president signed this one himself.

A week later Secretary Rusk talked with the British in Geneva. In his report Rusk noted that London did not exclude action but was not willing to go down that road until overt possibilities were exhausted. "For [the] present," Rusk admitted, "I do not believe covert action with or without [the] British is indicated." Rusk ended by asking the department to use diplomatic channels to ask the CIA's Frank Wisner to desist for the time being.

One thing President Kennedy demanded as a prerequisite for his decision had been an analysis of the possibilities and limitations of action. On March 15 the State Department completed an extensive policy paper. Its third option specified "a program designed to bring about the removal of Cheddi Jagan." Analysis in the paper indicates the project clearly envisioned "covert U.S. political action" and that British acquiescence (at a minimum) would be necessary. State recognized negative factors, conceding Adlai Stevenson's point that the United States must be prepared to pay heavily in world public opinion "if evidence were presented showing any U.S. covert activities." Even without such evidence, Russia and Cuba could be expected to make the most of allusions to earlier CIA operations in Latin America to diminish U.S. "credibility as a supporter of the principle of nonintervention."

The Guyana paper framed Anglo-American conversations in Washington, where the British survey mission reported its results. At the March 17 meeting, Deputy Undersecretary of State U. Alexis Johnson took pains to say the United States feared chaos and a Communist government, insisting on the need to work closely to avert catastrophe—code words to convince London to acquiesce in U.S. action if not rise to the occasion themselves. Reprising Dean Rusk's cautions of a month earlier, Johnson indicated that Washington saw Cheddi Jagan in the same light as Fidel Castro, saying, "We do not intend to be taken in twice." The British, on the other hand, reported that Guyana's large sugar corporations were not worried and mentioned that two of the biggest had no wish to become involved politically. One, the Bookers Group, "probably considered Jagan to be the best leader of the lot."

The State paper and the Washington talks became the basis for the deliberations of a shadowy unit called the Special Group, the highest U.S. government unit dealing with covert operations. When the Special Group met on March 20, Guyana was the third item on its agenda. The Group refined a CIA project proposal next sent to the British.

London's resistance to covert action weakened over time. When President Kennedy and Prime Minister Harold Macmillan met in May 1962, the British agreed to special arrangements for consultations with Washington on Guyana. At informal secret talks the Americans presented their action program. Macmillan still rejected the most energetic measures but decided he could abide some CIA efforts to manipulate Guyanese politics. By June, Arthur Schlesinger had told President Kennedy that "an independent British Guiana under Burnham (*if* Burnham will commit himself to a multiracial policy) would cause us many fewer problems than an independent British Guiana under Jagan."

Schlesinger intended his policy advice to guide Kennedy's decision on the covert action that Washington spooks advocated. The Central Intelligence Agency carried out many kinds of activities. Ones that aimed to influence the domestic affairs of other states were known as "political action." The Guyana project would be a political action. A variety of tactics might contribute to this kind of operation. The most obvious was to recruit—usually for pay—persons of influence in the target nation. Such opinion makers could include politicians, businessmen, labor leaders, and journalists—especially the latter two: labor leaders because they could put bodies in the street on demand, journalists because their stories in the print or broadcast media could sway people's beliefs. Barrages of such press coverage could be targeted to shape opinion, and if intelligence operatives had good enough connections, they could concoct the stories themselves, taking CIA's carefully crafted lines of argument and drumming them in by repetition. Judicious dollops of CIA money could help form or advance political parties and finance candidates at election time.

When subjects were aware of the role of American intelligence, they could be said to be "witting." Unwitting persons were those deliberately kept in the dark about the CIA role in what they were being asked to do. American intelligence operatives could pretend to be of other nationalities—a "false-flag" approach. But even if they revealed their true colors they would usually not identify themselves as CIA officers—they would be under "cover." The CIA command center in any country was called a "station," located within the U.S. embassy and headed by a station chief. An important station, or one with far-flung activities, would direct "bases" in other places within the country. Stations were typically staffed by officers under "light" cover—people supposed to be diplomats, commercial officials, or military rather than spies. Even deeper cover, undercover, were officers who pretended to have no connection with the U.S. government whatsoever. These persons were under "nonofficial cover." The Guyana operation would be conducted primarily by officers under nonofficial cover. The persons they recruited, agents or assets, evidently were mostly aware of the CIA origins of the plots they were carrying out. Agents were always left unwitting of CIA purposes, of course, but in a political action like Guyana, over time these became rather transparent.

The object was, as Arthur Schlesinger put it, to ensure that the government of an independent Guyana took the coloration that Washington desired, right down to who was in charge of it. To make that happen the CIA used agents of influence to create propaganda and place news that it wanted, labor agents to produce a visible opposition, and political agents to oppose those who the CIA decided were enemies of its desired outcome. Guyana would be a full-spectrum political action.

The Central Intelligence Agency suffered through tumult even as it began to focus on Guyana, for these were the months after its disastrous Bay of Pigs invasion of Cuba. There had been investigations, postmortems, a National Security Council policy review—every kind of inquiry. A generation of CIA leadership had been swept away, except, oddly enough, the agency's Western Hemisphere chief, the man who would have ultimate command of the Guyana project. Col. Joseph Caldwell King would be the go-to guy. King had spent his entire career in Latin America, doing studies on the Amazon water basin for Nelson D. Rockefeller before and into World War II, as an entrepreneur, and as a special agent of the U.S. Federal Bureau of Investigation. As entrepreneur, spurning contrary advice, King had opened a condom factory in ultra-Catholic Brazil, and made a considerable profit. Later he sold the plant to Johnson & Johnson and acquired stock that became ever more valuable as the company's stake in Latin America mushroomed. King became its vice president, selling in Argentina and Brazil. His military rank seems to have been honorific. In the early postwar period, when the FBI had been in charge of intelligence on Latin America, King joined the Bureau. In the late forties that role had been taken over by the new CIA, and King transferred to the agency. He soon became chief of its Western Hemisphere Division. When the agency overthrew the government of Guatemala in 1954, King was there. Wags called him "Jesus Christ," and he styled himself "JC," perhaps to assuage his anxiety at showing poorly next to the corps of Ivy Leaguers who dominated the CIA. King presided over the early part of the U.S. imbroglio in Cuba, when in fact the United States had been "taken in" the first time, as the Kennedy people kept telling the British. King escaped blame for the Bay of Pigs because it had been managed at a level above his pay grade, leaving him out of the loop. Some recall that officials feared his strongly conservative politics might skew the project. The Colonel had nonetheless been an advocate for ousting Castro, and in 1962 he saw Guyana as an opportunity to build a wall against *fidelista* influence extended into South America.

King's branch chief for this venture, a capable lieutenant, was Virginia H. Hall Goillot, among the most senior women in CIA's clandestine service. She *had* to be at that time, an era exceedingly difficult for women at the agency. Hall had lost a leg in World War II, then parachuted into France to work with the resistance, her prosthesis strapped to her body. She won the Distinguished Service Cross for that. In 1950 she married Paul Goillot, an OSS comrade with the resistance. She joined the CIA in 1951, originally as a branch officer for Western Europe, designing stay-behind networks for France. On the paramilitary staff in 1954 she too had worked on the Guatemala operation and had gone on to plan projects for Southeast Asia. Despite her experience and her medals, the legendary Hall had needed eleven years to obtain a one-level promotion to field grade. For the Guyana project she would have an important role.

On Guyana, Hall wrestled with the need to build capabilities inside the country. In early 1962 the CIA had no station in Georgetown and lacked direct contact with Jagan's opponent, Forbes Burnham. Hall recruited a Guyanese psychiatrist whose brother was an aide to Burnham. She sent CIA officer Joseph B. Smith to Barbados one weekend that February to meet the agent and his brother. Smith instructed the aide in tradecraft, including secret writing skills that Burnham's assistant could use to pass information. The Burnham link was made.

For this project there could be no question of resorting to a quasi-military operation or mounting a coup d'état. Guyana had no armed forces to draw into the game, and Cheddi Jagan's popularity remained such that, even after the Georgetown riots, no possibility existed for armed resistance, which in any case the British army would be bound to fight. The broad strategy was evident from the beginning: require an election, carry out a political maneuver to reduce Jagan's chances, then do everything possible to influence the outcome. The CIA had appropriate resources, including labor and international organizations. These took the lead in the scheme.

The Directorate for Operations* controlled the CIA's clandestine service and had the twin missions of espionage and covert operations. The Western Hemisphere Division and J. C. King worked for the Directorate for Operations (DO). So did the Covert Action Staff, locus of the agency's political warfare experts and its labor activists. By early 1962 the DO had a new boss, as did the CIA itself. The deputy director for operations, a professional intelligence officer, was Richard M. Helms, also not tarred by the Bay of Pigs because he had been careful to stay out of it. At one of their first meetings, new CIA director John McCone told Helms he would be the "man for Cuba." Because Cuba, by then seen as a dangerous exporter of revolution throughout Latin America, monopolized CIA effort, McCone's remark became shorthand for special attention to the hemisphere. Helms readily conceded that Central America and the Caribbean had been neglected ever since the creation of the agency. The demand for a Guyana covert action lay squarely within that framework, alongside a more ambitious project pursued directly against Cuba. These were among Helms's first projects as director of the DO.

Planning for Guyana depended upon a fresh Special National Intelligence Estimate (SNIE) prepared by CIA analysts in April 1962. This study looked at the Georgetown riots and concluded that racial conflict was likely to continue as the basic factor in Guyanese politics. That offered DO operators an obvious cleavage to exploit. The British were not about to resume direct rule, which estimators projected

---

* Created in 1951, this part of the CIA was known until 1973 as the Directorate for Plans in order to disguise its true function. Further, the unit's abbreviation followed the job title of its chief, the deputy director for plans (DDP). In 1973 this unit was retitled the Directorate for Operations (DO), the identity it retains today, and is headed by the CIA's deputy director for operations. To avoid confusion in this book, this element of the CIA will be called the Directorate for Operations throughout.

might triple their expenditures for the Commonwealth country. The analysis found L. Forbes Burnham, leader of the opposition PNC party, to be an "advocate of extremist measures in government." Jagan himself could *not* be determined to be a Marxist, and the SNIE assessed he would probably follow a policy of nonalignment in a postindependent Guyana. Both conclusions flew in the face of Washington's rationale for this operation, and both attracted little attention. Also ignored were the SNIE's warnings about Burnham's leadership weaknesses and the potential dangers of a government under his control. But the judgment that Burnham's party had "virtually no following" other than among "Negro ranks" held key importance. In the 1961 elections Burnham had polled 41 percent of the votes.

From an operational viewpoint the problem was to increase Burnham's attractiveness, cooperate with third-party movements such as the United Front, induce them into coalition with his PNC, and thus create possibilities for overcoming Jagan's popularity among the majority East Indian population. A measure that could substantially improve this picture would be to persuade the British to create an electoral system based upon proportional representation, in which minority votes in districts that would otherwise be won by Jagan's PPP would still count toward seating the opposition.

In June 1962 the Directorate for Operations hatched a plan. A CIA memorandum to the Special Group and the NSC staff director for intelligence, William H. Brubeck, summarized the concept. Aide Arthur Schlesinger, favorably impressed with Burnham on a Washington visit in May, told JFK in a June 21 memo, a week after the CIA paper, "I agree that the evidence shows increasingly that Jagan's heart is with the Communist world." On July 12 Dean Rusk recommended a program to Kennedy premised on the Jagan-as-Communist thesis.

In a covering note forwarding Rusk's memo, plus intelligence reports to the president, national security adviser McGeorge Bundy commented that a case against supporting Jagan existed, but the proposed tactics were murkier. "In particular," Bundy noted, "I think it is unproven that the CIA knows how to manipulate an election in British Guiana without a backfire." Schlesinger too joined the chorus, telling JFK the plan made him nervous, especially with prospects rated at less than fifty-fifty, asking, "Does CIA think they can carry out a really *covert* operation—i.e., an operation which, whatever suspicions Jagan might have, will leave no visible traces which he can cite before the world, whether he wins or loses, as evidence of U.S. intervention?" John McCone answered in a short paper on July 20, satisfying President Kennedy. Resistance evaporated.

But the British hurdle had yet to be surmounted. Kennedy met British ambassador Sir David Ormsby-Gore at Hyannis, Massachusetts, on July 21 and 22. He raised the Guyana question, telling the Crown's representative he wanted to know if Britain envisaged new elections, which "would provide opportunity for [a] government of different complexion to come to power through democratic process." On July 25 CIA director John McCone saw the President's Foreign Intelligence Advisory Board for a general review of the agency's covert financial support to political parties. McCone not only touched on the CIA's thoughts regarding Guyana, immediately afterward he discussed CIA labor operations and their relationship to American union groups, which would furnish the shock troops for the Guyana project.

Meanwhile Mac Bundy followed up Kennedy's sally with his own British counterpart, cabinet secretary Lord Hood, on August 6. Bundy emphasized urgency and warned against bogging down in endless talks. Kennedy accepted a proposal for a team of four officers from Britain's Secret Intelligence Service (SIS) to come to Washington a week later. On August 8 CIA's Helms and State's Alex Johnson agreed to bring matters to a head, forcing consideration of Guyanese political factors. Great Britain ultimately accepted the CIA project proposal and consented to provide SIS support.

London's most important contribution came in the fall of 1962 when the British set the date for a preindependence election in Guyana, later inducing the political parties to accept a formula for proportional representation in the national assembly. This improved Washington's odds for a favorable outcome. When NSC staffer Carl Kaysen told Mac Bundy the latest news on October 5, he noted about Guyana, "I think you know about the most interesting development here."

Now it was up to the CIA and SIS to get the ball rolling. The agency had long-standing ties to the American Federation of Labor (AFL), had played a central role in the 1949 creation of the International Confederation of Free Trade Unions (ICFTU), the Inter-American Regional Labor Organization (*Organización regional inter-Americano de trajabadores* or ORIT) in 1951, and the AFL's American Institute for Free Labor Development (AIFLD). During the fifties ORIT had been the most active in Guyana, encouraging that land's Trades Union Council to follow an anti-Communist line. But something more was needed. The ICFTU had a London-based affiliate, a secretariat for unions of government workers called the Public Services International (PSI). From 1958 the CIA had also had a relationship with the American Federal of State, County and Municipal Employees (AFSCME), the PSI's U.S. member, and the following year AFSCME set up a Latin American office for PSI. That unit became the cover for, and was headed by, CIA officer William H. McCabe, who liked to hand out cigarette lighters bearing the PSI logo and had photos of himself distributing food to Latin American peasants. McCabe had three years invested in labor work in Latin America, including in Guyana, where the CIA tried to sustain the labor unions opposed to Jagan. McCabe had been in Georgetown throughout the 1962 riots. Those who wondered at his apparent lack of union background were told McCabe was a PSI favorite. The PSI began offering advice to the Guyanese Trades Union Council, headed by East Indian Richard Ishmael, attendee of an AIFLD training course in Front Royal, Virginia. As a percentage of unionists, in the years before these events more Guyanese went through the AIFLD program—which included lectures on the dangers of communism—than citizens of any other Latin American nation.

With the British-mandated elections still far in the future, the CIA and SIS could build their project patiently. Records indicate expenditures for Guyana began in November 1962. That coincides with a program begun by AIFLD to build more than five hundred houses for Ishmael's Trades Union Council at a cost of $2 million. The agency's progress report circulated in mid-January 1963. Sending this to Kennedy for his weekend reading on January 26, Mac Bundy noted, in his precise handwriting, "It moves, moderately." Consular representatives reported that Jagan had the upper hand. But Burnham's party conducted almost no organizational activity.

Efforts to discredit Jagan included the United Front surfacing a document, the text of his "secret address" to a 1956 party conference. In the speech Jagan denounced associates just as Khrushchev had done in his secret talk to a Soviet party congress that year. The maneuver was designed to characterize Jagan as a Stalinist. Dissension among the ranks pleased the CIA and the United Front. At the international level the United States and the British acted to complicate economic difficulties by closing markets for Guyanese exports, primarily rice. By April 1963 Jagan's financial distress had become so serious that he wrote to Kennedy asking about the U.S. aid (promised as early as 1958) for road, drainage, and irrigation projects.

On April 15 Cord Meyer, responsible for CIA labor operations, briefed the President's Foreign Intelligence Advisory Board, including Guyana among his subjects. The centerpiece would be the general strike begun by the Trades Union Council with CIA support. Triggered by Jagan's introduction of a labor bill that would have given the government some powers over the unions, the strike continued for eighty days and became the biggest in Guyanese history.

Prime Minister Jagan calculated that the Trades Union Council would exhaust its strike fund in a month, after which the government could have its way. But Richard Ishmael met secretly with AFL-CIO officials, almost certainly including William McCabe, before declaring the strike. The foreigners promised help. The historians Robert Waters and Gordon Daniels have uncovered a sheaf of cables from McCabe and others reporting in great detail, and AIFLD paid salaries of eight Guyanese labor "interns" throughout the strike. The AFL-CIO alone spent $800,000. American documents reported by Waters and Daniels identify this as Operation Flypast.

Later investigations by British journalists concluded the CIA had furnished strike pay for the workers, distress funds, travel expenses for leaders, plus money for propaganda and a daily fifteen-minute radio broadcast. The agency funneled the money through the Gotham Foundation, which provided grants to AFSCME, McCabe's parent organization. Gene Meakins, a labor specialist, worked directly for the Trades Union Council, providing advice and editing radio scripts and a weekly newspaper. (Ex-agency officer Phillip Agee maintains that Meakins was a CIA man, though Meakins denies it. On the other hand, Meakins also claims that McCabe, well established as a CIA employee, had been nothing more than a dedicated labor organizer.) A CIA officer, perhaps Meakins, actually participated in talks between dockworkers and the government.

There were physical attacks on government officials, including Janet Jagan, minister of the interior. Richard Ishmael was identified in police reports as a member of a terror ring that plotted arson and bombings at government buildings (Forbes Burnham, also named in police reports, was acquitted when placed on trial). Troops of the elite British Coldstream Guards had to be called out to protect the unloading of Cuban freighters bearing food and a Russian merchant vessel loading export merchandise. Trying to maintain an image of evenhandedness, the British could not deny this assistance.

On June 21 President Kennedy reviewed the state of play. John McCone and Richard Helms attended for CIA, and Helms took notes. According to the notes, Helms opened with a briefing on the strike, commenting on Jagan's tough position with the Trades Union Council. Kennedy would provide aid to Guyana if it helped the CIA project, and anticipated another conversation with Prime Minister Macmillan. "It was clear," Helms wrote, "that the President regards British Guiana as the most important topic he has to discuss with the Prime Minister."

Dean Rusk flew to London in advance of the meeting, his goal to make clear that the British must not leave behind "a country with a Communist government in control," that London must unseat Jagan before independence. On June 30 Kennedy and Macmillan met at Birch Grove, England. Kennedy warned— twice—that the effect of having a Communist Guyana in addition to Cuba "would create irresistible pressures in the United States to strike militarily against Cuba."

This is astonishing. *Barely seven months after the Cuban Missile Crisis, which had brought the world close to nuclear war, a massive World War III between the United States and Russia, John Kennedy was threatening to start that war after all and place the onus for it on the British Crown.* The United States had made a public pledge not to invade Cuba as a consequence of the Missile Crisis. Aggressive overt action of this sort would reactivate the Russian guarantees to Castro that had made the crisis so dangerous. To do that on the excuse of the existence of the Jagan government in Guyana would have been both disproportionate and foolish.

The British could have seen through the subterfuge and turned Kennedy down. Instead they played straight, and the meeting concentrated on how to put a Forbes Burnham–led coalition in power. Intriguingly, William McCabe met with the Guyanese unionists within a day of the Kennedy-Macmillan decisions.

The first piece in the new maneuver was for London to provide that proportional representation would be the guiding formula in the upcoming Guyanese election. The British took that action in the fall of 1963. Cheddi Jagan's letter to Kennedy having gone unanswered, Jagan called in the American consul in Georgetown to say that he had seen Washington shift to a policy of "Jagan must go." The prime minister warned that his ouster could lead to a takeover by the extremists within his own party, saddling the United States with precisely the sort of Castroite situation it feared. Jagan then went to New York for the opening of the UN General Assembly and tried without success to meet with Ambassador Adlai Stevenson. No doubt Jagan understood the snub.

Meanwhile Washington conceived a fresh idea to dilute ethnic support for Jagan. In November, barely a week before President Kennedy's assassination in

Dallas, the State Department asked about the potential for a new East Indian–based political party, one different from Jagan's. The CIA replied on November 26 that the most suitable candidates to lead such a movement were reluctant to do so. In early December the agency followed up with a report that Burnham's PNC would favor such a party but do nothing to support it. If Great Britain resumed direct rule, there would be more scope for the new party. On December 6 Mac Bundy convened Helms and others and determined to pressure British and Canadian diplomats on the direct rule question. This endeavor failed.

In Georgetown, Jagan's People's Progressive Party saw its main chance in strong showings of public support. Continuing PPP marches and demonstrations coincided with the early 1964 Panamanian revolt against the U.S. authority in the Panama Canal Zone. That too led Washington to fear for the security of Guyana. Mac Bundy advised President Lyndon B. Johnson to tell the visiting British foreign secretary that he remained as concerned about Guyana as JFK had been. In February the Joint Chiefs of Staff reviewed U.S. contingency planning for military intervention in Guyana. The Chiefs expected that a battle group of ground troops could be inserted in twelve to twenty-seven hours, depending upon whether a situation involved no notice or a previous alert to U.S. forces.

By March pro-Jagan strikes had idled an estimated 30 percent of sugar plantation workers. The CIA reported Richard Ishmael's bitter complaints that his own organizers, with no protection, were unwilling to hold rallies. But on March 18 the CIA reported that Jagan's police were acting vigorously against intimidation and demonstrations. Violence increased again. By the end of April thirteen persons had died in strike-related incidents, most attributed to Jagan's PPP or its associated Guyana Agricultural Workers' Union. One of the dead was a British citizen.

Meanwhile the new-party initiative moved forward. On March 8 a group announced formation of a United Muslim Party. A week later came creation of the All-Indian League, an organization the CIA reported as "actually testing for support for the eventual formation of an anti-Jagan Hindu party." Agency undercover advisers were assigned to each party to encourage them to join forces. The CIA action achieved something of an undesired coup in early June when Forbes Burnham stood up in the assembly to propose a three-party coalition government. When the United Front refused to participate, the initiative collapsed (Jagan himself had made a counteroffer, not rejecting the proposal).

British authorities announced voting districts in mid-April, and voter registration took place in May. The CIA provided advice and support to the non-Jagan parties. In June the British monitor of the election certified the voter lists. The list for Georgetown contained fewer names (95 percent) than in the previous election. Other irregularities eventually turned up. There would be more absentee ballots cast by Guyanese overseas—votes more open to manipulation—than there were voters on the rolls.

Continuing violence frightened Guyanese and affected registrations. The CIA explored military training for some anti-Jagan activists and had a contingency plan to distribute arms. McGeorge Bundy approved it by telephone on May 7, a week after Helms proposed it. Caches of alleged PPP weapons were discovered by police, but it remains unclear whether this represented another CIA ploy. In late June, Jagan had to take his daughter out of school because of harassment from classmates. Five or ten homes were burning every day, and already sixty people had died. American diplomats in Georgetown believed that even troops could not now end the violence—they were too few and it was too widespread.

"No matter what I try to do," Cheddi Jagan told U.S. consul Delmar Carlson on May 25, "I can get nowhere. I am opposed by everyone, including the CIA which I suppose is the American Government. I laid my cards on the table to President Kennedy [in 1961], and he gave me to understand that he would help me but he didn't and I can only conclude that he was a liar or that he was influenced to change his decision."

The Guyanese leader made yet another bid for reconciliation. He called in Carlson several times over the last days of June. Jagan worried about Forbes Burnham.

"You don't know Burnham," Cheddi pleaded. "He'll cut my throat."

Prime Minister Jagan again suggested a coalition. He offered to sign an international treaty to neutralize Guyana in much the same fashion as Austria from 1945 to 1955. Jagan wanted to send an emissary to Washington to discuss the proposal, but his overture would not even be considered. The standard working group on Guyana convened at the State Department on June 30. It included Mac Bundy, Richard Helms from CIA, William R. Tyler of the State Department, and Bundy's special assistant, Gordon Chase. The officials agreed that "a dialogue with Jagan might conceivably cool down the . . . security problem" but doubted that Jagan would make important concessions. Washington rejected the approach in early July. In Georgetown, Carlson proved reluctant to inform Jagan. The same group plus additional officials, including NSC staff director for intelligence matters Peter Jessup, rejected an emissary again several weeks later. Finally Washington induced the *British* to tell the Guyanese that talks with the Americans had established that the United States saw no useful purpose in receiving an emissary.

The British themselves now pressed the issue of a national unity coalition of the three parties. When Gordon Chase approached him on the matter at the end of July, Mac Bundy returned the memo with his handwritten reply: "I'd stonewall for now."

When a Jagan political opponent came to Washington toward the end of August, Gordon Chase advised Bundy that to avoid the impression of being an American stooge, the Guyanese should not be accorded a meeting with the president.

By this time the British governor anticipated that even with proportional representation Cheddi Jagan's PPP might emerge with a small majority of the assembly. Washington told the British this would be unacceptable. By late August the CIA pronounced itself cautiously optimistic about the election, but in truth its political analysis fell short. A State-CIA meeting on Guyana took place on September 8, again optimistic. Several days later, with Desmond FitzGerald sitting in for the agency, this discussion continued. Bundy pressed for a contingency paper on measures if Jagan won. The CIA drafted a paper not long after, and Bundy discussed it with Helms and the State Department on September 17.

Meanwhile in Georgetown, after months of encouragement from CIA political action officers, Indian politician Balram Singh Rai decided to form a new Justice Party. For a month or so Rai appeared to do well, but then his effort sputtered to a halt. An internal document from Jagan's PPP, which the CIA acquired and reported late in August, declared that local elements hostile to the PPP had "secured international assistance in their efforts to overthrow the government," and that the "unity" of opposition forces "would not have availed were it not for U.S. intervention." The document recommended defusing such opposition elements as the Portuguese Roman Catholics plus overtures to the United States through Canada.

Forbes Burnham continued to plague all houses. He antagonized the British, remained in conflict with other opposition parties, and had a difficult time with the Americans as well. The U.S. consul in Georgetown reported to the Bundy-Helms-Tyler group on September 11 that he had tried to forge amicable relations with Burnham, but "it is tough to do so." Said the official, "Burnham, a racist and probably anti-white, remembers slights and repays them; at the same time, he takes advantage of people who treat him softly."

In short, by the fall of 1964, Cheddi Jagan had offered concessions, CIA's third-force movement had stalled, Burnham stood revealed as a treacherous ally, and the British worried that Jagan would win after all. Washington still had an opportunity to call off the CIA. It did not do so. Senior officials remained upbeat on the prospects for electoral victory.

Burnham campaign buttons produced in the United States and doubtless paid for by the agency now appeared in Georgetown. Gordon Chase told Mac Bundy that the CIA, "in a deniable and discreet way," had begun paying party workers. Violence escalated on all sides. A Justice Party station wagon was blown up, PNC meetings were fired upon, Jagan activists were roughed up or killed. In all, the campaign season brought with it almost 200 murders, a thousand persons injured, and about 15,000 people (more than 2,600 families) forced from their homes.

The December elections did not turn out as advertised. Cheddi Jagan won 47 percent of the vote, more than either the Americans or the British expected. Burnham trailed by almost thirteen thousand votes in spite of overseas ballots overwhelmingly favoring him. But because Jagan did not obtain an outright majority, a coalition would have to follow. The British governor simply refused Jagan the opportunity to put one together. A CIA officer elsewhere in South America noted in his diary on December 18, "a new victory for the station in British Guiana . . . largely due to CIA operations over the last five years to strengthen the anti-Jagan trade unions."

The British turned to Forbes Burnham to form the government. Burnham went on to rule like a dictator until he died in office, as racist and imperious as many had feared. Guyana's export industries of sugar, rice, and bauxite atrophied. By 1984 the wheel had come full circle and Burnham publicly accused Washington of trying to undermine his government by encouraging striking bauxite workers—shades of the CIA in 1963. Guyana did not have another free election until 1992. When it did, the nation elected Cheddi Jagan. Washington still had trouble coming up with a reasonable policy—Jagan had to reject an American nominated for ambassador who had been one of the labor leaders the CIA had arrayed against him. Ironically Cheddi Jagan would die in Washington, at Walter Reed Army Hospital in 1997, while still in office. Arthur Schlesinger said in retrospect, "We misunderstood the whole struggle down there. He wasn't a Communist. The British thought we were overreacting and indeed we were. The CIA decided that this was some great menace, and they got the bit between their teeth. But even if British Guiana had gone Communist, it's hard to see how it would be a threat."

The universe of covert operations only begins with political action. What the Central Intelligence Agency did in Guyana represents one kind of activity. Although the coordination and analysis of intelligence was the reason for the creation of the CIA, the agency derived its other identity—America's "Cold War agency"—from these covert projects. The political action in Guyana lay at about the halfway point on a spectrum from propaganda and influence peddling to violence (quasi-war), paramilitary operations, and support for military operations at the upper boundary. Many within the CIA and outside it saw covert operations as a third option between doing nothing and engaging in full-scale warfare. The story of covert operations is the saga of the third option, of these kinds of initiatives, though all cannot be treated in equal detail over the broad span of the CIA's history. The tale involves the men and women who made the operations happen; what was accomplished and what not; the impact of these activities on America's global quest for democracy—on its foreign policy, national security, and standing in the world; and the tension between the CIA's operations and the agency's accountability under a democratic form of government. This set of concerns will remain whether or not the Central Intelligence Agency survives as an entity in the post–September 11 world, because the perceived needs for and function of covert operations will continue.

Guyana was not the only CIA political action of its kind. Indeed it is among the least known. Of much greater renown is the agency's political action in Italy after World War II and over the decades afterward. There were many more such efforts. Political action involves all forms of activity that might contribute to a given outcome. Mechanisms include propaganda; subsidizing political parties, labor organizations, cultural groups, print and broadcast media, and other agents of influence; and sowing disinformation to discredit contrary messages. Political action may be viewed as the bread and butter of covert operations.

Some of these kinds of activities were also employed individually in long-term operations, such as the CIA's efforts to broadcast freedom, as it were, into Eastern Europe and the Soviet Union during much of the Cold War. Such efforts comprise the lowest end of the covert action spectrum.

Propaganda and psychological warfare remain at the heart of much that happens in political action. Often several of these types of projects are melded into a given operational initiative. The radio operations, for example, served a variety of different ends, simultaneously supporting various specific activities. At the global level, campaigns of several sorts may be in progress at the same time.

An intermediate form of initiative is the enlistment of officials or military officers in the target country to overthrow their government and install individuals more favorable to the covert actor. This fomenting of military coups d'état may involve aspects of political action as well as economic pressures and other more conventional foreign policy initiatives.

At the upper end of the spectrum are paramilitary operations, the use of armed force secretly supported by the covert actor to affect events in other nations. These operations may be full-scale wars and may also feature any or all of the other tools in the covert action kit. Paramilitary operations are the most significant variety of covert action and bear the greatest risks. Over time the character of this kind of activity has changed. Today the CIA often functions as a sort of middleman, or comprador, engaging the services of third parties, whether they be governments, security services, ethnic or political movements, or individuals. Military special operations forces have assumed increasing importance and supplanted the CIA in roles traditionally played by agency officers. The CIA nevertheless still supports these operations, as the next case study shows.

Purists might say that support of military operations is not paramilitary action, but the latter subsumes the former. Especially with the changing character of the world into the age of terrorism, military special operations have increasingly substituted for paramilitary action and must fall within the scope of this book. The growing predominance of nonstate actors today makes this element of the spectrum inescapable.

Other forms of activity have shaped covert action. Espionage provides key inputs for the secret warriors as, again, will be apparent from the next case. Intelligence analysis also provides guidance for operators. The CIA's "Great White Case Officer," Allen Dulles, once cited analysis as a check and balance on covert action. Strictly speaking this is not accurate, but the general point is that analysis establishes the dimensions of operational problems and indicates avenues of approach, as evident in the Guyana action. Parameters for covert activities are also set by congressional overseers in a process that has steadily grown more important.

Even at the lower end of the spectrum, covert action remains fraught with consequence for the peoples and nations involved. Covert operations have frequently involved transnational alliances with foreign intelligence services. These vital ties have proved critical in many instances, enough so that the saga of American covert operations provides a window on a number of companion intelligence services.

Time has transformed covert operations. Technological developments have changed the ways information moves, ideas are influenced, plans developed, spies operate. Devices have become more subtle, weapons more lethal, aircraft more capable, and so on. But there will always be room for error. The unanticipated, the unexpected event has great weight, the more so since the secrecy of these activities makes it difficult to apply conventional techniques when secret warriors get in trouble. That is what happened in the Iranian hostage rescue attempt of 1980.

The news came after the party broke up—in Georgia, near Fort Stewart, unwinding at the conclusion of a difficult military maneuver, one that certified the readiness of the recently created Special Forces Operational Detachment Delta. Modeled on an earlier maneuver conducted in the southwestern United States, Delta did so well it earned a commendation from the White House, which had monitored the entire affair. Delta's commander, Col. Charlie Beckwith, his top officers, FBI agents who had played terrorists in the drill, and CIA officers who had handled the intelligence side, celebrated over beers with Defense Intelligence Agency chief Gen. Samuel V. Wilson. After the liquor the group repaired to an all-night restaurant for a sumptuous breakfast. Beckwith finally stumbled into bed. He had hardly gotten to sleep when an aide phoned him—Iranian student radicals had taken over the U.S. embassy in Teheran, capturing the entire staff. It was November 4, 1979, the beginning of the Iranian hostage crisis.

Outside Washington another middle-of-the-night phone call awakened the director of the Central Intelligence Agency, Adm. Stansfield Turner. He was certain he was dreaming—Turner had gotten a similar call from the CIA duty officer seven months earlier when another Teheran demonstration had overrun the embassy. But this was no dream. In February the Iranian revolutionary government had ejected demonstrators and restored the embassy and the freedom of the U.S. diplomatic delegation. This time they did not. The former Shah of Iran had just been permitted to come to the United States for medical treatment, and tempers in Teheran were white hot. Admiral Turner went to CIA headquarters at Langley, Virginia, to prepare for a White House meeting. To his surprise, President Jimmy Carter waited a day before gathering his top officials in the White House Situation Room. After that three-hour skull session, national security adviser Zbigniew Brzezinski ordered preparations for a rescue mission.

Colonel Beckwith's unit would have the lead role. He sent his deputy, Maj. "Bucky" Burruss, plus a top planner to Washington to report to the Joint Chiefs of Staff (JCS). There they were told to obtain the latest information on the situation and present the concept for the mission. Moving a rescue force to Teheran posed obvious problems. The place lay far from any U.S. base, and a small American force would find it difficult to move among a teeming Iranian population, many of whom hated America as the "Great Satan."

At the White House, security adviser Brzezinski began holding daily sessions among top-level officials to deliberate on the proper course. For several months these continued without respite. Both he and President Carter kept close tabs on the progress of the rescue plan, which they kept out of the situation room brainstorming. Admiral Turner began every meeting by briefing the intelligence, then talk turned to diplomacy or coercion. After a week Turner noticed that certain officials stayed behind after the sessions and realized there were private discussions about what must be a rescue plan. Returning to his office on the seventh floor of CIA headquarters at Langley, Turner called Brzezinski, angrily objecting to being left out of the rescue planning, asking where the rescuers were going to get their intelligence if not from the CIA. Only then was the agency admitted to the inner sanctum of the rescue mission.

Neither JCS chairman Gen. David C. Jones nor Colonel Beckwith liked the initial plan. Both wanted more striking power. Delta had only 120 troopers. Yet every man and pound of equipment planners inserted to give the force more depth would have to be gotten to Teheran, where the hostages would have to be freed and evacuated. The constraints were tight indeed.

Just a week after the embassy seizure an air force special operations expert, Col. James H. Kyle, was summoned from his post in Albuquerque, New Mexico, to plan the air side of the mission, at first called Rice Bowl to suggest an Asian locale. Kyle became deputy commander of a joint task force cobbled together to carry out the operation under army Maj. Gen. James B. Vaught. Kyle thought Major Burruss, with his lock of unruly hair, looked like the cartoon character Dennis the Menace. Beckwith himself saw Burruss like the actor Robert Redford, handsome and rugged. Burruss emphasized that Delta needed to arrive in Teheran as a coherent unit, which ruled out any kind of parachute drop. A long-range helicopter flight soon emerged as the best option. Delta Force would furnish the muscle on the ground.

Colonel Beckwith moved his unit to a secure training ground, the same place used to marshal his earlier validation exercise. To execute this move secretly, Beckwith resorted to hiring rental cars.

President Jimmy Carter remained preoccupied with the hostages and the mission's success. The president's concern was well founded. An airline identified with the CIA had furnished the aircraft that flew the shah from Cairo to New York City. Although there were humanitarian reasons for Carter's action, the former Iranian dictator remained anathema to those who had become the new government of Iran. Brzezinski had conducted back-channel talks with moderate elements in the Teheran government, but the revelation of these contacts only added to the anger in Teheran. Among the consequences would be the demise of the moderate Iranian government and its replacement with one dominated by religious extremists.

The CIA had worries of its own. Even as controversy swirled over whether U.S. intelligence had failed to understand the revolutionary upheaval in Iran, the agency had the problem of the loss of its own people in Teheran as well as other official Americans and its offices, equipment, and records in the U.S. embassy. Beyond that the CIA faced the need to provide support for the rescue mission.

The agency had played a major role in the shah's Iran. Its station in Teheran when he fell had 125 persons assigned, a large contingent (though dwarfed by the 10,000 U.S. military personnel in Iran at the time). Americans had been evacuated, and only a tiny staff returned afterward. During the interval between the shah's fall and the embassy takeover, the CIA resorted to unusual tactics, using both official and undercover stations. The CIA station at the embassy, led by Thomas Ahearn, comprised just three operations officers and five persons overall. Howard Hart, with four agents, shuttled among CIA safe houses in Teheran, not so much a station as a clandestine network. Among their notable achievements was the exfiltration of "Raptor," a senior Iranian military officer, CIA's top spy in the shah's government. In the embassy takeover Ahearn and his people were captured, but Hart and his agents remained at large. They escaped and eventually turned up at agency headquarters where Hart became branch chief for Iran in the Near East Division of the Directorate for Operations.

Adm. Stansfield Turner, director of central intelligence under Carter, had a different headache in the form of six other Americans. Five of them, led by Consul General Robert Anders, had been in a building at the rear of the embassy when Iranian students began climbing the front wall, and had managed to escape. A sixth, agricultural attaché Lee Schatz, had an office outside the compound. These Americans took refuge at the Canadian embassy, shielded by Canadian ambassador Kenneth Taylor. Getting the six out of Iran posed critical questions for DCI Turner even as Ambassador Taylor and other brave Canadian diplomats hid the Americans in their homes. The Canadians offered to help in an escape attempt. In mid-December Turner approved participation by the Graphics and Authentication Branch of the CIA's Office of Technical Support, which had also been vital in the "Raptor" exfiltration. To test the difficulty of moving in and out of Teheran, branch chief Antonio J. Mendez carried out a covert operation of his own, creating a fake movie production company supposedly to film a motion picture in Iran. Others scouted out overland escape routes while Mendez focused on open travel through Teheran's Mehrabad airport. Even as Mendez set up his Hollywood company, "Studio Six Productions," his unit aided agency officers moving in and out of Teheran to prepare for the hostage rescue. Studio Six advertised in Hollywood trade publications, designed a logo, and solicited scripts (including one from Steven Spielberg) for a science fiction film set in the Middle East. Mehrabad, considered the quickest way out, became the route of choice, and Mendez and another officer flew into Teheran and prepared false passports for the escapees. They and their families left on January 28, 1980. To preclude reprisals, Ambassador Taylor left too, and Canada closed its embassy, evacuating all officials from Iran.

As final preparations for the escape proceeded, Admiral Turner reviewed the main rescue plan. Based upon seizing an airfield where helicopters could be refueled before heading to Teheran, the plan required holding that base for the duration of the mission, during which the Iranians might easily discover the operation and respond. Turner thought this far too risky and claims credit for the CIA in evolving the final rescue concept. Special operations experts advised simply landing in the Iranian desert to establish a refueling site and launching Rice Bowl from there. "Chuck Gilbert," a CIA aviation expert with extensive experience in Laos during the Southeast Asian war, spearheaded this effort. He had been assigned to the Iran task force as early as November 14. Within days the CIA had identified a site and prepared to fly a small aircraft into it to take soil samples that would establish whether the desert floor was hard enough to support the weight of all the participating aircraft. Turner ordered the plane pre-positioned at Rome and went to the White House, where he sold the concept to Carter and Brzezinski. The code name for the operation changed to Eagle Claw.

Intelligence remained a major sticking point. Special operations veterans of Eagle Claw condemn the intelligence as inferior and Turner as having been lukewarm at best. Turner disputes that. He later told Colonel Kyle that from the beginning of the crisis he spent most of his time on it. Charles G. Cogan, chief of the Near East Division, and Howard Hart would also have disputed complaints. The truth was, the CIA lacked sources in Teheran after the takeover, as Hart told the joint task force leaders. Creating fresh networks would be difficult.

Admiral Turner recalled former Teheran station chief George W. Cave from retirement to lead the advance team. Much of the work focused on trying to learn about Teheran from the outside, interviewing Iranians who had left or were traveling, combing their accounts for anything that would shed light on the hostages. In Rome, officer Floyd Paseman saw as many as a hundred Iranians a day to mine data. Out of all that he came up with just one who had real knowledge, developed during visits home, that could be used in the rescue mission.

Langley had reason to want the hostages freed—the Iranians had captured the CIA station in Teheran. They quickly identified Thomas Ahearn as its chief and kept him in solitary confinement. Although CIA records in Teheran had been evacuated when the shah fell, some were returned during the summer and fall, and new papers had gone into the files, which were supposed to have been destroyed or sent out after no more than three months. But they had accumulated anyway. When the embassy fell, station efforts to destroy its files were defeated by failure of a machine that reduced paper to pulp. Officers shredded documents, but the Iranian captors painstakingly reassembled them. They used these to single out William J. Daugherty, a case officer on his first tour, as another CIA person. Danger mounted daily.

The Iranians were an odd mix of student neophytes, fundamentalists, and anti-shah activists. Their slogans about the "Great Satan" were ubiquitous. Having captured sixty-six Americans in November, the Iranians released thirteen women and minority-group diplomats. But once the Iranians found Daugherty and charged two others, Malcolm Kalp and Phillip R. Ward, as CIA, the releases stopped.

By then Americans had begun actual rehearsals of Eagle Claw. Navy RH-53D helicopters were to be used for the movement, but these lacked sufficiently precise navigational gear, a failing remedied by the efforts of CIA's Chuck Gilbert. Marine pilots were to fly the craft because navy airmen lacked experience in long-distance flights over land. Delta Force, a separate unit of Rangers for airstrip security, and gasoline to fuel eight helicopters for their final stage of flight were to be delivered by MC-130 transport aircraft that met them at the remote desert site.

The site soon became known as Desert One. The copters would fly Delta to Desert Two, a staging base fifty miles from Teheran, then hide while the rescue took place. Colonel Beckwith and Delta Force would proceed into Teheran in trucks, free the hostages, escape in the helicopters to a third airfield to be taken over by U.S. Rangers, and the whole command would leave aboard MC-130s that returned to pick them up. Eagle Claw remained an extremely long-range mission, with the big MC-130s to fly from Egypt and the helicopters from the aircraft carrier *Nimitz* in the Indian Ocean.

The work in Iran to make all this feasible fell to the CIA. Admiral Turner's retiree, "Bob," was to be the inside man. Assisted by a fake identity crafted by Mendez's shop, Bob arrived in late December (the ease with which he transited through Mehrabad airport dictated the choice of that route for the Canadian exfiltration). Short, compact, and rugged-looking, Bob spoke a number of languages, though not Farsi, the language of Iran. He functioned effectively as a businessman starting a construction company. In meeting Colonel Beckwith, Bob's deliberate speech and mannerisms reminded the Delta commander of Anthony Quinn playing Zorba the Greek. Through Bob the CIA bought half a dozen English and two Mazda trucks and acquired a warehouse on the edge of Teheran to house them. The trucks were to be driven by Iranian agents the CIA recruited elsewhere and sent back home. One wealthy Iranian volunteer drove to Langley headquarters in a Mercedes but had no knowledge of the standard gearshifts of trucks and had to be trained stateside. Bob scouted out the Delta hide site (Desert Two) as well as the recovery airstrip to be used later. He left Teheran repeatedly to brief CIA officials in Rome or Athens. Bob personally advised Charlie Beckwith, but Beckwith wanted all the data rechecked by someone he trusted.

After the CIA rejected several Delta Force volunteers for a fresh Teheran scouting expedition, Maj. Richard Meadows asked for the assignment. Meadows became involved in the planning just a few days after the embassy seizure when Beckwith sent him to Washington to strengthen Delta's hand. A legendary Special Forces figure from the wars in Korea and Vietnam, Meadows now struck the CIA as an amateur with insufficient support and training—he could not master Portuguese for his cover identity. Admiral Turner, who saw the mission as a manifestation of distrust of the CIA, relented when Meadows threatened to go anyway. Strictly speaking, the Meadows mission was an egregious security error—he possessed detailed knowledge of the Eagle Claw plan. But Delta's previous lead candidate for the reconnaissance had been Major Burruss.

On March 10 Turner's deputy, Frank Carlucci, met task force chief General Vaught with the latest CIA data. There was also the problem of whether the Desert One strip, chosen from satellite photos, could bear the weight of the big MC-130s. That could only be verified on the spot. A reconnaissance mission would also install infrared runway lights that could be remotely activated to guide the aircraft landings. These were created by the CIA at the behest of Chuck Gilbert. At least three times JCS chairman Gen. David Jones, Admiral Turner, and security adviser Brzezinski appealed to President Carter to approve this preliminary mission.

At Camp David on March 22 the president received his first detailed briefing on the rescue plan. General Jones emphasized that Eagle Claw would be a highly complex operation. Carter preferred to await diplomatic developments but knew preparations were necessary. Stansfield Turner had pressed for permission to make the Desert One reconnaissance since January, and now Carter approved.

At Langley when he planned this expedition, Admiral Turner had been astonished to learn that his lead pilot, James Rhyne, had a peg leg, having lost one flying for the agency in Laos. Assured Rhyne was far and away the finest CIA airman, Turner scored this in the believe-it-or-not category and moved on. Copilot Bud McBroom was also a Southeast Asia veteran. They rendezvoused in Athens with air force Maj. John Carney and picked up a DeHavilland DH-6 Twin Otter modified for long range, taking it to Rome to load the CIA-designed strip lights. They went through Cairo and Masirah to Desert One, landing the night of March 31. Carney took soil samples and, aided by McBroom, installed the remote lighting. His worst problem would be orienting himself to the planned layout of the airstrip. While they were on the ground, no fewer than six vehicles drove past on the nearby highway. This was a bad omen. A second omen came at London's Heathrow airport while Carney waited with his samples for a Concorde flight home—two CIA officers appeared in the lounge and called out his real name, not his alias.

The scout mission confirmed that Desert One could be used. On April 7 President Carter held a meeting of the National Security Council. Secretary of State Cyrus Vance had opposed the foray for months, favoring UN mediation, but Carter brooked no further delay. The next day NSC staffer Gary Sick prepared a memo for Brzezinski picturing Eagle Claw as preferable to any other option. After a redraft, Brzezinski gave it to the president. As the exhausted Vance vacationed in Florida, Carter held a further NSC session on April 11 and approved the rescue. Vance demanded a hearing on his return. Unable to dissuade the president at their encounter, the secretary resigned effective after the Eagle Claw operation.

Meanwhile Major Meadows set out on the last-minute reconnaissance. He was given an Irish passport and identity as "Richard Keith." A Virginian, Meadows's Southern accent apparently struck the Iranians as Irish enough. He arrived in Teheran on April 21, three days before the scheduled start of Eagle Claw, just as Delta Force flew across the Atlantic to a staging base at Wadi Kena in southern Egypt. Meadows linked up with two Green Berets who had relatives in Teheran and were familiar with the region. They entered Iran separately and would be his drivers. There were tough moments, as when one of the men failed to stop at a roadblock and they had to talk their way past an enraged Iranian sergeant. But Meadows rechecked the Desert Two site, modified the planned hiding place, and used a satellite phone to tell Washington. At the last minute some workers showed up outside CIA's warehouse and began to dig up the street. Suitable bribes induced them to delay the work and fill the trench in again. The Iranian agent who had originally rented the garage now fled the country—a third bad omen.

The biggest question still remained—the exact location of the hostages. Just two days ahead of the operation, that was solved: the U.S. embassy chef, a Pakistani who had taught the Iranian occupiers to cook dishes suitable for the hostages, was suddenly allowed to leave the country. Flying out of Mehrabad, by chance the man sat next to a CIA undercover officer, who connected with him and got the cook to tell what he knew, instantly conveyed through CIA channels. Three hostages, including chargé d'affaires Bruce Laingen, were being held at the Iranian foreign ministry. The remaining fifty Americans were in the chancellery building in the U.S. compound. Howard Hart briefed the intelligence to Beckwith at Wadi Kena just four hours before Delta was to leave for Desert One. Hart was going on the rescue mission too.

Beckwith asked his air officer, the born-again Christian Maj. William Boykin, to say a prayer as troopers gathered. The blessing proved insufficient to overcome negative factors that determined the outcome. Despite the best efforts of CIA's Chuck Gilbert, who had gone with a senior airman to Diego Garcia and then to the *Nimitz* to check on the helicopters, one of the RH-53D choppers encountered navigational problems. Two more suffered mechanical failures in an intense dust storm during the flight to Desert One. There innocent Iranian passersby in a bus and trucks blundered into Delta on the ground, opening the door to a breach in Eagle Claw's security. Following the third helicopter abort, Colonel Beckwith considered that he no longer had enough ships to proceed. The joint task force commanders decided to terminate the operation. Then, in a horrible accident, one of the remaining choppers collided with an MC-130 aircraft. The fire that ensued, visible for miles in every direction, destroyed both craft and killed eight Americans. Losses would have been higher except for heroic efforts by several participants to save their comrades.

The hostage rescue had failed.

Iranian authorities quickly dispersed the American hostages, who would not again be together. Although Washington prepared plans for Operation Honey Bear, an expanded rescue mission, the Carter administration never again thought the intelligence good enough and did not overcome its uncertainties regarding a military special operation carried out at such long range. Meanwhile quiet negotiations with the Iranian government led to the release of the hostages on January 20, 1981, the day of Ronald Reagan's inauguration as President of the United States.

2

The Cold War Crucible

THE MEN IN THE YARD carried submachine guns. But they didn't threaten, just asked for food. The German farmer gave them some, and they left. No sooner were they gone than the farmer reported the incident to local authorities. The police at Wildenranna also received other reports of armed men in the woods along the Austrian border. Investigation quickly confirmed a band of some sort roaming the hills. Authorities at Wildenranna quickly asked central police headquarters at Passau to send reinforcements to help apprehend the intruders.

Thus began a dilemma for the Passau police command. The time was September 1947 in a Germany under occupation by the victorious Allied Powers. Passau lay in the American sector; police there reported to U.S. military officers. The news of an armed band north of the Inn River might signal some sort of aggressive move by the Russians. In any case German police were under standing orders: anything to do with foreign nationals belonged in the province of the Counter Intelligence Corps (CIC) of the U.S. Army. After a Passau police official telephoned American regional headquarters at Munich, the CIC decided to organize a manhunt in the hills. Agents drove to Waldkirchen and then fanned out toward the border, joining with German police who had, by now, also equipped themselves with submachine guns.

At three o'clock in the morning on September 10, one of the CIC search parties heard the voices of men in the forest. Soon they found the band, indeed a large group—almost forty men, sitting around a campfire, most of them singing. They wore Russian uniforms. American security officers carefully surrounded their camp and moved in.

The intruders put up no resistance. In fact they relaxed considerably when they learned the men apprehending them were Americans. Investigators discovered the band to be organized in military fashion. In addition to submachine guns the intruders had light machine guns and hand grenades. Like their uniforms, the equipment had been manufactured in the Soviet Union, and the men spoke what sounded like Russian. The strangers were disarmed and taken to Passau, then to a CIC base at Oberursel, outside Frankfurt. There the CIC brought in Russian intelligence specialists to work with the men. Thirty-five soldiers had been captured at the campsite. Four others, picked up in different places over the next few days, turned out to be from the same band. The U.S. Army put the affair under tight security.

The press reported some facts and more rumors. Even at this time, with Europe inured to displaced persons and prisoner exchanges between East and West, armed bands in Bavaria were uncommon enough to merit notice. A United Press reporter went to Passau a few days after and got a garbled version of the truth: the prisoners had told the CIC they were anti-Soviet partisans from the Ukraine. But speculation abounded: the captured men were Russian deserters; Polish guerrillas; or simply well-armed bandits. Ukrainian activists in the West, such as the pseudonymous Roman Rakhmanny in Canada, also sought access and got somewhat better information as, for that matter, did the Counter Intelligence Corps.

The CIC debriefed the men for more than three weeks. Interrogators satisfied themselves that the new arrivals were in fact Ukrainian partisans, their war against Russian forces still in progress in the Ukraine, Czechoslovakia, and southern Poland. The rebels provided considerable information about their movement, not to mention conditions in Eastern Europe. This intelligence CIC officers in Frankfurt worked into a report they circulated on October 5, 1947.

Under a leader named Khrin, reputedly one of the finest Ukrainian commanders, that spring the band had ambushed an armed convoy of Polish troops fighting alongside the Russians, killing the Polish vice minister of defense, General Karol Swierczewski. Later the Ukrainian Supreme Liberation Council had ordered Khrin's unit to make its way to the West in order to get the attention of the Allied intelligence services. Commander Khrin, wounded in both arms, did not make the long exodus, but his band succeeded in its mission.

Detailed information on anti-Soviet partisan activities in Eastern Europe struck the Americans as an intelligence windfall. Washington, however, saw the data as more than merely an opportunity to update its political perceptions of the Soviet Union. Instead, to some U.S. officials, the advent of the Ukrainian partisans signaled a chance for secret military action against Russia. The Ukrainian movement offered the opening for an offensive move in the Cold War, a classic covert operation along lines made familiar during World War II. The United States was just then creating a capability to engage in secret missions of all kinds, including covert operations.

Since that day in 1947, American secret wars have been carried out on almost every continent. These covert operations have involved tens of thousands of dead and wounded, thousands of native fighters, significant numbers of American clandestine agents, and even regular U.S. military forces. U.S. involvement has run the gamut from advice to arms, from support for invasions of independent nations to secret bombing in clandestine military operations; to the subsidizing of political parties, associations, or individuals; to the planting of misinformation by clandestine means.

The techniques for international coercion are not new, nor were they first developed by the United States. But American participation in World War II opened many eyes in Washington to the potential of special operations and provided a nucleus of personnel well versed in clandestine methods. The Cold War became the catalyst that brought methods and men together on missions that have been sometimes spectacular, often unfortunate, and occasionally surprising.

Early American intelligence officers benefited from the British example. During World War II the United States created an Office of Strategic Services (OSS) to perform all kinds of tasks. Under the irrepressible William J. "Wild Bill" Donovan, OSS functioned globally, with major commands in the Mediterranean, northern Europe, Burma, and China. OSS teams parachuted into France, Norway, the former Yugoslavia, and elsewhere; blew up bridges in the Balkans; worked with partisans in Italy; and led bands of tribesmen against the Japanese in Burma. The agency's psychological warfare experts crafted messages for enemy populations. OSS officers spied out the land and supplied incisive intelligence analyses to American commanders.

The U.S. military also acquired experience with secret operations during the war. Most often the military assisted operations, for example by covertly landing additional agents or supplies. The navy did this using submarines and PT boats, the air force with planes. The army actually ran guerrilla forces fighting the Japanese in the Philippines. The army and the Marine Corps established elite units for commando missions. The army's 5,307th Composite Unit, better known as Merrill's Marauders, played an important part in the Burma campaign, working closely with the OSS there. American psychological warfare units aimed to erode the morale of the enemy military.

The Burma campaign illustrates standard procedures for later secret wars in embryonic form. An OSS formation called Service Unit Detachment 101, sent to establish a base in India, began burrowing into areas occupied by the Japanese Empire. Agents from Detachment 101 infiltrated the Burmese hill country beginning in 1944, forged links with local Kachin tribesmen, and created a guerrilla movement against the Japanese. Weapons, supplies, and OSS officers parachuted into the jungle or were flown in by the planes of the "air commando groups" formed by the army air force. Radio broadcasts by Allied propaganda experts tried to spark hatred for Japan and hope for liberation by Allied forces working in tandem with the OSS and its brethren Allied agencies.

The OSS slowly built up the Kachin from local spy networks to roving patrols of fighters to organized guerrilla units. By 1944 the Kachin were fighting in conjunction with Merrill's Marauders and British Chindit brigades. More than ten thousand Kachin were fighting a year later, including a field force of seven battalions, each of almost five hundred fighters, led by the OSS. Legendary U.S. intelligence officers like Carl Eiffler and Joe Lazarsky got their starts in this very effort. Dozens of spies deep in the Japanese rear, plus about four hundred agents surveying nearby enemy positions, helped the Kachin units plan their missions. The Kachin in turn helped trap two powerful Japanese divisions during the final

Allied offensives in Burma, a brilliant climax to a very energetic campaign, the product of the efforts of just a few hundred Americans.

This became a remarkable achievement. Detachment 101 mobilized a military force more than thirty times its size, and used that capability to execute highly successful operations. Awarded a Presidential Unit Citation by the United States, the only OSS element so honored, Detachment 101 entered the lists of wartime legends.

Several features of the OSS tribal program are worth noting. Among them are the creation of formal units within the overall guerrilla force; the clearing of zones within the operating area to serve as local bases; the use of espionage nets to shield guerrillas and to find targets for them later; the use of outside bases for specialized training and major support; and the use of clandestine air supply and communication between local and outside bases. These techniques became essential features of secret warfare tactics. This type of clandestine operation came to be called paramilitary.

OSS also participated in the European theater under the patrician David K. E. Bruce. Teams assisted the escape of Allied airmen downed over the Continent, carried out commando raids, and cooperated with resistance fighters. One of the biggest OSS operations of the war came with the Normandy invasion of 1944. There the intelligence portion of the invasion plan, under the code name Sussex, called for special teams to be parachuted into France to supplement the resistance. The OSS, British Special Operations Executive (SOE), and French intelligence each contributed agents to form three-man "Jedburgh" teams sent to specific resistance networks. The Jedburghs parachuted in uniform but carried civilian clothes. They were backed up by Operational Groups, thirty-two-man strike teams for commando missions. More than five hundred OSS people went to the Continent in this campaign, including two future directors of the Central Intelligence Agency. Bill Colby led one of the ninety Jedburgh teams in France and later an Operational Group in Norway. William J. Casey masterminded the overall OSS effort to infiltrate Germany. There were also spy networks that produced other future CIA chieftains. In Switzerland the OSS nets were under Allen W. Dulles. Richard M. Helms spearheaded work in the Balkans. In later years Dulles and Helms also led the Central Intelligence Agency.

The European operations proved highly successful. The OSS alone had five hundred French and almost four hundred American agents in France by the time of the invasion. More than half the Americans with Jedburgh teams received decorations. Resistance operations are credited with slowing the German response to the Normandy landings and furnishing the Allies with vital intelligence. Casey's campaign got as many as two hundred agents directly into Germany, where they engaged almost entirely in espionage.

In addition to the OSS, the army's CIC had a parallel program on enemy territory through a much smaller network. This CIC activity had been under way since 1942. These army agents proved especially useful in Italy, where they helped identify Nazi efforts to penetrate pro-Allied Italian partisan groups.

World War II not only provided experience for the Americans, it formed and reinforced a certain way of thinking. The issues were black and white—to fight Hitler and Tojo, or not. Not to fight would have been an abdication of responsibility in the face of foreign aggression. Democracy hung in the balance against totalitarian dictatorship; President Franklin Delano Roosevelt made America the Arsenal of Democracy. After the war it became easy to transfer that Manichean hostility—and, for the intelligence types, their clandestine methods—to a newly perceived adversary. The target became the Soviet Union, or more formally, the Union of Soviet Socialist Republics—erstwhile ally recast as enemy due to ideological differences that had existed since the origins of that state in 1917.

This evolving hostility between the United States and the USSR did not matter at first. The surrender of Japan in August 1945 brought a scramble to demobilize the armies, one that extended to the intelligence service. The OSS had built up a strength of about thirteen thousand when President Harry Truman ordered its dissolution on September 20, 1945. Under the new arrangement, the parts of OSS that had dealt with analytical intelligence moved to the State Department. The detachments of clandestine officers went to the War Department as a new Strategic Services Unit (SSU) under Brig. Gen. John Magruder, the former OSS special warfare chief.

By early 1946 General Magruder's mandate—not so much to preserve or enlarge the SSU but mainly to liquidate it—had largely been accomplished. Former OSS officers who had served with the Jedburghs, the Kachin, and elsewhere went back to their homes, to law practices, to school, to the army. But Magruder also was responsible for producing fresh intelligence data. He and his deputies virtually begged army senior commanders to make use of their capabilities but were largely ignored. When Col. William W. Quinn took over the SSU in 1946, it had been reduced to fewer than two hundred persons working out of seven field stations in foreign countries.

In addition to the SSU, the army's Counter Intelligence Corps remained as a clandestine operations entity. Military Intelligence, or G-2, controlled the CIC. Given its role as the official intelligence branch of the army, G-2 was well situated to act in Eastern Europe and against the Soviet Union because of the army's presence in Germany, Austria, and Japan as part of the military occupation of those countries. The first American links with anti-Soviet Russian emigrés were forged by G-2. In a climate in which OSS verged on being dismantled, G-2 substituted for it and the CIC assumed a steadily more active role in what it called "positive intelligence" operations.

The 430th CIC Detachment, stationed in Austria, noted the shift in early 1947 when it recorded a change in emphasis from "denazification" to positive intelligence. In Austria the CIC operated "rat lines," clandestine transportation systems to spirit out of the country individuals of interest to U.S. intelligence. The CIC also had its own spy networks in Russian-occupied areas, including Austria, Czechoslovakia, and eastern Germany. It screened refugees, prepared cover stories to support its agents, and maintained relationships with other services. Al Ulmer, the SSU station chief for Vienna, had been with OSS. Once a new U.S. intelligence service emerged, the Central Intelligence Group, its first Vienna station chief, John H. Richardson, would be a former CIC man. Both were avid recruits for the Cold War crusade.

The same functions were carried out by the 970th (later the Sixty-sixth) CIC Detachment, with headquarters at Frankfurt in the American Occupation Zone of Germany. As agents this unit used certain notorious former Nazis in Germany such as Klaus Barbie. The shift in American priorities could be encapsulated in the life of netmaster Gordon Stewart, who headed the CIA station in 1948. A former OSS man, Stewart had come to Heidelberg to help in denazification but quickly began trolling Displaced Persons camps for sources to use against the Russians. He rode the rising wave of hostility to high office. A "Department of the Army Detachment," formed to handle interagency activities, eventually furnished cover for Stewart and his officers, who took over Barbie. It was the 970th CIC that handled the band of Ukrainian partisans.

On one level the partisans were identical to the masses of refugees, Displaced Persons (DPs), throughout Europe. By the fall of 1945 as many as seven million people were on the move, fleeing Soviet domination or driven from their homes by war damage. An equal number could be found in the Soviet Union or Russian-occupied Eastern Europe, and smaller numbers in the Mediterranean countries. Millions of former German soldiers joined the flow as they emerged from prisoner-of-war camps. Most were simply looking to settle somewhere safe, but many had nowhere to go and a major task for the United Nations during its early years was to house these DPs. Like the Ukrainian partisans, significant numbers of them came from lands swept by war and occupation and had information important to intelligence services, not least those of the United States. Screening DPs really meant identifying who was worth debriefing and, equally important, finding angry men and women who could be harnessed for clandestine missions. The Ukrainian partisans were prime candidates.

The Japanese attack on Pearl Harbor in 1941 that signaled U.S. entry into World War II had a fundamental influence on U.S. intelligence after the war. The assault had surprised American commanders. Investigations revealed a number of items that might have alerted leaders, but no one had been responsible for gathering and interpreting data at the national level. Thus Washington drew the lesson that the United States needed some sort of organization for intelligence, and it fell to President Harry Truman to work out the new schema.

Competing plans for a peacetime intelligence agency existed even before Truman abolished the OSS. Important issues dividing proponents of the various plans included the specific functions and degree of autonomy to be accorded such an agency. Truman's military advisers, the Joint Chiefs of Staff, favored an interagency group to supervise intelligence. The State Department proposed an arrangement that concerned only supervisory authority, which they wanted in the hands of the secretary of state. Members of the Office of Strategic Services proposed an independent agency but were not initially heeded.

Truman took part of the advice of his Joint Chiefs when on January 22, 1946, he issued a directive establishing a National Intelligence Authority (NIA) to oversee a Central Intelligence Group (CIG). The NIA, composed of the secretaries of state, war, and navy, plus Truman's personal representative, would monitor a director of central intelligence in charge of a CIG. Truman selected trusted individuals for both the DCI and his representative to the NIA, and he humorously referred to them as "personal snooper" and "director of centralized snooping." Truman's first DCI was Sidney W. Souers, a St. Louis businessman and presidential crony, proud of his reserve commission and his wartime service with naval intelligence. But Souers served only five months as director of central intelligence, though Truman convinced him to return as representative on the NIA and then the first executive secretary of the National Security Council. Army Chief of Staff Gen. Dwight D. Eisenhower recommended Charles H. Bonesteel, a top Pentagon planner, for the DCI job. Truman instead selected air force Lt. Gen. Hoyt S. Vandenberg. The president considered Vandenberg enough of a diplomat to get along with the State, War, and Navy departments.

Actually Vandenberg had been a combat commander, with minimal intelligence experience. But he was a good organizer and began to build the Central Intelligence Group. Under Souers, CIG had operated out of a suite of three rooms next door to the White House with fewer than 250 employees. Vandenberg soon established an office for research and evaluation plus administrative organs. In June 1946 he asked the National Intelligence Authority to give him responsibility for all U.S. foreign intelligence gathering, a preliminary to bringing the Strategic Services Unit back from the War Department. The proposal matched recommendations from an outside advisory group. Magruder's unit thus became the Office of Special Operations (OSO). By the close of 1946 there were about 800 officers in OSO alone, out of more than 1,800 total personnel in CIG. Between January and April 1947 the last holdouts, FBI agents in Latin America, transferred to the new intelligence group. General Vandenberg had plans to expand to several thousand officers over six months.

The peacetime intelligence agency grew quickly but remained a creation of the executive branch of government. The CIG had no basis in law. Already several bills dealing with intelligence matters had been proposed in Congress, and in 1946 the White House held discussions with CIG lawyers. Clark M. Clifford of the president's staff helped draft intelligence legislation. Vandenberg pushed for the bill and wanted Truman to announce creation of the agency in his 1947 State of the Union address. The president spoke to Clifford several times, expressing something close to outrage, though he went ahead with the initiative itself. Truman planned a reorganization of the entire military establishment, a proposal he sent to Congress in February 1947. Provision for the peacetime intelligence agency was included in the legislation, which became the National Security Act of 1947.

Through the 1947 law, Truman created a National Security Council to advise him on defense and foreign affairs. The separate War and Navy departments merged into a single Department of Defense, under which the air force also gained autonomy as an independent armed service. As for intelligence, the original proposal did no more than say that a Central Intelligence Agency would be formed. In the letter Truman sent to congressional leaders along with draft legislation, he did not even mention this aspect. Like the president, most congressmen concerned themselves mainly with parts of the bill unrelated to intelligence. Only late in congressional hearings did the intelligence initiative come up, and then attention centered on whether it would become some kind of secret police. Congressmen noted the lack of detail in the bill and amended it to prohibit the agency from possessing police powers.

Further amendments specified responsibilities for the new Central Intelligence Agency. Essentially Congress returned to Truman's January 1946 directive, extracting from it almost the exact language the president had used to assign functions. Under the National Security Act, the CIA was directly answerable to the president through the NSC. The law gave the CIA five duties: advising the NSC on intelligence; making recommendations on related matters; producing intelligence estimates and reports; performing "additional services of common concern" for the government-wide intelligence community; and "such other functions and duties related to intelligence affecting the national security as the National Security Council may from time to time direct."

This last provision has been said to convey legal authority for the conduct of secret warfare by the CIA. It should be noted, therefore, that the terms *covert operation, clandestine operation, paramilitary operation, secret operation*, and *special operation*, all euphemisms for secret warfare, appear nowhere in the law. Nor do the terms *political action, psychological warfare, propaganda, misinformation*, or *disinformation*. The phrase "such other functions" that appears in the 1947 act sought to cover unforeseen circumstances, but even there the legislative history of the law makes clear that Congress had not contemplated international coercion. The White House privately held a more expansive view. The "other functions" were purposely not specified but were expected to include covert operations. Clark Clifford notes of the language: "I reviewed this sentence carefully at the time, but could never have imagined that forty years later I would still be asked to testify before Congress as to its meaning and intent."

President Truman signed the legislation on July 26, 1947, and the National Security Act became law. Six weeks later, on September 8, the CIG became the Central Intelligence Agency. The CIA, thanks to General Vandenberg, had already become an expanding organization in search of roles and missions. It was at precisely this time that American officers in Germany apprehended the band of Ukrainian partisans. The Ukrainians were looking for help.

Conflict between the superpowers may not have been inevitable, but avoiding it in 1945 required more wisdom than either Russia or America commanded. Soviet

Generalissimo Joseph Stalin persisted in his obsession with defending Russian borders by means of a buffer zone of Soviet-dominated nations. In pursuit of this aim Stalin repeatedly broke agreements reached by the wartime allies concerning Eastern Europe. The West bristled. Soviet security concerns were regarded as a cloak for imperial conquest. Attitudes hardened on both sides. Crises over Soviet actions in taking over Romania and seeking egress through the Bosporus from Turkey seemed to confirm Russia's aggressive intentions. Truman explained to his secretary of state, James Byrnes, "I'm tired of babying the Soviets."

The succession of crises proved a watershed for public opinion in the United States. British wartime prime minister Sir Winston Churchill received a standing ovation at Westminster College, in Fulton, Missouri, when he declared in a speech, only a few days after one expired deadline:

> From Stettin in the Baltic to Trieste in the Adriatic, an Iron Curtain has descended across the Continent. Behind that line lie all the capitals of the ancient states of central and eastern Europe . . . all subject, in one form or another, not only to Soviet influence but to a very high and in some cases increasing measure of control from Moscow.

Early efforts at negotiation expired in the increasingly heated atmosphere. Within days of taking office in 1945, Truman spoke harshly to the Soviet foreign minister. Lend-Lease aid, which Americans had provided Russia since 1941, and the Soviets thought to extend, instead halted. In July 1945 Truman met with Stalin and British leaders at Potsdam, Germany. They talked of arrangements for Eastern Europe and the work of Allied Control Councils in the occupied countries, to be garrisoned until peace treaties were signed. After three top-level meetings—summit conferences if you will—over the years 1943–1945, no American president would again meet the Soviets at a summit for a decade.

In 1947 Soviet-American relations crossed another watershed. That February the British told American officials they would terminate foreign aid to Greece. Europe faced a cruel winter, the worst in decades, and the British government felt it could not continue supporting the Greeks, who had been receiving military and economic aid for more than two years. Meanwhile Greece had plunged into civil war—Communist insurgents threatened the right-wing royal government. President Truman approved a suggestion that the United States take over responsibility for Greece, adding aid to Turkey for good measure. In mid-March the State Department offered aid, which soon grew into substantial intervention in the Greek civil war.

This shift in Truman's policy toward countering Soviet moves proved more important than the aid itself. Under the new concept Soviet power had to be contained within the areas it had previously achieved dominance; further Russian expansion would be resisted. George F. Kennan, a foreign service officer, coined the term "containment," which was elevated to the status of the Truman Doctrine. In the containment enterprise the CIA became a key tool.

From the initial help to Greece and Turkey it would be but a short step to offering foreign aid more widely to European nations. Secretary of State George C.

Marshall expanded the offer in a commencement address at Harvard University on June 5, 1947. The Marshall Plan aimed at furthering containment by helping rebuild Europe, eliminating social conditions hospitable to the growth of communism. As an added benefit, rebuilt European economies could purchase American goods and services. The Marshall Plan became the first sustained foreign assistance program ever adopted by the United States. At the CIA the Marshall Plan became a device to disguise the provenance of money spent for propaganda and political action purposes, an institution that could help the agency exchange U.S. for local currencies, a way to hide CIA officers and a source of recruits to the agency's cause.

Soviet leaders were not wrong to view the Truman Doctrine and Marshall Plan as aimed at them. Stalin forbade occupied Eastern Europe to participate. The Czechs, whose political system the Russians had yet to subjugate, saw Marshall Plan aid as a counterweight to Soviet influence and initially responded to the American offer. Their maneuver led Stalin to consolidate Soviet control over Prague. Political pressures mounted until, in February 1948, a sort of constitutional coup took place. Non-Communist ministers in the Czech coalition government resigned, replaced by representatives of a minority party, the Czech Communist Party. Within a month a famous Czech patriot, Jan Masaryk, a prominent politician and official, died under highly suspicious circumstances.

These events in Czechoslovakia, plus the rising tide of hostility in America, now created a "war scare." The American high commissioner in Germany, Gen. Lucius D. Clay, cabled a warning on March 5, 1948, that war "may come with dramatic suddenness." Asked for its opinion, the CIA prepared a memorandum concluding that war was not in fact imminent, but it refused to predict beyond the following sixty days.

But in Germany matters came to a head. On the last day of March 1948 the Russians suddenly informed the West that they would impose travel restrictions on the three land corridors connecting the western sector of Berlin with the Allied occupation area of Bizonia. The restrictions went into effect at midnight, April 1. British and American trains en route to Berlin were halted at the Soviet zone boundary. The Allies shifted to aircraft for transport. On April 5 a British C-47 making its approach to the Berlin airfield at Gatow was destroyed when a Soviet fighter plane collided with it in midair. The Soviets apologized, but the Allies then ordered fighter escorts for their transport planes.

By July a full-scale blockade of Berlin had developed, lasting until May 12, 1949. During that time everything that arrived in West Berlin came by air in what would be called Operation Vittles: eighty tons the first day, within a month more than three thousand tons a day. During the blockade there were more than seven hundred incidents between Soviet and Allied aircraft; thirty-nine British, thirty-one American, and five German airmen were killed. The Cold War had begun in earnest.

The years 1945 to 1948 thus witnessed an accelerating cycle of misperception, provocation, and hostility on both sides. The wartime Big Four alliance became a thing of the past. Neither side saw much possibility for improving relations; Western leaders spoke of Soviet "aggression" and of the "captive nations" of Eastern Europe. President Truman looked to strike back at the Russians, and the CIA would be his instrument.

From its creation the CIA was caught in the shifting currents of the Cold War. In the fall of 1947 the first secretary of defense, James M. Forrestal, asked if the agency would be capable of undertaking secret political action and paramilitary campaigns on behalf of the United States. The CIA replied that it could complete any mission assigned it by the National Security Council and for which resources were made available.

At first the agency concentrated on building up capabilities. It occupied additional quarters in a complex of temporary buildings on northwest E Street in Washington, earlier the home of the Office of Strategic Services. Managed by a new director, Rear Adm. Roscoe H. Hillenkoetter, in its first year the CIA increased its budget by 60 percent and added hundreds of personnel. Stalwarts who had remained with the Office of Special Operations throughout its evolution from SSU to CIG to CIA began to see many old faces from OSS. A new wave of secret warriors appeared as well, young men and women who believed the Cold War to be the most important challenge of the age.

But in truth the CIA had yet to attain readiness for covert operations, and in important ways it lacked authority to engage in them. Responding to the initial Pentagon inquiries, Admiral Hillenkoetter had asked the CIA's legal counsel for an opinion as to whether the organization could conduct covert actions. General Counsel Lawrence R. Houston replied on September 25, 1947, arguing that the National Security Act failed to provide CIA the required legal authority. The famous language usually cited to justify covert operations was the provision that the CIA would fulfill such missions as the NSC might "from time to time" direct. But Houston noted that this provision was qualified by language that said the mission must be "related to intelligence." Covert operations had only the most tenuous relation to intelligence. Furthermore, Houston noted, Congress had clearly directed that the agency's chief mission was to coordinate intelligence reporting.

Houston did support one intelligence function related to covert operations already being performed. This was "acquisition of extensive indication on plans in Western Europe for [the] establishment of resistance elements in event of further extension of Communist control," including information on the training of agents, groups, radio operators, and their outside contacts. For secret propaganda and paramilitary missions, Houston felt, new offices would have to be established, entailing the procurement of "huge quantities" of all kinds of materials and involving large sums for expenses. The memo then declared that "we believe this would be an unauthorized use of the funds made available to CIA." If such operations were ordered by the NSC, Houston concluded, "it would, we feel, still be necessary to go to Congress for authority and funds."

Thirty-five years later Houston recalled that Hillenkoetter expressed concern at his opinion. The admiral asked whether there were offsetting considerations in the matter, whereupon the lawyer provided a second memorandum. Here Houston stated that "if the President, with his constitutional responsibilities for the conduct of foreign policy, gave the agency appropriate instructions and if Congress gave it the funds to carry them out, the agency had the legal capability of carrying out the covert actions involved."

Hillenkoetter took the problem to Truman. State Department policy planner George Kennan played a key role in pushing a proposal for secret propaganda. Kennan advised in December that Soviet covert operations threatened to defeat American foreign policy objectives absent this Cold War tool. He wanted a U.S. directorate for political warfare. At its very first meeting, on December 13, the National Security Council discussed a program for secret propaganda. The following day President Truman signed a directive, NSC-4/A, approving a secret propaganda program and assigning responsibility to the CIA. A week later Admiral Hillenkoetter ordered his OSO chief, Donald Galloway, to plan for a covert psychological campaign using existing CIA resources where possible. Galloway formed a Special Procedures Group within the Office of Special Operations in March 1948 to carry out the mission. Hillenkoetter instructed Galloway that the covert operations were intended to influence governments, groups, and individuals by all means short of physical, that they were to be kept distinct from all other U.S. government information activities, and that the program should move foreign public opinion so as to accomplish American objectives.

These decisions were made months before the Czech coup or the Berlin blockade. World developments only heightened American hostility and accelerated preparations for covert operations. While the United States talked about democracy, its policy goals were more immediate and often took other nations in a rather different direction. Italy became the first example.

Events in Italy crystallized all the talk of "political warfare." Mussolini's Italian fascist regime had been overthrown on the eve of surrender in World War II, and not long afterward the king abdicated. After the war came a republic, a parliamentary democracy. Going into elections scheduled for April 1948, the Italian radical left, in particular the Communist Party, were strong, with war recovery barely begun and massive unemployment benefiting their position. Truman sought to avoid a Communist victory at the Italian polls. In a report two months before the election, the CIA warned of a leftist bloc whose strength roughly equaled that of the centrist-moderate left government, but it held out the promise that interim U.S. aid could influence the electoral outcome. Truman's administration went into high gear to make that happen, committing $200 million in aid and supporting moderate and anti-Communist parties, especially the reigning Christian Democrats of Alcide de Gasperi.

Spooks intervened in this electoral drive, the first initiative of the CIA's Special Procedures Group. Some had worked with OSS in Italy and were reactivating old ties, others were neophytes, like F. Mark Wyatt, who had lived in

Italy before the war. The country fascinated him. The CIA threw him right into the breach. The agency approached de Gasperi with offers of cash, but the Italian insisted the Americans work with non-Communist parties across the board—including the socialists—not just his own people. Wyatt and others delivered suitcases of money at Rome hotels, supposedly chance encounters on the road, anywhere they could. Funds went to anti-Communist labor unions, corporations, religious movements, the right-wing Catholic Action, and more. The CIA financed campaign posters, ads, leaflets, media plants, and rallies. Results exceeded expectations—de Gasperi obtained an overwhelming majority in parliament, gaining against both left and right. Italy would be safe. Success also confirmed the utility of CIA covert operations.

George Kennan continued to press for a "special studies group," under State Department control, for things like the Italian operation. Admiral Hillenkoetter now advised the White House that the CIA could carry out covert activities with no change in the NSC-4/A directive. When State refused to go along with "this political warfare thing in any sane or sound manner," the CIA director threw up his hands—early in June 1948 Hillenkoetter told a Truman aide that Kennan could have it all: let State run the apparatus and let it have no connection whatever with the CIA. History might have been very different had that happened.

Instead President Truman, impressed by CIA's accomplishments in Italy, expanded not only the functions of the agency but those of the State and Defense departments plus the National Security Council. His policy directive, drafted primarily by Kennan, included both psychological warfare and paramilitary programs, here acknowledged for the first time. Truman signed the new directive, NSC-10/2, on June 18. Both kinds of missions would be carried out by a new organization taking operational orders from the CIA and its policy direction from a secret committee chaired by the director of central intelligence. Composed of representatives of the secretaries of state and defense along with the CIA's director, the secret committee became a unit of the National Security Council and worked directly for the president. Under this "10/2 Panel," soon also called the "Special Group," funds for the new organization would be included in the CIA budget while its director would be named by the secretary of state and approved by the NSC. According to the 10/2 directive, "the overt foreign activities of the US Government must be supplemented by covert operations."

Three features of the NSC-10/2 directive are crucial to the evolution of American covert operations. For the first time a presidential document specified a mechanism to approve and manage secret operations, making it responsible to the chief executive. Second, also for the first time, there appeared a definition of the genus. Finally, the CIA was again given the primary role, confirming the arrangement begun with NSC-4/A.

The covert missions were to involve more than psychological warfare, more even than secret wars. The new definition specified that covert operations included all activities sponsored or conducted by the United States either in support of friendly governments or against hostile ones, with the stipulation that they be "so planned and executed that any US Government responsibility for them is not evident to unauthorized persons and that if uncovered the US Government can plausibly disclaim any responsibility for them." The core of the 10/2 definition explained that

> such operations shall include any covert activities related to: propaganda, economic warfare; preventive direct action, including sabotage, anti-sabotage, demolition and evacuation measures; subversion against hostile states, including assistance to underground resistance movements, guerrillas and refugee liberation groups, and support of indigenous anti-communist elements in threatened countries of the free world.

Virtually the only thing left out is espionage. As far as intelligence is concerned, the scale ran to just short of "armed conflict by recognized military forces."

The definition of covert operations contained in NSC-10/2 endured for more than three decades. An Office of Special Projects, the new organization created to carry them out, later merged into the CIA, but the mechanism for presidential control prescribed by NSC-10/2 endures to this day.

George Kennan, who would later sour on this entire enterprise, remained an enthusiastic supporter of covert operations at their inception. It was Kennan whom the secretary of state placed on the 10/2 panel as the first representative of his department, and Kennan again who assembled the short list of nominees from whom the director was selected. At the head of that list Kennan put Frank G. Wisner, whom he did not know but who came highly recommended by Chip Bohlen (the State Department's other chief authority on the Soviet Union) and, reportedly, George C. Marshall. Frank Wisner, OSS veteran, was a man who favored aiding the "captive nations," and that included partisans like the Ukrainian People's Army. By some accounts Wisner had been a prominent advocate of creating the new covert action unit, though it remains a mystery how this could be true without his knowing Kennan. In any case, Wisner got the job and accepted it with alacrity. He met George Kennan soon enough. They spoke on the phone about whether balloons could be used to deliver propaganda leaflets over Eastern Europe. On August 6, 1948, they joined others to talk about making the NSC-10/2 mandate a reality. America's secret war had begun.

3

The Secret Warriors

IN AMERICA TODAY, when lawyers are so often disparaged as purveyors of litigation, the connection between law *firms* and spycraft is often overlooked. For the CIA in its formative years the existence of certain law firms held a key importance for the future of the agency. The only one of these entities to reach popular awareness is the law firm of Sullivan & Cromwell. Established in 1879, its founders were no longer around by the mid-twentieth century, but the firm comfortably retained William Nelson Cromwell's instinct for the jugular and his talent for attracting powerful clients, who in turn gave the firm's lawyers seats at some key passages of history. Cromwell, for example, represented the corporation that successfully arranged for the United States to take over and develop the Panama Canal. John Foster Dulles, another of the firm's lawyers, played a role at the Versailles peace conference at the end of World War I. His brother, Allen W. Dulles, who also had a bit part at Versailles, joined Sullivan & Cromwell in 1926, with Nazi German companies among his clients. During World War II, Allen went to Switzerland for the OSS and worked his German contacts to benefit U.S. intelligence. Foster's representation of the United Fruit Company later impacted directly upon CIA operations. These brothers presently became respectively director of central intelligence and secretary of state for President Dwight D. Eisenhower.

By no means was Sullivan & Cromwell the sole exemplar of this phenomenon. The other clear example is Donovan, Leisure, Newton and Lumbard, formed in 1929 by William J. Donovan, "Wild Bill" himself, executor of private missions on behalf of President Franklin Roosevelt and founder of the first U.S. intelligence agencies, the Coordinator of Information, then the Office of Strategic Services. After the war Donovan returned to his firm but continued to agitate for creation of the peacetime intelligence agency, and remained a strong supporter of the nascent CIA. The Donovan firm employed a number of former OSS people, some of whom went on to the Central Intelligence Agency. The most notable, OSS veteran William E. Colby, whom Donovan hired out of law school, would one day head the CIA.

Frank Gardiner Wisner had his own law firm connection. That came easily to Wisner, scion of the alliance between the two most patrician families of Laurel, Mississippi, holders of lumber interests that controlled that town. It was old money by the time Wisner became a teenager in the "Roaring Twenties." Despite the venturesome age, though Wisner left Mississippi he could not bring himself to leave the South. He put down roots in Virginia at private school and returned to attend the University of Virginia. Wisner excelled at track and field, at one time indulging Olympic ambitions as a runner. Virginia's genteel style suited Wisner so much that he went on to law school there, cultivating a haughty manner softened by a Mississippi twang that fit the bourbon he favored. He graduated third in his class, bringing an immediate offer from a Wall Street firm. The family money embarrassed Wisner, who could hardly summon the words to say "rich people" and would later put his government paychecks into a drawer, uncashed.

Wisner joined the firm of Carter, Ledyard, Milburn in 1934. Located three floors above the Donovan firm in the same building at 2 Wall Street in New York City, Carter, Ledyard did essentially the same work. Even older than Sullivan & Cromwell, the firm had been founded in 1854 by lawyers from New York City and Buffalo. James C. Carter, the Buffalo counsel, left after a few years to be replaced by John G. Milburn. The firm steadily expanded its general practice, perhaps its most notable account being American Express and its greatest claim to fame that in 1905 it had hired the young Franklin D. Roosevelt as an unpaid clerk. At Carter, Ledyard, Frank Wisner labored for seven years, eventually becoming a partner. There he met other associates and junior lawyers, including friends William H. Jackson and Gordon Gray, plus Tracy Barnes. Jackson, having just attained the exalted status of partner himself, had actually hired Wisner, the fledgling lawyer. With war clearly approaching in mid-1941, before Pearl Harbor, Wisner volunteered for the naval reserve. Gray metamorphosed into a psychological warfare expert; Jackson became a senior officer with army intelligence (G-2); Tracy Barnes served with the army air force and the OSS, later following Wisner into the CIA. Bill Jackson would conduct an outside review of their work and become a CIA boss when appointed deputy director of central intelligence. Gordon Gray would have his own piece to play as well.

Commissioned a naval reserve officer, Wisner's international legal experience quickly led to his being reassigned to the Office of Strategic Services. The OSS sent him to Cairo, then to Turkey, where in 1944 he opened an OSS station. As Nazi Germany retreated from its conquests and the Allies advanced, Wisner did too. He moved to Bucharest and from September 1944 ran the small CIA station there. Among other feats, Wisner organized the evacuation of American airmen held prisoner in Romania. The Soviet takeover of this country in January 1945 greatly affected him, for until then he had enthusiastically thrown himself into palace intrigues. That spring, as the Nazis collapsed, a German intelligence unit led by Reinhard Gehlen volunteered to spy for the Americans. Wisner now led the OSS detachment in Wiesbaden, Germany, that initially dealt with Gehlen. He then chaired the OSS committee that recommended the United States arrange to exploit

Gehlen. In this last assignment Wisner came under the command of Allen Dulles, up from Berne to supervise all OSS activity in Germany. The Washington desk officer responsible for their area, Richard M. Helms, also played a key role in what transpired.

Frank Wisner threw up his hands with army intelligence when superiors blocked his efforts to obtain bicycles for agents in the Soviet occupation zone. He returned to the law, but for this intense man, emotionally involved with this work, Wall Street seemed tame after OSS derring-do. Wisner occasionally lunched with Allen Dulles, himself back at Sullivan & Cromwell. Dulles, like Wild Bill Donovan, became a public figure agitating for the establishment of an intelligence agency. Wisner admired that and himself spoke out in favor of creating a mechanism for political warfare. In 1946 he took a considerable pay cut—not that it mattered to him—to return to government as deputy assistant secretary of state for the occupied territories. Early on he made a tour of the Displaced Persons camps in Germany. The post at State was one in which Wisner could exercise his expertise on Eastern Europe. Not coincidentally, his immediate boss had been a Carter, Ledyard client. Wisner and his wife Polly moved to Georgetown.

At home and at the office Wisner developed fresh connections with Washington movers—people like the State Department's Chip Bohlen, and Paul Nitze, just finished working on a massive study of aerial bombing—who had fingers in many policy pies. In any case, Wisner jumped at the opportunity to take charge of a new Cold War action group and soon found himself ensconced at CIA headquarters. Wisner glowed, hustling about the office and organizing impromptu races at Paul Nitze's lawn parties in which he would handicap himself by running backward.

The National Security Council approved Wisner's appointment on August 19, 1948. A week later, issuing the directive formally creating Wisner's organization, Admiral Hillenkoetter adopted the new name Office of Policy Coordination (OPC). The OPC went to war. Before year's end, Frank Wisner had already obtained a budget of $4.7 million, and he controlled seven overseas posts—or "stations" in the parlance of spies—with 302 persons on staff. The OPC had access to another fund more than twice as big from unused currency stabilization accounts at the Treasury Department, under agreements Wisner soon worked out within the government.

From "L" Building at headquarters, Wisner's web began to encircle the world. He knew well enough that time was needed to get up and running, but he simultaneously exhibited an impatience for action by his people in the field. The result became haphazard management, akin to a law firm, where the number of people on a case simply meant more billings. Wisner thought nothing of assigning the same task to several officers, then watching to see who came back with results. Meanwhile the OPC boss himself tore around tossing off more ideas for operations, which meant assignments. Hundreds of projects flowed from the OPC shop. Wisner needed people to carry them out. Within a year OPC had expanded to a staff of five hundred; by mid-1950 there would be another thousand on top of that.

George Kennan, who fancied the political warfare directorate as a tool in the containment kit, to be taken out only as required, reacted with horror as the OPC transformed itself into an active mechanism for foreign intervention. Kennan came to see the Office of Policy Coordination as a sort of Frankenstein monster and regretted his role in its creation.

By October 1948 Wisner had developed a general scheme for action. He envisioned more than a dozen different types of covert operations in four major categories: psychological warfare, political warfare, economic warfare, and what Wisner termed "preventive direct action." The gamut included everything from poison pen letters (under psychological warfare) to support of DPs and refugees, to preclusive commodities purchases and market manipulation, to support of resistance and guerrilla movements. The net effect would be to involve the Office of Policy Coordination in every imaginable sort of clandestine activity.

Proud of OPC's capabilities, particularly those for spreading propaganda and misinformation, Wisner began calling his network the "Wurlitzer," like the jukeboxes that carried many tunes. "Wisner's Wurlitzer" stuck as an identifier for the OPC propaganda apparatus and for his office as a whole. A number of other sobriquets also were soon applied around L Building, among the staff if not the spymasters. The OPC expanded steadily and soon had outposts in several of the other buildings, I, J, and K. The place became known as Cockroach Alley. Wisner would be recognized for his ability to make things happen and called "Wiz." His deputy became the "Ozzard of Wiz." There would be a psychological warfare staff under Joe Bryan, a Virginian after Wisner's own heart, who would be called the "Duke of Richmond." A romantic might have thought of it as Robin Hood and the Merry Men off to fight the despotic king, in this case Soviet dictator Joseph Stalin.

Stalin had mobilized the Soviet Union for World War II by fanning the flames of nationalism in his country. The theme of the invaded motherland became so prominent that World War II is still called the Great Patriotic War in Russia. But nationalism in service of the state, plus Soviet ideology, did not bridge the deep ethnic and cultural differences among the Russian peoples. The Soviet Union comprised a kaleidoscope of peoples and cultures governed from the center. The party papered over the differences in cultures, ranging from Muslim to Eastern Orthodox, and peoples, ranging from Ukrainians to Uzbeks and Asians. Stalin himself, a Georgian, came from the mountainous Caucasus region. The motherland theme in propaganda cloaked a "nationality problem" that predated Soviet rule to the beginning of Russian expansion under the tsars.

Minorities had resisted right along, notably Cossacks and Ukrainians. Many from these ethnic groups had fought with the Whites against the Communists during the Russian civil war. Ukrainian forces also allied with the Poles during the Russo-Polish war of 1920. Ukrainians then fought the Russians as German auxiliary troops in the Great Patriotic War itself. While the war as a whole might have ended in 1945, the Ukrainian guerrilla armies continued to fight. The Ukrainians discovered by the American CIC near Passau in 1947 were part of these forces. Another migration began with the Soviet victory in 1945, joining the waves of Displaced Persons: Russian deserters, defectors, former prisoners of war evading repatriation, and forced laborers, refilling the ranks of Russian emigré groups.

Beyond Soviet borders were the "satellite" states of Eastern Europe. These peoples too were not about to accept Soviet domination. In a military sense the Eastern European states were indeed "captive nations." Due to the stringent political and security controls the Soviets maintained in both Russia and Eastern Europe, the CIA quickly dubbed them "denied areas," places where intelligence operations could be conducted only with great difficulty and peril.

Organizing resistance in the denied areas initially seemed a simple matter of making contact with the right people. The captive nations, disaffected minorities, and groups of disillusioned social democrats and Communists provided fertile recruiting grounds, indeed irresistible ones, for Western intelligence officers as the Cold War intensified and the CIA received orders to begin a secret war against Soviet communism.

At an early meeting of the 10/2 panel on August 12, 1948, an NSC representative made clear that the Office of Policy Coordination should be controlled by the State Department during peacetime and the Pentagon in war. That disturbed Frank Wisner, the CIA member of the panel in whose office the group often met. The first representative for the secretary of defense, army Col. Ivan D. Yeaton, said little. In his turn, George Kennan demanded the State Department be given detailed information about objectives and methods to be employed in every proposed project involving a political decision. Instead Wisner effectively manipulated the system. The director of central intelligence had been vested with formal authority for OPC operations by the 10/2 directive. When he needed to, Wisner went to Admiral Hillenkoetter. The DCI, under pressure to produce action against the Russians, opposed little that OPC wished to do. Kennan soon left the panel, replaced by Robert Joyce, an advocate of increased covert action. After that, if there was a problem, Wisner could go to him. If stymied from both directions, Wisner would resort to the Pentagon, starved for intelligence on Russia and likely to support OPC initiatives.

The blockade of Berlin began only days after approval of NSC-10/2. The State Department, impressed with the results of CIA's impromptu intervention in the Italian general elections, and the CIA, then being criticized for failing to warn of a coup that had occurred in Bogotá, Colombia, were not inclined to challenge Wisner's maneuvers.

Much like the companion espionage staff in CIA's Office of Special Operations, OPC was divided into regional "divisions" and functional "staffs." The Eastern Europe Division handled operations in the denied areas of the Soviet bloc. Within the divisions were "branches," each responsible for a country or group, or for special applications. There were functional staffs for political action and psychological warfare. This has remained the pattern of organization at the CIA throughout its history.

Wisner had instructions not to poach on OSO territory. Since personnel from the espionage outfit were off limits to OPC recruiting, he turned instead to OSS veterans and the fresh crop of Ivy League college graduates just returned from the war—men whom Wisner's journalist friend Stewart Alsop called "the bold Easterners."

For his secret propaganda programs, Wisner's Wurlitzer included, at that stage, a shortwave radio transmitter acquired from the army, the first of a fleet of balloons used to carry leaflets over the denied areas, and a psychological warfare staff—a collection of practical jokers, creative misfits, and talented writers who blew off steam shooting BB guns at balloons in the office. At least one suffered a breakdown and was hauled off to St. Elizabeth's, a Washington mental hospital. The staff kept hatching plots to demoralize the Russians, everything from dropping superior Western trade goods over the Soviet Union, cueing unfortunate Soviet citizens to the shoddiness of Russian products; to huge-sized condoms (marked "Made in U.S.A." and "Medium") to engender penis envy. These proposals grew so outlandish that the CIA director threatened to close the shop down if Wisner brought him one more project involving balloons with payloads to drop.

The more serious schemes involved massive propaganda campaigns and radio broadcasting. To conceal CIA's hand in these efforts the OPC created visible public groups to whom the activities could be attributed. This was contemplated from the program's inception. Allen Dulles, who continued his lunches with Wisner and was soon asked by President Truman to participate in an outside review of U.S. intelligence for the National Security Council, talked with Wall Street colleagues and other acquaintances about forming such public groups. George Kennan made a similar proposal within the State Department, where Secretary Dean Acheson informally discussed the topic with several former American diplomats in late 1948 and early 1949. Among them was retired ambassador Joseph Grew, who in turn contacted Dewitt C. Poole, an OSS veteran and the senior American diplomat in Moscow at the time of the Russian civil war. In June 1949 Grew and Poole set up the National Committee for a Free Europe. Allen Dulles became its chairman of the executive committee. Such figures as the former high commissioner in Germany, Gen. Lucius D. Clay, joined Free Europe's board of directors.

The committee created a broadcasting subsidiary called Radio Free Europe (RFE) with corporate offices in New York. Internal RFE documents make out Kennan as the father of the enterprise. In its studios in Munich, the RFE employed Eastern European emigrés as broadcasters. RFE was secretly given Wisner's radio transmitter. A search began for more powerful equipment. The OPC kept in close touch, assigning a couple of officers to the Radio Free Europe staff in addition to Wisner's direct contact with many of its board members. Former OSS radio experts Peter Mero and Robert E. Lang helped select a transmission site near Frankfurt. The first RFE broadcast was a half-hour program beamed into Czechoslovakia on July

4, 1950. From that December RFE existed as a legal corporation. This and other broadcast units that followed became known to the CIA as "the Radios."

Russian adversaries were instantly alert to the dangers of the broadcasts and began to jam the radio frequencies that RFE used, as for two years they had already jammed the overt propaganda broadcast by the Voice of America. Truman's National Security Council contemplated a ring of transmitters surrounding Russia to alleviate the Voice of America problem, while the RFE solution became "saturation broadcasting," in which a series of increasingly powerful radio transmitters in different locations beamed the same programs to Eastern Europe simultaneously on varied frequencies. It took time to create a transmission array of that caliber, however. By 1952, when nine new transmitters went on-line, including one in Portugal, RFE approached critical mass. Saturation broadcasting began in earnest with Stalin's death in 1953 when RFE pulled out every stop to get the news to Eastern Europe. By then its Munich headquarters, at the edge of the Englischer Garten, contained almost two dozen studios. More than a hundred Americans and almost five hundred exiles worked there alongside a thousand local employees.

Wisner's Wurlitzer wanted a capability for beaming propaganda into Russia to match its RFE wing and proceeded in identical fashion. An American Committee for Liberation from Bolshevism (Amcomlib) started up in 1950 and was incorporated the following year. Franklin Lindsay put together its board of directors. Robert H. Dreher, who joined the CIA in 1951—as a naval reserve lieutenant he had been expelled from Russia on bogus spy charges three years before, but now made the allegation true—held up the agency's side in the creation of Radio Liberty. It first broadcast on March 1, 1953. This "Radio" had the same problems with the different Russian emigré groups that had bedeviled Wisner's secret warriors. The effort to impose some discipline upon the emigrés eventually led to the ending of CIA subsidies to the groups.

The Radios became important resources in the secret war against Russia. There was also the balloon program, which distributed printed materials. The first balloon was launched by an RFE crew from a German farm field in August 1951, the beginning of a stream that would deliver 400 *tons*—up to 300 million leaflets—over the denied areas. The balloon launch was attended, as if it were a ceremonial occasion, by RFE president C. D. Jackson, politician Harold Stassen, journalist Drew Pearson, representatives of the Radios, and emigré officials.

Creation of a capability for paramilitary operations became a key facet of Frank Wisner's OPC endeavor. Paramilitary efforts offered the most direct avenue to challenging Soviet power in the occupied territories and indeed in Russia itself. The paramilitary option had a defensive function as well. In the event of a Russian invasion that led to the conquest of Western Europe, the United States wanted to have stay-behind networks, similar to the European resistance in World War II, that would fight the Russians. If there was no invasion, the Americans still wanted to conduct paramilitary operations on the Russians' own ground of the denied areas.

The fledgling Central Intelligence Agency could not carry out these missions by itself and went to the Pentagon for assistance. A relationship with the Defense Department evolved despite some opposition. The secretary of the army initially prohibited assignment of army officers to the CIA on the grounds that he wanted his service to have nothing to do with covert operations. But in August 1948 the Joint Chiefs went on record declaring not only that guerrilla warfare be supported, under the direction of the NSC, but that the armed services form no special warfare units of their own, leaving the field by default to the newly created Office of Policy Coordination. Individual military men could be given special training, but OPC would be the only organization with a comprehensive capability to plan and conduct such missions. The military's interest became Frank Wisner's entrée for outflanking the 10/2 Panel when he encountered obstacles from CIA or State Department bosses.

In early August 1949 Wisner asked the army for extensive assistance, including the designation of an army officer to serve as chief of the OPC Guerrilla Warfare Group and the use of army facilities for CIA training. While the request for a detailee was later withdrawn, in mid-November OPC and army representatives agreed to use Fort Benning, Georgia, for CIA training. One of the OPC men at the conference was in fact on detached service from the army. He was Col. Richard G. Stilwell, who had served in Europe with the Ninetieth Infantry Division. As a military officer Stilwell played a major role in the CIA-army relationship.

There were also certain army assets in the field, especially in Germany, that would be useful to OPC. The main one was G-2's Counter Intelligence Corps, with its Sixty-sixth CIC Detachment at Stuttgart from September 1949. The Sixty-sixth CIC had the responsibility for screening Displaced Persons who would be the main source of OPC agent recruits. Some 42,000 people were screened by the Sixty-sixth during 1949 alone. As late as 1951, 500 defectors a month were coming from behind the Iron Curtain. The Sixty-sixth CIC also carried out "positive intelligence" missions in the Soviet zone, 2,211 of them in 1949, providing information useful to OPC in its preparation of secret missions.

Probably the most important resource that Frank Wisner pried from the army was an entire intelligence agency, a German one. This story stretches back to 1945, or October 1944 if counted from when the Germans began planning for their nation's collapse. Germany had had a military intelligence unit called Foreign Armies East that handled Soviet intelligence. As the end neared, the unit evacuated southwest toward the American armies. The director of Foreign Armies East, Reinhard Gehlen, ordered his files buried. He approached British intelligence about collaboration but they turned him down, though the British pumped those from Gehlen's unit whom they captured. The general then contrived to have himself taken by the

Americans. Gehlen offered to tell them everything he knew about Russia and bring together a cadre of his former top people to add to that intelligence. He also peddled those wartime files.

Gehlen, handled at first by the Counter Intelligence Corps in what was called Operation Rusty, became a case for the army's European intelligence chief, Brig. Gen. Edwin L. Sibert. Inexperienced with Russians, Sibert's G-2 interrogators found Gehlen's knowledge impressive. Transported to Washington in August 1945, the German went to Fort Hunt, near Mount Vernon, used throughout the war to house high-value prisoners. Extensive debriefings with G-2 and OSS took place there with Frank Wisner one of the inquisitors. There Gehlen began an alliance with the United States that ultimately took him back to Germany to create an intelligence unit working for G-2 and CIC. With the OSS abolished, central intelligence initially was not in on this play.

Creating an American relationship with Reinhard Gehlen provided an early illustration of a recurring theme in U.S. intelligence practice—making deals with the bad guys. With President Roosevelt having made World War II a struggle of democracy against dictatorship, victory over Germany entailed so-called denazification, the process of destroying the Nazi ideology not only by prosecuting top Nazis at war crimes trials but by prohibiting former Nazi officials from participating in the postwar political life of their country. So the question in 1945 became, how much of a Nazi was Reinhard Gehlen? The evidence on that issue is mixed. The German army did not equate to the Nazis or their party military and intelligence entities, and Gehlen is not known to have been a party member, but there was no doubt he protected staff who were, which under occupation rules disqualified him from service.

Gehlen is merely the exemplar. A long list of former Nazis, people like Josef Mengele, Klaus Barbie, Emil Augsburg, Gustav Hilger, Hans Herwarth, and many more, all formidable Nazis, evaded prosecution, were sometimes helped to escape on "rat line" routes kept open by U.S. intelligence, or even ended up working with the Americans. The CIA developed an entire operation called Project Bloodstone to exploit these Germans. The executive agent for Bloodstone was Wisner's man Carmel Offie. In each case authorities rationalized decisions with variations on the argument that a pact with the devil is good if it may help save heaven. That argument bears a cost for the United States when the need arises to demonstrate that professed democratic values truly drive U.S. policies. In the aftermath of World War II, U.S. decisions were consistently in favor of pacts with assorted devils. There were at least three major instances: Bloodstone, in which more than $5 million was directly spent to employ known Nazis on U.S. security projects; Operation Paperclip, in which former Nazi scientists were brought to the United States to continue developing technologies under American auspices; and Operation Rusty, the Gehlen organization. In each case Nazi connections of individuals were minimized and on occasion covered up. A number of those actions later backfired.

In view of the need to use individuals of ill repute, or defectors who needed to be brought into the country, or to have means to encourage recruitment of foreign nationals, the CIA sought to suspend immigration law in bringing people into the United States. In 1949 Congress modified the CIA portion of the National Security Act to permit the agency to bring up to 120 foreigners a year into the country outside normal immigration channels. Funds assigned the DCI for contingencies were also to be available to pay these people. The action taken with Reinhard Gehlen became an early example of this practice.

The Gehlen Organization was installed at Pullach, near Munich, in December 1947, at the time still working for the U.S. Army. Gehlen hired his specialists on the Soviets without regard for their pasts; some of his best had been Nazi party activists. Others were from the Nazi security services. No one seemed to bat an eye though the CIC carried out a secret monitoring effort for several years. The army's Counter Intelligence Corps initially assigned Col. Russell Philp to supervise Operation Rusty. The Central Intelligence Group had its own liaison, Samuel Brossard. The latter surveyed Gehlen's group, interviewing its deputy director, Eric Waldman, to make a recommendation as to whether CIG—soon CIA—should take over its care and feeding. Central intelligence initially rejected that course. Admiral Hillenkoetter even recommended that the Gehlen unit be abolished.

Yet by 1948 the Gehlen Organization was fully functional and the Soviet threat had become paramount. By then the army had begun winding down activities in Germany and wished to rid itself of Gehlen. Another policy review, conducted jointly by the army and CIA, became the order of the day. Col. Charles Bromley would be the chief army representative. The man from the CIA—also from the army actually, but in the reserve, having just joined the agency—was James M. Critchfield, a highly decorated wartime commander of an infantry battalion. In the last days of the war Critchfield had actually led his troops right past the mountain where Gehlen hid. Critchfield continued into Austria, where he returned later as a young colonel with the Counter Intelligence Corps. He joined the CIA in the summer of 1948. Richard Helms approved personnel assignments for Germany at the time, and Critchfield's file went to him. Helms felt he'd made an excellent choice. Critchfield's original assignment, to create an intelligence activity aimed at the Russians, morphed into the Gehlen review. Critchfield began that September at Pullach with no CIA or army input, no files, nothing. His army colleague soon dropped out. Gehlen and his assistants, Eric Waldman and Heinz Herre, were Critchfield's main points of contact. The CIA officer found no one among the three hundred in the organization at the time whose names appeared on the occupation authority's automatic arrest lists. He ended up filing a lengthy cable arguing there was little alternative to adopting the Gehlen Organization, though he cautioned that the CIA should study Gehlen's setup longer before deciding on closer connections. Frank Wisner volunteered to take up the account. The Office of Policy Coordination, unencumbered by CIA's fears about Gehlen, picked up where the army left off, and a formal agreement on cooperation went into effect in June 1949.

Code-named Marshall from his Vienna days, Jim Critchfield became the chief of base at Pullach. His deputy, Peer de Silva, had helped manage security for the atomic bomb project in World War II. Another, Henry Pleasants, had been a noted music critic and served with Critchfield in Vienna. The two once suggested to Critchfield that Gehlen be dumped. The base chief refused. Through Critchfield the CIA provided money, equipment, and advice for the Germans and passed on orders from Washington. The Organization in turn provided intelligence, both analysis and raw reports, from a few networks it imagined had been salvaged from the debris of the war. The "Org," as it was called—and this would be crucial for the CIA's secret war—provided training bases which would accommodate a variety of Eastern European and Soviet emigrés and defectors being groomed as agents or infiltrators. The CIA's secret armies began here.

American capabilities for covert operations came too late for some. In the Baltic states, where nationalist partisans waged a tragic struggle against the reimposition of Soviet control, the issue had largely been decided before Wisner's OPC got into the act. Western cooperation proved too little and too late. Nevertheless an attempt would be made. Wisner's move into paramilitary action was preceded by the British Secret Intelligence Service (SIS), whose Controller North became the first to make contact and give the Balts hope and support.

At the end of the war there had been a moment when news of the atomic bomb reached Lithuania. In Baltic cities one heard speculation that the Americans would hand Stalin an ultimatum and force Soviet withdrawal. To the enthralled partisans, it seemed freedom must lie around a single diplomatic bend. But Truman made no atomic threat; there was no rollback. In the words of an interested Lithuanian, "Reality methodically and pitilessly destroyed whatever hopes remained."

Stalin garrisoned Lithuania with strong forces, but the brunt of the struggle was borne by the Soviet secret police, which resorted to military assistance only in extraordinary circumstances. The Russians annexed the German port of Koenigsberg, which became Kaliningrad, and added Memel to Lithuania, renaming it Klaipeda. Soviet control measures confronted a people in turmoil. More than 150,000 were sent to the Gulags. Production "norms" for Lithuanian farmers and agricultural collectivization made paupers of many of the rest.

The Soviets countered the partisans with many measures, including amnesties, attacks, and ambitious "false flag" operations, in which entire Russian security units pretended to be partisan bands. Resistance reached a plateau in 1947. The largest recorded Lithuanian attack on a Russian post occurred in February 1948. But their strength was in decline—by 1950 the partisan BDPS had no more than five thousand fighters. Collectivization robbed the partisans of their food sources while the swelling ranks of Lithuanian Communists indicated that many people had decided to cast their lot with the Russians.

Without question the Baltic partisans could have used outside help. Before the close of 1945 the Lithuanians had contacts among the DPs. Some of these persons were in touch with Western intelligence, particularly the British. The Lithuanians had a regular courier service, mostly by land across Poland and East Germany. Little is known to have come immediately from these relations, though arms dealing is thought to have been going on in the Baltic. When, in 1947, the Swedish police set out to investigate a ring of rum runners, they wound up instead with a gun-smuggling operation involving deserters from the Soviet army. That August the Soviet newspaper *Pravda* accused the Estonian government-in-exile in Sweden of being a mere front for American espionage.

Moscow ought to have suspected the British. As early as 1943 the Secret Intelligence Service had sent an officer to Stockholm to recruit Balts. As with the Displaced Persons after the war, they found a ready pool of potential enlistees. Infiltration of SIS teams began in 1945. The experience was similar in all the Baltic nations. When the British gathered most Baltic refugees in a small number of DP camps among others of the same nationality, it made recruiting easier. British authorities also refused Stalin's demands to hand these DPs back to the Russians.

The British Controller Northern Area, Harry Lambton Carr, masterminded the SIS operation. Partisans who at first relied on leftover German and captured Russian weapons began to get help from British intelligence. The key Lithuanian resistance figures Stasys Zymantas and Walter Zilinskas were promised aid and helped organize opposition. The Soviets tumbled to the game toward the end of 1945 when they captured an SIS agent team, four Latvians who had landed on the Courland coast.

Russian security specialist Janis Lukasevics broke one of the Latvian prisoners, Vivuds Sveics, and induced the radio operator, Augusts Bergmanis, to cooperate. Lukasevics then initiated a deception effort, with Bergmanis radioing false reports of progress, asking for help and new teams—intercepted in turn. Sveics eventually returned to the West as an agent under *Russian* control, masquerading as a victorious partisan fighter, able to supply the Soviets with data on Balts receiving British training, SIS procedures, bases, and safe houses, and the covert supply network.

British intelligence had its own methods for recruiting and training agents for the Baltic secret war. It was not only the Russians who practiced false-flag operations. Making contact with the Balts, SIS officers usually pretended to be Swedish. The pretense would be maintained throughout training, the only exceptions being a few carefully selected recruits sent to Germany or Britain for specialized instruction. Carr and SIS chiefs reasoned that spies whom the Russians inserted among the Baltic emigrés would hold back from signing on with the Swedes in hopes of contacting SIS. Since the British occupation zone in Germany included the Baltic coast, from an early date Carr tried infiltrating agents by sea. This was preferable to airdrops, noisy and likely to attract the attention of authorities along the flight path. Landings from boats could be made silently and secretly.

London had a perfect force for sea infiltration. This was the Baltic fisheries patrol maintained by the Royal Navy beginning in 1949. Designed to protect local fishermen from interferences by Soviet naval vessels and to recover and disarm numerous mines strewn throughout the Baltic Sea during the war, the patrol consisted of minesweepers that were converted E-boats (patrol boats) taken over from the Germans at the end of the war. The British permitted these unarmed ships to wear the Royal Navy ensign. The SIS then enlisted a former German naval officer, Hans Helmut Klose, who had led a torpedo boat flotilla in the Baltic, to skipper their infiltration boat. Klose in turn recruited former comrades for his crew.

The Controller Northern Area ran the missions. Harry Carr needed eight months of negotiations with the Royal Navy and the British Foreign Office to secure all necessary permissions. A real problem was the tight British budget; for covert operations especially it was spread very thin—£500,000 was considered sufficient for the SIS according to one account. That was supposed to do not merely for Carr but for all British covert action programs. Here was where the Central Intelligence Agency could be quite helpful. In particular, Frank Wisner and his OPC had money to burn. Not only was Wisner liberally funded by three different agencies but a portion of Marshall Plan funds, up to 5 percent in each European country where it was active, were being set aside as so-called counterpart funds, which the OPC could spend without accounting.

The Americans were not ignorant of conditions in the Baltic states. President Truman himself, in a dramatic gesture near the close of 1946, congratulated a group of Estonian refugees who crossed the Atlantic in an old wooden sailing vessel and ordered the Immigration Service to ignore their lack of visas. Senator Millard E. Tydings of Maryland worked actively to publicize conditions in the Baltic states. More than twelve thousand Estonians in the DP camps signed a petition appealing for the freedom of their nation and sent it to Truman. Partisan activity peaked that same year. Before his death in 1948, Dr. Alfred Bilmanis, former Latvian minister to the United States, wrote a half-dozen works on the urgent needs of his country. The Lithuanians sent a partisan leader to the West to seek outside support. Juozas Luksa-Daumantas went to Britain and to America, where he wrote of partisan action behind the Iron Curtain. The Lithuanian-American Council, a prominent emigré group in the United States, in January 1947 made a public appeal for independence to the Allied Council of Foreign Ministers. The Lithuanians tried to meet with President Truman but were told he was unavailable. Washington, however, made strenuous assertions of support for democratic government in the Baltic states as elsewhere.

In May 1948 an official study group sent President Truman a report reflecting keen interest in these partisan actions. The report observed that "secret operations, particularly through support of resistance groups, provide one of the most important sources of secret intelligence." That August army staff officers advocated formation of a small planning group to fashion a war plan especially designed to "cause the people of Soviet Russia to overthrow their present totalitarian government and to render them all practicable assistance in this undertaking." But the army staff initiative went nowhere. Instead the OPC materialized under

Frank Wisner, and paramilitary operations came under Wisner's mandate for political warfare and preventive direct action.

The CIA joined British intelligence in the Baltic partisan struggle, using Wisner's OPC. Wisner in turn relied on Franklin A. Lindsay, his Eastern Europe Division chief. Recruited out of the Marshall Plan offices in Paris, Lindsay was another OSS veteran and one with real paramilitary experience—during the war he had worked in what was then Yugoslavia, arranging secret arms shipments, laboring in the fevered political canyon between right-wing and Communist partisans. It was Lindsay, together with a former State Department official, Charles Thayer, who had needled George Kennan with proposals for a political warfare organization as consultants to him in 1947–1948, so Lindsay can fairly be said to have contributed to the origins of OPC. But, enthralled by the Marshall Plan as an economic bootstrap for downtrodden Europe—as a Harvard grad student Lindsay had watched Marshall's speech pointing up the necessity for this program—Lindsay had gone to work with congressional foreign aid committees and then signed on with the plan managers. Wisner got to Lindsay and brought him into OPC in early 1949. At that time the British SIS solidified their contact with the Baltic forest brotherhood.

Lindsay and Wisner placed great trust in the Gehlen Organization. James Critchfield insists the Org never conducted operations, but in fact Gehlen's role proved vital from the start. The CIA, the SIS, and the German effort continued at least into the mid-1950s. Operations were mounted from the western zone of Germany, as was preliminary agent training, though certain specialties, such as parachute jumping, were taught in England and the United States. In the DP camps and among the Balt emigrés in Germany, Gehlen's agents roamed on behalf of OPC. The Org's talent scouts told the Americans whom to hire. The Germans had fewer language difficulties with the Balts, so they also did much of the basic instructing plus housekeeping at the bases. Some of the Balts suspected SIS motives in this project and were glad when the Americans came on board.

Gordon Stewart, the German station chief, worried after the first mission began, when on October 3, 1949, a team was parachuted into Lithuania by a Czech air crew working for OPC. Communications remained poor, the agents' messages garbled. Balts warned that the operation had been penetrated by the enemy. Stewart agreed, but the British resisted that view. In particular, one of the agents had come twice out of Russia, the ultimate denied area, with no difficulty. Harry Carr interpreted the Balts' suspicions as expressions of emigré politics. At the CIA, Harry Rositzke, chief of the Soviet Bloc Division, sided with Stewart. Arguments ensued.

In November 1950 Carr sailed to the United States aboard the ocean liner *Queen Mary*, brimming with proposals to increase the tempo of clandestine missions in Operation Jungle, as SIS had dubbed the enterprise. The CIA agreed. A fairly large pool of potential recruits existed. In western Germany alone the influx from the DP camps included twenty thousand Estonians, Latvians, and Lithuanians. The CIA also did some recruiting among emigrés living in the United States. Balts working for Lindsay earned $125 a week for three months of training, then

$100 per day when in the denied areas, with a bonus of $1,000 if their missions were judged successful. Few returned to claim the bonuses.

One early recruit to the CIA effort was Juozas Luksa, who parachuted back into Lithuania but soon died at the side of the forest brotherhood. The SIS sent in the team of Vitolds Berkis and Andrei Galdins in the spring of 1950. They succumbed to Soviet security troops masquerading as partisans. Between 1949 and 1951 the CIA reportedly parachuted several more agents, but results were poor. Accounts assert that about half the operatives survived, but known cases mostly encountered trouble of one sort or another. A team of four dropped into Lithuania by OPC in late April 1951, for example, were swept up almost immediately by Russian security. They had been housed in Stockholm, and their mission left from Munich. The Scandinavian Branch of OPC's Western Europe Division ran the Stockholm end. Branch chief Lou Scherer insisted that no leak had occurred on his watch. Had the betrayal taken place in Germany?

The CIA's concern became manifest about this time. The agency sent a delegation of seven officers to London, where they met with Harry Carr and other senior SIS officers concerned with the Baltic operations. Harry Rositzke led the group, and one of the more suspicious Balts accompanied the OPC team. Officers like Lindsay, Gerry Miller, the division chief for Western Europe, where the bases were located, and Lou Scherer, in whose jurisdiction much of the recruiting and support work was done, were under a cloud because of operational failures. With OPC plans for seaborne landings in the works, doubts had to be cleared up. Rositzke also raised questions regarding possible Russian penetration of Ukrainian resistance groups as well as British favoritism toward a group the CIA regarded as hidebound, which the CIA "baron," as division chiefs were nicknamed, saw as an obstacle to recruitment. The SIS controller reassured the Americans. Carr insisted SIS had as many concerns as the CIA and would take every precaution. Gerhardt Meyer, branch chief for the Baltic under Rositzke, came away unconvinced: "I feel I've just spent three days chewing cotton."

One of the earliest CIA landings was along the coast of Latvia on September 30, 1951. On that occasion Russians sighted the E-boat in territorial waters. Two Soviet destroyers gave chase, but Hans Klose maneuvered and his unarmed, unloaded E-boat outran her pursuers. The agent landed during this escapade later defected to the Russians. Major Lukasevics, the Soviet security mastermind, scored his greatest coup at this time when Harry Carr sent orders for agents Berkis and Galdins to return and bring along one of the partisan leaders. The Soviets fooled Berkis, convinced Galdins to remain in Lithuania (where they executed him), and inserted their own agent, Avritis Gailitis, as the purported forest brotherhood chief. Gailitis went completely unsuspected, regaling British case officers with phony exploits. Sandy McKibbin, the senior SIS officer involved, had been working with the Balts for more than seven years but did not detect the trick.

The partisan war sputtered to its futile end just as the CIA-SIS Baltic operation reached stride. The last battle in Latvia was recorded in February 1950. By that time the partisans in Estonia had been worn down to isolated bands and those in Lithuania reduced to fewer than five thousand. Although the Voice of America began broadcasting in Lithuanian in 1952, its appealing visions of democracy were at odds with the fact, evident to the remaining partisans, that the British and American agents were intent on intelligence missions and not helping them. Estonian appeals for arms brought just a few crates of pistols and submachine guns from the Gehlen Organization, along with two more agents. In Lithuania the national partisan army decided to disband in 1952. A few partisans continued to fight—there are reports of captures as late as 1960 and of deaths in action against Russians as late as 1964.

The CIA-SIS operation also petered out. Until 1956 agent teams went up the Baltic by boat. But after 1954 the Soviets planted a spy within the boat service too, while toward the end of 1955 the Royal Navy withdrew permission for German ships to use British naval ensigns, removing Hans Klose's cover. Then the new government of West Germany absorbed the Gehlen Organization and ordered a halt to its missions into Russia. Baltic partisan warfare proved not only futile but costly. Direct civilian casualties in the three states have been estimated at 75,000. Soviet losses are unknown. In Lithuania the partisans claim 80,000 Russian soldiers killed and somewhere between 4,000 and 12,000 Communist officials and local collaborators eliminated, while admitting losses of 30,000, including 90 percent of their cadres. The Soviets concede just a quarter of those losses but claim only the same number of partisans killed.

American intelligence followed these developments from operational bases in Germany and a monitoring station in Stockholm run by the Gehlen Organization. Reinhard Gehlen himself met Frank Wisner only once, a pro forma drop-in during Gehlen's 1951 visit to Washington. Beginning that April, Wisner's outfit had direct representation in Stockholm in the form of a field station established under William E. Colby, who had worked in Scandinavia for OSS at the end of World War II. His primary mission was to organize stay-behind networks in the region. These groups of agents would be activated only if the Soviets took over the country. The OPC station chief met many Eastern European and Balt emigrés, and talked for hours about conditions in their homelands—primarily, Colby recalled, to boost their morale and encourage them to maintain links with the resistance. A few were steered toward "the correct channels in Europe through which they could get support for anti-Communist activities." The Baltic partisan failure particularly upset Bill Colby, with its implications for his own attempts to create prospective resistance groups. The tight compartmentation of information within the CIA, especially regarding clandestine operations, precluded Colby from discovering that other secret wars throughout Europe were developing along much the same lines as the one he could see.

4

"The Kind of Experience We Need"

IN THE END it was not the Baltic coastal plain but the rugged Balkans that witnessed the first big CIA paramilitary operation. This plan, in conjunction with the British, aimed to unseat the Communist government of Albania, a small state on the eastern littoral of the Adriatic Sea. Geography made the campaign possible: Albania bordered on just two other nations, Greece and Yugoslavia, by 1949 both of them hostile to Stalin. So Albania's "Iron Curtain," isolated from the remainder of the Soviet bloc, became vulnerable. At the same time bases were available on the island of Malta and in Italy, both only a short distance away.

The CIA intended Albania to be a rollback of the Iron Curtain. To the degree a strategic rationale existed for this campaign, it lay in preventing Soviet access to warm-water ports, especially on the Adriatic, crucial to naval control of the central Mediterranean. At the moment the action began the CIA had intelligence that Soviet sailors and advisers were setting up a naval base there. The notion of creating an internal opposition to depose Enver Hoxha, wartime resistance leader who had risen to Communist dictator, came from the SIS. Small bands of commandos were to be infiltrated to set up local guerrilla groups, which could be coordinated and supported from the outside.

The plan, which the British called Operation Valuable and the CIA knew as BG/Fiend,* was discussed internally by the British in late 1948. British difficulties with Albania had begun with incidents two years earlier in which British warships were fired upon. Later a pair of destroyers were mined and sunk in the nar-

---

* Central Intelligence code names, or cryptonyms, have a two-letter combination preceding the name itself. The first element, in this case "BG," identifies a geographical area or functional purpose to which the name is assigned. Such alphabetic elements are frequently confusing, and this narrative will avoid them wherever possible. Also, the CIA term of art for an operation is "project," a word this narrative will use in that sense.

row Corfu Channel along the Albanian coast. Although the British Special Operations Executive (SOE) had armed and advised Enver Hoxha during the war, by 1949 London had decided to overthrow him. In February British foreign secretary Ernest Bevin agreed to the plan to "detach" Albania from the Soviet bloc. The Hoxha government, meanwhile, further encouraged British hostility by refusing to accept an International Court of Justice decision against Albania in the Corfu Channel case.

The British wanted American help, especially financial backing and the use of certain facilities. In March, William Hayter, a senior British intelligence officer, led a delegation of SIS and Foreign Office officials to Washington to argue for American support of Operation Valuable and to present a broad range of alternatives for the prosecution of the Cold War. The Americans responded with alacrity, and DCI Hillenkoetter consulted the 10/2 panel. A month later Frank Wisner took senior officials with him on a trip to London where the Albania plans were finalized. The deal would be sealed with a handshake over lunch at Buck's Club.

Coordinated by a joint committee in Washington, the British representatives for Project Valuable/Fiend were the SIS liaison man and their Balkan expert at the embassy. Americans included Robert Joyce, representing the State Department and its Policy Planning Staff, and James McCargar for the Office of Policy Coordination, whom Frank Lindsay assigned to take the lead. McCargar, a former diplomat pulled into quasi-covert work in his last assignments, had found the task so rewarding that he moved to the CIA. The first OPC field officer assigned would be Robert Low, a veteran of OSS/Cairo, who as a journalist had recently reported from the Balkans. The British initially provided almost all the manpower—it was the Brits who had people with Albania experience from the war, along with well-versed paramilitary experts. Lindsay, whose wartime OSS service had been in Yugoslavia, well knew that.

Hopes in Washington were high. Fiend was, Frank Wisner exclaimed to Joyce, "a clinical experiment to see whether larger rollback operations would be feasible elsewhere."

On his London visit that April, Wisner suggested the use of Wheelus Field, a U.S. air base in Libya, to mount the campaign. The British countered that Malta, a British possession, lay much closer to the objective. Malta became the training and boat base, though some supplies transited through Wheelus. Wisner ruefully told an SIS officer, "Whenever we want to subvert any place, we find that the British own an island within easy reach." British project director David Smiley flew out to the island in the spring. His cover was as deputy chief of staff to the commanding general. On Malta Smiley found an old castle, Fort Binjimma, suitable for a training center. Built during the Napoleonic wars, only a rough trail led to Binjimma, so strange eyes could be detected, while the place was large enough for the trainees and Smiley's staff. Smiley also procured a boat for agent landings, and SIS rented a villa on Corfu as an observation post. The SIS boss further induced a number of paramilitary experts from wartime days to participate, including Harold Perkins, who ran operations. Smiley supervised the training.

Feelers were put out in other directions as well. Yugoslavia, which had halted its aid to Greek leftist guerrillas and broken with Stalin in 1948, might participate. Although the Yugoslavs had approached the United States through CIA channels for military aid, and depended on this assistance to forestall any intervention by Russia, they decided they did not wish to increase Soviet hostility by acting against Albania. Exhausted by its civil war, Greece also wanted no part of Valuable/Fiend, though certain Greek generals tacitly assisted the CIA.

For Michael Burke the adventure began at the Algonquin Hotel. This New York landmark was famous in literary annals as the home of the "Vicious Circle," the luncheon group that had graced its Oak Room in prewar years and included such luminaries as Dorothy Parker, Harold Ross, Robert Benchley, Robert Sherwood, and Harpo Marx, among others. When Burke got a phone call from a man at OPC, he decided the restaurant would serve perfectly for a quiet meeting of spies. They arranged a lunch. The American authors and English character actors who frequented the Oak Room, Burke knew, would have laughed at the idea that the men at the next table were plotting the secret war.

Two men came up from Washington to talk with Burke. They had gotten his name from a friend, a former colleague with the Office of Strategic Services, most likely Frank Lindsay. A college football star at the University of Pennsylvania, during the war E. Michael Burke had served with the navy, been seconded to the OSS, and been sent into Italy with a team in connection with the surrender of that Axis nation. Toward the end of the war Burke had gone on to Yugoslavia and worked with Lindsay to support partisan activities. Another member of his team had been John Ringling North, of the circus family, providing Burke with connections in show business circles. He parlayed them into a postwar job as technical adviser to Warner Bros. studios on their 1946 film tribute to the OSS, *Cloak and Dagger*. Some believe Burke was the model for the role played by Gary Cooper in that movie. By 1949 Burke had established himself in the film industry but become restless. At the Algonquin lunch he had to suppress his excitement and let his CIA interlocutors talk him into coming to the agency as a contract officer.

The blandishments were spectacular—at least at lunch: multiple martinis, two bottles of fine wine, lobster salad, veal. The CIA men described the project in words that could have come straight from Frank Wisner: this was to be "an exploratory action, a clinical case," and close to Burke's experience. He volunteered. But the agency, so new it had scarcely thought through the requirements for clandestine operations, had no idea what cover identity Burke might use. It reassured him that Lindsay, who really had paramilitary experience, held the ultimate responsibility. Not to worry, Burke told the agency men, he'd provide his own cover. Michael Burke moved to Rome and pretended to be opening a new film company.

In Rome Burke began seeing Albanian exiles of different political colorations, with U.S. dollars the inducement to bury their differences. For their part the SIS called upon Julian Amery and Neil McLean, who had worked for SOE in Albania during the war, to sound out their old contacts in Rome, Athens, and Cairo. All were aware of the difficult path ahead. The exiles, Burke recalled, were "more a rallying point than a valid basis for a political revolution." Nevertheless the emigrés constituted the most important element of the project.

The politics of Project Fiend were byzantine. The most accessible Albanian leaders, those of the Balli Kombetar, or National Front, centered in Rome and Athens, had collaborated with the Germans and Italians in the war (though Balli had also waged partisan warfare against them). One leader had been interior minister under the Germans, directly implicated in a February 1944 massacre. Another had been justice minister for the Italian occupation government. At meetings in Rome in June and July 1949, Burke and Amery nonetheless brought Balli into the operation.

Immediately following those meetings, the Western spies flew to Cairo and called on exiled King Zog. Originally a tribal potentate in central Albania, Zog had seized power in a 1924 coup and several years later made himself king. Zog now had his own Legaliteti political movement, led by Ferhat Abbas. When Zog learned the West had already approached the Balli Kombetar, which opposed the monarchy, he furiously demanded the delegates leave.

Julian Amery saved the day, arguing that the time was not ripe to reestablish a kingdom. King Zog needed allies if he wished to attain that goal.

"He was like Talleyrand," recalled Wisner's representative, Robert Low. "I've never seen such diplomacy in my life."

Zog relented.

In Paris on August 26, Albanian exile leaders held a press conference, announcing formation of an Albanian National Committee. This group then secretly toured Britain. There OPC psychological warfare chief Joe Bryan helped the Albanians prepare press releases for their public launching. Bryan got a stay at the Ritz Hotel out of the endeavor, but the arguments among the Albanians proved so acrimonious that he considered the trip wasted.

The Albanians visited the United States more openly, sponsored by the OPC-funded Committee for a Free Europe. Acquiring American entry visas proved especially problematic given their history of collaboration with the Nazis and their lack of passports. Many of these same people had previously been denied entry. But OPC stepped in, arguing the visas were necessary for national security. The CIA did not care to be too closely involved, however; Bob Joyce reported to State, "My friends state that they would prefer not to approach the visa division directly in this case."

Eventually the Albanians got their documents, survived further misadventures with U.S. immigration officials in Canada, and arrived in America. They appeared in New York and Washington and on September 19, 1949, were received by Deputy Assistant Secretary of State Llewelyn E. Thompson. Two of the Albanians opened an office for the national committee in New York. There, on October 3, a senior Balli Kombetar politician, the seventy-year-old Midhat

Frasheri, died suddenly of a heart attack at the Lexington Hotel. Robert Low, called in by the police to identify the dead Albanian, had to explain his connection to Frasheri.

By coincidence, the same night the British boat *Stormie Seas* took two parties, totaling twenty partisans, across the Adriatic from Corfu to land in Albania. The "pixies," as SIS called the Albanians, had been training on Malta since July. This first foray met with disaster: four of the paramilitary men were killed, the others escaped into Greece. Albanian government security forces had evidently known the time and locations of the landings, and they were waiting.

One big problem with Operation Valuable, as it later turned out, was that one of the project's top men was a Soviet spy. That officer, H. A. R. "Kim" Philby, then beginning his tour as SIS liaison in Washington, held one of the two British seats on the joint coordination committee. But Philby did not reach America until a few days after the first pixie failure so he could not be charged with it, though the subsequent course of the Albanian project had much to do with the machinations of the British double agent.

The immediate problem for the secret warriors was to replace Frasheri at the head of the Albanian political organization. At OPC, Carmel Offie pushed strongly for the nationalist Hassan Dosti, who had collaborated with the Italian fascists during the war. Dosti proved to lack the political support to exercise this role. Offie himself soon left the CIA, an early example of a homosexual drummed out of the agency for fear of potential blackmail.

American and British leaders discussed Project Fiend at the highest level during Ernest Bevin's September 1949 visit to Washington. A CIA report concluded that "a purely internal Albanian uprising at this time is not indicated, and, if undertaken, would have little chance of success." Although presumably the CIA analysts were unaware of Valuable/Fiend, they noted nine weaknesses of the Hoxha government while highlighting greatly strengthened Soviet control measures plus continued improvement of Hoxha's 65,000-man army and 15,000-strong security force. Significantly, the report concluded, "the possibility of foreign intervention, in conjunction with widespread popular unrest and antigovernment hostility . . . represents a serious threat to the regime."

An Albanian campaign fit squarely with U.S. policy President Truman approved in December 1948, including an intent to "place the maximum strain on the Soviet structure of power and control, particularly on the relationships between Moscow and the satellite countries." The goals were given concrete expression in a basic policy paper on Eastern Europe on which Secretary of State Dean Acheson relied when speaking to Bevin. The policy provided for an ideological offensive on all fronts that "should be maintained not only on the overt but on the covert plane." In particular, "we should increase the support and refuge we may be able to offer to leaders and groups in these countries who are western-oriented."

In his conversation with Acheson, Bevin asked whether the United States basically agreed with the overthrow of the Hoxha government. Acheson replied in the affirmative.

"Are there," wondered the British foreign secretary, "any kings around that could be put in?"

The picture seemed less bright after the failed October landings. A December 1949 CIA report worried that loyalty to King Zog might be eclipsed by cleavages among the nationalist factions:

> The settlement of differences among the exiled Albanians to provide leadership and coordination is a prerequisite for any effective Albanian resistance against the Hoxha government. Not even this turn of affairs, however, would assure the achievement of any successful resistance without material aid from an outside power. This combination of factors necessary for the overthrow of the Hoxha regime is, as yet, lacking.

Political differences ultimately limited recruiting to strict quotas: 40 percent from the Balli Kombetar, 40 percent from Zog's Legaliteti, the rest from other factions.

After its disappointing beginning, Valuable/Fiend continued for years, consuming increasing resources. In 1950 the CIA began mounting its own pixie expeditions, forming a unit at Karlsfeld, Germany, called Company 400, an initiative begun by Carmel Offie. The unit started with about fifty Albanians but quintupled over time. The CIA set up bases there and in Greece. Seven Poles with wartime experience in Royal Air Force partisan-support units, led by the former Polish colonel Roman Rudkowski, were hired to fly transport aircraft. During the summer OPC used the planes for leaflet drops, with propaganda materials created by the CIA's new Psychological and Paramilitary Staff under Tracy Barnes, recently hired away from his law career. Crafters of the leaflets included E. Howard Hunt in an early CIA assignment. The first unilateral CIA pixie insertion occurred by airdrop in late November 1950—nine Albanians drawn from Company 400.

Kim Philby remained in Washington through the summer of 1951, when he came under suspicion and was recalled. Although doubts focused upon Philby as the result of the defections to Russia of two British diplomats, Guy Burgess and Donald Maclean, CIA's chief of counterintelligence may have wondered about the Albanian fiascoes as well. In the interim there had been a dozen infiltrations with almost fifty pixies. Virtually all those staged by sea or air had miscarried. In one spectacular failure in July 1951, with Philby already under investigation, three groups were parachuted in by OPC—one was obliterated on landing, one was surrounded in a house and burned alive, while two pixies of the last group of four were killed and the other two captured, with an embarrassing public trial in Albania that fall.

Only overland infiltration seemed to have any success. A group in September 1950 managed to survive for two months inside Albania but could raise no resistance. The most successful pixie was Hamit Matjani, a CIA favorite called the Tiger, who made fifteen incursions. He habitually moved overland and secretly. Matjani's sixteenth mission, a parachute drop, became his last. The Tiger and his party were ambushed by Hoxha security forces.

Matjani's last mission had actually been set up by Hoxha's own security men with Soviet advice. After capturing a radio and two officers of Zog's bodyguard in the spring of 1952, they forced the captives to use their radio to mislead the CIA with rosy reports of growing resistance and appeals for more aid—the same kind of deception with which the Soviets had succeeded in the Baltic. The SIS, frustrated by boat landing failures in the summer, withdrew completely. The Americans carried on, to drop Matjani to his death in May 1953.

The Hoxha government paraded captives for a week-long show trial in April 1954. Not even the CIA could continue after that. Frank Wisner had simply been wrong when he insisted to Philby at an early stage, "We'll get it right next time!"

Widespread disillusionment followed the Albanian experience, not least among the former "pixies." Halil Nerguti complains, "We were used as an experiment. We were a small part of a big game, pawns that could be sacrificed." Michael Burke, OPC station chief in Rome until 1951, voiced a general opinion when he observed, "In the end it was not possible to do without overt air and military support from England and the United States or somewhere. You couldn't do it just with the locals."

British officer David Smiley moved on to the elite military Special Air Service, then became a soldier of fortune. CIA ideologue E. Howard Hunt "welcomed" orders for transfer to the Western Hemisphere Division. Michael Burke, promoted from contract to regular CIA officer, went on to Germany where he ran agent drops directly into the Soviet Union.

It fell to the Southeast Europe Division chief, John H. Richardson, to liquidate Project Fiend. A wartime veteran of the Counter Intelligence Corps in Italy, Richardson had been renowned for his skill, tact, and the apparent ease with which he persuaded Italian townspeople to accept Allied military governments. Flying to Rome after the show-trial disaster, Richardson had the most delicate of missions. Joseph Leib, the Rome station chief, still believed in the adventure.

Richardson sat down over drinks with the station chief and got right to the point. Albanian activities would end immediately.

"Then," asked Leib, "it's all over?"

"All over."

"I don't know what they'll say about it in London." An aide accompanying Richardson noted that tears glistened amid the stubble on the overworked man's face.

Richardson responded gently, "London already knows."

The fighting in Albania may have been fierce, but some of the dirtiest, muddiest covert warfare took place right in Washington, D.C. There the Central Intelligence Agency quickly outgrew its buildings—four old ones at 2430 E Street, across from what is today the State Department, plus the four "temporary" ones down the slight hill and by the Reflecting Pool. Before long various cells of spooks were scattered in more than two dozen places around town. And as the Cold War heated up, so too did the pressures to do more. The number of ways CIA elements could stumble over one another grew steadily. Especially acute were the possibilities for foul-ups between Wisner's Office of Policy Coordination and the espionage mavens of the Office of Special Operations, headed by Brig. Gen. Robert A. Schow. Every time an OPC station opened in the field—and there were five new ones in the first year alone—the possibilities for confusion increased exponentially.

A host of reasons underlay the resentments between OPC and OSO. For one thing, Wisner's shop had been born rich: the OPC took over the unexpended funds of the CIA unit it replaced, made deals with the Treasury to use funds in other accounts, and got Marshall Plan money along with its own regular budgets. Agency wags joked about OPCers with their Jaguars while OSO officers drove broken-down Fords, but the humor betokened real differences. With the rush to build a capability for secret warfare, the usual hiring regulations had been suspended for OPC. Wisner frequently offered recruits employment at higher ranks, matching their civilian pay elsewhere.

General Schow's clandestine service people for the most part were from the Office of Strategic Services and stayed in intelligence through the lean years after 1945, considering themselves true professionals. Wisner's Wurlitzer had a proportion of former OSS officers, but they were coming back to spying after a time that had witnessed huge changes. They were the amateurs, cowboys with missionary zeal. Engaged in their campaigns of subversion and psychological warfare, Wisner's people viewed the OSO types as pedestrian, "'washerwomen gossiping over their laundry,'" as Frank Wisner colorfully put it.

The OSO remained under a strict CIA chain of command while Wisner played his games, with OPC suspended among Central Intelligence, the State Department, and the Pentagon. And in the field the key conflict remained the fact that both units wanted the same foreign folks on their payrolls. Stalwarts of OSO like Richard Helms felt Wisner's officers paid little attention to security discipline, coordination, or cover—key aspects of espionage tradecraft. Michael Burke's New York lunch in the early days of Project Fiend seems to bear that out.

As Admiral Hillenkoetter struggled to establish the CIA, officials of the National Security Council wrestled with how to control it. Secretary of Defense James Forrestal wanted supervision by the NSC executive secretary, at that time Sidney Souers, who had returned to Washington at President Truman's behest. Souers wanted no part of the job. He acerbically told Forrestal that if he'd wanted to manage intelligence he would still be the DCI. Hillenkoetter suggested that an outside panel be asked to review and report on U.S. intelligence management and missions. The president approved in January 1948. Allen Dulles, the Sullivan & Cromwell lawyer and intelligence activist, agreed to chair the panel. Forrestal made the appointment and, on Dulles's advice, those of two more members, William H. Jackson and Matthias F. Correa. All three were lawyers with wartime intelligence experience.

Completed over the summer and fall, the Dulles-Jackson-Correa report considered every aspect of U.S. intelligence practice and had much to do with the emergence of an integrated intelligence "community." It implicitly criticized Hillenkoetter, whose days after that were numbered. But beyond its conclusions on CIA leadership, on the community, on intelligence estimates, and on NSC supervision, the January 1949 report bore specific implications for the Office of Policy Coordination. Of course both Dulles and Jackson were friends of Wisner, and their report explicitly advocated strengthened covert action. Yet at the same time the study pointed to duplication and confusion between the Office of Policy Coordination and the Office of Special Operations. Truman's NSC ordered State and the Pentagon to collaborate on a paper that would turn the Dulles-Jackson-Correa report into a set of recommendations, completed and adopted by the National Security Council that July. One of these was that the CIA establish an "operations division" to include both OSO and OPC. Thus by the summer of 1949, even as Wisner's Wurlitzer took the field for covert operations in both Albania and the Soviet Union, President Truman's goals envisioned folding OPC more closely into the CIA. Reaching that goal turned out to require three years of hard work.

Hillenkoetter responded after about a month with a plan for the new directorate to bring together spies and secret warriors. The initiative required a revision of Truman's covert operations authority, NSC-10/2, the one that had cost the State Department and Pentagon direct control over Wisner's Wurlitzer. State took no action at all. The issue languished for months while OPC mounted missions in the field. Meanwhile the Soviet Union first tested an atomic bomb, marking a radical advance in its military technology. Truman ordered a full-scale policy review resulting in a now-famous paper, NSC-68. U.S. Cold War actions should ascend to a new level of intensity, according to NSC-68, including increased political and psychological warfare. While the cost of NSC-68 was still being calculated, in June 1950 North Korea invaded South Korea, initiating a bitter war. Within days of the attack Admiral Hillenkoetter requested sea duty, a neat solution to his replacement. The admiral soon left the CIA to command a cruiser division off the Korean coast. The onset of the Korean War triggered a whole new problem for the Office of Policy Coordination. Under the NSC-10/2 directive, in wartime the U.S. military would dictate missions for the secret warriors. But Korea, a limited war, did not engage the bulk of OPC resources, nor was it the main stage upon which the secret wars played. Suddenly even Frank Wisner had reason to demand changes in his NSC authority.

Truman already had Hillenkoetter's successor lined up. He was Lt. Gen. Walter Bedell Smith, the fifty-four-year-old officer who had been wartime chief of staff to Allied supreme commander Gen. Dwight D. Eisenhower. From 1946 to 1949 Smith had served as U.S. ambassador to Moscow. Now commanding the U.S. First Army, he was a reluctant recruit, repeatedly protesting his ignorance of intelligence work and advancing his health problems as an added objection. Smith had had several operations for ulcers, culminating in 1950 when doctors at Walter Reed Army Hospital removed most of his stomach. The Korean War began as the general recuperated. Truman prevailed on Smith, in view of the serious situation, to take on the CIA job. Sworn in on October 7, 1950, this no-nonsense DCI hit the intelligence community like a hurricane.

Walter Bedell Smith had the clout to make things happen and sufficient prestige among the U.S. military to knock down their opposition to CIA's role. The military intelligence units had resisted acknowledging the primacy of the director of central intelligence or fully participating in the community's board of directors, then known as the Intelligence Advisory Committee. Smith turned them into "a tame act at a circus," in the words of Paul Borel, a top CIA administrative officer. Smith performed similarly with respect to the Office of Policy Coordination, simply announcing he had taken full control. In view of his weak intelligence background, General Smith had demanded a deputy who made up for that shortcoming; the man appointed was William Harding Jackson, co-author of the 1949 CIA panel study and Frank Wisner's friend and former law partner. Jackson, Wisner, and CIA general counsel Lawrence Houston drafted new language for the NSC-10/2 directive, which they took to General Smith. Smith threw the paper in the trash. Wisner objected that he remained bound to the 10/2 panel. Smith told him to forget it—as DCI, the general said, he had all the authority necessary to direct OPC. The arrangements made in 1948 had been overtaken by events and were no longer valid.

As for Wisner's problem with wartime military control, in mid-December General Smith persuaded the National Security Council to suspend the relevant paragraph of the NSC-10/2 directive. He promised to draft a fresh revision and gave Wisner the task. The OPC chief consulted the interagency panel where, it should be noted, he had good friends: Bob Joyce still represented State while Gen. John Magruder, once head of the pre-CIA Strategic Services Unit, stood in for the Office of the Secretary of Defense. Admiral Leslie Stevens, member for the Joint Chiefs of Staff, had been naval attaché at the Moscow embassy when Bedell Smith headed that mission. Smith's review of the budget for 1951 sharpened the issue, for he found OPC planning covert operations far beyond anything envisioned in 1948, just because no one else was doing it. Seeking NSC guidance, Smith sent the White House a paper on the pace and scope of covert action. The JCS objected, and their paper went to the White House as well. It came back studded with scathing marginal notes in Truman's own hand, one of the few times Harry Truman ever commented in writing on intelligence matters. Meanwhile General Magruder told Secretary of Defense George Marshall that DCI Smith sought a fair solution. To avoid an open battle, Marshall had subordinates and JCS officers meet Bedell Smith and the 10/2 panelists to hammer out an answer. The Joint Chiefs went along with a formula under which they continued to send orders in wartime, but the contents were to be determined by the director of central intelligence. This arrangement would be codified in the revised directive NSC-10/5, which Truman approved in the fall of 1951.

There remained the internal struggle between the Office of Policy Coordination and the Office of Special Operations. Director Smith made a start at untangling the conflict by designating personal representatives whom he dispatched to the most important CIA stations abroad. These persons were in neither the OPC nor the OSO chains of command, but they were to be kept in the picture by both divisions and could alert General Smith when problems arose. Meanwhile at head-quarters Smith moved to impose coordination by making both offices report to a common boss: in January 1951 he created the Directorate for Plans (hereafter to be called the Directorate for Operations or DO). No doubt at the behest of Bill Jackson, General Smith brought in Allen Dulles, who for several months had been advising him as a consultant, as deputy director for operations (DDO).

Brains at CIA came up with the idea of bringing better cooperation between Wisner's Wurlitzer and the Office of Special Operations by collocating them. In March 1951 Wisner and the OSO chief, Gen. Willard G. Wyman, agreed. The gambit caused migraine headaches among administrative staff, faced with the need to make it work. The solution had matching branches of the two units along the same halls, directly across from each other. Management emptied successive floors within CIA buildings and moved OPC and OSO units to the new locations. But the wish could not make the reality: no one crossed the hallways. A different Smith, Joseph Burkholder Smith, joined OPC as a young officer in September 1951. He recalls that "OPC and OSO personnel, though located on opposite sides of the hall, did not cross each other's thresholds."

Meanwhile, DCI Smith's personal-representative arrangement did not work. The operating divisions kept cutting them out of the action. Only a few months after Dulles took over the DO, a formal complaint came from the field that Wis-ner's Wurlitzer was poaching on OSO turf. A fresh formula had to be devised. General Smith ordered William H. Jackson to survey both divisions. In May 1951, after completing his OPC study, Jackson recommended a single chain of command down to the station level. But Jackson's survey of OSO ran head on into Lyman B. Kirkpatrick, executive assistant to the DCI, who thought that OSO ought to be responsible for all contacts with agents or groups for any purpose, whether espionage or covert action, with OPC confined to activities that did not involve contact. Division chief Willard Wyman agreed and used a visit to Far East field stations that fall to reinforce the OSO message. When Wyman departed to take up an army assignment in Korea in December, Kirkpatrick succeeded him. The appointment became the latest of the personnel changes that eventually transformed the CIA: William H. Jackson left his post as deputy director of cen-tral intelligence, though he stayed on a few months as a consultant; Allen Dulles, who had been a consultant, replaced Jackson; and Frank Wisner moved up to be-come deputy director for operations. Col. Kilbourne Johnston took over as OPC chief.

Lyman Kirkpatrick also wanted DO staff kept to a minimum to avoid man-agers getting in the way of operators. Deputy Director Dulles reported this view to Smith—operations should be subordinated to espionage. But Bedell Smith had a predilection for covert operations. They were, in a favorite Smith phrase, "my dish of tea." On his deathbed the director recounted taking one especially nefarious suggestion to Harry Truman doubting its legality. On the spot the president wrote out an undated blanket pardon for his spy chieftain. In January 1952 General Smith signed a directive prepared by DDO Wisner mandating merger of the Office of Policy Coordination and the Office of Special Operations. The order ended months of rumors that had been grist for watercooler conversations throughout headquarters. At the moment of consolidation, the Office of Policy Coordination had forty-seven field stations and about six thousand personnel, slightly more than half of them overseas contractees. About half the OPC people worked for the Far East Division.

As an experiment, the small Latin America branches of both OPC and Special Operations joined together starting in August 1951, branch by branch, becoming the Western Hemisphere Division of the DO. That would be the first. Gen. Lucien K. Truscott, CIA's chief in Germany, saw Smith in early March and presented him with a scheme for integrating field stations of the two offices. Officials continued OSO's bitter rearguard struggle. One objection was that key spies' cover could be blown in the integration, another that staffs would resist the changes. Kirkpatrick tried again in May, proposing that the DO should have components for espionage, psychological warfare, and paramilitary activities, and that current chiefs would continue to lead their units. Kilbourne Johnston rejected that notion out of hand.

Finally Director Smith sent Kirkpatrick off to settle differences among warring spooks in the field and ordered Kirk's deputy, Richard M. Helms, to draft the new merger plan. One interpretation is that Helms followed direct orders from the DCI, another that Smith enlisted him to overcome the last vestiges of OSO opposition, yet a third that Helms understood resistance to be futile. Richard Helms would one day sit in the director's chair; his biographer has called him "the man who kept the secrets." In his memoirs Helms is completely silent about his role in the integration of the DO. Quintessential spy chief as opposed to secret warrior, Helms commented favorably on the people: "I was reminded of how much there was to be said for the way some OPC officers achieved so many of their objectives while hammering their service into shape."

General Smith issued the order in mid-July 1952, much of its text verbatim from the Helms paper. The July 15 directive, partly justification and part ordinance, argued that OSS and British experience during World War II as well as that of the CIA over the preceding three years showed the best arrangement to be a "single chain of command with a single set of administrative procedures," with the DDO as the director's deputy for all CIA clandestine activities. The Directorate for Operations would add staffs for long-range planning and review. The chief of operations under the DDO would act as chief of staff, eliminating duplication, and would be responsible for the field. The DO would have staff elements for secret intelligence and counterespionage, political and psychological warfare—the same functions formerly the province of the Office of Special Operations and the Office of Policy Coordination—plus paramilitary operations, technical support, and administration. The DO's paramilitary staff would be a fresh unit taking this function away from the former Wurlitzer.

Lyman Kirkpatrick, in Thailand to reconcile OSO and OPC station chiefs who had a little war going between themselves, suddenly got instructions to explain the DO changes and continue the trip, alerting others to the order. Kirkpatrick would become chief of operations of the DO, which meant functioning as deputy to Frank Wisner, the DDO. But Kirkpatrick never assumed the post. Before leaving Thailand, on July 20 Kirk suddenly fell ill. He turned out to have polio. After lengthy rehabilitation, he returned to the CIA in 1953 as inspector general. Richard Helms became acting chief of operations and would be formally appointed on February 26, 1953.

At the heart of the denied areas stood the Soviet Union itself. Even before there was a CIA, the Central Intelligence Group's orders were to collect data about Russia as unobtrusively and extensively as possible. The rush to make contacts among exiles and others with knowledge of the Soviet Union gave the emigrés a great incentive to produce information for American consumption, true and false. Pandering became so widespread the term "paper mill" was applied to networks that produced bogus intelligence. One emigré told the Gehlen people that nine-tenths of what the Americans were buying had been manufactured.

Still, CIA had no alternative except to deal with the exiles. The principal organizations were OUN and NTS. The *Ukrayinska Viyskova Orhaniztsiya* (UVO)—better known by its English-language rendering OUN, the Organization of Ukrainian Nationalists—the main Ukrainian nationalist grouping, had been founded by refugees in Paris in the early 1920s. From its beginning the Soviets considered OUN a threat. In the Ukraine, OUN established resistance groups and carried out occasional sabotage until World War II intervened. At that time nationalist Stepan Bandera was serving a life sentence for his murder of a Polish minister. Bandera escaped during the Germans' 1939 invasion of Poland to be elected head of OUN. Two years later the Germans invaded Russia, and Bandera and other OUN leaders appealed for Ukrainian freedom. Some saw the Ukrainians as associating themselves with German occupiers. Bandera became disillusioned with the Germans and was imprisoned by them, but he agreed to resume cooperation toward the end of the war. In late 1943, protected by German security, Bandera participated in a conference of ethnic minorities that set up an Anti-Bolshevik Front. In mid-1944 Bandera and other Ukrainians formed a Supreme Liberation Council to fight the Soviets.

During the Russo-German war OUN was armed by the Germans. Many Ukrainians fought in the auxiliaries. An entire division of the Nazis' Waffen SS, Sixteenth SS "Galicia," was composed of Ukrainians. Whole units of Ukrainians, German officers included, later formed the core of the UPA partisan army, the force behind the band of soldiers who appeared in Germany in 1947. Ukrainians claimed to have 50,000 soldiers in September 1944, scattered across the Ukraine, southern Poland, and eastern Czechoslovakia. From that summer, when the last German troops were driven from south Russia, OUN fought on its own. This was partisan warfare on a grand scale, and it did not end with V-E Day. Courier links increasingly broke down after May 1946, but in 1947 OUN leaders still claimed as many as 100,000 partisans under arms in eight large formations.

In 1946 Soviet officials demanded the extradition of Bandera, by then ensconced in the American occupation zone of Germany, as a war criminal. Instead he was kept under surveillance in an operation the CIC knew as Anyface, to prevent attempts against him. Warned to hide even though the CIC had information potentially implicating him in war crimes, Bandera disappeared. Americans told the Russians they had no idea of his whereabouts. Meanwhile Bandera's organization, with the help of British intelligence, reinvented the wartime Anti-Bolshevik Front as the Anti-Bolshevik Bloc of Nations (ABN), a multinational proto-fascist and essentially anti-democratic union that long outlasted the secret war against Russia.

Partisan struggle continued in the Ukraine, including those parts relocated within Poland and Czechoslovakia by Stalin's border changes. Ukrainians had suffered terribly in the Great Patriotic War—three million sent to Germany as forced labor, half that number still missing, two and a half million killed. There were plenty of reasons for them to support OUN and very few to welcome Stalin's return. Stalin's response was vigorous. He posted strong Red Army forces to the Ukraine. Party activists sent to the Ukraine and Moldavia (now Moldova) included Nikita Khrushchev, Leonid Brezhnev, and Konstantin Chernenko. Postwar work in south Russia became a stepping stone to power for many Soviet leaders. Marshal Georgi K. Zhukov went to command the Odessa Military District in July 1946. Zhukov had distinguished himself in the war and was perhaps Stalin's best general. Speculation at the time centered on the possibility that he was being demoted. Others maintain Zhukov's mission involved threatening Turkey, from which Russia wanted concessions. But State Department intelligence reports in 1947 observed that Zhukov was being used to stabilize the Ukraine. In fact, the local Communist Party headquarters at Odessa had burned down during riots there the preceding winter.

With Zhukov in command, military operations now assumed major proportions. Soviet and Eastern European reports in 1946 several times claimed the "liquidation" of hundreds of partisans, whom the Soviets typically tried to associate with the Nazis. In the spring of 1947 the Polish army, officered by Russians, began evacuating local populations. There were also coordinated attacks in the tri-border region by Polish, Czech, and Soviet forces. But OUN remained powerful. The partisans struck back when they machine-gunned the Polish vice minister of defense.

While Czech security strove to seal the border, they proved unable to prevent Ukrainian infiltration. That fall the Czech defense minister, Gen. Ludvik Svoboda, estimated that hundreds of partisans were still at large. The Poles claimed the elimination of six UPA "brigade groups" with two thousand partisans killed or captured. As for the Soviets, in a January 1948 speech reported by *Pravda*, Khrushchev declared, "The Ukrainian people have destroyed an insignificant bunch of Ukrainian nationalists and will annihilate the remnants of them." Referring to the partisans in his memoirs, Khrushchev concedes the "flare-ups" of fighting "sometimes amounted to war," and that partisan activity "became so serious that the Polish forces had to conduct full scale military operations."

But Khrushchev's January 1948 speech cloaked a struggle far from over. Members of the unit that escaped to Germany estimated OUN/UPA armed strength at between 50,000 and 200,000 soldiers. They also revealed details of the structure of the partisan forces: administratively organized into "regiments," with fighting units of platoon (40 men), company (150 men), and battalion (500 to 800 partisans) size. Most combat units were of company size and armed with light weapons, a half-dozen or more machine guns, and equal numbers of mortars.

This data about UPA capabilities did not prevent State Department intelligence from concluding that resistance no longer seemed serious. But it also did not prevent Ukrainian appeals. A conference of emigrés in New York appealed to President Truman on August 31, 1947: "Ukraine is fighting for its freedom by means of its powerful insurgent army. We endorse her fight for freedom on the grounds of the Atlantic Charter. We believe that Russian aggressiveness would lose its power if [the] Ukraine were liberated and acquired self rule."

In Washington there was growing interest in operations in the denied areas. A 1948 NSC study advocated ties with anti-Soviet groups as a prime means of acquiring information. The OPC began to move in 1949, with Frank Wisner demanding the Gehlen Organization get agents into Russia. Division chief Franklin Lindsay labored to get the project going. At the CIA's Office of Special Operations, Lindsay's opposite number, Harry Rositzke, looked at Pentagon wish lists as pie in the sky—they included up to two thousand agents on the ground in Russia.

But the hour was late in the Ukraine. Many UPA partisan companies were down to cadre strength. Although one unit conducted a daring five-week raid into Romania, Brig. Gen. Roman Shuchewycz, commander of the insurgent army, on September 3, 1949, ordered deactivation and conversion to an underground. The CIA's Ukraine operation began two days later, when two agents dropped by parachute after a flight from Germany across Central Europe.

Like so many others, this CIA project became a joint effort with the British. The Office of Policy Coordination differed with London over which emigré factions to back. SIS chose OUN. Officers at OPC believed the tide of history had turned against the partisans and preferred the Russian social democratic group National Labor Alliance, or NTS (*Natsionalno Trudovoi Soyuz*). The NTS formed in Belgrade in 1930, among emigrés of the first wave opposed to both Soviet and tsarist rule. It espoused parliamentary democracy. Like OUN, the NTS maintained courier services into Russia and tried to establish networks. Like Bandera, it had collaborated in the early days with the German wartime administration. But unlike OUN, NTS made no effort at partisan war. Rather, under Dr. Georgi S. Okolovich, the NTS ideologist Vladimir Poremski developed a "molecular theory," in which widening sectors of society would oppose the Communists and ultimately over-throw Soviet rule.

These views were advanced in pamphlets, in the NTS newspaper *Posev*, and on broadcasts of Radio Free Russia, the NTS station. An administrative headquarters was located in Paris and a field center in Frankfurt with more than two hundred personnel. The NTS recruited and trained its own agents near Frankfurt at Bad Homburg. The Russian emigrés already had relations with the Counter Intelligence Corps and Army G-2 as well as the Gehlen Organization and SIS. So it was easy for NTS to connect with the Office of Policy Coordination.

Soon the Russian project was in full swing. Frank Wisner's boys and the Gehlen Org did preliminary screening, recruiting the Russians under the same terms offered the Balts. Published estimates of the number of "special forces" agents trained before 1954 range up to five thousand. Most were members of labor units like the Albanian Company 400. This program functioned as a farm system, identifying suitable candidates for missions to denied areas. The number trained in the United States between 1948 and 1954, much lower, included at least two hundred persons with Nazi connections, people whom the State Department had to admit on grounds of national security.

The SIS took the lead in actual infiltration. According to Kim Philby, Anglo-American cooperation on denied-area schemes was chilly. On the Ukrainian situation, Philby recalls the CIA arguing that Stepan Bandera was anti-American, that OUN represented extreme nationalism with fascist overtones, and that anyway its roots were among the "old" emigration. A meeting in Washington, Philby asserts, between the responsible CIA officers and the SIS chief for Northern Europe, Harry Carr, ended with the sides openly accusing each other of "wholesale lying."

Philby claims the accusations were justified, on both sides!

London witnessed a conference at the highest level between the CIA and SIS in April 1951. Allen Dulles, now deputy director for plans and touring Europe to familiarize himself, seized the moment to coordinate with SIS. Dulles's staff encouraged the British to abandon Bandera. At the London conference Harry Carr flatly refused despite a weakened position—two SIS missions sent into Russia during 1950 had both disappeared without a trace.

The CIA and the British remained deadlocked, with the practical result that support continued for both the Ukrainians and the NTS. In 1951 the British dropped three parties of six agents each: into the Ukraine, the foothills of the Carpathians, and southern Poland. None ever reported back. At least one team consisted of veterans of the Nazis' SS "Galicia" Division. A CIA four-man unit was unproductive, as were several missions the secret warriors dispatched to the Ukraine and Moldavia. Remnants of OUN and Bandera forces held out in the Carpathians until 1952, but the bands were slowly tracked down.

Intelligence agents operated at grave disadvantage. The population was closely controlled and state security everywhere. It was only in 1951, apparently, that the CIA learned the printing processes the Russians used to produce internal passports and other documents. Planes to drop agents into denied areas were flown by the British through Cyprus and by the CIA through Greece and western Germany. But the partisans had been broken by the time agent teams began to arrive, so the underground proved unable to provide shelter.

The dilemmas were quite direct for Michael Burke. In 1951 the CIA contract officer, recalled from the Albania project, obtained a line slot at Frankfurt, Germany, on the Russian infiltration program. Burke missed the Mediterranean easiness of Rome and would not be much enamored of German rigidities, but the mission had precedence. He took charge of the CIA's biggest field operation, as Burke put it, "a large disparate body of Americans with varying skills and talents, dispersed in a dozen locations throughout the country, a myriad of ongoing activities of varying quality, and dozens of indigenous men and women agents ranging from individual couriers to organized resistance movements."

In May 1951 the CIA sent another army officer to Germany as Director Smith's personal representative. Gen. Lucien K. Truscott, Jr., thoroughly represented the Old Army. He had learned to play the bugle from the bugler in *his* father's cavalry regiment, then grew up to join the army, winning a battlefield commission in World War I. A forty-six-year-old Texan and a professional's professional, Truscott and Bedell Smith had both been at Fort Leavenworth in the mid-1930s, and in World War II Truscott had served briefly on Eisenhower's staff, which Smith headed. Truscott became one of the most successful U.S. commanders in Sicily, Italy, and France. He had had some unconventional warfare experience—with Lord Mountbatten at the Combined Operations Command at the time of the Dieppe raid and other commando actions—and went on to help found the American Rangers. Truscott had retired in 1947. Walter Bedell Smith induced him to return to Germany, where he had been an occupation commander shortly after the war.

Truscott had a natural ability for intelligence and a good nose for security. He quickly became concerned with agent losses in Russian operations. Investigating the CIA's relationships with the Gehlen Org and the NTS Russians, he found many ways the missions might be compromised. With Germany the CIA's biggest show—the station at Frankfurt comprised fourteen hundred officers at this time— weaknesses were serious business. When OPC and OSO consolidated in 1952, Truscott gained the power to issue orders in the agency's name. He initiated a formal inquiry. When Allen Dulles came through on a tour of CIA stations, Truscott used his briefing to warn of the collapse of infiltration operations. The general's prestige and known connections with Director Smith were such that he could make even Allen Dulles, who once walked out of a Truscott talk, sit down and listen to the rest of the gloomy news.

In late December 1952 came the collapse of yet another CIA-SIS joint operation, which ought to have given the Americans pause. This concerned Poland, where for years the spooks assumed they were in contact with an anti-Soviet underground called WIN (*Wolnosc I Niepodleglosc*, or Freedom and Independence). The roots lay in World War II when Polish resistance to the Nazis had been crushed in the 1944 Battle of Warsaw as Soviet armies stood by and watched. Stalin then proceeded to contrive a Soviet satellite state in Poland. The WIN consisted of Poles, mostly resistance veterans, as an anti-Soviet underground. But its first commander had been arrested and tried in a 1947 Soviet crackdown after the Americans and British cooperated in spiriting out of the country the former prime minister and other Polish nationalists. Why the intelligence services did not conclude that WIN had been destroyed right there remains a mystery. Around that time Harry Carr of SIS had approached Gen. Wladislaw Anders, Poland's wartime field commander on the Allied side, who naturally had WIN connections, and sought to forge links to the underground.

Poland seemed a logical theater for CIA political warfare, certainly a place to argue for democracy as against communism. WIN seemed the ideal instrument. Frank Lindsay powered up the Wurlitzer. The Poles sent couriers to the West, letters to emigré families, and radio messages to the Western intelligence services; they had, they said, five hundred WIN operatives, twenty thousand who could be mobilized, and a hundred thousand sympathizers. The WIN messages asked for money and supplies. The British and Americans did not know these messages were from the Russians, who were running WIN as a deception game.

In February 1949 the British bowed out of the affair. OPC then furnished all the money for WIN, more than a million dollars over three years. In 1951 Lindsay recruited John Bross, another of those former lawyers and OSS types, who had been a Jedburgh commando, to run the Polish business as his deputy. Bross also knew about CIA's German base since he came to the agency from a job as legal counsel to the U.S. high commissioner in Germany. Like others, Bross was completely fooled—once at a meeting he threw out the number 37,000 as a figure for Polish underground troops fighting the Soviets a month after the feared war for Europe began. In 1952 WIN asked for a list of the targets the CIA wanted destroyed in the event of that war, certainly something Russian intelligence would need to know. The CIA sent the list. Bross became queasy when WIN followed up by asking for an American general to be parachuted to the alleged underground to buck up its morale. Bross put his foot down. The Russians, knowing the game was up, blew the operation for its propaganda value. A star agent first recruited by the British revealed himself as a Russian spy, recounting how WIN had deceived the West. Then the Soviets staged a show trial of other WIN figures, hapless Poles whom the Russians had pulled in with this false-flag operation.

This latest failure, and the consolidation of the CIA's Directorate for Operations, were the end for Frank Lindsay. Burned out with the chain of disaster, Lindsay announced his departure. Allen Dulles asked him to write a paper on the lessons learned in all these covert actions. Dulles and Lindsay went over the draft one weekend day at Dulles's home. The conclusions, uniformly negative, reflected Lindsay's understanding of the Russians' tight security everywhere behind the Iron Curtain. Dulles could not abide this, but Lindsay stuck to his guns. He left for the Ford Foundation. His replacement as chief of DO's Eastern Europe Division would be John Bross. The CIA's secret war ground on.

There were many reasons for concern. Until 1951 the Soviets had the advantage of information from Philby, but he was not their only source. From 1950 on they received reports from Heinz Felfe, a senior officer of the Gehlen Org, plus Canadian spy Gordon Lonsdale. The Russians also used the flow of refugees and Displaced Persons, a main source of recruits for OPC and the SIS, to insert spies into Western operations. Among the most valuable was Capt. Nikita Khorunshy, who defected in Berlin in 1948, telling CIC his reason was love for a German girl. Like many Russian DPs, Khorunshy moved to Frankfurt. There he became associated with NTS. The emigrés relied on his recent knowledge of conditions in Russia and hired Khorunshy for their training school at Bad Homburg. Thus the Soviets had a spy at the very center of the operation run against them. Using intelligence from Khorunshy, they were able to supply agents with the specific qualifications sought by the Western services, spies who compromised their CIA missions. Khorunshy meanwhile, beginning in 1951, funneled the Soviets with a stream of data on individuals trained through the NTS–Gehlen Org–OPC network. He also suggested and provided the knowledge for an assassination attempt against NTS chief Okolovich. The betrayal of a 1953 team he had trained at Bad Homburg finally uncovered Khorunshy.

The CIA lost another sixteen agents in at least five missions during 1952 and 1953. British losses are still unknown, as are those of the Office of Special Operations, which ran its own agents into the denied areas. Each time the base dispatched one of CIA's aircraft to carry a team, it took a tremendous chance the plane would be downed behind the Iron Curtain. Agency officers agonized facing the go/no-go decisions for these flights. Although Khorunshy was arrested in 1954, the Soviets captured a solo agent plus yet another CIA team. Mike Burke estimated an agent's chances with all the best backup the CIA could furnish at no better than 50 percent. Whatever the odds, losses mounted with very little to show.

For their part, the Russians adopted Khorunshy's scheme to murder Dr. Okolovich. In February 1954 they sent two East Germans plus Capt. Nikolai I. Khoklov to Frankfurt to execute the NTS leader. Operation Rhine, as the Russians called their plot, miscarried when Khoklov repented and confessed to Okolovich instead of killing him. The extent to which NTS had by this time become subordinated to the CIA is suggested by the ease with which the Americans then took Khoklov away from NTS.

Michael Burke had had enough. Returning to Washington in April 1954, he went to dinner at Frank Wisner's P Street home. Allen Dulles also attended. Burke worried about the long flights over Eastern Europe needed to deposit agents in Russia. On the most recent intrusion the CIA plane had been intercepted by two Russian fighters over Hungary during its return. The plane had escaped into nearby clouds, but the sign was ominous—Russian radar coverage had become so wide and air units so numerous that the flights were exceedingly dangerous. Opinion at the CIA base turned against more attempts. Burke worried that headquarters avoided telling operators of dangers to their missions. He needed reassurance—

not only that CIA's commitment remained strong but that the president *wanted* the missions. His bosses gave Burke only standard arguments. Facing a headquarters tour, supporting a growing family, Michael Burke gave up the CIA. He went to the circus instead. Burke became an executive with Ringling Brothers, later with Madison Square Garden, and ended up as general manager of the New York Yankees. The CIA could not afford to lose officers like him.

Meanwhile the "Khoklov affair" became only one of a series of Soviet measures against emigré figures. Okolovich was beaten during an abortive kidnapping. NTS ideologist Poremski survived another miscarried murder attempt. The Russians were more successful with Ukrainian leader Lev Rebet, assassinated in 1957. Also killed were two senior Radio Free Europe broadcasters. This campaign climaxed on October 15, 1959, when Stepan Bandera died outside his Munich apartment building, dosed with cyanide from an ingeniously constructed gun.

Secret warfare against Russia ground to a halt. On a trip from Munich to Washington in 1953, Allen Dulles told one of his senior specialists on Soviet affairs, "At least we're getting the kind of experience we need for the next war."

Michael Burke, for one, could move on. Not so for many of the emigrés recruited by the CIA. One of the legacies of this secret war, the Anti-Bolshevik Bloc of Nations, went on to support dictators and help subvert democratic governments, the very antithesis of America's commitment to democracy. Along the way many idealistic people mobilized by the secret wars lost their lives. Reflecting on this period three decades later, State Department Balkans expert John C. Campbell commented: "What did we offer these people? We did not have any means really of supporting a revolt which might break out. I think we were responsible for the loss of some good, patriotic people from those countries because we gave them money and instructions."

5

The Covert Legions

IF HARRY TRUMAN had had his way, the deacon calling the shots in the secret wars would have been Gordon Gray. Gen. Walter Bedell Smith and William H. Jackson brought the word. Jackson, a Gray associate since the 1930s, represented the token of trust. General Smith told Gray that he, Smith, wanted Gray to succeed him as director of central intelligence and that service in a new NSC unit, the Psychological Strategy Board, would make him a logical choice to do so. Besides, said Smith, "The president is serious about setting up this board and we think that you are well-equipped to do it."

An insider's insider, Gordon Gray's discretion was exceeded only by his good sense. From the president's point of view, revising his NSC covert action directive had the purpose of designating a new subcommittee of the National Security Council as the lead authority on approvals. Gray would be chief of that unit. Truman knew Gray from service as assistant secretary and secretary of the army between 1947 and 1950. Gordon Gray left Washington but only theoretically—he became head of the University of North Carolina in February 1950 yet actually did not give up his army post until April, and even then he stayed on as a special assistant to the president until November. President Truman's summons became only the first of many callbacks for Gray, who served every president from Harry Truman to Gerald Ford.

Both brilliant and modest, Gray was the son of Bowman Gray, tobacco baron and chairman of the R. J. Reynolds Corporation. Bowman's son could have gone anywhere but chose the state college. Yale Law followed, and Gray worked a couple of years at Frank Wisner's Wall Street firm, Carter, Ledyard and Milburn. Then it was back to Winston-Salem where Gray hung out his shingle, then became a newspaper publisher. His two papers, the *Winston-Salem Journal* and the *Twin-Cities Sentinel*, and the radio station WSJS eventually morphed into a media empire. In 1937 Gray ran for state senator as a Democrat. He won reelection four years later. After Pearl Harbor Gray volunteered but refused a commission, entering the army as a private. The military gave Gray a commission anyway. He was assigned as intelligence and public affairs officer at Fort Benning before heading to Europe, where, as befitted his media experience, he set up propaganda radio broadcasts for Gen. Omar Bradley, including a powerful transmitter at Luxembourg City.

Shortly before Congress created the CIA, Gray, from his post with the army, nominated himself for director of central intelligence to replace Hoyt Vandenberg. This major departure from his usual manner suggests how serious Gray must have felt the international situation to be. President Truman chose Roscoe Hillenkoetter instead. Sidney Souers soured on Gray after that, but Truman had such confidence in the man that when it came time to set up the new NSC subcommittee, the president could not be dissuaded from appointing him. After Souers left Washington early in 1950, Gray had a clear field. Years later Souers told a CIA historian that he had had high expectations for the effectiveness of the Psychological Strategy Board until he learned who Truman had picked to lead it, making out the Gray appointment as some kind of patronage. Souers recalled complaining to the president, but it was already too late. Gray began by commuting to and from Chapel Hill once a week. He continued as university president throughout his new stint in Washington.

The task President Truman thought so important was to energize U.S. efforts in psychological warfare. Psywar remained a deep presidential interest, and indeed it lay behind the original Truman directive that started the CIA on its road to covert operations. Not only the agency had been involved. The State Department created a coordinating staff for "information"—Truman's lieutenants avoided use of the word *propaganda*—under the assistant secretary for public affairs. The Pentagon got into the act in early 1949, pressing Admiral Souers at the NSC to report on peacetime planning for wartime psychological warfare. That spring the NSC executive secretary circulated a draft directive mandating a fresh initiative, again located at State, which set up the Interagency Foreign Information Organization. Edward W. Barrett, a former *Newsweek* reporter, became the chairman. None of this satisfied the Defense Department, now worried about gaps between peacetime efforts and those contemplated in war. Barrett tried to mollify the Pentagon with a scheme for overt and covert psychological warfare activities plus domestic information and censorship. President Truman approved that proposal in March 1950. Thinking the problem solved, a few weeks later Truman announced a new American "Campaign of Truth" to be the antidote to Soviet propaganda.

While Truman struggled to regularize U.S. psychological warfare, the CIA, hardly indifferent, forged ahead with a plethora of initiatives. Youth organizations were funded to match those that received Soviet support. Labor unions were a special agency target, given the long histories and strength of Communist-affiliated labor units in Italy and France. The Committee for a Free Europe and Radio Free Europe remained major priorities. Frank Wisner personally attended planning conferences of these organizations in 1949 and 1950 and initialed their budgets. Allen Dulles, a former board member and the chairman of the Committee for a Free Europe, resolved not to abandon them. The agency still had problems—but CIA seems to have accepted that stimulating creativity required making certain allowances. These were people who in 1950 spent $34 million in Europe alone for their programs.

When Allen Dulles came to the CIA he hired a special assistant, Thomas D. Braden, a sturdy thirty-two-year-old Iowan who, before joining OSS, had fought with the British against Rommel in the Saharan desert. Afterward Braden and Stewart Alsop collaborated on an early book about OSS. Braden had advocated a peacetime intelligence agency. Then Dulles called him to CIA service. Unlike the usual Washington "special assistant," holding the boss's hand had little importance for Dulles's aides. His standard practice (Dulles would do it again with Dick Bissell) was to use assistants to handle certain projects outside usual channels. Dulles's outside projects concerned political and cultural warfare in Europe, and that became Braden's battlefield. He arranged CIA funding for women, youth, lawyers, and media to counter Russian efforts in these same fields.

Once Dulles had settled in as deputy director for operations, Braden suggested the creation of an International Organizations Division, putting his vest-pocket activities on a more formal basis. Frank Wisner reacted like a stuck pig—the unit cut across regional boundaries of his OPC branches, duplicating other works. Wisner vetoed the initiative. Tom Braden marched into Allen Dulles's office and handed in his resignation. Instead Dulles picked up the telephone, called Wisner, and told him to cease and desist. Braden formed his division. Once Wisner succeeded Dulles as DDO, Braden continued to rely on his direct link to the high boss, ignoring Wisner and going to Dulles whenever necessary. The International Organizations Division became one more CIA barony.

Suddenly the Korean War made concrete all the previous belly-thinking about peacetime/wartime distinctions in psychological warfare. State Department resources in the Far East had to be transferred to the regional supreme commander, Gen. Douglas MacArthur. Officials agreed on the need for a new independent agency, but the State Department, as it had in the days of the creation of the Office of Policy Coordination, wanted control, which both the CIA and Pentagon opposed. The wrangling continued through the fall and winter of 1950. President Truman scheduled this issue for the agenda of his National Security Council meeting on January 4, 1951, but the lengthy, desultory discussion settled nothing. Truman then gave NSC members one month to reconcile their differences. When that did not happen the president took psychological warfare off the NSC action list. He would settle the matter himself. And he did. On April 4 he issued orders establishing the Psychological Strategy Board (PSB).

A subcommittee of the National Security Council, the board actually looked very much like the 10/2 panel that monitored covert operations, with a central staff added. At the initial meeting on July 2 members agreed that the CIA would chair the group, which would direct agencies with regard to psychological warfare issues, coordinate and evaluate operations, and report to the NSC on effectiveness. The PSB staff, under Gordon Gray, constituted the central planning authority. In effect the PSB staff aimed to become the U.S. command center for psychological warfare.

But something went wrong along the way. General Smith sought a small elite staff to evaluate covert operations. In pushing for revision of the NSC-10/2 directive he wanted the Psychological Strategy Board to replace the 10/2 panel as approval authority. Psywar experts wanted a larger entity that actually *planned* operations, within the more rarified and arcane sector that was psywar. The best the PSB finally achieved was to help prevent interagency rivalries from crippling ongoing field efforts. Gray brought in OSS veteran Tracy L. Barnes as his deputy director. By 1952 the PSB staff had become the largest element of the National Security Council machinery, with a budget two and a half times bigger than that of the NSC staff itself. The CIA viewed the Psychological Strategy Board as a paper mill.

Gordon Gray tried to make the PSB work. Starting from three small buildings across Jackson Square from the White House, within months Gray moved the PSB to new offices in the K Building of the CIA headquarters complex. That put his people right in with the spooks and could have encouraged cooperation. Better than that, Gray had been Frank Wisner's colleague as a Wall Street lawyer. Deputy Tracy Barnes had also been with Wisner on Wall Street as well as Allen Dulles's subordinate at the OSS, and thus had relationships with key agency people. But Wisner had no intention of cooperating. He did not want the PSB as a command *or* an operating agency. He refused to go to PSB meetings even though Gray held them in the building next door. Wisner encouraged "Beetle" Smith, as the DCI was nicknamed, to form a covert action staff within the CIA that became central to operations approvals, keeping the PSB out of this action. That "murder board" let most proposals pass through.

The Psychological Strategy Board never established itself as the nerve center for covert action. The members were essentially the 10/2 panelists. An early representative of the secretary of defense, John Magruder, safeguarded Defense interests. The State Department repeatedly construed PSB inquiries as infringements on its interests too. General Smith was CIA's delegate, Frank Wisner the alternate. James E. Webb sat in for the State Department. Rear Adm. Leslie Stevens represented the Joint Chiefs of Staff and also handled military participation in covert operations. But the CIA consulted the board only when absolutely necessary, as when the agency needed PSB's help to get other agencies to lend a hand with its projects. Just one PSB staffer handled all the CIA liaison work. Of the mass of PSB paper, the documents on relations with the agency fill just one file. The CIA held back cards of its own, such as access to its library, upon which PSB staff depended, to encourage the board's staff to acquiesce. In the spring of 1952 the issue of the board's role in approving covert operations under NSC-10/5 came to a head. The CIA got its way. The Truman administration approved eighty-one covert operations during this period, few of them with more than cursory input from the Psychological Strategy Board.*

If Frank Wisner needed to know anything from the PSB he would go to Tracy Barnes, who became something of a CIA spy at the board. Thus, although Director Smith arranged through the board for other agencies to assist CIA in an expanded program of covert actions, the Cold War agency cut the PSB out of the loop. Gray protested, but only made Beetle Smith angry.

In November 1951 Gray began to host private luncheons of the PSB members where differences could be thrashed out before the monthly meetings. In December Gray held a briefing to show General Smith and DDO Wisner that the board would not trespass on agency turf. That didn't work either. Gray appealed to Smith to ensure that CIA representatives attended the meetings, but Smith refused. In January 1952 Gordon Gray resigned. He would be succeeded by Raymond B. Allen, president of the University of Washington. Allen's background in medical administration proved no challenge to the spooks, who did as they pleased. In mid-1952, Beetle Smith blew up when told that his agency had not cooperated with the Psychological Strategy Board. The final director of the PSB was Adm. Alan Kirk, who with his background in naval intelligence might have improved the CIA relationship. But by that time the White House had decided to have done with the board.

Evidence indicates that the Psychological Strategy Board failed as the U.S. high command for covert action due to the opposition of the line agencies, not because of Gordon Gray, as Sidney Souers would have it. The close relationship between psychological warfare and covert operations is further demonstrated by what happened to U.S. programs. Rather than restraining and coordinating propaganda and covert activities, the Psychological Strategy Board that Harry Truman created instead became a stimulant for an intensification of the Cold War.

The Psychological Strategy Board had a second problem, just as big, in the amorphous nature of its task "evaluating" and "coordinating" U.S. psywar plans. Gray's staff had orders to assemble overall, regional, country, and subject plans that the board could then review. Planning for propaganda and psychological warfare, and

---

* Despite the PSB's lack of impact on America's secret wars, or perhaps to shield its very success at avoiding subordination to the NSC-10/5 system, the CIA has very jealously guarded the records of the Psychological Strategy Board. In December 1988, after this author wrote about the PSB in a systematic way for the first time, the CIA sent a plane with a team of armed guards to Kansas City. The team went to the Truman Presidential Library in Independence, Missouri, seized the PSB records, and returned them to Washington. It became the first time in the history of the National Archives that a set of records processed under existing regulations and open to research had been withdrawn from public view. The CIA held on to the records for months, extracted several hundred documents from the set, and only then returned them to the Truman Library. It cannot have been the quality of the PSB's planning for psychological warfare that accounted for this degree of concern at Langley.

later monitoring national efforts in this regard, became the job of a PSB staff office. In one typical case, in August 1951 Director Gray suggested at a PSB meeting that the staff do an "inventory" paper surveying Cold War "weapons"—ranging from private media to government agencies to public associations—that could be used in political warfare. Then he set up the overall study with three panels: to examine the policy basis, the intelligence framework, and finally the actual inventory. First the intelligence component had to be dropped when it aroused CIA ire. The inventory panel's draft report, finished that fall, ran to a hundred pages. Director Gray made the group cut a quarter of the content but found the State Department willing to read only a *three*-page paper. The CIA and the Pentagon restricted themselves to bland comments. Gray resorted to putting out the full paper just before Christmas, labeling it as simply for information, not action.

More and more the pattern became one of fierce bureaucratic warfare. The State Department proved the worst offender, objecting that master plans were not practical and infringed on basic foreign policy. Gordon Gray countered that he would take the issue to Truman. State then went the other way, heaping work on the board, sending over mountains of papers, scheduling multitudinous meetings, briefings, and consultations with diplomats and returning ambassadors. The board became so inundated that "it could not think strategically, much less write a long-range concept." Gray finally gave up and concentrated on his university work, a job he kept through 1955.

The first comprehensive plan was for Germany, completed and sent to the PSB in the summer of 1952. Plans for other psychological operations aimed at reducing Communist Party electoral power in France and Italy, at influencing negotiations for a Korean cease-fire, at creating a pro-American disposition among Japanese, at carrying out "Doctrinal (Ideological) Warfare Against the USSR." Some PSB planners felt the CIA did not know enough about political differences among Soviet leaders for a sound psywar plan. They considered requesting a special national intelligence estimate on the subject. The PSB wanted a psychological warfare plan to be implemented upon the death of Stalin. That turned into a huge fight, and the plan would never be completed. Instead, when Joseph Stalin died in March 1953 the American response had to be cobbled together on the fly.

All the high-level interest, the encouragement of President Truman, and the advice of psychological warfare experts like Paul Linebarger never moved psywar technique beyond a relatively crude level. Linebarger, something of a guru in the field, had written a standard text on the subject and been the top consultant to OPC's Far East Division. He ran an orientation course to introduce new staff to this arcana, which the board ordered officials to attend and which the CIA hosted through at least six iterations. The agency's support for this endeavor constituted service it could trade on when the Psychological Strategy Board tried to clamp down.

Not that any of the training mattered. A plan for a "psychological offensive" against Russia, for example, is studded with moralistic rhetoric that sounds like a collection of homilies and themes. The three objectives in this plan were: to emphasize to Soviet rulers and peoples the reckless nature of their policy, to establish goodwill between the peoples of the two nations, and to widen the schism thought to exist between the Soviet people and their rulers. The propaganda themes suggested to reach these objectives included the following:

> The attempts of all tyrants to conquer the world have always failed. . . .
> Truth, mercy, pity, charity, love of family, hospitality, are some of the
> basic values which have always been dear to the Soviet peoples and . . .
> are held in common with the people of the free world, but in contempt
> by the Soviet rulers. . . . The U.S. is peace loving and honors the sover-
> eignty and integrity of peoples and nations [while, by contrast, Soviet]
> statements of possibility of peaceful co existence have been made only
> for the purpose of deceiving Soviet and other peoples. . . . [In Russia]
> first freedom of speech was lost, now freedom of silence.

There would be lots of other plans as well as advice from officials, spies, academics, advisory panels, and more. In Truman's era alone the Psychological Strategy Board accumulated more than 33,000 pages of records, much of them the minutiae of these plans, and most of that of about the same sophistication, or lack thereof. Henry A. Kissinger, an early PSB consultant, compiled an advisory report on Germany used in developing the psywar plan for that country. From Trieste to Thailand, from Sweden to Southeast Asia, from the "Potential Role of Wealthy Individuals in Foreign Countries" to "Moral Rearmament Events Around the World" to "Forest Problems in Africa, Near East and Southwest Asia," the PSB tried to build global influence. Plan "Torrential" concerned psychological operations during nuclear war, as if they would matter. Plan "Takeoff" tried to predetermine the spin to put on any possible collapse of truce talks to end the Korean War. Another stuffed file concerned "Doctrinal Warfare (Ideological)." Project "Engross" specified a program for "educating" escapees from behind the Iron Curtain while at the same time PSB crafted a plan to discredit Russian brainwashing.

The plans were usually written by ad hoc committees brought together for the purpose. For example, the contingency paper for spinning the Korean truce negotiations involved a group of seven: three persons from State, one from CIA, and one from each of the armed services. Several of these people had temporary duty assignments to PSB, the others simply went to the meetings. Perhaps it is not surprising that more than a year after State originally asked for this study it had yet to be completed. Through mid-1953 the Psychological Strategy Board set up thirty-six of these panels to draft forty-four different plans.

American democracy represented the best thing the United States had to offer the world, including its enemies in the Cold War. Not only that, Harry Truman and his successors believed in democracy, professed democratic ideals, enunciated the tenets of their faith, and were ready, when approached by such groups as the Balts, to issue ringing declarations of support. Yet somehow the psywar specialists failed in translating America's sincere credo into a compelling message. And the United States cheapened the coin of its appeal by covert actions that, to foreign populations, did not represent American policies democratically arrived at. At home the stagnant civil rights of minorities, the loyalty investigations and Mc-Carthyism of the 1950s, like the red-baiting of the left in later decades, offered America's adversaries ready targets for their own propaganda. Presidents employing the CIA as a Cold War agency, sending the spooks out to make the world safe for democracy, were, to use a baseball analogy, putting a batter in the box who already had one strike against him.

As for the State Department, Paul H. Nitze, now chief of the Policy Planning Staff, told Gordon Gray, "Look, you just forget about policy, that's not your business; we'll make the policy and then you can put it on your damn radio."

Others had hoped to have an easier time of it, namely the military experts on unconventional warfare, for whom Gordon Gray had toiled while still at the Pentagon. In the early postwar years there was little support for these methods in the armed forces. Army Ranger units and Merrill's Marauders of Burma fame were disbanded, as were the air force's air commandos. Psychological warfare capabilities existed only residually within the intelligence staffs of the various services. General Eisenhower, as army chief of staff until 1948, remembered his successes with psychological warfare in North Africa and Italy during the war, and the deception and unconventional warfare that had helped the D-Day invasion, and tried to preserve these capabilities. Maj. Gen. Robert A. McClure, who had been Ike's psywar expert, did his best to crusade for this capability. Even Eisenhower's orders proved insufficient to galvanize action. Some senior officers believed that covert psywar operations would not be accepted by the American people. McClure demurred.

The advocates of military psywar were helped by the appearance of NSC-4/A, which demonstrated presidential interest in the area of psychological warfare. The army began a staff study in January 1948 that led to the adoption that fall of a plan for establishing standardized psywar units plus staffs at all echelons of command.

Army proponents also tried to carve out larger roles for themselves. Gen. Albert C. Wedemeyer, chief of the army's Plans and Operations Division, thought the assignment of all "black" propaganda to the CIA was basically unsound. General McClure argued the army possessed a greater capability, in the form of outlets and audience, than even the State Department. A couple of years earlier, with the occupation forces in Germany, McClure had reported that his staffs controlled a full array of media: several dozen newspapers, six radio stations, more than a hundred magazines, every theater and movie screen (almost a thousand), and literally every one of the thousands of book, magazine, and newspaper kiosks in the country. Such a degree of penetration offered U.S. psychological warriors dominance as great as anything enjoyed by America's ideological enemies. Instead the occupation gradually lifted controls on the German media, and the U.S. military steadily dismantled its psywar units. Soon the subject was scarcely being taught in service schools. In 1950 there were only seven officers in the U.S. Army who specialized in psychological warfare.

As assistant secretary of the army, Gordon Gray encouraged the development of a psywar capability and made good use of studies by consultant Paul Linebarger that argued for better articulated capabilities in this area. Appeals for help from Frank Wisner at the CIA also had their uses within the army hierarchy. Gray went further, knocking heads together, demanding progress reports from the army chief of staff, Gen. J. Lawton Collins. All this predated Gray's duty at the Psychological Strategy Board.

There was also the issue of unconventional warfare capabilities or, as they are known today, special operations forces. At first paramilitary operations were considered part of the psywar function, the province of the army's intelligence (G-2) staff. The paramilitary side had been viewed with distaste by Gray's predecessor, Army secretary Kenneth Royall, who told a June 1948 meeting that he wanted his service to know nothing about covert operations. Prodded by Gray and others, Royall soon allowed participation in overt and even covert propaganda. By March 1949 Gray could tell his boss that "we are actually participating in Europe." Royall then designated Gray as the official to whom all covert matters would be taken.

Meanwhile the army staff acquired a "special warfare" section within its psywar area. Manned by veterans of Merrill's Marauders, OSS, and guerrilla commanders in the Philippines, the special warfare section laid down contingency plans for paramilitary actions, including, in the event of war in Europe, one to obstruct movement of Soviet reinforcements by activating a partisan force in Eastern Europe. A Joint Chiefs paper in August 1948 recommended the United States support guerrilla warfare under the policy direction of the NSC, envisioning the army acquiring means to carry out the plan. As already noted, Truman policy provided that the CIA have primary responsibility for covert operations during peacetime and the military in war.

Carrying out covert operations naturally meant real units and troops. The Joint Chiefs recommended against any sort of special warfare corps, instead favoring individual training within the services. Specialists would be on call to lead native guerrillas. But the army consulted with former OSS commander Col. Ray Peers on the formation of a Ranger Group, planned in early 1949 to include about 115 officers and 135 enlisted men. These "airborne reconnaissance agents" would be sent to theaters, army groups, and armies for specified missions. This was a step toward a special warfare corps, not away from it.

As elsewhere, the Korean War provided huge impetus. Troops in the field tried to run psywar leaflet campaigns against the North Koreans and then the Communist Chinese. Army commanders soon found inadequate the air force's use of occasional transport planes diverted from other work when available. After some Washington infighting, the air force moved ahead with the first actual special warfare units. Called Air Resupply and Communications (ARC) wings, three of these units were formed beginning in February 1951, stationed at bases in Great Britain, Libya, Okinawa, and Clark in the Philippines. A base in Alaska was planned but never activated. The ARC wings operated a wide variety of transport aircraft in exactly the same fashion as the wartime air commandos or the proprietary airline the

CIA bought known as Civil Air Transport. They engaged in disaster relief, conventional transport operations, and training flights in an attempt to disguise their real covert purpose. For example, when the U.S. Air Force began flying a regular passenger/cargo route from Clark Air Force Base in the Philippines to French Indochina in 1952, some of the missions went to the 581st Air Resupply and Communications Wing. Similarly, planes of the 580th Wing flying from Wheelus air base in Libya in the mid-1950s helped ferry critical fuel and chemical supplies to Turkey for the CIA's U-2 missions there.

The 581st Wing provides an excellent example of the relationship between the ARC wings and the Central Intelligence Agency. Activated in July 1951 after eleven months of training in Idaho, about a thousand airmen then moved to Clark Field. Commanded by Col. John K. Arnold, Jr., the 581st flew six different types of aircraft and helicopters, including black-painted B-29 bombers in a model configured for long-range air drops. Not long after reaching the Philippines, Colonel Arnold found himself summoned to Far East Air Force headquarters in Tokyo. Officers briefed Arnold on his unit's role in psychological warfare, dropping leaflets over the borderlands of North Korea and China. Two CIA men added authenticity to the scene.

"You're a marked man now," one of the CIA officers observed as they walked into the building.

The CIA contributed to the costs of running the ARC wing. James Darby, director of operations for the 581st, accompanied a CIA officer who made regular cash deliveries to the unit's finance section. According to reports, some airmen were actually CIA contacts or officers under cover, revealing themselves to comrades only many years later. Colonel Arnold knew there were CIA people in his unit but deliberately made no effort to find out more, reasoning that if captured he'd have no secrets to give away.

Arnold's choice turned out to be prescient. On January 12, 1953, the wing commander and a crew of thirteen flew one of their B-29s (tail number 44-62217) up to Yokota, where they picked up leaflets to drop over North Korea. This would be the 581st's first psywar mission in the war. "Stardust Four-Zero" became the radio call sign; the mission, to distribute the leaflets over six targets, should have taken less than half an hour. The B-29 would return to Yokota and reach Clark the following morning, where Arnold planned to relax with his wife May.

Everything went fine over the first targets, but at the last, near Korea's border with China, jet fighters intercepted them and damaged the plane so badly the crew had to bail out. At 11:16 P.M. Stardust Four-Zero radioed Mayday. The nearby city of Andung on the Yalu was the location of the Sixty-fourth Air Defense Corps, the main Russian unit participating in the war, which for several months had assigned some of its fighters to night duty. The Chinese are not known to have had night fighters at this time, but it is impossible to discover who shot down Arnold's B-29. The Russians regarded their participation in the war as secret, just as secret as CIA's relationship with the ARC wing, and never claimed credit for this success.

The incident provided a windfall for Communist propaganda. The shoot-down enabled Beijing to claim that U.S. forces were intruding into China. Inter-rogation of prisoners promised plentiful information. At least eleven of the crew were captured by Chinese troops and brought to Andung. Although three of Colonel Arnold's men remain unaccounted for (comrades believed they saw one in Chinese prisons), the airmen could detail the operation of the highly classified ARC wings. Colonel Arnold might know more, as might Maj. William H. Baumer, operations officer for the Ninety-first Strategic Reconnaissance Squadron, who had hitched a ride aboard Stardust Four-Zero to see for himself the difficulties of flights along the Yalu River zone. Baumer had definitely picked the wrong night to fly. After the Cold War, historians researching in previously secret Soviet records found messages sent in Russian intelligence channels, ask-ing and granting Russian intelligence help on interrogations of the U.S. airmen, later reporting that Moscow had gotten transcripts of Arnold's interrogations and other items.

The American airmen were moved by train to Shenyang and kept there two weeks, then taken to Beijing, where the real inquisition began. Chinese security kept the whole affair under wraps until November 1954, when Beijing decided to score a propaganda coup, holding a show trial of Arnold's crew and other CIA agents captured earlier. In his statement, no doubt made under duress, Colonel Arnold admitted what had been put in the indictment for the Chinese court: the 581st Wing's task, "besides psychological-warfare missions, is the introduction, supply, resupply, evacuation, or recovery of underground personnel."

Colonel Arnold was sentenced to ten years in prison, Major Baumer to eight, the other airmen to shorter periods. In fact, however, China released the Americans in the summer of 1955, when they were taken to a railway station near Hong Kong and handed over to a U.S. team headed by air force intelligence officer Delk Simp-son. CIA officers were right behind him, and CIA people were principals in the de-briefings of the returned airmen in Japan. Colonel Arnold was later sent to CIA headquarters to repeat his story. John Gittinger, a CIA psychologist, observed the interviews in Japan, determining how these Americans had borne up under captiv-ity. Meanwhile John Arnold's mission had outlasted his unit, for the air force had deactivated his ARC wing soon after the truce that ended the fighting in Korea.

Korea brought about not only a massive expansion in CIA activity—its budget doubled from 1951 to 1952—but wrought an increased separation between para-military operations and psychological warfare. Indeed for a time the latter pre-dominated, soaking up three-quarters of the agency's budget at the height of the war. But as the name "Wurlitzer" implied, Frank Wisner retained his deep com-mitment to psywar. Wisner's foot-dragging where the Psychological Strategy Board was concerned aimed specifically at protecting his own activities. Secret or "black" propaganda, as well as the partially attributable "grey" projects, were the particular province of OPC by order of the president under the NSC-4/A directive.

This became one more area where the sparks that flew off Wisner's table ignited important CIA initiatives.

The same support Wisner had lent the Committee for a Free Europe, the balloon leaflet efforts, and other projects now extended to Asia. The Committee for a Free Asia originated in 1951. An Asian analogue to Radio Free Europe was set up on Taiwan to beam programs onto the mainland. Radio Free Asia went on the air in May 1951 using leased facilities for shortwave broadcasts in several Chinese dialects and in English. Unfortunately the agency soon discovered through surveys that, for the most part, only Mao Zedong's party officials had radios; the CIA began aiming more at overseas Chinese in Southeast Asia. There is evidence of CIA subsidizing publications, labor movements, and youth and public interest groups, including the Committee of One Million Against the Admission of Communist China to the United Nations. The propaganda effort was nothing if not global.

In Europe the agency began funding all manner of cultural and political publishing activities, creating a certain overlap between OPC projects and those of Tom Braden. For example, Braden instructed two CIA officers in Paris, working with the Congress for Cultural Freedom, to keep their efforts from other agency staff. Thus Robert Thayer, who headed the OPC branch for France, remained unaware of this activity, Project Opera. As the Directorate for Operations emerged full blown from its fusion, the International Organizations Division under Braden held center field. Then activities became more transparent, at least within the DO.

One propaganda coup was mostly the product of Wisner's Wurlitzer. That was a movie version of George Orwell's novel *Animal Farm*. The OPC moved Howard Hunt into cultural operations after his Albania psywar assignment, and Hunt managed to secure film rights for *Animal Farm* from Orwell's widow. Carleton Alsop, a Hollywood producer and agent, and Finis Farr, a scriptwriter, both of them now with OPC's psywar shop, played key roles. The CIA then financed the animation and filming, which began in 1951, ensuring that its script ended with a more pointed allusion to Communist totalitarianism. Midway through this process the Psychological Strategy Board took over, having become the U.S. lead authority in this field. The PSB encouraged the CIA to seek film rights to another Orwell novel, *1984*, again one with Cold War propaganda potential if spun the right way. Changes to the story line of the film version of *1984* contravened Orwell's specific instructions. The movies were not ready for distribution until 1956, by which time both OPC and the PSB had passed from the scene.

Much of the work in the cultural field revolved around the deft floating of ideas where they might have intellectual and political impact; the strategic positioning of stories to attract the most attention and further circulation; the careful placement of people, whether cultural figures or leaders aligned with CIA, to maximize their ability to act; the intensive preparation for myriad conferences of youth and student associations, labor unions, and entities like the Congress for Cultural Freedom. Frances Stonor Saunders, the historian of CIA's cultural Cold War, recounts this story in great detail, at least as it concerns art and literature. It has been officially confirmed that the CIA funded the journal *Encounter* and subsidized publication of well over a thousand books before the end of 1967. A quarter of them were in English. Some involved direct collaboration between authors and CIA personnel, and more than one agency division involved itself in these operations.

The story of the CIA's relations with labor centers more on Jay Lovestone, former boss of the American Communist Party, who became an agency asset in a later incarnation as a labor activist. Like Allen Dulles, Lovestone ran with that elite group who periodically lunched with Frank Wisner. Overseen by agency counterintelligence guru James J. Angleton, Lovestone provided data that guided an entire category of CIA effort. At the moment of the inception of OPC, Lovestone had become executive secretary of the Free Trade Union Committee, a quasi-independent part of the American Federation of Labor and an obvious candidate for CIA recruitment. Indications are that by 1950 Lovestone's committee had almost quadrupled its previous annual spending as the result of CIA money. The funds were used for anti-Communist labor activities in European countries, one example being the International Center for Free Trade Unionists in Exile, based in Paris, a convenient labor counterpart to the assorted liberation fronts the CIA supported in the Balkans and Eastern Europe. Lovestone's committee contributed on other fronts as well, such as funds for the founding conference of the Congress for Cultural Freedom in 1950, probably an instance of serving as a conduit for laundering CIA funds.

An intense period in the relationship came at the end of 1950. On November 24, 1950, Walter Bedell Smith, Frank Wisner, and Carmel Offie met with Jay Lovestone and other union officials, including George Meany, the AFL president. DCI Smith, incredibly, thought the cash CIA channeled to Lovestone didn't constitute a subsidy to labor. Lovestone liked Offie; Wisner's assistant, under increasing fire at the agency, had officially been put on Lovestone's payroll a few months earlier (CIA continued to pay his salary). Lovestone also thought the CIA had been pinching pennies and behaving as if his committee was merely an agency proprietary. He thought OPC spent too much money on Italian unions and not enough on him. At the 1950 meeting Lovestone complained about the funding level, and Wisner countered by citing the amount the agency had actually given that year—$250,000, far more than the Free Trade Union Committee had received from its parent AFL.

Just a few months later Lovestone submitted even more ambitious proposals—the CIA should give him a larger amount permitting multiyear programs. By then Allen Dulles was pressing for Carmel Offie, whom he suspected of leaking CIA data to Lovestone, to be put on the shelf, activating a new channel (who eventually became Jim Angleton). Lovestone met Director Smith and senior officials again in April 1951, to no avail. Carmel Offie left the Lovestone committee two months later. The CIA subsidies for the Free Trade Unions Committee dried up, but not before the agency had handed out $464,000. Lovestone began to speak of the CIA as "Fizzland" and its officers as "Fizzheads," but he continued reporting and, from time to time, seeking cash for initiatives by later groups he worked with. The CIA, for its part, built deeper connections to the AFL and other labor groups.

With regard to the CIA and journalism, there was no single avenue. Instead a multifaceted association developed. Not only were journalistic positions valuable to the CIA as ostensible occupations for undercover agency officers, but the media remained a principal resource in the quest to plant stories and ideas. Project KM/Forget was the code name for a secret effort to insert stories in the media in one country, then resurface them elsewhere. There were many more like it. The CIA meanwhile grew ever more useful to the media as a font of background information for journalists and broadcasters. The relationship quickly became symbiotic. So entwined were the two sides that there would be virtual agency slots at media corporations. For its part the CIA assigned officers as liaisons with specific outlets. For example, through the 1950s Alfred C. Clark at the agency's New York office was CIA's link to the *New York Times*. His predecessor had been James Hunt, who opened a New York office for the CIG as early as December 1946. In the mid-1950s J. B. Love Reeves, a CIA liaison to other New York major media who was identified as meeting a variety of executives of broadcasting corporations and magazines including CBS, fulfilled the same function.

Carl Bernstein, who gained fame with Bob Woodward as *Washington Post* reporters who revealed the Watergate conspiracy of the Nixon administration, later wrote an exposé of the CIA and the media which asserted that the agency had used more than four hundred journalists as assets. The detailed investigation of U.S. intelligence by a Senate committee at that time supplied the number fifty as a total, while the CIA director of that era publicly admitted to three dozen. The *New York Times*, in a series of articles in December 1977, found that more than thirty but possibly as many as a hundred newsmen had worked as salaried CIA contract officers while reporting the news, that at least eighteen journalists had refused CIA recruitment offers, and that at least a dozen CIA officers had worked abroad under journalistic cover. The Senate investigation confirmed that more than a dozen U.S. news organizations or publishing houses had provided cover for CIA officers, though "a few" of these were not aware of that fact.

A typical charge of CIA involvement has been leveled at the *New York Times* reporter Sidney Gruson. But the agency itself held a different view. At the time of CIA's operation in Guatemala, the agency convinced itself that Gruson's stories aided its enemies. Efforts to get rid of Gruson went as high as Allen Dulles approaching the *Times*'s publisher.

The question of penetration in the media, not simply in the United States but globally, is central to any assessment of the efficacy of CIA psychological warfare action. The *Times* reports just cited found that allegations of CIA connections involved more than twenty major media organizations, that at times the agency Wurlitzer had had as many as eight hundred propaganda assets on the payroll, and that the CIA had infiltrated a dozen foreign news organizations and actually owned or subsidized fifty more, including newspapers, press agencies, and other communications entities. Agency entities or close relations, according to the *Times*, included Forum World Features, Continental Press Service, Editors Press Service, the Center for International Studies at MIT, and more. The CIA owned printing companies in Italy, India, and Japan, the newspaper *Daily American* in Rome (in which it held a controlling interest), plus others. Without more detailed analysis than is possible here, no conclusion can be drawn as to real effectiveness, but it can be confidently stated that these operations were large components of the U.S. clandestine program, vigorously pursued and waged over many years.

A project of the Tom Braden era characteristic of the agency's International Organizations Division was the funding of the National Student Association. This group of members of student governments at colleges throughout the United States, had been formed in 1947 at the University of Wisconsin. It forthrightly broke with the International Union of Students the following year when that organization refused to condemn the Soviet-inspired coup in Czechoslovakia, though with headquarters in Prague the IUS knew well enough what had really happened. (A Russian "student executive" with the group went on to head the Soviet KGB.) The CIA paid heed to the National Student Association after that, while the group took the initiative in helping create a non-Communist alternative, the International Student Conference, formed in 1950 at Stockholm.

Membership dues were not enough to fund the association and its worldwide counterpart, and grants were sparse, compared to Soviet funding for the competition. The NSA seemed too leftist during that era of McCarthyism. Neither the State Department nor Congress had any interest. One of the student founders subsequently joined the CIA, alerting bosses to the wealth of Russian aid going to the Prague-based competitors. Wisner's shop began to funnel a small amount of money to the National Student Association before the end of 1951, but Tom Braden multiplied and routinized this flow. Before it ended the CIA had given plenty of cash to the association in addition to paying for rent, supplies, and much else besides. Braden assigned his deputy, Cord Meyer, who had had pre-CIA experience with world peace association efforts, to supervise.

The National Student Association project worked this way: The student group held summer seminars each year, where the CIA combed the field for its preferences, then supported those people in the association's elections. Meyer and other agency apologists assert that the CIA made sure that only the NSA president and vice president were witting of the agency connection and that each year these newly elected officials could make the choice to end the relationship. The CIA money supposedly supported only the NSA's international efforts. That construction fails to show, however, that the agency had a first shot each year in influencing the choice of leadership; and that the group's leaders, confronting the prospect of losing a benefactor that took care of all their overhead costs should they decide to terminate the CIA link, may not have had a real choice.

During the National Student Association project, the CIA paid expenses for some 250 Americans to attend conferences of international youth groups, forming the core basis for U.S. delegations at meetings held in Vienna, Helsinki, and Moscow in the late 1950s and early 1960s. An American attending the Sixth World Youth Festival in Moscow in 1957 was specifically directed by the CIA to purchase samples of Soviet-manufactured items and report on Russian surveillance measures at the meeting. Attendees were debriefed more generally by CIA officers who mined them for what they could learn about Soviet intentions.

Braden's student project evinced methods common to similar CIA operations with a variety of ostensibly purely private groups. All this required money. Spreading money around without revealing its CIA origins proved a challenge. The Marshall Plan funds early on suggested the possibilities. Around 1951, recounts Richard Bissell, then a senior Marshall Plan administrator, he received a visit from Frank Wisner, whom he knew socially but with whom he had not previously done business. Wisner asked Bissell to help finance OPC operations by diverting a portion of the so-called counterpart funds the administrators controlled. This money, in local currencies, was contributed to the Plan by European countries in exchange for the assistance they received. Concerned with an apparently rising security threat to Europe in the wake of the Korean War, Bissell gave Wisner the money. The practice continued as OPC transitioned to the Directorate for Operations and until the Marshall Plan ended in 1952. Bissell moved on to the Ford Foundation, extremely concerned about foreign policy issues; the Ford Foundation began moving closer to the CIA orbit. Bissell believed the real Russian threat lay in internal subversion, not military action, especially in the Third World. This position quite matched CIA arguments.

Not long afterward Bissell became a CIA consultant. Among his assignments he helped Frank Lindsay on the study that examined how the Iron Curtain might be rolled back without war. The report ended up gathering dust on some shelf, but its most important consequence is the conclusion Bissell drew from it—psychological warfare by itself would never defeat Russia. The Ford Foundation began to commission work at MIT's Center for International Studies, the agency's academic think tank, set up by CIA and headed by a former agency deputy director. The CIA began moving cash through the Ford Foundation. In the mid-1950s, as the foundation came under the tutelage of H. Rowan Gaither, the flow increased and ramified. Conduits other than Ford were developed, foundations were set up as CIA shell corporations, and prominent individuals were used to represent undisclosed clients.

Use of this method mushroomed right into the 1960s. An internal agency study in 1966 found this technique "particularly effective for democratically-run membership organizations, which need to assure their own unwitting members and collaborators, as well as their hostile critics, that they have genuine, respectable, private sources of income." The funneling of money through legitimate foundations in fact became the most effective way to conceal CIA's role. Looking at major grants (at the time, more than ten thousand dollars) made by foundations other than the Big Three (Ford, Carnegie, and Rockefeller), the 1966 CIA review of grants made over the previous three years found the agency money involved in nearly *half* the awards for international activity and a *third* of those for scientific and social science initiatives. Of the total of seven hundred such grants, more than a hundred had been fully or partially funded by the Central Intelligence Agency.

Not only were the funding techniques important tools in CIA's bag of tricks, the projects they financed were weapons in the Cold War, often instruments of psychological warfare. But, like Richard Bissell, there were many in government who appreciated that psywar was not enough. Those officials, particularly the secret warriors, wanted real covert military capability. Forces for unconventional warfare could back up the CIA's psychological operations and its covert action and take over where they left off. Such forces soon joined America's covert legions.

An impetus for the creation of military units for special warfare was congressional action in 1950. Building on America's traditional commitment to freedom, and Washington's interest in the "captive nations," a proposed bill set aside funds for a legion of Eastern European emigrés who might be sent back into their countries. This Lodge Bill became Public Law 587, passed by the 81st Congress in June 1950, on the eve of the Korean War. It led the army to provide for the creation of a "Special Forces Regiment" of three battalions with a total of about 2,500 men, half of whom might be foreign recruits.

The Lodge Bill also envisioned an equal number of foreign enlistments in the U.S. Army. The military raised the ceiling to 12,500. But by August 1952 fewer than half that number had applied. Of those, just over 400 received required security clearances, and only half actually enlisted. Only 22 wound up assigned to the new Special Forces. The project would be revived as a bid to create an emigré force with a set-aside of $100 million introduced by Rep. Charles Kersten as an amendment to the Mutual Security Act of 1951. The concept would be accepted but never finally implemented.

While the emigré dream perhaps did not come to fruition, the Special Forces themselves did. Once again it was the Korean War that furnished the impetus. At army headquarters, increased need arising from the war, combined with continuing interest in psywar, led to establishment of an Office of the Chief of Psychological Warfare under the experienced leadership of Gen. Robert McClure. This office also had charge of "special warfare" planning. Although in 1950 only seven active army officers had specializations in psywar, by 1952 there were entire units devoted to radio and leaflet propaganda, and the army had set aside the personnel spaces for a new unit, the Tenth Special Forces Group. A year later the group had actually recruited and trained seventeen hundred officers and men.

A complement to the U.S. Army units also materialized. This was the creation of special units composed of Displaced Persons or citizens of the occupied countries. Recruits for the units made up the "labor battalions" referred to earlier in discussion of the Albania operation. Roughly forty thousand persons joined the battalions, living in military barracks, receiving some training, available to be armed. In 1953 the Eisenhower administration, responding to the Kersten initiative, considered broadening the labor battalions into a Volunteer Freedom Corps. Championed by psychological warfare expert C. D. Jackson, Ike's National Security Council talked over the concept several times and dreamed of a corps of as many as a quarter-million persons. A committee studied the proposition, but it was finally dropped amid diplomatic difficulties. In late 1954, Jackson attempted to revive the Freedom Corps, lobbying White House officials and Allen Dulles for months without success. Dwight Eisenhower showed interest in these schemes and did much to keep them alive, at least until the Hungarian revolution. As for Charles Kersten, in 1955 Allen Dulles tried to get his brother to enlist Kersten for a State Department job, and Foster countered by suggesting he be sponsored for membership on the Committee for a Free Europe board. The CIA's Dulles shot that down by adverting that Kersten's Cold War stance struck him as a bit too "overt."

The CIA had already created its own counterpart in the form of stay-behind networks, agent groups recruited and prepared ahead of time who were to be activated if the Russians overran Western Europe. Known today by the name "Gladio," after a title of an Italian component of this CIA network (among the first to be acknowledged, in the 1990s), there were perhaps five thousand members of these networks in all, including some in most Western European lands, to include the neutral countries Finland, Sweden, and Austria. Beginning in 1950 the groups provided yet another focus for OPC-OSO tension since OPC wanted action units for resistance while OSO wanted stay-behind networks of agents. Both CIA elements tried to recruit the same Europeans, who themselves frequently joined both sides of the CIA operation. Equipment for them was stockpiled in their countries. Many had orders to report to their bases only a month after their countries had fallen to the enemy.

In later years the Gladio networks became a positive embarrassment to the CIA because they constituted hotbeds of right-wing political action, engaging in actions from terrorist bombings to attempted coups d'état in Italy, Belgium, and elsewhere. (There would be specific fallout for the CIA in 1956, at the time of the Hungarian revolution, as we shall see.) The groups remained in being for decades—DO officer David Whipple, who later managed CIA operations in Western Europe, recalled that agent meetings and network exercises continued at the time he moved on to another assignment in 1979. Richard Helms, on the other hand, insists that the Gladio networks were dismantled before he came to the head of the CIA. "I had to sign off on all these projects," he told author Jonathan Kwitney. "What would have been the sense of keeping these operations so long?" Several nations ultimately held official inquiries into these clandestine activities. At the time the Gladio nets did nothing in the open. Daniele Ganser, the principal analyst of Gladio, presents evidence across many nations that Gladio networks amounted to anti-democratic elements in their own societies. If so, that is a telling judgment against a CIA in the service of a United States committed to making the world safe for democracy.

Meanwhile the presidential transition from Truman to Eisenhower brought change for the covert warriors. The Korean War was winding down, to end in a stalemate with the armistice signed on July 27, 1953, at Panmunjom. By then paramilitary operations in China were proceeding fitfully. Those in Korea ground to a halt slowly with mixed results. The Korean era still witnessed a substantial buildup of the means to carry out psychological warfare and covert operations, plus mechanisms to plan and manage them. Before the end of the conflict, veritable covert legions were ready to act on command. Operators like Frank Wisner and managers like Gordon Gray were equipped to make the most of available resources.

Through his unflagging enthusiasm for psychological warfare, President Harry Truman played a major role in this buildup. It occurred in secret while, in public, the political perception developed that the Truman foreign policy of "containment" stood helpless in the face of the global challenges of the Cold War. The way was open for someone offering a new direction, and Dwight Eisenhower, the Republican Party's candidate in the 1952 presidential election, did just that.

Eisenhower spoke often of the ideological struggle against communism; a recurrent theme of the 1952 electoral campaign was that the Truman administration had failed to wage this struggle. The Republican Party platform offered to "roll back" the Iron Curtain while Eisenhower promised to intensify the Cold War through such measures as removing the restrictions on Taiwan's Chiang Jieshi, unleashing him against the mainland, and strengthening propaganda efforts in Europe.

Eisenhower won the election. His victory rang in a new atmosphere at the CIA, where at least one intelligence officer felt the Republican platform read like the proposals he used to write at the OPC. The morning after the election, one of the senior paramilitary officers, home from Bangkok, pranced through the Directorate for Plans rooms shouting, "Now we'll finish off the goddamned Commie bastards!"

6

Bitter Fruits

MOST OFTEN the jangling telephone in the office of the president's appointments secretary brought new problems, the minor crises that made up a routine day. No doubt this was what was anticipated that early spring day in 1955 when John Earman, a special assistant to the director of central intelligence, came on the line. But Earman had a question, not a problem. It concerned an appointment with the president set for 9:50 A.M. on March 24. The meeting had been arranged to award the National Security Medal, the highest decoration given by the United States for intelligence work. A few months earlier, on December 15, 1954, President Eisenhower had signed a memorandum awarding the medal to CIA officer Kermit Roosevelt for the latter's role in a prime covert operation, the toppling of a legally constituted government in Iran.

Everything about the ceremony would be held very closely. The National Security Medal, itself a secret, could be awarded by the president at his discretion, unlike the military Medal of Honor, approved by Congress. Award citations and the medals are secret, kept in CIA vaults for the duration of an intelligence officer's career. The National Security Medal was not only secret, it was special. Kermit Roosevelt was only the fourth person to receive it.

It would not be the first time Roosevelt came to the White House, nor indeed his first brush with exotic adventures. The grandson of Rough Rider Theodore Roosevelt, some of Teddy's venturesomeness clearly had rubbed off on his progeny. In 1938, with rising danger of war, "Kim," as he was known, accompanied President Franklin Roosevelt's crony Vincent Astor on a Pacific island cruise-cum-spy mission in which they used a yachting expedition to survey Japanese docks, fuel depots, and airfields in the Marshall Islands. Astor had reported to FDR personally, and Kim went along for the evening with his cousin the president. Living in London a year later, Roosevelt felt so outraged at the Soviet Union's invasion of tiny Finland in the 1939–1940 "Winter War" that he recruited a Spanish Civil War–style international brigade—too late to help the Finns but a fine adventure all the same.

Months before Pearl Harbor, Kim joined the war information office that Wild Bill Donovan would turn into the OSS. Roosevelt's Ph.D. dissertation, on propaganda techniques in England's Glorious Revolution, had been just the thing to pique Donovan, who snapped Kim up from his job as a newly minted history instructor. One day Wild Bill asked Roosevelt what he thought about Iran, effectively giving Kim a portfolio he kept up through his career. He went to the Eastern Mediterranean with OSS boss Stephen Penrose, serving as a top intelligence evaluator. Roosevelt, then twenty-nine, first visited Palestine in 1944 and then went on to Iran. His cousin and fellow OSS/CIA stalwart, Archie Roosevelt, followed Kermit to northern Iran at the end of the war, affording a secondhand but still close look at the immediate postwar crisis in Iran, where the imperial government of Reza Shah Pahlavi survived as a constitutional monarchy.

Kermit Roosevelt served as a lead writer on the official history of the OSS, and he retreated to writing and academe afterward, returning to Iran repeatedly beginning in 1947, when he went back to research a book on Arabs and oil. Three years later Frank Wisner recruited Kim away from Harvard University. Roosevelt thought Wisner a scattershot, lacking depth and judgment, but he got on better with Tracy Barnes, a fellow Groton alumnus, or Miles Copeland, former Dixieland musician and CIC veteran from the war. Through Barnes, Kim quickly opened his own channel to Allen Dulles, the agency's new deputy director for operations.

It became clear to everyone that the Middle East would be Roosevelt's private preserve after a startling performance in Egypt. Kim knew Farouk, the king of semi-independent Egypt, from dealings during the war. The CIA sent him back. There Roosevelt reminded himself of his low opinion of Farouk, soon denigrated among agency insiders as the "Fat Fucker," and broadened his contacts to include the Free Officers' Movement, a revolutionary group whose reformist goals encompassed Farouk's overthrow. Chief among the officers was one Gamal Abdel Nasser. Project FF became the action against Farouk. In March 1952, Miles Copeland, acting for Kim, told several of the Free Officers that the United States was worried about increasing discontent in Egypt. The seed thus planted blossomed into a coup that summer. Nasser became a member of the resulting junta from which he emerged as Egyptian leader. Kim Roosevelt became Nasser's grey eminence, extending quiet CIA help and giving advice. Estimates are that the agency funneled $3 million into the Egyptian venture. Kim attempted to harness Arab nationalism to the American wagon of democracy but prudently faded into the background in the months after the coup to hide CIA's tracks. Agency operators understood the reasons for the anti-American rhetoric Nasser used with his public, but the State Department and White House did not, and the relationship soured. At least Roosevelt had tried. He would try again in Iran with results that, at least in the short run, turned out differently.

The award ceremony at the White House came off without a hitch. Roosevelt, his wife, and two children, entered the West Wing through a side entrance, avoiding press speculation. The appointment itself, just ten minutes before a session of the NSC, made it convenient for DCI Allen Dulles, Secretary of State John Foster Dulles, and Ambassador to Iran Loy Henderson to be present when President

Eisenhower strung the ribbon around Roosevelt's neck. The presentation indicated the esteem in which Ike held the intelligence community.

Iran had been a covert action writ large, solving a problem Eisenhower inherited from the Truman administration. The Iran problem arose from oil, though it had a Cold War overlay, specifically from British interest in Iranian oil. The CIA covert action represented the end result of an Anglo-Iranian oil crisis that had endured for two bitter years, drawing in the British government, the Royal Navy, the SIS, and then the United States. Great Britain had total control over the pumping, refining, and shipping of oil in southern Iran through the Anglo-Iranian Oil Company (AIOC). Under an agreement to expire in 1993, AIOC paid Iran rents and taxes plus salaries for Iranian employees. The money accounted for half of Iran's budget, but in fact AIOC paid more taxes to the *British* government than to the nation whose oil it pumped, and AIOC itself earned ten times what it paid Iran. Sure of their position, the British offered only cosmetic changes in a supplement to the agreement when it came up for renegotiation. Tensions heightened when the United States signed its own agreement with neighboring Saudi Arabia that recognized Saudi ownership of the oil and the corporation.

British suspicions of American interests in Iran persisted as a subtext in this affair, but were presumably swallowed by London and AIOC as the price for U.S. diplomatic support and for the covert operation that would follow. Nevertheless, as early as 1948 a group of American oil speculators formed Overseas Consultants in an effort to get control of oil production in *northern* Iran, where the AIOC had not sewn up its concession. Their legal counsel, interestingly enough, was Allen Dulles of Sullivan & Cromwell in his pre-CIA days. Kermit Roosevelt, who began traveling the Middle East for the CIA in 1950, was perfectly aware of American penetrations, British sensitivities, and Iranian politics.

Meanwhile the British contrived to have an Iranian parliamentary commission report nationalization of AIOC as completely infeasible. The prime minister presenting this conclusion to the Majlis read a statement that had clearly been inadequately translated from English into the Iranian language Farsi, and this linked him to British interests. He was shouted down and several weeks later, on March 7, 1951, shot dead as he knelt to pray in a mosque. Thus came to power a popular nationalist leader, Dr. Mohammad Mossadegh, who immediately presented a bill for government absorption of Anglo-Iranian. The bill became law, and on May 2 AIOC was taken over.

Because of its global interests, AIOC had a working relationship with SIS and soon demanded political action to change the government in Teheran to one willing to settle on favorable terms. Monty Woodhouse, the SIS station chief, arrived on the Teheran scene in August 1951, only a few weeks after Mossadegh's security service shut down AIOC's private intelligence net. Both Woodhouse and the Secret Service's controller for the Middle East, George K. Young, were amenable to action. They initiated schemes to discredit Mossadegh's leadership through psychological warfare, though without accomplishing much more than to make the Iranian prime minister aware of the British play. In mid-1952, when the Royal Navy actually seized a tanker carrying Iranian oil in violation of the British embargo, tensions reached fever pitch. Some weeks later Iran's monarch, the shah, responded by attempting to dismiss Mossadegh, appointing instead an elder politician in touch with British figures, including former SIS secret warrior Julian Amery. This maneuver failed. The Majlis reelected Mossadegh as prime minister, tying the shah's hands. The prime minister's National Front seemed to have overwhelming support.

London now shifted its stance on covert action. Young ginned up a plan to overthrow Mossadegh by means of a coup d'état. The SIS station began working actively with Iranian agents and arming tribes in the north like the Kurds. Suddenly in October the Mossadegh government cut diplomatic relations with Great Britain, closing down the SIS. Mossadegh's police also pursued key British agents and pro-shah figures in the armed forces. The SIS retreated to Cyprus and set up a rump Teheran station to observe as best they could. Norman Darbyshire took charge of the Cyprus/Iraq SIS detachment. Monty Woodhouse returned to London where he prepared a new plan, Operation Boot, that would finally be implemented. In November 1952 an SIS delegation showed the proposal to the CIA in Washington. Kim Roosevelt, traveling the Middle East as he often did, learned of Boot while stopping in London on his way home. "What they had in mind," Roosevelt would later write, "was nothing less than the overthrow of Mossadegh. . . .They wanted to start immediately. I had to explain that the project would require considerable clearance from my government."

While the Truman administration remained in office, official U.S. policy favored an amicable resolution of the AIOC matter. Thus nothing happened with the British proposal. But Truman had already become a lame duck and Eisenhower, working on his transition to the presidency, favored much more energetic covert operations. CIA director Walter Bedell Smith knew of British interest. Smith had been Eisenhower's chief of staff during the war. Not averse to exploring this British notion, Smith discussed it at a meeting in Washington that December even though Iran had not been on the agenda. The session brought together key CIA officers and SIS proponents. Agency participants included Kim Roosevelt, John H. Leavitt, chief of his Iran branch, Leavitt's deputy John W. Pendleton, and James A. Darling, chief of the Near East Division's paramilitary staff. Monty Woodhouse headed the British group.

Meanwhile Bedell Smith's days at the CIA came to an end. Eisenhower selected General Smith to serve as undersecretary of state, most likely to be the president's eyes and ears at the department. Ike replaced him at the agency, choosing Allen Dulles to be the new director of central intelligence. John Foster Dulles became secretary of state. The Iran covert action project began to move ahead.

Although Gordon Gray may have been disappointed he wasn't asked to head the agency, the truth was that Allen Dulles had had the inside track all along. As brother of the secretary of state, Dulles could avoid the squabbles endemic to Washington bureaucrats establishing a pecking order. As the deputy director he remained current on all matters related to the CIA. Dulles also had impeccable credentials in both diplomacy and intelligence, having served with the State Department from 1916 to 1926 and with OSS during World War II. With his ever-present pipe and professorial air, Dulles projected the perfect image for America's chief spy.

Allen Dulles's era began when he took an oath of office on February 23, 1953. Another SIS delegation, this one headed by British intelligence chief Sir John Sinclair, was in Washington at the time, its mission to plan a joint Iran operation. Allen Dulles had headed the Near East Division during his time at the State Department, and Sullivan & Cromwell represented AIOC's parent firm in the United States. Although he maintained a casual and noncommittal posture to the British, Dulles favored the idea of a joint operation.

Mossadegh appealed to the incoming administration for aid, not to settle with the "former oil company" but to develop resources. In 1952 the United States had provided $23.4 million in economic aid. But President Eisenhower's response on June 29, 1953, was that "it would be unfair to the American taxpayers for the United States government to extend any considerable amount of economic aid to Iran so long as Iran could have access to funds derived from the sale of its oil and oil products if a reasonable settlement were reached." Only military funds were offered.

In fact, however, four days before Ike's letter, Kim Roosevelt carried a twenty-two-page paper outlining objectives for an operation in Iran to a meeting in the office of the secretary of state. The paper condensed the much more detailed British plan left by SIS chief Sinclair. John Foster Dulles asked a few questions. Some State Department officers—for instance, Ambassador Loy Henderson—opposed the plan but now said nothing or made pro forma comments. Some CIA officers also thought little of it, notably Teheran station chief Roger Goiran, but they were not present and their views were not presented by Allen Dulles or Kermit Roosevelt. Secretary of Defense Charles Wilson, who knew only about those parts concerning the Iranian military, Kim described as "appropriately enthusiastic."

Allen Dulles asked Roosevelt to be sure to cover two items in his briefing, the prospective cost of the project and its "flap potential," or ability to cause controversy. Roosevelt estimated the price at no more than a couple hundred thousand dollars. On the flap potential, he proved ambiguous: if the spooks seriously miscalculated, the result could be disastrous in the Middle East, but on the other hand, the CIA division chief declared, if Project Ajax got the required support he did not see how it could fail.

The project amounted to a scheme frantically put together in Cyprus and Beirut. A few months earlier the CIA station in Teheran had reported inquiries from a senior Iranian general as to whether the United States might support a coup d'état against Prime Minister Mossadegh. In mid-March DO chief Frank Wisner had sent SIS a message informing the British that the agency now stood ready. As an interim measure the Iranian general received mild encouragement while headquarters and CIA station personnel brainstormed how to proceed. Donald N. Wilber, a part-time contract officer and Princeton archaeologist, and Miles Copeland, a veteran of the CIA's Egyptian adventure with Nasser, were the lead planners. Both were psychological warfare officers. Wilber had spent much of the preceding year in Iran running efforts against the Iranian Communist Party, the Tudeh.

On April 4 Allen Dulles approved a $1 million fund that the Teheran station could use to weaken Mossadegh. In Washington the first move came from the Art Staff, a unit of the DO's Paramilitary-Psychological Staff, which concocted a variety of anti-Mossadegh leaflets to be distributed in Iran. Planners traveled to Cyprus where, starting on May 13, they teamed up with SIS station chief Darbyshire to compile a paper describing the operation. They finished at the end of the month. The most delicate part came when the two intelligence agencies had to reveal exactly who their assets were in Iran. The British spooks were miffed that CIA's resources and money were so much greater and agency personnel more numerous, but they sat back to allow the Americans to take the lead.

Project Ajax envisioned a "quasi-legal overthrow" in which the CIA would manipulate public opinion into opposition and suborn members of the armed forces, the Majlis, religious figures, and businessmen. To induce the shah to dismiss Mossadegh, a series of emissaries would proceed to Teheran to persuade him to issue the appropriate decree, called a *firman*. At that point the agency would put crowds into the street to back up the shah's action and further pressure any wavering members of the Majlis. The Tudeh would be neutralized. The CIA would work through Iranian agents developed by the SIS plus its own people.

To support the plan the CIA had its analysts do an intelligence estimate, "Factors Involved in the Overthrow of Mossadegh," completed on April 16, which concluded that the project could work.

Wilber and Copeland carried the Ajax paper to Beirut. They met on June 10 with Kim Roosevelt, in from Washington, senior representative George Carroll, and CIA Teheran staff. The maitre d' at the St. George Hotel grille, a friend of Carroll's from his OSS days in Nice, gave them a quiet table and kept people away. Roosevelt took the paper on to London with only minor changes. On his last evening in Beirut he dined with the chief of the Lebanese security service, who tried hard to find out whether Kim would be going to Teheran, and had Pan American hold its London flight to have more time to ply Roosevelt with wine and questions.

British government and senior SIS officials approved. Roosevelt then went to Washington, where the agency circulated the plan on June 19. When the key interagency meeting took place six days later, John Foster Dulles's major concerns were not with the covert operation but whether the British government would agree on oil rights with the successor regime, and whether Washington would offer foreign aid in the aftermath. Ajax won approval. Kermit Roosevelt took charge of a CIA task force to carry out the project. This would be the real answer to Mossadegh's pleas for foreign assistance.

Compared to the protracted period of planning approval, Ajax's execution took place quickly. It was the struggle for control of the armed forces and police, together amounting to some 250,000 Iranians, that triggered the actual Iranian coup. In the spring of 1953 Mossadegh assumed the position of defense minister in his own cabinet and moved to supplant the shah as commander-in-chief. He appointed his own people to head the police and as chief of staff of the army. Quite likely these actions steeled the shah, who had failed to act decisively throughout the AIOC crisis, in his determination to rid himself of Mossadegh. In this case the Majlis refused Mossadegh's request for extended powers, leading the premier to dissolve parliament on July 19. A few days later major street demonstrations occurred in Teheran, said to be carried out by the Tudeh, against the Majlis.

The first emissary of the CIA/SIS consortium was the shah's sister, Princess Ashraf. Unpopular in Iran, she had gone to France, there to be contacted in mid-July by intelligence officers Darbyshire of SIS and Stephen Meade for CIA. The princess returned to Teheran without clearance from either the shah or the Mossadegh government, triggering a storm of controversy when she arrived on July 25. The shah refused to see her initially, but they met four days later. Ashraf told the Iranian chief of state that an emissary would come from London. That would be Asadollah Rashidian, one of several brothers of a wealthy Iranian shipping clan who were on the SIS payroll. To prove his bona fides, Rashidian asked the shah to select a phrase, those words to be broadcast over the BBC, a classic open code communication. The shah did so, and the British Broadcasting Corporation duly radioed the message. Rashidian, in turn, informed the shah that there would be an *American* emissary, Gen. H. Norman Schwarzkopf, known to the shah as trainer of his police a few years earlier. He had been recruited by DO Iran branch chief John Waller at the end of June. The general would give the shah the same assurances as had London's emissary, then ask him to issue the *firman* on Mossadegh, another ordering the army to remain loyal, and a letter declaring confidence in Gen. Fazollah Zahedi, the CIA/SIS candidate for Mossadegh's replacement. Schwarzkopf left for Teheran through Beirut on July 21, using the cover of a round-the-world tour. He met with the shah about ten days later. Reza Pahlavi still could not bring himself to do what had been asked. In fact the shah was so frightened of surveillance that he took the American general to a vast hall in the palace and pulled a table into the center of the room, whereupon both sat on top of it to talk.

Kim Roosevelt preceded Schwarzkopf by a few days. He entered under a false identity, making the road trip from Baghdad, crossing the border on July 19 at a dusty frontier station manned by a barely literate guard. Roosevelt stayed with a senior CIA man whose home had a swimming pool Kim found a great joy. He lay in the sun between sallies for meetings with CIA operatives and the shah. At the office the agent, Joseph Goodwin, laid in an inexhaustible supply of vodka. This was spy work with panache. To intensify tensions, the United States began deliberately avoiding meetings between its representatives and Iranian government officials. Ambassador Loy Henderson stayed away, in Salzberg, Austria, awaiting developments. Gen. Robert McClure, America's guru of military psychological warfare, who now headed the Teheran military mission, cooperated with Roosevelt quite pleasantly.

Meanwhile division baron Roosevelt replaced Roger Goiran. The bushy-haired station chief had long service in Teheran and had recruited quite an agent network, plus he had a good sense of the place. But Goiran all along had warned that the shah would be hesitant to move against Mossadegh. Kim Roosevelt saw him as a fanatic, a professorial type with a high-pitched voice who passionately backed Mossadegh out of a sense of guilt. Why that should be so, instead of a straight-line analysis from the CIA's most experienced man on the scene, is not evident. Roosevelt replaced him with Joe Goodwin. The Goiran recall was spun as an escalation of the confrontation with the Mossadegh government. Goiran left on August 2.

Just hours earlier Roosevelt had met the shah. The palace sent a car to pick Kim up at his vacation spa, bringing him to the palace at midnight. In the dead of night, through the gates the CIA man crouched down in the vehicle, pulling a blanket over his head. Kim had thought carefully about what to wear—grey oxford slacks, dark turtleneck, and Iranian-style sandals. The meeting went well enough and became the first of a series between the CIA and the shah, with a British agent sometimes alternating. Roosevelt assured the shah of both Eisenhower and Winston Churchill's personal support if he dismissed Mossadegh. They met again on August 3. The shah said he had never been an adventurer and would take no chances. He wanted more assurances from President Eisenhower. Ike made a last-minute insert into a speech he gave in Seattle and declared that the United States could not stand idly by while Iran fell to communism. Reassured, the shah still did nothing.

Working with a core of just a few CIA officers, Roosevelt activated SIS agent networks and those already serving the CIA. He used SIS communications through Cyprus for cables to Washington. Mossadegh's own schemes ran into trouble. His candidate for police chief bragged that he had a list of all British spies on the force. By the next morning the man had been gunned down. In desperation Mossadegh, a populist nationalist and in no sense a Communist, on August 8 opened trade talks with the Soviet Union. This news led President Eisenhower to issue the final go-ahead for Project Ajax.

The shah finally signed the *firmans* that fired Mossadegh, and appointed Zahedi as premier, but here there is some confusion as to the record. Kim Roosevelt recounts that the shah left with Queen Soraya for Ramsar, a resort town on Iran's Caspian Sea coast, without approving the decrees. The chief of the palace guard, Col. Nematollah Nasiri, went after him and finally induced the shah to sign. This is also the version in the CIA history. By some accounts Queen Soraya played a crucial last-minute role in stiffening the shah's resolve.

There is another account, however, by Prince Manucher Farmanfarmaian, an intimate of the Iranian ruler whose sister was Soraya's lady-in-waiting and who the shah customarily invited for hard-played volleyball games (which the prince detested). One such weekend at Ramsar, for example, the prince referred to as his Dien Bien Phu. In any case, on the afternoon of Sunday, August 9, Farmanfarmaian remembers, the shah and his intimates were enjoying tea and shade after volleyball, the emperor reading the newspaper, when the butler announced a visitor and the shah said to show him in. Dressed in a dark suit, the man offered the shah a document, and the Iranian emperor asked if anyone had a pen. Prince Farman-farmaian offered his. Reza Pahlavi signed the papers, handed back the pen, pronounced it a good one, and told the prince his pen would now be worth a lot of money, hoping it would bring them good luck as well. The document had been the decree appointing General Zahedi as prime minister, the stranger a CIA emissary. The prince then recalls the dinner conversation that day, clearly timing these events after the shah's departure for Ramsar.

The prince's story may be the weavings of a courtier or perhaps only part of a larger tapestry. In any case, the advance schedules prepared by Ajax planners supposed that August 14 would be the critical day. Allen Dulles and his wife Clover materialized in Rome. Dulles spent the night in the communications vault of the CIA's Rome station, hosted by station chief Gerry Miller. They were limited to talking Italian operations, however, because nothing happened in Iran.

Almost the only development of consequence in Teheran on the day of the long-anticipated coup was not an event but a demand—by the local plotters working with the CIA—that they would need $5 million immediately after acting. Kim Roosevelt and Joe Goodwin, already nervous about delays, were also told that nothing could be done until the night of the 15th. "The pool was no solace," Roosevelt records, "cigarettes and vodka-limes tasted awful."

Late in the afternoon of action-day, someone ratted out the plot. Mossadegh's chief of staff, Gen. Taghi Riahi, learned of the impending *firmans*. He alerted the First Armored Brigade to move that night and threw a cordon of troops around Mossadegh's house. By then Colonel Nasiri's Imperial Guard had sent squads to arrest prominent Mossadegh supporters, but they missed Riahi who had already gone to headquarters. Nasiri was arrested himself when he attempted to serve the first decree. In the morning Mossadegh went on the radio to announce that there had been an attempted coup but the government retained control.

The fat was in the fire. General Zahedi, having fled to a hideout outside Teheran, had put himself out of play. The general's son, Ardeshir Zahedi, later a top aide to the shah, stood beside the general throughout these days and denies Zahedi engaged in any foreign intrigues. Ardeshir took out an ad in the *New York Times* in May 2000 when the CIA history of Ajax was finally opened and the newspaper published a feature article based on it. Not only does the son deny Fazollah Zahedi's CIA connection, he insists no agency operation put his father into power, that in fact if there *was* such an operation, it failed. The CIA history shows that on August 16 a senior CIA officer spent much of the day in search of Ardeshir Zahedi to contact the general, who hid at the estate of a friend. Kim Roosevelt collected the general from his hideaway and brought him to the home of a CIA officer in Teheran. Later the CIA station compiled a public statement purportedly from Zahedi based on the direct advice of Ardeshir. The CIA's agents fabricated an interview with Zahedi as well. Donald Wilber's CIA account notes that Ardeshir Zahedi stayed with agency officers from August 16 on and his father from the next morning.

Mossadegh's National Front, plus the Tudeh, now began something of a psy-war competition with the CIA, the object being to convince Iranians that their side had the upper hand. The government put out press bulletins and held news conferences to insist that the plot had been broken up. Mossadegh had some success—at least one senior officer working with the CIA went to a foreign embassy to plead for asylum, believing Ajax had crashed. For its part the agency circulated cartoons and leaflets drawn up at headquarters, organized press coverage undermining Mossadegh's claims, and called in chits from anyone who owed the Americans—for example, one newspaper publisher who had been advanced the sum of $45,000. In one case CIA officers took two international journalists, including the *New York Times*'s Kennett Love, to an interview with General Zahedi. Joe Goodwin used the CIA station's radio to relay a message to the Associated Press in New York which asserted that "unofficial reports" acknowledged the anti-Mossadegh forces were armed with official decrees from the shah firing the prime minister and appointing General Zahedi in his place. Roosevelt and CIA officers ran around organizing street demonstrations of their own against Mossadegh.

Street protests by nationalists and by the Tudeh persisted. Up to six thousand pro-shah rioters recruited by the CIA then took to the streets as well. Eisenhower perceived Mossadegh's failure to suppress Tudeh demonstrations as coddling of Communists, as Mossadegh moving into the Soviet orbit. Ambassador Henderson arrived from Beirut on the 17th. He complained to Mossadegh, who answered by calling out the police. The next days brought lows and highs: CIA headquarters cabled regrets on the failure and advised Kim Roosevelt to leave Iran for his own safety. Instead Kim and George Carroll held a council of war, improvising a fresh plan. London rejected continuing appeals from SIS/Nicosia to permit its officers to proceed to Teheran. The shah secretly left the country for Rome the next morning. There he stayed at the same hotel as Allen Dulles, with obvious potential for direct contact.

Full-scale rioting broke out in Teheran on August 18 and 19. Several hundred people died in the violence. A friendly newspaper published the text of the shah's *firman* appointing Zahedi. Late on the 18th a CIA headquarters dispatch actually called off Ajax, and the SIS dispatched a similar instruction. But the tide had already begun to turn. Roosevelt got the Rashidian brothers and other agents to mobilize mobs in the streets while Iranians and CIA officers contacted army units throughout Iran to rally them to Zahedi. On the second day pro-shah tank units, informed by reporter Kennett Love of weak guard forces at the premier's house, attacked Mossadegh's residence. That morning Chief of Staff Riahi reluctantly informed Mossadegh he no longer controlled the army, and in fact pro-shah troops began to appear all over Teheran. Throughout the afternoon the CIA-backed forces consolidated their hold on the city. The shah returned from Italy and paraded in triumph through the streets of Teheran.

So ended Project Ajax, the first apparent U.S. covert victory. Kim Roosevelt received personal thanks from both Churchill and Eisenhower as well as the medal already noted. Aside from its direct cost, estimated at $10 million to $20 million—far more than the $100,000 or $200,000 originally estimated—Ajax had unfolded in a fashion following a scenario if not a precise plan.

The big winners were the shah and his henchmen, who gained absolute power, which they held for twenty-six years until swept away by a religious conservatism even more potent than the populism of Mossadegh. The United States, by participating in the coup, broke with its own tradition—and its declaratory policy—of unconditional support for democracy around the globe. Through support of the shah, the United States also committed itself irrevocably to his regime in a way that blinded Washington later when it should have recognized rising opposition. As for the cost to American taxpayers, Eisenhower approved $45 million in new funds soon after the Zahedi cabinet took office. The flow neared a billion dollars before the end of Ike's administration. The losers were the Iranian people; Mohammad Mossadegh, who was eventually captured and placed on trial; and, ironically, AIOC. Although Iranian oil production resumed in August 1954, the "former oil company's" claims were never fully resolved.

After the Iranian project, Kim Roosevelt returned to headquarters as assistant deputy director of the Directorate for Operations. Under Frank Wisner, Roosevelt led the political action staff and supervised that component's field operations. He tried to use a White House debriefing to critique Project Ajax.

"If we, the CIA, are ever going to try something like this again, we must be absolutely sure that the people and army want what we want.

"If not, you had better give the job to the Marines."

Roosevelt wrote later that John Foster Dulles did not want to hear such advice. This was true. Within weeks of that occasion, Roosevelt was offered command of a similar covert action being planned for Central America, in Guatemala.

Kim Roosevelt turned down this offer: inquiries showed that his criteria were not likely to be met in Guatemala. But he would not escape—instead, as a senior official of the DO he became a frequent participant in meetings held to consider the new plan. The Psychological Strategy Board, in its capacity as arbiter of America's secret war, approved the concept on August 12, 1953. Two weeks later a PSB luncheon further decided to give Guatemala the highest priority among U.S. initiatives.

Guatemala became the showcase for one of Allen Dulles's favorites, C. Tracy Barnes. A spook from the annals of the law, Barnes was a lot like Frank Wisner, another of those young hires by Carter, Ledyard and Milburn. Tracy had other social sacraments as well—Law Review at Harvard, Groton a year behind Dick Bissell. His undergraduate degree, from Yale, made Barnes a full-spectrum member of CIA's Ivy League clique. He had also married into money, which did not hurt, though his own family could hardly be described as poor.

The connection with Allen Dulles came with the Big War, which for Barnes embodied glory eternal. Commissioned and assigned to London, to the U.S. air attaché, Barnes strove to get into the field and transferred to Lord Mountbatten's Special Forces headquarters, then the OSS. He made parachute drops over British air bases for sport. Barnes twice dropped into France to work with the resistance. The second time he made it to Switzerland just ahead of German pursuers. There Allen Dulles reigned as OSS station chief. For the rest of the war Barnes did odd jobs for Dulles, most especially helping arrange the surrender of German troops in northern Italy, involving some pretty dangerous forays to meet undercover with Nazi officers who above ground were still fighting the war. The highlight was probably smuggling out the widow of Mussolini's foreign minister and the manuscript of his diaries. Dulles told others that Tracy Barnes was the bravest fellow he knew, and Barnes had a Silver Star and two French Croix de Guerres (one with Palm, the other with Star) to prove it.

With the peace, Barnes worked for a time with the National Labor Relations Board (preceding Bill Colby at that institution), then came home, as it were, spending three years with a Providence, Rhode Island law firm. It was Gordon Gray who brought Barnes back to Washington in 1950 as a special assistant to the secretary of the army. Gray left his position as secretary just as Barnes arrived, but Barnes stayed on under Clifford Alexander. A year later Gray reappeared as director of the Psychological Strategy Board and pulled Barnes in as deputy. By then Allen Dulles's star, rising meteorically over the agency, shone so bright that Barnes sought out the CIA official soon to be its boss. Tracy could see that the Strategy Board led nowhere in terms of power and influence. The nation's premier Cold War agency beckoned. Barnes moved over to CIA. A few months before TP/Ajax in Iran, Director Dulles put Barnes in charge of a new unit within the DO, the Paramilitary and Psychological Operations Staff, to coordinate the agency's most muscular Cold War activities.

The first key meeting on the Guatemala project took place in Frank Wisner's office around Labor Day 1953. Barnes and J. C. King of the Western Hemisphere (WH) Division went over the existing networks and operations in Central America. The agency already had a recruit for "our man in Guatemala," but his position remained weak, his assets outside the country negligible and those inside nonexistent, and his plan depended entirely upon anticipated popular support the CIA judged remote. Wisner could see formidable challenges.

The government in Guatemala, of a social democratic bent, had been elected in November 1950 with more than half the vote in a free election. President Jacobo Arbenz Guzman thereafter acquired even greater popularity. Peasants fully supported his ardent efforts to reform Guatemala's agriculture and economy.

Like the Iranian affair, the Guatemalan operation had its economic angle. This time an American firm, United Fruit, was involved. It too had used the law firm of Sullivan & Cromwell. United Fruit, the largest landowner in Guatemala, owned some 550,000 acres plus a controlling share of the country's only railroad. *La frutera*, as it was known, trembled at the Guatemalan government's land redistribution program. Beginning in February 1953 Arbenz expropriated almost 400,000 acres of land to parcel out to peasants. The Guatemalans offered compensation—twenty-five-year bonds at 3 percent guaranteed interest for the exact book value of the assets *la frutera* claimed for tax purposes. United Fruit rejected this settlement out of hand and, like AIOC, went to its home government for relief.

The lawyer Thomas G. Corcoran had been a lobbyist for Civil Air Transport and also for United Fruit. Tommy "The Cork" acted as intermediary now, selling *la frutera*'s scheme to the CIA. He met with Undersecretary Walter Bedell Smith that summer. Smith already knew of CIA's efforts and had no difficulty hearing out the lobbyist. A key difference would be that United Fruit, a principal purveyor of the charge that Jacobo Arbenz Guzman constituted a Communist threat to the Americas, and a participant in earlier plots, this time wanted nothing to do with the action itself.

Allen Dulles became the executive agent for Project PB/Success. He kept in close touch with the planning through personal assistants. Jim Hunt was Dulles's man for field operations, much as Tom Braden had been for international organizations. By the fall, definite action impended. The plan for Success, embodied in a September 11 paper, went right to Director Dulles. Based on the premise that the Guatemalan army, a poorly trained, indifferently equipped force of fewer than seven thousand troops, functioned as arbiter of the country's politics, Success aimed to inundate Guatemala with propaganda undermining loyalty to President Arbenz. At the same time the CIA would provide its own alternative, an ostensibly independent force under a former army officer, Col. Carlos Castillo-Armas. A CIA air force would bomb as necessary and drop leaflets while a CIA radio station purporting to be the voice of the rebels would convey the impression the movement had mass support. The concept envisioned the army defecting to Castillo-Armas as his rebel force entered Guatemala. In effect, the DO paper argued, "the task headed by the CIA calls for a general, over-all plan of combined overt and covert action of major proportions." The Directorate for Operations estimated the money required at $2.735 million. Dulles read the paper, as did the deputy director of central intelligence, air force General Charles P. Cabell. On September 15 he asked DDO Wisner for a brief memorandum to use with the Bureau of the Budget to obtain the necessary money.

The key conversations took place in Allen Dulles's own office. In mid-afternoon of Friday, September 18, the DCI brought together the players and many of the concerned observers. Those present, besides Dulles, included General Cabell, Frank Wisner, Tracy Barnes, Kermit Roosevelt, and J. C. King. Also on hand were Sherman Kent, the CIA's senior analyst, and Hans V. Tofte, returned from Korea to become Barnes's chief of operations. Allen Dulles told the group the basic plan seemed sound, and he'd already discussed it with several of the group.

Colonel King offered a detailed prospectus on the ground Project Success would need to traverse, commenting on CIA's stations in Central America, action needed to build up networks, psywar requirements, and personnel shifts. King advised that diplomatic measures could put pressure on Arbenz. The group agreed to press for State Department action. The colonel said he needed $50,000 right away. Allen Dulles replied he could have it at once. Washington planned to change some ambassadors in the area, and the group also talked about that. For Guatemala the CIA preferred a strong ambassador to work with the agency. Some also thought CIA station chief Birch O'Neil too cautious for a swashbuckling covert action, so pressure developed to transfer him also. Criticized as too ready to accept the ambassador's dictates, objecting to the use of propaganda created elsewhere, deficient in reporting on labor, and tolerating poor security, O'Neil's days were numbered. He would be replaced by John Doherty, cryptonym "Tranger." For Honduras, where the agency would locate some of its forward bases, especially a "black" radio station and certain air bases, the readiness of diplomats to work with the spooks was even more crucial. The CIA-State relationship also lay at the heart of the project where Nicaragua was concerned—there the CIA would have both ground and air bases and needed to move in tandem with the Nicaraguan government. Castillo-Armas, the Guatemalan rebel chief, had long been in touch with Nicaraguan leaders about their "friends to the North."

General Cabell advised Dulles to double the skimpy $300,000 programmed for unexpected developments ("contingencies"). Director Dulles, fine with that, rounded off the CIA project budget to a cool $3 million when he went to the White House to ask for the money.

Frank Wisner had the task of selecting the field commander for Project Success. Once Roosevelt turned the job down, Wisner got Allen Dulles to recall the Korea station chief, former army colonel Albert Haney. Haney had set up CIA guerrilla units in Korea, and Guatemala was to have a paramilitary component. The provenance of the appointment remains unclear: Hans Tofte, who became a Barnes protégé at CIA, had worked under Haney in Korea. Tofte himself had recently come on board and thus could have been pulling Haney in after him. Briefed in late October, Haney accepted on the spot. A few weeks later he proceeded to Opa Locka, Florida, to begin setting up a forward base code-named Lincoln. Haney exercised general supervision over CIA chiefs in the nations surrounding Guatemala plus direct control of forces assembled for Success. He took the pseudonym "Jerome B. Dunbar," and at a certain point Allen Dulles ordered that all cable traffic be sent to Lincoln for Dunbar, rather than to headquarters to be repeated to Opa Locka.

Al Haney had lots of problems. Many were with the CIA's own Western Hemisphere Division. Its director, like Haney, was a counterintelligence man, but from the FBI, not the army. Within the DO, Joseph Caldwell King's division had formal control over the stations Haney needed to use. King privately thought Project Success daffy and anyway did not want some task force poaching on his turf. Haney's deputy, Jacob Esterline, proved more equable and tried to play buffer between the two. Haney, soon endowed with his own nickname, "Brainy Haney," also raised hackles with Tracy Barnes, who tried to be decent and civilized where

Haney threw himself around like a loose cannon. Within his own task force, Haney quickly won the enmity of psywar chief Howard Hunt, with the two baiting each other over who drove the better car, for longer, or had achieved more (Haney claimed to have been the youngest bank vice president in America). To compensate, Frank Wisner devoted much time to Success, leaving a great deal of business in the hands of Dick Helms. Allen Dulles soon decided that Al Haney had to be insulated and his opportunities to rankle the top echelon limited. Dulles began flying Haney up for weekly private meetings at his Georgetown home. Richard Bissell, whom Dulles had brought in as a special assistant, also found himself acting as go-between, shuttling among Tracy Barnes, J. C. King, and Haney. Bissell soon concluded that Haney was doing a lot of the right things, he just rubbed people the wrong way.

More familiar with the area than Al Haney, whose experience had been in the Far East, King called in the task force chief one day to suggest a meeting with Tommy Corcoran. *La frutera* had plans and weapons CIA could use.

Haney did not like the idea and was blunt about it.

"If you think you can run this operation without United Fruit," King rasped, "you're crazy!"

Wisner and Allen Dulles, however, backed Haney and gave him a free hand.

In the end, United Fruit decided not to take part in Project Success. If the operation failed, the company would be grievously damaged, not only in Guatemala but globally. Agency representatives met with United Fruit officials in New York and elsewhere as the project revved up but found *la frutera* reluctant. It did wish to be informed, though, and Corcoran retained a liaison role, keeping *la frutera* executives up to date.

Despite United Fruit's preferences, in at least one respect the agency was carrying on with its program. That is, there had already been one CIA effort aimed at Guatemala, and that one *had* involved *la frutera*. Under a project code-named PB/Fortune in the waning months of the Truman administration, CIA had passed weapons to United Fruit for anti-Arbenz rebels. Project Fortune proved abortive, but the cast of PB/Success—Anastasio Somoza in Nicaragua, Honduran officials, and so forth—was almost identical. The main CIA operative would have been Colonel Castillo-Armas, and the CIA had been meeting with him since November 1951 and had had a contact officer assigned to him from the next year. Truman's secretary of state at the time, Dean Acheson, had objected, and the initiative had been put on hold. When the agency resumed the project the following summer, it changed the code name to Success.

By early October the Eisenhower administration had reached final agreement on dispatching John Peurifoy to Guatemala as ambassador. Whiting Willauer's name had already been entered on the list for a security clearance investigation, so he could be sent to Honduras as ambassador there. Peurifoy assumed his post late in 1953.

In November the CIA task force prepared an outline plan divided into five phases. The first stage would be staffing and assessment, by then well along. The

Guatemala station had been strengthened to almost a dozen, with three case officers under the station chief in the embassy and two undercover outside it. Honduras had only a pair of DO people in place, but seven were sent from Washington, Caracas, or Panama, and a couple more were awaiting approval by headquarters. Stage Two provided for "Preliminary Conditioning" of the target, with efforts to discredit Arbenz internationally and sow dissension at home, inducing defections. Project headquarters would move to the field, and cooperation agreements would be reached with Nicaragua, Honduras, and El Salvador. The initial delivery of fifteen tons of equipment for Castillo-Armas had already been prepared. Stage Three, to begin seventy-five days before D-Day, envisioned buildup of the mission forces and continued softening of the Guatemalan target. Stage Four, beginning at minus twenty-five days, CIA planners considered critical. Maximum economic pressure and an intensive rumor campaign were to sharpen divisions in the target, passive sabotage would become evident, and the CIA-backed paramilitary force would attain readiness. Stage Five would be the "Showdown." The plan enumerated a sixth stage, but that was to be the initial actions by the CIA-installed successor regime (to be "dramatic") and the termination of the project.

Reviewing the plans, Frank Wisner told Dulles they were vague, but this posed no difficulty since detailed plans would inevitably need to be modified later. Wisner recommended that Dulles approve PB/Success for execution. Director Dulles did just that. Eisenhower completed the circle on November 11, approving the money for the CIA operation.

Allen Dulles had the agency senior leadership in his office for one of those late-afternoon sessions he seems to have preferred for sensitive business. It was November 16, 1953. Present were General Cabell, Frank Wisner, Tracy Barnes, Kermit Roosevelt, and J. C. King. Dulles worried that President Eisenhower wanted quick results. The historians Richard Immerman and David Barrett have shown that the White House itself was being pressed by Congress. "This is a top priority operation for the whole agency and is the most important thing we are doing," the CIA director exhorted. Then Dulles averred, "I am under pressure by others to get on with this."

Success moved forward, though not without developments portending an outcome different from its name. The CIA organization for the project, which Richard Helms confirmed in mid-November, still had not completely filled out. Some doubted the fealty of Nicaraguan dictator Anastasio Somoza, and J. C. King wanted to use the first arms delivery to Castillo-Armas, based in Nicaragua, to deepen Somoza's commitment. Another part of the plan involved using U.S. military assistance officers from several Central American countries, but the Pentagon resisted—the assistant to the secretary of defense for special operations refused to permit CIA to bring the military into the plan. Hans Tofte took that frustration to Tracy Barnes, but the PP Staff chief could do no better. One of the oil companies told the CIA it would be feasible secretly and gradually to reduce stocks of fuel in

Guatemala to a point where an oil crisis would result, but company executives refused to proceed without cooperation from competitors. Later the State Department refused to intervene, fearing any multicorporation move would be identified as U.S.-inspired.

Just before Christmas command post Lincoln went operational at Opa Locka. Al Haney covered several walls of his operations center with a complex flow chart tracking the many distinct parts of Success, showing current status and what needed doing before other portions of the project could move ahead. The charts impressed Richard Bissell when Dulles's man went to Florida on his ever-more-numerous visits. In mounting fury, King complained that Haney considered himself directly under the DCI and that psychological warfare had been critically slowed by obstructions, such as a two-month delay in moving mimeograph machines to Castillo-Armas, as well as Lincoln's intention to craft its own psywar plan regardless of what had already been arranged.

In late January 1954 there occurred an enormous security breach. Arbenz police recruited a Panamanian diplomat, Jorge Delgado, an associate of Castillo-Armas who had functioned as a courier. Delgado gave the government copies of correspondence between the rebel leader and others, including Somoza, and for several months he acted as a double agent, furnishing the Arbenz people even more data. Delgado was present, for example on January 12, 1954, when the first CIA "black" aircraft landed in Nicaragua with weapons. Based on the Delgado material, the Guatemalans arrested an individual who was the principal link between Castillo-Armas and the supposed internal opposition. This internal front happened to be notional, essentially nonexistent, but the agent network was real. The Arbenz government presented the Delgado material to the Organization of American States, to other Central American governments, and turned it into a white paper released to condemn American intervention.

The CIA went into high gear to neutralize these developments, attempting to paint Delgado as a known fabricator. Meanwhile Castillo-Armas, pulled in to meet with CIA officers at an Opa Locka safe house, responded indignantly to suggestions that his own organization might have been the source. He denied any need for a security review.

The U.S. embassy in Guatemala City kept up unremitting pressure on Arbenz throughout these events. Ambassador Peurifoy set the tone in January 1954 when he told a reporter for *Time* magazine that "public opinion" in the United States might "force" actions "to prevent Guatemala from falling into the lap of international Communism." The CIA prepared the groundwork as quietly as possible. Henry Heckscher, a key operative from Berlin, posed as a European coffee buyer to move covertly inside the country. Later his role expanded to inducing defections from the local military.

Project Success became the first real CIA covert operation for David Atlee Phillips, brought in after a harrowing brush with Florida police (who arrested him for trying to spend an allegedly bogus check) that almost broke his CIA cover and ended his clandestine career. He came before Tracy Barnes and E. Howard Hunt for vetting. Phillips, an amateur actor as well as a journalist, originally recruited in Chile four years earlier, had a flair for colorful language but was no dummy. He put the key question to Tracy Barnes at their first meeting: "But Arbenz became president in a free election," Phillips pointed out. "What right do we have to help someone topple his government?" Barnes evaded the question.

Project Success political action kicked off after the Arbenz white paper. Chief political operator E. Howard Hunt masterminded this aspect. Dave Phillips was assigned to run the "black" radio station. Phillips began with a field trip where he contrived to meet Henry Heckscher. The coffee buyer's professionalism and skill were legendary at CIA, but when Phillips checked, not much of Heckscher's information proved useful. In April, Phillips and several Guatemalan acolytes prepared a dilapidated dairy barn at Santa Fe in rural Honduras as the clandestine "Voice of Liberation" radio, CIA code name Sherwood. In Guatemala City an anti-Communist student newspaper, *El Rebelde*, began publishing weekly, "supported and partially controlled by CIA," as agency documents acknowledge. An agent network code-named Essence waged a political handbill and poster war against the Arbenz government. The most successful endeavor, the "32" campaign, involved planting stickers or painting walls with this number, a reference to an article of the Guatemalan constitution prohibiting foreign political parties—thus an attack on the Guatemalan Communists. In El Salvador a Castillo-Armas-directed emigré publication also received CIA money. Agency press assets throughout Central America began planting stories designed to further the political-psychological program.

In Washington, Whiting Willauer received his CIA briefings on February 8, the bulk of the time devoted to the DO programs. Soon the newly minted ambassador, his appointment encouraged by Tommy Corcoran, was in Honduras arranging for the "rebel" air force. Willauer, until then a senior manager with CIA's Civil Air Transport, reported to Claire Chennault in a letter that he worked day and night to arrange training sites and instructors plus air crews for the rebel air force, and to keep the Honduran government "in line so they would allow this revolutionary activity to continue." Later, participants acknowledged that if some of the Guatemalan rebel aircraft had been shot down, surviving pilots would have been found speaking Chinese. The lead pilot, a former navy ace, seconded by another navy vet, were backed by a variety of aircrew. A total of about a dozen aircraft were assembled, including three bombers plus P-47 and P-51 fighter-bombers.

Willauer gave the CIA advice on airmen, on the timing of increasingly frequent "black" flights (night was best), and on which local officials were or needed to be apprised of the American activity. Visiting home on two occasions, Willauer went to CIA headquarters to convey his views directly. The ambassador spoke of Project Success with Honduran officials ranging from the president to the air force chief of staff. By mid-April CIA officials were concerned, admitting they had never thought Willauer "would be projected into first-hand discussion of details of this operation."

The State Department publicly termed the charge that Americans had a role in the Castillo-Armas plans "ridiculous." At that very moment Guatemalan exiles, assorted Latin Americans, and American soldiers of fortune were training in CIA camps in Nicaragua and the Panama Canal Zone. Arms and equipment now arrived in a steady stream aboard huge U.S. Air Force C-124 transports borrowed by the CIA, their markings painted out. Colonel Castillo-Armas himself lived in a house in Managua directly across the street from the first secretary of the U.S. embassy. On February 10 Al Haney held a conference at Lincoln to check all aspects. While those things the CIA could control proceeded relatively smoothly, denunciations by Arbenz posed a major problem, as did the loss of agent networks swept up by Guatemalan security. Communications traffic brought another headache— Project Success had resulted in a fivefold increase in priority messages sent from the United States to American missions in Central and South America. Anyone with a competent radio watch on the CIA could detect the swell. Little could be done other than to try to send more messages by courier or pouch, not possible in an urgent situation. That eventuality arose almost immediately. Leaving his apartment one day, a Castillo-Armas lieutenant left behind a batch of secret messages. Compromised were *all* the basic cryptonyms and pseudonyms, not just for Success but for the CIA at large. Two of the cables had been from CIA headquarters, the rest from Haney. Fortunately for the secret warriors the leak did not reach the ears of the Guatemalan government.

The big attraction in March 1954 was diplomatic—the conference of the Organization of American States, where the United States pushed for a condemnation of Communist penetration of the hemisphere and the Guatemalans decried American intervention. Secretary of State John Foster Dulles delivered a speech prepared in consultation with his brother, the CIA director.

Beneath the surface the plot boiled. Agency progress reports noted that the logistics arrangements were on track, far enough advanced that one of two C-124s CIA had borrowed from the air force could be returned. Eventually 433 tons of arms and equipment were delivered by airlift. Agency officers, increasingly mistrustful of Castillo-Armas, explored an anti-Communist "structure" that excluded him. Cost estimates for the Sherwood radio project had firmed up to the degree that Al Haney decided to base the Guatemalan announcers and scriptwriters in Florida instead of Honduras, sending prerecorded tapes that would then be broadcast. Sherwood's radio equipment arrived aboard a late March black flight. Meanwhile the State Department developed cold feet about direct U.S. involvement. Jake Esterline of the task force believed the diplomats had dug in to defend the principle of noninterference in internal affairs of states, and told Lincoln to watch out. On March 16 Frank Wisner met with Dick Helms, Tracy Barnes, J. C. King, and others for a high-level review. Haney warned that delaying D-Day would cause morale problems and weather difficulties. Wisner saw no need to change the tempo. What mattered was not to get caught.

One Project Success preparation with sinister connotations was the creation of a list of Guatemalans "for disposal by [the] Junta Group," evidently requested by Al Haney. A similar list had been compiled for Project Fortune, and this, renewed, formed the basis for the draft list of March 1954. "Rip" Robertson took it to Opa Locka to be checked against CIA biographic data. Decades later agency researchers established that no one had actually been assassinated on the basis of these lists, but they would have eerie echoes for the CIA in Indonesia and Vietnam.

Director Dulles visited Station Lincoln on March 31. The spy chieftain expressed himself much impressed with the briefings he received on the operation and apparent competence of the personnel.

"Continue the good work and give 'em hell!" Allen Dulles exhorted.

Toward the end Dulles turned to Lincoln's chief of security and asked him to tell Haney, who was absent, that the DCI "meant exactly what he said when he referred to this project as the most vitally important one in the Agency."

In April the public who paid attention to Central America were diverted by a plot to assassinate Nicaraguan leader Somoza. This would be attributed to the "Caribbean Legion," a loosely organized leftist anti-totalitarian entity. As a movement the Legion had peaked in the late 1940s and had never enjoyed the regimented structure implied in its name. It had, however, received some support from Arbenz's predecessor as president of Guatemala. The CIA propagandists now made strenuous efforts to pin the attempted assassination on Arbenz. Behind the scenes, Rip Robertson's paramilitary boys began smuggling packets of CIA equipment across the Guatemalan border to four anti-Arbenz sabotage teams. Frank Wisner also approved the final timetable for the attack phase, plus a fresh psywar initiative to help justify the operation: the CIA would configure a phony Soviet bloc arms shipment to Guatemala and contrive to make the world believe the weapons had been landed from a Soviet submarine.

A tiff between the CIA and State Department now endangered Project Success: DDCI General Cabell assured senior diplomats on April 10 that no black flights into Honduras would occur until State studied the situation. The agency, which had already scheduled fifteen such flights, made one the following night anyway. Investigation showed that Al Haney had instructed his air officer to disregard the DCI's no-go cable. Secretary of State Dulles could not then protect his brother's agency from the fury of diplomats scorned; within days the CIA was told to report on the impact that postponement or cancellation of PB/Success might have. Wisner's defense combined elements that would be employed once again when the identical question arose during the CIA's operation against Cuba: cancellation entailed the danger of open recrimination from the CIA's Guatemalans, effectively exposing the CIA's hand; it would worsen U.S. relations with Nicaragua and Honduras (and lend comfort to Arbenz); it would leave Washington with "the $64-question"—what to do about Guatemala; and have adverse morale effects to boot.

While this impasse continued, the CIA resumed black flights at a rate of *two* per day. Where Wisner, King, Esterline, and others had been furious at the earlier violation of the flight ban, the absence of protest this time suggests that headquarters supported Haney's resumption of deliveries. If the CIA irrevocably committed, the State Department would have that much more trouble shutting it down. For his part, on April 24 DDO Wisner mounted a full defense of the project in a paper refocusing the operation. In retrospect his handiwork is notable for its utter misappreciation of Guatemalans' willingness to rise against Arbenz (while rightly rejecting Castillo-Armas estimates of forty thousand adherents, Wisner projected somewhere between six thousand and nineteen thousand partisans; in reality *no* Guatemalans would rebel). At this point the State Department backed off.

A few days later a full headquarters delegation visited Opa Locka in triumph. Frank Wisner, Tracy Barnes, and Richard Bissell all went on this trip to Lincoln. The DDO hastened to give the bottom line: "We have the full green light and the go-ahead," Wisner declared.

The god of operations cautioned that the approval relieved no one of the responsibility to conduct Success so as to minimize any chance of attribution to the United States. False trails had not been sufficiently developed—for example, provision had been made for a minor arms purchase from Rafael Trujillo in the Dominican Republic, which could be used later as an answer to the question of where Castillo-Armas had gotten all those guns. Wisner wanted more of the same. He also wanted to see Lincoln's documentation on the strength of the anti-Arbenz opposition—despite what he had written a few days earlier, "Headquarters had never received a clear and concise statement of what the plans are with respect to what takes place on D-Day." Referring to Allen Dulles, or perhaps even to President Eisenhower, Wisner remarked, "The boss has to be satisfied that we have what it takes."

Among themselves, Wisner talked with Barnes about a paper for Assistant Secretary Henry Holland at the State Department to illustrate what Project Success had accomplished other than those aspects that concerned the diplomat. At a meeting once they were back in Washington, Dick Bissell spoke of a different paper, one that might show how much time had been wasted as a result of the fight with the State Department. Helms, King, and Kermit Roosevelt sat silently around the table.

The CIA's big psywar victory came soon afterward. Project Washtub, the attempt to plant a cache of arms and make it seem like the work of the Russians, carefully surfaced in early May. Reporting cables crowed that when Somoza called in the diplomats and reporters to look at the weapons, conveniently marked with hammer and sickle, even the U.S. ambassador was taken in. The French ambassador, who had been in Greece during the civil war there, readily confirmed the weapons as being of Soviet bloc manufacture. In early May Tracy Barnes, who had begun spending most of his time at Lincoln or making the rounds of other forward bases, returned to headquarters for consultations. The meetings in the DDO's office that followed included Dick Helms, Dick Bissell, Kim Roosevelt, J. C. King, and Jake Esterline, among others. Wisner hammered home the dictum that black flights into Honduras would go only with the okay of Allen Dulles or General Cabell. Barnes described the status of the various PB/Success elements. The CIA project seemed to be moving ahead smartly.

One action by the Arbenz government did play into the preparations for Success. The Guatemalans turned to Czechoslovakia to buy 2,000 tons of arms from the Skoda works. Washington learned of the move when an agent in Poland reported the loading of the weapons aboard a freighter at Szczecin. The ship turned out to be the 4,900-ton Swedish vessel *Alfhem*, which eluded several attempts at interception and reached Puerto Barrios on May 15, 1954. The phony Washtub weapons and the real ones from *Alfhem* permitted the United States to argue that the Russians were indeed penetrating Latin America. President Eisenhower promptly initiated Operation Hardrock Baker, a naval blockade of Guatemala. The blockade was illegal under international law, but no one had standing to oppose it. The *Alfhem* affair brought a windfall for Howard Hunt's propaganda experts. Radio Sherwood went on the air on May 1 and went to town on the arms cache and the freighter. Then, in the only real defection sparked by the CIA, former Guatemalan air force chief Rodolfo Mendoza left the country with the former U.S. air attaché who had been at CIA the day before departing for Central America. The supposed defection became grist for Dave Phillips's radio mill. The Arbenz government made a significant error, taking the government radio station off the air for installation of a new antenna. For several weeks the "Voice of Liberation" became the only show in town.

Later, Guatemalan police made a series of arrests. Eisenhower refers to these in his memoirs as a "reign of terror," and government killings of the opposition. At the time CIA reported that the wave of arrests probably resulted from Guatemalan search of the home of CIA's agent "Semantic" on May 30. Piero Gleijeses, the foremost historian of Guatemalan politics in this period, concludes that several hundred were arrested and at least seventy-five killed, including persons who had nothing to do with the CIA conspiracy. But, equally deplorable, Eisenhower made out the Arbenz government as "agents of international Communism in Guatemala [who] continued their efforts to penetrate and subvert their neighboring Central American states, using consular agents for their political purposes and fomenting political assassinations and strikes." Aside from individual arrests of opposition figures, and the ambiguous role of Guatemala in the alleged assassination plot against Somoza, there is no evidence to sustain the charges.

The *Alfhem* affair led to the first military action of the project. Headquarters ordered a sabotage action; CIA paramilitary man Rip Robertson wanted to go into Puerto Barrios with frogmen to sink the Swedish ship with explosives. Washington turned him down. Instead Robertson got orders to send saboteurs from the CIA-backed "liberation army" to blow up trains carrying the equipment. Robertson led the team despite orders that no Americans were to be involved. The saboteurs laid explosives on the railroad track, but the detonators, drenched in a downpour, fizzled. The CIA team then shot at one of the trains. They could not stop the ten-train convoy. One anti-Arbenz soldier died, as did one of Robertson's strikers. Two later commando attacks also failed. With the gloves off came increasing pressure, from Haney and others, for air missions. Lincoln wanted to mix some bombing with leaflet drops. Barnes preferred to smuggle leaflets into the country and have them distributed by anti-Arbenz activists, giving the impression of a widespread rebellion.

After all this trouble, the Czech weapons proved of little use to the Guatemalan army. They included large-caliber cannon designed to be mounted on railway carriages, of limited value on Guatemala's nominal railroad network. The *Alfhem* had carried anti-tank guns, though there were no tanks in Central American armies. Only a small fraction of the World War II–vintage British and German small arms arrived in working order. Eisenhower might think Arbenz a Communist, but clearly the real Communists were no friends to Guatemala. The Czechs took the government's cash and delivered useless weapons. In a supreme irony, the arms enabled Eisenhower to declare that Guatemala had become an "outpost" of "the Communist dictatorship" on the American continent.

On May 23 the navy received orders to conduct surveillance of shipping near Guatemalan ports. The next day Ike told a party of congressional leaders he was ordering the navy to stop "suspicious" foreign-flag vessels on the high seas. Thus began Hardrock Baker. *Alfhem* herself was intercepted on the return voyage and escorted to Key West for a thorough search. The Dutch government lodged an official protest after a Dutch ship was boarded on June 4 at San Juan, Puerto Rico. Later it was decided that no more ships would be boarded without specific State Department authorization. James Hagerty, Eisenhower's press secretary, wrote in his diary on June 19, "I think the State Department made a bad mistake, particularly with the British, in attempting to search ships going to Guatemala. . . . As a matter of fact, we were at war with the British in 1812 over the same principle."

Project Success was already in its final phase. Howard Hunt's propaganda featured cartoons, posters, pamphlets, and more than two hundred articles based on CIA materials placed in the Latin press by the United States Information Agency. The military plan had to be changed at the last moment when Salvadoran officials refused to allow the invasion to be mounted from their country. At the beginning of June, Tracy Barnes argued that the paramilitary plan as originally conceived could no longer be carried out. As late as June 16 a meeting at CIA headquarters considered cancellation or postponement of Project Success, with Wisner willing to entertain a hiatus for reevaluation if moving forward seemed to invite catastrophe.

The final plan based the rebels in Honduras. Castillo-Armas made his invasion two days later, riding in an old station wagon accompanied by a few trucks. Only about 140 soldiers were with him, though several additional forces entered Guatemala at other points. The same day Arbenz held a mass rally at a stadium in Guatemala City, which CIA aircraft buzzed and leafleted. One rebel patrol tried to hook through El Salvador, but the soldiers were arrested by Salvadoran border guards and freed only with difficulty by CIA-inspired corruption. In all there were perhaps 400 rebel troops. Castillo-Armas advanced to a church six miles into Guatemala, then halted. He awaited the popular revolution that was supposed to support him. From there the main force would march overland and capture the railroad station at Zacapa, a Guatemalan military garrison, while several boat-loads of men made for the Caribbean port of Puerto Barrios. Both places, plus Guatemala City, would be bombed by the CIA air force.

But no popular uprising appeared. Castillo-Armas did not march even the few miles to Zacapa. Another of his units was defeated in a small skirmish, and the biggest action of the campaign, also an insignificant battle, proved no better than a standoff. The seaborne force sent to capture Puerto Barrios also failed. The CIA, myopically optimistic, reported to President Eisenhower on June 20 that Castillo-Armas had taken in as many soldiers as had joined him, for a total of more than six hundred armed men.

All now depended on Whiting Willauer's rebel air force. It had run a number of bombing and leafleting missions since the first day of the invasion. A raid that caused some damage at Puerto Barrios involved a hand grenade and a stick of dy-namite. Another pilot missed his target and ran out of gas, crash landing across the Mexican border. The CIA operation could have been exposed right there, as it was an American national, William Beall, taken into custody. But the agency managed to get him released quietly, and Project Success survived the flap. Two more planes were hit by small-arms fire and could not be repaired. The CIA air force seemed no more effective than the "liberation army."

Allen Dulles got the bad news on June 20 from Al Haney. The rebel air force could not operate more than four planes at a time. Losses made the difficulty greater; the supply of high-explosive bombs was limited, so pilots resorted to dropping smoke bombs, leaflets, even empty Coca-Cola bottles, which made a noise much like the explosion of a bomb.

Haney reported that Nicaragua's Somoza had offered two of his own P-51 fighter-bombers to make up rebel losses, but only if the United States replaced his aircraft. This sounded simple until State's assistant secretary for Latin America in-sisted on a presidential decision.

On the afternoon of June 22, Eisenhower met Allen and Foster Dulles at the White House. Henry Holland entered the office carrying several legal tomes. But legality had ceased to be the issue.

The president turned to Allen Dulles. "What do you think Castillo's chances would be without the aircraft?"

Dulles replied without hesitation. "About zero."

"Suppose we supply the aircraft," Eisenhower pressed, "what would be the chances then?"

"About twenty percent."

Mainly because of the important psychological impact of air support, Ike agreed to the request. The Somoza "rebel" planes were in action the next day, and air attacks became the CIA's main activity.

The bombing led to the worst scare of Project Success. The British were an-gered over American boarding and search of ships at sea. Then the CIA bombed and sank a British merchant vessel. The ship was the *Springfjord*, which had sailed from the Nicaraguan Pacific port of San Jose. Tacho Somoza feared the vessel carried gasoline, with which the Guatemalans might fuel their trucks and airplanes to attack Nicaragua and exact retribution for Somoza's help to the CIA.

Somoza turned to Rip Robertson, top CIA officer at the airfield, and demanded the ship be stopped. Robertson asked Lincoln for orders, but his cable arrived at two in the morning. Al Haney and Tracy Barnes refused. They told Robertson to use another method—frogmen or a commando raid.

This infuriated Somoza, who thundered, "If you use my airfields, you take my orders!"

Robertson, also disappointed by the orders to desist, ordered up one of the fighter-bombers. Fifteen minutes out of base, the plane found *Springfjord* and hit her with a five-hundred-pound bomb. Fortunately no one was hurt, and the ship sank slowly enough for officers and crew to abandon her. *Springfjord*, it was later learned, had carried only coffee and cotton.

When news of the sinking reached Washington it destroyed the cordial atmosphere Ike sought for a summit conference he was hosting for British leaders. Frank Wisner left immediately for the British embassy to offer personal apologies. The agency investigated circumstances of the incident in October 1954 and confirmed the ship had been sunk on Robertson's orders without authorization from either Lincoln or CIA headquarters, by one of the air arm's American pilots. The British allowed themselves to be mollified, and the CIA later quietly reimbursed Lloyd's of London, insurers of the *Springfjord*, the $1.5 million they had paid out on the ship. Colonel King of the agency continued meeting Assistant Secretary Holland on this matter as late as the spring of 1956.

In the heat of action, however, *Springfjord*'s sinking had a significant psychological impact on the Guatemalans. The bombing broke the political situation wide open. Apparently the Guatemalan military began thinking the CIA would stop at nothing to oust Arbenz. The army began to consider a coup. Arbenz received an ultimatum and resigned before the day was out, taking refuge at the Mexican embassy and asking for political asylum. Project Success achieved its aim after all.

Despite the success of this unintended strike, the *Springfjord* incident had a rather different effect for CIA. It convinced Eisenhower of the need for more rigorous control over covert action, leading to establishment of a senior review group similar to Truman's 10/2 panel. The final price tag for Guatemala—though the CIA has only admitted to the original $3 million budget expense—came in considerably higher. That figure does not include the money paid out on the *Springfjord* incident, the cost of replacing Somoza's aircraft, hardware taken from CIA stockpiles, or subsidies that followed the coup d'état. The actual number is probably at least double the projected cost.

Al Haney's era in covert operations came to an end; no further major assignments came his way. Rip Robertson, branded a "cowboy" after *Springfjord*, saw Allen Dulles, who fired him. In a 1966 interview with *New York Times* reporters, Richard Bissell conceded that the action "went beyond the established limits of policy." Frank Wisner and Tracy Barnes celebrated. Barnes would be rewarded with stewardship of the station in West Germany, one of the CIA's front-line jobs. Howard Hunt's services were considered necessary for CIA's political action efforts in Japan. Dave Phillips, who believed the PB/Success psywar effort had been the engine of victory, went on to greater things in the WH Division.

In retrospect, and with more of the true record now open to view, it seems perplexing that the Central Intelligence Agency, and indeed secret warriors in many places, for decades held out Iran and Guatemala as models of successful covert action. The inner stories reveal that both Projects Ajax and Success skirted with failure. At some point in each case the CIA came close to canceling the operation. The projects may be said to have succeeded despite themselves, not marched forward according to meticulous plans. Gaps in CIA knowledge of local conditions, unrealistic expectations, fixation on a certain worldview, the personal weaknesses of CIA allies, the competing interests of groups working with the secret warriors, the physical properties of weapons and equipment, and the limitations of tradecraft all number among the reasons why success hovered at the edge of failure. The deep secrecy in which CIA held the stories of the covert actions served to disguise this characteristic and to hinder, even long afterward, careful evaluation of the strategy.

At the time CIA thought it had done rather nicely with the Iranian and Guatemalan operations, so well, in fact, that within months the agency was deliberately leaking certain details of both to the writers Richard and Gladys Harkness for a series of favorable articles. Eisenhower's memoirs employ only the thinnest of linguistic disguises in discussing these two crises, calling CIA agents in Teheran "representatives" of the United States government, and saying of Guatemala that the United States had to do something. Allen Dulles is even more forthright in his book *The Craft of Intelligence*:

> In Iran, a Mossadegh, and in Guatemala, an Arbenz had come to power through the usual processes of government and not by any Communist coup as in Czechoslovakia. Neither man at the time disclosed the intention of creating a Communist state. When this purpose became clear, support from outside was given to loyal anti-Communist elements in the respective countries, in the one case to the Shah's supporters; in the other, to a group of Guatemalan patriots. In each case the danger was successfully met.

But was the danger met, or did it ever exist? In the Cold War vision of a two-camp world, there was little room for indigenous nationalisms. Not only did the United States act readily against nations like Iran and Guatemala, those ventures were initiated regardless of the countries' efforts to maintain friendly relations with the United States. The CIA operations made a mockery of the oft-reiterated American principle of nonintervention in the internal affairs of states.

The Central Intelligence Agency, unleashed in the name of democracy— democracy as defined by American foreign policy, which came to mean governments that assumed pro-American stances—actually encouraged the opposite. No elections occurred in Iran between the 1953 CIA operation and 1960; thereafter parliament existed at the pleasure of the shah. In Guatemala after 1954 the republic was abolished. A new constitution was adopted only in 1965, but that was soon suspended by military rulers. In fact the excesses of the ruling oligarchy became such that the United States itself, under the Carter administration, finally halted virtually all foreign aid to the country. Over the long haul the covert actions did not produce the results advertised.

In both Iran and Guatemala the United States received credit from world public opinion for creating dictatorships, not democracies. In the short term, though, these covert operations seemed to be shining successes. So while the fruit might prove bitter in the long run, Eisenhower felt encouraged to try more of the same.

7

Adventures in Asia

CHOOSING SIDES may have been a dilemma for people in Europe, but in the Far East that quandary was multiplied a thousandfold. In China cooperation between Nationalist and Communist parties broke down soon after the defeat of Japan; Jiang Jieshi and Mao Zedong merely resumed their interrupted competition for power. All over Asia the Cold War proved especially pernicious. Religious and nationalist movements recast China, India, and Southeast Asia as actors in a global ideological struggle; dominion hung in the balance.

The United States participated in the struggle from the beginning. After abortive efforts to mediate between Chinese factions, President Truman aligned the United States with Jiang Jieshi against the Communists. Mao Zedong's field armies nevertheless swept through mainland China. The Nationalist collapse climaxed in 1949 when the Chinese Communists overran Beijing and south China despite American military and economic aid to Jiang, and at precisely the time when U.S. covert action capabilities were coalescing within the CIA and the Pentagon.

Washington soon considered exploiting the still tenuous Communist control of the mainland, using new Nationalist bases on islands off the coast. The Korean War injected tremendous momentum into the program; in turn this expansion eventually created a headache for the secret war managers. But, aside from their policy implications, the clandestine campaigns enjoyed only indifferent success. More important, the intelligence buildup that occurred greatly expanded CIA capability for, and interest in, covert actions of all sorts.

Driven from the mainland, Jiang Jieshi's* nationalist forces established themselves on the islands offshore, chiefly Taiwan. The Chinese Communists had no

* Since the era of these covert operations, China has changed its written language. The new rendering, called *pinyin*, is intended to be more phonetic than the traditional. In a historical account such as this, however, the new system can generate confusion. In general this narrative will render place names, with which readers may be familiar, in the modern form while retaining the traditional rendering for historical figures, with the exceptions of the major figures well known to history. Thus Mao Tse-tung will be Mao Zedong, Chiang Kai-shek will be Jiang Jieshi, Peking will be Beijing, and Fukien appears as Fujian—but Li Tsung-jen remains in the traditional form.

navy to speak of and no experience with amphibious war. Only small vessels, mostly junks, were even available to be commandeered. Mao's armies made one great effort, in early 1950, to fight their way onto Hainan, the next-largest island to Taiwan. They succeeded after ten invasions and considerable casualties when, as had so often happened on the mainland, the morale of the Nationalist troops broke. Superior force was no guarantee against defeat; Jiang ordered the Nationalist survivors back to Taiwan. Although there were fears the Communists would follow, an invasion of Taiwan was a much more difficult proposition and was not attempted.

Proposals for covert action predated Nationalist defeat in the civil war. Jiang had gone to Taiwan in early 1949, resigning the presidency in favor of his vice president, General Li Tsung-jen, who tried to negotiate with Mao. That spring Claire Chennault, a retired American officer who had commanded the Flying Tigers during the Sino-Japanese war and afterward organized the private airline called Civil Air Transport (CAT), which initially operated in China, went to Washington with a proposal for U.S. support to a Nationalist bastion in southern China plus covert aid to guerrilla forces loyal to Li Tsung-jen. Chennault's airline had fallen on hard times, and he sought help for it as well.

The State Department was not much interested in the Chennault plan, so the former general pursued his other agenda. Chennault went to Thomas Corcoran, his business partner in Civil Air Transport. Corcoran put Chennault in contact with CIA officers, culminating in a series of meetings during the summer of 1949. By August Chennault was talking to Col. Richard G. Stilwell, chief of the Far East Division of OPC. Wisner's Wurlitzer thought an airline like Civil Air Transport could provide an important covert asset, and it had an interest in military aid as well. President Truman simultaneously directed the State Department to reexamine the feasibility of Chennault's plan.

Before these deliberations could be completed, Nationalist resistance on the mainland disintegrated, forcing a shift to operations mounted from outside China. Civil Air Transport acquired greater prominence. In early October the CIA received an analysis of the Chennault plan from George Kennan which took no position on the project but nevertheless allowed Wisner to contend that State had approved it. Civil Air Transport was enlisted in the secret war, flying its first CIA mission on October 10, 1949. Tommy Corcoran, on behalf of CAT, and Emmet D. Echols of CIA's Office of Finances signed a formal agreement on the 1st of November.

Meanwhile, on October 28 a detailed proposal for covert operations in China from Gen. John Magruder went to the secretary of defense. Magruder, citing his experience as chief of the Strategic Services Unit, advocated active operations. Secretary of Defense Louis Johnson forwarded the proposal and an accompanying memorandum from Wisner to the president. Harry Truman expressed interest, but the collapse of resistance on the mainland temporarily halted the project.

This became a defining moment for Civil Air Transport. Founded in 1946 by Chennault and Whiting Willauer, CAT had made its living flying troops, supplies, and dignitaries in the Chinese civil war. The airline's performance in 1948 was impressive: 34 million ton-miles; almost a quarter-million passengers carried; about 90,000 tons of cargo consigned. By mid-1949, however, runaway inflation in China plus the Nationalist disintegration brought CAT face-to-face with disaster. The CIA put a half-million dollars in hard currency into CAT, $200,000 of it up front. The airline used the cash to relocate to Taiwan with corporate headquarters in Hong Kong, ending the chaos of existence on the mainland. (Chennault's friendship with Jiang Jieshi meant the end of CAT domestic air service once the Communists took over.) But CIA money did not solve the underlying market problems for Civil Air Transport, which would be forced to go back to the agency again and again until the spooks virtually owned the airline.

Access to a fleet of transport aircraft became a great boon for the CIA. In Europe air missions had to be run ad hoc or through the U.S. and British air forces. Missions required delicate interagency discussion, sometimes a little horse trading too. In Asia with CAT, the Office of Policy Coordination could dispense with politics. Occasionally there came a question whether CAT crews would volunteer for flights, but since Willauer's pilots flaunted their skills and can-do attitude, this rarely became a problem.

The first arms request came from Gen. Ma Pu-fang, a Muslim leader in northwest China, thought to have fifty thousand troops. Aid to Muslims is the only covert action known to have been specifically mentioned by President Truman at a November 1949 meeting on assistance to anti-Communist Chinese. But before shipments could be organized, General Ma went down in defeat. Gathering his fortune of $1.5 million in gold bars, Ma Pu-fang escaped on a CAT plane, then left on a pilgrimage to Mecca.

Recruits for missions to the mainland had to be found. This was not difficult because the Nationalists ardently wished to return; Jiang sounded the keynote in a speech in which he promised to go "back to the Mainland," a theme he dwelt on throughout the 1950s, adopted as a slogan by the pro-Taiwan "China Lobby" in the United States.

Yet there were difficulties in Asia, not unlike those the CIA encountered in Europe. Among the Nationalists were factions, all of them hoping to corner U.S. aid. Alfred T. Cox, the OPC officer sent to Hong Kong to represent CIA at Civil Air Transport headquarters, worked as a sort of broker between the United States and the squabbling factions. Li Tsung-jen, whose "Third Force" resistance based itself in Hong Kong, hoped to become CIA's exclusive Chinese ally, but the agency dealt with every group it could find.

Chinese politics embarrassed Washington from the beginning. Immediately upon leaving the mainland in December 1949, sixty-year-old acting president Li went to New York for medical treatment. Invited by President Truman for an official visit, Li Tsung-jen claimed to have almost 200,000 guerrillas loyal to him, mostly in southwest China. In a memorandum of February 22, 1950, he proposed a four-point program, including guerrilla warfare; underground activities; penetration of overseas Chinese; and mobilization of liberal elements dissatisfied with both the Communists and the Nationalists. As acting president of China, Li Tsung-jen stayed at the official Blair House residence. President Truman planned a formal reception for Li, a luncheon to be held on March 2. But the day before, in Taiwan, Jiang Jieshi suddenly declared himself ruler of China and resumed the presidency. Instantly deprived of power, Li remained in the United States, competing with Jiang for influence among ethnic Chinese. This political competition continued for decades.

Despite internal struggle, OPC officers continued to think Li Tsung-jen offered a viable alternative, his Third Force untainted by either communism or the corruption of the Nationalist government. The OPC Far East Division chief of operations, James G. L. Kellis, worried that backing both factions only robbed the United States of sincerity. Because Jiang Jieshi controlled the offshore islands—the potential bases for secret war—there was ultimately no choice but to support him if the CIA wanted a secret war against Mao.

The China campaign was masterminded by the Far East Division. The unit, a microcosm of the early CIA, was itself a forest of cliques. One came from the army's World War II Ninetieth Infantry Division, another from the OSS in Burma. Wisner's Far East Division chief, Richard G. Stilwell, on detached service from the army, had headed the Ninetieth Division's operations staff. His China branch chief, William E. Depuy, his primary logistics officer, Gilbert Strickler, and the commanders of the CIA detachments on two different offshore islands critical to the campaign, Edward S. Hamilton and Lon Redman, were all Ninetieth Division veterans. Jim Kellis had been with OSS in Turkey and Greece. Ray Peers, the chief of the OPC station on Taiwan, had fought with OSS Detachment 101 in Burma during the war. Stilwell's deputy, Desmond FitzGerald, another former officer who served in Burma, had been an adviser to the Nationalist army. The president of the CIA proprietary company set up to furnish cover for the Chinese project, Charles E. Johnston, had spent World War II in China. Robert J. Delaney, deputy and eventual successor to Peers; Rodney Gilbert, the psywar chief on Taiwan; and such case officers as Frank Holober and Philip Montgomery all had had wartime experience in either China or Burma, where Chinese Nationalist forces had also fought. These were small circles, bands of CIA brothers looking out for one another.

Korean hostilities reinvigorated the China programs, especially after the November 1950 People's Republic of China intervention in the war. Decisions in Washington sharpened the Far East command problem by expanding the scope of covert activities. In early 1951 a National Security Council policy paper endorsed a vigorous program of covert operations to aid anti-Communist guerrilla forces. Late that year Truman asked what more could be done to hurt Beijing. Disruption of Chinese supply lines became an explicit goal in an NSC directive that the president approved at the end of the year.

Having kept its options open, the CIA began to put in place the elements for a secret war against China. The cover would be an ostensible private company, in reality owned by the CIA—Western Enterprises Incorporated (WEI), a legal entity in Pittsburgh, Pennsylvania. Frank Brick, a lawyer who happened to be another Ninetieth Division veteran, filed the papers. An office opened on Taiwan in early 1951, with the first CIA officers arriving that March. Claire Chennault met them at the airport, and senior people were put up at the Grand Hotel. Some called headquarters the Guest House, others referred to WEI as Western Auto. New agency people passed through Pittsburgh to process their WEI paperwork, with corporate head Charles Johnston acquiring the moniker "Pittsburgh Charlie." Training and operational bases followed in southern Taiwan and on other offshore islands.

Western Enterprises became the bailiwick of Ray Peers, a first-rate organizer. Peers missed few tricks, including bringing along his former OSS mess sergeant, a chef apprentice at New York's Waldorf-Astoria Hotel, whose genius with food made the Guest House a destination for American diplomats, military officers, and all manner of visiting spooks. The good relations thus created served when Peers needed help himself. Western Enterprises soon acquired a fleet of a half-dozen boats, mostly junks but also some fast patrol craft. Civil Air Transport furnished flight services both to forward bases and for the parachute training of Chinese guerrillas. The unit soon began putting out tentacles to small islands off the mainland, most importantly Xiamen and the Tachen Islands. Detachments of Western Enterprises were placed in these forward positions. The CIA also created a network of coast-watchers to detect and follow ships transiting the Taiwan Straits.

Shipping activities most resembled the old OSS derring-do. In December 1950 Washington began a total embargo of trade to China. Several hundred items were prohibited—more than for the Soviet Union—and placed on a contraband list. Although the State Department opposed the move as likely to increase Chinese dependence on Russia, the Pentagon and CIA likened it as cutting into Chinese capabilities. A big part of enforcement would be Nationalist naval patrols from Taiwan, but the CIA carried on its own secret campaign using the Western Enterprises fleet. Air scouts, CIA coast-watchers, and Nationalist intelligence reports alerted agency marauders, who took to their own patrol boats or junks to intercept. The coast-watchers worked in small teams which landed on uninhabited islands and stayed out of sight, occasionally collecting information from friendly fishermen.

China had little merchant shipping of its own at the time, but there were extensive imports. At least one Polish and two Russian tankers were stopped at various times, and the CIA collected its first sample of Soviet jet fuel from one of these boardings. There could also be diplomatic headaches. Great Britain and France, though allied with the United States, recognized Communist China and traded with it. Agency marauders stopped British ships just like others, handing them over to the Nationalists, who seized cargoes with aplomb. British warships countered by occasionally escorting their own merchantmen bound for mainland ports. On at least one occasion a British destroyer forced a CIA attack boat to abandon its attempt to halt one of these merchant craft.

Project Stole was a covert attempt to block Indian medical supplies from reaching Mao's China. The aid, including makings for three full field hospitals, was packed on a Norwegian freighter. Stole proposed to stop the shipment at all costs, and the CIA earmarked a million dollars for the effort. Hans Tofte met with other OPC Far East station chiefs in Tokyo to plan the heist. At one point in Hong Kong, Al Cox made sabotage preparations under the noses of British authorities for when the Norwegian vessel docked there. The freighter bypassed Hong Kong. Tofte went through WEI to approach Jiang Jieshi, who happily lent his patrol boats, which intercepted the freighter on the high seas. Cox and his CIA agents were hidden below deck when the Nationalist gunboats commandeered the cargo.

After the Korean War began, President Truman declared the Taiwan Straits neutralized. He started a U.S. naval patrol there with a cruiser and a couple of destroyers. In principle the patrol aimed to close the straits both to Chinese Communist attacks on Taiwan and to Nationalist forays onto the mainland. While this complicated the CIA mission, it increased the value of the islands since these were already on the mainland side. Thus in practice the island bases leapfrogged the blockade, enabling the Nationalists to hit the mainland in spite of the supposed neutralization. By the end of 1950 there were 65,000 Nationalist troops on the offshore islands. These garrisons shielded the CIA detachments as they trained guerrilla units on these same islands.

To accomplish its aims the CIA's secret warriors obviously needed to work with the Nationalists. This meant Chinese intelligence agencies. Useful to this purpose was that Western Enterprises boss Ray Peers had gone into China immediately after World War II to liaise with Chinese intelligence. By now the legendary Chinese spy chieftain Tai Li, whom Peers had known, had passed from the scene. His successors competed intensely against one another. The official resistance unit, the Continental Operations Department *(Ta-lu Kung-tso Ch'u)*, answered to Tai Li's successor, Gen. Cheng Kai-min. But, from the CIA's point of view, this unit controlled few critical assets. Both the bases on the offshore islands and the remaining forces on the mainland—cavalry in the wilds of western China—were under the primary Nationalist intelligence entity, the Secrets Preservation Bureau *(Pao-mi Chu)* of Gen. Mao Jen-feng. Not only did General Mao, who had close ties with Madame Jiang Jieshi, head the intelligence unit, Jiang appointed him a member of the Political Action Committee, the Chinese equivalent of Washington's Special Group, which coordinated Nationalist intelligence under Jiang's son, Chiang Ching-kuo. Peers found himself dealing with both senior generals as well as Ching-kuo and Madame Jiang. In fact Madame Jiang appeared among the spooks so often, from hosting dinners to participating in inspections, that she should be credited with her own role in the secret war. Beyond simple competition between spy services lay an additional layer of sensitivity—Chiang Ching-kuo competed with Madame Jiang as chief lieutenant to the generalissimo and guardian of Jiang's legacy, and to position himself as rightful heir. Meanwhile American ambassador Carl Rankin felt that all these spy games among the offshore islands were simply diversions from the real business of running Taiwan. Ray Peers needed all his diplomatic skills for the job.

Another challenge in those early days was the cleavage between CIA's Office of Policy Coordination and its Office of Special Operations. Under navy cover, Robert J. Myers headed the OSO station on Taiwan, and his organization considered OPC schemes to land troops on the mainland as delusional. At the same time Peer's officers felt OSO intelligence support of their paramilitary effort to be pathetically inadequate. Yet even as OSO denigrated the campaign, Myers dabbled in it, visiting different offshore islands with Chinese spy chiefs, making Western Enterprises people suspicious of OSO competitors. The OSO helped OPC's Larry St. George set up the first coast-watcher networks, but tension continued between the CIA elements.

The American military became one more source of competition. A U.S. military advisory group went to Taiwan after Truman neutralized the straits. In May 1951 the group numbered only four hundred, and the flow of U.S. weapons and training had just begun. But soon the Americans were supplying destroyers, amphibious ships, jet aircraft, and much else, and the number of advisers reached into the thousands (an additional reason why CIA found it easy to disguise its officers under navy cover). The Nationalist military soon found they could play off the military advisers and Western Enterprises against each other.

After CIA secret warriors took up their places on the offshore islands, they began to recruit troops. The units were distinct from the Nationalist armies. Although called "guerrillas," these formations had standard infantry training, equipment, and organization. Edward S. Hamilton, among the Ninetieth Division stalwarts, headed the OPC detachment on Xiamen, where the CIA formed two battalions of guerrillas. Special scout troops received parachute training under Lou Rucker. Frank Holober handled intelligence for mission planning. The initial operation went off in September 1951 when a Nationalist guerrilla unit went ashore on the mainland to create a base inland where supplies and more troops were to land to expand the cleared area. Instead the Nationalists sought out a fight. The People's Liberation Army (PLA) concentrated forces and wiped out the interlopers.

Western Enterprises went on recruiting guerrillas and achieved a psywar coup by inserting anti-Communist leaflets into letters captured by a patrol, after which the letters were put back into the mail system from Hong Kong. Chinese commanders carried out some operations on their own while Hamilton plotted a fresh mission. That came in October when raiders landed on a small island lightly held by the Chinese Communists. With that mission under their belts, a more ambitious raid took place on December 7 on the island of Nanri Dao, not far from Fuzhou. The operation proved completely successful except that the Nationalist general leading it was shot in the head as he peered over a rock. Island targets were the most desirable since the Communists themselves had difficulty sending reinforcements to the points under attack.

In early 1952 the Joint Chiefs of Staff ordered the navy to provide the CIA with ships and facilities for coastal landings on the mainland in addition to Korea. Joint planners at the Pentagon, in deference to the loyalties commanded by Li Tsung-jen, argued that the United States should support *all* anti-Communist Chinese. That February the Joint Strategic Planning Committee recommended a $300 million budget for covert operations onto the mainland. Regarding CIA's association with Jiang Jieshi's faction, the military planners warned, "Covert activity within China would be unlikely to overthrow the Chinese communist regime in the absence of an effective counter revolutionary movement, a political program, a clear-cut organization and competent leadership, none of which the Chinese Nationalists appear capable of providing at this time."

In the summer the raiders returned to previous targets for a new round of attacks. Against strict instructions, CIA radioman Roger McCarthy went ashore on one of these raids. Among several others, the most successful took place in October, the target again Nanri Dao. The Nationalists conducted their largest naval action since retreating to Taiwan, using warships given them by the United States, and sent along four thousand regular troops plus a thousand guerrillas. Western Enterprises supplied little but intelligence backup, and CIA people stayed home when the raid was carried out. The Nationalists not only reached their goals, they stood back and took on a wave of Communist reinforcements, inflicting many casualties and capturing almost a thousand prisoners. Jiang Jieshi's propagandists announced that they had conducted fifteen raids on the mainland that year and gave glowing accounts of results.

When the CIA created its unified Directorate for Plans, China operations came under new pressures. Ray Peers returned to the army, replaced by another detached military officer, his deputy, Lt. Col. Robert J. Delaney. Total CIA personnel on Taiwan at this time were estimated at six hundred. The long-standing animosity between DO elements expressed itself with the intel boys fearing the paramilitary specialists were getting in the way of collecting real information, and the knuckle-draggers scoffing at OSO concerns. But in the DO merger the Far East Division went to OSO—its boss Lloyd George became chief of the unified division. Dick Stilwell went back to the army.

The CIA established a North Asia Command to consolidate control over its various operations against the Chinese run from Japan, Korea, the offshore islands, and Thailand. By then Frank Wisner had created an international network including elements in Singapore and Burma, and on the Pacific island of Saipan, all serviced by CAT, with navy cooperation on sea transport. George went off to be deputy chief of the command under Adm. Leslie Stevens. They issued a plan to stand down the paramilitary effort in favor of intensified intelligence collection plus support to non-CIA Nationalist Chinese efforts. George Aurell took over the DO Far East Division.

Meanwhile separate programs to aid Manchurian guerrillas not loyal to Jiang continued under CIA. This operation, known as Tropic to Civil Air Transport pilots, used CAT crews flying out of Japan at night in unmarked C-47s. The Yale College class of 1951 was heavily recruited for the program, recalls John T. Downey, who joined the CIA after graduation. Assigned to set up resistance in Kirin province, Downey visited Saipan in 1952 to select a four-man unit, Team Wen, parachuted into Manchuria in July. That November 29, Downey and Richard G. Fecteau, with the CIA only five months, plus a CAT flight crew, were forced down in China while attempting to recover an agent sent to observe the team at work. The failure of this flight and capture of Downey and Fecteau by the Communists essentially brought a halt both to the Manchuria program and to many China operations. The CIA, extremely concerned that others might also be vulnerable to capture, renewed its strict instructions that American officers were not to participate in incursions. The two CIA men were eventually brought before the same Chinese show trial that judged the psywar B-29 crew captured months later. Downey remained imprisoned in China until 1973 and Fecteau until 1971.

Along the Chinese coast, arguments among CIA officers were very different. Rather than struggling over phasing out the paramilitary mission, the men at the front debated whether the raids ought to be small-scale or racheted up to major quasi-conventional operations. A new CIA detachment leader on Tachen, Robert H. Barrow, a Marine seconded to the agency, held out for the big missions. Subordinate Robert Dillon objected that Western Enterprises would be hard-pressed to supply the needed landing craft or artillery, and that Jiang Jieshi's government had not shown the requisite determination. Dillon asserted that as a civilian he could understand both the military and political aspects—he intended to transfer to the Foreign Service and might one day be an ambassador.

"Yeah," Major Barrow guffawed, "and I'm going to be commandant of the whole damn Marine Corps!"

In fact both men were right. Robert Barrow went on to become commandant of the Marine Corps. Dillon proved correct when the Nationalists mounted a really big raid and it flopped. By now Dwight Eisenhower had come to office and unleashed the Chinese Nationalists by ending the neutralization of the Taiwan Straits. The raid involved not only the guerrillas but every Nationalist armed service, coordinated by the "other" Nationalist spy service, the Continental Operations Department. Robert Barrow participated as Ed Hamilton supervised and Frank Holober watched for Western Enterprises chief Delaney. A paratroop drop and a guerrilla landing on Dongshan were supposed to drive the Chinese Communists into the arms of Nationalist regulars. Madame Jiang attended the dress briefing. In the actual operation the airdrop miscarried as a number of its planes were forced to abort due to mechanical failures. The amphibious landing by regular troops turned into a nightmare when the tide, supposed to be coming in, was not. Landing craft never got closer than a mile from the beach, leaving hapless invaders to wade or slog ashore through mud. The CIA guerrillas hit the beach in fairly good order but found the Communists responding much more rapidly than in the past and quickly marshaling forces to quash the landing. The Nationalists managed to withdraw and took some prisoners, but there was no victory. This landing was more akin to the Baltic or Albanian CIA failures than the heroic Normandy invasion.

Psychological warfare also remained active. Balloons carried by prevailing winds gave way to leaflet drops from aircraft. The experience of Colonel Arnold and his air force B-29 are but one example. Some flights were made by Civil Air Transport, others by the Nationalist air force. According to one account, in 1953 leaflet flights averaged thirty a month, and 300 million pieces of Nationalist or CIA propaganda were loosed over mainland China.

In accordance with the CIA reorganization plan, detachments on White Dog, Baiquan, and Xiamen progressively pulled back. Western Enterprises disappeared in 1953. Charles Johnston, the original "Pittsburgh Charlie" himself, came to close down the mission. Americans shifted to using cover with a new Naval Technical Training Center, a variant of the naval cover assignments that OSO officers had sported from the beginning of the program. Beijing, still concerned about bases on the offshore islands, launched a succession of international crises beginning in late 1954 at Mazu. A couple of months later U.S. warships and Nationalist craft evacuated more than six thousand troops and civilians from Mazu, among them the final CIA contingent. At Xiamen the People's Liberation Army began an "Artillery War" that endured for years, the first of almost half a million cannon shells falling on the island, disrupting guerrilla bases at any hour. It became even more difficult to raid the China coast.

Training for the agency's special missions remained a perennial concern. Both Chinese and Korean recruits went to a secret CIA base for advanced instruction. Located in the mid–Pacific Ocean, on the island of Saipan, the facility provided a secluded and secure location. Actually, by using the island, the United States violated international law, since Saipan was technically a United Nations dependency, part of the Trust Territory of the Pacific Islands, merely administered by the United States. When supervision of the trust went from military to civilian hands in 1951–1952, the navy successfully fought a Department of the Interior plan to place trust headquarters on Saipan, preserving CIA's security.

The CIA used a military designation, Naval Technical Training Unit, for its cover. Cost of the base is estimated at $28 million. Recruits arrived by night, flown in on C-47 aircraft like those of Civil Air Transport. New arrivals were blindfolded on arrival, then driven to the base. But the CIA facility had been built on the highest mountain on the island, with surroundings plainly visible to the trainees. The standard of living and style of construction on the rest of the island bore little relation to the concrete barracks and tract houses of the CIA base, and there were periodic emergencies when the "Naval Technical Training Unit" had to be quickly sanitized and closed before visits of UN trusteeship commissioners. The estimate of Chinese recruits is imprecise—only some "hundreds" are cited. After training, the recruits returned to operating bases for their missions. These included commando raids, sabotage, and liaison with local anti-Communist resistance groups. John Downey's choice of the team for his Manchuria mission is typical of the practice. Later in the decade the Saipan base would come in handy again in the CIA's Tibetan covert operation. In 1960 the secret warriors considered using Saipan to train some of their Cuban exile fighters.

The United States continued hiding the Saipan base from public view, very probably due to the international legal violations inherent in its use. As late as

1967 the White House responded vapidly when a University of Illinois professor asked about CIA training on Saipan.

One of the largest CIA operations in China began in early February 1951. Known to Civil Air Transport as Project Paper, it was nothing less than an invasion by Nationalist guerrillas based in the Shan states of northern Burma. This paramilitary effort was carried out in the face of the Burmese government and created an unnecessary international controversy. It also led to organized Nationalist Chinese involvement in heroin traffic that continues to this day.

Project Paper relied upon Li Mi, another of Jiang Jieshi's many generals. He escaped when his army disintegrated in battle and made his way in disguise to Yunnan province, where Li took command of the Nationalist Eighth Army at Kunming. During 1950 Li slowly retreated toward the border as the PLA approached.

About fifteen hundred of Li Mi's troops withdrew into Indochina where the French disarmed the lot and interned them. But the French had an army there while Burma (now Myanmar) had few military forces, and those were fully occupied against revolting Keren tribesmen. Li Mi headed for Burma and easily crossed the border with more than two thousand men from the Nationalist 97th and 193rd Divisions. The general himself went to Hong Kong but soon rejoined his troops. In Burma the Chinese built a base camp, drafting Shan tribesmen for labor and to fill their ranks, and contacted local Chinese smugglers. Despite clashes with the Burmese army that forced a few hundred more Nationalists into French internment in Laos, before the close of 1950 Li almost doubled his strength. A World War II–vintage airstrip at Mong Hsat, refurbished by the Nationalists, became Li Mi's new base, graced with a huge portrait of Jiang Jieshi, bamboo barracks, and a hilltop headquarters of imported wood and concrete. Within a year the Li Mi forces had almost doubled again.

Project Paper intended to reequip Li Mi's band for a return to Yunnan. Civil Air Transport, using three planes to begin with, parachuted instructors and weapons to the Chinese in northern Burma. Soon CAT had a regular supply flow. Aircraft flew from a CAT detachment at Bangkok, with personnel shuttled from Taiwan and weapons from a CIA depot on Okinawa. Soon planes were landing at Mong Hsat. The whole operation was coordinated by Alfred Cox, OPC's chief of station at Hong Kong, and Sherman B. Joost in Bangkok. The Burmese government learned of this support when its own intelligence officers, watching the Chinese, witnessed five of the supply drops.

The CIA ingeniously provided cover through a parallel project to train and equip paramilitary forces for Thailand. In Miami the CIA chartered a company just like WEI, the Overseas Southeast Asia Supply Company—Sea Supply as it was familiarly known—with a $38 million government contract to support the Thai. Its cable address, "Hachet," gave commercial cover to CIA officers working with both the Thais and Chinese. Before the end of 1953 Sea Supply had two hundred employees, and about eighty more Americans in the embassy in Thailand worked overtly as advisers. By then almost five thousand Thai soldiers had been trained and equipped. Whatever happened to Li Mi, the Thai did very well from the bargain. Assistance to Li Mi and the existence of Sea Supply were open secrets in Bangkok. Sherman Joost, as a team leader with the OSS in Burma during the war, did not much mind the attention. It was a welcome change from the frustrations of Taiwan-based China operations, from which he had been reassigned to Paper.

Meanwhile Li Mi began calling his forces the Yunnan Province Anti-Communist National Salvation Army. A first invasion of Yunnan occurred in May 1951, in two columns with two thousand men, accompanied by CIA officers and regular supply drops. The Nationalists advanced a few dozen miles into Yunnan but were out again within a month. Li Mi's column, defeated, retreated precipitately, while the second force, hearing this news, fell back as well. In July Li Mi sent subordinate Liu Kuo-chuan on a second incursion, which was driven off by local Communist Chinese units. This time the Communists needed just a week.

The failure should have occasioned a critical review of the Li Mi operation. Indeed Li returned to Taiwan for consultations with the Nationalist government, but the outcome was a decision to strengthen the effort. David M. Key, U.S. ambassador to Burma, reported from Rangoon that the Burmese knew of Americans in the area and of the use of U.S. equipment by the Nationalists. He concluded that "this adventure has cost us heavily in terms of Burmese goodwill and trust." Nevertheless, at the CIA Richard Stilwell insisted that support to Li Mi had been insufficient. Ambassador Key resigned.

The CIA brought in a new logistics director, James A. Garrison, to manage the now substantial arms flow to Taiwan, Thailand, and Burma. American engineers were sent in to improve Mong Hsat airstrip. Then CAT began an even larger airlift no longer confined to parachute drops. Some seven hundred Nationalist troops from Taiwan reinforced Li Mi, whose strength by 1952 had grown to twelve thousand.

Open controversy erupted in late December 1951 when Beijing publicly charged the United States with ferrying Nationalist soldiers from Taiwan to Burma. The charges were repeated by Soviet diplomats in a United Nations political committee. The controversy bubbled despite several U.S. denials, including one by Secretary Dean Acheson, and a statement by an American UN delegate that the Nationalists had simply failed to honor their pledge to remove troops from Burma. The Burmese UN delegate agreed that Li Mi was receiving outside aid; Nationalist denials were countered by copies of actual orders from Jiang Jieshi to Li Mi that had been captured by the Burmese army. In the midst of the controversy, the *New York Times* reported on February 11, 1952, that witnesses had seen Li Mi's soldiers brandishing brand-new American weapons. Two months later Burmese sources reported that Americans, including ex-military fliers, were the ones smuggling arms to Li Mi. The Burmese army broke up a seaborne shipment of more men and arms to the Nationalists but could never discover whether this had been a Jiang Jieshi or a CIA maneuver. In 1952 the government declared martial law for northern Burma and opened large-scale military operations against the Nationalists.

Still, the United States persisted in its denials. To lessen the visibility of the issue, Jiang asked Li Mi to return to Taiwan. To explain the Nationalists' arms, reports were leaked that Li Mi's men had sold opium to finance their activities. It is not clear whether the United States at this stage encouraged the drug trafficking to preserve cover for the CIA operation, but Chinese sales of drugs from Burma have been an important source of cash ever since and a pernicious practice that cost America far more than it gained from any Nationalist military activities.

No matter how threadbare the cover story, denials continued. The true facts were so closely held within CIA that the agency's analysis branch was not told of them. Nor, by and large, was the State Department. The U.S. ambassador to India, Chester Bowles, received CIA assurances that there was no American aid to Li Mi. As Asian governments increasingly refused to accept these claims, Bowles was reduced to arguing that no American administration could afford to halt the arms flow during an election year for fear of being accused of coddling communism. Meanwhile when several white men with the Li Mi troops were killed in battle with the Burmese army, their bodies yielded diaries and notebooks with home addresses in Washington and New York City.

Passing through Washington en route to his new assignment as ambassador in Rangoon, the diplomat William J. Sebald received similar assurances that Li Mi was receiving no U.S. aid. When Sebald attempted to repeat the disclaimer at a diplomatic reception, Burmese army chief of staff Ne Win replied, "Mr. Ambassador, I have it cold. If I were you, I'd just keep quiet."

In the summer of 1952 Li Mi returned to Burma to lead a second invasion of Yunnan. That August 2,100 Nationalists marched 60 miles into China before being driven out. This became the last of the remarkably inept invasions. Instead the Nationalists turned against the Burmese government. Li Mi guarded his Burma base with more troops than he used in his Yunnan incursions. Now he forged links with anti-government Keren tribesmen and even the Burmese Communist Party. In the fall of 1952 Li crossed the Salween River in a major offensive against the Burmese army. His drug trafficking soared.

Not only would Li Mi be ineffective, his ventures led to the ruin of U.S. relations with Burma for most of the decade. Whereas in 1952 the Burmese refused to demand a UN investigation, believing that neither superpower would accept its conclusions, the next year Rangoon tabled a resolution branding the Chinese presence an act of aggression. When the United States opposed the motion, Prime Minister U Nu unilaterally terminated all American aid programs in his country. The Nationalists hardly disguised their connection to the Li Mi forces—in 1955 Jiang Jieshi sent his former commander of forces on Mazu Island to Burma as Li Mi's deputy.

The Li Mi operation had been dear to some CIA officers, a special favorite of Desmond FitzGerald, deputy chief of OPC's Far East Division. When Stilwell returned to the army, FitzGerald soldiered on under his replacement, Lloyd George. With the OSO-OPC merger and creation of the Directorate for Operations, George Aurell succeeded to the top job at the Far East Division. He left the decisions mostly to "Des." Subordinates felt that Aurell avoided going out on a limb while his deputy, like Frank Wisner, sparked an idea a minute. Educated at private schools and Harvard College—at Groton he had been a classmate of Tracy Barnes—the forty-two-year-old FitzGerald often served as a conduit for project proposals. He pursued Cold War confrontation with romantic fervor, preventing cancellation of Project Paper following Li Mi's 1951 debacle. A year later, with nothing to show but failure, plus an international uproar over the intervention, FitzGerald had little alternative but to acquiesce in dismantling the activity, a headache for FE/4, the branch of Far East Division that handled both Burma and Thailand.

This evaluation of the Li Mi operation was given to Chester Bowles by an Indonesian cabinet minister in April 1953:

> What could be more ridiculous than to allow American arms to be used to build up the power of a renegade group totally incapable of inflicting any damage on the Communist Chinese, but fully capable of thwarting the democratic Burman government's effort to crush her own communist rebellion and bring order to a troubled nation?

Six years later, in May 1959, intelligence officers would tell a U.S. president that the Chinese Nationalists in Burma caused "nothing but difficulty." They embarrassed a government that Washington by then considered more favorably, and gave the Chinese Communists a pretext for intervention in Burma. "In short," according to the synopsis furnished to President Eisenhower, "they make trouble for our friends but do not have sufficient capability to even tie down significant ChiCom forces."

William J. Donovan, wartime chief of OSS and Eisenhower's appointment in 1953 as ambassador to Thailand, oversaw the attempt to clean up the Li Mi mess. This repatriation of Chinese Nationalists from northern Burma came at the express wish of the Burmese government. Li Mi returned to Taiwan in October 1952, but his soldiers stayed. A four-power conference in Bangkok among Burma, Thailand, Nationalist China, and the United States agreed to remove them. This led to Operation Repat, a Civil Air Transport airlift of Chinese who crossed from northern Burma to Thailand and were then flown to Taiwan.

An initial group of 50 Nationalist soldiers entered Thailand on November 8, 1953, with no weapons but bearing a seven-foot portrait of Jiang Jieshi. Flights began the next day; CAT used C-46 aircraft with extra fuel tanks flying at maximum range. In an initial phase almost 2,000 troops and several hundred dependents reached Taiwan. In the second phase, February–March 1954, another 3,000 Nationalists with 500 dependents departed. People flown out later brought the total to about 5,600 soldiers and more than a thousand dependents. Each one cost the United States $128 paid to a CIA proprietary.

Something of a farce, Repat included evacuees who were Shan and Lahu tribesmen, not Chinese, and dependents swelled the numbers without ameliorating

Burma's security problem. In addition, the many troops brought out many fewer weapons—a thousand rifles, sixty-nine machine guns, and twenty-two mortars— some of them antique pieces, not the modern arms the CIA had given Li Mi. Numerous evacuees contrived to return to Burma. The Nationalists maintained forces in Burma no longer under CIA control. These later grew to as many as twelve thousand and continued their drug trafficking right into the 1980s.

Significant changes now occurred in the Taiwan Straits. The Seventh Fleet had had orders to bar the straits to forces of both sides. Eisenhower changed the order to block only Beijing, freeing Jiang to attack the mainland. In early 1953 the United States gave the Nationalists their first jet aircraft (F-84 fighters) and sanctioned an expansion of the Nationalist Marine Corps to three brigades, tripling Jiang's amphibious force.

In connection with the jet deal the Nationalists agreed not to use their American weapons, particularly aircraft, on offensive missions without first consulting with the United States. But Jiang sought no approval several months later, in July 1953, when he committed the planes to support a Nationalist raiding force. Jiang's chief of staff apologized, claiming dire emergency: the raiders were being driven into the sea and needed to buy time for an orderly withdrawal. The Nationalists promised it would not happen again, but in June 1954 Jiang's navy used its American-supplied destroyers to seize a Soviet tanker on the high seas between Luzon and Formosa. The Eisenhower administration assumed a posture of studied neutrality.

Overall, apart from its creation of a support network, the CIA's paramilitary campaign against China produced paltry results. There had been some military impact in Korea, though this was limited because the large partisan units materialized only after the most active, mobile phase of the war. Agency operations in Manchuria and Yunnan were almost totally ineffective. Moreover they prompted stringent Communist security measures, so may even have impeded the CIA's developing intelligence sources in China. As in the Burma project, some CIA efforts proved positively detrimental to larger U.S. foreign policy interests, and those along the China coast contributed to the inception of the series of crises in the Taiwan Straits that repeatedly brought America near war with China during the 1950s. Covert action irritated the Chinese without producing any American advantage in the Cold War.

Among the important covert operations of the period in Asia is one that combined political action with psychological warfare and limited military involvement to defeat an armed resistance and put a pro–United States leader in power. This took place in the Philippines. Again the initiative would be antithetical to stated U.S. principles in support of democracy.

The Philippines became independent at the end of 1946. At the time there were a number of partisan groups that had actively fought Japanese occupiers with U.S. help during World War II. One, the Hukbalahap (called Huks), an amalgam of peasant-based groups and Filipino Communists, formed a National Peasants Union and then a coalition group, the Democratic Alliance, to contest the 1946 elections. There the Alliance won all the congressional seats for key parts of the island of Luzon, but President Manuel Roxas alleged fraud and refused to seat the delegates. The Huks resumed fighting under wartime leader Luis Taruc. In 1947 the United States signed a military base agreement with the new Republic of the Philippines, providing for naval and air bases in exchange for U.S. foreign aid and military assistance. Military advisers naturally were concerned about the Huk uprising and spent much time and effort to bring the Philippine army a victory over the guerrillas. The government called its strategy the "mailed fist." This approach did little to defuse the resistance. Newly elevated president Elpidio Quirino (formerly the vice president) enticed the Huks into negotiations in 1948, but these proved abortive.

Enter the CIA. The agency had a station in Manila, of course, and a base at Subic Bay, which had become a major U.S. Navy installation. The OPC station chief, a detailee from the air force, Maj. Gen. Edward G. Lansdale, had a natural affinity for political psychological warfare. He became the darling of psywar experts. The major's background had been in advertising—product lines like soft drinks and blue jeans—and he had lived in Hollywood, attending UCLA. Lansdale had served with the OSS, returned to the army, and transferred to the air force. In the Philippines the forty-three-year-old psywar whiz found a perfect vehicle in Ramon Magsaysay, the Filipino defense minister appointed by Quirino in the summer of 1950.

Magsaysay, a Filipino congressman and wartime guerrilla fighter who came from a poor part of Luzon, had a more evolved view of the resistance. He began a land redistribution program financed through a government corporation to wean the peasants away from the Huks. Magsaysay also benefited from internal fissures in the rebellion—a split between Taruc and the Philippine Communists, many of whose top leaders had been captured in Manila police raids. Lansdale began promoting Magsaysay using all the resources of the Wisner Wurlitzer, eventually making the Filipino a larger-than-life figure.

In the conflict Lansdale added psywar to the standard military protection measures. He used massive sound amplifiers on airplanes to saturate Huk areas with prerecorded messages or simply noise that capitalized on peasant superstitions to instill fear. The land program was adapted to encourage defections from the Huks. The CIA also installed a New York political operator, Gabe Kaplan, to create a movement to influence voting, beginning with the Philippine congressional elections of 1951. Lansdale engineered a supposedly grassroots movement to draft Magsaysay for the presidential election. George Aurell worried about the CIA's growing involvement in nation-building, but Des FitzGerald forged ahead with gusto. Ramon Magsaysay won the 1953 elections, but that proved only the beginning. The CIA remained a player in Filipino elections through the rest of the decade. Magsaysay died in a plane crash four years later, and by the time of the 1957 election George Aurell had become station chief in

Manila. The CIA could not decide who to support in that contest. John Richardson replaced Aurell in time for the next congressional elections, and this time there were CIA favorites.

Manila became an important agency base for Far East operations, particularly its China Mission, which transferred there from Japan in 1955. Led by Desmond FitzGerald, who had desperately wanted a field assignment, the mission purported to be a theater command for actions aimed at Beijing. It never succeeded. The barons at headquarters disliked having anyone come between them and their station chiefs, while the latter wanted to operate, not deal with some supernumerary, and they wanted to go to the highest level at headquarters, which meant the Far East Division chief. The China mission became moribund, much as had the Psychological Strategy Board. FitzGerald finally returned to Washington, succeeding Tracy Barnes as head of the DO's Political/Paramilitary Staff, slightly reorganized after Guatemala.

Meanwhile the Huk rebellion sputtered on but came close to disappearing. By 1954 almost ten thousand persons had died, half that number were prisoners, and a couple of thousand more were wounded. An almost equal number had been induced to give up by land offers and other measures. Luis Taruc himself surrendered in May 1954, about the same time Edward Lansdale was promoted for his work in the Philippines. But no grass grew under Lansdale's feet. He had already moved on to a new secret war.

Vietnam became another theater for the CIA. Known as French Indochina, after World War II the countries of Vietnam, Laos, and Cambodia were caught up in revolution. France had ruled them as a colony from the late nineteenth century, but independence movements steadily evolved, and with the end of the war they openly opposed the restoration of French colonial rule. In Vietnam the Communist party's Viet Minh front formed a government in August 1945 and issued a declaration of independence remarkably similar to that of the Americans in 1776. Vietnamese leader Ho Chi Minh sent letters to President Truman soliciting aid for his fledgling reach toward nationhood. Americans of the OSS and other military intelligence units briefly worked in Indochina then, and these Americans had high expectations for Vietnamese self-government. The Viet Minh ran the country for seventeen months before French armies and the Vietnamese began warring over the new Vietnam. France proved quite successful at painting the Viet Minh as little more than satraps of monolithic Russian communism while the United States also worried about the weakness of France in the post-1945 world. The result was that when U.S. involvement in the Far East burgeoned, French Indochina became one scene of the action. What seemed to some as new American initiatives in the Cold War inevitably appeared to others as U.S. support of French colonialism—the opposite of slogans about democracy and self-determination.

The Central Intelligence Agency first sent people to Vietnam as part of the U.S. legation that opened in Saigon in the summer of 1950. Two years later the agency's presence expanded to northern Vietnam, with an officer heading a base in Hanoi. Jurisdiction fell to the same branch of the Far East Division that handled Li Mi in Burma. In mid-1951 Truman approved a policy for cooperating with friendly governments in operations against guerrillas, the kind of warfare central to the Indochina conflict. About that time the agency suggested to the French commander-in-chief that he form partisan units behind Viet Minh lines, following much the same formula the CIA had applied in Korea. The French were not enthusiastic. The issue came up again in mid-1952 when the French applied for more aid to create Vietnamese light infantry battalions. French generals continued to resist the CIA proposals; more precisely, the French created a mixed airborne commando force unilaterally, with no U.S. participation.

A widening U.S. paramilitary effort began with secret discussions in 1953. Strapped for money and facing the escalating cost of their war, the French asked for additional military aid, including for "special warfare," and the new Eisenhower administration agreed. Ike's condition was that the French agree to U.S. help on secret warfare. Ed Lansdale participated in the military group that surveyed Vietnam in the course of these deliberations. The French ran the partisan units behind enemy lines in the north. In the south there were two religious movements or "sects," the Cao Dai and Hoa Hao, and also a band of river pirates, the Binh Xuyen, private armies financed by French intelligence. There is evidence that the French, in briefing a senior CIA officer about their activities in Saigon in December 1953, offered the CIA a role in control over these forces in return for additional aid money. The briefing was repeated for another CIA official in March 1954, but the offer was rejected. Nevertheless there were Saigon rumors of American contacts with the private armies, especially after late 1953, when two women connected with the U.S. embassy were found dead in a jeep on a rubber plantation close to Cao Dai headquarters. In another incident, also hushed up for diplomatic reasons, a consul at the embassy, stopped for an identity check at a bridge, was found to have plastic explosives in his car trunk. But Joe Smith, a young Far East Division officer, believes that Saigon station agents refused to contact the religious minorities because they were Catholics and considered the groups blasphemous.

American special warfare experts were also active in northern Vietnam. In the north the French had about ten thousand partisans in nineteen separate bands. This increase over previous levels was encouraged by the Americans. Beginning in December 1953 two U.S. Army officers were permanently assigned to the French special warfare command to handle requests for equipment. Obscurely titled Detachment P of the 8533rd Army Attaché Unit (Special Foreign Assignment), another U.S. covert office appeared in Hanoi to furnish combat intelligence for the partisan operations. Maj. Roger Trinquier, the French commander, visited Korea to observe American-organized partisan activities there. By February 15, 1954, the American ambassador to Vietnam was reporting that "we are already making [a] contribution to increased French practice of 'unconventional warfare.'"

President Eisenhower was not satisfied with the progress. In a June 1954 letter to friend and fellow general Alfred M. Gruenther, then serving in France with
NATO, Ike complained that the French had rebuffed most American offers of the
kind "that would tend to keep our participation in the background, but could nevertheless be very effective. I refer to our efforts to get a good guerrilla organization going in the region."

Early agency involvement included Civil Air Transport as well. The CAT action flowed from the military aid program, which loaned the French some C-119
"Flying Boxcar" transports. Twenty-one CAT pilots familiarized themselves with
the C-119 at the air force base at Ashiya, Japan. The whole class went to Indochina,
where they actually outnumbered the French crews given C-119 orientation at
Clark Air Force Base. The CAT people brought everything they needed, down to
their own refrigerator and supply of bottled beer. The first CAT flight in Indochina
was a supply lift to an entrenched camp in Laos on May 6, 1953. Within the year a
gaggle of two dozen CAT pilots would be caught up in the French debacle at Dien
Bien Phu. The CAT crews performed combat missions while a full squadron of U.S.
Air Force C-119s—its pilots often moonlighting with CAT—flew ostensibly less
dangerous flights to support the French. The air force people, housed at a hotel in
Haiphong, got help from the CIA base chief in Hanoi. For a time their messages
moved on CIA radio circuits. At least one of the air force pilots, Allen Pope, resigned to join CAT, which paid a lot more for essentially the same work.

Beginning in late 1953 the French tried to break the Viet Minh by tempting
them to attack a strong mountain camp at Dien Bien Phu. Squaw II became CAT's
name for its Dien Bien Phu airlift (Squaw I having been the Laotian mission in the
spring). In all the CIA proprietary flew 684 times to the mountain camp. Chief pilot
Paul R. Holden was wounded by anti-aircraft fire on his fifth mission. The top flier
was A. L. Judkins with 64 flights, next was Steve A. Kusak with 59. Pilots recall the
flak over Dien Bien Phu as being as heavy as anything they encountered in World
War II. Kusak himself was flying a mission alongside James B. McGovern on May
6, 1954, when McGovern was shot down in his C-119. Nicknamed "Earthquake Mc-
Goon" after a popular comic strip character, McGovern died just hours before the final collapse of the French at Dien Bien Phu, one year to the day after CAT had first
flown in Indochina. McGovern's body and other artifacts were discovered in 2002
at a crash site in Laos, almost five decades after his plane went down, by Americans
searching for those still missing in action from the U.S. war in Vietnam.

At one point in the Dien Bien Phu crisis the French asked Washington for the
loan of some B-29 bombers. The United States discussed encouraging the French
to add an air component to their Foreign Legion, which could be given B-29s, and
which American crews could then be encouraged to join. But the option was impractical given the immediacy of the crisis.

The Eisenhower administration was nevertheless so impressed with CAT per-
formance that it considered creating an entity to fly combat aircraft and help the
French. At the request of the NSC Operations Coordinating Board, the staff of Gen.
Graves B. Erskine, assistant to the secretary of defense for special operations, pre-

pared a plan. The concept provided for an International Volunteer Air Group (IVAG) that could be "sponsored" by France or some Asian government. The unit would have several squadrons of F-86 jet fighters, and there was talk of giving it B-29s as well. Only eight months would be necessary to set up IVAG, officials were told, at an initial cost of $130 million and an annual operating cost of $200 million.

Although first discussed in the context of Indochina, IVAG could possibly have had much wider covert applications, and this potential was clearly perceived by the Pentagon special warfare planners: "such a unit will always be useful as a ready striking force in the event of renewed aggression in any part of the Far East. Without it no air striking force exists which can be employed on short notice in circumstances where it is undesirable to employ official U.S. air power." In the event of a declared war the IVAG could be "officially inducted into the U.S. Air Force as an additional wing," a clear allusion to Claire Chennault's Flying Tigers.

Pentagon planners believed that "creation of an IVAG is consonant with and within the framework of U.S. national policy" but felt the project required "NSC affirmation" and an opinion from the attorney general that confirmed the legality of enlistment by U.S. civilian and military volunteers.

The original plan called for creation of the unit before the end of the 1954 rainy season in Indochina, but the National Security Council made no decision. The United States considered a private firm, Aviation International Limited, to recruit American aircraft mechanics to assist the French air force in Indochina, but used military personnel over the short term. The first Indochina war ended soon after.

The OCB recommendation to form an International Volunteer Air Group was nevertheless taken up that summer. The NSC approved it on August 18, 1954. Although the end of the Indochina war briefly shelved the IVAG plan, it became the responsibility of the CIA with the Pentagon's Office of Special Operations. Proponents of a "foreign legion" air force were never able to work out the problems of cover or basing, however, and these finally scuttled the plan. Nevertheless this exercise established an NSC-approved role for the kind of covert air force the CIA had just utilized in Guatemala and would again resort to in the Far East.

French defeat at Dien Bien Phu led to a negotiated settlement at Geneva which provided for a temporary division of Vietnam into two "regroupment zones" which became known, respectively, as North and South Vietnam. The partisans in the North ended up being taken over by the CIA after all. In June 1954 an agency special unit, ten men under Col. Edward G. Lansdale, arrived under cover as the "Saigon Military Mission." They worked independently of John Anderton's Saigon station. Geneva provided for a two-year hiatus after which elections were to be held to reunify the nation. Lansdale's mission, specifically for operations, had that much time to prepare the ground.

Lucien Conein, the mission's deputy for the North, took on the partisans. He managed to smuggle a few shipments of weapons and explosives into North Vietnam under cover of the French withdrawal, and carried out some psywar actions, but he had no capability for long-term support. By 1956 the last of Conein's projects had failed.

The secret warriors were more successful in South Vietnam. There Lansdale established a close friendship with the politician Ngo Dinh Diem. When President Eisenhower sent a new U.S. envoy to Saigon in late 1954, Gen. J. Lawton Collins, he received a briefing from Frank Wisner, Richard Bissell, and Pearre Cabell advising him to make full use of Lansdale in the struggle for power in the South. Later Allen Dulles secretly visited Saigon and was squired about town by Lansdale, reminding him of the excitement of wartime Switzerland. Beginning in January 1955 the CIA stopped giving the French cash to pay for the political-religious sect armies. Instead Lansdale funneled the money to Diem, who took over the sects and made them his first power base. The tab amounted to tens of thousands of dollars a month and increased steadily. Several additional CIA subsidies went directly to Diem's palace contingency fund, used to pay off politicians and for similar purposes. A visiting agency officer saw so much cash passing through the station he told a colleague in Singapore that this kind of money in Malaya could have ended the entire Communist movement simply by handing every ethnic Chinese radical a first-class airline ticket to China.

Diem consolidated his power in Saigon by neutralizing first the pro-French army, then the powerful sects. Lansdale stood with him every step of the way, privately visiting sect leaders, enlisting them in key coups, carrying Diem's messages and money, and contriving stumbling blocks to obstruct French maneuvers. Lansdale advised Diem, often daily. But the Saigon leader failed to deliver on promises of political reforms he made to the Americans. Eisenhower's envoy and friend, General Collins, finally decided to end U.S. support, at which point Lansdale used a CIA back channel to alert his bosses. In Washington, Allen and Foster Dulles conspired to undercut the Collins policy. It was Collins, not Lansdale, who would be replaced. Lansdale also convinced Diem to claim nation status for the southern regroupment zone. In October 1955 Lansdale was awarded the National Security Medal, as Kim Roosevelt had been before him.

The Geneva settlement provided for all-Vietnam elections in July 1956, which Eisenhower feared would reunify the country under North Vietnamese leadership. The administration encouraged South Vietnam to reject the elections. While Diem thus cast the die for a second Indochina war—in which both special warfare and the CIA would play a large part—the United States saw its new Southeast Asian ally in Cold War terms. Thus American planners designed the South Vietnamese army against a conventional military threat. The basic strategy embodied in U.S. 1955 war plans set the CIA to retard an enemy advance through Laos while the U.S. Pacific Fleet made coastal raids with special warfare units to harry a Communist advance down from North Vietnam. But when war returned to Vietnam it took the form of an internal uprising against Ngo Dinh Diem. The Americans prepared themselves and the South Vietnamese for the wrong threat. All this was of a piece with the evolution of the CIA's secret wars in Asia, which grew far beyond the Korean conflict. True to expectations, Dwight Eisenhower greatly expanded the playing field. Covert operations in East Asia proceeded with exuberance, an exuberance matched elsewhere by the Central Intelligence Agency.

8

"Acceptable Norms of Human Conduct Do Not Apply"

AS ONE OF the CIA's Princeton Group of consultants, Richard Bissell spent his final months before actually joining the agency circulating his latest policy prescription among key players. The true weakness in America's defenses, he argued, lay not in any inability to face Soviet invasion of Western Europe but in the Third World, where Bissell feared revolutions would ultimately be exploited by Moscow. The CIA's activities in Indochina and the Philippines had aimed directly at this threat. But to Bissell's surprise—indeed to that of the CIA itself—the first real crisis of the Eisenhower era erupted in the middle of Europe, Germany specifically, and nowhere else.

One catalyst of events was Stalin's death in March 1953. While Radio Free Europe, then Radio Liberty, busied itself with saturation broadcasts and the Psychological Strategy Board hurriedly cobbled together an overall response, Russian spy chief Lavrenti Beria briefly held power in Moscow, loosening the reins of Soviet control in Eastern Europe. In East Germany, recently clobbered with production quotas that further increased hopelessness, the liberalization betokened a new right of protest. In mid-June construction workers in East Berlin began work slowdowns that blossomed into demonstrations. Protests reached peak intensity, and workers made plans for a public march on June 17. The news spread throughout East Germany by word of mouth, but also courtesy of Radio in the American Sector (RIAS). Although not an appendage of Wisner's Wurlitzer, RIAS did the same work for the U.S. high commissioner in Germany, with eight Americans and 650 Germans on its Berlin staff. East Germans made the demonstration a spectacle never before seen behind the Iron Curtain. Documents in Russian and former East German archives released after the Cold War show that East German authorities and Soviet occupiers lost their nerve. Two entire armored divisions entered East Berlin. Strikes and labor protests continued for the next two days.

The CIA had recently issued a National Intelligence Estimate specifically to predict the impact of the Beria "peace offensive" on Germany. But looking at

Berlin, the analysts concentrated on the possibility of something like the Berlin Blockade, that is, Soviet harassment against the West. No one expected internal unrest. At the CIA's Berlin Base, led by William K. Harvey, surprised intelligence officers scrambled for any information they could get, and obtained much of it from RIAS broadcasts, as did many in both East and West Berlin. The CIA had lost track of Soviet forces in East Germany, with frantic confusion the result.

Only Harvey's deputy, Henry Heckscher, himself German-born, understood the demonstrations' threat to Communist power in the East. Heckscher argued that the CIA should give the strikers weapons from the agency's stockpile in West Berlin. David Murphy, a subordinate at the Berlin base, denies that the field submitted any request to approve CIA intervention, citing the recollections of Tom Polgar and Gordon Stewart, both senior officers in the overall German program. Murphy notes that General Truscott, to whom Polgar was a deputy, would have fired anyone who suggested such a thing. Other Berlin base officers recall that Bill Harvey, not Heckscher, sent a cable recommending a U.S. show of force, not arms to the East Berliners. Alerting American troops in Germany might have put the Russians on warning.

The cable reached CIA headquarters after Allen Dulles had left for the day. Division chief John Bross bucked it up the line to Wisner. A military alert, beyond the ken of the agency, would have to go through Eisenhower. In this fast-moving situation Washington had little possibility of acting in time. Wisner rejected Bill Harvey's suggestion. A paper prepared at the Psychological Strategy Board on June 17 noted that John Foster Dulles's State Department had a similarly cautious attitude.

On June 19 Allen Dulles briefed the NSC on the riots and similar protests in Czechoslovakia. Then C. D. Jackson speculated on exploiting events for propaganda purposes. President Eisenhower interjected that if the United States intervened to fan the flames of discontent, the heads that rolled would be those of America's friends.

Jackson argued that the riots might be the bell pealing disintegration of the Soviet empire, but the president's view prevailed. Ike saw supplying arms as inviting the slaughter of the protesters. The United States could not risk major war with the Russians, one that might well go nuclear. Washington's only official action was to offer food aid.

Soviet secret reports found in the archives decades afterward estimated the number of rioters in East Berlin on June 17 at 66,000, about 10,000 of them actually from *West* Berlin. Over the following weeks about 10,000 East Germans fled to the West. Almost 3,000 people were arrested and a hundred were killed or wounded in street clashes.

During the summer and fall the Psychological Strategy Board prepared a plan to take advantage of unrest in Eastern Europe. Eisenhower approved an NSC policy paper with both short-term and long-range measures toward this end. Among the long-term actions, CIA had primary responsibility for a program to implement the Volunteer Freedom Corps initiative, training and equipping underground organizations capable of launching large-scale raids or sustained warfare when directed to do so.

The president also ordered an overall strategic review, dubbed the "Solarium" study for the White House indoor garden where the panelists met and presented the final report. Three task forces assembled, each to argue for a particular line of action. The "rollback" approach was subsumed in Solarium's "Alternative C," designed "to increase efforts to disturb and weaken the Soviet bloc," attacking the "Communist apparatus" worldwide and missing no opportunities "to confuse and unbalance our enemy."

The Task Force C program foresaw preparations for atomic warfare, expediting development in the Volunteer Freedom Corps, and the employment of Chinese Nationalist troops, first against Hainan Island, then the mainland. Planners estimated costs at about $60 billion for the first two years, declining to $45 billion subsequently, with perhaps another $5 billion needed if the program led to new hostilities in Korea.

George Kennan, chief of the Task Force A panel, argued eloquently for the alternative of "containment" as offering lower costs and less risk of war with Russia.

Eisenhower took Kennan's point. The president jumped up and said he wished to summarize. Rollback, Ike said, would strain American alliances and represented "a departure from our traditional concepts of war and peace." He chose to restrict military spending and avoid greater risk of atomic war. Option B—continuing previous policies—did not interest the president.

Few have noticed that Ike did not select a pure strategy. Containment, Kennan's option A, he mixed with elements of the Task Force C program, in particular covert action. That this was the decision is clear from the record of the NSC meeting on July 30, 1953, where participants discussing the Solarium results explicitly raised the possibilities for action in Guatemala, Iran, and Albania.

Allen Dulles noted that he had already sent a CIA paper on Albania to the Psychological Strategy Board. Dulles also asked the National Security Council to make new policy decisions, presumably for U.S. action in Guatemala. Only in the case of Albania did President Eisenhower inject a cautionary note, "because of the question of who gets it and who gets hurt." Both the Guatemala and Iran covert actions were carried out, as already recounted.

Dwight Eisenhower, a general with broad military experience, seemed better equipped than Harry Truman to judge the feasibility of covert action. As president he accepted the Cold War rationale, encouraging covert operations as an integral part of the conflict, even as he managed intelligence better than many presidents before him and since. The record shows President Eisenhower intimately involved in the secret war. The story of how Ike managed to do this while preserving his claim to know nothing demonstrates masterful command of ponderous organizations as well as a tightly drawn doctrine of "plausible deniability." Ike's key lay in the use of his staff, a habit he no doubt acquired in the military.

At the strategic nuclear level, Eisenhower did much to resist a stampeding arms race, though his achievement has been tarnished in recent years by revelation of his delegations of authority to use nuclear weapons. But as the man who institutionalized covert operations, Ike does not emerge as the moderate, even liberal, Republican seen in historical reappraisals. It is apparent—and now largely accepted by historians—that Eisenhower *relied* upon covert operations instead of, and in preference to, conventional military force. He institutionalized covert operations precisely by creating mechanisms to manage them. The president did this even while the Indochina and Guatemala ventures were in progress, and he sustained the effort to control global clandestine operations.

President Eisenhower began his quest for a new system for covert action during the heady days of 1954 when Ajax shone as the CIA's crowning achievement. Ike wanted to replace Truman's top-secret NSC order which prescribed the procedure for approval. Truman's 10/5 panel, the Psychological Strategy Board, had endorsed covert operations informally, but the Truman directive merely gave the group authority to regulate the Office of Policy Coordination. Eisenhower abolished the PSB in the summer of 1953, making the Truman directive obsolete. With the OPC merged into the CIA's Directorate for Operations, the Iran and Guatemala covert operations were approved in ad hoc fashion. Eisenhower's new order, signed on March 15, 1954, and numbered NSC-5412, brought the system into sync with the new structure. In his directive, Ike for the first time gave formal powers to his management mechanism for secret wars.

Yet within three short months the CIA, without orders, sank a ship off San Jose, Guatemala, a vessel moreover, belonging to an American ally.

To enhance morale, President Eisenhower openly expressed satisfaction to the CIA's Guatemala secret warriors, but privately he determined to get an independent review. Staff members approached retired air force Gen. James H. Doolittle, who agreed to lead a study group. Ike's final instructions in a letter on July 26, 1954, three days before his White House reception for the Project Success team, asked for a comprehensive review of the factors of personnel, security, cost, and efficiency of covert operations, along with an assessment of how to "equate the costs of the overall efforts to the results achieved." The panel would report to Eisenhower personally on how "to improve the conduct of these operations."

Jimmy Doolittle was a good choice. Dynamic leader of the airmen who had bombed Japan in 1942, immortalized in the book and movie *30 Seconds Over Tokyo*, Doolittle had experienced wartime special operations and understood them. Doolittle knew Ike from Britain in 1944 when he had been a subordinate air commander. He met with Eisenhower in early July 1954, then sat down with William B. Franke, Morris Hadley, and William B. Pawley to perform the review.

Doolittle's committee held its first meeting at CIA headquarters on July 14. It received extensive briefings from the agency, State, the Office of the Secretary of Defense, the armed services, the FBI, and the Bureau of the Budget. By July 29

Doolittle had assembled a staff and had his review in full swing. After seeing both Allen Dulles and Frank Wisner, Doolittle and consultant J. Patrick Coyne inspected CIA installations in Western Europe in mid-September. On September 30 the "Report of the Special Study Group on Covert Activities" went to the president.

The Doolittle Report gave solid support to the rationale for the secret war. Its second paragraph stated quite baldly:

> As long as it remains national policy, another important requirement is an aggressive covert psychological, political and paramilitary organization more effective, more unique and, if necessary, more ruthless than that employed by the enemy. No one should be permitted to stand in the way of the prompt, efficient and secure accomplishment of this mission.

So serious was the conflict with communism that "there are no rules in such a game. Hitherto acceptable norms of human conduct do not apply." The secret warriors could have asked for no better.

But Doolittle's report also criticized performance in several areas. It concluded that the agency's staff of five thousand could be reduced 10 percent without impact. (Only in 1959–1960 did CIA budgets provide for reductions—of about 1 percent.) The "fusion" of the old OPC and OSO Doolittle termed a "shotgun marriage." The report warned that the "Cold War functions" of the Directorate for Operations overshadowed its espionage role, and the committee recommended the DO be reorganized into a viable "Cold War shop." Dulles should be given more support on covert action, with staff provided by the National Security Council for better implementation of NSC-5412.

These recommendations were controversial. Eisenhower asked Doolittle to discuss them with Allen Dulles personally. Doolittle did so, then saw Ike on October 19 and told him the study was a constructive critique. He thought Dulles's basic problem was organizational—the CIA had grown "like topsy," but neither its director nor Frank Wisner were especially good organizers.

Doolittle remarked that Allen Dulles had taken personal criticism pretty well but fought for his staff people "to the point of becoming emotional." Doolittle cited their mutual comrade, Walter Bedell Smith, who had once said that Allen was "too emotional to be in this critical spot" and that "his emotionalism was far worse than it appeared on the surface."

Eisenhower replied, "We must remember that here is one of the most peculiar types of operation any government can have, and it probably takes a strange kind of genius to run it."

The president also defended his CIA director: he had not seen Allen Dulles "show the slightest disturbance." Furthermore Allen had important contacts throughout the world.

Doolittle tried one more tack, referring to the relationship between the DCI and the secretary of state. Having brothers in these two posts created problems that "it would be better not to have exist."

Eisenhower resisted strenuously. He had appointed Allen Dulles in full knowledge of the relationship, Ike said. It did not disturb him because CIA's work was partly an extension of State's job, and because a confidential relationship between the two brothers "is a good thing." "I'm not going to be able to change Allen," observed the president. "I have two alternatives, either to get rid of him and appoint someone who will assert more authority or keep him with his limitations. I'd rather have Allen as my chief intelligence officer with his limitations than anyone else I know."

What the president did instead was work hard to implement his system. First he tried to do this through the Operations Coordinating Board (OCB), a subgroup under the NSC supposed to focus on implementation, the successor to the Psychological Strategy Board. The presidential directive gave the OCB authority over covert operations. But OCB was not senior enough to be making decisions on projects, and it included more officials than ought to be concerned with secret war. So on March 12, 1955, in a revised NSC-5412/1, Eisenhower created a new Planning Coordination Group to be advised in advance of all major covert operations. It would be "the normal channel for giving policy approval for such programs as well as for securing coordination of support therefor."

This remained inadequate. In delineating the CIA's responsibility to seek project approval, the directive mentioned "need to know"; the agency interpreted this to mean that not all elements of a plan had to be briefed or approved. When CIA insisted it had been completely forthcoming, Eisenhower countered by setting up a panel of designees of the White House, State, and the Pentagon plus the DCI. Ike's designee was his special assistant for national security affairs. This committee was so high-powered there could be no question of its "need to know." It became known as the 5412 Group after the directive that established it, NSC-5412/2 of December 28, 1955, or informally as the "Special Group."

Any problems with a project went to the president through his special assistant, who spoke with the voice of the boss. Eisenhower preserved "deniability" by not actually participating in the 5412 Group, but he remained in constant contact with each member. The president also held White House postmortems, like those following Iran and Guatemala, along with semi-annual reviews of ongoing and planned projects that the CIA presented to the full NSC.

Eisenhower's commitment to the Cold War is clearly demonstrated in NSC-5412/2. The directive provided the secret warriors with the broadest possible charter, the breadth of which is still worth quoting in its entirety:

> 3. The NSC has determined that such covert operations shall to the greatest extent practicable, in the light of U.S. and Soviet capabilities and taking into account the risk of war, be designed to:
>
> a. Create and exploit troublesome problems for International Communism, impair relations between the USSR and Communist China and between them and their satellites, complicate control within the USSR, Communist China and their satellites, and retard the growth of the military and economic potential of the Soviet bloc.

b. Discredit the prestige and ideology of International Communism, and reduce the strength of its parties and other elements.

c. Counter any threat of a party or individuals directly or indirectly responsive to Communist control to achieve dominant power in a free world country.

d. Reduce International Communist control over any areas of the world.

e. Strengthen the orientation toward the United States of the peoples and nations of the free world, accentuate, wherever possible, the identity of interest between such peoples and nations and the United States as well as favoring, where appropriate, those groups genuinely advocating or believing in the advancement of such mutual interests, and increase the capacity and will of such peoples and nations to resist International Communism.

f. In accordance with established policies and to the extent practicable in areas dominated or threatened by International Communism, develop underground resistance and facilitate covert and guerrilla operations and ensure availability of those forces in the event of war, including wherever practicable provision of a base upon which the military may expand these forces in time of war within active theaters of operations as well as provide for stay behind assets and escape and evasion facilities.

This turgid prose encompassed a universe of possibilities. The CIA spent decades exploring them.

One critical controversy concerned legislative oversight of the intelligence function. The executive branch itself posed the issue in 1955 when another study group under the Hoover Commission, mandated by Eisenhower, looked at the situation. Gen. Mark Clark, an old army colleague of the president's, led the study and took a jaundiced view. Clark recommended a congressional joint committee on intelligence, similar to the panel that watched over atomic energy. Soon there were a score of bills before Congress proposing to regulate intelligence, including one by Democratic Senator Mike Mansfield of Montana with no fewer than thirty-four co-sponsors.

Although Ike had requested the Hoover Commission's report, he rejected Clark's recommendation and moved to head off the Mansfield Bill. His dual response embodied formation of the President's Board of Consultants on Foreign Intelligence Activities (PBCFIA), a citizen consulting group working directly for him, plus supporting supervision by existing secret subcommittees of armed services panels in both houses of Congress. The subcommittees gave form to amorphous arrangements. The Senate defeated the Mansfield Bill by a vote of 59 to 27. More than a dozen co-sponsors turned against their bill on the floor, as well as all the members of the armed services intelligence subcommittee. For years bills similar to Mansfield's were introduced at every session of Congress but repeatedly tabled or vanquished.

Despite the more formal structure, this could not be called oversight. Intelligence officers had no duty to cooperate with PBCFIA, strictly a presidential advisory group, or to keep the congressional subcommittees fully and currently informed of their activities. Agency directors appeared with budget requests, and the CIA would answer explicit questions if asked, but no one volunteered anything.

Contacts on programs, as opposed to briefings on questions of intelligence analysis, were kept to a minimum. According to official records, in 1955 and 1956 the CIA provided just one briefing to the Senate's armed services subcommittee, with none at all in 1957. The average for the decade from 1955 on works out to fewer than two a year.

Such encounters as occurred were hampered by CIA's obsession to protect itself and its "sources and methods" on security grounds. Real reasons could be quite different. On one occasion in the 1950s, when Allen Dulles expected tough inquiries as a result of successful Soviet penetration of a CIA covert operation, the director told his assembled DO division chiefs, "Well, I guess I'll have to fudge the truth a little." With a twinkle in his eye, Dulles averred that he would admit the full truth to the subcommittee chairman, "that is, if [he] wants to know." On another occasion, he commented to his assistants, "I'll just tell them a few war stories."

If anything, the legislators made it easy for the secret warriors. Senior senators and congressmen on these subcommittees appreciated their access to the world of the spooks. Republican Senator Leverett Saltonstall of Massachusetts once expressed a typical attitude when he commented: "It is not a question of reluctance on the part of CIA officials to speak to us. Instead it is a question of our reluctance, if you will, to seek information and knowledge on subjects which I personally, as a Member of Congress and as a citizen, would rather not have."

As for the President's Board of Consultants, Eisenhower relied upon the group not so much as the watchdog he alluded to but as collaborators on the stuff of intelligence. The best way to think of the board would be as efficiency experts. Ike underlined this by his selection for PBCFIA's first chairman, Dr. James R. Killian, then the White House science adviser. The Killian Board, as it was often referred to, included other notable scientists, military men (among them General Doolittle), and a few captains of industry. It stimulated advances in intelligence technology but in these early years had little impact on covert action.

So the secret warriors marched on, led by their president, insulated from outside inquiry, ordered to stir up trouble for the enemy—a Cold War agency with a mission. There remained questions of capability—an area in which Eisenhower would make extensive use of his private consultants but one where the president himself would have to engage.

While President Eisenhower struggled to manage covert action, secret wars continued aplenty. The mid-fifties were a high point for secret warriors in Europe, especially in the use of pure psychological warfare to complicate Soviet control of Eastern Europe. The Americans took advantage of spontaneous outbursts of resistance within the Soviet satellites, the closest the Eisenhower administration ever came to fulfilling its commitment to "roll back" the Iron Curtain.

If some had had their way, more than propaganda would have been involved. The CIA and the British had used Russians and Ukrainians for espionage and liaison behind the Iron Curtain. Eastern Europeans could be found in the army's Tenth Special Forces, their entry facilitated by the 1950 Lodge Bill and an amendment to the 1951 Mutual Security Act that set aside specific funds for an army unit of Eastern Europeans. But aside from exiles integrated into Special Forces, the army did nothing with the mandate with which it had been saddled. Russian propagandists had a field day accusing the United States of subversion. Frank Wisner told Tracy Barnes in the winter of 1951 that the United States was taking a beating on this question. Congress nevertheless appropriated money in several budgets which the army did not use.

When Eisenhower became president he tried to persuade the army to cooperate on the Eastern European unit. Instead his army general officer friends told him the many reasons they thought the unit could not function effectively.

"Fellows, tell me this," Ike countered, "just how high does a fellow have to go in this outfit before he can call the shots?"

But army leaders continued to balk at creation of an Eastern European unit. The CIA then took the lead, recruiting what amounted to an American foreign legion. Hundreds of Eastern Europeans, hired, trained, and led by a Yugoslav exile, awaited orders to go home and fight. The code name Red Sox/Red Cap has been linked to this project. According to CIA officer James J. Angleton, the exile force ensured the CIA's ability to act in an East Berlin–style crisis of Soviet control.

President Eisenhower prescribed strategy quite strictly through a series of National Security Council directives. For Eastern Europe the governing orders were a general policy series along with the directive, "U.S. Objectives and Actions to Exploit the Unrest in the Satellite States," adopted in the wake of the East Berlin riots. In February 1955 there followed "Exploitation of Soviet and European Satellite Vulnerabilities." The administration reviewed progress on achieving the objectives of this latter policy at the end of that year. Thereafter, in July 1956, Ike adopted a revised directive. By then events already in motion triggered a renewed crisis in Eastern Europe.

The 1956 crisis originated in Moscow, not Washington. In late February Nikita Khrushchev, consolidating his power as Stalin's successor, criticized the deceased dictator in a secret speech to the Twentieth Congress of the Soviet Communist Party. Khrushchev laid bare corruption and rigidity in Stalinism to discredit his Politburo rivals. The speech became an important lever in the Cold War. Here the leader of Russia admitted grave flaws in leadership. The speech even discussed Stalin's personal interventions in the affairs of Hungary and Yugoslavia that led to an open split with the Yugoslavs, at least, who were driven into the hands of Washington. Khrushchev offered a new "socialist legality." Here was political dynamite.

Khrushchev's political maneuver succeeded, but the text of his remarks reached the CIA. It materialized after Allen Dulles ordered a search, which, he writes, "I have always regarded as one of the major coups of my tour of duty." One copy came from a Polish Communist and another courtesy of the Israeli intelligence service Mossad. A further copy seems to have come from contacts on the Italian left. The text sat on Frank Wisner's desk in the DO lair, I Building, "Quarters Eye," by April 1956. The CIA undertook careful authentication both internally and with trusted academic Kremlinologists. Ray Cline, then chief of the Office of Current Intelligence, judged the Khrushchev text reliable.

Use of the Khrushchev speech quickly became a point of contention, however. Cline recommended publishing it as a psychological warfare move. Frank Wisner favored selective secret use to mobilize active East European resistance. The question was decided at a very high level. Ray Cline recalls laboring with Dulles on a talk the DCI would deliver. It was a Saturday, June 2, 1956. Dulles suddenly interrupted this work, swung his chair around, and looked intently at the intelligence analyst.

"Wisner says you think we ought to release the secret Khrushchev speech."

Cline related his reasoning. He writes that "the old man" had a twinkle in his eye when he answered, "By golly, I am going to make a policy decision!"

Allen Dulles phoned Wisner and told the DDO he had given the matter great thought and had decided the speech should be printed.

This version is suitably romantic, but the fact is that three days earlier, on May 31, Dulles had given a copy of the speech to national security adviser Dillon Anderson asking that secrecy be kept "pending a decision as to what, if any, public use should be made of this document." It is inconceivable that Anderson did not go to the president on a matter of this importance. If Cline quotes Allen Dulles accurately, the DCI may have amused himself by hoodwinking his own OCI chief about a decision he had not made. This rendition infuriated Jim Angleton, case officer for the Israeli agents who helped with the Khrushchev speech. In retirement Angleton denounced the Cline account. The counterintelligence expert stayed true to form in believing that Frank Wisner's option of secretly using the speech to foment resistance represented the proper course.

Meanwhile the Khrushchev speech appeared in the press on June 4, 1956, the result of Eisenhower's decision. That began a hot summer and fall in Eastern Europe.

The consequences of the Khrushchev relations played into the CIA's ongoing propaganda campaign. With saturation broadcasts RFE had moved ahead to specially targeted initiatives. Operation Veto, inaugurated in early 1954, encouraged long-term resistance to the Soviets, especially in Hungary. Operation Focus succeeded Veto. Both urged Hungarians to demand concessions from their Communist government. The CIA "Radio" beamed broadcasts into Hungary for twenty hours each day as the "Voice of Free Hungary," supplemented by balloon leafleting, which peaked in 1954–1955 and had a major role in Focus. By this time RFE had a substantial capacity to exploit Khrushchev's words. Surveys later showed that more than 80 percent of Hungarians listened to Radio Free Europe while 20 percent also got information from the balloon leaflets. According to the CIA's own postmortem, in the four months between publication of the secret speech and the Hungarian revolution, Radio Free Europe exploited it heavily.

There were also riots in Poznan, Poland, in reaction to the news of Khrushchev's "destalinization." With these came the return of the Communist faction of Wladyslaw Gomulka, a leader purged earlier for his belief in the existence of many roads toward socialism. Soviet troops deployed momentarily but Gomulka, threatening an open break with the Warsaw Pact, convinced Khrushchev to back down. Jan Nowak, heading RFE's Polish broadcasters, kept the reporting low key, avoiding exacerbating the crisis. The Russian leader visited Poland and defused the issue. Khrushchev also went to Yugoslavia, where his talks led to a declaration that there *were* multiple roads to socialism. This too was featured on RFE. The news electrified Hungary.

The CIA knew it had a problem. Eisenhower's directives set a strategy of vigorous challenge to Soviet control. But the agency's Eastern European exile legions, as Jim Angleton later confirmed, were far from ready. The Gladio arms caches could not be drawn down either—if this crisis brought war they would be needed. And the Radios had no action capability. In short, CIA faced a huge gap between the course it urged on the Eastern Europeans and its ability to offer practical assistance.

About to embark on an inspection trip to Europe, Frank Wisner had Al Ulmer out to his vacation home on Maryland's eastern shore. Though Ulmer now worked in the FE Division, he had headed stations in Athens and Vienna and had an idea of the enormity of the situation. The two men could only scratch their heads in frustration. Some sources maintain Wisner mentioned possible arms shipments to Hungarian rebels when he saw Richard Bissell at Quarters Eye after the weekend. Bissell's own account completely ignores the Hungarian crisis. Others note a private meeting where Foster Dulles overruled his own diplomatic experts and brother Allen, who advised having U.S. forces hold military maneuvers in Austria. White House records show this option never reached the NSC table.

On October 23 demonstrators swept through Budapest demanding a new government under Imre Nagy, a previously purged Hungarian Communist. Reinstalled as premier, Nagy's opponents continued to control the party. RFE broadcasts encouraged Hungarians to press the Nagy regime on liberalization. Nagy sponsored reforms but, despite his resistance, party leaders invited Soviet forces to restore order. Agency psywar boss Cord Meyer, who had supervised RFE since 1954, awakened the morning of October 24 to a phone call from Dulles, who ordered him to headquarters immediately.

"All hell has broken loose in Budapest," Dulles thundered.

In Paris by now, Frank Wisner gathered high-powered field officers to brainstorm a plan. They included William Durkee, a deputy to Meyer who had handled

RFE almost from its inception; Michael Josselson, a CIA specialist on cultural operations; James MacCargar, with a Free Europe unit; Karl Kalassay, a Hungarian specialist; and William E. Griffith, political director for Radio Free Europe. They produced no fresh ideas. MacCargar brought in a former senior Hungarian politician and sent him to Vienna to contact figures at home, but that resulted in little more than exhortations. Wisner proceeded to Germany. Tracy Barnes found the DO chief so tightly wound he feared a nervous breakdown.

Arrests by Hungarian secret police triggered widening revolt. Outraged citizens in the village of Magyarovar murdered members of one security detachment. But then ten thousand Russian troops entered Budapest. Within days street fighting engulfed the capital and the provinces. The story in CIA lore is that officers in Budapest scribbled reports lying on the floor of the U.S. embassy with bullets whizzing above their heads. RFE covered the events too, though according to the CIA postmortem, "no RFE broadcast to Hungary before the revolution could be considered as inciting armed revolt," and none promised U.S. military intervention.

Some Hungarian exiles on RFE's staff could not resist statements about Western support, inflating Hungarian hopes of help. In an RFE programming review, Bill Griffith noted that an October 27 broadcast "fairly clearly implies that foreign aid will be forthcoming if resistance forces succeed in establishing a central authority." The next day: "Hungarians must continue to fight vigorously because this will have a great effect on the handling of the . . . question by the Security Council." On October 30: "Imre Nagy has not enough Hungarian blood to reign."

On Radio Budapest, Nagy appealed for outside aid. Jeffrey Blyth, Budapest correspondent for the London *Daily Mail*, encountered a large crowd of Hungarians near the Danube one day. They watched the sky. Blyth heard people asking, "Where are the Americans? Where are the British? When are they coming?"

On November 4 RFE broadcaster Zoltan Thury commented, "In the Western capitals a practical manifestation of Western sympathy is expected at any hour." The RFE review Bill Griffith conducted declared this broadcast to have been the worst break of all with the Radio's policy directives. But Thury's daughter Eva later countered that Griffith himself had set the policy for RFE's Hungarians and that on November 4 and over the following days he made himself scarce at its Munich headquarters. Griffith's postmortem tried to shift blame onto Hungary desk chief Andor Gellért, in poor health during this period, who delegated virtually all his script approval powers to others, among them subordinates who practically never attended morning staff meetings. That may be, but Griffith himself bore responsibility on such management issues. Sig Mickelson, a president of the Free Europe Committee and foremost historian of RFE, sees the Radio as having dealt with the crisis with "an excess of exuberance."

Lawrence de Neufville, formerly CIA's man on the production of the movie *Animal Farm*, had been with RFE since 1954. De Neufville termed the entire guidance exercise a sham and delusion: "Radio Free Europe was regularly sending guidances to Washington and Munich about its broadcasts, but it was all just mud in your eye, because they simply ignored their own guidances." Even worse, though the CIA had a full department dedicated to translating journals and broadcasts from Eastern Europe, no one bothered to do the same for RFE broadcasts, so no one really had any idea what Radio Free Europe had actually *said*. When C. D. Jackson wanted to see some transcripts, they had to be translated specially for him.

The Russians withdrew temporarily at the end of October but surged back not long afterward with a full-scale mechanized offensive. Griffith mentioned the withdrawal in an October 28 memorandum. Notes of Soviet Politburo meetings show Khrushchev briefly considering a deal with Nagy, but the complaints of members and the views of Yuri Andropov, Russian ambassador in Budapest, canceled that possibility. Griffith's sanguine report was overtaken by events.

Assistance to the rebels became an immediate question at CIA, as it had been in the East Berlin episode. The crisis caught the Directorate for Operations unprepared. The most Allen Dulles would do—a recommendation to Eisenhower that the U.S. send a humanitarian medical unit to Hungary—amounted to an unfeasible proposition. The military risk to Western Europe from an intervention had not changed since 1953, and the president's answer had to be the same. On two separate occasions in the Hungarian crisis, Ike rejected proposals to airdrop arms. The second came after the Hungarians themselves went on the air with a radio appeal for CIA help. Eisenhower ended the debate, asserting that Hungary was "as inaccessible to us as Tibet."

The Russians moved in on November 4 with more than 200,000 troops and over 2,500 armored vehicles, reconquering Budapest by November 8 and the rest of the country before the end of the month.

The Eisenhower administration, meanwhile, largely diverted by the unfolding Anglo-French intervention at Suez, had less and less time to consider the Hungarian situation.

Frank Wisner, impatient to be on the scene, reached Vienna on November 7. His Mississippi drawl boomed at the CIA station. The deputy chief of station at Vienna, Peer de Silva, saw little to do—events moved faster than the CIA could keep up with. Station officers like William B. Hood, an espionage specialist, and John Mapother, a political action man, looked on in horror. The day after Wisner reached Vienna, Soviet tanks completed their conquest of Budapest. Fictionalized accounts by former CIA officers suggest that agency people in Hungary were caught up in the events of the rebellion and barely escaped across the Austrian border, helping those they could. Vice President Richard Nixon and former OSS chief Wild Bill Donovan, like Wisner, came to Vienna to see for themselves, receiving some of the fugitives. Nixon went to the border one night. There he asked Budapest students whether RFE and the Voice of America had encouraged their rebellion. The Hungarians answered with a simple yes.

Almost 200,000 refugees made it to Austria. Casualty estimates ranged up to 30,000 dead and 50,000 injured. Nagy, his heroic former defense minister, and more than 200 others would be executed. Some 30,000 Hungarian refugees fled to the United States where they were received at a special facility at Camp Kilmer in

New Jersey. Army intelligence set up a debriefing center there, where interrogators led by Dorothy Matlack tried to find out all they could about events in Communist-dominated Hungary.

Eisenhower's decisions affected the secret warriors' morale. The DO officers saw in Hungary "exactly the end for which the agency's paramilitary capability was designed." Some felt intervention could have been carried out without war against Russia. In passing up that opportunity, Bill Colby recollects, "we demonstrated that 'liberation' was not our policy when the chips were down in Eastern Europe." Similarly, writes Harry Rositzke, "it was clear that the steady barrage of assurances that the West was firmly opposed to the continuing Communist exploitation of subject peoples could not fail to give RFE's listeners the hope that the United States would come to their aid."

Wisner too, in a way, broke on the Hungarian anvil. After one night at the border, watching the wink of machine-gun fire as Soviet forces tried to halt the refugees, Wisner bitterly proceeded to Rome, where deputy station chief Bill Colby, like Barnes in Germany, found him close to a breakdown. In fact the DDO could hardly continue. Back home Wisner went duck hunting. On December 16, suffering chills, he checked into a hospital. His fever soared to 106 degrees; he had hepatitis. Sometimes attributed to a meal of bad clams, the illness had much to do with Wisner's sheer exhaustion. Deputy Richard Helms filled in during his recovery.

Eisenhower ordered Allen Dulles to do a formal analysis of Radio Free Europe's part in the Hungarian business. The director assigned this task to Cord Meyer. With the help of two Hungarian-speaking analysts, Meyer made a full survey of RFE broadcasts. His conclusion: "I am satisfied that RFE did not plan, direct, or attempt to provoke the Hungarian rebellion." Dulles forwarded the four-page report of his political action staff to the president on November 20.

The highlighted passage on the White House copy, among the paragraphs of justification for RFE, read, "A few of the scripts reviewed do indicate that RFE occasionally went beyond the authorized factual broadcasting of the demands of the patriot radio stations within Hungary to identify itself with these demands and to urge their achievement." Further, "there was some evidence of attempts by RFE to provide tactical advice to the patriots as to the course the rebellion should take and the individuals best qualified to lead it." The RFE broadcasts, said one conclusion, "went beyond specific guidances" though the uprising itself resulted from Soviet repression rather than RFE broadcasts or Free Europe leaflets.

Eisenhower ended blunderbuss psywar campaigns like Operation Focus, tightened corporate control over RFE broadcasting decisions, and ordered an end to the balloon leaflet program.

The last loose end was the CIA's "liberation army." Upon returning to duty, Frank Wisner again enthused about initiating a resistance project, now in Czechoslovakia, but he also obsessed over starting a rebellion that might fail spectacularly and reveal CIA's hand. Even Allen Dulles saw that danger. Ike ordered Gen. Lucien Truscott to dismantle the liberation force. Some emigrés joined the U.S. Army where they ended up with Special Forces and found themselves in places as distant as Laos. Others stayed in Europe, where the NTS and OUN-R plots still boiled. In Germany, 1958 would be the high point for a mysterious organization called the Battlegroup Against Inhumanity (*Kampfgruppe gegen Unmenschlichkeit*). Drawing funding from the Crusade for Freedom, the conduit established to finance RFE, the "battlegroup" would be linked to several 1958 commando-style raids in East Germany, including a failed attempt to blow up the Elbe bridge at Wismar. These and earlier actions aroused such controversy that the organization disbanded a year later. The agency's capabilities for paramilitary warfare in Eastern Europe and the Soviet Union never returned.

Hungary left bitterness all around. At the CIA, as Bill Colby put it, "whatever doubt may have existed in the Agency about Washington's policy in matters like this vanished." East Europeans now knew that American claims to support resistance were merely rhetorical. In the White House, growing awareness of the sensitivity of these activities led to reduced emphasis on psychological warfare. Hungary demonstrated that the plain existence of certain capabilities can create controversy, even in the absence of any effort to do so.

President Eisenhower put as much stock as any of his predecessors—perhaps more than many—in extolling democratic values. Arguments for democracy were pervasive in the psychological warfare ploys he favored. In Europe in the 1950s Ike put democracy at the core of his secret war against Russia, articulated overtly through the United States Information Agency and the Voice of America, but most especially covertly through the Radios. Yet Hungary showed the audiences of those preachings, beyond question, that when their efforts to reach for the values the Americans professed were challenged, the U.S. response would be predicated on power considerations, not democratic beliefs. Realization that people in Eastern Europe and elsewhere could see this undoubtedly contributed to the malaise at CIA in the wake of the Hungarian crisis. But there were other fish to fry.

The President's Board of Consultants on Foreign Intelligence Activities, commonly known by the name of its chairman, James R. Killian, could look into any aspect of intelligence activity, on its own initiative or at Eisenhower's request. They were to report annually. The Killian Board met bimonthly, many traveling to Washington at their own expense to render this service. Killian was an inspired choice in this era of burgeoning technological developments, supporting strong scientific representation. His experts—people like Edwin Land, William O. Baker, and Charles Stark Draper—gave U.S. intelligence absolutely crucial suggestions for the U-2 spyplane; its successor, the SR-71; National Security Agency communications interception, and more. But PBCFIA interest extended to covert operations as well.

At its first meeting with the CIA, the watchdog committee endured eight hours of an agency briefing—densely packed details on intelligence collection, analysis, and covert operations. Agency Inspector Gen. Lyman Kirkpatrick, responsible for all dealings with the board, recalled that first encounter as "brutal," and writes that it "was in truth a saturation effort." But Kirk could not head off an initiative to examine covert action. David K. E. Bruce, the respected diplomat who had led OSS operations in the European theater during the war, and Robert A. Lovett, a former secretary of defense, took a hard look.

Frank Wisner feared the inquiry. Well he might. With sophisticated understanding of the secret world, Bruce went to the heart of the matter. The secret warriors could be "buccaneers," Bruce found, chalking up credits for success but no debits for failure, with approvals made in pro forma fashion. Between frustrating the Russians and keeping the rest of the world Western oriented, any operation could seem important. The bright, young secret warriors needed to justify their existence, but once past approvals, no one had any idea what was going on except them. Bruce and Lovett expressed certainty that no one who had helped launch the secret war in 1948 had foreseen these consequences. Easy approvals brought messy realities. Wisner defended the DO, arguing as he left for Europe (just before Hungary) that "informality does not mean irresponsibility."

Bruce and Lovett also worried about coordination between the CIA and the Pentagon, observing that someone high in government should be calculating the long-range wisdom of these operations. The Bruce-Lovett paper went to Eisenhower at the end of 1956, advising Ike to order the CIA and the Pentagon to integrate their war plans, have CIA make more thoughtful plans to work in a post-nuclear-exchange environment, and achieve better synchronization between CIA's "black" propaganda and those "unattributed" grey activities carried out by the United States Information Agency.

The Killian Board told Eisenhower, both in writing and at a December 20, 1956, meeting, that it rejected the procedures for implementing covert action. Projects became the exclusive preserve of the CIA, 5412 Group approvals were too informal, and, in particular, "as far as we have been able to determine there is no real joint staffing of any clandestine project."

A month later Ike met with his top officials in the Cabinet Room at the White House to hash out the issues. Director Dulles said he favored joint approval, but not if that meant people all over government could pore over the projects. The president took the CIA's side—5412 programs could not be staffed throughout the agencies. Ike questioned bringing more people into the process. Eisenhower's national security adviser suggested a limited compromise—the 5412 Group members could each designate staff assistants, and only those officials would see the proposals. Ike agreed. He went on to say he had become "increasingly concerned about the security of such matters." John Foster Dulles added that he did not think he should have to tell anyone about covert action unless he wanted to, and used the example of suggestions to his brother, Allen, that he would not want known at State. The secretary of defense asked whether covert action should be separated from espionage. Both Killian and Allen Dulles responded no, the question had been looked at many times and always rejected.

Eisenhower extended the mantle of plausible deniability by interjecting that things in the "5412 field" were better not known by the president *or* his top secretaries, "so they could be in a position to disavow them if necessary." Ike wanted to know about the idea for a program but nothing of its details. Besides, he said later, "If something really hot [is] proposed, it [will] be discussed in a meeting in this room."

In a written response to the Killian Board a week later the CIA accepted its recommendation on 5412 matters. In early March the Special Group itself noted that proposals within established policies did not need "joint staffing," but agreed that those outside the boundaries could be handled in a new way. The Special Group's March 4, 1957, agreement actually constitutes the first written requirement for the Central Intelligence Agency to circulate proposal papers in advance of covert action approvals.

Months later, when the NSC considered ordering the Joint Chiefs to undertake a study of limited warfare and Director Dulles wanted the CIA to be included, the Council's notetaker drily recorded: "The President replied facetiously that he, of course, had no knowledge of covert operations."

Another Killian Board initiative—getting Ike to make Allen Dulles use a chief of staff—the CIA steadfastly opposed. The president sided again with Dulles. He did have Allen bring Lucien Truscott back in yet one more incarnation, this time as a sort of in-house liaison between the clandestine and analytical sides of the agency.

During this period, and championed by Allen Dulles, the CIA sought funds for and began work on a new headquarters complex at Langley, Virginia, eight miles from downtown Washington. President Eisenhower encouraged the agency to relocate even farther from the capital, precisely because of his fears of the consequences of nuclear war. Focused on its day-to-day need to labor in the vineyards of government, the agency refused.

Eisenhower worried about controlling the secret warriors but pursued his Cold War with gusto. The very rush of events made it difficult to go back over old ground. The 5412 Group provided semi-annual presentations of the covert program, but it remained impossible to exercise constant control. Initiative became crucial to protecting the president's interests. Like many bureaucracies, however, 5412 reacted to recommendations rather than exerted positive leadership. The real initiative lay in the hands of the Central Intelligence Agency, which, in fulfillment of the 5412/2 objectives, launched more covert ventures around the world. These eventually took President Eisenhower to the very brink of the CIA mess he feared. The locale would not be Russia or even Eastern Europe. Ike's headache began in the Third World.

9

Archipelago

HUNGARY may have been in crisis, but the Middle East fell into full-scale war. Powerful distractions drew Dwight Eisenhower away from Europe. The known issues—the Anglo-French invasion of the Suez, and the collusion of those powers with Israel, which simultaneously launched its 1956 war on Egypt—certainly monopolized attention at the National Security Council. But Suez represented only the tip of the iceberg, and much that lay below the surface involved the secret warriors. Paltry results did not dampen their ardor.

One plan originated months before Suez. A CIA contract officer, assigned for cover purposes to the Operations Coordinating Board, heard the code name Straggle at an Anglo-American intelligence conference. It had been dropped by George K. Young, deputy chief of British intelligence, in connection with a Middle East project the CIA man had never heard of. In Washington he discovered that a planning task force called Omega had already formed at State. In fact President Eisenhower had approved this project in late March 1956. Allen Dulles called the secretary of state on March 22 saying he had something urgent. The next morning before noon, John Foster Dulles hosted a group at his home to hash over the Middle East. Foster's guests included Allen, Kim Roosevelt, and James Angleton.

Unfamiliar with the chain of command, the CIA officer, Wilbur C. Eveland, thought

> That plans to undertake a coup in Syria were centered in the Department of State struck me as highly unusual. I'd expected to see papers referring to NSC policy decisions and instructions that the OCB coordinate carrying them out. Instead, it seemed, the decision had been made by the Secretary of State, and the Omega planners were in charge of following through.

Kermit Roosevelt completed the scheme with George Young in London in April. Foster Dulles considered the final Omega paper on May 23. Shortly thereafter Eveland, an experienced Middle East hand, got orders to scout possibilities on the ground. He had two months. In July Roosevelt flew to Jordan on an assignment related to the project.

American secret warriors had been operating in the Middle East since before the creation of the CIA. In Syria specifically, Stephen Meade, a military attaché and soon-to-be CIA detailee, helped Syrian officers plan an early military coup. Miles Copeland, among the original CIA political action specialists, assisted. But the officers they backed held power for barely a few months, after which the secret warriors forged an alliance with a new regime. That group, in turn, was overthrown by a left-wing military coup in 1954. Copeland, meanwhile, had been diverted to a private consulting company, though he returned to head the DO political action staff. In Egypt, Nasser's increasing power, steadfast Arab nationalism, and progressively radical reforms soured Washington. When the Egyptian leader went on to advocate Third World neutralism, declare a pan-Arab United Arab Republic, and make arms and aid deals with the Communist bloc, he incurred the wrath of John Foster Dulles. Kim Roosevelt tried and failed to induce Nasser to change course. As Syrian leaders showed signs of moving toward the Egyptian orbit, especially interest in joining the United Arab Republic, their nation went back on the CIA hit list.

Before the end of 1954 the agency was in touch with the officer who assassinated Syria's leader the following year. Although there is no evidence of Washington's complicity in this regime change, the Syrian public linked the United States to these events and moved closer to Nasser. Thus arose Plan Alpha, an Anglo-American design. By late 1955, Foster Dulles had set his mind on new leadership in Damascus but wanted it to appear to have come from within. That, of course, meant covert action. President Eisenhower and Dulles took up the matter with British leaders early in 1956, leading to the general Middle East plan Omega and its Syrian component, Project Wakeful.

All this happened before Suez, a crisis that would be exceedingly uncomfortable for Eisenhower. In July 1956 Nasser nationalized the Suez Canal. The CIA's Cairo station under James Eichelberger had no advance warning. The Egyptian move brought outrage in Britain. France saw Nasser as allied to the revolutionaries it was fighting in Algeria, and joined with the British in a military scheme to invade Egypt and retake the canal. To provide the excuse, the French enlisted Israel to make its own attack, permitting Anglo-French invaders to pose as arbiters separating the warring sides. The maneuver, patently colonialist in its aim of restoring British dominion over the canal, would conflict directly with America's rhetoric of democracy and self-determination.

Unlike Hungary, which erupted suddenly and took place simultaneously, the Suez dilemma confronted Eisenhower throughout the summer and fall of 1956. While his administration plotted coups with the British in Syria, the connection threatened to associate the United States with British neocolonialism. Ike strove to avert a British military action by negotiations, but neither the British nor the Egyptians were mollified. By September 1956 U.S. intelligence believed an Anglo-French military move likely if negotiations failed. Kim Roosevelt picked up more hints from British officials at the United Nations. On September 12 the CIA created a special interagency group, code-named the Paramount Committee, to track Middle East developments full time. Agency U-2 aircraft flew over Anglo-French bases, returning photos of invasion preparations. Later the U-2s by chance captured the very moment of the British bombing of Egyptian airfields. The war began with the Israeli attack on October 29, with the Anglo-French intervention a few days later. Equipped with the CIA's intelligence, Eisenhower felt obliged to veto the Anglo-French resolution at the UN Security Council that would have given legal justification for the intervention.

Operation Wakeful, known to the British SIS as Straggle, led to a complete disaster. The basic idea had been to trigger a coup by Syrian officers and forestall the leftist Ba'ath Party. Scattered evidence indicates the plan centered on encouraging a revolt among Druze tribesmen, combined with a border crisis with Turkey. The British manipulated the CIA into timing the operation for precisely the time of Suez. At the end of October the CIA paid out $165,000 to one Syrian agent, but there could be no question of moving ahead once the British invaded Egypt. The Syrian and Iraqi agents became convinced the Americans were merely assisting the action against Nasser's Egypt.

Howard ("Rocky") Stone resurrected the Syrian coup in 1957 as Operation Wappen. The CIA in Beirut coordinated a covert working group composed of representatives of SIS plus Iraqi, Jordanian, and Lebanese intelligence services. Rocky, one of the officers who had worked with Kim Roosevelt on Ajax, had spent a year at headquarters and then gone to the Sudan, where he helped right a sour relationship with its military dictator. Arriving at Damascus in April 1957, Stone found Washington demanding fresh action. He relied on deputy Arthur Close and subordinate Frank Jetton. The plot involved suborning the commander of the Syrian armor school, who would position his tanks around Damascus, after which other units should side with the plotters. There were meetings at a CIA safe house and at Stone's home, and a reported $3 million changed hands. The agency talked to former Syrian president Adib Shishakli, considered an unacceptable ally in the 1956 coup plan. At the key moment, a summer night that August, Stone invited a couple of embassy secretaries to accompany the group at his house so the gathering would look like a party.

This time Syrian security had been on to the plot from the beginning. Stone's agents simply walked up to the desk of intelligence chief Lt. Col. Abdul Hamid Sarraj, named the CIA officers, and turned in their agency money. Rocky Stone and Frank Jetton, caught red-handed, were exposed in the Syrian press and expelled from the country. In its August 26, 1957, issue, *Time* magazine nevertheless dismissed reports of the U.S.-sponsored coup as Soviet propaganda.

Questions remain regarding CIA participation in Iraq. In 1958 the Iraqi monarchy fell to yet another military coup. A few days before, Frank Wisner confidently told a State Department colleague that the Iraqi public might not like the government but there were few activists to do anything about it. Ike's chief of staff, Sherman Adams, agrees that the agency gave no warning of the coup. Washington saw the officers who took control as Soviet clients.

In April 1959 Eisenhower set up an interagency group to consider covert options to prevent a Communist takeover of Iraq. British documents have John Foster Dulles on record from a year earlier speculating that the "Mossadegh example" might be the way to handle the Iraq situation. Six months later came an attempted assassination of the Iraqi leader, Abdul Karim Qasim.

This maneuver became a step in the rise of Saddam Hussein, then a junior officer in the Iraqi army, a participant in the attempted murder. Some versions picture Saddam as a CIA agent, others as an Egyptian one, yet others as a last-minute hire and simply a Ba'ath activist. More conspiratorial views hold that Saddam took payments from an Egyptian attaché, or that his CIA contact, an Iraqi dentist, had parallel ties to the Egyptians. Unlike the 1958 coup, which took the CIA by surprise, the agency knew of the attempted murder. Saddam, who failed, fled to Egypt and only returned years later. By one account it would only be in Egypt that Saddam got in touch with the CIA. Collusion reached everywhere. Iraqi exiles in Beirut bragged of their CIA connections—one told anyone who would listen that he had Allen Dulles's private telephone number. Other evidence suggests the CIA again took measures to incapacitate or eliminate Qasim in 1960, and that it was involved in the coup that overthrew him in 1963. James Critchfield has been cited as making the initial recruitments for the 1963 coup. A senior Iraqi official in the successor government openly averred, "We came to power on a CIA train."

"I spent most of my time," recalls Miles Copeland, "helping Kim Roosevelt to pick up the pieces after collisions with Egypt and other Middle Eastern governments caused by Secretary Dulles' insistence on policies and lines of action that both State and CIA field people knew would be disastrous." Indeed Foster pursued the secret war with the same zeal and energy he displayed in covering distances heading for diplomatic meetings, making himself the most-traveled secretary of state in American history to that time. Of course Foster kept close tabs on covert action through brother Allen, the DCI. His role has yet to be fully appreciated. The Suez and Hungary crises brought a hiatus when Foster, suffering acute abdominal pain, was found to have colon cancer. He had surgery at Walter Reed Medical Center, then convalesced at his Hobe Sound vacation home in Florida. But by 1957 Dulles had returned to the fray.

On many fronts the State Department now cooperated closely with the secret warriors. Psychological warfare particularly was pursued covertly by State through its United States Information Agency, including Voice of America radio (and later television) broadcasting, working in tandem with the CIA Radios. The USIA also had libraries in many countries, field offices, and sponsored cultural events and speakers.

In Japan, for example, Psychological Strategy Board plans dictated support for the center-right Liberal Democratic Party. The USIA quietly invested in Japanese movies and television. By 1955 unattributed USIA money had financed six feature films and supported open broadcasts of more than eighteen thousand hours of radio, the equivalent of beaming on two frequencies twenty-four hours a day for a year. The USIA effort tried to influence, or at least neutralize, progressive tendencies among the Japanese intelligentsia. The CIA supplemented and extended these programs, with psywar experts like Howard Hunt crafting seductive scripts for Radio Free Asia. The agency-funded Asia Foundation sponsored its own Japanese commentators, and there were labor operations plus political payoffs—made easier in Japan where it was a social custom to pay citizens for their votes. Agency funding of the Liberal Democrats has been acknowledged by Al Ulmer, the FE Division baron of the time. The extent of CIA activity remains shrouded in secrecy even decades later, but the acting CIA director, in a 1995 letter to the *New York Times*, did not even attempt to deny the support, retreating to the threadbare argument that the CIA needed to keep faith with recipients of the covert aid.

The agencies marched together in many places. In Italy, where CIA political action built toward a May 1958 election, the USIA operation grew as large as that of the secret warriors. Tracy Barnes and then Miles Copeland headed the CIA political action staff, their projects as unusual as attempting to insert astrologers into the entourages of foreign leaders known to rely on the occult, or forging links with such cultural movements as moral rearmament.

John Foster Dulles kept the State Department out of the more exotic chicanery but turned a benign eye toward the whole endeavor. Dulles remained an abrasive, rigid figure in an administration that accentuated pragmatism, his advantage mainly the outlook he shared with President Eisenhower. The secretary of state had already gone into physical decline—he would die of cancer in January 1959—and continuing crises took a great toll on Foster's remaining strength. But before that happened Dulles would become the prime mover in a major CIA covert operation, one, for that matter, not very far from Japan.

In his own recollections of the presidency, Dwight Eisenhower mentions Achmed Sukarno of Indonesia exactly once: Eisenhower remarks that he had not seen Sukarno in years. This comment, in describing why Ike felt justified in rejecting a 1960 plea by Sukarno and other leaders for talks between the United States and the Soviet Union, reveals nothing about how the president used the CIA to get rid of the Indonesian leader. In fact, Ike's general dissatisfaction with Indonesia led to a paramilitary operation designed to overthrow the government, much as in Iran or Guatemala. In his 1960 appeal for superpower detente, Sukarno spoke from the experience of having been caught between the adversaries.

Son of a minister, John Foster Dulles behaved as if choosing one of the Cold War camps was the moral duty of nations. Sukarno's unpardonable offense had been to reject this division of the world into camps, espousing another way—neutralism—an association of "nonaligned" nations. Dulles steadfastly opposed nonalignment. The People's Republic of China had had a big role at the 1955 conference in Bandung, at which Sukarno launched the nonaligned movement, and China's emergence from diplomatic isolation here especially galled Foster. At the

Geneva conference a year earlier, after all, Dulles refused even to shake hands with Chinese foreign minister Zhou Enlai. His disposition blinded Dulles to real opportunities for improving relations. When another of the nonaligned leaders, Premier U Nu of Burma, visited Beijing in 1957, for example, he offered to intercede for the Americans. The Chinese indicated they would be willing to release the imprisoned CIA officers John Downey and Richard Fecteau in exchange for nothing more than permitting journalists to visit the People's Republic and report on the "New China." But Dulles refused, and the CIA men languished for decades. Worse, Dulles turned on Sukarno and leaped at suggestions for a covert operation aimed at the Indonesian.

The cultural and geographic nature of his land made Sukarno vulnerable. A Dutch colony for almost four centuries, Indonesia was a mélange of Muslim, tribal animistic, and Buddhist influences. The different social groups were isolated by geography—Indonesia being a vast archipelago of six big and about three thousand small islands forming an arc from the tip of the Malay Peninsula to the Philippines. Independence came in the rush of decolonization after World War II. For Indonesians, the problem lay in transforming this kaleidoscopic society into a unified nation-state.

Sukarno had been a prominent wartime nationalist, then active in the postwar resistance to the Dutch. The natural choice for president, at once pragmatic and visionary, Sukarno was no Communist. Indeed he outlawed the Indonesian Communist Party following an abortive coup attempt in 1949. Sukarno turned away from the armed forces too after a political play by army leader Col. Abdul Haris Nasution three years later. He walked a tightrope among the many political factions. Economic chaos reigned amid political struggle. Rubber, tin, and oil were major export products, but prices for the first two fluctuated widely in the early 1950s while oil production fell. Factionalism grew so rampant that by 1956 parliament had not yet ratified government budgets for the first years of the decade.

For its initial project the CIA tried political action. Indonesian elections were scheduled for September 1955. Kermit Roosevelt approved a program memorandum requesting a million dollars. The memorandum, just a few paragraphs long, completely lacked the detail of need, plan, and expected results required under Eisenhower's 5412 system. Yet the project sailed through and the money went to benefit the progressive Muslim Masjumi Party. Exchanging the dollars for Indonesian rupiah on the Hong Kong black market, the CIA quadrupled its money. But in the elections the Communists, who received more than six million votes, almost a fifth of the total cast, far outstripped the Masjumi. Sukarno then appeared to confirm American fears by making official visits to China, Russia, and other Eastern European countries. The CIA cast about for ideas.

Again Frank Wisner set the pace. One day toward the end of 1956, he said to the chief of the DO's Far East Division, "I think it's time we held Sukarno's feet to the fire."

Wisner's subordinate, Al Ulmer, returned to his office with word that new arrangements for Sukarno were a priority. One officer with the Indonesia branch,

FE/5, recalls being told that "if some plan for doing this were not forthcoming, Santa might fill our stockings with assignments to far worse jobs." The Far East Division was the biggest in the DO at the time, so Ulmer had plenty of choices in the matter.

As it happened, Alfred C. Ulmer, Jr., knew paramilitary operations but little about Asia. Ulmer had begun with the navy, transferred to OSS, earned the Bronze Star, and stayed on with intelligence even before the advent of CIA. His work as station chief in Greece impressed Wisner, who had brought Ulmer to headquarters in 1955 and promoted him to chief of the division.

Ulmer depended on FE/5 to develop a plan. At just this juncture opportunity seemed to blossom. Military commanders in western and northern Sumatra, Indonesia's largest island, frustrated by changes, declared themselves independent and not bound to the national military command. The colonels who began this revolt in December 1956 used their troops to smuggle goods through Singapore. The revolt widened in March 1957 when the commander at Manado, in South Sulawesi province, declared a state of emergency and replaced the civilian government. There, on Celebes Island, a Charter of Common Struggle (*Piagam Perjuangan Semesta*) or, in the Indonesian acronym, PERMESTA, emerged as the rebel alliance. This term soon identified the entire movement. PERMESTA became an open rebellion after April 6, 1957, when twenty-nine army soldiers died in a clash on Celebes.

The CIA had several avenues to reach the plotters. Richard Bissell, still special assistant to Allen Dulles, recalls that some Indonesians had approached the agency at least two years earlier. He observes, "I think it's fair to say all the people the Agency dealt with eventually ended up as opponents of Sukarno." These contacts may have come through the Indonesian military attaché in Washington, who later defected. In addition, CIA officer James Smith, Jr., went to Sumatra to contact the colonels. The United States also conducted training for the Indonesian national police, in the course of which came quiet attempts to recruit promising candidates.

A contact in April 1957 through a local channel from two of the more prominent colonels intrigued the CIA. Ahmad Husein of central Sumatra was one. The other, Maludin Simbolon, passed over for army chief of staff in favor of Nasution in 1954, now commanded northern Sumatra. The colonels wished to meet with a CIA man. The desk officer took the cable from Djakarta station chief Valentine Goodell to Ulmer's home one Sunday morning. Ulmer immediately imposed top security, restricting knowledge to just nine persons at the CIA.

With some trepidation, as there had been no 5412 Group approval of an operation, Ulmer persuaded Dulles and Wisner to let him follow up. A meeting took place; the Indonesians wanted U.S. weapons. This left FE/5 in a quandary since it lacked approval. After an unsuccessful try at arranging a private arms deal, the CIA determined to seek appropriate authority.

Sukarno helped the Eisenhower administration decide to support PERMESTA. In February 1957 the Indonesian president gave a speech asserting that "Western style" democracy had proved inadequate in Indonesia. Sukarno declared that political parties should disband in the interest of the nation, leaving a system of "guided democracy"—authoritarian rule by the president, assisted by an advisory council Sukarno himself would appoint. Washington read the speech as a thinly disguised initiative to bring the Communist Party into association with the president. To top it all, Sukarno then welcomed Soviet leader Kliment Voroshilov for a stay of more than two months in Indonesia. In May Eisenhower flatly rejected Sukarno's request to visit.

That fall Australian foreign minister Richard Casey came to Washington for alliance discussions. He held private meetings with both Allen and John Foster Dulles, and had both of them in some of the conference talks, the DCI at Casey's insistence. The CIA director told the Australian minister his agency had secret contact with the rebels. Allen Dulles is reported as saying, ". . . the breakup of Indonesia should not be regarded as an objective, but only as something which might have to be accepted as a last resort."

Allen Dulles seems to have been ambivalent about this scheme. He kept in touch, sometimes at home in midnight phone conversations with Ulmer. But over time Dulles questioned the dedication of the Indonesians. The CIA director began acting more as commentator at the NSC and less the secret warrior wearing a bit in his teeth. Dulles increasingly delegated Indonesia to deputy Charles Cabell. In turn, General Cabell employed Richard Bissell as point man. Bissell arranged a few U-2 flights to gather data. The main center for planning moved to the State Department, where meetings of an NSC special interagency committee were chaired by State's intelligence director Hugh S. Cumming.

The Indonesia project is unique in revealing John Foster Dulles's leading role in the secret war. The secretary, in New York for the UN General Assembly, learned of the final go-ahead from Allen on September 16, 1957. Only Foster's side of the exchange has been recorded:

"Then you got the green light otherwise?"

"Is this the West and not the East end?"

"Nearer us?"

"OK."

Hugh Cumming's committee paper on Indonesia became the lead item of business at NSC on September 23. It recommended that the United States "continue the present pattern of our formal relations, but so . . . adjust our programs and activities as to give greater emphasis to support of non-Communist forces in the outer islands, while continuing attempts to produce action by non-Communist elements on Java." The council ordered new planning, a process that led directly to Project Haik, as the Indonesia operation would be called. The Joint Chiefs of Staff complained that the concept conceded Java, the most important part of the country. They advised extending a small amount of military aid, enough to drive a wedge between the Indonesian military and Sukarno without affecting its real capability against the rebels should they remain loyal to the government. But the

Chiefs never followed up, and they grudgingly approved with those actions necessary to Haik. Before the end of September the formal policy logically entailed
execution of the CIA's covert operation.

At Far East Division the mood became ecstatic. Al Ulmer exclaimed,
"We'll drive Lebanon off the front page!" The branch, FE/5, felt approval meant
they could rely on the Pacific Fleet for arms shipped the right way. State imposed certain restrictions: there could be only one team of Americans on the
ground—one officer plus his radio operator. Des FitzGerald thought such a tiny
commitment portended failure. His doubts were not to be ignored since, as FE's
top paramilitary expert, he carried much of the load. Once colleagues saw Des,
who loved being at the center of the action, blowing cold on Indonesia, that sent
a distinct signal.

When DDO Wisner hand-carried a simple voucher to the director's office, authorizing $10 million for Haik, Allen Dulles, it is reported, signed with a flourish.
The initial outlay would be $843,000 that CIA paymasters disbursed in November
1957.

From that moment Foster Dulles spoke to his brother frequently about Haik.
Foster overruled his own ambassador in Jakarta, John Allison, who had learned of
CIA contact with the rebels and argued against involvement. As had been the case
with the American ambassador to Burma during the Li Mi affair, Allison was then
deliberately misinformed about the extent of CIA activity.

Foster Dulles called Allen on November 29, though, to tell the DCI of an "extremely significant" cable from Allison that involved a "complete reversal"—the
ambassador now advised action. Foster said, "What was happening there was that
one by one they were gradually being eliminated. Our assets were gradually
shrinking. Today we have substantial assets with which to deal. We will, however,
have only half those assets six months from now."

The degree of Foster Dulles's involvement again emerged the next day when
hand grenades were thrown at Sukarno as he left a school fund-raiser in the company of children, an assassination attempt by Muslim fanatics unrelated to PERME-
STA. Although Sukarno escaped, ten persons died and forty-eight children were injured. The question of sending condolences Foster resolved by telling Allen,
"Probably the failure to do it would look suspicious, but the Sec[retary] said he
wanted to be sure it was handled in a routine way."

In early December difficulties arose with the British. At Singapore, CIA station chief James P. Collins maintained liaison with British intelligence, headquar-
tered at Phoenix Park. Rebel emissaries came to Singapore to meet Collins at the
close of 1957, and the CIA officer had to sneak around, hiding from SIS. Singapore was the ideal arms conduit, but the British blocked CIA efforts. The agency
had already begun preparing a weapons delivery to PERMESTA on Sumatra. This
would be easiest if routed through Singapore.

Allen Dulles went to Foster while senior British officials were in Washington
for discussions. The secretary remarked, "If this thing goes on the way it is we will
have something across there which will be pretty bad." Foster then called his un-

dersecretary, Christian Herter, and told him that the CIA chief was quite upset with the British. Foster wondered why London resisted action and whether the Australians and Dutch could be mobilized to bring pressure. Secretary Dulles said "what he would like to do is see things get to a point where we could plausibly withdraw our recognition of the Sukarno government and give it to the dissident elements on Sumatra and land forces to protect the life and property of Americans; use this as an excuse to bring about a major shift there . . . we may never have a better opportunity." On December 12 Hugh Cumming told Foster he hoped the secretary "will get the British with us in Indonesia. MI 6 [SIS] wants to move and cooperate with CIA."

The Americans won their point. A few months later SIS officers were standing alongside CIA people at the Singapore airport control tower as the reception committee for aircraft returning from arms deliveries.

Meanwhile the Americans moved big time but set up the action through bases in the Philippines. Eisenhower had mentioned "having some amphibious equipment," as Foster Dulles reminded a Pentagon official on December 7, and the navy came up with the landing ship dock *Thomaston*. The vessel, loaded with a pair of barges bearing arms for eight thousand troops, sailed for Sumatra. Simultaneously Al Ulmer sent John Mason, chief of his air branch, to the Philippines to board the submarine *Bluegill* and watch the unloading, taking photographs.

Allen Dulles, pleased at the successful delivery, told his brother on January 15, "Everything is going all right on the other matter on the other side of the world." They seemed unaware that, due to poor coordination, bazookas (an effective heavy weapon) had been left out of the shipment, which would cost the rebels dearly when government troops attacked them later.

The CIA now inserted observers on Sumatra. Political specialist James Smith handled one of the colonels. Dean Almy, with cover as U.S. consul in Medan, watched the fence-sitters. Fravel Brown, a China ops veteran, plus his radioman made up the team with the rebels at Padang. In a token of the changed British attitude, Brown reached his post through Singapore.

Brown's reports became the DCI's basis for a last-minute appraisal on January 31 that mostly echoed the optimistic view. The fourteen-page paper argued that the "Padang group" seemed assured of backing from at least one major political movement, that the group believed Sukarno to be weakened and felt it could obtain "Western, particularly US support."

Intelligence declared that "the group, in present circumstances, believes it could successfully resist any military action by forces loyal to the central government." The CIA knew in advance of a rebel ultimatum, which it predicted would be delivered "on or about 5 February," but critically miscalculated in judging Sukarno would not pressure the outer islands; CIA assumed the Padang group would have the advantage there and that "at a minimum," PERMESTA could launch "fairly widespread guerrilla warfare" on Java. The agency hedged only noting "we are unable to estimate the outcome" of a fight and in its observation that the conclusions applied only until Sukarno received substantial Soviet military aid.

Secretary Dulles worried about the rebels' long delay declaring themselves. "During the stalling period the present regime is going to get a lot of stuff," Foster told Allen on February 4. With Indonesia up for discussion at the NSC, it is not surprising that "the subject of Archipelago" came up again on the 5th between the secretary and the DCI.

On February 6 Allen Dulles told the National Security Council that matters were reaching a climax. The CIA now expected the rebel ultimatum in two days. It would actually be broadcast over the radio on the 10th. Director Dulles furnished forty-eight hours' advance notice. At State, Secretary Dulles called Hugh Cumming to demand results. Cumming had two officials brief Foster in greater detail but stopped them before they could broach the CIA action. Indeed Foster Dulles and Cumming had mulled over operational aspects for months but they needed to keep the circle of knowledge tight.

Events moved inexorably ahead in Indonesia. Sukarno left to travel overseas. While in Osaka, Japan, the colonels came into the open. They sent an emissary with the ultimatum to abandon "guided democracy" and a list of acceptable cabinet ministers, promising support if these persons were appointed. Sukarno refused. On February 15 PERMESTA proclaimed a rebel government comprising figures from Sumatra, Sulawesi, and Java, though the rebels had little strength on the latter island.

Now the secretary of state developed doubts about justification, as he told Allen in a darker moment on February 21. The United States had no treaty or congressional authority to become involved in civil war. The CIA chief warned that the rebel colonels could not go on indefinitely. Foster ruminated that Washington could recognize PERMESTA as a belligerent and then sell it weapons.

The CIA Far East Division had expected that 5412 Group approval would bring full cooperation, but the navy continued to drag its feet. Adm. Arleigh Burke, chief of naval operations, simply did not press the issue. The navy provided the landing ship and submarine for initial moves, then took weeks to send warships to Singapore to give the United States an intervention capability. Where an aircraft carrier and a heavy cruiser were envisioned as the core of the force, the navy finally dispatched just two destroyers. The CIA had repeatedly gone over cooperation with the sailors in December and January. The reality proved intensely disappointing. On February 22 both Allen Dulles and Christian Herter again raised this matter with Burke.

About this time aerial reconnaissance disclosed Indonesian site preparations for a bomber-length airstrip on the island of Natuna Besar, north of Sumatra. At the Pacific Command, Adm. Felix Stump now feared Sukarno might allow Russian bombers use of the facility. Navy resistance suddenly melted. The navy began aerial photo missions to support Project Haik.

Naval flights created a possibility for compromise of the project. Plausible deniability had begun to evaporate. In the field it finally did. The first airborne weapons delivery to Sumatra took place on February 23. Packed on Okinawa by CIA officer James McElroy, and coordinated from Clark Air Force Base by John

Mason's deputy, Garfield Thorsrud, plus Roger McCarthy, the loads were put aboard two Civil Air Transport C-46 aircraft. Both pilots—Paul R. Holden and William D. Gaddie—were veterans of the CIA airlift to Dien Bien Phu. When they landed to refuel in Thailand, Thai soldiers boarded the planes and started pulling apart the containers, a breach of security contained only with difficulty. Meanwhile the PERMESTA colonels arranged an arms deal with the Chinese Nationalists about this time, and a Chinese military mission appeared in Sulawesi.

When word of arms shipments reached the American embassy at Djakarta, it embarrassed John Allison, who still advocated accommodation with the Indonesian government. Accounts differ on whether Allison asked for a transfer or was simply ordered out of the country. Secretary Dulles sent Allison to Czechoslovakia. The ambassador speculated in retrospect that Sukarno had "disgusted" Foster. Allison had his moment, passing through Washington en route to Prague. He stopped at the CIA for a debriefing. The intelligence officers listened carefully and were polite. Afterward, a senior CIA man walked the ambassador to his car and said, "You should know that several of us here agreed with your reports and recommendations from Djakarta. I think you will be proved right in the end."

Indonesia dominated talk around the table at the White House, with discussions at fourteen of the seventeen National Security Council meetings between November 1957 and March 1958; keeping talk of it out of the Cabinet Room proved almost impossible. In at least one instance, the NSC meeting of February 27, conversation skirted the thin line separating the overt and covert tracks of "Archipelago," as Foster euphemistically referred to Project Haik. Allen Dulles opined that the colonels had moved too quickly. Although Sukarno's forces had yet to make a major attack, and CIA speculated that he doubted his troops' loyalty, the rebels had not evaluated their own strength very well. "The great problem confronting us," the CIA chieftain told the NSC, "is how far we go into the matter." If the rebels failed, Allen Dulles feared—he expressed fair certainty—that Indonesia would go over to communism. President Eisenhower responded that if a Communist takeover really threatened, Washington would have to intervene. John Foster Dulles then interjected that U.S. chances were better since there existed an "indigenous government" on Sumatra.

The notes of a telephone call Foster made to Allen Dulles at 4:20 P.M. that afternoon are worth quoting at length:

> The Secretary said he does not know whether the talk this a.m. about the area should lead to greater activity. Allen said he is talking about it now. You reach a point where it is extremely difficult to do much more without showing your hand. The Secretary thinks if it is going to work we should take some risk of showing our hand. They agreed it is the last chance. The Secretary mentioned buying stuff in the Philippines. Allen said the question of delivery is difficult. They can get it in only the way we do it. Allen said they are going ahead. We are ready to give them a bird as soon as they can eat it. We are pushing ahead as daringly as we

can. It is a vigorous program and they are very happy with it and cooperate very well. The Secretary just wanted him to know he has the feeling we can't play too safely here and we have to take some risk because it looks to him it is the best chance we have. Allen is glad to hear it.

Arms deliveries alerted Frank Wisner to leave for Singapore, there to command the archipelago operation in the field. The CIA station had been augmented for the project. Through Scott Breckinridge, its liaison officer in Australia, the CIA also pressed the Australians to do something about journalists writing on the U.S. role in Indonesia. The Philippines became prime base for Haik. Navy submarines left from Subic Bay while airdrops were staged from a CIA compound at Clark under Paul Gottke. The agency enlisted the services of several hundred Americans, Poles, Filipinos, and Nationalist Chinese to maintain and fly a small fleet of transport aircraft, P-51 fighters and B-26 bombers. Some of these planes and crews later moved forward to Manado on Sulawesi. Although only about a dozen aircraft were involved, this represented the International Volunteer Air Group in action.

The Indonesian government now began taking strong measures. Chief of Staff Nasution dismissed six rebel colonels, and more discharges followed. Nasution declared that force would be used, and a week later a warship maneuvered ostentatiously off Padang. Radio stations were bombed by government planes. In another conversation, on March 4, CIA boss Dulles told the secretary of state of his terrible fear the United States would have to halt Project Haik. Allen assured Foster he had not as yet issued any such orders.

John Foster Dulles attempted to prevent the American role in Indonesia from becoming public knowledge. In appearances before Congress in March and April he insisted that the United States had not intervened but had followed international law. At press conferences he described the rebellion as an internal matter and said Washington would not permit arms sales to either side. The revolt should be dealt with by Indonesians "without intrusion from without."

On March 6 Allen Dulles told the NSC that Sukarno had delayed in order to put his own forces into position to move against them. Allen dismissed his brother's hopeful doubts as to whether Sukarno's troops had the stomach for battle. The CIA had good access since the officer Nasution had put in charge happened to be close friends with an American attaché. A week later Sukarno troops landed on the Sumatran coast. On March 11, within hours of a CIA arms delivery, government planes struck the drop zone. Troops landed there and seized most of the weapons. The Sukarno forces briefly held CIA officer Brown, who insisted he was merely one of hundreds of Americans on Sumatra working for oil companies, and then made his escape.

Director Dulles reported to the NSC on March 13, telling the group that General Nasution personally coordinated several columns converging on Padang. About two weeks later a CIA seaplane reached Sumatra with the first actual troop training mission. Officers Anthony Poshepny and James Haase plus a radioman joined Pat Landry, already in place for almost a month. But the training seemed fruitless—the CIA team drew up a schedule, then no one came. Dean Almy, senior officer on Sumatra, believes the secret warriors progressively became enmeshed in the rebel cause.

President Eisenhower wanted a full workup of the intelligence, and on March 27 Allen Dulles presented a lengthy White House briefing. After describing the terrain, the CIA assessed rebel strength on Sumatra as much weaker than Nasution's forces. The navy sent urgent orders to its reconnaissance squadrons in the Pacific, and that day three aircraft flew photo missions over Indonesia. One of them, an AJ-2P Savage piloted by Sy Mendenhall, suffered damage while flying over a PERMESTA base in Sulawesi. The incident, with the plane forced to make an emergency landing in the Philippines, brought another flap.

On April 8 the *Chicago Daily News* published an article on American airdrops to the rebels, triggering more consternation in Washington. Secrecy continued only because the *Daily News* story never spread more widely. Anxious to shore up the rebellion, CIA's General Cabell made proposals that went too far even for Secretary Dulles. Not satisfied with what they heard from the U.S. Pacific Command regarding its capabilities, Allen Dulles sent Cabell to Honolulu to investigate. Meanwhile the Sukarno forces made steady progress. On April 14 Allen told the NSC he expected an amphibious assault on Padang any day.

Eisenhower mused that the rebels really needed a submarine or two to parry the invasion fleet. The navy had subs on the scene, notably the *Bluegill* and *Tang*, but these received no orders to intervene.

Usually Ike held NSC meetings on Tuesdays. The session of April 14 came a day early. What happened instead on Tuesday was a fateful decision for CIA to take its gloves off. Director Dulles had been alerted by presidential aide Andrew Goodpaster of "the Boss'[s] deep interest particularly re use of American personnel." Dulles shot back that his secret warriors were about at the limit of their authority. Allen called Foster, telling his brother of Ike's concern.

"We are reaching the hour of decision," Allen declared. Foster replied that they needed to find a political basis to make the covert operation an overt one.

Allen went alone to the White House, Foster took two aides. Would the United States recognize PERMESTA as the government or a belligerent? That afternoon, in one of several phone calls with Allen, Foster remarked that the rebels might fight harder if they saw prospects. Should the CIA tell them the United States might accord recognition if they beat back Sukarno's attack? Could Washington end its restriction on paramilitary teams? Could CIA employ people other than its own? What military assistance could be brought to bear? Eisenhower looked to the idea of "soldiers of fortune" as his avenue to preserve plausible denial, and on April 15 he emphasized that he wanted no U.S. personnel detached from CIA service for the sole purpose of working in Indonesia, but that CIA proprietary personnel like Civil Air Transport pilots would be unobjectionable.

Secretary Dulles suggested stronger intervention might be necessary—without overt support the rebels could fail. But Foster undercut his own argument, opposing American troops in Sumatra to protect U.S. citizens and the oil fields there. The CIA came away with a green light to stage activities under the "soldier of fortune" rubric. Reporters at a news conference that day asked about diplomatic recognition for the rebels. John Foster Dulles tried to be both obscure and optimistic.

This action came too late for PERMESTA on Sumatra. Sukarno's landings took place as foreseen. Allen telephoned Foster on April 17 to report the invasion under way. Among the rebels, some units changed sides; often troops simply ran away. A real battle for Padang, which fell after three days, sealed the rebel defeat. The CIA training team made a hazardous trek to a stretch of unoccupied coast to commandeer a boat and head out to sea, where they were retrieved by the *Tang*. The cover story that they were big-game hunters caught in the crossfire of the rebellion had to be as ludicrous as the one they had used on land—Poshepny had said the CIA team were scientists hunting exotic butterflies.

Allen Dulles informed Foster on April 23 that the rebels seemed to have no fight in them. Foster actually speculated on whether the United States should now switch sides and back Sukarno. Aghast, the CIA director cautioned against such a move as premature. Agency officials lifted the original limitation of one team with the rebels. But white faces were not enough—the rebels lacked backbone. Anthony Poshepny had already met Tibetan trainees—fierce partisans. He found the Indonesians quite tame. Frank Wisner agonized in Singapore.

Reliance on a movement neither cohesive nor unified was to be a key error in Project Haik. The PERMESTA colonels opposed rule from Java, but their political program revealed their motivation as personal. That envisioned a loose federation of regions, essentially major islands and groups of islands in the archipelago. The regions were to retain most of their income, giving only a little to a central government. The plan would have served well in warlord China.

The same separatism the CIA exploited to create Haik ensured that the rebel movement could not function as an alliance. Difficulties due to the geographic dispersion of the islands precluded joint action. A mismatch also existed between the ideological commitment of CIA's secret warriors and the less lofty aims of the colonels. This kind of mistake had also been made in Guatemala, but that time Arbenz had panicked. Sukarno stood his ground.

Another pervasive problem lay in the disparity in means between the rebels and the Indonesian government. Sukarno had a navy, an air force, Marines, paratroops. The rebel colonels had local forces but not much more. The light weapons and ammunition the Americans delivered by submarine or airdrop did not make up the difference.

Regarding diplomatic recognition, Hugh Cumming's people had assembled a paper that showed only weak legal grounds for such a move. Then came the battle of Padang and rebel defeat. Allen Dulles gave Foster details in a lunchtime phone call. Foster remarked that Sukarno's invasion "has happened with far greater efficiency, speed and precision than he had expected." Allen, not surprised at the defeat, warned, "We have to be careful not to get too far out on a limb." A few days later Foster speculated on recognizing a Sumatran state, but Allen advised waiting. Sure enough, on April 28 word came that "the East is boiling." The last rebel capital of Sumatra fell on May 4.

The CIA did what it could to stiffen the rebellion. With the end on Sumatra the rebel capital moved to Manado on Sulawesi. A most conspicuous facet remained the rebel air force. Indonesian airmen stayed loyal to Sukarno, making it hard to explain how a PERMESTA air force had materialized almost overnight. Of course these were the men of Civil Air Transport, or, more precisely, CAT aircrews who left the proprietary to keep the CIA hand hidden. There were also Chinese Nationalists, Poles, and one Hungarian who had worked directly for the CIA; plus a couple of Filipino pilots, who earned more each month than the Philippines paid in a year. At Clark airbase the U.S. Air Force in 1957 had declared surplus some seventy-three B-26 bombers, twin-engine propeller-driven aircraft. Phased out of U.S. service or returned by France after Indochina, the planes had good range and load. The CIA selected three of the bombers and acquired several P-51 fighters from the Philippines, which had converted to jet fighters.

The U.S. Air Force refurbished the planes for the agency, arming the bombers with nose cowlings covering half a dozen heavy-caliber machine guns, with an equal number emplaced in the wings. Agency officer Cecil Cartwright supervised air operations. A separate airlift run by Thorsrud and McCarthy used larger cargo planes to deliver weapons. When all had been prepared, the aircraft moved to a base at Manado.

"Rebels" were first reported as bombing Bandung in late March. But the initial CIA air strike came against Makassar on April 13. Two B-26 bombers participated and one of them crashed, killing two Polish aircrew. The plane would be replaced but not the pilots. The Poles were not used again in Project Haik. Instead the CIA brought in two more Civil Air Transport pilots, Allen L. Pope and William H. Beale, to fly the remaining B-26s. Filipinos Antonio Dedal and Rex Reyes flew the P-51s. More than a dozen raids followed. When the airmen seemed close to exhaustion, Richard Bissell actually reached down into his U-2 spyplane unit to recruit two more pilots, Carmine Vito and James Cherbonneaux. The security breach if either were captured would have been enormous, and for that very reason they were never permitted on a combat mission. Nationalist Chinese helped with air services, staying to work with PERMESTA even after the CIA left and, for a time, flying their own B-26 bomber.

In the April 28 attack on the oil port of Balikpapan, a British tanker suffered hits along with an Indonesian gunboat, a virtual replay of the CIA snafu with the freighter *Springfjord* during the Guatemala operation. Rebel troops from Manado seized Morotai and its airfield to bring more targets into range of the P-51s, as Director Dulles told the NSC on May 1. Allen ruefully admitted, in a reference to foreign ships, that the attacks had been "almost too effective in certain instances." Targets included Makassar, Morotai, Balikpapan, and Ambon. On other occasions ships were attacked at sea.

The danger of CIA exposure continued to be extremely high. Indonesian intelligence learned a fair amount and tried to discredit PERMESTA. Sukarno propaganda reported airdrops on several occasions, at least once linking the Australian air force to a flight. The government accused American and Chinese "adventurers" of working for the rebels and later announced it had sent Washington a list naming names.

In response, President Eisenhower at his news conference of April 30 commented publicly for the first time. Ike declared that the United States remained neutral and added, "Now on the other hand, every rebellion that I have ever heard of has its soldiers of fortune." Ike felt he had done so well that he called Foster to brag, the only time during the entire operation that the two discussed Project Haik on the telephone. Foster Dulles followed up the next day, saying the United States had no legal obligation to control American soldiers of fortune.

The soldier-of-fortune argument turned out to be disastrous. On May 18 a rebel B-26 bomber attacked Ambon, hitting a crowded village marketplace where people were on their way to church. This tenth raid on Ambon found ready government defenses. Damaged over its next target, an airfield, the bomber's right wing caught fire. The crew bailed out and were captured. The bombardier was Indonesian but the pilot an American, Allen Lawrence Pope. Within the day, Washington knew of Pope's detention. General Cabell told Foster Dulles the CIA had "a lot of confidence in the man." Pope had flown in Korea and helped the French in Indochina, including fifty-seven missions to Dien Bien Phu. In Saigon in December 1957 he had been recruited for the Indonesia operation. His first PERMESTA mission took place in March 1958.

Director Dulles met with his brother to discuss the setback, taking Pearre Cabell with him. Despite the danger, they argued for another strike at the same target. Sukarno and Nasution were preparing to attack the last rebel strongholds. Secretary Dulles shot back that either the rebels had to succeed in winning political support or the United States would have to consider intervention. Pinprick air raids were not about to do the job. On May 19 Foster separately discussed the Pope shoot-down in phone calls with Allen, Cabell, and his Far East assistant secretary, Walter S. Robertson. The latter remarked that perhaps the time had come to bring the Australians up to date on Project Haik.

The loss of Pope's B-26, bad as it had been, marked only part of an even worse day. There had been a second bomber on the mission, one that confronted an Indonesian interceptor and crashed on landing. That left the rebels with no effective air arm since several days earlier Sukarno's planes had successfully wiped out the rebel's C-54s and the CIA's P-51s on the ground. Allen Dulles and Pearre Cabell met Foster late that afternoon at the secretary's home. Field commanders were now pressing for attacks to blunt Nasution's buildup in eastern Indonesia. Foster insisted the Indonesians' political front had to be more coherent or, again, there must be overt intervention. Covert operations had run their course. At Quarters Eye, Director Dulles reluctantly told John Mason's deputy, James Glerum, "We're pulling the plug." Three successive headquarters cables were necessary to get the field people to understand Haik had truly reached its end.

Suddenly, on May 20, John Foster Dulles stood before the press to say the rebellion should be resolved without foreign involvement.

The next day Allen Dulles sent the secretary of state a note confirming the U.S. people had all been pulled out. Separately Allen added the text of a letter from Sumual, one of the colonels, who had seen off the agency's men, declaring his Indonesians would fight to the end, expressing the surety they would meet again and again, "anywhere this struggle is being fought and more especially when the chances of winning it are seemingly very thin." Foster acknowledged the rebel leader had lofty sentiments he put in an inspiring way.

Certain its pilots could stand up to torture, the CIA "sanitized" its B-26 bombers to prevent them being linked to U.S. inventories, and the pilots underwent strip searches to ensure they carried no incriminating evidence. The Americans did not think Sukarno could prove Allen Pope's official relationship. But the pilot had concealed papers aboard the aircraft. The Indonesians captured Pope's flight log, air force and CAT identification cards, his contract, and a post exchange privilege card for Clark Air Force Base. On May 27 the papers, and Pope, appeared before the world press at Djakarta. Both Eisenhower and Foster Dulles had been caught in a lie.

Some reports suggest that the CIA secretly assembled a team at Clark to snatch Allen Pope out of his Indonesian prison. Supposedly agents would smuggle him an escape suit and he would be lifted out by an ingenious ground-air pickup system; but the mission was never attempted.

The Pope shoot-down spelled the end for "Archipelago." An officer at FE/5 heard Allen Dulles use the phrase "we must disengage" as the director ordered a stand-down for CIA's field force. The CIA phase of PERMESTA's revolt ended with the fall of Manado to Sukarno forces on June 26. The final result strengthened his hand; in the words of the historian Brian May: "The American intervention was a gift to Sukarno." The Indonesians fought on for years in a sort of low-intensity harassment campaign. So long as the Nationalist Chinese stayed with them, they had some outside backing. After that the rebels depended on proceeds from smuggling and whatever they could raise from sympathizers. The smuggling annoyed the British, who had to live on in Malaya after the CIA went home, and whose officials were supposed to enforce the law impartially.

Haik strained relations with the British and Australian intelligence services, but no one at CIA was cashiered. The man who made the original contact with the colonels, given his choice of posts, took London. Al Ulmer headed to a prestige post as station chief in Paris. A prime undercover officer went on to Algeria. Desmond FitzGerald got the Far East Division. Even Allen Pope, tried in December 1959 and sentenced to life in an Indonesian prison, would fly again for the CIA.

The disaster did finally sap the strength of Frank Wisner. Returning from Singapore in June, at the airport Wisner encountered Des FitzGerald, who found him alternately disconnected or aggressive. Even Frank's wife Polly saw the problem, and she quietly asked FitzGerald and Gordon Gray for help. His biographer, Evan Thomas, believes Wisner succumbed to manic depression. One day in September Wisner basically went berserk. Agency employees were astonished to see him led away in a straightjacket. Following a lengthy recovery, Wisner became London chief of station. Richard Bissell succeeded him as CIA's new deputy director for operations.

The advent of Richard Bissell changed many things for the Directorate for Operations, but one stayed the same: the worries of the president's watchdogs, again expressed within a few short months. Reporting at the end of October, they made veiled reference to Frank Wisner's departure, then went on: "this unfortunate situation highlights the necessity for reviewing, and perhaps recasting, some of the virtually autonomous functions presently assigned" to the DO. The Hull Board—Jim Killian's place as chairman now taken by retired general John E. Hull—especially objected to the Directorate for Operations being solely responsible for review of its own activities. This evaluation function—which also applied to the review of covert action proposals before they went to the 5412 Group—made the CIA the arbiter of what covert operations were suitable and how to carry them out, plus the effective judge of how well they had been executed. This same ground had been plowed by David Bruce and Robert Lovett two years earlier.

General Hull and others made these points to President Eisenhower when the PBCFIA met with him on December 16, 1958. They urged Ike to take the function away from the CIA, especially for political-psychological and paramilitary operations. Project Haik served as an example of how things could go wrong. Robert Lovett, co-author of the board's previous covert action study, pressed Eisenhower to transfer review authority to the 5412 Group. Gordon Gray, recently named national security adviser, noted the group had not been very active reviewers in the past—actually it mostly had just sat back to listen when CIA appeared twice a year to run down a laundry list of covert ops. President Eisenhower insisted his 5412 Group should meet as a court, implying a capacity to review operations. He then told Gray to study the entire relationship between the CIA and the 5412 Group and report back.

What happened next had less to do with Indonesia than the president's desire to fine-tune his staff organization. Although angry about the Haik fiasco, Ike had had changes in the works for a long time. The CIA did act on some issues. Lyman Kirkpatrick and the new DDO, Bissell, instituted a broad reexamination of the DO mission. They abolished its internal inspection and review staff. In a February 16, 1959, memo Director Dulles maintained that his people took into account all available intelligence before starting a project, thus guarding against self-serving data. Dulles argued that the Hull Board had an exaggerated notion of DO autonomy. The last point is interesting in that one of its members, Jimmy Doolittle, had expressly advocated expanded operations a few years earlier. Dulles held out Bissell's survey as a response to the Hull Board, asking the president to wait and see what came of this effort.

By July Bissell had finished his inquiry, and in response Dulles made a few changes. Based on the survey's observation that actions to overthrow governments required constant liaison with the White House and State Department, Dulles relocated approval authority at a higher level in the DO. Actions might also necessitate clandestine logistics, air support, and paramilitary efforts beyond the ken of an area division, so the survey advocated the use of a "task force" for such activities. A task force already existed within the Western Hemisphere Division for the Caribbean, but this arrangement the survey viewed as woefully inadequate.

Bissell appointed an assistant DO just for the psychological warfare and paramilitary areas. The staffs for these activities were regrouped into an Operational Services unit. The work of the DO inspection staff he transferred to the CIA inspector general. Tracy Barnes returned from Germany to be the assistant DDO. John Bross, a friend of Bissell's since prep school days, became special assistant for the reorganization. Bissell also inaugurated a formal DO planning staff he put under Edward Stanulis.

The Hull Board withheld judgment. Later the CIA split up its old Near East and Africa Division, making the Africa branch a division in its own right, and the rump a reformed Near East and South Asia Division. In May 1960 the board nevertheless told President Eisenhower that ways could be found to organize the DO along more efficient lines.

Ike's watchdogs were dissatisfied with Dulles's reforms. One man with a good view of this interplay, White House national security official Karl G. Harr, later recalled, "We used to say, 'Well, Allen Dulles, he's not a good administrator or a bad administrator, he's innocent of administration.'"

Executive control had become even more important. Rather than shrinking after the Korean War, the Directorate for Operations grew. On Dulles's watch the DO added a thousand personnel slots plus an equal number of support staff in the directorate and elsewhere at CIA. The Cold War unit spent 54 percent of CIA's money. By 1958 there were also seven thousand *military* personnel *outside* the agency whose jobs centered on assisting CIA activities worldwide.

Such operations as Project Haik required close cooperation between the military and the agency, making the nature of their formal relationship an important issue. The Pentagon-CIA link ran through the 5412 Group, whose staff the CIA provided. One of the Hull Board proposals recommended enlarging the 5412 staff to include more people from State and the Pentagon.

Everything depended on the 5412 Group.

Gordon Gray made the 5412 Group his special concern. Having once hoped to become director of central intelligence, Gray had seen his chances expire with the end of Harry Truman's administration, but he had returned. He made himself indispensable to Eisenhower and impressed Ike tremendously with his calm demeanor, efficiency, and discretion. In 1953 he took the political heat for the Oppenheimer security clearance cancellation. At the Office of Defense Mobilization,

Gray had supervised the Gaither Report in 1957. When Robert Cutler, Ike's special assistant for national security affairs, left the White House to return to his Boston bank, the president turned to Gray, a Democrat, to fill this important post. Thus Gordon Gray had suddenly catapulted over the DCI. Now he helped Eisenhower run the CIA.

As the president's special assistant (a post today known as the national security adviser), Gordon Gray became Ike's voice on the 5412 Group, observing the CIA in action. Although Allen Dulles officially functioned only as adviser, Gray found that the Special Group exercised virtually no initiative, which left the field largely to the DCI. The special assistant openly raised his doubts at the December 1958 meeting.

After Christmas Eisenhower met privately with Dulles and Gray, now studying the CIA–5412 Group relationship. Ike laid great stress on managing intelligence and clandestine operations, with the Hull Board and the 5412 Group reporting directly to him. The system *had* to work because its purpose was "to obviate any tendency for Congressional groups and their staffs to get into these activities."

Allen Dulles made appropriate conciliatory comments, but Gordon Gray demurred. The semi-annual covert operations review took place on January 15, 1959. Four days later Gray sent a memo of "random thoughts" to Allen Dulles, the secretary of state, and the Pentagon representative on 5412. Gray's criticisms were not random at all. They included these issues: only four or five of the projects mentioned had been discussed by the 5412 Group within the preceding six months; a better sense of mission was necessary; "the criteria with respect to what matters shall come before the Group are ill-defined and fuzzy"; 5412 needed procedures to evaluate operations in addition to approving them; and, "I strongly believe that the President would expect some initiative" from the group.

Eisenhower agreed. In an effort to deal with these problems, on December 26, 1958, the president had asked the group to have regular weekly meetings in place of the occasional ones that had been the rule. At one of Gray's regular briefings to Eisenhower, on June 22, 1959, "the President . . . referred to one particular activity which he was disturbed about but said that he assumed it had been approved by the 5412 Group. I [Gray] reported that it had not been approved by the Group within the last eleven months."

Finally, relations between the Pentagon and CIA remained a point of controversy. The CIA actually dealt with three different parts of the Pentagon: International Security Affairs represented the secretary of defense; the Joint Chiefs of Staff provided military input, and Ike had made the chairman a 5412 Group member in 1957; direct coordination of execution, as well as military "cover" support, continued in the hands of an assistant to the secretary of defense for special operations. Since the Truman period this officer had been Marine Lt. Gen. Graves B. Erskine, in whom Secretary of Defense Neil H. McElroy had complete confidence. McElroy's successor, Thomas S. Gates, Jr., in office from December 1959 and through the remainder of Ike's presidency, had been a naval reserve officer off

Iwo Jima in 1945. Graves Erskine had commanded the Third Marine Division there. Erskine had direct access to President Eisenhower when necessary. An officer on Erskine's staff, air force Col. Fletcher Prouty, recounts that the copy of NSC-5412/2 filed with them contained the president's handwritten notation that equipment delivered to the CIA be limited to that absolutely necessary for the specific covert operation approved.

The Hull Board criticized many facets of Pentagon involvement and raised the possibility of a single focal point, preferably under the Joint Chiefs. Eisenhower retorted that this got the military into political matters. He resisted letting the 5412 Group into actual implementation. So, in effect, Ike ended by defending his existing arrangements for covert action.

President Eisenhower continued wrestling with dilemmas of control versus security and plausible deniability. Ultimately he could not solve them, though failures like those in Syria and Indonesia must have spurred him, as did political pressure for congressional oversight. But the 5412 Group was not the answer—there was no one, really, to *question* covert operations. So long as the managers believed in the efficacy of Cold War activities, approvals would be easy no matter what the policy machinery. This unquestioning belief led to the most difficult paramilitary action yet mounted by the secret warriors, a partisan war on the high plains of Asia.

10

The War for the Roof
of the World

DES FITZGERALD'S ENTHUSIASM became vital to the next big campaign. Not only did this one involve many of the same secret warriors as the failed adventure in Indonesia, the project cut across the boundaries of the CIA's own feudal baronies. The locale, Tibet, could be considered part of China or of the Indian subcontinent. In the DO's division of the world, China belonged to FitzGerald's barony, the Far East Division (FE), the subcontinent to the Near East Division (NE),* now under Jim Critchfield. A project in Tibet depended on logistics and training bases that FitzGerald ran, but the theater of activity could be reached overland, at least by the CIA, only from places where Critchfield held sway. This could have triggered tremendous infighting among the secret warriors. That it did not resulted partly from the affinity CIA barons developed for the Tibetans, partly from operational necessity, and also from new methods the CIA had put in place a couple of years earlier.

In his efforts to cope with the global presence of Soviet spies and diplomats, Allen Dulles had earlier begun superimposing missions to counter the Russians on local CIA stations the world over. Soon he also added people to cover the added workload. Thus a station working for the FE Division, or for that matter NE, would also be responding to the Soviet Russia Division. In 1956 the CIA initiated a similar system to counter China where there were populations of overseas Chinese residents, and that included India. This routinized the special arrangements previously required for FE to carry out activity in the NE area. Jim Critchfield did not mind having some of his people act primarily in support of FE, and Des FitzGerald took full advantage.

---

* This name, like our usage with the Directorate for Operations in place of that for Plans, is adopted here for consistency and to avoid confusion. As recounted in the last chapter, until 1959 Africa formed part of the assignment of this DO division and figured in its name, Near East and Africa Division, though the Indian subcontinent remained within its purview.

High in the Himalaya Mountains, Tibet had by turns been a theocracy or a Chinese vassal state, sometimes both at once. Through the first half of the twentieth century Tibet preserved its status as an independent nation largely due to its virtual inaccessibility. The Communist takeover in China included new efforts to subjugate Tibet. In this early period the CIA connection had already begun to figure—in fact the agency's first death in the line of duty, a combat death if you will, was of Douglas S. Mackiernan, Jr., an officer under State Department cover who had operated equipment to detect Soviet atomic tests in Xinjiang.

Late in 1949 Mackiernan began a journey into Tibet but perished at its border in April 1950. Given the fall of the Nationalists, U.S. desire to resist the Communists, and Tibetan appeals for aid, there is some question whether the trek originated as a sort of survey of military aid requirements. He never reached Lhasa, the Tibetan capital. A companion who survived, Frank Bessac, though apparently an agency contract officer, had no knowledge of their actual mission. Bessac eventually reached Calcutta where the CIA base chief, Frederick Latrash, debriefed him on meetings with the Tibetan religious ruler, the Dalai Lama.

Signs in Lhasa were ominous. A sacred object, a gilded wooden dragon, began to drip water from its mouth. The People's Liberation Army approached Yunnan in the summer of 1950, then Tibet. A belated effort to create an effective army with military aid from India never had time to succeed. In August the PLA Eighteenth Army defeated a tiny Tibetan force that was feudal in nature: a handful of ancient guns, the Dalai Lama's personal guard, and armed monks and farmers. Briefly fleeing, the Dalai Lama agreed to a Chinese administration.

After Tibet's occupation by the lowland or "Han" Chinese, the first question for the Americans was how to learn anything at all about that mountain land. India provided some information at first, but with the advent of John Foster Dulles the Indians became less and less cooperative.

Nestled in the foothills of the Indian Himalayas lies the village of Kalimpong. A dot on a map within the triangle formed by the junction of the borders of Nepal, Sikkim, and Bhutan, Kalimpong remains virtually unknown to outsiders. Tourists coming to see the mountains visit the Nepalese capital Katmandu. If they venture near Kalimpong it is usually to see another Indian town, the tea center Darjeeling. Typically those who do reach the area are more interested in Tibet, for the village is a main point on the trail to Lhasa. After the Chinese takeover of Tibet, the CIA's interest was rather more direct: as early as 1951 Latrash's successor in Calcutta, Robert Linn, appeared in Kalimpong seeking to speak with Tibetans.

In 1953 Chinese road surveyors in the province of Kham on the eastern Tibetan plateau began talking of reform. The Tibetan governor, Rapgya Pangdatsang, could find no support in Lhasa, however. The Dalai Lama wished to avoid confrontation. A year later, when the Chinese began establishing cooperative farms, fighting began with the Khampa, fierce and skillful horsemen who became very effective partisans.

In the spring of 1955, pretending to be a tourist, an American came to Kalimpong. Not what he seemed, he was an unnamed official of an unnamed U.S. agency.

Perhaps Kalimpong was not what it seemed either. The village had become a focus of dispute between India and China. Beijing complained that Kalimpong served as a base for resistance to Communist rule in Tibet. Indian Prime Minister Jawaharlal Nehru told his parliament as early as September 1953 that "a nest of spies" had taken root there. Agents came from every country, said the prime minister. "Sometimes I begin to doubt whether the greater part of the population of Kalimpong does not consist of foreign spies."

The American of 1955 could have been a diplomat or a spy. He is not further identified by the man who tells the story, George N. Patterson, a Scottish missionary who worked in eastern Tibet, spoke the language, wrote several books about the country, and resided in Kalimpong. One of a small group of Westerners who knew anything about Tibet, Patterson was enchanted with the country and was well known in Tibetan political circles, including those of the Dalai Lama. As Patterson tells it, the American came to him. Most probably a spy—John Turner, the CIA's latest man in Calcutta, would have been the likely candidate. Turner had actually grown up in Darjeeling. He was quite familiar with the setup. Patterson acted as translator in several meetings over four days. This was not the first spy to try to reach the Tibetans through Patterson. The preceding year an Indian intelligence officer had appeared, asking for contacts willing to discuss anti-Chinese resistance.

The Tibetan Rapgya Pandatsang, a moderate politician, had outlined his difficulties for Indian officials much as he now did for the CIA. The American, sympathetic, stressed problems of supplying equipment over the Himalayas, and said Indian cooperation would be essential. According to Patterson, the American went on to draw up a ten-year assistance program designed to overthrow the Chinese in Tibet after the first five. The American said a special U.S. agent would be sent who had no contact with the embassy but would handle Tibetan affairs.

Tibet became one more situation where the secret warriors used local resistance movements to American advantage. This time there could be no question of the United States supporting democracy—Tibet had been a semi-feudal theocracy for centuries. Tibetans were quite happy with the Dalai Lama. The most that could be claimed for the U.S. action would be that it supported self-determination for Tibetans. Traditionally conservative, the Tibetans were both politically and culturally distinct from the Han Chinese, of whom Communists were merely the latest political shading.

The tragedy for Tibetan independence lay in the relative strengths of the Chinese Communists and Nationalists. Whereas Jiang Jieshi lacked the strength to be more than first among warlord equals, Mao Zedong's movement, unified and determined to control every corner of China, triumphed. The new mandarins had a program, tremendous energy, and the People's Liberation Army. There was ultimately no way to keep the lowlanders out of Tibet. And the Han had no use for a barter economy. Once the Han arrived, moreover, primitive Tibetans faced an enemy with modern implements of war.

Tibet was scarcely prepared for modernization. The "roof of the world," a land of monasteries—more than three thousand of them—nomads, and small towns, had long been ruled by a hierarchy of monks advised by a small commercial elite. Nothing less than the godhead, the incarnation of Buddha, chosen as a child by wise monks after tests, signs, and meditation, the Dalai Lama sat at the top. In this land, policy followed portent.

Communist rule proved wrenching. Friction between the Chinese Communists and the Tibetan theocracy developed rapidly. The Chinese soon alienated Tibetans by establishing work "norms"; by attempts to place portions of Tibet within other provinces; and by their forcible mustering of several thousand Tibetan children for education in the lowlands as party cadres. Tibetan resistance was inevitable.

A major Chinese difficulty in Tibet was an utter lack of infrastructure. There were no railroads, roads, or even airfields, a condition that precluded rapid economic development and also prohibited military operations using modern equipment. The Chinese set out to remedy this with massive construction efforts—roads to Lhasa across the ancient Tibetan provinces of Amdo and Kham. These represented tremendous engineering feats; the Kham road, for example, crossed fourteen mountain ranges and seven rivers, including the headwaters of the Mekong and Yangtze, at an average altitude of thirteen thousand feet. When the road reached Lhasa in 1954, the price of tea declined 30 percent while a box of matches, previously dear enough to command a whole sheep, fell to just two pounds of raw wool. Such effects were unwanted changes to Tibetans.

Early in 1955 the Chinese arrested Lobsang Tsewong, an Amdo leader who spoke against the new inequities. When a unit of 200 PLA troops arrived to restore order in mountainous Golok, tribesmen disarmed them, cut off their noses, then sent them back as a warning. The Goloks joined forces with Dorji Pasang, a chieftain of more than 100,000 families, already fighting for several years. The PLA sent large detachments to eastern Tibet. One force of several regiments met the united Amdo rebels. Routed, the Chinese lost 7,000 or 8,000 troops.

Even today it is not yet possible to provide a detailed analysis of the Washington decision-making on Tibet. The records remain security-classified. Tibet remains "buried in the lore of the CIA as one of those successes that are not talked about," according to Fletcher Prouty, who managed secret air missions for General Erskine's Office of Special Operations. Evidence indicates a steady growth in CIA interest from the time of the Kalimpong meetings recounted by George Patterson. Former CIA officers recall that Sam Halpern, a Far East Division officer and executive assistant to the division chief, believed the impetus for the operation, quickly dubbed Project ST/Circus, came most strongly from John Foster Dulles, seconded by his undersecretary, Herbert Hoover, Jr. Halpern cites the intent as harassment of the Chinese Communists, not support for Tibetan independence. My own conversations with Halpern confirm this view.

Thomas Parrott, who worked directly for the 5412 Group as its CIA-provided staff officer, adds that State merely recorded its nonopposition to the operation, whereupon Allen Dulles insisted upon an affirmative endorsement. That followed.

In late 1956 the chief of FE/2, the China Branch of the Far East Division, designated a full-time DO desk officer for Tibet for the first time. That man, John Reagan, had worked in Japan with FitzGerald on China actions and before that had been a paramilitary veteran of Korea. Not long afterward the wealthy Tibetan trader and now resistance leader, Gompo Tashi, renewed contacts with the Americans and selected Tibetans for CIA training outside their country. The Tibetans joined up in February 1957.

Headquarters emphasis on Tibet shifted slightly when John L. Hart took over FE/2. But it was Hart who planned for active operations. The Project Circus task force formed in July under Frank Holober, a key operative on Taiwan during projects against mainland China. Holober wrote the proposal the 5412 Group considered when starting the Tibetan project. The first cost estimate came to a mere $500,000 to set up a Tibetan unit. Approval by the 5412 Group still cannot be pinpointed. The outcome, however, can. Rebel leaders were told that the United States was considering a move in Tibet, but the decision depended upon what the CIA learned from initial scouts. Frank Wisner insisted that the first agents confine themselves to gathering intelligence. On August 21 a CIA U-2 spyplane took photos of Tibet for the first time.

Continued reluctance to reveal CIA operations in Tibet undoubtedly relates to the later improvement of U.S. relations with the People's Republic. Today it is thought indelicate to draw attention to an effort to stir up trouble for that nation. Refusal to open the record on Tibet is ironic given the many failures that pepper CIA's paramilitary record, since the war for "the roof of the world" was among the more profitable operations, at least in intelligence terms. Despite CIA reticence, a fair description of the dimensions of the Tibet operation is possible.

In 1956 the American Society for a Free Asia, the ostensibly private lobby group that, like its European counterpart, had been set up with CIA help, sponsored a U.S. lecture tour by Thubten Norbu, an ex-abbot and the Dalai Lama's eldest brother. Norbu made more visits over the next few years to speak of the rebellion. That February simultaneous attacks occurred at several points in Tibet so widely separated that coordination seems to have been necessary. Chinese propaganda charges of American meddling in Tibet began around this time, and some observers put the initial U.S. air deliveries to this period—but as noted, accounts of CIA veterans date the inception later. Frank Holober recalls the agency as already having begun annual subsidies of $180,000 to Gyalo Thondup, but the money went for political, not paramilitary, action. At the time the Dalai Lama remained in India, still being wooed by Chinese officials to induce him to return to Lhasa. That return marked the occasion for the kickoff of Project Circus.

At Kalimpong a number of young Tibetans were agitating for national resistance. John Hoskins came to the village and took the men Gompo Tashi had selected, eight, to be smuggled out through East Pakistan (now Bangladesh). John Reagan came to India to supervise. The Tibetans went by unmarked plane through Taiwan to Saipan. There they underwent a full round of CIA training. Roger McCarthy, one of the Saipan instructors, recalls that the CIA team had precious little time to prepare for the Tibetan recruits. Eli Popovich found the Tibetans a challenge—tough and strong, but an odd mixture of warrior and mystic. The Dalai Lama's brother Norbu attended part of this training and impressed the agency's Harry Mustakos with his concern for the lives of ants in a bathroom they were cleaning. The same Tibetans who agonized over ants would be fierce fighters and demand more sophisticated weaponry from the CIA. They won the hearts of agency people with their beguiling combination of simplicity, determination, and precision.

A succession of Tibetan trainees followed the first group. Recruits often took a month to negotiate the trails, either to Kalimpong or to Assam and thence through India. The Pangda brothers had made a fortune using the trails during World War II, smuggling arms to Jiang. They had a well-established network, including a warehouse at Kalimpong, suddenly reopened. Recruits traveled to Calcutta by train, where the link was a contact address. CAT planes flew to Taiwan with refueling stops at Bangkok and Hong Kong. The planes' blinds remained drawn.

In camp, the recruits from Kham and Amdo were shown a new world of weapons and devices unknown in Tibet. The tribesmen were highly proficient soldiers, their cavalry universally feared by the PLA. Yet the Tibetan language had no word for "cavalry." Skilled horsemen, the Tibetans had thirty different words for parts of a horse's harness but none for the harness as a whole. The language had different words for specific species but none for "tree"; there were scores of terms for depths of trance or meditation but none for "sleep." The new military objects Tibetans encountered led to the words "skyboat" for airplane and "skycloth" for parachute.

Some recruits transcended their lack of experience with Western technology to become radio specialists. Men who hardly knew what electricity was learned to beam broadcasts, send Morse code, and encrypt messages. Others became weapons experts or air-ground coordinators who could mark drop zones for supply missions. The recruits were eventually divided into three groups: one to retrace its steps and become unit leaders with the partisans; one to remain as instructors and translators; and one selected for special missions and given further training. From early 1959 the CIA moved its program to the United States, to a newly opened facility at Camp Hale, near Leadville, Colorado.

The Tibet operation occurred within the larger framework of the secret war against China. In this conflict Taipei was an important CIA station with a broad range of activities, its centrality reemphasized after the Taiwan Straits crises of 1954–1955 and 1958. Jiang Jieshi still dreamed of returning to the mainland. The Nationalists infiltrated agents at a rate of one or two a month throughout the period. The CIA tried to keep Project Circus separate from its other China operations because Jiang also coveted Tibet. Thus, though the CIA had well-trained

Nationalist aircrews, it could not touch them for Tibet airdrops. When a fresh CIA project was proposed to initiate resistance in Chinese provinces that might coordinate with the Tibetans, the initiative had to be rejected due to the enmity between Tibetans and Han Chinese.

During the 1958 crisis, Rear Adm. Roland N. Smoot, commander of the U.S. military mission on Taiwan, observed the Nationalist training of special forces, some five thousand of them. Chiang Ching-kuo described an ambitious plan to land the troops along the mainland coast. While the Americans refused to help this effort, they did support boat or midget submarine landings of commando parties of a dozen to twenty men. Boat groups usually left from Quemoy, the submarines from Taiwan.

The CIA station chief in Taiwan from early 1958 to June 1962, Ray Cline, became a close personal friend of Chiang Ching-kuo. They talked dozens of times about Nationalist units and agents on the mainland—about two hundred in all during these years. But Ralph McGehee, an officer in Cline's station, has no recollection of a single exchange regarding Tibet operations. The accomplishments of agents, largely replaced in 1960 with overhead reconnaissance, paled next to the product of Nationalist pilots trained to fly U-2s under the military aid program. The photographic evidence came back to the CIA for interpretation. The station's Tibetan involvement remained restricted to training even though that state was considered part of China. The Tibetan project went forward under the direct control of the CIA station in India.

Although in its early years the rebellion remained confined to eastern Tibet, Chinese actions virtually ensured its spread. The reduction of the Litang monastery became a key provocation. In late February 1956, in the third week of Tibetan New Year celebrations, the PLA suddenly laid siege to the monastery. Litang—crowded with house monks, a couple thousand more in for the festivities, plus merchants and townspeople, about eight thousand people in all—put up stiff resistance. The Chinese besieged the place for sixty-four days, culminating in a strike by jet bombers, the first in the Tibetan war. The next day the PLA occupied Litang. Many were butchered. A few thousand escaped. Litang began a Chinese scorched-earth strategy designed to break the theocracy. Instead Tibetans united to resist them.

For the Chinese Communists, the Tibet war was a struggle for control of roads. The roads were the substance as well as the symbol of Mao's arrival. Throughout the provinces, posts defended the roads at twenty-mile intervals. Just manning these required forty thousand PLA troops plus half that number of militia. The roads determined the capabilities of the PLA. They quickly became the main target for the *ten dzong ma mi*, Tibet's "soldiers of the fortress of the faith." Raids increased in scale. Estimates in 1957 credited the main Tibetan force with eighty thousand partisans, with another ten thousand bandits or local tribesmen also arrayed against the Chinese.

One of Chou Enlai's promises to the Dalai Lama had been a withdrawal. A few party cadres pulled out, but many more Han specialists and farmers came to Tibet in a sort of colonization program. The PLA removed most soldiers from central Tibet, but instead of transporting them to China proper, the army reinforced in Kham and Amdo, to a level of more than 100,000. Soon the PLA had fourteen divisions fighting the partisans. The Chinese strengthened their supply system in 1957 by opening a major truck maintenance shop in Lhasa.

Not even these measures stemmed partisan success, especially by the Khampa, who by 1958 claimed to have ejected the Han from all of southeastern Tibet. A partisan leader visiting Kalimpong claimed forty thousand PLA soldiers killed in battle. After September 1957 CIA radio teams provided direct communication. In central Tibet a partisan unit under Amdo Leshe, recipient of some of the earliest American airdrops, fought in the Lhoka district, guarding the pack trail down to Kalimpong, upon which the rebels depended for the bulk of their ammunition. Leshe had radio contact with Taiwan. The CIA-trained Tibetans were a couple of self-contained teams, one to link with Gompo Tashi, the other to a resistance area.

Warfare brought cleavages to Tibetan society. Nonviolent Buddhist Tibetans had a moral problem in choosing war against the Han. The PLA helped resolve these qualms by bombing monasteries, beginning with Litang. Ultimately even the monks took sides. The Panchen Lama, Tibet's second most important religious leader, cast his lot with the Chinese. But most lamas took the rebel side. This was the case at the Drepung monastery, one of Tibet's largest, which sheltered survivors after the Litang siege. At the Drepung, a monk remembers, "I saw the [rebel] weapons, guns and rifles, come in by night. Night after night."

At first the weapons were not from the CIA. Project Circus air operations, code name Barnum, initially ran on a shoestring, planned by "Gar" Thorsrud of FE Division air branch. The landing of the two agents Athar and Lhotse, with the first air mission on October 20, 1957, required a modified B-17 aircraft flown from Taiwan. Agency officer Roger McCarthy went along to mind them. Thorsrud, as he would also do in Project Haik, used expatriate Polish fliers brought out from Wiesbaden. A month later the CIA dropped three more agents into Tibet.

These ad hoc procedures were insufficient for the long haul. The air force had abolished its ARC wings in 1956, with leftovers of the unit that had been at Clark airbase moved to Okinawa, where it became the innocuously titled 322nd Troop Carrier Squadron Medium (Special). This unit used a mix of aircraft including B-29s. Its super-spooky Detachment 1, which the CIA favored and financed, flew a rebuilt C-118 plus a couple of C-54s. Reconstruction using parts from many aircraft made them untraceable, and they were modified for long distance, high-altitude flight. The value of air force cooperation with the CIA is shown by the January 1958 agency commendation awarded to Col. Fletcher Prouty, air deputy at the Pentagon's Office of Special Operations. For the first Tibet supply drop in July 1958, the agency replaced an air force crew with one from CAT. In a revealing cultural change once the flights began, clothing made of parachute material began to supplement scarce cotton in Tibet.

Getting those cases of weapons into the Himalayas became easier with developments in aircraft technology. At the time of the Hungarian crisis President Eisenhower thought that nation was as inaccessible as Tibet. But in December 1956 the C-130 Hercules, produced by Lockheed, began flying for the U.S. Air Force, and more than anything else it made possible the expansion of the secret war. This remarkable airplane could make the extended flights (more than 2,400 miles from Bangkok) and still carry significant loads—up to 22 tons for a late-model C-130E, almost five times the payload of the C-118.

Civil Air Transport did not own any of these aircraft and leased none before its March 1959 transformation into Air America. Its two hundred missions over the Chinese mainland before 1961 include ST/Barnum flights, but with B-17, C-54, or C-118 aircraft until late in the game. Such C-130s as flew in the Far East belonged to the air force, in fact to the spooky 322nd Squadron. General Erskine controlled them from the Pentagon. Deputy director Cabell of the CIA approached air force General Curtis LeMay to secure use of the aircraft, then borrowed them from Erskine for missions. More than a year passed in making the necessary preparations.

Highly qualified crews were vital on Tibet flights. These had to be made at low altitude, ascending the Himalayas and then finding remote drop zones without benefit of radio navigation beacons, unreliable at these distances. Navigators used star fixes instead. Atmospheric conditions made late fall months optimal. Range considerations dictated routes entering China from Vietnam, or else staging through airfields in Thailand or East Pakistan. Emergency landings in India were possible but not to be counted on. A typical flight would carry palletized cargo for a drop and perhaps some Tibetans to be parachuted. Crews comprised the pilot, usually two copilots, a pair of navigators, a crew chief, and a CIA control party of four. At least a dozen former forest firefighters, "smoke jumpers" in the trade, joined the agency for the operation. Many called themselves the "Missoula Mafia," for their Montana origins. Project Barnum included forty-four of these highly dangerous missions.

The CIA's ignominious failure in Indonesia became a perverse boon to the Tibet secret war. Stocks of weapons and equipment the agency had assembled were rendered superfluous—but became available to the Tibetan resistance, just now becoming a unified national movement. Their battle flag, first raised on June 16, 1958, appeared before a portrait of the Dalai Lama. The force would be known as the *Tensung Tangla Magar*, the National Volunteer Defense Army (NVDA). Its creation ushered in the most intense phase of the Tibetan war. Just a few weeks later Frank Holober traveled to India to meet secretly with the Tibetan agent Athar. The Khampa and the CIA were about to go for broke.

Although the NVDA was a unified resistance army, opposition to the Han had yet to become universal. The fighters were still drawn mostly from Kham and Amdo. Resistance in central Tibet was largely held in check by one man—the Dalai Lama. The new phase of the secret war began with a struggle for the heart of that man.

Tenzin Gyatso, the fourteenth Dalai Lama, embodied the spirit and wisdom of his people. According to tradition the Dalai Lama, as well as his colleague the Panchen Lama, are venerated as incarnations of the founder of lamaism in Tibet (in about 1400 C.E.).

Tenzin Gyatso tried not to take sides. He worked with the Chinese to the extent necessary but several times refused to call out the Tibetan army to help the PLA. On the other hand the Dalai Lama denounced resistance, advising Tibetans not to get involved. Gyatso permitted the dismissal of his own cabinet in favor of officials more acceptable to the Han. The NVDA leadership knew the Dalai Lama must be enlisted for any effective national resistance, and by early 1959, many lamas also believed him a virtual prisoner in Lhasa. Tibetans wanted to save the Dalai Lama.

Late in 1958 the NVDA began an offensive into central Tibet. Eschewing their usual marauding tactics, the partisans attacked Han garrisons. By December PLA posts within twenty-five miles of Lhasa were being raided. In late January or early February 1959 the PLA garrison at Tsetang, thirty miles from Lhasa, fell to the Tibetans. For the first time the NVDA had a presence close to the capital. The Chinese sought to make the Dalai Lama a hostage. They invited the Tibetan leader to a "dramatic presentation" at the compound of the PLA Military Area Command, headed by Gen. Tan Kuan-san. Senior advisers to the Dalai Lama, some secretly supporting the NVDA, interpreted this as a device to capture the political-religious leader. They urged him not to attend.

The Dalai Lama made excuses not to go to the Chinese compound—then a crowd surrounded the Norbulinka palace where he was then staying. On March 10, 1959, thirty thousand Tibetans demonstrated, shouting that their religious leader must be protected. One Chinese collaborator in the street died, stoned to death. Over the following days tension mounted with mass demonstrations. The PLA garrison of perhaps forty thousand troops strengthened its fortifications around Lhasa. Tenzin Gyatso later wrote, "I felt as if I were standing between two volcanoes, each likely to erupt at any moment."

On March 15 Chinese troops appeared outside the Dalai Lama's abode. His guards had to be kept from shooting. On the 17th, as the Tibetan leader met with his cabinet, two mortar shells exploded nearby. That fateful Tuesday the Dalai Lama fled. That night, in three groups, the leader, his immediate family, and senior advisers escaped. Tenzin Gyatso left disguised as a common soldier of the guard. In order to avoid attracting attention the group carried nothing with them. Over subsequent days between eight thousand and thirteen thousand citizens left Lhasa. On March 20 General Tan ordered open hostilities, stimulating the exodus. Only then did the Chinese command realize that the Dalai Lama had gone.

The French explorer and scholar Michel Peissel describes these events as "one of the strangest and most ill-understood coups of recent times." Under its top leader, Gen. Gompo Tashi Andrugtsang, the NVDA offensive drove within miles of the capital, timed precisely to place a protective force near Lhasa just as the Dalai Lama left. Partisan units formed a rear guard behind the party throughout its trek to the Indian border region and also created a diversion northeast of Lhasa, confusing PLA searchers.

On November 1, 1958, Gordon Gray sent a note to NSC executive secretary James Lay. It read, "If, as a result of the new social experiment in Communist China, there should be some sort of revolt, is our policy clear as to what course of action we would follow?"

In fact Washington had anticipated only limited potential from the Tibetan rebellion, as indeed from any operations against the People's Republic of China. That spring the administration pointedly rejected a Nationalist Chinese proposal for a paramilitary effort parallel to Project Circus. A secret survey of the possibilities for uprisings done for Eisenhower in the summer of 1959 by Assistant Secretary of State for Far Eastern Affairs J. Graham Parsons made this clear. Regarding Tibet the survey predicted that

> if the Tibetans are able to maintain their resistance movement in the face of large scale Chinese Communist suppression efforts, other border area minorities might be emboldened to carry out dissident activities. However, the Chinese Communists probably have the capability of preventing prolonged rebellion, except in the most isolated areas, and of containing it.

At the same time peasant uprisings in central China were deemed unlikely. Further, the survey judged the Nationalists greatly exaggerated their ability to intervene on the mainland, though the State Department believed it "by no means suicidal" of Jiang Jieshi to contemplate such raids.

Despite limited possibilities, the 5412 Group considered Gordon Gray's question in secret deliberations. Classified memoranda from Allen Dulles to President Eisenhower dated January 22 and March 3, 1959, concerned Tibet. The president's staff secretary reported from CIA and State intelligence reports that "the Tibetan uprisings apparently have resulted in a considerable loss of prestige for Communist China in India."

India's opinion was crucial since Nehru had turned aside the Dalai Lama's request for political asylum three years earlier. In July 1958 the Chinese again made issue with the Indians over the use of Kalimpong as a center of resistance. But by then Nehru too had chosen sides, and he rejected the Chinese charge. In New Delhi parliamentary debates ignited by the Dalai Lama's journey, the prime minister went out of his way to defend Tibetans living at Kalimpong, denying the village was a "command center" of the NVDA effort.

One exchange in a debate on April 2, 1959, is especially revealing. After Nehru talked about Kalimpong, the member Nath Pai asked, "What is the Home Ministry doing about it? It seems to be absolutely ineffective."

Nehru replied, "The Home Ministry or the External Affairs Ministry are not at all worried about the situation."

Member Hem Barua then asked incredulously, "They allow the spies to [conduct] espionage?"

"Absolutely yes," said Nehru.

In another debate Nehru explained that India's first news of the events at Lhasa had been a message from the consul general on March 10, which had arrived the next day. But the New Delhi journal *Statesman* reported in its issue of March 2, before anything had happened in Lhasa, that there would be a coup and that the Dalai Lama would flee that city on March 17.

American ambassador Ellsworth Bunker kept Washington apprised, but the best information came from the CIA. During this period Gen. Charles Cabell or Desmond FitzGerald was on the phone with Gordon Gray almost daily. On March 17 the president learned the Chinese had ordered an all-out attack and that the Khampa had captured a sizable PLA outpost a week earlier. On March 23 Dulles informed Eisenhower that the Dalai Lama had left Lhasa on the 17th, and the CIA compared his travel route to its appreciation of the centers of rebel armed strength.

The CIA furnished an American-trained Tibetan radio operator with an agency RS-1 radio to the Dalai Lama's party—or, more precisely, when agent Athar Norbu learned the Dalai Lama was on the move, he left NVDA headquarters with a small guard force, joining the ruler's group. Athar set up repeated airdrops of supplies (crucial since the Dalai Lama had left Lhasa with nothing), enabled the party to communicate with nearby NVDA units (CIA officer John Knaus maintains the Tibetan agents were in communication *only* with CIA headquarters), and provided daily reports to the CIA beginning March 25. Branch chief John Hart tracked developments at headquarters, helpful since the Circus task force had just been taken over by Roger McCarthy, who had still to get up to speed.

The Dalai Lama wrinkled his nose at the heavily armed tribesmen surrounding him. Armaments were a distasteful necessity. He especially frowned at one guerrilla, his own cook, who carried a bazooka and enthusiastically sought out a target, at one point loosing several shells at a fancied Chinese military position. Tibet's leader watched his cook reload, so awkwardly the man surely would have been killed in a real fight. As the party neared India, the CIA radio operators passed on the Dalai Lama's request for asylum. The message reached Washington in the dead of night on a Saturday, March 28. FitzGerald immediately ordered it forwarded to New Delhi.

Also along for the Dalai Lama's ride were Tibetan filmmakers whose material the CIA later assembled into a motion picture, including footage of airdrops from C-130s, supply containers falling in the snow, scenes of the escape and the trek, and other suitable footage. Fletcher Prouty thought the movie an impressive piece of CIA propaganda.

On April 1, just as the Dalai Lama's party entered India, Eisenhower in Washington learned, "We have informed Embassy New Delhi we think the US should take no action with respect to Tibetan refugees which would diminish the effect the revolt appears to be having in India."

A message from the Tibetans, received on April 2, contained an important plea: "You must help us as soon as possible and send us weapons for 30,000 men by airplane." The message sparked action in Washington. The National Security Council, which had not discussed Tibet since June 20, 1957, suddenly met on the subject in March, twice in April, and again in June 1959. A thirteen-page classified CIA report, a letter from Allen Dulles to the president, and a cable reporting the Dalai Lama's views to the White House appeared before the NSC meeting on April 23. Dulles's letter concerned the Dalai Lama's determination to resist the Chinese. Meanwhile, on April 21, field commander Gompo Tashi ordered the NVDA to abandon positions in the Lhoka district defended to permit the Dalai Lama's escape.

One of the CIA's few admissions on covert operations before a congressional committee came during this period, when Director Dulles could contribute to the propaganda offensive on Tibet. Appearing at a closed session of the Senate Foreign Relations Committee in late April, Dulles spoke of the Dalai Lama's escape, in the course of that discussion revealing that the CIA had known of his progress from its communicators and had forwarded his request for asylum to Nehru. The CIA director also averred that the agency remained in close contact with the Dalai Lama's two brothers. Dulles admitted the Chinese were attacking and were victorious, and he compared the Tibetan people to the Hungarians of 1956.

Tibetan sources maintain that the Eisenhower administration made important decisions in May 1959. This correlates with available records. Gordon Gray showed Ike a CIA proposal to move Project Circus to a higher intensity even before the Dalai Lama left his country. On April 25 White House aide Andrew Goodpaster asked Director Dulles for data the president could examine at leisure. The same day Dulles got the CIA to revise the paper on Tibetan operations he had sent over a couple of days earlier. The paper—the guts of which remain classified—concludes by observing that the Tibetan resistance, heavily engaged, had little food or ammunition left. The CIA director briefed the NSC a few days after.

The Joint Chiefs of Staff weighed in when officials met on May 8 to work out details of the stepped-up Tibet program. The Chiefs too wanted "affirmative and positive action in support of the Tibetan people." Aid to refugees went on the agenda. Now, however, the State Department began dragging its feet, warning of adverse consequences if America established herself as protector of the Dalai Lama. Even refugee assistance, the diplomats felt, could be given only if it remained covert. On June 4, when the NSC again pored over the dilemmas of Tibet, the split between the military and diplomats came into the open. By then intense Chinese attacks south of Lhasa were pushing Gompo Tashi's troops back.

Allen Dulles reported on May 7 that arms shipments were being prepared, but their dispatch was hindered by a dearth of data on the locations of Tibetan units. Suddenly, on May 12 and 14, U-2 missions flew over the country, the first since the early planning for Project Circus. The vast majority of the CIA supply flights to Tibet took place over a ten-month period beginning in May 1959, though the agency never succeeded in making all the missions it programmed. Bissell's U-2s took more pictures on September 3, 4, and 9. Ten days later a C-118 inserted an agent team that found the Chinese in complete control of their area and had to trek down to India. Three more teams followed and successfully met up with the NVDA. Supply drops by C-118 in October and November deposited hundreds of rifles plus ammunition and heavy weapons. Another U-2 mission took place in November. The C-130 flights began in December, instantly doubling weapons deliveries and increasing ammunition supplies manyfold. Air force Maj. Harry C. Aderholt devised techniques to increase C-130 payloads by almost half a dozen tons, enriching supply loads even more. The high point occurred in early January 1960 when, on two different nights, no fewer than seven American planes attempted to deliver their loads. Gompo Tashi harnessed hundreds of mules to carry away the supplies. In all the United States parachuted four hundred tons of equipment to the Tibetans.

Expansion of the CIA program brought the training of Tibetans to the United States. Five groups totaling nearly seven hundred trainees were planned (though not achieved). Tibetans flew into Peterson Field, six miles east of Colorado Springs, and moved by buses with blacked-out windows to a site at Camp Hale, situated at an altitude above ten thousand feet, about the closest the CIA could come to the rarefied air of Tibet. Partisans arrived on Globemaster transports. They were never told they were in the United States, though at least one group, taken to the CIA's training facility The Farm, and to Quantico for classroom work, were perfectly aware of where they were.

Used in World War II to train the Ninety-ninth Ski Battalion, which furnished some personnel the OSS then sent to Norway, as well as mountain troops who served in Italy and Alaska, Camp Hale had been dismantled by the few hundred German prisoners also kept there. What was left the army used for winter maneuvers until 1956. It seemed an ideal location for a CIA facility. Tom Fosmire became top trainer, seconded by a staff of about a dozen who included several more veterans of the Indonesian adventure and at least one Balt. Tony Poe, soon to become notorious in Laos, taught weapons. John Knaus, an operational analyst for the DO, had spent several years detached to the United States Information Agency (another example of the connections between CIA's black and USIA's grey propaganda). He would later take over the Project Circus task force.

To discourage curiosity a cover story that unspecified "atomic tests" (though not explosions) would be conducted at the reopened base was provided to the *Denver Post* and appeared on July 16, 1959. Local utility companies were asked to give a day's notice before sending linemen to service poles in the vicinity. Finally, guards were ordered to shoot to kill if they encountered unauthorized persons.

While training proceeded, the Dalai Lama took his cause to the United Nations, where no Tibetan discussion had occurred in nine years. Ireland and Malaya offered a resolution condemning China for genocide. Despite its secret paramilitary support for the Tibetans, the United States wished to stay in the background. Secretary of State Christian Herter asked UN Ambassador Henry Cabot Lodge to lay low. Meeting with the Dalai Lama in India, diplomat Winthrop Brown as much as told him that Washington preferred he not bring up the sovereignty issue in any UN debate but rather concentrate on China's human rights record. Washington did not permit the Dalai Lama to enter the country.

The rate at which the diplomatic initiative gained momentum surprised the State Department. Herter feared the UN resolution on genocide would fail and that the defeat would be a serious setback. He opposed "a resolution recognizing [Tibet's] independence or sovereignty," instead suggesting "a slap on the wrist" for the Chinese. Secretary Herter told Lodge he had informed a British diplomat that "all we wanted to do was to have this thing come in as mild a resolution as possible." American interests were not identical to those of the Tibetans. Washington's espousal of self-determination around the globe did not extend to the CIA's allies in its anti-Chinese secret war.

The UN General Assembly passed a resolution in October 1959 expressing concern that human rights were being suppressed in Tibet. The vote was 45 to 9, with 26 abstentions, among them the British. The Soviet bloc voted solidly against the resolution. There was not a word about independence or sovereignty, the primary aims of the Tibetans.

Fighting continued unabated inside Tibet. In Lhasa alone during 1959, according to PLA documents, 87,000 people died. That year, the Tibetan year of the Earth Pig, the PLA tried once and for all to cut the trails into Tibet from Kalimpong. The Chinese began a two-and-a-half-year pacification effort. Toward the end of 1959 a few hundred Soviet advisers were reported in Tibet for the first time.

Dwight Eisenhower visited India late in 1959 but found it inexpedient to meet the Dalai Lama. Before the trip C. D. Jackson, a friend of Allen Dulles as well as Ike, sought to intervene after speaking to a case officer, but the CIA director dissuaded him. Des FitzGerald bore the brunt of Dulles's anger at what he fancied was unauthorized action by some agency cowboy. A few Khampa actually went to New Delhi hoping to deliver a letter to Eisenhower, but all requests were rebuffed. Ike, however, did accept certain gifts sent through CIA channels by Tibetan leader Gompo Tashi: a Khampa knife, charm box, articles of clothing. Tashi added a letter pleading for help, ending on this note:

> We Tibetans have determined to fight to the last against the Chinese Communists with full weapons of modern warfare as there is no alternative left to us except to fight. We see no other Powers other than the United States which is [sic] capable of giving us help in every respects [sic] to free Tibet from the domination of Red China. The situation has become very serious like a patient about to die. Under the circumstances as stated above, with a heavy heart, we appeal to your Excellency to impart necessary instructions about the best possible course for us to follow.

Americans acknowledged the gifts orally, but because Tashi had not used "channels considered by the Embassy to give him official status," no other reply was deemed necessary. Eisenhower preserved his deniability. The following year Washington again discouraged the Dalai Lama's request to come to America.

Secret plans proceeded despite this refusal to associate with the Tibetans. Before his NSC meeting on February 4, 1960, the president met with a group including Gordon Gray, Herter, Allen Dulles, Cabell, and Desmond FitzGerald. Director Dulles described recent supply deliveries but also Chinese success in finding the better-armed, less mobile rebels. Dulles asked Eisenhower to approve continuation of Circus. Ike wondered if Tibetan resistance simply increased repression. Des FitzGerald countered that no brutality could be greater than what the Han were already doing. Secretary of State Herter added that the project certainly harassed Beijing. Ike okayed another push.

But Beijing pushed back. Already on the offensive, Chinese troops launched new attacks within weeks of Eisenhower's decision. The heavier weapons the CIA had supplied the Tibetans paradoxically made them somewhat less mobile, and the Chinese had more of the territory already under control. Tibetan bands were caught in several places. In one fight the PLA claimed to have killed eight hundred of an NVDA force of several thousand. By late spring two CIA teams with the partisans had to flee to India, and four CIA radio teams were wiped out. Only six of almost twenty CIA-trained agents survived. Just then another event in the intelligence world brought a complete halt to U.S. air support. On May 1, 1960, the Russians shot down a CIA U-2 plane deep inside the Soviet Union. President Eisenhower ordered a halt to all intrusions into Communist airspace. That included the C-130 flights into Tibet.

One estimate is that the CIA equipped fourteen thousand "soldiers of the fortress of the faith," almost all the active male population still fighting in the high Himalayas. Supplying the NVDA without aircraft seemed impossible, but the agency attacked the task efficiently. The project needed new tactics, proposed by Gyalo Thondup, who saw the promise of the ancient principality of Mustang, between Tibet and Nepal, as a base from which Tibetans could radiate into the countryside as small bands, not large units. Des FitzGerald surmised that aircraft could still be useful if they did not enter China. At an Interpol conference that summer, Dick Bissell's chief of operations, Richard Helms, cleared the concept with Indian intelligence. The liaison was required because some Tibetans were now to train in India. Meanwhile the International Jurists Commission set up by the UN released its conclusion that China had indeed attempted genocide in Tibet, giving the CIA program added momentum.

On September 15, 1960, the 5412 Group convened just before a National Security Council meeting. According to a brief record note, "As a result of the discussion the DCI said he would reorient his thinking to some extent" and come back with an alternative. The key would be to limit the visibility of Mustang, switching to caravans moving overland. This meant a loss of volume delivery, but the agency had little choice—at least CIA could use the stockpiles it had accumulated in

Okinawa, Taiwan, and Thailand. Des FitzGerald and Roger McCarthy did the heavy lifting on planning. The agency also began monthly subsidies to the Dalai Lama totaling $1.7 million a year that continued into the 1960s. Just before the 1960 elections CIA's General Cabell updated the Special Group on Tibet, adding comments about Cuba, another CIA project by then in full swing.

One veteran recalls that on Election Day, Far East chief FitzGerald learned of Eisenhower's vow that Richard Nixon, if elected, would continue Circus. Instead the presidency went to John F. Kennedy. Evidence suggests officials handed the project over to the Kennedy transition team several weeks later, though Ike himself did not sit down with the president-elect until December 6. Eisenhower specifically recalls that Allen Dulles had already briefed Kennedy on a number of international matters, including the Far East. In fact, at a discussion with Gray and Eisenhower on the morning of November 25, "Mr. Dulles reported to the President on certain consultations he had had with respect to projected undertakings in Tibet and received further guidance." Thus Eisenhower passed on the Tibetan secret war. Now Kennedy would decide.

The New Delhi locus of the Tibet effort raised both diplomatic and intelligence problems. The DO's Near East Division, restive at the independence of officers in India who worked with the Tibetans, made trouble for them. That affected John Hoskins and Howard T. Bane, brought in to insulate Hoskins from the CIA station chief, now Harry Rositzke, who took a jaundiced view of Project Circus. Meanwhile John Kennedy's ambassador to India would be Harvard economist John Kenneth Galbraith. Before leaving for his post on March 27, 1961, Galbraith discussed CIA operations in India with Richard Bissell. There was an element of irony in this meeting of two economists, one perhaps the foremost Keynesian, the other a man who had long resisted Keynesian arguments but ended up administering Keynesian-style foreign and military aid, first for the Marshall Plan, now for the CIA. Bissell showed Galbraith the list of projects, many of which bothered the ambassador. A couple of weeks earlier President Kennedy had authorized CIA airdrops to Mustang. Now Galbraith found them distressing.

Galbraith determined to stop these "spooky activities," Tibet among them. The ambassador thought the partisans "deeply unhygienic tribesmen." Galbraith ordered his country team to make a full investigation of CIA activities one of its first moves. He recalls that Harry Rositzke made little effort to defend the program. As for himself, the ambassador writes, "I was not troubled by an open mind. I was convinced that most of the projects proposed would be useless for their own anticommunist purposes and were capable, when known, of doing us great damage as well."

Galbraith started from behind, as JFK had already approved supply flights, and a pair of them took place even as the new ambassador prepared to leave for New Delhi. One dropped equipment over Mustang, the other one more CIA team inside Tibet. But Galbraith persisted. He took his views to Washington in May 1961, where he found Kennedy subdued by CIA failure in Cuba. He argued with the president, Bobby Kennedy, and McGeorge Bundy, and put his objections to

Dulles and Bissell, telling them Kennedy had been sympathetic to ending the project.

But Galbraith's efforts were not wholly successful. He did not get Circus canceled. The partisans had achieved the status of an ally. Kennedy, the man who challenged Americans to do what they could for their country in the Cold War, could not abandon one of the few active resistance efforts against Mao Zedong. Ambassador Galbraith would be permitted to shut down CIA activities aimed at the Indian Communist Party, but the Tibetan program lasted somewhat longer. Kennedy did rule out further flights into Tibet.

Everything depended on Mustang. The camp, a mountain stronghold northwest of the Nepalese capital of Katmandu, began growing in late 1960. Under the new formula the NVDA fighters were to be gathered in companies, more formal units to escape the tribal and clan rivalries that had previously reduced their effectiveness. But when Tibetans learned their forces were gathering at Mustang, a migration from all over India began. That meant publicity and potential security breaches. CIA officers tried in vain to curtail the migration, though they had more success blocking access to the camp. Tibetan families settled nearby.

In October 1961 the NVDA achieved a great success. A raiding party led by the Indian-trained partisan Ragra, sent to disrupt traffic along the Amdo road, wiped out the Chinese in a light truck. Among the dead they found a deputy regimental commander. The bags of documents they captured, sixteen hundred pages in all, included reports on the 1959 Lhasa uprising, material on the Sino-Soviet split, and a file of issues of the "Bulletin of Activities of the General Political Department of the People's Liberation Army" (*Kung-tso T'ung-hsun*), a secret journal for PLA commissars covering the period January to August 1961. A CIA officer personally retrieved the material and carried it to Washington, where Allen Dulles proudly exhibited the documents to the Special Group a month later. The political journal would be translated and opened to American scholars by the State Department in August 1963. This windfall is the reason Ray Cline records that Tibet "resulted in a bonanza of valuable substantive intelligence."

Meanwhile the CIA sent political action specialist Howard Stone, last seen in Syria, to head a beefed-up station in Katmandu. The agency also created a new proprietary airline, Air Nepal. Long Air America flights from Bangkok to Mustang used this cover. Light planes did short-range work from Katmandu. Of this Galbraith comments, "I was especially disturbed by [this] particularly insane enterprise." He believed that later, in conjunction with Bobby Kennedy, he finally cut the Nepalese connection.

A December 1961 incident demonstrated beyond doubt that the Tibet program continued. On the morning of December 7 deep snow and icy roads around Camp Hale delayed Don Cesare's bus of Tibetans bound for Peterson Field. Rather than flying away at night, the Tibetans reached the field after dawn. Airfield employees saw the Globemaster sitting on the apron and strange men milling about. The local sheriff raced over with two deputies. To preserve secrecy, army soldiers held forty-seven Americans at gunpoint, including the sheriff, then told them it would be a federal crime to talk about it, all in the name of a dubious national security. The story made local radio the next morning. By afternoon it was in the *Colorado Springs Gazette*, and it stayed out of the *New York Times* only due to personal appeals from Secretary of Defense Robert McNamara. Snafus like this one had terminated projects before, Indonesia being a case in point. The Peterson incident was even more serious in its way—the CIA is proscribed by law from operating inside the United States and has no authority to detain citizens to protect secrecy. The major flap in Washington ended Roger McCarthy's tenure as chief of the task force. He was replaced by John Knaus, a former Camp Hale trainer and a sophisticated, well-spoken secret warrior who would write a history of the resistance. In that book Knaus fails to mention the Peterson incident at all.

With Mustang the pattern of operations changed completely. The virtual end of airdrops and Chinese dominance of the trails above Kalimpong made it impossible to wage large-scale operations. Meanwhile Mustang itself proved so remote that sustained forays were not possible. Gyen Yeshe replaced Gompo Tashi, his clumsy methods an annoyance. The resistance, reduced to less than seven thousand, then to less than two thousand, became a war of expeditions and patrols, with access to Tibet each time more difficult.

The CIA made several more air missions, but permissions became bureaucratic battles the secret warriors found as tough as fighting the PLA. The document scoop in 1961 won one of these battles, but CIA lost most of what it had gained after India's 1962 border war with China, when W. Averell Harriman made a diplomatic tour of the region and sided with Galbraith. Not even Des FitzGerald, Jim Critchfield, and John Knaus, who were among his entourage, could turn Harriman aside. The diplomat finally backed FitzGerald's fallback proposal, an alliance among CIA, Indian intelligence, and the Tibetans. As the Mustang force diminished, most of the partisans enlisted in the Indians' border commando unit, which eventually far exceeded the resistance in size. Indian intelligence also set up a joint headquarters. A communications center was established at Orissa by 1963, and a combined headquarters in New Delhi by early 1964, all paid for by CIA. The Indian intelligence people met weekly with CIA and NVDA representatives. Indians were supposed to command, but they never permitted the partisans to do anything big. A virtual revolt among the Tibetans eventually resulted.

Washington's secret warriors reoriented their program again. High-level talks with Gyen Yeshe and senior leaders in the summer of 1963 found CIA managers insisting that the Tibetans return to their country as a condition for support. Kennedy simply would not authorize deliveries inside neutral Nepal. The Tibetans countered with a proposal to split their strength among both places. A couple of months later William E. Colby, now the chief of the DO Far East Division, carried a fresh proposal to the Special Group. Colby argued for a switch to targeted raids aimed at specific objectives, warning of significant losses. In 1964 the Special Group approved a scheme to continue giving the Tibet issue a high international profile but with a reduced emphasis on military activity. Payments to the Dalai Lama continued, while for the most part the resistance received CIA cash only. A final weapons airdrop took place at Mustang in May 1965. But the leading edge of the CIA effort now shifted to Ithaca, New York, to Cornell University, where the agency sponsored Tibetans learning English, writing, and international relations in the hope they could become spokespersons for their cause.

In the end, Washington abandoned the Tibetans. By 1968 the CIA had told the Special Group that no current operations justified the Tibetan forces at Mustang. The few telephone taps the CIA wanted could easily be managed by a much smaller effort. The following year the secret warriors told the Tibetans that the United States would end its support. Another blow in 1969 was the retirement of Gyalo Thondup. With the U.S. rapprochement of 1972, Mao Zedong demanded an end to the charade. When the king of Nepal visited Beijing in November 1973, Mao concerted action (John Knaus is not convinced this was the case). The next year the Nepalese, with information from the disaffected Gyen Yeshi and arrangements with the PLA to patrol their side of the border, put ten thousand royal troops up against Mustang, including Gurkhas just as fierce as any Khampa. The top commander escaped with the NVDA archives and a small escort, only to be killed in a later ambush. Seven other Tibetan leaders surrendered at Mustang and sat in a Katmandu jail until pardoned by the king in 1981. It was the end of the Khampa rebellion.

From the beginning Washington knew that Tibet could never be more than a large-scale harassment of the People's Republic of China. To achieve this the CIA promised liberation to the Tibetans, caught up in their hopes and dreams, who suffered prolonged agony in this war. Tibet also became a searing experience for CIA paramilitary experts, who learned the language and customs of the country and became emotionally attached to its struggle, only to have to close down the project later. They saw the darker side of the CIA's intelligence "bonanza." John Knaus concedes "a certain operational hubris" and acknowledges that for the secret warriors, preserving the project becomes almost an end in itself, endowing the covert action with momentum and excitement.

Troubled by questions about the CIA's role, Knaus sought out the Dalai Lama, Gyalo Thondup, Lhamo Tsering, and other key Tibetans to ask whether the secret warriors had done the right thing. Knaus's sense of relief when most of the Tibetans accepted the American actions is almost palpable. But in truth, despite the CIA's intelligence successes in Tibet, America's reputation as guarantor of national self-determination gained nothing from its refusal to support Tibetan nationalism on the international stage.

For Tibetans, more than a hundred thousand of whom became refugees from their country, there would be one mitigating factor—defeat took many years; they could adjust gradually to the trauma. In Cuba, the CIA's next paramilitary disaster, trauma would be a matter of seventy-two hours of hell.

11

"Another Black Hole of Calcutta"

AT CIA HEADQUARTERS the New Year 1959 struck in a quite subdued fashion as a number of key people sat around a table awaiting news from Havana. Fletcher Prouty represented the Pentagon at this séance, which took place the day and the hour that Richard Bissell officially assumed the office of deputy director for operations. For months the agency had followed events in Cuba in growing fear of the disintegration of America's cozy position there. Military dictator Fulgencio Batista had been unable to quell the rebellion that spread rapidly across the island, just ninety miles from U.S. shores. Batista's main opponents, the socialist July 26th Movement of Fidel Castro, successful in every endeavor, appeared to be marching on Havana. Despite sanguine CIA analysts who argued Batista's solid hold on power, President Eisenhower approved measures to forestall a Castro government in Cuba.

Ike's mind, influenced by Florida businessman and dabbler in the secret world William D. Pawley, began focusing on anti-Castro schemes late in 1958. That November Pawley, who owned the Havana bus company, had founded the Cuban airline, and fancied himself an activist, hosted several persons, including CIA Western Hemisphere Division chief J. C. King, at his Miami home. No stranger to the agency, Pawley had helped in the Guatemala operation and participated in the Doolittle report. Now he advocated Batista's resignation in favor of a Cuban leadership not as radical as Castro, and Eisenhower let him try. Pawley traveled to Havana in early December to feel out Cuban politicians. King and another CIA officer went along. But the moment had already passed. "In Cuba the rebel drive is retaining its momentum," noted the president's intelligence briefing for December 29. "Many high-ranking officers in the armed forces are said to be making preparations to leave."

For its part the CIA became involved in at least four different plots. Colonel Prouty's group at Quarters Eye on December 31, 1958, sat there because a U.S.

aircraft, a Helio-Courier from Key West, flew a clandestine mission to Cuba. Washington wished to find Cubans to whom it could deliver arms, a "third force" non-Castroite movement. The mission required backstopping—in case of a problem, a spare Helio waited in Washington. A large C-54 had been summoned from Europe, and its cargo of weapons would be packed by the day after New Year's. The flight went as planned, but no "third force" existed.

Central Intelligence Agency officers who had succumbed to the fervor of the anti-Batista revolution, such as William Caldwell, station chief when Castro's movement first became entrenched, had given way to more hardened attitudes. The current chief of station, James Noel, sided with Ambassador Earl Smith, who stood solidly against Castro. The station warned of Batista's vulnerability even as the CIA tried its eleventh-hour effort.

On December 23 Allen Dulles told the NSC that Batista's days were numbered and that Cuban Communists could be expected in any Castro government. Gordon Gray watched as a December 30 meeting canvassed possibilities. Senior diplomats, more favorable toward Castro than Ambassador Smith, nevertheless would not oppose third-force efforts. Of course Batista knew his position had become untenable—days earlier a general strike had given a frightening illustration of how unpopular the dictator had become. The question preoccupying everyone was what Batista would now do. Prouty's group on New Year's Eve understandably sat in an atmosphere of expectancy.

In Havana that night Fulgencio Batista y Zaldivar's New Year's party seemed unusually subdued. Guests ate *arroz con pollo* served by military aides in dress uniforms, a few drank champagne, most coffee. The atmosphere is captured well by a scene in the movie *The Godfather, Part II*. Until that day, December 31, 1958, Batista's last in power, the guests had been the rich and powerful of Cuba. Some of the sixty visitors knew or suspected Batista might flee.

Castro's irresistible forces were descending from the Sierra Maestra Mountains where the struggle had begun two years earlier. At first his guerrillas had been contained by the Cuban army. But Batista's corrupt and oppressive dictatorship increasingly lost support. Cubans flocked to Castro's July 26th Movement (M-26, or *Movimiento del veinte-seis de julio*), which took its name from the date of an unsuccessful revolt Castro had once led. The M-26 guerrillas spread out from the Sierra, creating fronts in several parts of Cuba. Those who cared could see the handwriting on the wall.

Batista, no fool, knew what portended. The dictator's brief appearance at his reception came around midnight. He handed power to his commanders. Then Batista's family and closest associates left for the airport. Aboard three airplanes the group took flight. Batista left the Camp Columbia base at 2:40 in the morning of January 1, 1959. David A. Phillips, now a part-time CIA undercover agent in Havana, sat in his backyard as the aircraft flew over. Phillips immediately informed superiors, some of whom at first did not believe the news.

At that moment the M-26 unit closest to Havana, a column at Santa Clara under Argentine *commandante* Ernesto "Che" Guevara, was 150 miles away. Che slept atop the hood of his jeep. He got the news seven hours after Batista fled. Guevara immediately ordered a road march. His force arrived in Havana the next morning and drove directly to the La Cabana fortress, whose garrison of 15,000 men dwarfed Che's small M-26 column.

The M-26 *commandante* walked up to La Cabana's iron drawbridge. There he shouted, "I am the Che, Guevara. I want to talk to your chief."

A few moments later a government jeep rolled out of the fortress. The occupant, an army major, unholstered his pistol and handed it to Guevara.

"We are not interested in fighting. It is not necessary now."

The Cuban civil war ended there. A few days later David Phillips stood in the crowd as Fidel Castro entered Havana in a triumphal motorcade.

Washington's efforts to shore up the dictatorship, and then to force Batista into reforms that might stave off Castro, left the Cubans in no doubt as to U.S. policy. The change in government on January 2, 1959, could have ushered in both a new beginning and an opportunity for U.S. relations with Havana. Castro, suspicious from the outset, did little to make that happen. Eisenhower failed to grasp the opening both because of discomfort with Fidel and a certain impatience. Events led to a spectacular covert operation, an episode that would blacken America's reputation as a proponent of democracy.

The origins of the hostility that persists between the United States and Cuba has faded into the mists of time. Note therefore that in 1959 (notwithstanding Castro's pronouncements decades later) Fidel Castro had not become a Communist nor his July 26th Movement a Communist Party. Nor did Castro bring Communists into government. According to a 1958 CIA report, the Cuban Communist Party favored general strike tactics, not the M-26 armed insurgency. Argentina, Brazil, Chile, and Mexico all had Communist parties four or more times larger than Cuba's. Castro's own movement also far outnumbered the Cuban Communist Party.

Relating to the Castro government, Eisenhower began with a wait-and-see attitude. The CIA's initial assessment explained Batista's fall by citing corruption and his consequent lack of public support. Allen Dulles is said to have taken this report and personally rewritten it. A paper Dulles forwarded to State in February 1959, not at all complimentary to Castro, called the situation "far from stable." The paper asserted that the M-26 group lacked "dynamic positive leadership," saw it "floundering," its difficulties magnified by "the relative youth and inexperience of a great many top leaders." Thus "the glamour of the Sierra Maestra and the straggly beards is rapidly wearing off . . ."

Fidel visited Washington in April for a speech to the American Society of Newspaper Editors. He did not meet Eisenhower but spoke to State Department officials and with Vice President Richard Nixon, who thought Fidel sincere but reported, "He is either incredibly naive about communism or under communist discipline." The State Department analysis read:

With regard to his position on communism and the cold war struggle, Castro cautiously indicated that Cuba would remain in the western camp. However his position here must still be regarded as uncertain. He did go sufficiently far in his declarations to be vulnerable to the criticism of radicals among his supporters.

On his own copy of the State Department analysis Eisenhower wrote, "We will check in a year!"

Castro did have a problem, but with Cuban conservatives, not the radicals. By and large the landed, monied families had been tied to the Batista forces. Fearful of the revolution, they left in droves, taking their dollars with them. Within two weeks of Castro's assumption of power in Havana, the CIA had set up an office in Miami, a field activity of its Domestic Contacts Division, to keep watch on the arriving refugees, headed by Justin F. Gleichauf, the sole agency officer involved. Miami presently became the largest station in the CIA's global network, on a par with Bonn during the Soviet operations or Taiwan at the height of China activities.

By December 1959 there were a hundred thousand Cuban emigrés in the United States alone. Without these skilled technicians, doctors, and lawyers—and their money—Cuba had little capital to diversify away from sugar, whose market centered in the United States and was regulated by a quota system. Meanwhile under Batista the Mafia had controlled gambling at the Havana hotels. *The Godfather, Part II* illustrates this also. The Mafia left when Castro prohibited gambling, drying up another source of capital. Expropriation, as attempted by Mossadegh in Iran and Arbenz in Guatemala, became the *fidelista* solution. An element of irony existed here since Castro's father had once worked for United Fruit. In any case, in the fall of 1959 Fidel promulgated a decree for nationalization. That December the first American concern was "intervened," as the Cubans called it. In 1960 the sugar plantations and Havana hotels followed. Land reform accelerated with the nationalization of large holdings, beginning with the Castro family plantation. It is said Fidel's mother never forgave him. *Fidelistas* failed to offer compensation to owners, worsening the injury.

Eisenhower feared *fidelista* exportation of revolution. There were reports of a "legion" created for this purpose. During 1959 and 1960 small, armed groups invaded Panama, Guatemala, and the Dominican Republic, much as Castro himself had sailed to Cuba to establish his base in the Sierra Maestra. The rebels were citizens of their own countries. While some received Cuban assistance, they were in no sense directed by Castro. In fact the "invasion" of the Dominican Republic was carried out from Puerto Rico, a U.S. territory.

The American government, even the CIA, recognized these factors to some degree. On November 5, 1959, Deputy Director Charles Cabell told a Senate judiciary subcommittee that neither the Cuban Communists nor the CIA considered Castro a Communist, that the Cuban Communist Party sought to influence Castro but did not control him. Cabell also downplayed *fidelista* participation in revolutionary expeditions, pointing out these were not organized or dominated by

Cubans. He also conceded that "anti-Communists have an interest in rumors which will increase our alarm over the Communist influence in Cuba."

As Cabell spoke on Capitol Hill, at Foggy Bottom Secretary of State Christian Herter put finishing touches to a paper he sent Ike the same day. The memo proposed four measures on Cuba. These included doing nothing to help Castro consolidate power; a propaganda campaign to promote the American concept of democracy; encouraging opposition to Castro both in Cuba and elsewhere while avoiding any impression Washington was pressuring him; and preserving mutual interests for the United States and a "reformed" Cuban government.

Herter ended on a revealing note: "In view of the special sensitivity of Latin America to United States 'intervention,' I would propose that the existence and substance of this current policy statement be held on a very strict 'need to know' basis."

Dwight Eisenhower accepted the proposals and also the secrecy, as Andrew Goodpaster told Herter on November 9. At the White House, knowledge would be confined to Goodpaster himself, Ike's son John S. D. Eisenhower, Gordon Gray, and one confidential secretary. When Gray proposed that the Hull Board be brought into the circle, Allen Dulles shot that one down fast. In April 1959 the president had been willing to wait a year; now, six months later, Eisenhower approved measures that led to a secret war.

The CIA already had its answer: in August 1959 discussions had begun on creating a paramilitary capability for Latin America. Studies ensued, with a recommendation that the DO's Western Hemisphere Division set up a staff and move to acquire an airline usable in the region.

Meanwhile the secret warriors also intervened to help put Castro in the penalty box. On November 24 Allen Dulles saw the British ambassador and asked that Great Britain resist Cuban attempts to buy weapons, in particular Hawker Hunter jets then under negotiation. The ambassador's cable noted Dulles saying: "He hoped that any refusal by us to supply arms would directly lead to a Soviet-bloc offer to supply. Then he might be able to do something." Dulles said Castro "had a streak of lunacy" and speculated that his leadership might last eight months or so, though if Fidel endured this "testing time" he might remain in power for a number of years. Director Dulles conceded that "there was at present no opposition to Castro . . . capable of action."

Several strange incidents occurred in Cuba around this time. On February 19 an American-piloted plane blew up while flying over the España sugar refinery in Matanzas province. A month later, near Matanzas town, two Americans were captured in another plane crash. The captives, William L. Schergales and Howard Rundquist, injured, were hospitalized; one asserted that the Castro government had hired them. The story could have been true or, just as likely, a bit of disinformation repeated by the American press.

There was also an incident in Havana harbor. The Pan American dock, already nationalized, was unloading the French motor vessel La Coubre, carrying general cargo plus ammunition purchased from Belgium. On March 4, without warning, a blast blew away the ship's bow and most of its superstructure. Secondary explosions ignited the stacked munitions; flames quickly spread. All the firefighters in Havana barely contained the blaze before it reached the nearby Tallapiedra electric plant. More than a hundred people were killed or injured. Castro blamed the Americans; Washington denied it. The only sure fact remained that the Compagnie Trans-Atlantique Française had lost a merchantman. A week later the Cubans expropriated their first three sugar mills.

From their offices around the Reflecting Pool, CIA officials were on the case. The DO had had an officer, Edward A. Stanulis, planning full-time for CIA action in Latin American contingencies since September. Cuba became his number one priority. That November the agency ordered that operations were to be based on the premise that Cuba had a non-Communist government, but that instruction swiftly went into the round file. Director Dulles asserted in a December 4 speech that Latin Communists would use nationalism as a slogan to justify breaking ties with the United States. Just a week later J. C. King sent Dulles a memorandum insisting that Castro's "'far left' dictatorship" not be permitted to stand. The WH Division chief advocated a range of actions, among them that "thorough consideration be given to the elimination of Fidel Castro . . . [which] would greatly accelerate the fall of the present government." Allen Dulles, not yet willing to go that far, crossed out King's word "elimination," substituting "removal from Cuba." The core of the paper recommended the CIA train a cadre of Cubans who would assemble other exiles in a Latin American country, after which they would infiltrate Cuba to lead anti-Castro dissidents. This formed the heart of the eventual Cuba paramilitary plan.

Allen Dulles took the anti-Castro project to the 5412 Group on January 13, 1960. State questioned moving in the absence of solid internal opposition. Dulles acknowledged this criticism but emphasized the CIA would try to open a wedge for an opposition. Yet "over the long run," Dulles observed, "the U.S. will not be able to tolerate the Castro regime in Cuba."

The 5412 Group conditionally approved. Examination of Special Group records by a Senate committee in the 1970s shows that Dulles recommended that the CIA prepare plans to effect Castro's fall. Five days later at Quarters Eye a dozen people met with J. C. King to create a Cuba task force. The unit became the fourth branch of King's division, WH/4 in CIA usage. Eighteen persons were assigned to WH/4 at headquarters, twenty at the Havana station, and two more under diplomatic cover at the U.S. consulate in Santiago, Cuba.

Jacob D. Esterline became chief of the task force. A Burma OSS veteran, Esterline had graduated from the University of Pennsylvania and wanted to be a lawyer. Recalled to service during the Korea years, he had been noticed among names on an assignment list by Ray Peers, who had him seconded to the CIA. The agency used Esterline at its Fort Benning training camp, then sent him to the Western Hemisphere Division in 1953. Esterline had never had anything to do with

Latin America yet suddenly found himself deputy chief of the Guatemala coup task force. After that Esterline served as chief of station in Guatemala, then went to Venezuela as station chief, to rebuild networks decimated in another coup. He learned of plans of Venezuelan groups to protest a visit by Vice President Richard M. Nixon and attempted to persuade Washington to cancel the visit, or at least warn Nixon, but got nowhere. Then he witnessed a state visit by Fidel Castro, received by rapturous crowds in Caracas. Frank Wisner passed through town about then, and Esterline told him that if the agency decided to do anything about Castro, he wanted in. Now Esterline found himself selected chief of the Cuban task force.

Early planning focused on several concepts. A guerrilla-leader ploy involved twenty to thirty Cubans who would return to the island, much as the CIA did in Tibet. A second plan aimed to disrupt the Cuban economy by sabotage of such targets as sugar refineries. Director Dulles carried that idea to the 5412 Group on February 17, and it became the first one he presented to President Eisenhower. Direct action to eliminate Fidel and Raul Castro and Che Guevara formed a third possibility.

Director Dulles met with the president and Gordon Gray. Accompanied by aides, Dulles went armed with color schematic drawings of sugar refineries and presented a harassment plan, explaining how CIA proposed to disrupt production.

Eisenhower listened patiently.

"Allen, this is fine," Ike interjected, "but if you're going to make any move against Castro, don't just fool around with sugar refineries. Let's get a program that will really do something about Castro."

"Yes, sir!" Dulles responded.

On March 9 the WH/4 task force held its first meeting. J. C. King upstaged Esterline, telling the audience that Director Dulles would shortly take a project paper to the 5412 Group. King worried that the CIA could not use certain U.S. islands for psychological warfare or paramilitary purposes, and that leaders of friendly nations were not yet willing to "stick their necks out further to support an operation directed at the overthrow of the Castro regime." Presidential approval could remove some of those obstacles.

Colonel King exaggerated when he told his officers there were prospects for a Cuban attack on the U.S. naval base at Guantanamo Bay, and he stretched evidence to say Latin leaders feared they would soon be victims of Cuban exploitation; but Allen Dulles used similar reasoning presenting the Cuba paper at 5412. King also noted that unless the top *fidelistas* could be eliminated in one "package," the operation might be a drawn-out affair in which Castro could be overthrown by force. The plan crafted by Jake Esterline and Richard C. Drain envisioned an exile force gathered over a period of months.

A White House meeting on March 10 touched on these themes. Cuba appeared ninth on a long agenda. The NSC considered suspending the doctrine of nonintervention in Latin America in the event communism dominated or threatened any of its nations. A policy paper advised sanctions against any Latin state that even established close ties with the Soviet bloc. In the Cuba discussion the

NSC Planning Board foresaw no clear prospect for good relations with Castro. The board favored economic warfare, eliminating subsidies on Cuban sugar. Further, Washington should convince the Organization of American States (OAS) to cast Cuba as a hemispheric problem, eliminating a key obstacle to action. Adm. Arleigh Burke, attending as chief of naval operations, wanted someone to unite the anti-Castro factions. Many of those around Fidel were worse than the "Maximum Leader" himself, Burke felt, and therefore "any plan for removal of Cuban leaders should be a package deal." Allen Dulles observed that the eligible leaders were no longer in Cuba and noted CIA had a design to deal with Castro.

"We might have another Black Hole of Calcutta in Cuba," Ike remarked.*

Soon Director Dulles had his plan—the Esterline-Drain paper, a scheme he unveiled on March 14 after the annual review of 5412 activities. Based on the discussion, Quarters Eye did a quick revision titled "A Program of Action Against the Castro Regime," dated March 16, 1960. The objective was "to bring about the replacement of the Castro regime with one more devoted to the interests of the Cuban people and more acceptable to the U.S. in such a manner as to avoid any appearance of U.S. intervention." The essence would be "to induce, support, and so far as possible direct action, both inside and outside of Cuba, by selected groups" with whom the CIA already had contact. The plan envisioned that "since a crisis inevitably entailing drastic action in or toward Cuba could be provoked by circumstances beyond the control of the U.S. before the covert action program has accomplished its objective, every effort will be made to carry it out in such a way as progressively to improve the capability of the U.S. to act in a crisis."

The secret warriors felt they could create "a responsible, appealing and unified Cuban opposition" located outside Cuba, after which "a powerful propaganda offensive can be initiated in the name of the declared opposition." To undermine Castro's popular support, a semi-covert "grey" radio station would broadcast on long- and shortwave bands and, in the original proposal, would be located on Swan Island, northeast of Honduras. The propaganda would be supplemented by Miami commercial stations and clandestine leaflets distributed in Cuba. The CIA reported progress toward creation of a covert apparatus inside Cuba, "responsive to the orders and directions of the 'exile' opposition." The agency estimated it could have an organization up and running within sixty days.

Although Esterline and Drain presented their concept in fair detail, the CIA's budget estimate did not provide for the size of force eventually reached. The first budget projections called for $2.5 million over two years, far less than eventually spent. The concept received the code name JM/Ate;† the Pentagon would know it as Project Pluto.

---

* In India in 1756 the Nawab of Bengal, resisting British encroachments, had captured Calcutta and imprisoned Englishmen in the "Black Hole," a storeroom in the fort. Dozens died before the East India Company recaptured the city. Eisenhower used the phrase to make out Castro as an oppressor.
† In actuality the original cryptonym was JM/Arc, but this would be compromised in December, replaced with Ate. To avoid confusion this narrative will adopt the later nomenclature.

The paragraph on military action from the Project Ate concept is worth quoting at length:

> Preparations have already been made for the development of an adequate paramilitary force outside of Cuba, together with mechanisms for the necessary logistical support of covert military operations on the island. Initially a cadre of leaders will be recruited after careful screening and trained as paramilitary instructors. In a second phase a number of paramilitary cadres will be trained at secure locations outside of the United States so as to be available for immediate deployment into Cuba to organize, train, and lead resistance forces recruited there after the establishment of one or more centers of resistance.

Preparations would take six to eight months. At 5412 Gordon Gray had complained about the extended schedule and wondered about a crash program. Now the agency reported that a limited air capability "already exists under CIA control" and could be expanded. Within two months the secret warriors could supplement this with a force under deep cover in a third country; and the exile organization would be functional within Cuba, which the agency saw as providing hard intelligence, arranging the landing or exfiltration of agents, inducing the defection of individuals as directed, doing the distribution of "illegal propaganda."

The project paper commented on problems of cover also. The secret warriors made clear that "all actions undertaken by the CIA in support and on behalf of the opposition council will, of course, be explained as activities of that entity." And, in a reference to persons like William D. Pawley, the agency's Cuba paper further explained that it would "make use of a carefully screened group of U.S. businessmen with a stated interest in Cuban affairs." Such people could act as a funding mechanism, and CIA personnel could be documented as their representatives. Money from private sources would also help disguise the agency's hand. Allen Dulles's proposal noted $100,000 in pledges already made by Pawley and others. The secret war managers now estimated the Cuba project would cost $4.4 million.

On March 17 in the afternoon, President Eisenhower took the unusual step of convening the 5412 Group, plus other senior officials, in the Oval Office. Eisenhower accepted the CIA's Cuban project. Not before some discussion, however. Once Allen Dulles presented the basic plan, Bissell did most of the talking. Bissell, whose skills lay elsewhere, and who had appointed Tracy Barnes his assistant precisely because of the latter's abilities as a salesman, did well enough here. The exile slogan would be to "restore the revolution." Most likely they would be located in Puerto Rico, though Mexico would be better in the unlikely event the Mexican government would agree. The group of American businessmen would be in New York. The paramilitary force, Allen Dulles interjected, would require eight months and begin with a cadre of leaders outside Cuba.

The spy chiefs took the approval back to Quarters Eye. Allen Dulles had barely begun his introductory remarks when he had to take a call from the president. The group waited. Bissell, silent, worked through a stack of cables. General

Cabell slouched in a chair. Gossip over a Georgetown party occupied Tracy Barnes and Richard Helms. Colonel King of WH Division did not even attend. Lesser fry fidgeted. The scene could have served as metaphor for what was to come. Dulles reported the president's go-ahead. Ike wanted everyone prepared to swear they had never heard of this scheme—the great problem would be leaks. Those, it turned out, would be just one headache.

Ike awaited results on Castro. Allen Dulles came to the National Security Council time after time to report that Castro was expropriating properties or putting Cuban newspapers under government control, yet popular support for the Maximum Leader stayed high. By early April 1960 the CIA task force began producing daily progress reports. In May the government completed nationalization of the United Fruit Company's 272,000 acres of cane fields, though for the moment *la frutera* held on to its two mills. On June 3 Tracy Barnes attended a meeting at Foggy Bottom that considered retaliation in kind—persuading U.S. oil companies to stop refining crude for Castro at their Cuban refineries. Three weeks later Charles Cabell briefed Vice President Nixon on the latest developments. Dick Bissell and J. C. King were on hand to take questions. That nothing had weakened Castro was the most disturbing aspect of CIA's presentation, Nixon declared, demanding OAS action plus economic sanctions.

A few days later a large group met at the State Department to mull over economic measures. OAS approval remained problematical, and pushing to isolate Cuba in that organization might harm U.S. regional allies. Arguments about support for right-wing versus leftist dictators further complicated the issue. General Cabell and Colonel King again represented the agency. Secretary of State Herter questioned them elliptically. Cabell expressed general satisfaction with CIA progress on its covert operation but warned that Castro's popularity remained undiminished. Economic warfare would be necessary to Project Ate, Cabell observed.

Around the end of June, Ike told Gordon Gray he could not remember the details of the March 17 discussion where he had approved the Cuba project. Gray reminded the president of what Allen Dulles had proposed, then reported "the current thinking as to the timetable of various events." Weeks later, with Eisenhower at Newport, Rhode Island, Gray told him of a fresh CIA bid to expand the exile force, use Guatemalan bases, and enlarge the budget accordingly.

By August Esterline's task force had reworked its plan and presented it in a new memorandum to the president. The key meeting took place at the White House on August 18. Present were Allen Dulles, NSC officials, the chairman of the Joint Chiefs of Staff, and Treasury Secretary Robert Anderson, who coordinated trade policy on Cuba. After talk of the U-2 affair, which had consumed Eisenhower since May, the group turned to Ate. Allen Dulles cited success in creating a Cuban political front, the FRD, so far based in Mexico. The CIA director also extolled Radio Swan, now on the air, its broadcasts attacking Trujillo in addition to Castro. Cuba had already begun jamming its transmissions. At Fort Gulick in Panama the CIA had trained a cadre of twenty or more exiles who would go to Guatemala and help instruct five hundred more men. Several dozen radio operators were also learning their trade. Dulles noted that he now needed U.S. military people to assist in training.

Secretary of Defense Thomas Gates, not happy, shot back that the training did not concern him as much as the possibility that the U.S. military might find themselves going over the beaches into Cuba. Richard Bissell deflected his objection—only fifteen or twenty people were involved, most of them already on assignment to CIA. They would be concerned primarily with the movement of aircraft. Bissell commented, "There would be no conceivable hazard involved and they would get no closer to para-military operations than the airstrip in Guatemala." Gen. Lyman Lemnitzer, the JCS chairman, saw no difficulty with the military trainers.

Deputy Director Bissell also spoke of the Cuban exile force. He expected they could be ready for action by November and would constitute "a standby force preferably of non-Americans with special forces type training." Secretary Gates renewed his objection. Hot debate over the use of Americans as part of the force ended with Allen Dulles, who said the decision could be put aside and reexamined by the CIA with the Joint Chiefs.

Gordon Gray added that an abortive project would be worse than none—it would be unwise to mount any action without the determination to see it through. If a backup force were necessary, this should be considered fully now. Director Dulles still wished to defer the issue.

The operational concept centered on the internal resistance to Castro. It might succeed without "outside help," Bissell noted. Some B-26 bombers would have Cuban exile pilots, and they could fly in support of the "local resistance." They would be supplied by air and sea, and some exiles would be sent to stiffen them. The CIA had identified a dozen anti-Castro or "alleged groups" with potential. If these failed to unseat Castro, the backup force would capture an island off the Cuban coast, such as the Isle of Pines, which could become the ostensible resistance base. Allen Dulles admitted the project had blown through its budget: the CIA now thought in terms of $10 million more than already set aside.

If everyone believed JM/Ate had a good chance, Eisenhower was for it. Cost posed no obstacle: Ike declared "he would defend this kind of action against all comers and . . . if we could be sure of freeing the Cubans from this incubus, $25 million might be a small price to pay."

So money became the next issue. After the meeting Dulles visited Maurice Stans, director of the Bureau of the Budget, to ask that the funds be included in CIA's request for fiscal year 1962.

"It is needed," the DCI explained, "to supply and train somewhere in Central America a group of exile Cubans who are preparing for a guerrilla invasion to overthrow Castro." The director refused to supply documentation to support his demands. Stans protested. "It's none of your damn business!" Allen Dulles angrily retorted. "If you question my authority go to the President and ask him."

Stans did exactly that. Dwight Eisenhower soothed him with an explanation: "I authorized Dulles to spend that money but I did not authorize any specific military action by the anti-Castro Cubans. That will have to come later and I won't give it an OK unless I'm convinced it is essential and I'm convinced it won't fail." Stans went back and wrote $15 million into the CIA budget. Ike probably rued that day.

One piece of the Cuba scheme was held so tightly that only a handful knew about it: Dick Bissell had a whole other track under way. During the spring there had been talk of neutralizing Castro—J. C. King's comments in an early memo and at a March staff meeting are examples—but not much had been done. Bissell made that talk into something real.

Only days before President Eisenhower approved the original JM/Ate program, Tracy Barnes had been at dinner at Senator John F. Kennedy's Georgetown home. John Bross, now Bissell's top planner, also attended. The star attraction was the Englishman, former spy, and author of the James Bond thrillers, Ian Fleming. Asked about Castro, Fleming ruminated that what he would do would be discredit the Cuban leader, subject him to ridicule, harping on Cubans' fascination with money, religion, and sex. A huge Fleming fan, like Allen Dulles himself, Barnes passed this vague notion along, and early the next morning Dulles telephoned the home where Fleming was staying.

But the historian Evan Thomas is correct to note that it remains impossible to connect the Fleming suggestions and the early CIA program by anything more than suggestion. Under orders from President Lyndon B. Johnson, in 1967 the Central Intelligence Agency's inspector general carried out a full internal investigation of efforts to kill Castro, and the same ground was later plowed by a presidential commission (the Rockefeller Commission), a Senate investigating committee (the Church Committee) in 1975, and a House of Representatives committee (Select Committee on Assassinations) in 1979. Both the internal and independent investigations found CIA plots against Castro beginning around this time, and found the early ones focused on somehow discrediting the Cuban leader. One plot envisioned radioactive chemicals sprinkled in Castro's shoes, presumably during a scheduled visit to Chile, which would cause his hair to fall out, robbing the image of Castro's virility. The CIA had agents on the staff of a radio station on Castro's itinerary; Fidel unaccountably canceled the visit.

Much more concrete was what occurred following Eisenhower's decisions of August 18. Deputy Director Bissell called up Col. Sheffield Edwards and asked him to drop by. Edwards, another of the ex-FBI folk at the agency, headed the Office of Security, part of the CIA Directorate for Support. Bissell asked Edwards to contact the Mafia, whose gambling profits from Havana casinos had disappeared as Castro prohibited the practice. Edwards undertook to do so. This track of the Cuba operation remained entirely separate from the exile project. Jacob Esterline knew of the plot but had no knowledge of the planning. Its purpose was assassination.

Later inquiries into the plots go to considerable lengths to determine whether Allen Dulles approved the scheme. Dulles died in 1969 before the plots became known. Edwards passed away in 1975, never clarifying this point. Richard Bissell, who died in 1994, is exceedingly sparse on the murder plots in his memoirs, but claims *he* first learned of the Mafia approach *from Edwards*. The CIA inspector general in 1967 was quite specific that it was Bissell who *asked* Edwards to get involved. Edwards and other figures in these events all recalled specific exchanges with Bissell, who professed not to remember any of them. His generic stance with investigators was that he did not recall but that some such contacts must have occurred. Bissell's memoir remark that "I had no desire to become personally involved" is certainly correct, but the antecedent, that "The idea did not originate with me (as some authors and historians have claimed it did)," can only be true in the sense that Bissell had been asked (by someone higher up) to take care of this matter.

It has been established that Colonel Edwards personally briefed Director Dulles and General Cabell about a month after initiating the Mafia contact. In Bissell's presence, Edwards used elliptical terms to refer to the plot, updating the CIA chieftain and his deputy. Bissell personally handled the details. But a key point, never made, is that as DDO Richard Bissell had *no* authority over an officer from the Support directorate. For Bissell to have asked Edwards to do *anything* required sanction from Director Dulles.

Of course Richard Bissell had no experience dealing with the Mafia, as he acknowledges, and that, plus his high-ranking CIA position, were good reasons for him not to become directly involved. Rather, Colonel Edwards asked his deputy, James P. O'Connell, to find someone with the right connections. Among their officers, Robert Cunningham knew a detective named Robert A. Maheu who did. O'Connell and Cunningham, like Edwards, were FBI men who had come to the agency and Maheu, also former FBI, had done contract work for the CIA. Maheu had let go his CIA retainer by this point but remained happy to work with the agency, and Shef Edwards told Bissell he had a man with suitable underworld contacts. The Dulles briefing happened then. The CIA inspector general's comment on this point: "It is appropriate to conjecture as to just what the Director did approve. It is safe to conclude, given the men participating and the general subject of the meeting, that there was little likelihood of misunderstanding." Maheu approached Mafia go-between Johnny Roselli.

Bob Maheu and Jim O'Connell went to Miami the week of September 23, and Maheu alone met with "Sam Gold," later identified as Salvatore ("Sam") Giancana. He in turn introduced the CIA cutout to his courier "Joe," who turned out to be Santos Trafficante. The agency offered $150,000 to take out Castro. O'Connell never met the Mafiosi himself, no doubt to avoid any direct link between the CIA and the Mafia. O'Connell, who headed the Operational Support Branch of Sheffield's office, happened to be very senior for a case officer, another indication of the sensitivity of this initiative. In fact only three persons at the CIA— O'Connell, Edwards, and Bissell—were fully apprised of the plot.

Meanwhile at headquarters, Colonel Edwards went to the Technical Services Division (TSD) of his directorate, the scientists who concocted exotic weapons and equipment for the agency, where chief Cornelius Roosevelt fielded his request. But the doctor who headed the operations division of the Office of Medical Services made notes indicating that on August 16 he was asked for a box of Cuban cigars impregnated with lethal chemicals. The cigars were ready by October but not delivered until four months later. Jake Esterline recalled keeping a box of poisoned cigars in his safe for months until disposing of it. Roosevelt and O'Connell remember the cigar scheme as having been considered but rejected.

Edwards next turned to TSD for poison capsules, bacteria in liquid form. What he got would be solid white pills. When the support chief tested one, it lay inert at the bottom of a glass of water. Unacceptable. Other capsules were crafted, tested on monkeys, and worked. A pencil was also hollowed out and prepared as a device with which to smuggle capsules into Cuba. The CIA inspector general proved unable to determine exactly when the capsules reached O'Connell, who passed them to Johnny Roselli for Trafficante, but this happened in February 1961 or later. By then the plot had already failed. The Mafia's man in Havana, Juan Orta, director general of Castro's personal office, had been slated as the hit man to poison Castro. Orta had apparently gotten into Trafficante's pocket by taking bribes on casino licenses back in Batista days, but Fidel fired him on January 26. After that the CIA had no way to deliver a poison.

Trafficante briefly favored using a prominent exile, identified as Tony Varona, as an assassin, but that too fell through, though O'Connell and Edwards told the inspector general money went to Varona for the job. When Jake Esterline learned this he went through the roof, properly insisting that anti-Castro leaders could not be involved in any such plot. In the spring of 1961 Edwards had word sent to Roselli that the project had gone onto the back burner. There would be no neutralizing Castro. The Cuban operation would have to succeed on its own.

A different story of the vendetta against Castro is told by the Cuban exiles themselves. For the most part the exiles ardently believe, with some justification, that they created a resistance of which the CIA took advantage. As agency reports noted soon after Batista's fall, the romance of the revolution wore off quickly, and by the spring of 1959 disillusioned Cubans, scattered at first but gradually building links, began to oppose Castro. The Communist question—whether the Maximum Leader was one or not—predominated for them. Cuban government repression and property seizures drove more and more into opposition.

In February 1959 fifty men went back into the Sierra Maestra under Manuel Artime, a former Batista military commander who had sided with Castro. Styling themselves "*commandos rurales,*" they taught reading to illiterate peasants. Several contingents of these workers for the revolution made progress until Havana ordered them to substitute the teaching of Marxist doctrine. That became the last straw for yet more Cubans. By the summer, opponents had begun to coalesce.

Dominican dictator Trujillo backed a plot against Fidel that August, but the *fi-delistas* broke it up, then purged the army of all former Batista elements. By October the "red terror" had progressed, with Havana ordering the arrest of remaining *commandos rurales* as well as such revolutionary leaders as Huber Matos, now accused of fomenting revolt against Castro. Days later came the death of another of the most-admired *commandantes*, Camilo Cienfuegos, who disappeared under mysterious circumstances after arresting Matos.

In November 1959 Dr. Manuel Francisco Artime and other military men organized one anti-Castro group. A month later Rogelio Gonzalez-Corso, Higinio "Niño" Diaz, and others created a fresh umbrella organization, the *Movimiento de recuperación revolucionario* (MRR), soon to be a mainstay of the resistance. On February 5, 1960, students in Havana mounted a public protest against visiting Russian minister Mikoyan, and guerrilla activities began in the Escambray Mountains a few weeks later. Commandante Evelio Duque became a key rebel field commander, and Gonzalez-Corso, who took the *nom de guerre* "Francisco," the central underground coordinator. By April the MRR network extended to all the provinces. Francisco became the main coordinator among a profusion of rebel movements sprouting everywhere. In July the newly created *Frente revolucionario democrático* (FRD) voted Francisco its national chief in Cuba. Six weeks later, desperate for supplies, Francisco secretly made his way to the United States to try to synchronize the internal resistance with outside aid. Gonzalez-Corso certainly encountered the CIA, not just the exile organizations, for he returned to Cuba on a U.S. submarine, bearing gifts for his fiancée Dulce Carrera-Justiz.

What opposition existed inside Cuba remained uncertain. Nino Diaz's band in the hills outside Guantanamo never had a battle. Diaz, lamenting the shortage of recruits, soon turned up in Miami to make cause with the exiles. Artime's underground dissipated after his letter of resignation appeared on the front page of a Havana newspaper. Artime went into hiding and arranged for the Americans to smuggle him off the island. Cuban engineer Manuel Ray, who had been M-26 underground boss for Havana and then Castro's minister of public works, also claimed to be organizing a network and wanted CIA help.

While Francisco attempted to coordinate with the anti-Castro forces outside Cuba, deputy Lino B. Fernandez took over. Calling himself "Ojeda," Fernandez passed along important intelligence that MRR agents acquired. Ojeda had to deal with another rebel *commandante*, Plinio Prieto, who insisted he had contact with the Americans and direct support from the CIA. Prieto wanted to be taken to the rebels in the Escambray. Ojeda did as asked.

Years later Lino Fernandez recalled this period painfully. The resistance did not call the CIA, rather the reverse. Resistance member Rafael Quintero makes the same point: he went to the United States to get someone, anyone, to agree to help. He had not been looking for a CIA connection. Ojeda insisted he had conversations with agency people still in Cuba—Jim Noel continued to head the Havana station until the United States withdrew its embassy in January 1961—but rejected their approach.

"The CIA men wanted to put in our hands the Batista people—members of the army. We didn't like that," Fernandez related at a 1996 conference. "We were against Batista. We were fighting against Batista for seven years. . . . There was no *way* we were using the Batista army."

Cubans struggled to create a resistance, said the former guerrilla chieftain, making his point a different way, but the CIA "tried to create *another* internal resistance without taking the trouble to find out what was already there." Or again, "The CIA tried to invent, to fabricate, an opposition inside Cuba at the same time . . . there was already a growing resistance movement." Rafael Quintero recalls being asked by the CIA in March 1960 how many Cubans were actively against Castro; he put the number at five thousand. Outside, in Miami, Manuel Artime began enlisting volunteers who trained, hopefully but rather unrealistically, to join the internal resistance.

But attitudes toward Batista, and Castro's communism, remained inextricably intertwined, and not only for the Cubans. Many anti-Castro activists drew the line at working with others they saw as tainted from the Batista years. Manual Artime drew some of that opprobrium. Conversely, others rejected figures they saw as too close to Castro or his brand of socialism. Manuel Ray, a founder of the MRR, was especially controversial in that way. As the result of such cleavages, only in the very last days before the CIA's invasion did the agency's political action people succeed in inducing the Cubans to widen their political council to include Ray. Typically, by that time agency analyst Gleichauff at the Miami field office had identified no fewer than *seven hundred* distinct anti-Castro groups functioning in Florida. Also typically, an American diplomat in the Havana embassy recalls Jim Noel as keeping silent about Manuel Ray at meetings while in the corridors the CIA station chief repeatedly tarred the man as a socialist, insisting the United States could not work with him. Yet task force boss Esterline thought the station chief liked Ray. Noel himself told the historian Peter Wyden of his fondness for Ray, claiming to have helped smuggle him out of Cuba and to have engineered the compromise that brought Ray into the Cuban exile coalition.

An anti-Castro opposition certainly existed, but the Cubans themselves, both the internal resistance and the exiles, never succeeded in making it unified or cohesive. For its part the Central Intelligence Agency, spurred on by Castro government measures—Fidel finished nationalizing U.S. businesses in October, almost 550 of them—hastened to complete arrangements for the secret war. But the CIA succumbed to the same cleavages as rent the Cubans. It had a whale of a job trying to make Eisenhower's covert action a reality.

Immediate activity at Quarters Eye followed President Eisenhower's August decision. The first move became securing a Central American base to prepare the Cuban exiles. As Guatemala station chief years before, Esterline knew the prominent Alejos family, of whom Roberto Alejos owned a mountain plantation he called Helvetia, a large, secluded locale. Esterline had his successor, Robert K.

Davis, approach Alejos, who proved quite amenable. The task force chief cleared the move with the secret war managers. Dulles, Bissell, and others asked him to be front man with the Guatemalans. Esterline met Alejos in Miami, then both flew to Guatemala City aboard an agency aircraft, "black" in CIA parlance, leaving secretly and entering illegally. On a mission with the knowledge of the ambassador but no contact with the embassy (except through Davis), the WH/4 chief negotiated an agreement with Guatemalan president Miguel Ydigoras Fuentes allowing the CIA to train troops in his country. The Guatemalans had no problem making a deal—not only did they owe the CIA for their place in power, Esterline told them the exiles would be in their country for just two months. The Helvetia plantation became known as Camp Trax.

At the offices of WH/4 Jake Esterline listened while Allen Dulles laid down parameters for Project Ate. Dick Bissell supplied detail. Tracy Barnes, Bissell's associate director, supervised. Richard Helms sat quietly—rather out of character—frequently looking at his fingernails. Soon Helms stopped coming to project meetings altogether. Beyond his help in drafting the March project proposal, work on a few early cables, and a peripheral role in one of the aircraft incidents, the DO's chief of operations stayed away from JM/Ate. Helms read none of the daily message traffic, consulted no one on WH/4 staffing, made no comment on the plans.

Whether Helms absented himself or was purposely cut out remains obscure even today. In memoirs Bissell concedes his uneasy relationship with Helms and attributes the standoffishness to that. In *his* reminiscences Helms writes only elliptically of feelings regarding the project, piggybacking off the Bissell memoir to assert that no one ought to have needed the months it took to appreciate the difficulty of creating a World War II–style resistance (as Bissell complains), and that the most appropriate CIA role would have been the recruiting of agents in Castro's government who could help blunt Cuban efforts to export revolution. Biographer Thomas Powers attributes Helms's silence to distaste for and opposition to the plan. Helms focused on running clandestine activities, leaving Cuba entirely to others. Bissell, blaming his own managerial style, later expressed regret at not having taken Helms more seriously.

Unlike Helms, Richard Bissell had complete faith in Project Ate. His experience with Guatemala had given the DDO a "lively appreciation" of the seeming susceptibility of Latin societies to subversion. This "inherent vulnerability," and CIA's wealth of know-how as a result of Success and Ajax, furnished the basis for action, making Cuba "another suitable and manageable target." By August Esterline's people had progressed enough to uncover political fissures among the anti-Castro Cubans—charges of Batista taint embroiled the very first cadre sent to Florida's Useppa island for leadership training, and the unpleasantness replicated itself when the agency opened Camp Trax. Tensions also arose between the exiles and the CIA, whom they saw as imposing a *different* politics on them. And there were the technical headaches of mounting various maritime and aerial operations.

The result that Dick Bissell writes of—"a thorough education in the difficulty of establishing an effective guerrilla organization"—is what Helms thinks the

DDO ought to have known beforehand. By then Bissell, immersed to his ears, could not turn back. Moreover the onus remained on his shoulders—as the secret warrior put it to an interviewer in 1976: "In the preparations for and conduct [of] the Boy [sic] of Pigs, there were an awful lot of operational decisions that I couldn't possibly take back to Allen."

Tracy Barnes also believed in the Cuba project. Helms is acerbic on the subject of Barnes. The consummate spy, Helms saw Barnes as someone who could never quite "get the hang of secret operations," rather like failing despite endless effort to master a foreign language. Barnes, in Helms's view, had turned in totally unremarkable performances as chief of station in posts in Germany and London and, promoted by Dulles's boosterism, remained blissfully unaware of his inadequacies. He was, Helms devastatingly notes, "a man of Allen Dulles's imagination." Similarly, the CIA official historian considers that Barnes larded the files with numerous memoranda that went over well-trodden ground, contributing little—in fact that Barnes had engaged in "verbal diarrhea." Yet with Richard Bissell preoccupied on many fronts—spy satellites, a new-generation reconnaissance aircraft, U-2 affair investigations to which Bissell had to respond, and *another* CIA covert operation ramping up in Africa—the Cuba project became a special province for Barnes.

When Cuba was over and the dust had settled, there would be an internal inquiry by Inspector General Lyman Kirkpatrick, different from the ones on the anti-Castro plots. One of Kirkpatrick's big criticisms would be that the project had not been staffed by the best agency people. Helms agreed. So does agency historian Jack Pfeiffer. It should have been simple to prevent the division chiefs, the CIA's barons, from filling the Cuba task force with underproducing case officers by setting a requirement that a certain percentage of assignees have both a set rank and top performance ratings. Helms himself warned off Tom Polgar when the latter consulted him on a posting to head the task force. Jim Critchfield, the Middle East baron, also spurned an offer to lead the venture.

Back in April, with the Cuba project beginning to gain momentum, Director Dulles had insisted on the best people, but he did not do enough to provide the right staff. The personnel system that was created enabled Jake Esterline to ask for particular officers, and if denied, to appeal to Tracy Barnes, who took requests to Bissell. As early as April 22 Barnes told the DO chief personnel officer of the WH/4 priority. A month later that official sent the barons a memo demanding help. At the DO weekly staff meeting after the president's August decision, the personnel chief reiterated the rules to the barons. Division chiefs were to bring disputes to him or Barnes. The problem lay specifically with the DO—Jack Pfeiffer points out that the agency's Directorate for Support assigned excellent people. Pfeiffer blames CIA procedures for task forces and notes that the entire arrangement was scrapped after this operation.

Even by August, Esterline still had a good dozen senior officer vacancies, and his project kept growing. Paramilitary chief Col. Jack Hawkins joined up in September. By October, when WH/4 finally reached to within a few people of its 235 anticipated staff, the task force added another 130 slots. The counterintelligence chief at Miami base never did get a case officer assistant. In October there were exactly four CIA trainers at Camp Trax. Its total agency staff numbered nine. Trax lacked any counterintelligence officer for a long time while Radio Swan spent months looking for an announcer. Late in October Hawkins renewed the request for Green Beret instructors. The Special Forces trainers, whom President Eisenhower approved in August, reached the CIA camps only in January 1961. The inspector general would record that almost half of those in the top tiers of WH/4 ranked in the bottom third of agency performance ratings, with about 20 percent in the lowest tenth.

The list of underachievers could have started with Tracy Barnes except that, given his post as associate director of the DO, Barnes had an inevitable role. Nevertheless this criticism of the Cuba affair is overblown. Jake Esterline led a task force many of whose key slots were filled by people renowned in their specialties, either in Project Success or elsewhere. Take the political action staff: Howard Hunt and Dave Phillips were known political operators, and Jerry Droller was well esteemed, though despised for his ambition and without Latin American experience.

The task force also included Jim Noel, former Havana station chief; his deputy; the Cuba desk officer from WH Division; and others. The air boss was Col. Stanley Beerli, CIA's top airman and the mastermind behind U-2 operations. His field assistant, Gar Thorsrud, came from the Tibet project and Indonesia before that. Esterline's deputy, Ed Stanulis, had been top planner for the Western Hemisphere Division. Dick Drain, chief of operations, fresh from service in Greece, had held the same job at the station, and had psychological operations experience in the Eisenhower White House (with Nelson Rockefeller). He knew no Spanish, though, and the closest he'd ever come to Latin America was punching cows in Arizona in 1940.

The top trainer at Camp Trax was an army Special Forces lieutenant colonel, Frank Egan; and the field commander, Hawkins, had participated in World War II amphibious landings and had been guerrilla commander against the Japanese in the Philippines. In Korea he had led a rifle battalion in the invasion of Inchon.

Esterline could navigate the system and ask for people by name. One, Rip Robertson, had been persona non grata to J. C. King after sinking the British freighter during the Guatemala operation, but enlisting Rip as a contract officer did not require King's approval. Esterline thought highly of Robertson and didn't mind bringing him back. Anticipating the need to embark the exile force, as well as for an airfield as close to Cuba as possible, CIA planners decided Nicaragua offered the best possibilities. Robertson used his connections with dictator Anastasio Somoza to obtain a base at Puerto Cabezas on Nicaragua's Atlantic coast. The contract officer became an amphibious warfare trainer, case officer aboard the landing ship *Barbara J.*

Another fresh face was Grayston L. Lynch. A Special Forces captain, Lynch had been on his way to Laos with another program when an army friend, a liaison with CIA, put him in touch with Desmond FitzGerald. The CIA's Far East baron began the process of recruiting Lynch, but somewhere in the bowels of bureaucracy the hire simply got lost. Returning from Laos late in 1960, Lynch saw his friend who immediately pulled him into the Cuba group. Lynch jumped through all the personnel hoops to enter on duty at CIA in less than a day. He worked for field commander Jack Hawkins, the intrepid Marine. Hawkins employed Lynch to train Cuban frogmen and later as case officer aboard the landing ship *Blagar*.

Action began in the air. Colonel Beerli managed overhead imagery of Cuba. That meant the U-2. Beerli slated a first mission for the same weekend that Francis Gary Powers was shot down over Russia. In early August the CIA acquired cheaply—for exactly $307,506.10—all outstanding shares of the faltering Southern Air Transport. The air cargo firm had four acres of property in Florida, owned one C-46 aircraft, and leased another. Planes and crews from Air America, the new incarnation of Civil Air Transport (reorganized in 1959), arrived to beef up the line. It shuttled between Guatemala and a former navy airfield at Opa-Locka, Florida, where the CIA concentrated its Miami-area activities.

Bob Davis prepared the airstrip at Retalhuleu, near Camp Trax, which became the exile base. He contracted an American company active in Guatemala. Eventually the strip, slowed by rain through the summer, received its first airplanes. The work, completed for $1.8 million, cost almost double its budget. Esterline discounted profiteering: the construction had been a fine job completed during the worst season, and the airstrip became active in time to receive the first CIA arms shipments. It would be called the "Hilton" to distinguish it from the spartan facilities at Trax.

Esterline's air staff eventually numbered fourteen. Cuban exiles were recruited as pilots and aircrew—almost a hundred were screened but not all signed up. Gar Thorsrud at Retalhuleu put together five transport and seventeen bomber crews. After August the CIA hired almost eighty Americans from Maj. Gen. George R. Doster's Alabama Air National Guard. They reached Hilton early in December. The CIA also obtained planes from the Guard, including fifteen B-26 bombers, five C-46 transports, and seven C-54 transports. The CIA had wanted B-25s, considering the other aircraft inferior, but could not find any.

For maritime activities the CIA acquired another proprietary, a defunct company in the Florida Keys called Mineral Carriers, Inc. Some early sea missions encountered Cuban patrol boats, leading to demands for a well-equipped mother ship for small boats plying Cuban waters. The agency used Mineral Carriers as cover for two landing ships, *Blagar* and *Barbara J*, which it bought for $140,000 and then spent twice that much to modify. The ships were converted Landing Craft Infantry (LCIs) left over from World War II, displacing some 250 tons and capable of carrying 200 personnel. The CIA bought its first boat, the *Metusa Time*, in the summer and made its first nautical foray on September 28, landing several hundred pounds of equipment on a Cuban beach and picking up two men to bring back to Miami.

A second boat, *Sea Gull*, became a nightmare. Bought from an oil-rig service outfit for $111,000, the boat broke down within yards of its dock and then spent months under repair, consuming the full effort of one of the Miami base maritime specialists. Repaired just in time for a diversionary mission in conjunction with the invasion, *Sea Gull* did little for Miami base. A third CIA boat, the 110-foot *Tejana*, became the workhorse of the effort, though she became active only in February 1961. In one month *Tejana* carried more materiel to Cuba than *all* the previous CIA and Cuban exile cruises put together.

Eisenhower's August decision upped the ante across the board. Cuban exiles began arriving at Camp Trax only to have to build facilities for the big base the CIA envisioned because the Alejos plantation had none. Thus little actual training had been accomplished when the Eisenhower administration, looking at Castro's large military versus the small CIA force, decided on something more. Told to set up a dozen infiltration teams to link up with the Cuban resistance, Colonel Hawkins now got orders to form a larger, conventionally armed unit to back up the teams. On August 22 the lead group of infiltration trainees from Panama, including Manuel Artime, Jose Perez San Roman, Rafael Quintero, and others, arrived at Trax base. By the 27th quite a few exiles were present. Soon there were 160. Weapons arrived late in September along with a shadowy staff that included Eastern Europeans, Mexicans, Chinese, and even a Filipino, Jose Valeriano, who had begun his CIA contract work with Ed Lansdale years earlier. Esterline recalls being "knocked off" his original timetable in August or September but not being much concerned.

In the fall of 1960 CIA analysts reported Soviet-bloc deliveries of equipment to Cuba, including tanks, armored personnel carriers, field guns, and mortars. Castro had increased the size of the Cuban army by half and had a good 200,000 militia.

Richard Bissell spoke to Jake Esterline and Jack Hawkins, arguing several times that if the project relied so much on a landing force, this needed to be larger. Colonel Hawkins, complacent, agreed. "I would talk it to Esterline and Hawkins, and I don't think Esterline bought this view, either as completely or as soon as I did," Bissell told a CIA interviewer later. "I remember the feeling that I was well ahead of King, perhaps—certainly Jake—in the belief that we had to place nearly exclusive reliance for the initial phase on whatever force it was possible to land." Esterline, also worried about Castro's military, preferred to go immediately to the active phase, sending in as many Cubans as the CIA had ready, perhaps landing from an LST and marching them into the Escambray. Even if they failed it would simply have been one more round of the resistance war, not an obvious CIA-backed invasion.

Bissell wanted another thousand or fifteen hundred exile troops and eventually forced that change, but the expansion meant even more CIA people. Bissell recalls, "By late fall 1960, I was greatly concerned that senior officers involved in the operation were overworked and that we were running out of appropriate personnel to fill all the positions." In fact, by the time the Cuban invasion actually occurred, WH/4 would be staffed by almost six hundred CIA officers.

On Halloween, over Director Dulles's signature, headquarters sent revised orders. They contained a new concept: no more than sixty in the infiltration teams;

everyone else would join an "assault force" that would consist of "one or more infantry battalions," its mission "to seize and defend lodgment in target by amphibious and airborne assault." Instructed to count on fifteen hundred men, and told that WH/4 knew the larger operation needed several more months' preparation, Colonel Hawkins should tell the Cubans that a "bigger scale strike" would be better. A reserve unit of several hundred Guatemalans with their own officers, who could be landed behind the Cuban assault unit, also figured in the scheme. The cable noted that the concept had tentative approval from Allen Dulles and that White House approval impended.

On November 3, a few days before the 1960 presidential election, the 5412 Group went over the Cuba project at length. General Cabell attended for the CIA, and Brig. Gen. Edward Lansdale represented the Office of Special Operations of the Pentagon. With his usual care, Gordon Gray pushed members to report status. The Pentagon worried about the large Castro militia, and State's man conjured the image of a ticking clock—he could foresee, said Livingston Merchant, "that there would occur a point in time beyond which covert intervention would not do the job." The group also mulled over assassinating Castro, though for security, or because he did not know, or for other reasons, General Cabell gave the impression the agency had nothing afoot in this area.

There can be no doubt the revised CIA plan amounted to an invasion. The 5412 Group resisted it, making the issue one of a CIA operation as against a combined agency-military one. But the invasion plan went forward, restricted to about half the several thousand Bissell had pushed for. Eisenhower approved. Trax learned the news on November 4. When CIA first briefed the navy on the plan just before 5412, it was the combat unit option that the secret warriors described. Dwight D. Eisenhower, not John F. Kennedy, holds the responsibility here.

A "third force" in the Cuban context meant moderate July 26th Movement adherents who rejected Castro's move to the left. It so happened, however, that WH/4's political action chiefs held opposing views. For Project Ate/Pluto, Howard Hunt wanted no M-26 people no matter how moderate. Gerry Droller, on the other hand, did not much care about the political coloration of recruits. There was continual friction between the two on the subject of whom to enlist, and personal antipathy between them. Droller held the title as WH/4 political action chief, but Hunt had the forward assignment and a reputation honed not just in Guatemala but in Lansdale's Philippines project and elsewhere. Droller got a leg up when Hunt visited Mexico City to meet with the FRD there and lost a briefcase full of secret documents (Hunt blamed one of his agents, but that hardly mattered). On the other hand, Hunt actually visited Havana that summer, which the headquarters-bound Droller could not do.

The search for a surrogate Cuban political movement centered in Miami. Robert Reynolds opened the CIA base there on May 25, 1960. Known as JM/Ash, the base masqueraded as the Coral Gables branch of a New York headhunter firm with a Pentagon contract. Reynolds had to play the buffer between Hunt and Droller. An eleven-year agency veteran, Reynolds had served in Mexico and Argentina, spoke Spanish, and headed the Cuba branch of the DO's Western Hemisphere Division when Castro took power. He knew Esterline from the OSS in Burma in World War II, a nexus that united many on this project. Among the first people selected for the WH/4 task force, Reynolds had another headache besides the Hunt-Droller conflict—a second-in-command who outranked him—but Bob had been Esterline's original deputy and the acknowledged area expert. The arrangement worked fine.

Hunt and Droller were something else. Howard Hunt, a contemporary, had entered on duty at CIA in 1949 just a month after Reynolds. The senior of two political officers at Miami base, Hunt held the reins. Gerry Droller worked out of Washington, liaising to the supposed committee of interested businessmen, and posed as a steel tycoon when visiting Miami. Droller's crude behavior and plantation-master style, with his Teuton accent and specialty in European operations, gave Hunt excuses to put Droller on a tight leash. That applied especially after Droller, as "Frank Bender," held a meeting in a Miami hotel room so boisterous that the next-door neighbor, a stenographer whose brother worked for the FBI, took full notes. The FBI then asked the CIA about this plotting. Meanwhile Hunt exercised his political proclivities. Droller alienated some Cubans, Hunt cut off others. All this did not add up to a happy political alliance. Esterline favored Droller, whom he considered much more reliable than Hunt, but thought Droller his own worst enemy.

Critics of the Cuban fiasco point out that the selection of the FRD excluded more than a hundred other factions. Even so, the *Frente* were an acrimonious bunch, hardly less contentious than Hunt and Droller themselves. When the CIA helped Manuel Ray flee Cuba, the *Frente* split fiercely over whether Ray should be included. The FRD leadership also wanted huge amounts of money. Their budget demands added up to $740,000 a month.

Political action people at the agency guided the *Frente*. Control became a critical issue among the Cuban exiles, leading to the very divisiveness the CIA had sought to avoid. Howard Hunt despised "Manolo" Ray and tried to minimize CIA support for Ray's political group. Washington had to knock heads both to bring the Cubans together and get Hunt to stand aside. With CIA pouring $130,000 a month into the *Frente* alone—a lot less than the Cubans wanted—and a total action budget of perhaps a half-million, there was plenty to fight over.

Agency officers plugged potential leaks in Florida. Already Manuel Artime's MRR efforts had threatened disclosure. In the summer of 1960 local residents near Homestead saw Cubans drilling and heard their loudspeakers at a farm. As a joke someone threw firecrackers into the compound. The exiles thought they were under attack and poured forth, guns blazing. After one prankster was wounded and several Cubans arrested, only federal intervention convinced local officials to drop charges. But a Miami newspaper got wind of the episode, including CIA's connection to the exiles. In Washington, Allen Dulles received reporter Stanley Karnow and his bureau chief and induced them to kill the story.

The press also learned of the CIA communications complex, opened in June at the former Richmond Naval Air Station, leased from the University of Miami. This became a hugely visible element. For instance, where Bob Reynolds, even by the fall, had only a couple of political action people and a couple of paramilitary experts, he had forty-four communications specialists at Opa-Locka, more than the rest of the CIA base altogether.

Meanwhile, with growing numbers of exiles and trainers the CIA's cover story broke down elsewhere too. Early recruits dealt with Americans who insisted they were working privately. After August the scale of Trax, the activities there, and the close cooperation of U.S. officials in Panama and Guatemala made an official connection impossible to deny. By late August *New York Times* reporter Tad Szulc, in Costa Rica covering an OAS conference, learned of the CIA project from Cuban friends. Dissuaded from writing a story once he checked with the State Department, Szulc stayed interested. On October 30 the Guatemala City daily *La Hora* published an article based on bragging by Cuban exile political types that revealed Trax's existence. Picked up by *Hispanic American Report*, a regional studies newsletter by Ronald Hilton of Stanford University, the report tipped off Havana. The Stanford piece, in turn, led to an editorial in the November 19, 1960, issue of *The Nation*.

Miami base had other problems too. Bob Reynolds received his basic instructions in early October. Supposed to personally supervise any project activities in the area, and draw on any CIA facilities, personnel, or resources there, Reynolds had responsibility but vague authority. The Droller-Hunt fight reflected the basic dynamic—key activities were reserved to WH/4 while Miami repeatedly found itself relegated to a support role. The boat operations ran out of Miami, for example, but headquarters, not Reynolds, decided when and how they would be carried out. For air operations Miami functioned only as a letter box, recording resistance requests, passing them up to Esterline, then informing the Cuban resistance of the response. In fact staff sections in Miami had their own channels to headquarters, bypassing the base chief entirely.

On agents the standards were even more confusing. Since most Cubans belonged to one or another group, lines of communication ran to Camp Trax, Miami, and Cuba. Howard Hunt had a claim to use agents as political operatives rather than spies. And Quarters Eye had its call as well—when the U.S. embassy pulled out of Havana, Miami base got orders to take over its networks, but instead they were run directly out of WH/4. No doubt this related to the fact that Jim Noel had gone to Washington. Once again Miami became a letter box. Morale suffered accordingly. Many felt Miami should be a true CIA station, with support from Quarters Eye rather than the other way around: Miami performing menial tasks to backstop the Cuba task force.

Personnel at the Miami base were fewer than needed even to cope with the jobs it did have. Reynolds got his first paramilitary expert in June and a second that summer. Richard Bissell repeatedly questioned why Miami needed any at all, suspicious that Reynolds merely duplicated work elsewhere. Late in August Bissell asked Barnes and Helms to look into whether Miami (and Panama) were over-staffed. Only in September did Miami base get an intelligence specialist, and there would be a long lag in running up the counterespionage section. Reynolds got no photo intelligence because no one at JM/Ash held the necessary clearances. His two maritime specialists were overwhelmed with the boats and infiltrators.

Bob Reynolds repeatedly pressed WM/4 for clarification of his mission, or sufficient authority to execute it. By December he was begging for "discretion for operational action." Several months later, "the base would welcome more precise requirements for its agents . . . in the interest of making more efficient use of them." In his eventual end-of-mission report the Miami chief observed that future denied-area operations should either be firmly vested in a forward base or run from headquarters, but that divided command during Ate/Pluto resulted in competitive relationships to no purpose. By then Reynolds had 160 CIA officers on his rolls, almost half communications people, many of the rest spinning their wheels. The one key relationship that did exist remained that between CIA's political action officers and the Cuban exile leaders.

While exile politicians argued, the Cuban resistance struggled on. At least Ray had a real group in the MRR. Failure to work more closely with him, and with "Francisco," "Ojeda," and the MRR underground, proved one more crucial error. Another guerrilla band in the Escambray Mountains of Oriente was led by M-26 veteran Capt. Manuel Beaton. With several hundred men, Beaton might have accomplished something, though critics derided his band as little more than a collection of relatives. The exiles bragged of a thousand or more guerrillas in the Escambray. The first CIA supply drop came by C-54 in early October. This plane was hit, lost an engine, then went off course while the crew slept and its automatic pilot drifted. They barely made a crash landing in Mexico, where the CIA project came close to being blown once more.

Airdrops into Cuba became the bread-and-butter work of Retalhuleu base. During the first phase of the project there would be thirty supply missions, only four of them judged successful. There were also more emergency landings—in Mexico, Jamaica, and the Cayman Islands. In the Jamaica incident the snafu went entirely unnoticed by CIA. *Frente* radio monitors heard the emergency message, and exiles warned the secret warriors of the disaster. Worse, when the pilot telephoned the agency's Guatemala emergency number, officers said they had never heard of him. Only swift action by the *Frente* security chief saved the day: he spoke to the crew in Jamaica and convinced them to return.

The air system seemed sluggish and lacked responsiveness. Requests went through Miami base, which had no role in the missions but had to hold the bag when it came to smoothing the feathers of enraged guerrilla leaders. Here the WH/4 task force too functioned merely as a letter box. Colonel Beerli's Development Projects Division had the real action. A month into his assignment, Hawkins had seen enough to write a blistering memo detailing shortcomings and demanding change. Richard Bissell responded with a pair of directives that essentially confirmed the existing setup; Colonel Beerli continued in charge. When Beerli's people acted on Cuban matters they would be considered part of WH/4, code-named JM/Glow. This simply gave the air staffers extra hats to use rather than subordinating the Beerli unit to Esterline, which had been Hawkins's recommendation. With its own communications, the air staff acted on its own authority and had access to Bissell independent of WH/4. Bissell routinely dealt with Beerli on the U-2 and SR-71 programs, had no qualms about the arrangement, and felt it preserved the division's ability to function outside the Cuban context.

In addition, every proposed flight had to be recommended by General Cabell who had long worked this side of the street, and approved by the 5412 Group, inserting inevitable lags in the CIA's ability to act in a timely fashion. Only around November did Esterline succeed in getting Beerli to designate a single staffer, George Gaines, as focal point for all project-related air ops matters.

Success remained elusive, and much of what passed for it really did not make the grade. Pilot Eddie Ferrer flew eleven times to Cuba before registering a good drop. The frustration became palpable. The resistance felt the same. One mission rated successful took place on December 30. Four days earlier Miami base learned that one of the CIA-trained agents who had infiltrated back into Cuba wanted an equipment drop on his *finca*, or farm, the most convenient location. He specified what he needed and how it should be packed, as well as the location and layout of the drop zone. The request went to Esterline, who passed it to Stan Beerli.

Approval procedures naturally led to a meeting in General Cabell's office. Beerli explained the mission and had finished when the CIA deputy director asked how much cargo space the shipment consumed. Told the cargo represented a small proportion of capacity, Cabell ordered the load topped off with rice and beans. Dick Drain, startled, warned Cabell that the plane's task was to deliver the specific items requested. Propaganda chief Dave Phillips interjected that Cuba had no shortage of rice and beans. But Cabell wanted to be "forward leaning."

"Drop the rice and beans," he ordered Esterline.

The next day Quarters Eye sent word to tell the agent he would receive the shipment as he had requested. But the air staff, in cables not cleared with Esterline, added allotments of 800 pounds each of rice and beans, and 160 pounds of lard in addition to the 1,500 pounds of weapons the agent needed. They also threw in 200 pounds of leaflets for propaganda. When a C-54 flew the mission, the plane tarried too long in the area, showed lights, loosed leaflets onto the agent's farm, and dropped almost a ton of supplies the Cubans did not want and could not handle. The agent actually left Cuba in February and went to Miami to denounce the air operation, cancel a follow-up drop, and say he would accept no more CIA airdrops no matter the content. The agent felt the CIA had simply endangered him.

For some time afterward at CIA, General Cabell would be known as "Old Rice and Beans" while many agency folk picked up "forward leaning" for their lexicon. General Cabell leaves this episode unmentioned in his memoir.

Seaborne supply had its own difficulties: the CIA did not even have a maritime unit. The agency had always borrowed from the U.S. Navy. Once the project began, boat operations were improvised. Cubans themselves were quicker off the mark, with Cuban-owned boats *Reefer* and *Wasp* beginning supply deliveries in September 1960. Typically CIA case officers like Rudy Enders arranged supplies to haul, or coordinated the Miami end of operations to exfiltrate anti-Castro people or insert agents. Around November the agency actually acquired the *Wasp* from its Cuban owners. In 1960 a dozen Cuban or CIA boat missions took place off Cuba. Throughout the period before the invasion, boats carried fifty-one agents, radio operators, or rebel leaders and extracted seventy-nine persons. Early in 1961 Castro imported fast patrol boats and radars from Russia to block the boat activities.

Around December 1960 Castro's Fuerzas Armadas Revoluccionarias (FAR) became actively involved in a major counterinsurgency campaign against the Escambray, beginning a blockade to force hungry guerrillas to emerge in search of food, when they would be captured or killed. By the spring of 1961 the FAR blockade had the guerrillas starving. In all, aircraft dropped almost fourteen tons of materials. Perhaps a third actually reached the rebels while boats landed almost four times as much, again with some seized by Castro forces. This amounted to very thin gruel, and at some point there were probably rebels wishing the CIA had in fact dropped rice and beans to them. The failures perplexed Jake Esterline and his officers.

Meanwhile the analytical component of CIA, the Directorate of Intelligence, had been cut completely out of the action. From Esterline on down, no one in the DO was allowed to request any intelligence analysis that might even suggest what impended for Cuba. The analysts did not "need to know" about the uprising. As a result they could not furnish effective support to the paramilitary planners.

The chief analyst, Deputy Director Robert Amory, Jr., went to many of the same Georgetown parties as the secret warriors but, even privately, heard nothing about JM/Ate. Washington gossip being what it is, Amory undoubtedly found out. He also sat through a Capitol Hill briefing on January 6, 1961, where Allen Dulles presented the Senate CIA subcommittee some details on the Cuban project. But Amory had no standing to supply reports that might call the project into question. The U.S. Intelligence Board analyzed Soviet aid to Cuba in November 1960 and February 1961, but without deeper knowledge of CIA plans their reporting failed to tell WH/4 much of what it needed to know about Castro's capabilities both against the resistance and an invasion.

To cap it all, the CIA from Trax intervened in Guatemalan politics. On November 14 a number of army officers revolted against President Miguel Ydigoras Fuentes, who had allowed the CIA into his country. Dick Bissell awoke to a 3:30 A.M. phone call from the duty officer at Quarters Eye: a dispatch had just come in from Lt. Col. Frank Egan at Trax, conveying Ydigoras's demand for the CIA Cubans to help him. Bissell spoke to the State Department, only to learn the diplomats would not decide until later in the day. Egan needed an answer in an hour. Bissell cabled Egan on his own authority permitting the use of CIA pilots but not the exile troops. He recalls no evidence the troops were ever used. But President

Eisenhower was later briefed that Cubans deployed to Guatemala City and Puerto Barrios, disarming the rebels. It seems that two planeloads flew to the affected places but never got off the aircraft. Cuban veterans like Felix Rodriguez have spoken and written about the intervention. The U.S. Navy also responded, dispatching Amphibious Squadron Ten to the Caribbean with the helicopter carrier *Boxer*, five destroyers, and a contingent of two thousand Marines.

President Ydigoras survived and with him CIA's privileges in Guatemala. But Ydigoras became restive as the CIA Cubans overstayed their allotted two months. The agency asked for two more; after that, Esterline used his frequent trips to assuage the Guatemalan leader.

The CIA contributed to rupturing secrecy. In his effort to recruit Cubans in Miami, Howard Hunt took photos of Trax. The pictures got wide distribution and found their way into the *Miami Herald*. Publication outraged Esterline. Hunt's effort to sanitize the photos did little to disguise their true meaning. Sets of the pictures even reached the Cuban government—the Ministry of Information gave them to a Havana newspaper.

In Eisenhower's councils after November 1960, it would be implausible to argue that Project Ate/Pluto remained secret. The most that could be claimed was that details of it were still hidden. Total surprise became impossible.

President Eisenhower had to be frustrated with leaks, the repeated recasting of the operation, and the OAS's complete rejection of sanctions against Havana. Bilateral trade became the one area where Eisenhower pretty much had his way. Ike beamed at the performance of Bob Anderson, coordinator of U.S. economic actions. In mid-March 1960 the United States revoked export licenses already issued for a sale of helicopters. Two months later Eisenhower terminated all existing aid. In July he drastically reduced the quota for Cuban sugar after amendment of the law permitted such revisions. On October 14 Fidel completed nationalizing the Cuban sugar industry. The administration answered by embargoing almost all trade. Political relations deteriorated. Twice during 1960 U.S. Ambassador Phillip Bonsal was recalled from Havana for "consultations." After Castro demanded withdrawal of half the embassy personnel, the United States, on January 3, 1961, broke diplomatic relations. The final message from Jim Noel's CIA station in Havana went out about noon that day, reporting his code materials destroyed.

The rupture of relations occurred after the Cuban project expanded yet again. The new concept, aired in Allen Dulles's office the week after the 1960 presidential election, envisioned a conventional amphibious landing. The Cuban exiles could establish a beachhead, declare a provisional government, then call for American help. The plan for an invasion went to the 5412 Group on November 16, to President-elect John F. Kennedy two days later, and to Eisenhower on the 29th.

Ike made no final decision, but he demanded expedited preparations. At the meeting of November 29, which included many of the same people who sat on 5412, he questioned the boldness and imagination behind the project, given the necessity for plausible deniability, as well as whether actions were effective. The president repeated the concerns of William D. Pawley, who had complained to Eisenhower about the size of the operation and the political character of the *Frente*. (Pawley, a presidential crony, sided with Howard Hunt's view of exile leadership as too far left.) Ike showed his unhappiness. Referring to the transition, he said he did not wish to be "in the position of turning over the government in the midst of a developing emergency."

If a "developing emergency" existed, no fault lay with Eisenhower's intelligence overseers. More than three dozen 5412 Group meetings touched on Cuba between the project approval and the end of the Eisenhower administration. From November 1960 on, eight to ten of these involved detailed discussion. On December 8 the CIA mounted a full-scale briefing. Jack Hawkins described the conventional invasion option, including the latest developments. Hawkins detailed a concept including an amphibious landing on the Cuban coast preceded by airstrikes, to seize and hold a beachhead, then draw dissident elements to join up, hopefully triggering a general uprising. There would be extensive air preparation—up to a hundred flights a month for many weeks, some of them bombing missions.

The landing force would be a heavily armed unit of 600 to 750 exiles with U.S. training and equipment. Frank Egan described the Cuban force at Camp Trax and its superior motivation and leadership. Egan felt these exiles would have no trouble exacting a heavy toll among Castro's larger forces. The 5412 Group issued no formal approval but encouraged the CIA to proceed.

The agency complained anew of Pentagon foot-dragging, specifically the refusal of Special Forces personnel for temporary duty in training the exiles. It was true. Since August the Office of Special Operations, which advised the secretary of defense on covert operations, had been registering objections; both Graves Erskine and Ed Lansdale voiced criticism. Lansdale was especially acerbic in his comments to Undersecretary James H. Douglas, who represented the Pentagon at Cuba meetings. In the discussion of December 8, Douglas agreed to recommend the release of twenty-seven Special Forces advisers but made clear that the Pentagon in no way supported CIA's plan. Lansdale spoke up, but Allen Dulles interrupted to say he was not a principal on this committee. Undersecretary Douglas countered that the Group should indeed listen. Months later, when CIA air boss Stan Beerli told an investigating panel that the agency had had to fight for every single thing it got out of the Pentagon, the complaint really referred to Lansdale and his colleague Fletcher Prouty.

President Eisenhower worried about synchronization among the U.S. agencies. At Ike's November meeting he created a coordinating panel with a senior official from the State Department plus one from the agency. The conversation took place immediately after the president spoke to William Pawley, who had wanted a single coordinator and proposed himself for the job. Instead Ike went for the panel. The State Department nominated Whiting Willauer, Dick Bissell chose Tracy Barnes. On December 7 the president approved. These men handled everything related to Ate. Willauer, the chairman, who had done so well in maintaining the Honduras base for the CIA's Guatemala coup, was recalled from Costa Rica, ostensibly as special deputy to Thomas Mann, the assistant secretary for Latin America. He usually took the CIA side in disputes. The Special Group itself continued to furnish overall guidance.

At Willauer's first meeting with his focal group the ambassador's vision emerged as even more expansive than CIA's—five to ten thousand Latino volunteers to train in the United States and get rid of Castro. A Pentagon representative listened aghast. Willauer also called attention very early on to the skimpy air side of the project—his experience with Civil Air Transport showed here.

The leaders of the secret war gathered again on January 3, 1961, to discuss progress as well as the rupture of diplomatic relations with Cuba. Bissell reported that Ydigoras wanted CIA forces out of Guatemala by March 1. The exiles' own morale would suffer if they did not soon see action. The time problem also applied at the OAS, observed Willauer. American bases, unacceptable to Eisenhower, were the only suitable alternative. No one spoke of the difficulties of CIA's Miami base, the ineffective aerial supply, the lack of visible strengthening of resistance on Cuba, or the continuing popularity of Castro, and precious little would be said of the deep enmities among exile leaders. Participants instead emphasized their confidence in the troops. Gordon Gray mentioned a report calling the Cubans the best army in Latin America. Although he saw some equipment shortages, Joint Chiefs chairman Gen. Lyman Lemnitzer agreed. Within weeks, frustrated, these wonderful exile troops would mutiny.

President Eisenhower summarized: the two reasonable alternatives were to support the Cubans to go in March, or abandon the operation.

Exactly seven days later the *New York Times* published an account of Cuban exiles training in Guatemala.

Did the president bequeath his successor a "developing emergency"?

Eisenhower's presidency ended with the Cuban project at mid-course. *But* during his final months in office, and especially after the election that Kennedy won, Eisenhower had sparked a remarkable surge in preparations, including a much-expanded operational concept. Then he left Jack Kennedy to choose between the tough alternatives Ike had summed up on January 3. Only two days before Kennedy's inauguration, Eisenhower's councils were still grappling with problems that could only be passed on. The horns of the dilemma were even clearer then: Whiting Willauer wrote a memo on January 18 that explicitly said the Cuba project might not succeed under existing plans, that to proceed *assumed* the United States stood ready to intervene. The next morning, at the last Eisenhower-Kennedy meeting of the transition, Ike turned to Cuba. According to Clark Clifford's notes, the president insisted that the United States had to support "to the utmost" those who struggled against Castro, and that responsible action meant "to do whatever is necessary."

The postmortem conducted later by a panel under Gen. Maxwell Taylor concluded that it had been incumbent on the president, at the latest by November–December 1960, to make the basic decision as to how far the United States was willing to go.

By not confronting that choice himself, Dwight Eisenhower left questions history has yet to confront openly. Rather, given events that actually took place on Kennedy's watch, and JFK's forthright acceptance of responsibility, historians have repeatedly presented the Cuba fiasco as a pure artifact of the Kennedy presidency. But Kennedy's people implicitly trusted the secret warriors. Eisenhower had been at the apex of the secret war for eight years; he knew better. He knew the difficulties of the 5412 Group, the CIA's penchant for avoiding implementation review once approvals were given, and the conflicts between military and civilian intelligence agencies. Ike knew the status of Project Ate and its specific problems. Until the moment JFK took his oath, President Eisenhower could have shut down the project with a few words. But he didn't. Ike believed in the secret war.

The declassified records of the Cuba meetings during Eisenhower's final months reveal that the arguments given Kennedy were well rehearsed. Many knew the weaknesses in the CIA's plan. Castro's forces were clearly more powerful than the exiles could muster. The point had also been noted, by the State Department on January 3 and most recently by Willauer on the 18th, that American forces would have to back up the invasion. The conditions for success simply had not been created.

President Eisenhower's stated motive—to counter a leftist or Communist Fidel Castro—evolved despite the lack of Cuban diplomatic relations with the Soviet Union. Actual exchanges of Cuban and Soviet diplomats occurred only during the summer of 1960, when the CIA already had its project in motion. The rise of U.S. hostility in many ways resembles the tragic enmity Eisenhower permitted to develop toward Nasser and Egypt, with peremptory choices for covert action, dismissals of the foreign leaders' words and deeds, and an almost willful refusal to understand their positions. The net result put America on the wrong side of its own advocacy of national self-determination. Covert actions to impose regime change, even if successful, also put Washington in a poor position to insist that America stood for democracy.

The question of direct American involvement in Ate/Pluto also illustrates the control system gone awry. That no Americans were to be involved in combat remained a fundamental assumption. After the fiasco in Indonesia it is doubtful whether Ike would have accepted any direct involvement. But before the end of his administration, Americans were flying with the exile air force, and CIA officers were commanding the rebel LCI mother ships.

Eisenhower told Max Taylor just weeks after the Cuban operation went down that he held no responsibility, he'd never approved any invasion. Two years after Kennedy's death, Eisenhower repeated the claim in interviews and in his memoir *Waging Peace*: he had never approved a plan because the exiles never had a unified political leadership. According to Ike there had been a "program" but no plan. This recollection is supported by his son and other White House staff. Yet the date on the CIA's plan for a conventional invasion near Trinidad, Cuba, is December 6, 1960. There was a D-Day too—March 1961—as well as a specific timetable for invasion-related events.

Eisenhower's memory is correct only in a technical sense: he withheld sanction due to the problems with Project Ate. But he personally participated in numerous deliberations on the Cuba plan—throwing plausible deniability to the wind—and pushed for more action. He *did* approve an invasion-dependent scheme, and he knew that John Kennedy would have to execute or cancel it. Ike also knew that Kennedy lacked the detailed understanding that might have guided a decision. Eisenhower's not acting to halt the operation essentially constituted approval.

At numerous meetings, Gordon Gray remembers, the president repeated one of his mantras: "Now boys," Ike would say, "if you don't intend to go through with this, let's stop talking about it." Eisenhower did not take his own advice. Within months the result would crash atop the secret warriors' enterprise like a ton of bricks.

12

The Bay of Pigs:
Failure at Playa Girón

THE CUBA OPERATION almost never came off, and in every way it would have been better if it had not. Each day Castro grew more entrenched and his militia more numerous and better armed. Each day the exiles lost a little credibility. But Jake Esterline and his bosses, aware of the stakes, had no intention of moving against Castro until their exile force had been fully prepared, and the U.S. military trainers reached Camp Trax only late in the game. Jack Hawkins needed a solid, on-the-ground evaluation of the Cuban force. General Lemnitzer could say whatever he liked at White House meetings, but his were paper assessments based on figures for equipment and such. Hawkins and Esterline realized that many of the Cubans' weapons had just been issued, and the exile unit, swollen every day by new recruits, no longer actually met U.S. military standards. Agency trainers like Napoleon Valeriano and William Buckley knew a lot but lacked the up-to-date awareness of the professional military. Without Special Forces trainers, the CIA believed their Cubans would not be set until the fall of 1961. The Cubans thought themselves plenty ready and viewed American higher-ups, if not their immediate supervisors, with increasing suspicion and scorn, especially the Filipino trainer Valeriano.

Exile veterans often romanticize this Guatemala training phase. The truth was different. At Retalhuleu Cuban pilots resented the handling of air operations and their exclusion from the base's little social club. The failures of flights to succor the resistance lowered morale even more. A number of the Cuban airmen staged a strike to protest conditions. They were taken away, not to be seen again. At Camp Trax the Cubans also abhorred their conditions. The American trainers lived in Roberto Alejos's plantation *hacienda* atop the hill. The training necessarily remained perfunctory until weapons were distributed. On January 13 Lt. Col. David Crowe finally arrived with almost forty Special Forces soldiers. Meanwhile divisions sharpened between exiles from the student groups and those of the former Cuban military. When the Cubans tried to elect their own leader, the Americans insisted on selecting him instead. The CIA chose Jose ("Pepe") San Roman, an officer of the old Batista army trained in the United States at Fort Benning and elsewhere. San Roman had led a military revolt against Batista and been imprisoned, but that did not excuse him in the eyes of the purists.

What the CIA saw as ensuring a professional cadre, many Cubans viewed as against the very principles of democracy for which they wanted to fight. While Trax boss "Colonel Frank"—army Lt. Col. Frank Egan—was in Washington, the exiles had it out. San Roman assembled the brigade, told the men they would be going to Cuba under his command, and asked those who did not wish to follow him to step to the right. Almost half the existing force, 230 men, including every person in the planned second and third battalions, took that step. Egan returned to face protesters' demands.

In interviews and oral histories, many participants pass over this January 1961 near mutiny. In his book-length account of the Bay of Pigs, CIA contract officer Grayston Lynch fails even to mention the brigade mutiny. Francisco Molina of the Second Battalion is one of the exceptions, but he remembers "some problems in Guatemala" as a coup d'état against the *Frente*. Battalion commander Hugo Sueiro describes events simply as "political turmoil at the camp." Francisco Hernandez, another Second Battalion participant, recalls fearing that their officers were taking CIA orders, not those of the Cuban political leadership, and that was what caused the trouble. A hundred exiles remained adamant even after mediating a working arrangement. The agency, among other things, agreed to banish trainer Valeriano, whose role had much diminished anyway with the arrival of the Special Forces. Cuban holdouts were kept in tents for two weeks of the rainy season. Then Howard Hunt and several *frente* political leaders visited Trax and exhorted them. The FRD people told the men the CIA were there to help, disguising the degree to which, in fact, the brigade existed as a CIA creation.

In a deft political move, Jose San Roman resigned, reenlisting as a private. Egan defended Pepe and reinstated him as brigade commander. A dozen hard-core *refusniks* were sequestered, in fact kept prisoner, until the Cuban operation had ended. Pepe San Roman gradually gained the confidence of the remaining Cubans, even those who had seen him as a *batistiano*. The CIA's selection had been a good one. Manuel Artime, resident political authority of the FRD—and liaison with the Americans—also helped end the controversy. It had happened for reasons that had everything to do with what made Ate a CIA project rather than an exile improvisation.

Meanwhile, the exiles suffered their first training casualty. Carlos Rodriguez Santana, recruit number 2,506, fell to his death during a march through the mountains. In memory of him the Cubans adopted the unit designation Brigade 2506. San Roman commanded a force that eventually totaled about fourteen hundred men. Beginning with the Second Battalion, the brigade units went successively to a lowland base for intensive unit training.

The brigade contained six small "battalions" and a heavy weapons group. Men of the First Battalion trained as paratroopers, getting up at three or four in the morning for even more strenuous exercises. The Fourth Battalion made up a small armored force with five M-41A2 tanks, plus trucks mounting .50-caliber machine guns. The tank detachment actually trained at the U.S. Army base at Fort Knox and never met their comrades until the invasion. The weapons unit contained 4.2-inch mortars, 3.5-inch bazookas, and 57- and 75-millimeter recoilless rifles. The "battalions" ranged from 167 to 185 men, somewhat fewer than a standard rifle company in the U.S. Army. There also existed a commando force under "Niño" Diaz of 168 men, who would make a diversion at another point on the Cuban coast just before the main landing. They too trained separately, as did the brigade frogmen, in Louisiana; landing craft crew trained in the Florida Keys or Puerto Rico.

Finally, there was the exile air force under the nominal command of Maj. Manuel Villafaña. The air group numbered more than 150 Cubans and an equal number of Americans, both as aircrew and in support roles. The combat element consisted of sixteen B-26 bombers, the air transport unit of eight C-46s and six C-54s.

Richard Bissell expected to reinforce the Brigade 2506 beachhead once the invasion began. About 500 Cubans gathered in the Miami area, of whom 162 joined the brigade before it left Guatemala. The rest would fly into the battle area once the exiles set up an air base. The invasion force carried extra weapons for 4,000 volunteers and expected to enlist numerous *campesinos*. These would flesh out San Roman's small battalions.

Meanwhile problems with the Cubans seemed to grow almost daily. Besides discussions in Miami and Havana newspapers, a major leak appeared in the *New York Times* in a January 10, 1961, article by Paul Kennedy. In yet another sign of rapidly eroding secrecy, in its January 27, 1961, issue *Time* magazine printed a photograph of Cuban rebel aircraft sitting on the ground at the Retalhuleu base. The Guatemalan government began insisting the CIA Cuban unit leave the country. Something had to give.

A different and huge obstacle lay in the fact that Dwight D. Eisenhower no longer commanded the secret warriors. John Fitzgerald Kennedy had won the 1960 presidential election on November 6, 1960, defeating Richard M. Nixon. Had Nixon won, the secret warriors would have been in no doubt about their Cuba project. Nixon lacked Eisenhower's professional mastery of the craft of intelligence, but he had been an enthusiastic supporter from the outset. Kennedy remained an unknown quantity. Or not. Allen Dulles did know the new president—he had met Jack in April 1955 at Palm Beach. Good friends with Kennedy's father Joe (Dulles biographer Peter Grose maintains that Allen knew Joe Kennedy mainly by reputation, but Dulles himself insisted, in a 1964 oral history with Tom Braden, that he knew Joe Kennedy "quite well" from his days at the law), Dulles befriended Palm Beach neighbors of Jack's father. The neighbors' home on North Ocean Boulevard lay up the street from the Kennedy compound, so Dulles could hardly miss the Kennedys on his visits. Dulles met Jack as the Massachusetts politician recuperated at Palm Beach from an illness, working on what would be his best-selling book *Profiles in Courage*. Dulles knew Jack Kennedy as a devotee of spy fiction, and knew him well enough that Jacqueline Kennedy made Allen a present of one of Ian Fleming's early James Bond novels, *From Russia with Love*. Dulles liked it so much he joined the legion of Fleming fans and bought the next Bond novels himself.

Of course there were occasional contacts with Congressman, then Senator Kennedy on official business. And Allen Dulles, Richard Bissell, and other senior CIA people also encountered Kennedy on the Washington social scene. Dulles, Bissell, and Kennedy, for example, all shared friendship with newspaper columnist Joe Alsop. Robert Amory, the agency's deputy director for intelligence, had met Kennedy while an undergraduate in college, and while not close, always found him cordial when he encountered Kennedy on Capitol Hill.

Dick Bissell had his own Kennedy moment, which he speculates resulted from an Alsop comment to Jack. The candidate invited Bissell to his Senate office and asked his views on a range of issues. Bissell answered but made it clear he still worked for Eisenhower and could do nothing of an active nature. Kennedy asked Bissell to give him ideas that might be fed into the campaign, but the CIA official, pressed by the daily string of emergencies, never got around to it. Bob Amory's impression was that Kennedy regarded Bissell as one of the four or five brightest people in the government.

During the 1960 presidential campaign, Allen Dulles briefed JFK on international matters in general, including the Cuba situation, but Kennedy had not been privy to the covert plan. As a matter of policy, Dulles later put it, "I did not brief candidates on secret operations which were destined to come out in the future." Richard Nixon, not so sure, pressed Allen after his first briefing, admonishing Dulles to tell Kennedy nothing. Indications are that Dulles had mentioned a covert capability designed to bring political pressure on Castro, and the Swan Island radio activity, but nothing more. The reports Dulles sent President Eisenhower after each of his briefings are sparse on detail and indicate simply inclusion of the subject of Cuba. Many years later, agency historians preparing a history of presidential candidate briefings noted: "A search of CIA records has failed to confirm that Dulles briefed Kennedy on the status of Cuban covert action planning in either of their two sessions held before the election in 1960." In contrast to the first Kennedy briefing, at Hyannis in July, the second took place in impromptu fashion on September 17, when Dulles, interrupted at a Georgetown dinner, was asked to meet JFK and spoke to him privately for about half an hour. There could not have been time to tour the world horizon *and* cover covert operations.

But nothing could convince Richard Nixon. In mid-October, during the climactic phase of a series of televised debates between the candidates, Nixon denounced Castro in a speech, declared his patience exhausted, and advocated a quarantine of Cuba. The Cuba issue resounded in the debates, in which Nixon painted Kennedy as soft on communism. Responding to that charge, on October 20 the Kennedy campaign put out a statement demanding support for Cuban "fighters for freedom," blaming the U.S. government for providing "virtually no support" to the "non-Batista democratic forces in exile, and in Cuba itself, who offer eventual hope of overthrowing Castro." Drafted by Kennedy aide Richard Goodwin, who had tried to get JFK on the telephone the night before but found him asleep, the statement went out, further enraging Nixon. At their last debate Kennedy took up the October 20 statement, but Nixon, who later insisted he was trying to preserve the secrecy of the CIA operation, attacked the position as reckless. He asserted that American backing for the exiles would not work, would be condemned by the UN, and amounted to an invitation for Russian involvement in Latin America.

Nixon insisted afterward that Kennedy must have known and had stolen a march in the debate, forcing him to oppose the administration's actual policy as "dangerously irresponsible." Within government Vice President Nixon demanded to learn what Kennedy had been told of the CIA plan. By his account in a memoir, within the hour aide Fred Seaton reported to Nixon that Allen Dulles had indeed told Kennedy. By the CIA director's account, Eisenhower political wizard Wilton B. Persons phoned and Dulles informed him he *had* briefed JFK "on Cuba" but failed to clarify that he referred to events on the island, not Project Ate. Nixon later attributed defeat in the 1960 election, in part, to the unnatural stance adopted regarding Castro. In his book *Six Crises*, Nixon wrote that the newspapers had reported contemporaneously, in July, of Dulles briefing JFK about Cuba, and that he had corroborated his suspicions by speaking to knowledgeable people (Fred Seaton). On publication of Nixon's book in 1962 the Kennedy White House averred that the two-and-a-quarter-hour CIA briefing had not dealt with the Cuban operation. In a battle of press releases, Nixon countered that he had personally researched the matter, adding that Ike's orders had been that Kennedy should be as well briefed as the vice president.

In an April 1962 interview with television reporter Eric Sevareid, Allen Dulles called the whole episode "an honest misunderstanding." Recently declassified records of the phone conversations of his successor, John McCone, who dealt with both Dulles and the White House during this controversy, and advised Kennedy officials on their public statement, indicate that private approaches were made to Nixon but did not dissuade him. Dulles told McCone—accurately—that Kennedy could not have known of the invasion plan because as of the date of the debate (October 20) there *was* no such plan. It would be adopted about two weeks later.

Nevertheless Nixon's analysis in the debate itself proved exactly correct: the enterprise he himself had pushed was indeed "dangerously irresponsible."

"Freedom fighters" happened to be the exact term used in Eisenhower's secret councils to refer to the Cuban exiles. As a matter of fact, secret warriors recount that in the final weeks before the election, Nixon encouraged a slowdown in the expectation he would be taking over. Then, having lost, the vice president egged Ike on to accelerate the project. Task force chief Esterline told a CIA interviewer in 1975, "I blame Nixon far more than I do Kennedy for the equivocation and the loss of time . . . that led to the ultimate disaster."

The flap over Kennedy's Cuba statement was the first of four decisions that in the eyes of history seem to have taken authorship away from Dwight Eisenhower and placed it squarely in John F. Kennedy's basket. The second was Kennedy's actions during the final preparations.

Allen Dulles and Richard Bissell visited JFK at Palm Beach on November 18, 1960. *Now* they broached the Cuba project. The meeting took place outside, near the swimming pool, where a big table permitted them to lay out maps. Bissell described the plan for almost an hour, including the invasion (thus Eisenhower's authorship). Bissell recalls: "The plan, as we outlined it to him, did contemplate some form of landing of a significant force to act as a catalyst in inducing, ultimately, a revolutionary situation in Cuba."

The CIA briefing papers note that points prepared for presentation included Eisenhower's original project approval, the political action efforts already under way, propaganda publications and radio broadcasts, and a range of paramilitary phases. The briefing included discussion of the early guerrilla phase; a second phase with a combined sea-air assault coordinated with guerrilla activity; and a final phase that provided for a possible airborne assault on Havana as well as the contingency for U.S. military intervention if necessary; also the timing and numbers of men and items of equipment to be sent. The CIA explicitly noted that it did not believe resistance activity in Cuba could unseat Castro without outside action. Dulles and Bissell avoided soliciting an approval, and the president-elect volunteered none. The CIA officials also spent time discussing covert activities in the Dominican Republic, elsewhere in Central America, Venezuela, and Tibet.

Afterward the pipe-toting DCI took Kennedy into the back garden for a private conversation. Bissell stayed on the terrace. Soon after the top bosses returned, Tracy Barnes told Howard Hunt that JFK had given a "qualified go ahead."

Meanwhile Kennedy proceeded to rob himself of the machinery Ike had created to control the secret warriors. Kennedy's White House arrangements dismantled much of the Eisenhower NSC systems. The device of the 5412 Group, in theory intact (by March it would have had three sessions), in practice took a backseat to meetings at which JFK personally presided. More than ever before, the new NSC staff transacted business directly. Kennedy never consulted Ike's White House staff secretary, Andrew Goodpaster, who had the relevant information at his fingertips. Kennedy also abolished the President's Board of Consultants on Foreign Intelligence Activities, the one entity supposedly intended for intelligence oversight. Finally, in an action with special impact on interagency coordination for the Cuba operation, on February 8 the Willauer-Barnes group passed out of existence.

John Fitzgerald Kennedy swept into office with confidence that belied his narrow electoral victory. Although his "New Frontier" offered fresh visions of America's role in the world, real policies on questions like Cuba changed not a whit. Instead Kennedy eliminated staff offices he thought had stifled action; he did not see the positive value of those institutions. JFK would have no staffs senior enough to do things on their own and no board capable of providing a second opinion. No doubt thinking he was moving away from a certain (fancied) passivity, with which critics had tarred the Eisenhower administration, Kennedy exercised direct leadership. He made no changes whatever in the upper management of the CIA. Project Ate also continued, though those close to Kennedy insist the young president had a certain ambivalence about it.

The secret war went on as before, the difference being that mechanisms established to control it disappeared. The most obvious continuity between the Eisenhower and Kennedy administrations was Cuba. That project decisively demonstrated the fallacy of abolishing controls over the intelligence community.

Robert Amory stunned colleagues when he attended one of the Kennedy inaugural celebrations, a Camelot costume ball, as Fidel Castro. Some secret warriors saw that as a serious security breach. But Amory didn't care. He had a point to make. Of course, on one level Amory could not break secrecy—as chief of the Directorate for Intelligence he led a CIA unit with no official knowledge of the Cuba project. Roger Hilsman, whom Kennedy appointed to head the State Department's Bureau of Intelligence and Research, believes both he and Amory were cut out of the loop on Cuba precisely because the secret warriors feared they would oppose the operation. Be that as it may, Amory knew. The DI chief at that time held responsibility for the Photographic Interpretation Center that processed all overhead imagery for U.S. intelligence. Its head, Art Lundahl, kept Amory apprised of the pictures passing through his shop. Photos of the Cuban coast were worthy of comment to the boss.

Robert Amory, Jr., a solid Republican, the type who would run for office in Massachusetts, a Democratic state, did not shrink from expressing doubts to this new tribe of Democrats. Amory had already seen the depths of failure. Hungary, several years into his watch at the DI, had affected Amory deeply. In atonement, he and his wife Mary subsequently sponsored a Hungarian refugee into the United States. Amory had no desire for the same thing to happen to the anti-Castro Cubans. He also had a lot more experience with invasions than *anyone* involved in the Cuba project. In World War II Amory had been a landing-craft operator, finishing the war as a colonel in charge of a whole regiment of the vessels, a veteran of twenty-six assault landings in the South Pacific, many of about the same dimension as the planned CIA operation. Jack Hawkins, the actual invasion boss, had participated in exactly two, the massive Iwo Jima endeavor, where the United States had held all the cards and put ashore many thousands of troops, and the large Inchon operation in Korea. Amory thought Hawkins "just didn't know beans about what a small self-contained beachhead would be like." The Cuba plan failed Amory's smell test. But no one consulted him. Perhaps they were scared off by his Castro costume.

Amory, far from alone in his view, represented the element at CIA that was skeptical about the Cuba project. Some doubted the internal resistance could cripple Castro, others questioned that outcome even if the CIA sent in its exile brigade—in other words, they found the project dubious even with CIA at full stretch. Another DI unit was the Office of National Estimates (ONE), which produced the community's official flagship reports, the National Intelligence Estimates. Without bringing it into the circle of knowledge on the plan, Dulles and Bissell asked ONE to assess Castro's grip on power. ONE's memorandum in late January could not have been reassuring to the secret warriors. The analysts judged that time was not on Washington's side, that Castro had successfully consolidated his control.

Barely a couple of weeks earlier Director Dulles had participated in the final reunion of President Eisenhower and his Hull Board watchdog group. The board had long complained that the Directorate for Operations did not incorporate intelligence analyses into its covert action plans. Dulles had defended his agency—and did so again at this January 1961 meeting—responding that the DO used intelligence estimates in all phases of planning. But in fact the ONE report had no discernible impact on the Cuba plan. Equally important, there is no evidence Allen Dulles did anything to ensure that it did.

Two days after the inauguration, Project Ate received its first airing before the gaggle of officials who were Kennedy's men. National security adviser McGeorge Bundy, Secretary of Defense Robert S. McNamara, Secretary of State Dean Rusk, and a host of others endured a long briefing where Brig. Gen. David W. Gray went over the Cuba project in eye-opening detail. For most the day brought their first knowledge that the United States had already created a secret army of Cuban exiles. Gray had poster-size charts and noted that U.S. participation was expected to be necessary.

President Kennedy attended a full-dress presentation a week after the inaugural. While his Palm Beach conversation had been exploratory, the White House meeting on January 28 was specific. He listened as Allen Dulles mentioned what would soon be called the "disposal problem," that the Cuban brigade had to get out of Guatemala soon, and what then? Dulles also told of Castro's growing military power and, somewhat more fancifully, "a great increase . . . in popular opposition." Discussion focused not so much on the invasion plan as on a comparison of that with six alternatives, including economic warfare or direct U.S. intervention. The official record notes the conclusion: "No course of action currently authorized by the United States Government will be effective in reaching the agreed national goal of overthrowing the Castro regime."

"It was very ethereal," Bobby Kennedy recalled a few months later, but what stuck in his mind is that he remembers being told "it would be impossible to successfully overthrow Castro because of his control over his armed forces and the country in general, unless you had the invading force backed up by intervention by U.S. forces." JFK received the ONE estimate judging time to be on Castro's side. Kennedy ordered intensified political action, sabotage, overflights by CIA U-2 aircraft; and State Department preparation of an anti-Castro propaganda plan to be implemented throughout Latin America. He discovered that the U.S. military had not considered the feasibility of Project Ate and directed the Joint Chiefs of Staff to do such a review.

Events began to move swiftly. A few days after Kennedy's orders, the JCS were officially briefed on the CIA's plan for the conventional invasion. This provided for a landing on the south coast, near the town of Trinidad and the Escambray Mountains. The Joint Chiefs' official opinion, after a few days of study by a committee led by Brigadier General Gray, appeared in a paper titled "Military Evaluation of the CIA Paramilitary Plan—Cuba."

The seventeen conclusions in the JCS paper indicated continuing differences. On one hand, the military judged that if the airborne drop were successful, it would take several days for Castro to react to the landing, and thus, despite its shortcomings, the CIA had a fair chance of success. On the other hand, the Chiefs concluded that the Cuban army could reduce the beachhead. What constituted a fair chance? General Gray put it at 30-70. No one he heard went any higher than 40-60. Others estimated the chances *against* achieving surprise at a whopping 85-15.

The military's warning implied the need for rapid breakout from the landing site. But the CIA's own view, articulated by Jack Hawkins in a January 4, 1961, report for Esterline, "Policy Decisions Required for Conduct of Strike Operations Against Government of Cuba," held quite the opposite: Brigade 2506 should try to survive on the beachhead and *not* break out until the time became opportune or the United States intervened. Indeed, CIA planned to fly in Cuban politicians to form a provisional government while agency planners arranged for supply landings for a month on the beachhead. The conflicting views of military and CIA were not reconciled, and President Kennedy now lacked the supervisory staffs to tell him that.

Allen Dulles meanwhile curried favor among the Kennedy people. At several morning staff meetings Dulles referred to the need to gain their confidence. One confidence-building measure came early in February when Dulles, a member of the exclusive Alibi Club, used that venue to host a dinner for key White House staff and top CIA spooks. Just over a block from the NSC staff offices, the Alibi Club, founded in 1884 by disaffected members of another Washington institution (the Metropolitan Club), has an unlisted telephone on a stand with a list of excuses next to it and the prices for each. The Alibi prided itself on decorating with oddments and things donated by members—just fifty at this time. Besides Dulles, future CIA directors Richard Helms, William J. Casey, and William Webster would all be members. Helms's comment that "Very little plotting goes on at the Alibi Club" clearly does not apply to this evening in February 1961. Bissell brought down the house at this basic get-acquainted session, introducing himself by declaring, "I'm your man-eating shark!" But, even from this dinner, the secret warriors did not come away unscathed—someone asked them why the United States had gotten into so much trouble in the Indonesia operation, Project Haik.

American intervention remained a sensitive matter. CIA understood the need to disable Cuban air forces that could disrupt the exile landing. Although a program of exile air strikes had been laid on, the secret warriors knew that Castro possessed some jet fighters. The exiles had no comparable aircraft. Support by jets, the most obvious form that U.S. intervention might take, had been mentioned both by CIA officers and Whiting Willauer. Kennedy rejected it, and the CIA knew of his reluctance.

On February 9 Adm. Robert L. Dennison, commander of the navy's Atlantic Fleet, sought clarification. At a discussion with Kennedy the admiral asked, "Am I likely to be involved in a bail-out operation?"

"No," replied the president. If there were any problems, the exiles would fade into the hinterland; American forces need not become overtly involved.

The next day Dennison received a directive from Joint Chiefs chairman Lemnitzer defining the scope and restrictions on navy support, clearly to be minimal.

By mid-February Esterline knew that Ate could not make the planned invasion date of March 5; Washington delayed it a month. The Guatemalans were asked to accept the delay. The military used this time to send three colonels to inspect Camp Trax and Retalhuleu. They assessed the brigade to be in good shape, but the odds were against surprise. The air evaluation stated that one Castro plane with .50-caliber machine guns could sink most or all the fleet, so if there were no surprise the operation would fail. Without air superiority, the invasion would also fail.

On February 17 the brass had it out. By now the CIA had a paper arguing that the Cuban exiles could not infiltrate Cuba as guerrillas without huge losses, forfeiting effectiveness and being unable to rendezvous to conduct operations. In effect the disposal problem could best be solved by sending the brigade to invade Cuba. Bissell later recalled talk of loading the Cubans onto ships which, if not able to sail for Cuba after a reasonable time, could be escorted to a U.S. naval base (Guantanamo or Roosevelt Roads in Puerto Rico), and the exiles disarmed and set loose. No one wanted to think of the consequences of that. (Jake Esterline years later recorded that no one, from JFK on down, ever asked the WH/4 task force to develop a stand-down plan.) At the February 17 meeting Bissell stressed the need to decide when and how to surface the *Frente* political leaders. Secretary Rusk became the main adversary, arguing that the schedule left him little time to stoke up OAS support for regime change. Kennedy, having seen reports of Castro's jet aircraft, asked if these were a result of the CIA effort. The reply was both encouraging and not: Castro's jets had belonged to Batista, but if the United States waited much longer the Cubans would be receiving Russian jets, as they were already getting tanks and guns.

In contrast to later decades, when Congress and the CIA tussled endlessly over current notification of covert operations, Allen Dulles told legislators about the Bay of Pigs in advance. On March 10 he appeared before the secret subcommittee of the House Armed Services Committee and informed the overseers not only of the timing of the original decision ("just about a year ago now") but of the CIA's efforts with the exile *Frente*. General Cabell followed to describe the exile army and air force. Answering questions, Dulles added that resistance to Castro would have to be sparked from the outside. Cabell claimed that increasing the size of the exile force would mean a lowering of military standards. The CIA deputy director also revealed the plan to seize and hold a position in Cuba rather than fan out to join the guerrillas. Legislators questioned size and feasibility. No one told the CIA it should forget about its invasion.

How could the president interpret the conflicting reports that reached him? In the Oval Office one day Kennedy turned to Allen Dulles, asking him about the odds. The DCI alluded to his conversation with Eisenhower during Project Success. "I stood right here at Ike's desk," said Dulles, "and told him I was certain our Guatemalan operation would succeed, and, Mr. President, the prospects for this plan are even better than they were for that one."

Despite his doubts, Kennedy, McGeorge Bundy thought, kept looking for ways to make Ate work. Allen Dulles encouraged the president, treating him to another recitation of the disposal problem: "Don't forget . . . we will have to transfer [the Cuban exiles] to the United States, and we can't have them wandering around the country telling everyone what they have been doing." Arthur Schlesinger believes that Washington's desire to keep Project Ate going owed much to the embarrassment that would attend its cancellation. At Bissell's full-dress presentation of the plan for an invasion at Trinidad in Cuba on March 11,* Dean Rusk again voiced objections. Rusk wanted an airfield there big enough to handle B-26 bombers so that strikes against Castro's bases could be said to be coming from Trinidad. Told the field was not that long, Rusk wondered if the CIA could airdrop a bulldozer to lengthen it.

"If I ever made a suggestion like that to Mr. Dulles," Esterline interjected, "I should be summarily fired." The Cuba task force chief wore out his White House welcome that day.

JFK saw a daylight landing at a Cuban city as a "spectacular" invasion and asked for an alternative, convincing some that he sold out the Cubans that day. But Kennedy nevertheless issued a directive stating that he expected to approve the invasion. People outside the White House have a very different view of Kennedy's decision: reducing the visibility of the invasion, an action tantamount to diminishing its chance of success, had roots in the president's ambivalence. Kennedy's decision on the "visibility" of the invasion is the second of the choices that have marked him with authorship of this disaster.

Commentators on the Cuban operation often write of the Trinidad plan as if it represented a solution, that is, Project Ate would have been successful if only the CIA's exiles had gone into Trinidad instead of their eventual target. But there were no panaceas. In fact the secret warriors overstated the possibilities at Trinidad while underestimating Castro's defensive potential. An agent reported several thousand Cubans around the city ready to take up arms against Castro. With no means to cross-check, DO operatives took the dubious figure at face

---

* Not to be confused with the island of Trinidad off the coast of Venezuela.

value. Meanwhile Castro, who had no spies in Guatemala but plenty in Miami, and whose security services carefully followed media accounts of exile activity, *expected* the CIA invasion at Trinidad. Where the Pentagon and CIA held that the nearest Castro militia or FAR troops were a hundred miles away, and evaluated their response capacity as a single battalion on the first day, Castro himself revealed at a 2001 conference that the FAR had concentrated two full brigades (six times the force) backed by thirty heavy cannon right at Trinidad, with observation posts overlooking the bay and preregistered artillery targets. Without counting Castro reinforcements, Brigade 2506 would have been landing against superior forces in prepared positions.

But Trinidad, a big town, violated President Kennedy's edict to reduce "visibility." On March 12 Esterline got orders to redraft. In a frantic all-night work session, Jack Hawkins surveyed the Cuban coast for localities that met three criteria: not easily accessible to Castro forces; having an airfield capable of accommodating B-26 and C-54 aircraft, one that could be captured on the first day; and close to suitable beaches. Only a few places matched some of these criteria, and just one met them all: the Bay of Pigs, about eighty miles west of Trinidad. Two days later the paramilitary planners presented the Bay of Pigs option to the Joint Chiefs.

On March 15 both options were outlined at the White House. JFK, to Schlesinger's mind, listened somberly, again rejecting Trinidad as a "World War II assault operation." He ordered the Bay of Pigs plan to be reoriented for a night as opposed to a dawn landing. No one told Kennedy that the United States had never carried out a major nighttime invasion. Other profile-lowering measures included halting rebel resupply flights at the end of March and cancellation of leaflet drops until after the landing. The CIA, whose chance of victory depended on mobilizing the Cuban population, foolishly accepted the flight stand-down, stopping the supply flow to the resistance. JFK also wanted to be able to call off the invasion up to the day before it happened.

Finally it all came down to the people President Kennedy assembled in the Cabinet Room on April 5, his last real opportunity to cancel the invasion. Kennedy went around the table to poll participants. Fulbright adamantly opposed Ate, but the center of gravity was Adolf A. Berle, a former senior diplomat whom JFK had brought back to review Latin America policy. Esterline saw Berle as a strong supporter. Earlier, in a furious battle of memos, Dick Bissell had crossed swords with Tom Mann, the assistant secretary of state for Latin America. Now, like Mann, Berle delivered a lengthy disquisition, with a lot of "con" but a good deal of "pro" too. Asked where he finally stood, Berle declared, "I say, 'let 'er rip!'"

At this point task force chief Esterline returned to Guatemala for one final visit to the camps. As a morale booster he brought along rebel leader Jose Miro Cardona. The men flew black, out of Miami, crewed by some of the CIA's Polish pilots. The secret flight became embarrassing when Cardona suffered a seizure as the plane neared Guatemala City. Oxygen had to be administered. Esterline sweated bricks that they would not need a hospital, which would have meant explaining their presence in Guatemala.

President Kennedy continued wrestling with the go/no-go decision for a few more days, consulting Arthur Schlesinger again, but finally gave way. Kennedy even intervened with the *New York Times* when he learned the paper had a major exposé of the Cuba plan by reporter Tad Szulc ready to go to press on April 10. The president persuaded publisher Arthur Hays Sulzberger to downplay the story, though he failed to get it spiked.

The image of the United States in world public opinion had to be considered. Self-determination had been bedrock American foreign policy since Woodrow Wilson. Plausible deniability remained necessary precisely so that leaders might deny U.S. involvement. At an important forum for world opinion, the United Nations General Assembly, then in session in New York City, a Cuba debate already figured on the agenda. Kennedy had appointed Adlai Stevenson his ambassador to the UN and believed Stevenson's integrity to be a vital asset. Kennedy ordered Arthur Schlesinger to brief the ambassador together with CIA and State Department people.

Schlesinger arrived late for the meeting in Stevenson's suite at the Waldorf Astoria Hotel on the morning of Saturday, April 8. As a consequence, Tracy Barnes, CIA's man, did most of the talking. Steeped in the agency's "need to know" tradition, and despite close friendships with Stevenson's senior assistants and his own acquaintance with the ambassador, Barnes imparted minimal information: this would be an all-Cuban affair merely helped by the United States, not a word about air strikes or other details. True, Bissell had told Barnes to say as little as possible, but Barnes made it impossible for Stevenson to play his role effectively. Barnes's reticence was probably encouraged by the ambassador's reaction—Stevenson doubted JFK had thought through the issues. Within days the effect of Tracy Barnes's inadequate briefing became painfully apparent.

Meanwhile Project Ate accelerated. Two final postponements resulted in an invasion set for April 17. On April 1 Admiral Dennison received marching orders in a Joint Chiefs memorandum. The navy reinforced Guantanamo in case Castro should move against it, and Adm. Arleigh Burke, chief of naval operations, quietly put two battalions of Marines on transports in the area just in case. Dennison provided a flotilla built around the carrier *Essex*. Destroyers *Eaton* and *Murray*, with superior navigation gear, would accompany the invasion fleet to the Bay of Pigs while amphibious ship *San Marcos* carried the exile landing craft with their vehicles and some supplies. A submarine would carry out a diversion at a point off Pinar del Rio, at the other end of Cuba. Dennison's instructions were to avoid association with the exile fleet.

The Cubans sailed not from Guatemala but from Puerto Cabezas, Nicaragua, code-named Trampoline. The rebel navy began assembling early in April, starting with the CIA's *Blagar* and *Barbara J.* Five merchant vessels of the Garcia Shipping Company, chartered by the CIA, carried the bulk of Brigade 2506. When Grayston Lynch, whose ship arrived at the port on April 1, viewed aerial photos of the new landing site at the Bay of Pigs and the nearby village of Playa Girón, he saw coral reefs. Photo interpreters told Lynch he was wrong. Cubans on his ship actually knew the reefs and confirmed to the CIA contract officer they existed. A brigade doctor pointed out the reefs to Colonel Egan during the final briefings. The Trax base commander insisted they were looking at clouds. The disaster proceeded to unfold with the scripted style of a Kabuki play.

The secret warriors worried about JFK's inflexibility on the invasion. They knew well enough the signs of an operation gone awry. Esterline's section chiefs assembled on April 9, right after his return from the Guatemala visit and just before Hawkins went to Puerto Cabezas for the brigade embarkation. Bissell had called the meeting. At the last moment Doris Mirage, his secretary, phoned to say the DDO would be delayed. The group repaired to an agency hangout, Napoleon's, a restaurant on Connecticut Avenue. Jim Flannery, one of Bissell's special assistants, went with them. They began with martinis and went on to brandy before task force operations chief Richard Drain raised the forbidden question: "Have any of you entertained the notion that this damned thing might not work?" The last-minute switch in the target area boded ill.

Drain suggested they could just not go back to work. Had the Cuba task force walked off the job in the middle of the pre-invasion workup, that would surely have ended Project Ate. Some looked uncomfortable; Jack Hawkins was angry. No one said anything. Finally Jake Esterline chimed in, "Let's go back."

When one of the group asked why, the task force chief replied, with great emphasis, "Because we're good soldiers, that's why."

Within a week Esterline and Hawkins would be at Richard Bissell's house trying to resign.

On April 10 the exile force began moving from Trax and the other bases. At Trampoline 316 support personnel, including 159 Americans, assisted in loading. The ship *Rio Escondido*, slowed by propeller damage from a log when departing New Orleans, sailed on April 11, the fastest vessels on the night of 13/14. Tracy Barnes and a senior paramilitary man went to New York on April 12 to inform the Cuban politicians. By this time the *Frente* had widened to include Manolo Ray, unacceptable to Howard Hunt. Hunt finally had to be relieved and relegated to work with Dave Phillips and the propaganda unit.

President Kennedy still reserved his final decision, with an option to cancel the invasion up to twenty-four hours before the landing. Although a military man sent to observe loading reported the situation chaotic and the shipping inadequate, the president's qualms were resolved by a cable from Jack Hawkins:

MY OBSERVATIONS HAVE INCREASED MY CONFIDENCE IN THE ABILITY OF THIS FORCE TO ACCOMPLISH NOT ONLY INITIAL COMBAT MISSIONS BUT ALSO THE ULTIMATE OBJECTIVE, THE OVERTHROW OF CASTRO. THE BRIGADE AND BATTALION COMMANDERS NOW KNOW ALL DETAILS OF THE PLAN AND ARE VERY ENTHUSIASTIC. THESE OFFICERS ARE YOUNG, VIGOROUS, INTELLIGENT, AND MOTIVATED WITH A FANATICAL URGE TO BEGIN BATTLE. . . . THEY SAY THEY KNOW THEIR PEOPLE AND BELIEVE AFTER THEY HAVE INFLICTED ONE SERIOUS DEFEAT

UPON THE OPPOSITION FORCES, THE LATTER WILL MELT AWAY FROM
CASTRO. . . . I SHARE THEIR CONFIDENCE.

THE BRIGADE IS . . . MORE HEAVILY ARMED AND BETTER EQUIPPED IN
SOME RESPECTS THAN U.S. INFANTRY UNITS. THE MEN HAVE RE-
CEIVED . . . MORE FIRING EXPERIENCE THAN U.S. TROOPS WOULD
NORMALLY RECEIVE. I WAS IMPRESSED WITH THE SERIOUS ATTITUDE
OF THE MEN.

Kennedy gave the go-ahead. When it was all over and the brigade leaders returned
from captivity, reporter Haynes Johnson showed them the cable. Unanimously the
exiles insisted that they were told nothing about the actual plan until the final moment of embarkation.

The effort to destroy Castro's air force was the first, crucial action of Project Ate.
It carried the code name JM/Fury. If not eliminated, FAR airplanes posed a
tremendous threat. Castro's inventory included six B-26 bombers, four T-33 jet
trainers modified to be fighters, and two to four British Sea Fury fighters. Principal bases were at Havana and Santiago. A surprise air attack scheduled two days
before the invasion would seem to do the trick, and any remaining planes would
be bombed at dawn after the landing. That was the plan. A follow-up strike the day
before the invasion dropped out of the planning.

There was no lack of warnings on the criticality of this element. On their way
to a late White House meeting, General Gray asked Tracy Barnes whether the senior officials had ever been told that the full air preparation was a necessity. Barnes
admitted not but told Gray not to worry, yet never did anything about it. Similarly
Richard Bissell brought in air force Gen. Leo Geary for a last-minute assessment.
Geary concluded that the air plan would be adequate only if implemented in all its
aspects. Bissell made choices that precluded that possibility.

The CIA hoped to conceal the exiles' hand, claiming the air strikes were by
Castro defectors. To this end the agency acquired two extra B-26 bombers simply
to fly from Nicaragua to Florida where the pilots would retail the cover story. Sixteen bombers would hit six Cuban air bases in the real attack.

When Kennedy continued insisting on reducing visibility, Bissell, on his
own, halved the initial strike force. Gar Thorsrud had to scale back targets, to only
main airfields, to be hit by eight bombers. These reductions in the planned air missions were a major reason for doubts among Esterline's staff.

The mission proved successful as far as it went. The exile planes achieved
surprise. Shortly after dawn on April 15, 1961, about half of Castro's air force was
smashed.

Jake Esterline telephoned Bissell and said he and Jack Hawkins absolutely
had to sit down with him and talk. They appeared on Bissell's doorstep in the
Glover Park neighborhood of Washington. Esterline took the cutbacks in Project
Ate to their logical conclusion: there remained no good faith expectation for suc-

cess. He and Hawkins wanted to resign. Bissell questioned their loyalty and shamed them into staying on. In 1975, speaking to CIA interviewer Jack Pfeiffer, Bissell professed not to recall this at all. Esterline and Hawkins together did an interview with the historian Peter Kornbluh in 1996. In it the former task force chief declared, "I am forced to a very unhappy conclusion and that is that he [Bissell] was lying down and lying up for reasons that I don't yet totally understand."

Almost immediately the bombing cover story began unraveling. The exile planes from Nicaragua reached Florida as planned. One landed at Opa-Locka, the other at Miami International Airport where its pilot, Mario Zuñiga, recited the pre-arranged tale that he was a disaffected FAR pilot. Photographed by the press, pictures of Zuñiga's B-26 were flashed almost immediately to New York, where the United Nations had turned to Cuba.

The pictures clearly showed FAR markings, which the CIA had thoughtfully painted on the aircraft. Adlai Stevenson exhibited them in the debate, using the photos to deny U.S. complicity. But the photos showed too much—the Miami B-26 had a special nose assembly with machine guns, devised for the Indonesia operation; Castro's B-26s had plastic noses for a bombardier. An enterprising reporter discovered that the bomber's guns were taped up and thus could not have been fired. It also strained credulity that a group of spontaneous defectors could launch a simultaneous strike at different bases. In addition, Henry Raymont, the UPI reporter in Havana, saw the attack planes and confirmed they had no markings. Exposed as a fabrication, Stevenson's statement flopped. The ambassador realized that Tracy Barnes had deceived him. Embarrassed, Kennedy sent McGeorge Bundy to New York with a fuller account for Stevenson.

President Kennedy tamped down the next round of CIA bombings to avoid a UN debacle. Then he directed Mac Bundy to issue fresh orders to Dulles, Rusk, and McNamara prohibiting any employment of U.S. forces. In addition: "The specific plan for paramilitary support, Nestor, has been rejected, and the President does not wish further planning of any such operations for an invasion of Cuba. There will be quiet disengagement from associations developed in connection with Nestor." But Kennedy was too late to cancel the next part of the CIA plan—a diversionary landing in Oriente province that night.

Meanwhile Col. Stanley Beerli at the CIA's Air Operations Center planned a follow-up air strike to neutralize the remainder of Castro's air force. Communications intelligence indicated that Castro's last aircraft had regrouped at San Antonio base. Beerli and his assistants selected targets from the latest U-2 photographs. Then fate again intervened, in the person of CIA Deputy Director Charles Cabell.

This was his moment. In seven years at the agency, Cabell had seen good times and bad. As DDCI he had helped create the CIA as we know it. General Cabell had come from the air force, a long-service reconnaissance man and one of its early photo interpretation experts. At one time he had been in charge of setting intelligence requirements for his service, and he had headed air intelligence too. Cabell had twice worked for the Joint Chiefs of Staff, including during the Korean War, so he knew the interservice arena. A master pilot, he had briefly commanded a bomber group in the campaign against Germany. Somehow Central Casting had come up with Cabell as the prototype for a figure that became a fixture at CIA: the savvy officer who could fill in the intel types on what they needed and get CIA the things it wanted. A down-home sort, Cabell liked Westerns, the tropics, and Mexican cooking. Cuba should have been right up his alley. Instead he presided over one of the project's key operational failures.

Allen Dulles, as part of the cover, had a speaking engagement in Puerto Rico that he had accepted long before, so Cabell had command that weekend. His arrangement with Dulles provided for the two to be interchangeable, each cognizant of all aspects of CIA business. In addition, Cabell chaired the CIA Watch Committee and could comment authoritatively on current intelligence. He considered himself on top of the case.

Returning from an April 16 golf date in sport shirt and slacks, General Cabell heard that Quarters Eye had gotten the final "go" for the invasion by telephone at 1 P.M. Cabell reviewed the plans. He learned of Beerli's latest air strike, asking if it had been approved. Aware of the UN embarrassment, Cabell wanted to check with Dean Rusk even though Beerli insisted everything was fine. About 9:30 P.M., McGeorge Bundy, alerted by Rusk, called with JFK's decision that no further strikes be launched until Brigade 2506 captured an airstrip inside Cuba. The net effect cut air support to the missions already flown rather than the forty-odd flights once programmed (but not in fact proposed to the president, who had only been asked to approve strikes on D-2 and on D-Day).

The order struck Cabell "like a falling bomb." He thought the go-ahead included all subsidiary measures, such as the air strike. At this point Richard Bissell entered. The DDO demanded reconsideration. He and Cabell rushed to Rusk's office, appealing to him. General Cabell knew air like a cook knows beans, and advanced a series of reasons why Castro's airfields should be struck. Rusk rejected their entreaties, except for allowing the exile air force to fly support over the beaches. Both CIA officials protested vigorously; Rusk finally phoned the president and put their arguments to him. Cabell concedes that Rusk rendered his points accurately. JFK again rejected the air strike. In history this refusal became the third factor in assigning Kennedy the full blame for the Cuba failure.

A veteran of bombing campaigns, General Cabell knew their weaknesses and, well steeped in the JM/Ate plan, knew that it hinged on success in taking out Castro's air force. He also recounts his understanding that the invasion could no longer be called off. With the strikes he believed the operation to be risky but feasible. Now the president wanted to reject a measure Cabell considered absolutely vital. Yet he declined Rusk's offer to speak directly to the president. That was Cabell's error, not Kennedy's. "I don't think there's any point," the general said. Rusk held out the phone to Bissell. "I think I agree with that," the DO director added. Cabell felt pressed for time with everything that needed doing at headquarters. Only later, in retrospect, did he ask himself if one says "no" when asked to speak to the president. In his memoir Bissell would write: "Today I view this decision of Cabell's and mine as a major mistake. For the record, we should have spoken to the president and made as strong a case as possible on behalf of the operation and the welfare of the brigade."

Returning to the agency, the CIA officials went directly to the WH/4 offices to report the denial of their appeal. Bissell let Cabell tell the bad news. "There's been a little change in our marching orders," Cabell said. They would have to go "headsy, headsy." Esterline and others were dumbfounded. The room rang with expressions of frustration.

Jack Hawkins hit the table with his fist. "Goddamn it, this is criminal negligence."

Jake Esterline added tightly, "This is the goddamnest thing I have ever heard of."

Tracy Barnes drafted the "FLASH" precedence cable to Trampoline canceling the air attack. Gar Thorsrud received it just half an hour before the strike aircraft were to launch. Some pilots were already in their cockpits. General Cabell is proud that no one suggested a bit of foot-dragging to let the strike go through. By 4 A.M. he and Bissell were speaking to Rusk again, on the telephone, begging for authorization to have U.S. Navy aircraft fly air cover for the invasion fleet and support over the beachhead. Cabell met Rusk in the latter's apartment at the Park-Sheraton Hotel. Rusk opened the door in his bathrobe. This time Rusk insisted that Cabell speak to the president, and the White House switchboard reached JFK at his Glen Ora, Virginia, estate. After a brief exchange, Rusk got on the phone, then conveyed Kennedy's refusal.

Missions would be restricted to direct support over the beaches on the first day. There would be thirteen exile B-26 sorties, none of them against FAR bases. Castro's air force got its chance.

Another narrative of these events is that of the Cubans, both enthusiastic supporters of Fidel Castro and those who sought to unseat him. Castro quite consciously used the CIA secret war and Washington's overt hostile measures as proof of the need for his countrymen to pull together for the revolution. What clearer demonstration could there be than a CIA invasion? The anti-Castro resistance could be— and was—attributed to the Americans because it had CIA help. Reasonable Cubans could argue the realities. The invasion was another matter: such an act could *only* happen at the instigation of the "Yanquis." The hand of the CIA became Castro's best organizing tool. The anti-Castro Cubans, meanwhile, had their own angle. Exile fighter Alfredo Duran forthrightly told the retrospective Musgrove Plantation conference in 1996, "The feeling among the people in the brigade was that we were using the CIA, not the CIA using us; that we had a purpose and the purpose was going back to Cuba." The contending forces clashed at Playa Girón, as the Cuban revolutionaries know the Bay of Pigs battle, and they view its outcome as a victory for the Cuban people.

Much depended on the internal resistance. Over rum and dominos in Miami, or drinking beers in the spartan bar at Puerto Cabezas, Cuban exiles spent endless hours on this, probably even more than Kennedy, whose deliberations often ranged over the subject. Even the *fidelistas* concede the revolt began early and burned on. Project Ate's original purpose was precisely as a line of support to the resistance. The revolution applied unevenly across Cuba. In some places cadres made mistakes, in some they lacked a correct political analysis, in others the new bosses succumbed to the same corruption as the old ones.

Agrarian reform could be a double-edged tool: one could demand bribes to delay seizing the land just as easily as take it over. Las Villas province figured in CIA reports as strongly anti-Castro. Someone put the number 70 percent to that opposition, though opinion polls were a rarity in 1961 in Cuba, and certainly the agency never had permission to take any. Jake Esterline commented later that a poll would have been more useful than the spy reports he got out of Cuba. Las Villas happened to be one of the places the *fidelistas* had gotten off to a bad start, where peasants were run off their land or shaken down around Sagua la Grande and Sanctí Spiritus. There had also been difficulties with the literacy programs (Cuba had a million people then who could not read or were only semi-literate), and Cuban *guajiros* can only have been shaken when Castro's *commandantes* pulled the teachers back. Las Villas contained the Escambray Mountains. There had been no land reform at all. Both Trinidad and Playa Girón were in Las Villas, Trinidad below the Escambray, the Bay of Pigs to the west, closer to Havana.

One thing the CIA got right was to plot the invasion in the Cuban province most hostile to Fidel. But clandestine supply efforts reflected no strong consciousness of this. Almost half of everything landed by sea went to Havana province. Of the rest, the vast majority went to Matanzas, with Las Villas left somewhere behind along with Pinar del Rio and Camaguey.

The switch to the Bay of Pigs moved the scene of action to the sparsely populated Playa Girón. And by the same token that Castro's troops could access the site only along a few roads, it would be virtually impossible for any *campesinos* who wanted to join Brigade 2506 to reach it. The depth of optimism in the plans is nevertheless shown by the fact that CIA's two LCIs carried weapons for an additional fifteen hundred recruits while a merchant vessel scheduled to arrive a fortnight after the landing bore arms for thirteen thousand more fighters. In actuality perhaps fifty Cubans joined the assault unit once it landed.

When Cubans (on all sides) thought about the resistance, they generally focused on either the fighters in the Escambray or the underground in Havana. "Ojeda," Lino Fernandez, ran from pillar to post to coordinate, especially once Castro's security services captured his chief "Francisco." The latter, not overly pleased with the American support resulting from his 1960 mission to Miami, did the best he could. The internal resistance developed suspicions of the CIA greater even than those of Brigade 2506. Supply deliveries (or the lack of them) were suspect, so too the radio plan, in which all operators communicated exclusively to Miami, where Bob Reynolds held all the threads in his hand. According to Jose Basulto, who ran a network around Santiago de Cuba, radio operators began making private arrangements, complete with rudimentary codes, so that if necessary they could cut the CIA out of the loop.

Operating in Havana had its advantages. The big city made it easier for resistance members to get around. In addition, boats and planes still maintained travel schedules from Havana to the United States. That made it possible to infiltrate agents legally and created a ready escape route. Carlos Gonzalez Vidal, the rebel who firebombed the El Encanto department store, carried out that action on condition he be evacuated to the United States immediately afterward. His capture at Barracoa Beach in the middle of the night resulted from suspicions of local militia when they saw a flashlight shined out to sea. Felix Rodriguez, among those Cubans who infiltrated on behalf of the CIA, stayed clear of the security services. Enrique Baloyra ran the intelligence section of the student group DRE and saw Castro's State Security officers on the street all the time. The resistance had to work clandestinely, burrowing deeper as its net of safe houses shrank. Baloyra believed the resistance was not able to rise up but saw no reason to think time was on Fidel's side.

A rough index of the degree of opposition to Fidel may be its size, though that is virtually impossible to determine. A figure of 5,000 to 6,000 seems to encompass the estimates of observers ranging from Lino Fernandez to Castro himself. The CIA's final pre-invasion policy paper puts the number at 7,000. On the other hand, one measure to indicate support for Castro might be the "committees for the defense of the revolution," which the *fidelistas* set up as mobilization and surveillance mechanisms feeding information to State Security. More than 100,000 of these committees were created, down to where each big building in Havana had its own.

There *were* resistance networks within Cuba. The first CIA agent to return to Cuba (he entered legally), Manuel Reyes Garcia, managed to operate freely right through the invasion. Similarly, Felix Rodriguez worked around Santa Clara and persisted for five months past the failure at Playa Girón, finally escaping to the Venezuelan embassy where, accorded immunity, he stayed until permitted to leave Cuba. Miguel Orozco Crespo headed the infiltration teams the CIA simultaneously formed when it decided to expand the exile force to a brigade. Eighty men were earmarked for the teams. The first infiltrated on February 14, 1961. Two more were to have entered toward the end of that month, but trouble aboard the LCI *Barbara J*—a sit-down and hunger strike—aborted the mission. Most of Crespo's teams did try to infiltrate, and other singleton agents were dispatched direct from Miami. According to official CIA records, as of March 10, 1961, thirty-two men of this unit had entered Cuba. Four more agents went through Guantanamo on March 29. Around the time of the invasion, the CIA believed it had put in the field some thirty paramilitary people, thirty-one intelligence agents, and thirteen active (plus four reserve) radio operators. They covered much of the island of Cuba.

Castro's security services worked around the clock. Police ranged throughout Havana, backed by militia. The secret service were the iron fist. State Security is a bit of a misnomer—that organization would be created only *after* the CIA invasion—but the G-2, an artifact of the FAR, already had a reputation for dedication and relentlessness. Grayston Lynch called the G-2 "almost a Caribbean branch of the KGB," trained and equipped by the Russians and a first-rate service. That would be true only later. Richard Helms had a better characterization: "Cuban intelligence was not world class but it had the significant advantages of area knowledge, a level of domestic political support, the latent ethnic loyalty of some Cubans living abroad, and the excellent help offered by the KGB and GRU officers on assignment in Havana."

Fidelista security scored its coups. A beach landing by two dozen rebels of Rolando Masferrer's group in early 1961 was pursued and tracked down by a couple of thousand militia. An airdrop near Trinidad in September 1960 flushed out much of the MRR network in that sector. Prime Minister Castro initiated a program of economic and social development for the Escambray, an indication that security needed help in those mountains. Plinio Prieto's group fell to the *fidelistas* in October. Former July 26th figures who had gone over to the anti-Castro forces, Jesus Carreras and William Morgan (an American), were arrested and executed around that time. Another American, John M. Spiritus, condemned as a CIA agent, went to prison. That would be about when Castro had Huber Matos arrested as well. In March 1961 two leaders of an anti-Castro group were apprehended just days after arriving. On March 18 the police arrested "Francisco," the internal resistance chief Rogelio Gonzalez Corzo. In the last weeks before the invasion, according to a Cuban history of Playa Girón, security captured about two-thirds (twenty-three of thirty-five) of the agents attempting illegal infiltrations. Richard Bissell noted later to a CIA interviewer that Cuban agents were typically caught within a day of landing on the island.

The resistance did achieve certain results. As the CIA tabulated them, between October 1960 and April 1961 anti-Castro rebels bombed or set fire to the Havana power plant, a major department store and five others, a sugar refinery, two dairies, the railroad and bus terminals, a militia barracks, 40 tobacco drying barns, and "twenty-one Communist homes." They destroyed a microwave station, derailed half a dozen trains (and bombed another), and hit numerous power transformers. There were 200 bombings in all, mostly nuisances, 800 sugar-cane fires (reportedly destroying 300,000 tons of cane), and 150 other fires. Some of the worst damage, including the firebombing of El Encanto (where an exploded incendiary device found afterward had been stamped "U.S. Army"), a couple of former Woolworth stores, the power station, one of the refineries, and several warehouses, occurred in a wave of violence just before the CIA invasion.

Key to the prospects for CIA's Project Ate was the armed resistance, which centered in Las Villas province, especially the Escambray. Member groups of the Cuban front were urged to send people to the Escambray to join the rebel bands while CIA infiltrations inserted agents to organize in towns around the mountains. Las Villas suffered when it came to seaborne supply shipments, but airdrop missions were more numerous. Of course, because many airdrops failed for one reason or another, the bottom line would show the Escambray front generally shortchanged. The CIA sent an agent, "*Commandante* Augusto" (Jose Ramon Rui-sanchez), to coordinate the front, but he passed the assignment to Evelio Duque, whose personality clashed with other leaders, including the commander of the largest rebel column.

In December 1960, recognizing the growing guerrilla capability, Castro ordered a special pacification campaign in the Escambray. Operation "*Jaula*" (Cage) involved forty thousand to fifty thousand troops and militia. Fidel wanted the farmers mobilized and ordered new efforts to expand literacy. Volunteer teachers, engineers with electric generators for villages that had never had so much as a lightbulb, propaganda units that showed movies—all contributed. On January 5 CIA weapons dropped to the rebels were successfully recovered by Castro forces. The next day *fidelista* troops captured a rebel camp. But guerrilla fighters were active too. The rebels in the Escambray gradually grew to number several thousand fighters.

The *fidelistas* attempted to accelerate their cleanup of the Escambray so as to avoid facing multiple threats when the CIA invaders arrived. The limitations of the militia precluded success; still, several of the guerrilla columns were smashed (a State Security historian claims twenty-five groups of rebels were defeated by the end of March) while Duque and some of his top officers fled Cuba. But Castro could not keep up the pressure—according to Victor Dreke, among the more ideological *fidelista* field commanders, many militia were workers and peasants who volunteered and were not paid. Once the workers really needed money, or the peasants' crops were ripe for the harvest, they needed to return to civil life. In early April the government ordered seventy militia battalions back to their home districts.

Secret warriors worried about the internal resistance but stopped air and sea missions that nurtured it during the final weeks before the invasion. Later the CIA took rebel cries for help during those weeks as evidence of the strength of the movement. From March 22 until the day of the landing there were more than a dozen requests from resistance forces for airdrops to an alleged five thousand guerrillas. During the battle and over the next days requests arrived for the support of more than three thousand rebels. Interestingly, only four hundred of these fighters were in Las Villas. There is no evidence on how real these figures were, how much they were exaggerated for the CIA's benefit, or, for that matter, whether the agency counted troops twice or more when recording these figures.

Fidel knew of the CIA operation and took steps to find out more. As early as October 1960 a G-2 officer went to Costa Rica to gather data there. Other reports came from Mexico City and Florida. Many were mistaken or exaggerated. In September, for example, Cuban intelligence heard of a mass insertion of CIA agent teams about to happen. It never did. In early November Havana learned that the CIA Cubans were moving from Camp Trax to Puerto Cabezas. That did not occur until April 1961. Numbers were estimated at six thousand, even up to fifteen thousand—ten times Brigade 2506's true strength. On CIA airplanes the worst exaggerations were that the exiles had jets and B-29 bombers. Other reports

were more accurate. One detailed the split among the Kennedy people over moving ahead with Ate, with fair detail on who favored what. A January 1961 report
contained more than two dozen pages on CIA preparations. Most disturbing—
especially to Jake Esterline, who found out only when it was all over—an April
13 cable from the Soviet embassy in Mexico City reported the invasion imminent, in fact for the 17th, which it was.

Meeting on April 14 with Soviet Ambassador Sergei M. Kudryavtsev, Che
Guevara remarked that "the danger of invasion of the country by large beachheads
of the external counterrevolutionary forces has now in all likelihood receded." Although Che proved wrong, his comment shows Havana to be aware of CIA's plan
for a large-scale invasion. Fidel, his minister of defense Raul Castro, and the
Cuban general staff had examined the possibilities in detail, as Castro recounted at
the fortieth anniversary conference held in 2001 in Havana. Castro also revealed
what he had genuinely feared—a widespread series of guerrilla landings to link up
with the resistance. Of course the CIA had abandoned that option months earlier
at Richard Bissell's insistence.

Cuban military dispositions at the moment of the invasion indicate no
knowledge of immediate CIA objectives. The FAR had broken up the huge force
it concentrated for the Escambray encirclement. Only a small detachment of militia guarded Playa Girón. The nearest real unit, nothing more than a militia battalion, camped at Central Australia, a sugar refinery more than twenty miles
away. In fact, Fidel Castro noted in 2001, the locale and timing of the invasion
were excellent.

The CIA bombing of Castro's airfields two days ahead of the invasion served
as a clear warning to Havana. Castro staged a huge rally in the city, proclaiming
Cuba's determination to stand up to Washington. And for the first time he publicly
declared the revolution a socialist one. Simultaneously Cuban security apprehended every dissident and rebel they knew of, along with plenty of Cubans who
happened to be in the wrong place at the wrong time. Lino Fernandez, coordinator of the resistance after "Francisco," disappeared into jail. More than 20,000
people were arrested, with estimates as high as 100,000 or 250,000. As a result, internal resistance was swept from the board before the invasion even began.

Plans for a diversion in Oriente under Niño Diaz might have fooled Castro.
With Cuba alerted by the bombing, the Diaz landing would have been the next
news, and Havana could have gone for it. But the ploy never happened. The Garcia Lines ship *La Plata* and the CIA boats *Sea Gull* and *Tejana* carried the assault
unit. A week before, the frogmen supposed to guide Diaz's troops to the beach
perished in an accident with a hand grenade. Now substitutes approached the
shore, thirty miles from Guantanamo, only to see Cuban soldiers on the beach.
Another try the next night failed; heavy seas and the rocky beach were blamed.
Jake Esterline groused that two men with a canoe had scared Diaz off. (Esterline's
are not the only speculations: Cuban Gen. Fabian Escalante writes that Diaz's
true purpose was to excuse U.S. intervention by making a phony attack on Guantanamo Bay.)

Another diversion, off Pinar del Rio at the opposite end of Cuba, involved a submarine, flares, a few shells, plus electronic emissions. Castro feared a landing there and would have believed in it. After the big Havana rally on April 16 he sent Che Guevara to rally the defenses. Guevara wounded himself when his pistol discharged by mistake. Later, when Fidel got reports of a landing, he could see Brigade 2506 in front of him at Girón and dismissed them.

Plans to activate the resistance by inserting coded messages into the broadcasts of David Phillip's Radio Swan collapsed with the Cuban security crackdown. Phillip's extensive propaganda program—he had no fewer than twelve *million* leaflets stockpiled to induce the *campesinos* to rise and join Brigade 2506 or the resistance—went fallow as the leaflets sat in warehouses. First, on Kennedy's orders, the CIA canceled its air missions starting several weeks before the landing, then, once the invasion happened, it was entirely preoccupied with air support.

Networks in Havana were gone, those in the rest of Cuba heavily impacted. All this left fighters like Jose Basulto high and dry. On the day of the bombing Basulto had been at Manzanillo preparing for an expected arms delivery. When he returned to Santiago, avoiding the air base—among CIA's targets—Basulto found most of his agents arrested. His network had only a few submachine guns and six pounds of explosives, scarcely enough to dent Castro's army. On the day of the invasion Basulto and his closest remaining companions went on a beach outing to Siboney, cavorting in the waves. They figured they had done what they could. Now everything depended on Assault Brigade 2506.

Grayston Lynch's ship *Blagar* carried the brigade commander and staff. Lynch had not known Jose Peres San Roman, but by the end of the voyage he respected the wiry Cuban commander. They spent much of the night of April 15 closeted in the wardroom talking over the difficulties the brigade faced. Lynch gave San Roman pointers on fighting Castro's Russian-made tanks, not to mention the use of his own armor. The fleet of four ships and two LCIs arrived off the Bay of Pigs on schedule. There they met the U.S. Navy's *San Marcos*. The big Landing Ship Dock launched craft bearing the brigade's trucks and tanks, and one to pick up the Cuban crews and distribute them to the craft. Then the CIA landing craft operators withdrew to the *San Marcos*, which steamed away. The Cuban invasion fleet split into elements to approach each of its landing beaches. It was just before midnight and the beginning of April 17, 1961.

Except for three large craft with the vehicles and four for personnel, all brought by the American amphibious ship, the Cubans relied on small fiberglass boats with outboard motors. These had been a headache for Lynch and Gar Thorsrud, who installed and tested the motors back at Puerto Cabezas, because an officer from the Joint Chiefs insisted on erroneous steering installations and fuel mixtures. Lynch had finally gone along just to get the man off their backs. Now the motors failed and slowed down the operation.

At least the beaches were marked—against orders that no Americans were to be involved, Rip Robertson and Grayston Lynch led frogmen ashore to accomplish this. As CIA case officer aboard the command ship, Lynch took it upon himself to make the final decision on beach conditions and therefore crewed a launch carrying frogmen. The intruders encountered a reef a foot below the surface about a hundred yards from the surf line. The tide was still coming in. At the landing point it seemed like Cuban locals were partying, so Lynch steered to starboard. As they cleared the coral one of the lights to mark the beach went on, twice, apparently the victim of a short circuit. A frogman finally sat on it to suppress the illumination. But Comrade Mariano Mustelier's militia post at Playa Girón saw the light and sent two *milicianos* in a jeep to investigate. The vehicle came up in front of the CIA team and shone its headlights directly at them. Grayston Lynch, agency contract officer, became the first to open fire at the Bay of Pigs, emptying half a magazine into the jeep. His frogmen joined in. Interrogating captured *milicianos* later, Brigade 2506 intelligence learned that the militia thought they'd seen a lost fishing boat and were trying to guide it in. But the firefight gave away the invasion. Playa Girón went dark. Mustelier radioed the news to Central Australia. So much for the element of surprise.

At the head of the Bay of Pigs lay the village of Playa Larga. There Jose San Roman hoped to block the causeway across the swamp from Central Australia. The LCI *Barbara J* and the Garcia Lines ship *Houston* arrived off Playa Larga about 2 A.M. Rip Robertson and three Cuban frogmen did their own shore reconnaissance, then began landing the Second Battalion. Comrade Gonzalez Sucro, patrolling with five *milicianos*, saw shadows and demanded a halt. Quickly another firefight began.

Commandante Jose Ramon Fernandez, one of Castro's best field commanders, awakened by Fidel between 2 and 3 A.M., received four calls from the Maximum Leader before he could dress and get on the road. Fernandez would take over at Central Australia and seal the causeway exit. Castro had been at general staff headquarters, "Point One," on Saturday morning when the exile B-26 bombers hit his airfields; he had no intention of being caught flatfooted. By 3:15 he had swung into action. In less than an hour the radio posts at Playa Girón and Playa Larga fell silent. Fidel took personal control. He ordered the command at Santa Clara to send Battalion 117 to Covadonga, another of the several exits from the Bay of Pigs area, placing it under Commandante Filiberto Olivera Moya. By morning Fernandez could see the first reinforcements, militia of Battalions 223 and 219 from Matanzas, and expected the cadets from one of the training schools he commanded. Capt. Orlando Pupo headed toward Playa Girón from the east along the coast. Red Beach at Playa Larga endured its first air attack from a Castro B-26 as early as 6:20 A.M.

The parachute drop of Brigade 2506's First Battalion came soon after dawn. These men were to block Castro troops from both Central Australia and Covadonga. They landed in a mass drop, leaping from half a dozen C-46 aircraft and one C-54, escorted by four exile bombers. The drop scattered. This was not Normandy. Eddie Ferrer, for example, came under fire from *milicianos* in a jeep and released his paratroops a few miles short of their drop zone.

Off the beaches, disorganization happened for another reason. Gray Lynch, called back to *Blagar* after a short time ashore, found a CIA dispatch warning him that Castro's air force still had planes. The danger to the invasion fleet dictated they put ashore as much as possible before dawn, then clear the area. Frantic activity ensued. Some landing boats could not start their motors, courtesy of the Joint Chiefs of Staff supervisor back at Puerto Cabezas. Others hung up on the reefs while, as the tide fell, unloading came to a halt.

Dawn found most of the brigade ashore but with far less than the planned amount of supplies. The invasion fleet remained off the beaches. That was when Castro's air force made its appearance: in two strikes, at 6:30 and at 9 A.M., his planes hit the ships. Nilo Carreras's Sea Fury fighter scored rocket hits on the transport *Houston*. Carreras hit below the waterline, otherwise the ship might well have exploded since she carried ammunition. She also had aboard the 130 men of Ricardo Montero's Fifth Battalion. The survivors swam ashore without equipment, into the salt marshes of the Zapata Peninsula, across the bay from the brigade positions. Off Playa Girón, Sea Fury aircraft sank the *Rio Escondido*. It went down with the brigade's communications van and aviation gasoline for use at the Girón airstrip.

At Playa Larga, Hugo Sueiro's Second Battalion got ashore in good order. With Brigade 2506's impaired communications, however, hours passed before Sueiro could tell Pepe San Roman at Girón. The battalion at Playa Larga, in position to reinforce the paratroops near Central Australia, received no orders. By the time San Roman established radio contact, yet another CIA error was becoming evident.

Among key assumptions throughout the planning had been that Castro would need days to react. Exile officers were told before embarkation that there would be no resistance at the Bay of Pigs, that FAR would require until D+2, the second day after the invasion, to mount significant opposition. Bissell, Hawkins, and other planners repeatedly used this estimate. Their confidence was striking given their ignorance of conditions in Cuba. Admiral Dennison, in his own planning, had submitted a list of ninety specific questions on Castro forces, and twenty-nine on the Cuban resistance, as early as December 1960; less than a dozen were answered. The secret warriors had been wrong about the reefs; they were also wrong that no Castro forces would be in the area. About a hundred militia guarded Girón and vicinity and a larger force, Battalion 339 at Central Australia, had already begun to pressure the paratroops north of Playa Larga.

At the time of the first invasion scare in December, Castro's mobilization orders had created great confusion. Later repeated scares created a highly efficient system, however, and Castro had two days after the air attack to put his units in motion. This time there were no mistakes. By 9 A.M. Commandante Fernandez at Central Australia had his troops from the Matanzas Militia School, sending them forward without dismounting from their trucks. Large forces, including armor, deployed against the exile brigade from the first day. Before evening the paratroop roadblocks had been driven back toward Playa Larga, and Castro's forces could begin to attack down the causeway to the head of the bay.

Ultimately some twenty thousand troops assembled against the invasion force. Intending a night counterattack, Fidel appeared at Central Australia, directing operations, calling all over, using an old, hand-cranked black telephone. He called his brother Raul, telling the defense minister, "You're missing the party!" He ordered "a hell of a barrage." Fernandez pushed his troops down the causeway. By early morning of the second day, April 18, the exiles at Playa Larga were desperate as FAR tanks approached. Meanwhile the paratroop roadblocks near Covadonga on the opposite flank of the bridgehead were also in retreat.

In the evening Allen Dulles returned from his expedition to Puerto Rico. No doubt the Young Presidents' Association, whom he had addressed, appreciated his remarks, but the director had been out of pocket at a critical moment. Richard Drain met Dulles at Baltimore's Friendship Airport. Drain quickly passed along the gist—the invasion hung by a thread. Their drive to Washington passed mostly in silence.

Brigade 2506 had no real chance. On the second day San Roman's troops were driven back on all fronts. San Roman sent his deputy commander, Erneido Oliva, to Playa Larga with some troops and a couple of tanks. Oliva took over the defense and put up a good fight. But the village had become impossible to hold, and the brigade's troops fell back to Girón. The biggest success of April 18, an air strike against the Castro column advancing from Playa Larga, became known as the "slaughter of the Lost Battalion," as many of the 339th Militia and their trucks expired under Oliva's fire and the strikes, disrupting the FAR's advance. Castro had assembled two dozen tanks and self-propelled guns, and the B-26 strikes knocked out seven of them.

The Cuban exile pilots of Major Villafaña's air force were demoralized after losing four planes on D-Day (two more made forced landings) and run ragged from flying constant missions. They tried a night attack on Castro's air base at San Antonio but could not find it in the dark and overcast. Next morning McGeorge Bundy warned JFK to expect CIA pleading for air help. Bundy noted that assistance would be hard to deny because the Cuban exiles needed it, but the real issue lay in whether to reopen the question of U.S. intervention. He advised Kennedy to wipe out Castro's air force, "by neutrally-painted U.S. planes if necessary," but to "let the battle go its way." The president made a different choice: he authorized navy air cover, but for an area away from the combat zone. Kennedy's refusal to engage U.S. Navy aircraft in support of the CIA Cubans is the fourth decision that saddled this president with responsibility for the Bay of Pigs.

Faced with the problems at Trampoline, Richard Bissell quietly removed the prohibition on Americans flying missions. CIA contract pilots flew two of the nine sorties on April 18. Each flight could spend only about twenty minutes over the

Bay of Pigs, which added up to very limited capability. Castro's jets, closer to their bases, had a lot more air potential in addition to outperforming the B-26s.

Once more that night the principals debated air support at the White House. Kennedy left a state dinner to participate. The arguments and potential consequences were familiar, but the danger to the CIA Cubans had risen dramatically. JFK agreed to a halfhearted measure: U.S. jets could fly cover but under such restrictions that they could do little.

On April 19, the third day, Americans piloted six of the seven aircraft sent over the Bay of Pigs. Two American-crewed planes were lost, killing Riley Shamburger, Wade C. Gray, Willard Ray, and Leo F. Baker. They were American casualties in a war which, according to President Kennedy as recently as his news conference of a week earlier, occurred strictly between Cubans.

By the third day Brigade 2506 had virtually exhausted its ammunition. The ships of the invasion fleet, carrying the supplies, had scattered. They were rounded up by Dennison's warships. Grayston Lynch and Rip Robertson aboard *Blagar* and *Barbara J* stayed together, and *Blagar* shot down FAR aircraft. Amid frantic appeals from Pepe San Roman and the CIA, President Kennedy came closer than ever to intervention. American jets made intermittent overflights from the *Essex*. On Wednesday the 19th, destroyers *Eaton* and *Murray* closed in toward shore with orders to take off survivors. San Roman sent a last, plaintive message, then shot at his radio. The navy found twenty-six survivors. Lynch and Robertson took their LCIs to search for *brigadista* escapees. Castro's artillerymen sighted in on the U.S. warships and prepared to fire, but Jose Ramon Fernandez, and then Castro himself, ordered them to stand down.

Twenty-two of the exiles endured an odyssey by sailboat to land in Mexico. The remains of Brigade 2506, including San Roman, political chief Manuel Artime, and deputy Erneido Oliva, scattered into the swamps and were rounded up one by one. Castro's forces killed 114 brigade soldiers and captured 1,214. Havana admits to suffering 178 dead while exile sources claim inflicting losses of 1,600 killed in action and 2,000 wounded.

As the cables flowed into the WH/4 command post, disaster glaringly evident, the task force ground to a halt. Esterline and his top people had been living on cots at Quarters Eye for a few days, manning the center round the clock. Now they reacted from exhaustion and despair. Esterline groaned. Dick Drain threw up into a wastebasket. Ed Stanulis scratched his wrists so hard they bled.

At one of the numerous Washington discussions of limiting damage from the defeat, the Joint Chiefs were amazed to hear Bissell say, after all the talk of how an uprising would overthrow Castro, that the brigade could not switch to guerrilla-style fighting. President Kennedy finally conceded, raising his hand up just under his nose, "We're already in it up to here."

Richard Nixon and Dwight Eisenhower had a special interest in the outcome of the Cuban operation. Nixon planned a foreign policy address in Chicago and had arranged for a CIA briefing through Kennedy. Allen Dulles made the presentation at Nixon's Washington home on April 19. The CIA director appeared an hour and half late. Nervous and shaken, Dulles seemed almost desperate. Nixon asked if the agency man wanted a drink.

"I certainly would," Allen replied, "I really need one. This is the worst day of my life!"

Nixon, who read the newspapers better than most and could not miss Cuba splashed all over the front pages, asked what was wrong. Dulles blurted, "Everything is lost, the Cuban invasion is a total failure."

In a rush the DCI sketched developments, blaming Kennedy's "nervous aides" for getting JFK to compromise Project Ate with changes like dropping the air strikes. "I should have told him that we must not fail." Allen stared at the floor. "I came close to doing so but I didn't."

"It was the greatest mistake of my life!" Dulles repeated.

Nixon heard President Kennedy's version directly, in a telephone call and an afternoon chat at the White House. The conversations were mercifully silent on Nixon's own role in this fiasco.

Allen Dulles faced the music with Eisenhower on Friday, April 21. Conciliatory, Ike reassured the shattered DCI. Prelude to a weekend the Eisenhowers had been invited to spend at Camp David with the Kennedys, the briefing cued the former president to the inside story. Ike and Mamie helicoptered over from Gettysburg anticipating a social visit, but JFK opened with business and walked Ike over to the terrace at Aspen Lodge.

President Kennedy did not quibble. "The chief apparent causes of failure," JFK told Eisenhower, "were gaps in our intelligence, plus what may have been some errors in shiploading, timing, and tactics."

By their own accounts, in his moment of disaster Nixon and Eisenhower encouraged Kennedy to pursue Fidel Castro. Richard Nixon advised the president to find a "proper legal cover" and then "go in," exactly the kind of thing to fuel conspiracy theories like Fabian Escalante's—that the United States might stage a fake attack on Guantanamo Bay and then invade Cuba. Eisenhower told Kennedy he'd support "anything that had as its objective the prevention of communist entry and solidification of bases in the Western hemisphere."

Neither the new administration nor the old understood that implacable American hostility had precisely the wrong effect on Cuba, driving Castro into the arms of the Russians.

Six weeks later Ike received another detailed account of the Bay of Pigs from his friend William D. Pawley, whose information came from a *brigadista* escapee. Pawley also recounted what he had learned of White House meetings during the invasion. In an allusion to John Kennedy's 1956 book *Profiles in Courage*, Eisenhower wrote in his diary that "if true, this story could be called a '"Profile in Timidity and Indecision.'"

Ike sealed up the notes, plus an accompanying map. The envelope would only be opened years later by archivists working on his papers.

Fidel Castro also had an interest in the outcome of the secret warriors' big play, and for more than the obvious reasons. The failure of Project Ate stymied, and for the moment halted, American efforts to unseat him, but it also had a number of additional consequences. Central Intelligence Agency involvement in an open effort to depose Castro demonstrated beyond the shadow of a doubt that U.S. actions were far from the American rhetoric of self-determination. The operation put Washington squarely in violation of international law. The Bay of Pigs furnished concrete evidence for the "Yanqui" imperialism Fidel loved to excoriate.

For American leaders who professed concern that the "Cuban model" might spread through the Western Hemisphere, failure validated that model and lent it credibility across Latin America. Washington had seen Castro's prestige in Latin America as a diminishing quantity. The Bay of Pigs reversed that. Here a Latin leader had stood up to the United States. Whether democracy or dictatorship, Fidel's government had been sustained, and the CIA operation had united Cuba in support of it. That gave Castro an important organizing tool.

Playa Girón became an enduring feature of Fidel's public statements, his leadership in the affair a piece of his heroic persona. And the evident hostility of the United States encouraged the radicalization of Cuba, both in defense and as a response.

American intervention also put Cuba squarely on the table of Cold War conflict. That meant greatly increased aid from a Soviet Union pursuing its side of that competition. The U.S. threat also gave the Russians reasons to provide that aid for free, a key consideration for Castro, whose economy faltered due to his nationalizations, the U.S. sanctions, and global trade conditions. For many years after the Bay of Pigs, Cuba got a free ride from Moscow.

Most of these consequences had been perfectly predictable. But Washington restricted its deliberations to the instrumental and short-term questions, such as the exile "disposal" problem or the amount of time needed to gain support at the OAS. This is among the most serious failures of all, and it lies squarely on the desks of Presidents Eisenhower and Kennedy.

One other thing John Kennedy told Dwight Eisenhower: there would be an investigation. Indeed, an investigation could not be avoided, and in fact more than one. Gen. Maxwell D. Taylor presided over the first committee, which called itself the Green Board. Robert F. Kennedy represented his brother, the president. Allen Dulles guarded the interests of the Central Intelligence Agency. Adm. Arleigh Burke watched out for the navy. The board held twenty hearings with participants from Bissell on down, including *brigadista* escapees and politicians.

Grayston Lynch and Rip Robertson appeared, literally plucked off a navy destroyer in the Caribbean and shuttled to Washington. A series of special courier flights through Jacksonville, then a suite at the Shoreham Hotel and new custom-tailored suits were laid on for the case officers, who were watched by CIA minders, then closely pumped by the committee. Lynch, astonished to learn of the Washington end of the operation during lengthy debriefing with WH/4, made up his mind that the Taylor committee intended to produce a useless whitewash once he heard the line of questioning pursued by JFK's brother Bobby.

The declassified transcripts of Taylor panel testimony do reveal an odd circumspection. It could hardly have been otherwise. The details of the air strikes, the plans for Trinidad versus the Bay of Pigs, the military's review of the CIA plans— all were examined over and again. How these were handled set off Gray Lynch. But other central questions were not confronted at all. Allen Dulles mounted a preemptive defense of the CIA: at one session he remarked that he favored reassigning paramilitary activities to the Pentagon.

The committee eventually attributed failure to a mistaken belief that this large operation could be conducted with plausible deniability; to a lack of coordination among U.S. agencies; to the attempt to command from a distance, with headquarters at Washington. The panel concluded that the guerrilla option had not really been available to the exiles, and that the plan Project Ate had had "a marginal character . . . which increased with each additional limitation." By not actually rejecting the CIA plan, the Joint Chiefs seemed to have approved it and thus bore a measure of responsibility. Everyone had failed to do the things possible to ensure success.

On May 16, 1961, General Taylor made one presentation of his committee's report to President Kennedy at a luncheon. This would be a private session, and all panel members except Admiral Burke were there. Bobby Kennedy shone. From the CIA were Allen Dulles, General Cabell, and Richard Bissell. On June 13 Taylor's group again discussed their final conclusions with Kennedy. Bissell remembers the occasion as an evening in the upstairs sitting room of the White House. At Quarters Eye the morning staff meeting on the 14th found Dulles reporting that there would be just one copy of the study and it would stay with the president. Bissell thought that a splendid idea since any leaks could not then be blamed on the CIA, but he wanted a copy for agency files since it represented the best available account of the Bay of Pigs.

The CIA came out looking much better than it should have. Bissell himself agreed, telling an agency interviewer in 1975 that the Taylor report had been "very fair," "reasonable," and "mild." The report said nothing of the absurdity of using an invasion plan cobbled together in just a few days, a month before execution, and very little about the military feasibility of committing fifteen hundred Cuban exiles in a beachhead area forty miles wide, against a military establishment numbering in the hundreds of thousands. The report even observed, "We do not feel that any failure of intelligence contributed significantly to the defeat," though it conceded that the data had not been perfect and the effectiveness of Castro's military forces "not entirely anticipated or foreseen." Agency historian Jack Pfeiffer, author of CIA's four-volume official account of Project Ate, and other agency veterans have been highly critical of the Taylor report, seeing Bobby Kennedy's role as having been to ensure that outcome. But the plain facts show a wide array of basic errors in CIA's implementation of the project.

In its recommendations, the Taylor report discussed possible establishment of a "Strategic Resources Group," consisting of a chairman, the DCI, and the undersecretaries of state and defense—nothing less than the old 5412 Group resuscitated. The report also recommended, following Dulles, that the armed services be accorded primary responsibility for paramilitary operations, with the Joint Chiefs of Staff the normal avenue for presidential advice, and that an inventory be made of U.S. paramilitary assets.

President Kennedy responded to the recommendations of the Taylor committee with several National Security Action Memoranda in late June. One appointed the chairman of the Joint Chiefs as the president's main adviser for "military type" actions in time of peace as well as of war. Another ordered the inventory of U.S. assets for covert warfare. The third we will return to in a moment.

In early May Kennedy revived his oversight unit—not the 5412 Group but the President's Foreign Intelligence Advisory Board. The prominent citizens group, to which Dr. James Killian returned as chairman, and Clark Clifford and Gordon Gray were soon appointed, met an unprecedented twenty-five times between May and December 1961. They pressed for details on the CIA's covert operations. At their very first session, on May 15, Allen Dulles made a point of suggesting that the Killian Board look into the future relationship of the CIA to paramilitary activities—an allusion to his new line that these ought to be handed over to the armed services. President Kennedy joined the meeting in progress. He now felt someone at the White House should be "constantly in touch with and on top of covert operations," observing that Congress believed this to be already the case. That exchange led into a fresh discussion of the failure of the 1958 Indonesia project. The Cuban fiasco, Jack Kennedy rasped, represented "Indonesia all over again."

Another of Allen Dulles's comments raised eyebrows on the board. The CIA director suggested that the PFIAB also look at the agency's use of proprietaries like Radio Free Europe and others. Clark Clifford cast a withering eye on Dulles and quietly said he had been on the Radio Free Europe board of directors for three years but here, now, learned for the first time that it had any connection to the CIA. Dr. Edwin Land professed himself "both shocked and indignant" to hear that RFE was a proprietary. Land, incidentally, had been a member of Eisenhower's watchdog board since its inception.

Director Dulles reiterated his idea that the paramilitary function be handed off at another Killian Board session on May 25. The third of President Kennedy's June NSAMs did exactly that.

At the May 25 PFIAB meeting, Gen. James Doolittle, who had once advised Ike that CIA covert action should be as ruthless as those of the Soviets, this time said it looked like the "covert operations dog is wagging the intelligence tail," and that needed to be reversed. In July national security adviser McGeorge Bundy told the board that the president, General Taylor, and himself had recently sat through a two-hour presentation on current CIA covert action by Dulles and Bissell. In October, handing over a summary outlining CIA proprietaries and cover organizations,

Allen Dulles began to shut the door on information again, telling the Killian Board that CIA violated its principle of compartmentation by giving up this data. He said nothing of the agency's embarrassment that the list of entities presumably unknown to the board went on for seventeen pages. The PFIAB executive secretary assured the director that they took greater precautions with CIA data than the agency itself.

The PFIAB submitted many recommendations in 1961, some of them on covert operations from the board's own Bay of Pigs postmortem. Among these were advice that the CIA increase its intelligence work and deemphasize covert action; devise a means of eliminating low-potential programs; consider moving covert activity outside the agency; and consider relocating the DO outside Washington, perhaps to New York or elsewhere. Ninety percent of PFIAB recommendations are said to have been effected. These were not.

Meanwhile investigation of the Bay of Pigs also proceeded within the CIA itself. Just two years earlier, responding to criticism of the Directorate for Operations that the Hull Board had offered President Eisenhower, Dulles had ended the DO role in reviewing its own covert activities and assigned this function solely to the CIA inspector general. Now the IG looked at the Bay of Pigs, the first major review under the new system.

Inspector General Lyman Kirkpatrick, with his staff of about a dozen investigators, assembled a detailed picture of the CIA side of the affair. Studying the paper trail and talking to more than 125 people, the inquisitors touched the points made by the Taylor panel but went far beyond it in terms of criticizing the secret warriors' assumptions about Castro's vulnerability, arrangements for equipment and training, the changes in the planning, the agency's operational security, and the management of JM/Ate. Stung by Kirkpatrick's powerful arguments, DO officers struck back with claims that Kirkpatrick had been motivated by personal reasons—animosity for Bissell after being passed over for deputy director for operations—and thus his report amounted to a hatchet job. Even college friend Tom Parrott took that view. Dick Bissell raised the issue himself in a 1967 interview:

> . . . the then Inspector General was known to be, to I think everyone who knew him, extremely ambitious. He was an individual who, as I felt well before this incident, was not above using his reports and his analysis of situations to exert an influence in the direction that he chose, and these directions were, not always but sometimes, tied up with his personal ambitions. I think in this case he had a number of purposes he was trying to serve, more or less of that character.

In a wheelchair, afflicted with the polio he had contracted while on duty for the agency, not long after the report Kirkpatrick was shunted to a different CIA post.

Dark gossip attended the preparation of the IG report, but uproar followed its October 1961 completion. By then a new director held the reins at CIA. Despite the direct relationship between the mess and his own appointment, John A. McCone gave Kirkpatrick's report short shrift when the IG presented it on November 20. He met Kirkpatrick and remarked that the report gave a false picture, suggesting that the CIA alone had responsibility for the failure. Then he arranged for the inspector general to supply an additional memo pointing a finger at the "U.S. Government" (that is, the Kennedy administration). McCone also promised the DO that its rejoinder would be bound together with the report, and he needled Bissell more than once on the DO's progress in compiling this response. Largely the work of Tracy Barnes and practically as long as the IG report itself, that paper went to the director on January 18, 1962. Denunciations of the report were also filed separately: by Allen Dulles, by Bissell, by Charles Pearre Cabell; by Barnes (in addition to his work on the DO response paper), and by three Cuba task force officers. All these circulated with Kirkpatrick's report, then Director McCone had the copies collected. McCone had all save one destroyed.

Years later in his memoirs, Richard Bissell reconsidered his view on the Kirkpatrick report. The IG's conclusion that the Cuba project had been inadequately staffed the former deputy director now termed "probably correct." As for Kirkpatrick's critique of the decision process, Bissell now wrote that

> much of his characterization was fair, but I have never felt that inadequate paperwork or staffing had much to do with whatever misconceptions arose. The shortcomings of our procedure were mainly attributable to keeping the circle of knowledgeable participants as small as possible. I will say, however, that I found our procedures refreshing in contrast to the stuffy discussions and negotiations that went on among the National Security Council's staff members during the Eisenhower years.

Dick Helms, who had a better opinion of Lyman Kirkpatrick's critique, also sided with McCone in holding the Kennedy people to blame for sloppy decisions, even while he noted the project could not have succeeded on its own terms.

There is no question that the Cuba debacle stripped away the CIA's luster, especially that of the Directorate of Operations. Although the CIA might not have looked so bad in the Taylor report, Kennedy had considered Allen Dulles a master spy and a political asset, and now he did not. At lunch with Arthur Schlesinger and James Reston during the last days of Project Ate, the president remarked, "Dulles is a legendary figure and it's hard to work with legendary figures." He kept Allen on until completion of a new CIA headquarters building in Langley, Virginia, the construction of which had been one of Dulles's great dreams, then let him go.

Director Dulles retired to write a book, *The Craft of Intelligence*, in which the passage explaining the Bay of Pigs contains barely a few lines. Later he reacted angrily to publication of the Schlesinger and Theodore Sorensen memoirs on Kennedy, with their descriptions of the president's concerns about the CIA plans. Dulles wrote drafts of a reply, hundreds of pages, never published. The rebuttal shows that CIA officers consciously abetted Kennedy's ignorance in the expectation that, when the chips were down, JFK would have to go along with whatever the agency needed in order to save the exiles. Without the pressures of defending current programs, the former CIA director admitted to failing to ensure that Kennedy understood that air cover had become an absolute prerequisite for success, and to failure to protest repeated orders to reduce the noise level of the operation, so as to avoid hardening the president's leanings against it. Dulles, who rejected Kirkpatrick's IG report, accepts its key criticisms in his drafts. His successor John McCone would have added one more: in 1986 McCone told Dick Bissell that a big mistake had been Dulles's absence from the scene, going to Puerto Rico. Dulles himself saw no problem with this maneuver.

Among smaller fry, Grayston Lynch in a 1998 memoir published a fierce diatribe aimed primarily at Schlesinger, Sorensen, and the journalist Haynes Johnson. In common with a number of CIA veterans, Lynch sees in those accounts the same whitewash as in the Taylor report. The on-scene CIA officer, Lynch defends the stalwart fighters of Brigade 2506 and places the onus of responsibility squarely on Kennedy's shoulders. Lynch has certain details wrong (Bissell, not JFK, halved the initial strike against Castro's air bases, though based on understanding the president wanted less "noise"; there was not—at least in Washington councils*— a plan for a campaign of five or more major strikes before the invasion; it *was* true that internal uprising held a significant role in CIA's concept; Castro did not mistake the U.S. deception in Pinar del Rio for the true invasion), but his core argument is that if the *brigadistas* had ruled the air, the operation would have ended with the downfall of Fidel Castro. Agency Deputy Director Charles Cabell makes the same argument. This is sheer speculation.

At best the CIA air force might have denied Castro forces entry into the Girón area, more likely it could have done no more than make the FAR assault slower and costlier. Brigade 2506 would still have had to get *out*, through a far superior Cuban army which the terrain would then have favored just as it helped the exiles in defense. A completely hidden obstacle would have been a species of crab native to Girón. The thousands of crabs crushed while crossing the roads, their razor-sharp shells often covering roads several feet deep, would have sliced the tires of the brigade's vehicles. Beyond the beachhead, victory would still have required the Cuban people to change sides.

Lynch and Cabell's contention is representative of a view held by participants ranging from Jack Hawkins to exile pilot Eddie Ferrer, to observers like John McCone. But bombers were not about to conquer Havana. Air superiority was necessary for success, not a guarantee of victory. Aircraft, certainly not in the types and numbers available to the CIA, could not destroy Castro's army. Meanwhile the internal resistance, weak and far away, had no chance to link up with the brigade. The Cuban people were the key factor, and the CIA lacked the capacity to wean them from the romance of the Revolution.

Any one failure would have wrecked this complex plan, while every single element had to go right for it to have had even a chance of success. The CIA's proj-

---

* Such a strike program appears in a schedule provided by Gar Thorsrud's people at Puerto Cabezas but not in the JM/Ate planning documents that President Kennedy considered a month before the invasion.

ect had been marginal at best, from the beginning. Dwight Eisenhower and the agency share the blame for that.

Richard Bissell had been considered the leading candidate to succeed Dulles as the DCI; instead his star went into eclipse. Kennedy famously told him that if America had had a parliamentary government he, the president, would resign, but given the presidential system, Bissell had to go instead. John McCone came on board to replace Dulles in November 1961, and then Bissell resigned. Shortly thereafter McCone's first wife died, and the new director felt he needed some stability. He phoned Bissell from California, where McCone attended the funeral, and asked the DO to stay until he returned. In early 1962, with the president's blessing, Bobby Kennedy met with Bissell and said he and McCone wanted the erstwhile secret warrior to go back to dealing in his strong suit, starting up a new Directorate for Research (really science and technology) that the agency was about to create. Bissell declined. He left to head a think tank, the Institute for Defense Analyses in Alexandria, Virginia. There were no farewell parties or ceremonial leavetakings.

Tracy Barnes's career flamed out too. Gossip about the botched briefing of Stevenson spread throughout the agency, infuriating Barnes, who felt he had not lied and that the UN ambassador could have asked questions. The atmosphere soured so much that, a few months later, a junior officer had no compunction about standing up at a staff meeting Barnes conducted to declare that it would really help the DO if Barnes, Bissell, and John Bross all walked the plank. The staffer was shunted to a job at the Pentagon, but Barnes moved over to become division chief of the newly established Domestic Operations Division. E. Howard Hunt became a subordinate.

Gen. Charles Pearre Cabell returned to the air force in December 1961. John Bross, like Helms, held little regard for Tracy Barnes's tradecraft, and his loyalties ran to Bissell. Lyman Kirkpatrick, removed as inspector general, became the CIA's executive director, another of McCone's new posts, but found the job a sinecure. He left in 1964 to become an academic. Robert Amory departed the agency for the White House in 1962, becoming head of the international division of the Bureau of the Budget and its resident expert on intelligence. Dick Drain tried to get as far away as he could, and went to Nairobi as chief of station. Later he turned up in Saigon at the height of the Vietnam War, serving as deputy chief of the largest CIA station in the world. Other agency careers appeared unaffected but in the long run sputtered out. Gar Thorsrud shifted to one of the proprietaries and worked out of a disguised CIA air base at Marana, Arizona, retiring in the mid-1960s. Gerry Droller was promoted to special assistant for political action for the WH Division while Jake Esterline became its chief of operations. They soon had their hands back in with the Guyana affair. Esterline received only a couple more, pro forma, promotions during his career and ended up as chief of base in Miami. At the time of Watergate, the Miami post embroiled Esterline in hot water again, for some of the CIA's Cubans would be characters in that scandal. Worn out, Esterline retired in mid-1973.

By and large, however, the Bay of Pigs proved to be more benign for CIA personnel than participation in later agency muck-ups: only a few dozen officers retired, few were cashiered, no one went to jail.

Thenceforth Kennedy kept the CIA at arm's length. Langley became more than a headquarters complex across the Potomac River, it was shorthand for an alliance of secret warriors the president viewed warily. JFK told aides of his desire to "splinter" the CIA "into a thousand pieces and scatter [it] to the winds." But the actual shake-up proved less extreme.

13

Cold War and Counterrevolution

THE NOTORIOUS Cuba project had been a crossover operation, a CIA covert action begun under one president and continued by another. There are lots more. Tibet, of course. Another, a tragic page from the history of Africa, took place in Zaire, formerly the Belgian Congo, with the arrival of independence. This American operation occurred against a backdrop of intense political strife and Belgium's residual colonial ambitions.

Trouble swiftly followed independence day, June 30, 1960. The Belgians had done as little as possible to prepare the Congolese, to the extent that, for example, there were a mere thirteen college graduates and no African officers in the Congolese army. The basic strategy conceded independence but ensured that Belgians would be needed to *operate* all Congolese institutions. The Belgian commander of the Congolese army, Gen. Emile Janssens, hammered home the point at a meeting with African soldiers where he wrote on a blackboard "*avant independance = apres independance.*" The colonial relationship would endure.

After just five days the Congolese army revolted against their Belgian officers at Thysville, ninety miles from the capital. There, at Camp Hardy, a main base of the army, the *Force Publique*, the Belgians were locked up. Frantic stories of rapes, looting, and unrest in army units in Elisabethville and the capital, Leopoldville, sparked concern. A day of panic in Leopoldville occurred on July 8. Both the British and the French embassies evacuated some personnel. Several thousand Europeans fled across the Congo River to Brazzaville in the Congo Republic. Then rebel armed boats blocked the river.

The revolt naturally triggered a response by the infant government of the Congo. Prime Minister Patrice Lumumba attempted to restore order. He dismissed General Janssens, then all Belgian officers in the *Force Publique*, more than eleven hundred of them, promoting native soldiers to replace them. Lumumba, chief of the *Mouvement National Congolais*, was a young radical, a charismatic black of pan-African sentiment and one of the Congo's few college graduates. In May 1960 elections, Lumumba's party had won thirty-five seats to become the largest in the parliament and the only one with deputies elected from most provinces. The Belgians preferred to avoid a Lumumba cabinet, but the government inevitably coalesced around the largest party.

While the popular Lumumba had a following, the army revolt allowed the Belgians to present his government as ineffective and to intervene with Belgian paratroops on July 10 to restore order. In various attempts to obtain countervailing assistance, Lumumba and Congolese President Joseph Kasavubu appealed for United Nations protection, the cabinet asked for American help, and Lumumba requested Soviet assistance. The United Nations, with Eisenhower's support, passed a resolution to assist the Congo. A UN security force that would eventually amount to nineteen thousand troops from thirty different European, Asian, and African nations deployed to the Congo. The maneuvers for foreign support drew the United States and the Soviet Union into the local situation, in effect bringing the Cold War to Africa.

Washington had little if any knowledge to make the choices it did. It did not know that Lumumba had made a deal with an American mining company before his appeal to the Soviets. Perhaps naively, Lumumba believed the deal cleared the way for him to request Russian help too. The United States did not know that the Congolese independence movement, two years before Lumumba, had already solicited Moscow's aid and that the Russians had said no—a decision that rose to the Politburo level and was made by Soviet leader Nikita Khrushchev. The U.S. embassy in Leopoldville obtained the overwhelming majority of its information (90 percent by some estimates) from Belgian sources, who protected their own interests. Americans relied upon those few Congolese conversant in French. No one at the embassy spoke Limbashi, the tribal language of the *Force Publique*.

Lawrence Devlin, the CIA's station chief in Leopoldville, is a case in point. On the day of independence, living with his wife in Paris, Devlin knew little of the Congo. For a time he had been assigned to Brussels, introduced to a few of the people involved (according to one source Devlin met Joseph Mobutu when that gentleman worked in Brussels as a press spokesman). He spoke French, and that was it. Headquarters ordered Devlin to the Congo by fastest available means. He arrived in Leopoldville to be detained by Congolese soldiers, who handed the CIA man a pistol and made him play Russian roulette for their amusement. That scene became Devlin's initiation to the Congo. The CIA station, nonexistent at first, was then fashioned from personnel pulled from wherever. By September the station chief had just three case officers, all temporary duty, one from the Middle East, the others seconded from the Far East Division.

Similarly the CIA base at Elisabethville (today Lubumbashi) had just one officer, John Anderton, plus a communications man. Much too senior, Anderton had headed large CIA stations and just returned from a long tour in the Far East. But Ike had taken Allen Dulles aside at a cocktail party and asked if he had someone at Elisabethville—he did not. Allen told Ike he did. The CIA had to cover Dulles's affirmation. Anderton had been assigned simply because he was available and spoke French. The base had no networks or agents.

Washington did not like Lumumba and encouraged opposition, especially from the more moderate President Kasavubu. American diplomats in Leopoldville reported negatively on Lumumba's initiatives. Policy hardened rapidly after Devlin cabled on August 18 that both the embassy and his station believed the Congo to be experiencing a "CLASSIC COMMUNIST EFFORT TAKEOVER GOVERNMENT." In Washington that day, President Eisenhower told the National Security Council that there could be no question of one man forcing the United Nations (and the United States) out of the Congo. Ike's declaration, it should be noted, came within hours of his final go-ahead on the Cuba project. His wording struck NSC staffer Robert H. Johnson as something like a presidential order for an assassination. A week later Gordon Gray reminded the 5412 Group of the need for vigorous direct action in the Congo.

The DO's Africa Division, barely a year old at the time, looked toward its first big operation. Chief Bronson Tweedy, his wartime background in naval intelligence with later CIA service in Bern, Vienna, and London, stood ready to go. "Brons" in his time had coordinated a few covert actions with the British but, like Devlin, knew nothing of Africa. He crafted what the CIA called Project Wizard, which began as a political action to neutralize Patrice Lumumba. Tweedy anticipated Devlin's "classic takeover" message with one reporting that he had begun to seek approval for a covert operation. Bissell answered Devlin immediately after the president's NSC outburst, sending instructions plus permission to proceed.

Patrice Lumumba's appeal to the Soviet Union actually occurred on August 21, three days *after* Washington's decision.

In a fresh cable on August 26, following Gray's exchange with 5412, Director Dulles declared that Lumumba's removal had become an urgent objective. The phrase "in high quarters" in that cable would have been understood by CIA officers as a reference to the president. Usually such cables were reviewed by the relevant deputy director. Preparing to testify before investigators of the Church Committee in 1975, Richard Bissell, shown a copy of this dispatch, was astonished to see that it had been released by Richard Helms, not himself. In fact Bissell had been on vacation; Helms had sent it in his stead. In his memoirs Bissell recalls his return to duty, when Allen Dulles explained that *he* had written the cable, just after a meeting where Eisenhower and his advisers had explored the subject at length.

Bissell met with Tweedy about planning a murder using poison, and with CIA scientist Sidney Gottlieb about neutralizing an unnamed African leader. Brons assumed Bissell had authority to issue these orders. The division chief set up a special security compartment, "PROP," for all information on the operation. CIA scientist Gottlieb descended on Leopoldville (today Kinshasa) in late September, slugged in cable traffic as "Joe from Paris," or "Joseph Braun" (and pseudonymously called "Joseph Scheider" by the Senate investigators), another in the sudden influx of agency officers. Gottlieb came bearing exotic poison and a plan to murder Lumumba, separate from and in addition to Project Wizard, itself quickly approved by the 5412 Group. As with the Castro plots, senior participants have denied any presidential connection with assassinations in the Congo, but the Senate investigation amply demonstrates that, approved or not, this plotting actually happened.

Larry Devlin remained in the dark about the scheme, though for more than a month it had been plain that the agency wished to get rid of Lumumba. Devlin mulled this over with David W. Doyle, one of his case officers. Doyle suggested using a high-powered rifle with telescopic sight, pointing out a couple of the CIA men were crack shots. By Doyle's account the whole idea infuriated Devlin, a good Catholic, who regarded it as completely immoral. Doyle believes Devlin rejected the Washington-hatched assassination plots, but he lacks direct knowledge—in September Devlin sent Doyle forward to Katanga to replace Anderton at Elisabethville.

David Doyle could not arrive in Katanga soon enough for the base chief. Anderton's files turned out to consist entirely of his demands to be relieved.

Devlin ("Victor Hedgman" to the Church Committee) got direct orders to prepare for the arrival of someone who would identify himself fully with instructions that must be carried out, and to mention this operation to no one. This is consistent with the station chief rejecting the Lumumba murder plot earlier. Gottlieb was the person referred to. Two days before Gottlieb's arrival, Allen Dulles sent another personal cable to the station. Not taking Gottlieb's word, Devlin queried Quarters Eye—nothing in his training or experience had prepared him for a murder order. Asking about the authority, Devlin was told the order came from the president. Fifteen years later he told congressional investigators that he promptly received confirmation. Devlin mentioned shooting as an alternative. He stalled, threw up obstacles—his assets were not good enough, an "airtight op" would be impossible, he would need to use one of the station's most sensitive agents. By then it was early October. The agent swore himself ready to help but was lukewarm to the plot. Meanwhile the aged poison lost its potency. A CIA officer tossed the stuff into the Congo River (there are also reports it remained sealed in a safe in the CIA station). Gottlieb left on October 5. Bronson Tweedy finally cabled Devlin that he would send a "third country national operative." Headquarters also thought about sending a senior agency officer on direct assignment for this mission—a CIA James Bond—or a commando group to snatch Lumumba.

The Africa Division did in fact send a senior officer to Leopoldville in October 1960. Justin O'Donnell ("Michael Mulroney" in the Church Committee report) told congressional investigators that Dick Bissell asked him to go to kill Lumumba. O'Donnell rejected the mission for the same reasons as Devlin. He also suggested that such a conspiracy hatched in Washington would be a federal felony. O'Donnell went, but only to attempt to draw Lumumba out of his security envelope so that someone else might have a chance at him.

Richard Bissell and Bronson Tweedy both denied having any recollection of these events. Both, however, took the tack that such things could have happened, their memories simply were poor. When this investigation took place Bissell was sixty-six years old, Brons Tweedy fifty-one. (Allen Dulles could not be interviewed—he had died in 1969.)

In 1960, as Americans made up their minds about Lumumba, the Belgians continued to occupy parts of the country, notably Katanga province with many of the Congo's most valuable mineral resources. Urged by the Belgians, Katangese politician Moise Tshombe attempted to secede with his province. The slow arrival of the UN force allowed the Katanga secession to bring the Congo to the brink of civil war.

Political cleavages deepened in September when President Kasavubu fired Lumumba's cabinet, using Katanga as justification. The Americans had made their choice—the 5412 Group approved covert financial support for Kasavubu on September 1, four days before this constitutional coup. Lumumba reacted by attempting to dismiss the president, creating an impasse resolved only when parliament annulled both actions.

Joseph Mobutu would be the wild card. A former journalist, army noncommissioned officer, and member of Lumumba's party, the twenty-nine-year-old Mobutu became an instant "colonel" after the army revolt. Lumumba installed him as chief of staff. American diplomats and CIA officers, especially Larry Devlin, cultivated Mobutu for weeks. On September 14 Mobutu launched a military coup, declaring his intent as "neutralizing" Kasavubu, Lumumba, and all the politicians for the rest of the year. Two Project Wizard local assets featured in the structure with which Mobutu replaced the cabinet, and another became Congolese security chief. When former CIA aide Victor Marchetti wrote in the early 1970s that in the Congo the agency had bought and sold politicians, he was exactly correct. On October 6 Quarters Eye cabled Devlin that it had new plans for Project Wizard, to include "ARMS, SUPPLIES AND PERHAPS SOME TRAINING TO ANTI-LUMUMBA RESISTANCE GROUPS." On October 27 the 5412 Group okayed another $250,000 fund to drum up support for Mobutu. A month later the moguls of the secret war made the further decision to arm the Mobutu forces.

Lumumba became the prime target. Mobutu hoped to supplant him with American help. Allen Dulles favored any solution that excluded Lumumba, whom he regarded as a "harrowing" figure, undoubtedly "bought" by the Communists. At the CIA a branch formerly responsible for DO activity in several African lands suddenly became the Congo task force, led by Edward O. Welles, a gung-ho secret warrior who had fought alongside the British in the Balkans and Middle East and in the Special Boat Service. There is no available, open evidence as to Welles's knowledge of the CIA's targeting of Lumumba. But on November 21 the third-country national, still known in agency lore only by his cryptonym, QJ/WIN, arrived in Leopoldville to participate in the plot. Before he could get to work the situation changed.

Weeks earlier Lumumba had asked for UN protection, and the UN created an envelope around Government House that amounted to incarceration. Frustrated by oppressive security, Lumumba escaped, aided by sympathetic guards. He made for

Stanleyville in Orientale province, evading other UN troops. But he never arrived. Slowed by rain, unable to resist the crowds in every village who demanded he speak to them, the leader found himself critically delayed. Surveillance reports from CIA evidently aided in his capture on December 1 by Mobutu forces. On December 12, Moishe Tshombe declared his secessionist state in Katanga. QJ/WIN left the Congo in late December, but not before the slapstick touch of another CIA asset, WI/ROGUE, attempting to recruit *him* for an attempt against Lumumba.

The degree of CIA complicity in the consequent murder of Lumumba remains disputed. Not so the Belgian role. They too played the game of states, and Brussels had huge stakes in the Congo, especially in Katanga. By official account Belgian intelligence services spent $6 million to destabilize Lumumba's government. They marked Lumumba a liability and conspired against him. Researcher Ludo De Witte pieced together so much of the Belgian story in the 1990s that publication of his book forced both a government inquiry and a parliamentary investigation. In February 2002 the Belgian government issued an official apology, accepting moral responsibility in Lumumba's death and establishing a democracy fund in his memory. The United States has taken no such action.

Lumumba was brutally beaten, then killed, on January 17, 1961. The CIA payroll included the Congolese official who signed the arrest warrant. Lawrence Devlin told the Church Committee that the station had close connections to "several sources" who knew the truth about Lumumba because they made the decisions, but that those people had not acted under CIA direction. The cable traffic reveals that the agency had current information on Lumumba's condition and movements in captivity during January 1961. The cables also show that Devlin feared an imminent coup in Lumumba's favor, making action urgent. Moved by plane, Lumumba was diverted in mid-flight to Katanga—Moise Tshombe, formerly a Lumumbist, had switched sides. Base chief David Doyle observes that the Katangese leader above all was a "realist." Opportunist might be a better description.

Doyle expresses himself as frustrated at Lumumba's sudden materialization on the Elisabethville scene, imprisoned or not, beaten or not. When Doyle learned of the leader's presence, apparently two days later, he sent Devlin this dispatch: "THANKS FOR PATRICE. HAD WE KNOWN HE WAS COMING WE'D HAVE BAKED A SNAKE." The cable mistakenly noted that there were no plans to liquidate Lumumba.

The base chief missed the entire play on the unfortunate Congolese leader's death, and Doyle worried he would be sacked. But the message to Devlin apparently appealed to Allen Dulles's sense of humor. A political cartoon arrived in a pouch from Ed Welles: it showed two Texans baking a snake. Doyle then realized he would be safe.

Not so Patrice Lumumba. The nationalist had been tortured and killed the night after landing at Elisabethville. Belgian officers and Katangese officials participated. Several Belgian soldiers were actually in the firing squad, and Belgian officers with command of Katangese police and security forces did nothing to countermand any of these actions. Stories of CIA people, such as Devlin, driving around with Lumumba's body in the trunk of their car appear apocryphal.

A few days later John F. Kennedy became thirty-fifth President of the United States. For almost a month after that, the Congolese leader's fate remained the best-kept secret in the Congo. JFK reacted with shock and anguish when he learned of Lumumba's death on February 13. Only two days before that the 5412 Group—now Kennedy's Special Group—had granted another half-million dollars for the Congo project.

Dealing with Patrice Lumumba had taken months. Exorcising his ghost in the Congo required years of fighting, never to be fully accomplished.

Kennedy's State Department advisers proposed an activist role. The CIA, left out, protested to McGeorge Bundy. Allen Dulles sent Bundy a letter on February 5 warning that the agency's views had not been taken into account. Bundy reassured Dulles: President Kennedy, well aware of the circumstances, would ensure the CIA a hearing. Arthur Schlesinger relates that JFK saw the UN in the Congo as filling a power vacuum, in the absence of which there would be a Soviet-American confrontation. That view hinged on a certain analysis of Soviet motives. The young president had an opportunity here to shift from the Eisenhower policy, removing the Cold War context and crafting an African New Deal. Officials held divided views—even within State, Africa Bureau people generally favored a softer approach than the Europeanists—and a "Katanga Lobby" existed in Congress and among the public. But JFK approved the activists' program. Backing Leopoldville would be framed as supporting reunification of the Congo, no doubt more palatable to newly independent African states but no different in substance from Eisenhower's approach. The road to democracy in the Congo did not lie through Washington.

Mobutu's ban on political activity expired with the new year. Soon Kasavubu announced a new prime minister and cabinet while Mobutu remained the strongman. This uneasy coalition prevailed for five years—the figurehead Kasavubu plus a succession of prime ministers—until Mobutu emerged from the shadows with a coup that established his open domination. Cyrille Adoula, most prominent of the cabinet heads, would take the heat for the suppression of Katanga. In typical Congolese fashion, the emergence of Adoula automatically alienated other factions and stimulated more separatist movements.

The scale of the Congo project necessitated close cooperation between the CIA and the U.S. military. The effort was massive: by May 1961 the air force had lifted 20,000 UN troops and 6,000 tons of equipment; the navy had brought in another 5,000 UN troops while taking home 2,600. Assistance to Leopoldville included eighteen helicopters, ten C-47 aircraft, and five larger C-119s. At its full stride the CIA burned money at a rate of a million dollars a day. Adoula received substantial agency support.

Washington attained its goal—a friendly government in Leopoldville—but the price amounted to disintegration of the country. With creation of yet another secessionist regime in southern Kasai province there were no less than four "nations" in the Congo. The U.S. role became one of reinforcing Leopoldville until the UN forces or the Congolese army could reunite the land. The UN peacekeeping force came under criticism as a cat's paw for the Americans.

Intelligence reporting clearly showed the portents: the Belgians both intransigent and engaged, with their own angle to play; the Mobutu-Adoula faction hoping to divert secessionists with temporary alliances while enlisting the UN to disarm Tshombe, after which Mobutu's own troops could clean up; the European nations uneasy with the international measures taken. For many months CIA analysts—perhaps kept in the dark by the DO—failed to perceive Mobutu's power, consistently identifying Adoula as the main Congolese player. In weekly tracking reports on events the analysts followed the separatist "nations," constantly featuring Adoula as the instigator of Leopoldville's maneuvers to take them down.

One element that helped keep Mobutu in the background is that his Congolese National Army would not fight. Or, more properly, that the army was riven by the same crosscutting loyalties of tribe and clan that afflicted Congolese politics, with the result that it was often the instrument of secession rather than the solution to national disintegration. Katanga got most of the attention in the world's eye while the CIA turned its gaze elsewhere. Specifically the agency feared Antoine Gizenga, who laid claim to the mantle of Lumumba. Gizenga had visited Russia and studied in Prague, impressing Washington as Moscow's man in Africa. He led a secessionist regime in Orientale province, based in Stanleyville.

Gizenga's "nation" fell to a combination of CIA action, the man's own ineptitude, and Adoula's maneuvers. The agency soon appreciated that Gizenga's key weaknesses were money and arms. He bought the loyalty of "Gizengist" units of the Congolese military with weapons and cash, making backing critical. Reports were that Gizenga had the best-paid army in the Congo. The CIA discovered the Russians were sending Gizenga cash—in U.S. dollars—and weapons. Washington deliberated on blocking the flow. On June 8 the Special Group considered an action proposal. Allen Dulles warned of political dangers while State and the Pentagon favored moving ahead. Mac Bundy concluded he had to take the issue to the president. Kennedy approved.

Gizenga's arms deliveries were disrupted by the agency cleverly and successfully. The CIA knew that Czechoslovakia had begun sending merchant vessels to the Sudan—unusual in that almost all Soviet Bloc trade had previously gone to West Africa. The CIA also knew that much of the tiny Czech merchant fleet consisted of ships transferred by Beijing, with Chinese crews and possibly secretly under Chinese control. Beijing had taken a very friendly position toward African independence movements, especially in the Congo. The Sudan associated itself closely with Egypt's Nasser, who the CIA estimated wanted to play a leading role in Afro-Asian circles and favored Gizenga in the Congo. Sleuthing established that a Czech ship, probably one of the Chinese-crewed vessels, was carrying a cargo of arms to the Sudan ultimately bound for Gizenga. Washington considered asking the Sudan to embargo the shipment but, given the Nasser connection, rejected that approach in favor of public exposure. With some judicious payoffs in Port Sudan, the crane unloading the Czech-flag vessel slipped as it carried the second pallet, spilling crates all over the dock. Some broke open to scatter Soviet-made rifles everywhere. The shipment, consigned as Red Cross refugee aid, was revealed as weapons. The Sudanese confiscated all of it, halting Gizenga's arms supplies.

Meanwhile in Cairo, where Gizenga maintained an office, the CIA discovered a Russian plan to send the Congolese $1 million in U.S. currency. Agents were able to learn the itinerary of the courier Gizenga sent to pick up the money. Larry Devlin arranged a surprise—again in the Sudan. Thanks to more bribes the courier, carrying a third of the cash in a suitcase, was summoned for customs inspection in Khartoum. Terrified, he contrived to leave the suitcase in a bathroom. The CIA recovered it, making a profit on the operation. Gizenga's difficulties were greatly magnified. When his soldiers began holding up tribesmen to get their money, "Gizengist" sentiment diminished rapidly.

Adoula supplied the next maneuver, getting Gizenga to accept the offer of a vice premiership in the government, apparently without thinking through the politics of this deal. This connection with the Leopoldville government tarnished Gizenga's Lumumbist credentials and enabled Adoula to demand his presence in the capital. Gizenga went on the lam instead, disappearing from Stanleyville, living for weeks in the bush so no official papers could be served on him, virtually halting his political activity. A fall 1961 conference where Gizenga had hoped to form a new national party flopped as a result, and Adoula was able to get the national assembly to vote to summon Gizenga to the capital.

The next phase of this struggle was overshadowed by events in Katanga. Mobutu's troops failed in an attempt to take the province outright. In September came an outbreak of fighting between Tshombe's Katangese troops and UN forces. This led to a forgotten chapter in the sordid story of the Congo, the death of UN Secretary General Dag Hammarskjöld, who came to mediate. The secretary general, a Swede, worried about events and the degree to which the UN seemed compromised by taking sides in this strife. On one leg of his shuttle, Hammarskjöld was to meet with Moishe Tshombe. Approaching the airfield at Ndola (just across the border, in what is now Zambia) on September 17, the secretary general's DC-6B aircraft crashed, killing Hammarskjöld and thirteen others. Subordinates believed that Katangese mercenaries shot down the plane. Since the Belgian *Union Miniere* financed much of Tshombe's mercenary force at the time, this conclusion again implicates the Belgians. Others insist the aircraft crashed due to mechanical failure and maintenance faults.

Tshombe had beaten Mobutu's troops thanks to his Western mercenary force and a jet fighter that gave him aerial superiority over Katanga. President Kennedy reluctantly issued an order that the United States would supply jet aircraft if they could not be gotten elsewhere, but Washington was saved from that escalation when Sweden and India sent planes of their own. Incidents between Tshombe troops and the UN multiplied. An uneasy truce lasted some weeks. Now CIA's Bronson Tweedy came to Katanga for a personal survey. He and Jim Doyle, longtime friends (their fathers had been at Princeton together), helped put out a fire burning a train filled with ammunition whose explosion might have destroyed much of Elisabethville. A December Special National Intelligence Estimate found that the question of reintegrating Katanga had become so critical as to threaten the Adoula government.

Almost simultaneously the truce collapsed as the UN went on the offensive. At the critical moment Tshombe was away on a trip to Paris and Brazil, where he went for a conference of the Moral Rearmament movement—unwittingly observed by CIA's political operatives. Washington sent C-130 transports to move UN reinforcements to Katanga. Tshombe's troops and mercenaries fought a pitched battle for Elisabethville and were largely driven from the city, but the UN was unable to secure much more than its headquarters, the airfield, and other major installations. A fresh political accommodation would be negotiated among the UN, Tshombe, and Adoula. Tshombe disputed and violated its terms for many months. Amid the horror of Katanga, Mobutu and Adoula took advantage to arrest Antoine Gizenga, whom they sent to jail. The Soviet media protested. In January 1962 UN forces captured Gizenga's capital at Stanleyville. Within the year, in the topsy-turvy of Congolese politics, the national assembly would be demanding Gizenga's release.

In an April 1962 television interview, former CIA director Allen Dulles admitted that his CIA and the United States had overestimated the degree to which the Russians had involved themselves in the Congo. The premise of the entire venture had been mistaken.

The Katanga stalemate continued for more than a year. A Special National Intelligence Estimate prepared at the agency in May 1962 found the reintegration of Katanga essential to the future of the Congo but the obstacles to action unchanged. That November the State Department's intelligence unit filed a lengthy research memorandum that made no judgment on the wisdom of military action but warned against abandoning the United Nations. The UN came up with a reintegration plan, but Tshombe stalled, then rejected it. In December, with Kennedy's National Security Council Executive Committee, the fabled EXCOM, discussing Congo at the same meetings where it considered the aftermath of the Cuban Missile Crisis, Kennedy demanded a fresh assessment of UN military capability in the context of a new U.S. "Operating Plan for the Congo." Only a week later fighting broke out between UN forces and the Katangese. Tshombe's secessionist state collapsed. In his turn he too went to prison. But, as Cord Meyer explained to the President's Foreign Intelligence Advisory Board on April 15, 1963, the CIA's project in the Congo continued. The messy Congolese affair boiled on.

The Cuban operation represented the summit of a certain type of paramilitary action. The Congolese project showcased a new style of combined CIA-military activity. The frantic era of the OPC and the early CIA were gone. Paramilitary plans in Frank Wisner's time frequently involved grand schemes carried out against foreign governments. Kennedy's administration brought a shift toward operations in collaboration with established governments, aimed at real or imagined domestic enemies. There were still exceptions, of course, the Guyana project among the most prominent. The failure in Cuba contributed to the change of emphasis, demonstrating anew the resilience of target governments. Yet the change was in the wind before the first frogmen stepped ashore at Playa Girón, propelled by a shift in view at the top level of the U.S. executive.

National security policy during the Eisenhower administration combined CIA's active paramilitary campaigns with a "New Look" military strategy that was radical in a different way. Ike's policy rested upon the enormous power of nuclear weapons, the assumption that future wars would be nuclear, and a desire to maintain the American economy, which Eisenhower felt could not grow in the face of large military budgets. Thus his rigid and often arbitrary ceilings on defense spending. With atomic power emphasized, the ceilings required reductions elsewhere. These could only come from conventional forces. The Eisenhower period witnessed cutbacks in the army and Marine Corps. Many opposed Ike's policy, especially the army brass. One chief of staff resigned over the issue. With notable exceptions, other army generals also opposed the New Look, but Ike carefully satisfied the navy and air force, appointing Joint Chiefs chairmen who supported him. The army argued in isolation.

The CIA was the one shop with a common interest in the army's limited-war capability. Paramilitary operations were limited wars, possible contingencies for the employment of conventional force. As early as 1955 the CIA commissioned a study, Project Brushfire, of the political, psychological, economic, and sociological factors that affected "peripheral wars." The Center for International Studies, under economist Max Millikan at the Massachusetts Institute of Technology, conducted the study. Brushfire became one of a series of research contracts that CIA gave the MIT institute, which it had originally funded. On his copy of an information memo regarding Brushfire, Eisenhower's Joint Chiefs chairman commented, "I think the answers are so plain that it is a waste of money."

When Eisenhower in early 1958 ordered a policy review on limited war versus full-scale conflict, the CIA wanted to be involved. John Foster Dulles sought to discourage brother Allen's participation, saying the agency should be concerned with intelligence questions, not "operational" ones. Director Dulles allowed himself to be mollified by promises that the CIA would be permitted into operational aspects on some later occasion.

Further limited-war studies followed, and the CIA contributed, but its interests were scarcely known outside government while army officers trumpeted their opposition to the New Look to whomever would listen. The most prominent army spokesman was chief of staff Gen. Maxwell Taylor. Specifically, Taylor asserted that a strategy of massive nuclear retaliation could not counter "brushfire" wars, and that a strategy of "flexible response" could meet conflict at any level of intensity. At the CIA, which saw paramilitary action as a rung on the conflict ladder, the secret warriors undoubtedly cheered. But at the White House, Eisenhower gave short shrift to Taylor's views. The general retired to write a book that advocated forces to meet the full spectrum of contingencies, brushfire wars as well as big ones.

No doubt Tracy Barnes, agonizing over the Bay of Pigs, paid little attention when a letter crossed his desk on the last day of that disaster. From James E. Cross at the Institute for Defense Analysis, the missive commented on what Barnes had said about another CIA initiative, a study group on the deterrence of guerrilla warfare. Cross believed that officials already understood this problem; they had to be told how to make the most of assets in threatened areas. The study group had held a couple of working meetings. A draft paper on limited war, written by the CIA's Jim Critchfield, already sat on desks at Quarters Eye. Both Allen Dulles and Richard Bissell read it before the landing at Playa Girón, and it received other circulation at CIA as well. One of Critchfield's recommendations provided for a survey of assets for unconventional warfare and paramilitary operations. All this moved fast precisely because the CIA, in building bridges to the new president's inner sanctum, had seen Kennedy's deep interest. Like two comets on intersecting trajectories, the rise of Maxwell Taylor would coincide with JFK's demand for action on counterinsurgency.

After the Bay of Pigs failed, the inadequacy of efforts in the field of low-intensity warfare were glaringly evident. Fears that Russia would encourage "wars of national liberation" heightened concerns about the need to deter guerrilla warfare. Kennedy wanted someone to answer a Khrushchev speech on these conflicts and settled on his self-professed man of ideas, Walt W. Rostow, then the deputy national security adviser. By mid-June both the president and NSC staff were working over the proposed text of a presentation Rostow would make at the Special Warfare Center at Fort Bragg, North Carolina. Two weeks later President Kennedy approved a directive providing for a government-wide evaluation of paramilitary requirements. This led to a top-secret summer study that combined the themes of deterring guerrilla warfare, limited war, counterinsurgency, and paramilitary operations. Walt Rostow watched this exercise closely. Another sparkplug, the study's formal chairman, was Richard Bissell.

In early July a luncheon took place at CIA where Bissell set the direction for his policy review. He told Rostow, and Bissell's initial overview paper borrowed heavily from Walt's speech text, *very* well known once Rostow gave the talk at Fort Bragg. At the Pentagon, Ed Lansdale also prepared a paper, the first of several, which recited in bald numbers the staffing levels in special warfare units. In mid-July Allen Dulles reported that CIA had begun coordinating with Lansdale on future paramilitary requirements.

Closely watched at the White House, Bissell's study became almost his swan song with the CIA. In contrast to pre-Cuba days, he now listened hard to what the White House had to say. From the NSC staff, Robert Komer suggested language for portions of the report, while from Maxwell Taylor's staff Col. Julian Ewell, the general's *éminence grise*, soaked up Bissell's comments and gave back Taylor's responses. Bissell's paper grew odd tentacles in successive drafts over the fall of 1961. Presenting an update on covert action procedures to Kennedy's recreated Killian Board, Bissell suddenly spoke of regaining public confidence in CIA covert action by revealing the existence of the Special Group, much as Eisenhower had once revealed the Killian Board itself.

At another point Bob Komer did a summary of Bissell's paper in which he inserted the recommendation to vest high-level authority in the Special Group, which Taylor headed. That measure did not appear in Bissell's original, which his assistant John Bross distributed on November 21. Although Komer assured Bissell that his summary changed nothing in the paper, he told his boss, McGeorge Bundy, "I took advantage of Walt's imminent departure [Rostow would leave the NSC staff for the State Department] to press for what I think is the most logical solution, i.e., to tag Taylor and the Special Group with this task." Bissell let this pass without comment.

Everyone had an agenda. Walt Rostow wanted to center U.S. thinking about dissident movements and insurgencies within the framework of stages of economic growth. The CIA deputy focused his interest on the agency's role in such events. As Bissell put it,

> A general problem in threatened underdeveloped countries is that of developing and strengthening the basic governmental and social institutions that are prerequisites to modernization. In some cases, as in the Congo, the local leadership is responsive to the need for change but lacks the background and competence to take needed steps on its own. In other cases, a frustrating and exasperating problem in countries severely plagued by Communist political and military subversion . . . is the reluctance—bordering on blind obstinacy—of the governmental leaders to admit the need for reform. In both cases the traditional and internationally accepted tools of government-to-government diplomacy . . . are unlikely by themselves to provide the guidance or the resources to achieve the reforms and changes essential to winning broad-based popular support for the national regime. In such situations the broad range of covert action measures available to us offers our best and only chance of increasing our leverage and achieving needed changes in time.

Bissell foresaw a "suitable covert operational methodology" that would involve "funding and guidance channels of bona fide private international or regional organizations," particularly labor, youth, farm, or veterans groups; confidential relationships with local political leaders ("non-attributably backstopped"); and covertly funded consultants to local regimes.

There could also be a CIA role strengthening internal security and defense. "Offensive countermeasures" would be "primarily intended as spoiling operations," including cross-border operations. With a finely honed sense of the dangers inherent in this, the paper admitted such tactics would become "almost unpredictably dangerous" if the adversary believed there existed a possibility he or she might be overthrown or lose territory. And, "The advantage is lost if an offensive operation against the aggressor is conducted in such a manner as to compel him to regard it as a formal act of war." A further important theme—which fed back to Walt Rostow's advocacy—was that "public expression would be given to the rationale."

On December 8 the final counter–guerrilla warfare task force paper contained Dick Bissell's statement of the techniques the Kennedy administration imagined would make the world safe for democracy. It also met Robert Komer's agenda, saying, "Because of its responsibilities in directly related fields and because the agencies chiefly concerned are already represented on it, expansion of the mandate of the NSC Special Group seems the most effective way to carry out this function." The Special Group would designate threatened countries, and for each of them Washington would form a task force to ensure optimal use of resources.

Richard Bissell's last act would thus be to move Kennedy to reorganize his machinery for covert action. In fact the Special Group talked over the Bissell report on December 14. General Taylor formalized the early ad hoc procedures, drafting a directive that JFK approved on January 18, 1962. Because there has been confusion about Kennedy's leadership of the secret war, this structure is worth underlining: The president established the Special Group (CI)—the abbreviation stood for "counterinsurgency"—to formulate plans on guerrilla warfare matters, in any country so designated. The existing Special Group—formerly the 5412 Group—on Cold War matters continued (the nomenclature had now been reversed: "5412" became the insider jargon). A *third* Special Group also appeared, the Special Group (Augmented). The difference was that Max Taylor chaired the 5412 Group existing since Harry Truman's day while Bobby Kennedy skippered the Special Group (Augmented), identical save for his addition and its specific focus on Cuba.

Maxwell Taylor had been a paratrooper. In the army in his time, paratroopers were considered a military elite—thoroughly modern and flexible officers. Solidly cast in this "Airborne" mold, Max Taylor was unusual, just as Kennedy thought. More typical were the army officers who throughout the 1950s hindered the development of Special Forces. The Tenth Special Forces Group had been in place at Fort Bragg since June 1952. In September 1953 it was supplemented by the Seventy-seventh Group, which remained in the United States while almost eight hundred men of the Tenth Group deployed to western Germany, where they occupied an old German army base at Bad Tolz in Bavaria. This expansion coincided with the return of the Korean War veterans, a major source of Special Forces recruits. Subsequent growth slowed to a snail's pace as anxious army generals preserved conventional units as best they could within the New Look budgets. Preoccupied with adjusting to nuclear war, the brass had little time for advocates of unconventional warfare.

The German deployment became the first giant step. At Bad Tolz the Tenth Special Forces planned for partisan campaigns in Eastern Europe and showed what they could do in NATO maneuvers. Detachments sent from the United States to other nations to help in training inaugurated a Special Forces role that has endured ever since. A permanent presence in the Far East began in 1956 when provisional teams went to Hawaii, then to Okinawa. In June 1957 this became the First Special Forces Group. Special Forces began missions to Laos as early as 1959, and in 1960 they appeared in South Vietnam, training Vietnamese rangers at the invitation of President Ngo Dinh Diem.

A wave of disillusionment swept through Special Forces, as at the CIA, when Eisenhower took no action during the Hungarian revolt. The unconventional warfare experts also smarted from their encounters with the army bureaucracy, which banned the wearing of Special Forces' semi-official headgear, the green beret. Dedication was a valued attribute in a Special Forces soldier, but a person needed a lot to stay in the teams at that time. By 1960 Special Forces groups had tripled but amounted to only about two thousand troops, fewer than the personnel spaces the army had allocated in its 1952 decision to maintain a single unconventional warfare unit.

As military formations go, a Special Forces "group" represented something new. One component, an administrative base, served the needs of many distributed teams, called "operational detachments." From group headquarters a C Team provided control and intelligence support for a large area while a B Team did the same for a region. The operational detachment was the A Team. These had a wide range of skilled experts for technical and medical services and combat leadership. The basic concept called for an A Team essentially leading a large partisan force or providing a training cadre. Special Forces recruited experienced officers and noncommissioned officers (NCOs), selected only the best, and then cross-trained team members in several of the required skills. During the 1950s this was quite necessary since many of the teams had but a fraction of their authorized complements.

The notion of Special Forces commands for regions and countries, with A Teams for field forces, clearly aimed at organizing resistance to an adversary's military advance or occupation. The essential function, similar to the CIA's stay-behind nets, was to harass and disrupt. But because of the expertise of their members, the A Teams were also highly suited for the training mission and for command of friendly irregular units within friendly territory. The latter became a key task in counterinsurgency. Here Special Forces at last found the role that sustained it through the Vietnam era and after.

This only became evident later. Good fortune came to Special Forces with the election of John F. Kennedy. Within days of JFK's inauguration one of the president's NSC staff, Walt Rostow, began questioning the adequacy of army training for war against guerrillas. Special Forces already ran counterinsurgency courses at its headquarters in Fort Bragg. These emphasized the economic, social, political, and psychological origins of war. Special Forces seemed to be on top of the subject, and President Kennedy saw a major role for Special Forces' knowledge in "brushfire" wars.

A few months later Rostow went to Fort Bragg to address the students of the Special Warfare Center, his speech approved by Kennedy. Rostow's speech put guerrilla war in the context of global underdevelopment, a sort of crisis of modernization. Although Rostow commended the students for reading Lenin, Guevara, and Mao Zedong, he insisted that guerrilla war dated to long before the Russian Revolution. "Guerrilla warfare," as Rostow put it, "is not a form of military and psychological magic created by the Communist." Rather, "we confront in guerrilla warfare in the underdeveloped areas a systematic attempt by the Communists to impose a serious disease on those societies attempting the transition to modernization." America's central task would be "to protect the independence of the revolutionary process now going forward." Guerrilla warfare "is powerful and effective only when we do not put our minds clearly to work on how to deal with it."

Kennedy perceived Special Forces to have done just that. Rostow returned to Bragg in late 1961, this time accompanying the president on a personal tour of the Special Warfare Center. Its commander, Brig. Gen. William Yarborough, took a calculated risk and greeted Kennedy wearing the proscribed green beret. The president came and saw, spoke supportively, and helped Special Forces gain new impetus. On April 11, 1962, JFK released an official message to the army, calling the green beret "a symbol of excellence, a badge of courage, a mark of distinction in the fight for freedom." Henceforth Special Forces would be known as Green Berets, with official regulations to govern their size and color and how they should be worn. In a remarkable expansion of the franchise, decades later the entire U.S. Army clamored for berets of their own and now wear this headgear in varied colors and devices.

From the beginning of Kennedy's presidency a rapid expansion of Special Forces occurred. In March 1961 the army doubled the number of units. Now groups specialized geographically—the Tenth Group for Europe; the First for Asia; a new Eighth Group for Latin America; and Third and Sixth groups for Africa and Middle East assignments. The Seventy-seventh Special Forces Group became the Seventh. Authorized strength doubled to fifteen hundred soldiers per group. Psychological warfare units also increased, in early 1965, to three battalions and two companies plus detachments. By November 30, 1964, the strength of army special warfare units stood at more than eleven thousand.

In Germany the Tenth Group retained its mission of infiltrating the Soviet bloc. The theater war plan, OPLAN 10-1, according to revelations in the British press, in 1962 provided for the Tenth Group to disperse into forty-nine guerrilla warfare zones throughout Eastern Europe. Its A Teams were each credited with the ability to mobilize a partisan battalion every month, for a potential resistance force of almost eighty thousand within six months, according to the estimates of the Special Operations Task Force Europe.

In its concentration on behind-the-lines wartime activity, the Tenth Group became an exception. Green Berets working other areas of the globe focused more on counterinsurgency and military assistance. The future looked bright. "For the first time in United States history," said army spokesmen in an informational publication, "this [guerrilla organizing and psychological warfare] capability has been made available before it is needed. Through it the Army now has one more weapon which can be applied with discrimination in any kind of warfare."

There were air force special forces too. These provided support, especially airlift. The air force called its approach to special forces the "air commando" concept. An "air commando" unit contained a little bit of everything—medium and light transport aircraft plus fighter-bombers. The same unit could supply partisans, make air strikes in their support, and maintain physical contact by flying light planes onto small airstrips. The ARC wings had continued the tradition, but the air force had abolished them. Had the Khampa partisans possessed such capabilities in Tibet, the PLA might never have been able to overcome them.

Air commandos were eclipsed in Eisenhower's budget-conscious air force. Faced with expensive bomber and missile programs, little interest remained. Tactical commanders were preoccupied with their transition to supersonic jet fighters. Even air transport leaders had bigger ticket programs like the C-130 Hercules or the large jet C-141 Starlifter. The air commandos fell nebulously somewhere among the functional responsibilities of the various air force commands.

Despite all obstacles, a start was made in the late 1950s with the formation of a small, secret organization within the service. As with the army, Kennedy galvanized the air force. In March 1961, responding to instructions that each service examine how it could contribute to counterinsurgency, air force headquarters ordered the Tactical Air Command to create an experimental counterinsurgency unit along air commando lines.

Very soon thereafter, on April 14, 1961, the air force activated the 4400th Combat Crew Training Squadron under Col. Benjamin H. King at Eglin Air Force Base, Florida. The unit based its planes at nearby Hurlbut Field. Initially they included sixteen C-47s, eight B-26s, and eight T-28 Texans, propeller-driven training aircraft converted to carry bombs or rockets and machine guns. Nicknamed the "Jungle Jim" unit, the 4400th began with 350 airmen and the dual mission of training indigenous aircrews and participating in combat.

Meanwhile, for top-secret airlift missions over longer distances the Military Airlift Command established special E-Flights in certain of its C-130 squadrons. The unit for the Far East, for example, was E-Flight of the Twenty-first Troop Carrier Squadron on Okinawa, formed in late 1961 with four or five C-130s, already involved in the Tibet operation.

In April 1962 the air force dispensed with euphemisms and reactivated its First Air Commando Squadron, a formation that traced its lineage directly back to March 1944 in Burma. The squadron later expanded to a wing, supplemented by more combat crew training squadrons, a combat support group, and, at Eglin, the Special Air Warfare School. All these capabilities were controlled by a Special Warfare Division at USAF headquarters. Long before this stage arrived, the original Jungle Jim unit had gone into action in Southeast Asia.

Changes also came within the Pentagon. The Office of Special Operations transformed itself after the Bay of Pigs. Although OSO representatives such as Ed
Lansdale had raised objections to the Cuba project, the Joint Chiefs were appor-
tioned some blame in the failure. Secretary of Defense Robert McNamara, none
too happy, wanted streamlining. Graves Erskine ran a tight ship, but perhaps there
was just too much work for a single office.

At that time the OSO truly functioned as an intelligence focal point. It handled liaison and everything else from allocating forces to covert projects, to military personnel for detached service at CIA, to cover arrangements, to Pentagon
participation in reconnaissance satellite development. McNamara was told that he
did not really need a special assistant for these matters. Suddenly, the day after the
final defeat of the Cuban exiles at the Bay of Pigs, most of the OSO personnel
were reassigned to other military tasks.

Some OSO officers feared that Lansdale might take over the special assistant's functions. After all, he had been deputy to General Erskine and one of the
foremost proponents of counterinsurgency. But there were questions as to whether
Lansdale knew much about satellites and other technical intelligence issues.

The Joint Chiefs of Staff set the stage in late July 1961 when they asked for
guidance on peacetime support to the Central Intelligence Agency. An existing
agreement from 1957 now seemed obsolete. The officers need not have worried.
When OSO disappeared, McNamara assigned its technical responsibilities to the director of defense research and engineering. Under his August 7 directive, deception
responsibilities went to a special planning office within the navy. Lansdale retained
a small staff to handle only special activities. On September 12 Lansdale defined the
terrain in a paper to the Chiefs and all the service secretaries: routine matters could
be handled by those already assigned to liaise between the military and CIA, but
anything requiring policy discussion or major participation would go to his office.

Some credit Erskine with achieving this division of tasks. A new unit, the spe-
cial assistant for counterinsurgency and special activities (SACSA) is what finally
emerged. In any case, Ed Lansdale did not succeed to the OSO empire. Pulled into
a renewed Cuba adventure, Lansdale disappeared. A Marine general had headed
OSO, and now another Marine became SACSA. With an eye cocked toward the
White House, the Marine Corps gave the post to an officer who had served with
Jack Kennedy in the South Pacific during World War II, Maj. Gen. Victor "Brute"
Krulak. Jack Hawkins came back from the CIA to become his assistant. Both were
skeptical of the covert operations that followed the Bay of Pigs, especially
Hawkins. But on counterinsurgency SACSA proved very active, and Maxwell Tay-
lor's Special Group (CI) made sure it stayed that way. Army civilian executive
Joseph A. Califano, Jr., came to think Krulak's nickname very well chosen.

Dick Bissell had been an enthusiastic supporter of counterinsurgency, leading
the 1961 summer study. His successor, Richard McGarah Helms, was not so

much so. A professional from the espionage establishment, Helms had been poised for this job for a decade. He had been the go-to guy for spies, heading the division that covered Germany during creation of the CIA-Gehlen Organization alliance and the heady years of that country as base for penetration missions behind the Iron Curtain. He had dutifully played second fiddle to Wisner, then Bissell. Now Helms began the meteoric rise that took him to the top of the CIA in the span of a few years. Despite his proclivities, in the process Helms would preside over a peak in the secret war, the years from Kennedy to the Nixon-Kissinger era.

Helms took over an expanding DO but one inflicted with self-doubt. Already a stream of defectors had begun to sow fears of a Russian mole at a high level within the CIA. And there were the covert action failures—which nevertheless did not impede the growth of DO capabilities. The directorate remained the largest component of the agency, a thousand stronger than when Ike took office, spending 54 percent of CIA's budget. An extra thousand CIA personnel supported DO's work. Field stations in Africa increased by half between 1959 and 1963, reflecting the rise of Tweedy's Africa Division. Impelled by Cuban projects, personnel in the Western Hemisphere Division grew 40 percent between 1961 and 1965. After that the focus would shift to Southeast Asia.

A few weeks before Helms became DDO the CIA general counsel, Lawrence Houston, put on record his opinion regarding the legal basis for covert action, admitting that "there is no statutory authorization to any agency for the conduct of such activities." No explicit prohibition existed either, Houston added, and "some of the covert Cold War operations are related to intelligence within a broad interpretation" of the National Security Act of 1947. Examining the language of the law, the CIA lawyer specifically conceded its failure to cover paramilitary operations— the clause that read "such other duties and functions" in the act, always cited in this regard, was explicitly tied to "*intelligence* affecting the national security." Thus, wrote Houston in this January 15, 1962, memorandum, "it would be stretching that section too far to include a Guatemala or a Cuba even though intelligence and counterintelligence are essential to such activities."

Houston's conclusion: "Therefore, the Executive Branch under the direction of the President was acting without specific statutory authorization, and CIA was the agent selected for their conduct."

Defending the government's conduct in these paramilitary operations, the CIA general counsel was reduced to arguing that "it can be said that the Congress as a whole knows that money is appropriated to CIA and knows that generally a portion of it goes for clandestine activities. To this extent we say that we have Congressional approval of these activities." Thus the CIA's own legal counsel saw no general mandate for paramilitary operations or political action, no specific authorization, and only the weak claim that Congress had approved by means of appropriating money. It is worth noting that a parallel argument that Congress had in effect approved a declaration of war by appropriating money for the Vietnam War would be ruled invalid by the courts.

Larry Houston believed it was for the administration to decide what and how many Cold War activities. Prodded by Bobby Kennedy and Max Taylor, it did. Under procedures adopted after the Bay of Pigs, any project costing more than $3 million had to be approved. The CIA could conduct operations budgeted for less than $250,000 on its own. After October 1962 the Special Group expected to be appraised of *every* covert project.

From the beginning of Kennedy's presidency to the fall of 1962, according to the Special Group's own records, it approved 550 covert operations. During the first half of 1963 it sanctioned another 23 actions (out of 35 proposed). Figures given to the congressional investigators in 1975—163 covert operations between January 1961 and November 1963, compared to 104 approved during the Eisenhower years—evidently count only activities above a certain threshold. Even so, a later internal audit found that in 1961–1962 the Special Group considered only about 16 percent of operations actually initiated.

The gains from these activities were limited. On the one hand, Kennedy tightened his control; on the other, he brought the locus of responsibility closer to the White House. McGeorge Bundy recalls:

> In 1961 I listened with a beginner's credulity to the arguments of the eager operatives who promoted what became the Bay of Pigs. . . . Through the next two years and more, I watched with increasing skepticism as the Kennedy Administration kept the pressure on the CIA for more and better—if smaller—covert operations.
>
> I think I played a small part—his own learning from experience was much more important—in President Kennedy's growing recognition that covert action simply did not work and caused more trouble than it was worth.

Kennedy's demise ended the potential for a change in policy. And Mac Bundy failed to stem the rising tide of project proposals.

But DDO Helms faced a new difficulty when Kennedy reduced the autonomy enjoyed by CIA stations. The degree of control an ambassador should have over CIA operations in his assigned country had been a touchy issue for years. The experiences of Chester Bowles in India, William Sebald in Burma, and John Allison in Indonesia illustrate the problem. Wise station chiefs kept their ambassadors informed, as Jacob Esterline had done with Tom Mann in Guatemala (when Mann had been ambassador to El Salvador), but this had been voluntary. After a 1958 interagency study, Eisenhower gave the CIA virtually complete autonomy, directing that the ambassador's writ stopped at the station chief's door. The spooks, not the diplomats, sat in the driver's seat.

President Kennedy reversed this policy. Among the PFIAB recommendations of 1961 had been one that ambassadors be fully informed of CIA activities in their countries. Kennedy agreed. State Department official U. Alexis Johnson drafted a letter for JFK's signature, dispatched in May 1961. The Kennedy letter established a "country team" concept: CIA could sit on embassy senior councils but the ambassador would be the authority. John Kenneth Galbraith's troubles with the CIA in India show that State's authority still had far to go.

As deputy director for operations, Dick Helms also had to contend with a new boss. John Alex McCone took over as director of central intelligence in November 1961. A Californian, and from outside the agency, the fifty-nine-year-old McCone opened to widespread suspicion but left with many regarding him as one of the greats. Archie Roosevelt, Kermit's cousin, newly returned from a tour in Madrid, looked at McCone and saw in him "just the director the Agency needed at this critical point." McCone had plentiful experience as a corporate manager, including some relevant to agency interests, such as CEO of a shipping company, but he was an engineer and entrepreneur. McCone understood power in Washington too, having been chairman of Eisenhower's Atomic Energy Commission and an air force official during the Truman years. A self-made millionaire, he would be immune to fear of losing his job.

Director McCone had a problem on covert operations with the President's Foreign Intelligence Advisory Board. After the Bay of Pigs the president instructed the board to monitor this aspect more closely. Allen Dulles had begun swinging the door back, telling PFIAB that he had violated secrecy rules by handing over data, but McCone tried to close the door all the way. Alex, as he liked to be called, refused to furnish data on Special Group matters, using the excuse that these were his own to pursue. Neither Jim Killian nor fellow board members accepted that the president's panel should be denied data for inquiries on behalf of the chief executive.

So began a fight that lasted over a year. Board staff approached McCone's deputy, Gen. Marshall Carter, to schedule a briefing. Carter delayed. A week later he refused. The briefing, finally scheduled for June 1962, was then canceled the day before. The board received dollops of information from time to time—a presentation on Laos here, a comment on the Congo there—to placate them. McCone told Killian he had spoken to the president and JFK agreed with him. Killian shot back that he'd talk to Jack Kennedy himself. National security adviser McGeorge Bundy, a member of the Special Group in his White House capacity, agreed with Killian. On June 24 Jim Killian had dinner with Alex McCone and hammered out a compromise—the DCI would present a briefing book specially prepared by the CIA. For the first time the agency worked up a guide to ongoing covert activity.

As it turned out, the McCone-Killian compromise was only a tactical retreat. First the CIA proposed to brief only those covert operations that involved aerial reconnaissance—one way to sort out big fry from the small fish—but when it came to the latest Cuba project, PFIAB found (because the CIA had not briefed on it) that no overall plan seemed to exist. By late 1962 the Killian Board wanted access to Special Group records. This happened in the wake of the Cuban Missile Crisis, where JFK ordered Killian to produce a specific postmortem. Director McCone could hardly resist. The CIA tried to get away with exhibiting only records on aerial surveillance of Cuba. Again on March 25, 1963, McCone told Kennedy the Killian Board reports created a misleading record that might leak and be "very damaging" to the agency. Kennedy answered that the advice of an independent board seemed invaluable to him; as for the rest, "he thought the Board's record of discretion was excellent." Typical of the CIA approach would be the PFIAB meeting of April 23, where Lyman Kirkpatrick asked that discussion on the Cuba operation exclude diplomat Sterling Cottrell, who headed the government's interagency Cuba task force, because he too was not supposed to know about it.

As PFIAB chairman, James Killian created—and his successor Clark Clifford continued—a subcommittee on covert operations. This group finally received the agency's general briefings. The panel included Gordon Gray, returned in a new incarnation; William Langer, historian and senior CIA analyst from early in its history; and retired diplomat Robert Murphy. In early April they received Cord Meyer, chief of CIA's International Organizations Division, a logical official to inform the group on actions in Latin America other than Cuba, which involved a good deal of labor and political work, such as the project then under way in Guyana. Bob Murphy, not impressed, told the full panel that Meyer's presentation consisted of "light touches." Meyer conveyed the impression that covert operations were of "such routine nature" that they did not rise to the level of importance that PFIAB "attached to covert action operations and requirements."

This ploy did not work. A few weeks later the Clifford Board demanded and received full data on Cuba, as they did again in June, when Clifford asked member James Doolittle to survey areas where the CIA had *not* implemented PFIAB recommendations Kennedy had approved. A fresh briefing in September featured CIA's big guns, not just Meyer but Richard Helms and Des FitzGerald. In September and November John McCone at PFIAB defended the CIA's role in South Vietnam against publicly reported charges of meddling in Saigon politics. Among other things, he denied that the agency had anything to do with the coup d'état that overthrew South Vietnamese leader Ngo Dinh Diem.

Board members became increasingly concerned about the system's self-correcting ability. They found none. At an early meeting one member remarked how impressed he had been—possibly a result of the Bay of Pigs postmortems going on just then—with how the Special Group could monitor implementation. But then they heard Max Taylor say his group had no such capacity, a judgment seconded on another occasion by State Department Special Group member U. Alexis Johnson. Queried in September 1963 by Langer's covert action panel, Thomas Hughes of the State intelligence unit noted that the department usually received project proposals only at the last minute, just before the Special Group had to decide on them. The CIA admitted this practice and justified it saying that McCone insisted on reviewing these documents before he would allow them out of Langley. The Clifford Board remained unhappy.

Beyond PFIAB, McCone had problems managing the components of CIA's far-flung intelligence empire. The covers and contacts staff had placed people in journalism, broadcasting, business, and academe. Within the Pentagon itself there were between seven hundred and a thousand "units" that supported or provided cover for the CIA, ranging from post boxes and telephones to full-scale formations with men and equipment.

A singular headache was the array of CIA proprietaries. When McCone succeeded Dulles, preparations were already in place for the latest addition to the proprietaries, what became a complex of insurance and investment companies formed to handle contract agents' and survivors' benefits arising from the Cuban affair. Helms set up a Domestic Operations Division to manage the proprietaries, including this one. It also ran a program that picked up odd bits of intelligence by interviewing Americans who traveled to the denied-area countries or foreign nationals resident in the United States. An inspector general review of the unit in the mid-1960s found haphazard financial direction of the proprietaries by the division.

Fittingly, perhaps, Tracy Barnes became chief of the Domestic Operations Division, and Howard Hunt a senior staffer. Another was Hans Tofte, who finally brought Barnes down by getting the agency in the newspapers again under dubious circumstances. A junior CIA officer, looking at an apartment Tofte offered to rent, saw secret documents in Tofte's home and reported the security violation. Agency minders carted away several boxes of materials Tofte had taken from the office. Matters got out of hand when Tofte alleged that the security officers had stolen jewelry from his wife. He sued the CIA, with attendant negative publicity. Tofte lost the case and his job. Barnes retired soon thereafter.

Then there was Air America. Aviation law changes in Taiwan had posed obstacles for Civil Air Transport. The CIA had already been moving in the direction of reorganization. In 1957 it created the Pacific Corporation, a Delaware-registered holding company, taking over assets of the shadowy American Airedale Corporation, then formed Air America under it in 1959. Pacific Corporation had headquarters in Washington and field offices in Taipei. Air America was the ostensibly private charter firm under its slogan, "Anything, Anywhere, Anytime . . . Professionally!" A rump CAT remained on Taiwan as a Chinese domestic airline while extensive maintenance facilities were spun off as Air Asia. Pacific Corporation held residual interests. This proprietary was massive: at its height Pacific Corporation employed 20,000 people, more than the CIA itself. Air America directly employed 5,600, up to 8,000 if support personnel are counted, and owned or leased 167 aircraft. In 1970 it averaged 30,000 flights per month. In 1973 its Pentagon contracts amounted to more than $41 million.

Much smaller but still significant was Southern Air Transport, which grew enough to have semi-autonomous corporate divisions for Atlantic and Pacific operations. This company both owned and leased DC-6 or C-54 propeller-driven transports, Boeing 727 jets, and the civilian version of Lockheed's C-130. One example of the shell games played here is a DC-6A aircraft (tail number N89BL) originally owned by American Airlines. In June 1960 World Airways bought the plane, leasing it the same day to Southern Air, which that day leased it on to Air America. At other times Air America lent money to Southern Air. As support for the war in Southeast Asia loomed larger, Southern Air won a $3.7 million air force contract to move cargo and passengers on interisland routes in the Pacific.

Another important air proprietary was Intermountain Aviation. Centered at an airstrip in Marana, Arizona, northwest of Tucson, Intermountain had been formed in the late 1950s as an aircraft modification and maintenance activity, originally the Sonora Flying Service. It acquired Marana from Beiser Aviation Corporation. The base had long been a center for air force crew training, and the CIA soon used it for this as well. Once succeeding in making their first solo flights, pilots were dunked in the swimming pool that featured among the base's amenities. Tibetan partisans went there to learn how to parachute. After the Bay of Pigs, Gar Thorsrud showed up at Marana as president of Intermountain. His chief lieutenants, Connie M. Seigrist and Douglas R. Price, had been his deputies at Trampoline in the Cuba project. Intermountain furnished the B-17 aircraft—a CIA plane first acquired for Indonesia—used in the James Bond movie *Thunderball* for a thrilling scene in which the spy is picked up from the sea. In 1966 more than a hundred B-26 bombers sat on the apron ready to refurbish for operations. Extending our example of CIA's aircraft shell games, in 1967 the DC-6A previously mentioned was re-registered to Intermountain Aviation.

Managing the proprietaries, including many more than mentioned here, was a formidable task. The CIA used a combination of interlocking boards of directors plus agency personnel working under cover. George A. Doole, a former Pan Am pilot who joined the agency in the early 1950s, is the best known. When Air America was formed, Doole became an equal shareholder with Pacific Corporation, though the majority shareholders by far were Taiwanese persons, who themselves may have been stand-ins for the agency. Headquarters management was vested in the Domestic Operations Division. On February 5, 1963, Director McCone created an Executive Committee for Air Proprietary Operations to get a handle on at least some of the empire. Lawrence Houston chaired the EXCOMAIR, which included representatives of the DO and the CIA comptroller. Houston had saved the CAT relationship by recommending it be continued back in 1956, when the 5412 Group considered liquidating the proprietary, without which Indonesia, Tibet, and Cuba would not even have been possible. Now he experienced the real headaches involved. EXCOMAIR administered the proprietaries directly, effectively taking them away from Tracy Barnes's division.

In 1968 the agency's inspector general, by then Gordon Stewart, conducted a study of the air proprietaries. Although some of his own staff protested that Stewart's criticisms went too far, it is reported—strikingly—that the CIA could not establish exactly how many aircraft it owned.

As DCI, John McCone made no pretense to micromanagement. A California businessman, he understood that experts like Houston and Helms knew their jobs better than he could hope to. McCone gave his component chiefs much more freedom than had Allen Dulles. Richard Helms appreciated that. As DDO, Helms encouraged CIA efforts in Africa, Latin America, and Southeast Asia. By the mid-1960s Helms had almost as many people working in the DO as in the entire State

Department—more than a third of CIA's personnel. A former officer records that almost 2,000 covert action experts were on board, as against 4,200 working in espionage or other clandestine service functions. The bulk of the paramilitary people were in the Special Operations Division. The DO had about 4,800 officers in the area divisions. Far East was the largest with about 1,500, Africa the smallest with just 300 officers. Apart from the DCI's contingency fund, the Directorate for Operations spent almost 60 percent of the CIA's budget. A lot of that money went to pursue Washington's vendetta against Fidel Castro.

14

The Secret War Against Castro

FOR ED LANSDALE, Kennedy's presidency became a roller-coaster ride, fraught with threat and opportunity, up one moment, down the next. Lansdale's promotion to brigadier general, recently confirmed, was capped by suggestions that he be made the next U.S. ambassador to South Vietnam. That possibility evaporated with objections variously attributed to Dean Rusk or Robert McNamara. Certainly the fifty-three-year-old warrior had his troubles with the secretary of defense. Lansdale once described the last time McNamara allowed him to deliver a brief about Vietnam: trying to give some sense of the unique character of that conflict, the secret warrior brought a sack into McNamara's office, held it above the desk, and dumped an array of knives, pistols, punji sticks, and similar exotica on its surface. The display only scandalized the secretary of defense. But Lansdale's forte had always been propaganda—back to advertising before World War II. McNamara's shock proved insufficient to move him to dismiss Lansdale, so the air force general stayed on. For their part, Max Taylor and Walt Rostow failed to keep Lansdale off their mission to survey the South Vietnam situation in the fall of 1961.

Because of his position, Lansdale was pulled into the anti-Castro enterprise he had advised against. As early as May, Dick Bissell told Lansdale of the CIA's newest plan to keep the heat on Castro. In retirement the general later conjectured that his involvement with Cuba had damaged his career most. If there was one thing he could take back, that would have been it. But in 1961 Ed Lansdale answered the summons of the White House.

Complaints about the handling of the Bay of Pigs brought no end to the secret war against Castro. If anything, the administration redoubled its efforts. *Brigadistas* still roamed the Zapata swamps when Bobby Kennedy sent Jack a memorandum calling for new action. Even during the interval of stocktaking the NSC affirmed the intent to get rid of Castro, and the CIA strove to rebuild its covert capability against Cuba. The agency had a new proposal within a month of the failure. That summer the president put aide Richard Goodwin in charge of a group to review proposals for new measures. In the fall the Special Group reviewed the situation.

The CIA, overwhelmed by the travail of its move to a new headquarters complex at Langley, nevertheless furnished Maxwell Taylor's committee a full read-out on Cuba. According to the CIA, the anti-Castro political groups were becoming more realistic, though Miro Cardona, being subsidized to the tune of $90,000 a month, still represented a problem. Exile groups were providing recruits for paramilitary training, and the CIA had a thirty-five man commando unit, the rump of the Niño Diaz element of the Cuban brigade, ready for action. Propaganda efforts were in the best shape. Radio Swan continued its broadcasts. CIA had gotten its programming onto dozens of stations in Latin America and several in Florida as well. A ship for pirate radio broadcasts to Cuba had also become available. The agency had about a dozen agents or communicators ready to infiltrate, and retained contact with twenty-six more in Cuba, mostly in the Havana area. The CIA carefully added that some anti-Castro Cubans were carrying out sabotage missions in Cuba without its support. Its own plans were for minor actions; any major missions would be cleared with the Special Group.

At that stage Jack Kennedy took a hand. With his brother Bobby the president discussed a "command operation" inside Cuba. According to journalist Don Bohning's careful account, the impetus may have come from the outside, from reporter Tad Szulc, no less. Szulc was running around Washington lobbying for renewed covert operations, even telling a friend, diplomat Robert Hurwitch, that he hoped to see the president. Szulc in fact did see JFK. How much of this was Szulc, how much Kennedy, and how much Richard Goodwin, for that matter, is not clear. Goodwin sent the president a memo at the beginning of November that analyzed the idea as "the only effective way to handle an all-out attack on the Cuban problem."

Goodwin believed. Assistant counsel to the president, he had talked with Bissell about a renewed covert program since a month after the Bay of Pigs disaster, taking Tracy Barnes's suggestions for deliberations of his task force. Goodwin then had an uncanny encounter with Che Guevara at a Latin American conference in Uruguay that summer, at which Che had *thanked* the Kennedy man for the Bay of Pigs, now a boon to Castro's efforts to consolidate control. "The beauty of such an operation over the next few months," Goodwin had written, "is that we cannot lose." Either the CIA would unseat Castro or it would end up with a stronger underground, better propaganda, and a clearer idea of Castro's power. But Goodwin recommended against CIA leadership, reckoning that it should be headed by Robert Kennedy. Goodwin helped Tad Szulc in his quest to see administration higher-ups. Over a period of a few days in early November, Szulc met with both Bobby and Jack Kennedy. Szulc's meeting with the president is reported to have been at the suggestion of his brother.

President Kennedy handled this situation carefully. Szulc, one of those journalists who had ferreted out the Bay of Pigs plans, had excellent contacts in Cuba and had proven himself an acute observer. That summer he had reported through Arthur Schlesinger a private conversation with Castro after the Bay of Pigs. The only other person present at his Oval Office chat with the president late on the morning of November 9 was Goodwin. Kennedy sat in his rocking chair, Goodwin on the sofa. JFK mostly asked questions. According to his own notes of this conversation, Szulc told the president that "Castro thought [that] despite the Bay of Pigs, JFK was the only American politician with whom he could deal in terms of improved relations." Kennedy expressed no interest in that. Instead he asked how strong Castro seemed, whether new covert operations made sense, things like that. The president felt the need to control the CIA, to make it impossible for the agency to "construct another operation like the Bay of Pigs." He said something about setting up a "special group on Cuba."

Suddenly Kennedy leaned forward in his chair.

"What would you think if I ordered Castro to be assassinated?" the president asked.

Taken aback, Tad Szulc replied that it would be a terrible idea: such a scheme could only make Castro stronger. Kennedy said he had only been testing. He felt the same way, but he'd been under "terrific pressure" to go ahead with a murder plot. The United States, the president declared, "morally must not be part[y] to assassinations."

Tad Szulc made no use of this information. But Kennedy went ahead and did what *he* had told the reporter, *all* of it. Lansdale received his own call to the White House around this time—he called it "the late fall of 1961." The timing narrows considerably because a Lansdale memo to McNamara on November 25 shows him already at work on Cuba. Lansdale made out that his assignment had been vague, but it was to be done directly for the president, and Kennedy personally asked him to do it. Lansdale would "look over the situation vis a vis the U.S. in Cuba and . . . see if I had any ideas."

Lansdale reported back within days. He estimated Castro's overthrow to be possible, but the Cuban sugar crop should be attacked at once and Fidel should be kept so busy with internal problems that he would have no time to stir up trouble in Latin America. Robert McNamara and Bobby Kennedy sat in. A Goodwin note on November 22 indicates the secret warrior had already put these thoughts to paper.

When Maxwell Taylor convened the Special Group that same day, he groused that Edward Lansdale ought to be in another part of the world, a reference to the proposal that the general go to Saigon as ambassador. That Taylor, who had struggled to exclude Lansdale from his own recent Vietnam inspection trip, and then to minimize Lansdale's role on it, should want him for ambassador is striking. Several days later in a memo to McNamara, Lansdale actually *thanked* him for nixing that proposition: "I am most grateful for your decision last week protesting the idea of my going out to Vietnam 'to hold Diem's hand,'" Lansdale wrote. The task that really needed doing, he noted, was "working to get a certain special project, of interest to the President, off dead center." This byplay puts a far different light on the received history of Lansdale's candidacy for ambassador.

Sam Halpern, whom Lansdale had known since the early 1950s, had recently been reassigned to the Cuba branch. Lansdale asked him for a cryptonym for the new Cuba project. In an effort to obscure the project, Halpern looked at a list of code names set aside for Thailand. He selected Mongoose.

Edward Lansdale became the man of Project Mongoose, planning and supervising this covert action. A presidential directive on November 30 declared Kennedy's determination to "use our available assets to go ahead with the discussed project in order to help Cuba overthrow the communist regime." The Pentagon, State Department, and CIA were to designate representatives to help Lansdale, and each should have "effective operational control over all aspects of their Department's [sic] operations dealing with Cuba." On a single sheet of paper President Kennedy cast the die for his vendetta.

Robert Kennedy quickly emerged as field marshal of this renewed secret war, though corridor gossip gave Lansdale that role, even nicknaming him "FM." Almost daily Lansdale informed Bobby—in quick handwritten notes, memoranda, hallway conversations, on the phone—of progress in the operation. Before a Special Group session in early December, for example, Lansdale frankly told RFK, "I decided to lay it right on the line on what it will take to win against the communist team." He anticipated problems: "I'm not sanguine that even a heavy whip will put the right spirit into bureaucrats, but doggone it we have to work with what we have." A month later Lansdale asked the attorney general to personally make clear to Edward R. Murrow, head of the U.S. Information Agency, Lansdale's authority to give him orders. A week after that Lansdale warned Bobby of his presentation to the Special Group. When Lansdale actually presented the Mongoose plan on January 18, 1962, he again supplied the first copies to Robert and John F. Kennedy.

Lansdale presented an elaborate proposal. He divided the new Cuba operation into six phases, to end with Castro's overthrow. Like an escalation ladder, the phases began with intelligence gathering and proceeded through more strenuous actions. Lansdale included almost three dozen separate elements, from establishing pathfinder agents, then bases, then clandestine headquarters, to actions like sabotage or work slowdowns, to open revolt. One item anticipated defections of Castro's henchmen; another, attacks on revolutionary cadre, including key leaders. The Special Group consensus viewed this as a good start but wanted it broken into a more explicit schedule. The next day Bobby Kennedy convened Lansdale's assistants, with CIA deputy director Marshall Carter attending for the agency. RFK delivered an exhortation: action on Cuba required not merely Lansdale's effort but theirs, and they were to use every resource at their command, spare no expense. This had become the chief priority of the United States. Bobby quoted his brother, the president: "The final chapter on Cuba has yet to be written."

By February Lansdale had completed a fresh version that timed his phases to culminate in October 1962. McGeorge Bundy's doodles and notes reveal that the Special Group (Augmented) talked over the number of Cuban exiles ready to fight, teams necessary for various operations, transportation needs and hardware for a voice of the Cuban movement, and that old bugaboo, the point when the United States might intervene. Arrangements now fell into place quickly. Guidelines for Mongoose, dated March 5 and prepared by Maxwell Taylor, instructed the secret warriors to proceed in such fashion as to permit disengagement. General

Lansdale would continue as project chief. The CIA next day promised to ensure a steady flow of intelligence on Cuba—this flaw of the Bay of Pigs would be avoided. Secret warriors actually hired the Zogby firm to conduct an opinion poll in Latin America identifying countries where propaganda gains against Castro were possible and issues the CIA could use to that end.

All the work built to a meeting with Kennedy in the Oval Office on the afternoon of March 14, 1962. Everyone was there, including the Joint Chiefs chairman and representatives of Robert McNamara and Dean Rusk. Just before the president entered, Lansdale told the group that Taylor's guidelines would preclude success. Taylor emphasized the need to gather intelligence. President Kennedy, as he had done before the Bay of Pigs, shut off discussion of U.S. intervention. The group nevertheless considered certain military support for the CIA and contemplated sabotage plans for Mongoose. A lot rode on knocking out Castro's patrol boats. JFK congratulated his warriors on what they had accomplished, complained about the danger the press might guess what impended, and wondered if the United States should refuse further Cuban immigration. The president reassured his warriors: he wanted them to carry on.

Waiting in the anteroom during the key Mongoose meeting were CIA officers Richard Helms and William K. Harvey. Lansdale had asked John McCone to let them in, but the CIA director nixed the idea. McCone had made Dick Helms his lieutenant for Cuba, and the new deputy director for operations spent part of every day on the issue. Excluding the DDO and the task force chief was highly unusual. McCone may have wanted to keep the play in his own hands, or he may have anticipated the fight over guidelines and wanted no witnesses. Or perhaps, like Jack and Bobby, McCone felt CIA had made a poor showing and wished to keep as low a profile as possible.

The fact was that the CIA had begun reconstituting quite quickly after the Bay of Pigs, something not evident to the Cuban agents left to flap in the wind as Castro's security services hunted them down, but true nonetheless. Records of DCI morning staff meetings indicate the agency began planning new activities for Cuba within weeks of the disaster. By May 19 it had a proposal. The agency offered a revised plan in July with a price tag of $13 million.

Arthur Schlesinger complained to Dick Goodwin, the White House commissar of the secret war on Castro, that the CIA's notion of island-wide resistance under its own banner represented a focus on convenience rather than pathways to success. The same discrimination against the non-Castro left and favoritism for the *batistianos* that had characterized the Bay of Pigs remained pervasive. "It is a fallacy," Schlesinger warned, "to suppose that clandestine activity can be carried out in a political vacuum." That August, Kennedy approved the scheme anyway. By September the idea was that the CIA would act through Cuban groups with potential for effective political opposition, and that covert activity would destroy important economic targets.

Kennedy's National Security Council formally adopted the goal of ousting Castro and considered means ranging from a naval blockade to an international Caribbean Security Force to strong economic sanctions, with the CIA one more arrow in Kennedy's quiver. The military dreamed up deception schemes that would establish a justification to invade Cuba, and updated its contingency plans.

In mid-December 1961 John McCone had to explain to JFK when the press reported a new covert operations snafu: the eight-man team intended to carry out Operation Whale had suffered an engine failure and aborted their mission, and their boat had been rescued by the Coast Guard. A couple of the agents were picked up by a passing freighter, leading to press attention when panicked operatives tried to hush up the episode. Eyes must have widened when McCone said that he could not establish who had given orders for that raid.

Plenty of CIA laundry would have to be washed at the Special Group (Augmented). But the Kennedys kept CIA under the lash. Where Max Taylor told them to proceed in a low key, Bobby Kennedy insisted no time, money, or effort be spared. He met the managers at his Justice Department office to drive the point home. By January 1962 he had begun regular sessions to prod the bureaucracy.

The Central Intelligence Agency maintained its Miami base in a colonial-style building on the south campus of the University of Miami. Bob Reynolds left, temporarily replaced by Robert Davis. The former Guatemala chief stepped on toes at Jay Gleichauf's refugee reception center, a major source of recruits and information on conditions inside Cuba. Next the CIA dispatched Albert L. Cox. Best known for his role in acquiring and managing Civil Air Transport, Cox had been an OSS commando in Italy and France, had run operations against the Red Chinese from Hong Kong, had managed CAT during its campaign at Dien Bien Phu, and had since worked in staff positions at headquarters. Cox had been chief of the paramilitary branch of CIA's Covert Action Staff. But though Cox could put pieces back together, some doubted his dedication. He stood among those at the agency who had entertained hopes for Castro at the beginning, and very early on had even advocated cooperating with the Cuban leader.

About the time CIA moved to Langley, William K. Harvey, task force boss, learned that a colleague from Berlin was back in town. Harvey summoned Theodore G. Shackley and sent him to Miami to report on what the base needed to be reconstituted as a full CIA station. Shackley spent a few weeks looking over the situation, then filed his report. Harvey then appointed him chief of operations under Cox.

Ted Shackley insinuates that Al Cox somehow was not serious. He records the man as absent when he arrived, and suggests the chief turned up only intermittently afterward. When Harvey came to review an operational schedule and Cox did not show up, Shackley notes, his reign ended. But it is equally likely that Harvey did not believe Cox had his heart in Mongoose, or that Cox thought this venture fated. Howard Hunt claims to have turned down an offer to lead the station, but there is no evidence for that. Hunt had been tarred by the Bay of Pigs fiasco and had no relationship with Harvey. On the other hand, Harvey had no problem asking Shackley, former Berlin base chief, to do the job. In May 1962 Harvey's man took up the position. He had local knowledge—Ted Shackley came from Palm Beach and became known as the "Blond Ghost" while playing football at his high school. This game would be much bigger.

The star of Lansdale's operation had made his mark in the shadows in Washington and Berlin. A storied legend, forty-six-year-old Bill Harvey held the distinction of having suspected Kim Philby as a Soviet mole even as the Britisher bamboozled CIA counterspy James Angleton. He had then run the agency's Berlin base for seven years. Shackley had been his protégé, doing Polish operations out of Berlin. During his time Harvey had witnessed the East Berlin riots, supervised the Berlin Tunnel operation (in which the CIA and the NSA had tapped a major Russian telephone cable, recording secret conversations), and conducted a host of retail spy games. Among those who transferred from the FBI to CIA in its first years, Harvey stood out as someone who could go up against the best Russian spies. He was a lawyer, but unlike the Ivy Leaguers at the top of the DO, his degree came from Indiana University in his home state. Some thought Harvey inspired, others reviled him as a paranoid or a pedestrian drunk and womanizer, but many had strong opinions on this short, stocky Hoosier.

In early 1960 Richard Bissell ordered Harvey to create an ultra-secret unit for "executive action"—assassination—known simply by its agency cryptonym, ZR/Rifle. As far as is known, ZR/Rifle had only one field agent, the obscure QJ/Win, who turned up in the Congo later that year (Justin O'Donnell, the officer sent to the Congo to help deal with Lumumba, was Harvey's deputy). To disguise Harvey's role, Bissell located his unit within the CIA's in-house code-breaking staff, for which the CIA officer supposedly qualified as a result of the Berlin Tunnel affair. A sloppy dresser, Harvey nevertheless inspired awe among those who knew he sported pistols in his pockets, even at headquarters. Harvey had had guns in his desk as early as Berlin—a violation of agency regulations—but always managed to have good reasons for it, the latest being that he knew so much he could not permit himself to be taken.

At one of General Lansdale's sessions with Jack Kennedy, the president had marveled that he seemed to be America's James Bond. Not so, Lansdale shot back, the real Bond was at CIA and named Bill Harvey. Kennedy asked to meet this larger-than-life figure, which led to a séance at the White House where the dapper president shook hands with the disheveled secret warrior. As Lansdale told the story, the Secret Service had to relieve Harvey of his pistols. Harvey himself denied ever carrying guns to the White House.

Harvey had a hand in the assassination plots against Castro. Tad Szulc is not the only one with whom JFK discussed murdering Fidel. Kennedy raised the same subject with Florida Senator George Smathers in the guise of asking what he thought the reaction might be in Latin America. Smathers reacted much as had Szulc, and Kennedy's response, also identical, was that he completely agreed. But during this same period members of CIA's Board of National Estimates were directed to write a paper on that subject, *and* in early October, acting on specific instructions from Maxwell Taylor, the executive secretary of the Special Group asked Taylor's assistant to develop a contingency plan: "what was wanted was a plan against the contingency that Castro would in some way or another be removed from the Cuban scene."

The Special Group official, CIA officer Thomas A. Parrott, reported back that he had told Tracy Barnes that "an up-to-date report be furnished as soon as possible on what is going on and what is being planned." Parrott then added, "I did not tell Mr. Barnes of Presidential interest."

Coincidentally or not, on November 15 Bill Harvey, the ZR/Rifle chief, received orders to take over the Mafia operation that had lain dormant since January. Shortly thereafter Harvey was also asked to head the CIA's in-house task force on Cuba. On the morning of January 18, 1962, a few hours before presenting Mongoose to the Special Group (Augmented), Lansdale sent Attorney General Kennedy a note which said: "My review does not include the sensitive work I have reported to you. I felt that you preferred informing the President privately."

Bill Harvey acquired more poison capsules from CIA's Technical Services Division for Mafioso Johnny Rosselli in April 1962, two months after getting a hand-over from Sheffield Edwards. Harvey and Edwards's deputy went to New York to see Rosselli at the Savoy Plaza Hotel, and Harvey alone went to Miami a couple of weeks later to hand over the poison. Cuban exile leader Tony Varona, the actor in this plot, asked for high-powered rifles and money, and would be given those as well. But Harvey didn't think much of this operation, nor did Dick Helms when he looked at it. Helms told Harvey to shut down the Mafia hit squad. Harvey could halt CIA support but had no way to stop Tony Varona.

At the Justice Department, Robert Kennedy presided over FBI investigations of organized crime in the United States. Through wiretaps, informers, and other means, veiled references to the Mafia's CIA alliance emerged. The FBI investigation terminated in the spring of 1962, once CIA security officers objected to it. As attorney general, Robert Kennedy received a formal briefing on May 7, the first time he is on record as learning about assassination plots. Sheffield Edwards rejected Bobby's demand for a written report—that wasn't CIA practice for a sensitive operation. Bobby made a show of being surprised.

Did the Kennedys know? Did John F. Kennedy order Castro's murder? Did Robert Kennedy supervise? Did both of them cover their tracks? In 1975 the Church Committee decided it lacked evidence to conclude that Eisenhower or Kennedy (or Lyndon Johnson) had ordered an assassination. But scattered in its report, the depositions of the Rockefeller Commission, and other documents, the evidence and chronology are highly suggestive. Readers can draw their own conclusions.

Meanwhile at Langley, Bill Harvey called his staff Task Force W—the last for William Walker, a nineteenth-century American adventurer who had cut a swath across Central America. Miami station went under the cover of Zenith Technical Enterprises, or JM/Wave by its agency designator. The walls were graced with phony charts purporting to display sales and production trends, even a certificate for contributions to charity. Theodore Shackley's JM/Wave had 112 exiles on board from the beginning, plus 40 CIA officers at Zenith and 39 more in Opa-Locka. At any given time there were a dozen or more Special Forces with the exile commandos. Bob Moore, later Gordon Campbell, were his deputies. David Morales led the paramilitary staff, Jack Corris took charge of support, Seymour Bolton headed the political action staff. The station eventually grew larger than the one that supported the Bay of Pigs invasion. Soon Shackley had a huge operation, with an annual budget of more than $50 million, a dozen buildings at Opa-Locka alone, over a hundred leased vehicles, several thousand Cuban agents, and more than 600 American employees.

Wary of skimping, the Mongoose planners wanted real resources: use of an air force bombing range for demolition training, three USAF transports and a pair of seaplane aircraft for air missions, several light planes for liaison work, a couple of Coast Guard cutters, half a dozen PT boats, even two large navy vessels (Landing Ship Docks) and two submarines. The navy and air force crews were to be "sheep-dipped"—in CIA practice, a cover measure separating the individuals from any official government connection, and in this case something that would have applied to hundreds of personnel. Clearly Mongoose would have had the same deniability problems as the Bay of Pigs had it ever gotten that far along.

Instead Project Mongoose proceeded in a most haphazard fashion. Paramilitary activities occurred more or less openly, cloaked by the array of Miami Cuban groups. Conducting the operation from the United States compelled the CIA to create liaisons with federal, state, and local authorities, including police and the customs service. It also involved numerous violations of law ranging from CIA's National Security Act charter to the Neutrality Act, to statutes on firearms possession and perjury. A frequent task for JM/Wave staff became bailing out or otherwise rescuing CIA or Cuban personnel who had run afoul of the law.

Ted Shackley forged ahead. Beginning in March he set up the first infiltration teams, each of half a dozen Cubans. But Washington's priorities emphasized intelligence collection. The military worried about wasting time on preliminaries, the CIA about Bobby's micromanagement, Lansdale about putting collection ahead of action. He tried to use a March 16 meeting of the Special Group (Augmented) and the president to alter the orders. Prompted by McCone, Lansdale commented that the priorities tied CIA's hands if sudden developments created opportunity. When the Joint Chiefs chairman added that plans for intervention were ready, President Kennedy shot them both down. Later Bill Harvey wrote Director McCone, siding with those objecting to the tight control. Typically, on March 21 Bobby told the group that the president stood ready to do whatever necessary.

But a certain schizophrenic quality applied: the Kennedys restricted the operation to intelligence gathering, then continued to wonder why Castro still reigned. Conversely, with intelligence gathering emphasized, few operatives in the field were in fact specialized in spying. Trainees were overwhelmingly paramilitary types, with few collection experts.

The JM/Wave people reflected the trainees: Shackley's assistant Thomas Clines and CIA men like Rudy Enders, George French, Robert Wall, Edwin Wilson, and Harold Chipman were all paramilitary officers. French, a demolition expert, loved to blow things up. Rip Robertson and Grayston Lynch were back, leading units comprising many teams of Cubans. A CIA contract officer records that, with the word "paramilitary" declared verboten after the Bay of Pigs, they were now part of the Special Operations Division. The Miami operating base, set up under the station's aegis, lagged on maritime capability throughout Mongoose, in spite of the efforts of Gordon Campbell and Rudy Enders. Training the commandos proved easier than finding boats to move them. Motorboats sailing from Miami and throughout the Florida Keys made up the core. The station's maritime branch has been described as "huge," but the Special Operations Division remained the largest element.

On March 12, 1962, Team Cobra infiltrated Pinar del Rio province, creating a network active for some time. In June AM/Torrid went into Oriente, but most of it left in a few months. The one remaining agent and a fresh radioman set up in Santiago de Cuba as a spy mission. Mongoose's major achievements were few.

Use of the anti-Castro groups proved a double-edged sword. As paramilitary operations succeeded one another, many of them beyond the exiles' capacity, cover became increasingly threadbare. Cuban groups enjoyed the cachet of their ties with the United States, but in the longer run exposure of their CIA links made it harder to claim political legitimacy. "CIA front" became a charge used to discredit many groups, not least by Castro.

A more immediate problem was that the CIA's relations with the exile groups precluded agency control in the covert war. Cubans striving to gain credibility with the CIA carried out some attacks. Other raids the CIA canceled were made anyway by angry exiles who felt themselves denied a chance to strike. It could be difficult to determine if CIA had ordered an action at all. Reporter Tad Szulc made a fresh appearance, accompanying Cubans on a raid—his connections ran to the exiles, not the CIA. *Life* magazine photographers went on another. Businessman William Pawley financed at least one raid. Others by groups like the Second Naval Guerrilla or Alpha 66 had nothing to do with CIA. But once the agency had furnished training or equipment, Castro could charge the CIA with the raids, independent or not.

The covert action exacerbated Cold War tensions as well. Expansion of Soviet military aid to Cuba followed the Bay of Pigs, as did the attempt by Khrushchev to extend a Soviet nuclear umbrella over the Caribbean island. The Russian buildup that ended in the missile crisis had its roots in strategic considerations, but Castro might not have accepted Soviet nuclear weapons in Cuba were it not for the American threat.

Intelligence support improved from what it had been a year earlier but continued to exhibit difficulties. Ray Cline, CIA's deputy director for intelligence after Amory, knew of every aspect of Mongoose save assassination plots. John McCone told him, and updated him too. The DCI occasionally took Cline along to meetings as well. McCone solicited his advice and permitted Cline to discuss matters with his analysts. Although the DI did not write papers for the project, knowledge enabled Cline to pose questions for analysts in such a way that their products were helpful to Mongoose planners. But the problems with the myriad exile

groups were mystifying, and they overlapped boundaries between political operatives and those who were supposed to evaluate Castro's chances.

Diplomatic support also lagged. In June Lansdale and Bobby Kennedy maneuvered the State Department into agreeing to make action proposals. Bobby
now chafed at the restrictions he had set, telling John McCone that Mongoose had
lots of data but little to show. At the time, Mongoose remained mired in Phase
One. Lansdale worried that the agencies were protecting their interests and that he,
as a mere "chief of operations," would be unable to knock heads together. He persuaded Bill Harvey and the CIA to prepare a revised "Alternate Course B," then
went to Bobby Kennedy to discuss "B+." The latest plan aimed at strengthening
the atmosphere of resistance in Cuba. Teams of three to five fighters would infiltrate all over Cuba, a strike force of about fifty commandos would conduct sabotage missions, and a wide variety of psychological warfare, propaganda, and other
means would be used to sharpen fears. Lansdale cut back Bill Harvey's prospectus, which had called for several times more fighters in the commando teams. The
attorney general approved the plan; the Special Group did not. They were swayed
by John McCone, who held out the specter of the Hungarian revolt and warned
that the United States risked the same kind of slaughter. In the context of the rapid
buildup of Soviet forces, already begun, McCone's argument had merit. Lansdale
disagreed. Revolt against Castro had to come from the Cuban people, he believed,
and the more visible CIA's role the less likely that would be.

Once the exiles were mounting sabotage missions on their own, it became
even more difficult to restrain Cubans working for Task Force W. President
Kennedy reviewed the final version of Plan B+ and approved it on August 20. The
materials given him explicitly stated that the CIA program had no possibility of
overthrowing Castro. In early September the Special Group (Augmented) approved Phase Two raids against Cuba. Lansdale's list of tasks had grown to more
than fifty. But when Harvey recommended a commando strike at a power plant,
the group discouraged it. Harvey erupted in a shouting match with the attorney
general. The principals had long noticed Harvey's inebriation, especially after
lunchtime, and there had been quiet remarks behind his back. After this fight with
Bobby, Harvey became persona non grata. Dick Helms or the Task Force W
deputy chief, Bruce Cheever, had to substitute for him.

Around this time Ted Shackley got his chance to meet John F. Kennedy. At
Langley for a day to review the September infiltration schedule, Director McCone
took Shackley along to see the president. McCone figured the station chief could
provide a view from the trenches. Kennedy asked a few questions—about espionage, not paramilitary raids.

The project peaked in the months separating the Bay of Pigs from the Cuban
Missile Crisis. The numerous attempts to infiltrate agents were mostly failures.
Several more assassination schemes were all abortive. Cargoes of Cuban sugar
were contaminated with chemicals in San Juan, Puerto Rico, and other ports. Shipments of machinery and spare parts en route to Cuba were sabotaged. Infiltration
became the bread and butter of the effort—exile Felix Rodriguez claims to have
personally landed ten *tons* of equipment in Cuba during the year before the mis-

sile crisis. There were commando strikes on Cuban railroads, oil and sugar refineries, and factories. Photographic intelligence expert Dino Brugioni recalls Bill
Harvey almost as an enemy, believing that the analysts spied on him. But Harvey
lied about results—as evident from the overhead photography. Confronted with
pictures that showed no damage to a building supposedly bombed, Harvey retorted
the photos did not show the inside of the structure, and he demanded that photo interpreters be sent to Miami to brief. Brugioni recounts that this sort of thing happened again and again. Harvey finally thundered, "What in the hell does a bunch
of quacks know about covert operations?"

Bobby Kennedy's enthusiasm won the support of many who were disgruntled
by the Bay of Pigs fiasco. Rip Robertson was one. Robertson thought little of
politicians but met RFK during the Taylor Committee investigation and returned
to tell the exiles that Bobby was all right. At one point Robertson led a mission
where the team was to sabotage the Matahambre mine, Cuba's largest, by setting
explosive charges on conveyors and key equipment. The mission came off, but
nothing happened. Cuban security found the devices and disarmed them. Ted
Shackley decided the Cuban who had set the timers botched the job. Another time
Robertson offered money if a raider returned with the ear of an enemy. The man
brought back two. Robertson served throughout the secret war against Cuba.

In a way the exile groups forced Kennedy's hand with one of their freelance
strikes. Acting on information that Czech and Soviet officers partied on Friday
nights at Havana's Blanquita Hotel, exiles decided to make a raid; six Cubans
crammed a speedboat with two .50-caliber machine guns, a 20-millimeter cannon,
and a recoilless rifle. On August 24 they entered the suburban harbor of Miramar,
sailed close enough to the Blanquita to see the lights in the ballroom and the uniforms, and shelled the place. The group involved, the Student Revolutionary Directorate (DRE), continued on CIA's payroll. One of the raiders, Jose Basulto,
would continue to lead similarly independent forays against Cuba for decades.

Meanwhile Washington's belly-thumping culminated in a series of meetings,
in the JCS Operations Room on August 8 or 9, and at the State Department on August 10. At the last of these, John McCone recollected in 1967, when CIA Inspector General John Earman looked into the matter, someone talked about the need to
"liquidate" top Cuban officials including Castro. McCone insists he protested instantly, that he went to Bob McNamara's office right afterward* and reiterated the
protest (McNamara reportedly in full agreement), and that no such suggestion ever
received serious consideration at the Special Group (Augmented). But—and here
assassination rears its ugly head again—the paper General Lansdale sent his
agency managers *after* the August 10 meeting assigned Bill Harvey to write a paper on CIA's role, listing under the rubric of "Political" the aspect of "splitting the
regime, including liquidation of leaders." Bill Harvey went ballistic, calling Lansdale's office. The field marshal not there, Harvey screamed at Frank Hand, Lansdale's deputy, denouncing the stupidity of putting this in a document. The next day

---

* McCone special assistant Walter Elder remembers this as a telephone call from CIA headquarters,
and as taking place a day or two later.

He protested to Richard Helms. Harvey made clear that *Robert McNamara had himself brought up the question of assassination* in Rusk's office on August 10. Staff took the Lansdale memo and whited out the offending phrase, but it survived in Harvey's note to Helms.

In Lansdale's deposition for Rockefeller Commission investigators in 1975, lawyer David W. Belin asked if he remembered those words. Lansdale did not, and doubted his memory would be refreshed. "I just don't recall anything at all on liquidation of leaders," Lansdale said. Nor did he remember Frank Hand telling him about Harvey's phone call, or calling the CIA man to say the correction had been made. "It might have happened," Lansdale added, "but I don't recall." His recollection improved before the Church Committee, where Lansdale testified that the idea had been shot down on August 10 but that he had included it in instructions to Harvey because "it might be a possibility someplace down the road."

More sharp argument erupted at a Mongoose meeting on October 4. There the attorney general archly said that "higher authority" worried about the meager results and he, RFK, wanted massive activity. John McCone countered that the NSC had been holding the forces back. Bobby Kennedy retorted that, to the contrary, the Special Group had "urged and insisted upon action by the Lansdale operating organization" and that no specified action had ever been rejected at the NSC level. White House squawks were for particular reasons: in the case of frogmen landing in Eastern Cuba, the men had been *Americans*; in another instance, at the Miramar hotel, the action had been irresponsible. A major strike at Matahambre had been the objective of three failed missions. Lansdale told the group that half a dozen new raids were planned and another strike on the major target would be added. Some talked of mining Cuban territorial waters. The October 4 meeting concluded that "more dynamic action was indicated."

General Lansdale approached Bobby Kennedy in mid-October for a renewed initiative centered around Manolo Ray. Only political warfare would trigger Cuban revolt, he reiterated. He appended a scheme to have a submarine surface and fire star shells over Cuba on All Souls Day night, igniting Cuban superstitions, coupled with the CIA spreading rumors of portents of Castro's fall. Tom Parrott thought this ridiculous—the CIA talking about the Second Coming, saying Christ opposed Castro—he called it "Elimination by Illumination." In 1975 Lansdale reacted furiously to Parrott's characterization, claiming he had never heard of the scheme, but in truth the secret warrior proposed this psychological mission in a memo on October 15, 1962.

A day earlier a CIA U-2 reconnaissance plane flying over Cuba had taken photographs showing equipment associated with Soviet nuclear missiles. This flight had been laid on as a result of reports from Mongoose, but the ensuing Cuban Missile Crisis would sweep away the CIA project. When Dick Helms arrived at Robert Kennedy's office the morning of October 16 to deal with certain legal matters, Bobby already knew of the photos. That afternoon the Special Group (Augmented) would have evaluated Mongoose to date, a review Helms dreaded, but now the attorney general had to help deal with Soviet missiles in

Cuba. Bobby went ahead with the Mongoose meeting to preserve an appearance of normalcy. Every bit as bloody as Helms feared, the review featured Robert Kennedy again declaring the president's anger and discouragement. Acting for recently married John McCone, in California on his honeymoon, Deputy Director Gen. Marshall S. Carter presented a fresh CIA paper on sabotage. Two CIA Cuban teams were ashore at that moment, and other minor achievements were cited, but the rest was for the future. Bobby liked the CIA paper but insisted he would now begin meeting *every morning* with Lansdale and the Mongoose coordinators in search of results. In fact the greatest results ever achieved by the CIA project were the emplacement of the agent nets whose reports helped the U-2 spyplanes find the Soviet missiles.

Beginning that day, Robert Kennedy sat with his brother and others through almost continuous sessions of the ad hoc "executive committee" of the National Security Council (EXCOM). They considered diplomatic approaches to the Russians, an invasion of Cuba, blockade, or bombing of the missiles. Their central problem became getting the Russians to take those missiles out of Cuba without starting World War III. They needed to avoid anything that might provoke a Soviet or Cuban military response. In this context the Kennedys' constant pushing for actions in Mongoose became inimical to the larger objective.

The secret warriors had their own solutions for the Cuban crisis. They continued to act in accordance with Bobby's open orders, confirmed as recently as October 16. At the State Department, Robert A. Hurwitch, assistant for Cuban affairs, wanted exile pilots to bomb the missiles, using unmarked planes for ostensible attacks on oil refineries. Bobby himself, according to some evidence, pondered staging a provocation like the sinking of the *Maine* at the outset of the Spanish-American War, discussing it with Cuban leader Roberto San Roman, brother of one of the Brigade 2506 commanders, and Rafael Quintero, a CIA commando he met during negotiations to free the *brigadistas*.

Task Force W still pursued the Mongoose directive for action and moved to put commando teams in Cuba. The Special Group (Augmented) debated objectives. Finding Russian nuclear storage bunkers had the highest priority. Bill Harvey thought the teams could scout for U.S. invaders.

At Miami station the situation was thoroughly confused. Ted Shackley had seen a stream of orders for more than a week. His exile teams were on edge. Felix Rodriguez, for example, had been accosted by case officer Thomas Clines and asked to volunteer for a parachute drop to place a radio beacon to guide a bombing raid, then was placed in a safe house without even the opportunity to pick up his wife from work. Sequestered in pre-mission lockdown, the commandos needed surety. Shackley had twenty missions scheduled—nineteen were paramilitary and one for intelligence gathering—utilizing all his teams. The JM/Wave chief begged Langley, sending a long dispatch. Part of it read: "BELIEVE FLUCTUATIONS IN GO AND STOP ORDERS OVER PAST SEVEN DAYS HAVE BEEN SUCH THAT WE ARE SITTING ON EXPLOSIVE HUMAN SITUATION WHICH COULD BLOW AT ANY TIME WITHIN NEXT FORTY-EIGHT HOURS." The station chief reminded headquarters that his fifty commandos were fully trained, ready to go, and would not remain under control unless Washington made up its mind. "THERE IS IN MY JUDGMENT NO MIDDLE GROUND ON THIS ISSUE."

Thus in the middle of the missile crisis, Ted Shackley threw the Kennedys this hot potato, amounting to the "disposal" problem all over again, that very pernicious feature of the Bay of Pigs. And Shackley wanted to go. Admitting he had not considered political realities, that he viewed matters from a nuts-and-bolts perspective, Shackley pumped for a decision. A commando landing at the height of the crisis, with both sides on hair-trigger alert, could have touched off World War III.

Bill Harvey took the Shackley cable and forwarded it to Ed Lansdale. General Lansdale circulated the text to the Special Group (Augmented).

Three of the teams had *already left* in submarines for the north coast of Cuba. Six more were to infiltrate from submarines or drop by air. The others would follow. Exile Rafael Quintero wanted assurances and phoned the attorney general. RFK, facing the horrifying prospect of nuclear war, suddenly ceased being the gung-ho advocate of covert action.

Bobby Kennedy later recorded an oral history in which he recounts looking into this matter to find that top CIA officials were unaware of the missions. In view of Shackley's cable, that is not possible. In fact on the morning of October 26 the EXCOM discussed the operations and McCone personally briefed the landings. President Kennedy and McGeorge Bundy both spoke of reorienting Mongoose. In any case, Bobby went to Langley and denounced everyone, especially Bill Harvey. On October 30 the White House halted all Mongoose operations. Lansdale went to Miami to ride herd on Shackley. There was no more talk, as there had been on October 4, of mining Cuban harbors. Director McCone soon packed Bill Harvey off to Rome as station chief, getting him out of the line of fire.

All this time the exile prisoners from the Bay of Pigs continued to languish in Cuban prisons. Hurt by the embargo in place since January 1961, Castro offered to trade them for medicines, tractors, spare parts, and such things. Desultory exchanges on the prospect occurred into 1962. After the missile crisis, Castro lowered his price while the administration threw its weight behind efforts to raise $53 million worth of medical equipment, drugs, and baby food for the deal. Lawyer James A. Donovan, who had arranged the trade of Soviet spy Rudolf Abel for CIA U-2 pilot Francis Gary Powers, negotiated the exchange.

The final agreement on the prisoner trade was made on December 22, 1962. Altogether 1,179 veterans of Brigade 2506 returned to the United States. In a covert twist to this game, CIA assassination plotters bought a scuba diving suit for Donovan to present to Castro as a gift. At Langley's Technical Services Division, scientists impregnated the suit with a fungus to trigger a chronic skin disease, and the breathing apparatus with a tuberculosis bacillus. The suit was carried to Donovan by an unwitting lawyer, John Nolan, who learned of the ploy during the investigations of the 1970s.

"Can you imagine," recalls Nolan, "I mean, can you imagine? Here is Jim Donovan—the guy who has already done his stuff once, a guy the Other Side trusts—down in Cuba, trying to cut a deal, very tough negotiations, very delicate discussions, everything has got to be above-board because Fidel holds all the cards and the Company is setting Donovan up—not even telling him, keeping him unwitting—to hand Fidel Castro this nice big germ bag."

Fortunately the American lawyer, witting or not, took the precaution of replacing the diving suit with one he bought himself.

Castro returned the prisoners, including twenty non-brigade CIA agents.

The superpowers eventually resolved the missile crisis at a high level. The Soviets removed their offensive weapons from Cuba; the Americans later dismantled similarly threatening forward-based systems in Turkey. President Kennedy publicly promised not to invade Cuba. As for the covert forces in play, the CIA received orders to reorganize yet again. By the time of the crisis, Richard Helms had already decided on Harvey's replacement. He needed someone of sufficient stature to overawe field officers and show them their project continued as a priority, someone who knew the inner workings at Langley as well. Helms selected Desmond FitzGerald, the Asian expert. To get Des and avoid the impression that the Far East baron had taken a demotion to lead a mere task force, the Mongoose unit became the DO Special Affairs Staff, and Des simultaneously a deputy chief of the WH Division responsible for Cuban matters. General Lansdale left his post as well, elevating FitzGerald to direct command. To give him someone who knew the players, Jacob Esterline became his chief of operations.

President Kennedy also revamped White House controls. Instead of Robert Kennedy taking the lead role, the National Security Council became more directly involved. Aspects of the Cuban project figured in EXCOM discussions in late 1962 and early 1963, and in a few sessions of the NSC proper. Thereafter the Special Group (Augmented) handed over its role as prime manager to an NSC "Standing Group" chaired by McGeorge Bundy.

The Standing Group worked as Kennedy's utility infielders. In 1962 it had handled the very delicate matter of Katanga and the Congo. Mostly the group supervised routine matters such as policy on Algeria, backstopping negotiations with Spain, plans for nuclear weapons dispersal, or establishing a worldwide network to communicate with manned spacecraft in orbit. Those functions now covered its highly serious assignment directing the Cuba project. Sudden location of Cuba decisions to this obscure NSC appendage may explain why even today the secret war after the missile crisis has received little attention.

One question was policy toward the Cuban exile brigade. Castro government statements pointedly feared a new larger, better-equipped exile brigade. The United States denied such a plan, but in fact there was another exile initiative organized by the American military. It created a special Cuban volunteer program in July 1961, though most of the influx took place only after the *brigadistas* returned.

McNamara's deputy, Roswell Gilpatric, had told the Mongoose meeting of October 4, 1962, that the Pentagon had made progress. When JFK spoke to the *brigadistas* at the Orange Bowl in December, the army's Cuba program formed his core element. What to do with the brigade figured at the EXCOM meeting of January 25, 1963. The NSC Standing Group had reviewed the issue the day before. Under the group a Cuba Coordinating Committee handled day-to-day activity. As the issues were summarized for Vice President Johnson by his military adviser, "the basic decision must be made as to whether an invasion of Cuba, directly or indirectly, is to be supported, or whether, in a lesser sense, serious provocations or incidents should be a part of the basic policy. When this decision is made, the disposition of the Cuban Brigade can more easily be determined."

Joseph Califano managed the project on behalf of Secretary of the Army Cyrus R. Vance. A special assistant, Califano was serious about the care and feeding of the Cubans. Bobby or Jack Kennedy, it seemed, was on the phone to Califano almost every day about Cuban recruiting. As exile liaison, he dealt with one of the heros of Girón, Erneido Oliva. On the army side, Califano employed two experienced lieutenant colonels, James Patchall for covert operations, and Alexander M. Haig, Jr., to take care of the brigade. Haig found officers who would have merited promotion in any army but others who attained positions in Brigade 2506 on the basis of social standing. These status cases were the hardest. In early 1963 the program took in 200 exiles a week. Almost 3,000 enlisted, and 2,600 Cubans completed U.S. military training. The army leaped at the opportunity to bring in the Cubans, the air force trod slowly, and Bobby Kennedy had to knock the navy into line. As had happened with Quintero during the missile crisis, exiles who disagreed with Califano's actions often took their cases to Bobby, who did not hesitate to reverse orders, even his own.

Califano deputized for Vance, who almost never attended, in representing the Pentagon on the Cuba Coordinating Committee, nominally chaired by the State Department's man but in actuality dominated by Bobby Kennedy. As before, many of the meetings took place in the attorney general's office. Mongoose merely moved further underground. Joe Califano found some of the proposals bizarre. Balloon leaflet schemes were the least of it; here there were serious suggestions to use radio broadcasts to get all Cubans to turn on their water faucets at the same time, things like that. Attaching incendiary devices to bats, whose timed fuzes would ignite buildings as the bats roosted, was another idea. Notions of parachuting saboteurs trained at U.S. military bases, who if captured would have directly implicated the United States, were only slightly less dangerous. As for the bats, they would have had to be transported by U.S. aircraft. Reflecting later on this period, Calfano decided he had become embroiled in "Keystone Kop capers."

On February 18 Vance and Califano, fictive committee chairman Sterling Cottrell, and others met President Kennedy in the Oval Office. Colonel King attended for the CIA. General Krulak represented SACSA. Kennedy sat in his rocking chair, facing the fireplace. Vance presented a paper arguing for a range of actions against Castro. He and Cottrell began arguing over which were appropriate, whereupon JFK stood up and left.

Independent exile raids remained a problem. In 1962, despite the existence of hundreds of boats that probably carried out thousands of cruises, U.S. Customs, the Coast Guard, and other authorities apprehended exactly four boats and fifty Cubans. Very likely these seizures were intended as lessons to the others to follow the orders of their CIA controllers. In January 1963 Des FitzGerald went to Miami and supposedly urged all U.S. authorities—not just Customs and the Coast Guard but the police also—to crack down on the independents. Yet raids in March twice caused serious damage to Soviet merchant ships, leading to diplomatic protests. In a letter discussed at the NSC on March 29, Secretary Rusk declared, "I am concerned that hit-and-run raids by Cuban exiles may create incidents which work to the disadvantage of our national interest. Increased frequency of these forays could raise a host of problems over which we would not have control."

The CIA, refocusing, had almost finished training a new team of frogmen for underwater demolition, and had two paramilitary teams in readiness—in all about 50 exiles with operational experience. As of early April no harassment missions were under way. Propaganda broadcasts into Cuba ran at 270 hours a week, and the most ambitious activity, a "subtle sabotage program," featured about 50,000 pieces of mail per month sent anonymously to Cubans from throughout the Hispanic world encouraging resistance or defections. Agency subsidies to Cuban political groups continued at a rate of $250,000 a month. Also under way were technological developments—the General Dynamics Corporation had a contract to design a shallow-draft boat for inshore work that would be faster than anything in Castro's navy—but those seemed nowhere near fruition.

Des FitzGerald had worries too—the Cuban response to one exile pinprick exposed a CIA mothership in the same area, working with small boats to put operatives ashore. Another time the *fidelistas* followed some exiles back to their forward base in the British Caymans, seizing commandos and equipment. International incidents and British intervention became complicating factors.

On April Fool's Day the coordinating committee demanded action anew. Jack and Bobby convened top officials at the White House two days later to hash out the issue. Both the CIA and Pentagon were present in force: Helms and FitzGerald for the agency, Vance and Califano for the Department of Defense. McGeorge Bundy guarded the president's interests. Observers included Tom Parrott, Ralph Dungan, and Robert Hurwitch. Prodded by JFK, Des FitzGerald admitted that raids were accomplishing nothing beyond building morale. Kennedy actually didn't mind that, he said, as long as the exiles stopped the incessant press conferences where they fought for credit. Mac Bundy added that the Special Group had decided the raids were not worth the effort. Bobby revisited escalation—he wanted to know the prospects for larger raids of a hundred to five hundred exiles. Joe Califano could hardly believe what he was hearing. Bobby was obsessed, Califano thought: "The intensity I had admired in his dealing with [Southern politicians on civil rights] now struck me as vengeful." Both he and Vance left the meeting deeply troubled.

During April the Standing Group began meeting weekly in the White House Situation Room. Now Bundy plunged into the project with typical *élan*. Beyond surveillance of Cuba to monitor Soviet forces and weapons, and covert action to damage Castro's economy, there were new concerns: isolating Cuba from the Free World and countering Castroite subversion. Bundy at least allowed the possibility of improving relations with Castro, but deliberations never went there. Instead Kennedy had the full NSC consider the newest menu on April 20, and four days later Robert McNamara told the group that Castro's position would only improve if the United States took no additional measures. John McCone followed up, saying CIA projected Castro would be stronger in a year or two. This was the moment to act. The agency had completed fresh proposals for covert harassment and sabotage, already approved by the coordinating committee. Bobby Kennedy proposed the U.S. aim at ousting Castro within eighteen months, causing as much trouble as possible in the meantime. This amounted to Mongoose all over again.

The director of central intelligence described the possibilities starkly. McCone doubted the CIA could overthrow Castro or that diplomacy might detach him from Moscow, though he did not mind trying. But he wanted the Soviets (and their weapons) out of Cuba. The director felt that "we must not, under any circumstance, dismiss the possibility of a second confrontation of a type encountered last October." He had "the same feeling about the presence of SAMs in Cuba now as I did last fall." Carefully planned sabotage could magnify Cuban problems but not bring down Fidel. McCone's reasoning is worth quoting:

> Low-level sabotage, such as minor crop destruction activities, interruption of transportation, etc., will be annoying. Successful major sabotage from within and without will, in my opinion, add to the problems created by the economic [blockade] measures. This will be particularly true as the flow of spare parts to essential plants (such as power plants) is effectively shut off. A combination of economic pressure and large-scale sabotage will hurt Castro seriously, but it will not bring him down. In addition a variety of other actions can be effectively carried out which would seriously impair relationships between Castro and Latin American countries.

The CIA director also wanted to amplify and play back any criticisms Cuban and Soviet leaders might make of each other, to create divisions between them, and carry out an effective misinformation program.

Among subjects discussed in this NSC policy review was "conditions without Castro, assuming Castro would be assassinated or die." A few days later, on the agenda for the next Standing Group meeting, the death of Castro was listed as a contingency that could lead to the accomplishment of wider political objectives.*

---

* In the Church Committee's report *Alleged Assassination Plots* (p. 171), this is mentioned as part of a category comprising events not initiated by the United States, but the original record, declassified in 1996, shows that that statement is not correct. Two of the four contingencies (Castro's death or a Hungary-style repression) could have been triggered by U.S. actions, and the introduction to the language on the agenda memo says nothing about foreign initiation. McGeorge Bundy's cover note, incidentally, adds that the memo "speaks in circumlocution on one or two sensitive points."

At that meeting Bob McNamara, taking McCone's point, acknowledged that small-scale sabotage had little potential. Afterward Bundy asked CIA for its assessment of Cuba after Castro's death. The Board of National Estimates did that report. Bundy also instructed the agency to study effective interference with the Cuban economy.

On May 28 the NSC Standing Group listened to FitzGerald present his fresh covert action plans. There were two: a general plan and a specific option dealing with Cuban oil supplies. Director McCone provided the preface, introducing his new task force chief with the remark that America needed to heighten hardship in Cuba, and that measures to that end plus sabotage might create such desperation that Fidel's *commandantes* would get rid of him. McCone was prepared for the CIA role in this to become apparent. McNamara reiterated his earlier stance that sabotage would be insufficient. Desmond FitzGerald remarked that a new sabotage program could begin by the new-moon period of July.

Bobby Kennedy entered the Situation Room as FitzGerald ended his briefing. The attorney general did not care whether Washington believed it could bring down Castro or not; something had to be done about Fidel.

Des FitzGerald revised his proposal based on the Standing Group discussions. His June 8 revision built on the assumption there would be no major U.S. intervention, and included only things the CIA could do. But the plan integrated existing projects and some new ones into an overall program including intelligence collection, propaganda, stimulation of disaffection in Cuba, economic denial, sabotage, and support of autonomous exile resistance. It proposed hit-and-run attacks against selected targets, specifically the Cuban electric power industry, its oil facilities, transportation, and manufacturing assets.

Several weeks into the project, Des FitzGerald returned to the NSC Standing Group to update them. The agency planned two operations for the anniversary of Castro's revolution, July 26. These were postponed to avoid conflicting with U.S.-Soviet negotiations on a nuclear test-ban treaty, scheduled for a few days later. Soon Ted Shackley's JM/Wave was preparing a dozen or so missions every month. Yet straws were already in the wind. Special Forces officer Bradley Ayers, training an exile unit in the Florida Keys, enthusiastically received a visit from Bobby Kennedy. Not long after, he received orders to stand down.

But the exile brigade notion had not disappeared. In fact the really novel feature of Kennedy's June decision was to switch to a stance backing "autonomous" raids, in other words, abandoning the pretense of impeding the exiles. Manuel Artime, returned from prison in Cuba, was the prime mover in the reinvigorated effort. An actual "brigade" became the centerpiece of Artime's scheme, to be based in Central America, stage raids on Cuba, and ultimately move there. This would have been the Bay of Pigs all over again, with the exiles supposedly calling the shots. Rafael Quintero scouted out locations for the base. Luis Somoza, Nicaraguan dictator, offered his cooperation. Manuel Artime and other prominent exiles completed their arrangements, moving by early August. They set up shop near the town of El Bluff. Soon they began bombing Cuba. Langley sent Jake Esterline to Panama as station chief, placing him where he could coordinate training services and other help for Artime.

Public speculation of CIA involvement ran high. The public was right: Langley had assigned Henry Heckscher as case officer to Artime, subsidizing him at $50,000 to $100,000 a month, though for the more limited purpose of encouraging a revolt by Castro's armed forces. Heckscher held monthly meetings with Artime, often accompanied by Quintero, usually in the United States though never Miami. Another indication of CIA support was what happened when Artime and Quintero tried to recruit Felix Rodriguez to run their communications. They promised him a demonstration of their U.S. government backing. Rodriguez, one of those who had enlisted under the special army program, was at Fort Benning as a army lieutenant. He demanded radio training right there, on the base, instead of his normal duties. Two gentlemen promptly showed up at Benning to give him the instruction.

On July 16 Desmond FitzGerald reported to the Standing Group on the "brigade" in Central America. (Actually the brigade was located in the United States—Erneido Oliva had gotten permission to pull together all the Cubans in the army and create a single combat unit. The "brigade" in Nicaragua never grew larger than about four hundred exiles.) The press already connected Bobby Kennedy to Artime and others in the operation—again correctly. Bobby suggested floating so many rumors that no one would be able to distinguish truth from fiction. John McCone agreed that could be done. Washington considered putting out an official statement denying any relationship with exile hit-and-run raids, but RFK opposed that, and his word carried.

Actually the raids gave the CIA good cover for its own activities. In the Magic City, Shackley invented a phony Cuban exile group, Commandos Mambises, to take credit for CIA raids. With deputy David Morales and paramilitary officer Bob Simons, he set up a frogman team for clandestine missions, kept outside and separate from the commando forces. On August 18 and 19 gunboats struck the Cuban oil facilities at Casilda and a plant at Santa Lucia. Desmond FitzGerald had specifically made Casilda a target in his original April plan while Santa Lucia fell squarely within the target categories CIA had proposed. Shackley had an agent claim credit in behalf of the fake group, even predicting the Santa Lucia strike in advance to gain credibility.

According to Shackley, this device worked like a charm. But Gordon Chase, Bundy's NSC staffer for intelligence, told the security adviser, "Even the connoisseurs in Miami seemed to pay relatively little attention to the two CIA-sponsored attacks." Within weeks the Bundy staff was congratulating itself on the excellent operational security of the August raids, and Chase wrote a paper for the Special Group on the continued need for secrecy, using the August raids as an example. Suddenly the White House wanted secrecy, not publicity. Ted Shackley's unit made only three more raids on Cuba.

By now McGeorge Bundy wore many hats, among them chairman of the Special Group, where he succeeded Maxwell Taylor. General Taylor had given up the post in 1962 when appointed to head the JCS. On October 3 Bundy's Special Group adopted a menu of nine additional CIA missions, and on the 24th a schedule for the period from November through January 1964, including thirteen raids, among them missions against an electric plant, an oil refinery, and a sugar refinery. Within Califano's army office, Al Haig processed the paperwork and passed it along. Bundy held the reins there too, apparently none too successfully since it seems that just five direct CIA raids occurred between the summer of 1963 and the spring of the following year—the strikes by Shackley's phony exiles. Then the agency's focus shifted.

Desmond FitzGerald briefed the PFIAB on the program in early September. More Catholic than the pope, the board encouraged the spooks. Another FitzGerald briefing, on September 25, aimed at bringing around the Joint Chiefs of Staff. This culminated a series of contacts at Joe Califano's request in which FitzGerald let out bits of CIA's story and asked for help. For some time the Pentagon had been less than enthusiastic about the secret war. A typical military view held that the Bay of Pigs—and Mongoose—were failures because they lacked the expertise and capability that regular forces could bring to the table. In July, Califano's office had compiled a detailed analysis of where the secret warriors had been and what they needed to win, concluding the program held no promise, not even a moderate chance of success. The FitzGerald briefings began soon thereafter.

Presidential decisions back in April had given the military a wider support role, particularly in Artime's autonomous "brigade," and the series of strikes these exiles carried out through the fall seemed to bear out Pentagon opinions. An August bombing raid, well equipped and coordinated, the subject of much media speculation, was actually attributed to Shackley's Commandos Mambises. A second autonomous initiative began to create a force under Manolo Ray. But the inertia level remained high and relations with the CIA delicate. On one occasion Califano met FitzGerald in Miami at his hotel. Des opened the door, put his finger to his lips, proceeded to turn on the radio full blast and run every water tap in the room, and then whispered in Joe's ear. Califano thought he had stumbled onto the set of a spy movie. It was no way to do business.

The other track of the Cuba operation—assassination—continued throughout. Soon after FitzGerald came on board there was a scheme to get Fidel with an exploding seashell. Sam Halpern, whom Des retained, questioned the legality of the enterprise when he learned about it, and took the matter to CIA counsel Lawrence Houston. The lawyers decided that if the project had been authorized by the president and attorney general, it must be legal. The seashell plot, never realistic (how to make sure Fidel picked up the right shell?), collapsed by itself. But new possibilities arose. FitzGerald's plans hinged on encouraging a coup against Castro by the Cuban military. That formed the operational goal of the June plan. When Des briefed the Joint Chiefs in September, one theme was how the CIA had begun studying the ways German generals had plotted against Hitler during World War II. Langley asked the Pentagon to assemble all its data on Castro's officer corps.

From Miami, Ted Shackley's foreign intelligence chief, Nestor Sanchez, spent a good deal of time traveling Latin America and chatting up Cuban officers. The Pentagon intelligence was grist for his mill. One officer, Maj. Rolando Cubela Secades, met with the CIA in Mexico City as early as 1961. Over the months there were repeated indications he might wish to defect. Cubela, in Spain as the Cuban military attaché, could travel freely and met other CIA officers in Helsinki during the Mongoose period. He became a CIA agent code-named AM/LASH. Nestor Sanchez pursued FitzGerald's ambition to trigger a coup. Returned to Langley, the Cuba chief assigned Sanchez as case officer to AM/LASH, whom he met in Brazil in September 1963. Cubela spoke of an anti-Communist circle in the Cuban military—music to the CIA's ears—but most of them were loyal to Fidel, or they were afraid.

The Cuban went on to Paris. Although he told the CIA that he wished to get away from politics and wanted nothing more to do with Sanchez, the agency officer followed him to the French capital. A sympathetic character, Nestor Sanchez claimed descent from the conquistadors and spoke fluent Spanish. He could trade on war stories from Korea, where Sanchez had started out with the agency in 1951, and he had been deputy station chief in Guatemala City during Project Success. He was a veteran of a dozen years with the CIA, with service in Latin America and the turbulent Middle East of the 1950s, and able to talk Cubela out of cutting ties. Instead Cubela turned the conversation to getting rid of people—only in that way could a coup ever succeed. Sanchez later maintained that Fidel himself was not mentioned.

But AM/LASH proved no easy sell. Cubela feared the United States would walk away from a plot, as it had from Brigade 2506. He wanted assurances from a senior U.S. official—AM/LASH specified Robert F. Kennedy. He also wanted weapons—high-powered rifles with telescopic sights. Sanchez had no authority to make deals but passed on the demands. After Cubela's second request to meet with a top official, on October 17, DDO Richard Helms cleared Des FitzGerald to follow up, with instructions to present himself as the personal representative of Robert Kennedy. FitzGerald's counterintelligence chief warned him that AM/LASH might be an imposter working for Castro's G-2, but the ebullient spook brooked no objections. The meeting took place in Paris on October 29; Nestor Sanchez interpreted. FitzGerald's field report and Sam Halpern agree that they avoided mention of an actual operation. Nevertheless, Rolando Cubela demanded equipment support, and the CIA provided it.

Scientists at Langley crafted a poison pen using a toxic chemical injection. Nestor Sanchez went to Paris to hand over the instrument. He met Rolando Cubela again on November 22. Only hours later President John F. Kennedy fell to the bullets of assassin Lee Harvey Oswald in Dallas, Texas.

At the moment of Kennedy's murder, Des FitzGerald sat in Georgetown's City Tavern Club, at lunch with a foreign diplomat who fed the agency snippets of gossip. When the Cuba task force chief heard of the assassination he thought immediately of Cubela and the Castro murder plot. He hoped there was no connection. Sam Halpern drove FitzGerald back to Langley afterward, the chief sat white as a sheet. They discussed Cubela.

That moment marked the effective end of the CIA's assassination plots, though the Cubela affair dragged on. The CIA gave weapons to Cubela, and there were fights between Langley and Miami station over the shipments, with several sums of money handed over. Manuel Artime independently contacted Cubela in late 1964 and received CIA money to fund the Cubela plot. In March 1966 Castro's security services arrested AM/LASH, who was sentenced to twenty-five years in prison. The CIA murder plot received no mention at the trial, though the Artime contacts figured prominently. When the Rockefeller Commission and the Church Committee investigated this affair in 1975, Joe Califano learned that his suspicions about why the CIA needed all that biographical intelligence had been correct.

Meanwhile John Kennedy's successor, Lyndon Baines Johnson, brought a fresh perspective to the White House. LBJ may not have known that Kennedy had begun to put out peace feelers toward Castro, but he certainly felt less committed to the secret war. Al Haig believes it a fact that President Johnson understood JFK's assassination as the result of the murder plots, and LBJ made comments at several times suggesting that was true. The new president also voiced doubts regarding Cuban exile groups, including Artime with his brigade in Nicaragua.

President Johnson ordered curtailment of the U.S. military's Cuban enlistment program. For Joseph Califano the consequence would be a very painful reunion on February 24, 1964, with Erneido Oliva, who made the last of many appeals to use the Cuban assault brigade against Castro. Oliva slumped into his chair when Califano rejected the idea. A few days later Oliva and several others resigned. Fewer than 150 Cubans volunteered for the special Cuban program between the beginning of 1964 and the end of April 1965. Oliva went to Thanksgiving dinner at Califano's home. Later he returned to the U.S. Army Reserve, from which he finally retired as a brigadier general. But the intentions of the several thousand Cuban recruits clearly show from the fact that only 61 of them continued in U.S. service after training. In November 1965 the initiative would be phased out.

The Cuban operation began dying as sensitivity to the problems of control increased. Around the time Califano saw Oliva, Des FitzGerald sent McCone a paper that went over the options without adding anything. In March Des reported again on the status of the Artime and Ray autonomous operations, extolling their deniability and using a fresh version of the "disposal" argument—should the United States terminate its support the exiles would probably just go on, especially Ray's group. The secret warrior anticipated that the groups would be ready to become active in two or three months.

On April 7 Lyndon Johnson held a White House review. McGeorge Bundy recommended continuing the economic blockade, propaganda, and intelligence gathering, but he wanted discussion of the future of sabotage missions, both the CIA's and the exiles' autonomous ones. John McCone referred to FitzGerald's "integrated" program to argue the marginal value of doing just some things. President Johnson had doubts. McCone insisted the United States still wanted Castro's *commandantes* to rise up. "He was deadly serious about all this," Ray Cline remembered. "It was crucial to have Cuban communism a failure. If we couldn't destroy it . . . we ought to make it as unattractive as possible by making it a poor show economically for the Cuban people." FitzGerald spoke of the nonagency exile activities. Robert McNamara reiterated what, for him, had now become a hard conclusion: the covert program had no chance. The real question for McNamara had become what should be Washington's overall policy toward Cuba.

President Johnson would hold more of these discussions, but the question of bringing the Cuban actions to a halt had been squarely posed. In May LBJ adopted his basic stance of cutting back the Cuba project. About the same time Artime's group conducted its first significant raid—on a sugar mill—and Ray tried a highly publicized infiltration. Ray never made it. Mechanical breakdowns on boats and a variety of other excuses were advanced to explain why. As for the Artime group, in two years it attempted fourteen operations and completed four. None of this impressed the White House. Gordon Chase fed Mac Bundy a stream of new objections on both diplomatic and political grounds. On June 18 the Special Group decided against immediate changes, but shortly afterward came charges of corruption among the Artime group, on which the CIA had already spent $5 million. Langley decided the charges were groundless, but the episode did nothing to increase confidence. The Johnson White House steadily backed away from the exiles.

Secret warriors like Ted Shackley never gave up. The Miami station chief deplored the "on-again, off-again orders we began getting from Washington." Kept on the leash, his commandos began drifting away. Shackley still felt he had units that "could have waged an effective guerrilla campaign in Cuba" if only "the strategy from Washington had been more resolute and sustained." In an account preoccupied with strikes, raids, and condemnations of those he worked for, Shackley never pauses to explain how his Cuba operations, any more than the many, many previous failures, would bring down Castro, who had now consolidated his leadership and built a strong, well-equipped military.

Official support only encouraged the Cubans. In the new atmosphere the CIA on June 10, 1964, reported that the exiles had their own plan to assassinate Castro—Artime's links to Rolando Cubela. The Special Group pondered this a week later. In the face of McCone's comment that it must all be Miami cocktail party talk, the wizards of the secret war decided to alert the FBI and the Justice Department: Washington could not permit any such plot to be carried out. The ground had shifted that much.

Periodic NSC discussions and autonomous exile strikes continued through late 1965, but Cuba was increasingly left behind. Scattered data indicates at least one CIA infiltration operation that year but not much else. A flurry of Special Group deliberations on Cuba took place during the summer, and Mac Bundy forwarded a CIA paper to President Johnson. This framed an LBJ decision to cut back still more. Support to the "brigade" in Nicaragua ended. CIA bases in the Florida Keys closed one by one. The Cuba task force stayed alive—Dave Phillips succeeded FitzGerald and eventually Jim Flannery followed him—but the project accomplished little. As long as the exiles continued plotting and the agency needed to know, plus hold the hands of Cubans who wanted it, Miami station stayed active.

As Cuba operations wound down, agency logistics wizard Jim Garrison* took Jake Esterline with him on a visit to a secret CIA supply dump in the Midwest. Esterline thought he had better things to do, but Garrison dragooned him into the trip. The stockpiles were vast—cases of rifles, heavy weapons, assorted equipment, row upon row.

"See all of that?" rasped Garrison, "You made me buy that, you bugger!"

Esterline ended his career in Miami, running JM/Wave years after Shackley had left, primarily as a social services provider.

Through their Cuban project the secret warriors created a cadre with military skills, one that far outlasted the CIA operations themselves. As the Johnson administration changed gears, pursuing Castro in Africa and South America, those Cubans became a fresh legion at Washington's command. The secret war against Castro spilled over onto new fronts.

Africa became the next theater in the secret war, or, more precisely, it returned to the forefront of Langley's concerns. Barely had the Congo been reunified when, in the summer of 1963, a new rebellion commenced in that country, led by another former minister, Pierre Mulele. The CIA learned that Mulele had been in China for an extended period, presumably for instruction, thus believing him to be a Communist agent. That fall his troops began attacking Mobutu in Mulele's home province. This could not have been worse for Leopoldville—the UN was withdrawing even as Mobutu's army remained far from effective. The rebellion known for Mulele, or as the Simba Rebellion for the word "lion" in Swahili, rapidly grew. Representing LBJ, diplomat Averell Harriman visited the Congo in March 1964, promising more U.S. aid.

Secret warriors faced a new problem. The CIA's best chance—and Mobutu's—lay in a new undercover air effort. This had been built gradually, starting with the import of some T-6 trainer planes from Italy. The addition of weapons pods converted the aircraft to the ground-support role. The first mission was flown from a strip in Kwilu province in February. After Harriman's visit the air project accelerated. Better T-28 aircraft came, along with pilots the CIA had sent to Intermountain Aviation to check out in the planes. John Merriman, Intermountain trainer on this project, became the chief of operations for the Congo air effort.

---

* No relation to the New Orleans district attorney who acquired fame in the 1960s pursuing tendrils of the alleged plots against John F. Kennedy.

Joining him were Air America pilots Ed Dearborn and Don Coney and many Cubans, among them Gus Ponzoa, leading fifteen Cuban pilots in the T-28 unit. After that came a formation of B-26 bombers led by Joaquin ("Jack") Varela, a top flier with CIA B-26s. The U.S. Air Force transferred the bombers to a classified project on June 26, the last aircraft of this type it gave to the CIA.

Exactly a month later Merriman became the first casualty of the CIA air campaign when he broke rules prohibiting combat missions by Americans to take up a T-28 against a reported Simba truck convoy. His wingmen were Ponzoa and Varela, both Bay of Pigs veterans. His plane hit, Merriman nursed it to a crash landing but was injured so badly he died a few weeks later.

In June Mobutu installed a new cabinet under Moishe Tshombe, summoned from exile. The CIA saw few favorable signs, though it reported Katanga stable. Two months later, however, a Special National Intelligence Estimate frankly admitted that "regional dissidence and violence have assumed serious proportions, even by Congolese standards, and produced the threat of a total breakdown in governmental authority." Tshombe's prospects were put at no better than fifty-fifty, and if he fell there was no telling where it might end. Days later rebels seized Stanleyville and made hostage all whites, including the American consul, his assistant, CIA base chief David Grinwis and his two radiomen, fifteen other Americans, and hundreds of Europeans, including missionaries, nuns, and mining engineers.

The need for a force to defeat the rebellion had become acute. The best Congolese army elements were now white soldiers of fortune, principally of English and Belgian extraction, proud to call themselves mercenaries. A few hundred of them made up a small battalion called Five Commando under the South African Col. Mike Hoare. It remains unclear what role the CIA had in financing Five Commando—available documents, principally an INR review of CIA African activities in 1964, have had their guts excised (though indicating political payoffs as large as ever)—and at that stage the Belgian mining companies still reigned. Still, Five Commando and the CIA air force spearheaded a Stanleyville relief effort. While the American and British embassies kept their distance, U.S. military attaché Col. Knut Raudstein happily talked to Hoare and went on the mission. Varela's CIA aircraft were crucial in breaking up ambushes and supporting the commandos, with the first B-26 combat mission on August 21. As Hoare neared Stanleyville it seemed he might be too late. The Great Powers took a hand. In Operation *Dragon Rouge* (Red Dragon) late in November, Belgian paratroops flown in by the U.S. Air Force captured Stanleyville to free the hostages. Use of Special Forces had been considered but rejected. More than two thousand foreign nationals were evacuated to Leopoldville. Stanleyville now became the main base for air operations in the northeast Congo.

Through all this the agency had been deathly afraid for its people in Stanleyville and needed to replace the staff. Richard L. Holm, just returned from Laos where he had watched the Ho Chi Minh Trail, transferred to the Africa Division and was preparing for assignment to North Africa when suddenly diverted. Holm had been taking French lessons from Colette, Larry Devlin's wife, and often spoke of the Congo with the former station chief, who now told division baron Glen Fields that Holm would be a good fellow for Stanleyville. The neophyte Africanist arrived in December, but his would be a short tour—on February 17 Holm flew with a T-28 attack mission. Two planes were trapped by a weather front. Holm's aircraft crashed. He survived horrible burns, rescued and cared for by villagers using native medicine. Case officer Charles Cogan saw Holm on his return and marveled at his survival. Several years of rehabilitation were necessary before he could return to duty. Cuban pilot Juan Tunon of the second plane was never seen again. Later missionary reports established that Tunon had been captured by the Simba, killed, and eaten.

The Congo became a bloody project for the agency. Several months after Holm's serious injury a CIA contract officer, Bill Wyrozemski, working out of Albertville, died in a head-on collision with a Congolese army truck.

Meanwhile Che Guevara turned up. According to Piero Gleijeses, the foremost historian of Cuba in Africa, Fidel Castro convinced Che to make Africa a waystation on his quest to carry the revolution to Latin America, where the ground had yet to become fertile for uprising. Fidel promised that he would continue preparations while Che fought. The *commandante* traveled through Eastern Europe and Algeria to Tanzania, where he connected with the Simbas. The Congolese were embarrassed, fearing international reaction to news of Che in Africa. Meanwhile Castro combed his forces for blacks whom he sent as a special unit. Victor Dreke, perhaps the most senior black, became Che's second and led the unit to Africa. They infiltrated from Tanzania across Lake Tanganyika. From April to November 1965 the Cuban column worked in Orientale province. Their first battle occurred in late June.

The CIA learned of the Cubans in September. Even then no one really believed Che was there. Special Forces now sent advisers and teams. At one point station chief Benjamin H. Cushing volunteered CIA funding for Mobutu's entire mercenary effort. He rejected the offer. Although the Simba enclave where Che fought became stronger for a time, Mobutu forces began an offensive at the end of September. Meanwhile the Cubans' base in Algeria disappeared with the overthrow of the Ben Bella government, and in October the Organization of African Unity, which contributed money and arms to the Simbas, halted its support. Che could read the tea leaves as well as anyone. Dreke recalls, "At a certain point we realized the thing was lost, that the Congolese themselves had made a decision to end the fighting." The Cubans withdrew into Tanzania.

In 1965 the impatient Mobutu launched a new coup and installed himself as national leader. He renamed Leopoldville as Kinshasa. The Congo he renamed Zaire in 1971. Hoare's Five Commando continued to fight for Mobutu for another five years, but the rebellion had peaked. More mercenary units were added. Moishe Tshombe went into exile again. Lured from Madrid in 1967 to meet ostensible backers on a Mediterranean island, his airplane was hijacked to Algiers and Tshombe imprisoned. (Tshombe died two years later. He may have been poisoned.) That July the mercenaries revolted. The United States quickly deployed a

Joint Task Force Congo with several C-130 aircraft and 150 men that flew Congolese troops to fight the mercenaries. Inept Congolese army efforts allowed the mercenaries to hold out for a few months, but the issue was never in doubt, and eventually they were driven across the border.

In both the Stanleyville airdrop and the 1967 episode, the Johnson administration avoided notifying Congress of the use of force and U.S. participation. Dean Rusk spoke to a few senior members privately, a measure increasingly common with all manner of covert operations.

Through all of this the CIA air unit remained absolutely vital. Agency officers determined the missions. The unit would have been familiar to any Bay of Pigs veteran, or, for that matter, any American airman from "Jungle Jim." It included ten C-47 transports, eight or nine B-26 bombers, and eight of the light T-28 fighter-bombers. The Cuban pilots were hired by one of those ubiquitous Miami corporations, Caribbean Aero Marine (Caramar). If employed under conditions similar to Five Commando, the pilots would have been on six-month contracts. They called themselves the "Cuban Volunteer Group" led by Réné Garcia. Often gathering at a favorite restaurant, the Pizzeria, humorists joked that a couple of hand grenades of an evening could wipe out the Zairian air force.

Mobutu had no pilots of his own until the CIA deployed its more advanced aircraft and handed the T-6s back to the Zairian government. In October 1964 a new unit of mercenaries became active under a South African, Jerry Purren, known as Twenty-one Squadron. The CIA air force became Twenty-two Squadron.

Belgian pilots and maintenance crews worked the transport planes; the combat aircraft were repaired by the Western International Ground Maintenance Organization (WIGMO), a Lichtenstein corporation employing fifty to a hundred European mechanics. When more mercenaries were hired later to run patrol boats on Lake Tanganyika, WIGMO maintained the warships. The CIA flew the vessels in pieces into Albertville, where they were reconstructed and put on the lake. An American SEAL officer from Vietnam, Lt. James Hawes, supervised the activity. WIGMO continued to work with the Mobutu government through 1969.

In mid-1966 there were only a dozen Cuban pilots, but they accounted for the vast majority of the air support in Zaire. Public interest grew after the *New York Times* ran a major series on the CIA in which it discussed the agency putting an "instant air force" in the Congo. Washington decided to begin phasing out the Congo project about that time, according to Cyrus Vance, and the first of the B-26s left the Congo in February 1966. As late as August 1967 the Special Group approved recruitment of additional Cuban pilots for the Congo. This would be the final contingent. After the air operations ended, Réné Garcia stayed to become Mobutu's personal pilot, flying the Zairian dictator wherever he wanted for another sixteen years. Mobutu died in 1997. In classic Congolese style, Laurent Kabila, a Simba leader of the 1960s, would rule the Republic of the Congo (the name has been revived) for several years at the end of the century.

The agency continued to face off with Fidel Castro, who did not give up on Africa after his misfortune in the Congo. Simultaneously with Che's expedition, Castro sent another column under Commandante Jorge Risquet to Congo-Brazzaville, the nation on the opposite bank of the Congo River from Mobutu's Zaire, and a former French colony. The 250 Cubans in Risquet's force had multiple purposes. They served as a potential reserve for Guevara until his operation evaporated. In 1966 Risquet's doctors organized the first vaccination campaign ever carried out in the country. Another aim, continuing in revolutionary solidarity, was to train fighters for leftist groups in Angola, where an independence movement fought Portugal to liberate that African colony. The fighters returned to the Angolan enclave of Cabinda, or by boat to Angola proper. In June 1966 the Cuban unit broke up a military coup against the Brazzaville government. About six months later the Risquet column returned to Cuba aboard a Russian vessel. A smaller Cuban training mission remained behind, still working with the Angolan independence movement known as the MPLA.

A few Cubans went undercover and entered Cabinda to work directly with the rebel movement. When leaders planned an attack on a Portuguese fort, a larger Cuban force participated, and the Cubans even contributed four artillery guns to the Angolan revolution.

Suddenly B-26 bombers and Cuban exile pilots showed on the Portuguese side in Angola. That these were private adventures is cast into doubt by the indictment of the CIA proprietary Intermountain Aviation for illegally exporting B-26 bombers to Portuguese Africa. This affair began in April 1965 when executives of a Tucson, Arizona, firm called Aero Associates approached a British pilot about ferrying ten B-26 aircraft to Portugal.

The first transfer went smoothly, but on a second flight the pilot John R. Hawke, forced by bad weather to land at Washington, D.C., suddenly suffered engine trouble on his approach. He flew over the White House, prohibited air space. Questioned by federal officials, Hawke used a code word ("Sparrow") he had been given for an emergency and was released. He completed the flight, as well as five more. In Miami in September 1965, however, federal officers arrested Hawke, who went to trial in the fall of 1966 along with Gregory Board of Aero and middleman Henri Mari de Marin de Montmarin. The men were accused of violating U.S. arms export laws. The trial took place in Rochester, New York, where Hawke had stopped on U.S. soil during his first ferry mission.

Defense lawyers subpoenaed CIA general counsel Lawrence Houston, requiring his testimony. Although Houston denied any CIA connection with the arms shipments, he affirmed that the agency had known of each B-26 transfer days in advance. A CIA document admitted in evidence, dated May 25, 1965— that is, very early in the project—specified that Portugal had acquired twenty of the B-26 bombers, which were to be modified in Canada with long-range fuel tanks. Former agency officials identified the source of the planes as Intermountain

Aviation and Evergreen International, the CIA proprietaries. The defendants were acquitted.

Many covert action proposals emanate from CIA headquarters. But many others come from the State Department or agency people in the field. In Africa in the mid-1960s, according to a survey by the State Department's Bureau of Intelligence and Research, the larger number came from the field, the smallest from Langley. Of all the continents where it engaged, the CIA stretched the most in Africa. Despite its expansion on this continent from 1959, the combination of many former colonies attaining independence and the lack of area specialists left the agency playing catch-up. The Africa Division handled some nations remotely by sending officers from other posts—undercover operatives covering an itinerary like traveling salesmen. This was not only Langley's problem. The INR survey makes clear that increases in CIA capabilities corresponded roughly to State's own drive to cope with the blossoming of Africa.

The two agencies frequently clashed over field versus Washington initiatives, or ends and means. There were also fights within agencies. For example, when the field proposed that the CIA recruit rebel Holden Roberto in Portuguese Angola, Langley came together on the opportunity but the State Department split, its Africa Bureau supporting the idea strongly while Europeanists opposed it. Four distinct proposals to fund Roberto were tabled during 1964, but the Special Group finally deferred action at John McCone's request. Yet the CIA and Africanists ultimately won; Roberto went on the payroll. Although the Congo absorbed much of the Africa Division's capability, tentacles soon reached many other places. Angola was one. Another, political action in Somalia, the Special Group approved in February 1964. The project lasted three years. The Special Group reportedly considered a State Department proposal to supply arms to certain groups in Tanzania, where secret-war wizards saw President Julius Nyerere as a problem, in the summer of 1964. There is no current evidence on process or outcome.

Like Nyerere, Washington viewed Ghana's leader Kwame Nkrumah as a troublemaker. The CIA's role in Ghana seems to have flowed from both Washington and the field. A nationalist hero and first president of independent Ghana, Nkrumah had an uneasy relationship with the United States. Educated in missionary schools and in the segregationist America of the thirties and forties, he learned his Marxism there, influenced by the racial attitudes of the day. He was no Moscow puppet. Nkrumah called his program "African Socialism." Turbulent Ghanaian politics soured Nkrumah, who became increasingly dictatorial after assassination attempts in 1962 and 1964. He introduced press censorship, dismissed the supreme court, and imprisoned many opponents. Ghana's economy went into deficit as prices for its cocoa plunged. Nkrumah attributed the hardship to the former colonial power, Great Britain, and to the United States. Washington blamed Nkrumah for anti-American agitation in Ghana. American aid for a dam on the Upper Volta River and to develop new economic resources in aluminum hung in the balance.

Nkrumah attributed the January 1964 assassination attempt to the CIA. The Johnson administration stepped carefully around this thorny question, with U.S. Ambassador William P. Mahoney assuring LBJ that his country team—including CIA—was fully under control, and the CIA denying any role. In February 1964 Nkrumah sent Johnson a letter asserting that there were "two conflicting establishments" representing the United States, the diplomatic mission and the CIA, which "seems to devote all its attention to fomenting ill-will, misunderstanding and even clandestine and subversive activities among our people, to the impairment of the good relations which exist between our two governments." Johnson conveyed reassurances on the CIA both in his response and through Ambassador Mahoney, who reportedly told Nkrumah that the five CIA officers in the station at Accra were under his strict supervision.

But Washington's record was not entirely innocent. As early as February 6, 1964, Dean Rusk asked John McCone about suitable candidates to head a post-Nkrumah government, and they discussed the very general who was eventually to move against the Ghanaian. The two men speculated on the possibility of concocting a covert operation in concert with the British. When the State Department proposed an action program it had the explicit purpose of slowing Nkrumah's leftward political evolution. The proposal was to actively undermine him by threatening to halt aid to the Volta River project, recognizing opponents, and using psychological warfare and other means to diminish his support. President Johnson deliberated on this program at the exact moment Nkrumah sent his letter protesting CIA subversion.

LBJ went ahead with the Volta dam aid, but he may well have approved undermining Nkrumah. During a home visit in March 1965 Ambassador Mahoney met with Director McCone and AF Division deputy chief John Waller. They specifically discussed a coup plot in Ghana hatched by police and military figures, including Gen. Joseph A. Ankrah, the same man McCone and Rusk had considered a year earlier. Evidence indicates the Ghanaian military's plans were well known to the CIA, which reported on them more than half a dozen times in 1965. As yet there is no evidence of direct CIA involvement from documents. What we do have is a series of confident predictions of a coup from both the ambassador—who accurately foresaw that Nkrumah would be replaced by a military junta within a year—and NSC staffer Robert W. Komer. That summer Nkrumah detected the coup plot and cashiered Ankrah. The Ghanaian generals, their peripatetic plots more than a year old, were temporarily stymied.

Kwame Nkrumah strove for a role on the world stage, trying to be a peacemaker and help end the Vietnam War. This annoyed Washington, especially when Nkrumah tried to intercede between the British and Guyana's Cheddi Jagan. He also made unwelcome overtures in the Middle East. In the summer of 1965 Nkrumah sent diplomatic envoys to North Vietnam, suggesting that he himself visit early the following year. He tacked on visits to Burma and the People's Republic of China. According to CIA political operative Miles Copeland, under whom the agency had begun an effort to plant astrologers on world leaders known to favor the occult, a CIA occult agent may have had a role in convincing Nkrumah to plan this trip.

In 1965 Nkrumah published a book, *Neo-Colonialism: The Last Stage of Imperialism*, which must have raised hackles in Washington. Then came an overt move toward Moscow—Nkrumah accepted Soviet arms and training for his presidential guard. The last straw may have come when the CIA reported that a Soviet arms shipment was on its way to Ghana.

William Mahoney left Accra for good in the summer of 1965, and for eight months there was no U.S. ambassador. Station chief Howard T. Bane had a much freer hand. Bane proposed the CIA sponsor a coup. The views of Africa Division chief Glen Fields are not known, but he had been amenable to the Congo, and his deputy John Waller had made his mark in the 1953 CIA coup in Iran. The Special Group turned them down. Bane thought that shortsighted, and as a colleague later put it, he had "no patience for management of which he was not a part."

Howard Bane, another man who came to Africa from the DO Far East Division, had an affinity for the military and determination to go with it. A knuckle-dragger, in Korea he had run a net to rescue downed fliers. In India he had back-stopped the Tibet project, insulating it from the jaundiced Harry Rositzke. He wet his teeth in Africa heading the CIA station in Kenya. Not phased by the Special Group's rejection, the tobacco-chewing, cigar-smoking Bane took advantage of his instructions to keep a close watch on the Ghanaian military. With a complement variously reported at ten or up to three dozen case officers, Bane exploited his military contacts.

A few winks and nods from Bane betokened U.S. support to Ghanaian soldiers. With just a pair of brigades, both based in Accra, there were not that many to convince. Bane had time to suggest that Langley send a few officers from the CIA Special Operations Division, who could not only concretize the impression of support but use the coup to purloin documents and code materials from the Chinese embassy in Accra, a unilateral operation under cover of the coup. Headquarters spurned him again. But in mid-January 1966 Bane reported that a rash of coups elsewhere in Africa had reenthused Ghanaian officers, and on February 17 came concrete indications of a plot, Operation Cold Chop. Twenty-four hours before the coup, Bane reported the military planned it for the time Nkrumah was out of the country. President Nkrumah left Ghana on February 22, the coup occurred on the 24th. General Ankrah returned to head the resulting junta.

That the coup actually surprised Washington is suggested by Bob Komer's memo to LBJ a month later, in which he suggested to Johnson that "The coup in Ghana is another example of a fortuitous windfall." Walt Rostow later told historian David Rooney that the CIA knew the plotters, but "We did not throw a match in the haystack." Yet Langley credited Accra station with an assist. Howard Bane wound up as chief of operations for the AF Division.

In Tanzania, meanwhile, Che Guevara tarried for months after leaving the Congo. There he turned his diaries into a narrative, seeking to understand what had gone wrong. He stayed in Dar-es-Salaam until early 1966, when a top DGI official came to give Guevara the latest assessment of prospects for revolution in each Latin American country. Guevara really wanted to fight in Argentina, but security services there had suppressed dissident networks. In Peru the CIA and the government had foreclosed the option. That left Bolivia as the major prospect. Che's hope lay in what he called a *foco*, literally a focus or a lighthouse, in practice an exemplar activity that could lead the masses to rally to the revolution, much as Castro's small July 26th Movement had brought the end of Batista.

Guevara's ploy confronted a transformed Western Hemisphere Division at CIA. By 1966 it had shrunk to become smaller than the Miami station during Mongoose. About a hundred officers served at Langley and twice that many in the field. Its largest station, Mexico City under long-service boss Winston Scott, single-handedly absorbed 15 percent of the division budget. The largest branch continued to be that for Cuba, but this had shrunk to just thirty officers. Division chief William V. Broe, a Far East specialist, had been drafted after a tour as station chief in Tokyo. Jake Esterline had now risen to deputy chief of division. Still on board after all these years was Gerry Droller, chief of the covert action staff. Thomas Polgar, a European expert and most recently CIA's boss in Vienna, headed the Foreign Intelligence Staff. They had $37 million to play with in the fiscal 1967 budget.

The top of the agency had been transformed also. Two directors had come and gone—John McCone over disputes with the president, William F. Raborn perhaps for lack of them. But in 1965, when President Johnson appointed Admiral Raborn, he simultaneously made Richard Helms deputy director of central intelligence. His departure for the Seventh Floor left the Directorate of Operations in need of a chief. Raborn let Helms choose. For DO boss the selection was between Helms's longtime associate Thomas Karamessines and Desmond FitzGerald. When Des saw what had happened, he marched into Helms's office to bid for the job. Karamessines did nothing. Helms chose FitzGerald, who thus arrived to head the CIA's clandestine service. Helms exacted the promise that FitzGerald would weed out useless covert operations. Cuba projects took another hit.

Subtle change came to the Special Group. Lyndon Johnson made this his own in June 1964 with an NSAM that retitled the unit. Now it became the 303 Committee, named for its establishing directive. The committee met weekly or more frequently if necessary. Occasionally projects were approved in a telephone conference. The CIA sent papers in advance, and members arrived prepared to discuss them. The primacy of the national security adviser as chairman had become established. Until February 1966 this would be Mac Bundy, for a month or so after that Robert Komer, then the chairman became Walt W. Rostow.

The chairman informed President Johnson to an extent that only the two of them knew. But if the 303 Committee could not agree, or an operation involved great risks, LBJ would convene their seniors—McNamara, Rusk, and the CIA director—to discuss the matter directly. Deputy Undersecretary of State U. Alexis

Johnson represented the State Department during some of this period, and writes that he always tried to put himself in the shoes of the president. For his efforts he acquired the nickname "Dr. No." But the State Department backed many projects, and the 303 Commmittee approved a large share of the proposals laid before it. Alex Johnson writes, "I would say we reached a firm decision in all but a few cases."

Bolivia would be one of the easy ones. During the Kennedy years Washington gradually began mixing itself into the politics of this Andean country. A paper prepared for the Special Group (CI) in September 1962 acknowledged the leftist politics of La Paz and viewed any threat as arising primarily from local leaders wanting to maximize power in the style of Chinese warlords. In 1963 intelligence reports found Bolivia to be one of the most highly armed Latin nations, where many had guns at home and the government handed out weapons to various labor and peasant groups. Where Washington took umbrage at the Venezuelan case, it did nothing about Bolivia.

Nothing except political action, that is. In August 1963 the Special Group approved secret funds for Washington's favorite party in Bolivia's 1964 elections. Between 1963 and 1965 the CIA spent $1.2 million to support peasant organizations and youth groups, and for propaganda. The leftists won, but not by enough to avoid a coalition that included the American favorites, the MNR (*Movimiento nacional revolucionario*). Then in November 1964 Gen. Rene Barrientos Ortuño, a vice president in the coalition, launched a military coup that swept away the leftists. Two months later the 303 Committee approved more cash for Barrientos to fulfill election promises. Records indicate that the general was aware of the CIA source of the money. Then, in the face of political opposition, Barrientos jailed opponents and canceled elections. The 303 Committee nevertheless authorized more payments in July 1965 and again in March 1966, before a new election in which Barrientos triumphed. All this kept Gerry Droller very busy. Not only the Cubans were engaged in Bolivia.

It is fair to say that by this time the Central Intelligence Agency had a fixation on Che Guevara. Slow to appreciate emerging differences between Fidel and Che, the CIA produced analyses of economic policy disputes between the two in the fall of 1965 when Guevara had already gone to Africa. The paper, by analyst Brian Latell, caught the flavor of the disputes, but the agency would not accept what its Africa field officers and their Cuban exile operators were saying—that Che fought against *them*. There were other "Che sightings" too, resulting in Langley's determination to get him at all costs. But not everyone believed—as late as May 1967 Des FitzGerald told the visiting U.S. ambassador to Bolivia that Guevara was dead and buried in an unmarked grave in the Dominican Republic.

Despite FitzGerald's observation to Ambassador Douglas Henderson, the CIA's secret war against Guevara came to a head in Bolivia, and in 1967. Che had arrived in the country late the preceding year, heavily disguised and using an Uruguayan passport. For all his theorizing on revolution, Guevara chose badly in establishing this *foco*. Yes, Bolivia featured great poverty; yes, the country suffered from adverse economic conditions—its tin exports, the main cash source, were greatly affected by falling global prices; yes, the high Andes seemed a secondary issue to Washington. But all that failed to translate into readiness for revolution. Three major weaknesses crippled Guevara's effort. First, in planting his guerrilla band in the countryside, Che never forged links with dissidents in La Paz and other cities. Second, in the jungle Che cut himself off from the restive tin miners. Finally, in Che's countryside the peasantry proved sparse and, worse, afraid to commit to revolutionary activity. Che's Bolivian diaries repeatedly note peasants as terrified or terrorized; few of them joined. Tactical errors abounded too—Che knew much less about the wilderness where he operated than demanded in his own theories for revolution. He remained far too optimistic, and when *compañeros* made these points or wished to leave, Che would not have it.

The latent weaknesses did not prevent Che Guevara from enjoying a period of success. General Barrientos remained ignorant of the threat. Vague rumors floated into La Paz of partisans in the jungle. The CIA station under John Tilton perked up, among the first to believe the tales of Cubans, and then of Che, but beyond Broe at WH Division it seemed hard to convince anyone at Langley.

Through the first half of 1967 Guevara's small band (only about sixty men) feared hunger more than Bolivian troops, and their attacks succeeded. Toward the end of March they ambushed a Bolivian patrol and inflicted severe casualties. Then La Paz began to pay attention. Barrientos called in Ambassador Henderson and handed him a request for U.S. supplies. On April 28 the Bolivian military signed an agreement with the U.S. mission in La Paz to permit a Special Forces mobile training team to instruct the Bolivian Second Ranger Battalion. In early July Che captured a village and its army garrison, a high point in his campaign.

The key intelligence breakthroughs came in mid-March when two Bolivians deserted Che's band, giving the army details on the Guevara unit, and on April 20 when security services picked up French journalist Regis Debray and an American photographer named George Roth. This incident rose to the level of a Bolivian military triumph when reported to LBJ in his President's Daily Brief: "Troops have scored their first victories against the guerrillas. Twice last week army patrols hit guerrilla bands, inflicting casualties and taking prisoners." The prisoners were Debray and Roth. In a way the reported success was real, for under hostile interrogation both men gave up more data. CIA officers intervened with the Bolivians to moderate the treatment of Debray. A mysterious woman, Tania, variously reported as an East German, Russian, or Cuban agent, or a revolutionary groupie, had originally conveyed Debray to Che and stayed on with Guevara's band. Debray, a French Communist and revolutionary theoretician in his own right, later wrote at length about Che in Bolivia, and something of a cottage industry has developed around the question of who betrayed Guevara. In the mythologies that surround these events, Debray, Debray's Bolivian lawyer, Tania, La Paz Communist cells, Castro, Cuban agents, and Bolivian deserters have all been charged with the crucial betrayal, similar to theories of the Kennedy assassination.

Meanwhile the Washington merry-go-round continued. On May 11 Walt Rostow told LBJ—likely based on Debray's interrogations—that Che could really be in Bolivia and not dead, "as the intelligence community, with the passage of time, has been more and more inclined to believe." On May 25 CIA cables added that Castro could open a new front where the borders of Bolivia, Peru, and Brazil met. Days later Rostow pitched his note to Johnson as if Che *had been* in Bolivia but had left. The CIA report on June 14 stated, "Ernesto 'Che' Guevara [deleted] is personally directing Bolivian guerrilla activities and has been physically present with the guerrillas." But a DIA report stated that Guevara had recently been executed in Cuba. As of mid-July the La Paz embassy itself remained uncertain, making the reluctance at senior levels of the Central Intelligence Agency more understandable.

The mystery solved itself over the summer. Victor Marchetti, a special assistant to Richard Helms, records that his chief was another who did not credit the Guevara-Bolivia thesis. Despite Helms's and FitzGerald's doubts, Bill Broe ordered some Special Operations Division people sent to La Paz. As a result, in June the division set up an unusual unit within Tilton's station to concentrate on Guevara. Tilton, who had been a case officer in two Latin countries, realized the need to genuflect to Bolivian attitudes about arrogant Americans, and all three members would be Cuban contract agents, exile veterans of the Bay of Pigs. Not long afterward, reacting to Che's village raid, Bolivian army troops discovered Guevara's base camp. There they found photos of Che in his Bolivian disguise. When examined closely, several features resembled Guevara, and a couple of smudged fingerprints clinched the case. Captured documents identified others as Cubans too, including some thought to have been with Che in Africa.

Suddenly the equation changed, not in La Paz but in Washington. At his northern Virginia vacation home in The Plains that July, Des FitzGerald collapsed playing tennis one afternoon and died. Tom Karamessines succeeded to leadership of the DO. It fell to Karamessines to take the news to Helms. Although Helms still refused to believe, he could no longer simply dismiss the evidence on Che, and he authorized a stronger CIA effort.

In early August Felix Rodriguez and Gustavo Villoldo arrived in La Paz and began their special mission, joined by a third Cuban agent. They met with Interior Minister Antonio Arguedas, who gave them cover identities as captains in his ministry. At the end of the month came a true Bolivian victory: a mountain battle where Guevara's band was caught and lost a third of its force, including Tania, with a key Cuban lieutenant captured. Rodriguez and a Bolivian officer questioned Che's aide.

Meanwhile U.S. Special Forces completed training the Bolivian Second Rangers, which took the field in mid-September. After about ten days they caught Che's band near the village of La Higuera. The CIA's Felix Rodriguez joined the Rangers to provide tactical advice. Operations continued near the village until October 8, when the Rangers caught up to the guerrilla band one more time. There Capt. Gary Prado Salmon's company captured Che Guevara. The guerrilla commander, wounded in the leg, could not flee.

With the notorious Che in custody, the immediate issue for the CIA became obtaining intelligence from the *fidelista*. Here the agency's interests clashed with the Bolivian desire to see Guevara dead. During the long pursuit both Ambassador Henderson and station chief Tilton tried to convince Barrientos that if Che were captured he should be brought to La Paz for interrogation. Barrientos demurred, afraid of the unrest that could accompany Che's arrival, captive or not. When the moment came, Tilton was on leave and Henderson knew nothing.

Felix Rodriguez and the Bolivian field commander took a helicopter from their tactical headquarters to La Higuera. Afraid he could not convince the Bolivians to spare Guevara, Rodriguez left a message for retransmission to Langley through the station in Paraguay. He thought that an embassy official sent to the scene might have better luck. Langley got word too late. Rodriguez photographed Che's papers, including his Bolivian diary, and talked to the Argentinian revolutionary. Che proved quite willing to discuss revolution but refused to answer questions about his mission. Then came a call on the field telephone. The Bolivian officers were away. Rodriguez answered in his cover identity as a captain of the Interior Ministry. He heard the code numbers that ordered Guevara's execution. Rodriguez passed the order along. Sgt. Jaime Teran did the deed. Later the Bolivians moved the body to a hospital at Vallegrande, where CIA contract officer Gustavo Villoldo got in the act. Villoldo appeared in pictures beside Che's body and gave journalists the impression he supervised the activity. That became the first public knowledge the CIA had had anything to do with Che Guevara's death. In a macabre touch the Bolivians cut off Guevara's head and hands and disposed of the body. Photographs of the dead Che proved an embarrassing *faux pas*.

Washington experienced a few days of confusion while the particulars were tied down and Guevara identified. Walt Rostow, at a meeting where the initial cable appeared, snapped his pencil in half and beamed. His memos to LBJ over the next days exhibited increasing confidence, until on October 11 he presented the event as discouraging potential guerrillas. Rostow exulted: "It marks the passing of another of the aggressive, romantic revolutionaries like Sukarno, Nkrumah, Ben Bella—and reinforces this trend."

Che's Bolivian diary soon acquired a life of its own. Before his death the 303 Committee actually discussed the handling of documents expected to be captured and agreed on a cover story—that the Bolivians had asked the United States to analyze these materials. It is a fair inference that the Special Group later specifically considered what to do with the diary, though evidence that might establish this remains classified. In any case, various versions of the diary appeared during the summer of 1968, including one released by Castro. How Havana might have acquired a copy of Guevara's Bolivia diary became a mystery unraveled by Antonio Arguedas, the interior minister. Arguedas suddenly disappeared—he had gone to Chile and asked for asylum, but instead the Chileans handed him over to the CIA station in Santiago. Langley sent Nick Lenderis, his original recruiter, to talk some sense into the man. The CIA then followed and accommodated Arguedas as he traveled to London, New York, and Lima, Peru. The Bolivian gave a series of press conferences in which he not only revealed giving the diary to Castro but that he himself had been a CIA agent, charging the agency with interfering in the internal affairs of his country. Arguedas finally returned to La Paz to stand trial, survived an assassination attempt, fled to Mexico, and turned up in Havana in 1970, bearing Che's death mask and embalmed hands. Not long afterward John Tilton, the former station chief, was sent to Vietnam as the last director of the notorious Phoenix program.

The meaning of the long struggle against Castro for America's Wilsonian ideals of self-determination and democracy is debatable. No one elected Fidel Castro, true enough. And the professed goal of the Cuba project had been to get rid of him, after which Cubans themselves could decide who their leaders would be. The agency supported Cuban exiles who wanted that. But the CIA had also supported Fulgencio Batista, and no one had elected him either, except in trumped-up plebiscites intended to consolidate his control. Nor were Joseph Mobutu or René Barrientos elected to the posts they held. Democratic values did not run deeply among those whom Washington backed in its secret wars. What remained true would be that Washington warned against socialist ideals. A truly democratic policy cannot exclude any political belief, and in this sense the secret war fell far wide of the Wilsonian vision. As for Cold War issues, it was never true that all those enemies marched to the tune of Moscow drummers. It would be more accurate to say that Washington chose sides in the countries where it intervened, then cloaked those conflicts in the trappings of ideological warfare, justifying its interventions in the name of democracy. These were purposeful choices, not accidental ones.

The secret war against Castro shows the warriors at full stride—created under Truman, enhanced by Eisenhower, built up by Kennedy, enthused by the potential of counterinsurgency strategy. By the 1960s both capabilities and contingencies were in place. The Congo became one front in a global competition, Cuba a second. Two such campaigns conducted simultaneously formed quite an achievement, but even more impressive is that both went on in concert with a third sustained effort in Vietnam as well as other CIA operations. The secret warriors had truly achieved a global reach.

15

War in Southeast Asia

ALTHOUGH NOT CUT from the same cloth as Maxwell Taylor, Ed Lansdale also considered himself something of a theorist. Managing Operation Mongoose and backstopping covert action at the Pentagon took Lansdale away from his primary interest, counterinsurgency (CI). For a decade after his work in the Philippines, Lansdale continued to advocate psychological warfare and other CI techniques. He expounded what he called the "demotic" strategy, an approach especially aimed at the popular will, its goal the same as "winning hearts and minds."

Lansdale occasionally got the chance to articulate his vision. In 1959, after Eisenhower ordered air force C-130s to fly construction equipment to certain upland villages in Laos, Lansdale toured, adding the Philippines and Vietnam to his itinerary, then wrote a long report on the potential of "civic action." A skilled harmonica player, he believed in the armed patrol with a guitarist, helping build village dispensaries and schools, giving medical help to villagers, and employing other tactics designed to win popular sympathy. Lansdale argued his case strongly, and he had extra credibility as architect of the successful Huk campaign for which he had won the National Security Medal.

General Lansdale also happened to be the American behind the ascendancy of South Vietnamese President Ngo Dinh Diem. Despite his fervor, Lansdale's remained a controversial strategy until the advent of Jack Kennedy. Even within CIA, where political action had become a credo, many preferred direct measures. At the beginning of 1961, a few weeks before Kennedy's inauguration, Lansdale went to Saigon for a fresh assessment. He found the Diem government losing its dynamism in the countryside while guerrilla warfare spread and the army floundered. Diem had barely survived a coup two months earlier. The U.S. military advisory group, with which Lansdale had once served, remained too hampered by restrictions to have much impact.

Lansdale spent a little over two weeks in Vietnam. He spoke with Diem and other Vietnamese as well as embassy people. Compiling his report on the plane to Washington, Lansdale submitted it on January 17. In Saigon he had found American and Vietnamese officials who talked like the French and Vietnamese in Hanoi in 1953–1954. He saw Vietnam as under "intense psychological attack"; 1961 would be a fateful year, and "Vietnam is in a critical condition and [we] should treat it as a combat area of the cold war, as an area requiring emergency treatment."

Lansdale's report presented his vision of an operation "changed sufficiently to free these Americans to do the job that needs doing." His answer was to select "the best people you have"—in Lansdale's opinion, "a hard core of experienced Americans who know and really like Asia and the Asians"—and give them a free hand. A new ambassador should be sent immediately as well as "a mature American" to conduct "political operations to start creating a Vietnamese-style foundation for more democratic government."

This report created a stir in Washington. Walt Rostow showed it to President Kennedy days after he entered office. Busy, Kennedy didn't want to read it. Rostow told him he should. Kennedy looked up when he had finished.

"This is the worst one we've got, isn't it?" asked JFK curiously. "You know, Eisenhower never mentioned it. He talked at length about Laos, but never uttered the word Vietnam."

The secretary of defense wanted to hear from the author himself. Robert McNamara asked Lansdale around. "Somehow I found him very hard to talk to," recalled Lansdale later. "Watching his face as I talked, I got the feeling that he didn't understand me."

Several attempts to assign Lansdale to Vietnam were blocked until 1965 when Ambassador Henry Cabot Lodge overrode all opposition. In the meantime Ed Lansdale retired after Mongoose. In Vietnam, psychological warfare would be strictly an adjunct to conventional force.

President Kennedy formed a committee to canvass Vietnam alternatives. Given the Pentagon's status as the biggest player, McNamara deputy Roswell Gilpatric chaired the group. The Gilpatric committee faced a difficult task: many of its members had entered with the new administration and were just finding their balance. Gilpatric's own recollection is that "none of us . . . who were charged with the responsibility for this area, had any preparation for this problem. What we didn't comprehend was the inability of the Vietnamese to absorb our doctrine, to think and to organize the way we did." Still, the Gilpatric group came to President Kennedy on May 6, 1961, with a list more than forty items long.

Kennedy's decisions set a course for the American experience in Vietnam. Between doing nothing or committing U.S. forces, JFK chose graduated expansion of effort, beginning a cycle repeated many times. On May 11 Kennedy approved some of the Gilpatric recommendations. The United States expanded its advisory group and paid to increase South Vietnamese forces. Of particular importance for the secret warriors, the program included deployment to Vietnam of a provisional Special Forces group of Green Berets plus a mandate to "expand present operations in the field of intelligence, unconventional warfare, and political-psychological activities."

Kennedy also searched for a strategic concept he could use in this growing conflict. Counterinsurgency theory suggested population resettlement, leading to "strategic hamlets" and many subsequent variants. Geography suggested sealing off South Vietnamese borders, preventing infiltration from the North or through Laos. The border-control approach, touted as early as May 1961 by Robert Komer, a CIA analyst on duty with the NSC staff, became a pillar of the U.S. concept. With its twin, pacification, it provided the foundatiom for U.S. strategy throughout the Vietnam War. North Vietnam countered with the Ho Chi Minh Trail, begun in 1959, which moved cadres to the battlefields of the South. Supplies traveled down the trail and went by sea as well.

In November 1961 Kennedy faced a recommendation for a commitment of regular U.S. troops, this time from Maxwell Taylor and Walt Rostow, just returned from a survey trip on Kennedy's behalf. General Taylor tried to prevent Ed Lansdale from participating, but McNamara insisted he go to perform a special assignment—helping the Bissell study of resources for unconventional warfare. The Taylor-Rostow report included options for a "radical" increase in the numbers of Green Berets, and "increased covert offensive operations in the North as well as in Laos and South Vietnam." President Kennedy rejected the troop request while approving almost everything else, including covert action.

Indeed more secret warriors were reaching South Vietnam. The same day he sent Taylor and Rostow to Saigon, JFK ordered out the 4400th Combat Crew Training Squadron, the special air warfare "Jungle Jim" unit, operational on November 16, 1961. It flew missions under the code name Farm Gate. The deployment figured in a wider expansion. America's assistance group grew from fewer than 700 when JFK entered the White House to more than 12,000 by mid-1962. There were U.S. supply units to support the Vietnamese, U.S. helicopter units to fly them to battle, the Special Forces, plus navy, air force, and Marine Corps detachments. Farm Gate retained its clandestine status while semi-clandestine air force units followed: Mule Team to fly short-range air transport, Ranch Hand (at first called Hades) which dumped toxic chemicals to defoliate the countryside, and more. The Vietnam contingent could hardly be called a "group" anymore; it became the Military Assistance Command Vietnam (MACV), continuing to grow to about 22,000 by 1964.

Despite this plentiful support, conditions in South Vietnam deteriorated. The Vietnamese never seemed to catch the elusive National Liberation Front (NLF) rebels. It was evident by 1963 that Diem had lost most of his remaining political support, in particular when his brother, Ngo Dinh Nhu, began using force to quell demonstrations by Buddhists, the majority religious movement. South Vietnamese army officers felt the crisis made it impossible to prosecute the war. In Saigon, talk of a coup filled the air.

Those early days in Vietnam, much like Korea in years past, were an adventure for Americans. In the beginning it had been Ed Lansdale who established the close

U.S. relationship with Vietnamese authorities. When he left at the end of 1956 the liaison role remained a major activity of the CIA station at Saigon. Later that role grew. The CIA wanted its own sources among South Vietnamese politicians. By 1960 the agency had the best information outside the presidential palace, save perhaps for the NLF intelligence networks. Indeed, in a 1960 coup attempt, CIA officers were in contact with both sides throughout. This caused some difficulty for station chief William E. Colby when Diem's brother Nhu found out. Threatened with arrest or worse, CIA officer George Carver had to be spirited out of Saigon. A second officer, Ed Regan, was pulled out temporarily until the Vietnamese cooled off.

Another task on the CIA's list was to infiltrate North Vietnam using Vietnamese special forces (formed in 1958) or paramilitary teams recruited by the CIA. Allen Dulles briefed Kennedy on the initiative early in 1961, and the president ordered intensification of the effort. Bill Colby created Project Tiger for this mission. The agency quickly gave up on Saigon special forces—they ran operations only inside South Vietnam. Instead the CIA recruited its own Vietnamese commandos. Colby, with his experience on Soviet programs and with the OSS in France and Norway, ought to have been the first to question feasibility here, but he forged ahead. North Vietnam had excellent security services. Colby tried to send agents, both singleton spies and teams, by sea and air. Ed Regan and Russ Miller trained the commandos assiduously. Navy detailees to the CIA prepared the boat crews. The South Vietnamese air force manned CIA planes for airdrops. But Hanoi swept up every team and even mounted a show trial late in 1961 of a Saigon aircrew captured when their plane crashed on a resupply flight. More than 200 commandos were lost in Project Tiger. McGeorge Bundy warned Kennedy in 1963 that the missions involved most of the dangers common to those in denied areas. But the U.S. military took over and continued five more years, losing 450 more South Vietnamese to no effect. Hanoi had penetrated the program from the beginning.

Col. Gilbert Layton of the army ran the Combined Services Division of Colby's CIA station, controlling Project Tiger and other paramilitary efforts. "Chink" Layton, originally detailed to the CIA, had joined the agency in 1950 and participated in many of the projects of that era. Like Colby, he had set up "stay-behind" networks (in Germany). He had been an instructor on Saipan, had an earlier tour in Saigon and one in Turkey, and had been liaison between the army and the CIA's Tibetan training center at Camp Hale. The fifty-year-old Layton knew a losing proposition when he saw one but proved unable to change the luck of Project Tiger.

Chink Layton, Colby, and other CIA officers had far greater success with a paramilitary effort in South Vietnam's Central Highlands, organizing armed forces among the tribal minorities. For self-defense, an upland counterpart of "strategic hamlets," then for border control, the tribal units became the basis for a striking force. Called the Village Defense Program by the CIA, and Civilian Irregular Defense Groups (CIDGs) by the military, the units had fortified base camps and Green Beret leadership. Until November 1962 the CIDG program was entirely a CIA project; thereafter operational command shifted to MACV, though the agency continued to foot the bill. All responsibility went to the military in a 1963 phase-out of CIA activity known as Operation Switchback. By the time Colonel Layton transferred to Thailand in 1965 the CIDGs were well established. They comprised eighty base camps.

By then, Colby had left too. At Langley he succeeded Desmond FitzGerald as chief of the DO's Far East Division. John H. Richardson followed Colby in Saigon. From the army's Counter Intelligence Corps, Richardson had been an authentic espionage hero in 1944–1945, instrumental in capturing a notorious German spy in Italy. "Jocko" Richardson stayed at CIC after the war, switched to the Central Intelligence Group, then CIA. It was Richardson who, in the denouement of the Albanian project, had shut down the operating bases. He had worked Vienna and Trieste, and moved to Saigon from Manila. Colby introduced Richardson to Ngo Dinh Nhu, now head of Diem's intelligence services. A gregarious man who had been a classmate of Richard Nixon's at Whittier College, Jocko, like Chink Layton, spoke four or five languages, including French, indispensable in Saigon. Richardson got on quite well with Nhu, but he was ham-handed—typically, Jocko moved into a house that had been the headquarters for torturers of the French (and then Saigonese) *Surété* and was thought to be haunted, then wondered why Vietnamese would not visit him there.

With a style not unlike John McCone, who let subordinates carve out empires as long as they did not cross the boss, Richardson waded into the morass. The Saigon station was no longer the homogeneous unit of forty that Bill Colby had squired. The paramilitary crowd made up one circle, the espionage crew another. Since 1961 there had also been a communications intelligence circle while the demands of war swelled the station with a growing cadre of analysts. Then there were the political action people. One of the agency's political specialists played a key role in the demise of Ngo Dinh Diem. Lucien Conein, his cover as a lieutenant colonel assigned to the Vietnamese Interior Ministry, but whose real function involved contact with the Vietnamese generals, had also been a member of Lansdale's 1954–1956 mission.

The biggest empire within the CIA station was Richardson's own. His problem lay not with the Saigonese but with U.S. authorities. Convinced that Diem's time had run out, Washington tried desperately to get him to broaden his government. The assistant secretary of state for Far Eastern affairs, Roger Hilsman, evidently with preliminary authorization but while President Kennedy was out of town, drafted a cable backing a coup suggested by Vietnamese generals. Nhu's special forces had just made bloody, widely condemned attacks on Buddhist pagodas. That became the last straw. A cable on August 26, 1963, instructed Conein and CIA officer Alphonse G. Spero to tell the generals the United States would not oppose a coup if it had good chances of success. Richardson reported the maneuver through CIA channels.

McCone went on to oppose the coup initiative, soon joined by Taylor, McNamara, and Vice President Lyndon Johnson. Washington scuttled the Hilsman cable. McCone, Colby, and others spiked the initiative, but Kennedy still insisted Nhu must go. If Diem would not fire his brother, the United States would look for alternatives.

But Ambassador Henry Cabot Lodge felt that John Richardson had undermined him. The ambassador insisted on transferring the station chief. He specifically wanted Ed Lansdale to replace Jocko. Then Nhu too sold out the CIA boss, having a newspaper identify the station chief in print. Abruptly recalled on October 5, Richardson was done. For a time the Vietnamese generals backed down, but two days before Richardson's hurried recall they told Conein of new coup plans. That coup took place on November 1, 1963. The CIA put up $40,000 for expenses, which Conein carried in a briefcase. Diem and Nhu died in custody of the plotters the next day. Thanks to Conein, the CIA had had a front-row seat to the coup planning if not its precise timing, of which the embassy received just minutes' warning. Assassination seemed epidemic in November 1963. Three weeks later President Kennedy fell to the sniper's rifle in Dallas.

Asked almost two decades later for his opinion of U.S. support for the Diem coup, Edward Lansdale replied, "I think we should never have done it. We destroyed the Vietnamese Constitution, not we, but the people we were working with, threw it in the waste basket." Indeed, CIA support flew in the face of America's commitment to democracy and left the United States embroiled in a war that it remained ill suited for, could not win, and could not walk away from. Washington's search for military effectiveness stood revealed as deeper than its support for democracy. Those who argue that Jack Kennedy would have withdrawn from Vietnam have never been able to get past the consequences of the Diem coup, which President Kennedy, after all, supported. The maneuver eliminated all possible flexibility in U.S. policy. As for the suggestion that the CIA ought to be excused on the basis of its opposition to the coup, this is based on the secret record of its (excessive) policy role rather than the discoverable one of its agents on the street in Saigon. As a practical matter, public and world opinion would be dictated by the discoverable record, not the secret one.

Several more coups occurred before 1967, when Gen. Nguyen Van Thieu and Air Marshal Nguyen Cao Ky consolidated control in Saigon. Langley's political action people made numerous efforts to deepen political support for the regime. Washington repeatedly encouraged Thieu and Ky, as it had Diem, to broaden their base and construct a democracy, but the South Vietnamese institutions created in 1966–1967 never blossomed, and the Saigon regime's failure never resulted in sanctions from Washington. That too says something about the U.S. commitment to democracy.

Soon after the Diem coup, Bill Colby arrived in Saigon to pick up the pieces. He had John Richardson to dinner the night before leaving Washington. His priority was to replace the station chief. Colby called on Peer de Silva, recently dispatched to Hong Kong after a long tour as CIA chief in Korea, where he too had seen a coup up close. De Silva had a strong background in espionage against denied areas, and had run security for the atomic bomb project. He and Colby had over-lapped for part of a year at Columbia University. Director McCone approved de Silva's appointment about the time Kennedy died, then made the suggestion to in-coming President Lyndon Johnson and recalled de Silva to Washington. He took de Silva to meet the president. LBJ wanted only the best for Saigon. De Silva be-came the first of a succession of CIA chieftains drawn from top agency ranks.

In consonance with John Kennedy's decisions after the Bay of Pigs, the CIA had been ordered to get out of the paramilitary business. That became the origin of Operation Switchback, which turned over the agency's montagnard CIDGs to the military command in Vietnam. But the prohibition lasted less than a year. A direc-tive already in draft form when LBJ became president provided for unilateral U.S. pressures against North Vietnam, a program of covert military action called OPLAN 34-A. Langley's Far East baron Bill Colby went to Honolulu within weeks of Diem's downfall to discuss this with U.S. military commanders. Colby now op-posed missions of the sort he had carried out in Project Tiger, but the CIA view would be overridden. President Johnson approved OPLAN 34-A. The CIA boat base at Da Nang, handed over to the military under Switchback early in 1964, would be expanded to support 34-A. Quite soon the military's Studies and Observation Group (SOG), with orders for commando attacks along the North Vietnamese coast as part of 34-A, added its own version of the infiltration program. The CIA supplied intelligence and specialized support to these activities as long as they continued.

The 34-A operations led to the next major escalation of the U.S. war in Vietnam. On the last night of July 1964 occurred a raid by fast, heavily armed Swift boats, attacking North Vietnamese facilities on the islands of Hon Me and Hon Ngu in the Gulf of Tonkin. The Hon Me raid coincided with another U.S. intelligence ac-tivity, a "De Soto" patrol into the Gulf. De Soto patrols were U.S. Navy collection efforts for communications intercepts. Ships on these operations carried enhanced radio equipment. De Soto patrols had been pursued off the coasts of China, the So-viet Union, and North Korea. President Kennedy had approved a similar program for North Vietnam in 1962, when the first patrol was conducted. A second De Soto mission took place in 1963, and the destroyer *Craig* made an intercept cruise in the Gulf in March 1964. In any case, the destroyer *Maddox* was on a De Soto pa-trol when Swift boats passed her, the 34-A raiders returning to base. That evening the *Maddox* steamed past the recently shelled islands.

The North Vietnamese sent out torpedo boats which attacked the *Maddox* in international waters the next afternoon. They were driven off with one sunk and the others damaged. President Johnson then deliberately ordered the *Maddox* back into the Gulf of Tonkin, accompanied by another destroyer, the *C. Turner Joy.* Two nights later the two destroyers mistook instrument readings for another attack. President Johnson retaliated with carrier air strikes on North Vietnam. He then went to Congress for a resolution supporting his action, and on August 7, 1964, the legislature approved the Gulf of Tonkin Resolution. President Johnson then relied on the resolution in place of a declaration of war.

McGeorge Bundy's immediate problem became what to do with De Soto. As a reconnaissance project De Soto patrols were approved by the Special Group, which Bundy chaired. Because of LBJ's extreme sensitivity to Vietnam developments, the president took up this question directly. Both De Soto and 34-A operations halted while Johnson considered policy. The Joint Chiefs argued for action, bombing North Vietnam and relaxing restrictions on American forces. Maxwell Taylor, ambassador to South Vietnam since July, favored waiting to see if the Vietnamese political situation stabilized. Like Kennedy before him, Johnson selected less than the maximum option: resume De Soto patrols and 34-A; reinforce Farm Gate with heavier jet bombers. Thus operations like De Soto and 34-A, which were provocative, were approved not on their merits but as alternatives to greater provocation.

Meanwhile on the ground the CIA recovered its earlier momentum. In search of some means to counter the National Liberation Front in the villages, several agency officers innovated armed bands of villagers who within months accounted for the killing of hundreds of guerrillas. De Silva's deputy, Gordon Jorgensen, soon called the units People's Action Teams. A variant of the same idea took root in the Mekong Delta, sparked by Stewart Methven, reassigned from Laos. The paramilitary specialist "Rip" Robertson presently materialized in Vietnam to work in these programs. In the Central Highlands the CIDG effort continued to expand. In June 1964 Mac Bundy asked Director McCone to turn back the clock to before Switchback, to have the CIA reenter Vietnam, as it were. In March 1965 McCone presented a consolidated program of a dozen projects the CIA proposed to conduct. The agency essentially defined the role it assumed throughout the Vietnam War.

The secret war on the western flank of South Vietnam, among the rugged mountains and high plains of Laos, represented a complementary effort to isolate the battlefield in the South. Paramilitary action and political manipulation in Laos attained heights never before achieved. In previous efforts the CIA had always been hampered in one way or another: actions were impeded by U.S. reluctance to show its hand, as with Cuba or in Albania; or by lack of truly popular indigenous groups, as in Indonesia or the People's Republic of China; or by the absence of suitable support bases, as in Tibet. In South Vietnam the Pentagon had a better claim to command.

Laos was different. There was no difficulty in defining the mission for the secret warriors—insurgency was increasing in South Vietnam, and the North used Laos to move to the battle area. Thus Laos became the front line in the struggle. Bases were plentiful both there and in neighboring Thailand, another American ally. At the same time the American military was excluded from Laos by the 1954 Geneva Accords on Indochina, which allowed only the French to advise the Royal

Laotian Government (RLG). In Laos the CIA had the field all to itself, with the military supporting its actions, rather than the other way around.

After the 1954 agreement, Laos had had a chance for independence with stability. A little country with a small political elite, leaders of all persuasions were well known to one another, many related. Prime examples were two princes of the royal blood, Souphanouvong, a leader of the Communist movement, and his half-brother Souvanna Phouma, a proponent of neutralism. The French had residual influence in Laos while the American presence, established after Geneva, grew slowly through the 1950s.

The Eisenhower administration had no mind to accept a neutralist solution. Much as he did with Sukarno, Nehru, and Nasser, Ike insisted that Laos side with the West in the Cold War and spent two years discouraging formation of a coalition government. American aid began in 1955. By 1960 the United States had provided Laos more than $250 million, two-thirds of it to pay the entire cost of maintaining RLG armed forces.

The CIA station played a critical role in political action. Showing their predilection for "third force" options, the secret warriors backed a pro-American Committee for the Defense of National Interests (CDNI), formed after a 1958 electoral upset in which Souphanouvong's party gained the majority of the seats contested while the prince himself was elected by the largest margin in every district of the country. The young people who formed CDNI were called *les jeunes*. In the Laotian political capital, Vientiane, many of them represented the Junior Chamber of Commerce, and they were reformist but conservative, anti-Communist, and had the rare advantage of crossing clan and party lines. It quickly became an open secret that American special services supported CDNI. The 1958 elections were supposed to complete reintegrating the nation, which was under military control by different factions, just like warlord China. The socialist Lao People's Front (*Neo Lao Hak Xat*, or NLHX) and especially its parent, the Laotian Communists, or Pathet Lao, dominated in two provinces. In November 1958 Prince Souphanouvong accepted the king's authority, and Pathet Lao troops in these provinces joined the Royal Lao Armed Forces (RLAF) while the NLHX was to be represented in a neutralist coalition under Souvanna Phouma. But the accord disintegrated when the Souvanna cabinet fell in July 1958.

Suddenly *les jeunes* took center stage, gaining seats in a cabinet formed in August even though some ministers had lost their elections. Pathet Lao ministers were dismissed. Trouble quickly followed within the RLAF as the Pathet Lao troops revolted, rekindling the Laotian civil war. The Eisenhower administration increased aid when fighting resumed, and increased it again as conflict deepened. The CIA station, the American conduit to CDNI, grew especially important in the U.S. embassy.

All was not well there. The ambassador favored Souvanna's neutralist solution and considered his policy had been sabotaged by the CIA. Station chief Henry Heckscher refused to tell his boss about some agency activities. Ambassador Horace Smith took his grievance to Allen Dulles early in 1959, demanding Heckscher's transfer. The DCI knew of Heckscher's arrogance but also his resourcefulness. Dulles backed the station chief and at the end of his tour even assigned Heckscher to northeast Thailand, where he mounted cross-border operations into Laos. Taking that into consideration, Heckscher outlasted his ambassador, for Smith was replaced in the summer of 1960 by Winthrop G. Brown, a former Wall Street lawyer and ambassador to New Delhi.

Only three weeks after Brown's arrival, the pro-U.S. government was overthrown by the paratroops of Captain Kong Le. A veteran of the French campaign for Dien Bien Phu, Kong Le remained inscrutable to most Americans, who disbelieved neutralist declarations and harbored the theory that he must be a Communist or "fellow traveler." American perceptions aside, Kong Le became the strongman and asked Souvanna Phouma to form a new cabinet. Winthrop Brown counseled Washington to cooperate with Souvanna, the most pro-Western leader sustainable in Laos. Brown believed that CIA station chief Gordon L. Jorgensen agreed.

In fact the Eisenhower administration was pursuing its own game in Laos, with the CIA at the center of it and Jorgensen squarely on board. Eisenhower sent in a covert military advisory group euphemistically called the Program Evaluation Office. Beginning in the summer of 1959 Ike added more than a hundred Special Forces men under the code name "White Star." Grayston Lynch, the CIA boat man, first connected with the agency while in Laos with this unit. White Star worked with the RLAF whose strongman, Gen. Phoumi Nosavan, one of the *jeunes*, denounced neutralism and launched a coup that toppled Souvanna. The CIA had a case officer with Phoumi, John Hasey, who lived next door and shared his aspirations. At the same time Campbell James worked directly with Souvanna.

Not merely playing both sides of this street, the agency took steps to recruit the Hmong tribe in the Annamite mountains. Stewart Methven, who had arrived from Japan in the summer of 1959, met Hmong military commander Vang Pao at the hut of Filipino medical staff. Over a series of visits Methven convinced the Hmong leader to ally with the CIA. This became Project Momentum.

On the surface Washington supported Vientiane, but secretly it backed Phoumi and recruited a Hmong secret army—actually called that, the "*armée clandestine*." Desmond FitzGerald dropped in to survey the scene. Toward the end of 1960, John N. Irwin, representing the Pentagon on the 5412 Group, visited southern Laos and talked with Phoumi. A second Irwin trip occurred before Kennedy took office. The Americans began channeling aid to Phoumi, bypassing the Vientiane government. The CIA induced Phoumi to pass supplies to the Hmong, who swore allegiance to the general. Reports of a North Vietnamese invasion of Laos following a trumped-up border incident were used to justify further aid increases.

Fleeing Vientiane after Phoumi's coup, Souvanna Phouma and Kong Le made an alliance with the Pathet Lao. A little over two weeks later, on December 4, 1960, the Soviet Union began to airlift military supplies to the Kong Le–Pathet Lao forces, and the Pathet Lao started an offensive of their own. Political intrigue had turned Laos, the Land of a Million Elephants, into a Cold War battleground.

The effect of U.S. actions would be to undercut the delicate political balance in the country, hardly conducive to democracy. Souvanna Phouma said of a senior U.S. official, and by extension of American policy, that he "understood nothing about Asia and nothing about Laos."

President Eisenhower's decisions clearly indicate his concept of Laos as a secret war. Aside from White Star and the Hmong, he approved the movement of B-26 bombers to Thailand, not immediately used in Laos because of the need to assemble non-American crews. Ten lighter T-6 strike aircraft were also approved, initially without bombs, to be flown by Laotian pilots. The aircraft were provided by the Thais, then replaced by the United States. By January 4, 1961, Air America had plans to have mechanics in Vientiane service the Laotian air fleet. Air America also flew White Star troopers around Laos, and enabled CIA officers to shuttle between Phoumi and the Hmong. Fifteen Air America craft at Bangkok were flying one thousand tons of supplies a month into Laos. Ike ordered a naval task force bearing Marines into position for intervention in Laos and placed them on a high state of alert.

Laos figured among the main topics at Ike's transition discussions with Kennedy. Eisenhower warned Khrushchev that the United States intended to ensure that the "legitimate government" of Laos stayed in power. At a morning meeting on Laos on December 31, 1960, Ike joked that perhaps the time had come to use existing plans for airborne alert of the Strategic Air Command. In parting he told the group, which included Allen Dulles and Gordon Gray, "We must not allow Laos to fall to the Communists, even if it involves war."

President Kennedy thought Laos no place for major conflict. In office he used coercive diplomacy, threatening with U.S. force and briefly converting the Program Evaluation Office into an open advisory group, but he aimed for international accord. With the help of Averell Harriman, Roger Hilsman, and Dean Rusk, Kennedy achieved his aim. When Phoumi Nosavan stood in the way, his American assistance evaporated and his CIA link, Jack Hasey, disappeared, sent to the Congo despite opposition from Desmond FitzGerald and Bill Colby. Kennedy's Special Group made that decision themselves on February 5, 1962.

It was Harriman who engineered the cutoff of Phoumi. A loyal Democrat and senior statesman, Harriman carried weight with Jack Kennedy, and he tried for a credible Laotian neutralization agreement. Harriman also knew what he wanted—when CIA officers in Vientiane briefed him on Laotian politics and claimed popular support for Phoumi, the president's irascible envoy turned off his hearing aid in the middle of the meeting.

Diplomacy led Harriman to Geneva, where an international conference reached agreement in 1962, though in the end neither side observed it. What also flowed from the accord—the installation of a coalition government in Vientiane under Prime Minister Souvanna Phouma—proved to be the one lasting achievement of the negotiation.

Washington laughed with scorn at North Vietnamese assertions that all their forces had withdrawn from Laos: only *forty* enemy soldiers passed the international commission's border checkpoints. But the United States violated the agreement too, continuing to supply and command the Hmong secret army. Two agency officers, Anthony Poshepny and Vinton Lawrence, established a CIA base at the Hmong center of Long Tieng. In the spring of 1963 the assassination of neutralist Laotian officials led to a fresh outbreak of fighting. Now the Pathet Lao attacked the neutralist forces, who eventually joined the RLAF. The war resumed. Souvanna Phouma secretly asked for U.S. help, and President Kennedy agreed. In late 1963 Kennedy designated the CIA as "executive agent" for the Laotian paramilitary effort.

The largest tribal mobilization of all, the very foundation of the CIA's secret war in Laos, was that of the Hmong, or, as they were then known, the Meo. This word is a bastardization of the Chinese name Miao used for this mountain people, but it is a pejorative. The tribes respect no borders and are found in Laos, China, and North Vietnam. Generations of French and American secret warriors knew them as Meo, a proud but friendly people who practiced slash-and-burn farming, raising poppies for opium, with villages in the mountain valleys.

It was probably inevitable that the Hmong would be dragged into the American war. Their poppies had had hidden effects on conflict in Indochina since the French war, when both sides had used opium money, though the Hmong mostly sided with the French under the leadership of Touby Lyfoung, a pro-French notable and the first of his tribe to graduate college. Touby's Hmong fought for the French, comprising the bulk of the partisan force that vainly attempted to save Dien Bien Phu. Vang Pao, a veteran of that debacle, led a French commando unit on the fruitless expedition. Where Touby Lyfoung functioned as potentate and tribal politician, Vang remained a military commander. When Stewart Methven met him in 1959, Vang held the allegiance of many (though not all) clans and could deliver on promises of recruits.

Feeling too old for another war, Touby left the main leadership role to Vang Pao. While some Hmong sided with the Pathet Lao (clan leader Fay Dang becoming a member of the Pathet Lao central committee), Touby and Vang Pao made their alliance with the CIA, not directly supporting Phoumi but waging a parallel war. Before Kennedy took office there were already 2,500 Hmong in the secret army. Within months the number had almost quadrupled. Vang drew his cadres from the half-dozen ethnic Hmong battalions in the RLAF, which merely enraged Laotian officials. Kong Le forces soon attacked. Vang Pao lost his own village, forced to retreat into the surrounding mountains. Worst of all, the Plain of Jars airfield also fell, endangering supplies. The Pathet Lao joined the Kong Le offensive and threatened the entire Hmong tribal area. The spring and summer of 1961 witnessed a Hmong mass exodus. Whole villages moved. More than 70,000 people trekked into the mountains to make new homes. Without a crop already in the ground, the Hmong were threatened with starvation in their new homes.

Several Americans were vitally important in the Hmong future. When the CIA's Methven left for South Vietnam—FitzGerald had promised him his choice of posts but reneged at the last moment—Methven handed the Hmong account over to Bill Lair, a thirty-five-year-old officer who spent much of the 1950s in Thailand as a CIA case officer to the Thai Police Aerial Recovery Unit (PARU). He too had watched the French debacle at Dien Bien Phu and thus appreciated Hmong fighting qualities. Lair ran Project Momentum for almost a decade and had the contacts with the Thai that were crucial to secure the assistance of PARU teams, the link between secret army units in the field and distant CIA managers. Known as "Cigar" in agency cable traffic, Lair ran the entire secret army with eight other CIA officers, a White Star team (soon withdrawn), and a hundred PARU Thai.

A second American organized the system that would revictual the *armée clandestine* for the next eleven years. Maj. Harry C. Aderholt, commander of the air force's small, unconventional warfare detachment on Okinawa in 1959–1960, helped the CIA on air operations in Tibet and Southeast Asia. Aderholt went to Vientiane in early 1960 to set up a light plane service from the Laotian capital to Phong Saly town, where a tiny landing strip was carved into the side of a mountain. Working with Vang Pao, "Heinie" Aderholt surveyed northern Laos for a network of similar airstrips, soon called Lima Sites, and stayed for two years to oversee their construction. Aderholt also helped the CIA find suitable aircraft such as the Pilatus Porter (Helio U-10 in U.S. service) that could use the smallest Lima Sites.

A third American, Edgar M. Buell of the U.S. Agency for International Development, became a legend in Laos. Buell initiated airdrops of rice into the mountains, indiscriminate "blind" drops at first since the whereabouts of the Hmong were unknown for several months. "Pop" Buell left his embassy desk to parachute into the mountains. He spent two months walking the forests, personally contacting Hmong villages. Those that agreed to follow Vang Pao he listed for regular rice drops, supplies of seeds and tools, medicine, and so forth.

In December 1961 the Hmong opened two new bases farther west, at Long Tieng (LS-30/98) and Sam Thong (LS-20), which became the main centers of the secret army. Long Tieng served as Vang Pao's headquarters, a major mountain commercial center with a Hmong population of forty thousand. The CIA created a base there initially staffed by Anthony Poshepny and Vint Lawrence, who remained after the 1962 Geneva agreement, told to stay out of sight. Known by its radio "handle," Sky, Long Tieng became the nerve center of the secret war.

Sam Thong became the administrative, medical, and education center. Consolidation continued through the mid-sixties. A modern hospital and the first Hmong high school were both established there. The Geneva agreement had little effect on CIA support. Air America continued regular humanitarian flights. Even before fighting resumed in the spring of 1963 the agency had directed Air America to make almost a dozen flights specifically to deliver weapons euphemized as "dirty rice." Ingeniously, the CIA met requirements for "withdrawal" of foreign troops by pulling its people back to Thailand, from which they would simply fly to their jobs in Laos with Air America shuttles each morning.

For the CIA, Project Momentum became a model of "nation-building," the political action approach fostering civic institutions in hopes that grateful clients would then cooperate with American policies. But nation-building among the Hmong, as with the montagnards in South Vietnam, brought political problems. The CIA effectively created nations within nations. Activities were possible only to the degree the central government extended autonomy to tribal peoples. Saigon triggered a montagnard political crisis in 1964–1965 precisely by reducing the autonomy accorded tribes in the Central Highlands. The CIA's relative success with Vang Pao resulted from Vientiane's being too weak to exert similar authority. From the American strategic standpoint, however, keeping the Vientiane government weak to enable the secret army flew in the face of fostering a national government that could defeat the Pathet Lao. Rather, in recognition of Hmong autonomy, Vang Pao received repeated RLAF promotions and was treated as the commander of an RLAF military region while Touby Lyfoung became a minister in the Royal Laotian Government. Despite such tokens, the lowland Lao never trusted the Hmong.

Vang Pao struck his greatest blow to date in 1963, in a raid that destroyed a Pathet Lao supply road, dynamiting a full kilometer and sending sections tumbling down a mountainside. Cable traffic suggests that Vang Pao moved without CIA approval, and ahead of any Pathet Lao attacks. It was not the first time CIA troops acted beyond the secret warriors' control, nor would it be the last.

The *armée clandestine* grew to thirty thousand troops. Vang Pao and the CIA worked out a program to increase striking power: a third of the Hmong formed Special Guerrilla Units (SGUs), partisan battalions supported by bazookas and a few heavy mortars. These became the regular forces in Vang Pao's army. They were later supplied with 75- and even 105-millimeter guns, the latter usually lifted from mountaintop to mountaintop by Air America helicopters and used to fire down into Pathet Lao posts.

Air America provided the airlift under contract to USAID. Lima Site techniques were perfected to the point that C-130s could disgorge entire palletized cargoes in quick flybys. Smaller Air America planes relayed cargo to outlying sites. Each morning Sky handed out assignments to the fleet as the planes entered Laotian airspace. Sometimes Air America hauled passengers, often fuel for the stocks at the Lima Sites or additional cargo for distribution. Sky frequently assigned as many as four or five successive missions a day to the light transports.

Secret warfare in Laos assumed the dynamic, free-wheeling style of Sky air operations. The epitome was embodied by Tony Poe, who attained legendary stature in the war. Identified by his CIA cryptonym "Pin," Poe (really Anthony Poshepny) went everywhere with a boxer's mouthguard in his pocket, always ready for a fight. Tony came from the big CIA Thailand base at Takhli to be senior adviser to Vang Pao, or Sky chief. Poe transferred up from the Cambodian border, where he had been working with anti-government rebels. An alumnus of the Camp Peary class of 1953 and a veteran of Indonesia, Saipan, and Camp Hale, Poe had an extensive paramilitary resumé. At Long Tieng he presided over intensification of the struggle. Vint Lawrence manned the base while Poe ranged out with Hmong SGUs. The Laotian operation heated up.

Status as a CIA project greatly facilitated the *armée clandestine* mobilization in Laos. Supplies were disguised in aid to Thailand and the RLAF. Money was hidden in military assistance, USAID, and CIA budgets. In fact the main obstacle proved to be funding. The expansion of the secret army after 1964 could not be accomplished without noticeable increases. Although the agency budget remained secret, the small CIA subcommittees of Congress had to approve the higher requests. To obtain that approval the CIA relied on its recognized role in counterinsurgency plus its vital contacts in Laos and Thailand. The agency also spiced up its presentation. Langley desk officer Ralph McGehee, handling Thai matters at headquarters after a tour in the field, recalls being flattered one day when division chief Colby invited him to present parts of the CIA case. Des FitzGerald approved the briefing and asked Congress to fund more than a hundred secret army units. Vang Pao actually had only a couple dozen small-size formations at the time, but at Langley, McGehee and other DO officers performed a paper reorganization, endowing the Hmong overnight with the required number of units, each of just a few men. McGehee felt remorse over the falsification, but the subcommittees approved the money. Congress as a whole never explicitly considered the Laos request. For Richard Helms, who became director of central intelligence in 1966, congressional inattention freed him to do a job. The Central Intelligence Agency settled down to fight a real war in Laos. The question remained how long it could stay secret.

By now the system had assumed its final form. The ambassador had the last word. Aware of CIA's major projects, ambassadors were then consulted on each activity that went outside embassy guidelines. He retained specific approval authority for air operations other than armed reconnaissance over the Ho Chi Minh Trail. Since Project Momentum relied upon close cooperation between the Hmong and the air force, the CIA was in the ambassador's office all the time. He became a key player in the Southeast Asia Coordinating Committee, which brought together the American ambassadors, military commanders, and intelligence chiefs in Laos, South Vietnam, and Thailand.

Ambassador Leonard Unger had the helm during the initial phase of the Laotian war. Fluent in both Thai and Lao, deeply interested in the Land of a Million Elephants, Unger successfully protected Souvanna when coup attempts were made against him. Although his successor calls Unger "a most reluctant militarist," the escalation of CIA's secret war came on his watch. William H. Sullivan followed Unger. While Sullivan had been a senior member of the U.S. negotiating team at Geneva, in Laos he became an enthusiastic field marshal of the secret war. "There wasn't a bag of rice dropped in Laos he didn't know about," said William P. Bundy of Sullivan. G. McMurtrie Godley replaced Sullivan in 1969. He actually *earned* the nickname "field marshal."

The embassy had a small air staff that maintained approved target lists, processed requests for new authorities, and coordinated among the ambassador, the CIA, and air force commanders in Thailand and South Vietnam. Emergency requests often came through the station chief. He supervised at least three parallel programs. One, out of the embassy, assisted the Laotian government directly. A second set of initiatives, in tandem with U.S. forces in South Vietnam, sought to obstruct the Ho Chi Minh Trail where it crossed through the southern panhandle of Laos. One of these, Project Hardnose, looked to place roadwatch teams to report on movements along the trail. Two more CIA officers, Michael Deuel and Michael Maloney, died working on Hardnose in October 1965 when their helicopter crashed in the jungle. The third initiative was Project Momentum.

Although only a few dozen CIA officers labored full time on Momentum, the project actually spun an exceedingly complex web. The command center had been located in Thailand, just across the border at the airfield of Udorn. There Bill Lair and his deputy, Pat Landry, gave orders to Vang Pao's secret army. They arranged for Air America to support the Hmong and for air strikes to back its operations. Their air boss through the late sixties was Maj. Richard Secord of the air force. For his goals and operational approvals, Lair referred to the CIA station chief in Vientiane. For supplies, Thai volunteers to work with the *armée clandestine*, and air missions, Lair dealt with the U.S. command and CIA station in Thailand. Through much of this period the station chief in Bangkok was "Red" Jantzen, whom Lair had known for more than a decade. Jantzen would be followed by Peer de Silva and Lou Lapham, both former Saigon chiefs.

Relations between the field command and the CIA station in Vientiane varied. The agency's chiefs of station had different styles and manners. Gordon Jorgensen left for Saigon in 1962. Charles S. Whitehurst presided over the re-ignition of the Laotian war. He brought the Langley perspective, having headed the FE Division branches for Cambodia and Laos, but much of his field experience had been in China operations. Douglas S. Blaufarb, come to CIA from a career at the Voice of America and the U.S. Information Service, cut his teeth in covert operations setting up radio nets for the Albania project. He believed in adaptive response and mostly gave Lair a free hand. Ted Shackley received the Vientiane posting as reward for his service on the Cuba front. As Shackley arrived in the summer of 1966, the Mekong River suddenly spilled over its banks, inundating Vientiane, in some places rising the equivalent of four stories—an ominous sign. Only incredible ingenuity enabled the Americans to keep the embassy open.

Shackley viewed covert action as a "third option" and saw Project Momentum as an alternative to using U.S. troops, fielding an army for a fraction of the cost. He wanted to control everything. Shackley hurled the secret army into major confrontations with the Pathet Lao and the North Vietnamese. On his watch Vang Pao's Hmong began to sustain serious losses. Lawrence Devlin came to Laos at the end of 1968 when Shackley moved to Saigon. Hugh Tovar helped endow the Hmong with their own miniature air force of T-28s. Vang Pao's losses continued to accelerate during Tovar's tenure. Tovar arrived in 1970, when combat had intensified and Hmong force levels were falling. He introduced Thai troops in artillery and even infantry roles, all the while denying there was any secret war, even after reporters revealed the existence of Long Tieng and Sam Thong. During Devlin's time enemy troops actually threatened Long Tieng, with pitched battles for the ridge that dominated it.

As Richard Helms puts it, "The agency . . . was flat out in its effort to keep the tribes viable militarily." In his later memoir Helms would call Laos "the war we won." Working flat out meant about 250 Americans either in Laos or commuting to their assignments; air force personnel permanently assigned to Long Tieng; and a budget that grew to $300 million a year. In keeping with covert operations etiquette, Ambassador Sullivan issued strict orders for Americans to stay out of combat. He says that "when I found those orders were willfully disobeyed, I peremptorily removed [offenders] from the country." But despite Sullivan's orders, the CIA station appears to have taken little action against such "cowboys" as Tony Poe, who reportedly suffered more than a dozen wounds in assorted firefights and once made a fantastic thirty-mile trek to safety carrying a wounded native comrade. Disciplining Poe meant giving him another assignment to a different tribal strike force, the Yao in northern Laos, where he sent patrols into Burma and China.

Air America made it all happen. In South Vietnam alone, by late 1965 the proprietary moved 1,650 tons of cargo a month with a fleet of more than 50 planes, among them two dozen C-54s, C-46s, and C-47s. The load increased to 2,500 tons a month in 1967–1968. In Laos the relative war effort of the United States and the Royal Laotian Government can be measured in monthly airlift tonnage. The Laotian air force averaged 400 tons a month in 1966; Air America moved 6,000 tons plus 16,000 passengers.

Air America had facilities at Bangkok, Takhli, and Udorn, with maintenance performed at Vientiane and Udon, the site of a major proprietary base. The Air America helicopter fleet began at Udon with the transfer of sixteen air force H-34s in March 1961. In addition to their general aviation role the helicopters were vital for air rescue. During the first years of U.S. bombing, Air America rescued four times as many airmen as the air force.

Pilots were supposed to fly during time off from work on regular flight routes. They were paid bonuses, given tax advantages, and could clear upward of $40,000 a year, a huge sum at the time. As in the Congo, Air America folk in Vientiane had their favorite watering hole; here it was the bar called the Purple Porpoise. Hazardous flying, with clouds, sudden mists, and rain, plus enemy guns, justified the pay. Of four Air America C-130 crews trained in the mid-sixties, only one remained in 1970. Destinations—the Lima Sites—were frequently tiny, tricky airfields. Long Tieng, with a paved runway, good navigation beacons, and an all-weather landing system, was an exception, but it was often merely the first stop of the day. Sky had a sophisticated communications center as well as the Hmong propaganda outlet "Radio of the Union of the Lao Races." The CIA base at Sky funneled orders to Vang Pao, sent others to the Thai teams that accompanied the Hmong Special Guerrilla Units, and ensured supply deliveries. Vint Lawrence left

Laos and the CIA for a career as a cartoonist. When Tony Poe went up-country, new blood took over at Long Tieng. By late 1966 press reports of Americans in the field with the Laotians were eroding the plausible deniability of the secret war in Laos.

With the intensification of the war came growth of the CIA proprietary that fed it. Flying Tiger, by way of comparison, had been the largest private air charter airline in the world when Air America was formed. In 1968 Flying Tiger had twenty-eight aircraft with slightly more than two thousand employees, whereas Air America had almost two hundred planes and four times as many workers. In February 1969 the Air America fleet in Thailand consisted of twenty-nine helicopters, twenty light planes, and nineteen medium transports. That unit alone was larger than Flying Tiger.

The demand for air tonnage in Laos led to an anomaly in secret warfare—competition. Continental Air Services hired away an Air America manager, then sought some of the same USAID contracts. Because legal action to preserve Air America monopoly threatened to reveal its ownership, Continental Air got some of the work. Continental accumulated a couple of dozen aircraft in Thailand by 1968, including C-46 and C-47 transports. In addition, contract work would be done by Bangkok-based Bird Air, and beginning in late 1967 the CIA and USAID got together to buy Vang Pao two old C-47s, the beginning of the Hmong leader's private air force.

"Air America did a magnificent job," comments division chief Bill Colby, "but it was not a combat air force." Attacks in support of the Hmong were carried out from Thailand by air force T-28s in "Jungle Jim"–type units. A few of these planes were given to the RLAF to lend credence to the cover. The T-28 force eventually attained a strength of a hundred fighter-bombers in the Fifty-sixth Special Operations Wing. Heinie Aderholt had a further Laotian incarnation as leader of this formation. The fighter-bombers were supplemented by a wide range of U.S. Air Force gunships, first the AC-47, later the improved AC-119 and AC-130 models.

Vang Pao's tactical combination remained his Special Guerrilla Units plus "air," as he called it. Omnipresent airpower did succeed for a long time, and once the Hmong got their own air unit, its pilots' familiarity with the terrain made "air" even more effective. But Hmong objectives sometimes diverged from American ones. A staff officer with the Thirteenth Air Force in Thailand recalls an occasion when his commander, informed the Hmong had hit a target on his prohibited list, demanded Vang Pao's immediate appearance so he could be chewed out. Told the United States had no control over Vang's planes, the general demanded their gasoline and munitions be cut off. The air force had no authority to do that either.

Apparent success greatly pleased Washington. The Hmong program became something of a showcase. In August 1964 LBJ ostentatiously received Pop Buell at the White House. The Hmong New Year in 1966 was attended by the King of Laos and the diplomatic corps. In 1968, as a gift, Vang Pao gave President Johnson an ornate flintlock musket of Hmong antiquity. On two occasions the Americans rewarded Vang with secret visits to the United States. On one of these trips

VP, as Americans affectionately called him, toured the Green Beret training center at Fort Bragg. The agency sent Stewart Methven to be his escort officer. During the other trip, Vang went to colonial Williamsburg and Disneyland. With six wives at Long Tieng, the Hmong chief had a lot of shopping to do. At Disneyland the CIA reciprocated Vang's gift with a replica Zorro costume. Vang Pao actually wore this outfit to boost morale during a battle in Laos.

The campaign against the Ho Chi Minh Trail gave the *armée clandestine* a new mission. Accurate bombing required precise navigation, leading the air force to put a radio beacon atop Phou Pha Thi, a Hmong sacred place and one of the tallest mountains in Laos. Later the United States added a radar and based helicopters there for rescue missions. Phou Pha Thi became Lima Site 85. Pony Express, an air force helicopter lift activity, moved 150 tons of equipment to the site for the radar installation and the dozen Americans necessary to operate the equipment. Vang Pao's Hmong were to defend the facility. Bill Lair warned that the Lima Site could not be defended against serious attack, but the managers of the air war, who wanted to use the radar's precision targeting ability, overrode all objections.

Phou Pha Thi did not escape Hanoi's attention. It made a concerted effort to neutralize this installation. In one of the few recorded instances of North Vietnamese bombing, in January 1968, two of four Soviet built AN-2 biplanes, modified to carry bombs, were shot down attempting to bomb LS-85, one actually by an Air America pilot firing a rifle from his helicopter.

This battle punctuated Ted Shackley's final months as station chief. The blond ghost from Cuba and Berlin rode close herd on Project Momentum, installing his own man, Thomas G. Clines, as deputy chief at Udorn. Bob Blake and Richard Secord still ran the air branch. Secord, who liked to think he and Clines a great team, watched the aerial photography as Hanoi's troops closed in on the mountaintop. He called repeatedly for air strikes to halt the buildup. Lair took those warnings to heart, but the readout on Clines and Shackley is more confused. Deputy station chief James R. Lilley (who left Laos two months before this battle) records Shackley warning that LS-85 could not be held beyond March 10. Others believe Shackley oddly complacent. Air strikes would be too few and too late. The Hmong SGUs guarding the base were driven off—two of their CIA advisers, a forward air controller, and five of the radar technicians barely escaped in a desperate helicopter evacuation—and the battle unfolded with the inevitability of a Greek tragedy. On the night of March 10–11, 1968, the radar base fell. Ten Americans disappeared, and one of those escaping died of gunshot wounds aboard the helicopter. For Jim Lilley, writing thirty years later, the Phou Pha Thi battle "still conjures up wishful thinking of what could have been avoided."

Vang Pao's secret army attained its peak strength during this period. It numbered forty thousand soldiers, mostly local defense forces but about fifteen thousand grouped in Special Guerrilla Units. Yet the North Vietnamese matched their strength. Soon roughly two divisions of Hanoi's army regularly fought in northern Laos, quite frequently against the Hmong. They made regular forays against Skyline Ridge that overlooked Long Tieng. The spooks had Laos wired for sound and filled its air with photo reconnaissance planes. In at least one case, according to Shackley, CIA even planted radio beacons on a Pathet Lao unit and completely monitored its movements. A cycle of operations developed: during the dry season the North Vietnamese attacked the Hmong in the mountains and the RLAF on the Plain of Jars, capturing many positions. When the wet season came, Vang Pao would counterattack and recapture much of the lost terrain.

By this time the CIA had an actual barracks and team house at Long Tieng. Vince Shields had become chief of base, Pat Landry succeeded Bill Lair. Lao sources report that the CIA now backstopped Vang Pao with a command team of three. About thirty more Americans assisted in training, and there were a couple of dozen paramilitary specialists with the SGUs, now being brigaded together as mobile groups to increase their firepower. Agency teams with the Special Guerrilla Units varied from four to twelve men. The CIA advisers, mostly contract officers from the U.S. military under what the agency called its "Jewel" Program—men like James L. Adkins, John Stockwell, James Parker, and Wilbur Greene—lived in the team house when at base, then went into the field with the Hmong. Aside from Long Tieng, there were three other CIA indoctrination bases in Laos and a major training facility in Thailand, where Hmong could undergo unit exercises without the danger of combat.

James R. Lilley puts the total CIA contingent at this point at some 250. Officially the U.S. embassy had 70 "assistant military attachés." There were also 73 Americans with Continental Air Services and 207 with Air America. In 1970 the Nixon administration admitted to almost a thousand Americans in Laos, including more than 200 military, almost 400 government employees, and more than that number of contractor personnel. According to CIA officer Victor Marchetti, rank-and-file CIA people were becoming less enamored with Laos, not because they objected to the operation but because it had become unwieldy and obvious rather than sophisticated and secret.

A few were concerned with mounting losses. Until 1969 the air force had been lucky—only three helicopters had been shot down in Laos, and all but one of the aircrew were rescued. Now luck ran out. In a year six large air force CH-3 helicopters were downed and a seventh destroyed on the ground, half the total of choppers of this type lost in Laos during the entire war. The Nixon administration admitted to more than two hundred dead in Laos, with about that number missing. The CIA's deaths now included Louis Ojibway, Wilbur Greene, Wayne McNulty, John Kearns, and John Peterson, one of them in North Vietnam.

Richard Helms finally made a visit to Laos in September 1970. Station chief Larry Devlin squired him around the country. He realized the war had grown—Hmong units now had to be larger to move safely; the North Vietnamese had begun using tanks and artillery; Vang Pao was literally running out of men. The wrecked C-47 that Helms and Devlin shot past as their twin-engine Volpar landed at Long Tieng symbolized the danger that lurked if Hanoi should gain control of the Skyline Ridge. Vang Pao impressed Helms with his command presence, but the Hmong leader had been reduced to recruiting "child soldiers," boys of thirteen or fourteen. Only Thai mercenaries now kept up the numbers of troops in the Hmong mobile groups.

Perhaps the continuing losses had something to do with the change of heart, a most important one, that occurred in Congress. Political backing for the Indochina war had waned, support for Laos especially. At one time or another fifty senators had been informed of the CIA program, but one by one they jumped off the boat.

A case in point was Senator Stuart Symington of Missouri, whose help had been especially important given his membership on the CIA subcommittee.

Symington had backed the Laotian war. On a visit to Laos and Thailand in 1966, the senator said good things to pilots and embassy people about the efficiency of the secret war. He encouraged the CIA to tell its story and listened in the Armed Services Committee on October 5, 1967, when Theodore Shackley palavered for two hours about where fighting took place and how much it cost. The CIA put soldiers on Laotian battlefields for a fraction of the price of the U.S. military effort in South Vietnam. Symington made that observation, and Shackley agreed. Richard Helms sat to one side taking it all in.

Two years later Stuart Symington steered a different course. At hearings on U.S. worldwide commitments he demanded explanations, asserting that the United States was "waging war" in Laos and had been for years. Said Symington, "It is time the American people were told more of the facts."

At this October 1969 hearing, Senator Symington nudged William H. Sullivan into the admission that there was no formal U.S. obligation to the Hmong.

In his own testimony Richard Helms refused to be drawn out on the authority for this covert "war," reiterating the "such other functions" language in the 1947 National Security Act. In an October 30, 1969, memorandum to Director Helms, General Counsel Lawrence Houston argued that CIA had "no combatants as such" in Laos, and that "I know of no definition . . . which would consider our activities in Laos as 'waging war.'" Although the CIA lawyer carefully noted that "from 1947 on my position has been that this is a rather doubtful statutory authority on which to hang our paramilitary activities," he advised Helms, "I think you were exactly right to stick to the language of the National Security Act."

Symington felt he had reason to be exasperated with the agency's disingenuousness. As the senator put it, "I have never seen a country engage in so many devious undertakings as this."

Helms, for his part, fastened on Symington's change of heart as dishonesty. In a 1981 interview, Helms said, "When Senator Stuart Symington got up and started talking about a 'secret war,' he knew far better than that." In his later memoir, Helms adds that the senator had been briefed several times on the CIA program and had even been Ted Shackley's houseguest during his visit. Others also held out Symington as a blackguard. In the 1980s former Deputy Director for Intelligence R. Jack Smith published a novel in which Senator Symington was the thinly disguised villain. Agency officials had a deaf ear for the corrosive effects of secrecy on public support for their endeavor.

Drug trafficking in Laos constituted an element that helped sour key figures in Washington. It has already been noted that the Hmong raised poppies. Processed in laboratories, those poppies could become opium, heroin, morphine, or other powerful drugs, some hallucinogenic, many addictive. The lucrative drug trade became pervasive in northern Laos as it was in upper Burma and Thailand. Indeed, the area is known as the Golden Triangle for exactly this reason.

When the CIA decided to run a war in northern Laos, the drugs came with it; there was no way to avoid them. The Chinese in Burma, the old Li Mi band, bought some of the poppies and moved them across the border in caravans. Lowland Lao and Thai bought more. But when the airplanes came they introduced an incomparably more efficient means of transportation.

By the mid-sixties CIA officers were reporting intelligence on the movement of drugs. The agency passed the data on to drug enforcement authorities but not much else was done about it. Even this seemed too much for some. On one occasion Helms told Senator John Stennis, chairman of the Armed Services Committee, of this CIA reporting.

Stennis paused, shook his head, then said, "I'm not sure you people ought to be getting involved in things like that. I don't know that that's a proper activity for you."

"Well, Mr. Chairman," replied the CIA director, "how could we possibly not help the United States government when we've got such a hideous drug problem in this country?"

Helms insists the CIA helped, but its attitude was ambivalent at best. Tony Poe, for example, threatened to throw out of his plane anyone carrying drugs, but he did nothing about caravan traffic or drug laboratories in his sectors. Nor could the CIA do anything to prevent the Hmong's own use of drugs, prevalent in their culture. A few attempts were made to encourage the Hmong to raise other cash crops instead of poppies, but the return on growing potatoes, meager by comparison, made the substitution absurd. There are unconfirmed but persistent reports that CIA officers were disciplined when they took such actions as destroying drug labs.

A prohibition against smuggling on Air America planes had been in place since 1957. But enforcement depended on the pilot, and the only remedy was to land at the nearest airfield and put offenders with drugs off the plane. When Air America crews themselves ran drugs, there was nothing to stop them. Not until early 1972 did the proprietary set up a Security Inspection Service, and even then it operated only at large installations.

Moreover there was competition. Some of those running drugs are said to have been among the most senior commanders of the RLAF. Drugs moved on Lao military and private air carriers. Air America crews faced a daily temptation of huge profits for smuggling small packages.

In the summer and fall of 1972, when Hugh Tovar led the CIA station in Vientiane, the agency's inspector general, spurred by detailed revelations in a book the agency tried to suppress, *The Politics of Heroin in Southeast Asia*, began a formal investigation. Scott D. Breckinridge of the IG office participated in the team of officers who began in Hong Kong and spent more than two weeks at eleven agency facilities, interviewing more than a hundred CIA, State, USAID, Pentagon, Air America, and other employees. Their report, "Investigation of the Drug Situation in Southeast Asia," found no evidence that the CIA or any of its senior officers had ever permitted drug traffic "as a matter of policy." There had been individual cases of smuggling, but the persons involved were said to have been promptly disciplined. The Hmong, curiously, are presented as having had little to export.

While exonerating the agency (and claiming its critics discredited), Breckinridge's account of these events confirms every charge aimed at CIA's allies: Laotian generals did participate, drugs moved on military aircraft—and boats; laboratories were photographed; the agency even discovered schedules for planned shipments to South Vietnam. The episode is represented as a success, in isolation, as if the criminal activities of allies did not reflect on the agency. A few years later a CIA officer serving in Burma witnessed an IG inquiry on another matter and came away singularly unimpressed: "IGs, hoping for plum assignments, have a personal stake in not rocking the boat. I never again trusted an IG investigation until the inspector general position became presidentially appointed and congressionally approved."

In any case, despite the denials, drugs moved. Ambassador Godley arranged for one senior Laotian officer to be fired. No more. Breckinridge reached the conclusion that the CIA could not have achieved much more against the drug traffic than it did. This points directly to a key weakness of covert operations: making alliances with indigenous groups inevitably involves buying into their less wholesome features. This in turn may help discredit CIA programs as well as the larger aims of American policy.

In turning against the Laotian secret war, Senator Symington and others in Washington were reacting to factors other than the military situation. Drugs were a major problem in the United States and had real military implications in South Vietnam, where American soldiers were becoming addicted in increasing numbers. Officials who believed the military situation in Laos could be divorced from all other matters were simply wrong.

In Vientiane and Washington the situation looked quite serious by 1970. With Hanoi and the Pathet Lao pressing against the Plain of Jars and the Hmong areas, Ambassador Godley asked for massive strikes by B-52 bombers. By now Washington was at loggerheads over "secrecy" in the Laotian war. Symington pressed for release of the full transcript of his hearing. The Nixon administration sanitized this so heavily as to make it misleading, whereupon Symington refused to issue the document. The request for air strikes came in this charged political context. Fearing leaks from the Pentagon about B-52s in Laos, Secretary of Defense Melvin Laird opposed the option so as to create a record of rejecting it. Secretary of State William P. Rogers also resisted the plan. According to Henry Kissinger, national security adviser to Richard Nixon, Laird wanted the strikes put into a super-secret program whose records would be falsified. Such B-52 missions were already under way in Cambodia.

Growing congressional opposition and increasing enemy success sharpened Washington's problem. "We were caught," recounts Kissinger of the Washington policymakers, "between officials seeking to protect the American forces for which they felt a responsibility and a merciless Congressional onslaught that rattled those officials."

Toward the middle of February the Royal Laotian Government appealed for B-52 strikes. Kissinger recommended the attack at a meeting with the president, Laird, Dick Helms, and the Joint Chiefs' acting chairman. Richard Nixon approved strikes if the Pathet Lao advanced. Within twenty-four hours the condition had been met; an attack with three B-52 bombers took place on the night of February 17–18. More followed, yet Vang Pao relinquished his last positions on the Plain of Jars.

Strikes by the B-52s were enough, in Kissinger's phrase, "to trigger the domestic outcry." Senators Eugene McCarthy and Frank Church, along with Senate majority leader Mike Mansfield, deplored the escalation. By February 25 Symington, with Mansfield and Senators Charles Mathias, Albert Gore, John Sherman Cooper, and Charles Percy, were demanding full release of the Laos hearing transcripts.

Within hours the Laos war was secret no more. The story broke at Long Tieng and on press tickers the world over. Making the scoop proved as easy as walking down a mountain. Journalists had chartered an Air America plane to Sam Thong, the USAID center. The secret warriors were proud of their civic action programs and wanted to show the place off. But three reporters were much more interested in Long Tieng and the *armée clandestine*. They walked out of Sam Thong and down the trail to Long Tieng, leaving behind the official tour. One reporter actually entered the base and watched for two hours before being challenged by a Laotian colonel, then questioned by an American. All were taken into custody and put on a plane to Vientiane. Ambassador Godley was furious, but it was too late. For the first time Long Tieng had been observed by outsiders. Landings and takeoffs from the Lima Site were clocked at one a minute. Air traffic was so intense that planes and helicopters had to form a holding pattern. The reporters saw windowless buildings sprouting numerous radio aerials and tall men wearing civilian clothes but carrying automatic weapons. They knew the men were Americans when they discovered the base had an air-conditioned American-style officers club with panoramic glass windows. Beginning with the *Los Angeles Times*, the Long Tieng story appeared everywhere.

In the Senate, Symington asked the administration to bring Ambassador Godley back to testify. Foreign Relations Committee chairman J. William Fulbright went ahead and put on the record information the Nixon people had been trying to keep secret: that Helms had admitted in testimony that CIA used USAID cover in Laos. Fulbright added that the embassy's Rural Development Annex recruited partisan soldiers and native agents while the mysterious Special Requirements Office did logistics. Further details were added in April 1970 when continuing pressure forced the administration to relent and release the 1969 congressional testimony.

Any chance of limiting the damage was lost when Nixon ordered an invasion of Cambodia. Further Laos hearings were scheduled by the Senate Foreign Relations Committee. Angry senators ruled out allowing testimony in executive session. This record would be in the open. These political events plus the military developments in Laos marked a tidal shift in the secret war.

In late 1971 Senator Symington sponsored an amendment to the appropriations bill that set a ceiling of $350 million for all U.S. funds spent in Laos. This level prevailed in 1972, though it increased to $375 million for the next year. Tovar's field officers were having trouble keeping the North Vietnamese off Skyline Ridge. By that time Indochina peace negotiations were in full swing, leading to the Paris agreements of January 1973. For Laos these provided a coalition government, like that intended in 1958, except that the Pathet Lao had grown considerably stronger. Fourteen years of warfare accomplished none of the original U.S. goals. Vang Pao became a big loser in the settlement, which ended American air support for the secret army.

The cease-fire was to go into effect at noon on February 22, 1973, when Vang faced a renewed North Vietnamese offensive. Several outposts were under attack as the cease-fire neared. The Hmong general made a last appeal to the CIA. In reply he was handed a message from the chief of unit at Sky: "As we discussed previously, USAF support would cease as of 1200, 22 February. I confirmed this . . . today by talking with CRICKET, the [airborne command post] in this area. USAF were under instructions to clear Lao air space."

Disgusted, Vang Pao kicked the dirt and showed the message to nearby reporters.

Leaving Laos, one of the last shifts of American command planes radioed back, "Good bye and see you next war."

One of Long Tieng's outposts fell two and a half hours later. The last CIA advisers left aboard Air America. Hugh Tovar soon left Laos also. Vang Pao, on his own, walked a road that could lead only to exile.

Beginning in 1973 the new Laotian government pressured Air America to cease operations. The CIA proprietary did halt flights to hundreds of airfields and gave a dozen C-123 transports to the Laotian air force. Many Air America employees at Udon were laid off. After a Laotian prohibition on its operations, Air America closed up shop in June 1974. The Udon facilities were taken over by Thai Airways Aircraft Maintenance Company.

The results of CIA's postmortems on Laos are not known. One view is that of Douglas Blaufarb, Laos station chief in the mid-sixties. Blaufarb, who defended the Hmong against press criticism in the *New York Times* in 1971, continued to believe that the tribe had a right to fight for its future, their struggle misunderstood in the United States, in part precisely because of secrecy. In mobilizing the Hmong, the United States incurred an "undoubted moral obligation" which it could not meet. Blaufarb also believes the war effort was hampered by the predominance of the American military in Southeast Asia, which constantly menaced the independence of the ambassador in Vientiane. Finally, argues this former CIA officer, the improvised nature of the secret war led to an open-ended campaign without clear aims other than general U.S. objectives in Indochina.

Of course general U.S. objectives in Southeast Asia revolved around South Vietnam. The CIA labored long and hard there—on building a political base for the Saigon government, on pacification, on unconventional warfare programs. The guerrillas made the war real at the end of March 1965 when they detonated a car bomb just outside the U.S. embassy in Saigon. Station chief Peer de Silva, badly wounded, lost an eye. Agency secretary Barbara Robbins died while several more persons from the typing pool and at least two case officers, like de Silva, were wounded. Eleazar Williams stepped into the breach to act as station chief until Langley promoted Gordon Jorgensen. During that interval President Johnson decided to commit U.S. troops to combat in South Vietnam, and the war intensified.

Under LBJ's dictum that the first team should go to Vietnam, and given the dominance of Cuban operations in the early 1960s, CIA's next station chief was John L. Hart, from the Cuba task force. Hart came to Saigon early in 1966, a forty-five-year-old man with broad experience. He had had a hand in Wisner's Wurlitzer, doing political action in Italy, but also paramilitary work in the Korean War and the Tibetan operation, where he had been in charge when the Dalai Lama escaped the country. Hart had headed CIA stations in Thailand in the early 1950s, and in Morocco later. Far East Division chief Bill Colby had several things in common with Hart: both had been born in the United States and raised abroad, in Hart's case Albania and Iraq as the son of a diplomat; both served in Italy; and Hart had been born in Minneapolis, across the river from Colby in its twin city, St. Paul. By all accounts the agency's Asia baron had no problem with the new Saigon station chief.

Some recall that John Hart had little stomach for paramilitary operations. But he had participated in several, and it would be on his watch that the CIA went into high gear on fresh projects, opening a training center at Vung Tau for counter-terror team recruits. By the spring of 1966 there were more than three thousand armed men in several programs. Hart also emphasized political action, providing funds and specialists to South Vietnamese labor unions and certain parties, and expertise to Vietnamese writing a new constitution. In 1966–1967 South Vietnam held national assembly and then presidential elections with CIA backing it all the way. The elections were less about democracy than about solidifying the power of the Vietnamese generals.

For much of this period Ed Lansdale resided in Saigon in one last incarnation, this time as a sort of factotum for the ambassador but actually as a conduit for his South Vietnamese contacts. Lansdale functioned as intelligence collector par excellence. He left soon after the enemy's 1968 Tet offensive. Bill Colby and

John Hart shared Lansdale's perception that the road to success lay in winning the hearts and minds of the Vietnamese people. Colby peddled that line incessantly in Washington, in policy papers and in his advice to superiors, with Hart a kindred spirit. But the headaches involved were legion. The United States did not even know how many South Vietnamese there *were*, even just in Saigon, much less how to gain their allegiance. As Hart later recorded, "We had only the vaguest notion of how many people lived in that benighted country and there was certainly no way of taking a census in the midst of war." Hart tried his best. In fact, one of his pacification initiatives in 1966 was to create "census grievance" teams—trained at Vung Tau—dispersed into the villages to find out not only how many people there were but what they were saying about Saigon and who had sided with the National Liberation Front.

Hart approved the appointment of a set of regional CIA chiefs for South Vietnam's military command zones, who could connect with the Saigon Police Special Branch in their areas and take care of other agency activities. The regional officers were followed by CIA people appointed for each South Vietnamese province.

Nelson Brickham, Hart's chief of operations, came to him with an even more ambitious proposal, one to keep book on the bad guys—essentially to create a database on just who belonged to the NLF and where they stood in its parallel hierarchy. After the consideration at Langley—not only by Colby but by Helms and the agency's new special assistant for Vietnam affairs, Phillip Carver—this would be called Intelligence Coordination and Exploitation (ICEX), a direct predecessor to the Phoenix Program. Hart, temporarily sidelined by eye problems (a detached retina suffered while playing tennis), did not participate in the late 1967 meetings that actually created Phoenix, which aimed to combine the understanding of the NLF supposedly developed by ICEX with efforts aimed at neutralization. Under Phoenix there were to be interrogation centers in each province, and later district, to collect even more data. A new paramilitary force, the Provincial Reconnaissance Units, became the CIA's enforcement mechanism, but South Vietnamese police and military units were also involved.

Phoenix was up and running in the spring of 1968, but by then Hart had left, replaced by his deputy, Lou Lapham. It formed part of a fresh organization, Civil Operations and Rural Development Support (CORDS), that united all pacification programs. By then William E. Colby had returned to Saigon, sent by LBJ to be deputy chief of CORDS. Colby succeeded to the top job when his boss, Robert Komer—also an old CIA hand—became U.S. ambassador to Turkey. As a result it would be Colby who presided over CORDS and Phoenix. Although much would be accomplished on pacification, the Phoenix Program became highly controversial due to human rights violations, the problem of huge numbers of South Vietnamese political prisoners, and its inability to develop the information necessary to attack the higher levels of the NLF infrastructure.

Most frequently Phoenix functioned as a vehicle for Saigon officials to engage in extortion, eliminate their rivals, or solidify power. While tens of thousands of alleged NLF cadres were "neutralized" under Phoenix, the number of senior

Liberation Front officials swept up were a mere handful. Colby worked hard to inject discipline and legal processes into the effort, but he was never able to control it. In the meantime Phoenix became a political football in the United States, leading to a series of congressional hearings, much like those on Laos, in which Colby was beset by critics. He returned to the United States in 1971, his future at every turn dogged by participation in this program.

Phoenix piled up some impressive statistics. During 1969 alone, it "neutralized" just under twenty thousand NLF suspects, of whom more than six thousand died. In 1971 Colby told a Senate hearing that there had been more than twenty thousand killed in all, almost thirty thousand people imprisoned, and about eighteen thousand converted into Saigon agents. Not to be outdone, the South Vietnamese claimed more than forty thousand dead suspects. But when questions arose over the legality of these operations, even under Vietnamese law, authorities rapidly retreated to an admission that 87 percent of the supposed cadres had perished in the course of regular military operations.

From 1969 through 1972 Theodore Shackley led the CIA station in Saigon. Given that CORDS's purpose fit classic definitions of political action, and that Colby's organization held formal responsibility here, room for conflict with Shackley existed. In particular the two groups competed over who would run the most promising agents recruited in the course of Phoenix. The CIA had first dibs as the nation's front-line intelligence agency. That led to temptation among CORDS advisers to keep secret their best spies so as to avoid having them taken over. Vietnam intelligence suffered as a consequence.

Possibly the most contentious matter to arise during Shackley's time in Saigon was the conflict with army Special Forces over the so-called Green Beret Affair, the June 1969 execution—or murder—of a Vietnamese agent working for Special Forces at Nha Trang. Killed after a long, inconclusive interrogation, on grounds he might be a spy for Hanoi, the case came to the attention of U.S. commander Gen. Creighton V. Abrams, who ordered a full investigation. Counter Intelligence Corps inquiries traced orders for the killing up the chain of command to the head of the Fifth Special Forces Group, Col. Robert B. Rheault, and he plus a number of Green Berets were remanded for courts martial. Their defense was that CIA—Shackley and the agency's regional officer-in-charge, Dean Almy—had demanded the murder.

Lawyers threatened to subpoena Shackley, Almy, and Richard Helms. During preliminary hearings, the agency began sending its people off on temporary duty assignments so they would be unavailable. The issue rose to the highest levels: memoranda from CIA general counsel Lawrence Houston, meetings between counsel for the agency and the army, even a session of the United States Intelligence Board at which the murder was the only subject, no notes were permitted, and all backbenchers were kept out—unprecedented in U.S. intelligence history. The army dropped all charges without ever going to trial.

Saigon politics per se remained within Shackley's purview, and there would be another presidential election in 1971. To both Colby's and Shackley's credit, their differences remained relatively minor.

Another intelligence mission, principally involving Special Forces, particularly MACSOG, was prisoner rescue, under the code name Bright Light. The most spectacular mission was a raid carried out quite close to Hanoi in November 1970. It hit a complex near the town of Sontay, where Americans were thought to be held. The raid, Operation Ivory Coast, came off without a hitch, unlike the later Iranian hostage rescue fiasco, but it illustrated a different problem with these kinds of missions: no prisoners were found. Intelligence on prisoner locations in rescue missions was always uncertain. Twenty-eight more rescues were attempted after Sontay. Of the total of 119 missions undertaken between 1966 and 1973, fully 98 were raids. The rescue missions freed several hundred South Vietnamese soldiers and 60 civilians but only one American prisoner, and he died shortly afterward from wounds inflicted at the last moment by his captors. Raids might be spectacular, but they were not about to determine the outcome of the war. That could only be done on the ground, in the South, and the prospects dimmed every day.

Thomas Polgar followed Shackley in Saigon, taking over in January 1972. A European specialist with no Asian experience whatever, recently posted in Latin America, Polgar did pretty well, but the war had already gone bad. Hanoi staged a huge offensive that year, finally driving the United States out of the conflict, at least in terms of military involvement. The Paris cease-fire agreement sealed the fate of the Saigon regime. Polgar presided over thirty more months of battles that pitted Saigon, on its own, against Hanoi. In some respects the CIA role actually grew with the U.S. military out of the game, but the South Vietnamese gradually lost ground until, in March 1975, their defenses collapsed. Over two frantic months the issue became the evacuation of South Vietnamese, including the agency's assets. Many were left behind, along with the Saigon station's records, which fell into Hanoi's hands when the U.S. embassy was captured on April 30, 1975. Frank Snepp, Polgar's top analyst, has left a searing account of the CIA's final days in-country, and others have also described those terrible weeks when a few CIA officers saved some Vietnamese, often heroically, but the larger defeat remained inexorable. The fall of Saigon brought the end of the wars.

The secret wars in Southeast Asia represented many things to many people. To some they were laboratories to test techniques, to others a political morass at the edge of the Vietnam quagmire. These many years later the full story of secret operations in Southeast Asia is still untold. To some Americans, Laos symbolized government secrecy used to cloak doubtful legality. To many, Vietnam symbolized power illegitimately unleashed and inevitably defeated. To most, all this seemed a terrible mistake. Yet even as these events unfolded, the Central Intelligence Agency had more going on, at home as well as around the globe.

16

Global Reach

BLESSED WITH a perfect background for an internationalist, Richard McGarrah Helms could have been a diplomat, a banker, or a military officer. His maternal grandfather, an international banker, lived in Basel, Switzerland. His father had been an executive with the Aluminum Company of America. But Helms chose to be a spy. Born on Philadelphia's Main Line, as a boy Helms lived in New York City and New Jersey. Herman Helms saved the family the horrors of the Great Depression by cashing out of the stock market before the crash, affording Helms opportunities denied to many among his generation. Herman and Marion Helms wanted their children to have an international education and moved them to Europe, just as Dick finished his junior year at a private high school. Helms summered in France, spent a year at the Swiss prep school Le Rosey, then another at a German *gymnasium* in Freiburg. Skiing, soccer, and crew soaked up his time, and much of the rest was spent trying to understand geometry taught in French or Latin taught in German. Helms needed a tutor for the Latin, given that Williams College, the family school, required four years of the language but the *gymnasium* did not teach it. After a late bout with chicken pox—acquired during a family trip to Italy—Helms arrived at Williams in the fall of 1931.

Aside from inducing the college to accept his dual major in English and history, Helms learned a lesson for later life. As editor of the newspaper he wrote an editorial advocating ending both the Latin requirement and compulsory attendance at chapel. The world crashed down then, with demands he be expelled for expressing such heresy. Helms had been an excellent student—he would graduate magna cum laude with a Phi Beta Kappa key—and survived this confrontation. No doubt the memory of his Williams experience helped him in certain CIA controversies.

But the spy life came later. Richard Helms wanted to be a journalist or lawyer. He toyed with Harvard Law School but instead took a job with the United Press in London. His later assignment to Berlin led to an unforgettable lunch in 1936 with Adolf Hitler and other Nazi luminaries. Helms also saw the nadir of journalism—being scooped by the rival Associated Press on reporting the Nazi

Party rallies at Nuremberg. And he covered the Olympics where American athlete Jesse Owens won the two-hundred-meter dash. Helms hoped to have his own newspaper one day and left the United Press to learn the business end of journalism with the *Indianapolis Times*, where he became advertising manager. While in Indianapolis he married Julia B. Shields, recently divorced from the founder of one of the larger grooming products firms of the day.

World War II brought a sea change for Dick Helms as for so many others. A former United Press boss, now with the OSS, asked Dick to join him, but nothing came of that. Helms volunteered for the naval reserve and ended up at Harvard after all—as an officer trainee. Detailed to the navy's anti-submarine warfare staff, after just a few weeks Helms was simply detached to the OSS one Sunday morning. Two weeks of training, assignment to the OSS planning unit, and long hours monitoring the counterintelligence program from Washington led Helms to do everything he could to get into the field. In early 1945 that finally happened when he went to London, where William J. Casey led OSS efforts to penetrate Germany. Dick Helms never returned to journalism.

The London job opened Helms to the inner sanctum of operations, bewitched him, and brought him to his life's work. He shared an apartment with Casey and became the spy's spy, a master of clandestine espionage in Europe, for which education and experience equipped him perfectly. He soon moved to Paris with Casey, continuing the work. By the end of the war, Helms was an established expert on Germany. When OSS sent a mission into the defeated nation, Helms went along. Allen Dulles, supposed to head the unit, stayed in Switzerland to wind up affairs there while his deputy focused on management, leaving Dick Helms the key field officer. Helms met many who became towering figures in the CIA, including not only Dulles and Casey but Walter Bedell Smith, Frank Wisner, Gordon Stewart, Peter Sichel, Rolf Kingsley, and such fellow travelers as Robert Joyce, intelligence officers and diplomats who played major roles in the agency's covert actions.

Like many of them, Richard Helms stayed on when the OSS became the Strategic Services Unit, and then through its meanderings until it emerged as the Central Intelligence Agency. Already in a senior position, Helms rose to become the CIA's staff chief, then division chief for Germany, responsible for a major theater of the secret war. He only went on to greater glory. By the 1950s Helms had a reasonable expectation of selection as chief of the Directorate for Operations, but then Allen Dulles passed him over for Wisner. Helms served as chief of operations. Active and engaged, Helms told a group of officers, "My job is to hold an umbrella over you fellows and catch the crap so you can get on with your operating."

When it became impossible for Wisner to continue as DDO, Dick Helms, who had already twice acted in that position, held the strongest claim to the job, but Dulles selected Richard Bissell instead. The spy maven thought of resigning. Near the end of his life, Dulles told Helms that not making him DDO had been his worst mistake. Dulles's choice reflected Eisenhower's predilection for covert operations. But after the Bay of Pigs, the man who kept the secrets could not be denied.

In early 1962 the forty-nine-year-old Helms, affable and precise, became deputy director for operations in his own right. In the Congo, Laos, South Vietnam, and South America, Helms showed he could play the covert action game as well as anyone, and he ably seconded John McCone in this pursuit. The CIA director sometimes took Helms to meetings at the White House, and at one of these he introduced the DDO to the president.

With Lyndon Johnson, John McCone never achieved anything like the rapport he had had with Jack Kennedy. Johnson remained slightly suspicious. A man of the Senate, LBJ probably resented how McCone threw his weight around on Capitol Hill in 1963, at the time the Senate debated an arms-control agreement (the Partial Test Ban Treaty), staking out a political position and even lending CIA analysts to those who believed as he did. McCone's penchant for policy advice also irked Johnson. LBJ increasingly cut out face time in the Oval Office, which annoyed McCone. By early 1965 John McCone, at loggerheads with LBJ over Vietnam and access, had had enough. That April he quit.

A few days later Johnson aide Marvin Watson telephoned Helms at Langley and asked him over the next morning. The Secret Service ushered Richard Helms into the Oval Office, and when LBJ got off the telephone he announced to the startled spook that John McCone had resigned. President Johnson appointed Vice Admiral William F. Raborn as successor. But Raborn, a Navy rocket specialist, knew nothing whatever about intelligence. Johnson wanted him backed up by someone with real knowledge of the agency's work. Richard Helms was that man. On April 28, 1965, he became deputy director for central intelligence.

Returning from the LBJ Ranch after the appointments were announced, the president told Helms that he and Raborn were to shake up the agency. LBJ must have liked what he saw. Little more than a year later, when Johnson decided he wanted no more of Red Raborn, he elevated Dick Helms. Raborn displeased LBJ in a different way, by doing what the president asked and *keeping away* from him. The CIA director was not helped by a low-level campaign of guttersniping from agency people and their allies, annoyed at this neophyte on the Seventh Floor. President Johnson named Vice Admiral Rufus Taylor as DDCI. "I thought he had the personality of a dead mackerel," an LBJ lieutenant was later quoted as saying of Helms. "But he certainly had the respect of the president."

Johnson appointed Helms on June 18, 1966. Ten days later the Senate confirmed him, and he was sworn in on June 30. One of the longest-running tenures of any director of central intelligence began that day.

Helms became the first CIA director to have to deal with a major flap over CIA domestic activity. Allen Dulles and his predecessors had had problems with paramilitary operations abroad, or with the agency's perceived intelligence failures, but it would be on Helms's watch that domestic activities attracted attention and quickly made waves. The unraveling can be said to have begun in the spring of 1966 with publication in the *New York Times* of articles on U.S. intelligence. Both the CIA and the White House were forewarned about the series by some of the people the reporters spoke to. The agency even sent out an all-hands cable instructing stations how to respond to local questioners. When the *Times* began publishing, stations reported back what parts of the stories were getting the most attention in their countries. The CIA subcommittee of the House Armed Services Committee asked for and received an agency briefing on the articles. Most of the material dealt with older chestnuts: the power of secret intelligence in general, the Bay of Pigs, the Congo, and so on; but there were hints of other issues. Probably most important, the stories challenged some Americans who were involved with certain CIA secret activities.

Key here were the officers of the National Student Association (NSA). Nongovernment and nonpartisan, the NSA functioned as an umbrella group of mainly student organizations at various colleges. The agency's International Organizations Division had seen the NSA as a counterweight to Soviet-sponsored youth groups in the 1950s. Although sensibilities had changed, impelled especially by growing opposition to the Vietnam War, the NSA had remained active in the cultural Cold War. Into the 1960s the CIA paid for NSA international activities, arranged for its offices in the Dupont Circle section of Washington (the group had a rent-free fifteen-year lease for space on S Street, Northwest), and contributed to the upkeep of its senior officials. The CIA also funded summer seminars for student leaders and used them to spot talent for recruitment. By some accounts, agency cash, channeled through friendly foundations, amounted to $3.3 million. Even at the time this information surfaced, membership dues accounted for just $18,000 of an $800,000 NSA budget. After 1962, when CIA's International Organizations Division merged into its Covert Action Staff, that unit ran the student project.

Later investigation established that the CIA had made operational use of some of the students on their foreign sojourns. One, on an NSA scholarship as an exchange student in Poland, had to be pulled out for fear he would be picked up as an American spy. More frequently the agency simply asked students to keep a watchful eye during their trips and tell what they had seen.

By 1965 NSA leaders were uncomfortable with the CIA relationship. The press revelations of 1966 soured them still more. Shortly before the *Times* series on the CIA, NSA president Phil Sherburne told his director of development, Michael Wood, of the CIA's role. Not all were witting—Cord Meyer of the Covert Action Staff made sure of that, monitoring NSA elections, revealing agency backing only to the association president and its vice president for international affairs. When Wood learned of the connection he was scandalized. He first tried to replace the CIA money, contacting Vice President Hubert H. Humphrey, who did some fund-raising but had little success. Association officials attempted to dissuade Wood, who saw their pleas as bribery. Wood then told others at NSA of the CIA connection and began talking to the San Francisco–based magazine of political commentary, *Ramparts*. The magazine had already raised eyebrows at Langley with an exposé reporting that the CIA had hired Michigan State University to furnish assistance to the South Vietnamese police. Very much against the Johnson administration and strongly anti-war, *Ramparts* saw the opportunity to make a powerful statement against covert action by revealing the CIA-NSA links. Subsequent events would test Helms's umbrella theory of management.

The Johnson administration became perfectly aware of this brewing cauldron of trouble. By May 1966, within a month of the *Times* revelations, Director Helms sent the White House information about *Ramparts* and its editor, Robert Scheer. The White House wanted more, and Helms initiated an investigation of the magazine's alleged Communist ties, using its own files and those of the FBI. There were none to find. The agency reluctantly reported this to national security adviser Walt Rostow.

Cord Meyer, whose name appeared in the ensuing flap, writes of this almost as if he were an innocent bystander implicated by NSA's irresponsible young radicals. In fact the CIA, *before* the event, acted preemptively to limit the damage. A special assistant to the deputy director of operations, ordered to pull together the data on *Ramparts*, progressed to schemes to wreck the magazine. Langley considered asking the Internal Revenue Service to audit *Ramparts*'s tax returns but dropped that idea. Edmund Applewhite, a seventeen-year agency veteran of literary bent, who had once worked with Buckminster Fuller, coordinated these schemes for the DO. Applewhite told a later interviewer, "I had all sorts of dirty tricks to hurt their circulation and financing. . . . We were not in the least inhibited by the fact that the CIA had no internal role in the United States." Later Applewhite was promoted to deputy inspector general of the CIA and decorated with the Intelligence Medal of Merit.

In early January 1967 Langley picked up rumors in New York publishing circles that a *Ramparts* piece on the agency and the National Student Association, written by Marcus Raskin, had been scheduled and would focus on CIA subversion of American youth—hardly an image in the democratic mold. About the same time the agency intercepted a letter from an unknown organization, probably contrived, mailed from Vienna, still a spy haven. The letter alleged that the CIA employed someone in the coordinating secretariat of the International Student Conference in Brussels, with purloined documents from secretariat files that seemed to substantiate the charge. The NSA was a Conference affiliate. This permitted Langley counterspy James Angleton to assert that the entire matter was a Soviet disinformation plot. Had CIA followed Angleton's advice it would have been even less prepared for the coming storm.

Instead Cord Meyer instructed James Kiley, his case officer for the NSA, to turn off the money spigot. At least the agency would be able to deny a current relationship.

On Monday, February 13, Director Helms was in Albuquerque after a long day of inspections. With CIA weapons experts, Helms had gone west to visit the Nevada nuclear test site and Los Alamos, where the bomb designers held sway. Now he got a White House cable ordering him back to Washington immediately. Helms drily writes that this became "one of my darkest days."

Aides quickly found that there were no commercial flights available, and it took an hour to arrange through Air Branch for a proprietary, possibly Intermountain Aviation, to send an aircraft to take Helms to the capital. On the long flight the DCI pondered how he might have offended Lyndon Johnson, or what else could be wrong. Doubt festered when the White House took hours to return the call Helms put in as soon as he reached his Seventh Floor office. Helms, who liked a scotch before dinner, must have needed several that day.

In fact Helms had done nothing to trigger this episode. Rather, it marked the onset of the *Ramparts* flap. A week earlier presidential political aide Douglass Cater had been sitting in his White House office when his phone, too, rang. In that case it had been National Student Association president W. Eugene Groves seeking an appointment. Cater, one of the original founders of the NSA—a couple of dozen student idealists who began with a conference at the University of Wisconsin in the late 1940s—followed the group with interest. Now he expected some declaration on Vietnam. Instead Groves told Cater that *Ramparts* had gone to press with its article. As soon as the man left, Cater dictated a note to President Johnson.

Then the phone rang again, the direct line from the president.

"Well, aren't you the lucky one," LBJ drawled. "You let that fellow come into your office and lay a big, fat turd right in your lap."

Cater well knew what portended here. He had been an addressee on CIA memoranda about *Ramparts* and Robert Scheer the previous summer, and had himself written papers that circulated within the White House. As a former NSA member he could also see the implication of the charges of student complicity with the agency. Cater rushed in to see the president; Johnson glowered impatiently. Cater argued they ought to use the week left before *Ramparts* hit the newsstands to prepare a response. Cater made private inquiries and determined that NSA funding had been approved by the Psychological Strategy Board, and that "no one raised a warning or monitored the runaway growth of this enterprise." Other details of White House activity remain obscure, but the summons to Helms came the day *before* the flap began—when *Ramparts* discussed its findings in full-page ads in both the *New York Times* and the *Washington Post*, and front-page stories in both newspapers covered the issue. As soon as that happened, the State Department held a press conference and confirmed the essence of the charges, as acting secretary Nicolas de B. Katzenbach had explained to LBJ he would do. Reporters caught up to Allen Dulles and asked about the CIA funding. Dulles replied the money had been well spent.

President Johnson never held a White House meeting on how to proceed, allowing the agency to dangle on a limb, but Richard Helms acknowledges that the student association flap was a CIA problem "from start to finish." LBJ now instructed the agency to cease all subsidies to youth or student groups and ordered a policy review of CIA relationships with educational and private voluntary organizations. Helms read in the newspaper that he would be a member.

Like the Taylor Board after the Bay of Pigs, the 1967 policy review group was no impartial, objective panel. Its members were Helms, Nicholas Katzenbach, who had actually coordinated the public response, and John W. Gardner, the secretary of health, education, and welfare. They met in Katzenbach's office, Helms and Gardner on a sofa, the acting secretary behind his desk. Helms recalled sharp debate and occasional frost but no hostility. In five weeks they hammered out a policy that the United States halt all such covert assistance but develop a fresh initiative to support worthy groups openly. The National Student Association would be the sole entity mentioned in their report, which noted that "no useful purpose would be served by detailing any other CIA programs of assistance to private American voluntary organizations." Of course an equally vulnerable target, Radio Free Europe/Radio Liberty, lay behind that language.

Helms chafed at the order to desist from aid to *all* organizations, but he understood the rationale and believed they had headed off a full-scale congressional investigation by these measures. He would nonetheless be called to testify. Georgia Senator Richard B. Russell, a member of the CIA subcommittee of the Armed Services Committee, took some of the wind out of the storm when he revealed that he had known all along and approved of the CIA subsidies.

Gene Groves dismissed the Katzenbach Report as a whitewash, but he nevertheless faced NSA members, demands that he be impeached for the CIA link. Doug Cater came to his own conclusions: "Secrecy has a self-destructive potential which cannot stay the long course, especially when pitted against this country's passion for publicity." When the secret warriors took umbrage at revelation of the Laotian war, they had already had two years in which to learn the very lesson then repeated.

Exposure of the CIA role in the National Student Association marked not the end but the beginning of controversy. The agency had no one to blame but itself for what happened next. The media jumped enthusiastically into the fray. Further news stories about the NSA connection obliged Gene Groves to make declarations he would have preferred to avoid while others positioned themselves around the debate. As soon as reporters began to delve into the NSA-CIA relationship they uncovered the bigger story. The foundations that Langley had used to fund the NSA were the same that served as its conduit to the Congress for Cultural Freedom and Radio Free Europe. This bit of sloppy tradecraft left two key CIA political action projects vulnerable to discovery by inquiry into the student group. Worse, the cat was already out of the bag: eight foundations CIA used had been publicly identified in congressional hearings several years earlier.

Embarrassed at the time, Langley had not done enough to alter its arrangements. One of Cord Meyer's subordinates, the chief of his program evaluation group, had pushed for more secure channels but accomplished little. Thus reporters who followed leads to the foundations financing the students almost immediately found CIA donations to Radio Free Europe, Radio Liberty, and other projects. Soon the papers were filled with diagrams tying the Central Intelligence Agency to a variety of ostensibly private institutions—not just the "radios" but cultural groups, the Asia Foundation, and more. Langley had been funneling $10 million a year into labor, youth, and cultural activities overseas. This was major blown cover.

Cord Meyer, who had a tin ear for the politics of intelligence, regarded what happened as an act of unilateral political disarmament but is silent on his role in the tradecraft failure.

The truth is that the Radio Free Europe link had already begun to fray. The astonishment of PFIAB members when they learned of CIA and Radio Free Europe has already been recounted. No doubt knowledge of links to Radio Liberty (RL) had a similar impact. These were huge entities with costs to match—a special assistant to Helms put the annual expense for RFE/RL at $30 to $35 million, with the agency footing 90 percent. Each year RFE held a big fund-raising drive, relying on donated space and air time for advertising, in which Americans were told that without their contributions, efforts to encourage democracy in Eastern Europe could be crippled. Presidents supported these campaigns at CIA's behest. John F. Kennedy hosted and spoke at a White House luncheon for the RFE campaign on October 25, 1963, his remarks prepared by Cord Meyer, who wanted Kennedy to say that RFE redressed an "imbalance" between a Free World entirely open to Communist propaganda and a Soviet Bloc "largely closed to information and to Western thought." What Meyer did not wish to say openly had equal significance: a section heading for JFK's remarks, "Capitalizing on Communist Dissension"— which could have revealed RFE's CIA propaganda mission—had been crossed out and replaced with "Source of Bloc Information."

In November 1964 Meyer negotiated dates with Mac Bundy for President Lyndon Johnson to appear at a similar event. At Langley, Meyer and Helms assumed that Johnson supported the radios. But LBJ became restive at participating even before the 1967 meltdown. Some months earlier another of these events got onto his schedule without, as he saw it, his agreement. Because the commitment had been made, LBJ kept it, but on December 20, 1966, Johnson sent Director Helms a note instructing him: "Please take steps to make sure that I don't get committed on any fund raising projects in the future."

Then came the *Ramparts* affair and its further revelations. Under the Katzenbach guidelines the administration moved to sever ties with Radio Free Europe. The CIA wanted to provide RFE/RL a large final payment, but this did not erase the flap potential. On May 5 White House media specialist Robert E. Kintner informed the president that ABC News now had the goods on CIA-RFE and intended to use them. Kintner forwarded a paper from Helms that mentioned CIA's idea of a golden parachute, which would at least eliminate current funding problems. The CIA argued that the radios were not really private voluntary organizations like the National Student Association but were agency proprietaries working under CIA control—a complete negation of the arguments used to solicit public donations. When the news appeared, CIA's Radio Free Europe connection garnered wide attention. By November the president had had his fill. After one of his Tuesday Lunches, LBJ spoke privately with Dick Helms.

"I won't fund those radios of yours any longer," Johnson declared.

The CIA director, completely flustered, reacted. "You can't do that!" Helms replied. Aghast at his trespass of decorum, Helms stood mute, then began reciting reasons why the radios were so important. After a few minutes LBJ interrupted and said he would go along if Helms got congressional cooperation without any White House assistance. Helms took on the job.

It took weeks to line up friendly legislators, apprise them of the situation, and enlist their support. Helms then informed President Johnson. It did not hurt that Georgia Senator Richard B. Russell, a close friend of LBJ's, became one of the strongest backers. The RFE/RL issue consumed almost the entire Special Group meeting on December 15. Using a concept of "surge funding," the CIA proposed to give the radios enough to last through mid-1969. One unusual aspect concerned how the radios should handle their tax liability with the Internal Revenue Service with their covert CIA income now in the open. The secret war wizards also wanted to preserve the CIA's role setting policy for the radios. How that could be maintained once Langley no longer funded them remained unclear.

So a new era dawned for the radios. Helms testified for the budgets before the CIA subcommittee of the Senate Appropriations Committee. He encountered opposition from the chairman, Louisiana Democrat Allen Ellender, skeptical of the effectiveness of broadcasts into Russia, but Senator Russell and other supporters carried the day.

Toward the end of 1968 the PFIAB urged Johnson to push for congressional support of one or more publicly financed institutions that would take care of the "radios." The crunch came in 1969 when funds were depleted. The last Johnson budget contained new money, but the president cut it, intending to present the lowest overall request possible. Public fund-raising that year, fueled by $20 million in advertising, netted a mere $100,000. The administration of Richard Nixon, with Henry A. Kissinger as national security adviser, were unwavering Cold Warriors and had no qualms about funding. The CIA money did not disappear after all. By this time U. Alexis Johnson, returned to Washington as undersecretary of state, sat on the Nixon administration's Special Group. He recalls hard work as the group kept track of the "CIA Orphans," as he calls them, and sent budget proposals to Congress. Johnson believes the Special Group agencies "could have been more aggressive in persuading the Congress to fund some of these programs overtly."

The *Ramparts* flap marked a sea change for the agency, ending Frank Wisner's fabled Wurlitzer. Two years later Cord Meyer went to London as chief of station, his service rewarded by Dick Helms with the Distinguished Intelligence Medal. In 1972 Robert H. Dreher, who had been the CIA's sparkplug on Radio Liberty, went into retirement.

In January 1971 New Jersey Senator Clifford Case proposed legislation creating a Board for International Broadcasting to oversee the radios. For the first time a government official, not merely the media, acknowledged the CIA link to the radios. Case pointed out that the agency had put several hundred million dollars into RFE/RL without Congress ever formally considering the expenditure. The Case proposal provided $30 million for 1972 and temporary policy guidance from the State Department until the board became established. Hearings before Fulbright's Senate Foreign Relations Committee featured repeated testimony from Alex Johnson. Fulbright remained suspicious of the radios as propaganda outlets but could find no malfeasance or other grounds to build an opposition to the legislation, which passed later that year. A funding proposal in March 1972 gave the radios $36 million for that year. The international board finally materialized at the end of 1973.

The 1967 controversies fed public concern about the U.S. government's use of covert operations and its control of intelligence in general. Eisenhower had established what had now become the PFIAB, and he called it a watchdog group, specifically to head off congressional efforts to substitute a formal oversight mechanism for the secret subcommittees. Failure at the Bay of Pigs led Kennedy to tighten executive controls, but his measures were invisible to the public. Dick Bissell had suggested surfacing the Special Group and describing its role, which would have replayed Ike's strategy of the fifties, but that idea went nowhere.

Until the *New York Times* series in 1966, Langley had followed a strategy of attempting to discredit or minimize public discussion of intelligence issues, particularly those regarding covert operations, while promoting its own achievements. Shortly after the Bay of Pigs, author Andrew Tully published a book that portrayed the agency favorably. His work contained information that must have come from Langley, no doubt to counteract the negative publicity from the Cuban failure. The major exposés of the CIA that emerged during that period, Haynes Johnson's *The Bay of Pigs* and David Wise and Thomas B. Ross's *The Invisible Government*, both in 1964, were each the subject of high-level agency deliberations on how to neutralize them. The director of central intelligence discussed the Wise and Ross book directly with the president.

Perhaps it is not surprising that those few academics and observers who followed intelligence at the time stood for greater openness and oversight. As early as 1958 Harry Howe Ransom had gone on record in favor of a joint congressional committee. Paul W. Blackstock, in his 1964 book *The Strategy of Subversion*, renewed the debate. Both argued that oversight had become necessary. Blackstock viewed controls as helping legitimate intelligence, part of a process to counteract the dangers of blowback from these activities.

Congress had its own concerns, and some of its members listened to the public debate. In particular, Senators Eugene McCarthy, Mike Mansfield, and J. William Fulbright became active in a renewed drive for oversight. McCarthy introduced legislation for several years running. His best chance came in 1966 on the heels of the *Times* series. Mike Mansfield, the Senate majority leader, summoned top legislators to discuss the bill in late May. The legislation to create a Senate oversight panel had been favorably reported out of committee. Mansfield wanted to avoid a fight on the Senate floor. Bill Fulbright offered the compromise of setting up *another* secret subcommittee under the Foreign Relations Committee. If the private citizens who comprised PFIAB could be told all about secret operations, he insisted, why did the Foreign Relations Committee remain out of the loop?

Richard Russell rejected any subcommittee, and the CIA remained strongly opposed to all oversight formulas. President Johnson's national security adviser told him of the impasse early in June. Mansfield and minority leader Senator Everett Dirksen met with LBJ on June 2. The president resisted broadening CIA reporting to the Senate. Mansfield developed a further compromise that added a couple of members of the Foreign Relations Committee to existing CIA subcommittees. Significantly, LBJ assigned his political aide Harry C. McPherson, Jr., to handle this, not national security adviser Walt Rostow or the NSC staffer on intelligence, Peter Jessup. McPherson asked Johnson to stay out of the matter.

Although advised to steer clear, LBJ, like Eisenhower, worked behind the scenes for the status quo. As early as the fall of 1965 a presidential directive reaffirming the role of PFIAB had been prepared, which, as McGeorge Bundy put it, "we plan to use . . . as appropriate with Congressional leaders when there is any question about our effective supervision of the Intelligence Community." The paper proved useless when the issue actually arose, because Fulbright and others were angry precisely because PFIAB was being given material denied to Congress. When NSC aide Rostow, who replaced Bundy, told Johnson that an unhappy Fulbright did not understand why Foreign Relations should be denied access, the president scrawled across the bottom of his copy of the report, "Because they leak!"

LBJ backed up the strong opposition of DCI William F. Raborn. A few weeks later, when Richard Helms succeeded to the top job at CIA, advice continued to flow from White House political assistant Bill Moyers. The strategy worked out in meetings and phone calls between McPherson and Senator Russell involved watering down the McCarthy resolution, which lost its provisions for a staff and a budget and action by a certain date, and became merely an addition to the existing secret subcommittee. In response to a further letter from Fulbright, the CIA again refused information to the Foreign Relations Committee. Russell came out strongly against the bill, and once Russell and McPherson determined they had the votes to defeat it, they insisted on bringing it up for a vote. With Dirksen's Republican minority plus the weight Russell threw into the scales, Senator McCarthy's resolution was defeated by a vote of 61 to 28 that July. To mollify proponents, Russell invited Fulbright and the ranking Republican member of his committee to sit with the secret subcommittee the following year when the CIA went to Capitol Hill for a detailed presentation on Laos. Richard Helms later became a good friend of Senator Eugene McCarthy.

Following this episode, the CIA's contacts with Congress increased somewhat: between 1965 and 1974, on the average, the Senate Armed Services Committee received three briefings a year; the Senate Appropriations Committee and the House Armed Services Committee, four. Congressional attitudes were still lackadaisical. The House unit held no meetings at all in 1971 or 1972, while in 1967 the CIA appropriation breezed past both House and Senate after a single legislator visited Langley to observe a rehearsal of the budget presentation.

The CIA took advantage. In 1966 Helms went to Capitol Hill with his deputy director for science and technology and a collection of fancy spy gadgets, successfully deflecting discussion of real issues. Similarly Helms gave the following advice to his special assistant on Vietnam affairs, George Carver, before Carver's first appearance on the Hill: "Don't waffle, don't ramble and don't guess. When you're getting into an area you feel you can't discuss, you tell them. But you also tell them as succinctly as possible the answer to the question they asked. Not the question they should have asked."

"Oversight" thus remained entirely in the hands of the PFIAB. Clark Clifford's panel concerned itself primarily with efficiency, not legality. Many of its inquiries during LBJ's last years concerned aircraft shoot-down incidents in which, as in the U-2 episode, planes had blundered into foreign airspace. Its most prominent postmortem would be that done after the Tet Offensive in Vietnam. The group did one study of intelligence organization—too late for LBJ to do anything about it—during Johnson's final months. On covert operations this report said, "the group believes that . . . procedures for the initiation and control of covert operations by the appropriate policymakers are now both effective and flexible," but warned this would change if permitted to "become a formal ritual." The report found improving secrecy the basic task since most covert operations that failed had been exposed, and often "highly adverse political consequences at home and abroad" flowed from such revelation. Thus, "If in years past the assessment of the feasibility of secrecy had been more accurate many of the covert activities that were ultimately compromised would not have been initiated and others would have been terminated earlier." These were pious words indeed in view of the observation a couple of pages later that "it is rarely possible to keep large operations secret for long if at all, and their compromise is usually dramatic." The ultimate conclusion was that covert operations should be restricted to those that offered substantial chances for success, in which "the government [is] prepared to accept the consequences of compromise."

By the 1960s a concern with secrecy had supplanted the previous dedication to plausible deniability in discussions of covert action. The presidential advice quoted here is representative of a wide array of CIA and other government commentaries. The Bay of Pigs, the Congo, and other events had effectively eroded plausible deniability, resulting in a stand for a general assertion of secrecy.

The people who made the choices, of course, were the members of the 303 Committee, LBJ's renamed Special Group. Secretary of State Dean Rusk may not speak for all the principals who participated as secret war managers, but his remarks are eyebrow-raising. "I look back with chagrin at my performance as a statutory member of the National Security Council charged with overseeing CIA activities," Rusk wrote in 1990. LBJ sometimes called them together, but that happened when their surrogates on 303 could not agree. The secret war, Rusk believes, should have been a focus for "we permanent NSC members—not our substitutes." Rusk himself never asked to review either, nor did the principals ever draw up the agendas or stop to review "what was actually being done, rather than just consider items placed on the agenda." The former secretary of state decided that control ought not to be left to subordinates or congressional committees: "We learned the hard way."

In actuality the 303 Committee's approach had not changed since Kennedy's day. If anything, Lyndon Johnson practiced covert techniques even more enthusiastically. Between November 1963 and February 1967 the 303 Committee approved 142 covert action proposals, an average of 5.25 per month. That compares to 4.8 approvals per month from Kennedy's Special Group. During the decade beginning in 1965 some 32 percent of approved covert actions were for election support in foreign countries, 29 percent for media or propaganda activity, and 23 percent for paramilitary operations or arms transfers, the remainder for assorted projects.

The Central Intelligence Agency professed to believe executive control was strong. According to a February 1967 agency memorandum:

> The policy arbiters have questioned CIA presentations, amended them and, on occasion, denied them outright. The record shows that the Group/Committee, in some instances, has overridden objections from the DCI and instructed the Agency to carry out certain activities. . . . Objections by State have resulted in amendment or rejection of election proposals, suggestions for air proprietaries, and support plans for foreign governments. . . . The Committee has suggested areas where covert action is needed, has decided that another element of government should undertake a proposed action, imposed caveats and turned down specific proposals for CIA action from Ambassadors in the field.

This is a carefully circumscribed description, one that suggests more restraint than actually exercised, as the following will show. In addition, the language indicates a fair amount of tinkering with proposals. That represented an effort to bring sound management to covert action, but, as noted elsewhere, it also brought responsibility that much closer to the president.

Although this narrative has detailed a welter of 303 Committee meetings (including those of its predecessors) on a variety of subjects, all pertain to specific covert actions, and while the totality clearly conveys the extent to which this NSC unit managed the secret war, it fails to convey the breadth and depth of the work. A quick survey of 303 business will aid in understanding its importance.

One staple of the work was the joint reconnaissance program. Each month the officials responsible for spyplanes, satellites, De Soto patrols, and assorted other technical collection programs listed the missions planned and placed it before the 303 Committee. Significant modifications were also considered. When President Johnson wished to reveal the existence of the CIA/air force supersonic reconnaissance plane OXCART (SR-71) in 1964, the Special Group pondered that proposal. In 1967 when the CIA wanted to use OXCART over North Vietnam ("Black Orchid"), the group considered that too. No one hesitated to dictate alterations. At a November 1967 session, for example, the 303 Committee changed the date for one "Burning Sun" collection mission and modified the closest point of approach to enemy territory planned for another. Peripheral flights around Cuba, missions over North Korea, electronic intelligence "tickler" flights against the Soviet Bloc, the resumption of De Soto patrols after the Gulf of Tonkin, the *Liberty* and *Pueblo* affairs—all concerned the 303 Committee. The project to place nuclear-powered detection gear in the Indian Himalayas to monitor Chinese weapons development came before 303, as did the continuation of U.S. intelligence ground stations in Iran, Pakistan, and Ethiopia. The group did not deal in espionage.

From the beginning of 1967 through May 1968 the 303 Committee handled five proposals for specialized use of submarines, seven for the U-2, eight for OXCART, five for other aviation assets, and eight for scientific or technical collection programs, most in the Far East.

During the Vietnam War the 303 Committee approved similar monthly program proposals for OPLAN 34-A pressures against North Vietnam as well as for cross-border patrols into Cambodia, Laos, and North Vietnam. In connection with the Gulf of Tonkin incident, former NSC staffer Francis Bator recently reminded the author that it would have been a 303 Committee responsibility to ensure that, unless intended, there was no conflict between the 34-A attacks along the North Vietnamese coast and the De Soto patrol taking place at the same time. Records are still not available to answer that question.

The Special Group also monitored implementation of covert programs. In the six months through mid-1968, for example, 303 considered eighteen different status reports on assorted covert actions. During that period there were no fewer than thirty requests for project renewals. A former member who had served on the Special Group told a Council on Foreign Relations symposium in January 1968 that the 303 Committee had been notably deficient in reviewing ongoing projects. These figures seem to bear out that observation.

Several of the status reports to 303 concerned Guyana. In March 1967 the CIA proposed a new covert operation to influence the next election there. The 303 Committee approved the plan on April 7. This included monthly payments to Forbes Burnham, ostensibly to help him with party organization. Delmar Carlson, by this time ambassador, met directly with Burnham as early as that June, and the record of their conversation shows they explicitly discussed how overseas votes in the election would be manipulated, even to the numbers of votes for different parties that Burnham would allow. The record indicates that Washington had a say in this. The United States tried, without success, to moderate Burnham's behavior. The 303 Committee could have halted the money flow. It did not. Between 1962 and 1968 the CIA spent more than $2 million on Guyana capers. In December 16, 1968, elections Burnham's party won an absolute majority in the Guyanese parliament.

Approving the consolidated budget for covert operations, an annual exercise, always generated heat. A special issue in the summer of 1966 was the degree to which the White House Bureau of the Budget—Bob Amory, the former CIA man, was chief examiner—could involve itself in the details of the projects, and 303 engaged Amory in protracted negotiations. But the bureau was Lyndon Johnson's budget traffic cop, and this exchange could end only one way.

White House matters arose time and again with PFIAB inquiries. Some Special Group meetings with the board have already been recounted. In the summer of 1968 the PFIAB asked what 303 procedures prevented it from simply being a rubber stamp. Clearly the board aimed to discover how well 303 reviewed projects, what it learned from this, and what was the practical effect. Judging from Dean Rusk's comment, the answer could not be flattering.

Specific issues preoccupied the 303 Committee from week to week. In November 1967 the group immersed itself in forward planning for the CIA Laos program through 1969. *Ramparts* and other 1967 controversies did not entirely close off youth initiatives—in March 1968 the 303 members authorized CIA to run an operation at the World Youth Festival to be held in Bulgaria that summer. A month later the Special Group, back on Vietnam, considered a move to expand CIA's Provincial Reconnaissance Units. Over the seventeen months beginning in January 1967 the committee dealt with twenty-three projects for Africa, thirty-three for Latin America, fifteen for Europe, fourteen for Asia, and two for the Middle East. 303 rejected a half-dozen. According to a 303 memo to PFIAB, the paucity of Middle East projects followed from the Six-day War, whose aftermath precluded the political action projects that had formed the bulk of CIA's effort in the region.

Sometimes 303 matters were kicked upstairs to the president. In the 1967 controversies over CIA funding, for example, these items first came before 303. That July, Rusk signaled his desire to bring one to LBJ's Tuesday Lunch national security meetings. As Dick Helms pointed out to Walt Rostow, Rusk worried about the fallout in Congress if the operation were blown, not the project itself or its objectives. That December Nick Katzenbach told 303 that Rusk "had not been overcome with enthusiasm" for Operation Night Bolt, a scheme to send SEALs to reconnoiter Haiphong harbor. Walt Rostow agreed to take it up at the next Tuesday Lunch.

An illustration of the 303 process exists in the matter of CIA political action in Italy. This program came before the 303 Committee in June 1965. In two meetings that month the Special Group considered another year's subsidy. Complicated by Italy's multiparty political system, making necessary a welter of CIA approaches to different groups, sometimes with cross-cutting interests, the secret war managers decided to go ahead. Mac Bundy expressed his private doubts to President Johnson, who demanded a review of the Italian program. Early in August Bundy reported back that JFK had thought the payments excessive, that CIA political action specialists believed the United States was not getting its money's worth, and that subsidies had been declining for that reason. There had been a spike upward in 1963, an Italian election year. But the subsidies were nevertheless significant, and Italians had been telling CIA contacts they needed a lot more. Bundy recommended funding what the 303 Committee had already approved, with the CIA to tell Italian politicians they would not get more unless they could show the money was really needed and could be used effectively.

When the program came up for renewal in 1966, American diplomats in Italy told Alex Johnson, State's 303 representative, that another election was coming and could be especially important. Proposals before 303 actually provided a cut of one-third. Efforts were made to structure subsidies so they went to specific recipients for specific activities in support of U.S. objectives. The committee restored the money on the understanding that CIA subsidies would be phased out after the election and disappear by 1968. The 303 Committee approved final subsidies on August 22, 1967. In all, between 1958 and 1968 the CIA's leading Italian recipients received some $26 million, with another $11.3 million going to other political parties. Total cost of CIA political action in Italy from the 1948 elections to the termination of the program added up to $65.1 million.

Even on a set of projects the secret war managers wanted to eliminate, it had taken three years and a lot more money to close them out. The parallels to the golden parachute arrangements made with the students, the radios, and the Asia Foundation are evident. Proponents could always resort to the argument that CIA assets left in the lurch would be unable to fulfill Washington's objectives or, worse, might turn against the United States. It remained easier to initiate covert actions than to terminate them, even with tough management. Any weakening and a project would reappear on the Special Group agenda, as happened with Italy. Lyndon Johnson's successors encountered the same basic dynamics.

Lyndon Johnson had been a president with a passion for domestic policy. Proud of instituting the social programs he called the Great Society, LBJ viewed foreign affairs as problems that came with his job. He was keenly disappointed with the Indochina war, which absorbed ever greater time, energy, and the economic resources he preferred to invest in domestic programs, not to mention the idealism of American youth, which might have transformed the nation. The growth of controversy and opposition to the war ultimately cast a pall over Johnson's political future. In the spring of 1968 the president decided he would not run for reelection. The strongest candidate in the resulting free-for-all, and the victor in the November elections, was Richard Milhous Nixon.

Like Johnson, Nixon stood ready to use the full potential of his office, even to seize power for it. This has led observers to term these years the era of "the imperial presidency." Unlike LBJ, Nixon was primarily interested in foreign policy. He was also suspicious of the bureaucracy and wanted policymaking centered in the White House. Paradoxically, though Nixon preoccupied himself with details he wished to be seen as above the policy fray. This made his choice of staff crucial, especially the adviser for national security and his NSC staff. For his purposes, Nixon's selection of Henry A. Kissinger as security adviser proved inspired. Adept at maneuvers and at fighting in the political alleyways of Washington, Kissinger, a former Harvard professor, became the operator Nixon wanted.

Nixon's dominance of American foreign policy would be outlasted by Kissinger's, in the end by two and a half years. At the outset, however, there was no question as to Richard Nixon's primacy. His remarkable comeback became the prelude to an increased global role for the United States.

From his eight years as vice president under Eisenhower, Nixon had acquired a broad understanding of covert action. He now took command of ongoing projects in Southeast Asia, initiating new ones there, in the Near East, and in Latin America.

Although Richard Nixon learned much of what he knew about leadership from President Eisenhower, there were fundamental differences between the two. Ike tried to be subtle, to work with a hidden hand. Nixon preferred dramatic decisions yielding sensational results. Also, whereas Eisenhower used covert action extensively, Nixon's efforts here proved somewhat more restrained. In Vietnam, Richard Nixon's program remained robust. In 1969, for example, a major 303 Committee issue, on which Nixon repeatedly prodded Kissinger and Helms, was CIA initiation of fresh psychological warfare efforts in North Vietnam. But growing controversy, not least over the secret war in Laos, held Nixon back. Covert operations would be initiated elsewhere, however, and Nixon's reticence about starting them did not prevent him from demanding extravagant results.

Nixon's proclivities were reinforced by a group assembled by old line Wurlitzer-man Franklin A. Lindsay. Out of the business for years now, at least directly (he became head of the Itek Corporation, a prime contractor for equipment used in U.S. spy satellites), Lindsay took up the reins again briefly in 1967–1968 to lead a study group on the utility of covert operations, their work relevant to whomever might win the elections of 1968. That happened to be Richard Nixon. Under the aegis of Harvard's Center for International Affairs, Lindsay's group included old warhorses Richard Bissell and Lyman Kirkpatrick, former officials Abram Chayes and Adam Yarmolinsky, and such academics as Samuel P. Huntington, Richard E. Neustadt, Lucien Pye, Roger D. Fisher, Edwin O. Reischauer, and Max Millikin. The group finalized its report in December 1968 and gave it to Henry Kissinger's transition team.

Dispensing with traditional plausible deniability, the Lindsay group advised the president to concern himself directly with covert operations. In a passage that no doubt resounded for Kissinger, the report advised Nixon to assign a senior aide with direct access to the president to oversee all covert operations. Kissinger in fact got that task in his role as national security adviser. The Lindsay group viewed Richard Helms as an effective CIA director and saw no need to change leadership at Langley—again the course Nixon adopted. On the other hand, it felt the DCI should be enjoined to say "no" more frequently when proposals did not seem viable.

No immediate program changes seemed necessary, except that the group pushed hard for public funding of Radio Free Europe and Radio Liberty. In general the Lindsay report found that covert operations had little capacity to achieve important objectives and were best suited to tactical situations for short-term gains. Costs included the danger that Americans would see their country as engaging in "dirty tricks" abroad, the weakening of American constitutional checks and balances through their being bypassed in these activities, and damage to the international system from the evident U.S. disrespect for the legitimate interests of other governments: "The character of such secret intervention makes it difficult for the United States to justify it and reconcile it with the general principles of international behavior for which we stand."

Whether these activities were exposed or not, there were risks and costs, the Lindsay report concluded. And it affirmed, as had previous reviews, that large-scale operations rarely remain secret. Nevertheless a major reason to engage in these activities remained the need to do things covertly. The cautious approach here was quite evident. In a 1974 survey ranging over the many examinations of intelligence through the years, the CIA characterized the Lindsay report as concluding there was no need of additional supervision, simply stricter internal controls. Langley's own study for the new administration made out covert operations as "designed to discredit the prestige and ideology of International Communism and reduce its control over any areas of the world, and conversely to strengthen the orientation toward the U.S. of the peoples of the free world."

Director of Central Intelligence Richard Helms may have been gratified by the Lindsay group's recommendation that President-elect Nixon keep him on, but in truth the Helms's appointment was a done deal. After his first transition meeting with Nixon at the LBJ Ranch, Lyndon Johnson pulled Helms aside and told him that Nixon had asked and that he, Johnson, had commended Helms as an effective spy boss. Later Nixon summoned Helms to New York's Hotel Pierre for a lookover. Henry Kissinger, already with the president-elect, had known Helms since the Berlin crisis of 1961 and seconded the recommendation. Although Nixon did not announce his selection until December 18, from mid-November Helms knew he would be continuing at the CIA.

Nixon reappointed Helms, but president and chief spook were never comfortable together. Richard Nixon's memoirs say nothing of his opinion on Helms, but there are numerous disparaging comments in Nixon's conversations recorded on tape. Helms had met Nixon as far back as the Hungarian uprising, when he briefed the vice president before Nixon's visit to Austria. They did not cross paths again until now. Helms had no illusions: reappointment, he writes, "did not shake my longstanding impression of Nixon's antipathy for the agency." Kissinger records that Nixon suspected Helms of being close to circles that included some of his worst critics. That may be true, but in fact there were few people with whom Nixon *was* comfortable, Kissinger included.

The president intended to keep the CIA at arm's length, initially even excluding its director from his National Security Council meetings. Reminded that, by law, the DCI advised the Council on intelligence, Nixon relented enough to permit Helms to brief the NSC, after which he was to leave. That clumsy procedure left the principals without answers to any question they thought up after Helms's departure, and lasted fewer than two months. Nixon smoothed the rough edge by inviting everyone on the NSC to lunch with him after their next meeting. Helms then entered the fold, never knowing whether the president had merely forgotten his previous dictum. Later Helms learned that Defense Secretary Melvin Laird, whom Nixon needed and dared not cross, had issued an ultimatum that the DCI be included. But Kissinger demanded that all CIA material—intelligence, operations, *anything*—go to the president only through him.

Nixon continued to hold against Helms and the Central Intelligence Agency what he fancied had been their responsibility for his loss of the 1960 election against John F. Kennedy—Langley's supposed leak to Kennedy on Bay of Pigs plans—and he acted against the agency where possible. Nixon forced the CIA to reduce its overseas staff, eroding its covert capability, and he cut the agency's budget. Later Nixon demanded that the CIA declassify documents on the Diem assassination and the Bay of Pigs which the president thought might discredit political opponents. When Helms refused, it became another black mark against him and the agency.

But on the afternoon of March 7, 1969, Nixon helicoptered to Langley with Helms to address senior officials of the CIA in the agency's large, dome-shaped auditorium, "The Bubble." As is common in such ceremonial pep talks, the president painted the role of the CIA in the most glowing terms. "I look upon this organization," Nixon declared, "as not one which is necessary for the conduct of conflict or war, or call it what you may, but in the final analysis . . . one of the great instruments of our Government for the preservation of peace, for the avoidance of war, and for the development of a society in which this kind of thing would not be as necessary, if necessary at all."

Referring to the "call it what you may" war, Nixon said: "I think the American people need to understand the need for this foreign policy option."

But there was little hope by 1969 that the public attitude toward covert operations would be as permissive as when Nixon had been vice president, before the Bay of Pigs, the Congo, Vietnam, the National Student Association, Radio Free Europe, and so on. The 303 Committee approved continued funding for selected Soviet emigré groups and activities early in the Nixon administration. Then came the Green Beret murder case in Vietnam and revelations of the Laotian secret war. In October 1969 Kissinger issued a directive in Nixon's name requiring covert actions normally approved by the 303 Committee to be reviewed every year. Two months later, extending Kennedy's and Johnson's practice, Nixon reaffirmed that ambassadors were the leaders of the U.S. missions in their countries, to be kept in the picture on all CIA activities.

As became the standard in the Nixon White House, the president's men then kept ambassadors, and much of the rest of the government, in ignorance of what the chief executive had in mind. Thus in opening relations with the People's Republic of China, for example, Henry Kissinger and Alexander Haig, his deputy, made a series of 1971 secret trips to prepare Nixon's way for a ceremonial visit to Beijing a few months later.

The China secret affected CIA directly. In December 1971 Beijing suddenly released Richard G. Fecteau, one of the agency officers captured back in 1952, as a goodwill gesture. Langley had no idea why this happened, and the second CIA prisoner, John T. Downey, stayed in jail, though with a reduced sentence. When the CIA learned of Nixon's China trip it begged for help on its other prisoner. At the time Downey's mother, ill, had little chance of surviving until the man's sentence ran out. Meeting with Chinese leader Zhou Enlai on February 25, 1972, Nixon indeed mentioned Downey. Zhou commented optimistically on a possible release, though he noted the absence of precedent for this between nations with no diplomatic relations. Nothing happened. By November Downey's mother had been confined to an old-age home. NSC staff asked Nixon to revisit the issue. The president used a news conference to admit publicly for the first time that Downey and Fecteau had been CIA officers and apologize for their presence in China. Beijing released John Downey in March 1973.

For more than two decades, since the inception of covert operations in Harry Truman's time, it had been assumed that a certain duplicity went with the territory. This formed the essence of the concept of "plausible deniability." But the rationale had always been to prevent knowledge of the actions becoming available to the targets, in the case of minor endeavors, or the American public in larger ones. No one ever intended to deny information to leaders in the U.S. government. Propelled by the growing controversy over covert operations, however, Nixon and Kissinger contrived to do exactly that, elevating duplicity to a virtual management principle. Since the inception of the technique, the problem of controlling covert operations had been a thorny one. We have seen the efforts of Truman, Eisenhower, Kennedy, and Johnson. Nixon too made his changes. According to Kissinger, the change came because the 303 Committee had been identified in a 1969 news story.

In fact the reconstituted NSC Special Group expanded to include the attorney general John N. Mitchell, Nixon's close friend and former law partner. Undoubtedly Mitchell joined the Special Group as a personal watchdog to keep an eye on Kissinger, whom Nixon did not entirely trust. Other Special Group members saw little reason for his inclusion. Mitchell rarely spoke at meetings and instead played with his pipe.

Nixon formalized the change on February 17, 1970, in National Security Decision Memorandum (NSDM) 40. The Special Group became the 40 Committee. The NSDM also rescinded NSC-5412/2 with its anti-Soviet rationale. Instead Nixon's directive stated, "I have determined that it is essential to the defense and security of the United States and its efforts for world peace that the overt foreign activities of the U.S. Government continue to be supplemented by covert action operations."

Under NSDM-40 the Special Group was to approve "all" major and politically sensitive covert action programs and the joint reconnaissance schedule, and to review covert programs annually. The review requirement responded to criticisms of the Johnson-era 303 Committee and represented one of the few substantive changes in NSDM-40. To fulfill CIA's role, at Langley the DO's Missions and Programs Staff developed the justification and objective memoranda for 40 Committee approval. This staff also became the center for operational planning. A reorganized covert action staff also replaced the previous one in the area of political and psychological operations.

Having carefully set up this framework, Nixon and Kissinger proceeded to ignore it. The most frequent occasions for 40 Committee meetings became those for project review. U. Alexis Johnson, back on the group again, writes, "It is true that during the Nixon administration the President and CIA bypassed the Committee on sensitive topics." When Nixon gave his first go-ahead on covert arms to Cambodia, he ordered Kissinger to say nothing to the 40 Committee. At the very same time the Special Group had on its plate a similar clandestine arms initiative, to supply rifles to the King of Jordan, so this was not a matter of excluding a certain type of activity. Everyone from the Special Group to the secretary of state lived in ignorance of the Chile initiative called Track II, even though the group considered almost two dozen other aspects of covert action in Chile. Similarly the 40 Committee would not be consulted on the project shortly to be described, a paramilitary effort among the Kurds of Iraq.

Among decisions that can be traced to the 40 Committee, those on collection figure prominently. Overhead and satellite reconnaissance targeting, submarine incursions into foreign territorial waters, and the *Glomar Explorer*'s attempt to raise a Soviet missile submarine from the floor of the Pacific Ocean were discussed by the 40 Committee. A project to spend $10 million to influence the Italian elections in 1972, much like the budgets approved for Chile, went through the full approval process, by then pretty much routinized. Another routine function was the approval of subsidies to certain foreign leaders—reportedly half a dozen were on the CIA payroll, including King Hussein of Jordan. Thus it came as no surprise when secret-war managers were asked to approve $20,000 to be handed to President Bokassa of the Central African Republic, who had received certain documents (believed forged) impugning American motives and threatened to break relations with the United States. The 40 Committee was used on everyday decisions but not for the big plays.

Henry Kissinger chaired the 40 Committee. He set the meetings and agendas, assisted by a single CIA staffer. Only principals could attend; Henry was the ultimate arbiter. The first official manual on covert operations, prepared by the CIA in 1972, observed that only about a quarter would be considered by the 40 Committee. Excluded were not only many minor, unimportant operations but virtually all the major, sensitive ones.

One technique Kissinger used to minimize the committee's impact was to have as few meetings as possible. He liked to poll by telephone on the dubious theory members had better uses for their time. Beyond the question of what could be more important than running the nation's covert action program, it cannot have escaped notice in the Kissinger NSC that phone calls permitted fewer records to be kept, and allowed Kissinger to take on other officials one by one. Avoiding meetings also prevented the kind of give-and-take that would have allowed officials to realize what was going on. In 1972 the 40 Committee met only once. In 1973 and 1974 it adopted more than three dozen decisions without meeting to discuss any actual covert action program.

The essential activity became focusing covert activity more tightly on exact foreign policy goals. In Southeast Asia, Latin America, and the Middle East, action continued on something like the old scale, but across the board, spending declined in most geographic and functional areas. Mostly due to Vietnam, the cost of paramilitary operations reached a peak in 1970, but after 1972 it declined even in the Far East. By 1973 the CIA director could report that only 5 percent of the agency's budget was spent for covert action. At the same time a relatively high proportion of projects—over a quarter—were defined as major operations. How Kissinger supposed the 40 Committee could review every major operation every year without ever meeting can only be imagined.

The Special Group had never been so moribund. This might not have been so costly had other oversight mechanisms functioned more effectively. They did not. The President's Foreign Intelligence Advisory Board, which Nixon reconstituted by executive order on March 20, 1969, remained the sole alternative. Maxwell Taylor, the first chairman, was in declining health and left after about a year, succeeded by Adm. George W. Anderson, under whom PFIAB became decidedly more political. In the style of the Nixon White House, PFIAB members like lawyer Franklin B. Lincoln, *Los Angeles Times* magnate Franklin D. Murphy, New York governor Nelson Rockefeller, and former diplomat Robert Murphy took their concerns directly to the president. In the six years of Nixon's presidency the board met with the president only eight times. Nixon sometimes convened smaller groups, but at his behest, not theirs. A senior PFIAB official recalls that the board exercised no watchdog function. An NSC staffer of the period observed that in her experience, in two and a half years across the hall she never saw the door open to PFIAB's suite in the Old Executive Office Building.

The board retained some classy, dedicated members, in particular Gordon Gray, William O. Baker, and Edwin H. Land, who worked selflessly and hard, but they labored in isolation. Gray headed a small subcommittee on clandestine collection. Baker and Land continued to focus on technical issues. Possibly PFIAB's greatest achievement during this period came in their area, where Baker and Land fought for a next-generation photographic satellite with digital readout capability, opposed by the air force.

Governor Rockefeller headed the subcommittee on covert operations, and there is little indication he ever saw one he did not like. Bob Murphy once suggested assassinating Ho Chi Minh—the CIA rejected that out of hand. (Murphy often played the devil's advocate, saying things just to see how people would respond.) The aged Ho died late in 1969. Agency officers were highly critical of Murphy. Some said, in a play on the title of his memoir, that Murphy was a warrior among diplomats. Admiral Anderson, a nitpicker, went after the CIA on its Soviet estimates, which he regarded as insufficiently alarming, and put his effort into writing alternative, more somber, papers. Staff thought Anderson's presence a bad influence. Later additions to the board included California governor Ronald Reagan, who seems to have left no tracks; scientist Edward Teller, very active but held in contempt by Baker and Land; and Texas governor John Connally, who propelled PFIAB into its first-ever study of economic intelligence collection and had powerful influence on the president.

Richard Helms dealt straightforwardly with the board. Typically PFIAB staff would tell Helms before a board session about the nature of the meeting, and the CIA director would come prepared to discuss the subject. Helms showed up with a single aide, in stark contrast to the military, whose generals appeared with full entourages. Henry Kissinger and Gen. Alexander M. Haig usually sat in on PFIAB's meetings with the president. Kissinger, or sometimes the board's executive secretary, prepared information papers for Nixon before the meetings.

Richard Nixon used the board for chores that might have little to do with intelligence. Early on the president assigned PFIAB to assess the Russian-designed AK-47 assault rifle against the American M-16. Later tasks included examining the capabilities of the Soviet SA-7 "Strella," a shoulder-fired anti-aircraft missile, or commenting on a U.S. sale of tanks to Turkey. There would be a six-month-long study of the intelligence failure on North Vietnamese supply shipments through Cambodia. Sometimes Kissinger made the assignments, but he carefully emphasized that he acted for the president. In June 1970 Nixon met the board, opening with a long soliloquy on foreign policy in the Middle East, then asked PFIAB to make an East Asian inspection trip and render a report in the style of those that British consultant Sir Robert Thompson had supplied to Nixon about Vietnam. The board did just that and had one of its smaller group meetings with the president on July 18. Admiral Anderson had focused on military affairs, Gordon Gray on intelligence, Frank Murphy on pacification issues, and Robert Murphy on political matters.

Board executive secretary Gerard P. Burke accompanied the group on this trip. A National Security Agency officer with long service as chief of staff to Gen. Marshall Carter, a good friend of Max Taylor's, Burke came to PFIAB as deputy to J. Patrick Coyne, whom he then replaced. Burke's experience had been in the missile intelligence field, and his initial purpose was to give the board depth on its review of the Soviet estimates. Now Burke was pulled into everything. For a time he felt himself virtually commuting to Vietnam since that subject came up at every single PFIAB meeting.

During the 1970 tour Burke sat by the window as board members talked to Lon Nol in Cambodia, and he took notes when they spoke to Souvanna Phouma in Laos. They visited Long Tieng and saw Vang Pao's Hmong army. Enormously impressed that a war directed by a few CIA field hands seemed to be working while the one led by all the generals in Vietnam looked like a lost cause, Burke appreciated the incredible mess. But there was little time—or staff—to study the issues well on those ten-countries-in-ten-days inspections. The group was unable to look into the Phoenix Program. Gordon Gray studied drug use by American soldiers in South Vietnam, yet the PFIAB remained entirely unaware of drug running by U.S. allies in Laos. A year later, Burke recalls, the board never heard of and did not see the CIA inspector general's report on the Laotian drug traffic.

The talking points that Kissinger prepared when the PFIAB group returned indicate the White House interest here. Nixon, aside from Vietnam, should ask whether Lon Nol really commanded or if he reflected the confidence of ignorance. As for Indonesia, where PFIAB had met with Suharto and his intelligence chiefs, Kissinger wanted Nixon to ask "On Cambodia, did he [Suharto] emphasize the importance of Indonesia's maintaining its appearance of neutrality? Or did he emphasize the need to save the Lon Nol government?" Clearly Nixon's intent here had been to use PFIAB to feel out Suharto's willingness to engage more deeply as surrogate for the United States in Cambodia.

A May 1972 meeting record shows the board in its more traditional role. Nixon apologized for not meeting PFIAB more frequently. Their conversation touched on the Soviet estimates, on net assessment, on overhead reconnaissance, human intelligence collection, and on economic intelligence. Nixon asked the board to study the capabilities of U.S. versus Russian conventional weapons. Covert operations were nowhere in the conversation. At this very moment Nixon had resumed pressing the CIA for covert action against Hanoi while the agency had moved into high gear on a paramilitary initiative with the Kurds in Iraq.

Any potential the Foreign Intelligence Advisory Board might have had as an oversight mechanism on covert operations was vitiated by the Nixon administration's Machiavellian secrecy. For example, at one point Kissinger himself asked the PFIAB to examine the situation in Chile, where the socialist Salvador Allende had just been elected president, to see whether the CIA had failed to propose measures that might have prevented this. Yet Kissinger then refused the board access to 40 Committee minutes and NSC records that would have shown covert actions had been approved and carried out. The PFIAB review ended right there.

In another instance Gordon Gray supervised an inquiry into U.S. counterintelligence. Closely watched by both the CIA and FBI, Gray ran a full-spectrum review, including visits to key overseas facilities, without encountering the deleterious impact of the hunt for alleged Soviet "moles" that had been tearing apart the CIA for years. Gray's report contained no criticism whatever of Langley counterspy James J. Angleton, the operator behind the witch hunt. The CIA blackout of PFIAB necessary to achieve that result must have been massive.

After leaving the board, Robert Murphy chaired a presidential commission on the U.S. government and foreign relations. The commission's overview volume, in its discussion of intelligence issues, included remarks about PFIAB immediately following its conclusion that the president's role remained crucial: "We believe the Board should play a larger role—the steady, external and independent oversight of the performance of the foreign intelligence community as a whole." Nelson Rockefeller, who chaired another presidential commission in the mid-1970s, also reported that the board's role should be strengthened. These were commentaries on their experience with PFIAB during the Nixon years.

Meanwhile Richard Nixon lost his ability to wield power even as he concentrated it in the Oval Office. "Watergate" is an ugly name from the Nixon years, a product of his 1972 reelection campaign. It is important to the CIA because of the participation of Bay of Pigs veterans, not only Cuban exiles like Bernard Barker but CIA officers like Howard Hunt. Agency security specialist James W. McCord, Jr., like Hunt, collected his paycheck at the White House. When the public learned that the CIA had helped Hunt's White House schemes, had prepared certain psychological profiles of Americans at the request of the White House, and that virtually the same Watergate cast had carried out illegal break-ins on White House instructions, the CIA knew it had a major political problem.

Most troublesome of all, Nixon tried to use the agency to shut down the FBI's investigation. Langley resisted, but whatever it had or had not done, the inquiries and the drawn-out investigation were certain to damage the agency. Richard Helms designated Executive Director William E. Colby as point man for Watergate matters. Director Helms, during his final months, and Gen. Vernon A. Walters, who held the post of DDCI from 1972 to 1976, spent a great deal of time defending the CIA from White House demands or the Watergate investigation and others that succeeded it.

Watergate, and especially the CIA's refusal to enlist in the White House political cover operation, provided grist for Nixon's reflexive antipathy for Richard Helms. By September 1972 the president was telling his chief of staff, H. R. Haldeman, that Helms had to go. Nixon also spoke of cutting the CIA back by as much as 40 percent. A couple of weeks after Nixon's victory in the November election he summoned Helms to Camp David. The spy anticipated budget business and armed himself with the usual briefing papers. Instead Haldeman ushered Helms into the presidential presence and Nixon, after awkward small talk, broached his desire for fresh faces. The conversation turned to Helms's future, and the two agreed on the CIA director's suggestion that he be appointed ambassador to Iran. Helms recounts that he has no idea why that country popped into his head. He left believing he had won a single concession: the move would be delayed until the end of March 1973, when Helms reached the agency's mandatory retirement age.

Bob Haldeman records in his diary for November 20, 1972, the fateful day at Camp David, that Helms recommended either Bill Colby or Tom Karamessines as his successor. Except for the Teheran appointment, none of what Helms discussed that day would come to pass. Rather, in early February 1973, among other appointments, Nixon announced his selection of James R. Schlesinger as director of central intelligence. The president had reached outside the agency. And the accelerated dismissal of Helms, which barely gave the departing director time to arrange a farewell ceremony, Haldeman attributed to simple error.

Nixon-era covert operations proceeded despite this political infighting. One nation to feel the weight of Nixon's covert option was Iraq, especially the Kurds in Kurdistan in the north of the country. This secret war essentially involved the United States doing a favor for the Shah of Iran.

The Kurds were a nomadic people, a loose confederation of some forty tribes who earnestly desired nationhood. They were spread out across the borders of five countries: Iraq, Iran, Syria, Turkey, and the Soviet Union. As early as 1948 a CIA estimate observed, "The mountain tribes known as the Kurds are now and will continue to be a factor of some importance in any strategic estimate of Near East affairs." Periodically, Kurds had fought the Turks, Iraqis, and Iranians in quest of their freedom—*sarbasti* in the Kurdish tongue. Shortly after World War II, Kurds cooperated with the Russians to set up a short-lived tribal "republic" in northern Iran. After a 1958 coup in Baghdad, the Iraqi government began cutting back Kurdish autonomy. The tribes took the field in a partisan war in which long campaigns alternated with cease-fires. Mullah Mustapha Barzani, a tribal potentate since 1945, led the main forces. Finally, from sheer exhaustion, in early 1970 the Iraqis and Kurds reached a settlement.

Peace might have reigned except for Iran. The Iranians were engaged in several border disputes with Iraq, including an acrimonious one over the international boundary in the Tigris River, which had changed course in such a way as to put the main shipping channel used by the Iraqis into an area claimed by Iran. The Shah of Iran feared the end of the Kurdish war would bring more direct confrontation between Iran and Iraq. He stirred up trouble for the Iraqi government—by then in the hands of Saddam Hussein. The shah offered money and weapons for Kurds to resume their fight. Dissatisfied with Saddam's implementation of the 1970 settlement, outraged by an assassination attempt against Barzani, the Kurds were tempted but also distrusted the shah. Barzani would consider the shah's offer only with a U.S. guarantee that Iran would not cut off the Kurdish resistance. In March 1972 Jordanian King Hussein forwarded Barzani's request for the guarantee to Nixon.

Teheran had already made two overtures to Washington, and concern grew when a high-level Soviet delegation visited Iraq that April and reached an arms deal with Saddam. In May Nixon and Kissinger made an official visit to Iran, immediately after the Moscow summit where the first strategic nuclear arms agreements with Russia were completed. In Teheran, John B. Connally, another Nixon political associate, told the shah that Washington could help the Kurds. The CIA handled the American side through its station in Teheran.

Kissinger set up the U.S. apparatus for the Kurdish secret war. He records Washington's goals as raising the costs to Baghdad of controlling Kurdistan, improving Kurdish bargaining power, and convincing Saddam to respect his Kurdish minority as well as Iranian security concerns. Kissinger military aide Col. Richard A. Kennedy met with the CIA and one of Barzani's sons on the Kurds' requests. A staff assistant, Alfred L. Atherton, Jr., became the NSC staff focal point. Nixon signed the authorizing directive on August 1. No 40 Committee meeting took place to analyze the project.

At first the Nixon directive provided for covert support of $5 million. The CIA provided $1 million worth of captured Soviet weapons and ammunition, and it remains unclear whether this formed part of the budgeted program or, like the initial CIA arms to Cambodia, occurred off the books. British covert aid also figured. The Israelis were helping the Kurds too, and had been since 1965. Together the three countries funded the secret war at a level of $1 million a month. These involvements were dwarfed by that of the shah. Armed with this assistance, the Kurds raised a hundred thousand partisan troops called *peshmerga*, a larger force than Mustapha Barzani had ever fielded. They engaged large Iraqi forces, including more than ninety thousand regular troops with twelve hundred tanks and two hundred guns, plus auxiliaries. By October the CIA could report that the Kurds were engaging much of the Iraqi army.

In 1973 the secret war intensified, along with demands for money. That March the CIA proposed an increase—one of James R. Schlesinger's few moves on the covert action front—which Kissinger backed and Nixon approved. Kissinger reports the shah's covert aid at about $30 million, and Iran began giving the Kurds heavy artillery as well.

Then the Iraqis joined other Arab states against Israel in the October 1973 "Yom Kippur War." Two Iraqi armored divisions and parts of two infantry divisions deployed into Syria, almost half of Baghdad's forces. Henry Kissinger's description of this intervention is of a piece with much of his writing: in his first volume of memoirs Kissinger puts the Iraqi expeditionary force at one division, about a third of its size. In his last volume, published long after the history of the October war had been well documented, Kissinger reduces the Iraqi force to a single brigade, a small fraction of the actual. Kissinger in fact argues that restricting the size of Saddam Hussein's force in the October war was an important achievement of the covert operation with the Kurds. But Baghdad clearly discounted a Kurdish offensive at the time of the war. Seeking to take pressure off their own front in Syria, Israeli advisers told the Kurds that now was the time for a big attack on Saddam. Barzani thought this a good idea and asked Washington about it. The CIA opposed any move. On October 16, 1973, Kissinger instructed the CIA director to tell the Kurds not to attack. Barzani relented. Kissinger's response thus flew in the face of his claimed achievement.

In the spring of 1974 the Iraqis launched a new offensive against the Kurds from more advantageous positions seized a year earlier. Barzani asked for new aid: $180 million to achieve Kurdish autonomy, or twice that amount to build an infrastructure to support independence. Even the lesser amount exceeded the entire CIA covert operations budget at the time. The CIA director—by then Dick Helms had gone to Iran as ambassador, Schlesinger had left, and William E. Colby was the boss—argued against any increase in aid to the Kurds. Kissinger viewed Colby as an isolated voice among a multitude who agreed the Kurds would be unable to defeat the Iraqis at prevailing levels of support. Kissinger asked Ambassador Helms and deputy national security adviser Gen. Brent Scowcroft to develop an alternate proposal, and they came back with a figure of $8 million. Another $1 million in overt refugee aid completed the U.S. package. The British and Israelis (together contributing about $7 million a year) maintained their assistance. Helms helped convince the shah to double his aid to $75 million.

Kissinger accuses the CIA secret warriors of dragging their feet on the program while acknowledging that this moment in fact provided the opportunity for a real review of the policy. Kissinger admits he was too preoccupied with other issues to focus. Barzani and the Kurds, Henry writes, were poor guides, exuberant one moment but warning of defeat the next. The shah, dangerously, had gone to the extent of sending auxiliary troops into Iraq to fight in *peshmerga* uniform. Then Director Colby warned that Barzani's headquarters and best supply route to Iran were being threatened by Iraqi advances. Colby advised cutting back—the CIA had already given the Kurds almost $20 million, including more than 1,250 tons of weapons and ammunition. Rather than rethink the program, Kissinger cooked up a deal with the Israelis, who were happy to exchange Russian weapons they had captured in the October war for new American ones, to the tune of another $28 million.

Under unrelenting military pressure from Saddam Hussein's forces, by early 1975 the Kurds were in trouble. By now Washington estimated that only Iranian military intervention could save them, and that course would require at least two divisions of troops and cost $300 million. The shah had no intention of doing that. In February 1975 he began negotiating a border settlement with Saddam.

For the shah the Kurds were but a single card to play. Teheran and Baghdad bridged some of their differences, leading to a modus vivendi in March. Simultaneously the shah halted his aid, stopped free passage for CIA arms shipments, and closed his borders to Barzani's *peshmerga*. The next day the Iraqis began a full-scale offensive.

On March 10 the Kurds sent CIA an anguished appeal: "OUR PEOPLE'S FATE IN UNPRECEDENTED DANGER. COMPLETE DESTRUCTION HANGING OVER OUR HEAD. NO EXPLANATION FOR ALL THIS. WE APPEAL YOU AND U.S. GOVERNMENT INTERVENE ACCORDING TO YOUR PROMISES." Barzani also sent a personal letter to Kissinger, by now secretary of state in addition to his White House post: "We feel . . . that the United States has a moral and political responsibility toward our people who have committed themselves to your country's policy."

Arthur Callahan, Teheran station chief, in forwarding the Kurdish appeals, desperately asked if Langley had been in touch with Kissinger's office. He warned, "IF [THE UNITED STATES] DOES NOT HANDLE THIS SITUATION DEFTLY

IN A WAY WHICH WILL AVOID GIVING THE KURDS THE IMPRESSION THAT WE ARE ABANDONING THEM THEY ARE LIKELY TO GO PUBLIC. IRAN'S ACTION HAD NOT ONLY SHATTERED THEIR POLITICAL HOPES, IT ENDANGERS [THE] LIVES OF THOUSANDS." Kissinger made no reply. Callahan had not only offered options for a response but argued it was the right thing to do. He was left holding the bag. In Kissinger's version the station had all along sided with headquarters in resisting escalation and now succumbed to feelings of guilt. As many as 200,000 Kurdish refugees poured into Iran, many of them to be forcibly repatriated. None were admitted to the United States.

Pressed on the abandonment of the Kurds, a senior U.S. official famously retorted, "Covert action should not be confused with missionary work." Columnist William Safire became the first to identify this callous official as Henry Kissinger.

In retrospect Kissinger calls the public's horror over our sordid role in this covert action disaster "another of those episodes in self-flagellation." But this had nothing to do with narcissistic atonement for the exuberant optimism of the 1960s, as Kissinger goes on. He himself concedes that the pros and cons of the operation "seem much more balanced than they did at the time," and that "we probably should have analyzed more carefully the disparate motives of the anti-Iraqi coalition together with the consequences of one of the partners jumping ship." The truth is the Kurdish paramilitary action was pure realpolitik, and it rose and fell on considerations that had nothing to do with the Kurds or their desires for independence and democracy. Indeed, realpolitik was and remained at the heart of U.S. maintenance and development of covert action capabilities.

This period became a time of change for the secret warriors. James Schlesinger, a defense analyst with no intelligence experience other than his work on a management study for Nixon in 1970–1971, first replaced Richard Helms. Schlesinger moved over to secretary of defense after only five months at Langley, but in that short time he presided over important changes.

Within the agency itself, Schlesinger tried in a more measured way to fulfill the president's expectations for cutbacks. Convinced that much of the dead wood lay in the Directorate for Operations, the DCI concentrated there. Personnel began to fall as about a thousand officers were retired, asked to resign, or fired. Many of these people were paramilitary specialists. The actual reduction amounted to about 7 percent, not the 40 percent Nixon once spoke of. The covert action budget had been in decline since Laos funding had been taken away from the CIA and given to the Pentagon. The old Directorate for Plans disappeared, becoming, more appropriately, the Directorate for Operations (DO). Thomas Karamessines went into retirement with his colleague and friend Richard Helms, replaced as DDO by Bill Colby, and, when Colby swiftly moved up to the top job, by William Nelson, a Colby protégé.

Another change begun by Helms continued under Schlesinger, to be completed by Colby. This was the reorganization of the air proprietaries. A DCI directive in 1972 ordered that Air America be maintained only through the end of the Indochina war, that Southern Air Transport be sold and its Pacific Division immediately liquidated. The CIA divested Air America in stages. The firm E-Systems, a Texas corporation, bought Air Asia, the massive Taiwan maintenance facility. Air America planes and other assets were sold off one by one. By 1975 the parent Pacific Corporation had been reduced to eleven hundred employees. Final disposition of Air America was completed by mid-1976. The CIA expected to realize $20 million from the transactions.

A former owner of Southern Air Transport bid for the corporation and offered $5.6 million. Helms approved the sale during his last month as DCI, and the Southern Air board concurred. But other air freight companies objected, and one offered $7.5 million. Schlesinger rejected this bid. As acting director, Colby ordered final liquidation on July 31, 1973, but the former owner made a further counteroffer. The sale closed on the last day of 1973. There were later repercussions when the owner himself then liquidated Southern Air, violating a contract clause against windfall profits. The CIA sued and won a judgment of $1.3 million, in the course of that litigation admitting its ownership of Southern Air Transport. Ultimate losers were the SAT employees whose jobs evaporated.

The CIA also liquidated Intermountain Aviation in 1973, selling its airfield complex to Evergreen Aviation Corporation. In a clever touch, agency lawyers retained the same Phoenix firm that first took the Miranda case to trial for the legal work on the sale. Because Evergreen continued to do the same kinds of work as its predecessor, including for the CIA, it had never been clear that this was not simply a fresh agency proprietary cover. Evergreen invested some $24 million in the Marana base over the next decades, turning it into the largest aircraft storage facility in the world.

Meanwhile William E. Colby received the nod to follow Schlesinger as director of central intelligence. During Colby's confirmation hearings before the Senate Armed Services Committee, Old West–style "Wanted" posters sprouted on walls all over Washington. This mimicked a technique used in the Phoenix Program. The posters featured an ace of spades—used by Americans in Vietnam to connote death or killing—within which was a sketch of Colby's face. The DCI made sure that CIA's Office of Security did nothing about the posters.

Bill Colby's agency still had a global reach. But storm clouds were already gathering. The accumulating revelations of CIA actions over the years, many of them controversial, built public concern about the Cold War functions of this agency. For years the public remained quiescent, sedated by the assurances of presidents that the CIA acted in America's name to support its democratic values and combat the Russians on Cold War battlefronts. Mostly Americans had let it go at that. But the seeds that would bring those happy assumptions crashing down had already been sown. Not only could they not be recovered, but the reaping was about to begin. Colby took over at just that moment, September 1973, and the unraveling began in Latin America.

17

The Southern Cone

RICHARD NIXON and Henry Kissinger's most maligned covert enterprise took place in Chile, where they encouraged dictatorship over democracy, sanctioning a lapse in democratic rule that endured for two decades. But in truth the Chile case has broader meaning, for Nixon and Kissinger came on the scene late in the game, when U.S. intervention in Chilean politics had been under way for some time, one more facet of Washington's effort to guide the political evolution of an entire continent. What Nixon and Kissinger did escalated the CIA involvement. This operation spanned the terms of three American presidents—Kennedy and Johnson before Nixon—and the crossover illustrates an important aspect of political action: projects initiated for a specific purpose at a moment in time have often turned into open-ended campaigns from which extrication becomes difficult. We have seen this phenomenon at work in Italy and Guyana, but Chile provides the best-documented example as well as an illustration of the dangers associated with these activities. The adventure in Chile set the stage for a challenge to the very existence of the Central Intelligence Agency.

Political action in Chile in the Kennedy-Johnson era has been known ever since the Nixon operations sparked intensive investigations in the mid-1970s, but the breadth of the earlier involvement has been obscured by its characterization as simply "an" intervention in the 1964 Chilean presidential election. In fact the CIA functioned as the U.S. government's action agency for a wide-ranging program to shape Chilean politics that went on for more than a decade. That the CIA would lead a democracy into dictatorship no doubt never occurred to the secret war managers who started down this road, but that is how it turned out.

An American ally for many years, proud of its tradition of more than a century of democracy, Chile originally declared its independence from the Spanish Crown in 1810. Several features distinguished the history of Chile. First, unlike much of Latin America, where military rule and coups were quite common, the military in Chile found the climate inhospitable for intervention in politics. One coup in 1927 brought military rule for fewer than four years until, his government discredited, the *caudillo* resigned and slunk away. After ineffectual efforts to form a stable government, a couple of more coups in 1932, and further political posturing, the military gave way to civil administration. From 1932 until John Kennedy's day, Chilean democracy remained vibrant.

The second important fact is that Chilean democracy reigned in the face of economic problems. Large landholdings impeded agricultural growth while lack of capital restricted the exploitation of Chile's rich natural resources, especially copper, and opened the door to foreign investors who ended up with a major stake in Chile's economy. Fluctuations in world prices prevented Chile, like Bolivia, from enjoying the full benefits of its mineral riches.

These persistent problems led directly to the third feature of the Chilean scene: politicians promising radical reforms were the norm, not an aberration. Only one president in modern Chilean history had been elected on an openly conservative platform while between 1938 and 1953 the Chilean Communist and Socialist parties constantly served in government. In short, when John F. Kennedy took office in the United States, Chilean politics had long had a reformist character embracing a wide political spectrum.

Arthur M. Schlesinger, Jr., credits John Kennedy with sophisticated understanding of the evolution of Latin America. Kennedy's biographer sees JFK as well aware of the breakdown of oligarchies, the impossibility of saving the old order, even of avoiding the trap of favoring right-wing regimes, as he finds Eisenhower was prone to do. Kennedy wanted to chart a different course. Schlesinger describes at length how JFK came to his "Alliance for Progress," a sort of combination Marshall Plan and social/political program for Latin America. Kennedy outlined this initiative and gave it a name in Tampa, Florida, in October 1960. Among the tenets of that speech—Schlesinger quotes it—stood "'unequivocal support to democracy' and opposition to dictatorship." Once established in the White House, President Kennedy gave substance to the initiative and sent a delegation to an inter-American gathering at Punta del Este, Uruguay. This same conference became the setting for the confrontation, already recounted, between Che Guevara and JFK's Latin America man Richard Goodwin. The conference's joint declaration explicitly made a series of pledges, the first of them: "To improve and strengthen democratic institutions through application of the principle of self-determination by the people."

President Kennedy may have understood the realities of Latin political development, but the language of fine promises stopped at the hard edge of purpose once Kennedy decided to go after Fidel Castro. Washington counted its friends and marked its supposed enemies. There would be a second conference at Punta del Este in early 1962, by which time Washington had begun shopping for support to eject Cuba from the OAS. Chile under President Jorge Alessandri, a moderate in office since 1958, refused to participate. Just a few weeks later suggestions for projects in Chile went to Kennedy's Special Group.

These would be the first of many CIA projects in this land in the Southern Cone of South America. If the United States could get the right people elected to the Chilean National Assembly, the government in Santiago could act against Cuba without fear of domestic consequences. In early April 1962 the CIA put two fresh ideas before the Special Group, one to strengthen the organization of Chile's Christian Democrats, the party considered most in tune with U.S. interests; the other to help the Radical Party, a movement farther to the right. Initially the Special Group approved $50,000. That merely turned on the spigot. Before the summer ended, the group approved another $180,000 for the Christian Democrats alone.

A pair of decisions in early 1963 provided more cash to the Radical Party. That failed to keep the Radicals from losing their place as the country's largest political grouping in municipal elections in the spring. The Christian Democrats henceforth became the agency's main bet. And bet Langley did. On August 30, 1963, the Special Group continued the Chilean political action payments. More than a dozen proposals in all gained approval during the first two years.

One such project came directly from the president. Kennedy, attending a meeting of Harvard's Board of Overseers, spoke to fellow member David Rockefeller about enlisting big business to fight Castro. Spurred by Kennedy administration guarantees of investments, Rockefeller formed the Business Group for Latin America, which ultimately enlisted more than three dozen multinational corporations. In the same way the CIA conducted relations with labor or cultural groups, Langley assigned a case officer full time to handle the Business Group (the first of these left to work directly for the organization). The Business Group provided cover for CIA officers and contributed to political action, serving as a conduit for agency funds. Meanwhile, in Chile's uncertain economic climate, by 1967 the investment insurance had cost American taxpayers $600 million.

From the U.S. perspective, Chile no longer seemed a potential addition to Washington's anti-Castro mobilization. The existing Chilean government had presided over ballooning foreign debt while huge inflation sapped peoples' salaries. The influx of foreign investment seemed more like a fire sale of the national patrimony. At the same time the Socialist/Communist coalition had barely been defeated in the previous election. Another presidential election impended. Suddenly Washington saw CIA political action as a necessity.

The opposition would be formidable. Salvador Allende Gossens, scion of a clan of prominence, studied medicine but loved politics, and in 1933 broke his family's tradition of ties to the Radicals by helping found the Socialist Party. Allende became a Socialist leader in Valparaiso, first elected to the Chamber of Deputies, the lower house of the assembly, in 1937. Two years later he appeared in national government for the first time as minister of public health. Allende innovated public policy, creating a national health care system and contributing to Chile's social security system. In 1943 he became secretary general of the Socialists. From the mid-1940s Allende began broadening the left, beginning with cooperation between the Socialists and Chilean Communists. In the 1952 presidential election, Allende's first, he finished last in a field of four candidates. Ariel Dorfman, the noted Chilean poet, has written that he began hearing Allende's name as a young man in the mid-fifties, ranked with such leaders as the Argentinian Arturo Frondisi or the Guyanese Cheddi Jagan. In the 1958 elections Allende lost again, but barely—the margin of his defeat wafer thin. By 1964 there could be no doubt that Salvador Allende was the man to beat.

None of this came as any surprise to the secret warriors. They put the groundwork in place late the year before. On December 19, 1963, the Special Group approved a onetime payment to a Chilean democratic front that included Radicals, conservatives, and liberals. At the same time senior Christian Democratic Party (CDP) operatives were in Washington, meeting the CIA's J. C. King to tout their candidate Eduardo Frei Montalva and beg for agency money to fill their campaign coffers. Colonel King, receptive to these entreaties, on Christmas Eve sent Director John McCone a proposal memorandum. The bid involved half a million dollars, quite a present. McCone wanted to hear more. Just before New Year's, Hank Knocke, his executive assistant, asked King to clarify a few points. The baron represented the CDP as the fastest-growing party in Chile and the only one able to beat the Communists among their own base constituency. The concept ruled out any possibility the agency might influence CDP policy because Langley's money would have to be unattributable and Frei unwitting. But King nevertheless expected Frei to move in directions the United States favored.

Washington's deliberations took time, in part because this set of decisions marked the transition from Kennedy to Johnson. As the secret-war wizards deliberated, the price tag went up. When Frei's emissaries pursued their request again, in Santiago with U.S. embassy officials in March 1964, the CDP wanted a million dollars. The White House viewed this with equanimity. Ralph A. Dungan, a Kennedy holdover and political adviser whose special interest was Latin America and who would soon go to Santiago as ambassador, told Mac Bundy that he would not balk at $750,000. Dungan promised to talk to Desmond FitzGerald and find out exactly how much cash was at stake. The CIA now said it had no money for this project. The Special Group would have to approve use of the DCI's contingency fund. Bundy convened the group in the White House Situation Room on April 2, but deliberations failed to settle doubts. The group did okay CIA's own plan for propaganda and political action during the election campaign.

At this point FitzGerald, who had replaced King as Latin America baron, visited Santiago for a personal reconnaissance. He closeted himself with station chief Rudolph Gomez, reviewing CIA assets and operational possibilities apart from the CDP. Rudy Gomez, formerly Colonel King's deputy, had good lines to Langley and knew of King's earlier contacts with Chilean politicos. He set up a meeting for Des to hear the party's needs directly. That took place on May 5. In an unrelated but troubling development, a few days earlier, while complaining to a U.S. diplomat of a blabbermouth associate, Eduardo Frei revealed that he was not, after all, unwitting of the CIA.

Richard Helms related what FitzGerald had learned to the Special Group, which met again on May 14, directing McCone to disburse $1.25 million from his contingency fund for the project. A small portion would be aimed at the Radical

Party, but most went to support Frei. There would be no CIA task force, but an interagency group that periodically reviewed political payments would monitor the election operation. At Langley, Helms began daily sessions with deputy Tom Karamessines, familiar with political action from his days in Greece; FitzGerald; and the DO's Chile branch officers.

The rapidity with which the agency swung into gear once fresh money flowed indicates that Rudy Gomez had worked overtime to prepare this campaign. Television not being well established in Chile at that time, radio figured importantly. By June a CIA propaganda group had produced a series of political advertisements, purchasing air time to broadcast them twenty times a day on Santiago and local Chilean stations. Agency assets at several Chilean radio stations, capable of direct action, began inserting items in daily news broadcasts, reports picked up and recycled by dozens of local stations. Cartoonists sketched anti-Communist drawings lampooning opponents that were printed on posters, several thousand of which went out every day. Hundreds of thousands of copies of a pastoral letter by Pope Pius XI, written years before, were reproduced with the notation "printed by citizens without political affiliation." In other countries the CIA inserted more stories in media or solicited dire warnings from figures opposing Allende rule. In Chile these were reported as legitimate news. And there was "black" propaganda, scurrilous items purportedly from Communist or Socialist sources to discredit their supposed authors. In all, the propaganda operations cost $3 million. Langley considered the scare campaign the best part of its Chile operation.

Gomez conducted a second political project distinct from the CIA's help to the CDP. This effort tried to dissuade the Radical Party from serious participation in the election. The agency wished to avoid drawing votes away from Frei or the possibility that the Radicals might throw their support to the Socialists.

Finally there was popular political mobilization, enlisting blocs of voters, interest groups, and the like—recognizable from any American election—which the CIA did on its own, independently of Frei's party. The agency supported an anti-Communist womens' group, and it pursued at least two projects with Chilean labor unions and another with the Business Group.

Conversely, when rumblings of discontent arose within the Chilean military, among whom some officers might have opposed a Socialist taking office, the CIA shut them down tight. Rudy Gomez used an intermediary to caution one circle of Chilean officers. When another group asked if the United States might support a coup d'état, Gomez told them to forget it.

In late July the 303 Committee, Johnson's renamed Special Group, released a further half-million dollars to maintain momentum. The U.S. government also received offers from private corporations of cash to use against Salvador Allende, but 303 rejected those at the time. Before the campaign ended the CIA would spend $2.6 million in direct support of Eduardo Frei's Christian Democratic Party. The cost per favorable vote cast in the Chilean election came in higher than what the combined Democratic and Republican parties in the United States spent per vote in the U.S. presidential election of 1964. In the September 4 election Frei won

55.7 percent of the vote, outpolling Allende's 39 percent. The CIA emerged triumphant.

The dust had barely settled when, less than a month after the victory, the secret-war managers argued over whether to use the leverage gained by support of Frei. At a State Department–CIA brainstorming session on October 1, FitzGerald confessed his displeasure with rumors that the departing U.S. ambassador had advised Rusk against any such maneuver.

FitzGerald apparently had no specific skullduggery in mind. "It's the atmosphere of mistrust that bothers me," Des declared.

"Don't worry," quipped State's assistant secretary for Latin America, Thomas Mann. "I trust you."

The CIA investment in Chile, ever growing, had to be protected. With National Assembly elections impending, the 303 Committee bought a fresh proposal, jointly produced by Ralph Dungan and his agency station chief, to help selected candidates. On February 5, 1965, the group allocated another $175,000 (Richard Helms records this at a half-million dollars) for covert assistance in the March elections. Again the results were pleasing. More than a dozen Communists and Socialists succumbed while nine Christian Democratic politicians won their races. The vote gave the CDP more senators than anyone else and an absolute majority in the Chamber of Deputies.

Too many Chileans knew something about what the CIA had done. Probably no one—Frei's top people included—knew everything, but so many had been enlisted that plenty held some piece of the puzzle. Inevitably suspicions found expression. Termination of the latest project in the summer of 1965 did not end the danger. The agency shut down lines to Jesuit priests who had been considered useful. But ongoing CIA projects, including both the CDP funding and a separate attempt to induce Socialist deputies toward softer goals instead of Communist ones, continued through the year. The agency also dealt with a cabinet-level official. And CIA, in its persistent effort to blunt Communist organizational advantages, conducted an urban project among the slums of Santiago. Any of these could have broached, blowing Langley's cover.

Left-wing journalists in Chile speculated on what the Central Intelligence Agency had been up to. By late 1965 Salvador Allende had heard enough that he felt confident, when interviewed by the *New York Times*, in charging "outside forces," including the United States, with responsibility for his defeat in the presidential election.

For many months Chilean politics reverberated with charges and countercharges of electoral meddling. For the spooks this could be dismissed as unimportant, but it threatened to break into major controversy if the right information came into play. Revelation of Project Camelot illustrated the problem. A Pentagon social science research effort, Camelot tried to identify factors that could be exploited in counterinsurgency. It triggered instant dispute when first uncovered in Chile. Events elsewhere in Latin America sharpened the threat. Widespread but unconfirmed charges that the CIA had backed the military coup in Brazil in 1964 caused suspicion, and there were the reports of CIA action against Che Guevara in Bolivia. More concrete charges from Bolivian cabinet minister Antonio Arguedas soon gave form to Chileans' shadowy fears.

The next CIA project initiated in Chile aimed at countering the threat of exposure. It expanded the agency's capacity to generate countervailing propaganda. Station chief James B. Nolan merged earlier propaganda units into a new structure in 1967, improving efficiency and security.

Fresh leadership now came to the American embassy in Santiago. In June 1967 Edward M. Korry took over as ambassador. His marching orders, direct from President Johnson—Korry later recalled—were to prevent Salvador Allende from coming to power. But the ambassador had particular ideas on America's role. He had no desire to play proconsul, telling that directly to Frei. He wanted nothing to do with praetorianism—Korry radically cut back the U.S. military mission, heavily restricted CIA contact with the Chilean military, and at a certain point ordered the station to seek his personal approval for any approach to senior Chilean officers. Later Korry extended that rule to the agency's dealings with cabinet ministers as well.

Shortly after Korry's arrival the agency's Jim Nolan gave way to Henry D. Heckscher, moving over from Tokyo, as station chief. Heckscher, something of a CIA legend, had done it all—Soviet operations from Berlin, covert action in Guatemala, nation building in Laos, working with the Cuban exiles, lately media manipulation in Japan. Santiago, something of a prestige post, would be his last before retirement. Arrogant though resourceful, Heckscher had a difficult time with Ed Korry, himself something of a prima donna. Heckscher, who saw the Frei government as moving to the left, disdained Korry's view that Frei's CDP was the best deal the United States could achieve: a non-Communist party with enough of a modernist approach to retain a congressional majority. The station chief also had another, more elemental problem: by the close of 1967 not a single officer remained in Santiago who had worked on the early projects and knew the players and backstory.

As Ambassador Korry took up the reins, the agency began moving again. The 303 Committee laid out another $30,000 to strengthen the right wing of the Radical Party. Keith Wheelock, one of the new CIA officers, became the field man on this initiative. Korry himself instigated another. Looking ahead to congressional elections in 1969, he proposed a classic support operation. The 303 Committee put up $350,000 in July 1968. (Later, in the 1970s, Korry contended that all CIA projects had been pared to the bone just before Richard Nixon entered office. That does not track with this 303 decision, the largest single addition to the CIA Chile budget since the Frei election.)

Heckscher chose the races to play in and the candidates to back, then the CIA did its thing. In eight months of intensive politicking the agency used the methods that had served it so well, but the thread had run out. Chile's gross national product did not grow at all in 1967, and in the next year, when the cost of living rose almost a quarter—and international aid (both U.S. and multilateral) faltered—the

GNP increased less than 1 percent. Incumbent Eduardo Frei had to pay a price, and his CDP paid it. Heckscher's project became a pyrrhic victory: considered an operational success because the targeted races went CIA's way, the election yielded a net loss for Christian Democrats. Both the far-right National Party and the left gained seats, leaving the CDP vulnerable, ending its absolute majority. Heckscher no doubt was further alarmed when Frei reopened the terms of trade with American copper companies, settled two years earlier. Frei also canceled a much-anticipated visit by Governor Nelson Rockefeller. Thus was the stage set for a new Chilean presidential election, and for the Nixon administration that would confront it.

To some degree what Washington feared from a Socialist victory in Chile became inevitable no matter who won the election. Conversely, among some officials in the new Nixon administration the apprehensions of Allende went farther than the possible. The CIA component responsible for drafting the National Intelligence Estimates captured this conundrum well. In a 1969 NIE the Board of National Estimates considered the prospects for Chile. Abbott E. Smith, chairman at that time, had a reputation as a genial generalist, a former professor who had written American political history. Smith had excellent analysts at his command, plus an office of draftsmen and -women, among whom resided the best expertise. At the time Washington was consumed with a different dispute over estimates, one about Soviet nuclear missiles, so initially there were few with a stake in the Southern Cone. The 1969 NIE on Chile thus emerged with little acrimony. The paper concluded that *any* new Chilean president would move in the direction of expanding relations with the Socialist and Communist world. The left, the estimators believed, had a fifty-fifty chance of winning. An Allende administration might move faster, but the NIE also found that Salvador Allende specifically, needing to preserve his relationship with the United States as well as Chilean nationalism, would hesitate to move too far toward Havana or Moscow. Ambassador Korry strongly disputed this and protested the NIE conclusions in a series of cables to Washington.

There was more. In another estimate a year earlier, the BNE had surveyed conditions in Latin America. That NIE found that pent-up desire for improvement, the beginnings of development, and the weakening of oligarchies and military regimes had already made trends irreversible. As an assistant to Director Helms put it, "forces for change in the developing Latin nations were so powerful as to be beyond outside manipulation."

To listen to top analysts, a laid-back approach might have been the best course. But that certainly would not have pleased Korry and Heckscher in Santiago; or the DO at Langley, where branch chief Tom Gilligan had been grinding out papers warning of Allende; not to mention those at the White House. The Helms aide Victor Marchetti notes: "As is so often the case within the government, the most careful advance analysis was either ignored or simply rejected when the time came to make a decision on a specific issue."

The opportunity for choice arose in the spring of 1969. About six weeks after Chile's March elections the 303 Committee met to discuss Chilean projects. The group decided to end CIA's effort in the Santiago slums—the agency simply could not compete with Allende's Popular Front (literally "Popular Unity," or *Unidad Popular* in Spanish, yielding the acronym "UP"), the alliance between Chilean Socialists and Communists, in those neighborhoods. At this 303 session CIA Director Helms asked what the U.S. intended to do about the coming presidential election. The agency carefully noted that political action, if desired, needed to be prepared almost immediately. The 303 Committee ordered a propaganda workshop to sharpen capabilities but deferred any immediate decision. The agency reassigned Tom Gilligan to Portugal.

One reason the 303 Committee came to no decision was opposition from the State Department. Henry Kissinger accuses State's Latin American bureau of living in a world in which it "could not bring itself to face Chilean political realities." Kissinger asserts that no Chilean Christian Democrat stood any chance in the upcoming contest. Frei, though personally popular, could not succeed himself under the Chilean constitution. But Kissinger's account misleads by what it fails to say: far from not facing Chilean realities, the State Department's reluctance stemmed from a different reality it had very much in mind. Acutely conscious of the Chileans' sensitivity to U.S. political interference, State worried that any whiff of a CIA operation would make an Allende victory inevitable. They had a reasonable argument. If any skullduggery took place in connection with the Chilean election, far better it be an internal Chilean affair. Kissinger dismisses this view with the comment that "a great college term paper could have been written on that subject." In fact the differences demonstrate that, when policy came down to the concrete question of which leader in a country a U.S. administration preferred, Washington never was able to resolve the contradiction between its methods and America's international commitment to democracy.

Henry Kissinger accepts some blame for Chile, but not for reconciling the policy contradiction. Kissinger feels he should have forced action, sooner, from Washington's Cold War agency, the CIA. He admits to failing to focus on Chile until late in the game, 1970. As usual, Kissinger pleads the press of other events. The truth was, as he had told Chilean diplomats the year before, "I am not interested in, nor do I know anything about, the southern portion of the world from the Pyrenees on down."

Kissinger indulges in a convoluted disquisition on how items appeared on the 303 (later the 40 Committee) agenda, to buttress a claim that he somehow did not know of suggestions for covert action in Chile. According to Kissinger, the CIA proposed issues but deferred placing them until settling differences with the State Department. It is true that CIA prepared the 303 proposal papers based on conversations with State. But the implication that Latin America bureau foot-dragging at State kept Chile off the agenda is inaccurate. Kissinger admits that agendas were fixed after consultation with him, that the CIA warned more than once that Chile preparations needed to be made in advance, and that, in fact, *he* put Chile on the agenda. Richard Helms affirms that Langley spoke loudly and often on the need to prepare. Since the subject did come up at 303 within months of Nixon taking office, the question becomes why it did not return for a year.

Attributing the failure to Charles A. Meyer, State's Latin America assistant secretary, is not sufficient. Kissinger demanded that the department's outgoing cables get his clearance. Former diplomats and NSC staff have commented, in many contexts, on the awkwardness of this process, under which they spent long hours in Henry's outer office awaiting approvals. Thus Meyer's dispatches to Korry, answering the ambassador's repeated warnings on Allende, came before Kissinger, who must have been aware of the issues.

Another aspect is the hostility between Korry and CIA chief Heckscher, who for a very long time could not agree on a covert action proposal. Heckscher heavily favored Jorge Alessandri but could not get a hearing from the ambassador. He wore Korry down only in December 1969, using the argument that unless they did something they would have no answer later, when people asked what had been done to prevent Allende's victory. The two then suggested an election project. At this point State's qualms did figure—the department nixed the proposal because it envisioned support for the CDP, which State believed did not have a practical chance, and because it thought mere money insufficient to help Alessandri, candidate of the rightist National Party. Korry and Hechscher revised their plan, which State and CIA reviewed. They wrote a paper with both agencies' views. On March 25, 1970, it came before the 40 Committee.

Henry Kissinger suddenly swung into action, startling the group. "I don't see why the United States should stand by and let Chile go communist merely due to the stupidity of its own people," Henry declared. He complains in his memoirs that CIA-State private exchanges had kept him in the dark about the proposal for four months, and then that the 40 Committee approved the "grand sum" of $135,000, as if Dr. Kissinger had not been reviewing the cable traffic, had no role in the deliberations, no ability to impose a larger budget, and no capacity to discover what impended—none of which was true. Thus Kissinger's ultimate objection reeks of hindsight:

> Had I believed in the spring and summer of 1970 that there was a significant likelihood of an Allende victory, I would have an obligation to the President to give him an opportunity to consider a covert program of 1964 proportions, including the backing of a single candidate. I was resentful that this option had been foreclosed without even being discussed.

Kissinger's motives were complex. Richard Nixon exhibited concern and also responded to U.S. corporations, in danger of losing their guaranteed investments and highly agitated. Kissinger was always sensitive to Nixon's cares. Roger Morris, a sort of handyman on the NSC staff at this time, believes that Kissinger actually saw Allende as a greater threat than Castro: "I don't think anybody in the government understood how ideological Kissinger was about Chile." On the other hand, Henry has been quoted at least twice in 1969 essentially telling Chileans that their hemisphere held no importance. Kissinger was also bent on dominating the State Department, concentrating control in his White House office, and Chile could be used to that end. With a *failed* anti-Allende operation—one ensured by underfunding—Kissinger could argue the dangers of leaving policy in the hands of the State Department.

Whatever the original motive, Washington was soon carried away by polling data that showed Alessandri ahead of Allende, with the supposition he might be defeated. On June 27 the 40 Committee added another $300,000 to the pot. State still argued against Korry's latest idea, a two-phase proposal which included a contingency plan in case the election went to the Chilean congress, required if no candidate won more than half the votes. State, along with all the other agencies on the Special Group, approved the cash. Langley ordered Heckscher to sharpen his propaganda and aim it more directly at Allende.

The late hour did not prevent the CIA from accomplishing a great deal in Chile. Nor did the 40 Committee's stance against backing a specific candidate preclude exactly that activity—the International Telephone and Telegraph (ITT) Corporation put $350,000 of its own money into the election. John McCone, former CIA director, was now a member of the ITT board, well aware of business offers to help during the 1964 election, and ready to suggest this anew. He knew exactly whom to talk to at Langley. Still an agency consultant, McCone met Helms twice at CIA and another time at home in California. He put ITT board chairman Harold Geneen in touch with CIA Western Hemisphere Division chief William V. Broe. Other corporations matched the funds. In ITT's case, its representatives in Santiago dealt directly with Heckscher, who furnished contacts. Bill Broe told the other companies where to put their money, which amounted to the same thing as the CIA actually backing candidates. More than $1.1 million went for political action in the 1970 Chilean election, not on a par with the Frei cycle but hardly insignificant, and most of it went to candidates, not for the spoiling operation. Kissinger maintains that he remained ignorant of the corporate funds at play.

Henry Heckscher aimed a half-dozen covert action projects toward shaping the election. Agency officers like Donald H. Winters were primary operatives. One project, a scare campaign, tried to make Allende out as a Stalinist. Another aimed to neutralize the Radical Party whose voters might go for Allende; this involved actual subsidies to a political group. Projects placing press and radio items were reaching five million people a day. The spooks tried to separate Socialists from Communists in the *Unidad Popular*, and to split the Communists from the national labor confederation. Sign-painting teams worked the streets by night, scrawling graffiti to suggest that Allende would send people to firing squads ("*al paredon*" was the slogan), and slapping up posters linking him to the Soviet invasion of Czechoslovakia, picturing tanks in the streets of Santiago. Other themes came right out of psywar texts: Allende would end religious freedom in Chile; his victory would undermine the family. Heckscher made such use of his assets that they became dangerously exposed and would later be of limited utility.

Among the most vital resources was the Chilean paper *El Mercurio*, the country's biggest daily with a circulation of several hundred thousand. Published by Augustín Edwards, who owned a couple more papers and much else besides, *El Mercurio* was Chile's newspaper of record. Long had the agency wooed it. Although details remain shrouded in secrecy, official reports indicate the CIA's penetration extended through the 1960s, beginning with a single reporter. More joined the CIA payroll, some agents became editors. By the late sixties the agency could plant news in *El Mercurio* along with an occasional editorial, so in the 1970 campaign this "enabled the Station to generate more than one editorial per day based on CIA guidance." Material here had a multiplier effect since it influenced other papers as well as radio news broadcasts throughout Chile.

Henry Kissinger convened the 40 Committee on August 7 to review progress. By now the situation did not seem so favorable. Poll data had been skewed. Allende gained ground despite the best the CIA could do. Kissinger asserts that the election now appeared so tight that no new action could make any difference. An official CIA review in September 2000 notes that "High-level concern in the Nixon Administration resulted in the development of a more aggressive covert action initiative." The issue before the 40 Committee that day, Kissinger writes, was whether to explore preventing Allende from taking office if he won. This measure, considered risky, went on hold. The CIA report suggests otherwise.

Evidence suggests that Chile policy became hostage to Henry Kissinger's effort to centralize control in the White House. Just before the 40 Committee met, the security adviser complained to Nixon chief of staff H. R. Haldeman that Secretary of State William P. Rogers was out to get him, to sabotage "all our systems and our foreign policy." Not long afterward, Nixon endured a couple of days of frantic Kissinger phone calls, with Henry incensed the president had invited Rogers to Camp David. Nixon began talking to Bob Haldeman about a "Kissinger problem." That happened the day before Kissinger convened his senior review group, the most powerful NSC unit (other than the president meeting with the full Council) to debate the results of a pair of government studies, one on Latin America, the other, Chile. The security adviser now hedged the outcome of the Chilean election and asked for a paper for Nixon's decision on policy toward an Allende Chile.

Meanwhile Langley published a fresh NIE. This estimate predicted that an Allende government would almost certainly recognize Cuba, challenge U.S. interests in the hemisphere, and accelerate measures affecting U.S. multinational corporations. The NIE became fodder for those pushing for a last-ditch anti-Allende maneuver.

As Washington moved ahead, the game in Chile went to the next level. On September 4 Chilean voters gave the plurality to Salvador Allende, though his margin of victory proved so narrow it forced the congressional runoff. Reaction along the Potomac was instantaneous. The election had been on a Friday. Early Saturday morning Helms and top officials gathered in the CIA operations center to follow the results, their mood funerary. Kissinger summoned the 40 Committee for Tuesday. In the interim he demanded State get him Korry's advice.

America's man in Santiago replied that there remained little chance to defeat Allende, that to be caught in the act would be disastrous, that Eduardo Frei's participation was essential (and unlikely) in any blocking scenario, and that Washington should accommodate itself to an Allende government. Then a remote event intruded—on Sunday in the Middle East, Palestinians began hijacking airliners and flying them to Jordan. Not only a major distraction, the crisis suggested a need for U.S. action somewhere else to demonstrate toughness.

What Kissinger heard at the 40 Committee confirmed the judgment of the embassy in Santiago. Latin American baron Bill Broe started by agreeing with Korry's assessment, highlighting some of his points. The CIA man felt the decision not yet ripe and recommended that Korry and Heckscher "probe all possible aspects of feasible actions" and report back. Discussion became heated. Director Helms expressed his view that the Chilean opposition would evaporate once Allende took office, and the Chilean Marxist would quickly neutralize the police and army, leaving no rallying point. Helms made no policy recommendation but gave his intelligence judgment: "a military *golpe* against Allende would have little success unless undertaken soon." The Pentagon agreed: to be effective, action had to be in the "very near future." Alex Johnson and Charlie Meyer warned that intervening against Allende's election might result in civil war in Chile.

Henry Kissinger and John Mitchell doubted that "once Allende is in the presidency there will be anyone capable of organizing any real counterforce against him." Ignoring the State Department's warning, Kissinger used Chile to further his drive for control and show Nixon's resolve. He ended the session by directing that Korry report immediately on the pros and cons of a coup with U.S. assistance, and the prospects for a Chilean political opposition.

Edward Korry believes that he lost credibility in the Nixon White House when he advised against adventures in Santiago. There existed an important counterweight to Korry—International Telephone and Telegraph. Within days of the election, ITT began reaching directly into the White House, speaking to Kissinger's NSC staff aides for Latin America among others. When the 40 Committee met again on September 14, in the face of Korry's advice the secret war managers voted $250,000 for a campaign to influence the Chilean Congress runoff. Helms recalls the atmosphere as "grouchy." Its main decision, described as a "Rube Goldberg" gambit—an awkward and patched-together mechanism that achieves an unlikely result—would become known as "Track I."

Richard Nixon, a friend of Pepsi corporate president Donald M. Kendall, took a telephone call from him. Kendall told Nixon that a friend, Augustín Edwards, publisher of *El Mercurio*, wanted to talk to people in the White House. Nixon knew Edwards and needed little convincing. To him Allende represented something like what Castro had been for Kennedy. Years afterward, in a celebrated television interview with David Frost, Nixon rationalized that the addition of Chile to Cuba would have made Latin America a "Red Sandwich," a variant on the domino theory alleged to apply to Southeast Asia.

Nixon told Edwards and Kendall to see Kissinger. Nixon does not recall specifically but concedes it quite possible that he told his people to see the Chilean publisher. The next morning, September 15, Edwards and Kendall breakfasted with Kissinger and John Mitchell. Edwards pleaded for help. Later he saw Richard Helms at a downtown Washington hotel to convey the same message. Nixon ordered Kissinger to get Helms over to the White House. That afternoon, before heading to Kansas City for a speech, Nixon spoke with Helms, Kissinger, and Mitchell.

The president minced no words. As Helms penciled notes, seated to the right of Nixon's desk, the president told the CIA to take Allende down. Make a *golpe*, Nixon said. Even if the chances were just one in ten, he wanted to do it. Echoing LBJ to the CIA on Vietnam, Nixon wanted the best men, full time, and he told Helms he could have $10 million, more if necessary. As for Chile, the president said, "Make the economy scream!" Nixon wanted to see a plan within forty-eight hours.

"If I ever carried a marshal's baton in my knapsack out of the Oval Office," Helms later commented, "it was that day." He then told Senate investigators, "My heart sank over this meeting, because . . . the possibility of bringing off something like this seemed to me at that time to be just as remote as anything could be."

Nixon also told Director Helms to keep the whole project secret from just about everyone.

Secretaries Rogers and Laird, Ambassador Korry, station chief Heckscher—all were to be kept in the dark. Even at Langley knowledge was to be restricted. The 40 Committee, whose writ to approve *all* covert operations Nixon had recently affirmed, would not be informed of this one. Helms thought it the tightest clamp-down he had experienced since World War II. Tom Karamessines speculated to Senate investigators that the restrictions were designed to avoid State's objections or reflected a concern over secrecy. In a sworn statement to the same investigating committee, Richard Nixon declared he did not recall ordering secrecy, but he conceded that "It was my opinion that any effort to bring about a political defeat of Mr. Allende could succeed only if the participation of the CIA was not disclosed," and Nixon admits ordering the embassy in Santiago cut out of the loop.

Within twenty-four hours the White House was swept up in a further distraction as CIA reported signs that the Russians were about to open a naval base in Cuba. For Kissinger, Chile became just part of his "autumn of crisis." The last-ditch attempt to head off an Allende presidency has come down to history as "Track II," as Tom Karamessines dubbed it, an effort that led to the death of the de facto commander of the Chilean army. The CIA knew this mission as Project FU/Belt. It would not be Langley's finest hour.

In his golden years, secret warrior David A. Phillips used to meet his good buddies for lunch or dinner to chew over their exploits. Their watering hole, a good Cuban restaurant called Omega in the Adams-Morgan neighborhood of Washington, is gone now, its place taken by a supermarket. The atmosphere at those lunches, languid and nostalgic, differed diametrically from Phillips's reality those days in 1970. Nine months into a tour as station chief in Brazil, Phillips suddenly received orders to take the next available flight to Washington and tell associates that he would be away several weeks for a promotion board. Phillips knew something was up, speculating it might be Chile, but on his long trip he dismissed the thought. Chile had become a crash priority. Phillips would be in charge of the task force for Project Belt.

Returning to Langley after his fateful encounter with the president, Director Helms called together senior people to develop a plan to show Nixon. Early the next morning, Helms gathered the group, including his deputy, Gen. Robert Cushman, and his executive director, Col. "Red" White. From the DO were big guns: Karamessines and his associate DDO, Cord Meyer; the region's baron, Bill Broe; deputy division chief Jim Flannery; and a few subordinates. Helms told the secret warriors they had ten million to spend, and put Karamessines in command. There would be a task force of the best people, with Colonel White to make all necessary arrangements, and Phillips as lead operations officer.

The CIA director recalls the meeting as "bleak," with no one holding out any great hope of a successful plan, the only apparent avenue being a military coup. Cord Meyer recalls he and Karamessines were stunned. "We were surprised by what we were being ordered to do," Meyer writes. "Much as we feared an Allende presidency, the idea of a military overthrow had not occurred to us as a feasible solution." Little time remained for an operation; the CIA station had been discouraging military action and would suddenly be reversing course; they knew of no Chilean officers ready to act against Allende. Helms had to meet Kissinger again on the 18th to detail CIA's plan. He could not just tell the security adviser that the risks were great and the action impossible. That day Langley began a march into the valley of death.

When Helms saw Kissinger again their conversation on Track II was perfunctory. Rather, the national security adviser expressed himself as more concerned with economic pressures that could be brought to bear. John McCone had seen Kissinger and Helms and conveyed his corporation's concern. Kissinger's staffer Viron Vaky had also talked with ITT executives the day before. The economic pressures would feature in the 40 Committee track, and they would endure long after Allende took power.

The final Chilean runoff, set for October 24, 1970, loomed in Santiago. That gave the agency barely a month. Karamessines would direct the project and liaise with the White House. For Helms this also offered a private channel to the State Department: Karamessines and William P. Rogers had been young lawyers together in racket-busting days on Thomas E. Dewey's district attorney staff in the 1930s. Karamessines also practiced very strict compartmentation, for example keeping the DI ignorant, thus being a good man to enforce the secrecy instructions.

Dave Phillips found himself pressed into service. Barely had he gotten an ID badge with access to appropriate headquarters areas when deputy chief Flannery pulled Phillips aside to brief him. Phillips relates that he could hardly believe the assignment. He and Flannery agreed that they could not buy the Chilean Congress for $25 million, much less $250,000. Flannery had served with Phillips several times in the past and now led him carefully to the appropriate conclusion—they needed a *golpe*. Both men saw poor prospects. Phillips recounted, "The odds [were] unacceptable, it [was] something that [was] not going to work, and we were going to be burned if we [got] into it." Karamessines found his colleagues universally agreed. "Problem is, Helms has marching orders," Flannery said. Helms, Karamessines, Broe, and Phillips all testified later to intense White House pressure. As Flannery told investigators, "There was just no question we had to make this effort, no matter what the odds were."

Track II was very closely held at Langley. Except for Broe, Flannery, and the Chile branch chief, no one at WH Division needed to know. Dave Phillips fibbed about his sudden appearance, though the promotion board story must have worn thin when he slept in the building—quite unusual. There was talk of running Phillips's task force directly out of Karamessines's office, but that would have been a tip-off. Instead they were put in a mail room. At least it adjoined the WH Division front office. Phillips experienced ethical doubts, partly due to what he knew about Chile and Allende, but also because the secrecy forced him into false positions. His staff mixed experienced people with some young officers, most important among them John J. Devine, called "Jack," a former high school teacher from Philadelphia on his first DO assignment. Devine converted the overnight cables from Santiago into reports his superiors could fathom in the morning.

Determined not to be completely idiotic, Phillips broke one rule early, bringing in Henry Heckscher. The station chief went on record as early as September 23 noting strong reasons to suppose the Chilean military would acquiesce in Salvador Allende's presidency. Heckscher warned that the Chilean commander, Gen. Réné Schneider, a strict constitutionalist, had firm control and would permit no intervention in politics. The parameters of action were quite narrow as Heckscher saw them, while options were limited. He was called to Washington and politely read the riot act. Langley instructed its station chief merely to report, not to fill his cables with argumentation.

Santiago military attaché Col. Paul Wimert, used as a go-between with Chilean officers of several factions, had to know too, and Heckscher would control him. Otherwise the twelve-person station would be bypassed. Instead Phillips mounted his emergency effort with agents sent from outside the country. All would act as "false flag" agents—pretending to act for someone other than CIA. One, Tony Sforza, had cover as a professional gambler, an Argentinian with business interests. Among his other agency exploits, Sforza had been the CIA's debriefer of Fidel Castro's sister Juanita in Mexico City in the summer of 1964. Another, Bruce MacMaster, masqueraded as a representative of the Ford Foundation and other institutions—a violation of CIA regulations in place since the National Student Association scandal. There were two more of these agents, whose communications to Phillips ran through an undercover officer at a safe house in Santiago, to Buenos

Aires, then to Langley. Ambassador Korry, left to believe that Track I amounted to everything the United States did in Chile, would eventually be furious.

As the task force put its network in place, Dave Phillips crafted his operations plan. On September 27 he sent it to Henry Heckscher. The agency intended to create a coup climate, including political, psychological, and economic warfare—ITT had already raised this aspect with Kissinger, and corporate documents mention a possible million-dollar fund for bribes or other purposes—but Phillips believed the key would be psychological warfare within Chile. The intent would be to create a pretext for action, and pressure would be put on President Eduardo Frei to either manage a coup or get out of the way. The seeds of failure are already visible in this dispatch, which began by noting, "WE ACCEPT AS HYPOTHESIS THAT FREI WILL PROBABLY NOT MOVE."

On September 29 William Broe of WH Division met with ITT executives. Corporate documents revealed in the scandal that later surrounded this business intervention in foreign policy include the executive's cable recounting the Broe meeting to ITT's chairman. The CIA baron told the corporate executives that the agency had taken certain steps but wanted "additional help aimed at inducing economic collapse." Langley's concept included having banks refuse to renew loans and companies drag their feet on deliveries and payments; savings banks relocate corporate accounts; and the withdrawal of technical help. The CIA even wanted ITT to approach other corporations in its behalf. ITT would do what it could but refused to recruit for Langley's economic war. As Broe met with ITT executive E. J. Gerrity, Tom Karamessines phoned chairman Harold Geneen and ranged over the same ground. McCone got updates from ITT's people. In 1970–1971 there would be more than three dozen CIA contacts with ITT.

Meanwhile the agency's false-flag officers had decided the Chileans they were talking to were useless. Korry learned of the contacts and again prohibited them. The same day at the 40 Committee, Kissinger ordered that Korry's prohibition be canceled. On October 7 Phillips directed Heckscher to approach the Chilean military himself. Langley's desperation is evident in this cable, where the task force chief demands creating some sort of coup climate, starting a rumor mill if the left could not be provoked into furnishing a pretext. A status report a few days layer noted that Heckscher, passing word that the United States would support any military move, had heard in at least two places that there were no such prospects. Ambassador Korry visited Washington at this point. Meeting Nixon in the Oval Office on October 12, Korry frankly averred that nothing could prevent Allende's assuming office and that the embassy should retool for the new era. Korry saw Kissinger's eyes bulge.

As for Track I, there were four sessions of the 40 Committee in the month between mid-September and mid-October. All wrestled with the scant potential for any coup or parliamentary maneuver to shut out Allende. On October 14 the CIA told the group that no coup climate existed in Santiago. Ambassador Korry attended this session and added his agreement. Kissinger reflected that there seemed to be little left to do.

Tom Karamessines met Nixon, Kissinger, or NSC deputy Alexander Haig six to ten times over the month Track II was most active. His briefings of Nixon were uniformly negative. Investigators reportedly concluded—but did not publish—that Al Haig served as the de facto manager for Track II at the White House. Haig says nothing at all about Chile in his memoirs. Karamessines's key encounter took place on October 15, with fewer than ten days left until the runoff in Santiago. The DDO carried a short paper in which the agency argued that a moderate U.S. stance would afford Allende "a fertile atmosphere" for ties to the West, while a tough posture would accelerate Chile's move toward the Communist camp, and in any event a failed coup would, from a U.S. perspective, range from bad to awful.

Kissinger and Haig listened as Karamessines evaluated the plotters' chances as less than one in twenty. The security adviser reluctantly decided to instruct Langley to desist but preserve CIA assets and keep the pressure on, hitting "every Allende weak spot in sight—now, after the 24th of October, after 5 November [Chilean inauguration day], and into the future." Karamessines and Phillips translated these orders into instructions for the Santiago station. Langley's cable declared:

IT IS FIRM AND CONTINUING POLICY THAT ALLENDE BE OVERTHROWN BY A COUP. IT WOULD BE MUCH PREFERABLE TO HAVE THIS TRANSPIRE PRIOR TO 24 OCTOBER BUT EFFORTS IN THIS REGARD WILL CONTINUE VIGOROUSLY BEYOND THIS DATE. WE ARE TO CONTINUE TO GENERATE MAXIMUM PRESSURE TOWARD THIS END USING EVERY APPROPRIATE RESOURCE.

Kissinger and Haig later testified that coup planning had been terminated on October 15. In his memoirs, Kissinger quotes himself telling Nixon, "I saw Karamessines today. That looks hopeless. I turned it off. Nothing would be worse than an abortive coup." Henry notes that the president agreed. The security adviser adds, "When I ordered coup plotting turned off on October 15, 1970, Nixon, Haig and I considered it to be the end of both Track I and Track II." Orders to preserve assets, Kissinger maintains, were for the "clearly remote" chance that might make action possible. This version does not comport with the declassified record. The orders were intended to produce an opportunity, not respond to one.

On the ground in Santiago, Bruce MacMasters and Tony Sforza were in touch with plotters headed by Gen. Roberto Viaux Marambio. So was Colonel Wimert from the embassy. Viaux used both channels to demand money and weapons. For a time Wimert carried riding boots stuffed with cash in the trunk of his car. On October 19 several machine guns were sent to Santiago by diplomatic pouch. Viaux was to kidnap General Schneider, setting off events that would forestall the runoff vote. He received the CIA's desist order but pressed on, and weapons were given to him after this order. Agency cables later provided to Senate investigators show continuing White House concern over progress. Two attempts were botched. Instead, on October 22 a different group of officers (which, however, included some of the same people) murdered Schneider. The assassination created a backlash in Santiago, increasing Salvador Allende's vote on October 24 when Congress elected him president of Chile.

Kissinger would like the public to believe that his order ended covert action in Chile, but that is simply false. Karamessines testified: "As far as I was concerned . . . what we were told to do was to continue our efforts. Stay alert, and to do what we could to contribute to the eventual achievement of the objectives and purposes of Track II. . . . I don't think it is proper to say that Track II was ended." Similarly, ITT executives discussed their follow-up with John McCone. They would take it to Kissinger and the State Department. Kissinger himself proceeded with the Chile policy review he had ordered in August, and that led to a Nixon decision within days of Allende's inauguration. Washington's policy had an important covert aspect.

An intelligence memo prepared for the policy review pointed out that the United States had no real security interests in Chile. But the options paper assumed Allende's anti-American bias and that the Chilean president would establish authoritarian rule. Demonstrating its isolation in Nixon's councils, the State Department left open the question of what U.S. objectives vis-à-vis Chile should be while the Pentagon demanded that the goal be to prevent "establishment by the Allende government of an authoritarian Marxist regime, prevention of the regime's falling under Communist control, and prevention of its influencing the rest of Latin America."

Henry Kissinger picked up right there. His briefing for the president on November 5 baldly declared, in underlined text: "The election of Allende as President of Chile poses for us one of the most serious challenges ever faced in this hemisphere." In Kissinger's judgment the risks in doing nothing outweighed those of adopting a hostile strategy. Although he conceded that Allende had legitimacy, and that "we are strongly on record in support of self-determination and respect for free election," Kissinger advocated preventing Chile's new president from consolidating power. He warned against a modus vivendi with Allende (termed "essentially State's position"), and advocated a hostile approach. Henry advised Nixon to decide that "we will oppose Allende as strongly as we can," and to make that clear at the NSC in order to forestall "a steady drift toward the *modus vivendi* approach."

Nixon began that NSC meeting by asking Director Helms for an intelligence update. The CIA chieftain summarized the Chilean election and its political background, attributing the "immobilism" of those who had not opposed Allende to a process in which "the Chilean people was softened up and conditioned for six years to accept revolutionary language, not only coming from the Communists and Socialists, but generated by the ruling Christian Democrats themselves." Helms talked as if there had been no CIA political action in Chile during that time. He found that Allende knew how to achieve his aims and would move slowly against foreign investors at first. U.S. investment insurance could potentially cost taxpayers more than $600 million, representing the majority of the $800 million book value of direct American investment in Chile at the time. Helms recited a clandestine report that Allende had promised Latin revolutionaries to support them once he attained power. But Helms dismissed the Cold War threat: "Moscow is showing caution in dealing with the new government. In turn, the Chilean Socialists will want to avoid excessive dependence on Moscow."

According to records of this meeting, Kissinger then told the council that *no* clear choice existed, though he had certainly stated one to Richard Nixon the day before. Secretary Rogers spoke next, favoring an economic squeeze on Allende. Secretary of Defense Melvin Laird added, "We have to do everything we can to hurt him and to bring him down." Technical experts observed that declining prices for copper, which Chile depended on for 80 percent of its export income, would hurt. Nixon immediately ordered studies of the amount of stockpiled copper the United States could sell off. The word "destabilize," used here merely in regard to copper prices, eventually described Washington's overall intent toward Allende. The president himself insisted that the United States increase military assistance to the Chileans while giving Allende "cold Turkey [sic]" on economic aid. Nixon himself said, "Make sure that EXIM [the Export-Import Bank] and the international organizations toughen up."

Three days later, in Nixon's name, Henry Kissinger signed a directive that ordered "the public posture of the United States will be correct but cool," which excluded further bilateral aid and quietly brought "maximum feasible influence to bear" on international banks to limit credit to Chile. The U.S. would warn multinationals of its concerns about Allende but also seek to reduce vulnerability to corporate losses, terminating or reducing existing investment guarantees. In short, "the United States will seek to maximize pressures on the Allende government."

In his memoirs Kissinger indulges in creative accounting to deny—and he does it explicitly—that Washington tried to destabilize Chile. Kissinger asserts that "What our opponents called destabilization was in fact an effort to help the institutions of civil democratic society survive Allende's pressures to destroy them," and he insists there was no attempt to overthrow Allende, only a strategy in anticipation of Chilean elections in 1976. Yet the word "destabilize" was first used not by some woolly protester but at the Cabinet Room table in the White House two days after Allende's inauguration. The problem with Kissinger's protestations is that the record is quite clear. The story it tells is not the one Kissinger would like to believe.

By late November the 40 Committee had begun reviewing a covert action program designed to advance the new Nixon policy. It quickly approved a plan and a "contingency" budget. On November 19 the covert program for Chile was the top item on the 40 Committee agenda. William Broe reported the program consisted of "a number of political actions designed to divide and weaken the Allende government," a dozen in all. The budget, $750,000, amounted to double what the CIA had had for the elections themselves.

Henry Kissinger told Richard Nixon on November 25 that the plan included assisting friendly Chilean media and using selected outlets to play up Allende's faults, enlarging contacts among the Chilean military, supporting non-Marxist opposition groups, and—Kissinger repeated the language Bill Broe had used at the 40 Committee—not preserving a moderate opposition but dividing and weakening the Allende coalition, that is, destabilization. In January 1971 the secret-war managers increased the covert action budget to $1.24 million. In March an American, Howard C. Edwards, accused of participation in an international scheme to lower the price of copper, was apprehended by Chilean police. Chilean sources identified Edwards as a Bay of Pigs veteran who had worked in Czechoslovakia during the Prague Spring. Over the first half of 1971 the 40 Committee approved another half-million dollars for direct support to Chilean Christian Democrats.

By July, before new Chilean congressional elections, the war managers decided to commit $150,000 to subsidize opposition candidates. Their vision of Chile contrasted markedly with intelligence analysts—a month later a fresh Chile NIE pictured the Soviets as cautious about Allende, his relations with Cuba as distant, and the leadership in Santiago as careful not to subordinate national interests to those of any Communist power. Salvador Allende had long had a relationship with Fidel Castro, the estimate observed, yet had studiously avoided "excessive overtures" to Fidel. In Kissinger's account he makes a point of Castro's month-long visit not long after the election, but Ambassador Nathaniel Davis's memoir actually shows that contacts between Castro and Allende were noticeably cool. While nationalization of industry dominated U.S.-Chilean relations, the NIE concluded that Allende seemed to wish to avoid confrontation. In all, this portrait of Chile showed a socialist leadership anxious to preserve friendship with Washington while pursuing economic reforms.

From the summer of 1971, when the multilateral aid units, stymied by U.S. vetoes, began denying loans, Allende's problems sharpened. Every penny fall in the price of copper cost Chile $14 million in earnings. Within two months of Allende's inauguration, foreign lines of credit available to Chile dropped from $230 to $30 million. Allende's political headaches, covertly fomented by the CIA, were already serious.

At the Santiago station, Heckscher had been replaced by Raymond A. Warren about a month after Track II failed. Quite familiar with Chile, where he had spent five years in the 1950s, Ray Warren had worked in labor and political operations. A veteran of the Guatemala operation PB/Success and the Bolivian political actions in the early sixties, Warren had formerly been deputy chief of WH Division. He had a strong station, including Don Winters, who stayed on as deputy chief and had also served in Guatemala and Nicaragua. New additions included Frederic W. Latrash, under AID cover, another Project Success foot soldier, who had been sent to Ghana after Nkrumah's overthrow. From Washington came Jack Devine, the Chile task force gopher, now on media operations, who could supply the Langley perspective; and James E. Anderson, whose cover was as a consular officer for the embassy. Holdovers included John B. Tipton, Arnold M. Isaacs, Fred Shaner, and Val Moss. There would be a clandestine operations group of four, a propaganda group with several more case officers, a paramilitary group, and a unit working specifically against Cubans and agents of other Communist states.

Ambassador Korry also left Santiago. Korry had tried unsuccessfully to steer between the White House and La Moneda, the Chilean presidential palace, encouraging Washington to maintain a "soft" attitude toward Allende while telling the Chilean leader he *had* to toe the line in relations with the United States. Kissinger wanted Korry out right away, and he wanted the failure to prevent Allende's victory associated with the State Department and Korry, not with the White House. Al Haig advised Kissinger that the White House seemed fairly clean but that the CIA could be caught out and the blame blow back that way. In February and March 1971 the issue of Korry's replacement came up at the White House. Secretary Rogers wanted to relieve him. Haig cautioned Kissinger *not* simply to get rid of the troublesome envoy. "He holds a great many secrets, including the fact that the President both directly and through you communicated to him some extremely sensitive guidance," Haig wrote. "I can think of nothing more embarrassing to the Administration than thrusting a former columnist who is totally alienated from the President and yourself . . . into the world without a means of livelihood." Rogers's treatment of Korry even Haig found "shabby."

In April 1971 Ambassador Korry completed a report on the failed election operation, which presumably dotted i's and crossed t's. On Haig's instructions the Kissinger NSC staff handled the report outside normal channels, preventing it from leaving any footprints in the NSC filing system. Haig also acted to suppress a Chile postmortem by the President's Foreign Intelligence Advisory Board.

That October, Korry's ride came to an end. His successor, career diplomat Nathaniel Davis, proved an acute observer but had a limited role. Economic assistance halted; USAID funds dried up; the United States prevented loans to Chile by multilateral sources like the World Bank and even discouraged them from private institutions. Funds for the Chilean military, on the other hand, were continued and increased, a none too subtle hint to the officers.

As Chile's economic problems worsened, the CIA's sting was illustrated by the measures Allende took to shut out the newspaper *El Mercurio*. In the fall of 1971 that became the focus of Kissinger and the 40 Committee. Based on a new CIA proposal, the Nixon administration approved a $700,000 subsidy. Agency payments to *El Mercurio* in fact quadrupled during the Nixon years. Covert action funds approved by the 40 Committee during the destabilization dwarfed anything spent before, including the expensive campaign of 1964: $2.8 million in fiscal 1971, $2.9 million in 1972, and $1.68 million in 1973. The CIA actually spent $7.5 million in that period.

American activities helped polarize Chilean politics. Economic woes turned the middle class against Allende and eroded the neutrality of the armed forces. Ultra-left groups resorted to violence, with Cuban weapons brought into Chile, and a desperate Allende at the eleventh hour moved to arm loyal workers. The Nixon administration monitored developments closely, bugging the Chilean embassy in Washington. In November 1971 the agency could finally report whisperings of restiveness among the Chilean military, and it tried to lay out the criteria to use in discussing the mechanics of a coup. Santiago station's penetration of the military had grown so deep that WH Division deputy Jim Flannery on December 1 asked Warren to go slow—the contacts could easily become known while the CIA actually lacked 40 Committee approval to proceed with a coup. The station, Flannery cabled, should report history, not make it.

Ambassador Davis had to exercise constant vigilance over CIA initiatives. Despite the "country team" concept, the constant White House proclivity was to cut out the embassy. Some things Davis learned only from reading the Senate investigative report a few years later. Several CIA sources confirm that money to Chilean political parties often moved through "third country" conduits—European parties or other Latin countries. Davis had trouble learning of those. His worst moment with Ray Warren came over this subsidizing, when CIA started routing cash through a Chilean politician and Warren refused to tell the ambassador who it was. In a "highly charged discussion," Davis told Warren he "would not be blind-sided"—if he discovered a Chilean he dealt with had become a CIA conduit without his knowledge, there would be hell to pay. Davis gave Warren twenty-four hours to think about it. The next day the CIA officer told the ambassador of the new conduit.

President Allende inevitably made mistakes. Proceeding with plans for the nationalization of industries, necessary to his domestic program, further stoked Washington's hostility. The personal edge to this shows in the half-dozen break-ins that took place at the Chilean embassy in Washington in the spring and early summer of 1972, when the White House "Plumbers" unit of Watergate fame ransacked the offices of Ambassador Orlando Letelier.

A new National Intelligence Estimate in June 1972 continued to see Chilean restraint in foreign relations, and maintained that Chilean democracy had held up well under the Allende government. A halt in U.S. exports now cut off the flow of spare parts, with serious consequences. Unrest began to reach fever pitch in the fall of 1972, when the truckers union began a series of national strikes, halting virtually all transportation in Chile for months on end. In days the economy lost millions of dollars. A few months later strikes that began with a key episode at the Teniente Mine, taken over from Kennecott, crippled the copper industry. The miners at Teniente received assistance from the American Institute for Free Labor Development (AIFLD), whose country director for Chile, Robert J. O'Neill, acknowledged in retirement that he had been a CIA officer.

Despite the widespread chaos, Allende's Popular Unity gained in the March 1973 elections—eight more seats in Congress on a plurality of 43.4 percent. There have been efforts to picture this election as an anti-Allende victory, saying the assembly came in just short of what was required to impeach the president, but these appraisals carefully avoid mention of the UP gains and hence the dynamic of the electoral shift.

Theodore Shackley, who took over the WH Division in May 1972, was embroiled in Chile from the start. Shackley opened a direct channel to the publisher of *El Mercurio* through Augustín Edwards's lawyer, meeting him several times in Washington. The baron also coordinated damage control with ITT officials, whose machinations in Chile burst into public in 1972 with leaked ITT documents. Opposition from both Ray Warren and Nathaniel Davis forced Shackley to cancel a planned field trip to Santiago. The Cuban DGI had a good station in Chile under Juan Carretero Ibañez, who had been the Havana coordinator for Che Guevara in Bolivia, and could have discovered Shackley's presence. Knowledge that CIA's man of Mongoose, Laos, and Vietnam was in Santiago would certainly have cued Allende's security services to the dangers that impended.

Shackley became the first secret warrior able to sit down with State colleagues to discuss a coup that might actually work. By October 1972 the agency was confident enough to predict that U.S. help would be unnecessary when the coup occurred. In fact by May 1973 the bugs at the Chilean embassy in Washington no longer worked, but the CIA had Santiago wired for sound. A coup was so likely that Shackley again ordered Ray Warren to reduce contact with the Chilean military to avoid the CIA being linked with any *golpe*. Warren protested: the station had responsibility to warn of a coup and could hardly do that without access. Shackley confirmed his instructions—culpability had become more important than prediction.

At Langley at the same time, Shackley reviewed the covert action program for the DCI, suggesting additional measures. Among these were payments of $350,000 for the CDP and $200,000 to the National Party. About $35,000 also went to *Patria y Libertad* (Fatherland and Liberty), a right-wing group so extreme that, according to Shackley, he, Warren, and Davis all concurred on stopping the cash flowing to it. In June Ted Shackley moved up to DDO, replacing Bill Colby. His successor was David A. Phillips, only ten months into a tour in Venezuela. It seemed Phillips was always being called back from places he was stationed.

The covert action moved ahead smartly. The State Department filed objections in a July 25 memorandum from its Latin American Bureau. Ray Cline, now State's INR director, undercut criticisms, recommending forging ahead. On August 20 the 40 Committee approved the latest proposals. Several days later Santiago station asked for subsidies to particular groups. For fiscal year 1974 the 40 Committee allocated $1.1 million; CIA had spent only $231,000 of that money when the coup actually happened.

Strikes introduced the last act of the drama. Decades later it remains impossible to say how the truckers and miners were able to sustain a year-long series of walkouts forsaking their own livelihoods. The truckers union had no appreciable strike fund. Rumors at the time were that the strikers were financed by the Americans or Brazilians. AIFLD is thought to have passed money and certainly provided advice. State and CIA officials denied to Congress that they had anything to do with the strikes. Dave Phillips rejects CIA complicity, as does the 2000 CIA report, though this acknowledges that Chilean groups funded by the agency may have passed along a certain amount of cash. In 1974, when journalist Seymour Hersh alleged CIA funding in the *New York Times*, quoting agency sources among others, his articles triggered a veritable flap in the White House.

Until 1973 the Chilean armed forces were largely quiescent under the leadership of commander-in-chief Gen. Carlos Prats. As his political difficulties grew, Allende bought military loyalty in part by bringing Prats into his government. On June 29 loyalist forces crushed a coup attempt by officers inspired by *Patria y Libertad*. The CIA passed the word. Ecstatic, Kissinger reported the first news to Nixon, then had to report failure. President Allende tried to enhance military participation in his cabinet, but the generals and admirals were now reluctant to join. About a month after the abortive coup, assailants murdered Allende's naval aide. In August discontent surfaced in the form of a demonstration outside Prats's home by officers' wives. Prats resigned.

Gen. Augusto Pinochet had helped quell the June *golpe*. He is said to have expressed indignation. The CIA, unlike their experience in Indonesia in 1965, had a good line on the general. Impressions of him at a dinner in August 1971, and his opinions on Allende a year later, made their way into agency cables. By September 1972 Pinochet had expressed the view that Allende had lost his ability to lead. The general served as army chief of staff, and after the Prats resignation became acting commander-in-chief. Previously considered a constitutionalist, it was Pinochet who led the military coup against Allende.

Santiago station officer Jack Devine sat to lunch at DaCarla, a popular Italian restaurant in Santiago, on September 9, when a colleague told him his wife urgently needed to talk. Devine called home, to be told in cryptic terms that a source, about to leave the country to avoid the coup, said it would happen on September 11. The navy would make the first move. By evening Devine had confirmed the tip and discovered the time of initiation. His cable, written into a report, went to Nixon and Kissinger on September 10. Devine became the first to have the correct information, but Washington already knew—attachés in Santiago had reported the impending *golpe* on September 7. A report in Defense Intelligence Agency files shows this data circulated the next day. The Americans had Santiago well wired indeed. Devine and Don Winters disagree on how high U.S. contacts went in the military, with Devine believing there was no access to the decision-makers, but the intelligence reports settle the question.

On the 11th, Warren's station was fully staffed but locked down on the seventh floor of the embassy. Warren had a lookout across the street with a view of the palace. Actually the post was the hotel room of a young officer sent temporarily to Santiago, who had been debating the chief for weeks on the date of the prospective coup. She thought it impossible before Christmas. When the coup began she went up to Warren, kissed him on both cheeks, and said, "Merry Christmas!" Station officers staffed the lookout and an open telephone line. General Pinochet led the *golpe* and became chief of the junta that wrested control from the Chilean government. By mid-afternoon it was over. La Moneda was bombed and attacked during the coup. Salvador Allende committed suicide.

At the White House, Richard Nixon was delighted but concerned. When Henry Kissinger phoned him with the news, the president quickly asserted, "Our hand doesn't show on this one, though."

The national security adviser, careful as ever, replied, "We didn't do it. I mean we helped them—created the conditions as great as possible."

Next day Kissinger convened his crisis management unit, the Washington Special Actions Group, in the Situation Room. William E. Colby, newly minted CIA director, led off by describing the situation in Santiago, but Kissinger concentrated on culpability and consequences. He ordered the return of U.S. Navy vessels in the area, without touching at Chilean ports. He talked of loan credits, aid amounts, and other items necessary to get the Chilean economy running again. After what Nixon considered a decent interval, the United States recognized Gen. Augusto Pinochet's military junta as the legitimate government. Recognition came just a week after Kissinger told the Senate that the administration had decided *not* to rush into this action.

The occasion for Kissinger's statement had been his confirmation hearing for the additional post of secretary of state. The national security adviser testified before the Foreign Relations Committee six days after the coup. Among other things, Kissinger told the senators that there had been total confusion at the White House when Pinochet forces moved against Allende, including within his Washington Special Actions Group; that the CIA had had nothing to do with the coup; that he knew nothing about the Chile activities of the CIA-backed labor unit AIFLD (which would have come before Kissinger's 40 Committee); and that "it is incorrect to say that we cut off the credit" to Allende's government. Kissinger told the senators he had said to Ambassador Davis some days before, in discussing endemic reports of coup plotting, "Just make sure none of our Embassy personnel has anything to do directly or indirectly with any of the plotters, if there are any plotters, in response to any approaches."

Kissinger and Nathaniel Davis assert that Allende created the opposition through his own actions. While it is true the social changes introduced by Popular Unity triggered fear and doubt among many Chileans, such assertions beg the U.S. involvement. American money fueled a drumroll of Chilean media criticism and the coalescing of right-wing groups, like *Patria y Libertad*, which spearheaded anti-Allende forces. Former Ambassador Korry estimates Track II led to nine different assassination plots, including one against himself.

The outcome in Chile ultimately hinged on the attitude of the armed forces, and it had been made abundantly clear to the Chilean military that U.S. friendship was not to be had by supporting constitutional government. It is also not clear that the American military had no involvement. American attachés were in the field with Chilean units. Several naval vessels were off the coast for UNITAS (an annual naval exercise by the United States and Latin nations), and one of these is reported to have landed a Navy SEAL team. As part of the same maneuver, the United States deployed thirty-two aircraft to the nearby Argentine base at Mendon. Finally, on the day of the coup, an electronic intelligence aircraft was flying over the Andes, variously reported to have relayed communications among the coup plotters or recorded them for U.S. intelligence. This last action would have been impossible without forewarning. As Kissinger spoke to the senators, anti-American protesters were demonstrating in Argentina to protest the U.S. role in the coup.

The Pinochet junta immediately declared a state of siege and began a widespread campaign of repression. It justified its actions by alleging that the military had acted to forestall an ultra-left coup. Mass arrests swept Santiago and elsewhere. Two sports stadiums were crammed with prisoners, jails filled to overloading. Some enemies were shot on sight in the street. The CIA station filed preliminary reports that more than thirteen thousand persons had been arrested, somewhere between two thousand and ten thousand killed. There have been estimates of up to eighty thousand dead, but in later years the numbers have dwindled to something less than CIA's October 1973 estimate of four thousand.

The prisoners, roughly handled and singled out by hooded informers in scenes that might have come right out of the *Battle of Algiers*, existed in a state of complete terror. About two dozen American citizens were caught up in the dragnet. Some were freed quickly, others languished in Chilean hands for days or weeks. At least two Americans, Charles E. Horman and Frank Teruggi, died at the hands of the Chilean military. Teruggi's body was found by CIA officer James E. Anderson, acting in his consular cover role. Washington made little effort to seek explanations, apologies, or compensation for the American families.

Former Allende government senior officials were imprisoned on Dawson's Island off the far southern tip of the continent, a bleak and forbidding place even in this Chilean springtime. Mary Helen Spooner's study of Pinochet's regime contains an excruciating account of how the wives of several officials, personal friends of Pinochet under the old order, begged him for the return of their husbands. One of the women, Isabel Morel de Letelier, wife of the former defense minister, Orlando Letelier, would see her husband again—Orlando came back after almost exactly a year. Her colleague Moy de Toha—both had confronted Pinochet in his own office within a week of the coup—would be heartbroken. Her husband, former Interior and Defense Minister Jose Toha, perished in captivity. In the summer of 1975, almost two years after the coup, nearly half the original prisoners on Dawson's Island remained in captivity.

Gen. Carlos Prats, warned the junta would kill him, tried to telephone General Pinochet, to be told he was not available. Prats knew a setup when he saw one. The general took his wife, found loyal officers at a nearby air force base, flew to a point near the Argentine border, and escaped to freedom. In Buenos Aires Prats began work on a memoir which, given what had happened in Chile, could only be an explosive political document.

The Santiago junta now began to build its own spook network, ultimately creating a secret police organization, called DINA, under Col. Manuel Contreras Sepulveda. Conceived as a Chilean version of the CIA but focused on domestic matters, DINA supplemented the intelligence units of the three armed services and a combined counterespionage unit that already existed. All of them played central roles in the Pinochet repression. Contreras quickly established a foreign operations entity called the Brigada Exterior. Among its first projects was the assassination of General Prats. For a time Prats enjoyed the protection of Argentinian authorities, but in the summer of 1974 this was withdrawn. One night that September, explosives destroyed Prats's car as it entered his garage. Mrs. Prats burned to death; the general died from a severed leg and other injuries. This success encouraged Pinochet to inaugurate a wider campaign against persons considered subversives both inside and outside Chile.

Augusto Pinochet proved acutely sensitive to charges of being an American puppet, and he accepted aid without bending an iota to Washington's views. Simultaneously the CIA, already subjected to intense inquiries regarding its activities in Chile, resolved to go slow with the new regime. There remained the ongoing covert actions approved as recently as a month before the coup. These were placed on hold. In February 1974 *El Mercurio* associates were told of the end of their subsidy. At about the same time the 40 Committee considered a proposal to fund the CDP. Kissinger comfortably rejected the suggestion. David Popper, new ambassador to Chile, responded to a personal appeal from Eduardo Frei by requesting a final payment, approved in June. Some CIA officers, aghast at Pinochet's path, wished to turn against him the covert weapons that had been used on Allende. Instead the agency closed out operations in Santiago. As Peter Kornbluh, the closest observer of U.S. actions in Chile, writes, "Now that Allende was dead, the rationale for covert action to 'preserve Chile's democratic institutions' no longer seemed important to U.S. policy makers—even as the regime that overthrew him was systematically dismantling those very institutions."

The deputy director for central intelligence, Gen. Vernon Walters, came to Santiago in March 1974 to assay Pinochet's spies. With him were the brass of WH Division. The Americans talked of help to Chile on foreign threats but acknowledged this could be adapted to the alleged internal challenge. A new station chief came at this time. Stewart D. Burton went on picnics with Colonel Contreras and within a year recruited him as a CIA source. A special agency team arrived in Santiago in August and stayed for months training DINA, during the very period the Chileans worked up to their assassination of General Prats.

In the summer of 1975 Contreras visited the United States twice. On both trips he saw Walters, once for lunch in the executive dining room at Langley. That October Contreras hosted a conference in Santiago for heads of the spy agencies of the Southern Cone. A formal "convention" a month later created a multinational anti-subversive campaign called Operation Condor. The intelligence agencies of Uruguay, Paraguay, Argentina, Bolivia, and Chile, later joined by Brazil, Ecuador, and Peru, shared information, exchanged representatives, informed one another when dissidents were expelled, and coordinated propaganda.

There would be murders or attempted assassinations in Costa Rica, Mexico, France, Portugal, Argentina, and on the streets of Washington, D.C., where Orlando

Letelier died when his car blew up in Sheridan Circle, just across the street from the Chilean embassy, in September 1976. An American citizen, Ronni Moffitt, died with him, and her husband Michael suffered injuries. The reluctance of U.S. authorities to investigate links between the Letelier assassination and DINA is a measure of the collusion at that point between Washington and Chile. Condor became in effect a terrorist network, a characterization only rendered stronger when DINA began working with anti-Castro Cubans. The number of victims has yet to be established, but incidents continued through 1980.

Through its actions in Chile the Central Intelligence Agency contributed to the inception of this horror. The agency undoubtedly learned something of Condor from its spy Contreras, and declassified documents show the United States officially aware of the operation from March 1976. As Condor proceeded, the CIA learned a great deal more from its sources in the participating countries, yet it rarely intervened to stop them. U.S. agencies resisted the appropriate conclusion, as did Henry Kissinger, who actually visited Santiago in 1976 for an OAS meeting and delivered a notably weak speech about human rights. In particular there is clear evidence that the Letelier assassination could have been prevented but was not. The sad end of Washington's asserted intention to uphold democracy in Chile was to inaugurate a dictatorship that endured for a decade and a half and to bring terrorism to American shores.

The consequences of the Chilean adventure were perfectly visible at the time. Indeed the CIA itself pointed them out. In June 1975 the National Intelligence Officer for Latin America issued a fresh NIE on prospects for Chile. The estimate observed: "Allende's ouster and death and the repression that followed provided fertile ground for an international campaign designed to discredit the military government and embarrass the US." Russia and Cuba exploited the propaganda issue, but progressive political movements everywhere pointed to Chile as evidence not of America's commitment to democracy but its drive to imperialism. Said the National Intelligence Estimate: "To many, Chile has replaced Vietnam as a 'cause celebre.'" Chile had become "an international pariah at heavy cost to its international, political, and economic interests." Nixon and Kissinger gave their enemies this issue on a silver platter. Their actions now embroiled the secret warriors in the political fight of their lives, not on some distant battlefield but in the United States itself.

Adm. Elmo Zumwalt, chief of naval operations in the first Nixon administration, retired believing that the manner in which Richard Nixon and Henry Kissinger conducted foreign policy, shrouding their personal motives in secrecy and chicanery, left booby traps everywhere. Chile was a prime example. Almost every aspect of the secret war against Chilean democracy contained seeds for controversy, both over policy writ large and over the tactics of America's Cold War agency, the CIA. The Nixon people were sitting on a basket of hand grenades with loose safety pins. And they were doing this in a climate in which other political and national security developments—Watergate, Vietnam, the Phoenix Program, Laos, revelations of CIA use of private institutions—had already eroded the credibility of official denials and the faith of the American people.

The first fissure on Chile operations began with columnist Jack Anderson. The journalist acquired copies of ITT memos and cablegrams, some of them cited earlier, demonstrating that the multinational corporation had intervened with the Nixon White House and acted in concert with the CIA. On March 21, 1972, Anderson published the first of a series of syndicated columns on the CIA, ITT, and Chile. Suddenly the issue of political intervention in democratic elections appeared on the public agenda.

Some secret warriors, adherents of the cult of secrecy, like to believe that each time revelations like these come before the public, the act is traitorous and the actor someone out to get their organization. The reality is that leaks come from the inside, usually from the top, and are fueled, first, by officials seeking to push policy in a certain direction, or by persons embarrassed by U.S. actions and unwilling to be a party to them. The ITT Chile documents are a case in point. By several accounts they had been floating around Washington for a year and a half. They had been given to the Senate Foreign Relations Committee and to journalists, Jack Anderson among them, who initially used the documents for articles attacking Salvador Allende. What changed between 1970 and 1972 was the public perception of the Nixon administration as manipulators of information.

Richard Helms quotes Bill Fulbright as warning him around the time of Tracks I and II that if he learned of that kind of thing, he would blow it wide open. Yet Fulbright did nothing with the ITT documents (or with the Pentagon Papers, which he received during the same period). But Nixon and Kissinger's cavalier treatment of Foreign Relations Committee inquiries into the U.S. role in Laos, plus their handling of various congressional resolutions designed to limit U.S. activity in Vietnam, consumed all remaining tolerance. In 1972, when Jack Anderson brought the CIA-ITT connection into the open, Fulbright took action. He sanctioned an inquiry into the role of multinational corporations by a subcommittee under Idaho senator Frank Church. That inquiry zeroed in on Chile where Church, chairman of Fulbright's subcommittee on Latin America, had a particular interest.

The net result was that the CIA's destabilization of Chile proceeded in the field while that very initiative came under a public spotlight, the subject of congressional inquiry at home. To say the situation was explosive merely acknowledged the facts.

After his 1972 reelection, Nixon's appointment of Helms as ambassador to Iran effectively got the CIA masterspy out of the way. Nevertheless Helms and William Broe were obliged to testify in early 1973 to Church's subcommittee. Broe, by this time inspector general of the agency, seemed so consumed with the confrontation that his work suffered. Richard Helms came under additional questioning in both public and closed hearings as Fulbright's committee considered his nomination for ambassador. Always loyal to the chain of command, Helms, in view of Nixon's instructions about secrecy on Chile, denied in sworn testimony that the CIA had tried to overthrow its government.

In his memoirs Helms speculates that Fulbright was trying to push his way into an oversight role in intelligence, previously denied by Senator Russell and President Johnson, as shown earlier. (Russell had since died.) Helms is probably right that Fulbright's desire contributed to his stance in 1972–1973, but more important was the deteriorating relationship between Congress and the Nixon White House. Scott D. Breckinridge of the CIA's inspector general's office points out that the senators violated guidelines their staffs had set with Langley for the Hill appearances—a further indication of the breakdown. The Helms testimony became yet another hand grenade threatening to explode, both at Langley and the White House.

By no means completely ignorant of CIA involvement in Chile, Congress had been told of Chile activities various times. Some were larger-scale briefings that included Chile; sometimes individual members, senators, or staff were informed. In all, the subject had come up about forty times between 1964 and 1973, half of these including talk of money released for Chilean covert action. Congress already had data contrary to Helms's assertion of innocence, and Church's subcommittee got more from ITT representatives. They swiftly asked Langley to respond to five specific questions. The agency took the line that the Helms testimony had been accurate. Anticipating that response would be inadequate, Theodore Shackley recommended outflanking the criticisms by a private approach to Senator Henry Jackson to get the Armed Services Committee to intervene, on grounds CIA "sources and methods" needed protection. Agency leaders rejected this course. Instead James Schlesinger and Bill Colby sat together in March, affirming Helms's original declaration. That begged the question of the agency's role in the destabilization. Another hand grenade had been put in the basket.

Through the hot summer of 1973 Washington boiled even as the Chilean truckers' strike took Allende's presidency to the edge. Media speculation on CIA backing became a continuing theme, to which Congress responded with more questions. A dozen more CIA briefings on Chile took place between March 1973 and December of the next year. Bill Colby, now DCI in his own right, sat in the hot seat on October 11, 1973, to deny to a House committee that CIA had had any role in the strike or the coup. Another hand grenade.

Among those dissatisfied with Langley's descriptions was Massachusetts Representative Michael J. Harrington. The congressman demanded more open discussion. Langley tried to walk a tightrope between the contending demands of Congress and the Nixon White House. In an effort to be able to say that Congress had been properly briefed, CIA director Colby went to a friendly interlocutor, Representative Lucien N. Nedzi, Democrat from Michigan and chairman of the CIA subcommittee of the House Armed Services Committee, and arranged for an appearance. On April 22, 1974, Colby and Latin America baron David Phillips appeared at a "hearing" of the subcommittee. Director Colby danced around the issues, according to Harrington, spending about a third of his time on Kennedy-Johnson era programs and most of the rest discussing generic tactics, not the substance of the Nixon project, though it is evident Colby gave up some budget figures. At the end of the session Colby privately told Nedzi of Track II, keeping it out of the written record. The CIA would be able to say it had fully informed Congress after the fact. That June Harrington read the proceedings and used them for letters to colleagues and to Senator Fulbright advocating full-scale public hearings on the CIA in Chile, and also for a letter to the editor of the *New York Times*.

Agency defenders accuse Harrington, in using Colby's information, of breaking House rules against publication without prior approval (of material given Congress in closed, executive session). In fact a congressman filed a formal complaint against him for this transgression. When the House of Representatives looked into the matter, however, the charge had to be dismissed. Nedzi had been the sole member present to take Colby's testimony, had not officially called a hearing, and had had no quorum to close the hearing, hence it had never been "closed" under House rules. Harrington had no obligation to seek approval. Langley had tripped over its own cleverness.

This became the first Chile hand grenade to explode. Harrington had no success on hearings, but a few months later he put much of the same information into a pair of resolutions of inquiry he tabled in the House of Representatives, that would have obliged the president and the secretary of state to produce data on the economic measures against Allende. The Harrington letters also gave Senator Fulbright an opportunity to press again for a joint oversight committee for Congress to monitor the CIA.

In the meantime Richard Nixon's Watergate problems had escalated to fever pitch with a Supreme Court decision that required him to give up Oval Office audiotapes—providing incontrovertible evidence he had conspired to cover up his machinations in the 1972 election. The House of Representatives voted three articles of impeachment. On August 8, 1974, Nixon resigned. Vice President Gerald R. Ford succeeded him.

By now Langley's efforts at damage control were rapidly being overtaken by events. Shutting down the Harrington inquiry could not have saved the secret warriors. In June the New York publisher Alfred A. Knopf released the book *The CIA and the Cult of Intelligence* by Victor Marchetti and John D. Marks. As a result of legal action by the CIA and the Nixon White House, the book appeared with more than 160 deletions, including roughly a third of its commentary on Chile. Among the deletions alleged to have been necessary on national security grounds was Henry Kissinger's improvident remark disparaging the sovereign right of the Chilean people to their election results. Knopf and the authors went to court to force release of the material. Legal discovery, court arguments, and the to-ing and fro-ing surrounding the entire affair furnished many new opportunities for leaks. Seymour Hersh, investigative journalist for the *New York Times*, then transitioning from reporting Watergate to covering intelligence issues, acquired this story and the paper printed it on September 11, including Kissinger's soon-notorious comment. No doubt the secretary of state hit the ceiling.

Although Hersh represented only the leading edge of a drumbeat of press coverage on Chile, his stories quickly became more hand grenades. So were those of Laurence Stern of the *Washington Post*. Both published pieces on September 8 revealing the Harrington letters. On September 12 Hersh wrote that Senator Frank Church intended to press the Chile issue. A week later, when Secretary Kissinger sat before the Senate Foreign Relations Committee to testify on Russia, Church diverted the discussion to Chile. Kissinger had to work hard to keep the exchange innocuous. On September 16 the *Times* front-paged a Hersh article portraying Kissinger as chief strategist on Chile and the economic blockade. Four days later the paper carried as second lead a Hersh piece linking the CIA to the strikes. That day Director Colby spoke twice on the telephone to Kissinger, denying the story, later warning him of Hersh's next article. On September 21 Hersh's theme would be Kissinger in present tense—that he had omitted CIA involvement with Chilean labor and trade unions in briefings to Congress and to colleagues in the Ford administration in just the past week. Three days later Hersh reported that the Nixon administration had decided in 1971 to escalate actions against Allende.

To say that Hersh's reports raised eyebrows in the Ford White House would be understatement. They forced President Ford into an official disclosure. At a September 16 news conference Ford *admitted* there had been a CIA covert action: "The [CIA] effort was made to help and assist in the preservation of opposition newspapers and electronic media and to preserve opposition political parties." Ford carefully denied involvement in the coup. He characterized covert actions as necessary "to help implement foreign policy and protect national security," and justified them on grounds the Communist nations spent more on this kind of activity than the United States. Spy chieftain William Colby followed with a letter to the *Times* two days later. Referring specifically to Harrington, Colby denied ever using the term "destabilization," which the congressman had. Scott Breckinridge, Nathaniel Davis, and others seize upon this point to discredit critics, apparently unaware the word had first been used in Nixon's own cabinet room on November 6, 1970.

Kissinger's staff at both Foggy Bottom and the White House went into high gear to counter Chile revelations, in particular the Hersh stories. Deputy Secretary Lawrence Eagleburger told Kissinger that Hersh would continue and that Henry himself was "the ultimate target." Eagleburger got Nathaniel Davis and former Santiago deputy ambassador Harry Shlaudeman to draft a strong denial *to be released by the Central Intelligence Agency*. Davis would separately put one out from the State Department. Eagleburger argued in another memo to Kissinger that the unusual gambit of bringing out the denial through the CIA would be more effective and would pacify "Hill interests who want a series of hearings on the issue." Bill Colby volunteered to issue such a denial when talking to deputy national security adviser Brent Scowcroft on September 23. Langley ultimately did not issue the denial. Davis is silent about this episode in his own memoirs. Kissinger also says nothing about the attempt to counter Hersh, aiming his barbs instead at Colby.

By then Director Colby had his hands full, for the matter of the Helms Chile testimony came to a head. One of Hersh's articles, on September 17, noted that staff on Fulbright's committee were pressing for Richard Helms, William V. Broe, and two State officials to be cited for contempt of Congress for their 1973 testimony. What Hersh did not know is that, within the secret world of Langley, this dovetailed with completion of an inquiry by the inspector general begun when the CIA chiefs repeatedly had had to defend the Helms-Broe testimony.

Broe, briefly the IG, could not be in the position of rejecting an inquiry that involved him personally, and approved the study shortly before leaving the agency. The inquiry droned on for a year and a half. One participant came out of retirement for the task. Another, Thomas C. Lawlor, an analyst from the Office of Current Intelligence who had previously served on detail with the IG, discovered papers from early reviewers that used the word "perjury." Superiors gave more weight to the view that Helms had been sandbagged when senators went beyond agreed guidelines, but Lawlor did a straight review. After consulting with the general counsel's office on the legal definition of perjury, he decided the testimony before the multinationals subcommittee had indeed been problematical. On September 5, 1974, a draft paper sent to the IG stated: "There is reason to believe that perjury was committed and that the Agency was aware of that fact," and that "some of the statements in Mr. Helms's [confirmation] testimony seem not to be in full accord with the facts. Mr. Helms's testimony is significant here because it was subsequently cited by the Agency as authoritative."

Superiors tried to get the word "perjury" expunged from the paper and did get the analyst to remove passages pertinent to an ITT legal case (attempting to recover its Chilean investments from the U.S. government). But the panel stood on its interpretation. The IG passed the paper to Colby with the comment that General Counsel John Warner should provide a second opinion. Warner asked for further examination by a three-officer panel, two lawyers plus Lawlor. They agreed with the original review. Warner added an analysis refuting that conclusion. According to Colby's note for the record on September 25, Warner found no clear evidence of perjury in the testimony. Colby decided not to refer the matter to the Justice Department.

The legal panel insisted on meeting with the CIA director and did so. Regulations required the referral, they maintained, so CIA's obligation was to let Justice make the final determination. Hiding the issue only increased the chance of later leaks and a bigger explosion. In the climate of September 1974 that seemed a reasonable proposition. Colby nonetheless held the line for two more months, amidst threats of resignation. The last defense was a 1954 CIA-Justice agreement governing what could be withheld from Justice Department scrutiny. Colby sought to discover whether that exempted Helms. On December 21 he met with Acting Attorney General Laurence Silberman, who asserted jurisdiction, making Langley yield up the case files. Helms and a faction of stalwarts never forgave Bill Colby this supposed betrayal. Indicted in 1977 for perjured testimony, Richard Helms pleaded no contest to the charges and got off with a two-year suspended sentence and a $2,000 fine. Another Chile hand grenade had exploded.

In 1974 the atmosphere became superheated. Late in October radio broadcaster Daniel Schorr of CBS reported that State had opposed the Chile intervention, citing Ray Cline, the INR director, who now sang a different tune. Contrary to what he wrote in later memoirs, at the time Henry Kissinger ordered an immediate review of 40 Committee files and then leaked several documents to the media on which Cline's marginal notes indicated that he had favored stronger, not weaker action. Kissinger himself gave Schorr an interview denying the allegation. Days later Hersh reported, based on 40 Committee documents, that the CIA had still been asking for cash for Chilean rightists in the summer of 1973. Apart from anything else, *current* covert action data had been deliberately leaked to settle political scores.

Henry Kissinger's concern for his reputation certainly inflicted considerable damage on U.S. national security, both then and later. Forced to acknowledge CIA actions to congressional investigators, Kissinger, in his memoirs, then castigated the bureaucracy for failing to execute the orders he initially denied having given. Kissinger's sensitivity is apparent even after decades. In 2003 a fresh account of the Chile affair appeared, written by Peter Kornbluh and based on the declassified records, showing Kissinger in a poor light. The former official now orchestrated efforts to discredit this work through negative reviews, pressuring the Council on Foreign Relations to influence the publication of letters commenting on its own review. Historian Kenneth Maxwell, author of the review in the Council's publication, the journal *Foreign Affairs*, and editor of the journal's Latin America review section for more than a decade, resigned after being denied the opportunity to respond to Kissinger associates. Maxwell had liked the Kornbluh study more than Kissinger wanted.

Nasty political infighting in Washington through the fall of 1974, combined with Watergate and Vietnam, created tinderbox conditions. Oversight of U.S. intelligence, an issue that stood in the wings, had already been suggested by the Chile debate. When Seymour Hersh published a further revelation just before Christmas—that the CIA had conducted domestic operations against the anti-war movement in the U.S.—the conflagration ignited. Within weeks a presidential commission, a Senate investigating committee, and another in the House of Representatives were all created to look into the CIA. Called a rogue elephant, the Central Intelligence Agency faced the fight of its life.

18

From "Rogue Elephant" to Resurrection

A SIMPLE TELEPHONE CALL triggered the tempest. Seymour Hersh phoned Director Colby on December 18, 1974, to say he had it from several sources that the CIA had carried out a massive intelligence operation against American opponents of the Vietnam War, including break-ins, mail intercepts, wiretapping, and surveillance. Colby saw Hersh and tried to explain that his data reflected distorted fragments of different projects, all within the agency's charter. He insisted that such activities had ceased under 1973 directives that made plain the CIA would stay within the strict letter of the law. Colby felt Hersh had blown his information out of proportion. Hersh did not see it that way. His article was splashed across three columns of the front page of the Sunday *New York Times* on December 22. The headline read: "HUGE CIA OPERATION REPORTED IN U.S. AGAINST ANTIWAR FORCES, OTHER DISSIDENTS IN NIXON YEARS."

The immediate consequence, as Colby himself concedes, became "a press and political firestorm." He remembers the events as "ruining not only the Christmas season for me but nearly all of the next year as well." Colby arrived on the Seventh Floor at Langley just in time to face this explosion. The ground had been well prepared by the Nixon-Ford administrations. Watergate, plus their disingenuous handling of explanations for U.S. activity in Laos and Chile, fueled what became a season of inquiry. The political controversy ushered in a decade of turmoil for the Central Intelligence Agency.

In all the years since passage of the National Security Act of 1947, presidents had successfully warded off further legal codification of intelligence duties, responsibilities, and restrictions. On a certain level it is not surprising that Richard Helms had felt confident in deliberately misleading Congress on Chile. But the pressure built a little each time the White House avoided reforms, until by 1974 the pot boiled. Indeed it was red hot. The CIA's Cold War mystique had eroded, and with it Langley's protection from scrutiny. Bill Colby's troubles had a lot to do with the White House.

Attitudes began changing in the late 1960s, but the pace accelerated in the Nixon years and by now public confidence had reached a low ebb. Historian Kathryn Olmstead has reported 1975 polling data from the Gallup organization which show barely 14 percent of Americans held a highly favorable view of the CIA. Among well-educated college students, that level was halved. Two years earlier support—already anemic—had stood at 23 percent. The hand grenades from Chile and Southeast Asia were taking their toll.

Despite occasional flaps, the Central Intelligence Agency had been very lucky for a very long time. None of more than two hundred legislative measures intended to oversee or restrict it introduced before 1974 ever passed. Now, however, bad feeling predominated in Congress. In an amendment to the foreign aid bill that year, Democratic Senator Harold Hughes of Iowa and Democratic Congressman Leo B. Ryan of California successfully sponsored legislation to require reporting of significant covert operations to relevant committees of Congress. In practice this worked out to eight committees with more than 160 members plus senior staffs. Commenting on the Hughes-Ryan Amendment, President Ford focused on the danger of leaks rather than the advantages of oversight. Then Bill Colby got that phone call from Sy Hersh.

President Ford was flying to Vail, Colorado, for some skiing when Colby warned him of the imminent Hersh story on CIA domestic activities. The spy chief, speaking to Air Force One over an open line, a radio patch through the White House switchboard, had to be most circumspect. Ford immediately demanded a report. Later that day he responded to growing press inquiries by declaring he had asked Henry Kissinger, as NSC adviser, to obtain Colby's report.

Bill Colby's bad year got off to a rousing start that Christmas Eve. That evening he crossed the Potomac to visit Kissinger at the State Department. In the two days since the Hersh article, the CIA director had assembled a memorandum describing how the *New York Times* story had exaggerated. But there was fire behind the smoke, as Colby had to admit. In fact Hersh had uncovered some of the major CIA abuses recounted in the "Family Jewels" compilation Jim Schlesinger had ordered. This document gathered together allegations of illegal or questionable activities observed by employees throughout the agency. It happened that Kissinger had never been briefed on the "Family Jewels," completed as Colby replaced Schlesinger at Langley.

At last Colby went ahead with his briefing, then handed Kissinger a copy of the report. It noted allegations of CIA assassination efforts against foreign political leaders such as Castro, Ngo Dinh Diem, and Dominican dictator Rafael Trujillo. Kissinger flipped quickly through the pages but slowed when he came to the part about assassinations. He stopped and looked up.

"Well, Bill, when Hersh's story first came out I thought you should have flatly denied it as totally wrong," said Kissinger, "but now I see why you couldn't."

The next day Kissinger wrote to Ford explaining that besides the items in Colby's report, there were other CIA actions that raised questions of judgment on moral issues. He took Colby's thirty-page account to Vail to show the president. Kissinger favored an inquiry, one confined to a narrow scope.

There were no White House denials, and Ford said nothing to support the CIA. There were no official statements from the agency or Colby. The only refutation came on Christmas Day from Richard Helms, a source who increasingly lacked credibility.

Director Colby wished to save the agency but without lying or doing anything illegal. That meant sitting tight for the inevitable investigations. The first would be Ford's, with parameters worked out among advisers Richard Cheney and Donald H. Rumsfeld along with Kissinger. Taking the route of a White House investigation enabled President Ford to show leadership, set the limits himself, and potentially head off other inquiries. White House staff drafted an order for the panel, gave Ford lists of prospective commissioners, and sounded out those people on their willingness to serve. Most of this took place while Ford still vacationed.

When the president returned to the White House he saw the key people. On January 4, 1975, in the Oval Office, he led off with Henry Kissinger, who told Ford that the outpouring of press accounts since Christmas represented merely the tip of an iceberg.

"If they come out, blood will flow," Kissinger said.

The national security adviser added that Richard Helms had confirmed the worst. In a veiled reference to Project Mongoose and the plotting against Castro, Kissinger went on, "For example, Robert Kennedy personally managed the operation on the assassination of Castro."

Immediately afterward Ford saw Helms. The discomfort level, if anything, exceeded that of the president's talk the previous day with Director Colby. Aware of his exposure to criminal indictment in the Chile perjury, Helms also knew of the proposed commission. Ford assured Helms he automatically assumed the CIA man had done the right thing. Helms responded that he would defend himself. Perhaps threateningly, the former top spook warned, "A lot of dead cats are going to come out." But he used the phrase again later, in the context of the more general controversy now raging.

"Frankly, we are in a mess," Ford admitted.

"I think the mood of the country is ghastly," Helms agreed. "I feel deeply for you, Mr. President."

Helms supported the presidential commission and made the constructive suggestion that FBI activities also be included in its purview. Ford replied he would think about that, but in fact his commission stood ready to go and he gave it no instructions to look beyond the CIA. Ford wanted the commission to stay within its charter. Given the political climate he did not think he could guarantee this.

Publicly Gerald Ford declared he would not tolerate illegal activities by intelligence agencies. He said Colby had given assurances that no such activities still existed, and announced a commission under Vice President Nelson Rockefeller. Of course Rockefeller, who had headed the PFIAB subcommittee on covert operations, could be depended on to ride herd on the members, and their mandate ended with the domestic abuses the press had reported. Rockefeller would do a very good job.

Meanwhile Colby testified before the CIA subcommittee of Senate Appropriations on January 15. Pressed for his response to the charges of skullduggery swirling about, Colby's opening statement reprised his report to President Ford. The committee, given the political climate, took the unprecedented step of releasing his testimony. Kissinger and others condemn Colby, essentially claiming the CIA chief put out this material without White House approval, but the spy chief was simply recounting what Ford had known since Vail. Colby also undoubtedly went to Capitol Hill expecting that the statement would be tightly guarded. The secret subcommittees had never before taken such action. This in itself shows the political sensitivity of the time.

In view of public opinion, Congress would not leave the field to the Rockefeller Commission. Very swiftly it established its own investigative committees. The Senate approved its panel on January 27 by a vote of 82 to 4, naming a Select Committee to Study Governmental Operations with Respect to Intelligence Activities. Frank Church would chair the fourteen-member group. The House set up a ten-member panel in February, but this became embroiled in disputes and would be replaced months later by a slightly larger Select Committee on Intelligence led by New York Democrat Otis G. Pike. So began what has become known as the "Year of Intelligence."

In his memoir, *A Time to Heal*, Gerald Ford writes as if the Year of Intelligence should be blamed on journalists and congressional committees who wanted to look at *"everything* in the files." Ford is correct that the Watergate atmosphere contributed to the intensity of the inquiries, but the CIA abuses were scarcely incidental. There would have been no controversy without questionable activity.

From the instant of first exposure to the "Family Jewels," President Ford's major concern remained leaks. This is the one point he returns to repeatedly in his memoir, and it certainly preoccupied him in office. The terms of reference for Rockefeller were carefully drawn in an effort to avoid the most sensitive areas, like assassinations. But Ford and Kissinger had no such control over the congressional investigations, though the White House did develop lines to friendly members or staff that afforded some ability to influence committee activity, or at least find out what they were up to. It was a mistake to suppose that the investigations were merely an annoyance, and improper at that. In fact the very existence of the CIA hung in the balance.

Obviously it would be impossible for the commission and committees to investigate without collecting data, or for them to report without revealing details.

The White House saw the inquiries as a major threat. The intelligence community at large—beyond the CIA—reacted in like manner. Withholding documents and witnesses, or restricting testimony by officials, certain to arouse ire, only encouraged leaks. Yet that became the main tactic utilized by the White House and the agencies. Arguing the need to preserve the secrecy of agency "sources and methods," then stretching that category to cover every conceivable bit of information, the spooks fought a rearguard action through the corridors of Capitol Hill, Langley, and the other centers of U.S. intelligence. Kissinger aligned himself with the most extreme keepers of the secret vaults.

Director Colby, who saw more clearly the danger that the CIA might be swept away if it failed to give at least the appearance of cooperation, was vilified for his efforts and ultimately forced to resign. That, plus his role in the Helms perjury case, tarnished Colby's reputation for many secret warriors. Others, frustrated that anyone would question the DCI's ability to lead the CIA, felt he "handled the grilling with aplomb." The inquiries involved only certain persons at the agency, effectively compartmenting the grief from others at Langley. The inspector general actually commissioned a poll and interviewed a significant fraction of agency employees, demonstrating that morale remained high, except among the top echelon.

The charges against the CIA became the stuff of lunchtime conversation in the agency cafeteria, "but few expressed any real concern for the future." Richard Holm, who now headed China operations for the recently renamed East Asia Division, recalls that "we did our jobs while struggling with the substance of some of the revelations." Staff working directly with the inquisitors were even more upbeat. Scott Breckinridge of the IG office felt the agency in pretty good shape. Hank Knocke, liaison to both Rockefeller and Church, who told Breckinridge the job had cost him among colleagues, reminisced later, "I was proud to be among those who worked . . . in defining the terms for improved oversight and accountability."

Those who thought the CIA's wounds self-inflicted objected to the inquiries. Duane Clarridge, for example, then chief of operations in the Near East and South Asian Division, said of Colby, "He betrayed his own because he didn't try." The coalescence of pro-Helms and pro-Colby factions at headquarters created a cleavage that rent the CIA of the 1970s.

This is not the place for a full treatment of the investigations of the Year of Intelligence. But it is important to understand the interplay as it affected covert operations. Contrary to assertions that Director Colby said what he pleased and ignored the White House, Ford's staff actually kept close control. The president's political advisers looked after general attitudes while lawyer Phillip Buchen followed daily developments. Controls became even tighter that fall when Ford set up a committee under John Marsh that met daily to coordinate strategy against the investigations. Kissinger's NSC staff reviewed the release of every CIA internal history the Church Committee asked for. Robert McFarlane, then a subordinate on the NSC staff, ruled against Church seeing many of the documents and expressed reservations about more, including some quite innocuous ones. Ford and his NSC reviewed Colby's proposed testimony on covert operations, and the DCI went to the White House immediately after that hearing to report on what had been said. In June the White House adopted explicit guidelines on dealing with covert operations data, and modified them later.

In May, Ford's advisers, faced with the Church Committee schedule of formal hearings on covert operations, decided the CIA director should brief only, not testify, and only the leaders of the committee. Deep in the hole politically, Ford proved unable to make that stick. Instead Colby was told what he could discuss: Cuba, but only the Bay of Pigs; the Congo, but only the late war period; Chile, but not after 1971; Korea, but only until 1952. Russian, Greek, and Indonesian involvements apparently seemed nonthreatening to the White House, and unfettered discussion of those was permissible. Other covert operations were out of bounds altogether.

Director Colby, far from being off the reservation, cooperated. He wanted to "sanitize" documents given to the Rockefeller Commission, only to be overruled by the White House. He assigned Scott Breckinridge of the IG office, an original author of the 1967 report on assassination plots, to dissuade the Rockefeller staff from looking too hard at this. Breckinridge ran afoul of David Belin, but judging from the absence of the subject in the commission's report, the effort succeeded.

For the congressional committees, Colby's original arrangements created four levels of increasing secrecy regarding materials. Only basic historical data would be given freely. More sensitive data would be sanitized before shown; the investigators could get only the expurgated versions. At the third level the inquisitors had to visit CIA headquarters, where "fondling files" were housed in the IG office—investigators could make notes only, copying was prohibited, and notes were reviewed by CIA before being let out of the building. The most secret data Colby restricted to indirect reference—it could be used only for briefings or briefs. This included everything about presidents' orders and much about covert action. When inquisitors proved adept at identifying documents sourced in CIA histories, asking to see them, Colby added word-for-word review to his restrictions.

Proposing fresh guidelines to the NSC late in June, Colby anticipated that the investigators might be satiated with in-depth briefings—but of just those programs the CIA selected to typify categories. The agency would offer only a few documents to amplify oral presentations. Again those could be read only at Langley. Everything pertaining to the president, 40 Committee, and the like would be removed from the files, and the White House could review each case before CIA made it available. Colby hoped to satisfy the inquisitors with the National Student Association case, Laos, and Indonesia. President Ford agreed at the time.

A key index of Bill Colby's basic approach is that he tried—and failed—to keep the "Family Jewels" out of play. The measure his detractors prefer is based on a comment Vice President Rockefeller made after a session with Rocky's commission. Rockefeller asked whether Colby ought to be telling so much, as if the CIA did not have an obligation to fully inform a presidential commission, and as if the commission had no legal responsibility to conduct a full inquiry. Indeed it had already overridden CIA's attempt to expurgate documents given to it. No one who makes this criticism notes Rockefeller's role on covert action at PFIAB or the political vulnerability hanging over the vice president as a consequence.

By way of contrast, Gerald Ford himself was responsible for the leak that put the most sensitive covert action issue on the table. At a luncheon with newspaper editors on January 16, 1975, Ford mentioned assassination plots in describing why he had given Rockefeller a narrow assignment. Television reporter Daniel Schorr quickly picked up the gossip about this and confronted Colby with a direct question at the end of February. Colby could not deny the fact, though he did deny any plots in the United States and refused to discuss cases. That news appeared to a public uproar, with Ford forced to expand the remit of Rockefeller's commission to cover assassination allegations, and the Senate also obliged to widen the scope of Church's inquiry.

Reflecting Ford's interests, the entirety of the text on assassinations that eventually appeared in the Rockefeller Commission report concerned whether CIA officers or contract employees had had any role in the murder of John F. Kennedy. This happened in spite of the personal efforts of staff director David Belin, who conducted this portion of the inquiry, deposed a variety of witnesses, and pulled together documents from the agency and elsewhere. Belin's preliminary report, nearly a hundred typescript pages, ended up on the cutting-room floor, its discussion of CIA plots against Castro, Trujillo, Lumumba, and Ngo Dinh Diem kept from the public. President Ford had the source materials turned over to him.

Like Bill Colby with the "Family Jewels," in the political climate of 1975 Jerry Ford could not hold this line. Instead, several days after he released the Rockefeller Commission's report, the president told a news conference that he would turn the assassination files over to the Church Committee. Confining Belin's inquiry turned into a mistake: Ford had no control over the Church Committee's treatment of the same subject. The CIA went to court to force the committee to remove certain names from its report—which in most instances Church did voluntarily. On October 31 President Ford wrote members asking that the entire report be kept secret. Several weeks later, after acrimonious debate on the Senate floor, the committee released the report on its own authority.

Refusals to supply data often occurred in the open, to be reported in the press. One of the worst instances happened with Henry Kissinger and the Pike Committee, which went to the full House of Representatives to secure subpoenas. The subpoenas were voted. The CIA's own lawyers concluded that the documents at issue could not be protected, but Kissinger gave up the papers only when he was about to be cited for contempt of Congress. Before the end the House voted seven subpoenas, but Ford's administration surrendered materials on only a few. Three it rejected, including one addressed by name to Kissinger to supply copies of all State Department recommendations to the NSC on covert operations since January 30, 1961. The second also concerned covert action while the third related to intelligence on arms control.

Ford's opinion is that the Pike Committee went out of its way "to stick it to Kissinger." After consulting with the attorney general, the president intervened on

November 19, 1975, writing Otis Pike that the subpoenaed documents had been legitimately withheld. The committee responded by voting to cite Kissinger for contempt, a measure that went to the full House in December. President Ford compromised, releasing some materials.

Counterattack came in early January 1976 when White House aides told the congressional committees that if they hoped to obtain information in the future as oversight panels, staffs would have to be reduced and stiff penalties adopted for leaks, penalties to include expulsion from Congress. For its part the CIA recommended numerous deletions from the Pike Report for reasons of national security. A number were accepted, but Pike's committee rejected about 150 of the proposed deletions. Ford prevailed upon the full House not to release the report. Some 246 representatives voted to suppress it, 124 for its release.

When television reporter Daniel Schorr asked for his reaction, Speaker of the House Thomas P. "Tip" O'Neill, Jr., said, "This is an election year, and they're getting a lot of flak about leaks, and they're going to vote their American Legion posts."

But the Pike Report did leak, and major portions appeared in a New York weekly, *The Village Voice*. A couple of hundred copies of the report had gone to an assortment of congressional and executive offices. No culprit ever emerged, though it was established the initial leak had been to Daniel Schorr.

Again, Gerald Ford might have done better with the original House committee. The first chairman, Representative Lucien Nedzi, came from the president's home state and had been the leader of the secret subcommittee. Nedzi's position on the House investigation disintegrated, in fact, when it became known that Colby had briefed the Michigan congressman on that portion of the "Family Jewels" concerning assassination, but Nedzi had told none of his colleagues. Nedzi would not even be a member of the panel that finally conducted the inquiry.

Frank Church, a liberal Democrat with presidential aspirations, hoped to ride the intelligence investigations to national prominence, positioning himself as a dark horse for 1976, with a solid bid for the presidency possible in 1980. Be that as it may, his investigation proceeded quietly and systematically. Plenty of material was withheld from the Senate committee, but Senator Church knew where to look. The Idaho Democrat had been a member of the Foreign Relations Committee when the CIA spurned that body in 1966. He participated in the Laos hearings of 1967 and 1969. Church had also been chairman of the subcommittee on Multinational Corporations to which Richard Helms had lied about CIA involvement in Chile. Ambitious or not, the senator determined to follow up several of these subjects.

For its interim report on alleged assassination plots, the Church Committee conducted numerous interviews, held sixty days of hearings, and accumulated more than eight thousand pages of sworn testimony. Some witnesses were reinterviewed on the basis of later information. For its review of covert operations, the committee received fourteen CIA briefings and conducted more than a hundred staff interviews, among them thirteen former ambassadors and a dozen CIA chiefs of station. The investigation continued past its original September 1975 deadline. Sixty professional staff assisted. A final report, approved and released in April 1976, ran to many volumes plus detailed staff studies. There were also seven volumes of hearings, an interim report on the assassination plots, and a case study of covert action in Chile. Six additional case studies on covert operations remained classified at the request of the CIA.

The significant conclusion from all this: Congress had failed to provide necessary statutes. Intelligence needed a constitutional framework. Presidents had made excessive and sometimes self-defeating use of covert operations while inadequate legislative attention had been given to budgets. The committee recommended that overall CIA budget figures be made public so that annual budget debates could be realistic. The fundamental issue remained one of balancing secrecy with American democracy. Church's committee, and Pike's as well, recommended the creation of permanent oversight units on intelligence. Both houses established such committees in 1976. The Central Intelligence Agency entered a new era of formal legislative oversight.

From the millions of words in the hearings, findings, and recommendations of the Church Committee, one phrase in particular stuck in the minds of many who heard it: one day Frank Church wondered out loud whether the CIA had not become a "rogue elephant." Government officials spent years living down that damning epithet.

Church's opinion after the investigation by his committee was that U.S. capabilities for covert action should be sharply circumscribed. Most of his colleagues would not go that far.

Referring to the secret warriors in comments appended to his committee's report, Church expressed this view: "Certainly we do not need a regiment of cloak-and-dagger men, earning their campaign ribbons and, indeed, their promotions by planning new exploits throughout the world. Theirs is a self-generating enterprise." With capability in place, pressures on presidents to use it, the senator believed, became immense. Of this activism the senator wrote, "I must lay the blame, in large measure, to the fantasy that it lay within our power to control other countries through the covert manipulation of their affairs. It formed part of a greater illusion that entrapped and enthralled our presidents—the illusion of American omnipotence."

Church's opinion would undoubtedly be strengthened by yet another CIA venture, a covert action in Africa, carried out even as the investigations worked toward their finales. This was called Project IA/Feature. Like the Congo, Feature intended to influence events in an African colony headed for independence. This time the target was the Portuguese colony of Angola, immediately south of Zaire.

The Angola affair really began in Portugal with the April 1974 leftist military coup that overthrew a long-standing dictatorship. Portugal had been warring against indigenous independence movements in Angola and other African colonies. The new Portuguese government had no stomach for this fight, and Lisbon announced its withdrawal from Africa. Angola represented a classic case of colonial underdevelopment. It would become independent on November 11, 1975. Until then, under the "Alvor agreement" Portugal negotiated with the three rebel movements that January, a coalition government would prepare elections. The fact that few Portuguese settlers intended to stay on complicated the situation, as did the existence of Angolan oil production in a section of the country, Cabinda, isolated from the rest.

Each of the three rebel movements had its own armed forces, and they were left to fight it out among themselves. Tribally based, the movements' political competition had ethnic overtones as well. The Popular Movement for the Liberation of Angola (MPLA by its Portuguese initials), the National Front for the Liberation of Angola (FNLA), and the National Union for the Total Independence of Angola (UNITA) all espoused vaguely socialist ideologies, were left of center, and all had taken cash and guns from Communist nations. MPLA had the strongest political organization, appealing to the Mbundu tribe, founded in 1956 as an offshoot of the Angolan Communist Party. FNLA came from the Bakongo, of about 700,000, more than half of whom fled to Zaire during the Portuguese resistance war. Holden Roberto, an educated Christian of peasant stock, had founded FNLA in 1954. The CIA had known him since 1953 and put him on its payroll in 1966, in part to counter the Chinese Communists, who were already helping FNLA. Jonas Savimbi, Roberto's chief lieutenant, broke away at that time to form UNITA among the Ovimbundo, Angola's largest tribe. The groups waged parallel wars against Portuguese colonialists but were not allied in any way.

Except for Vietnam and the Cold War, Angola might have reached independence without anyone taking notice. Kissinger credits Zambian leader Kenneth Kaunda in an April 1975 visit with convincing him and Ford that the MPLA could not be permitted to win Angola with Russian arms—the Cold War argument. Another interpretation of U.S. intervention is that Washington, concerned by the perception of its weakness after Vietnam, chose Angola to show its strength. The truth lies somewhere between and is a good deal messier.

A huge amount of juggling has concealed the record on Angola. Kissinger himself records that Kaunda's claims—that African leaders agreed with his stand—proved completely misleading. Kaunda in fact had supported the MPLA but a faction that lost out, giving him motive. But the secretary of state learned this later, and "none of this changed the basic challenge, which was Soviet intervention on a scale not seen in Africa for fifteen years." Kissinger writes of an airlift of Soviet weapons to a nearby country for transshipment and a flow by sea "said to involve two dozen ships." This version both fudges the chronology and is a gigantic exaggeration, essentially a fiction. Kissinger may have focused on the Soviets later, but the evidence suggests that at least initially the affair had more to do with who controlled the oil production of Angola's Cabinda enclave.

During the Angolan revolution the CIA had played both sides, selling the Portuguese B-26 bombers and permitting them to recruit Cuban exile pilots for the planes while paying Holden Roberto as an intelligence source. When the Portuguese coup took place, Langley created a special task force for Portugal, not Angola. The connection to Roberto had been maintained at a low level, but in 1974 the CIA increased its support to $1,000 a month. At the time the FNLA's main backing came from China, arming Roberto's troops and training them in Zaire, with a unit of more than a hundred military advisers in camps that dictator Joseph Mobutu allowed Roberto to establish. This became the first time where the United States and Communist China worked together on a covert operation in a third country.

Within days of the Alvor agreement, the 40 Committee approved the provision to Roberto's FNLA of $300,000 but rejected a suggestion for another $100,000 to Savimbi. President Ford quickly approved. The project amounted to a political action, enabling FNLA to get a leg up in the move toward elections. The CIA funded a printing press for a newspaper, equipment for a radio station, and fifty thousand election-style campaign buttons. Deputy national security adviser William Hyland argues that the cash scarcely raised a wave in Angola, but the fact of CIA support betokened a relationship that Roberto could flaunt, and *that* was the key factor. Buoyed by the support, Roberto in February 1975 ordered his troops to attack MPLA cadres in the capital, Luanda, and in northern Angola. In one instance in early March, fifty unarmed MPLA activists were gunned down. These attacks ended any possibility of coalition government. A second round of FNLA attacks in Luanda tempted fate.

Thus both the initial CIA subsidy and the outbreak of fighting predated any appeals from Kaunda to Ford and Kissinger, and combat began with the U.S.-backed FNLA movement, not with the MPLA. In addition, Zairian Joseph Mobutu, who funded a separatist movement in Cabinda, began stirring up trouble there as well. As early as October 1974, Mobutu's planes started flying FNLA soldiers to Luanda.

At this juncture the Soviets took a hand, resuming aid to the MPLA, which they had terminated several years earlier. Moscow had favored the same MPLA faction as Kenneth Kaunda, which lost out to leader Augustinho Neto. The breakaway Communist nation Yugoslavia (with which Washington had fairly good relations) became the sole socialist country to help MPLA during this period. Moving into the post-Portuguese-war struggle, Neto appealed for help, but the Russians initially did nothing. Then they talked of equipping a special unit for the MPLA, but the idea embodied two thousand troops, not Neto's whole army, of which this would have been a small fraction. In addition the Soviets wanted to train those soldiers in Russia, not in Angola. These schemes are tiny compared to claims of Soviet arms aid made by defenders of the U.S. intervention. As for the timing, definitive records are still lacking, but indications are that Moscow began thinking about this aid at about the same time Washington put together the CIA political action. Weapons began arriving between March and May. The assistance included a couple of aircraft loads to Luanda, but most of it came on a pair of ships. Two, not two dozen.

The MPLA had long had friendly relations with Castro, and not long after the Soviets sent help, Havana followed suit with a small contingent of Cuban advisers. A few Cuban observers and negotiators reached Angola early on, but the work of historian Piero Gleijeses shows conclusively that Cuban military trainers arrived only around August 1975.

Washington had already swung into action. About the end of April Henry Kissinger asked for an options paper. Bill Hyland sees Kissinger's involvement as "late and hesitant," yet these moves predate the Cuban advisers. One 40 Committee discussion after the January project involved arms aid, but nothing had yet come of it. Nathaniel Davis, returned from Chile and now assistant secretary of state for African affairs, answered Kissinger with a pair of memoranda: on May 1 advising against covert aid for Jonas Savimbi, which he felt could not remain secret; and six days later cautioning against pre-independence shenanigans in Angola. Upon returning from a familiarization visit, Davis repeated his warning. Kissinger nevertheless insisted on the interagency review, conducted by a group under Davis. They submitted their options paper and an associated study (NSSM-224) on June 13.

The majority opposed intervention; instead the Davis panel held out for diplomatic efforts to encourage settlement among the factions. This reflected a basic understanding that Angola was an African, not a Cold War, problem. Intervention carried high risk of exposure with negative effects in Angola, across Africa, and in relations with Portugal; it offered only limited benefits and potentially contributed to increased Soviet involvement. Davis warned that the United States would have to reckon with "probable disclosure" and argued that "at most we would be in a position to commit limited resources, and buy marginal influence."

The June 13 report of the Davis group framed a stark choice for President Ford. By then another outbreak of fighting had occurred in Luanda, sparked this time by Neto's increasingly powerful MPLA. Events had begun to move against U.S. ally Roberto. According to the Pike Committee, which studied Angola in some detail, the Davis group's prime recommendation disappeared from its report "at the direction of National Security Council aides." The course was presented to the NSC as merely one policy option, others being to do nothing or make a substantial intervention.

In preparation for a National Security Council meeting, Secretary Kissinger sent two senior Africanists to the front-line states to survey the situation. They returned to tell the secretary that Mobutu favored intervention in support of the FNLA and would help with his own forces. The Kissinger memoirs artfully describe his encounter with the diplomats without mentioning at all the NSC meeting—a fateful one—that took place the same afternoon. Secretary Kissinger's briefing memorandum for Ford conceded that U.S. interests were "important but not vital," and noted Mobutu's push for intervention. Contrary to Kissinger's recitation of Zambian leader Kenneth Kaunda's position, in this paper he notes that Zambia (and Tanzania) "can be expected to continue to work for a peaceful settlement." The Kissinger briefing made out the diplomatic option as only an opening move—

everyone agreed on that, but afterward the choice would still be between a neutral attitude or stepped-up involvement. Kissinger's discussion of the latter lays bare his preference:

> *Active support* of the FNLA and/or UNITA could enable us to check the momentum of leftist forces and to facilitate assertion of control by pro-Western moderates but would involve considerable risks. Assistance would have to be covert or channeled through third parties. We would be involving ourselves in a match with the Soviets, yet we do not enjoy the same freedom to raise the level of support as do the Soviets.
>
> In addition to our substantive interest in the outcome, playing an active role would demonstrate that events in Southeast Asia have not lessened our determination to protect our interests. In sum, we face an opportunity—albeit with substantial risks—to preempt the probable loss to communism of a key developing country at a time of great uncertainty over our will and determination to remain the preeminent leader and defender of freedom in the West.

The NSC meeting itself opened with Director Colby describing the situation in Angola. Colby warned of the MPLA-FNLA standoff in Luanda. New fighting could break out at any time, he said, while Cabinda "remains a tinderbox" where MPLA had a slight edge but Mobutu-supported separatists also figured in the equation. The text on Soviet military aid is deleted from the currently available declassified version of the document, but its placement and length suggest that the CIA had no evidence of the huge arms shipments claimed by Kissinger. Moreover, *there is no mention at all of alleged Cuban troops in Angola.* President Ford's questions show that he knew very little of this West African nation. Kissinger jumped in, raised the specter of the Congo from the early 1960s (where, as seen earlier, the Soviets had been misrepresented as meddling), then remarked that "Soviet arms shipments have reversed the situation." The secretary of state expressed himself as "not in wild agreement" with any of the proposed options, but he discounted neutrality as giving away the game to Neto's MPLA, and a diplomatic approach as a sign of weakness.

Kissinger's comment on covert action is deleted but probably favorable since immediately afterward President Ford asks if there are specific proposals for "grants in the arms area." Ford also says that diplomacy would be "naive." The group does recognize Kaunda's encouragement of U.S. intervention. Defense Secretary James Schlesinger then cautions that "if we do something, we must have some confidence that we can win, or we should stay neutral." Schlesinger saw Holden Roberto as "not a strong horse." The consensus bypassed this point to agree to "keep Roberto and Savimbi viable and keep the options open," as William Clements, Schlesinger's deputy, expressed it. Bill Colby promised action proposals within five days.

Kissinger and Colby agreed that in African wars those who controlled a nation's capital usually won. The CIA chief added that the educated classes in Angola were concentrated around Luanda and tended to support MPLA. For Kissinger this was one more reason to ramp up a CIA program. In early July, just as Langley completed options for Project Feature, another round of fighting erupted in Luanda. The MPLA drove its adversaries out for good. That presence in the capital—the condition for success that Kissinger himself had framed for the president—had now been lost made no difference at all to his drive to jump-start the covert operation.

Action now moved to the 40 Committee. Assistant Secretary Davis prepared a fresh dissent paper for Undersecretary Joseph J. Sisco. The oil in Cabinda, in which Gulf had a $300 million interest, remained the only significant American stake, Davis argued. He agreed with Kissinger's view that if the United States did anything at all it had to do it quickly and massively, decisively. Davis simply doubted this could be done, pointing to the CIA's own paper which made clear that the United States could not win in the best of circumstances, and argued that in these particular ones the Soviets were freer to escalate than the United States. The diplomat warned against leaks, raised questions regarding the legality of the contemplated method of weapons delivery (they would be given to Mobutu, who would hand the rebels U.S. weapons he already had), and questioned a premise in the CIA paper that arming Holden Roberto and Jonas Savimbi would discourage them from engaging in a civil war. Nate Davis's colleague William G. Hyland, who now headed the Bureau of Intelligence and Research, dismissed the paper as the usual State Department carping.

Meeting on July 14, Kissinger's 40 Committee directed the CIA to finalize details within forty-eight hours. Langley should use the CIA director's contingency account so as to avoid the need for the Ford administration to ask Congress for money. That would have meant explaining a paramilitary intervention to the same legislators then busily investigating the CIA. The top leadership at Langley opposed Project Feature—the CIA, like the State Department, worried about exposure while estimating a $100 million price tag, an amount not available in the DCI's contingency fund. While Langley refined details the press reported FNLA forces completely driven from Luanda, and the CIA received new data on Soviet arms shipments—more and heavier weapons flowing into MPLA hands. Assistant Secretary Davis made one more try at turning Kissinger away from his determination to proceed.

On July 17 the 40 Committee blessed the project. Henry Kissinger took the proposal to President Ford, along with Davis's dissent paper. Kissinger quotes himself as favoring action and urging the president to study the dissent. Ford merely wondered why Davis was so vehement. Kissinger warned he had "massive problems within" State over the program and expected Davis to resign and the program to leak. Ford approved an initial $7 million the next morning. A million of that went directly to Mobutu, not to any of the Angolan rebel groups. Nathaniel Davis indeed resigned when he learned of the go-ahead. In a replay of the Haig-Kissinger ploy with Ed Korry in Chile, Kissinger kept Davis on the reservation and out of media hands by convincing him to become ambassador to Switzerland.

The CIA, which had advised against Track II in Chile and the Kurdish operation, again received distressing marching orders. That it proposed a plan at all was used by Kissinger in 1976 Senate testimony to argue that "the CIA recommended the operation and supported it." This is in marked contrast to Kissinger's recollections, where he takes every available opportunity to castigate the agency as loathe to participate in covert action. Put another way, Kissinger's constant railing about CIA reluctance to engage, plus the fact that Langley did conduct all these operations, demonstrates quite directly that the Central Intelligence Agency, far from being a rogue elephant, functioned under purposeful presidential control.

One reason Director Colby was so lukewarm is that he knew the difficulties involved. Project Feature, just a few months after the final denouement in Vietnam, found the agency still licking its wounds. The Special Operations Group, Langley's paramilitary experts, had been reduced under DCI James Schlesinger, and they had no recent African experience. As of late 1974 the agency had fewer than ten black case officers. Some saw the Africa Division of the DO, still the smallest, as having its hands full watching dozens of nations. A 1971 policy review chaired by the State Department, according to a subordinate officer, concluded that the CIA had been useless in Africa and recommended closing the division. Its baron, James Potts, strongly supported Feature. Potts came to the Africa Division from a four-year tour as station chief in Athens, where Langley's headaches were from Greek colonels who had taken over the government amid public suspicions of CIA collusion. It had been his second Greek assignment, and Potts had tired of political action. Angola offered fresh terrain and a new mission.

Project Feature proceeded under very high priority, so urgent in fact that a first planeload of weapons went off to the FNLA, via Zaire, before Langley even formed a task force and before the Portuguese withdrew from the airfield that received them. By August 9 two more loads had been sent on air force C-141 transports while CIA assembled a shipload of supplies.

Director Colby chaired an interagency group to oversee Feature. Kissinger objects to that procedure, crediting the spy chief with an insufficiently aggressive attitude and CIA with lacking a "sense of tactical feasibility" and being "attracted to dramatic ploys rather than to a coherent long-term strategy." The national security adviser observes that he and Ford ought to have put someone in the White House in charge—CIA management would have been okay for espionage or a political action but "it made no sense with respect to military operations on the scale now unfolding."

These are specious objections. Langley had just ended secret wars in Kurdistan and in Laos and Vietnam, both of which involved long-term strategy over a decade and a half; and it had worked against Cuba for half a decade and in Tibet longer than that. Except for Project Mongoose, the standard had *always* been for CIA management, and if Angola *had* been intended as a new Mongoose, Kissinger and Ford were in real trouble, for that kind of effort was simply not possible amid the controversies of the Year of Intelligence. If that seemed problematical, the problem should have been apparent to the White House at the time. If the White

House had been in charge, this would not have freed Ford from clearing a more muscular approach with Congress. Kissinger quotes himself telling the 40 Committee there were "'no rewards for losing with moderation,'" by way of explaining that he held a "most liberal interpretation" of the formal directive, which was simply "to establish a balance of power in Angola, as a prelude to negotiations." In other words, Kissinger's—notorious—posturing should be taken as the guidance rather than the actual directive. Moreover the monies actually approved for Project Feature were consonant with the formal objectives, not the expansive goals Kissinger asserts retrospectively.

One level below Colby's management group, Langley's Angola task force was somewhat unusual. Appointed chief, John Stockwell was a twelve-year veteran and old Africa hand who had also served in Southeast Asia. The agency's equivalent of a colonel, relatively junior for the job, Stockwell held a slot normally reserved for generals. Judging from Stockwell's account, Jim Potts then ran it— the division chief rather than DDO William Nelson. Potts, his deputy George Costello, and Stockwell prepared detailed plans right up to the last minute. On July 27 President Ford upped the ante, approving another $8 million for the program.

The CIA principals gathered in Nelson's office to review the plans for the Colby working group. When Costello suggested that the moment had come to determine how far the CIA should go, DDO Nelson spoke up: "Gentlemen, we've been given a job to do. Let's not sit around wringing our hands." Colby carried the latest plan to the 40 Committee on August 8.

John Stockwell, sent on a fact-finding mission to Zaire and Angola, visited both Holden Roberto and Jonas Savimbi. The latter seemed by far the more credible opponent for the MPLA. French intelligence chief Alexandre de Marenches agreed. So did the British, apparently, and a British corporate aircraft flew the CIA officer to Savimbi's headquarters. De Marenches, not so fortunate, had to send one of his SDECE officers on a trek of more than a thousand miles just to put key questions to the UNITA leader. Savimbi had the strongest movement. An inspiring leader, his political organization was competent and had grass roots. Much of Roberto's support resided in Zaire. On August 20, while Stockwell observed the FNLA and UNITA, President Ford authorized an additional $10.7 million for Feature. By the time the task force chief reappeared at Langley, the project had momentum. In all, Langley put about a hundred secret warriors into this battle for black Africa.

Mobutu would be critical. With MPLA in control of Angola's main seaports and railroad, CIA supplies could enter only through Zaire (or South Africa). In addition, Holden Roberto had his FNLA base camps in Zaire and resided there too. In fact Roberto showed no inclination to leave his comfortable villa for the front, something of which the United States was well aware (Roberto had not been in Angola in years)—Jim Schlesinger even mentioned this at the key meeting with President Ford. Mobutu had Roberto in tow and to some extent used FNLA as a cat's paw to advance his own interests in Angola.

Stewart Methven, chief of station in Kinshasa, handled relations with the FNLA and Mobutu. Methven, a covert project man par excellence, a member of the first class to graduate from Camp Peary, was a Langley legend. His exploits in Southeast Asia ranged from training Diem's spooks in the 1950s, to work on the montagnard scout program and the counterterror teams, to pacification and political action. But Methven had earned the greatest acclaim in recruiting Vang Pao for the secret war in Laos. He had been controller for Vietnamese officer and politico Tran Ngoc Chau, who became such a political thorn to Nguyen Van Thieu that the Saigon leader had him jailed. The CIA failed to protect Chau, and the Young Turk blew Methven's cover. That upset the spy's son, who learned of his father's occupation in the *New York Times.* By then deputy station chief in Indonesia, Methven watched as General Suharto began secretly helping Nixon in Cambodia, with supply shipments to the pro-U.S. side. John Stockwell fought alongside the Hmong in Laos, and also had Vietnam service in common with Methven, but their relations quickly soured over Project Feature. Stockwell saw Methven as far too willing to pander to Joseph Mobutu, presiding over payoffs and barely concealed bribes—like ice plants and boats for Zairian officials—while standing aside as Mobutu used FNLA aid to reequip his own military. Stockwell also saw Jim Potts as weak for failing to rein in the station chief in Kinshasa.

Meanwhile Methven solved the problem of an air force by the simple expedient of rewarding defectors who brought airplanes with them. Eight assorted light planes were contracted, commandeered, or diverted. In one instance Methven went along with Mobutu's demands for $2 million from CIA to buy a Zairian C-130 worth less than a third of that, though Langley rejected the scam. The Americans also acquired a pair of Swift boats for the FNLA to run off Cabinda. The boats, 140 trucks, several hundred radios, and 70 mortars sailed on August 30 from Charlestown for Africa aboard the freighter *American Champion.* Project deliveries to Zaire also included a dozen M-113 armored personnel carriers and almost 20,000 automatic rifles. Soon there would be a munitions stockpile in Kinshasa of 1,500 tons. But corruption reigned: Zairian shipments to the rebels included no armored vehicles, fewer than half the number of modern rifles the CIA gave Mobutu, and more than 12,000 old M-1 carbines. The FNLA ultimately received supplies at a rate of ten tons per day, much of it old and worn out. As on other occasions, the agency made its cash go farther by undervaluing the weapons, for example pricing an M-1 carbine at $7.55 or a .45-caliber automatic pistol at $5.00.

Langley fooled itself, supposing the Zairian weapons somehow hid its hand. Mobutu's involvement simply invited attack on the rebel rear base in Zaire while reducing the effectiveness of rebel forces. Meanwhile China continued to train the FNLA almost until independence day. When Roberto's troops failed to show much striking power in northern Angola, Mobutu sent in two of his paracommando battalions plus some Panhard armored cars in return for more CIA arms. Half the twelve hundred troops Mobutu sent into Angola deserted. His army turned back after suffering only about fifty casualties.

The secret warriors also tried to substitute propaganda for boots on the ground. Fully a third of the Feature task force were psywar specialists, their effort code-named Project IA/Cadmus. In Kinshasa they planted stories in the two major newspapers, *Elimo* and *Salongo*. The same thing happened in Lusaka, the Zambian capital. Whatever favorable development could be seized upon was converted into leaflets printed on a mimeograph in Kinshasa. Planes dropped them inside Angola. In at least one case MPLA radio in Luanda took CIA leaflets and broadcast them verbatim. At Langley a committee compiled press guidance for the State Department, several paragraphs each day with the themes that should be pushed. Often the stories were completely made up—in one instance a lurid tale of Cuban soldiers raping and pillaging, complete with the accounts of victims. The Cubans were supposed to have been taken and executed by a firing squad of women. Another story told of UNITA capturing Soviet advisers when they took a village. Looking for evidence of Communist presence, and ignorant of African superstitions about spirits (Stockwell believes that women, especially, would never have participated in killings), the press gave such stories great play. When journalists—more than fifty of them—tried to follow up the stories, they found nothing. Savimbi admitted to reporters that UNITA had no Cuban or Russian prisoners and had never been near the village named in the accounts. The propaganda coup evaporated.

The station chief in Lusaka, Robert Hultslander, dealt with UNITA. Despite liking Savimbi, Hultslander eventually came to agree with the U.S. consul in Luanda that the MPLA were, in fact, better qualified to govern the country. Theoretically no Americans were to work inside Angola. But Hultslander got a Special Forces training team in mufti to instruct UNITA recruits. This would be critical since, at the outset of Project Feature, Savimbi's forces numbered only a few hundred. CIA communications experts were also located with both UNITA and FNLA, handling not only Feature cable traffic but training rebel radio operators. More ominously, South Africa, both through its armed forces (SADF) and its intelligence service, the Bureau of State Security (BOSS), intervened as well. Early on South African troops occupied a hydroelectric dam in southern Angola. Then BOSS quietly sent money and arms to UNITA. This meant that the CIA and the secret warriors of the white minority regime worked hand in hand in a covert operation in the heart of black Africa, which automatically put Washington on the wrong side of African nationalism, to devastating political effect. All the propaganda the agency generated so assiduously could not alter that reality.

Langley coordinated war strategy with BOSS, permitted high-level talks with BOSS officials in Washington, and sent UNITA some arms through South Africa. The CIA paid for gasoline to move SADF armored cars to help Savimbi. Plans were in process to procure a C-130 transport and some helicopters to be given to SADF for its UNITA supply flights. In October the South Africans asked for help acquiring 155-millimeter artillery shells they claimed were needed in Angola.

Stockwell's account maintains that Africa Division chief Potts entertained even wider cooperation with the South Africans. These were stifled by staunch

State Department opposition. The diplomats upheld the Kennedy administration's arms embargo on South Africa and quashed suggestions for major collaboration. State proved right in the fall, when journalists confirmed the presence of South African troops with UNITA. Instant black African revulsion toward the Western-supported factions followed. This dealt Project Feature's political action component an irreparable blow.

Ironically, one of the diplomats who closely questioned CIA plans for Angola was Frank Wisner, Jr., son of the legendary secret warrior. Another cautious diplomat was Edward Mulcahy, State's representative on the Colby working group, who quietly threatened to resign if Potts went ahead with the South Africans.

South Africa escalated its involvement in the fall of 1975, sending a force that included armored cars plus associated logistics. Task Force Zulu, its commander code-named Rommel (an Afrikaner, Col. Koos van Heerden), was more powerful than Savimbi's entire army at the time. Zulu became Savimbi's spearhead. Typically the South African Operation Savannah was passed off as a UNITA offensive and the SADF troops, if anyone asked, as mercenaries. Savannah became the most successful military action mounted against the MPLA. Rommel advanced rapidly while another SADF task force joined Savimbi at his headquarters. Within two weeks Zulu captured the major port in southern Angola and threatened the port at Lobito and the Benguela railroad, one of Angola's few major transport systems.

The South Africans were good fighters. With them UNITA gained much of Benguela province. Neto turned to his Soviet allies. Moscow increased its shipments, allowing MPLA troops to introduce potent artillery rockets during the summer and 76-millimeter guns about this time. The Cuban military mission became active in late August, planning to operate four training detachments, and Cuban advisers of one of these first participated in combat toward the end of October—a few dozen men compared to the Zulu force of well over a thousand. Lobito fell on November 7, four days before independence. Kinshasa newspapers praised the fighting abilities of FNLA and UNITA.

The Zulu force represented one prong of a pincer attack toward Luanda. Roberto's FNLA was the other. Stiffened by more than a hundred Portuguese mercenaries—their recruitment financed by the CIA—the FNLA advanced on Luanda from the north. Finally inside Angola, Roberto got a bit of South African help too: advisers and some guns in early November. South African sources report a small CIA contingent with Roberto as well. The American consul and all remaining U.S. diplomats left the capital at this time.

Through exhaustive research Piero Gleijeses established that Fidel Castro decided to commit combat troops to Angola on November 4, the same day Havana sent a hundred heavy weapons experts that the Angolans had wanted for months. (Kissinger both greatly exaggerates the pace and timing of the Cuban commitment and wildly underreports the South African involvement.) The first men of an elite battalion left for Luanda several days later aboard two aircraft. Gleijeses believes Castro moved when he appreciated that South Africa had really intervened. The Cuban unit went into the lines defending Luanda from the FNLA. The MPLA and the

Cubans blunted Roberto's attack. The South African advance also stalled with ambushes set by the few Cubans facing them, who destroyed bridges and then defended the only other paved road to Luanda.

Henry Kissinger cites a CIA report to the 40 Committee on November 5 as showing that the FNLA and UNITA were on the cusp of victory. But what he quotes shows a static picture: a list of a list of ports and provincial capitals controlled. The report itself notes the factor already beginning to swing the pendulum: the "heavy" commitment of Soviet equipment, armor, and trainers, plus Cuban combat troops. Secretary Kissinger adverts that "we" interpreted Moscow's moves as harassment, not policy, and "therefore judged that Moscow would recoil once the United States asserted an important national interest." Kissinger miscalculated, not the CIA.

On independence day, November 11, there were about seven hundred Cubans in Angola. In an emergency airlift and sealift called Operation Carlotta, Cuban volunteers came in large numbers: the remainder of the elite battalion almost immediately (this unit halted SADF's Zulu force), a thousand artillerymen in early December, several thousand more by the new year, up to fifteen thousand in all by the spring of 1976.

Between the end of October and November 18, according to the CIA, more than twenty Russian aircraft delivered arms to the MPLA. After Ford and Kissinger appealed to Moscow, the Soviet airlift halted on December 10, not to be resumed for weeks, without affecting the military balance. There could be no plainer demonstration of rebel weakness.

Estimated Soviet aid stood at $100 million in December 1975, and four times that amount by March. Weapons delivered included fifty T-54 tanks, 122-millimeter artillery, and MIG jet fighters. Moscow had always had this capacity but no reason to engage so deeply until its client seemed menaced. The Soviet-bloc response anticipated in Washington's original deliberations had come to pass.

In northern Angola the FNLA failed to capture the isolated enclave of Cabinda, seat of Angolan oil production. Cubans and MPLA forces began to push back the FNLA. Holden Roberto tried to raise more mercenaries to stiffen his army. Roberto offered a million dollars for a "parachute regiment." Soldier of fortune John Banks received advances to recruit in England. In the United States the recruiter was David Floyd Bufkin, a former pilot and California crop duster, variously reported to have received cash from either Roberto or the CIA. Mercenary recruiting used the grapevine plus ads in newspapers. Bufkin also appeared on television and advertised in the action magazine *Soldier of Fortune*. Roberto's "parachute regiment" ultimately received 140 British and seven American recruits, some with no military experience at all. Twenty-three arrived too late and were sent home. Another group was rejected as unsuitable.

The Central Intelligence Agency engaged in a parallel effort to recruit in Portugal, yielding several hundred men for FNLA. Through French intelligence, which also contributed ammunition, four helicopters, and its own agents, the CIA contacted longtime soldier of fortune Robert Denard, who recruited twenty mercenaries for UNITA. Another forty went to UNITA from BOSS. Instructions prohibiting Americans from working inside Angola were spurned by a fresh army mobile training team at FNLA headquarters.

Washington viewed the worsening situation with alarm. On November 27 President Ford authorized another $7 million for Project Feature. That exhausted the CIA director's contingency fund. Any more had to come from Congress. Langley prepared options for the 40 Committee alternatively priced at $28 million, $60 million, or $100 million. Director Colby, now a lame duck awaiting replacement, recommended the first program. Ed Mulcahy of State personally carried the options paper to Kissinger before the latter departed on a ten-day trip to China with Ford.

Later Mulcahy, unable to tell the working group just what Kissinger had decided, said, "He read it. Then he grunted and walked out of his office."

"Grunted?" asked Potts incredulously.

"Yeah, like, unnph!"

They were reduced to trying to figure out what an affirmative "unnph" might sound like.

Kissinger is silent about this exchange. He writes that he backed the $60 million option. Ford approved the CIA's recommendation. This revolved around "reprogramming"—taking money from one government account and moving it to another—which applied to amounts of less than $50 million and could be done with the approval of appropriations committee chairmen alone. But the $28 million gambit was blocked.

In the Year of Intelligence, Congress had ceased to be a rubber stamp. It also knew a lot more about Project Feature than earlier secret wars—a result of the Hughes-Ryan reporting requirements. The CIA first informed both House and Senate members and staffs beginning a week after Ford's presidential finding, though not the full eight committees required. In particular, on August 4 Director Colby briefed Democratic Senator Dick Clark of Iowa shortly before Clark left on a fact-finding mission to Africa. The senator, chairman of the African Affairs subcommittee of the Foreign Relations panel, feared the intentions behind the project. What Clark saw led him to suspect U.S. collusion with South Africa. He returned determined to do something. South African intervention and the collapse of the rebel offensives only sharpened Clark's resolve. At just this time the executive came to Congress for the Angola money.

Meanwhile public exposure, delayed by the secrecy of Colby's CIA briefings, inevitably occurred. Congressmen had sworn silence on what they learned in thirty-five briefings from the DCI in 1975–1976. The first leaks appeared in the *Washington Post* and the *New York Times* in late September to no apparent effect. They were muted by the continuing CIA-manufactured propaganda, a case of blowback in which agency foreign activities affected American politics. Even afterward, in his congressional appearances, Colby continued claiming that no CIA weapons were going directly to the guerrillas and that no Americans were involved inside Angola. The operative words were "directly" and "inside." Henry Kissinger lent his own hand, testifying to the Church Committee on November 21 that CIA involvement in Angola was purely to bring about negotiations.

The subterfuge finally collapsed. On December 5 Ed Mulcahy came late to a hearing at Senator Clark's subcommittee. The CIA witness, William E. Nelson, went first. Nelson, a Colby protégé, probably feared his own days numbered, as Ford had suddenly fired Colby a month earlier. Having spent most of his career in the Far East Division, including a long tour on Taiwan at the nadir of China operations, Nelson knew the downside of covert action. By December an insider could certainly view Angola as trending in that direction. For whatever reason, Bill Nelson suddenly admitted the truth about Project Feature.

Then Mulcahy arrived and laid out the agreed version that minimized U.S. actions. Senator Clark confronted Mulcahy with Nelson's testimony, revealing the lie. Capitol Hill buzzed. Legislation to terminate the project was the result.

In 1994, in a debate waged on the letters page of the *Washington Post*, former CIA baron James Potts attributed the legislation to a complete outsider, the academic Gerald J. Bender. The true story revolves around California Democrat Alan Cranston, the Senate majority whip at the time. Cranston wrote an amendment in conjunction with his aide, William E. Jackson, Jr. They relied on Bender for expertise on Angolan history and politics, but he had no other role. Meanwhile Democrat John Tunney, junior senator from California, faced tough competition for re-election in 1976, beginning with the nomination. Cranston permitted Tunney to present the provision in his own name, and they attached it to the Pentagon appropriations bill.

President Ford lobbied hard to defeat the Tunney Amendment. He made telephone calls, had newly promoted national security adviser Brent Scowcroft assemble a chronology designed to show how little had been done, and threw his congressional liaison staff into the fray. Ford directed Kissinger to postpone a trip to Moscow in part to oppose the legislation, which prohibited expenditure of any money for Angola not specifically appropriated, thus ruling out the reprogramming ploy that Ford counted on. After debate in the Senate, Tunney's amendment passed by a considerable margin (54 to 22). In a statement Ford complained of the grave consequences of abandoning responsibility.

Ford's statement laid groundwork for a counterattack when the bill came before the House. But on December 21 a provocative article appeared on the front page of the *New York Times*. This time Seymour Hersh had details of Feature plus the story of Ambassador Davis's resignation. Driven by more leaks, discussion of Angola mushroomed. Ford simultaneously engaged in a very public fight with the committees investigating intelligence over whether their reports and findings could go to the public, including a specific study of Angola from the Pike Committee. The Church Committee had recently released its report on CIA assassination plots, opening many eyes and increasing Ford's political difficulties on Angola.

As the House bill moved forward, the president pulled out all the stops. Press secretary Ron Nessen's notes of January 1976 briefings indicate careful parsing of

Angola questions, and marching orders to reiterate Ford's position. On various occasions Nessen's instructions were to claim that Washington knew nothing of South African troops, that there had been no U.S. recruiting of mercenaries (tightened to become a denial of recruiting *Americans*), that Congress had been fully informed on all covert matters, that he had nothing to say, or that he had nothing to say beyond Ford's and Kissinger's comments. When White House counts indicated probable defeat, the president himself phoned House leaders to delay the vote. Talking points prepared by Scowcroft's staff show the Kissinger visit to Moscow now served to excuse postponement, and that a delay of even a few days was considered helpful for the CIA to move arms and for the United States to explore alternate sources. Ford got his delay but the Tunney Amendment passed the House. President Ford reluctantly signed it into law on February 9, 1976. So intent is Kissinger on shifting blame that he argues "with victory for the Cuban and Soviet forces in Angola, the geopolitical context for SALT [nuclear arms control] was gone."*

Calamity befell the FNLA mercenaries. Generally an undisciplined lot, they arrived to a dilapidated bus, ratty clothes, and tatty weapons, as Dave Tomkins recalls. There were no maps. The mercenaries were led by a self-styled "colonel," an enlisted veteran of the British Parachute Regiment, who called himself Costas Gheorghiu. Unbalanced in the opinion of some, a good trooper according to others, he had only fifty or sixty men. Tomkins understood that they, plus some black troops with them, were the entire FNLA army in northern Angola. They never had a battle. He never saw a Cuban. Gheorghiu cut a swath of murder and rampage across Zaire and Angola, culminating in the execution for alleged desertion and misconduct of more than a dozen men by their own comrades.

Others died as well. Among them was a real paramilitary expert, well regarded at Langley—George Bacon III, a Green Beret who had served in Vietnam in 1968–1969 and done a tour for CIA with the Hmong, using the agency cryptonym Kayak, in 1972–1973. Bacon received an intelligence medal for Laos but quit in disgust at what he perceived to be American betrayal of South Vietnam. He was a "cowboy" in the CIA tradition and enthusiastic about Angola.

The mercenaries' demise came when the MPLA decided to advance and Gheorghiu tried to ambush them. Many were captured including Gheorghiu, wounded, and three Americans. In Luanda the Angolan government put them on trial. The self-styled colonel, American Daniel Gearhart, and two others were condemned to death. Nine men received long prison sentences, with sixteen-year terms

---

* In fact, Kissinger's difficulties on nuclear arms control derived from a set of problems that had little to do with Angola: differences over the coverage of specific weapons systems, fears of compliance, a decline in political support related to Kissinger's own overselling of his achievements, Soviet intransigence over Jewish emigration, Kissinger's struggles with the Pentagon over what U.S. weapons systems should be constrained, and general suspicions of the Soviet Union. Angola had a role in distrust of the Soviets, but a small one compared to other issues. The counterfactual here—that Moscow would have agreed to nuclear weapons limits if only it had looked like the CIA was winning in Angola—is so absurd it clearly demonstrates the emptiness of this argument.

for Americans Gustavo Grillo, a Marine Corps veteran of the Battle of Hue; and Gary Acker, also a Vietnam veteran. The State Department barely acknowledged these men and made few efforts to secure their release. Grillo and Acker were finally freed in an Angola–South African prisoner exchange in 1982. Surviving mercenaries complained about CIA severance pay. Mobutu simply pocketed final payments given him for Roberto and Savimbi.

The South Africans continued destabilizing Angola. Thoroughly disillusioned, CIA officer John Stockwell resigned and went public. With this fiasco so recently revealed, it is not so surprising that Senator Church made strong charges on covert action in his committee's final report. Church also called Henry Kissinger a "compulsive interventionist."

The Tunney Amendment, attached to a specific budget bill, would soon expire. Senator Dick Clark took a hand and proposed permanent legislation. It would be reported out of the Senate Foreign Relations Committee unanimously—highly unusual—and passed by large majorities in both houses of Congress in mid-1976. The Clark Amendment made the restriction an enduring one. In April 1977, after the changeover to the administration of President Jimmy Carter, another White House meeting centered on what to do about Angola. Afterward the CIA director went to Senator Clark with a proposal to funnel the rebels weapons through France. Clark would have none of it, and the episode embarrassed President Carter, who publicly claimed he had only learned of this covert action scheme from the newspapers. That proved the end of Angola operations for an entire presidency.

The Senate Select Committee on Intelligence went on to do a yearlong investigation of Project Feature. In the spring of 1978 it concluded that the Ford administration had misled Congress on the scope of the operation, not revealing some activities and mischaracterizing others. Documented with cable traffic and official papers, the study confirmed that the CIA had indeed spent more than a million dollars to recruit mercenaries, that despite standing orders U.S. personnel *had* served inside Angola, and that the CIA had been much closer to the South Africans than admitted. The committee also singled out Henry Kissinger's November 21, 1975, testimony to the Church Committee as especially misleading. The Central Intelligence Agency denied the charges and tried to show congressional overseers where it had briefed various matters. Colby maintained that the CIA had not conducted Angola the way it had Laos. Kissinger dismissed the inquiry as a smear job.

Project Feature, a product of White House determination, had been a dismal failure. Those who attribute causation of the Angolan war to Moscow and Havana typically downplay the effect of the initial CIA program, which inflated Holden Roberto enough to think he could break up the national unity coalition before independence. Apologists also fudge the timing: the attacks that broke up the coalition preceded Soviet arms. Thus they overplay the Cold War aspect. U.S. intervention brought the Cold War to Angola, not the other way around. While Langley made operational errors in its effort—like supposing the initial program would have no fallout—the major mistakes were of policy. Conceiving Mobutu as an effective ally and siding with the South Africans were decisions that undermined the entire project. The CIA correctly anticipated the Soviet response to U.S. intervention and opposed the paramilitary program it was nevertheless ordered to conduct.

Those who argue the CIA could have won in Angola if only Congress had not cut off the money flow cannot get around the weaknesses of cooperating with Zaire and the deadliness of the alliance with the Afrikaner regime. In addition, U.S. ignorance of Angolan conditions and its fixation on Roberto (given his lack of popular support) created more obstacles to covert success. The United States lacked an infrastructure for a decisive intervention, and geography precluded backing Roberto and Savimbi except through other states. Scale of the program is not the real question: the proper comparison is between the $100 million or so spent by Moscow in 1975 with the CIA's $32 million in Angola, $100 million in Zaire *plus* the funds committed by South Africa (substantial), Zaire, France, Britain, and the People's Republic of China. Those numbers are not currently discoverable, but the total likely outweighs the Soviet-Cuban expenditures.

The story of Angola is that Gerald Ford and Henry Kissinger heard lots of advice to steer clear yet chose to head straight for disaster. As for America and democracy, the Ford administration acted against it. There is no doubt that Roberto's FNLA, Savimbi's UNITA, and Neto's MPLA were in an uncomfortable coalition, but at least they *were* in coalition and had the opportunity to fight out differences at the ballot box. Giving Roberto the advantage of CIA political action helped spark a civil war, and wading into that conflict not only proved shortsighted but placed the United States on the wrong side of African nationalism. In addition the Ford-Kissinger decisions further complicated their problems right in Washington, D.C., creating important new restrictions for the secret warriors.

The events of the Year of Intelligence touched off a struggle to regulate U.S. intelligence, an effort that has ebbed and flowed ever since. "Oversight" is the game, which the executive branch, claiming there is too much of it, has on the whole played more successfully than Congress. Legislators on Capitol Hill, having created reporting requirements through Hughes-Ryan, strengthened their monitoring by replacing the secret CIA subcommittees with permanent committees in both houses of Congress.

Oversight did not bring the end of covert action, however. On February 15, 1976, newly minted CIA director George H. W. Bush refused to say whether the Angola project had ended. In a later interview Bush commented, "What happened in Angola was that a properly conceived program, one signed off by the policymakers and reported in accordance with law to the congressional intelligence committees, was leaked and once it was leaked it was aborted." He then went on, "I think there is a role for covert action somewhere between inactivity and sending in troops."

During the Ford administration there were also covert actions in Portugal and in the Malagasy Republic, where an American ambassador who had been a career

CIA officer was expelled following a puzzling series of musical-chairs military coups. Former agency officers take credit for putting in place a constitutional government. But the 1975 constitution promulgated for the democratic republic permitted only a single political party and remained in place until the fall of the government in 1991. To this day the Malagasy project continues classified.

Oversight simply meant that covert actions were reported and justified by a "presidential finding," formally known as a Memorandum of Notification. Hughes-Ryan specified that all significant or anticipated actions by the CIA not for intelligence-gathering purposes be so covered. The executive tried to limit oversight, particularly where covert operations were concerned. In December 1975 special counsel Mitchell Rogovin of the agency gave the House Permanent Select Committee on Intelligence a detailed explication of CIA's position, in which Langley construed a statutory basis for its activities. The argument was that covert activities lay within the "inherent powers" of the president; they had been conducted by presidents long before a CIA existed, thus the agency was not attempting to assert new powers. Rogovin also referred to the "such other functions" provision in the 1947 act, arguing Congress had never objected to these practices and had always approved agency budgets.

These claims are undercut by the legal opinions of the CIA general counsel rendered on several occasions since 1947. Congress obtained a copy of a paper prepared in 1974 for the general counsel's office, which took much the same position as had counsel Lawrence Houston: the National Security Act "functions" language applied to intelligence gathering; extending it to covert operations strained the law. The paper added that covert operations were an implementation of policy, a shared power under the Constitution.

Paradoxically, by laying out reporting requirements for covert operations, the Hughes-Ryan Amendment could be seen as authorizing them in the name of Congress.

Whatever animosities Bill Colby had attracted, he had at least been a CIA professional. When George H. W. Bush took the helm at the end of January 1976 there were grave doubts. A Republican politician from Texas, Bush overcame those doubts, appearing at staff meetings in shirtsleeves and professing an "aw shucks" attitude. His mixture of quick appreciation and practical problem-solving won many converts. Richard Holm, for one, had been a Colby supporter but came away a fan of Bush. Genuine concern for the rank and file plus the international awareness Bush had honed as ambassador to the United Nations and to Beijing were the roots of his success. Although not a great manager of the CIA's analytical role, or major advocate of covert operations, Bush's sensitivity to public relations and connections returned stability to Langley, with an impression of White House support and a regeneration of agency morale.

In a move that curried favor among one agency faction, throughout his time as DCI Bush resisted Justice Department demands to turn over materials pertaining to Chile and ITT, the evidence necessary for its determination on whether to prosecute Richard Helms.

Within weeks of Bush entering the director's suite, President Ford issued an executive order on the intelligence community. Billed at the time as a major reorganization, in fact the move amounted to minor tweaking, its main purpose to head off congressional action on a CIA charter. The executive order responded partly to the excesses revealed during the Year of Intelligence, partly to a set of a dozen suggestions Bush had made as he prepared to take over. In early 1976 Ford's Executive Order 11905 became the first public regulation ever to describe the function of U.S. intelligence and restrictions on it. The order prohibited assassinations, enshrining directives Colby had issued. It replaced the 40 Committee with an Operations Advisory Group, placing decisions in the hands of cabinet members, not deputies. The attorney general continued as a member while the White House budget director became an observer. Telephone concurrences, at least, were prohibited. Covert operations were defined as those intended to further U.S. policies abroad. Ford also put fresh people on PFIAB. The CIA would concentrate administrative functions under a new deputy and elevate its community role with a second.

At Langley, Director Bush turned the improbable trick of raising morale while purging the leadership. Inside half a year Bush changed eleven of the top fourteen CIA officials. Some he transferred, a few he promoted, others retired, and Bush brought in a couple from the outside.

When he spoke of "excesses," Bush typically referred to outside investigations of CIA, not his agency's activities, deploring the effects of the Washington spectacle on CIA relations with foreign services. To reinvigorate those associations Bush tried to convey an impression of receptivity and keep hands off foreign operations. On his watch the intelligence services of the Southern Cone nations moved strongly on Operation Condor—and assassinated Orlando Letelier in Washington. Nor did the docket stop there. In fact during the Bush period actions against dissidents in the United States were carried out by the intelligence services of Iran, the Philippines, South Korea, and Israel. The CIA itself recruited Panamanian Manuel Noriega.

There remained the matter of the Directorate for Operations. The DO still seemed bloated from the Vietnam War. The question of realigning it remained a major agenda item. A consensus on the need to do this had existed at the CIA since Schlesinger's time. In 1974 a management study for Colby had advised the agency to shed its covert operations mission. Another, completed in 1976, recommended cutting the DO by 1,350 officers over a five-year period. That spring deputy director William Nelson sent Bush a memo about moving ahead on reductions. As Nelson later described this incident to journalists:

> There were a lot of people in the [DO] who were marginal performers. The low middle. We needed quality, not quantity. I told him that the lower 25 percent should be identified and should be encouraged to seek other employment. . . . I said we owed these people a lot but not a lifetime job.

Bush would think about it, he told Nelson, but he put the paper in the round file. Although Director Bush never disavowed reductions, he made no move to initiate them. A few months later he selected E. Henry Knocke over Nelson to be deputy director of central intelligence. Nelson retired. That opened up the DDO position, for which Bush chose William Wells.

A broadly experienced officer from the old OSS cadre, Wells had been close to both Bill Colby and Tom Karamessines, and had spent his agency career on Far East operations after selling kerosene lamps in China before the big war. Representative of the very group who stood to be phased out, Wells happily went along with Bush doing nothing to reduce personnel. As associate DDO, meanwhile, Bush elevated secret warrior Theodore Shackley.

In a memoir published at this time, Ray Cline advocated taking the covert operations function away from the CIA and giving it to the Pentagon. George Bush opposed that course in interviews, insisting the mission belonged to the agency.

By far the most serious situation to confront Bush during his time at Langley was the Lebanese civil war. Fighting broke out there in the spring of 1975 and was stilled temporarily by Syrian mediation and then intervention; but a year later the Maronite Christian and Muslim sects were back at arms. Next to Indochina, this had become Langley's biggest headache. In 1975 division chief David Blee promoted his deputy, Clair George, to chief of station in Beirut, then considered a prestige assignment. George, a skilled street man, relaxed as a ballroom dancer where many spooks played tennis. He needed all his dexterity in Beirut, a maelstrom. On June 16, 1976, the new American ambassador, Francis E. Meloy, Jr., died under a hail of bullets on his way to his very first meeting with the president-elect of Lebanon. With him perished his driver and the embassy's economic counselor. George scrambled to figure out whether the murders had been some insane mistake or an act aimed at the United States. It turned out that Meloy had been abducted before being killed. The next day President Ford held an NSC meeting to consider evacuating Americans from Lebanon. Director Bush briefed the CIA's latest information, which looked pretty bleak. Ford decided to pull out.

The evacuation would be carried out by the U.S. Navy. The CIA scored a coup here because it had established a relationship with the Palestine Liberation Organization (PLO), and PLO security forces now furnished protection for the maneuver. Bush had already ordered evacuation of CIA families from Beirut; now Clair George had to pull out the agency officers themselves. The operations center at Langley set up a special area just to monitor the pullout. In the middle of the night Bush came to watch along with anxious DO officers. The move was completely successful. For a time the Beirut station worked out of Athens. That fall the Arab League placed a deterrent force in Lebanon, which became the origin of a Syrian occupation that endured for three decades. The CIA returned to Beirut.

Jerry Ford faced the Lebanese crisis in the middle of his political campaign for the election of 1976. He lost that election to Governor James Earl "Jimmy" Carter of Georgia. During the hard-fought campaign Carter several times indicated suspicion of the CIA. A climate of apprehension prevailed at Langley when he came to office. As for George Bush, the director made a bid to stay on as DCI, but Carter wanted his own man in charge. There would be a new broom at the head of the Central Intelligence Agency.

Much of 1976 passed as Congress set up machinery for intelligence oversight. Legislation containing intelligence charters was considered during the Carter administration in 1978 and 1980, but it never passed. Meanwhile congressional support for regulatory action on intelligence peaked during Carter's middle years. When charters were taken up at hearings, the vast majority of CIA professionals testified against excessive restrictions on covert action. Witnesses at various hearings included such figures as George H. W. Bush, John McCone, Richard Helms, Bill Colby, Hank Knoche, Dick Bissell, Tom Karamessines, David Atlee Phillips, and Gen. Richard G. Stilwell. They undoubtedly believed they had achieved a signal victory in avoiding CIA charter legislation.

Outpacing a laggardly Congress, the White House seized the initiative on intelligence reform. President Jimmy Carter continued Ford's practice of intelligence regulation through executive order with one he signed in 1978. The assassination ban continued. The decision-making body became the Special Coordinating Committee of the NSC, with essentially the same membership. The covert action definition narrowed somewhat to include only those "conducted abroad" in support of national foreign policy objectives. Typical activities approved by the SCC during the period included the provision of training and special communications equipment to the leaders of Egypt and the Sudan for their personal security, and an anti-Cuba propaganda campaign in the Horn of Africa.

Hank Knocke stayed on for six months into the Carter administration. He later recalled that when presidential findings were signed, copies went to the congressional oversight committees. "I never presented a finding to any of these committees," says Knocke, "but what there wasn't a whole range of questions and answers covering an hour or two. And usually a lot of fulminating—like, who in the world wants to do thus and so?"

The White House created a fresh mechanism to monitor operations, called the Intelligence Oversight Board (IOB). Much later, in the heat of the Iran-Contra affair, it would be revealed that the IOB, essentially moribund, had never conducted an investigation. Two of its three members though, former ambassador Robert Murphy and Leo Cherne, came right out of PFIAB, Cherne having been its most recent chairman. James Farmer ran the IOB for Carter. The Foreign Intelligence Advisory Board itself was abolished by the president.

At first the Carter administration had no great appetite for covert action, postponing the day of reckoning between congressional oversight and executive power. President Carter nevertheless defended executive primacy. He supported legislation to repeal Hughes-Ryan and reduce CIA reporting to the two specialized intelligence committees of Congress. Carter also made use of a gambit innovated by Kissinger and Ford—blanket findings to justify in advance all covert operations concerning terrorism, narcotics, and counterintelligence. From the oversight standpoint, once this device became accepted it shrank the scope for program review in these areas.

As in many matters during his years in the White House, Carter was frustrated in his first choice for CIA director. Theodore Sorensen, Carter's nominee, had to withdraw when his nomination ran into strident congressional opposition. Next Carter turned to Adm. Stansfield Turner, a naval officer, then NATO commander in Italy. Turner and Carter had been classmates at Annapolis. Although regulations forced him to retire from the navy to accept the offer, Turner took the DCI job. A novice at intelligence, the admiral provided strong, reformist leadership.

Despite being able, Turner was an outsider at Langley and remained unpopular. He gained no friends when, like Porter Goss early in the twenty-first century, Turner showed up with a coterie, mostly former naval officers, as his inner staff. One, Rusty Williams, did a global evaluation of the Directorate for Operations, visiting stations, poking into all manner of things. The rumor mill buzzed with accusations that the DCI's man regaled the front office with innuendo about people's escapades on station.

Any chance of Turner's being accepted evaporated with the staffing reductions he needed to meet budget limits. Although the DO passed its evaluation, those personnel studies from the Bush era had still to be faced. When the director asked Bill Wells what ought to be done, the DDO did not oppose reduction. Admiral Turner actually cut back planned staff reductions by more than a third. To cut the time of hysteria, the DCI shortened the layoffs from five years to two. While more than eight hundred staff slots were dropped, the DCI insisted these be almost entirely from headquarters. (Some sources report a quarter were field positions, Turner says none.) The remainder were support jobs.

Most of the reduction came from early retirement and attrition, with real firings minimal. The admiral actually forced only about 150 officers into retirement—Cord Meyer being one example—and fired just 17. Although the DO declined from its Vietnam War peak of about 7,500 to roughly 4,750, that total is rather close to strength in the mid-sixties (5,500). There were actually more reductions under Schlesinger and Colby than under Turner.

But the handling of the cutback was abysmal. Turner allowed himself to be convinced that CIA would avoid legal liability by simply serving up pink slips rather than graciously commending officers' service, which might furnish grounds to question the personnel actions. Retirements were dictated by edict. Personnel officers went through their files and culled the oldest and the bottom 5 percent of performers, the latter by taking the lowest-ranked officers within their grade levels. The old hands were the most numerous (92 percent of those let go were over age forty), with the most experience and usually at least one language. Some young officers were victimized. At least one, dismissed from a European station, hired Mitchell Rogovin (back in private practice), showed that his rankings had been based on differences with a station chief who wrote his efficiency reports, and was eventually rehired to avoid the lawsuit he threatened.

Inexperienced at Langley, the admiral did not know he had been set up. Turner's strategy gained the DCI no friends and alienated the clandestine service. President Carter could not miss the torrent of complaints reflected in media reporting. He asked Pennsylvania governor William Scranton to look into the CIA personnel mess. Scranton gave Admiral Turner a pass. That did not stop officers from blaming him. Many would agree with the DO's Floyd Paseman who writes, "Our collection capability was decimated." Turner would argue it had been improved. Some sided with him. Tom Gilligan, who had served both in stations and undercover, believes that "Turner's decision to make the cuts evenly from top to bottom made more sense than the plan proposed by [DO] management." Turner himself, in retrospect, believes he should have done the same as George Bush—nothing—and passed the problem on.

The cutback issue played out over years. So did an unsavory scandal over former DO officer Edwin P. Wilson that began a few weeks after Turner became DCI. The Wilson scandal added to criticisms of the admiral, who felt obliged in the course of it to replace DDCI Hank Knocke and discipline Ted Shackley, a Wilson associate, as well as fire a couple of other officers. That did not add to his luster.

Then there is the denouement of the Helms affair. Admiral Turner found Helms very defensive when they met. Little wonder. The forces that had stalled the Justice Department in this matter were eroding. Prosecutors had impaneled a grand jury late in 1976. As Carter took office, Helms was told he was a target of the inquiry. The secret document issue persisted into the fall of 1977—the CIA had turned over sixty documents to Justice, but they could not be given to the grand jury until declassified, and Bush had stalled that. There is no evidence whether Turner had a direct role, but the Helms indictment went forward in September. That November Helms pleaded no contest to two counts of perjury. Declared guilty, he received a suspended sentence and a fine, collected from former comrades in cash donations one afternoon at a country club lunch. No matter Turner's role, he could not but suffer as CIA veterans bristled at the treatment meted out to Helms.

It is to Director Turner's credit that he persisted and did what he could to make the community responsive and responsible. In the DO, Turner brought forward John N. McMahon, whose background lay in technical intelligence. On a temporary assignment in charge of the intelligence community staff, he impressed the DCI so much that in 1978 Turner had McMahon replace Bill Wells. Everywhere Turner sought to manage the colossus. Clandestine service gadfly Duane Clarridge, never slow to criticize weakness, credits Turner with trying to transform the DDO into the lead manager of a directorate, leaving behind his traditional role as "nominal 'chief spy.'" McMahon as DDO played his own part, among other things reinvigorating field training for operations officers at Camp Peary and personally selecting graduates' assignments. Admiral Turner conceded in later interviews that he had not paid as much attention to the DO as the service wanted, but he certainly had not ignored it. Still, the former DCI recalls, "Being confident that the organization was not *out* of control was not the same as feeling that it was adequately *under* control."

As for congressional oversight, Stansfield Turner felt it a positive benefit to the CIA—a view decidedly unconventional at that time. He strongly resisted prior notification of covert operations to Congress. He also advocated restricting reporting to the intelligence committees and adopted harsh strictures against leaks. Most of this Congress yielded with the Intelligence Oversight Act of 1980, passed as an amendment to the fiscal 1981 budget, repealing Hughes-Ryan. Congress did insist on being "fully and currently informed," and got some definition of elements that belonged in a proper finding. Senators who wanted a comprehensive intelligence charter gave up.

As one of his policy review initiatives, President Carter ordered a study of intelligence, completed in February 1977. Although it centered on resource allocation and the responsiveness to the president and other consumers, the review gave some attention to covert operations. The chief consequence was an expression of interest in developing a new standard doctrine, but the paper saw procedures for controlling action as adequate. The Carter review also observed that the procedures, not only maintained, might "perhaps [be] put into statute." The administration's willingness to concede on this issue remained untested.

Meanwhile the DO stayed in business. Leery of covert operations as Carter may have been, his national security adviser Zbigniew Brzezinski demanded action. Robert M. Gates served during this period successively as CIA analyst, special assistant to Turner, and NSC staff director for intelligence. Gates dealt with both Brzezinski and his deputy, David Aaron. He recalls, "The most frequent criticism of CIA that I heard . . . was its lack of enthusiasm for covert action and its lack of imagination and boldness in implementing the President's 'findings.'" Preoccupied with his duties as manager of the intelligence community as a whole, Admiral Turner left the covert action role to his deputy Frank Carlucci.

Within two months of his arrival at the White House Brzezinski, who had a major interest in nationality questions as an avenue to the breakup of the Soviet Union, had already begun insisting on new propaganda efforts to reach into Russia. These White House demands were slow to gather momentum, in part because Brzezinski first tried to work through CIA's Soviet/East European Division, whose expertise lay in running spies. Richard F. Stolz headed the division at the time, and he not only numbered among the anointed spy chiefs but had several successful espionage penetrations against the Russians active at that time.

Once Brzezinski connected with the Covert Action Staff, propaganda projects began to move. Paul Henze, seconded from CIA to the NSC staff to help Brzezinski on intelligence, had an extensive background in propaganda and political action and helped refine these programs. Underground literature that Soviet dissidents knew as *samizdat* received a boost from CIA xerox machines. Russian exiles in Western Europe and elsewhere got help from the agency for more formal publishing efforts. Toward the end of 1977 the agency established that the Russians were running their own propaganda operation to stoke up anti-nuclear opposition in Western Europe. Langley worked to expose Moscow's activity through British journalists and others.

Findings were also approved for operations against a pro-Cuban government in Grenada, a political action in Jamaica, and actions in Nicaragua and El Salvador as those governments faced Marxist guerrilla movements. Some of these findings occasioned strong objections when they were described to the oversight committees in Congress, but there is no recorded instance in which a covert action was called off due to such complaints. In late 1979 President Carter signed a finding authorizing the CIA to block Cuban activities throughout Latin America.

Turner wanted capability in reserve and wished to avoid squandering it on insignificant moves. He preferred highly directed operations, such as one mounted in an East African country to recover certain equipment from a downed aircraft. Carlucci has been especially identified with a paramilitary venture in concert with the British and, for the first time, Saudi Arabia, that began in South Yemen in February 1979 when that country attacked North Yemen. Turner is reported to have thought this project ridiculous, but others forged ahead. Vice President Walter Mondale, formerly a senator and a member of the Church Committee, supported the effort. The CIA recruited several dozen Yemenis and formed two strike teams, one of which ended up in Yemeni prisons, the other withdrawn. Secret warriors terminated the operation at that point. The United States also sent $390 million in military aid to North Yemen and eventually helped broker an uneasy unification of the two states in 1990.

By 1980 the pendulum had swung from restraining the "rogue elephant" to "unleashing" the CIA. International events as well as public opinion account for much of the impetus for the shift. Four developments especially affected the debate over the role of covert operations and controls over them: the advent of human rights as a foreign policy focus, the rising incidence of terrorism, the fall of the Shah of Iran, and the Soviet invasion of Afghanistan.

Human rights, the enshrinement of which proved to be Jimmy Carter's foreign policy legacy, at first appears antithetical to covert action, indeed not a policy issue at all. Certainly many at the time resisted thinking of human rights abroad as a policy goal or issue. But in fact the goal could easily be manipulated to cloak cynical aims, as Zbigniew Brzezinski did with his effort to destabilize Russia through its nationalities. The succeeding Reagan administration would be especially adept at this exercise, used to justify covert action.

The rise of terrorism, on which the Carter administration took a hard line, led to renewed attention to military special warfare forces. This ended the post-Vietnam doldrums of Special Forces. These had fallen to only 3,600 in three groups, all deployed in the United States, with detachments in Europe and the Far East plus a battalion in Panama. Reserve and National Guard units assumed the bulk of the special warfare mission, with a force level of 5,800. Anti-terrorism provided a new rationale, much as counterinsurgency had under Kennedy. With the support of chief of staff Gen. Edward C. "Shy" Meyer, the army formed two elite commando units, Blue Light and Delta. These initiatives received personal attention from Brzezinski.

The third development was the fall of the Shah of Iran—what followed in its wake. Policymakers and intelligence analysts either refused to recognize the shah's growing vulnerability or could not agree on what to do. Carter at one point complained to Turner, Brzezinski, and Secretary of State Cyrus Vance about the poor quality of political intelligence he received. Similarly, more detailed criticism emerged from a House intelligence committee study, repeated extensively in the press and by opinion leaders.

The Iranian crisis of 1978–1980 ended by calling into question U.S. special warfare capability. Diplomats were unable to preserve friendly relations with the Islamic Republic under the Ayatollah Khomeini. As already recounted, Iranian militants took over the U.S. embassy on November 4, 1979. National security adviser Brzezinski ordered preparation of a rescue mission. Secretary of State Vance strongly resisted a resort to force. In Teheran the militants released thirteen black and women hostages, and later they freed one man, Richard Queen, who had contracted multiple sclerosis during captivity. Otherwise diplomatic efforts were of no avail. On January 29, 1980, when the Canadians smuggled six Americans out of their embassy in Teheran, Director Turner gave no prior notice to the intelligence committees, who were briefed hours after the Americans were out of the country. That pushing at the envelope of newly established congressional oversight, allowed to pass at the time, became characteristic of the system.

The losses at Desert One, the failed helicopter rescue mission, obliged Carter, through Secretary of Defense Harold Brown and the Joint Chiefs, to reveal the existence of Operation Eagle Claw. The Carter administration faced ridicule from many quarters. Cyrus Vance, who perhaps had earned the right to criticize, remained charitably silent. Nevertheless Carter continued to maintain a military option as part of his search for a way out of the hostage crisis.

Gen. James Vaught continued leading the joint task force, which prepared a larger-scale plan, Honey Badger. Vaught had some of the best covert operations people around. His air commander, Brig. Gen. Richard V. Secord, had worked on supplies to the Kurds, been a sparkplug in Laos, and had special operations experience going back to "Jungle Jim." Secord had also been air advisory group boss in Iran from 1975 to 1978. Vaught's chief operations planner, Col. Robert C. Dutton, held three Distinguished Flying Crosses for his exploits flying out of Thailand in the Vietnam War. Dutton had served under Secord in Iran. The joint task force staff worked in unison. Individual will and a desire to get the hostages out overcame Pentagon politics, in this case the services' demands that each be part of the task force.

Some criticisms of Eagle Claw centered on inadequate planning. There had not been enough helicopters; the requirement to use a "unit" precluded a Pentagon-wide search for the best pilots; the many exercises had never included a complete rehearsal of all phases of the operation. Honey Badger was to correct these deficiencies. Even worse than before, however, the problem was intelligence. The Iranians dispersed the hostages and redoubled their vigilance. In desperation and in hope, the United States turned to expatriate Iranians, who flocked to volunteer their contacts. One who did this was Albert Hakim, to the extent of putting his Multitech Corporation, which still functioned in Teheran, at the disposal of the Americans. The degree to which Iranian exiles considered this patriotic may be gauged from the fact that Hakim went to General Secord after having been turned down by him for lucrative business contracts. Now Secord put Hakim in touch with air force intelligence.

A flood of reports came from Hakim and the other sources. General Secord remembers hundreds. But no one ever pinned down the hostage locations because there was no way to check the reports (and because the Iranians began moving the hostages around Teheran, keeping them in small groups). Uncertainty continued, with the joint task force in constant consultation with the CIA. In October 1980 Langley suddenly announced it had new information, presenting an elaborate briefing. Secord called this the "Eureka" briefing because of the abrupt claim that CIA had all the answers—this might just be someone's wild idea. Joint task force intelligence had no information to corroborate Langley's view. General Secord actually escalated this dispute up the chain of command to the White House, where Carter policymakers were reminded of the insoluble intelligence problems of the rescue option.

By comparison, the military side was in much better shape. The Honey Badger force stood ready from August 1980. Whenever there was fair consensus on the intelligence picture, Dutton and the operations staff put together a new plan. General Vaught's forces conducted at least six major exercises rehearsing successive versions of Honey Badger. The secret warriors also made a start toward filling the void of in-place assets with the army's formation of a Foreign Operations Group (FOG), a unit to facilitate deep-cover missions, soon renamed the Intelligence Support Activity. Air force HH-53 helicopters, with better avionics to navigate through sandstorms, were substituted for the navy craft used in Eagle Claw.

As preparations continued, costs mounted. Honey Badger was of such importance, however, that General Vaught spent the money and only then went to the services to tell each how much it owed. They intended to go to Congress later to seek a supplemental appropriation. But Honey Badger never went down. Instead diplomatic prospects improved, an accommodation was arranged, and after 444 days of captivity the Americans were released on January 20, 1981. Subsequent debriefing of the hostages by joint task force intelligence showed that the "Eureka" data had indeed been mistaken.

Fiasco in the Iran hostage crisis crystallized opinion on the need to strengthen special warfare capabilities. As Stansfield Turner put it, "The talent necessary for covert action is available in the CIA and it must be preserved." The military wanted capability at the Pentagon.

At this juncture, as Washington began to resurrect covert action, another international development intervened, the Soviet invasion of Afghanistan in December

1979. Langley, already involved in a minor key, immediately prepared plans for operations and gave prior notice to the congressional committees. The first known Hill briefings on this subject took place on January 9, 1980. Langley's representatives were Frank Carlucci and John N. McMahon, the director of operations. The secret warriors were back in the saddle.

19

The Mountains of Allah

EVERYTHING IS TRIBAL. Tribes and clans exist not just as ethnic or national group-ings, like the tribes of Afghanistan or Iraq, but by self-selection. The Central Intel-ligence Agency itself is a collection of clans. Alan D. Fiers, Jr., an agency Middle East specialist, put the thought well in a 1991 appearance before the Senate Select Committee on Intelligence. "The CIA is a family," Fiers declared, and went on: "The DO particularly is a family . . . the DO is like—is broken down into clans: the Middle East clan, the Latin American clan, the Far East clan, the European-Soviet clan. . . . The bonds of mutual experience aren't there outside the clan." Fiers ran into trouble during the Reagan years, and there are differing opinions on him among the tribes at Langley and outside them, but his description of the social tex-ture rings true.

Often covert operations cut across clan boundaries. The clan might not have the right tradition or skills, some special qualification becomes necessary, or per-haps the president orders the CIA director to deploy his best people regardless of their "home" divisions. Paramilitary experts are a clan of their own and may be needed. Political action and propaganda skills more likely exist within the divi-sion. The operations in Angola, Vietnam and Laos, Congo and the Bay of Pigs—all involved bringing people in from outside the clan, and perhaps a price had to be paid for that.

Afghanistan would be unusual in being led almost exclusively by the clan, in this case the DO's Near East (NE) Division. Moreover the division developed the project in tandem with the Iranian hostage mission, which added to its burden. Af-ter April 1980, with burgeoning criticism of the failed hostage rescue, the clan had even more need to succeed.

Jimmy Carter recalls the Soviet invasion of Afghanistan as a shock "to a world which yearned for peace." The background is more complex and perhaps more sinister than Carter's simple sentiment. The Russians had not simply invaded a neutral or enemy country. Rather, a pro-Soviet regime had been in power in

Afghanistan since 1973, when a prince of the royal blood carried out a coup d'état against a king traveling in Europe. Even before, under the monarchy, Afghanistan had had a close trading relationship with Russia, its most important commercial partner. The Russians gave foreign aid to Afghanistan as early as 1956. By the time of the Soviet "invasion," that aid had grown to $2.5 billion. Most of it had been economic, from taxis in the capital of Kabul to a road from the Russian border. America too had given aid, for dam projects and a national highway, and President Dwight D. Eisenhower once visited Kabul for an afternoon.

Sardar Mohammed Daoud assumed the title of president after his coup, but the Soviet Union and Afghan Communists regarded him as pro-Western. As early as June 1975 tribal rebel forces attempted to overthrow Daoud, staging an uprising in the Panshir Valley. In April 1978 he was brought down by force, by the People's Democratic Party of Afghanistan, the Communist Party of the land, itself divided into two major factions.

Power in Kabul suddenly seemed limited when it came to solving thorny problems, not least the insurgency among Muslim fundamentalist groups and certain tribes that began soon after the Daoud coup. The first permanent rebel base coalesced as early as May 1978. Meanwhile one of the Communist factions, rent by internal discord, convinced itself that the others did not know the way forward. One faction, the Parcham ("Banner") became isolated within the movement, neutralized during 1978, its leader banished to Prague as ambassador. Parcham figures were accused of CIA connections, and more than two dozen alleged conspiracies were supposedly discovered during this purge.

On February 14, 1979, the kidnapping of U.S. Ambassador Adolph Dubs in Kabul set off alarm bells in Washington. An experienced diplomat, Dubs had earlier been in Moscow under close surveillance by the KGB. According to Russian defector Vasiliy Mitrokhin, Soviet intelligence decided Dubs had CIA affiliations. In any case he was grabbed off the street by persons who demanded the release of others held in Afghan jails. Rather than negotiate, the Afghans launched an assault on the hotel room where Dubs was held. Their people went in with Russian equipment, including flak jackets and weapons, and with senior Soviet officials downstairs in the lobby, including the KGB's security chief, the top Russian adviser to the Afghan police, and the second secretary of the Soviet embassy. Dubs perished in the intense gunfire that ensued. Certain things obscured what had just occurred, including the execution of surviving captors, prevention of forensic analysis of the crime scene, blocking of access to American investigators, and planting of evidence. It is not possible to say whether this was a conspiracy or whether, if so, it was of Russian or Afghan origin.

Meanwhile the purge of Parcham did nothing to solve the power struggle. The two top leaders of the other Communist faction, called the Khalq, remained at each other's throats. Titular boss of the now Democratic Republic of Afghanistan (DRA), Nur Mohammed Taraki had been the original founder of Khalq, which united with Parcham to form the Afghan Party as far back as 1965. Taraki had been a representative in the Daoudist legislature. Taraki's deputy Hafizullah Amin, given a supervisory role over the DRA's secret police, became the key instigator of the purge. Amin concentrated control over the army, the security services, and the government. The Russians scrambled to save their Afghan agents or those they considered vital for the effective functioning of the DRA. In the summer of 1979 the Soviets learned that Amin also sought authority over the $400 million Afghanistan had in foreign banks.

The tribal insurgency continued unabated, leading the government to ask for Russian help. In Washington the Carter administration saw Russian aid to such countries as Angola, Ethiopia, and Somalia as adventurism, and spoke of an "Arc of Crisis" in East Africa and the Indian Ocean. With a Russian client state in trouble in Afghanistan, it appeared the ideal moment to repay the Soviets in what Carter officials saw as their own coin. The Dubs murder seemed to demand a response. Zbigniew Brzezinski, Carter's ebullient national security adviser, quickly instructed the CIA to produce options for Afghan action.

When Langley reached into its bag of tricks it would not be whistling in the dark, at least not entirely. The CIA had a liaison relationship with Pakistani military intelligence and, through them, Afghan tribesmen. Other U.S. agencies were feeling around too. As early as January 1979 an officer of the U.S. Drug Enforcement Administration met with Afghan resistance figures at Lahore. Subsequent encounters took place in other Pakistani cities. The DEA's interest lay in stemming the flow of heroin from Afghanistan, drugs helping finance the resistance, but the CIA could use the same contacts to develop a covert operation.

Ambassador Dubs cautioned Washington that it might lose more associating with rebel warlords than could be gained from these contacts, but in February the CIA reported new signs of unrest. By March 5 Admiral Turner had a list of options for Brzezinski. The next day the NSC discussed whether to aid Afghan rebels. Ten days later, on March 18, during a visit to Moscow by the Communist prime minister of Afghanistan, the Democratic Republic first asked for direct Soviet intervention. The Kabul government, facing new uprisings, including a revolt of elements of the Afghan army, made a series of pleas that Moscow turned down one after another, even though Russian advisers were killed in these risings. In Washington on March 30 the NSC Special Coordinating Committee (SCC), Carter's Special Group, revisited the question of a CIA paramilitary operation. Pentagon official Walter Slocum told the restricted meeting there might be value in such an effort. A week later the full SCC met to consider it.

The CIA meanwhile fleshed out the initial plan with more analysis. Just a couple of days after the SCC session, White House staffer Paul Henze began complaining of foot-dragging at Langley. On April 6 the SCC went over a gamut ranging from minor propaganda to a high-end initiative that included training and support. The consensus favored a "nonlethal" program. Langley prepared a draft presidential finding and returned it to the White House. The lethargy lay there, not at Langley. By the end of April the CIA had completed a set of data on Afghan ethnic and religious groups which it could use for a major study of the resistance. Only on July 3 did Carter approve the finding.

The American program began with supplies of food and clothing, helping the resistance without greatly committing the United States. Brzezinski wanted more, but with President Carter due to see Russian leaders in Vienna, a forceful course in South Asia had to wait. The summit duly took place, and Carter signed an arms limitation treaty with Soviet leader Leonid Brezhnev. Shortly after his return the CIA paramilitary options came forward. Brzezinski bragged to French reporters in a 1998 interview that on the day of Carter's finding he wrote the president a memo predicting that a paramilitary program in Afghanistan would force the Russians into full-scale intervention.

The initial stake of just half a million dollars lasted barely six weeks. It had to be raised. Agency officers picked up the DEA channels to the resistance and were quickly in touch with several major groups. By September 28 the CIA station in New Delhi had cabled Langley more than once about recruiting suitable fighters, soon popularly known as the *mujahedeen*.

Authorization for the CIA to engage in a covert action also meant informing Congress. That happened on July 19 when officials briefed the Senate intelligence committee on findings that respectively covered Afghanistan and Grenada.

Meanwhile Moscow had sent the DRA government armed helicopters and transport models but resisted appeals for troops. In May *mujahedeen* mounted armed uprisings in several provinces, with government troops hard pressed to meet them. Moscow worried about the safety of its aircraft, and after lengthy deliberation sent a battalion of paratroopers to the base at Bagram, near Kabul. Washington soon learned of this from cables that gave an accurate count of the total of Russian military advisers, mentioning the troops (and some aircraft mechanics) at Bagram, and recording that the Russians either sported civilian clothes or Afghan uniforms. On July 20, despite Soviet aid, rebels in one province threatened its capital. Two Russian advisers were killed. In early August an Afghan airborne regiment rebelled in Kabul, its mutiny suppressed with difficulty. Only a week later a full Afghan division was bloodied in a pitched battle with insurgents.

The evident inability to cope with the resistance concerned both Moscow and Kabul. The Russians advised the Kabul government to get rid of Hafizullah Amin, the minister who was concentrating so much power in his own hands. There were doubts (never resolved) whether Amin—who had studied in the United States at Columbia University—had, in fact, been recruited by the CIA.* Other Russians

---

* One CIA officer remembers having seen a report, possibly Indian, that associated Amin with the Asia Society. At the time the Indians had close relations with Moscow and may have passed along this data. If so, and if the KGB believed it, this would be an instance of blowback from the CIA public institution activities exposed in 1967. An American diplomat at Kabul at the time of the Soviet intervention reports that Ambassador Dubs specifically asked the CIA station chief if Amin worked as an agent and received assurances he did not. The diplomat himself had five meetings with Amin at various times and found him uniformly hostile to the United States.

thought him mentally unstable. While Taraki visited Havana and Moscow and heard Brezhnev's direct warning, Amin alleged an assassination attempt by ministers he called an anti-party group. Instead of Amin being forced out, on September 14 he carried out a coup, placing President Taraki under house arrest and later moving him to a prison, where he would be strangled to death a few weeks later. At that time there was a further coup attempt by the Afghan army, a last ditch effort by Khalq loyalists that was put down in bloody fighting.

According to some Russian accounts, the Amin government understood the difficulties of defeating the rebellion and tried to settle with some resistance groups, in particular the Islamic fundamentalists of Gulbudhin Hekmatyar. The coup attempt, the October countercoup, and the *mujahedeen* talks Moscow took as evidence of Amin's lack of responsiveness and his willingness to bargain away the Soviet investment. The Soviet general staff, anticipating a Politburo decision, began preparing for intervention, though senior generals counseled the leadership against any military move.

Meanwhile, by October Washington had already begun to seek foreign support for broader covert action. In Saudi Arabia the U.S. ambassador learned the Saudis were ready to extend assistance to the *mujahedeen*, previously held back to oblige the resistance to unite. The Americans and Saudis agreed that Riyadh would match CIA funds. On December 17 the Special Coordinating Committee met to finalize the next stage of the Afghan project. The CIA would furnish weapons, improve rebel communications and logistics, and conduct worldwide propaganda against the DRA and its Soviet backers. This occurred a week *before* the Russian invasion.

During the long months of 1979 the Soviet Politburo considered a massive commitment of ground troops in Afghanistan almost a dozen times, repeatedly rejecting it. Now the reaction would be emotional, not principled. The defense minister and Politburo members who specialized in ideological matters became key advocates for military intervention, and that is what Moscow decided. On December 12, in a series of consultations with Politburo members in various combinations, Moscow made its decision to send troops to "A"—Afghanistan. Soviet sources argue that if either or both Brezhnev or Nikolai Kosygin had been in better health at this time, the idea would have been rejected again.

The invasion began just after Christmas. Plans were for 52,000 troops of the Fortieth Army to cross the border from the southern Soviet Union. One target was Hafizullah Amin. On December 6 the Russians sent a lead element of *spetznaz* special forces ahead to Bagram to carry out a secret mission in the event of intervention. They were to neutralize Amin in a commando raid. The *spetznaz* were successful; Amin was murdered in the presidential palace ("Objective Oak") in the bloodiest battle of the intervention. The Russians were more favorably disposed toward Amin's successor, Parcham leader Babrak Karmal.

The Soviet intervention unnerved those who saw Russian imperialists reaching for the Persian Gulf. The shah once told Richard Helms that if it were a question of Russia reaching the Gulf, he would take over that area first. Those in the

United States who feared a blitzkrieg aimed at the Persian Gulf saw it as a prelude to worse—attack across the North German plain, perhaps the onset of World War III. President Carter came under wide criticism for permitting the Russians to surprise America like this. Carter told a reporter on New Year's Eve that the Soviet action affected his thinking more profoundly than anything during his time in the White House.

But these claims entirely fail to take into account the CIA's intelligence reporting and the hidden U.S. policy of conducting a CIA paramilitary operation, one that Brzezinski, at least, *expected* to trigger Soviet intervention. Carter telescoped these developments when he told undergraduate students at Emory University in 1982 that a covert program had been the best way to punish the Soviets short of "going to war, which wasn't feasible."

The Soviet intervention represented not so much the blitzkrieg portrayed in U.S. news reports as a slow slide into a quagmire. The surprise displayed in the media was absent within the administration, all along aware of both CIA and State Department reporting of the number of Soviet advisers, their initial commitment of troops disguised as Afghan government soldiers, and so on. The United States detected the Russian buildup prior to invasion, their increased state of alert, even the introduction of Russian *spetzuaz* into Kabul. American insight on the Soviet move extended to knowledge of the ethnic composition of the Russian forces—the CIA reported the presence of numbers of Tadjiks, Uzbeks, and other Central Asian ethnic soldiers in the Fortieth Army. The CIA's warning experts conducted a postmortem on the Russian invasion and concluded that, while the agency did not predict its precise size or timing, because of the synergistic performance of communications and photographic intelligence, the CIA had provided at least ten days' advance notice.

The American policy of acting against the Russians continued and deepened. On December 27, 1979, the day the Russians intervened, President Carter signed a fresh finding permitting the CIA to furnish more weapons aid. Zbigniew Brzezinski held more than twenty sessions of the SCC in the wake of the Soviet intervention, assembling an array of sanctions that Carter then added. Senior CIA analysts completed a paper in January 1980 which viewed Moscow as creating a zone of security around the USSR. The paper suggested the United States could make this expensive, supporting groups on the basis of ability to inflict Russian losses. Written by a Soviet specialist with no Middle East experience, the paper warned that failure in Afghanistan would result in Middle Eastern countries drifting toward the Soviet orbit.

The initial shipment of CIA weapons, a cargo of old British rifles from Egypt, arrived in Pakistan on January 10. Two weeks later President Carter enunciated a doctrine that would bear his name: the United States would regard any attempt by an outside power (such as the Soviet Union) to gain control of the Persian Gulf region as an assault on its vital interests.

Zbigniew Brzezinski wrote later that his main concern had been "to make sure that the Soviets paid some price for their invasion." Brzezinski's involvement extended to traveling to Saudi Arabia, where he confirmed the Saudi alliance with the CIA. His muscular approach combined with President Carter's fury to exact a steep price: deep cuts in American grain sales to Russia; a U.S. boycott of the 1980 Olympics, scheduled to be held in Russia; and withdrawal of the SALT II nuclear arms control treaty from Senate ratification. Agency political action experts dreamed up a scheme to bring Afghan partisans to New York to testify at the United Nations, but this plan foundered on fears of violating the prohibition against CIA activities inside the United States. Meanwhile Jimmy Carter paid a political price of his own, aside from any costs imposed on the Soviets—Afghanistan seemed one more bit of evidence for dark pictures of Cold War imbalance painted by Republican leaders. Carter could not stem the tide that elected Ronald Reagan president in November 1980.

The CIA's Afghan project belonged to NE. Charles G. Cogan, the DO's Middle East baron since 1979, had panache and dramatic flair along with his experience. Cogan had been in India, in the Congo at the height of the sixties troubles, and chief of station in Amman, Jordan, in 1970, when Palestinian forces tried to oust King Hussein. His horseback riding with the Jordanian king, much like Ray Cline's or Red Jantzen's drinking bouts with Taiwanese and Thai rulers, helped forge close links between the CIA and the Jordanians. For Afghanistan, Cogan's marching orders were to meld the parallel support given by the Saudis, Chinese, and Egyptians. Cogan's worst headache would be the hostility the U.S. military incurred in the Iran hostage rescue. Associate DDO John Stein functioned as top supervisor. Previously chief of station in Libya, Stein emerged from the Iran disaster untarred, and he had dealt with the Egyptians. The Afghan task force chief, John MacGaffin, also came with extensive Middle East experience. His unit, technically the South Asia Operations Group, gradually expanded to peak strength, only fourteen officers.

The CIA could not act through the U.S. embassy in Afghanistan—small, closely watched, and with no possibility of contact with the *mujahedeen* resistance, largely based in Pakistan. Kabul functioned primarily as a listening post: CIA and U.S. diplomats there took the pulse of the Soviet and Afghan government war effort.

The action took place in Pakistan. Under John Reagan the CIA station in Islamabad maintained close contact with the Pakistani government, in particular its Inter-Services Intelligence (ISI) department, headed by Lt. Gen. Akhtar Abdul Rahman. With the ISI, which had an Afghan branch and detachments along the border in northwestern Pakistan, the CIA did business with the *mujahedeen* through a base at Peshawar, beneath the Khyber Pass, forty miles from the Afghan border. The CIA base at Peshawar, always small, never resembled the huge bases the agency had grown in Berlin or Frankfurt at the height of the European secret wars, or that in Miami at the time of Mongoose. Peshawar base and Islamabad station together numbered just about forty CIA officers. With task force staff at Langley plus Cogan's NE people, and even some DI analysts thrown in, there were fewer than a hundred officers pushing the Afghan program.

John McMahon would be astonished at what presently occurred in the Hindu Kush. The agency's deputy director for operations, McMahon, knew nothing about the Near East. His baptism of fire had been the Iranian hostage crisis. He had earned good marks there for helping infiltrate the Delta Force agents, but he well knew the military antipathy for the agency. McMahon responded by turning prodigious energy to making sure Afghanistan went smoothly. Admiral Turner's successor, William J. Casey, later called McMahon the "father" of the Afghan secret war.

The sleekness of the CIA commitment did not mean this project proceeded without the major support common in paramilitary operations. Rather it would be the Pakistani ISI that provided the muscle. Its Afghan Bureau consisted of officers posted from throughout the Pakistani military. The bureau did much for the resistance. The ISI funneled the military aid, allocating percentages to the various *mujahedeen* groups; the Pakistanis transshipped the aid from points of entry to the rebels; and the bureau gave the *muj* intelligence to use inside Afghanistan. The data came partly from the ISI and partly from British intelligence (SIS), but most came from the CIA. Under its most active director, Brig. Gen. Mohammad Youssaf, who served from 1983 to 1987, the Afghan Bureau opened camps to train the *mujahedeen*. Youssaf also sent ISI commando teams on special missions with the *muj* and tried to coordinate forces from different rebel groups for joint attacks on Afghan or Russian troops.

Rebel bands typically formed from calls by clan elders or tribal leaders, who appointed their commanders. When the CIA studied Afghan ethnic groups in the spring of 1980 it found that Pashtuns made up more than half the population and that fierce animosities split the clans, including those between Sunni and Shiite Muslims. The agency calculated that these divisions would impede a unified front or strategy. A September paper from the CIA's Office of Political Analysis reported literally hundreds of tribes, representing more than a dozen major groups, in numbers ranging from a few thousand to hundreds of thousands of people.

One of the Russian problems was that the very reforms Afghan Communists and Moscow apparatchiks considered essential to bringing Afghanistan into the twentieth century were anathema to the tribes. Within months the Russians estimated that hundreds of rebel bands were active, with fighters totaling between twelve and twenty thousand. Before the end of the year Russian leader Leonid Brezhnev would say during a visit to India that the conditions that had forced his country to intervene had not disappeared. Afghan Communist leader Babrak Karmal charged in November that his country was being subjected to armed aggression from Iran and Pakistan.

The first CIA weapons entered the pipeline while time remained to prepare for their use. Nothing moves in Afghanistan during the early months of the year, when the snows are so deep and the winds are so cold that the struggle is to survive.

In 1980 the British sent some Special Air Service soldiers to observe *muj* operations. With the thaw the *muj* took the field.

Not long after taking office the Reagan administration began moving on Afghanistan. New CIA director William J. Casey presented the project as part of a menu of covert actions to stymie the Russians. President Reagan approved the finding in March 1981. At that time Reagan first used the term "freedom fighters" for the Afghan *mujahedeen*. Later he applied it to all rebels the world over that CIA would support. Reagan's secretary of defense, Caspar Weinberger, quickly advocated new arms for the guerrillas. That spring Director Casey made the first of what became annual pilgrimages to the Near East. Casey visited the king of Saudi Arabia and his intelligence chief, Prince Turki-al-Faisal, plus the leader of Pakistan, military strongman Gen. Mohammad Zia ul-Haq. The CIA's project could not proceed if these men softened in their commitment. The Saudis continued matching U.S. contributions to the rebels, and General Zia fronted for the CIA in equipping the *mujahedeen*.

Chuck Cogan accompanied Bill Casey on every Near East trip during his time in charge of the division. He found General Zia a true believer. Zia feared Soviet encroachment, saw their intervention as such a move, and dearly wanted to strike back. When Casey visited Zia at home, the Pakistani put a map on his coffee table and superimposed on it a red triangle template to represent the Soviet thrust. Zia broke off only to play with his daughter when she wandered into the room. According to Cogan, Casey came away more than impressed, grousing at the American media for "distorting" Zia's image. Unmentioned went the reason for U.S. concern with Pakistan—Zia's nuclear weapons program, an issue since Carter's day. Zia and General Akhtar of ISI, who lived next door, represented a common front.

Casey left Islamabad if anything more convinced than Jimmy Carter had been of Soviet perfidy. The CIA director ordered up a Special National Intelligence Estimate on the Soviet threat to Pakistan. Completed in August 1981, the report foresaw Russian political pressures on Islamabad, but analysts refused to predict anything like a Soviet invasion. They expected that the Russians, the Afghan government, or both might make small raids against insurgent camps or artillery or air strikes across the border, but that "any prolonged occupation of even a small part of Pakistan is unlikely within the coming year."

To pursue the Afghan project and a panoply of new CIA secret wars, Bill Casey needed to put his own house in order. He believed John McMahon was not aggressive enough to head the Directorate for Operations. When Richard Allen, Reagan's first national security adviser, ordered a covert operation to disable a floating drydock the Soviets had put in the Somali port of Berbera, McMahon objected to this act of war, and the DO chief's star suddenly set. He was shifted to head the agency's analysis directorate. At Langley, CIA insiders favored John Stein for his replacement, but Casey chose Max Hugel, a business associate with no intelligence experience whatever. Casey briefly made Hugel a top adviser, then appointed him DDO. But before the job could be finalized, it evaporated in a controversy over Hugel's insider stock transactions.

The end result for the DO was that John Stein took over after all. But John McMahon, whom Casey wanted to shunt aside, reappeared in a new incarnation, resulting from a different case of personnel turbulence: Casey had appointed a navy vice admiral, Bobby Ray Inman, as his deputy director of central intelligence, second man for the entire community. Admiral Inman was restive, not so willing to cut corners as the CIA director, much more dedicated to traditional missions, closely connected to congressional overseer Senator Barry Goldwater. He watched Casey's secret wars with mounting anxiety. In mid-1982 Inman resigned to pursue a career in computers. Casey, by then already under attack as a covert action cowboy, suddenly saw John McMahon as a desirable DDCI—his presence suggested the agency would remain within legal bounds. Deputy Director McMahon would have a further impact on the Afghan covert action.

In its first year the Reagan administration doubled the size of the previous CIA budget for the Afghan project. Once the Saudis matched that, Pakistan's ISI had real money to play with. In August 1981 five of the largest rebel groups formed an alliance whose center of gravity resided in a council located at Peshawar, beyond reach of the Russian enemy. Fearful a unified command would impede its ability to manipulate the warlords, the ISI undermined the initiative. By that summer there were roughly 45,000 *mujahedeen* fighters. Through the year the rebel groups averaged almost 500 attacks a month. According to Soviet figures more than 500 vehicles were destroyed that year and 4,550 security troops killed. In one province (Kunduz) the government controlled only 10 percent of the villages.

The Soviets and Afghan Communists initially enjoyed greater success with their respective intelligence services. The Russian KGB, reprising its tactics in the Baltic uprisings of the 1940s and '50s, formed false-flag units. The most important of these, code-named Cascade, pretended to be *mujahedeen* bands. The 150-odd soldiers in each such security unit gained the confidence of rebels who revealed themselves only to be eliminated. The Afghan KHAD agency tried to block trails into the country with some success, using its 5,000 border troops. KGB officers were attached to KHAD in increasing numbers, first a staff at headquarters, then groups of 10 to 15 advisers in each of the 29 provinces. In 1981 the Russians received even greater powers to intervene in Afghan affairs. Najibullah, the KHAD chief (many Afghans use one name), raised no objections. Toward the end of 1981, in an effort to devise new tactics, KGB chief Boris Kryuchkov visited Kabul with Soviet Defense Minister Dmitri Ustinov. Babrak Karmal also met top Russians at Tashkent that December. No one had a solution. The KHAD grew enormously: from 700 at the time of the Russian invasion to more than 16,000 by 1982, but its heavy hand did little to stem the rebellion.

The war sputtered on. Karmal continued the Communist Party infighting, with a PDPA congress in the spring of 1982 marking the final triumph of the Parcham faction over the Khalq. Arab countries played the major role in assistance to the rebels, though ultimately they were eclipsed by the CIA, except for the Saudis, who continued to match the United States dollar for dollar. But Iran gave significant aid to Sunni Muslim groups at least until 1983, especially Gulbudhin Hekmatyar's Hesbe-e-Islami, and to Shiite Muslims along the Iranian border. Egypt sold arms and donated some also. Others put up money or permitted rebel groups to open offices and recruit for the *mujahedeen*. The most fundamentalist groups, like Hekmatyar's, also had some success in making direct approaches to Muslim countries for certain support.

Pakistan sustained its role, with Peshawar and the nearby city of Quetta as the front-line bases. The ISI's Afghan Bureau made allocations among the rebel groups at coordinating meetings held quarterly. The ISI director General Akhtar presided, with the chief of the bureau, and that of the parallel bureau Akhtar created to move the supplies, plus their staffs. CIA and Saudi money went into ISI bank accounts. Aid in kind, such as weapons, the donors purchased directly and brought into the country (until 1985 it remained a firm rule that mostly Communist-bloc weapons would be given to the *muj*). The amounts of both cash and weapons given to each group varied depending on performance, but only two of the seven key groups in the rebel alliance were not fundamentalist, and ISI played favorites. One major rebel leader, Ahmed Shah Massoud in the Panshir Valley, was not in the alliance. The net effect was that roughly two-thirds of aid went to the most radical religious groups.

The CIA got weapons wherever it could. Most of those from European and Middle Eastern countries transited Saudi Arabia by air or entered the Pakistani port of Karachi. The U.S. Air Force did the airlifting out of Dhahran, where a CIA officer acted as liaison. When the Pakistani air force tried to participate, it had trouble with landing or overflight rights, in spite of Saudi Arabia's cooperation and CIA's presence at the airbase. A contingent of three, later five, CIA officers at Rawalpindi monitored storage and shipment inside Pakistan. Certain items, like rockets from China, came to Pakistan directly from their countries of origin.

At first rebel commanders went to ISI depots with pony trains to pick up equipment stockpiled for them. But the arrangement proved cumbersome. The CIA bought and delivered animals to the rebels, but stocks of local ponies soon dried up. Langley sought the advice of mule experts like Dr. Melvin Bradley of the University of Missouri, and bought mules in his state and shipped them to Pakistan, but the Missouri mules were not used to the climate and wore out quickly. Some Chinese ponies were employed, but a better expedient proved to be mules from Argentina, where the *pampas* and Andean mountain living favored animals better adapted to the mountains of Afghanistan. The Pakistanis eventually hired traders who provided their own animals for a fee. Of course the fees rose every season, and ISI's transport department still had to bring the materials to the border depots. A typical mule load was a couple of sacks of corn meal and perhaps four rockets or recoilless rifle rounds.

Timing was also a problem: ISI officials complained the CIA never seemed to realize that when the snows melted each year in the spring (usually April), the pack trains could hardly move, so supplies needed to be brought in early to compensate.

The traders crossed a highly permeable border—more than two hundred trails cut through the mountains that lined it. Neither Afghan troops in the 1980s nor Pakistani guards in the war on terror of the twenty-first century have sealed this border. In November 1982 the Defense Intelligence Agency argued that even a major increase in Russian troops (fifty thousand men) would not enable the Soviets to seal off Afghanistan permanently from the outside world. In the 1980s permeability worked in the CIA's favor, later it would not.

The tribes on the land were the key to effective supply, and these took a cut of whatever moved through their territory, fees that multiplied as supplies went farther. *Mujahedeen* deep inside Afghanistan received barely half what they had been consigned. Rebel leaders preferred cash, which they could use for almost anything at local bazaars. About 40 percent of shipments crossed the border in the vicinity of Peshawar and another 20 percent near Quetta, not far from the huge underground base the rebels established in the caves of Zhawar.

The sole alternative would have been to parachute supplies to the rebels. Brigadier General Youssaf of ISI maintained that airdrops were nonsensical. Drops meant using U.S. aircraft in a Russian war theater and thus posed a danger of direct U.S.-Soviet confrontation, a chance heightened by the large number of flights necessary. The parachute method also opened the possibility of U.S. aircraft losses in a CIA covert operation. Lacking proprietaries the size of Air America, by the 1980s not even Langley could conduct projects on the scale of Afghanistan as aerial endeavors. Langley agreed. Chuck Cogan later characterized those who called for U.S. airdrops as living in a dreamworld.

On the whole the supply situation remained uneven. In late 1982 the Defense Intelligence Agency reported that major rebel groups possessed ammunition and modern assault rifles but lacked heavy weapons, especially machine guns, mortars, anti-aircraft guns or missiles, anti-tank weapons, and radio equipment. The difficulties were mainly for smaller rebel groups or those in isolated positions, such as Massoud in the Panshir Valley. This is consistent with what Pakistanis say about how they allocated the weapons. But ISI shortchanged groups not in its favor. For instance, there are reports that the rebels were given about 400,000 modern Soviet-type assault rifles; yet, according to Washington lobbyists for the *muj*, one of the main groups received just 4,000 modern weapons by 1983, along with almost twice that number of old Lee-Enfield rifles. This minor-key firepower compared poorly to what the Russians had or even what other rebel groups were receiving. Over the same period a rebel group that had had 13 machine guns in 1982 possessed 250 by the spring of 1984.

A major difference between the covert actions of the Reagan era and earlier CIA activities is that in the 1980s varied rebel groups deliberately lobbied Washington, not to build support but to get what they viewed as a fair share of cash and weapons. Law firms or public relations consultants did some of this work, as did activists for the cause. This was true for Afghans, Nicaraguans, Angolans, and so on. The Cubans had formed activist groups outside CIA projects, for which they solicited money and support. Only in the Reagan years were there public efforts to promote CIA programs.

Divisions rent the administration over the numbers and kinds of weapons to furnish the *mujahedeen*, perhaps making the solicitation important. This was true even at Langley, where Bill Casey, a true believer, never actually made his mind up on the goals of the operation. John McMahon supported the covert project but doubted the United States could achieve anything unless it had a diplomatic policy to encourage Soviet withdrawal. That ranged him against those who wanted to make Afghanistan Russia's Vietnam, a group that sometimes included Casey, or those who wanted outright victory, including some in the Pentagon, Congress, and on the CIA's project task force. According to Robert Gates, there were also those who feared greater effort would trigger a massive Soviet response and a slaughter. Existing findings made the project a harassment effort, and that was what the congressional committees were told. Intelligence reports estimated that Moscow spent forty dollars for every one from the CIA.

Analysts at the Directorate for Intelligence held that the project could not achieve more than a disruptive effect on the Soviets, but Bob Gates, its chief from 1982 to 1986, did not. Gates repeatedly sent back reports to be reworked with additional argumentation on pitfalls for the Soviets in this war. Thus an April 1983 analysis by DI's Near East and South Asia office that found the *muj* incapable of expelling or defeating the Russians incurred Gates's ire.

Officials outside CIA, including former DDCI Vernon Walters, now ambassador to the UN, and Fred Iklé, undersecretary of defense for policy, rejected the limited vision of Afghan prospects. Richard Perle, Iklé's deputy, supported efforts by his assistant Elie D. Krakowski to seize control of the issue, which was far outside their portfolio. Krakowski recalled the Pentagon's goal as "the withdrawal of Soviet forces and the establishment of a stable Afghan government." Frank Carlucci, now deputy secretary of defense, and Nestor Sanchez, whom he had taken with him in the international security affairs field, gave helpful advice, though Sanchez would be especially useful on Central America. Pentagon efforts to carve out a policy role were simplified by President Reagan, who consistently refused to rule on the differences among his subordinates.

Langley's people did not see themselves as holding back the Afghan project. They had a full plate. Beyond the planning and weapons buying, options had to be cleared with General Zia, the Saudis, and other players. Chuck Cogan recalls an adrenaline rush when Bill Casey took over from Stan Turner, but to some degree escalation *had* to be incremental simply because the foundations needed to be laid. He feels that no one at CIA—at least initially—looked at Afghanistan as a bleeding ground, a Soviet Vietnam. That might have been the idea at the White House but not at Langley. When Howard Hart replaced John Reagan as station chief in Islamabad, Casey's instructions were simply to go out and kill Russians. Hart had won the Intelligence Star for his part in the Iran hostage rescue mission and had led the NE branch for Pakistan and Afghanistan at the inception of the project. Cogan selected him to lead the station on the basis of their shared experience. At a regional conference among station chiefs in late 1981, Hart convinced the NE baron to back the first of many escalations.

Hart cabled Langley on January 14, 1982, to put this on the table. Director Casey took the question to the Reagan administration's Special Group, called the National Security Planning Group (NSPG). They met late in February. According to Robert Gates, despite support from Frank Carlucci and Caspar Weinberger at the Pentagon, *and* from the State Department, not to mention Cogan's NE, the beefed-up project initially went nowhere. This seems possible only if Bill Casey did not in fact back it. Only after the Casey-Zia meeting that featured the red map overlay—which took place that April—did the DCI really begin to focus. Casey and Zia met again in late 1982 when the Pakistani leader again lectured the spy chief on his view of Russian objectives. The Gates memoir leaves the impression that Zia had to convince Casey of the need to move ahead. In addition, Gates quotes Casey as saying that Zia's goal centered on action "to keep the pot boiling, but not boil over," avoiding Soviet action against Pakistan. To the degree that Bill Casey accepted this, it put him in the camp of those who wished to use Afghanistan as a bleeding ground for Russians.

Progress did not satisfy the activists. Outside lobbyists reinforced those who sought victory. Several congressmen took up the mantle and pressed for legislation in favor of effective Afghan resistance. Democratic Congressman Charles Wilson of Texas waged what amounted to his own covert campaign against officials he thought insufficiently committed to the cause. Two he fastened on were Chuck Cogan and Howard Hart. By dint of repeated travel to Pakistan, Wilson forged his own links to top Pakistani leaders, including General Zia. He used these to encourage the Pakistanis to demand more than the CIA had programmed—more weapons and better ones too. Hart had good relations with Akhtar of ISI, but by 1983 there were being eclipsed as Wilson worked on Zia.

Budget levels on the covert program *were* affected by lobbying. The Reagan administration permitted itself to be moved even farther in directions it wanted to go. Reagan doubled what Carter had spent on Afghanistan. Congress, if anything, stayed ahead of the White House on the Afghan program. The CIA would ask for a couple of million dollars, Congress would appropriate twenty-five. Charlie Wilson became a sparkplug in this effort. The numbers only grew larger. In 1983 $30 million in CIA money ballooned with an extra $40 million in reprogrammed Pentagon funds demanded by Representative Wilson. Senior diplomat Nicolas Veliotis, Chuck Cogan's opposite number at State, recalled that colleagues handling the program had real worries whether they could handle the surging funds for the project.

The diplomatic policy that DDCI McMahon craved remained a nullity during this period. McMahon saw the CIA paramilitary effort as the fulcrum to open the door to agreement. A United Nations mediation effort under Diego Cordovez began early but proceeded fitfully. In 1983 it came a near breakthrough, with the UN drafting an agreed text, the Russians suggesting they were amenable to a conditional withdrawal, and the Reagan White House, preoccupied with Lebanon, permitting events to take their course. Instead the Pakistanis and Afghan rebels raised insurmountable objections. Diego Cordovez suspects that Casey may have encouraged that obstructionism. Army chief of staff Gen. Edward C. Meyer told Cordovez later, "Casey would *say* he wanted them out, but he actually wanted them to send more and more Russians down there and take casualties." By the time Secretary of State George Shultz made his first visit to Pakistan in July 1983, the diplomatic initiative had ground to a halt.

Big money, combined with funneling aid through third parties, led to any number of difficulties for the secret warriors, not least with the Pakistanis. In 1984, when the CIA program was again pumped up by $50 million in midstream, the agency sought huge amounts of weapons. Pakistani sources report that CIA logisticians suddenly produced a hundred thousand old Lee-Enfield rifles, apparently from India. Howard Hart had championed the Lee-Enfield weapons. These guns put something in rebel hands quickly and enabled the warlords to expand as fast as they could recruit fighters. The ISI protested—it had not requested the weapons and lacked storage for them. The agency merely answered that the shipment would be an advance on supplies for the following year. Of course that made ammunition an issue, and a Pakistani arms dealer got the CIA to buy thirty million rifle bullets at a premium. It turned out he procured the ammo from Pakistan's own stocks, put it on a boat, and sailed the ship around to make it appear to have come from elsewhere. Soon enough the ISI discovered Pakistani army stampings on the bullets, which then had to be remanufactured to eliminate the engraving—a cost of millions of dollars. The CIA's project had nearly ended before the last bullets were ready; the *muj* had long since switched to automatic weapons instead of these ancient bolt action rifles.

By 1984 Director Casey needed a new team. Beset by problems from other covert operations, Casey changed his DDO, moving Clair George over to lead the clandestine service. George in turn persuaded Casey to approve a comrade from the Africa Division, Bert Dunn, to head NE. Then came the matter of a task force chief. Alan Fiers, the lead candidate, still had a few months to run on a tour as station chief in Saudi Arabia. A fair-haired boy in Casey's estimation, Fiers had his detractors among the NE tribe. Meanwhile acting chief Gust Avrakotos had been deputy to MacGaffin from the early days and knew all the players, but he had fallen on the wrong side of colleague, now boss, Clair George. Avrakotos campaigned for the position and, one day when George was out of town, convinced associate DDO Ed Jushniewicz to appoint him, shutting out Fiers. Director Casey sent Fiers to lead his Central America task force. Avrakotos had ties to Charlie Wilson and quietly supported the move to a victory strategy.

During George Shultz's 1983 Pakistan visit, Zia had Akhtar of the ISI brief the visiting party on the status of operations. Akhtar reported that the resistance could control at will any portion of rural Afghanistan and that it dominated the

Afghan-Soviet border, inflicting heavy losses on the Russians. The reporting cable must have pleased Avrakotos, though Akhtar's next remark—that in spite of their losses the Soviets appeared prepared to continue their occupation indefinitely—offered a more ominous note.

By 1984 no part of Afghanistan was safe from the *muj*. Even Kabul, where KHAD headquarters was subjected to a rocket attack, the defense ministry had been bombed, and DRA officers kidnapped right off the streets, had become iffy. The constant menace of rocket attacks led the Russians and the Democratic Republic army to push a security perimeter out from the city. But in 1984 the CIA got hold of Chinese rockets with greater range and explosive power. The ISI sent along some of its commando teams as rebels staged attacks on the Soviet airbase at Bagram. Twenty-two planes were destroyed on the ground there and elsewhere. In one awesome strike a major ammunition dump containing more than thirty thousand tons of munitions exploded when hit by rockets. Enterprising ISI commanders videotaped the explosions; Casey delighted in showing these films at key moments when Afghan budgets were before Congress.

In 1984 the ISI presence with the rebels rose to two teams in the Bagram operation, seven around Kabul, and two more with *muj* groups near Jalalabad. In the latter part of the year rebels began to form units from their shifting bands, joining them to create "regiments," several of which were united in "fronts." Another mission was an attempt to block the Salang road tunnel, through which moved three-quarters of the Russians' supplies. Langley's experts advised ISI on the weight of explosives needed, which essentially required a truck bomb. The ISI tried several times to carry out this mission but proved unable to bring it together.

Meanwhile the CIA's relationship with the Pakistani ISI continued to be uncomfortable. Changing his team, Director Casey approved William Piekney for the station at Islamabad. Piekney pulled off some coups—notably the recovery of an intact Soviet gunship helicopter downed by the rebels—but his support at Langley wavered. Brig. Gen. Mohamad Youssaf of the Afghan Bureau continued as the effective field commander, yet on only a handful of occasions was he ever permitted into CIA safe houses in Peshawar. One irked him greatly—an urgent summons in the middle of the night, when Youssaf could not get his driver, got lost driving himself, then was told the Russians had learned of a rebel convoy hundreds of miles away. There was no way to know which warlord's band had been discovered, nor to get it a message, both of which Youssaf figured CIA ought to have known. The ISI leader loved the CIA's satellite photos and its radio intercepts but thought the secret warriors spent too much time spinning their wheels.

Bert Dunn, the incoming division chief, knew the Pakistani sensitivities. Dunn had led the CIA station in Baghdad during the early part of the Iraq-Iran War, and as a Special Forces officer with the army had served in both Pakistan and Afghanistan in the 1960s, monitoring U.S. military aid to the Pakistanis, with whom he had excellent contacts. But not even Dunn could calm the waters, undoubtedly because Washington and Islamabad had divergent objectives.

What the CIA did do was continue supplying intelligence. Some was very good indeed. The United States maintained its embassy in Kabul throughout the war. In April 1984 the DRA expelled the third secretary, Richard S. Vandiver, as persona non grata. Vandiver may or may not have been a spook, but a history of the agency's Directorate for Science and Technology establishes that the United States used its diplomatic pouch to move sensitive listening devices into the embassy, and official Michael Pillsbury confirms Washington had excellent data on Soviet moves starting from this time. It was at this point that the CIA's Afghan secret war entered its highest phase.

Bill Casey was a spy chieftain constantly on the run. His annual visits to the cockpit of the Afghan War typically lasted forty-eight hours or less. Much like the Washington emissaries who went to Saigon in such processions through the Vietnam War, these were the visits of someone who knew what he wanted, not one who wanted to learn the truth of the matter. Brigadier Youssaf first met Casey in the spring of 1984, when he and General Akhtar awaited the DCI's plane, a midnight-black painted C-141 Starlifter, at Pakistan's Chakala airbase. The ISI referred to the CIA director as "Mr. Black." Sometimes Casey brought his wife Sophia, sometimes his daughter. A couple of times he had John McMahon with him, but always NE chief Bert Dunn. The baron recalled that on these long flights, where the only people aboard were Dunn, Casey, one or two others, and the security detail, he really got to know the director.

There would be a perfunctory inspection or some demonstration of nifty new gadgets—in 1984 the ISI training camps were featured—then a command conference between allies. The Pakistanis frequently saw tension on the CIA side, for Casey, relentlessly enthusiastic, butted heads with more cautious line officers. Dunn seems to have been of two minds about Casey. The ISI were impressed when Casey overruled his people who thought some move unpractical or unwise. They nicknamed him "Cyclone." Some ISI wits preferred "Wanderer." Casey would blow through, then disappear into his plane for Saudi Arabia and a strategy session with its spy boss Prince Turki.

Casey on Afghanistan is difficult to read. Biographer Joseph Persico recounts that when John McMahon briefed Casey on the project for the first time, at the outset of the administration, the DCI shot back, "This is the kind of thing we should be doing—only more. I want to see one place on this globe, one spot where we can checkmate them and roll them back." Raising the specter of Hitler and Munich, Casey spoke of the dead in the secret war as saving lives in the long run. That should have put the CIA director squarely in the victory camp, but his actions never corresponded to those of a true believer. Rather, the DCI backed measures to draw out the Afghan project. Turning Afghanistan into a bleeding sore for Moscow might ultimately roll back the Russians, but it would take longer, cost more, exact a higher toll, and end ambiguously. Munich meant something different—rapid, decisive action in the short term. The strategic debate shows Casey's ambivalence sharply.

The controversy of the moment centered on providing the rebels better protection from Russian aircraft. Major options were Swiss-made Oerlikon anti-aircraft guns, Soviet shoulder-fired surface to air missiles (SAMs), a similar British SAM, or two different American SAMs. Charlie Wilson and congressional supporters of the *mujahedeen*, drawing from a secret paper John McMahon had sent to the Hill, had earmarked money specifically for the Swiss guns. These turned out to be heavy and awkward, difficult to move, and huge consumers of equally cumbersome ammunition. The guns ended up in static positions at rebel bases.

That left the missiles. The Russian SAMs, based on 1960s-vintage technology, were easy to counter, as the Soviet enemy well knew. They were not effective. The British SAM, called the Blowpipe, had problems of its own. Because it was an optically tracked weapon, the crew had to keep the enemy aircraft in sight during the missile's flight. In that interval the crew could be blown up or neutralized. The missile itself had reliability problems, according to the ISI, one of whose teams expended thirteen SAMs to no effect during one battle. The Afghan task force put $44 million of Saudi money into the Blowpipe because it could be spent without reference to congressional overseers, but the investment ended there.

So to the American SAMs, called "Stingers." The CIA's rule had been no U.S. weapons. Indeed the agency had a preference for Soviet-bloc weapons, for which the rebels could capture or buy ammunition as they fought. Going for American-made SAMs triggered a fight within the U.S. government that lasted more than a year. Officers worried about the security issue, about blowing CIA's cover by using a U.S. weapon, and about the potential for diversion to other governments or terrorist groups. The U.S. military, just beginning to introduce the Stinger, also showed itself reluctant to slow down deployment by sending missiles to Pakistan. Through much of this debate General Zia himself opposed U.S. weapons for the rebels to avoid provoking Moscow. When Brigadier Youssaf told visiting American-Afghan activists in 1984 that Stingers were needed, General Akhtar quickly summoned the group to hear a retraction.

The victory camp scored major points in late 1984 when the Senate passed a resolution in favor of greatly improving the equipment of the *muj*. In March 1985 President Reagan approved a national security directive that made it official policy to move beyond harassment toward victory. A new presidential finding accompanied the directive. Reflecting the exuberance, Undersecretary of Defense Fred Iklé at one meeting advocated cutting out the ISI middlemen by flying arms directly to the *muj*. Inevitably someone raised the danger of a Soviet-American confrontation starting World War III. Bertie Dunn's deputy, Thomas Twetten, attended this séance representing the agency, and told author Stephen Coll that Iklé had responded, "Hmmm, World War III—that's not such a bad idea." Iklé later claimed to Coll that he must have been kidding, but Twetten insists he heard the remark, and it silenced the room.

At the Pentagon Michael Pillsbury, an aide to Iklé, took the new finding as an opportunity to press for Stingers. Opposition remained strong. When Utah's Republican Senator Orrin Hatch visited Pakistan with a Senate delegation that summer, he took Pillsbury, a former staffer whom many regarded as a loose cannon, with him. They were to inspect a Pakistani army house along with General Zia. Before that encounter station chief Piekney, on instructions from Langley, told Hatch that Pillsbury could not attend. Senator Hatch demanded to speak directly to Director Casey and, when he got the CIA chief on the phone, induced him to relent. Casey apparently felt he had erred in agreeing to Pillsbury's participation, but he blamed the station chief. After that Piekney's stock at headquarters went into free fall.

At his meeting with the senators General Zia now said he favored the Stingers. Senator Hatch prevailed upon him to put this in a letter to Washington. Nudged by Zia, within a month Reagan approved an immediate shipment of a hundred Stingers while JCS, Pentagon, and State Department opposition melted. Brigadier Youssaf began to organize training for rebel gunners.

In October 1985 Bill Casey made another visit to the front, in company with John McMahon and Bert Dunn. General Zia again emphasized giving the rebels Stingers. Finally the logjam was broken. At a breakfast in early December, McMahon told Fred Iklé that the CIA would ship as many of the missiles as the Pentagon provided. When Zia saw Casey again in January 1986 he spoke of turning up the heat in the Afghan War. Director Casey waxed enthusiastic.

Major policy fights were simultaneously occurring on the Soviet side. In March 1985 the Soviet leadership changed, and Mikhail Gorbachev came to power. Gorbachev thought the Afghan intervention a mistake and had already hinted as much to Western diplomats. That July came a key discussion in Moscow. The Russians determined to change their Afghan strategy. The new concept, somewhat akin to what the United States had done in the last phase of the Vietnam War, amounted to "Afghanization." Gorbachev gave his generals two years maximum, preferably one, for a military solution, failing which Russia would get out. To give the generals what they needed the Politburo increased Soviet airpower and heavy firepower along with elite forces of paratroops and *spetznaz*. The DRA army assumed a larger share of offensive operations with the Russian elite forces as a spearhead; the bulk of Soviet troops would revert to a defensive role. A new leader for the Limited Group of Soviet Forces was brought in—Gen. Mikhail Zaitsev, previous commander of Russian armies in eastern Germany. Soviet troops in Afghanistan reached their greatest number, 108,000, not long after this policy review. A further Politburo meeting that October confirmed the plan.

The CIA received very good information on at least the initial stage of the Soviet strategic debate. An intelligence source code-named Veil provided access to Russian general staff material and other data. Renegade CIA officer Aldrich Ames began to spy for the KGB that summer. Source Veil dried up.

It is not clear how much the Soviet plan should be attributed to Gorbachev. Morton I. Abramowitz, then head of the Bureau of Intelligence and Research (INR) at the State Department, believes the Russian change of course was more like Jack Kennedy's Bay of Pigs—already in motion before the leader came onto the scene. Most interestingly, the CIA had already anticipated this Soviet strategy—in a major analysis by the DI in May. This five-year retrospective discussed the war's cost and Russian prospects. While Moscow had incurred substantial costs, the CIA felt Russia saw the price of remaining as more than the international costs of getting out. Rebel casualties (40,000) were estimated as far less than those of the Soviets and DRA (25,000 Russians, including 8,000 dead, plus 67,000 losses for the Kabul regime). In a guerrilla war, casualties to the rebel side usually greatly outnumber those for the counterinsurgents.

Langley's experts were not universally admired. But in this important survey the CIA had it exactly right: the agency did not believe Moscow foresaw early victory and the Russians were unlikely to make important progress during the next two years. The CIA expected Soviet reinforcements—five thousand to ten thousand (the actual would be closer to twenty thousand), primarily specialized troops—exactly what the Russians did. The American analysts did not think this could alter the outcome.

If the CIA erred in this analysis it was on the pessimistic side. The report noted, "We cannot rule out a more serious deterioration of the Soviet position in Afghanistan than we have estimated," and if that happened it "would result in a move not toward a political settlement but toward an expanded Soviet military commitment and a wider war."

An increase of 50,000 troops (three divisions) would require Soviet mobilization and an expanded logistical base and take many months to accomplish. It would also utilize the kinds of troops the Russians had found the least effective. An increase of 100,000 or 150,000 soldiers might enable the Russians to clear the cities and hold substantial portions of the countryside, while one of 200,000 to 400,000 offered a possibility of inroads against the rebellion—but the CIA doubted that that could be sustained. Moreover, "We believe this view underestimates insurgent morale and military performance . . . and exaggerates Moscow's effort to Sovietize the country."

The DI followed up in October with a study of the rebels, concluding that the divisions among the tribes were such that no near-term victory should be expected. Thus the CIA projected a stalemate.

The major *mujahedeen* initiative in 1985 came in southeast Afghanistan—an effort to capture the city of Khost. The campaign required coordination among the warlords, but personal and religious differences made cooperation impossible. Brigadier Youssaf attempted to knock heads together but failed. The Soviets, aware of the threat, mounted two major offensives. That led to the battle of Zhawar, a key receiving area for supplies from Quetta. The *muj* had developed it into a major base and training center, using bulldozers and explosives to open tunnels. Zhawar became a showcase for the rebels, with a hotel in one cave and others with a mosque, a communications center, repair shops and garages, an infirmary, and arms depots. The base had a permanently assigned unit, perhaps the first such formation of the resistance, equipped even with a captured Russian artillery piece and a couple of tanks manned by DRA defectors. During offensives the unit was hard-pressed. At the time of the second attack many rebel leaders were absent, on the Hadj, and one key commander died in the collapse of a tunnel. The Russians plus DRA forces captured most of Zhawar but could not hold it. The base remained in rebel hands and years later passed into those of the Taliban, until 2001 when U.S. troops in the war on terrorism finally took the place.

Supplies of rifles and missiles would not be the only sore points. Afghan task force paramilitary specialist Michael Vickers emphasized the mix of weapons and looked to where the resistance should be in a few years. Whether the rifles were Lee-Enfields or AK-47s seemed less vital than whether the warlords could supplement their firepower with heavy machine guns, mortars, and other weapons. Similarly a mixture of machine guns with the Oerlikons and SAMs provided the right set of capabilities. In fact the Russians would lose more aircraft and helicopters to machine guns than to missiles. The object was to drive the aircraft to high altitudes, robbing them of effectiveness, not to down planes. That was accomplished.

Other acrimonious disputes also arose. One concerned mines—first the weapons themselves, later mine-detection equipment. Both rebels and Soviets laid many thousands of mines during the war, and both progressed to new-generation nonmetallic versions. Later, as the rebels began assaulting defended positions, mine clearing became an issue. Around 1983, prodded by the war, the Pentagon began developing a device called "Lightfoot" to detect nonmetallic mines so they could be disarmed. Elie Krakowski recalls that the design work was completed in just a few months, but the military then had a devil of a time getting CIA to accept the product. The agency demanded lengthy tests. Lightfoot reached the field only in late 1985. Agency officers say the detection devices never worked properly. Krakowski insists the method was so effective it was used by the United States in the Gulf War. Another issue would be anti-tank weapons. Quite well supplied with armor, the Russians relied on tanks in every battle. Until 1987 the *muj* had only rudimentary means to fight them. Then the CIA brought in Italian-made anti-tank missiles, a measure that probably cost the Russians more than the Stingers. There were so many "ideal" weapons introduced at various times that one CIA officer took to calling them silver bullets.

Langley again revamped its high command for the secret war. John McMahon retired in February 1986, his post going to Robert Gates. Gust Avrakotos, the task force chief, an inside agitator for the victory camp, had been protected from Clair George by his connections with associate DDO Ed Juchniewicz and Congressman Wilson. But as CIA budgets increased radically, congressional backing became ever more important, so Director Casey built his own bridge to Wilson. Then Juchniewicz stepped down. Bert Dunn, his successor, had no dog in this race, and Avrakotos was banished to the Africa Division. In a significant breach of Langley's tribal cultures, the new Afghanistan Operations Group chief, Jack Devine, came from the Latin America crowd by way of a brief stint running the Iran Branch of NE. The division itself got a new baron when Tom Twetten succeeded Dunn.

Finally, the station chief at Islamabad moved on. At Langley one day in May 1986 Milton A. Bearden found himself in Clair George's Seventh Floor office. He hardly needed the weekend to decide. Milt Bearden became CIA's new field commander for the Afghan project. A Texan, Bearden had the advantage of coming from Charlie Wilson's home state.

About the time George appointed Bearden station chief, the Russians began their summer offensive. They concentrated on several provinces, tried to clear Khost again, and fought a new battle for Zhawar. The operations were standard, the results insignificant. The Russian military had failed. In Moscow Chairman Gorbachev came to the end of his patience. In a July speech he announced a limited withdrawal, and six Soviet regiments left the theater. Washington made an issue of claiming the Russians had offset the pullout by sending new reinforcements, but in fact the Soviet contingent in Afghanistan diminished by fifteen thousand troops and enough equipment for a mechanized brigade. Gorbachev had told mediator Diego Cordovez that the UN mission would ultimately be successful. Washington remained skeptical. In the summer of 1986 DRA officials prevented any progress in the negotiations, but Karmal, politically bankrupt, resigned. His successor Najibullah gradually softened. That December Najibullah went to Moscow where Gorbachev told him that Russia would be out of Afghanistan within two years. Deprived of source Veil, Washington needed that intelligence but did not get it.

Milt Bearden arrived in July 1986, just as the ISI was beginning to turn out rebels trained to use the Stinger missiles. The CIA had doubts about the effectiveness of the SAMs in *muj* hands, but the matter settled itself. In early September Stingers were used for the first time—and gunners hit three of the four helicopters targeted. Bill Casey, ecstatic, wanted to fly to Pakistan right away, but instead Bob Gates made the trip to familiarize himself with the front line in this secret war. During that visit the Iran-Contra affair began, calling Casey's entire enterprise into question. Through the controversy the Afghan project stood out as the jewel among Casey's wars, but beneath the surface it had begun to wind down.

"Uncle Milty," as Bearden was known, carried on. One key issue with the Stinger had been "accountability," which meant tracking the SAMs so they did not fall into the wrong hands. The CIA devised techniques for this, never perfect, but really the problem applied to every weapon down to the AK-47 rifle. Beginning in 1985 deliveries multiplied by a factor of ten. Sixty thousand *tons* of CIA weapons were floating around Pakistan. Bearden adopted a simple rule: if prices in the bazaars were much higher that what the CIA paid, that meant the market had not been flooded with rake-offs from agency shipments. He stayed cool.

Bearden never solved the problem of the warlords. He could have had some impact there—Uncle Milty had originally impressed Casey as station chief in Nigeria, then the Sudan, both nations riven by tribal differences, and he should have been sensitive to this issue. Bearden made some moves toward creating a rebel central command, only to be undermined by the Pakistanis. He left it at that. Field officers pushed for aid to Massoud, whom all agreed had the best troops and the most finely honed political sense. But that meant tangling with the ISI. Of course, with the huge expansion of aid the CIA might have demanded a revised distribution formula, but Bearden shied away from that too. He felt his orders were to beat the Russians, not quibble over which warlords were the most fundamentalist. Citations of the percentages of weapons given to rebel groups from the early and late war periods indicate shipments to the more radical groups actually increased. Bearden focused on sharpening the rebels' fighting edge. He had major differences with Brigadier Youssaf, who left ISI not long after the CIA man came to Islamabad.

In one area, that of the "Arab Afghans," Bearden had no control whatever. Early on the CIA had considered—and rejected—recruiting a corps from other Arab lands to fight in Afghanistan. Langley thought this unwise, as proved to be the case. But the secret warriors could not prevent Muslims getting the same idea, and it became a form of Arab radical chic to go fight the Russians in the mountains of Allah. There is no data on how many Arab Afghans took part in the war, but estimates hover around three thousand to five thousand. Fund-raising in Arab lands also became a source for the warlords, and by Soviet estimates brought in as much as $250 million annually by 1987. Much of this cash went to Peshawar and Quetta for medicine, food, and general assistance, and to fund the Arab Afghans themselves.

The young Saudi engineer Osama bin Laden, one of the Arab Afghans, began building an organization in Peshawar at this time. There is conflicting evidence on whether bin Laden actually fought in the war—perhaps in one battle is the consensus. There is little reason to doubt CIA assertions that it never helped him during the war. The secret warriors had no identifiable role with the Arab Afghans, and bin Laden was no more than a minor character at the time.

In the spring of 1987 Langley again changed its task force chief. Frank Anderson, a card-carrying Middle East warrior, became Bearden's new boss. Anderson spoke Arabic and had served in Yemen, Beirut, and North Africa, most recently as station chief in Morocco. He tried to keep up momentum with new weapons every few months, starting with the Milan anti-tank missiles. Anderson often felt like a supply sergeant. Congressional overseers once asked him what Washington could expect in terms of support from a future *muj* government, to which Anderson replied, "gratitude in the Afghan's dictionary is gonna be found somewhere after gimme and gotcha."

In April 1987 the *muj* mounted attacks into Russia. Moscow protested to Washington. In a maneuver worthy of CIA's peregrinations on Central America, DDO Clair George phoned Bearden to certify that the agency had had no role or knowledge of the attacks. The station chief probably did not know that exactly this sort of operation had been advocated by the Pentagon's Elie Krakowski in 1983 and by Bill Casey after that. Casey is said to have given ISI data on Soviet bases drawn from satellite photos. A year after the Russia attacks the KHAD or KGB struck back, blowing up a huge ammunition dump in Rawalpindi, Pakistan. Meanwhile a new director, Gen. Hamid Gul, took over ISI. The greatest change occurred in August 1988 when a C-130 crashed while carrying generals Zia and Akhtar as well as U.S. Ambassador Arnold L. Raphel. Pakistani elections then brought to power Benazir Bhutto, daughter of an earlier strongman. Once imprisoned by the ISI, Bhutto held them in little esteem. Her ascendancy increased prospects for negotiations, which began to move quickly. Diego Cordovez shuttled from New York to Geneva, Moscow, and Pakistan.

Frank Anderson felt his CIA project had no impact on the talks, but it was not in America's interest to permit the Russians to withdraw from their quagmire intact. With victory the goal, CIA budgets redoubled. Close to $300 million in 1984, by 1986 they stood at $700 million—and that funded only the CIA contribution. Adding Saudi money made the totals enormous. Soviet intelligence toted up the numbers in 1987 and came up with almost $2 billion. Humanitarian aid added close to a billion dollars through the decade. Estimates of total CIA spending on the Afghan project through 1991 (the United States gave the rebels a golden parachute) range up to $9 billion.

Robert Gates remarked at his 1991 confirmation hearings for CIA director that he would have grave doubts about the efficacy of covert operations, save for Afghanistan. That leads to the heart of the matter. Afghanistan supplanted Laos as the biggest paramilitary affair in CIA history up to then—and, more, an apparent success. By 1988 the Soviet military had stalled, its air effort neutralized by the *mujahedeen*'s SAM weapons. Russian troops could punch through but achieved nothing. In UN-mediated negotiations the Soviets agreed to a military withdrawal and carried it out. At 11:55 A.M. on February 15, 1989, Gen. Boris V. Gromov stepped back inside Russian territory, the last Soviet soldier to leave Afghanistan. Milt Bearden and Frank Anderson, breaking CIA standing orders not to cross the border, went to have their pictures taken at the same bridge where Gromov had exited.

But the Afghan War continued. Najibullah's Communist regime fought on, and both the CIA project and Russian aid halted only in 1992. The farewell gift of a generous allotment of arms to the factions—which CIA justified on grounds that the United States had a moral responsibility from mobilizing the tribes—served to fuel continuing civil war. A coalition government under a general of the former regime lasted about a year until the warlords fought again, over fundamentalist primacy in addition to political power. Ahmed Massoud and Gulbuddin Hekmatyar became enemies. Four battles for Kabul occurred, three of them *after* the Soviet withdrawal. Elections to be held in 1993 never took place. In the midst of the civil war a different, even more extreme fundamentalist force arose. The Taliban conquered Kabul and most of the country. Massoud—now allied with Najibullah's former general Dost—fought on. Before long they got help from the CIA *and* the Russians. The details of their war spill over into the story of the war on terrorism, but the facts make a mockery of pious arguments that the United States intervened to support democracy in Afghanistan, and the evaporation of American aid after the Russian withdrawal shows Washington's proclivity to discard pawns that outlive their usefulness.

It is not possible to conclude, as some like to say, that the Afghan War brought about the fall of the Soviet Union. The war *was* increasingly unpopular and costly in both blood and treasure, but its burden cannot be separated from pressures of waste, inefficiency, and cultural ennui. The Afghan War paled in comparison to Soviet economic and nationality problems. Ironically the immediate catalyst of the Communist downfall came with Gorbachev's attempt to craft a new union and the secession of the Baltic states, those theaters of long-ago CIA projects since terminated.

The Afghan operation also cost the CIA and the United States. Those at the CIA and elsewhere who worried that Stinger missiles given to the *muj* would show up on world arms markets proved exactly correct. At the height of the Iran-Contra affair, intermediaries for Teheran told CIA operative George Cave how pleased they were that the United States had begun supplying Stingers since they now had ten of them. As early as 1988 U.S. forces in the Persian Gulf, inspecting a motorboat belonging to the Iranian Revolutionary Guards, found two Stingers. During the CIA operation a thousand went to the Afghan guerrillas. About 350 are reported to have been fired. No doubt some were expended in training and others defective, but by the spring of 1994 estimates were that Afghan warlords still had at least 400 SAMs. Indeed the Stinger became such a prestige item that the warlords took to parading them on national holidays. Appeals to return unused missiles were useless. In 1994 the CIA began a new $65 million covert effort to buy back the same missiles it had given the guerrillas, apparently an enhancement of a CIA buyback program already under way. American demand fueled a surge in prices, fraud, and further corruption. Missiles that cost the U.S. army $35,000 each were being sought for $50,000 or $100,000, then $150,000, with limited success. Agency proprietary aircraft flew to Middle Eastern cities to bring back the SAMs thus acquired. It is reported that the CIA bought back perhaps 200 Stingers. A weapon that had a positive effect in one paramilitary campaign became a long-term security and terrorism headache.

Some Muslims who fought in Afghanistan left to seek new wars; others who admired the Afghan resistance from afar went there to learn the ways of the warrior under new terrorist lord Osama bin Laden. He is believed to have trained militants from more than forty countries, including Egypt, the Sudan, and Algeria, all of which had significant internal unrest from conflicts between fundamentalists and secular governments. The Algerian militants were blamed for a destructive series of bombings in France that began in early 1995, and the bin Laden strikes on the United States have become the stuff of new war.

Afghan Arabs have been identified fighting in Bosnia and in Azerbaijan and Tadjikistan of the former Soviet Union. There *is* a relationship between these horrors and the CIA war in Afghanistan, not in terms of responsibility but certainly in the empowerment of the perpetrators. One can debate the degree but not the fact.

The Afghan project underlines the point that successful covert operations offer only short-term benefits. Pakistan, one of the major U.S. allies in the Afghan effort, is now less stable than before, and U.S. aid did nothing to restrain the Pakistanis from forging their own nuclear weapons, or indeed from proliferating this technology to other lands. Its role as ally and frontline state vitiated Washington's leverage, leaving Islamabad to pursue its own aims, not just on weapons but in fomenting the same Muslim fundamentalism that has become so deadly. These results are incalculable.

American relations with China, another ally in the Afghan War, are not materially better as a result. Then there are the potential adverse effects of sophisticated American technology in the hands of terrorists, and U.S. interests threatened by armies of secret warriors rasied by the CIA. Taking the long view, Afghanistan is by no means an unalloyed victory for covert operations. By way of counterpoint, if there had never been a CIA secret war in Afghanistan, the Soviet Union would still have collapsed in the 1990s, perhaps not at the exact moment it did but undoubtedly within that decade.

Through all of this, or at least until his death late in Ronald Reagan's presidency, William J. Casey led an expansion of the CIA hailed at the time as its renaissance. Casey pushed for other covert action projects with a similarly anti-Soviet bent. Many of Langley's tribes would have their hands full during those years. To the secret warriors Bill Casey seemed the herald of a new age.

20

The Reagan Revolution

AT THE END of 1980 the members of President-elect Ronald Reagan's transition team unanimously believed there should be more covert action. William J. Casey, Reagan's 1980 campaign manager and his choice for CIA director, accepted this position though he largely ignored the transition report. The new director, a friend of the president and member of Reagan's informal "kitchen cabinet," made no bones about offering policy advice; by all indications, he rather enjoyed the role. Casey and Reagan were a close team. No director of central intelligence—except George J. Tenet in later years—ever spent more time with a president than Casey. Ronald Reagan saw his DCI as a loyal, tough, and competent adviser and an effective agent. Reagan appreciated Casey's political work and his personal achievements.

A Wall Street lawyer, Casey had grown wealthy on investments and from dispensing tax advice. An amateur historian, sometime president of the Export-Import Bank, and chairman of the Securities and Exchange Commission, Casey had also been one of the original secret warriors. In World War II he went into the Office of Strategic Services where he worked as an aide to Wild Bill Donovan. The OSS chief, in turn, sent Casey to London. There the acolyte helped organize the Jedburgh Program. In December 1944 Casey replaced David Bruce as OSS chief of secret intelligence for the European theater. He supervised the infiltration of OSS agents into Germany during the last days of the Third Reich. After the war Casey remained active in OSS veterans' associations and was appointed to the PFIAB by President Gerald Ford. To a newly elected Ronald Reagan looking for a CIA director, Bill Casey must have seemed a natural. Casey himself had wanted to be secretary of state but accepted the Langley appointment and ultimately decided he had the best job in Washington.

There was only one large problem, at first. That was poor speaking ability, which might not impress senators at a confirmation hearing. Casey could be well prepared for testimony, but that turned out to be the least of his difficulties. One irregularity after another emerged during the confirmation process, until Casey's chances appeared threatened.

Among these surprises was a political item from the Reagan-Carter election campaign that brewed into a significant scandal which pundits began calling "Debategate." Reagan and President Carter had appeared in several televised debates, formatted as joint press conferences, hosted by the League of Women Voters. Before the foreign policy debate a copy of Carter's briefing book was surreptitiously made and given to the Republicans. Reagan's staff used the book to prep him for what Carter might say. As Reagan's campaign manager, Bill Casey had kept the briefing book in his office safe. Several more things called into question Casey's judgment or integrity. His financial disclosure forms, necessary under post-Watergate laws, were incomplete and had to be amended. It also developed that Casey had not registered as a foreign agent as required by law during periods when he represented the government of Indonesia, and many others as well. Then it became known that he intended to continue managing his stock portfolio, which might create conflicts of interest for a CIA director.

After confirmation, judgment again became an issue in the summer of 1981 in the Hugel affair. This concerned Max Hugel, whom Casey personally brought into the agency as an assistant, then promoted to deputy director for operations. Hugel's attraction for Casey lay precisely in his *lack* of association with intelligence. As the CIA director explained to a friend, Gerald P. Carmen, Casey needed to break up the CIA Old Boys network, and only someone from the Outside could do that.

But Hugel did not last long. He resigned after allegations of insider stock transactions. This happened just two months into Hugel's tenure. Even after the initial disclosures, Bill Casey solidly backed his protégé, saying he had known Hugel as an honest man for twenty years. But once tape recordings surfaced of Hugel giving out business tips, Casey admitted to fewer than two years of more casual acquaintance. Hugel's legal problems later appeared as overblown allegations by associates, but as far as the CIA was concerned, the damage had been done. The appointment had shaken the clandestine service, which breathed a sigh of relief when the interloper departed.

Had he not had President Reagan's high regard, Bill Casey would probably have been swept away. As it was, Casey mended the fences he could, listing seventy former clients in financial disclosure statements, asserting he remembered nothing about Debategate, and eventually also agreeing to a blind trust for his stocks. At Langley Casey assembled the top CIA leadership in The Bubble to reassure them. Reagan defended Casey, commenting that the criticisms were merely personal. In August 1981 the Senate intelligence committee passed a recommendation judging "there is no basis for concluding Mr. Casey is unfit to serve" as CIA director.

Casey mollified the professionals with his next DDO. John Henry Stein, the man originally recommended by the transition team, was a forty-eight-year-old officer with two decades at the CIA. Director Casey's intentions were reflected in his instructions to the new DDO: concentrate on covert paramilitary and political action. Espionage and management could be left to an associate. Casey wanted to stress the critical role the spooks must play in the Reagan universe as well as motivate the best minds to see intelligence as necessary to national security. He anticipated difficulties with congressional overseers but believed these could be circumvented.

Langley did its best to follow the director's lead. Greater emphasis on recruitment led to a one-third increase in personnel, putting CIA back near its Vietnam-era peak. John Stein saved expertise in covert operations by bringing back eight hundred of the officers let go in the 1970s, most of them on contracts. Although spending for covert operations dropped to just 2 percent of CIA expenses, the base grew since the agency's budget more than doubled. From 1981 to 1984 the intelligence community's total allotment increased as much as a quarter. The military contributed to several programs while, by the 1980s, the radios were separately funded. CIA funds did not have to stretch as far.

The CIA under Casey moved into a phase of what enthusiasts saw as combat on Communist territory, fighting revolutionary movements anywhere the Reaganites perceived them as Communist-controlled—which meant almost everywhere. As he would put it in a 1986 speech, the United States had a window of opportunity to advance democracy. To do this, he declared an intent to match Soviet meddling: "Just as there is a classic formula for communist subversion and take-over, there is also a proven method of overthrowing repressive government that can be applied successfully in the Third World."

With its in-house capabilities plus its privatized or proprietary network, the CIA went to work. Director Casey advocated vigorous covert action. The president declared his support for "freedom fighters" everywhere and defended U.S. covert action. Casey backed operations that were talked down at Langley. John Stein resisted escalation in Nicaragua; John McMahon, Casey's DDCI after 1982, opposed the wrong kind of effort in Afghanistan, certain Libya plans, and renewed support for UNITA in Angola. For the most part Bill Casey got his way. By 1986, fueled especially by Afghanistan, the CIA's budget for covert operations surpassed its spending for espionage and clandestine collection for the first time in history.

Within the executive branch President Reagan worked to improve the climate for covert action. Reagan reestablished the President's Foreign Intelligence Advisory Board, which Carter had abolished, appointing conservatives who encouraged activism. Leo Cherne, a longtime Casey associate, who had chaired the PFIAB under Ford and in fact had been instrumental in bringing Casey onto the board at that time, returned as vice chairman. Anne Armstrong became chairwoman. Like Armstrong and Cherne, staff director Randall Fort, though sophisticated, wore his conservative credentials on his sleeve. The president populated his board with mostly like-minded characters, including Clare Booth Luce, Martin Anderson, W. Glenn Campbell, John S. Foster, Jr., Adm. Thomas Moorer, and William French Smith. On this board Henry Kissinger and Alan Greenspan passed for liberals. Only William O. Baker remained from the old cadre of PFIAB experts. He was joined by CIA space maven Albert Wheelon and airline magnate Robert Six.

In this administration the board was highly restricted. When the White House debated where to put PFIAB and how to fund it, the decision was to locate the board in its old offices on the fourth floor of the Old Executive Office Building, but the budget would come from money set aside for unanticipated needs. The Intelligence Oversight Board, with its minuscule $5 million budget, would be more than an order of magnitude ahead of PFIAB. There is no evidence of efforts to play watchdog; the advisers reviewed the great spy cases of the day, the Moscow embassy bugging mess, and disputes over satellite programs, but on covert action there is little trace of PFIAB. To the contrary, specific indications are that Director Casey encouraged President Reagan to purge the PFIAB in late 1985 in order to rid it of figures who questioned agency activities in Nicaragua. About half the board's twenty-one members were let go in a "streamlining" move, replaced with a fresh crop of conservatives.

Reagan also reorganized the National Security Council to create a National Security Planning Group (NSPG), a more restricted subcommittee of the NSC that included Vice President George Bush, the secretary of state, the secretary of defense, the DCI, the NSC adviser, and top political aides. Reagan's deputy secretaries committee, the old 40 Committee or Special Coordinating Committee at the heart of the secret war, was retitled the Crisis Pre-Planning Group (CPPG), then the Policy Coordination Group (PCG), also known as the 208 Committee for the room in the Old Executive Office Building in which it met weekly. The attorney general and OMB director, regular members of Carter's NSC Special Group, were relegated to occasional invitees.

Langley's proposals came in options papers passed around at the outset of a meeting and collected at the end. Final decision rested with the NSPG. Here the Reagan administration parted with its predecessors: Eisenhower had participated directly on the Bay of Pigs and the Congo, and Johnson on Cuba, but these had been ad hoc episodes. Under Ronald Reagan the president himself sat on the ultimate covert action decision body for the first time, eliminating the Special Group as a screen. In Reagan's day many decisions were made right in the Situation Room, at the NSPG table.

Reagan continued regulating intelligence activities by executive order. His version, Executive Order 12333, issued on December 4, 1981, contained a somewhat expanded definition of covert action, which it termed "special activities." The order reiterated existing prohibitions on assassinations and specifically provided that, except in time of war or by presidential direction, the CIA had full responsibility for "special activities." While domestic intelligence provisions attracted the bulk of public attention at the time, the order clearly referred to the NSC as "the highest Executive Branch entity that provides review of, guidance for and direction to" special activities.

Under these procedures Reagan had to sign Memoranda of Notification to justify each covert action and in order to authorize it at the policy level. Reagan issued general instructions affecting the CIA's role that were expressed in National Security Decision Directives (NSDDs), the authorization documents of his administration. These were supplemented by findings or secret annexes, such as in the 1985 Afghan escalation. Reagan approved covert action against Nicaragua in a November 1981 decision directive. About a year later he sanctioned Bill Casey's activist stance in an NSDD that ordered global covert operations to prevent nations from accepting the "Cuban model" as well as an NSDD that authorized a "public diplomacy" campaign that nevertheless had secret aspects. An important feature of the struggles over intelligence oversight that pitted Reagan against Congress during these years were controversies over the nature of presidential findings.

An uneasy relationship prevailed between the executive and Congress through much of the period. The Hugel affair and Casey's legal entanglements got the sides off badly. Nevertheless Arizona Senator Barry Goldwater, who chaired the Senate Select Committee on Intelligence, beginning in 1981 tried to protect Casey and minimize the intrusiveness of oversight. The committee supported the CIA in passage of the Intelligence Identities Protection Act in 1982 and in obtaining extra exemptions from the Freedom of Information Act two years later. But Langley took a jaundiced view, according to historian Frank J. Smist, Jr., who concludes that the CIA position (which he attributes to both Casey and Carter-era national security adviser Zbigniew Brzezinski) viewed the SSCI as compromising sensitive information and according oversight power to people with no expertise. Treatment of the House Permanent Select Committee on Intelligence was similar. The secret war in Nicaragua proved to be a particularly thorny area of dispute. But Bill Casey, confident in the capabilities of his secret warriors, had no qualms.

Proprietaries had long constituted a backbone of CIA covert capability. Under Casey's leadership they assumed greater importance. As before, aviation companies performed some of the most useful services, but the 1980s brought a great need for entities capable of moving money, currency trading, personnel services, and the quiet acquisition of various kinds of gear. The CIA had them all.

When Langley liquidated Southern Air Transport (SAT), its buyer, Stanley G. Williams, once SAT manager for the agency, initially went in directions CIA abhorred. Williams sold off most of SAT's assets, leading to contentious litigation. But mutual dependency proved too great—the CIA needed Southern Air, and SAT wanted Langley's business. Iranian air force contracts had comprised as much as 42 percent of SAT's work in 1978. The fall of the shah hurt SAT badly. Even with the Iranian deals, SAT posted a loss of $272,928 for that year. The Iranian account disappeared. Williams bailed out, selling Southern Air to lawyer James H. Bastian in 1979. He became its sole proprietor. Bastian had been SAT's legal counsel during its CIA years.

Southern Air Transport maintained headquarters and operating facilities in Miami and made a slow recovery. Operating revenue in 1982 totaled $9.8 million and profit $628,700. The next year Bastian brought in William G. Langton as president. Langton had previously worked for two other cargo carriers, Flying Tiger and Evergreen International. In 1984 SAT won $9.1 million in contracts from the Pentagon's Military Airlift Command, a figure that ballooned to $23.4 million a year later, out of total revenues of $38.9 million—60 percent of its business.

Southern Air's largest private account was as subcontractor to the Anglo-Irish firm IAS-Guernsey, to provide flight services to Marxist Angola. About three hundred flights were made in Angola between June and December of 1984 alone. Business increased further in 1985 after a competing company left Angola following destruction of one of its C-130-type aircraft on the ground in a guerrilla attack. That year SAT flew almost six hundred flights in Angola plus a hundred more from the United States to the Angolan port city of Benguela. At one point the State Department warned Southern Air against carrying Cuban soldiers on its flights, and SAT ceased doing so.

The charter company also worked for the U.S. government. Through 1986 the Military Airlift Command used eight SAT L-100s (civilianized versions of the C-130) daily for shuttles among bases in the United States. With the State Department, SAT had contracts for monthly flights to Havana to service the American Interests Section there, plus an arrangement to deliver humanitarian assistance to Nicaraguan rebels in Honduras.

Southern Air Transport remained strong through the 1980s. Its fleet expanded from three in 1983 to eight Boeing 707s plus 17 L-100s by 1986. At that time SAT employed 540 persons, including 96 pilots. The worst setbacks were two fatal crashes, the first in its history, on October 4, 1986, and April 8, 1987, both of L-100s flying for the Military Airlift Command. By way of comparison, as of 1982 only four private corporations (Standard Oil of California, Tenneco, Rockwell International, and Mobil Oil) possessed air fleets larger than SAT's.

In 1979 a former Air America chief pilot and hero of Desert One, James Rhyne, started a company called Aero Contractors. Over more than two decades, with a series of interlocking directorates and subsidiaries, it accumulated more than twenty aircraft and a major stake in an airport in Johnston County, North Carolina. Later investigation revealed corporate directors with fictitious names traced to post office boxes in Northern Virginia, Washington, D.C., or Maryland, plus a complex web of corporate cutouts. Research has yet to establish the operational role of Aero Contractors during this early period, though Rhyne advised some of the pilots recruited by private benefactors to work with the *contras*.

Another possible proprietary, or at least a company that provided services to CIA, worked out of a field at Middletown, Delaware. Summit Aviation specialized in aircraft brokerage and modification. Even former employees were uncertain of its status. During the Nicaraguan revolution of the late 1970s, Summit trained pilots for dictator Anastasio Somoza. In the eighties Summit Aviation was linked to aircraft the CIA used in El Salvador and Honduras, with planes prepared for the rebels fighting for CIA from Honduras, and with aircraft modifications for Southern Air Transport. In 1984 Summit received a grant from the Federal Aviation Administration to improve its airfield, enabling it to work on large multi-engine aircraft.

Caribbean-based St. Lucia Airways owned or leased two Boeing 707s and an L-100. One of its aircraft carried the shah from Egypt to the United States in 1978, the event that catalyzed the Iran hostage crisis. Revelations of secret U.S. arms deals with Iran brought new attention to St. Lucia with disclosure that a Boeing 707 making one of the deliveries bore company markings. St. Lucia denied involvement, but press investigation uncovered additional details. Another St. Lucia plane in fact carried U.S. weapons to Israel for transshipment to Iran. In 1985 an apparent St. Lucia L-100 was destroyed in Angola. The company denied any role in Angola, but its careful statement did not mention Zaire. Between January and April 1986 alone there were four flights from an American military base to an airfield in Zaire identified as a CIA supply point for UNITA rebels. These reportedly used a type of plane that exists solely in U.S. military inventories. Like SAT, St. Lucia did contract air work for the U.S. Military Airlift Command.

In 1984 a Honolulu investment adviser, Ronald Ray Rewald, charged with securities fraud, defended himself with the claim that his company, Bishop, Baldwin, Rewald, Dillingham & Wong, had been working for the CIA. The Rewald case, which may have been spurious, represented only the bare tip of the iceberg in terms of CIA corporate covers. Edwin Wilson's import-export operations are an example of the kinds of covers used to move arms and equipment, as is Associated Traders Corporation, which the CIA reportedly set up in 1969. Tetra Tech Corporation, brainchild of retired secret warrior James Critchfield, did security-related work in Middle Eastern nations where Critchfield had labored at the agency. During the first Bush administration a major scandal over a rash of bank failures revealed possible links between the CIA and no fewer than twenty-two savings banks, according to the *Houston Post*. In all these cases the CIA denied any role. Data remains too scanty to treat the issue of corporate covers with the depth it deserves. But the fact remains that, like the movie company CIA created to further operations in Iran during the hostage crisis, activities there and elsewhere depended on the use of these techniques.

The Reagan administration inherited a program, or at least a problem, in Iran. The hostages came home on Inauguration Day, but now there were plenty of expatriate Iranians in touch with the CIA, not least the shah, who wished nothing better than to return to Teheran. Reagan's behavior was "extremely schizoid," in the opinion of Iranian Mansur Rafizadeh, a former intelligence officer who worked with the CIA until 1983. Rafizadeh believes that American policymakers decided very early on to throw in their lot with the Ayatollah Khomeini, expecting that Muslim fundamentalism would be the best defense against communism in the Middle East.

Rafizadeh recounts that Bill Casey went to Ronald Reagan in September 1981 with a dual-track program. The president approved a yearlong tryout. The

CIA would fund disparate Iranian exile groups while simultaneously the United States would overlook Israeli arms shipments to Khomeini. On both tracks, gathering intelligence became the object. There is no evidence that the CIA itself sold arms to Iran at this stage. On the other hand, Langley proved quite adept at getting information from the exiles by putting them in competition with one another. Langley's controller was George Cave, fluent in Farsi and former station chief in both Teheran and Saudi Arabia.

Six or seven main exile circles were active, and the CIA developed them all. The German-based group of Adm. Ahmad Madani, commander of the former Imperial Iranian Navy, reportedly received several million dollars but insisted on complete control of its operations. The CIA, regarding Madani as too independent, eased him out. Many of the exiles were too busy squabbling to do much, but in 1982 the CIA reportedly began paying $100,000 a month to the Front for the Liberation of Iran, under Ali Amini in Paris. This included $20,000 to $30,000 for a new "radio," Radio Liberation (Radio Nejat), which broadcast four hours a day of anti-Khomeini programming from Egypt and became active in October 1982. The shah's son, Reza Pahlavi, cooperated with the FLI and appeared on an eleven-minute broadcast that overrode two Iranian domestic TV channels on September 5, 1986, probably FLI's greatest achievement. The CIA evidently provided miniaturized transmission equipment that made the disruption and substitution possible.

At the same time Langley curried favor with Khomeini. In late 1982 a Russian agent in Iran defected to the British, soon to be debriefed by CIA. The Russian spy, Vladimir Kuzichkin, provided data on the Communist Tudeh Party in Iran, including names of organizers. Langley passed the list to the Iranians, who executed most of its members before outlawing the Tudeh on May 4, 1983. According to Rafizadeh, the CIA did the same to some of the exile groups, passing their contacts in Iran to the Khomeini security services. As a result, Rafizadeh reports, more than a thousand persons were arrested or executed.

It is not clear that these diametrically opposed actions represented purposeful execution of a two-track policy. Mansur Rafizadeh believes this was the case, but an administration source saw U.S. actions as "groping through a maze," a series of actions without a policy.

The incoherence of U.S. policy comes into sharp focus when the question of relations between Washington and Iran is juxtaposed with the Islamic government's support for terrorists in Lebanon. Shiite Muslim militiamen in Beirut began a campaign of terror against the West, particularly the United States, when in 1983 Reagan abandoned neutrality in Lebanese factional infighting. The Shiite militia had close ties with Teheran; there was no détente with the "Great Satan," the United States. In a suicide attack on April 18, 1983, fanatics loaded a panel truck with explosives, rammed their way into the heavily defended U.S. embassy in Beirut, and blew it up. At that instant a CIA regional conference was going on inside; among the seventeen dead Americans (of sixty-three overall) were Robert C. Ames, the agency's national intelligence officer for the Near East and South

Asia, the station chief, his wife, and his deputy. Ames's hand would be found in the Mediterranean a mile offshore, still bearing his wedding ring. The blow energized Langley. The U.S. government began to crack down on arms shipments to Iran in Operation Staunch.

An even more ambitious dual operation, parallel truck bombings of the U.S. Marine and French military compounds in Beirut, followed on October 23, 1983. The toll mounted with 58 French and 241 American Marines dead plus another hundred injured, many grievously. Bombings continued—of the U.S. embassy in Kuwait, an Israeli military headquarters, and, on September 20, 1984, the American embassy in Beirut again, this time with a truck bomb that left 14 more dead. The Shiites also struck directly at the CIA again on March 16, 1984, kidnapping William Buckley, recently arrived station chief in this tough Middle Eastern city. Despite protective measures, the station chief was seized right off the street in Beirut and held by his captors for a year. He became the first of six American hostages taken in Lebanon.

Washington had a vital interest in all the hostages, and the CIA in Buckley even more. The continued captivity of his station chief amounted to an affront to Bill Casey. It was harder still for Clair E. George, now the DDO, himself the station chief in Beirut when two American diplomats were killed there during the Ford years.

Thoughts in Reagan's White House turned toward getting Khomeini to influence the Lebanese Shiites. An interagency study completed in October 1984 concluded that a new relationship could be forged only by Khomeini's successors. In April 1985 the NSC adviser learned from a consultant of Iranian interest in buying American weapons. The CIA entered the picture in May when Graham Fuller, Ames's successor, sent Bill Casey a memo that argued for "a bolder and perhaps riskier policy" on Iran that would at least ensure a greater U.S. voice in unfolding events. Casey sent the Fuller paper, intended for internal circulation, to the White House. But the CIA's official position, contained in a May 1985 update to the Iran Special National Intelligence Estimate, remained pessimistic: "Improvement of ties to the United States is not currently a policy option."

Israeli Foreign Ministry official David Kimche approached national security adviser Robert C. McFarlane two months later to ask if the United States might sell weapons to Iran. When McFarlane replied he thought not, the Israeli asked whether Washington would have any objection if Israel sold some of *its* American weapons, and if Israel could then replenish its stocks from the United States. The Kimche request led to an NSPG meeting at the White House on August 8 which appears to have given the Israelis a go-ahead.

A morass of deals with Iran followed, related both to reopening ties with Teheran and to recovering American hostages in Lebanon. Some used Iranian arms dealer Manucher Ghorbanifar, a man with a shadowy past of dealings with various security services, including Iranian, American, and Israeli. There were two Israeli arms deals, in September and November 1985, and the second time the Israelis bungled their shipment (routing it through Portugal without appropriate clearances) and appealed for U.S. help. This compromised the White House—McFarlane personally intervened with the Portuguese while the CIA had to provide an aircraft through Southern Air Transport.

Deputy Director John McMahon agonized over this use of CIA services without a presidential finding. Meanwhile McFarlane resigned in December, to be replaced by Adm. John M. Poindexter. At Christmastime Langley asked Poindexter for a finding to cover arms activity. Stanley Sporkin, CIA's top lawyer, wanted the finding to approve the CIA's November involvement retroactively. The CIA and NSC together drafted a document that Reagan approved on January 17, 1986. The finding contained orders that Congress *not* be informed and that it be carried out by private citizens as authorized agents of the United States. Such a private individual—Gen. Richard V. Secord—attended a meeting in the White House on January 11. There Secord met the CIA principals.

Through 1986 Secord negotiated deals, organized shipments, and supported the operations in progress. McFarlane, called back to go along on one mission in May, thought he could talk directly to the Iranians. He never did. A divergence developed: U.S. officials assumed that all the hostages would be released while the Iranians had no such idea. Secord's team spent the summer trying to open a second channel to Teheran, bypassing the Ghorbanifar link, now fully discredited.

A second channel was eventually opened and one further arms transaction arranged, but Ghorbanifar learned of it and struck back by blowing the operation's cover. The McFarlane visit to Teheran was revealed in a leaflet distributed there, and a few weeks later the story appeared in the Lebanese magazine *Al Shiraa*. The Iran arms deals, together with events simultaneously occurring in Nicaragua, ignited a firestorm in the United States that threatened the Reagan presidency.

Three hostages were released: the Reverend Benjamin Weir, Father Lawrence Jenco, and David P. Jacobsen. Reagan sold more than two thousand anti-tank missiles to Iran, plus spare parts and HAWK anti-aircraft missiles. But on the streets of Beirut the terrorists grabbed four more Americans plus British mediator Terry Waite. The CIA station chief, poor Bill Buckley, tortured for months to extract information, expired in the summer of 1986, leaving what is reputed to be a four-hundred page debriefing. Langley suffered grievous wounds. Meanwhile the NSC staffer managing the arms sales, Marine Lt. Col. Oliver North, had given the Iranians a sample of intelligence that might be available in a cooperative relationship with the United States.

The CIA strove to rebuild a network in Iran, running its operation through Frankfurt, Germany, where the steady flow of Iranian workers and migrants made it possible to access the expatriates without arousing suspicion. Some hold this to have been strictly an espionage ploy, others claim that the CIA attempted to set up a "stay behind" group to function against the ayatollahs as well as in case of Soviet conquest. A number of Iranians were recruited. As early as 1986 there were warnings that their communications with the agency had been compromised. Stephen W. Richter, the forty-four-year-old DO officer in charge, relied upon secret writing, an older method rather than the latest technology. Teheran had indeed penetrated his scheme. Beginning in 1988 Iranian authorities arrested more than thirty persons it convicted as CIA agents. Richter could do nothing. The Iranians blew the cover on this disaster in April 1989. The worst that happened to Richter was that he got chewed out during a meeting at headquarters.

Angola returned as a covert action during the Reagan years. The United States had been out of that country since the failure of Project Feature, but the Reaganites saw the United States as the patron of anti-Soviet action worldwide, a stance elevated to the "Reagan Doctrine"—and Angola remained frozen in the image of a Soviet satellite. Jonas Savimbi and UNITA had gone on fighting the MPLA with help from South Africa, and Savimbi certainly wanted to get the Americans back on board. He hired a high-powered Washington firm, Black Manafort Stone and Kelly, to do public relations. Despite the opprobrium of working alongside the South Africans, whose internal divisions were even sharper than in the 1970s, the Reaganites could not resist the lure. President Reagan told an NSPG meeting on November 12, 1985, "We want Savimbi to know the cavalry is coming." The main difficulty was a dispute between the administration and the intelligence committees over whether U.S. assistance ought to be covert or given openly, with Congress favoring the latter.

In early 1986 Savimbi made a highly publicized visit to the United States. The initial covert program provided $10 to $15 million, and UNITA received fifty Stinger anti-aircraft missiles. The materiel moved through an airfield at Kamina in southeastern Zaire, forwarded on CIA proprietary aircraft. Weapons shipments began in March 1986. In May the IAS-Guernsey company, managing flights by CIA proprietaries, protested that UNITA had fired on and damaged one of its C-130 aircraft. A couple of months later a delegation of Senate intelligence committee staff people visited, conferring with the CIA station chiefs in Zaire and South Africa. In December 1986 the MPLA announced that its forces had captured Stinger missiles from Savimbi's rebels.

The UNITA forces, spurred by renewed CIA aid, fought on. As early as 1984 Chester Crocker, the State Department's assistant secretary for Africa, by dint of talking to all interested parties, had begun a move toward a negotiated settlement to include a Cuban withdrawal, but Savimbi resisted a settlement. The CIA project to help him extended past the Reagan administration. Project budgets rose to about $50 million. Robert Gates claims that Secretary of State George Shultz supported the Angolan covert operation as a means of keeping the pressure on the Angolan (MPLA) government to come to agreement. Shultz himself writes that the CIA effectively posed an obstacle to settlement. In December 1988 the parties reached a pact that featured Cuban withdrawal, eventually completed in 1991. By that point a hundred thousand Angolans are believed to have died.

Among the other projects Reagan's secret warriors carried out, one of the least savory has to have been the project in Cambodia. This supposedly assisted only the non-Communist opposition, a tiny faction allied with the Khmer Rouge monster Pol Pot, with nonlethal aid sent through Thailand. In fact the play amounted to a shell game. Money given the non-Communist resistance eased the situation of the Khmer Rouge while simplifying China's problems as it backed Pol Pot. Initially only small amounts were involved, starting at $5 million and rising by only about half, though one account has Casey contemplating up to $12 million at a later stage, not far from initial funding for the Nicaragua project, after careful budget combing by CIA comptroller Daniel Childs. Media accounts put the Cambodia fund as high as $24 million. But little opposition existed in Cambodia. War had begun in 1978 when the Vietnamese invaded the country, outraged that the Khmer Rouge were massacring ethnic Vietnamese. The Cambodian resistance was attractive to the Reagan administration merely because it fought a Vietnamese-backed dictatorship. This project effectively put the United States in league with Pol Pot and Communist China, fueling the efforts of a political movement that had slaughtered two million of Cambodia's citizens. It did nothing for America's reputation as a bulwark of democracy.

Agency officer William Daugherty, who held a position in Langley's machinery for covert operations planning and approval after Iran and counterterror operations, writes that CIA officers and U.S. diplomats were all antagonistic to the Cambodia project. Cancellation followed. Robert Gates comments that Casey never warmed to the operation, that it remained a child of Shultz's State Department. Shultz says nothing of Cambodia at all. Small wonder.

Projects planned for Suriname and Mauritius were canceled because of administration or congressional opposition or blown cover, but there were plenty of others. Shultz shot down Suriname, where in 1983 Casey wanted to insert a couple of hundred *Korean* commandos to overthrow the dictator. That Langley could not find local recruits said everything. More than fifty covert operations were reportedly in progress by 1984, half in Central or South America, including both paramilitary action and espionage. This represented a 500 percent increase over the final year of the Carter administration. John McMahon's decision to retire in February 1986 came when the Crisis Pre-Planning Group approved the simultaneous escalation of four covert operations, Afghanistan, Nicaragua, Angola, and Cambodia.

Europe would not be ignored on Casey's watch either. Among the more lurid tales is that the CIA took advantage of the Soviet appetite for American technology by doctoring computers destined to control flows on a Russian natural gas pipeline, causing immense fires. Little evidence has emerged to back this story. More prosaic—and more effective—was the agency's effort to flood the Soviet Union with prohibited literature, especially miniature copies of the Bible and the dissident writings known as *samizdat*. French spy chieftain Alexandre de Marenches has taken credit for convincing Director Casey to move on this project, and the French certainly helped circulate the material. But Casey needed no encouragement, and Reagan backed him enthusiastically.

The CIA waged a similar campaign in Eastern Europe, especially Poland, the impetus following from the Soviet quasi-intervention there, the Polish imposition of martial law in December 1981, and the subsequent crackdown on the labor movement Solidarity. The AFL-CIO carried on a parallel effort directly with the union. The Catholic church also retained great influence in Catholic Poland, its efforts enhanced after Reagan's June 1982 meeting with Pope John Paul II, previously a Polish cardinal. That summer national security adviser William Clark called for options. Zbigniew Brzezinski, of Polish descent and expert in this matter, consulted with Casey on Poland and Eastern Europe more generally. The initiatives amounted to classic CIA political action. Langley's expenditures went for funding Solidarity, publishing texts, and printing presses and paper smuggled to assorted dissident groups, plus instructions and training where necessary.

Stimulated by the Reaganites, Radio Free Europe also had an important part to play. The old CIA radio had responded to the era of détente with visions of cutting back, changing its name, ending links to dissident networks, perhaps relocating its offices to the United States. Then the KGB masterminded a bombing of RFE headquarters in Munich. Its board wanted to use operating funds to make repairs. The Reagan White House saw an opportunity to energize the entire operation. John Lenczowski, Soviet specialist on the NSC staff, spearheaded the effort, proposing a $2.6 billion program to revamp RFE and scale up its activities. Everyone opposed him—the CIA, State, even the RFE board of directors. Finally he got the State Department to break with the pack—State's staffer for RFE recalls that senior officers, concerned with NSC's blocking of their negotiation efforts, decided to let Lenczowski have this victory so they could get on with their real work. The RFE program became part of the public diplomacy initiative President Reagan approved in 1982. Radio Free Europe broadcast freedom right through the decade, contributing its piece to the fall of the Iron Curtain.

By the time Casey's watch ended, the CIA's propaganda and political action staff had become quite active indeed. Besides its own projects, the CIA lent specialists out to the NSC and State Department units engaged in public diplomacy, especially for Latin America, and CIA money financed many of their efforts. But the staff had to depend on officers brought back from retirement. The unit's own senior staff numbered only a few dozen, among them just a handful of DO professionals, the rest being translators or analysts drafted from their normal work. As with the military's view of "combat arms" billets versus support roles, propaganda at the CIA carried less prestige than covert operations or intelligence gathering.

There can be no doubt of the popularity of covert action in Ronald Reagan's administration. By some lights Reagan exceeded even Dwight Eisenhower in his use of the technique. And Bill Casey was the instigator, constantly demanding fresh initiatives, taking odd suggestions and turning them into projects, encouraging the DO to be all it could be. All of this aimed at the Russians or Cubans, supposedly, except that so many Reagan secret wars targeted leftist governments more generally. No democracies resulted from any of the Third World operations. Projects in Europe can be judged successful except that the impact of CIA political action remains indeterminate. In Russia, where democracy has yet to become fully established, the CIA helped sharpen Soviet problems, but its contribution seems small. The structural weaknesses of communism and the cultural penetration of Western music and thought loom much larger in the end of the Soviet bloc. Broadly notable, however, is that political action seems to have been more effective than paramilitary interventions.

21

Bill Casey's War

WHAT IS STRIKING about the Nicaraguan secret war is Bill Casey's great fervor. Here the secret warriors had their chance to wage an all-out paramilitary campaign. Here the CIA, special warfare forces, the regular military, and the instruments of American economic power were combined to pressure a small Third World country. Langley recruited the fighters, pummeled them into political alliance, bought the weapons, and provided leadership. Green Berets and SEALs bestowed their practical expertise. The regular military built or improved bases, furnished some key support, and threatened the adversary by posturing in exercises on land and sea. The United States manipulated the levers of international financial assistance, as it had in Chile. The campaign exploited the presence and assistance of other nations and wed the classic elements of paramilitary and political action. Washington had every advantage.

Casey's fervor is all the more remarkable because the secret warriors divided over whether the covert actions were either feasible or necessary. Analysts like Robert Pastor and Anthony Lake, both former NSC staffers and one a future national security adviser, conclude that the CIA failed to appreciate the weakness of Anastasio Somoza's rule and the limited Marxist purity the revolutionaries would exhibit, but predictive failure does not justify covert action. Managua's new rulers did nothing inimical to U.S. interests. And the secret warriors, particularly after Chile, better knew the danger of actions taken on shaky policy grounds. Leftists headed the Nicaraguan government, specifically the *frente sandinista de liberación nacional* (FSLN), which came to power in 1979 at the head of the popular revolution that deposed Somoza. The dictator did not relinquish power without a struggle, naturally; Somoza's hillside bunker overlooking Managua had been the nerve center of a counterinsurgency war waged by the country's National Guard under his personal direction.

In the vernacular, the revolutionaries became known as Sandinistas; the National Guard and its allies, Somocistas. The Sandinistas were a coalition of five resistance groups, not a monolithic Communist or even a Marxist party. The ideology obscured traditional wellsprings of Nicaraguan politics that contributed to the

Sandinista revolution. Officials talked of a "mixed economy," but government control of prices and of much of the supply, plus graft (yet to be eradicated by the revolution), progressively eroded middle-class support for the FSLN.

President Carter approved a finding for a project against the Sandinistas in July 1979, in tandem with another aimed at Marxist guerrillas in El Salvador. The matter of Cuba must be central to any explanation for the Nicaragua covert action. Prodded by the State Department, a few months later Carter approved a broader finding to oppose Cuban activities throughout Latin America. Nestor Sanchez, then Latin America Division chief at CIA, proceeded without haste, trying to expose Sandinista connections to Cuba. Stansfield Turner worried that any hint the CIA backed opposition to the Sandinistas would backfire, enabling Havana to increase its involvement. But the Carter administration had not written off the Sandinistas and slated $120 million in foreign aid for Managua to provide a carrot to go with the stick. El Salvador seemed a thornier matter. To handle both these projects, in late 1980 Langley set up a Central America Task Force under Jerry Svat, an experienced DO officer.

Enter the Reaganites. Casey and Reagan were at one in their thinking about Nicaragua. Not only did President Reagan make the required decisions, he lent his personal influence to the secret warriors. In fact the covert aspect of "special activity" would be abandoned altogether in the attempt to coerce Nicaragua. White House determination to pursue the campaign ultimately led to international embarrassment of the United States, a showdown with Congress over intelligence oversight, and initiatives that took covert action outside whatever legal framework supports it, calling into question the role of the president himself. How all this came to pass illustrates many of the dangers of covert tactics.

The operation began soon after Reagan's inauguration. Just a month later Director Casey proposed a more extensive action—still focused on political and psychological warfare—to stop weapons shipments from Nicaragua to Salvadoran guerrillas. On March 9, 1981, Reagan approved this presidential finding. The finding went to the National Security Planning Group, which ordered detailed preparations. Bill Casey became the spear-carrier. During a visit to U.S. Southern Command headquarters in Panama that summer, briefings convinced Casey that the Sandinistas were sponsoring revolution elsewhere. The director determined to mount a vigorous secret war against them. When CIA's analysts estimated the Managua government could not be overthrown, Casey paid no attention. When leading secret warrior John Stein opposed the project and its expansion, Casey went around him. Senior analyst Robert M. Gates watched from the sidelines. Gates writes: "In virtually every covert action other than Central America, Casey was reasonably prudent—often even cautious—grumpily content to work through channels." Not here. In a notable breach of the tribal boundaries, Casey brought in Duane R. Clarridge, a Middle Eastern specialist, to head the DO's Latin America Division. This marked the beginning of a fateful alliance.

Those who got to know Bill Casey well, for example reporter Bob Woodward, credited him with considerable style. The agency's station chief in Rome shared that sense, if not Casey's taste: Duane Clarridge favored European-cut suits, showing a handkerchief from his pocket. A Panama hat often crowned his head. Cigars and brandy were his style too—here, at least, he matched Casey. Clarridge, familiarly called "Dewey," also liked red wine and, before Langley went dry, favored tastings with friends after the work of the day was done. The director encountered Dewey on one of his first jaunts, when Casey made a flash tour of CIA stations and Clarridge received him. The director traveled in company with Alan Wolfe, another of the Middle East clan and Dewey's old friend. The Rome spy chief lobbied Casey for Wolfe to be appointed DDO. Instead the director decided to shift Clarridge. Slated for a third year in Rome, the personnel drones first listed Clarridge to return to Langley as chief of the International Activities Division, then the European Division. John Stein happened to be another old friend of Clarridge's—they had gone through Army Reserve training together in their first days at the agency. When Stein stepped up to the DDO position, the new operations boss supported Clarridge. The European Division went to someone with more area experience. Then the Latin America Division opened up when Nestor Sanchez moved to the Pentagon.

Casey found Clarridge a real powerhouse. Gen. Robert Schweitzer, a true believer on the early Reagan NSC staff, thought no one who met Clarridge once could ever forget him. Arturo Cruz, Jr., a disillusioned Sandinista who went over to the rebels, felt Dewey's charm and witnessed his great appetite. Colleague Bert Dunn admired Clarridge from afar, though the two never actually served together. Dunn saw Clarridge as the first real case officer he ever met, and indeed that had been Dewey's forte. In Nepal, India, Turkey, Clarridge became an intrepid enlister of spies, not afraid to make a cold approach, the most difficult of recruitments. He believed in calculated risks. At headquarters Dewey had been a capable deputy to the barons he served. Until Nicaragua, he had also been lucky—he left Nepal before CIA's controversial basing of Tibetans there, left India before it turned to the Russians and went sour. Indeed Clarridge, who departed Rome on August 1, 1981, got out just before Italian leftist terrorists kidnapped a U.S. general, which would have scored a black mark for any station chief. Where those in the clandestine service aspired to fade into the crowd, the forty-nine-year-old Clarridge flaunted himself. As baron of the Nicaraguan war he drove a big sport-utility vehicle emblazoned with bumper stickers supporting the rebels.

Back at Langley, Dewey Clarridge had barely met the top people in his division when DDO Stein phoned. They were to meet the CIA director the next afternoon. Casey supplied a brief overview of the situation and told Clarridge to take a month or so and produce ideas on how to make it better. With absolutely no Latin experience and no command of Spanish, Clarridge offered enthusiasm. He took just a week to come back to the DCI. "My plan was simple," Clarridge writes, "1. Take the war to Nicaragua. 2. Start killing Cubans."

Bill Casey loved it.

Clarridge left with a mandate to draft a finding to cover the operation. Much of that work fell to Central America Task Force chief Jerry Svat. Intelligence showed that remnants of the Somoza forces were gathering in Honduras, talking of a march on Managua. They wanted to do the same thing to the Sandinistas that the FSLN had done to them. Other exiles, who opposed the "Somocista" National Guard, joined them in the summer of 1981 to form the *Fuerza democrática nicaraguense* (FDN). The CIA's project was to use the FDN. When the Latin baron told his station chiefs of the project, two, both Latin Americanists, objected. One was Jack Devine, who had watched as the agency got in trouble in Chile.

Casey's field marshal for the Nicaragua secret war takes pains to distance himself from his own dramatic description of CIA aims. Clarridge writes that the notion of killing Cubans amounted to part bravado, part pandering to Secretary of State Alexander Haig, whose policy was anti-Cuban to a fault. Indeed the CIA sought authority for this operation on the basis of interdicting arms supplies to guerrillas in El Salvador. But diplomacy could have accomplished that: the Sandinistas actually did halt shipments in the summer of 1981, when U.S. Ambassador Lawrence Pezzullo told Managua that aid money left from the Carter administration would be conditional on Sandinista behavior. Rather than building on that, the Reaganites noisily terminated all aid. Their offer on negotiations centered on Managua's surrender and Cuba's retreat.

The negotiation track became real only when Central American countries themselves created a framework for talks several years later. Declassified State Department cable traffic with the U.S. embassy in Honduras reveals that Washington, quite serious about *preventing* negotiations, pressured Honduras (and presumably the other isthmian nations) to agree only to regional groupings that rejected talking to the Sandinistas. The larger enterprise revealed in these U.S. maneuvers had to do with fighting Managua. Halting arms would be a by-product. This is important for several reasons. Most crucial, by cloaking its real aims behind the goal of arms interdiction, the Reagan administration introduced a confusion into its own activities that it never overcame. The limited goal precluded massive covert action. When such actions were attempted, they discredited Reagan's own assertions of intent. The goals also invited overseers of the secret war to hold the administration to its word, forcing the CIA into illegality as its action progressed, setting the stage for congressionally imposed termination. Not squarely facing these issues at the outset became a major error.

The Reagan White House was as vehemently anti-Castro as John Kennedy's. President Reagan believed that Cuban intervention fueled the Salvadoran civil war and that Nicaragua was the conduit for that support. Secretary of State Al Haig encouraged these views. Unable to strike directly at Cuba, the White House sought to "interdict" aid through Nicaragua. The Nicaragua campaign became a renewed manifestation of hostility toward Castro's Cuba. The extreme rhetoric employed to criticize Nicaragua showed U.S. determination to "get" Managua, in the Reagan administration view a surrogate for Havana. Killing Cubans was shorthand for overthrowing the Sandinistas. Ironically, there is no evidence that many Cubans were ever killed in the secret war on Nicaragua.

Most of the pieces were in place when Dewey Clarridge took his covert action project to the Restricted Interagency Group (RIG), the NSC unit responsible for Central America. Clarridge explained that the CIA would rely on the FDN and act through intermediaries, in this case Argentinians. Somocistas among the FDN would be ousted. Clarridge estimated a month and a half to implant a CIA base and logistics network, with activation two months after that. The CIA baron put the cost at about the same as a single top-of-the-line F-16 fighter jet. Diplomat Thomas Enders, who chaired the RIG, had seen the CIA in action in Cambodia in 1970. Confident of the agency, he nevertheless superimposed a diplomatic track to make it seem the Reagan administration was proceeding responsibly.

Director Casey went to the president. The Clarridge plan was discussed by the NSC in mid-November. Reagan approved the general policy in a National Security Decision Directive he signed on November 23, following with a presidential finding on December 1. The plan allowed the CIA to recruit a force of five hundred, possibly to be supplemented by another thousand Nicaraguan rebels being trained by the Argentines, and an initial budget of $19 million. The finding provided for the rebels to collect intelligence inside Nicaragua and carry out other missions. Clarridge's project, supposed to rely on third-country nationals, envisioned direct CIA paramilitary action against special targets. The plan aimed at eliminating "Cuban presence" and a Cuban-Nicaraguan "support structure" in Nicaragua.

The first order of business became assembling like-minded allies. Honduras, bordering Nicaragua to the north, fell in line quickly, turning a blind eye to anti-Nicaragua efforts. Costa Rica, to the south, would come later. After discussions (subsequently denied) with Reagan ambassador-at-large Vernon Walters, Argentina agreed to provide training and some advisers. In November, even before the finding had been signed, Clarridge took Svat and two other officers to Buenos Aires to hash out the details. The Argentines wanted to hear Washington say it would stay the course, that the CIA would not bug out when the going got rough. Dewey reassured them.

Langley's project utilized an opposition core of *contras* (the Spanish plural for "against") who fought a popular Sandinista government. In Miami, conservative labor leader Jose Francisco Cardenal and others formed the UDN (*Unión democrática nicaraguense*) and raised enough cash to buy two hundred weapons from local gun shops. Volunteers trained alongside anti-Castro Cuban enthusiasts at camps in south Florida. Former National Guardsmen could join if they accepted civilian leadership. The military chief of staff was a U.S. Air Force veteran.

Another group had closer ties to Somoza. This 15th of September Legion of several hundred National Guard veterans drew its name from the 1821 date of Nicaraguan independence from Spain. The legion, formed in May 1981, was said to be financed with hundreds of thousands of dollars from Luis Pallais Debayle, Somoza's cousin. It became active just as UDN established an office in Honduras.

Clarridge was not be the only one to go to Buenos Aires. Even before him several *contra* leaders met at Argentina's Military College with Col. Mario Davico, an aide to the chief of Argentine intelligence, then called Battalion 601. The Nicaraguans received $50,000 in fresh hundred-dollar bills and were told that more money and training would follow if the UDN, the Legion, and several smaller groups formed an alliance. This union produced the FDN. Further meetings followed in Miami, where Argentine Col. Jose Ollas, using the name Julio Villegas, told the Nicaraguans a three-way agreement had been made among the United States, Argentina, and Honduras to help them. Fifty *contras* went to Argentina for training, then became instructors at camps in Honduras. Ollas would be chief of logistics; another colonel, Osvaldo Rivera, the chief of operations, supervised a cadre of about fifty in Honduras.

The man who emerged as the top *contra* commander, Enrique V. Bermudez, a forty-seven-year-old colonel in the National Guard and a founder of the 15th of September Legion, initially served as second-in-command of the FDN forces. A Sandinista spokesman noted at the time that Bermudez had a clean record, which was not surprising—sent to Washington in 1975 for a course at the Inter-American Defense College, Bermudez had effectively been exiled by Somoza. He stayed on for three years as military attaché. When an army of Sandinistas and National Guard briefly seemed possible, as part of a transitional government in 1979, Bermudez was considered to lead it. He traced his own link to the Argentines to late 1980, when, he claimed, seventy to eighty Legionnaires received training in Argentina and were given $30,000.

Timing is important as it bears on the initiation of the paramilitary action. Bermudez made his claim in conversation with journalist Shirley Christian. Argentine participants, however, clearly date their activity to mid-1981. It is also at that time, August 1981, that the United States lost any opportunity for diplomatic accommodation, according to Ambassador Pezzullo. To Managua the U.S. demands seemed both excessive and imperious, with a halt in arms to El Salvador as a *precondition* to negotiation. In exchange for Nicaraguan concessions in five areas, the United States offered no more than strict enforcement of its neutrality laws. Incensed, the Sandinistas never even responded.

Most U.S. aid to Nicaragua stopped in March 1981, coincident with Reagan's first presidential finding. All remaining assistance ended that September. The Sandinistas further infuriated the State Department by denying they served as an avenue for arms and by their acceptance of Cuban help. Castro soon sent two thousand teachers and doctors. Reports of Cuban military advisers were current even during the Carter administration. But Washington cast the die for secret war against the Sandinistas in 1981, not before.

Before the CIA program began, the *contras* merely played at war. Their most serious effort had been the attempted destruction of a Nicaraguan airliner in Mexico City in December 1981. Now there was a possibility of real action. Covert aid made all the difference. The transformation, visible on the ground, took the *contra* bands to a higher level. In the early days the anti-Sandinista 15th of September Legion, led by Pedro Ortiz Centeño, numbered fewer than a dozen men with shotguns and .22-caliber pistols. As a sergeant with the National Guard's "Rattlesnake" Battalion, Ortiz Centeño took the *nom de guerre* "Suicide." Suicide liked to recount how they slipped across the border to assassinate Nicaraguan officials, but in fact his *contras* acquired a reputation only for robbery and indolence. In the eighteen months before July 1982, the Sandinista government recorded 45 gun battles but almost 250 cases of cattle rustling.

According to FDN chief of logistics Capt. Armando Lopez, the first CIA weapons arrived early in 1982. This shipment consisted of ninety-two Belgian automatic rifles, four machine guns, and two mortars. "We were all hugging," recalls Lopez, "we forgot about rank. We kissed our weapons. It seemed like a dream."

The first serious strikes occurred in mid-March when FDN units blew up two road bridges in northern Nicaragua. The next day the government declared a state of emergency. By the end of the month Managua could point to half a dozen instances of real or attempted sabotage. Problems also proliferated along the Atlantic coast, inhabited by Indians of the Miskito, Soma, and Rama peoples. The minorities of this region were not well integrated into the national polity; FSLN figures themselves admitted grave errors, including the jailing of a number of Indian leaders. In January 1982 Managua began resettling Indians from villages along the Coco River to camps farther from the Honduran border. This led to new anti-Sandinista forces—Misura (an acronym taken from the first letters of the tribes' names) and a later splinter group, Misurasata. Originally formed by the Sandinistas, Misura turned around after Miskito Stedman Fagoth Mueller, who fled to Honduras after revelation of his past service with Somoza, began to recruit armed bands there.

Clarridge and Svat had already been to Honduras to clear the way for a CIA base and local government cooperation. The Latin baron had promised an in-country unit by mid-January 1982. He delivered. The chief of station in the Honduran capital, Tegucigalpa, would observe the CIA operators, but the Nicaragua Operations Group worked directly with a base chief at El Aguacate, and with Langley. Still, the chief spent a great deal of time with *contras* in the Honduran capital.

Station chief Don Winters, another veteran of the Chile fiasco, ran interference with Ambassador John Negroponte, who took over the U.S. mission in "Tegu," as the Honduran capital was called, in late 1981. Negroponte, a former aide to Henry Kissinger, conducted the diplomacy, but he also keyed Washington to Honduran attitudes toward the *contras*, on ploys that might work, on talking points to use with the Hondurans, and on military aid. Negroponte's cable traffic, which has been declassified, shows he tried to counter unrest in Honduras and stimulate Honduran military cooperation with El Salvador, including several times when he coordinated U.S. helicopters to ferry Honduran troops to blocking positions along the borders of either Salvador or Nicaragua, and to respond to a hijacking incident. In contrast the ambassador was reluctant to intervene in human rights situations, including one where an American cleric "disappeared." Negro-ponte had a back channel for communications through the CIA, code-named "Red Baron."

The embassy had 150 personnel assigned; 176 military people assisted the Honduran armed forces, and 50 U.S. Air Force specialists staffed a radar that watched Nicaragua from a site known as Carrot Top on Isopo Mountain. The CIA station, not large, and the Aguacate base together had probably only a few dozen officers. In its early stages the entire Nicaragua program is reported to have been staffed by fewer than a hundred CIA people. Later the personnel in Honduras alone would be reported at that level. The agency also had significant representa-tion in El Salvador, including officers who were part of the *contra* program. For example, liaison in El Salvador arranged the use of Salvadoran air force facilities to launch a *contra* air attack on a Nicaraguan communications center.

Aguacate base started as nothing more than a dirt airstrip, 4,300 feet long with a shed on the side to service aircraft. When agency officers looked at the strip they groaned at what needed to be done. It was. The CIA rented the base from the Honduran air force, installed facilities, built a road to connect to the main *contra* camp at Las Vegas, and improved that as well.

Ray Doty became the first chief of base at Aguacate, Langley's local presence with the *contras*. Like Clarridge, neither Doty nor his chief engineer spoke Span-ish. They had cut their teeth in Laos with the *armée clandestine*. In fact Laos vet-erans permeated the paramilitary staff and provided the bulk of CIA leadership with the *contras*. All three of the Aguacate base chiefs and two of four Honduras station chiefs had been in Laos, along with many, many subordinates. That Clar-ridge found no difficulty mobilizing the requisite agency skills shows that Stans-field Turner's cutbacks of the late 1970s had not, in fact, crippled CIA capabilities the way so many charge. On the other hand, the predominance of Southeast Asia over Latin American expertise in the Nicaragua project hindered its success.

Meanwhile in Washington the Sandinistas seemed especially vulnerable due to internal dissension, economic weakness, minority dissatisfaction, and the pres-ence of *contra* groups across both northern and southern borders. American offi-cials tried to deny international loans to Managua and limit the impact of the "Contadora" group of Latin countries that sought to mediate. U.S. air, naval, and ground units began extensive exercises in Honduras and the waters off Nicaragua. Special Forces participated, as did engineer units, which built like mad, including improving the airfield at El Aguacate for the CIA program. Military aircraft flew *contra* supplies to this and other fields, as documented by a General Accounting Office report.

Headaches for Managua followed divisions among the Sandinistas them-selves. Some, even Sandinista leaders, went over to the opposition. One, Alfonso Robelo, had been among the nine-member Sandinista directorate. Another, Eden Pastora Gomez, a senior military officer, had become famous fighting Somoza un-der the name Commander Zero. Clarridge enlisted him in Acapulco in February 1982. Pastora demanded a weapons drop in Costa Rica as a token of CIA's sincerity. Clarridge returned to Washington, going straight from Dulles Airport to Langley to brief Casey. The deputy director, Adm. Bobby Inman, walked in on the conversation. He thought a weapons drop to rebel troops in a friendly country among the craziest ideas ever. But Casey approved it. The drop took place within the month. Pastora and Robelo moved to Costa Rica. In April Pastora announced formation of his opposition group ARDE (*Alianza revolucionaria democrática*). Immediately afterward Clarridge brought Pastora to Washington for a secret session with Bill Casey. The former *commandante*, spirited into the DCI's office by the private elevator that connects an underground parking facility with the director's Seventh Floor office, gave the CIA chieftain his own dog tags. Arturo Cruz, Jr., also soon aligned himself with the Pastora forces.

But as the paramilitary effort built steam, the United States lost its Argentine allies. This followed the 1982 Falklands War between Argentina and Britain, in which Reagan took the British side. That May Argentina withdrew from Central America, including Battalion 601 with the *contras*. Argentina's involvement was documented toward the end of 1982 when Hector Frances, a Battalion 601 officer in Costa Rica, gave testimony on his country's activities. In October Clarridge visited Buenos Aires one more time with Jerry Gruner, his new task force chief; Don Winters, the Tegu chief; and Honduran commander Gen. Gustavo Alavez. Argentine departure did not frazzle the CIA, which found the activities of Battalion 601 leaders obstructive. Director Casey made a trip around this time to Japan, and about a year later reports began of a mysterious Japanese presence among the Miskito rebels. Repeated allegations of Israeli assistance also surfaced. The Israelis openly sold arms to Honduras.

Hector Frances's revelations about the Argentine role stripped away much of what plausible deniability remained. In common with most large covert operations, Nicaragua was blown. As early as March 1982 major U.S. newspapers reported the operation and President Reagan's orders. Washington was shaken in early November when *Newsweek* magazine published a cover story on the Nicaraguan operation, replete with details from the *contra* camps, mention of the CIA, and speculation on the role of John Negroponte, described as the proconsul of the secret war. This flap tied up both State Department and CIA wires with cable traffic and featured State Department denials, while Negroponte and his friends wrote letters to the editor and publishers of *Newsweek* protesting the way he had been treated. The ambassador met with the Honduran president on November 4 to coordinate how each side would comment on the revelation. Even at that early date the Hondurans cautioned Negroponte that the *contras* would never amount to much. Before the end of the year the *New York Times* reported Nicaragua as Langley's biggest covert action in a decade. Journalists flocked to Central America, putting the *contras* under scrutiny unprecedented for a CIA project.

At this stage the CIA pressed for a broadened anti-Sandinista coalition. Even Clarridge acknowledged that the prevalence of Somocistas among FDN senior officials amounted to a negative. Langley's original marching orders specified the use of Nicaraguans who were both anti-Cuban and anti-Somoza. As a former National

Guardsman, Colonel Bermudez failed the test. In Miami in November 1982, CIA officers contacted a number of influential Nicaraguan exiles to discuss revamping the leadership. Exile leader Edgar Chamorro met CATF chief Gruner and his head of political operations, Joseph Fernandez, to plan a sort of congress of perhaps twenty leading Nicaraguans, in which Bermudez would merely be one voice. In early December a new FDN leadership board of eight civilians and five military men was unveiled at a Miami press conference. Chamorro became FDN public relations director, but all the exiles were primed first by CIA officers in a hotel room. It looked good to the media. The *New York Times* quoted Chamorro as saying, "We want to give democracy a chance in Nicaragua." The FDN board selected a recent exile, Adolfo Calero, as its chairman. Calero was soon known as the public face of the *contras*. Dewey Clarridge met the board a month later, going to Miami with Gruner and Fernandez in tow. The FDN publicized a twelve-point "peace initiative" actually written by Joe Fernandez.

With or without other countries, Reagan plowed resources into Casey's Nicaragua project. The initial CIA stake grew—to $21 million in fiscal 1983, then $24 million in fiscal 1984, for a total of about $80 million before Congress finally blocked funding. Director Casey made his first visit to the front in June 1982. Soon after that began the military exercises in which hundreds of American troops, especially engineers for construction, passed through Honduras. Green Berets reportedly numbered 114 by the summer of 1983. Delta Force operator Eric L. Haney, a Desert One veteran, recalls Honduras as having been like a second home for his unit in the 1980s. Costs were paid from Pentagon accounts without charge to the CIA, disguising the real price of the secret war.

Although there were few difficulties with resources, allies, or base areas, and though Managua was vulnerable, the *contras* achieved little in 1982. They succeeded only in building forces. The FDN claimed seven thousand troops in Honduras in early 1983; others credited only five thousand. There were also a couple of thousand Miskito in Honduras while Eden Pastora had another seven hundred soldiers in Costa Rica. Internal reports show the figures lower: Miskito and Pastora fighters actually counted in the statistic given out for FDN strength. The FDN put its troops into "task forces" that spent their time in camp or on forays into Nicaragua. The basic *contra* plan, to seize and hold territory inside Nicaragua, then declare a provisional government, never seemed to materialize.

Meanwhile the Honduran ally began to waver. John Negroponte repeatedly warned of this disastrous possibility, which he feared would convince Managua that the Sandinista revolution had become irreversible. In April 1983 Negroponte advocated pushing Eden Pastora hard to activate the southern front, raising the visibility of U.S. contacts with Calero, and doing more to gain the confidence of the intelligence committees of Congress, encouraging members to visit Central America. When the FDN once tried to get all its troops into the field, Negroponte suggested that the State Department's intelligence unit should draft a report specifically to be leaked—one that said the *contra* troops were all in Nicaragua, not Honduras. In May, using a CIA back channel, he warned that peace talks under the

"Contadora" initiative had adverse implications for the U.S. "special project." Negroponte's idea of U.S. goals for talks agreed with those who favored Managua's negotiated surrender.

Internal squabbling and shifting regional support were the true obstacles to *contra* progress. Pastora refused National Guard volunteers. He also refused to do much of anything else. The CIA cooked up a propaganda coup, producing a video of Pastora speaking which would be broadcast from a transmitter smuggled to a site near Managua. There the transmitter would drown out and replace Sandinista television. Task force executive assistant Linda Flohr directed the filming and sewed the ARDE flag on her own time at home. She could not even get Pastora to take off his fancy rings and Rolex watch for the taping.

The FDN had its own problems in struggles between factions favoring Nicaraguan civilians and those preferring Somocista leadership. There were delicate relations between the FDN and Miskito groups, shortchanged on supplies in favor of the *contras*. In addition the Honduran government feared both the FDN troops on its territory and Nicaraguan incursions to get at their base camps.

Among the troops, Colonel Bermudez demanded total fealty, physically intimidating those he thought not loyal enough. By the end of 1982, though he spent little time in the camps, Bermudez had become the unquestioned commander. Any remaining doubt concerned whether he would act independently. In Honduras the CIA-minted FDN board did not have the presence to exert much control. They made just one visit to the camps as a group. It would be the CIA, not FDN, that told Edgar Chamorro to move to Tegu and set up shop there. More often individuals went, but then they seemed emissaries, with Bermudez the reigning potentate. On one occasion several *contra* intelligence officers actually told FDN commissioners that Bermudez and his chief spook, Ricardo "Chino" Lau, the colonel's best friend, were plotting to kill them. The FDN directors could do nothing to investigate the charges, which Bermudez simply denied.

Allegations of human rights abuses inside Nicaragua actually reflected widespread injury as Bermudez stepped up the scale of FDN operations. Nicaragua suffered twelve disappearances in 1981, eleven in 1982, then twenty-two in February 1983 alone. Virtually all took place in provinces adjacent to Honduran camps. Some say it was common to kill captured Sandinista soldiers and militiamen. There were reports of looting and rapes, of action against coffee pickers, teachers, officials, and anyone in a vehicle. Some traced these practices to Argentine advice—holding up Argentina's "dirty war" of the 1970s as the model. Others saw *contra* terrorism resulting from the predominance of National Guardsmen accustomed to harsh methods during the civil war.

In a ploy to counter the negative human rights reports, John Negroponte decided to bring together *contra* leaders with American politicians. When a delegation from Representative Edward Boland's House Permanent Select Committee on Intelligence visited in late May 1983, Negroponte set up a meeting between the committee and Adolfo Calero. But when television journalist Peter Collins of ABC News followed the congressional people around town, any possibility of meeting clandestinely disappeared. Ambassador Negroponte then invited the HPSCI delegation and Calero to dinner at the embassy residence. Furious when he learned of the event, U.S. Ambassador Anthony Quainton in Managua cabled Negroponte on a CIA channel saying, "I HAVE MY DOUBTS ABOUT A DINNER AT THE EMBASSY RESIDENCE FOR A MAN WHO IS IN THE BUSINESS OF OVERTHROWING A NEIGHBORING GOVERNMENT." Negroponte defended the circumstances and explained his choice as the best of several unpleasant alternatives. The exchange confirms that, whatever the CIA and the administration were telling Congress about the objectives of the secret war being limited, privately no one doubted the true goal.

Given the origins of the anti-Sandinista opposition, the *contras* remained sensitive to accusations of association with the National Guard. Constantly striving to deny them, the rebels argued that only a small proportion of troops were Somocistas. They were right in that, mathematically, Guardsmen could not have made up the FDN force. The FDN troops numbered about two thousand in 1983 (publicly claiming seven thousand men) and perhaps six thousand in June 1984 (claiming as many as fifteen thousand). In the spring of 1987 *contra* leaders claimed a strength of sixteen thousand troops. Somoza's Guard had peaked at about eight thousand, of whom more than half fell into Sandinista hands before the end of the civil war. Reports were that several thousand soldiers remained in Nicaraguan prisons. A generally accepted estimate of the Guard proportion of the FDN forces is 20 percent.

These overall figures also obscure the leadership role of the Guard. Bermudez is the obvious example but only the tip of an iceberg. When reporter Christopher Dickey visited FDN camps in the spring of 1983, four of the five commanders he interviewed were not only National Guard but came from the same "Rattlesnake" battalion of Somoza forces. Column commander Suicide, also a "Rattlesnake" veteran, rose to command two thousand FDN troops while boasting to journalists of his murders and other deeds. Ricardo Lau, the spy chief, had been notorious for cruelty in Somoza's behalf while in the National Guard. Lau became an obstacle to *contra* unity when Eden Pastora cited him as an example of the worst kind of Somocista influence, refusing to join any united front in which Lau participated. Months after the FDN announced Lau's resignation, records propagandist Edgar Chamorro noted, "Lau was still the last person to talk to Bermudez at night and the first person to talk to him in the morning." Honduran authorities forced Lau to leave the country in late 1984. National Guard connections remained the Achilles' heel of the *contras*.

Of all the FDN directorate, Edgar Chamorro was in the best position to know the conditions in the field. Many directors spent time raising money for the cause, especially Adolfo Calero Portocarrero, a tower of energy who worked sixteen-hour days on trips to Europe, the United States, and Puerto Rico. Calero took the CIA and the exiles as his constituency. Some directors stayed in Miami. Chamorro set up in Tegucigalpa as the public voice of the FDN. There he wrote the releases and organized the visits of journalists to FDN camps. Soon his office alone was spending $2,000 a month to burnish the *contras'* democratic image.

One of Chamorro's projects became the drafting of a manual, *The Blue and White Book*, which discussed the meaning of social justice and democracy. This he distributed to FDN soldiers. Perhaps the political education could help counteract the brutality of the military leadership and the excesses of war. But the exhortations the troops received from FDN radio or the weekly newsletter *Commandos*, which Chamorro also ran, limited the impact of his manual.

Meanwhile FDN tried to clean up its act, disciplining a number of officers for egregious transgressions.

In the summer of 1983 a journalist asked Chamorro about FDN assassinations. Knowing the troops often mulled over murders and other atrocities, the propaganda chief admitted there had been some excesses. Human rights criticism resulted. *Contras* grumbled about Chamorro's admission, but the propaganda chief felt the FDN gained credibility from his forthrightness. The CIA took action after a Casey visit, initiating another manual for the *contras*. An agency contract officer, "John Kirkpatrick," wrote it. Kirkpatrick worked with Chamorro in Tegu several hours a day for weeks. A former Green Beret and veteran of Korea and Vietnam, Kirkpatrick drank too much and denounced FDN leaders while praising the troops. Chamorro thought him a character out of a Graham Greene novel.

The CIA manual, called *Psychological Operations in Guerrilla Warfare*, would lead to a major flap. Kirkpatrick relied on Vietnam experience and postulated approaches to insurgency. *Psychological Operations* reprinted verbatim portions of several lesson texts used at Fort Bragg in 1968 to train Green Berets. The manual did not shy from advocating deliberate terrorism. One passage spoke of hiring professional criminals. Another discussed the creation of "martyrs" for the cause, if necessary by arranging deaths of the *contras'* own fighters. Other sections dealt with selective violence, as in assassinating Sandinista officials in order to cow villagers. Later investigation disclosed that Ray Doty, Joe Fernandez, and about a dozen other DO officers had reviewed the manual, deleting what they thought offensive, but no one objected to the advice on assassinations, despite repeated DCI directives and the existing presidential ban.

Chamorro's doubts about Kirkpatrick were confirmed when, in November 1983, two thousand printed copies of *Psychological Operations* arrived at his office. The FDN propagandist caught the references to hiring criminals and to killing *contras*. Upset, he locked up the manuals and hired two boys to razor out the offending pages and glue in ones with innocuous material.

A year later the manual leaked. *Psychological Operations in Guerrilla Warfare*, with its text on "neutralization" implying assassination, stunned Americans. Congressman Edward Boland denounced it, and a storm of criticism disrupted President Reagan's reelection campaign. Reagan felt obliged to order immediate investigations by the PFIAB and the CIA inspector general. Additional investigations followed by the House intelligence committee. The Intelligence Oversight Board pretended to investigate. Again Casey's methods were called into question. Casey escaped the heat by reprimanding half a dozen officers, including chief of base Doty and political action chief Joe Fernandez. The reprimands meant nothing— Doty was promptly promoted to head CIA's International Activities Division.

In the field the *contra* war continued. From Honduran base camps the FDN mounted forays into Nicaragua with patrols of eighty troops and columns of a couple hundred. Suicide became a top commander controlling five columns. Possibly the height of activity came in early 1983 when the *contras* sent in columns of six hundred or eight hundred. The Miskitos were also active, and ARDE received new CIA aid: communications gear, supplies, and five hundred AK-47 assault rifles. Eden Pastora and Alfonso Robelo raised nearly two thousand ARDE troops before the end of the year while Miskito rebel strength peaked at about three thousand. Colonel Bermudez spent much of his time in Tegu, where the FDN had a radio station and a hospital. He planned a big push for the summer and fall, Operation Marathon. At Langley, Dewey Clarridge thought just two C-47s sufficient to re-supply the FDN columns—partisan warfare on the cheap, as it were.

Already clouds were gathering as the American public, never comfortable with the *contra* operation and distinctly disturbed by allegations of abuse, and Congress, suspicious at administration motives, expressed doubts. At his briefing of the Senate intelligence committee on the late 1981 finding, Director Casey faced questions from vice chairman Senator Daniel Patrick Moynihan, Democrat from New York. A year later, leak of an estimate predicting how long Managua could hold out brought anger that the administration *was* aiming to overthrow the Sandinistas. Congress went so far as to pass a prohibition sponsored by Democratic Representative Edward Boland of Massachusetts, part of the 1983 military budget, against use of funds to oust the Nicaraguan government. This became the first "Boland Amendment." Supposedly the CIA recognized this with a cable instructing officers to avoid any of a series of activities that could be prohibited. Director Casey went to national security adviser William P. Clark to say that he did not think an opinion from the attorney general necessary, but that the CIA would agree not to initiate operations unless ordered to do so. Clark okayed this idea. The result would be fancy footwork to evade Boland, not its observance.

At the beginning of 1983 Democratic Senator Patrick Leahy of Vermont, a member of the intelligence committee, decided to explore the facts on the ground, taking staff director Robert Simmons, a couple of others, and escorts from both CIA and the military. At the Tegu safe house from which he ran the war, Ray Doty told the party that his project focused solely on interdiction of arms traffic, but a wall map displayed *contra* maneuvers far in the interior of Nicaragua, nowhere near El Salvador. Doty denied any aim at Managua. Leahy heard at the embassy that the United States intended only negotiations, then Honduran Gen. Gustavo Alvarez told the senator the troops would be in Managua by Christmas. Leahy went on to Panama, where Dewey Clarridge, making a circuit of stations, had just visited. Leahy told the chief, former CATF boss Jerry Svat, that he wanted a briefing on the Nicaragua program. Svat replied that Clarridge had ordered him not to answer, then refused to handle any message to Casey from Leahy or Simmons. Just before the delegation had left Washington, John McMahon had pledged full CIA cooperation. Furious, Leahy threatened to call Casey on a nonsecure phone. Svat relented, and a cable went out late that night. By 6 A.M. the next morning Clarridge stood at Leahy's hotel room door. Clarridge fed the senator a line on why he'd been denied the brief—it all hinged on Panamanian dictator Manuel Noriega—but obviously this had nothing to do with arms interdiction. Clarridge's memoirs are silent about this incident.

The map Colonel Doty had exhibited in Tegu presupposed penetrations from the north and south to cut Nicaragua in half. But if the *contras* were doing anything out of Honduras, Pastora in Costa Rica remained totally passive. The agency pushed for action, Pastora repeatedly demanded supplies. The ARDE leader complained about what he received. In an odd throwback to the Bay of Pigs, the CIA dropped Pastora rice mixed with beans instead of separately. That infuriated Pastora. But he felt positively humiliated with the CIA drops of clothing. Pastora threatened to abandon the war. Clarridge had to smooth ruffled feathers. He came to San Jose, Costa Rica, and found that Pastora had left for the bush. Clarridge pursued up the San Juan River, but when Pastora found out he moved farther up-country. Clarridge finally caught up with the ARDE leader, who complained the uniforms were too big. The CIA baron shot back that they were standard size. Pastora associate Auturo Cruz, Jr., recounts what happened next:

> Pastora glared at the tall man from the CIA, as best he could from his lesser height, a full foot shorter than Maroni [Clarridge's pseudonym], and then the guerrilla commander abruptly pulled off his American-made pants to reveal his American-made undershorts—huge shorts tailored for the American body, shorts so large that they billowed down to Pastora's knees. Pastora stood in front of his men, underwear flapping at his knees.

Clarridge mollified the ARDE commander, playing Santa Claus, distributing watches and radios. Pastora agreed to resume the fight, but ARDE continued to do little. Clarridge writes of Pastora's charges that he received inferior equipment: "This was not true, but it remained a constant refrain of his throughout my association with him."

These operations were made possible by the aircraft the CIA procured through private companies. A McLean, Virginia, firm called Investair Leasing, with a fictitious corporate address at Dulles International Airport, bought five planes. Three were military O-2As, versions of a Cessna light plane, suddenly declared surplus in December 1983 and sent to Elephant Herd, a JCS "multiservice tasking" created specifically to provide weapons to the *contras* at minimal cost. Two identical planes—like the O-2As, taken from the New York Air National Guard—were simultaneously sold to El Salvador. In February 1984 the planes were armed with rocket pods by Summit Aviation at a Delaware airfield. Although there were claims that Elephant Herd provided all manner of items to the *contras*, in fact only the aircraft, a high-capacity automatic cannon, and some night-vision sights and scopes moved through this channel. In terms of volume, Israeli aid was far greater—in what would be called Operation Tipped Kettle, in 1983 Tel Aviv furnished $10 million worth of equipment captured in Lebanon from the PLO the previous year.

A La Jolla, California, company called Armairco has been linked with two light planes that crashed inside Nicaragua—one while raiding Managua in September 1983 and another O-2A shot down attacking Santa Clara a year later. Armairco is known to have bought Cessnas direct from the manufacturer. Established by a former army major, Armairco had an East Coast branch called Shenandoah Airleasing, which admitted that it "may well" do classifed mission work in Central America.

The FDN also received two old C-47 transports, provenance unknown, and at least one went to ARDE. Edgar Chamorro was derisive about these planes, telling a fellow FDN director to be sure to visit the National Air and Space Museum while in Washington, where he would see the same plane hanging from the ceiling. It is true that the C-47 had been flying for many years, but in the 1980s there were still twelve hundred of these planes in service, and it is difficult to see how resupply missions could occur without medium transports. Still, Chamorro's fears proved justified in March 1984 when an ARDE C-47 crashed in northern Costa Rica. An unidentified Caucasian died in the crash, possibly a CIA casualty.

There were confirmed CIA casualties in October 1984 when a twin-engine Cessna crashed outside the Salvadoran military airfield of Ilopango. An agency officer and three CIA contract agents were killed. Crammed with equipment, the plane had been on a night flight to intercept Sandinista communications. Other flights were made by army aviation detachments, and the code name Royal Duke was associated with similar air force flights from Honduran airfields.

An intimate relationship existed between the air operations, particularly, and U.S. military assistance to Honduras. When Gen. Paul Gorman took over Southern Command and made his first visit to Tegu in June 1983, Honduran commander Alvarez asked for help in improving eight airfields sufficiently to handle C-130-type aircraft. The fields were at San Lorenzo, Jamastran, Aguacate, Marcala, Cucuyaga, Puerto Lempira, Santa Barbara, and Copan. American forces on "maneuvers" in Honduras did the work. The Hondurans wanted the airfields to respond to possible Nicaraguan incursions, but five of the eight fields figured in the CIA campaign, with Aguacate its main base.

The *contra* air campaign did not amount to much—harrassment rather than real interdiction. Managua was raided a few times—once with key political effect in the U.S. Congress. Little significant damage occurred. At least two FDN planes were lost.

Eden Pastora sponsored an air raid on Managua on September 8, 1983. Two planes bombed the airport, one flying so low it disintegrated in the blast of its own bombs. Two ARDE airmen perished. Two U.S. senators, whom Bill Casey had encouraged to see Nicaragua for themselves, almost fell in the bombing. Democrat Gary Hart of Colorado and Republican William S. Cohen of Maine, their plane late, were in the air en route to Managua as the attack happened. Had the airliner been on time they would have been at Managua airport. The control tower and reception area, where the senators had scheduled a press conference, were extensively damaged, and dozens of people killed or injured. Cohen discovered during his visit that the Sandinistas had greatly reinforced the anti-aircraft defenses at the airport just before the attack.

The next day a T-28 aircraft ineffectually bombed the oil storage tanks at the major port of Corinto. About a dozen T-28 planes were in the Honduran air force. On October 3 an FDN supply flight was shot down by Sandinistas over northern Nicaragua. One man among that crew died, but two were taken prisoner; both had been National Guardsmen.

Nicaragua operations were indirectly responsible for other American deaths in Honduras. Army warrant officer Jeffrey Schwab died on January 11, 1984, when the helicopter he piloted toward Aguacate went off course into Nicaragua and was shot up by Sandinista soldiers. The following month, maneuvers led to the death of four Americans, with six others injured, including Green Berets. Two navy SEALs perished in a maneuver accident in December 1984. Six American and eight foreign journalists should be added to the military deaths. Casualties inside Nicaragua to 1984 totaled more than twelve thousand while *contra* losses are unknown.

Even more than Afghanistan, Nicaragua became Bill Casey's war. Where Reagan set the policy, the DCI executed it. But for Nicaragua, Casey went to Reagan, pushing him, encouraging his worst fears. Supervising Clarridge's planning, Casey overrode DO objections. In the field he oversaw arrangements of the case officers under Clarridge. The CIA director visited Tegucigalpa in the early summer of 1982 when the machinery was just moving into gear. At the height of controversy over human rights violations, in the summer of 1983, Director Casey again appeared in Honduras, and the guerrilla manual followed.

In his determined pursuit of Nicaragua covert actions, Casey ran afoul of Congress in a way unprecedented for a director of central intelligence. Having assured legislators that he would be open to the intelligence committees, Casey progressively terminated various kinds of reporting that had been routine. His disdain for oversight, no doubt reinforced by his painful confirmation, became well known at Langley. Dewey Clarridge added to Casey's concern, describing the way Senator Moynihan pushed at him when the CIA man went up to the Hill. Director Casey resolved to bring in a new broom to deal with Congress, for which he summoned Clair George, the associate deputy director for operations.

The House select committee had become especially suspicious. Still dominated by Democrats after the 1980 election, the House committee initiated the Boland Amendment in 1982 and 1983. This restriction passed into law as a secret clause of the fiscal 1983 appropriation. After one of these votes in July 1983, Reagan officials boldly answered that they had no intention of reducing aid to the rebels. Twice the House voted to terminate the *contra* program, saved only because friendly senators restored the CIA money when spending bills went to House-Senate conference committees.

By 1983, especially after the fiasco of the Leahy visit, it had become abundantly clear at Langley that the existing presidential finding needed amendment. The Senate intelligence committee told the CIA that May that the finding lacked specifics on what the project encompassed, the grounds for this action, and the objectives sought. The tension between the limited goal of arms interdiction and the much more extensive actual CIA activity invited probing. The act of drafting a new finding, with the briefings and solicitations of congressional opinion it required, might give Congress some sense of involvement. But at the same time Congress was promised a fresh finding to delimit the war more precisely, the CIA busily planned fresh escalation—mining ships in Nicaraguan harbors.

In May 1983 Washington informed Ambassador Negroponte of the quest for a new finding. On August 3 Director Casey appeared before the Senate committee to outline a draft. A week later he sent the reworked paper to national security adviser Clark and Secretary of State Shultz. For weeks the secret war managers refined the document. Clarridge showed it to Negroponte on September 12. The ambassador thought it too narrow, still focused almost exclusively on interdiction. Casey explained why—he wanted nothing that might jeopardize continued funding. Negroponte objected that a more comprehensive finding might actually attract broader support. This exchange illustrates how disjointed the war wizards had become.

The NSC discussed the orders on September 16; President Reagan approved several days later. The finding provided for U.S. support for paramilitary operations against Nicaragua. It broadened the project to include both arms and inducing "the Sandinistas and Cubans and their allies" to cease backing insurgents in the region. Nicaragua was to be robbed of the resources necessary to furnish such aid. The project was supposed to force Managua into genuine negotiations.

In the short term the CIA got what it wanted—Congress did not strengthen the Boland Amendment, though it kept spending on the Nicaragua war to the $24 million already appropriated, and warned that no more would be coming until the next fiscal year. But the fresh authority contained problems of its own. Economic warfare that impoverished Nicaragua could be seen as going much further than preventing Managua's help to revolution elsewhere. Several elements of the finding or the attached explanatory paper reveal a commitment to open-ended war. By including Cubans among the specified goals, authority had in fact been extended regardless of anything Managua might do. That negotiations were to be genuine and agreements verifiable set the stage for war despite peace talks. The Reagan administration also made itself the sole arbiter of the fulfillment of these conditions. Did the aim of promoting democracy include targeting the public support enjoyed by the Sandinista government? Text that remains excised from declassified versions of this finding leaves it unclear whether it permitted unilateral CIA operations, as were about to occur, or confined the agency to supporting others. Meanwhile the "others" had the explicit goal of overthrowing the Sandinistas, no matter what Reagan's finding might say, and the administration knew that very well.

For the longer term the September 1983 finding challenged congressional overseers of intelligence to decide they had been fooled. Already wary of a broadtracked finding, Casey attempted to assuage Congress with his explanatory paper. But, anticipating what soon happened, he warned that the $24 million budget would run out and that he expected to need another $14 million to get through the fiscal year. In explaining the finding to the Senate intelligence committee on September 20, Casey set one booby trap himself, saying: "The new finding . . . no longer expressly authorizes us to conduct paramilitary operations—but rather to provide support to Nicaraguan paramilitary resistance groups . . . we have less of a leadership role and more of a passive role."

The booby-trapped finding coupled with Casey's disastrous choice of congressional liaison produced a metastable solution. Clair George, of the DO fraternity since the Korean War, believed passionately in secrecy. George promised openness and made a show of it, inaugurating weekly lunches with the staff directors of the Senate and House committees. Robert Simmons at first thought the lunches a splendid device. But Simmons had been a direct witness to the burning of Patrick Leahy a few months earlier, and before long he saw himself being played too. Rob Simmons decided that George's idea of liaison amounted to the standard procedure of a clandestine service officer in a hostile country, with Congress the country and the CIA officer saying only what seemed politically necessary or strategically desirable. The flow of information, far from broadening, slowed to a trickle.

After two years of active warfare the *contras* could show no lasting success. A CIA timetable that envisioned "liberated zones" before the end of 1983 had gone badly awry, with the FDN failing to capture and hold towns. Casey did his best to gloss the facts, telling Congress that the Sandinistas might be overthrown in a year—skirting the edge of discourse that was legal under the Boland Amendment, a pitfall he escaped by insisting he had been misquoted. Casey's claim itself would also be discredited both by the American general commanding in Central America and by a leak that no intelligence estimates agreed with this assertion. Frustration led Casey to advocate the interdiction of Nicaragua's foreign trade by attacks on and the mining of its ports, an operation that took the secret war to a whole new level.

As Dewey Clarridge presents these events, Director Casey and he were equally concerned with the need to hit the Sandinistas harder. He quotes Casey: "Can't we get more pressure on these people?" But the resulting plan the agency's Latin baron describes was one to interdict seaborne arms shipments into El Salvador using gunboats—a measure that did not strike Nicaragua. Conversely, once Clarridge had the boats they never went after the arms trade, only attacking Nicaragua. And Clarridge muddies the water by claiming that CIA actions purporting to be against the arms traffic could force Managua to negotiate. This disingenuousness, even in retrospect, is necessary to maintain the appearance that CIA acted within the scope of the 1983 finding. Clarridge called his warships "Q-boats" after the disguised armed merchant cruisers used in both world wars. But they were not disguised at all. Others called them "Piranhas" after the predatory fish native to South America.

The Q-boats were manufactured in North Miami Beach by Cigarette Boats Racing, Inc.—two craft, thirty to forty feet long with Kevlar hulls and dual inboard motors, carrying grenade launchers and automatic cannon. The boats were large enough to carry, and lay, mines. They were capable of incredible speed—sixty-five knots. Sailors trained to use them on Roatan Island, off the northern Honduran coast. Bill Shepherd, a navy SEAL assigned to the DO, designed the configuration and monitored conversion. After all the work, there are *no* reports of Q-boats attacking vessels that were smuggling arms across the Gulf of Fonseca that separates Nicaragua from El Salvador. The U.S. Southern Command ran an operation to infiltrate the traffic, using Boston whalers on the Gulf of Fonseca led by a Delta Force operator. Southern Command discovered that much of the smuggling actually utilized boats belonging to Salvadorans. Clarridge records a *contra* commando raid on one of the coastal staging areas used for the traffic.

A second ploy was an air attack on a radio post the Nicaraguans used to intercept Salvadoran military messages to help the guerrillas and, some contend, relay their own traffic. *Contra* air commander Juan Gomez carried out the attack with a couple of planes flying out of the Salvadoran airbase at Ilopango.

Instead Langley's project quickly morphed away from interdiction—even before the September finding—into an effort to make the Nicaraguan economy scream. Secretary of State George Shultz recounts what happened. Shultz saw the NSC staff, not Casey, as trying to control Nicaragua policy, and believed if the United States lost the secret war it would be due to them. In late May 1983 he went to President Reagan, who agreed that Shultz should have the leading role on Central America. Then on May 28 Shultz received a cable informing him that the Crisis Pre-Planning Group had decided to mine a river on Nicaragua's eastern coast and have divers place limpet mines on ships in port. Shultz was dumbfounded.

Secret warriors' frustration had its mirror at the highest levels. Talk at the 208 Committee and the National Security Planning Group focused on how to break out of the cycle of military failure. On May 31 the NSPG reviewed the mine project. Shultz argued against the plan and insisted the CPPG had no decision authority, showing the directive that had created it. The CIA came in with a poor presentation, and Reagan rejected the project.

Like much that happened on Reagan's watch, the decision did not stick. Policy activists always thought they could go around the bureaucracy—and frequently succeeded. What Fred Iklé and Elie Krakowski had done on Afghanistan, Casey and Clarridge now did on Nicaragua. Early in July Casey went to Central America. With him he took Clarridge; DDCI John McMahon; the national intelligence officer for Latin America, John Horton; and another of the barons, International Activities Division chief Robert Magee. McMahon, representative of career professionals at CIA, wary about covert operations from Church Committee days, had learned to work in tandem with Congress, which opposed extravagant initiatives on Nicaragua. Bringing McMahon created an appearance of unity. Bob Magee returned to recruit Cuban exiles and other Latin Americans, whom the CIA would call "Unilaterally Controlled Latino Assets," or UCLAS. Soon afterward both *contras* and UCLAS began learning how to use limpet mines at Roatan island.

Casey then took a page from the Mongoose playbook—the CIA outfitted a mother ship. In the summer of 1983 Langley leased a vessel built to sustain offshore oil-rigs. The ship had a long, flat cargo deck sufficient for several helicopters. A pair of Q-boats could be launched or shipped by hydraulic ramps the agency installed. Given the time required for construction and the moment the mother ship went into action, acquisition of the ship and design and installation of its equipment had to have begun around the time of the NSPG meeting where Reagan *rejected* the CIA plan.

Edgar Chamorro records that Dewey Clarridge came to Honduras in July and told the *contra* high command that the CIA had decided to cut off Nicaragua's oil supplies—clearly unrelated to interdicting arms to El Salvador—and spoke of a plan "to sink ships" bearing oil for Nicaragua. The baron detailed several alternatives. Clarridge himself recounts going to the Restricted Interagency Group to advocate that the United States begin attacking selected economic targets. According to Clarridge, there were no objections, including from Secretary Shultz's representative, the RIG chairman. "Given the limited activity anticipated," Clarridge writes, "no one thought the decision needed ratification at an NSPG meeting." To recap, the CIA division chief, aware that the president had recently rejected the mining plan, here proposed a major escalation to directly attack the Nicaraguan economy and thought no approval from higher authority necessary. Moreover the CIA's Directorate of Intelligence also had no opportunity to comment on the potential of this plan, which angered Robert Gates as well.

Clarridge was correct in the sense that bringing Reagan on board would merely take time. At a briefing during the summer the president himself asked what could be done to hamper Nicaragua's oil. Suddenly the door opened wide. Bill Casey stood ready to recommend that the CIA attack Nicaraguan ports and ships carrying oil and other commodities. Not even a Shultz resignation threat could stop the project.

In the discussions at the White House, Bill Casey, "Cap" Weinberger, and George Shultz all recognized that Managua depended on imports, especially Soviet weapons and foreign oil. American military exercises in Central America had already featured naval task forces off the Nicaraguan coast; now NSPG members, harking back to Kennedy in the Cuban Missile Crisis, began talking of a blockade. That involved open use of force, however—an act of war. An administration having so much trouble just getting CIA funds approved in Congress had no chance of obtaining a declaration of war. Over at least two NSPG meetings, Robert

McFarlane recalls, they settled on mining Nicaraguan harbors rather than involving U.S. forces.

McFarlane says that Casey suggested the mining. Some preparatory work took place between the meetings, but the analysis, drawn narrowly, did not rise to the level of a real risk-cost study. The obvious rejoinder to mining—what would happen if mines sank a Russian ship?—surfaced at NSPG. The secret-war wizards resolved to produce mines not capable of sinking large ships. Of course this robbed the mining of its military rationale, and it affected legality as well, since international law permits only "effective" blockade. Ronald Reagan approved anyway. McFarlane concedes that the scheme was "not one of the happiest episodes" of Reagan's administration.

In the fall of 1983 Casey implemented the plan. The CIA itself carried out the attacks and mining of the ports. The mother ship acted as command post and carried raiding parties to distant targets. It also had armed helicopters to support raids. Commando parties consisted mostly of Latins and CIA contract agents for underwater demolition and specialized tasks. Contract employees piloted the helicopters while agency officers had complete command. On October 10, 1983, the mother ship conducted its first attack on the Nicaraguan Pacific Coast port of Corinto.

The assault reinforced a campaign begun earlier. There had already been two strikes at Puerto Sandino, a receiving point for oil deliveries, and the raid on a town on the Gulf of Fonseca, evidently a suspected transshipment point for arms to El Salvador. This action relied upon FDN commandos because it involved combat on the ground inside Nicaragua. The attempt had failed.

Then the CIA staged the attack on Corinto. The raid used the two speedboats, which crept in behind a Korean tanker and peeled off to fire at the shore. Eight storage tanks containing 3.4 million gallons of oil were set aflame. A freighter loaded with cooking oil suffered slight damage. The Exxon Corporation ordered its tankers to avoid Nicaraguan waters. On October 21 the campaign moved to the Atlantic coast after the mother ship transited the Panama Canal.

The CIA then raided Puerto Cabezas, known to an earlier generation of spooks as the operational base for the Bay of Pigs. With this CIA raid the secret war had come full circle for the people of one Nicaraguan village.

In late October the Sandinistas countered, declaring an offshore security zone twenty-five miles deep. Foreign aircraft and ships were to get permission to enter two weeks in advance. While the U.S. Navy observed territorial waters in conducting De Soto patrols, air force SR-71s ostentatiously broke the sound barrier over Nicaragua, hitting towns with unnerving sonic booms. In the face of growing shortages, the Sandinistas increased gasoline rationing. At Corinto 25,000 residents were temporarily forced from their homes by oil fires.

The CIA designed simple but effective mines whose prototype had been a sewer pipe stuffed with explosives, up to three hundred pounds of C-4 plastic. Tests took place at the Naval Surface Weapons Center, and about six hundred mines were fabricated and assembled in Honduras. The agency called them firecracker mines, but C-4 is powerful, and hundreds of pounds could do real damage.

Dewey Clarridge's account of the mine campaign is highly suspect. The Latin baron puts the timing toward the end of January 1984, telling a story of how for once he arrived home with time to reflect. Over a cigar and a tumbler of gin, Clarridge achieved sudden clarity:

> . . . it hit me. Sea mines were the solution. We should mine the harbors of Nicaragua, Corinto and the oil facility at Puerto Sandino in particular. The export season was coming up, and if we could block their shipping for even a short period, it would be enough of an economic hardship to bring them around.

The next morning Clarridge, alert to the political dangers of this course—he says—sent an officer to the library to look up the international law on mining. Clarridge concluded that nothing barred his proposed course of action.

Much of this rendition is questionable. First off, the mines *already existed*. The CIA and the navy needed time to manufacture and test the mines, and they were certainly created for a concrete purpose, not on the off-chance that someday someone would think up a use for them. Then there is the timing. Mines had been exploding under ships off the Nicaraguan coast since January 3. And the last of the NSPG meetings that considered mining before the fact had happened in December. The baron's private skull session most likely resulted from the NSPG meeting of January 6, where the group had agreed to try to force a decision against Nicaragua as soon as possible. On January 12 Casey informed Congress that the CIA proposed to empty its *contra* funding accounts immediately. The likely truth is that Clarridge merely resolved to escalate a mining campaign already in progress.

Also objectionable is the baron's reading of the international law on sea mines, the Hague Convention of October 18, 1907, titled "Convention Relative to the Laying of Automatic Submarine Contact Mines." The United States and Nicaragua were both parties to the treaty, which makes it illegal to mine the coast or ports of an enemy *even during times of war* for the sole purpose of intercepting commercial shipping, or to lay unanchored contact mines (unless configured to become inert at most an hour after being set). The treaty requires that the perpetrator act to preserve peaceful shipping and notify ship owners of danger zones. According to Clarridge, the convention applies only to free-floating mines. Few lawyers would agree, certainly not the International Court of Justice, which soon had to pronounce on the matter.

The mining aimed at a final coup de grace for the Nicaraguan port network. On January 3, 1984, Managua radio denounced the mines for the first time. Edgar Chamorro recalls being awakened by a CIA officer at two in the morning a couple of nights later. John Mallett, deputy chief of station in Tegu, handed Chamorro a press release the CIA had prepared in which the *contras* claimed responsibility for the mining. Several days afterward the FDN declared all Nicaraguan ports to be a "danger zone," no doubt to satisfy the Hague Convention.

A Japanese flag ship was the victim outside Corinto on January 3 and had to be towed back to port. This became the first of a dozen vessels of six nations damaged in the mining. On January 13 a Nicaraguan patrol boat struck another mine. There were also six raids on the port of Potosí on the Gulf of Fonseca, in at least one of which a CIA contract agent piloted an armed Hughes 500 chopper in combat. Rudy Enders, CIA paramilitary chief, directly supervised the operations. Listening to the radio chatter of one of these raids at the operations center on March 30, as Enders told Langley one of his Q-boats had stalled, Clarridge realized from the background noise that Enders actually sat in the helicopter. Dismayed, the baron could do little but curse. Puerto Sandino suffered attacks by speedboats supported by three helicopters. Clarridge describes the mining there on February 7 as the opening act of the mine campaign. On March 7 the CIA helicopters intervened again when the Q-boats were nearly trapped at San Juan del Sur. About seventy mines were laid during the campaign.

In view of the Boland Amendment, the CIA trod on thin ice indeed. Throughout the years of the burgeoning project Congress had become increasingly uncomfortable. Edgar Chamorro recounts, significantly, that the first CIA demands that the *contras* form a united front came during congressional debate over the Boland Amendment. Arizona Republican Senator Barry Goldwater, chairman of the intelligence committee since 1981, had been sympathetic to Reagan administration aims, but his relations with Langley soured somewhat in the controversy over the Casey appointment. Yet Goldwater, despite qualms, had been key to restoring CIA secret-war money, and the agency could ill afford to lose his support. The mining campaign destroyed it.

When the port campaign began, the CIA became curiously circumspect about its information to Congress. Bill Casey personally conducted the important briefings, so there is no doubt he aimed to do what he did. Perhaps Casey had merely been unintelligible—he was notorious all over town for his mumbling. The standard joke at Langley was that the director had no need for a scrambler phone since his speech came out already scrambled. Clair George complained to journalists that briefing upon briefing of Congress made no difference. Clarridge insists the agency made no effort to keep the mining secret, that CIA informed the oversight committees "as we were supposed to." He goes on: "At least the [House committee] had the decency to own up to the fact that they had been briefed, which is more than I can say for the Senate." The truth lies elsewhere.

First, the CIA used the *contras* both as cover for the mining and to mislead Congress. Early in its preparations, Langley reported that *contras* were training to use mines, then left overseers to assume the mining was FDN's when it would actually be a unilateral CIA project. The public claims about mining—made only by the *contras* and on CIA orders—reinforced that. To evade the budget cap, the mother ship was apparently funded directly out of the DCI's contingency account. Its presence at the big Corinto raid would not be disclosed for five months while combat action by CIA contract officers in January and March 1984 also went unacknowledged for months. It is not clear that Rudy Enders's direct participation was ever admitted.

Because self-serving statements were made—both by Casey in a CIA employee newsletter and by Robert McFarlane in a speech at the Naval Academy—

confusion surrounds the issue of the adequacy of CIA notification. A careful review is necessary. In January 1984 the Senate committee sought information, its interest piqued by CIA's intention to exhaust its Nicaragua budget. Senator Goldwater asked Rob Simmons to arrange a briefing for early February. Clair George, far from complying, tried and failed to get a postponement, whereupon Casey personally called Goldwater and got the date pushed back to March 8. Meanwhile Casey testified before the House committee on January 31 but not specifically on mining. The agency also arranged private briefings for Patrick Leahy and Rhode Island Democrat Claiborne Pell where mining was a topic. There is no evidence that officials went beyond their *contra* cover story.

By March the harbor mining had become controversial. Yet before the Senate overseers at the previously arranged March 8 session—and again five days later—Casey focused on a new CIA budget request for an extra $21 million, again not the mining, which the CIA referred to in a single sentence in a presentation of more than two hours, twenty-seven words in eighty-four pages of text. That reference stated merely that mines had been placed in Nicaraguan harbors by U.S.-backed groups—the CIA cover story recycled to its congressional overseers.

The agency tried to bypass Goldwater altogether and get the money direct from the CIA subunit of the Appropriations Committee, which had parallel responsibility. Headed by Alaska Republican Ted Stevens, a friend to Langley, the CIA subcommittee would have agreed except for vice chairman William Proxmire, the Wisconsin Democrat, who insisted on enforcing the Senate rule requiring the prior approval of the committee with substantive jurisdiction. When the Goldwater committee learned of the maneuver, all hell broke loose.

As for the House being "told" of the CIA mining, that happened on March 27 at a HPSCI hearing where Casey tried the same tack. Two committee members pressed him repeatedly on who was directing the mining until Casey admitted, "We are." Even today it is still not known whether the CIA director went beyond this image of a *contra* operation "directed" by CIA to disclose that the mining was a unilateral CIA effort.

Then Rob Simmons saw a March 30 Casey letter to Senator Pell that supplied additional detail on questions at his private briefing. The letter contained the phrase "Unilaterally Controlled Latino Assets." Before joining the Senate staff Simmons had worked in the DO for a decade. He knew the implication instantly. He understood plastic explosives too and figured "firecrackers" did not do justice to the power of the CIA mines. Simmons went to House staff chief Thomas Latimer and asked to see records of the CIA's briefings there, where he immediately found Casey's admission of a few days earlier. Simmons put the pieces together.

On April 2 Casey appeared combative before the Senate intelligence committee. Four days later Goldwater rose on the Senate floor to deliver a speech on the mining, mistakenly referring to classified information. Simmons had to stop him in mid-sentence. Later that afternoon the staff chief entered Goldwater's office to find the chairman in darkness, the shades drawn, pondering his blunder.

Simmons related his findings: "The CIA was directly involved in the mining. Casey withheld the information from us. The President personally gave the go-ahead to start the mining in the fall of 1983. Casey and McMahon admitted it. They claim they told us." The staffer described the limited briefings, adding that the context had been *contra* activity, not CIA operations. In his 1988 memoir Goldwater confirms that he too understood Casey to be talking about *contras*, not CIA. (Circumspection applied even within the administration—Secretary of State George Shultz asserts that he was also given the impression the *contras* were doing the mining.) Simmons felt the senator had been cut out because Casey feared he would try to talk Reagan out of the mining. Goldwater had pulled Casey's chestnuts out of the fire many times. He was devastated and bitter. On April 9 he fired off a letter to Casey frankly declaring, "I am pissed off!" When that leaked, Goldwater followed with a public statement that the "requirement of the law was not followed in this case. . . . I told Mr. Casey that this was no way to run a railroad."

Casey came to Capitol Hill the next day to denounce the SSCI complaints. Goldwater had left for a trip to the Far East, and now Langley went to full-court press. A piece in the CIA's internal newsletter asserted positively that the agency had fully informed Congress of its actions. Quietly, according to SSCI vice chairman Senator Daniel Patrick Moynihan of New York, spooks went to the *New York Times* to insinuate that Goldwater simply did not remember, that perhaps he was too old. Simmons is quoted as observing that these actions "can only be described as a domestic disinformation campaign against the U.S. Congress." Robert McFarlane capped the effort in his speech at Annapolis where he told the assembled midshipmen that every important detail of the mining had been shared fully.

The extravagant claims quickly disintegrated after vice chairman Moynihan resigned in protest. A slew of leaks revealed many particulars of the CIA's limited briefings. Goldwater returned and convinced Moynihan to withdraw his resignation, and Director Casey appeared contrite before the committee on April 26, promising better. Both Casey and McFarlane apologized. An SSCI annual report supplied chapter and verse on the deception. In the later Iran-Contra hearings, McFarlane testified under oath that the intelligence committees were not, in fact, informed of the mining as required by law.

In June 1984, prodded by the White House, CIA negotiated with Congress on the definition of reporting requirements. Langley agreed to give prior notice of covert actions that went beyond a finding, of anything requiring NSC or presidential approval, and on subjects in which the committees expressed interest. These so-called Casey Accords, which the director had not wanted to sign in the first place, had to be reaffirmed a year later.

To this day Dewey Clarridge remains defiant. He claims eleven separate briefings took place, implying that CIA disclosures were more than adequate. But four of those events were parts of the original deception, two concerned the budget end run, and three were Casey's after-the-fact explanations, leaving only the private contacts with Leahy and Pell. Clarridge wonders why those senators did not immediately tell their colleagues—a fair question—but he fails to discuss what promises of secrecy the CIA extracted from them.

Clarridge also terms the mining "just another operation consistent with a Presidential Finding," arguing that giving it special notice would have been "absurd" and claiming the distinction between a *contra* mining and a unilateral CIA action was "specious." The last point brings back the question of whether the September 1983 finding provided for CIA attacks. Director Casey himself had told the intelligence committee at the time that the authority *no longer permitted the CIA to engage in paramilitary operations.* The currently available declassified version of the finding contains nothing that disputes this. In sum, Clarridge's position is that this direct CIA action, which had both U.S. and international legal implications, required no special mention to overseers (and no approval from higher authority for American participation), and the question of whether it had been legal at all amounted to a side issue.

The CIA mining constituted a flagrant violation of international law. Not only did it obstruct freedom of the seas, the CIA specifically aimed at merchant shipping and issued no danger notices to mariners until mines had begun exploding; even then it released only the vague claims put out by the *contras*. Mining is a clearly defined act of war under the 1856 Treaty of Paris and the Hague Conventions of 1899 and 1907. This in turn raised questions regarding the CIA's authority under the War Powers Act. All this came to a head outside Corinto on March 20 when the Soviet tanker *Lugansk* hit a mine, wounding five sailors. In the scramble to contain this flap, CIA's John Mallett now told FDN leader Chamorro to deny that *contra* mines could have caused the damage. Giving that statement substance necessarily forced an end to the mining.

A year later Director Casey tried to assuage Senator Goldwater. When a professional group awarded the senator an achievement medal named for the eminent technologist William O. Baker, the CIA director went out of his way to give the speech honoring Goldwater. The senator's feelings can be imagined.

Dewey Clarridge asserts that one more month of mining would have driven Managua to the negotiating table. The claim is eerily reminiscent of U.S. officials talking about bombing North Vietnam, or prescient of Bush administration claims about victory in Iraq. That a Soviet vessel would be mined had been perfectly predictable. Blaming Congress or the press is what is specious—international furor plus danger of confrontation with Russia, not Barry Goldwater, are what made the mining unsustainable.

Domestic criticism gained a fierce intensity. Congress overwhelmingly passed a resolution condemning the U.S. action. Nicaragua brought suit against the United States in the International Court of Justice (ICJ). The Reagan administration suddenly felt compelled to reverse long-standing U.S. policy recognizing ICJ jurisdiction, with further adverse effects on world opinion. Among countries lodging protests, in addition to the Soviet Union, were allies Britain and France. The French debated sending a minesweeper to help Nicaragua clear its waters.

The mining caused Managua real damage. Toward the end of June, Nicaraguan Fisheries Minister Alfredo Alaníz stated that five fishermen had been killed, thirty injured, and thirteen fishing boats lost. With trade volume reduced, Nicaragua estimated it had lost $4.3 million in export income. Nicaragua's fishermen took the greatest risks as they swept the mines. At Corinto by May, damage was estimated at $9 million. More than thirty mines had been detonated, with a pair of improvised minesweepers sunk. At the United Nations only a veto by U.S. Ambassador Vernon Walters prevented passage of a Security Council condemnation of the United States.

At The Hague, Nicaragua filed suit with the International Court of Justice on April 9, 1984, charging U.S. violations of international law with the *contra* program in general and the harbor mining in particular. Although the United States renounced the Court's jurisdiction, it nevertheless submitted material condemning Nicaragua, such as reports from the propagandists of the Office of Public Diplomacy on Latin America and the Caribbean, an NSC-CIA political action unit housed within the State Department. The ICJ accepted these materials into evidence, but the American offerings did not overcome the testimony of witnesses like *contra* leader Edgar Chamorro and former CIA analyst David MacMichael, the evidence of the mining, or the *contra* manual *Psychological Operations in Guerrilla Warfare*. The ICJ found in favor of Nicaragua. The court determined that the United States had no right to seek the overthrow of the Sandinista government, no right to attack Nicaragua in the name of the self-defense of El Salvador, and no right to mine or attack ports. Only the American, British, and Japanese justices dissented from portions of the 11 to 3 decision rendered on June 27, 1986.

The Reagan administration dismissed the ICJ decision and vetoed a UN resolution designed to enforce the Court's findings. This blow underlined how little the U.S. action had to do with supporting democracy. The huge consequences compared with the limited risk that CIA planners envisioned in adopting the mining project shows how delusional the concept had been. Secretary of State George Shultz records quite straightforwardly, "The mining episode was a political disaster for the administration." Amazingly, Dewey Clarridge does not see that.

Meanwhile other aspects of the CIA project also encountered difficulties. The Miskito were essentially knocked out of the war. Brooklyn Rivera's faction of Indians reached an accommodation with Managua. Stedman Fagoth Mueller lost control over Misura, which stopped receiving supplies, Fagoth himself being expelled from Honduras. Then Colonel Bermudez's air force was set back when one of its two C-47 transports went down on a flight out of El Aguacate. All that was left was a C-54 that could not fly for lack of spare parts, and one last C-47 that Chamorro nicknamed the "rusty pelican." Honduras itself took a dimmer view of the *contras*, placing Washington under increasing pressure to sweeten the aid pot to Tegucigalpa so as to preserve friendliness toward the resistance.

Insofar as negotiations—which Clarridge professes were the aim—are concerned, the Contadora nations had scheduled talks for Manzanillo. A White House meeting on June 18, 1984, supposed to set out the U.S. negotiating position, produced NSC-driven terms that, in the opinion of the secretary of state, were intended to force the collapse of the talks at the very beginning.

After that, ARDE disintegrated. Eden Pastora and Alfonso Robelo had the one anti-Sandinista group with revolutionary credentials comparable to the Sandinistas. The ARDE facilities in Costa Rica included a radio station, a factory for making uniforms, several warehouses, and a fleet of about 150 vehicles. But Costa Rica guarded its neutrality in the Nicaraguan war and made some efforts to enforce it, arresting almost 100 ARDE members in late 1983 and seizing a shipment of refugee aid from Miami when gems turned up among the clothing. Seventeen Cuban Americans, thought to be en route to join Pastora, were ordered out of the country instead. Reports persisted of Pastora's group becoming involved in running cocaine for the Colombian cartels. When senior Pastora associates were implicated in a concrete drug-running scheme in October 1984, the CIA finally severed its relations with Pastora and informed Congress of allegations of ARDE connections with drug traffickers.

Still, ARDE had about three thousand troops. In early 1984 Pastora invaded Nicaragua, capturing the small town of San Juan del Norte. The Sandinistas redeployed and ejected Pastora. On May 30 he had a brush with death—in the form of a bomb built into a tape recorder at a news conference held at La Penca, in the bush. Both the FDN and the Sandinistas had motive for such an assassination attempt. By the time Pastora recovered, ARDE had lost steam. Then Pastora again fell victim, this time to injuries suffered in a helicopter crash.

Langley could cut off aid to ARDE, but it could not make the FDN effective. And its resources were swiftly drying up. The supplementary appropriation for Nicaragua fell on the rocks of the mining fiasco. The 1985 CIA budget for the *contras*—despite all Dewey Clarridge's venom and Goldwater's embarrassment—came out of committee in late May with a favorable recommendation, though predictably with more conditions. But that October, in the wake of the revelation of the nasty *contra* manual, Congress voted to halt all aid not specifically appropriated, plus any across-the-board assistance for at least six months.

The secret-war managers had anticipated these developments. As early as December 1983 an interagency working group recognized a strong probability the administration would be unable to get all the money it wanted, and the congressional spending limit imposed at that time confirmed the impression. The $21 million supplemental appropriation had been the first gambit to evade that restriction. A second, in February 1984, was National Security Adviser McFarlane's approach to the Israelis to see if they would take up the *contra* operation. Tel Aviv refused, albeit adding to its Operation Tipped Kettle stock of supplies for the rebels, which at least relieved the CIA of expenses it would otherwise have incurred.

At the height of the mining controversy, on March 27, 1984, Director Casey handed McFarlane a memo expecting failure to obtain the money, adding, "I am in full agreement that you should explore funding alternatives with the Israelis and perhaps others," and warning that CIA's cash would run out in mid-May. Casey sent Clarridge to South Africa, leaving immediately after the disastrous Senate hearing on April 10, to solicit aid there, but DDCI McMahon canceled the approach amid the controversy. Instead the South Africans were asked to help with aircraft, and Pretoria eventually leased some planes to Southern Air Transport, the CIA proprietary. In May came a first breakthrough—McFarlane met with Prince Bandar, the ambassador from Saudi Arabia. Already enmeshed with the CIA in Afghanistan, the Saudis agreed to contribute $1 million a month to the *contras*. The first of eight deposits was made to the Miami branch of a Cayman Islands bank in July. The money, in the name of Esther Morales, wife of a lawyer friend of Adolfo Calero, went to an FDN account.

In June came a crucial set of discussions within Reagan's inner sanctum. The group that met at the State Department on June 20 included both Casey and Clarridge, along with the other NSC principals and key players. Secretary Shultz listened in wonder as UN ambassador Jeane Kirkpatrick and others spoke of the continued possibility of securing CIA supplemental money and blaming Congress for losing Central America if the appropriation fell through. Shultz warned of the need for an option other than blame or alternate funding.

A few days later a similar scene played out in the White House Situation Room. The action had moved to the National Security Planning Group. Shultz spoke of the Manzanillo talks, and Casey construed the 1983 finding as *encouraging* "third country participation and support of this entire effort." Ambassador Kirkpatrick insisted the United States find the money for the *contras* so as not to be seen as abandoning them. Shultz cited presidential aide James Baker as saying that seeking money from third countries would be an impeachable offense. The secretary wanted an opinion from the attorney general, but others talked right past him. Casey agreed to a legal opinion, but one that made it clear the United States could seek the money. President Reagan observed that negotiations were desirable, but they should expect no concessions from Managua, and that *contra* money "is what will keep the pressure on Nicaragua." Vice President George H. W. Bush wondered how anyone could object to the United States looking for cash to support the rebels, but Bob McFarlane wound up by proposing that no one do anything about third-party support until the administration had the legal opinion and other information it needed. President Reagan had the last word: "If such a story gets out, we'll all be hanging by our thumbs in front of the White House until we find out who did it."

Following the June 25 NSPG, McFarlane's staff wrote a presidential directive that effectively shut down the diplomatic track. McFarlane, who, contrary to his own proposal at the meeting, had *already* solicited third-country cash from Saudi Arabia, had laid the basis for what became the Iran-Contra affair. The congressional imbroglio and international repercussions from the mining help explain

Ronald Reagan's motives, both in supporting the *contras* rhetorically and giving the coordination mission to his NSC staff. The sheer bravado of proceeding with a predetermined course regardless of the situation was breathtaking. The attitude would later be reprised in the deliberations of George W. Bush's administration in moving into the Iraq War in 2002–2003.

Meanwhile the fracas over the presidential finding led Reagan to revise procedures for covert action, finally formalized in a January 1985 national security decision. This order provided that all covert actions be authorized by written findings, that actions be reviewed periodically, and that the CIA be responsible for operational control of any covert action unless the president directed otherwise. As will be seen, these strictures were honored in the breach.

In the aftermath of the mining, Bob Gates sent Director Casey a penetrating commentary on agency performance. He told the CIA director that keeping Congress content in its knowledge of covert actions remained critical. Gates felt the task belonged to the deputy director for operations (DDO). Over several years John Stein and his associate director, Ed Juchniewicz, had been kept in the dark about some of Langley's activities, most prominently in Central America. Gates had previously complained to Stein on both Nicaraguan and Salvadoran issues only to find the DDO knew as little as he did. Casey subsequently shook up top brass at the CIA. Clair George, erstwhile congressional liaison, responsible for the lackluster CIA briefings on the mining, was promoted to DDO. If Gates thought that George in command of the clandestine service would fulfill the role he had delineated to the DCI, he was mistaken. And Gates's own information did not improve appreciably either—George and he were notably hostile.

Dewey Clarridge stepped up to become the DO's European baron. His replacement as Latin American Division chief, Al Wedemeyer, had a lot to handle with CIA funds now cut off. The new CATF chief, Alan D. Fiers, an import from the agency's Middle East clan, hardly knew what he had put in for. John Stein became inspector general. Bill Casey thought he was giving Stein a sinecure, but it did not turn out that way. For each of them the Nicaragua project would bite back.

Others tried hard to stay away. Offered the chance to take charge of the CATF's biggest branch, Tom Gilligan, who thought Reagan had bullied Congress into supporting the project and Congress had set rules designed to make it fail, opted instead for a zero-prestige slot as an agency recruiter in New England.

Joe Fernandez, the forty-seven-year-old task force political action chief, despite his reprimand for the *contra* psychological warfare manual, got the call to Costa Rica as station chief in San Jose. Fernandez was a stickler for detail. On the political action beat he had made sure even to wear clothes that might impress Edgar Chamorro. Born in New York but raised in Miami, very Catholic, Fernandez had seven children. Gilligan ran into him in a church parking lot one Sunday, shortly after walking away from assignment to the task force. Gilligan wondered why Fernandez would jump into the quagmire, especially since Joe had already served his time. Gilligan recalls: "Because, he said, that was where the action was and where he could have the most impact."

For Congress the *contra* manual became the last straw. It voted against a fresh demand for money, which the administration craftily contrived to have attached to a summer jobs bill, and then reenacted the Boland Amendment in stricter form, prohibiting Pentagon or intelligence community assistance to the *contras* as an amendment to the 1985 defense budget bill. In Honduras the CIA supply lines began to dry up. By June 1984 barely $1 million remained in CIA project accounts. Now Iran-Contra came to flower.

The *contras* shifted to a precarious hand-to-mouth existence. Columns remained in the base camps for months at a time. But President Reagan did not wish to give up this secret war. Reagan's effort to pursue the war led to a covert operation conducted from inside the White House, by the staff of the National Security Council. The result would be a bizarre tale of ideological fervor, greed, betrayal, and a controversy that eroded the power of Ronald Reagan.

22

Project Democracy

RONALD REAGAN'S CHOICE of an ambassador to the United Nations had been the most prominent woman among his campaign foreign policy advisers. Jeane J. Kirkpatrick came to Reagan's attention as a result of her article in the magazine *Commentary* in November 1979. In "Dictatorships and Double Standards," Kirkpatrick argued that there was a difference between dictators of the left and the right. She used the supposed distinction to hit at Carter administration policies, for example the president's refusal to support Nicaraguan dictator Anastasio Somoza. According to Kirkpatrick's reading of history, right-wing dictators are more respecting of human rights, do not create refugees, merely tolerate (rather than cause) social inequities, are more amenable to liberalization, and, of course, are more friendly to the United States. Revolutions, in this view, stem entirely from Soviet expansionism, not from historical forces.

Kirkpatrick's article became far more influential in the Reagan years than warranted by the quality of its reasoning or its presentation of facts (for example, she presented the mullahs' Iran as a Soviet client state). It provided a basis on which to rationalize support for right-wing dictatorships, whether democratic or Communist. The Reagan administration's rhetoric about global democracy, and its specific assertions that the Nicaraguan *contras* had a democratic character, owed a great deal to Kirkpatrick's logic, enabling officials to finesse facts with unsubstantiated claims of a normative type. Nicaragua held an election in 1984 but the Sandinistas won, so, according to Reagan acolytes, no democracy existed there. The *contra* leadership, composed entirely of persons who had never participated in an election, Reaganites portrayed as democratic.

By then Jeane Kirkpatrick had left the administration. Just to ensure the doctrine's author kept her hand in, Reagan appointed Kirkpatrick to the PFIAB after his 1985 purge. Ambassador Kirkpatrick had once visited Tegucigalpa, explicitly linking her theory to the Central American secret war. The CIA project together with the other Reagan-era covert operations were uniformly connected to the support for democratic values, even while detailed justifications for various actions spoke of Russia or Cuba. This remained true in the wake of the Nicaraguan harbor minings.

The *contras* tried to show optimism. Field commanders asserted that the FDN had never been in a better position. Political director Adolfo Calero, after defeat of the $14 million paramilitary aid request, declared, "I am confident we will pull through this crisis caused by the Congress." In fact there *had* been a disaster, and it had nothing to do with Congress. Langley cashed in all its chips for a high-risk operation. The disaffection of the Miskito and elimination of Eden Pastora removed FDN political rivals but reduced the threat to Managua. With no *contras* working from Costa Rica, the Nicaraguan military could focus on the Honduran border. As the Sandinistas reinforced the north, FDN columns were out of supplies from the CIA pipeline.

Calero's situation could hardly have looked more bleak. What reason had he for optimism?

Calero had the declarations of U.S. officials, from the CIA and the National Security Council staff, who met with him in Honduras in April at the height of the mining controversy. One was Dewey Clarridge. He introduced Marine Lt. Col. Oliver North of the NSC. North did the talking. The United States would not abandon the *contras*. He exuded confidence.

Colonel North's remarks were based on little more than a wish at the time, but the wish was Ronald Reagan's, and a president's desires carry great weight. North had been called in to see his boss, national security adviser Robert C. McFarlane, who told him and Donald R. Fortier, the deputy, to do whatever was necessary to ensure passage of the next *contra* appropriation. Fortier convened a high-level group to review the options. North held the *contras'* hands, keeping up faith and spirits.

Adolfo Calero threw himself into fund-raising. Cuban exiles were a major target. Restaurants and community centers in Miami and San Juan became locales for Calero and others to whip up sentiment and solicit checks. But the rebels could not raise enough. Calero estimated FDN needed $1 million a month to sustain itself, $1.5 million to expand. Rebel spokesmen, with Calero's approval, promised that within forty days the *contras* would establish an unbroken front from the Honduran border to Costa Rica. But that kind of money stayed beyond reach.

In Washington the United Nicaraguan Opposition (UNO), the umbrella group now masking the FDN, began shopping among high-powered lobbying firms. Gray and Company actually developed the public relations campaign, but Calero judged it too expensive. Although nothing developed from this contact, Gray employee Robert Owen became so dedicated to the cause that he put together his own support plan. Owen's scheme required twin tax-exempt entities, one for educational purposes, the other to raise money and seek influence. He showed this plan to Colonel North, whom he had met while working in the Senate in 1982. North encouraged Owen to visit Central America and scout out conditions there. Owen went to Costa Rica and Honduras in May 1984, spoke to *contra* leaders about money needs, and reported back to North at the Old Executive Office Building next door to the White House. This marked the beginning of an intense experience.

Intense is the word for Oliver Laurence North. He had been the most junior military officer sent to the NSC staff in 1981, but with the exception of Vice Adm. John Poindexter, North outlasted them all. He went to the political-military affairs section, where arms deals and crises are the stuff of daily duty. North seemed a logical choice to handle terrorism, where the administration had just begun defining policy. Colonel North marched into the vacuum, soon becoming a true focal point on the staff.

Another reason for North's longevity was Robert C. McFarlane. McFarlane came to the NSC in 1982, hired by William Clark as deputy national security adviser. When Clark moved on to the Department of the Interior in October 1983, McFarlane succeeded him as security adviser. Himself a former Marine colonel, Bob had a soft spot for North and thought of him almost as a son. He gave North primary responsibility for Latin American arms trading, and later for Nicaragua. "Ollie" North remained oddly defensive, as if he constantly felt the need to prove himself, to rise above his short stature (five feet, nine inches) or the lingering effects of wounds suffered in Vietnam and injuries from personal hijinks. Appearing as a character witness in the court-martial of a Marine buddy, North misrepresented himself as a pre-med in college, where in fact he had earned Ds in geometry and trigonometry. Other times he claimed that during his Okinawa tour he had commanded the "Special Operations Training Detachment," a unit that did not exist. Some remember North as a chronic name dropper. Others did not mind him so much. One woman who worked with Colonel North, mustering public support for the *contras*, saw him as "the occasional peacock among the roosters . . . with a hint of swagger about him."

For a time North's swagger seemed justified. He had a finger in every pie. It was North who in 1985 orchestrated the aerial interception of the *Achille Lauro* hijackers. Referring to the World War II interception and shoot-down of a Japanese navy commander, North had said, "We can do an Admiral Yamamoto." He was also involved in efforts against Muammar Gadhafi, and a central figure in the secret arms sales to Iran. All this plus his work for the *contras*, an activity he called Project Democracy.

Ollie's operations did not always come out so perfectly. As a midshipman at Annapolis he had used insurance money to buy a 427-horsepower Shelby Cobra painted Marine Corps green. When the academy had a field trip for midshipmen to Quantico, Ollie disdained the bus and organized his own car convoy. North's Shelby ran out of gas on the highway; he spent hours telephoning for emergency assistance. In the end, North's Project Democracy turned out very much like his Quantico trip.

North did not work in isolation. McFarlane, responsible to President Reagan, gave the orders. Reagan has said that he had nothing to do with arms shipments, but that he *did* support the *contras*, and that, as president, he remained unaffected by the Boland Amendment. Reagan certainly sustained the *contras* in numerous speeches, in an address to Congress, in receiving *contra* leaders at the White

House, in diplomatic talks with Saudi Arabian leaders, and in speaking at fund-raising events. Robert McFarlane's testimony is that he acted with the president's full authority. Reagan's order, as McFarlane put it to North and Donald Fortier, was to do anything necessary to win the next aid vote. Part of that amounted to keeping the *contra* force in being. That task went to Oliver North.

McFarlane himself performed a critical role. In meeting with counterparts from other countries, McFarlane mentioned *contra* funding as a dilemma facing the U.S. government. Help came from Saudi Arabia, which had never previously shown an interest in Central America, had no diplomatic relations with any country in the region, but had repeatedly invested in American covert action programs.

In the summer of 1984 Colonel North had Adolfo Calero in his office. Ollie asked for a bank account where money for the *contras* could be deposited. Calero provided an account number in a Cayman Islands bank, hoping for the best. In July came a deposit of $1 million in UNO's favor, followed by equal sums at monthly intervals through the year. After the third deposit, Calero began to believe, and UNO/FDN made plans. Seeing the president of Honduras on August 7, Ambassador John Negroponte told him that the FDN had funds from private sources.

At the interagency level the policy fights of 1983 had neutralized Reagan's Crisis Pre-Planning Group as a Nicaragua secret war command. Central American policy fell to the Restricted Interagency Group of senior officials. Ollie North represented the NSC staff at these meetings, chaired by the State Department representative, first Langhorne Motley, then Elliott Abrams. North also belonged to a three-person core group, a restricted RIG. The existence of this core group is disputed by Abrams, the purported chairman, though he admits its meetings took place, but the RIG figured widely in sworn testimony before Congress, a special prosecutor, and the courts. The third member of the core group was Alan Fiers, chief of the CIA's Central America Task Force. Abrams's logs show that these officials met seven times during the years 1985–1986, a period in which there were eighteen sessions of the full RIG.

Where Ollie North pushed so hard that some saw him as a loose cannon, Alan D. Fiers, Jr., remained a man of contradictions. Zealous and brash to a fault, presumably a good match for North, the CATF chief behaved with caution on Project Democracy. Fiers knew no Spanish, though he had a reputation as a fine linguist. A member of the agency's Middle East clan, Fiers was not entirely devoid of Latin experience, having been a Marine officer during the 1965 U.S. intervention in the Dominican Republic. Colleagues credited him with sharp political instincts, yet on Project Democracy he would be oddly ham-handed.

The CIA chief knew his way out of a tight situation. Admiral Turner had selected Fiers as station chief in Saudi Arabia just before Bill Casey came on board. Reagan's CIA director summoned Fiers and demanded to know why he should get the post and why he was any good at all. Fiers talked his way out of that one. Over four years in Riyadh he gained Casey's confidence, accompanying the DCI when he visited, preparing points for the spy chieftain's talks with Prince Turki as they coordinated the secret war for Afghanistan. By that time Fiers was slated to take over the Afghan task force. Instead Casey told Fiers he couldn't have the post; the DCI would not say what was in store. Fiers answered he would serve wherever Casey wanted him. A couple of days later the DDO, Clair George, phoned Fiers with his promotion to chief of the Central America Task Force.

Part of Fiers's caution can be attributed to the high politics of the Nicaraguan secret war. Just days after he took over CATF, controversy over the psychological warfare manual exploded over Washington. Casey had Fiers up to the Seventh Floor to demand the damage be limited—Ronald Reagan had dropped six points in the opinion polls and, with the election weeks away, something had to be done. Director Casey would issue reprimands. Fiers defended task force officers as best he could, but he could not do much. The episode led to his first appearance before the Senate intelligence committee. Fiers felt like "a cat being thrown into a clothes dryer."

Of course by then the CIA operation had been defunded as a result of the harbor mining. It fell to Fiers to figure out how to move forward. The Boland Amendment seemed clear enough, but Fiers soon discovered Ollie North's private operation. When North asked for CIA help, the CATF chief refused. Dewey Clarridge called Fiers to say things were afoot he knew nothing about, then advised him to collaborate with North. As far as Fiers could tell, the law restricted the NSC staff as much as the agency, and he took the issue to Latin baron Al Wedemeyer. Both went to see DDO George. Within a day or so the full group assembled in Casey's office, where the CIA director staged an elaborate ruse. By then, with Reagan re-elected, the problem of aiding the *contras* had acquired a long-term aspect. The episode demonstrates that Casey remained highly sensitive. Colonel North sat to the side. Director Casey turned to him.

"Ollie, Alan tells me you are operating in Central America. Is that true?" Casey asked.

He looked at Fiers. "Alan, tell Ollie what you told Clair."

Fiers did so, softening a few of the sharpest edges. Then Casey turned back to North: "Ollie, are you operating?"

Colonel North replied, "No sir, I am not operating."

Director Casey then intervened. "Good," he said. "I want you to understand that you are not to operate in Central America."

Alan Fiers emerged incredulous. He looked to Clair George for enlightenment. The DDO warned Fiers. George interpreted: "Sometime in the dark of night, Bill Casey has said, I will take care of Central America, just leave it to me. And what you saw go on in there was a charade."

"Jesus Christ, Clair," Fiers shot back, "if that is true then this will be worse than Watergate!"

Fiers determined to he a buffer between CATF officers and the controversies he expected from this project. Casey's fair-haired case officer had no idea how true his fears would be.

Assistant Secretary of State Elliott Abrams noticed rivalry between North and Fiers. That may have been for Bill Casey's ear. North clearly had a personal relationship with Casey, the first CIA director to have a hideaway office in the Old Executive Office Building, just down the hall from Ollie in Suite 302. On at least two occasions Casey visited North, another time he sent over a friend who wanted to make a *contra* donation, beer brewer Joseph Coors, and North talked the man into giving $60,000 for a light plane. How often North popped down to the DCI's office may never be known. In sworn testimony Bob McFarlane could not say whether Ollie followed his orders or Casey's. North's precise function for Casey remains a cipher, punctuated by reports that over 1984 and 1985 Bill Casey and Ollie North met UNO officials at a CIA safe house in Washington.

Always the back-alley brawler, Casey maintained a wide range of personal contacts for different purposes, some operational. Milt Bearden and Dewey Clarridge, the Afghan and Central America secret-war bosses, both had lines to the DCI. Similarly Casey brought back CIA's station chief in Managua from 1982 to 1984, Benjamin B. Wickham, Jr., as a special assistant, even working outside the agency on aspects of *contra* activity. North formed another such link, outside the purview of Fiers's CATF. Because the Boland Amendment expressly prohibited the CIA assisting the *contras*, a channel such as North's was essential if Casey wished to pursue the Nicaraguan war.

Casey built his bridge to Alan Fiers in November 1984. The task force chief was at home at dinner when the director called and inquired how things were going. Fiers asked Casey if he wanted the story plain or gilded. When Casey said he wanted it straight, Fiers told him prospects were terrible. They agreed to meet the next morning. At Langley, Fiers reiterated his conclusions: negotiations with Managua had gone nowhere (Fiers apparently was unaware that the administration intended these talks to fail), and the CIA had no strategy. Casey asked for a policy paper. When Fiers came back, Casey read the memo, then said he would take care of policy and Fiers should focus on operations. After that, Fiers too had a direct line to Casey. Fiers saw their relationship as akin to that between a father and son, reminiscent of McFarlane with North.

Fiers, far from being the only CIA official concerned about strategy, actually joined a long line of comrades. John McMahon told the Senate intelligence committee in 1991 that he had recommended that CIA hand off the *contra* project to the Pentagon even before the harbor mining. McMahon felt the secret war exceeded CIA capabilities. Similarly, about a month after Fiers's exchange with Casey, intelligence deputy Bob Gates took a hand with a memo to Casey in which he began, "it is time to talk absolutely straight about Nicaragua." Gates accepted the rationale for the war but noted that "the *Contras*, even with American support, cannot overthrow the Sandinista regime." Gates advocated creation of a *contra* provisional government which the United States would assist openly, including a blockade (a la the Cuban Missile Crisis, he termed it a "quarantine"), economic sanctions, and air strikes to destroy Sandinista capabilities. But Gates conceded that the "hard measures" he favored in this December 14, 1984, paper "probably are politically unacceptable." Bill Casey agreed with Gates's judgment. That left the field to the *contras* themselves.

Adolfo Calero wanted Colonel North's help, whether or not that included Casey. Calero would take help anywhere he could get it. The Cayman Islands account number he gave North also went to retired generals John K. Singlaub and Richard V. Secord. Singlaub had been to Honduras in March, impressed with the FDN camps and their need for modern anti-aircraft weapons. Singlaub would help raise cash for the rebel umbrella group UNO and later became Calero's best arms source. General Secord got the number when his company also made a donation.

In addition to the secret means there existed an open funding mechanism through conservative fund-raiser Carl R. Channell, whose National Endowment for the Preservation of Liberty collected more than $6 million. "Spitz" Channell courted donors quite successfully. With the White House, he arranged a series of NSC briefings for donors. President Reagan appeared twice in these sessions. On one occasion in the Roosevelt Room of the White House, Reagan's appearance came neatly sandwiched between talks by Elliott Abrams on general U.S. policy and a military briefing from Oliver North. Channell developed a one-two punch for likely prospects. He followed the gloom-and-doom with an appeal for a specific item the donor could contribute. The White House's Office of Public Liaison complemented Channell's effort with its own, with North as preferred speaker. The colonel asserted that those who opposed *contra* funding were mounting "the most sophisticated disinformation and active-measures campaign that we have seen in this country since Adolf Hitler." Elliott Abrams critiqued the story boards for Channell television ads. Channell consumed 35 percent or more of the donations on overhead or propaganda.

Ronald Reagan set the accent for the entire network with constant exhortations. In February 1985 and again later Reagan called the *contras* "brothers"; in March he termed Calero's crew "the moral equivalent of the founding fathers" and declared to America, "we owe them our help." Later he spoke of a Soviet "beachhead" in Nicaragua and called Sandinista leader Daniel Ortega, that July, "a little dictator who went to Moscow in his designer glasses." In case Managua missed the signal, on May 1 Reagan slapped a total trade embargo on Nicaragua.

The overriding question was money to sustain the *contras* through the next appropriation—so-called bridging funds. Here too Reagan played a role. Bud McFarlane took the cash problem to the Saudis during preparations for a visit by King Fahd. The Saudi king, accorded a private tête-à-tête with President Reagan, saw him in February 1985. No record exists of what they discussed, but shortly afterward the NSC staff learned that the Saudis would renew and even double their aid to UNO. Within a month the *contras* received about $24 million in three large deposits, bringing aggregate Saudi aid to roughly $32 million, comparable to what the CIA had been paying before the mining. Truly the Saudis at this moment permitted the *contras* to maintain their strength.

Beyond these connections, private sources helped Calero. A key operator was John K. Singlaub, who now headed the World Anti-Communist League and the United States Council for World Freedom. Singlaub had been deputy commander of U.S. forces in Korea during the Carter administration and had publicly criticized the president for considering withdrawals of American troops from that country. The confrontation with Carter led to Singlaub's transfer, and he retired to pursue his political beliefs in private life. General Singlaub, veteran of a long career much given to special warfare, had been detached to the CIA in its early days, serving in China as base chief in Mukden. There he forged relationships with the Nationalist Chinese that he now used to solicit funds or material aid, particularly air defense, for the *contras*. In the Korean War, Singlaub had been CIA's deputy chief of station. For the army in Vietnam, Singlaub had commanded MAC-SOG during the critical years 1966–1968. He still served as a Pentagon adviser. At least once he presented Casey with a proposal for a round-robin arms deal involving North Korea to provide the CIA with Soviet-style weapons.

Singlaub made direct approaches to South Korea and Taiwan, followed up by North and McFarlane sending another NSC staff member, Gaston J. Sigur. That brought UNO two donations of $1 million each. Singlaub would have gone for more save for the intervention of Elliott Abrams. The general's highly publicized private funding efforts in the United States proved much less lucrative, yielding $400,000 over two years. Singlaub gave Oliver North a *contra* weapons wish list which the Channell group used in fund-raising. Not least, John Singlaub had the contacts to bring Adolfo Calero the cheapest weapons and ammunition the FDN could buy anywhere.

Langley was aware of these developments. In February 1985 North discussed South Korean contributions with DDO Clair George. George also spoke to Alan Fiers about weapons being bought in China by Richard V. Secord. A year later, in April 1986, CIA reporting from Europe picked up indications of purchases in behalf of the *contras* by Secord agent Thomas Clines.

Finally, a constellation of minor benefactors were conjured by Reagan's appeals. The president likened them to the Abraham Lincoln Brigade in the Spanish Civil War. These included Refugee Relief International, which donated medical supplies, and Civilian Military Assistance, whose members went to Honduras to train FDN troops. These were "private patriotic Americans," as North called them. As General Singlaub told Ollie, all the press attention that went to him and groups like Civilian Military Assistance drew eyes away from Suite 302 of the Old Executive Office Building. Yet though Singlaub and the others prided themselves on patriotism, their services were not fundamentally different from, say, Ed Wilson in Libya. The secret wars spawned a generation of freelance cowboys. Project Democracy then brought the ultimate distortion, the Office of the President working directly with private citizens on a covert action.

It became apparent almost immediately in mid-1984 that the Nicaragua war had a new character. Colonel Bermudez's FDN columns disappeared from the field; Pastora took ARDE out of the fight. Not only did the single front line fail to materialize, there was nothing at all. The *contras* shifted to subsistence mode while reliance on the benefactors injected private agendas. Benefactor aims were not necessarily identical to those of FDN, President Reagan, or the NSC staff. The Hondurans, more skittish than ever, worried not only about the presence of *contra* base camps but the openness with which FDN paraded around Tegu. Fortunately Honduran commander General Alvarez left the scene, deposed by internal maneuvers, and his successors renewed their commitment to the *contra* enterprise. Ambassador Negroponte again midwifed this evolution, promising the FDN would be more discreet.

The Boland Amendment took effect on October 1, 1984, the first day of the new fiscal year. A final contingent of seventy-three CIA trainers left Honduras. Langley's orders to its stations were explicit:

FIELD STATIONS ARE TO CEASE AND DESIST WITH ACTIONS THAT CAN BE CONSTRUED TO BE PROVIDING ANY TYPE OF SUPPORT, EITHER DIRECT OR INDIRECT, TO THE VARIOUS ENTITIES WITH WHOM WE DEALT UNDER THE PROGRAM. ALL FUTURE CONTACTS WITH THOSE ENTITIES ARE, UNTIL FURTHER NOTICE, TO BE SOLELY, REPEAT SOLELY, FOR THE PURPOSE OF COLLECTING POSITIVE AND COUNTERINTELLIGENCE INFORMATION OF INTEREST TO THE UNITED STATES.

Now there were narrow limits on what the CIA could do. Langley's top analyst for Latin America, Robert Vickers, and Alan Fiers could no longer even *know* certain things. Soon after Boland took effect, Fiers rejected North's invitation to a meeting with Calero for this reason.

Bill Casey, however, continued to march to the beat of his own drummer. Casey would not discuss the *contra* aid with friend Joe Coors but had no hesitation sending him down the hall to donate money. Casey joked to North about contributing a million of his own. He saw Bud McFarlane in March 1985 specifically about third-country funding. Several months earlier the DCI had certified to Congress that the CIA had had no involvement in *contra* lobbying whatever. When the time came for Project Democracy to mount an airlift, Casey met with Gen. Richard Secord at North's suggestion, and Ollie later took Secord to see the DCI as well.

The CIA director ought to have been on warning. Not only had Bob Gates sent Casey personal advice to give the Nicaragua project away, Vickers produced an NIE in February 1985 on the prospects for Sandinista consolidation that warned of deficiencies in *contra* potential and even forecast declining effectiveness. Articles in the *National Intelligence Daily*, which Gates published, continued to highlight problems. Years later analysts accused Gates of slanting the books in favor of the rebels, but a 1990 inspector general study found that these products *had* been objective. Instead the IG faulted the small analytical unit within Fiers's task force, tarring it with warping and hyping the data, basing claims on deduction rather than evidence, and interfering with circulation of DI reports (where Gates was found to have fallen down was in failing to prevent these CATF interventions). In any event,

Casey and Fiers had to be engaged in wishful thinking to believe the *contras* were doing well.

As best as we can discern, Director Casey led Project Democracy. He used Oliver North as his field commander, juggling the pieces, carrying orders to the *contras* and the private benefactors. Casey separately called on Alan Fiers, whose CATF was handcuffed by the Boland Amendment, for intelligence and technical support. When diplomacy became necessary, North and Fiers could sway Elliott Abrams at the RIG. But both the *contras* and the benefactors had their own agendas, and the scheme was doomed from the start.

In late 1984 North asked General Secord, partners with Iranian-American Albert Hakim, to help with arms too. Secord told Hakim the President of the United States wanted their aid. Hakim accepted after assurances they would earn standard profits, with markups of 20 to 30 percent. Energy Resources, one of their web of companies, then brokered the biggest deal, an $11.3 million FDN order for ten thousand rifles of Soviet design, rocket-propelled grenades, mortars, and other equipment. The company managed to get Guatemalan end-user certificates and in December 1984 began buying the arms in Portugal and Poland. Secord gave Calero the impression that weapons were being sold to him at cost.

The best of Calero's deals by far was with General Singlaub, who worked with Barbara Studley of GeoMilTech. Singlaub arranged the deal early and took a long time to put it together, but for his $5.3 million Calero received another ten thousand assault rifles, lots of ammunition, and some SA-7 anti-aircraft missiles, possibly from North Korea. Where Secord's prices were slightly less than another competitor's, Singlaub's were cheaper by almost half. Barbara Studley may have lost money on the transaction. When his shipment reached Honduras in July 1985, a local representative of the competition met the vessel. Claiming to act for the officer to whom the cargo was consigned, the competitor was able to see documents that showed how little Singlaub had paid for the arms. He then tried to get Singlaub to sell *him* weapons at those prices. When Singlaub refused, the man threatened to block future shipments.

Infighting among arms dealers eventually sullied the White House itself, at a meeting among North, Secord, Singlaub, and Calero to discuss anti-aircraft weapons. Desperate to get SAMs, Bermudez had a Secord offer of $180,000 per set for British Blowpipes. Singlaub thought he could get the same missiles for $165,000, though he could not offer trainers. The deal went to Secord. When Singlaub complained, North conceded he had the better price, then went ahead to cut Singlaub out of future *contra* arms deals.

Actions prohibited by the Boland Amendment became a prominent feature of the North-Calero relationship. An important instance occurred in November 1984 when the arrival of Soviet-made gunship helicopters posed a new threat to the FDN columns. Calero wanted to attack El Bluff, the Atlantic port where the gunships arrived and were assembled and initially based. He called North on a secure line on November 5, then met with the NSC aide. In addition to a political strategy for coalition with Alfonso Robelo and Arturo Cruz, Calero talked to North about "borrowing" a T-33 jet from the Honduran air force that could hit El Bluff. A single plane strike would have been too limited, and Honduran cooperation was also a factor. This plan was dropped.

Ollie North asked McFarlane for permission to provide intelligence about El Bluff and went to the U.S. Southern Command (Gen. Paul F. Gorman) and the CIA's national intelligence officer for Latin America (Robert Vickers) to get the data. He assembled it into a package that Robert Owen carried to Honduras. Then Vickers found himself cut off from clandestine service data on events in Nicaragua.

In December a British paramilitary expert, David Walker, formerly commander of the Twenty-second Special Air Service regiment, met North and proposed a commando attack. North and Calero discussed the idea. Calero also consulted Singlaub about the concept, though not with specific details. A Walker associate entered Nicaragua to test the route but found such tight security around El Bluff that a raid seemed impossible. Calero abandoned the idea altogether. Although Walker received no immediate employment, he won a place on the team when Project Democracy expanded to include an airlift.

In February 1985 North asked Rob Owen to carry intelligence, including maps, to Calero. Owen met Colonel North just outside the White House Situation Room. The two discovered that the CATF had sent maps displayed on poster board, not at all suitable to be carried by a secret courier. North called Alan Fiers with some choice words on CIA competence. Langley sent a man to Dulles airport with a reformatted packet that Owen took to Honduras.

On a larger scale, North formulated a military plan to bring the *contras* victory. This involved the FDN seizing part of Nicaragua, declaring a provisional government, then holding fast. Puerto Cabezas was a likely target. The *contras'* Alamo-like stand would supposedly energize support for Reagan's policy, enable a U.S. naval blockade, and force Managua to fold. Elliott Abrams's RIG actually discussed this scheme, but the Pentagon and CIA both rejected it as nonsense. North nevertheless used the plan with prospective donors.

North busily suggested things the *contras* could do with all the money after the big Saudi donations, and warned Calero of the money's appearance. Owen carried another packet of intelligence to Calero in April while Ollie told McFarlane that Bermudez planned a big FDN offensive in June. The *contras* now claimed twelve thousand to fourteen thousand men in the field in eight regional commands (declassified U.S. cable traffic confirms only half this number). Despite the troops and the weapons bought by Calero, June was most notable for a shooting incident on the Costa Rican border. Nothing indicated an FDN offensive.

Bermudez's lack of results led to a council of war in July. A meeting at the Miami airport hotel involved Calero, Bermudez, General Secord, and Colonel North. Secord stated his opinion that without aircraft the *contras* "would be driven from the field and defeated in detail," and he volunteered to create an airlift.

Meanwhile, as quietly as North attempted to play his own role, the press picked up bits of the story and published accounts questioning Ollie's activities. Some in Congress noted the reports and began raising their own questions. At the

NSC, McFarlane received inquiries from Lee Hamilton of the House intelligence committee and Michael Barnes, chairman of the House Foreign Affairs Committee's Latin America subcommittee. These inquiries scared the White House. In answer to Hamilton, Bud McFarlane sent a letter drafted by North which asserted a "deep personal conviction" that no one on the NSC staff had violated Boland.

When the Barnes letter arrived, McFarlane and the president were at the Reagan Ranch. McFarlane later reviewed North's file and found at least a half-dozen memoranda that raised legal questions on NSC staff participation. Among them were the El Bluff plans, the transfers of intelligence, an abortive North scheme to pirate a Nicaraguan merchant vessel, NSC staff pressure to get the State Department to secure a multiple-entry visa for Singlaub's trips to Honduras, and more. Ollie managed to convince Bud that his activities were defensible. Again McFarlane signed a letter drafted by North, this one to Barnes, declaring "my actions, and those of my staff, have been in compliance with both the letter and the spirit of the law." Then McFarlane resorted to trickery in the face of Barnes's request for documents. McFarlane refused to surrender any papers or allow Barnes's staff access, but he invited the congressman to review documents at the White House if he wished. McFarlane then scheduled Barnes for just twenty minutes and used much of that time for verbal assurances. The problem memoranda lay to one side, immersed in a deep stack of paper in case Barnes asked to look at documents, but he did not. North squeaked by this test.

The Barnes letter also triggered an inquiry by the Intelligence Oversight Board, the legal watchdogs. Counsel Bretton G. Sciarone took charge. He had never practiced law and had passed the District of Columbia bar exam only to get the IOB job. He had no help save a secretary. This was his first opinion. Sciarone was handed the McFarlane assurance letters and had a five-minute conversation with North and a single forty-five-minute talk with NSC counsel Cdr. Paul Thompson. Thompson gave Sciarone documents to look at—but not to retain for study—and only to make notes. These *excluded* the problem memoranda. Based on this, Sciarone produced an opinion, routinely rubber-stamped by the IOB and issued on September 12, 1985. It found the NSC staff activity legal. At least twice, when Alan Fiers questioned NSC staff actions, Ollie North referred to the IOB opinion. Once North handed Fiers a copy, then took it back.

Thereafter the problem memoranda were carefully shielded: North made a list of their file locations and kept it taped to his computer. Once it began to appear there would be a real investigation, North checked the papers out of the NSC central registry and altered them, having his secretary type up revised versions. Whatever was in the IOB opinion, Oliver North knew he had a legal problem. Meanwhile the opinion did just what North wanted. Fiers would not be the sole victim of his deception. Ollie exhibited the opinion, on plain paper without letterhead or date, whenever anyone questioned the legality of his actions.

Bud McFarlane protected North from a congressional inquiry that would have halted the NSC *contra* program. No doubt this was a crucial moment in Project Democracy. Unchecked, the program moved ahead to creation of an airlift force, a unit that gave the White House all the attributes of a standard CIA paramilitary operation.

Supply headaches hampered *contra* action at every level. The Sandinistas did what they could to make the problem worse. In January 1985 they deployed two thousand troops on the Nicaraguan side of the border salient which contained most of the *contra* camps. With the soldiers came long-range rockets that could strike the *contra* main base at Las Vegas from inside Nicaragua. Ambassador Negroponte asked for aerial reconnaissance, which led to a Reagan administration appeal to Congress to let the CIA share intelligence with the *contras*. Negroponte also warned that if Reagan failed to obtain new money for the rebels, Honduran support would diminish. Already two thousand of the seven thousand *contras* were permanently immobilized, as many as were in Nicaragua, and the rest were able to operate only as supplies materialized. This did not satisfy the Hondurans. One evening in early February, talking in the library at the embassy residence, the Honduran chief of staff told Negroponte that the *contras* were in a race against time, caught between U.S. politics and Sandinista power.

For Colonel Bermudez and Aristedes Sanchez, chief of FDN logistics, supplying the camps in Honduras and moving stuff to columns in the field consumed their energies. They mostly bought food locally. Materiel for the columns in the field went into Nicaragua on the backs of men or mules. Men could not carry much, while mule trains could not be very long without impeding action, because the FDN had no secure rear area. This translated into patrols that could not stay out very long. Bermudez sent a few columns deep into Nicaragua to exert presence, but there rebel units typically made an ambush or two, set a few land mines, and trudged back to camp. The *contra* conflict remained a war of alarums and excursions, not a steady exertion of military pressure against an adversary. Congress had it on high authority, from Southern Command chief Gen. Paul Gorman, that the *contras* were incapable of overthrowing the Managua government.

One possibility was to give the *contras* real teeth by extending their reach and complicating the Sandinista strategic situation. This meant an airlift to get supplies to the front, and also doing something about Costa Rica, where the rebellion had fallen apart.

Until 1985 only the Miskito and ARDE operated from Costa Rica. By then both groups were quiescent. The Miskito, divided internally, felt they had been used by the FDN. ARDE had been crippled by the attempted assassination of Pastora plus charges that senior commanders were running drugs. The CIA and FDN both disliked Pastora. True, Alfonso Robelo joined UNO, but as chief of the ARDE political wing he had no troops. Without Pastora the followers drifted away. Any idea the FDN could step in and gain the allegiance of these rebels soon disappeared.

Calero tried to reactivate the southern front. He arranged with a pro-*contra* American farmer, John Hull, to use his land. After Robelo and Arturo Cruz joined

UNO there followed a protracted effort to woo the ARDE factions. Lack of equipment furnished ARDE's excuse; an airlift could alleviate that problem. But Secord believed that to get useful loads to the southern front in his twin-engine aircraft would require an airfield in Costa Rica to recover planes after their missions or for emergency landings. The idea of a Costa Rican airfield came up within a month of the decision for the airlift.

An airfield represented a new degree of involvement for the Costa Rican government. For the most part San Jose had been willing to wink at *contra* activities, making arrests or seizures in only the most egregious cases. Still, Costa Rica's official position remained one of neutrality. Allowing land to be used for an airfield was a positive act, an act of commission.

Ambassador Lewis Tambs was new to San Jose in the summer of 1985. Before leaving Washington, Tambs talked to Ollie North. Purporting to speak for the RIG, North gave Tambs the task of getting the southern front moving again. Elliott Abrams gave no such order, nor did Secretary Shultz in his written instructions, but Tambs evidently thought Colonel North's order the real one. In San Jose Tambs met CIA station chief Joe Fernandez, who told him of the need for an airfield at "Point West." Tambs told the Costa Ricans that an airfield benefited them—getting Fernando Chamorro's troops into Nicaragua would reduce the *contra* problem in Costa Rica. San Jose agreed.

General Secord turned to an air force comrade, Col. Richard B. Gadd, to supervise site preparations at Point West, which received the code name "Plantation." A Gadd company, Eagle Aviation Technology and Services received $100,000 for this work. Plantation possessed a 6,520-foot dirt strip, a barracks capable of housing perhaps thirty men, and an open-air shed. From the beginning there was a security breach just waiting to happen—the "secret" airstrip could be seen from the air by planes using the standard Pacific-side air approach to San Jose's airport.

A security breach did occur in the late fall. The instigator was Elliott Abrams on a visit to San Jose. Abrams sat with Tambs to listen as Joe Fernandez and two subordinates gave an hour-long briefing on Costa Rica activities. Not a word about Plantation. Abrams finally asked, "What about the airfield?" Both Abrams and Tambs saw the CIA station chief turn colors and thought he would have a coronary. Fernandez took Abrams aside, indicating his officers were not cleared to know about the airfield, and pointed out Plantation on a map.

With Plantation under construction (completed in the spring of 1986), only longer-range aircraft like C-130s could be used on air missions. Here again Secord turned to Gadd, who once boasted, "Give me an account number and I'll fly anything anywhere." He had done just that, including moving Task Force 160 helicopters to Barbados for the Grenada invasion, and flying Delta team units on exercises and missions.

The Reagan administration failed in a request for military aid for the *contras*, but it came back and won $27 million in "humanitarian" aid following an incredible series of gaffes by Sandinista leader Daniel Ortega Saavedra. When the State

Department had to administer this aid, Colonel North sent their newly formed Nicaraguan Humanitarian Assistance Office (NHAO) to Gadd for airlift services. As with Secord, he arranged these through Southern Air Transport, which made at least fourteen flights to the *contras*.

Gadd played a primary role in setting up the private benefactor airlift. He found the planes. Gadd almost bought some aircraft from the Venezuelan air force before he found better ones, two Canadian versions of the C-7 Caribou, along with a C-123K from Summit Aviation, acquired in March 1986. The C-123 was another security breach—so endemic to this operation—the same one used in a U.S. intrigue to entrap the Sandinistas in drug trafficking a year earlier.

To work the planes Gadd hired nine pilots, three loadmasters, and seven mechanics. The crews earned $3,000 a month. They had plenty of experience. The project manager—Secord called him chief pilot—William J. Cooper, had 25,000 hours in his flight logs and had been Air America's top pilot helping Vang Pao in Laos. The deputy, John McRainey, another Laos vet, had 19,000 hours of his own. McRainey, looking for a new gig, had gone to Air America buddy James Rhyne, who now ran the CIA proprietary Aero Contractors, but found the layout not to his liking. When McRainey asked about other prospects, Rhyne told him about the Secord-Gadd business. McRainey learned that CIA knew of the project, but it was not theirs. Rhyne advised him to be careful.

Other members were also Air America veterans. John Piowaty and Elmo Baker had flown in Vietnam. Baker had spent five years as an enemy prisoner. The youngest were Wallace B. "Buz" Sawyer and David Johnson, in their thirties. A British crew with David Walker, the former commando, as minimally capable loadmaster, and Iain Crawford for pilot, barely qualified on the C-123. Of the three American loadmasters, Eugene Hasenfus had flown with Cooper in Laos. All were nominally employed by a Quarryville, Pennsylvania, company called Corporate Air Services. The crews thought they worked for the CIA, as confirmed by Luis Posada Carriles during questioning by the FBI for the Iran-Contra special prosecutor. At the time McRainey thought they were the over-the-hill gang.

Meanwhile Cuban exile and CIA contract officer Felix Rodriguez—he of the Che Guevara hunt—had been in Argentina and the Middle East after Vietnam. He retired with back problems in 1976, but El Salvador brought Felix back. He wanted to apply a bomber-helicopter attack method he had innovated in the Mekong Delta in Vietnam. In December 1984–January 1985 Rodriguez made the rounds of Salvadoran and U.S. officials, including Don Gregg, friend and former CIA boss in Vietnam, who was now national security adviser to Vice President Bush. Felix met North. As part of his work for the Salvadorans, Felix held a commission in their air force and had free run of their base. North paid attention. That fall Ollie convinced him to add the task of liaison between the Salvadorans and the private benefactors. Working closely with Salvadoran air commander Gen. Rafael Bustillo, Rodriguez arranged for them to use Ilopango air base, soon code named Island.

Rodriguez had doubts about one operative, "Mr. Green," actually fellow Bay of Pigs and Mongoose veteran Rafael Quintero, who went between Sawyer's people and the higher-ups. Quintero had been close to Thomas Clines, Felix's former Mongoose case officer; both had worked with Ed Wilson and were on the danger list as far as Rodriguez knew. Then Rodriguez, who himself used the false identity "Max Gomez," learned that Clines had worked with Secord on *contra* arms deals, personally pocketing about a million dollars. Felix worried about the gloss that put on Project Democracy, thinking it was "the Wilson gang back in business." But Rodriguez himself had brought in a questionable character whom *he* trusted—Luis Posada, implicated in the 1976 bombing of a Cuban airliner in Barbados that had killed seventy-three people. Posada had worked for Venezuelan intelligence and Pinochet's DINA; he had been condemned to death in absentia in Venezuela for the airliner bombing.* Posada went underground, organizing Cuban exile groups, plotting to bomb *fidelistas* in Mexico City.

Rodriguez arranged for Posada to come to El Salvador under a false passport and got him a new identity. There Posada worked as general factotum and helper. He rented three houses in nice districts for Sawyer's pilots, and a hotel in San Salvador for visitors and the mechanics. He also handled the Enterprise's purchase of aviation fuel from the Salvadoran air force at Island. Once or twice Cooper took care of the gas when Posada could not make it, but the Cuban gained unquestioned control of the funds after a ham-fisted American outraged General Bustillo by dumping a wad of cash on his desk as if the purchase were some Mafia transaction. The private-benefactor operation was not one of pristine purity.

Project Democracy's aircraft were also not all they could be. Flying into Ilopango in February 1986, the first C-7 developed engine trouble and made a forced landing. The press reported the incident—yet another security breach at the outset of the airlift. The CIA's reluctance to furnish intelligence became another headache. Secord saw Bill Casey about this early in February. Both of them were too old, he said, to beat around the bush. "We want every bit of support we can get from you. But instead of that what we're getting is a lot of questions about the nature of our—of Gadd's organization." Casey made no promises. Secord complained that Alan Fiers, who was on his back, had no qualifications for the CATF job. Not only an Arabist, Fiers had no paramilitary experience, and the agency had few well-qualified people in its air branch. The officer Fiers had sent to see Dick Gadd, someone Secord knew from Laos, was not even an airman. Casey defended Fiers as sincere and dedicated, but the CIA contract officer disappeared, and North told Secord that Fiers seemed to have found religion. Secord heard rumors that Bill Casey had come down hard on the task force chief. Secord wanted regular updates on Sandinista troop movements and air defenses. Casey's reply has not been recorded, but shortly afterward the benefactors—and Joe Fer-

---

* Felix Rodriguez writes (*Shadow Warrior*, p. 240) that Posada's conviction had no basis in evidence. In fact, declassified CIA and FBI documents contain detailed accounts of several conversations among Posada and other plotters of the terrorist incident, on different occasions, venues, and evidently from different sources. In 2005 Venezuela demanded the extradition of Posada from the United States to face charges in this attack.

nandez in Costa Rica—received KL-43 on-line encryption devices that enabled North to communicate privately with them. Rafael Quintero took Fernandez the sophisticated coding device, produced by the National Security Agency. The first successful airdrop of lethal aid indeed received intelligence support cabled from CIA headquarters.

When Congress permitted intelligence cooperation, the agency used this cloak to deliver $13 million in communications gear. This was aid of a specific sort and allowed Calero to use UNO funds for other purposes. Moreover the CIA discovered as early as April 1986 that Joe Fernandez supported North's operation, but the agency took no steps to bring this fact to the attention of the oversight bodies. Again this represented the warriors in action—only a month earlier the agency's analysts had produced a fresh NIE, "Nicaragua: Prospects for the Insurgency," which once more found the *contras* in decline.

That April, when incoming division chief Jerry Gruner came through Central America to familiarize himself with the players and problems, Joe Fernandez asked for assurances that his connections to the benefactors were permitted by Boland. Gruner said he would check. Fernandez stunned Alan Fiers a month later when he raised the same issue at a regional session of agency chiefs. Fiers knew nothing about the links, and Gruner apparently had not mentioned it to him. On May 28 Fiers cabled Fernandez that Langley approved advice, communications equipment, and intelligence as okayed by headquarters, but no materiel or monetary aid. Afterward the CIA recruited and began training a *contra* radio operator to work the net from Island during supply flights. Until that happened Felix Rodriguez had this duty since he was the only one who could speak Spanish to preserve the fiction that the flights originated from the *contras* themselves.

The airlift's first great moment occurred in March 1986. A Sandinista infantry force pursued FDN troops across the border and made for the *contra* camps. The United States got Honduras to ask for assistance, whereupon an emergency aid grant of $20 million plus an airlift were laid on. Southern Command sent helicopters with U.S. crews to lift a Honduran infantry battalion into the area. One CIA pilot was badly injured in the crash of a helicopter surveying the combat zone.

Within days of the incursion, Project Democracy aircraft were flying supplies from Aguacate, the CIA base in Honduras. Buz Sawyer's logs show ten flights out of Aguacate between March 24 and 28 alone. In Nicaragua a Southern Air Transport (SAT) L-100 completed the first successful air resupply mission to a column inside the country.

Another SAT flight reached Aguacate on the evening of March 24. The SAT L-100 flew down from Dulles Airport with medical supplies and trusted courier Rob Owen, who watched the cargo compartment empty. Owen, hired by NHAO on the strength of a letter signed by Calero, Robelo, and Cruz, was to supervise the unloading of NHAO shipments because the Hondurans would not permit an American official do this. In fact he had another purpose: the L-100 was supposed to take on *contra* weapons at Aguacate and fly to Ilopango from where, the next night, it would make the first airdrop to the southern front. Ollie North asked

Owen to help because the SAT crew knew none of the contact people at the various points on this mission. This proved a dump from the start. Owen found no FDN weapons. The two CIA liaison men knew nothing of weapons, and *contra* representatives simply shrugged in ignorance. Owen went to the CIA chief of base, Jerry Adkins, who refused to call the Honduras station chief and get the FDN to release the arms. Finally Owen flew on to Island in an empty L-100. General Secord concluded that Adkins, as well as the agency's chief of station in El Salvador, were openly hostile to the private supply operation.

The next day at Ilopango came a meeting among Owen, Felix Rodriguez, Rafael Quintero, and Col. James Steele, the U.S. military advisory chief in El Salvador. They phoned Gadd, Secord, and North. Colonel Steele agreed to put through a secure call to Vincent Shields, the Honduras station chief. Ultimately they had to scrub the airdrop and scramble to inform the affected *contra* units. Another attempt took place on April 9 with an SAT L-100 that brought a load from New Orleans to Ilopango. The plane could not find the *contras* on the ground. Colonel Steele saw the frustration of the aircrew. When Secord wanted to try again, Steele insisted no mission be flown unless radio contact had first been established. Secord observed, "This is asinine—no black ops ever use this procedure." The drop finally took place.

By contrast with Honduras, in Costa Rica the private benefactors could get all the CIA help they wanted. Station chief Joe Fernandez had been involved since March 1985. Fernandez now used his KL-43 to report the successful L-100 delivery to the southern front. Ambassador Tambs knew that Fernandez had the KL-43 device. The diplomat allowed the station chief to go ahead participating in North's network. The other nodes on the net were North's NSC office, Secord, Gadd, Calero, Southern Air Transport, Rafael Quintero, and Felix Rodriguez. Fernandez subsequently provided intelligence on Sandinista air defenses and dispositions, weather conditions, and local liaison. Some of this might be permitted by the 1985 Intelligence Authorization Act, which allowed cooperation with the *contras*. But Fernandez went beyond that to become the contact point for the southern front *commandantes*. The CIA station chief even got into military planning, as demonstrated by his April 12 KL-43 message to North, in which he reported the L-100 drop, another drop for the Miskito, and the dispatch of new *contra* recruits forward with "ALL REMAINING CACHED LETHAL MATERIEL." As for future plans, Fernandez declared, "MY OBJECTIVE IS CREATION OF 2,500 MAN FORCE WHICH CAN STRIKE NORTHWEST AND LINK UP WITH QUICHÉ TO FORM SOLID SOUTHERN FORCE. LIKEWISE ENVISAGE FORMIDABLE OPPOSITION ON ATLANTIC COAST RESUPPLIED AT OR BY SEA."

This CIA cooperation on the southern front amounted to the best thing Project Democracy had going for it. The airlift remained sour, with accidents and abortive flights. April 1986 marked an intense spike in phone calls between Ollie North and Bill Casey. General Secord thought he could straighten things out and flew to Island on April 20, taking North and Gadd with him. Secord met the pilots at the Cooper house in San Salvador's Escalona district. There he told them that the British crew would make the flights into Nicaragua so that American nationals could not be captured. Secord and North went on to confer with Colonel Bermudez and Felix Rodriguez on anti-aircraft missiles for the FDN. Secord thought he might get ten launchers and twenty Blowpipes from Chile if Rodriguez could get Salvadoran end-user certificates. Rodriguez turned to North; the White House staffer made appropriate gestures. Bermudez complained of the old, slow aircraft in the lift unit. Ollie retorted that if he'd had the money he'd have bought an L-100. The planes were donated; the *contras* had to take what they could get. This conversation had fateful consequences, for Felix began thinking of the Secord aircraft as *contra* property. Rodriguez's early doubts about the operation became another path to the unraveling of Project Democracy.

Ronald Reagan still had that vision of hanging by his thumbs outside the White House unless he could get aid to the *contras*. The administration waited only as long as required by the existing legislation before going back to Congress with a fresh request. This time the secret war managers were determined to do it up right—no more half-assed shoestring appropriations that would force them back to the Hill after a few months. The request in February 1986 was for $100 million transferred from the Pentagon budget for the fiscal year beginning October 1. Bill Casey personally participated, presiding over congressional briefings at which the CIA used smear tactics in a classified paper, again collected once it was read. The paper characterized lobbying efforts in behalf of Managua by the consulting firm Agendas International as a disinformation and subversion campaign against the United States.

As Congress debated the money, President Reagan did something calculated to curry favor among the legislators whose votes he needed. With much fanfare, on March 14 the president sent a message to Congress on "Freedom, Regional Security, and Global Peace." White House spin doctors, including John Poindexter and Donald T. Regan, characterized the approach as essentially a repudiation of the Kirkpatrick doctrine that right-wing dictators are good. Henceforth the United States would oppose dictatorships of both right and left. Tyranny in any form supposedly became the enemy, democracy the goal, and the message claimed to be cooperating with a "democratic revolution" sweeping the world.

The text indeed said these things, but Reagan's message also contained apposite indicators or questionable assertions. His words on leftist regimes made his basic stance quite plain: "Soviet-style dictatorships, in short, are an almost unique threat to peace, both before and after they consolidate their rule." Pol Pot's Khmer Rouge killers in Cambodia, fighting against the Vietnamese-puppet government in Pnom Penh, were characterized as "democratic forces." The message also commented favorably about those with whom CIA worked in Afghanistan and Angola. As for the *contras*, Reagan's message contained the astonishing assertion that the rebels had been "holding their own—despite their lack of significant outside support"—a gambit to shame congressmen. The administration knew perfectly well that the *contras* had roughly as much "outside support" as the CIA had previously provided, and the White House itself had orchestrated that assistance. It also stretched credulity to assert Managua had a "Leninist regime" making war against its own people.

Reagan's message and the intensive lobbying proved inadequate. The House of Representatives rejected the $100 million CIA program, as it had every proposal for "lethal" assistance since the harbor mining. But now the Sandinistas became their own worst enemies. Later in 1986 leader Daniel Ortega made a movie star–like tour of Europe, seeking aid both in Western Europe and Russia, permitting Reagan to dub him a dictator in sunglasses. *That* was when Congress passed Reagan's $100 million program, to take effect on October 1. Once the budget passed in June, Alan Fiers held the first of several conversations with General Secord on whether the agency should take over the assets of the Enterprise, as Secord and Hakim dubbed their little empire. Ollie North warned Fiers to get ready.

Bill Casey took to the street in an effort to build public support. In a Denver speech on July 30 the CIA director warned, "We are only at the beginning of this struggle and we have to resist that old American tendency to expect instant and easy success." Casey expected the new money "to further turn up the heat on the Sandinistas" by expanding the number of *contra* troops and "opening new areas of operation." But "the Soviets and their Sandinista clients" would not "give up their toehold without a determined fight." The spy chief looked forward to seeing Moscow spending more to counter the insurgency than Washington did to support it.

After these many months, the name of the game in Washington was still "bridging" aid. This time the bridge had to reach from humanitarian aid, expired in March 1986, to the new program. Saudi Arabia had been a generous donor but had exhausted its interest. "Topfloor," in the radio parlance of Bill Cooper's crews, cast about for alternatives, as did the private benefactors. Gen. John Singlaub prepared a new approach to Taiwan, with which he'd been successful before. He was called off by Elliott Abrams. Taiwan did, however, donate another million dollars.

Ollie North dreamed up the scheme that brought fresh culpability into the White House. This was the diversion to the *contras* of money from the Iran arms sales. Ultimately the gambit involved only about $3.5 million, not the $12 million North anticipated, and that included the Secord aircraft and the Santa Elena airfield. Discovery of North's memo advocating diversion began the Iran-Contra affair when Justice Department lawyers found it in his safe on November 21, 1986.

The official U.S. government approach to solicit "bridging" aid from third countries was decided at an NSPG meeting on May 16. All the principals were present, including Reagan, Bush, Casey, Shultz, Weinberger, political advisers James A. Baker and Don Regan, plus a host of lesser lights. For the NSC staff North attended, along with Central America senior director Raymond Burghardt. Admiral Poindexter presented the situation as good but liable to change because *contra* funds were running out. Poindexter presented options: go to Congress for authority to reprogram other money, or seek third-country donors. Secretary Shultz initially favored solicitation. Bill Casey, perfectly aware of what had already been done, innocently asked if this had been tried before. Shultz, unaware of the Saudi funding until a bizarre telephone call from McFarlane that June, replied that a few unsuccessful approaches had been made. Others, also aware of the Saudi donations, pronounced solicitation worth exploring, including increased involvement by President Reagan. The NSPG decided that Secretary Shultz should make a list of candidate countries.

George Shultz gave the job to Elliott Abrams. Shultz had come a long way since September 1985, when, referring to North, he had instructed Abrams to "monitor Ollie." Now Shultz too was ready to seek donors. Interestingly enough, this episode goes entirely unmentioned in Shultz's memoirs. He instructed Abrams to avoid countries ruled by dictators and those dependent on U.S. aid. Abrams wanted donors to be oil magnates so they would have the requisite cash. He went to the assistant secretary for Middle Eastern affairs, Richard Murphy, who felt that none was suitable. The only other oil country Abrams could think of was Brunei, a tiny sultanate in Southeast Asia.

The original idea was to have George Shultz make the approach to the Sultan of Brunei during a visit. Extensive conversations among Shultz and top advisers on the secretary's plane crossing the Pacific convinced him to speak with the U.S. ambassador before talking with the sultan, and the ambassador, in turn, convinced the secretary not to make a solicitation.

Shultz decided instead that Elliott Abrams should handle the request, which was then arranged for August 8. Abrams contacted a high Brunei official in London. The two diplomats went for a walk in the park. Abrams began with his standard Central America speech, a talk he must have given a hundred times, then turned to the need for bridging aid. The sultan's emissary asked how much. Abrams reckoned NHAO had spent at a rate of $3 million a month, so he answered $10 million. The emissary replied that he did not have access to such amounts while traveling. Abrams handed him a three-by-five-inch file card with a typed bank account number. The assistant secretary's file card would later cause great diplomatic embarrassment. Abrams had gotten bank account numbers from both Alan Fiers at CIA and Colonel North at the NSC. The CIA provided a *contra* bank account in the Bahamas; North gave Secord's Lake Resources account in Geneva. Abrams used Ollie's number, but North's secretary inadvertently transposed two digits when typing. The Sultan of Brunei deposited $10 million on August 19. When Brunei asked Washington to confirm receipt of the cash, the United States proved unable to do so. The money had ended up in the account of a Swiss doctor. Lengthy legal proceedings had to be initiated to recover the money. Elliott Abrams was mistaken to suppose the CIA account more tainted than that of Lake Resources, with its involvement in shady arms deals and in the Iran weapons sales.

General Secord had all he could do to stay in touch with the players and movements of funds, arms, ships, and planes. For detailed management, Secord relied upon others. Tom Clines did the arms shipments to Central America. Air operations in

Central America were the province of Dick Gadd, but by the spring of 1986 he was pretty well burned out. Secord was doubly pleased at this time, therefore, to hear that his friend Col. Robert C. Dutton had retired from the air force. Secord had served with Dutton on the Iran hostage missions and trusted him implicitly. He immediately hired Dutton at STTGI as manager for the Project Democracy airlift.

Dutton came on at the beginning of May. Secord spoke of the legal situation at their very first encounter, handing Dutton a copy of Bretton Sciarone's sanitized IOB opinion which Secord considered sufficient "lawyering" to satisfy him. He told his manager to avoid violating the Neutrality Act by doing nothing on U.S. soil and by never delivering personnel, only things. Dutton immediately went to El Salvador to meet the people and see the equipment, carrying the legal opinion under his arm. There he reviewed ground rules with the crews. He emphasized William J. Cooper's role as air boss and restricted Rafael Quintero to support, with Felix Rodriguez a local facilitator. Dutton initially had a good impression of Rodriguez, though he came to think of Felix as a meddler. The aircrews sent mission reports to Dutton, who passed them to Secord and North, whom he saw as "co-commanders." By June Secord considered Rodriguez the project's biggest enemy, a leak waiting to happen. When TV reporters assembled an exposé of *contra* supply activities that summer where Secord's name surfaced for the first time, he felt the inside sources had to be either Rodriguez or hostile CIA officers.

The early intention to limit flights over Nicaragua to third-country nationals had to be abandoned in mid-June. The British crew had a pilot who had previously flown only helicopters. Moreover the crew's escapades in San Salvador drew unwanted attention plus a rebuke from Colonel Steele. David Walker's British were phased out; North and Secord decided to send Americans into Nicaragua. Here came another security breach waiting to happen. The private communications network was a breach already in progress, with top-secret KL-43 on-line encryption gear in the hands of people without clearances. Because his name had figured in the Wilson affair, Secord himself had failed to obtain a CIA clearance in 1983; his Pentagon clearances were later revoked after failure to file requisite disclosure papers. Bill Cooper, Calero, Quintero, and Rodriguez also lacked clearances. Their use of KL-43 units, operationally convenient, was illegal.

Beyond the use of secret encoding devices there were many ways in which the U.S. government made Project Democracy possible. Colonel Steele provided intelligence, weather data, and intervened several times when Dutton's people were locked out of Ilopango. Steele allowed Felix Rodriguez access to the KL-43, provided him a military car and advisory group identification, and made him deputy for the private benefactors. From the U.S. embassy Rodriguez received a powerful radio to communicate with the aircraft. Felix also got work crews to fix up his house, and the embassy expedited paperwork for Rafael Quintero. From the CIA came the vital cooperation of Joe Fernandez, who sent his drop-zone lists through Quintero and sometimes directly to STTGI.

The degree of CIA involvement held great interest for Secord and North, who pressed for more. On May 16, the same day the NSPG discussed cash solicitations,

North argued to Admiral Poindexter that the more visible Project Democracy became, with its planes, pilots, and weapons deliveries, the more inquisitive people would become. Steelhammer wrote, "We have to lift some of this onto the CIA." Rather than taking more, Langley seemed to want less—on May 21 Quintero informed Dutton that CIA officers were saying they could not talk to Secord's people at all. That applied to Bill Cooper's crew and presumably enjoined CIA's Joe Fernandez from helping. Secord went to North, who followed up with Langley, which remained cool for a time but later in the summer warmed up to the private benefactors.

In May North took Secord to a meeting with Bill Casey at his White House office. To Secord the discussion seemed part of an ongoing exchange. After insisting on the need to get CIA back into the field, Ollie complained of donations trailing off and mentioned a Middle East country where Secord had contacts he could solicit. Secord objected that he was not a U.S. official and that associates would not want to hear from private citizens. This was a far cry from his behavior with Calero in 1985, when he had claimed part credit for the Saudi donations. Asked how much he needed for the airlift, Secord estimated $10 million. This may have been what led North to put the Lake Resources account number on the file card for Elliott Abrams's Brunei caper. Secord again raised the issue of intelligence support from the agency.

Equipment continued to cause problems. Drainage was poor at the Costa Rican airfield, soggy from the rainy season. When Bill Cooper landed a C-123K there the first time, it sank into the mud. Poindexter learned this on June 10 from a computer email, or PROF, note, that Ollie left him. A week later an airdrop to the southern front failed when North and Joe Fernandez couldn't locate the rebels. In mid-June the managers decided to buy a second C-123K and a couple of spare engines after the first aircraft, ten miles off course due to faulty navigation equipment, hit trees and sheared away an engine. The plane managed to make Island safely, but the crew were almost killed. Pilot John Piowaty joined others to prepare a scathing letter indicting Enterprise aircraft maintenance.

The letter went to Felix Rodriguez. Felix had been in North's office in early May to say he wanted to bail out, but North sought to keep him. Later Dutton returned from an Ilopango visit to report that "Max is the only problem." Dutton felt Felix did not understand the concept of the operation. North asked Dutton to have Rodriguez come up to "Topfloor." Max Gomez presented himself at the Old Executive Office Building on June 25. Rodriguez had a problem just getting in the White House gate. That set the tone for the day, in which North accused him of violating security by talking about the airlift on open phone lines and claimed NSA intercepts to prove it. Rodriguez countered with the Piowaty letter. North looked at it and asked, "Is this a joke?" Felix replied that the writers had almost been killed. Dutton admitted he had not thought the incident worthy of North's attention.

Then Felix Rodriguez asked to speak to North alone. After Dutton left the room, Felix began, "Colonel, I have learned there is stealing going on here." North demurred.

Ollie turned to his television set, tuned to the congressional debate over the $100 million CIA project request. North pointed at the TV. "Those people want me," he said, "but they can't have me because the old man loves my [ass]."

Max Gomez would be isolated in San Salvador and slowly frozen out of Project Democracy.

Dutton made John Piowaty chief of maintenance.

The Enterprise sent its damaged C-123 to Southern Air Transport for repairs while the search for a second aircraft intensified. Cooper and a mechanic went to Evergreen Aviation to check out a new C-123K and had it at Island before the end of June. Cooper's crews also made their first successful airdrop to the southern front, with Buz Sawyer flying one of the Caribous. The C-7 had such a short range that after the drop it had to land at San Jose, Costa Rica, to refuel. The Costa Ricans had not given permission but relented. Joe Fernandez took care of it. That happened again on another flight.

Relations between Felix Rodriguez and the Enterprise worsened daily. Rodriguez asked what had happened to the Salvadoran end-user certificates he had provided for Blowpipe missiles, only to be told the deal had been delayed. He asked for the documents back. Secord did nothing. After late July there were a few more tense days, then Max Gomez was out of the operation altogether.

Leaving Project Democracy, Felix Rodriguez's actions permanently affected the Enterprise. He told Bermudez to consider Secord's planes FDN property. At Ilopango, Rodriguez arranged for armed guards on each flight to ensure that the planes did not divert from their missions. In Washington on August 8 Rodriguez met Donald Gregg, with some reason to suppose his remarks would reach Vice President George Bush, who had a real though still murky association with the Nicaraguan war. Bush had visited with *contra* commanders at Palmerola airfield when in Honduras in March 1985, and Gregg continued to keep him apprised of conditions in Central America. Rodriguez went over the ground he had covered with North. Felix charged, "Mr. Gadd is engaged in a ripoff." Gregg immediately called North's office and had Ollie's deputy listen to the "outrageous charges from my friend Felix." Gregg followed up in CIA and Pentagon channels a few days later. These charges created questions at high levels in the U.S. government. A few days later Lt. Col. Ralph Earl, North's deputy, along with Dutton, met with Col. James Steele. Dutton asked Steele to retrieve Rodriguez's KL-43. The colonel merely said he understood the problem.

The big break for Adolfo Calero came when Congress finally passed the $100 million *contra* aid appropriation effective with the new fiscal year. The NSC staff operators celebrated this long-awaited reprieve. But there was less to celebrate than met the eye—Ollie North had been quite correct that more people would become inquisitive as the Project Democracy airlift grew more visible. This covert operation began to unravel just as it reached full stride.

Below the surface there was more maneuvering. North and Secord conferred about Project Democracy's assets in the context of the CIA coming back into the

Nicaraguan secret war. Secord discussed this with Dutton, who wrote a paper summarizing assets and stating the options. The aircraft and field at Santa Elena plus other Enterprise holdings were estimated at $4.5 million. The options were to sell them, give them to the CIA, or lease them to the agency for $311,000 a month, more if the planes were used over fifty flying hours each. North raised the CIA purchase idea with Poindexter in July. At Langley Bob Gates, who had replaced John McMahon as DDCI and received explicit data on covert operations, also raised the question of CIA takeover of Enterprise assets. Alan Fiers objected that the planes and other equipment were decrepit and not suitable for the renewed CIA war effort.

Meanwhile numerous long-distance telephone calls between San Salvador and Washington complemented a very active flight program. Drop zones remained elusive, but in August Fernandez managed another mission to the southern front. Again the aircraft landed at San Jose, where Fernandez and the U.S. military chief handled permissions. Southern Front leaders now began to line up at Joe Fernandez's door with proposed drops.

But the flight program itself could potentially disrupt Project Democracy, not just from the fact of it but also because of what was carried. There were persistent reports of drug trafficking by the *contras*, with drugs transported by pilots returning stateside. The DEA actively investigated, including at Ilopango. In the 1990s the CIA inspector general looked into these reports. He could not substantiate them—for the northern front—but his conclusions were disputed by DEA agents and even alleged participants. Just one drug bust would have blown Project Democracy wide open.

Director Casey perhaps overlooked these developments. In declining health, Casey had much on his plate anyway, and the rumors of his sickness, so numerous they reached even Dick Secord's ear, preoccupied him. One night Casey called at home and asked Alan Fiers to lunch the next day. Their conversation proved unusual—Casey noted the rumors, tried to assure him they were false, then enlisted Fiers to knock them down.

Meanwhile Costa Rica installed a new government in May 1986. Its president had a peace plan to replace the stalled Contadora effort, and he put new teeth into neutrality. On September 3 police seized the Plantation airstrip and blocked its runway. North soon learned the Costa Ricans planned a news conference to reveal the base. He spoke to Elliott Abrams, who tracked down Ambassador Tambs on vacation, and the three held a midnight conference call. After that Tambs phoned President Oscar Arias Sanchez and persuaded him to cancel the revelation.

At the very moment North scampered to avoid a press notice that would have blown the project another way, Bob Dutton participated in what could have turned into a similar security breach. He had gone to Island on September 8 to get a feel for what the operations were like. As part of this visit Dutton went along on a supply flight, another abortive mission that found no one. It was rainy, the ceiling was barely 1,500 feet, the plane searched for an hour. By KL-43 on September 9, Dutton asked North for help in locating the southern front troops. Ollie replied that he would consult Joe Fernandez. But then the airlift got lucky. On September

13 Dutton reported on the KL-43 that Project Democracy had delivered 55,000 pounds of supplies in two days. Through the rest of the month perhaps seven loads were checked out of the warehouse for the southern front, and were dropped in ten to fifteen missions. Alan Fiers at Langley learned of the drops. North sent his deputy down to see.

When Dutton was reporting results to North, the White House man realized he had gone into Nicaragua. Ollie asked, "You went on that mission, didn't you?" North felt Dutton knew too much and prohibited him from flying. As with complaints to Felix Rodriguez about phone calls, this was symptomatic of North's great concern for small security issues while key clues were scattered in many places. A disgruntled participant or the passage of time both threatened to blow Project Democracy. Suddenly in September, project personnel were asked to sign secrecy agreements similar to those used by the CIA.

The time came on October 5, 1986. That day one of the C-123s had been laid on to deliver supplies to an FDN patrol called Sophia, the marker to be five smoke signals forming an L. Bill Cooper and Buz Sawyer piloted with Eugene Hasenfus as loadmaster. Cooper flew without standard evasive tactics against anti-aircraft missiles. That day his luck ran out. The plane overflew a Sandinista unit, was hit by a missile, and crashed. Hasenfus, even in Laos known for precautions to guard his safety, happened to be the only crewman wearing a parachute. He jumped and survived, only to be captured by the Nicaraguans. Unaware of the actual instigators of Project Democracy, Hasenfus told the Sandinistas his plane belonged to the CIA. The fat was in the fire.

In Washington the ruckus was enormous. The Reagan administration circled its wagons. Elliott Abrams's office tried to attribute the plane operation to General Singlaub and claimed the United States had nothing to do with it. Singlaub denied knowledge. The CIA denied any involvement whatsoever. At every step came fresh indications of ties to the U.S. government. Buz Sawyer's flight log, recovered from the wreckage, showed he had performed flights for the U.S. military with Southern Air. They also showed SAT personnel, including its president William Langton, along for some *contra* flights. Business cards in the wreckage suggested links to NHAO. The plane itself, tail number N4410F, was the same craft used in the drug-entrapment scheme perpetrated on the Sandinistas in 1984. Joe Fernandez wired Dutton demanding damage control. Ollie North, then John Poindexter, intervened with Justice to delay FBI and Customs Service investigation of Southern Air Transport, where the second Project Democracy C-123 sat. John McRainey flew the plane out for Island late at night when few could be watching.

Secord alleges that Langley decided to take over the Project Democracy assets. Ollie North met with CIA officials on October 9. The agency actually did purchase, for $1.2 million, the group's last weapons shipment, on the high seas en route to Central America when Hasenfus went down.

Official inquiries were inevitable. On October 8 Robert Gates appeared before the Senate intelligence committee. He insisted the CIA had nothing to do with the Hasenfus plane and gave background data on Cooper and Sawyer. The Senate Foreign Relations Committee set a hearing for October 10 and the House intelligence committee another four days later. At numerous Langley meetings officials tried to determine how to approach this testimony. Director Casey, DDO Clair George, and task force chief Alan Fiers decided George would be the primary respondent.

A cable with details on Felix Rodriguez reached George early enough to be included in his briefing book for the congressional appearances. But George ordered Fiers to edit out of his statement anything that might draw attention to the White House connections of the private benefactors. Fiers worried because the testimony said Secord had hired the same people and used the same bases as the former NHAO. Removing that would clearly be misleading if George were to tell Congress—as he did—that CIA knew nothing of the *contra* supply network. When Jerry Gruner told the DDO that Joe Fernandez admitted phone records would reveal many contacts between his CIA station and the Secord organization, George did not report that either. Far from knowing nothing of the benefactors, George actually had a former Secord employee in the DO air branch, hired after Secord complained to Casey. The man had helped set up the Ilopango base. Immediately after the Hasenfus shoot-down he had been ordered to make himself scarce and speak to no one. George offered his first set of denials on October 10.

On October 14 Clair George and Alan Fiers repeated their disclaimers to Congress. Norman J. Gardner, Jr., one of the DDO's special assistants, had just debriefed the air branch officer and sat among George's entourage as he feigned ignorance of the *contra* network. George denied knowing Secord or any of his people, and asserted he had learned of the supply operation only in the newspapers. Alan Fiers made similar denials—of knowing who "Max Gomez" really was, of knowing any private benefactors at all, of contact with the Secord base at Ilopango, of having discussed these activities with Oliver North. Elliott Abrams, who testified for State, also claimed no knowledge of or assistance to Secord and said he had first heard of the general in that day's press. At the Senate intelligence committee on December 3, George declared that he had learned of Richard Secord only after the fact. In a post hoc ass-covering attempt, on December 5 the CIA general counsel issued an opinion claiming that while contacts with the private benefactors might have been contrary to policy, they were not illegal. The opinion was a preemptive strike at the Boland Amendment, the first of many. In fact contact *was* the policy, and the policy was illegal.

All three officials were eventually indicted for providing false testimony to Congress. Fiers and Abrams pleaded guilty to reduced charges. Clair George was found guilty on two of ten counts in a second trial after a hung jury. George's testimony of October 14, a specific focus of the guilty findings, amply condemned him. A count of perjury for the December testimony was dismissed.

Meanwhile telephone records tied North explicitly to the action. Inquiries in El Salvador quickly revealed the pseudonym Max Gomez and then led to Donald Gregg in the Office of the Vice President. As if this weren't enough, the Iranian side of the Enterprise's activities simultaneously surfaced. Finally the discovery of a North memorandum discussing diversion of Iran arms funds to benefit the *contras* triggered the first of numerous investigations.

The revelation of the Iran side of the affair, beginning with articles in the Middle Eastern press, further busted administration efforts to keep the lid on. By November 10 the need for official acknowledgment had become so plain that President Reagan held a White House meeting to discuss a response. Several days later Reagan spoke to the nation in a televised address from the Oval Office, attacking "wildly speculative false stories" and characterizing the Iran arms sales as "small amounts of defensive weapons" that could fit in a single airplane—another untruth. And on November 19 at a news conference Reagan affirmed the accuracy of more claims that were false: that the United States had not traded weapons for hostages, that no third countries had been involved, that only two shipments had been made. He continued to minimize the sales, claiming that the weapons sold had been only about half the actual number, repeating the falsehood regarding the single aircraft load.

With the administration rushing to prepare for more congressional briefings and fresh CIA testimony—directly from William J. Casey—the hours now ticked too quickly for the secret-war wizards. James McCullough headed the DCI's executive staff at the time, with formal responsibility for drafting Casey's testimony. He believes the DCI might have muddled through had it not been for Casey's exhaustion and the brain tumor rapidly draining him. When the Iran revelations began, Casey, on a trip to Central America, had been out of pocket and unprepared. Clair George assigned two DO officers to make an initial review of the Iran side, which George briefed to Senate intelligence committee staffers on November 18, three days ahead of Casey's scheduled appearance.

McCullough and David Gries, Langley's congressional liaison, sat in on the briefing and came away amazed. They had known nothing of this. McCullough really hit the roof, however, when he found two of George's staff muttering about how he had *not* told the Senate intelligence people anything about the November 1985 arms shipment, which (as noted earlier) had not been supported by any presidential finding at all. Deputy Director of Central Intelligence Bob Gates had ordered that everything be included in the brief, and everyone thought it would be. No one understood why George had avoided telling Senate staff about this part.

Even as Langley's Seventh Floor went through gyrations trying to square testimony that might correct the record, differences developed on the accuracy of the proposed Casey testimony. The director, not a great moderator on his best days in McCullough's opinion, did a poor job reining in CIA barons who wanted to march off in many directions. Casey also proved ineffective at editing his testimony. George Shultz, who felt he was manfully battling the forces of darkness in this crisis for American democracy, had no confidence in CIA testimony that Langley would not permit him to see. Shultz demanded and received a penultimate draft the evening before Casey made his final changes and presented it. Shultz believed his main fight to be with an NSC staff that had developed an operational role, but Casey's CIA formed a mighty distraction. When Shultz finally saw the document it was laden with things he had not known—that the agency had kept from the State Department. For his part, Casey sent an "eyes only" letter to President Reagan, objecting to the secretary of state's "public pouting," demanding a "new pitcher," recommending that Reagan replace Shultz with someone like Jeane Kirkpatrick. At Langley Jim McCullough, dismayed when he saw the letter, objected to sending it. Casey's secretary told the staff director he held a copy—the original had already gone out.

That afternoon McCullough was startled again by White House chief of staff Don Regan, who came to Langley for an unprecedented visit to Director Casey in his Seventh Floor office. Unknown to McCullough, Attorney General Edwin Meese's investigators now had evidence that Oliver North had diverted Iran arms money to the *contras*. Shortly after Regan's one-on-one with Casey, the director, who had already spoken to Meese, left for home. He stopped at the White House for an NSPG. George Shultz found that session bizarre—officials spouting fantasy, talking of the Iran scheme as a correct policy that needed to continue, adding in for good measure a tilt toward Saddam Hussein in the Iran-Iraq War. Shultz quotes the president: "We are right!" Reagan pounded the table. "We had to take the opportunity! And we were successful!"

Reagan held a news conference on November 25 where Edwin Meese proceeded to tell the world of the diversion. The Iran-Contra affair had burst into the open. The controversy forced Reagan into a new clarification of procedures for approving and implementing covert operations, embodied in a directive issued on October 15. Its main point was to ensure that NSC staff had no role in carrying out these activities.

Iran-Contra also called into question the system of presidential findings. One arms sale had been completely unauthorized, justified only after the fact in a "retrospective" finding. Another action, Attorney General Meese would aver, had been authorized by a "mental" finding. Existing regulations already provided that all findings had to be written. Some Iran arms deals were not briefed to Congress for months, effectively an escalation of Casey's high-handed practices at the time of the Nicaragua mining. Through the remainder of the Reagan presidency there would be a frustrating dialogue between the White House (and CIA) and the oversight committees on the nature of findings. Congress succeeded in setting criteria for the information to be included in an MON, but the White House stonewalled on "timely" notification. Legislation to put into law a requirement that Congress be informed of any covert action within forty-eight hours passed the Senate in 1988 but stalled in the House. The issue was left for Reagan's successor.

If Bill Casey had survived he would surely have been prosecuted. Instead, on December 15, 1986, Casey suffered a seizure. Over the next few months he was in and out of hospitals. In May 1987 William J. Casey died. He never saw the final denouement. President Reagan would make many apologies, and Iran-Contra effectively turned him into a lame duck. Poindexter and North resigned. There would be congressional hearings aplenty, joint investigations, special prosecutors, trials. By the time Clair George had been convicted and Caspar Weinberger indicted, George H. W. Bush was president. On Christmas Eve 1992 Bush suddenly pardoned a series of figures, including Weinberger, George, Dewey Clarridge, Elliott Abrams, Robert McFarlane, and Alan Fiers. That marked the end of another broad season of inquiry.

Project Democracy never existed in a vacuum. The purpose had always been to reach the bright future when the CIA would fight again. Bill Casey wanted that, even if he sometimes played coy with Secord's operatives. The CIA did nothing to stop the benefactors, helped when it could, and did everything to get back into the action. The man supposed to mastermind the new age, James L. Adkins, CIA's latest project chief in Tegu, arrived on the scene in the summer of 1986. That rarity in the Nicaraguan war—a paramilitary man with Latin America experience—Adkins knew the political and legal dangers of the program and had tried to avoid this assignment. Eventually superiors had virtually put him on the plane, handing the fifty-two-year-old operations officer orders and a ticket. It must have appealed to Fiers, a former college football star, that Adkins had been an aspiring baseball pitcher, playing for a Milwaukee Braves farm club in the late 1950s. He had gone home to West Virginia and been a state trooper—an affinity point with Joe Fernandez, a detective sergeant with the Miami-Dade police department. Adkins had gone to college, then joined the CIA. Langley sent Adkins to Laos where he became an adviser to Vang Pao's *armée clandestine*. There he acquired a reputation, playing a key role in an offensive on the Plain of Jars.

By 1970 Adkins had had enough. He transferred to the Western Hemisphere Division of the DO and learned Spanish. He and Fernandez had been tag teamers, rising in the division, occupying increasingly senior posts at CIA stations throughout South America during the 1970s. Adkins had served in Santo Domingo and Pinochet's Chile. He emerged as station chief in Guyana—still under Forbes Burnham's dictatorship—in 1978. That proved fateful—the cult murder of a visiting congressman and mass poisoning called the Jonestown Massacre occurred on Adkins's watch, and the hearings that followed left him leery. The Nicaraguan war smelled of the same. Adkins rejected an early offer to participate, but he could not avoid temporary duty as a trainer in Honduras during the year of the mining. The ensuing controversy confirmed all his fears. Adkins joined the agency's Counterterrorism Group, about as far from Latin America as he could get, but even there superiors tagged him for the revamped secret war.

Jim Adkins arrived in Honduras in time to see the Secord operation establish itself, witness the increasingly tenuous relationship between the United States and Honduras, and get the flavor of the severe restrictions of the Boland Amendment.

After just a week in Tegu, Adkins told CIA station chief Vincent Shields, "This is the most fucked-up thing I've ever worked on!"

The Honduras relationship had become a major headache, though far above Adkins's pay grade. The Hondurans wanted much more economic and military aid than Reagan was willing to give. They pressed for jet aircraft, harping on the same intelligence about Nicaraguan MIGs that the Reaganites trotted out when the CIA program fell on hard times, a threat that never seemed to materialize. The Hondurans played the intel back at Washington. American diplomats tried to change the subject, focus on regional security, and enlist Tegucigalpa in a joint effort to train and teach both Honduran and Salvadoran army units. The first center had barely become active when the Hondurans stopped the program. That too they held hostage against more aid. The $100 million CIA aid program dwarfed everything the United States gave to the entire country surrounding the *contra* camps. Tegucigalpa constantly harped on the dangers posed by the camps on its territory, which contained the twin threats of encouraging a Nicaraguan invasion by their presence, or of an armed *contra* force that might intervene in Honduran politics. By this time John Negroponte had left Honduras. His successors, James A. Ferch and E. Everett Briggs, equally dedicated, never developed the same close relations with the Hondurans because the generals who collaborated with the United States during the early days had been swept away by political storms in Tegu.

Adkins fell afoul of both Honduran sensitivities and CIA legal prohibitions. Many *contra* camps were in a small area along the Nicaraguan border called the Las Trojes salient. CIA rules stipulated that everything entering the salient had to go overland. Only about twenty miles from Aguacate, the roads were so poor and the rains so bad it could take days to reach the camps. Visiting one of them in January 1986, Adkins found the freshly dug graves of children felled by an outbreak of measles. The victims could easily have been his own kids, living in a Tegu safe house. The agency could get vaccine in Tegucigalpa, but the overland route would take too long and the Nicaraguans regularly shelled the access road. The Boland restrictions prohibited helicopter flights within twenty miles of the border unless for intelligence gathering.

A few months earlier Langley had ordered Adkins to organize a rescue mission into Nicaragua, a deliberate violation of Boland to bring out American Indian activist Russell Means, engulfed in the war while visiting the Miskito. Means had gotten out under his own steam. The mission was scrubbed, but the contradiction remained—CIA had been willing to violate the law for political reasons but prohibited a humanitarian medical mission. Adkins decided to break the rules. He sent in medical supplies, and his helicopters brought out badly wounded *contras* for treatment at Aguacate or Tegu. Then he began to divert scout flights to the camps on their return, bringing back more wounded. On one occasion in November 1986 a flight transported military supplies.

For months the issue remained submerged. But in early 1987, after the CIA reentered the battle, Clair George and Alan Fiers came down to survey the new activity. They learned of the helicopter flights. Under the microscope of Iran-Contra,

George and Fiers felt obliged to bring the matter up in legal channels. Adkins told CIA Inspector General David Doherty that he would do the same thing again. Placed on leave, Adkins ended up going to ball games with Joe Fernandez while they both waited to learn their fates. They received reprimands and were fired by a new CIA director.

Political action remained a core of Langley's work throughout this period. To help make the *contras* more palatable to Congress, the agency brokered deals among UNO factions and between Calero's group and the Miskito. It is reported that several million CIA dollars supported UNO offices in Europe and Latin America, subsidized *contra* officials, and paid for their trips abroad. In early 1986, when the question was how to get Reagan's new *contra* aid through Congress, Langley was quite willing to help. A twelve-page CIA intelligence report in January tried to defend the *contras* against charges of human rights abuses by discrediting such allegations. Yet as early as February 1985 official Honduran government investigations had confirmed *contra* rights violations back to the beginning of the secret war. The result was that Congress earmarked $3 million of the new money specifically for a *contra* human rights independent prosecutor who would soon be bringing up *contra* commanders on atrocity charges.

Of course Langley had its own ideas for a renewed secret war. Those owed everything to Adkins. His operational plan envisioned a two-year effort divided into phases. *Contra* forces would form larger units, open new camps, and try to divide Nicaragua by cutting communications routes. The program included $70 million for military and $27 million for humanitarian aid. Activity would be coordinated by a renewed Nicaragua Operational Group under army Col. William C. Comee, Jr. A panel would oversee the CIA-military program. For one of its three members, President Reagan appointed Jeane Kirkpatrick.

Because of the proximity of Aguacate to Nicaragua and the restriction on flights close to the border, air missions were carried out from Swan Island, previously the location for the CIA's black radio during the Bay of Pigs. The air branch supervised procurement of Spanish aircraft, for which the agency hired former Rhodesian (Zimbabwean) pilots. One of the early endeavors involved a presumptive violation of restrictions on CIA domestic activity, when a hundred *contra* officers were sent for special training at Eglin Air Force Base in Florida. Meanwhile the *contras* lost Juan Gomez, their air force chief, and three more aircraft—a C-54, a C-47, and a twin-engine Beechcraft.

On the ground the issue remained in doubt. Calero claimed sixteen thousand troops, but the war went nowhere. A series of sabotage strikes in March 1987 by a commando group specially trained by the CIA only demonstrates the point. Arturo Cruz resigned from UNO. The Sandinistas mobilized upward of sixty thousand regulars and militia. Despite Elliott Abrams's promise that the *contras* would change the facts on the ground, the Sandinistas contained them. But with their big-budget support the *contras* were much stronger. In March 1988 the last major battle ended with the rebels stalemating a Sandinista offensive. Five years of paramilitary action and $300 million had not unseated them, and the administration spoke of a $105 million request for 1988. Still dissatisfied, Congress rejected the money. On February 3, 1988, the CIA operation permanently ended.

By then negotiations for a settlement of the Central American crisis were well under way. Managua signed a general agreement, as did the sides in the Salvadoran conflict, and reached a specific accommodation with the *contras*. Rebels regrouped into a number of zones, and UNO candidates won the next election. The Sandinistas were and remain the main political opposition. Integration of the former rebels into society continued to be problematic throughout the 1990s. The United States has essentially abandoned Nicaragua. What this says about Washington's commitment to democracy is an open question.

Bill Casey presided over a revitalization of the CIA's covert action capability. He was proud of that. But no one claims Nicaragua as a victory for covert operations. The many questions raised by Iran-Contra actually tightened controls over the agency. In his first appearance before the joint congressional committee investigating the affair, Richard V. Secord was led into an admission that the old Hughes-Ryan controls were appropriate. Casey's legacy would be the releashing of the CIA.

The worst aspect of direct White House involvement in a covert action was the squandering of a president's political capital on a marginal issue. The prestige of the presidency, openly committed to an effort at the very margins of legality in international relations, left Ronald Reagan damaged. Project Democracy muddied the waters further by skirting the law of the land. There are many wise reasons for eschewing such a policy.

President Reagan's campaign for *contra* aid came a far way from the days when Dwight Eisenhower refused even to meet with the Dalai Lama for fear of appearing to take sides. Even so, the new wave of paramilitary operations produced similarly indifferent results.

23

Full Circle

AN UNCOMFORTABLE INTERREGNUM followed Bill Casey's collapse. With Casey in and out of the hospital, Robert M. Gates served as acting DCI. On February 2, 1987, Casey resigned. The White House faced the sudden need to find a new director of central intelligence. Years before, at the outset of Ronald Reagan's presidency, Gates had told colleagues he wanted the top job. Now he came close to getting it. So close. The day Casey resigned, President Reagan nominated Gates as DCI in his own right. Perhaps the Reagan White House, beset by Iran-Contra, had not the energy or vision to seek out a new candidate for DCI. Or possibly Reagan saw Gates as a loyalist. Perhaps the call was for a professional but not someone with roots in the clandestine service. Gates fit that bill too. In any event, for a time it looked like Bob Gates would be moving into the director's office.

The Senate would have to approve the Gates nomination, but the White House had clearly felt out the ground there. In the 1986 off-year elections the Democrats regained control of Congress, making Oklahoma Senator David L. Boren chairman of the Senate Select Committee on Intelligence. Boren and a number of others reacted positively to the Gates nomination. Even Vermont's Pat Leahy saw the Gates appointment as a wise move. Opinion held that Gates would be asked tough questions on Iran-Contra but then confirmed.

Bob Gates put his best foot forward. There could be no denying his background as a superbly qualified intelligence officer. He had done that work for the air force and the CIA, beginning with Soviet nuclear weapons. He had seen diplomacy on the U.S. delegation to arms control talks. Gates had crafted the NIEs as an assistant national intelligence officer, as national intelligence officer, and later as ex officio chairman of the National Intelligence Council. He had done management as an assistant to a CIA director, an executive staff director, and as deputy director. Gates had headed one of the agency's tribes as deputy director for intelligence. He knew the White House, serving there under Jimmy Carter. As DDCI he had gotten a taste of covert operations and the clandestine service. In twenty-one years, in other words, Robert Gates had acquired wide agency experience. He had made some enemies, in particular as he handled intelligence reporting during the Reagan years, but in 1987 those people did not contest his nomination, which seemed unstoppable.

Except for Iran-Contra. Gates gave that his best shot too. Not coincidentally it became known that when he took over as acting director, Gates had recorded a classified video affirming that the CIA would act only under legal authorities and would never again do anything like the Iran arms shipments without a proper presidential finding. When hearings opened on February 17, Gates quickly made it known that he felt Iran-Contra had broken all the rules. He would resign if ordered to do something like that. Gates regretted not following up on the scattered indications of illegality he had perceived. But the nominee's assurances foundered on the rocks of the Iran-Contra investigations. A number of questions had yet to be answered then, including whether Gates had helped mislead Congress, the extent of his participation in concocting false chronologies, his role in efforts to have the CIA take over the Secord "Enterprise," when Gates learned of the diversion of funds to the *contras*, and what he had done once he knew it.

The more questions, the more Bob Gates's chances disappeared into the maw of assorted illegalities. Had Gates known of violations of the Arms Export Control Act? Had he known of the "retrospective" finding? What had he done? Again and again. At this point Congress created a joint committee to investigate Iran-Contra, and it did not expect answers for months. Then, on February 22, the public learned that in 1985 Gates had sent the White House a memorandum from one of his national intelligence officers advocating the improvement of relations with Iran through arms sales, a view at variance with existing estimates. Two days later the joint committee asked that Gates's nomination be put on hold. Senator Boren posed the alternatives of a vote or a withdrawal of the nomination while senior congressional leaders warned the White House that a fight over Gates would concentrate yet more attention on Iran-Contra. Reagan, who had just released a presidential commission report in an effort to put the scandal behind him, did not care to hear that.

Robert Gates decided to withdraw. The next day the administration took back the nomination. Gates issued a statement defending his actions during the Iran-Contra affair, denying he had covered up evidence or suppressed improprieties. Eventually the joint committee cleared Gates of illegal actions, and the Iran-Contra special prosecutor affirmed that conclusion, but there had been failings. Gates cites mitigating circumstances in his memoirs, where he writes:

> I would go over those points in my mind a thousand times in the months and years to come, but the criticisms still hit home. A thousand times I would go over the "might-have-beens" if I had raised more hell than I did with Casey about nonnotification of Congress, if I had demanded the NSC get out of covert action, if I had insisted that CIA not play by NSC rules, if I had been more aggressive with the DO in my first months as DDCI, if I had gone to the Attorney General.

It became Robert Gates's misfortune to be swept up in a web of illegality so immense it brought dangers of the impeachment of a president, which made Gates small fry indeed and virtually overnight neutered Ronald Reagan.

In withdrawing the Gates nomination, President Reagan simultaneously announced his appointment of William B. Webster to lead the agency. Webster liked to be called "Judge"—he had been a jurist on the federal bench, eventually on the Eighth Circuit Court of Appeals. Where CIA denizens begrudged Stansfield Turner his preferred title of admiral, no one held back with Judge Webster. Dedication to the law and to his native St. Louis, at least as deep as Turner's to the navy, had seen Webster through law school at Washington University, then a decade as a St. Louis attorney, another as a U.S. district attorney, and then the bench. In 1978 President Carter named Webster to head the FBI, the post he held when Reagan asked him to move to Langley. Three days shy of his fifty-third birthday, Judge Webster came with stellar reviews—squeaky clean, exactly what Reagan then needed. The Senate intelligence committee approved his nomination in early May, and the full Senate consented to it shortly thereafter. Judge Webster was sworn in immediately.

Bob Gates felt the weight of Iran-Contra lifted from his shoulders, only to hear from his brother that their father had just died. As Gates dealt with personal tragedy, Webster established himself at Langley. Again like Admiral Turner, Judge Webster brought in a coterie as his inner circle—this time of former FBI aides. That move scarcely endeared Webster to CIA staff, though he took some of the sting away by announcing Gates would remain DDCI.

The new CIA director had a background in government and even in the security field, where his time at the FBI had included notable investigations of corruption among congressmen, the Korean CIA, and, of course, Iran-Contra. In Webster's last months at the FBI the Bureau had looked into Southern Air Transport, the agency's quasi-proprietary. But Webster's knowledge of intelligence, mostly peripheral, resulted from participation in the National Foreign Intelligence Board, the DCI's committee of the directors of all the U.S. intelligence agencies. His background in foreign affairs, even thinner, did not help in the corridors at Langley.

Webster's tenure has received mixed reviews. Melissa Boyle Mahle, an officer with the DO's Near East Division, saw the Judge as isolating himself, managing rather than leading CIA, passing Olympian judgments, treating the agency as something dirty or infectious. "He did not lead the troops, or ever really try to get to know them," she writes. The chief of station in Brussels, Richard Holm, felt Webster never really fit in but nevertheless had been a good choice, and Holm was sorry when he left. Floyd Paseman, by 1987 a branch chief in the East Asia Division soon elevated to the management staff, believes Webster "did a terrific job of restoring the CIA's image." Dewey Clarridge asserts that Webster "didn't have the stomach for bold moves of any sort." Robert Gates acknowledges the criticisms but calls Webster a "godsend" to the CIA, observing that none of the complaints "amounted to a hill of beans compared to what he brought to CIA that May: leadership, the respect of Congress, and a sterling character."

An early test for Webster would be how he dealt with Iran-Contra. The Judge tried to fend off congressional efforts to substitute an "independent" inspector general for the CIA's in-house operation. Congress saw an IG report on the arms sales rendered in early 1987, and it paled next to the facts established in Capitol Hill's own investigations. Suggestions for an independent IG, appointed by the president and confirmed by the Senate, had been around since the Church Committee, along with the argument that typical IGs, feeling sidelined in that position and hoping for promotion out of it, had little incentive for deep inquiry. Republican Senator William S. Cohen of Maine, then vice chairman of the Senate intelligence committee, introduced a bill to create the independent IG shortly before Webster arrived. When Republican Senator Arlen Specter of Pennsylvania tabled a broader measure including the same provision, both Cohen and committee chairman David Boren supported it. Judge Webster argued that he had made extensive changes to the IG office and that the CIA did not need a statutory post, even asserting that he could groom officials for senior assignments while an independent IG might inhibit his duty to protect sources and methods. That worked for a time, but more proposals appeared until one passed Congress in 1989, signed into law by President Bush that November.

Meanwhile Judge Webster took his time on Iran-Contra particulars. Partly his reluctance was due to ambivalent feelings. George, Alan Fiers, and a couple of others received performance bonuses even now, though the DDO's was cut by half. Webster believed Clair George, a friend, innocent of any wrongdoing. Webster also knew that George H. W. Bush liked Dewey Clarridge. He did too, though concluding later that Clarridge had been a loose cannon, not always candid. Webster decided to reprimand Clarridge and drop him a grade, and transfer George. Both retired. But he fired Alan Fiers and secured resignations from Jim Adkins and Joe Fernandez. Later the DCI presented George with the National Intelligence Medal. Webster also prohibited CIA lawyers from defending agency personnel. Langley soon advised officers to take liability insurance in case they be called to account for their operations. Melissa Mahle, for one, felt fortunate to be nowhere near headquarters and, like others, tried to keep her head down.

While the Central Intelligence Agency struggled to regain its footing, dramatic changes were under way in the Cold War. Beset by economic problems, Russia moved rapidly toward accommodation with the United States. The change first became evident in nuclear arms control. Then Moscow publicized its change to a "defensive" military doctrine. In Afghanistan it invited the negotiations that led to its military withdrawal; in Angola it supported a similar negotiation that ended Cuban intervention. As developments occurred, the CIA's challenge to interpret what was happening in Russia became even greater due to the sudden disappearance of its agents, a result of the as yet unknown treason of agency officer Aldrich Ames and FBI special agent Robert Hanssen. Webster faced an urgent need to realign his Directorate for Operations.

Much had changed since Bill Casey. Despite the apparent success of paramilitary action in Afghanistan, covert operations were under assault from Iran-Contra. Russia had again become an enigma to the DO. Meanwhile the Middle East and terrorism loomed much larger as security problems while secret wars continued in Africa. Judge Webster needed someone he trusted at the DO's helm. Webster had graduated from Amherst College in 1947. Two years behind him followed a friend going to college on the GI Bill. Richard F. Stolz had fought in Europe with the 100th Infantry Division in World War II. Now an Old Hand at CIA, Stolz became Bill Webster's solution to the DO problem.

Actually recruited into the CIA by an Amherst classmate in 1950, Stolz had done his first tour in Trieste. A spy in the classic mold, not a covert operator, he had served not only in Yugoslavia but under diplomatic cover in Germany and Bulgaria. Considered a star, he made chief of station in Moscow in 1964. Stolz had closed out the Italian political action as chief of station in Rome from 1966 to 1969. In the 1970s he headed the CIA in Belgrade and DO's Western European Division and almost became deputy director then. But Stansfield Turner selected John McMahon over Stolz, whom he made baron of the Soviet Division. By the time Casey arrived, Dick Stolz held the premier supergrade post of station chief in London. Casey passed over Stolz a second time to choose Max Hugel, asking the fifty-six-year-old spy to come home as a handholder. Stolz would have none of it. He retired instead. Stolz consulted for the Casey CIA, which left him untarnished by Iran-Contra. Dewey Clarridge viewed Stolz as "somewhat timid operationally," others saw him as prudent. Either way his excellent relations with Judge Webster made Richard Stolz an effective DDO.

Probably Webster's most important initiative at CIA was to accept the concept of "fusion" and endow the method with concrete expression. The latest panacea in intelligence, fusion presumed that a real marriage of disciplines could generate payoffs greater than the contributions. At one level this meant bringing together all sources of data for step-shift gains in perspective. Another aspect of fusion was that it represented a new effort to break down walls between the clandestine service, the scientific wizards, and the intelligence analysts, who would be brigaded together in fusion "centers." Focused on specific functional areas instead of the largely geographic divisions that prevailed in the DO, the centers promised to enable operators to use a more comprehensive database for planning.

Judge Webster built on the efforts of Casey, who been the first to establish such a fusion unit. That entity, the Counterterrorism Center (CTC), had partly been foisted upon him by a presidential commission on terrorism headed by George H. W. Bush, which pushed for the unit in its report. The CIA had previously responded to this threat with a staff within the DO, then with a counterterrorism operations group, neither possessing the scope or resources of CTC. Dewey Clarridge claims some credit as well, having written a paper fleshing out the idea at the close of 1985, following terrorist attacks on the Rome and Vienna airports. The irrepressible Clarridge moved from DO's European Division to head CTC, backed by a finding enabling the CIA to take direct action to preempt terrorists.

Webster's contribution lay in broadening this effort, making the CTC a priority at the Directorate for Operations. In 1988–1989 the CIA director created new fusion centers to deal with international narcotics and counterintelligence. Dick Stolz played along, attempting to hold down the barons, who objected to being deprived of the officers and budget money siphoned off to the fusion centers. The division chiefs had plenty at stake in this battle and good means to fight it, for they essentially controlled the assignments and promotions of officers in their units. Word down the line in the clandestine service was that employees concerned about their prospects should be loath to work at the centers. The CTC started out with people and money for major operations, but Clarridge's successors could not maintain that momentum.

Although this moves a bit ahead of our story, Judge Webster took advantage of the collapse of Russia's Eastern European empire in 1989 to try to defuse the opposition to his changes. These events had great significance for DO missions. Webster and Stolz established a group of senior officers to brainstorm a strategic plan for the future directorate. Dick Holm, back from Brussels to run the Career Management Staff, played a key role. After weeks of heartache, Holm's group came up with a plan to sell within the DO, to the CIA as a whole, and on Capitol Hill. To Director Webster's relief, the plan acknowledged the role of fusion centers.

The proliferation of fusion centers continued through the 1990s, and tensions between the centers and line operators remain today, more than two decades since creation of the first of them. In fact the Intelligence Reform Act of 2004, by giving a new director of national intelligence the authority to create his own fusion centers (with a national CTC assigned to him by law), promises to reinvigorate this struggle.

Other immense changes lay in store for the United States and the Central Intelligence Agency. In November 1988 Americans elected George Herbert Walker Bush to become president. Barely a month later, fatefully on Pearl Harbor Day, December 7, Soviet leader Mikhail Gorbachev gave a speech at the UN General Assembly in which he publicly retreated from Cold War confrontation. Gorbachev announced major unilateral cuts in Soviet troops in East Germany, Eastern Europe more broadly, and even Mongolia, coupled with reductions in Russian military manpower. The speech included language suggesting that Eastern European nations were entitled to self-determination. Given the Soviet withdrawal from Afghanistan, Gorbachev's UN speech carried huge implications. Bush, the only President of the United States ever to have headed the CIA, moved cautiously, but the whole of his presidency would be dominated by the retraction of Soviet power and the eventual collapse of the Soviet Union.

The CIA too was wary of developments in Russia. Agency analysts had long foreseen growing problems, understood Gorbachev to be responding to a contracting economy while trying to preserve a version of Communist power, and pointed out specific fault lines in the Soviet situation. Analysts knew the Russians were spending large amounts sustaining foreign clients—the CIA projected Soviet expenditures from 1981 to 1986 to back Nicaragua, Afghanistan, and Angola alone at $13 billion, plus another $5 billion to $7 billion a year just for Cuba. But appreciating the motive forces in Gorbachev's evolving policy seems to have been too much for Langley. Briefing senators on the meaning of Gorbachev's speech, the national intelligence officer for the Soviet Union and key analysts, for example, portrayed the moves as tactical.

At the Directorate for Operations a similar attitude prevailed. Richard Stolz feared being taken in. Burton L. Gerber, a legendary case officer and street man in Eastern Europe and station chief in Moscow, now heading the Soviet and East European Division, had doubts too. Gerber questioned what CIA saw on the surface. One hint of change was that, miracle mirabilis, beginning in December 1987 the CIA began having its own sit-downs with Soviet intelligence, but the Russians certainly weren't giving away the store. Worry about a mole within the agency simultaneously focused the spooks even more than usual on spy-versus-spy espionage rather than the positive intelligence mission. As then Deputy Director Gates puts it, "the American government, including CIA, had no idea in January 1989 that a tidal wave of history was about to break upon us."

Gates soon left Langley—President Bush's national security adviser, Brent Scowcroft, asked him to the White House as deputy. President Bush also wanted his choice for director of central intelligence to signal confidence to the community and—no doubt recalling his own experience at Jimmy Carter's hands—wished to break the cycle of every president bringing in a fresh CIA director. He decided to keep Judge Webster. Gates's successor as DDCI would be Richard J. Kerr, again a professional drawn from the ranks of analysts. It would thus be Judge Webster and Richard Kerr who gazed in amazement as the tidal wave of history hit the beach. Meanwhile Bush engaged in a series of lengthy and sterile policy reviews. When the rubber hit the road at the end of the Cold War, American officials would be bystanders.

It took President Bush several months to move off dead center in his approach to Gorbachev and Eastern Europe. In mid-April 1989 the president ended certain trade restrictions on Poland and gave the first of several speeches on Poland, Eastern Europe, and Russia. By then the Polish military-Communist government had acknowledged its labor and democratic opposition by opening "round-table" talks with them, agreeing to free elections under a formula designed to preserve Communist control. Bush scheduled a visit to Poland. Perhaps the Eastern European upheaval beginning in Poland betokened in some way the CIA's propaganda there, though nothing it had done had the scope necessary to trigger a tidal wave. In any case, events in Poland were soon eclipsed by those in East Germany. By the time Bush reached Poland that July, East Germany had begun moving toward transformation, and Hungary had arrived, its Communist Party suddenly disavowing Leninism.

Restive East Germans began escaping to the West through Hungary or Czechoslovakia. Efforts to seal East Germany's borders brought mass public demonstrations that dwarfed the 1953 East Berlin riots. This time the Russians rejected intervention. Gorbachev gave no comfort to German Communists who wished to crush the mobs. Instead the East German government fell, and the cabinet that took over from them resigned in its turn. Their successors told East Germans they could leave the country without special permission. On the night of November 9–10 deliriously excited crowds in both East and West Berlin began tearing down the Wall piece by piece.

These events electrified Washington and the CIA. President Bush sat in his Oval Office when Brent Scowcroft entered to tell him that reports indicated the East German government had opened its border. It was mid-afternoon. They went into the study to watch live on television.

At Langley America's secret warriors took to the hallways. Excited gossip filled the air, champagne materialized, the spooks told war stories. Even the barons. Burton Gerber had moved that summer to squire the European Division, his place at the Russia House taken by Milton Bearden, a promotion for work in the Afghan War. Bearden heard from Richard Rolph, his station chief in East Berlin, that the border guards were really standing down, and people were crossing with alacrity. Rolph went out to mix in the crowds at Checkpoint Charlie. Bearden, like Bush, turned on the television, surfing between Cable News Network and the CIA's satellite access to German TV. Uncle Milty had made a point of going out onto the bridge over which the Russians had pulled out of Afghanistan; it would not be long until he made his own pilgrimage to Checkpoint Charlie.

Over the next months the Communist governments of Eastern Europe were swept away. Bulgaria, Czechoslovakia, Hungary, Poland, Romania, all went down. The Iron Curtain disappeared. These nations put in democratic governments, or at least as close to democratic as possible for societies raised on a diet of Marxism. Behind the questions of what the CIA knew and when, of whether Langley had "missed" the end of the Cold War and the collapse of the Soviet Union, lay an anomaly: America's premier Cold War agency had had only a bit part in the largest expansion of democracy to occur since the fall of the monarchies after World War I. Of course there had been agency operations in the East, but to claim great credit for the CIA in these events would be a significant distortion of reality. Instead, in 1989 as in 1953–1954, the agency created to fight the Russians continued to expend the vast majority of its money, talent, and effort in the Third World. As the Cold War ended, several of those Third World operations persisted, if not unabated, at least as a form of broken-backed secret war.

As with every president during the time of the CIA, George Bush inherited secret wars begun by predecessors. But he had an advantage only Lyndon Johnson had previously enjoyed—as a member of the preceding administration he had had the opportunity to know the origins and status of the actions. In Bush's case the primary theaters were Angola, Afghanistan, Libya, and Nicaragua. These secret wars entailed an assortment of headaches which left Ronald Reagan's successor to cope as best he could.

By 1989 Angola had begun implementation of a multilateral agreement that provided for South African and Cuban withdrawal and reconciliation among warring parties. Bush continued CIA funding for UNITA through at least two budget cycles. In 1990 the president vetoed the intelligence appropriation (retaining the preceding year's funding level) over a dispute on findings, as will be seen later. The second time around he kicked up a ruckus with the oversight committees to obtain a new peak appropriation, $80 million. Beyond that, evidence is sparse. Elections for a government were held, and the MPLA agreed to a coalition. But Jonas Savimbi, not satisfied with the outcome, had himself smuggled out of Luanda in a coffin and took up arms anew. Savimbi had key subordinates, including relatives, murdered. Whatever the purpose of the CIA's secret war in Angola, no one any longer could speak of democracy. The conflict had lost any claim to noble cause.

The Angolan war sputtered on for another decade. The United Nations brokered a new cease-fire and sent a peacekeeping force to the war-torn land. UNITA shot down a United Nations aircraft, South Africans resumed their covert intervention, Angolans starved, and amnesty offers to UNITA were spurned. Only Savimbi's death in battle in 2002 seems finally to have brought the conflict to a close. Had the Ford administration not begun this secret war, Angola might have been spared a quarter-century of misery. Had the Reagan administration not resumed the CIA covert operation, it is likely that Chester Crocker's diplomatic solution would have crystallized sooner, though there is no telling whether it would have stuck.

As for Afghanistan, Soviet withdrawal left the situation virtually unchanged. The *mujahedeen* remained pitted against Najibullah's Democratic Republic. The Russians sent Najibullah arms and cash, the CIA continued to support the *muj*. New weapons appeared on the battlefields, to the point that frustrated government forces, unable to strike down the resistance, began bombarding them with long-range missiles. President Bush made Afghanistan a subject of bilateral conversations between Washington and Moscow, as well as several personal meetings with Mikhail Gorbachev. Over time the superpowers agreed to stop their aid to the erstwhile proxies. The CIA handed over a final payment, a golden parachute, to the resistance.

Najibullah's control gradually weakened. His power was decisively compromised when a general and Uzbek warlord, Rashid Dostum, defected, shifting the balance of forces. By the time Kabul fell in 1992, Bush had disengaged the United States. Coup attempts began a new round of civil war between the Dostum-Masoud forces and the Peshawar-based resistance groups. Popular frustration with corruption and infighting among the warlords and fundamentalists led to the rise of new mullahs and an even more fundamentalist movement called the Taliban. Pakistani intelligence shifted their support to the Taliban, which introduced its own rocket attacks and went on to victory, conquering Kabul themselves in September 1996. They executed Najibullah, who had been sheltered by the United Nations. The Taliban admitted Osama bin Laden and his Al Qaeda. These events led directly to the terror war that continues today.

On Nicaragua President Bush steered a careful course. He believed in the necessity of a truce with Congress on the *contras*. The CIA's project had ended in

1988. Langley's division chief, Jerry Gruner, watched as diplomatic contacts led to partial agreements. Congress approved humanitarian aid to tide the rebels over into 1989, by which time Managua had scheduled elections for February 1990. Infighting among *contra* factions revealed fissures in the rebellion itself. Enrique Bermudez lost his commanding position, though he continued to function in that titular role. James Baker, secretary of state for Bush, refused to meet *contra* leaders, but he backed humanitarian aid through the Nicaraguan elections. Some leaders finally saw the president. Bush remained cool to their pleas.

The president took up the matter of Soviet arms with Gorbachev in their initial meetings as well as at the December 1989 Malta summit, to be told that Russia had halted shipments to Nicaragua. Cuba filled the void. American officials disputed the Soviet aid halt. Gruner and the CIA played a political action role in the elections themselves, fueled by $9 million in Bush administration electoral assistance. The Sandinistas lost, an outcome most U.S. officials had believed Managua would not permit. That says something about the Sandinistas too. International observers, headed by McGeorge Bundy and Sol Linowitz, pronounced the voting fair. In March 1990 there were slightly more than 6,000 *contra* troops in Nicaragua, among a total claimed force of about 15,000. These soldiers began regrouping and disarming, ending the long secret war. Between 8,500 and 11,500 *contra* rebels died in the CIA's secret war. Casualty figures for Nicaraguan civilians and the Sandinista military are not available.

The last of the crossover covert operations concerned Libya. Reagan had never abandoned his enmity for Muammar Gadhafi, though after previous misadventures he needed a new formula. Gadhafi furnished the means with a fiasco of his own, a strike into Chad in 1988 that ended with the capture of hundreds of Libyan soldiers. The CIA recruited six hundred of these men for a new strike force. They volunteered in order to stay out of prisoner camps. A fresh anti-Gadhafi political front formed under Abdel Moneim al-Huni, who rejected CIA overtures. The project had to be tied to royalist interests. Gradually a new CIA initiative evolved, stimulated by the bombing of Pan American flight 103 over Lockerbie, Scotland, in December 1988, attributed to Libya. But the moment never seemed right to commit this formation, even in 1990 when controversy surged over whether Gadhafi had produced chemical weapons. Late that year renewed fighting for control of the Chadian government exposed the unit, revealed to possess large stocks of U.S. weapons including Stinger missiles and dune buggies. This secret initiative turned into more of an embarrassment than anything else.

When Gadhafi demanded repatriation, the leaders of Chad ejected the Libyans. The soldiers went to Nigeria, then Zaire, aboard U.S. military aircraft. Colonel Mobutu expelled them when Congress halted U.S. aid for Zaire. In March 1991 about four hundred of the refugees went on to Kenya while the rest agreed to go home. Through the Libyan government-in-exile in Rome, Prince Idris agreed to care for the soldiers. Kenya suddenly received $5 million from the Bush administration, though aid to that country had been denied on human rights grounds.

In April 1992 the pretender to the Libyan throne died in London, mooting the entire exercise.

Like the operations themselves, the effort to regularize control of covert activity remained a work in progress. Bush pledged cooperation with the oversight committees, which refrained from enacting a law requiring notification within forty-eight hours. Bush substituted written assurances of "timely" notification. In October 1989 Bush told the committees that he would usually give notice within a few days but in some cases would rely upon his authority as commander-in-chief.

This did not sit well with congressmen, resulting in a 1990 effort to make the notification rules explicit. In an official account of its oversight efforts, the Senate reports that Bush officials assured them this measure would be acceptable. The 1991 intelligence budget bill contained the provision, which President Bush then trumped by pocket veto. The offending element was a part of the bill that defined covert operations so as to include "third party" activities. Bush asserted in a November 30, 1990, letter that "it is unclear exactly what sort of discussions with foreign governments would constitute reportable 'requests' under this provision," arguing that it could have a "chilling effect" on the U.S. government. Side assurances to the White House from the chairmen of both oversight committees were not satisfactory to Bush. Revised legislation passed Congress on July 31, 1991, but without settling the "third party" issue. Bush's successor, Bill Clinton, would be hoist on this petard a few years later.

Judge Webster may have been the most prominent casualty of the Gulf War. During the long interregnum between Saddam Hussein's invasion of Kuwait and the beginning of the coalition military campaign came a period of diplomacy and economic sanctions. In Capitol Hill debates and the struggle for public opinion, Webster was called upon to render opinions on the effectiveness of sanctions, Iraqi intent, and the balance of forces. Others seized on Webster's words as ammunition. This did not please Bush. Never that comfortable at Langley, Judge Webster decided he had had enough. He let a few weeks go by after the Gulf triumph, then stepped down. The DO shed few tears.

The White House announced the resignation on May 8, 1991. Appearing briefly with Webster, President Bush said he had yet to think of a successor but praised Robert Gates. That same day Bush summoned Gates to his cabin aboard Air Force One and asked if the former spook would accept the CIA nomination. Gates immediately agreed. He expected a painful confirmation process, and he got one. Iran-Contra investigations continued, and Bob Gates would not be definitively cleared until the special prosecutor's final report, still two years in the future. When Alan Fiers pleaded guilty in July 1991, Gates feared that Fiers would implicate him in some way. "The lowest point in my life came the day before the plea bargain was announced," Gates recalls. Acutely conscious of the fact that civil servants rarely rise to head their departments, Gates realized it had been a generation since Bill Colby had been confirmed. Gates had been close to some quite controversial people, from Kissinger to Casey. Then the summer of 1991 brought the final collapse of the Soviet Union, kicking off the debate as to whether the CIA had failed to predict it. Of course Gates had had a dominant role in CIA analysis of Russia for years. But this time, unlike 1987, Gates resolved to proceed with the confirmation process no matter what.

Charges that Robert Gates had politicized intelligence took center stage when confirmation hearings opened in September. At first an extended examination of the nominee was not planned. Marvin C. Ott, deputy director of the SSCI staff at the time, recalls that the predisposition to let Gates sail through created a staff presumption that there was nothing to look into. Committee staff and members were flummoxed by the appearance of a succession of analysts who gave chapter and verse on many Gates interventions in intelligence analysis. Reports on Afghanistan and Nicaragua were among those cited. Evidence emerged that current employees, reluctant to criticize openly, also saw Gates as an interventionist. Far from pro forma nomination hearings, those on Gates morphed into a major CIA inquiry.

The nominee presented a preemptive defense, attempting to disarm critics with examples of how he had simply tried to push analysts to back up their assertions, picturing some alleged interventions as his effort to tease out better reporting. Then a number of former analysts went before the committee to dispute that rendering, most notably Mel Goodman, who had been a colleague for years; Jennifer L. Glaudemans, a former Soviet analyst; and Harold P. Ford, one of the CIA's grand old men. Alan Fiers appeared as part of the committee's fairly extensive coverage of Iran-Contra, but his testimony did Gates no harm. Others supported the nomination. Gates himself returned for "something fairly dramatic," a round of follow-up testimony refuting critics. The hearings became the most extensive examination of U.S. intelligence since the Church and Pike investigations. Work at Langley ground to a halt as CIA officers watched every minute on television, much like Americans riveted by the O. J. Simpson murder trial.

The intelligence committee wrestled with its quandary. President Bush intervened, invoking party discipline to ensure that members backed the nominee. Ott believes Gates appealed to the White House for this measure. Committee chairman David Boren staged his own covert operation, acting impartially in the camera's eye while laboring in secret to build support for the nominee. Boren agreed to one of the most extensive committee reports on a nomination ever, in which his committee attempted to reconcile Gates's testimony with the charges against him. In Ott's view, this episode became the first time in a decade where partisanship reigned on the SSCI. Finally the committee approved Bush's appointee. Gates was confirmed early in November.

For all the drama of the hearings, the sequel did not live up to the fears of opponents. Director Gates strove to preserve flexibility as Langley marched into the post–Cold War era. He showed a healthy appreciation for the need to change, forming a whole range of task forces, fourteen in all, each to recommend changes in some aspect of CIA activity. A group on openness figured among them, advising that a swath of records be made public. In 1992 Gates spoke before a conference of diplomatic historians and promised that the agency would open up, even in regard to covert operations. As an earnest of its intentions, the CIA declassified large portions of the body of NIEs on the Soviet Union and that December sponsored a conference reflecting on the period. Stansfield Turner gave the keynote address.

One of the Gates study groups considered politicization. Although its instructions were drawn so narrowly it could conclude there had been none, Gates gathered a large contingent of officers in The Bubble in March 1992 to ventilate the issue. Directly confronting the matter that had clouded his confirmation, Gates squared the circle by acknowledging that whether or not there had been politicization in the past, it was a danger to be guarded against. The director declared his determination to find better ways to prevent policy-driven analysis.

Another task force focused on covert action. Among the novelties there, a delegation of senior clandestine services officers met with scholars at the Institute of Policy Studies, a leftist think tank, to solicit their views on directions the agency might take. They did not flinch when told the DCI ought to abolish the Directorate for Operations. Of course no such advice made its way into the final report, but DDO Thomas Twetten was placed on notice that the old days were gone. Twetten, one of the anointed, who thought nothing of rejecting a Freedom of Information Act request for Mongoose documents whose substance was already in the Church Committee report, was forced to retrench. The directorate consolidated operations in several African countries, closing a number of stations—a move that soon came back to haunt the agency.

A national center to target human intelligence assets flowed from Gates's concern for more spies. But DO officers in the field met with silence when they proposed new operations or recruitments. Iran-Contra showed that Langley would not back its officers in trouble, and now morale became difficult to sustain. One Latin American division field man told his mates, "Pay attention: this is the end of an era." Clandestine officer Melissa Mahle pictures the atmosphere well: "We were not listening. Operations officers felt they had been made the scapegoat of a failed White House policy. . . . We did not hear the call to do . . . business in a new way, in a way that would be more attuned to the attitudes of the post–Cold War 1990s." In a climate in which the agency's goal seemed to have been achieved, Robert Gates could not stem the retirements and resignations that began about then. The clandestine service denigrated him as a mere analyst who did not understand operations.

As far as covert action is concerned, Mahle makes the apt point that part of the CIA's problem was rooted in Reagan-era practice, in which covert operations were conducted openly and made the subject of political debate and partisan accusation, all to avoid explanations when projects did not go as advertised. She writes: "The CIA entered into a new phase of 'overt covert action,' a marvelous oxymoron that should join the ranks of 'jumbo shrimp' and 'military intelligence.'" The consequences of acting overtly included constant demands for specifics—from Congress, the press, the public, foreign governments—that meant secrecy headaches. Operational details could be exposed. Political tumult could terminate actions in midstream, magnifying the fear of abandonment of CIA's proxies. And overt action amplified tensions between CIA and the Pentagon too, as the special warfare community pressed for greater control. Worse, the CIA's role became that of bag man, hiring the proxies, whether foreign security services or local factions, as spearpoints for U.S. action. Paramilitary capabilities atrophied with cutbacks in the Special Activities Division. Operations also became less controllable as CIA steadily reduced its direct role.

The growing importance of proxies had implications for the use of covert action to implant democracy. To the old dilemma of shady means in service of lofty goals was added the spoiler of agents who acted in America's name with their own agendas, or those who took the CIA cash and wouldn't stay "bought." These problems were, and are, intractable.

As director, Robert Gates's vision involved gradual, planned change. He put teeth into the idea of support for military operations. One of the task forces worked on that alone. He tried to turn the agency toward the challenges of proliferation and transnational threats. Director Gates wanted more and better training for analysts, use of open source information, and techniques like competitive analysis. He ordered the revamping of CIA file systems. He opposed restructuring, including talk of a national agency for mapping and photographic interpretation, but agreed with the Pentagon on reforms at the National Reconnaissance Office. When Gates came to Langley, 60 percent of the CIA budget aimed at Russia; when he left that figure had dropped to 13 percent. But Gates never completed his mission. George H. W. Bush lost the 1992 election to William J. Clinton. A few days later, on November 7, Gates announced his retirement. He stayed only long enough for Clinton to choose his own director. During that interval, however, the lame duck President Bush took an action that brought Langley its first tragedy in the business of support for military operations (SMO).

December 9, 1992. If Americans remember anything about the United States in Somalia—other than the tragic battle popularized in the book and movie *Black Hawk Down*—it is the midnight invasion of this East African country where Marines landed in the glare of the lights of TV crews. The Somali operation was typical of U.S. military actions during the 1990s—"humanitarian interventions," in the lexicon. President Bush made the decision around Thanksgiving. Somalia had become a failed state, its government giving way to a coterie of warlords who overthrew Mohammed Siad Barré, Somali strongman for two decades. The warlords divided up the country, and Somalia plunged into chaos. The Bush administration had actually evacuated its embassy at Mogadishu, until then the Somali capital. Several thousand American citizens left at the same time the Gulf War military campaign began. By Bush's final days Somalia had declined further, with swaggering gunmen walking the streets and feared "technicals"—pickup trucks or four-wheel drive vehicles equipped with machine guns—doing whatever they wanted. International aid groups were unable to distribute food. The UN created a mission in the spring of 1992, but by fall the warlords were overawed no more. Somalis starved. Bush had lost his election but decided that a quick intervention could clear away the obstacles to relief aid. He could get the American troops out by Inauguration Day and leave the White House on the crest of a humanitarian triumph. Operation Restore Hope began there.

One reason the TV crews could set up on the beach was that the CIA cleared the way. Michael L. Shanklin, former deputy chief of station at Mogadishu, returned to help make this intervention possible. Langley had included Mogadishu among those African missions it closed, but now that would not wash. Shanklin arrived at an airfield north of the city with a CIA team to reactivate his old networks. Among his assets had been a top aide to Mohammed Farah Aideed, one of the most powerful warlords, who controlled much of Mogadishu. The man had been Shanklin's agent. Most likely using this channel, the CIA apprised Aideed of the impending U.S. intervention. The warlord agreed not to interfere. On December 3 the UN Security Council unanimously approved this expansion of its operation. Some 28,000 troops were slated for the operation, most of them American. The night of the landing, Shanklin's people watched the beaches confident there would be no shooting.

American troops quickly dispersed through Mogadishu, creating a main base at the international airport, by the sea. Heavy transports began arriving with army soldiers to bolster the Marines, and then foreign contingents. Troop convoys spread out into the interior, and detachments moved by sea to points on the Somali coast. The CIA facilitated these moves in the same way it had connected with Aideed. For example, a few days after the initial disembarkation, agency operatives teamed with U.S. diplomats and international peacekeepers to convince the Somalis guarding a large inland base not to contest its takeover, soon the center for helicopter missions to other towns. Similarly the chopper raid to Marka in January was carried off in exactly the same way. The first American death of the Somali operation was in fact a CIA assignee, Sgt. Larry Freedman of Delta Force, detached to work with the agency.

Conditions were never easy for the spooks. Unlike the military, who traveled in armed convoys or large helicopter lifts with lots of backup, CIA officers moved one or a few at a time, and never had the same priority for reinforcement. Shanklin confronted the chaos soon after the invasion, as he drove CIA's new station chief to meet an agent. Gunmen stopped them. One grabbed the fancy assault weapon Shanklin had in their vehicle. They did get away with their lives, and Shanklin's asset was so well connected he could actually recover the rifle. Still, as security deteriorated the CIA people were forced to surround themselves with protective details, which made clandestine movement virtually impossible. Mike Shanklin had one major advantage—as an African American he could at least blend in with the Somalis, preserving his freedom of action much longer than the others.

There would be no American withdrawal before Bill Clinton's inauguration. Instead the commitment endured for several more months. In March 1993 the UN set up a multinational force to replace the Americans, who continued to supply a large contingent, though most U.S. troops had left by May. Clinton exercised no personal supervision. His NSC Deputies Committee considered Somalia nine times before the climax of the action, but the president never pulled together his principals. By July, of about 21,000 troops the United States had nearly 4,000. Pakistan sent the largest contingent, almost 5,000 soldiers, followed by Italy (the former colonial power in Somalia) with 2,500, plus detachments from nineteen other nations. A Turkish general held the top command. Maj. Gen. Thomas M. Montgomery was the senior U.S. troop commander.

The UN also changed the mission. Where the peacekeepers had simply been directed to ensure that aid reached the people, now the UN wanted to help Somalia regain its footing as a nation. To accomplish this, the UN appointed a new special representative, an American, retired Adm. Jonathan T. Howe. Previously in the White House as deputy security adviser—Bob Gates's replacement—Admiral Howe had long had a predilection for force, an attitude that did not serve him well in Mogadishu—"The Dish," as the Somali city quickly became known to Americans.

Spooks and soldiers labored amid intense heat and blasting sun. The services did what they could to ease the passage. One American recalls the sexy voice of the woman disc jockey who entertained them in the mornings, serving up Top Forty hits on Armed Forces Radio: "99.9 FM Mogadishu, rockin' the Dish. Keep your head down and the volume up. And you thought the desert was hot!" Mike Shanklin, like others, performed brilliantly in an assignment he had hardly wanted. Code name Condor, Shanklin had had his share of heat and sun as a Marine major in Vietnam, only to put in more with the agency. As one of the DO's tiny cadre of black case officers, he had been certain of years in the sun and he had gotten them: Sudan, Algeria, Jordan, Chad, then Somalia the first time. Shanklin had had less than a week at Langley before being pressed into service for the Gulf War, then an abbreviated tour as station chief in Liberia. Shanklin's request was for a place where the water runs and the lights work. He thought he had gotten that—a plush slot in London with CIA's mission to the Brits. Then Shanklin had been pulled for this emergency mission to The Dish.

As the UN built up, Shanklin's relationships became complicated. The UN had an intelligence unit camouflaged as an information center. The U.S. Central Command built up its own Intelligence Support Element with eighty people. Then came the CIA station. At first it had been a couple of rooms in a ramshackle building in The Dish. Then it moved out near the base at the airport. Soon the station became ramified, with dozens of communications and technical specialists but never more than six case officers like Shanklin, all of whom were worked to the edge.

Langley's cadre for The Dish is interesting. The DO clearly chose security specialists over covert operators. Africa Division chief William R. Piekney, veteran of the mid-years of the Afghan War and now sitting among the barons, reached out to Garrett Jones, then completing a year's sabbatical at the Army War College. Jones had served in Africa, Europe, and the Middle East, but more to the point his thesis concerned intelligence support for UN peacekeeping, and he had been a Miami police officer. Jones was chief of station. His deputy, John Spinelli, code name Leopard, had also been a police officer, a New York City detective, before CIA. Plucked out of the Rome station, Spinelli knew nothing whatever about Africa but spoke native Italian, having been born and raised in Rome until he was twelve years old. That language was useful in The Dish, a former Italian colony. Jones went out in August 1993 aboard an agency shuttle, a nondescript C-47 the CIA had reconditioned with brand-new engines and state-of-the-art avionics. Spinelli met the plane. Condor would be their star operative.

By the time Garrett Jones arrived, the fat was already in the fire. Warlord Aideed, uncomfortable with the U.S. presence, became more and more hostile. UN officials tried to preserve a fair relationship. Their advice to Admiral Howe: do the same. One source told reporters of the outgoing U.S. military commander's comment to Howe: "Look, do not take on Aideed. You have to understand who the guy is in this country. You do not need to make him the enemy." But The Dish became tenser by the day. Aideed worried that other warlords were gaining on him by being less compliant. A CIA report on June 21 pictured Aideed as a canny opportunist and a disruptive force in Somali politics. In early June two dozen Pakistani soldiers had been killed from ambush by Aideed gunmen. The UN swiftly demanded the arrest and trial of the perpetrators.

The Pakistani soldiers had been attacked just after inspecting Aideed's headquarters and radio station. In Washington the NSC Deputies Committee adopted a four-phase operation aimed at Aideed. A week later the U.S. Tenth Mountain Division raided the radio station and command post. No Aideed. UN troops manned security cordons or raided weapons caches. The UN captured thirty "technicals" but no warlords, and a Moroccan battalion fell into an ambush. Howe then issued a warrant for Aideed's arrest, with a $25,000 cash reward. The raids and the warrant made the UN and the warlord adversaries, ensuring enmity. When Howe ordered another special operations mission, an air attack by heavily armed AC-130 gunships, the gloves came off.

Admiral Howe demanded U.S. reinforcements and a parallel effort to take down the warlord. American commanders also asked for heavy tanks. A July 19 CIA report placed responsibility for Somalia's predicament on Aideed's shoulders. Defense Secretary Les Aspin rejected the tanks but not a special mission force. Bill Clinton writes that Pentagon estimates were that the effort had only a fifty-fifty chance of success, and half that probability of taking Aideed alive, but he agreed anyway. In late August Task Force Ranger, a contingent of four hundred special ops troops with sixteen helicopters—a Delta Force element plus a company of Rangers—deployed to The Dish. Mortars shelled the airport as they landed.

Maj. Gen. William F. Garrison, Delta's commander, led the unit. Garrett Jones came to see him, telling Garrison that the CIA worked for him. Case officer "Buffalo" came with Task Force Ranger, as the intelligence support team under the SMO concept, and worked at their headquarters. Garrison sent one of his own people to the CIA station as liaison.

Years later Garrett Jones wrote an article he describes as the briefing he wishes he had given Task Force Ranger. Jones would have begun by noting the types of CIA people a soldier might meet, then the functions of a National Intelligence Support Team versus a station. The Dish, of course, had an improvised and very basic station. Protecting sources restricts the data CIA can give, while the likelihood of unforeseen necessities (like a rescue mission) requires that possibilities be reviewed at the outset, not in the heat of the moment. Everyone should expect spies to become compromised, ending key intelligence when needed most. And spooks and soldiers should at least use the same maps and be able to understand each other. All these things played out in the operation at Mogadishu called "Gothic Serpent." Jones might have added that CIA officers should avoid extravagant promises of cooperation, since ultimately they answered to Langley, not military commanders.

About the time Task Force Ranger reached The Dish, the CIA lost its prize agent. Playing Russian roulette with aides, the wrong chamber of his revolver came up when the man pointed the gun at his own head. Mike Shanklin tried to reconstitute the network under one of the aides, but deteriorating security now forced Condor to use a protective detail, fifteen men including four navy SEALS, restricting his mobility. The safe house Shanklin used in northern Mogadishu sprouted so many antennae that locals dubbed it the "CNN House." After a few weeks Condor heard that Aideed knew about him. Shanklin had to get out. Choppers picked up his team one night at a nearby soccer field.

General Garrison began new raids, blindingly demonstrating the poor intelligence while making his unit a laughingstock. The first went against a house Aideed supposedly frequented. Troopers roped down from the helicopters and captured the occupants—a bunch of UN relief workers and their Somali assistants. Then came an operation targeting the compound used by the Russians during the days of Siad Barré. The Rangers got into a firefight, but there were no warlords. The same happened on the next mission.

The CIA tried for better intelligence by radio monitoring. That didn't work either. Some recount that The Dish had regressed to the pre-electronic age, so no emissions were left to track. Others record that Aideed had switched to low-power handheld radios difficult to track. The warlord certainly minimized his use of radios anyway. Garrison went ahead with a raid on Aideed's radio broadcast facility. No kingpins there. On at least one occasion CIA informants were trapped in an artillery bombardment of Somali positions retaliating for attacks on the UN. Another time the CIA and military got into a fight over a "cross-border" mission, which the soldiers interpreted as an attack across a border while the spook was simply talking about putting a spy on a bus into the warlord-dominated zone.

John Spinelli came up with a fresh angle—news that a couple of Aideed bodyguards were ready to betray him for the reward money. They only had to be picked up and spirited out of the warlord zone. Jones had a bad feeling about the operation but left it up to his deputy. Spinelli scouted the area by chopper and returned with four CIA bodyguards early the next morning. In the interval Italian peacekeepers responsible for that sector began handing over to Nigerians, and the

Somalis attacked. Spinelli's jeeps were caught in the fighting. Spinelli was shot in the neck, a CIA casualty. General Garrison had him flown to Ramstein for treatment.

Mike Shanklin maintained contact with a couple of teams of gunmen who had worked for his network. When one spotted an Aideed lieutenant, the Rangers made a new raid. Troops arrived within half an hour, but the quarry had flown. Another Condor brainstorm resulted in the sole result of this campaign: Shanklin remembered a plan to have his top agent give Aideed a walking stick with a concealed tracking device. Condor asked Jones what had happened to the thing, and the station chief found it in a storeroom. Shanklin passed the stick to an agent, who gave it to an important aide, Osman Ato, an Aideed financier. The CIA used a helicopter to monitor movements of whoever had the walking stick. The chopper followed the device as a car stopped at a gas station below, and Delta made an instant drop-in, capturing Ato.

Admiral Howe radiated optimism, the only higher-up to do so. Others had a sense of foreboding. A fresh four-point plan approved by the NSC Deputies Committee on August 16 seemed less sanguine than the old one. Garrett Jones saw a report from headquarters titled "Looming Foreign Policy Disaster." Langley pressured the station to advise on U.S. operations and intentions, which left Jones angry at being asked to spy on his own side instead of the enemy. In October, a few days after the Ato capture, he cabled Bill Piekney an "eyes only" message complaining that the Delta Force had been misused, that the myopic focus on Aideed would not solve Somali problems, and that Jonathan Howe had no idea what he was doing. "THINGS ARE BAD AND GETTING WORSE," the cable began. Piekney told the station chief to shut up and get on with it. The next day came the battle of Mogadishu.

"Cheetah," one of Jones's scarce case officers, was in charge of the newest network, based on a splinter group from Aideed's forces. Early on October 3 Cheetah reported a gathering of Aideed's top aides. "Wart Hog," the CIA officer now heading the Delta support team, radioed that the agent should indicate the building by stopping his car next to it and putting up the hood. The agent complied. Garrison ordered a raid. Jones, standing next to him, cabled this to Langley, but the initial reports were all good. In the space of minutes success turned to disaster as a chopper, damaged, went down, and for hours the focus became saving its crew and security team, then the men who went to rescue them. More helicopters were lost or damaged, as were vehicles from the quick-reaction forces sent in on the ground. Today it is believed that an early action of the Al Qaeda terrorists had been to train Aideed's gunmen on tactics against copters.

The next morning General Garrison presided over a gloomy review at his command post. Military action to rescue the missing was ruled out. Sending out choppers to call the men's names on loudspeakers, trivial as it seemed, became the choice. The military and spooks turned to the UN representative present, Kenneth L. Cain, who felt like the first time he had been called upon in law school. Cain said his job was to listen to the options and report to the UN command.

"Why don't you go talk to some imam and ask him for help?" Garrett Jones sneered.

Cain thought the station chief's expression was one of disgust.

Eighteen American troopers were killed and another eighty-four wounded in the disastrous gun battle. Another American, one of the chopper pilots, was captured and his body dragged through the streets. It was recovered afterward only by making a deal with Aideed. The United States would refrain from further retaliation.

Task Force Ranger now packed up and went home. Admiral Howe left too, replaced by his predecessor Robert Oakley, who had gotten along with Aideed, and the UN command made a truce with the warlords. When the UN pulled out of The Dish in 1995 their information unit left behind several boxes of U.S. intelligence documents, causing more heartache at Langley. In a way it had been Saigon all over again, albeit on a small scale.

A senior officer from the Latin America division replaced Garrett Jones, who retired in 1997. John Spinelli resigned in March 1998 after failing to get the CIA to change its disability rules to match those of other federal agencies. He later went to court to force that change. At last report that litigation continued. Mike Shanklin received an Intelligence Star for his bravery, left the agency, then had his security clearance stripped because he could not pass a lie detector test. The test broke down beginning with questions about his wife, an Italian doctor he had met in The Dish and consoled over the loss of her companion, his former star agent. Two Medals of Honor were awarded to U.S. fighters in the battle.

The Senate Armed Services Committee and the President's Foreign Intelligence Advisory Board both decided after study that the intelligence support in Somalia had been as good as could be expected. It was the policy that had failed. Bill Clinton recalls that "the battle of Mogadishu haunted me." Only afterward did Clinton convene his full National Security Council on the subject for the first time. The Dish became his Bay of Pigs. "The Somalia tragedy shocked Clinton into taking control of his foreign policy and his bureaucracy," NSC executive secretary Nancy Soderberg writes. "Mogadishu was a strategic setback," notes Clinton's national security adviser, Anthony Lake, "not only in perceptions of the United States abroad, but in our confidence at home." Lake recalls the battle as the worst moment of the first term of Clinton's presidency. All three use the image of the Bay of Pigs.

The President's Foreign Intelligence Advisory Board had been in decline since Ronald Reagan's day. The first President Bush had left the board alone for a year, then cut it back by more than half in a replay of Reagan's 1985 purge. The revamped six-member board he placed under former Senator John G. Tower. Bush selected strong members with good grounding in intelligence work. They included a former deputy director of central intelligence, a director of the National Security Agency, a CIA estimator and NSC staff official, plus a couple of technologists, one of whom, John M. Deutch, would presently head the CIA himself. But the board left as few tracks as the Bush-era Intelligence Oversight Board, headed by a political figure, former Governor James Thompson of Illinois.

President Clinton retained both institutions, appointing Adm. William J. Crowe, a former chairman of the Joint Chiefs of Staff, to lead the PFIAB. Like Reagan, Clinton had a tendency to use board membership as a political reward. Among his appointments was Zoe E. Baird, soon after she failed to attain the post of attorney general. On the other hand the Clinton PFIAB did real work. Its postmortem on the Mogadishu disaster has been noted. Somalia brought more changes than the board anticipated—the failure forced Les Aspin to resign as secretary of defense, and Bill Clinton then gave him the board chairmanship. Admiral Crowe went to London as U.S. ambassador to the Court of St. James. The Aspin appointment led to one of the most important developments of the decade for U.S. intelligence.

Energetic and hyperactive, Aspin had no intention of slowing down. Instead he wanted to make PFIAB the center for thinking about post–Cold War intelligence restructuring. In this he had competition, for projecting the future shape of the community concerned many. The House intelligence committee, several Washington think tanks, and the Council on Foreign Relations each had their own vision. Former officials like the NSA's William Odom advocated reorganization too, then or later. But Les Aspin used the Somalia disaster to press Clinton for either a PFIAB study or a presidential commission made up entirely or primarily of board members.

Even on this idea Aspin had competitors. Four months after Mogadishu the FBI arrested CIA officer Aldrich Ames, whom agency counterspies had finally identified as the man responsible for many agent losses.* The Ames arrest focused enormous attention on the DO and led to demands for a review for quite different reasons. Virginia Republican Senator John W. Warner stood out among those who called for an examination. Warner, one of the few to have looked deeply at the Mogadishu debacle from an oversight standpoint, had actually stood in front of Garrett Jones and complimented him on the job CIA had done in The Dish. Now, in the wake of Ames, he wanted a shakedown.

Clinton had no stomach for a policy review of U.S. intelligence. He rejected the PFIAB study and did nothing until Warner provided for a presidential commission in the bill authorizing the CIA budget. The administration opposed this too until Aspin offered a compromise that became law. Les Aspin himself became chairman of the commission and John Warner a member. Including Aspin, seven of seventeen members were on PFIAB.

Although Clinton gave Les Aspin a broad role in the review, the president's delays—he waited months before making his selections—showed reluctance to

---

* The initial impression that Ames had been the only source of these losses would itself fall to subsequent evaluations. Suspicion later centered on FBI special agent Robert Hanssen, who would not be arrested until February 2001. Most recently CIA experts like Milton Bearden have expressed a belief that even Ames and Hanssen, taken together with Ed Howard, do not account for all the agent losses.

engage these issues. Aspin moved on his own, finally starting the review process in February 1995. Three months later the chairman suffered a stroke, a coma set in, and then Les Aspin lay dead. President Clinton brought in Harold Brown, a noted technologist and former secretary of defense in the Carter administration. The review became known as the Aspin-Brown Commission.

The group wrote its report by the due date and put out 150 pages of closely reasoned text plus appendices. Readers gleaned that intelligence would be crucial in the new world and that there needed to be international cooperation along with coordinated response to global issues. Aspin-Brown advocated a new "national" agency, one to bring the photo interpreters and map experts together. There would be plenty of text on policy guidance, space reconnaissance, technical collection, even oversight. But the twin concerns of the initiators were virtually invisible in the final report: both covert operations and counterintelligence were submerged in snippets of text within general treatises on broad issues.

In its final report Aspin-Brown acknowledged that covert action remained the most controversial activity but recommended that the capability be maintained to give presidents an option short of military force. The commissioners cited most witnesses, as well as the 1975 Rockefeller Commission, to support covert action for specific U.S. policy goals and subject to careful processes of approval.

The commission offered the caveats that covert methods should be no more aggressive than needed to accomplish the objective, and that actions should be undertaken only where compelling reasons precluded disclosure of U.S. involvement. The commissioners elsewhere conceded criticism that the Directorate for Operations had become parochial and insular, calling that a cliché and recommending the CIA rotate DO officers through outside assignments. They defended covert action by crediting it with success in thwarting terrorist incidents, smashing drug cartels, and attaining goals without resort to the military. The two or three pages on this were dwarfed by the many devoted to organizational issues (where only minor reforms made the final report) and the dozens on intelligence collection means, technical and otherwise. Accounts by commission staff make clear that talk about covert action by the commissioners, witnesses, and staff had been lively, extensive, and disputatious, much more so than reflected in the actual report.

Among the hearings before the commission was a day, July 14, 1995, that could reasonably have been called "Seventh Floor Day." Four of the five witnesses had been either the DCI or deputy (the fifth had been deputy director for intelligence). They included Dick Helms, Judge Webster, John McMahon, and R. James Woolsey. Woolsey? The commission would hear from the sitting director of central intelligence several weeks later, but the truth is that the sun of Clinton's first DCI had risen and set in the relatively brief interval between his inauguration and this commission review.

Jim Woolsey, a Democrat at the time, and a lawyer, was an outside import to Langley. He knew a certain amount about spy satellites as a defense intellectual active on nuclear issues, but his closest brush with the CIA had come in 1989, when Woolsey in his legal role represented Charlie Allen trying to buck a reprimand for Iran-Contra. The term "neoconservative" was coming into use then, but in 1992 Woolsey would have been better recognized as a Jackson Democrat, one of the acolytes of Washington State's Henry Jackson, a conservative on defense. He had sat on presidential commissions during the Reagan era, when Brent Scowcroft brought Woolsey onto a group studying nuclear forces. He and Scowcroft collaborated on articles advocating strategic force solutions, and early in the first Bush administration Scowcroft had tried to tap Woolsey to shepherd a policy review on that subject. Woolsey had been a negotiator on force reductions in Europe. He had also served as undersecretary of the navy in the Carter administration, counsel to the Arms Control and Disarmament Agency, briefly a member of the Kissinger NSC staff, and an army officer during Vietnam days.

Woolsey contributed policy advice to Michael Dukakis's presidential campaign in 1988 and did the same for Clinton in 1992. That summer Sandy Berger, who coordinated national security for the campaign, brought together a group with—as Clinton himself puts it in his memoir—"more robust views on national security and defense than our party typically projected." The group, which endorsed Clinton, included Woolsey. The candidate listened and satisfied himself that his conservative flank had been covered. Clinton recounts that he wanted to appoint House intelligence committee chairman Dave McCurdy as DCI, but McCurdy refused. The congressman probably recommended Woolsey in his stead—McCurdy headed an advocacy group in which Woolsey participated as his second. Woolsey had also known Les Aspin since 1971 and several times contributed to Aspin political campaigns. In any event, just before Christmas Sandy Berger summoned Jim Woolsey to Little Rock for what the Washington lawyer expected to be a consultation on whom to appoint to head the CIA. Instead Clinton offered the job to him.

R. James Woolsey got off on the wrong foot, and his situation only worsened. He proved both unlucky and unskilled as DCI. The Mogadishu debacle had already begun building. Barely a week before Woolsey's confirmation hearing a Pakistani extremist went on a shooting spree at the road intersection outside CIA headquarters, throwing Langley into a rage as two agency officers died and three were wounded merely for stopping at a red light.

The new director knew enough to warn Congress that a garden of snakes had replaced the single dragon as the threat in the post–Cold War world. But Woolsey used that analogy to argue that Americans, instead of enjoying a Cold War dividend—a reduction in U.S. intelligence budgets—ought to spend as much or more. Director Woolsey gave token support to Clinton plans to cut intelligence spending by a billion dollars the first year, toward an overall reduction of $7 billion over five years, but he really wanted something very different. The DCI got into a table-pounding exchange with Congress in May at a secret hearing where he sputtered that reductions would gut the agency.

Soon Jim Woolsey would hardly be on speaking terms with Dave McCurdy or his successor, Representative Dan Glickman. Woolsey's relations with Senate committee chairman Dennis DeConcini deteriorated even more. The DCI proved wooden with the spooks, endearing no one when he had an encrypted lock installed on his office door at Langley. He raised hackles among the secrecy cult when he announced that the CIA would declassify Cold War records, including those from covert action. That he merely repeated Bob Gates's promise made little difference. Plain hysteria followed his initiating personnel cuts—a government-wide review by Vice President Al Gore ordered them, but Woolsey wanted them deeper and quicker. Actually Woolsey directed the cuts *away* from the DO, but few secret warriors paid any attention to that.

The DCI did no better with the White House. Several times Woolsey tried to take the President's Daily Brief to Clinton, only to be ignored. National security adviser Anthony Lake and Sandy Berger, now deputy, also gave the CIA short shrift. Journalists attributed their attitude to experience (for Lake, at least) in the Nixon White House. When a small plane crashed on White House grounds in 1993, wags joked it was Woolsey trying to get in to see the president. Woolsey showed how bad it was when he began telling the joke on himself.

Barely had Woolsey become comfortable on the Seventh Floor when controversy broke out over the CIA and Haiti. Troubles on that Caribbean island had been brewing for months. In fact Americans trapped in The Dish consoled themselves by listening to the news from Haiti. A military coup against the government of Jean Bertrand Aristide brought matters to a head. Questions arose about links between the CIA and the groups of thugs and militia spearheading the violence, plus Haitian officers involved with drug runners. The chief thug had been a CIA asset. Then Brian Latell, a senior CIA analyst, briefed Congress on an agency psychological profile of Aristide, noting that he was mentally unstable and had been in a Canadian psychiatric hospital. That could not be confirmed. Woolsey gamely pretended there was no egg on Langley's face, telling a TV audience the CIA had been pretty good on Haiti. At the White House, Nancy Soderberg of the NSC staff scored the Aristide profile "a textbook case of the politicization of intelligence." Meanwhile the Mogadishu chickens came home to roost. Director Woolsey packed DO boss Tom Twetten off to London, replacing him with Hugh E. "Ted" Price, then the chief of the fusion center for counterespionage. Within months the arrest of Aldrich Ames called Price's leadership of the spy hunt into question.

Director Woolsey defended Price, and he spent a good deal of energy on the Directorate for Operations. The DO still consumed more than half the CIA budget, reported at $3 billion at this time, but was widely seen as afflicted with low morale. Covert action fell to 5 percent of DO spending. The four-to-five-month paramilitary course at Camp Peary was cut back. The directorate closed fifteen stations in Africa. Of course, that still left something on the order of a hundred CIA stations. Over a few years' time more than half a dozen station chiefs were replaced for cause, though some of the causes were trumped up. In Cyprus a chief had stolen a religious icon; in Bonn the German government asked for the recall; in Paris the French did the same; in Peru a station chief drew a pistol on his own staff. The subjects—or victims, depending on one's point of view—included Richard Holm and Milt Bearden.

In Jamaica a woman chief of station, Janine Brookner, was replaced after reporting one of her officers for abusing his wife. Denied promotion, her reputation sullied by dark gossip, Brookner filed suit. The agency had already begun a "glass ceiling" study that eventually confirmed anecdotes like Brookner's: women at the CIA were routinely denied promotions and desirable assignments compared with their male colleagues. For every CIA female masterspy there were a dozen Brookners. It took until 1994—in the Latin America Division—for a woman to become a DO baron. A class-action suit resulted. Both suits were settled against the agency because Woolsey wanted them off his desk—but they went on his blotter. Field officers like Melissa Mahle tread exceedingly softly, even distancing themselves from complaints if they wished to stay active. And African Americans? About this time there are reported to have been barely two dozen active black case officers among a DO cadre of eighteen hundred to two thousand. No wonder the directorate had to close stations in Africa.

Meanwhile the newly empowered CIA inspector general investigated CIA's handling of the Ames case and rendered his report in September 1994. He found no fewer than twenty-three officers at fault, starting at the top. The IG's cast of culprits skewered the ranks of the agency: directors Casey, Webster, and Gates; DDOs Clair George and Jack Devine; division chief Burton Gerber. The directors had handled the investigation on their watches; the barons had mostly dealt with Ames when he had been assigned to them. Ted Price held inevitable responsibility as chief counterspy. For months Woolsey had been larding speeches with claims of his aggressive response to the Ames case. But when the IG report appeared the director disciplined only half those cited, just seven on the active roster. Acknowledging that Price had dropped the ball on the notorious mole, Woolsey reprimanded the clandestine service chief but kept him on. Spooks began calling the day Woolsey acted on the IG report "Whitewash Wednesday."

Finally came intelligence reform. Jim Woolsey opposed what became the Aspin-Brown review, yet while talking of the post–Cold War world, in almost two years there is little evidence he moved to realign either the operations or the intelligence directorate. Similarly, Ted Price got credit in press releases for reforms that are not evident. When creation of a review commission began to look certain, Director Woolsey tried to head it off with an internal review of the DO and DI. Congress would not be put off.

At home just before Christmas 1994, Woolsey's family confronted him about how the CIA job took away from time together, and prevailed upon him to change. Woolsey called up President Clinton and said he would have to leave the CIA. Bill Clinton had a regular circus with the DCI post—filling it remained a headache. Vice Adm. William O. Studeman, the DDCI, acted in the post during the interregnum. Clinton first nominated air force Gen. Michael P. Carns, who withdrew in March 1995 with the same problem Zoe Baird had had—employing household help without meeting U.S. labor and/or immigration law. Then the president asked

John M. Deutch, previously a PFIAB member. Deutch, the deputy secretary of defense, wanted to be secretary and turned Clinton down, but after the Carns mess he relented. He was confirmed and sworn in that May. Ted Price saw the writing on the wall and retired. Just as these changes were grinding forward, in Iraq came the final collapse of Langley's latest secret war.

In one form or another the CIA's shadow war against Saddam Hussein went on for years, without quite the ferocity of its struggle with Fidel Castro but with a similar doggedness punctuated by failure. The fight began in the Gulf War, continued as a paramilitary effort, then faded into political action. It began with the first President Bush, who at the outset of the Gulf War compared Saddam to Adolf Hitler, and as hostilities unfolded virtually invited the Iraqi people to overthrow their dictator. As coalition armies smashed the Iraqi forces, the extra effort required to take Baghdad and dispose of Hussein would have been a mere incremental addition, but Bush rejected that course. In retirement he told TV interviewer David Frost in December 1995 that he had miscalculated by anticipating Hussein's demise. In fact in his diary the president had written of Hussein at the time of the war, "Hope to see the madman is gone."

Many Iraqis took Bush at his word. Expecting the United States would help in an endeavor it had invited, they took up arms. The Marsh Arabs in southern Iraq, the Kurds in the north, and elements of the Iraqi military all fought. The Iranian People's Mujahedeen helped Shiite rebels. For weeks beginning in March 1991 the battle ebbed and flowed, with the issue never really in doubt. Saddam had begun pulling his vaunted Republican Guard out of the Kuwaiti front soon enough to keep it substantially intact, and those troops became his trump cards against the rebellions. A CIA report on March 16 laid out several possible scenarios, including the fall of the dictator and emergence of a pro-Iranian Shiite state, but it noted that Saddam had the upper hand. That never changed. Iraq lacked prominent leaders who might supplant the dictator. Several hundred thousand Iraqis are believed to have perished in the fighting.

President Bush may have intended more than is apparent on the face of this history. There are at least two accounts that assert a White House decision in the very first days of the Gulf War to take down Saddam by means of a covert operation. But the only actions known to have happened were those contributing to the war itself—the economic and psychological warfare and the arming of a Kuwaiti resistance. During the uprising, what President Bush did would be more overt: in conjunction with London the United States imposed "No Fly Zones" over northern and southern Iraq, preventing Saddam from using his air force against the rebels, and Bush began Operation Provide Comfort to send relief to the Kurds. Washington also continued economic sanctions in hopes of further weakening Saddam, and later in conjunction with UN disarmament measures. From Capitol Hill and the media came calls to break the ban on assassinations in order to kill Saddam—a "silver bullet" solution as it were.

The evidence suggests that President Bush, agonizing over the plight of the Iraqis and the relationship between the rebellion and his own exhortations, decided to resort to covert action *after* March 1991. Langley's reports clearly suggested an opening—a March 16 intelligence memorandum, prepared by Winston P. Wiley's Iraq cell of NESA, observed that

> The wars with Iran and over Kuwait have almost certainly cost Saddam military support. We believe many officers and men must harbor considerable resentment against him for giving away the gains acquired in the costly war with Iran and for nearly destroying Iraq's military capability in the Kuwait war.

Thus a key to undermining Saddam might lie in the Iraqi military. The problem would be to neutralize Hussein's Republican Guard, his best troops, and his airpower.

The broad concept seems to have been that if an Iraqi rebellion broke out, one of Saddam's generals would take the opportunity to shoot him, and that would be that. A presidential finding resulted. When the draft memorandum of notification crossed the desk of Middle East baron Frank Anderson in May 1991, he wrote in the margin of his copy, "I don't like this." That summer the agency weighed in again with an SNIE that pointed to the intense internal—especially military—and other pressures on Saddam. Deputy Director for Intelligence Richard Kerr took the unusual measure of adding a personal note that drew attention to the estimate's discussion of Saddam's vulnerabilities. While many in the community warned that an Iraqi successor regime might not be very different from Saddam's, and some—primarily INR—observed that his regime might crumble suddenly due to its own weaknesses, and though there may have been reluctance at NE Division, these things did not halt the move toward covert action. President Bush signed a lethal finding in October 1991. The project had initial funding of $15 million. Langley formed an Iraq Operations Group within Anderson's division.

To a considerable degree the No Fly Zones could neutralize Saddam's airpower, one key to the success of this project. In September U.S. officials informed Saudi Arabia of the deployment of eighty additional aircraft for possible punitive strikes, plus missile batteries to protect against Iraqi counterattacks. The Saudis seem to have been reluctant to go along, but the evidence is not clear—there are reports that Riyadh encouraged this initiative, though preferring to spread the risk by having some forces based in Kuwait or Jordan. In November 1991 Bush assured King Fahd that the United States would maintain sufficient power in the region to defeat Iraq.

Just as Bob Gates went back to the CIA, his NSC Deputies Committee asked the JCS to consider how to cope with the Iraqi military. The Joint Chiefs were to plan for the contingency of Iraqi commanders making a desperate plea for help, no doubt predicated on their rising against Saddam. Gen. Colin Powell, the JCS chairman, warned against excessive optimism when the Deputies Committee debated the issue on December 12. Powell believed success impossible unless the United

States stood ready to use ground troops. Brent Scowcroft apparently argued that airpower could negate Saddam's core capabilities. Thereafter planning was pulled into the White House.

Director Gates traveled to Cairo and Riyadh in February 1992. Immediately before that trip, Iraqi dissident factions first met in Damascus. Under cover of a CIA familiarization tour, Gates saw Egyptian and Saudi officials about Iraq. National security adviser Scowcroft is reported to have approved Gates's talking points. Another version has it that the CIA director solicited views on dealing with Saddam without offering a U.S. plan. Soon afterward Egypt and Syria publicly declared they would not participate in any covert operation. But intelligence chiefs of Syria, Saudi Arabia, and Iran then convened in Damascus to hammer out a common front. They were unable to do so. These three lands all had reasons to hate Saddam. Although they could not agree on an active operation, they began supporting the Muslim fundamentalists of the Supreme Council for the Islamic Revolution in Iraq.

Meanwhile the CIA began to rev up Iraqi dissident groups. Langley hired the Rendon Group, a Washington public relations firm that had helped the U.S. government with propaganda on Panama and on Kuwait during the Gulf War, to make the dissident movement real, funneling $326,000 a month to Rendon for this purpose. The propagandists and the CIA encouraged a range of exile groups to attend a congress in Vienna in mid-June 1992, where the Iraqi National Congress (INC) was created and Ahmad Chalabi elected its head. DDO Thomas Twetten said of the INC exiles, "They needed a lot of help and didn't know where to start." Rendon spread the exiles' words around the globe in a massive anti-Saddam campaign.

In the spring Director Gates secretly visited Jordan, where King Hussein, the former CIA asset (not related to Saddam), wanted no part of an Iraq covert operation but agreed to give the agency a free hand in his country. After that the former Baghdad station worked out of Amman. Obstacles remained formidable. An NIE issued shortly before the Vienna congress found Saddam stronger than ever and likely to remain in control for at least another year. About then the House intelligence committee, in its markup of the CIA budget, pumped up funding for Iraq to $40 million. Serious covert action impended.

The exile groups were happy to pocket CIA money. Beyond that they were apparently told the United States would support ousting Saddam but were not promised direct CIA help. The lukewarm Middle East response to Washington's invitation seems to have cooled Bush. The agency was not involved when in early July 1992 word began filtering out, initially through the exiles, of some kind of military rebellion followed by Saddam's massive crackdown. Each day the gloom deepened. An assassination had miscarried. A military *putsch* either had been attempted or had been discovered by Saddam's security; forces involved included Republican Guards, among them the original commander of this organization. The supersecret Special Security Organization, which Saddam created after the 1991 uprisings, had defeated the action. Saddam locked down the army—no units permitted to move for any reason. Those arrested and imprisoned—or worse—included a former chief of staff, heroes of the Iran-Iraq War, a number of generals, a prime minister's son, senior diplomats, and many others.

After the abortive *putsch,* the CIA focused on the dissidents. There were uneasy relations between Chalabi's INC and another umbrella group, the London-based Iraqi National Accord of Ayad Allawi, backed by the British Secret Intelligence Service. In October 1992 at Irbil in the Kurdish zone, the CIA brought the INC together with the Kurds and the fundamentalist Supreme Council for the Islamic Revolution in Iraq. For the moment Allawi was excluded. Soon the rumor came out of London, from an Iraqi exile, that the CIA itself had given away the Iraqi military coup plot, right down to handing Saddam's henchmen a list of participants.

By then Bush's time had ended. Iraq became a crossover project handed on to the Clinton administration. In an end-of-term interview with the *Washington Post,* Brent Scowcroft reflected that ousting Saddam had never been "a major objective" of Bush policy in Iraq but that the effort had come "pretty close." Scowcroft observed the Iraqi generals that summer had failed because Saddam Hussein had "one of the most efficient security systems in the world."

The Clinton people were not much impressed. One later said: "The program was too fat, and all this front-end capitalization had been completed, and there was no coup plotting. There did not seem to be much prospect." They wanted to cut the Iraq project by half. Suddenly a fax campaign erupted, with appeal letters appearing all over Washington, particularly on Capitol Hill. Congress restored much of the money. An incident in 1993, when George H. W. Bush visited Kuwait to celebrate the Gulf War victory and became the target for an Iraqi assassination attempt, virtually assured the project's continuation. President Clinton struck the headquarters of Saddam's intelligence service with cruise missiles, but that merely framed his interim response.

Still, the unnamed Clinton official was right. Most of the CIA's cash went for the care and feeding of exiles. That might have been all right if the CIA had some prospect of depositing them in Baghdad, but they carried little weight as an alternative to Saddam. This open-ended program smacked of the long, futile bankrolling of Russian exiles in the West, which in the final analysis simply kept those people in business. The Iraqis were sincere enough, and made a start by their anti-Saddam messages to the Iraqi people. Langley tried to multiply the impact through its Rendon Group marketing. Thus the Iraq project attained the level of psychological warfare. But a fresh NIE in December 1993 explicitly noted that the Chalabi group "does not have the political or military clout needed to bring Saddam down or play an important role in a post-Saddam government." The estimate again concluded that Saddam was likely to stay in power, having defeated several attempts against him, though his vulnerabilities remained.

Ahmad Chalabi talked the talk amiably. He wrote a paper on the failings of the 1991 uprising and how that event, properly utilized, might have brought down Saddam. His paper became the INC's rallying point. After the Irbil meeting Chalabi began dividing his time between Kurdistan and the West, organizing in one place, lobbying in the others. Saddam's view of Chalabi's efforts may be gauged from the 1994 attempted bombing of the latter's house in Kurdistan.

Washington seemed divided and Langley far behind. According to CIA accounts, the State Department's regional director for Iraq had no interest even in being briefed on what the agency had on its plate. The NSC held no meetings on the subject. The CIA's Iraq Operations Group (IOG) adopted a wait-and-see attitude. In 1994 Stephen Richter replaced Frank Anderson at the head of the NE Division, agitating for action. Fred Turco, the IOG chief, agreed that Langley should at least test possibilities. His deputy, Robert Baer, plus a couple of SSCI staffers, visited Kurdistan that September. In late October Warren Marik led a CIA field team to follow up.

Among the generation of case officers who joined the agency after Vietnam, Marik spoke Turkish and could find his way around northern Iraq. Although it often seemed like slicing salami, Marik thought the Iraq project, code name DB/Achilles, might eventually shrink Saddam's span of control to Baghdad's city limits. Pressures for quick results, for a coup on a schedule, were what led the CIA astray. "We lost our way," Marik reflected later. Chalabi's plan looked to fit the demands for a schedule. Marik did not go up or down on the plan, but, an Afghan project veteran, he started providing weapons and training to INC activists. Langley did not order the training, but Fred Turco made no move to halt it either.

Marik's became the first of a succession of CIA teams in northern Iraq. Usually the Americans entered by truck from Turkey. Task force deputy Baer argued that CIA needed a permanent presence. He volunteered to set up a CIA base. Baer arrived in January 1995 under the pseudonym "Bob." A seventeen-year CIA veteran, Baer had served in India, Beirut, and elsewhere; a confirmed Middle East clansman, he had been deputy station chief in Morocco, most recently station chief in Tadjikistan; and had been with Dewey Clarridge in the early CTC. Teams rotating through Kurdistan on his watch varied from four to ten officers. In all about fifty CIA people made the trek.

Among his first tasks after arrival, Baer met with an Iraqi defector, Gen. Abdullah al-Shawani, a former commander of Saddam's special forces and of Turkmen ethnicity from Mosul. Shawani had defected earlier but had several brothers in Saddam's army, including one who led a Republican Guard unit. Here lay the potential answer to CIA's dilemma of how to neutralize Saddam's best troops—have the revolt come from their ranks. Shawani popped the Great Question: Would the United States support a coup if he launched one? Willing to take all the risks, the Iraqi nevertheless needed secure communications equipment plus assurances of immediate diplomatic recognition to prevent civil war. Baer, certain Langley would not respond to coup talk lacking details, was right. Stephen Richter pressed for more information.

Next came Chalabi and the Kurds. Baer had met the exile leader soon after joining the IOG. Chalabi had pressed for a permanent CIA presence. Now that "Bob" had arrived, Chalabi invited him to meet with a group that included the two main Kurdish factions. When the CIA man entered Chalabi's home, he found the

State Department's regional director already there. The diplomat, dropping by during an area tour, immediately left, with the Kurdish leaders following. Here lay another sore point: the Kurds, one faction headed by Masud Barzani, the other by Jalal Talabani, were at each other's throats, every so often with gunfire.

Chalabi decided the only way to bridge the differences was to have everyone fight Saddam. He activated his scheme for an uprising. For Project Achilles, Baer put Chalabi's initiative together with General Shawani's coup in the so-called Bob Plan. In Chalabi's scheme the Kurds would attack Iraqi army units opposite them, while in the south the Shiites would rise up anew. Saddam's army, according to Chalabi ready to revolt, could collapse within twenty-four hours. The other arrow in Baer's quiver, the coup, seemed complementary. Chalabi had one plan, while over the weeks Shawani divulged more details of his own: it hinged on Saddam retreating to his Tikrit stronghold where he would be toppled. A tank force would run interference while several army units combined to counter loyalists. Relatives commanded the coup forces and no one else knew anything, so security should be perfect.

So much for the concept. Director Deutch, Woolsey's successor, not only approved Project Achilles, he asked the task force to set markers to measure progress. Chalabi timed his uprising for March 4. As the appointed hour approached, the Kurdish differences, instead of disappearing, sharpened. The leak might have come there. Suddenly, in a move nearly unprecedented in the annals of CIA covert operations, an agency base chief in the field received a cable direct from the White House, from security adviser Tony Lake. It came the day before the planned uprising. The cable read: "THE ACTION YOU HAVE PLANNED FOR THIS WEEKEND HAS BEEN TOTALLY COMPROMISED. WE BELIEVE THERE IS A HIGH RISK OF FAILURE. ANY DECISION TO PROCEED WILL BE ON YOUR OWN." The message instructed Bob Baer to tell the plotters and confirm once he had done so.

Former NSC staffer Kenneth Pollack, who handled the Iraq account in 1995–1996, maintains that the covert operation had never been sanctioned by the White House, which might explain Lake's eleventh-hour intervention. But Baer specifically notes approval by Pollack's boss, senior director Martin Indyk, in January 1995. The truth here remains obscure.

Meanwhile the Kurds' Masud Barzani had little reason to trust the CIA—his father had been sold down the river on orders from Nixon and Kissinger. Now Barzani made common cause with Iran. Bob Baer saw Iranian gear with Barzani's fighters, even Iranian militia guarding Kurdish supply points. His faction seemed already to know of the Lake cable. At the last moment Barzani pulled out of the rising. Talabani, furious, made only perfunctory efforts. Chalabi went ahead—and the INC revealed its real weakness as very little happened.

Chalabi's effort fizzled. That left the coup. Saddam busted it. General Shawani saw failure all around and aborted his own effort. He took his family and fled to Syria. Robert Baer, ordered back to Washington, endured an FBI investigation for a potential violation of the ban on assassinations, since the Iraqi military would surely have killed Saddam. Langley hung its man out to dry. The NE baron and IOG staff distanced themselves from Baer as far as possible. But the CIA had never been direct participants, and Baer would be cleared after a year of misery.

Langley had an alternative to Chalabi—the Iraqi National Accord (INA), which British intelligence had been pushing on the CIA for months. The SIS believed Ayad Allawi had much deeper roots in Iraq and thus potential for action. The INA predated Chalabi's group and had never cottoned to them. Allawi stayed away from the "Bob Plan" and stepped up to the plate once it failed. If it wanted to accomplish anything, Langley had no choice except to go along. Not everyone at the agency agreed with the play-both-ends strategy. Warren Marik thought resorting to the INA amounted to using Saddam-like figures, since Allawi was a former official of Saddam's political party. But the task force and NE Division forged ahead. Stephen Richter one day went to the White House to brief the Allawi option to Clinton officials. Lake approved, contingent on the action being carried out by the summer of 1996 to avoid interference with the presidential election campaign that year.

The INA showed its mettle when adherents and disaffected officers stole radios from stockpiles of the Iraqi Fourth Army Corps in the south. Smuggled to Kurdistan, the gear could be used in military operations. The Accord also put broadcast transmitters onto the backs of trucks and beamed its messages into Saddam-land. There were car bombs in Baghdad, Tikrit, and other towns. Chief bomb maker Amneh al-Khadami, based at Suleimaniyeh in the Kurdish zone, assembled the bombs, and activists were paid to place them.

In March 1996 a former chief of staff of Saddam's army, Gen. Nizar Khazraji, defected and threw his support to the INA. There were other silent backers too, people like tribal leader Sheik Khamis Hassnawi or politician Abdul Jabar Kubaisi. Stephen Richter also convinced General Shawani to try his coup again, and had him coordinate plans with Allawi. Langley told Congress in May that Saddam's chances for holding power even one more year had diminished. Whether Director Deutch or NE baron Richter were the sources of this optimism, it was misplaced.

According to United Nations weapons inspector Scott Ritter, whose disarmament teams were primed to investigate concealment activities by Saddam's Special Security Organization, the CIA planned to use his inspections as trigger for the covert operation. Ritter believes that Richter actually cut back CIA support to the UN inspectors at one point in order to prevent them from getting ahead of the coup preparations.

But Saddam's intelligence service had penetrated the operation at an early stage. In January it reportedly captured the secure communications equipment used by Shawani. On June 26 the CIA Baghdad station in Jordan learned, in a call from Iraqi security on the agency's own satellite phones, that Saddam's henchmen knew all about the Shawani-Allawi project. Kubaisi fled the country. Others were apprehended by security services, more than two hundred, with eighty Accord members and dozens of Iraqi officers executed. In a TV extravaganza six months later, the Iraqi government televised the confessions of a number of the Allawi captives, portraying the Iraqi National Accord as an agency spy ring.

Now the Kurds began fighting each other again, breaking a 1995 truce. This time Jalal Talabani's faction switched sides to align with the Iranians while the Barzani forces sided with Saddam himself. The Iraqi army began attacking on August 17, 1996, the golden anniversary of the date when Barzani's father formed a Kurdish political movement for independence. The offensive gathered steam steadily. Bob Baer's successors, CIA officers at Irbil, fled across the Turkish border. Iraqi troops seized Chalabi's offices with their computers and files. Baghdad flung 30,000 to 40,000 troops and 350 tanks into Kurdish country.

Congressmen who had talked up the possibilities against Saddam suddenly wished to be quoted more skeptically. One told the *New York Times*, "Twenty million dollars to overthrow Saddam Hussein? *Please.*"

Several hundred Chalabi troops who had worked with the CIA retreated to the Turkish border hoping to be rescued. In fact American diplomats met with Masud Barzani and Turkish officials, arranging refugee status for former U.S. relief employees, everyone *except* the CIA fighters. Ultimately six thousand Kurds evacuated to Guam aboard U.S. military aircraft. Then, in May 1997, U.S. authorities *arrested* half a dozen of the erstwhile CIA fighters on immigration charges, suspecting that Saddam had used the refugee flow to send spies to the United States. The thoughts of officers like Fred Turco must have been dark indeed. Bob Baer had already decided to go public. And former CIA director Woolsey volunteered pro bono legal aid to the Iraqis. The case turned into a spectacle of secret evidence and murky charges.

Even this debacle did not end the sorry story of the Iraqi project, a sort of tar baby that proceeded in tandem with the overt U.S. and UN dealings with Baghdad on disarmament. As with the Vietnamese generals and Ngo Dinh Diem, Washington had talked of a coup, drew back, invited action against those it perceived as undesirable, then got involved in marginal plots. This evoked Vietnam. Unlike Saigon, which the CIA had had wired for sound, its sources in Iraq were minimal and news came secondhand. The repeated failures then compromised CIA's ability to recruit agents to provide real intelligence on Saddam's weapons of mass destruction.

Conservative groups in the United States continued to argue for aggressive moves against Saddam. Neoconservative Richard Perle actually gave a speech at the American Enterprise Institute denouncing CIA baron Stephen Richter—though not by name—demanding he be cashiered for incompetence. After 1998 elections returned Republican majorities in Congress, conservatives pushed for a *law* to enshrine the anti-Saddam operation. Congress voted $100 million for this purpose. President Clinton signed the legislation.

Neither the Chalabi nor the Allawi groups had the ability to topple Saddam, but they became the recipients of the U.S. cash. Payments to INC ceased after a couple of years when auditors found irregularities in its handling of funds, but that is when Ahmad Chalabi began feeding alarming claims of Saddam's alleged nuclear, chemical, and biological weapons to the Pentagon. Even when the CIA swore off the INC, the Defense Intelligence Agency picked it up, under the new presidency of George W. Bush, son of the Gulf War victor. Money for Chalabi continued in spite of a DIA review showing the reports were worthless, and until the Bush administration invaded Iraq in 2003 to overthrow Saddam by force.

The U.S. military flew Chalabi back to Baghdad and trained seventy INC activists as auxiliary troops. That number, compared to plans to recruit five thousand "Free Iraqi Forces," demonstrates the INC's actual weakness. Chalabi, who failed in an attempt to impose himself as mayor of Baghdad, sided with Shiite militants to reinvent his career. Linked to the ayatollahs of Iran, Chalabi would later be revealed as their spy, handing over secret U.S. code data. He became a figure in the U.S.-installed Iraqi provisional government. At this writing, after the Iraqi election of December 2005, Chalabi failed to gain any seats at all for his political party but may yet appear in Baghdad's government. As for Ayad Allawi, the Bush administration made him head of the transitional administration, and his small secular party won seats in a new parliament. Jalal Talabani became president of the provisional Iraqi regime and continues in that post. Masud Barzani is a powerful Kurdish party leader. The biggest winners of all were the Supreme Council for the Islamic Revolution in Iraq, the Shiites supported by Iran.

Stephen Richter's promise, tarnished by the Iraq operation, faded. Once spoken of as a leading candidate for DDO, the baron was passed over for that job. Still, he became head of the DO's Technology Management Group and received the Distinguished Intelligence Medal. Less exalted CIA officers did not do nearly as well. During George W. Bush's presidency, another baron was threatened with mayhem for warning against "Curveball," an INC operative purveying bogus data on Saddam's alleged weapons of mass destruction.

The Iraq operation of the Clinton years marked an important passage in another way. Here Congress arrived at partnership with the executive on mandates for covert action. Probably an inevitable consequence of "overt covert operations," the 1990s became an era when Congress could issue secret war orders with teeth in them. In a dim past, the age of Eisenhower and Truman, Congress had enacted law affecting covert action in Europe, and those presidents pretty much ignored the orders with impunity. During the 1980s, when Bill Casey and the Reagan folks came up with the "overt covert" formula, the powers of the Hill had been mostly negative ones. Congress could reject, as it did in Nicaragua. Charlie Wilson's Afghanistan had been the exception, and even he possessed few more means for enforcement than Charles Kersten had had three decades earlier. For all its imperfections, the system of congressional oversight had now progressed far enough that a president—and the Central Intelligence Agency—could no longer dismiss Congress out of hand. The congressionally ordered Iraq program, following upon years of CIA failure, made that quite clear. Haggling over the exact nature of the legislative-executive relationship lies behind all the major disputes of the 1990s, and the elaboration of rules of the road would be the key development of the turn of the century. This became as evident in covert operations as in other aspects of intelligence work.

24

The Struggle for Control

ONE OF THE thorniest dilemmas for American foreign policy in the 1990s was to deal with the consequences of the failure of Communist states in Europe. Russia is the obvious example, but far more consequential was the former Yugoslavia, a headache for the first Bush and Clinton, which embroiled the CIA, the White House, and Congress in a fresh fight over the definition of and rules for covert action. In fact the events of the mid-nineties probably represent the high-water mark for legislative oversight of intelligence, and to a certain extent a victory for the congressional overseers, as will be seen. Langley faced multiple masters and fateful choices. The U.S. intelligence community passed a further milestone on its road to . . . somewhere else—the uncharted waters it navigates today. All this began with a simple, seemingly straightforward mission. . . .

Yugoslavia was an artificial state from the beginning. Created in the wake of World War I from the detritus of the Hapsburg and Ottoman empires and the Serbian monarchy, Yugoslavia became an exemplar of the Wilsonian approach to nation-building. A pastiche of ethnic and cultural heritages and enclaves—between the wars there had been a half-dozen or more ethnically distinct educational systems—Yugoslavia had been held together by a combination of residual monarchic power and opposition to Italian encroachment. In Cold War Yugoslavia, the cult of the leader Josef Broz Tito and his national communism served the same end. Bosnian Muslims, long the disadvantaged population, began to gain status during the Tito period. Fear and envy of Muslims certainly figured in Serbian attitudes and, to a lesser degree, in Croatian ones.

The centrifugal forces in play at the end of the Cold War divided Yugoslavia, initially into two states, Serbia and a Bosnian confederation. In 1991 that confederation fractured into three mini-states at war, an entity composed of Bosnian Muslims, a Croatian state, and a satrap of Serbia. This bitter rivalry, the focus of ethnic cleansing—in fact the occasion for the coining of that term—powerfully challenged America's self-image and democratic idealism. As a locus of chaos on the fringe of Europe, the conflict in the former Yugoslavia also begged for the attention of nations pushing toward an idealized European Union.

The first Bush administration backed international efforts to suppress the conflict by means of a UN arms embargo. Toward the end of 1991 a cease-fire and initial negotiating framework were put in place in conjunction with a UN peace force. These proved ineffectual. In particular the lightly armed United Nations Protection Force, with virtually no authority, watched in horror as Bosnian Serbs killed Muslims, drove them from their homes, engaged in large-scale pogroms, and incarcerated people in concentration camps. The Serbian republic secretly armed Bosnian Serb forces, even providing cadres and intelligence support. In a Bosnian Serb siege of Sarajevo in 1992, shellings killed many innocents. During the U.S. election campaign candidate Bill Clinton spoke of lifting the arms embargo. Once Clinton became president, he needed to deliver on that promise.

Clinton policy began with "lift and strike," wonk shorthand for an approach that would end the arms embargo, enabling Muslim forces to catch up in armaments while the United States used the power of aerial bombardment to coerce Bosnian Serbs into observing cease-fire zones and other provisions to which they had agreed. President Clinton found little international support for lifting the embargo, though he obtained some backing for the "strike" element of the policy. The British and German approvals imposed many conditions: air strikes would have to be under NATO auspices, approved by both NATO member states and the UN, such a cumbersome procedure that at the height of the Sarajevo siege, when all agreed on the need for action, air strikes never materialized.

Nancy Soderberg, Clinton's NSC staff executive secretary, accompanied the president on a political trip in May 1993, shortly after the United States failed in an initial attempt to persuade the Europeans to back "lift and strike." Soderberg provides an account of discussions aboard Air Force One during that trip, where Clinton observed that top diplomat Warren Christopher should not give up. Soderberg advised Clinton he might get better results if he himself did some of the pushing. Convinced it was necessary to lift the arms embargo, Clinton fired up when British leaders indicated they might go for the "strike" portion of the policy but not the "lift."

Clinton's national security adviser, Anthony Lake, solidly on board for the policy, publicly advocated the equivalent of "lift and strike" as a political adviser before the election. In the administration, Soderberg watched with increasing appreciation as Lake maneuvered the bureaucracy to solve the real problem, which lay in the fact that Washington's own ducks were not in a row—the government had never resolved to put its *own* forces at risk in Bosnia, failing which it became difficult to ask others. There was an NSC Principals meeting on this in March 1993, but no agreement emerged.

That summer Clinton directed Lake to reexamine all options. The security adviser responded in July, asking the Pentagon how many U.S. troops would be necessary to end the siege of Sarajevo. Typically, the military generated plans for a huge deployment. Even after Lake visited the Defense Department to knock heads, the military still wanted 25,000 troops for the job. With opinion polls running against American participation in the UN force, and even more opposed to air strikes, such a troop commitment seemed politically impossible.

Lake wanted to coerce the Bosnian Serbs into freeing Sarajevo and other enclaves, and thought airpower could be tailored to that end. Clinton insisted that Muslims be able to choose whether to resist the Bosnian Serbs, and that meant the end of the embargo. Congress too pressured for an end while simultaneously opposing commitment of American forces. The CIA reported in the fall of 1993 that the Muslims were hard-pressed and that tens of thousands might not survive the winter. In September the Bosnian Muslim president, Alija Izetbegovic, addressed a plea to the United Nations for "lift and strike," then met with President Clinton to urge that Congress approve U.S. troops to guarantee the UN enforcement operation. Members of the House International Relations Committee warned Izetbegovic not to expect troops.

Meanwhile the Bosnian Muslims sought to evade the embargo. Early in 1993 Croat troops had seized a shipment of arms on an Iranian aircraft, early evidence that the ayatollahs had pitched in to help arm Islamist brothers. The traffic continued and broadened, with only occasional surface blips of incidents alerting the world to its existence. Eventually many nations would be identified as coming to Bosnian Muslim assistance, including Saudi Arabia (in for as much as $300 million), Turkey, Brunei, Germany, and others. These countries bought weapons from Malaysia, Germany, Brazil, Argentina, Chile, and others. Turkey is often pictured as having organized and served as conduit for the traffic. Bosnian Serbs received outside help too, most importantly from the Serb Republic but also from Greece and Israel.

The question of the arms flow brought the CIA into play. Diplomacy still advanced at a glacial pace. The European Union made new peace proposals. Newly confident with their weapons and arms deals, the Bosnian Muslims rejected them. A few months later the Croats halted more shipments and began fighting the Muslims. Washington hammered out a federation deal between Croats and Muslims, agreed to in March 1994. Muslim forces remained hard-pressed fighting Bosnian Serbs covertly backed by Serbian Republic troops. As Peter Galbraith, the U.S. ambassador to Croatia, later put it, "The Bosnian people, left unarmed against the Serb aggressors, had barely survived the winter of 1993–94. Without help we doubted they could last another year."

Washington did not lack for suggestions on action. At the very outset of Clinton's administration, diplomat Richard C. Holbrooke had written a paper identifying Bosnia as a key test of America's European policy, recognizing the arms flow, and recommending "that we allow covert arms supply to the Bosnian Muslims, *so that Bosnia's outside support no longer comes solely from the Islamic nations.*" A few months later commentator George Kenney publicized a menu of options that included, in addition to sending Western troops to enforce designated "safe havens" in Bosnia, initiating covert operations against Slobodan Milosevic, head of the Serbian Republic. In late 1993 and early 1994 a U.S. government official in

Croatia—probably Ambassador Galbraith—expressed interest in covert action to aid the Bosnian Muslims, telling the Croatians the United States would look the other way while arms went to the Muslims. Galbraith expected Iran to be the supplier. The DO, then under Tom Twetten, opposed an operation, according to a later Senate intelligence committee investigation, falsely informing State that a prohibition existed. Any proposal would need to come from the NSC or the president, policy concerns were attached, and hiding the U.S. hand would place it squarely in the arena of covert operations. Galbraith appeared unaware of the requirement for a presidential finding.

By the spring of 1994 Congress had legislation on its platter directing the Clinton administration to lift the arms embargo. In that connection Jeane J. Kirkpatrick and Morton I. Abramowitz published an exhortation to lift, arguing that America, having just presided over the creation of a new Bosnian federation, would be participating in its destruction if the embargo were left in place.

Behind the scenes a stream of cables and telephone calls from Peter Galbraith and the administration's special envoy to Bosnia, Charles Redman, warned that Croatian leaders would likely raise the issue of arms flow. Croatian President Franjo Tudjman indeed went to Galbraith to ask what the U.S. response would be if he opened supply lines to the Muslims, more or less in defiance of the embargo. Galbraith promptly asked Washington how to respond. At that moment Secretary of State Warren Christopher was absent on a diplomatic trip, so the question went to Deputy Secretary Strobe Talbott. The latter held discussions at the State Department, then consulted Christopher and security adviser Tony Lake. Talbott cited Galbraith as thinking the United States should show at least a yellow light on arms. Since a conversation with the president was vital under the circumstances, Talbott, a good friend and graduate school roommate of Clinton's at Oxford, seemed ideal to raise the matter.

President Clinton was leaving for California for the funeral of former President Richard Nixon. Lake invited Talbott to return aboard Air Force One on April 27. There the two officials engaged the president on Bosnia. Clinton agreed to de facto lifting of the embargo by ignoring violations. Galbraith was to inform the Croats he had no instructions, making him fear an attempt to sidestep the issue. He and Redman telephoned on April 29. Lake assistant Jane Watson took their call.

"Your instructions are to say you have no instructions," Watson told them. "When Tony passed the instructions on, he did it with a smile and a raised eyebrow."

Deputy Secretary Talbott later characterized the orders as clear and tart, and the ambassador executed them. Galbraith averred to Tudjman that he had no instructions. After checking with the NSC, with a figurative wink and nod Galbraith added that the Croatians should pay attention to what he had *not* said—"no." Then Redman, speaking with Tudjman's vice president, clarified the U.S. position by emphasizing that Clinton did not wish to be put in the position of explicitly saying yes or no.

On May 2 Tony Lake, trying to keep this entire matter off the books, told Redman the U.S. embassy in Zagreb need not file any cables on the exchanges. A couple of days later Talbott muddied the water, instructing Galbraith to file after all. When CIA Director Woolsey learned of this from his station chief in Zagreb, he hit the roof, taking his beef to a White House meeting: the ploy looked just like the covert action previously rejected. Talbott explained what had happened without giving away Clinton's explicit decision. That soon had further repercussions.

Within a week the U.S. Senate passed two amendments which, though mutually contradictory, clearly signaled its preference to lift the embargo. During the summer the Senate passed further legislation ordering the president to lift the embargo by November 15. There were fresh reports of arms traffic. At the end of July Richard Holbrooke took over as assistant secretary of state for European affairs and promptly tried to implement the actions suggested in his transition paper. Holbrooke put together a plan to give Bosnian Muslims as much as $50 million in arms delivered covertly, checking with State Department lawyers that the project was legal. As already true of the arms flow to the Muslims, the weapons would be solicited from third countries. Holbrooke promoted his plan with other officials.

Just weeks later Gen. Wesley Clark, newly appointed plans and policy director for the Joint Chiefs of Staff, visited the region at the tail end of a trip to Russia. In at least two different conversations, including one with President Izetbegovic, Clark spoke of arms and the implications of lifting the embargo. General Clark once mentioned potential U.S. willingness to encourage third-country participation. These remarks have been characterized as hypothetical, but they bear a palpable resemblance to Holbrooke's planning.

Then Ambassador Galbraith went to his CIA station chief in Zagreb and asked if $250 million in weapons would save the Bosnians. Developments convinced the station chief that nefarious schemes were afoot. In reports on the arms traffic, he began feeding Langley information on Galbraith's activities. A foot-high stack of CIA cables accumulated from this reporting. The DO, now under Ted Price, opposed Holbrooke's plan. Price warned the CIA director that a covert arms channel would be costly and inevitably become known. Jim Woolsey, reading the feed from Zagreb, his link to Lake very tenuous, feared the extent to which the NSC contemplated a covert operation, and the connection between Holbrooke's plan and Clark's conversations. In October 1994 Woolsey again complained about Bosnia policy. The CIA's doubts contributed directly to rejection of the Holbrooke plan by Lake and Secretary Christopher in early November.

The national security adviser went beyond simply rejecting Holbrooke's plan. He asked Anthony Harrington, head of Clinton's Intelligence Oversight Board (IOB), to investigate whether improper activity had taken place. There were three other IOB members: former NSA officials Ann Z. Caracristi and Gen. Lew A. Allen, and Harold W. Pote, plus a small staff. The IOB began its inquiry in December and in May 1995 produced a report that found no wrongdoing: only diplomatic activities had actually occurred, none of the covert projects had ever gone beyond planning, and much of the problem resulted from lack of communication on exactly what had been done. Of course poor relations were the very essence of Jim Woolsey's association with the White House, but by the time the IOB report emerged, Woolsey was gone. John Deutch now manned the ramparts at Langley. Where Anthony Lake and the NSC staff had perhaps been too busy for Woolsey, with the advent of Deutch their reluctance to deal with the DCI would reflect embarrassment.

As the IOB issued its report on U.S. diplomatic maneuvers around Bosnia's arms traffic, the situation in that unhappy country appeared more intractable than ever. A cease-fire had ended in April 1995. Serbs were shelling safe havens as well as Tuzla, where observers had spotted many "black" flights allegedly bearing arms. The siege of Sarajevo had entered its third year, longer now than the siege of Leningrad during World War II. The UN commander at Sarajevo issued an ultimatum to the Bosnian Serbs to withdraw their artillery from an exclusion zone around the city, and return weapons they had taken from collection sites. He called for NATO air strikes. In response, the Serbs took hostage almost four hundred UN peacekeepers.

Frantic to contrive an initiative, President Clinton scheduled an NSC meeting for Memorial Day, May 29, 1995. The entire national security leadership—except Richard Holbrooke, who married that weekend—went into continuous session. The Clinton arrangement for covert operations provided that projects be assembled by a Covert Action Planning Group within the DO, vetted by a Covert Action Review Group on behalf of the CIA director, then by the wider bureaucracy with an NSC unit called the Interagency Working Group for Covert Action. Finally the NSC Deputies Committee—Clinton's Special Group—would give a project the up or down sign. For Sarajevo all this would be compressed into a single weekend. No one got much sleep.

Officers at Langley saw Director Deutch and his new deputy for military support, Vice Adm. Dennis Blair, as involving the CIA in something they knew little about. A more charitable interpretation might be that the State Department and Pentagon, having taken the lead on covert planning for Bosnia in 1993–1994, were still ahead, and that Deutch and Blair, just arrived from the Pentagon, were content to let the military stay out front. In any event, the notion of "overt covert operations" widened the scope for military participation. Conferences over that weekend brainstormed a covert project that had the CIA working openly with the military to arm Bosnian Muslims and train fighters. Agency officer William J. Daugherty, staggered at the price tag, recorded it as "much greater than the gross national products of more than half the world's nations."

That venture, finally, would not be Clinton's solution. He resorted to bombing, an operation called Deliberate Force, combined with U.S. mediation by Richard Holbrooke that brokered a peace agreement signed at Dayton, Ohio. Toward the end of 1995 the arms embargo was lifted. President Clinton began a regular U.S.

military aid program, and a fresh sixty-thousand-soldier NATO force with a substantial U.S. contingent went to Bosnia. But John Deutch's stance during the deliberations was seen at Langley as evidence of inept leadership.

Technical intelligence collection remained Director Deutch's strong suit. His relationship with the Directorate of Operations went from bad to worse. Deutch came to Langley with the Intelligence Oversight Board actively investigating Bosnia. The Iraq project had gone up in smoke, making Robert Baer the target of a Justice Department inquiry. A month earlier a major flap had begun in Paris with the French accusing the CIA of economic spying against them, demanding the recall of renowned DO officer Richard Holm and several subordinates. Inspector General Frederick Hitz investigated that too. Deutch probably saw the DO as out of control.

John Deutch had played to Congress, talking of how he would keep the legislators closely involved and bring new accountability to the CIA. Meanwhile a fresh confrontation with the DO was already festering in Latin America, specifically Guatemala, where the old Eisenhower-era covert victory, Success, had turned to ashes. In a years-long civil war, Guatemalan forces had fought guerrillas, descending to wholesale eradication of Mayan Indian villages. Tens of thousands were killed. In 1992 a guerrilla leader, Efrain Bamaca Velasquez, disappeared. Married to the American Jennifer Harbury, Bamaca had been tortured and died under interrogation, his death faked and his real demise covered up. Within days of Bamaca's disappearance, the CIA station had reported it, plus the expectation his death would be falsified.

Harbury mounted a campaign to obtain justice, not only from the Guatemalans but for the U.S. government to acknowledge its own involvement. Under the glare of media lights it gradually emerged that a number of Americans, a dozen by official count, had disappeared in Guatemala since 1984. Stung by reports of human rights violations and Harbury's very public hunger strike, on March 30, 1995, President Clinton ordered his Intelligence Oversight Board to look into the Guatemala cases.

By the 1990s the principal value of CIA operations in Guatemala was to the war on drugs. Almost fifty tons of cocaine had been seized in transit there during the decade, and traffickers had been forced to turn to other avenues, substantially reducing this problem. The CIA had security links, giving the Guatemalan services $3.5 million a year as the decade opened (declining to $1 million by the mid-nineties). Assets included many of those involved in Guatemala's internal war. The open questions were the degree to which the drug war had compromised human rights, and the extent of CIA help to the Guatemalans in their war.

Langley had had human rights directives on the books since the Nicaraguan war. In 1989 these had been strengthened and linked to the assassination ban in CIA regulations: strictures were now extended to assets, and an agent's participation in such acts became grounds for termination. A year later the DO's Latin America Division reconfirmed the importance of human rights. At the time Guatemala had a priority second only to El Salvador on rights enforcement. In August 1992 division chief Terry Ward ordered all stations to screen new recruits for violations. Ward had been station chief in Honduras at the height of the *contra* war and could not have been unaware of the issue. But the Guatemala station delayed its review for almost a year and never completed it. The station changed hands as did the division—Ward left to become head man in Switzerland. In September 1994 his successor renewed orders for the review. The station terminated all but one delinquent agent early in 1995, and let go that asset soon thereafter.

Thus when John Deutch arrived the problem of tainted agents had presumably been cleaned up. Except that it had not—as the IOB would establish, until late 1994 the division never followed up on its orders for reviews, and the CIA's semi-annual reports to Congress on human rights violations exclusively emphasized positive developments. Yet the agency had been contemporaneously aware of several violations while one agent's participation in murder went unreported until after LA Division prodded the station to produce its review. No CIA officer saw the agent as a problem until then. Key allegations meriting briefing to Congress were not mentioned. Put differently, the matter had been of little importance at Langley.

As the media continued probing allegations of abuses, fresh fish were added to the stew. In September 1995 the IOB issued a preliminary report on CIA information to Congress while the agency's inspector general completed his own investigation. Director Deutch acted even though the IOB investigation was still in progress. Recalled from Switzerland, Terry Ward retired, as did Fred Brugger, the station chief judged to have withheld data, while already retired DDO Thomas Twetten received a letter from Deutch expressing concern at his lax management. A third DO officer was demoted. In all, eight persons received reprimands or letters of warning.*

The Directorate for Operations rose in virtual revolt. Many could not stomach dismissals on the basis of lack of candor. When Deutch called together agency personnel in The Bubble to announce his September 29 decisions, the crowd heckled him. The day Ward and Brugger were fired, spooks lined the hallways at Langley to shake hands. Officers ignored orders to disperse. It became a protest demonstration in the corridors of the CIA. After four hours security guards came to escort the unfortunates from the building. The clandestine service thought Ward and his colleague had been fired in the line of duty. A few years later, with a new DCI at the helm, Ward was called back and presented the Distinguished Intelligence Medal.

Probably the more important outcome of this episode would be guidelines on agent recruitment that the DCI issued after the Bamaca affair. These strengthened strictures on employing rights violators as agents. Much has been made of the restrictions, especially since the 9/11 attacks, as having tied CIA's hands. But

---

* Jennifer Harbury continued her quest and filed suit against the U.S. government, a suit that rose to the Supreme Court and was decided against Harbury in June 2002, finding that she had failed to sustain her claim that judicial access had been denied.

Director Deutch recognized at the time the need to employ spies of poor reputation; his regulations essentially provided that shady characters had to be approved by headquarters. Since Langley already routinely passed on recruitments, the regulations add only a shade of human rights emphasis. In 2002 the CIA issued an official announcement revealing that it had never, in fact, been prevented from hiring anyone as a result of the 1995 regulations.

These events taught operations officers that the Seventh Floor did not support the troops and accentuated the trend toward headquarters absorbing all important decisions. Melissa Mahle makes the relevant point that the burgeoning sophistication of the computer and the internet, which made possible instant communication between Langley and stations, added to the temptation to micromanage the field. John Deutch, by trade a mathematician and the innovator of cybernetic theory, might have been pleased, but DO people were not. Mahle records being encouraged to take out liability insurance. A million dollars' worth became a baseline figure. Frustration rose steadily, so high by 1999 that eight case officers sued the agency, charging that the CIA routinely discouraged their resort to lawyers in disciplinary matters and then failed to provide data necessary to a defense. "The field," Mahle writes, "became irrelevant." It is a further irony of history that the same lawyers who were warhorses of the secret war at the dawn of the CIA have become contributors to its risk-aversion.

Deutch cast his approach as "risk management," a term that could have come right out of cybernetic theory but that really meant arranging approvals so as to spread blame among the layers of the high command. It was not long before observers and former CIA officers began decrying the "risk averse" agency.

On straight management issues, Deutch also ruffled feathers. The director wanted his own man for DDO. At the time Jack Devine served as acting deputy director, the result of his post as associate, to which Woolsey had promoted him. The DO's favorite, Jack G. Downing, cut from the classic spy mold, was the only officer who had headed the stations in both Moscow and Beijing, and had been East Asia baron too. Devine, the Latin America expert, could have been DDO himself. Deutch passed over both to select David Cohen, a career CIA analyst whose only experience in operations had been a brief tour as head of the Office of Domestic Resources, not a cutting-edge DO position and a decade in the past to boot. Deutch sent Devine to London as station chief. Downing retired. Cohen proved inept at guarding DO interests.

Deutch brought Nora Slatkin with him from the Pentagon as executive director, the agency's senior management assistant. Many at CIA considered Slatkin a neophyte on intelligence and completely beholden to the top boss. Slatkin sightings and stories proliferated at Langley faster than the old Soviet Union had built nuclear weapons. The DO employed a special assistant just to keep track of her movements within the building and warn of her appearance. Among the bloating that went on during this period, Slatkin replaced the three-person unit supporting the executive director on covert action approvals with a staff of a dozen, all valuable DO officers then unavailable to the field.

The Covert Action Review Group became just one of many reforms, for Deutch pulled out the stops. He wanted officer participation, and many became involved. An agency that prided itself on being the least hidebound in Washington became a maze of hoops and ladders. One promise he delivered on would be improving the CIA relationship with Congress. Here he had a major assist from DDCI George J. Tenet, who came from the NSC staff where he had been top man for intelligence. Before that Tenet had spent a decade on Capitol Hill, mostly on the staff of the Senate intelligence committee, rising to become its director.

A couple of years earlier Woolsey had favored shutting CIA stations in Africa. Deutch talked of closing down much of the DO empire, preserving just major stations, in favor of technical collection that would presumably make up the gaps thus created. That changed. In April 1996 Deutch refused to promise Senate overseers that CIA would refrain from using journalists. By summer he spoke in Clinton's councils in favor of restructuring the remaining elements of the Iraqi covert project. In September Deutch began saying in speeches that he intended to increase CIA personnel assigned abroad and recruit more agents, and that he favored more covert operations. That November Deutch flew to Los Angeles for an unprecedented appearance at a town meeting to defend the DO against charges the CIA had colluded with drug traffickers in California and Central America. Having famously said that CIA officers were not as competent as the staffers he'd known at the Pentagon, in a departure interview with the *Washington Post* Deutch said, "I fired a lot of people. I certainly could have fired more . . . after a while, you have to ask, what are you accomplishing by doing it." At the end, Deutch felt, he and the denizens of Langley had begun singing from the same sheet of music.

Amid all the angst, CIA operations had to go on. The most important remained Bosnia. Agency planners discovered they had just four officers who spoke even passable Serbo-Croatian. H. K. Roy was one of them. Roy had seen the disintegration of Yugoslavia from the CIA station in Belgrade, had covered Kosovo, and had done an earlier mission in Bosnia. He had learned of the Lake-Galbraith arms ploy only a few months after it took place. In mid-1995 the DO selected him for Sarajevo as its first station chief. The "station," however, consisted of just one communications officer, a man who had been in on the chaos of The Dish, perhaps fitting preparation for Sarajevo. Roy helped pinpoint Serbian gun positions that would be destroyed in Operation Deliberate Force, and he reported on the massacre at Srebrenica. Then Roy discovered the downside of the Iranian arms traffic—the Iranians controlled Bosnia's interior ministry. He learned Iranian agents planned to kidnap him. Suddenly exfiltration became necessary.

At one point the situation grew so taut that Roy made his radioman promise to shoot him if they were about to be captured. In token to the complexities of the Deutch-era CIA, Roy had had to sign a waiver indemnifying the CIA in case he were disfigured on this mission (unlike, for example, Dick Holm in the Congo). Both Roy and his assistant realized that, if the eventuality arose, his comrade would have to convince agency lawyers that killing the station chief had been in Roy's best interest.

The Clinton administration eventually demanded—and received—the dismissal of the offending pro-Iranian minister as a condition for the military aid and training program it sponsored for Bosnia-Herzegovina.

Roy's was not the only exfiltration. Admiral Blair outraged the DO when he talked of agency sources to reporters, compromising several agents who then had to be moved to safety. Some CIA people also had to be redeployed. The cost reportedly came to $10 million. It is also said that a woman officer died in the line of duty in Bosnia.

Center stage now went to Support for Military Operations, the notorious SMO. Contingency operations, like Somalia, Haiti, and now Bosnia, were the major form of U.S. military activity. Admiral Blair presided over formation of a National Intelligence Support Team in tandem with Clinton's dispatch of an expeditionary force. In January 1996 the mission went into high gear. It included CIA operatives and analysts, military folk from the Defense Human Intelligence Service and DIA, NSA cryptologists, technologists, and communicators. Support included a U-2 detachment flying from southern France, early use of computer terrain-modeling, and the first use of the unmanned aerial vehicle known as Predator. The initial deployment was handled by a CIA team of fifteen under a junior officer. By all accounts the Predator did splendidly. When the military tried the same thing, they needed a unit of two hundred airmen headed by a colonel. Two of their eight Predators were lost within weeks.

The intelligence support team worked in Bosnia for the long term. Some variant of it continues there today. New intelligence teams became necessary in 1999 when Clinton moved on to confront the Serbian Republic directly in the Kosovo war. The highlight there, corrupted location data that led to the U.S. Air Force bombing the Chinese embassy in Belgrade, naturally became a matter of dispute. At least the Directorate for Operations rested easy—blame went to other segments of the intelligence community.

In November 1996 John Deutch resigned, following the tradition of allowing an incoming president—Bill Clinton returning for a second term—to choose his senior officials (Deutch held cabinet rank). He hoped to go to the Pentagon as secretary of defense. Instead Deutch received no post at all. In his memoir Clinton says that he "hated" to lose Deutch at CIA, but no other evidence exists to substantiate this. By then so much bad blood spotted the rafters that when computers at Deutch's home were found to contain unprotected classified information, CIA security officers were ready to throw the book at him. Deutch lost his CIA and (for a time) Pentagon security clearances, finally avoiding criminal prosecution only because of a presidential pardon. Nora Slatkin and five others were reprimanded for their handling of the original inquiries.

Capitol Hill watched all this closely. In fact the Senate Select Committee on Intelligence held four hearings before October 1996 just on the question of intelligence for intervention in Bosnia. That would be only one SSCI probe. Congress worked on intelligence reform legislation it put into CIA budget authorizations. Other areas of inquiry included examining the CIA role in Gulf War intelligence before the exposure of U.S. troops to potential toxic chemicals, the CIA's use of journalists and others, allegations of a CIA connection to *contra* drug trafficking, the claims upon the U.S. government by former South Vietnamese commandos who had fought for the CIA, the Bamaca case in Guatemala, intelligence for law enforcement, information security, the inspector general's office, organized crime in Russia, airborne and satellite reconnaissance, and more. The Senate intelligence committee also investigated terrorism issues, including the June 1996 bombing of the Khobar barracks in Saudi Arabia.

Counterintelligence continued to be a concern. Not only did the Aldrich Ames case still make waves, in November 1996, on Deutch's watch, the FBI arrested a DO counterintelligence officer, Harold Nicolson, who pled guilty to spying for the Russians.

In the time Dick Helms sat at the desk on the Seventh Floor, months' worth of CIA contacts with Congress could be listed in double-space typescript on just one or a few sheets of paper. That had not been the whole story, of course; there were a certain number of chats on the phone or at Washington parties. But by the 1990s contacts with Congress were running considerably higher than a thousand a year—and those were merely the official ones. Langley seriously discussed creating a regular intelligence periodical for Congress along the lines of the President's Daily Brief and similar reports.

Between January 1995 and September 1996 the SSCI received no fewer than 436 notifications of significant intelligence activities, not because so many covert operations were under way but because notification requirements expanded to encompass extremely minute actions. That too was an index of the rise of the congressional intelligence juggernaut. Conditions for notification, especially the definition of "current" notification, were also still controversial. In fact that issue figured in the most important SSCI inquiry of 1996, about Bosnian arms.

By far the key oversight action of this period with respect to covert operations was a series of inquiries into the Bosnian arms traffic. On April 5, 1996, the *Los Angeles Times* began publishing a succession of articles revealing the Lake-Galbraith maneuvers with their "no instruction" subterfuge. No fewer than six congressional committees took this up. In the House of Representatives, which had shifted to Republican control in the previous election, the incident offered an opportunity to score political points. (Some in the House probably saw a chance at payback for Iran-Contra.) The House International Relations Committee created a subcommittee and spent a million dollars on its inquiry. The SSCI developed identical information and reached the same conclusions in an investigation conducted in the normal order of its business. These were the most important of the congressional probes into the Bosnia affair, yet aside from generating heat and a huge report there was little to show for the effort.

For present purposes the Senate intelligence committee inquiry is the more relevant because it was completed and the report issued on November 7, 1996—still on Deutch's watch—and because President Clinton shortly thereafter nominated Anthony Lake as CIA director in his place. The Senate would have to confirm Lake, and the intelligence committee had jurisdiction. Here lay the ground on which the latest round of the legislative-executive struggle for control over U.S. intelligence was fought out.

Lurid press accounts pictured the Clinton White House as purposefully evading a UN embargo, in league with nasty Iranian ayatollahs. The Congress inevitably wanted to sink its teeth into that. Never mind that the Senate had pressured Clinton to lift the embargo, passing some of its legislation at the very moment of the Lake-Galbraith gambit, or that a few months later legislators actually moved to prohibit Clinton from enforcing it. The SSCI had several public hearings to question Peter Galbraith, Charles E. Redman, Strobe Talbott, and Richard Holbrooke; four more closed sessions were held plus six "informal" meetings. Witnesses included John Deutch, Jim Woolsey, the chairman of the JCS, the secretary of defense, and State and Defense department lawyers. Tony Lake appeared before an informal meeting, putting another crack in the dike presidents traditionally use to wall off their national security advisers from congressional scrutiny. Anthony S. Harrington of the IOB presented the board's conclusions to the senators as well.

Everyone insisted the Bosnia initiative had been a diplomatic maneuver, that impressions of a covert operation were mistaken, and that planning had never led to operations. The senators eventually accepted this view. The SSCI report argued that the administration would have been better off to inform participants of what had been afoot, and the report especially singled out lack of notification to Congress, which it deemed unacceptable. That led right back to the debate over "current" reporting of covert activity that had raged so long and so bitterly. The Senate committee also resurrected the issue of "third country" operations and notification responsibilities in those cases. Iran and others helping arm the Bosnian Muslims obviously fell under "third country" provisions, and the SSCI report reminded all that oversight in this area had yet to be perfected.

President Clinton's nomination of Tony Lake for CIA director afforded the Senate an instant opportunity to press its concerns and a position of advantage. John Deutch introduced Lake to CIA personnel and gave him a bear hug at an event in The Bubble, but that counted for little on the Hill. Not surprisingly, in the phone calls and informal meetings a nominee typically has before appearing—horse shows as it were—Lake told senators that the administration had erred in not informing Congress of the Bosnia ploy. He promised better. Lake also made the proper genuflections to legislative oversight, despite the secrecy he clearly had favored as national security adviser.

The senators had other concerns about Anthony Lake too. Some of them responded to Langley's doubts, given that Lake seemed to have had little time for CIA during his White House years. Lake mobilized support to counter such complaints. An anonymous "senior intelligence officer"—likely John Deutch—told the *New York Times*: "My experience with Tony Lake regarding secret operations, clandestine operations, and the clandestine service has been absolutely outstanding. I could not ask for more support. With respect to covert action programs, he's helped us focus them on the right things. That's had a dramatic and positive effect on my officer corps." This would have been news to Bob Baer, whose anti-Saddam coup Lake canceled the day before its execution.

At first the conventional wisdom held that Lake would be confirmed. Then questions arose over his stock portfolio, held a couple of years into the administration; then allegations that Lake had prevented the briefing of Congress on charges of secret Chinese campaign contributions in 1996; then others. Lake's promises to put his stocks in a blind trust had no impact.

The real issue, cloaked by the palaver, remained the legislative-executive balance of power over intelligence, exemplified by the Bosnia gambit. That became even clearer when SSCI chairman Richard Shelby, a Republican from Alabama, finally permitted confirmation hearings to begin—after three months had passed. Anthony Lake spoke of unvarnished intelligence. But senators' questions concentrated on Bosnia, the absent China briefing, Lake's belief that leakers were the same as spies, his opinion as to whether Alger Hiss had been a Communist—not much about the business of the CIA. While hitting Lake for suppressing data, Senator Shelby demanded and obtained access to the FBI background investigation for the Lake appointment—another indication of the balance of power.

When Shelby wanted another delay, supposedly to permit others to review the report, Lake threw up his hands. Bill Clinton recounts, "He was worn down after working seventy- and eighty-hour weeks for four years. And he didn't want to risk hurting the CIA with further delays. If it had been up to me, I would have carried on the fight for a year if that's what it took. . . . But I could see Tony had had enough." The former president comments, "I still regret the raw deal handed to Lake." Tony Lake withdrew his nomination with a testy letter to President Clinton, promptly released by the White House, calling the SSCI process a "political circus."

After the Lake episode Bill Clinton understood that the next director of central intelligence had to be someone who could please Congress and obtain confirmation from the Republican majority in the Senate. The president wanted someone acceptable to him, and it would not hurt at Langley if the candidate were in with, or at least known to, CIA officers. Several agency officers met the third criteria but not the others. The acting DCI, Deutch's deputy, fit every one. George Tenet had had two years to learn the ropes at Langley, and now he looked ready to step up. Tenet had got on well with Clinton while on the NSC staff, and he had extensive contacts on the Hill after years on the SSCI staff preceding that. A New York boy but close to the working class—his father owned a Greek deli—the sophistication Tenet had won the appreciation of the president, whose own rise from hardscrabble Arkansan to Oxford scholar held many similarities. President Clinton quickly named Tenet for DCI, and the nominee just as quickly won Senate confirmation.

George Tenet's time as director of central intelligence is too recent to appreciate fully, but it is worth comment as this narrative moves to a conclusion. Before that, however, something more on oversight. The rejection of Anthony Lake and the succession of George Tenet should be seen as a full victory for Capitol Hill.

But this would be no milestone in a triumphal procession; rather it represented a high-water mark. Almost immediately congressional sway began to recede.

Ultimately congressional control, even shared control, had to be unrealistic. The CIA answered to the president. Throughout the Cold War it had been the president's tool for international manipulation. This could only continue, due to the fact that Congress, by failing to pass an intelligence charter during the 1970s, had left existing ambiguities untouched. At no time since has there been sufficient unity of view, or a veto-proof majority of any political party, capable of imposing regimentation on the system.

Nor did every, or even most, legislators *want* control of intelligence. Many recognized that Congress had too many chiefs and lacked ability to sustain attention; it had not the necessary knowledge of programs, missions, and players. Its members might trip over important values. Many saw Congress as a partner with the executive in managing intelligence, with oversight the tool. None of this mattered. *Presidents* viewed every success of the overseers as diluting their authority. Tensions inherent to the system could be viewed as constitutional checks and balances except that the playing field, never level, awarded all advantage to the executive.

Take membership. Senators and congressmen most often came to the committees with no knowledge of intelligence and were subject to term limits. Even after these were extended, the limit required departure. Thus members arrived as a *tabula rasa*, affording the CIA and other agencies the opportunity to indoctrinate them. They learned gradually from experience. Plenty of matters came before the oversight committees revealing the reality as different from the ideal. Yet as members gained knowledge and experience, they were obliged to leave.

Then there are the staffs. Both the congressional committees have expert staffs, small in comparison to the entities they oversee. Neither staff comprises more than fifty or sixty persons. By the late 1990s, according to former SSCI deputy staff chief Marvin Ott, political loyalists predominated on the oversight staffs. Ott actually dates the decline to the Gates nomination and the hardball of the first Bush administration. Until 2000 the SSCI staff remained "unified," that is, staffers were not to represent political interests but simply to work the issues. The Senate staff had twenty-five slots for professionals—many of them former intelligence community employees—and thirty support staff. The staffs were often sympathetic to the agencies they monitored, full of friends, former colleagues, and fellow travelers. After the 2000 election the Republican Party invoked a clause in SSCI rules that permitted transformation of the staff to a partisan one.

The president has congressional liaison offices larger than the overseer staffs put together, plus insulators like the Intelligence Oversight Board and warning mechanisms such as the President's Foreign Intelligence Advisory Board. There are additional liaison resources at the CIA and the other agencies. A president is also able to invoke party loyalty to overcome a certain amount of opposition. And a president can make private deals with legislators to realize his goals. With an NSC staff to alert him to potential congressional encroachments, and command of the levers of power, presidents have the home field advantage on intelligence management. Congressional overseers frequently become one more pillar for presidential claims about the legitimacy of policy, not guardians of the public interest, part of the problem rather than the solution. Even in the Clinton era—where William J. Clinton is often accused of neglecting intelligence rather than managing it—the practical impact of presidential advantage was evident. This was nowhere plainer than on the watch of CIA Director George J. Tenet.

When Clinton nominated George Tenet for DCI, Senator Shelby immediately demanded the same access to Tenet's FBI file he had gotten for Anthony Lake. He did not receive it. That first, small sign of the pendulum swinging back attracted no attention at the time. Another was the rejection of a provision in the 1998 intelligence authorization act making it legal for a CIA employee to go directly to the oversight committees with evidence of wrongdoing, avoiding having to secure the permission of superiors. That had been the *only* mechanism by which the oversight committees had learned of the Guatemala (Bamaca) affair and certain Salvadoran human rights violations. A State Department officer lost his clearances and without them his job because he had gone to the SSCI on the Bamaca affair. Blissfully unaware of the shifting balance, the Senate intelligence committee smoothly handled Tenet's nomination.

The worst thing to emerge during George Tenet's confirmation proceedings was that the nominee's father, without his knowledge, had bought the family a condominium apartment in Athens. The DCI-designate hastened to build more bridges to congressional overseers. He had already brought in former House committee staff director Mark Lowenthal as a senior official. He soon encouraged Clinton to appoint Senate committee staff veteran L. Britt Snider as CIA inspector general. Keith Hall of the SSCI staff emerged as head of the National Reconnaissance Office. There were other examples as well. But Director Tenet moved even faster to widen channels to Bill Clinton.

Few outside professional circles knew much about George Tenet at the time. When the mass-circulation Sunday supplement *Parade* published a feature on John Deutch in November 1995, the magazine had put on its cover a plush portrait photo (which pictured Deutch standing behind Tenet and Nora Slatkin, his hands on their shoulders) that identified Tenet as DDO David Cohen. Tenet might never have made it to become CIA director—returning from Bosnia in 1996, the CIA plane flying him home from Dubrovnik was struck by a bird over the Atlantic, cracking the aircraft's windshield. The pilot barely succeeded in making a forced landing in Newfoundland.

But Tenet proved to have remarkable staying power. At forty-four he became the youngest director of central intelligence since James Schlesinger. Only Allen Dulles served longer as DCI. Only Dulles again, Dick Helms, and Tenet successfully negotiated the transition from a presidency of one party to that of another, and both Dulles and Helms had been professional intelligence officers while Tenet was not. Tenet, on the other hand, was the quintessential staff officer, assuming the coloration of those he served. His siding with Bill Clinton, perfectly logical, also shows the balance between Congress and the executive that existed at the time.

Unlike many staff people, George Tenet rose to lead. This began with his efforts to restore the CIA image, greatly tarnished in the public mind. Polling data for 1998 show that just over half of Americans had a positive view of the CIA. Langley held less of the public's esteem than any agency of the U.S. government except the Internal Revenue Service. Worse, these poll numbers were poorer than those for 1987, the height of the Iran-Contra affair. Director Tenet began by hosting an elaborate fiftieth-anniversary celebration for the agency, marked by receptions, conferences, and certain declassification actions.

Among other things, Tenet created a "Trailblazer" award, first given to fifty individuals deemed crucial to U.S. intelligence. He greatly expanded CIA's program of assigning "officers-in-residence" to universities, helping increase public awareness and educating students on the agency and its cohorts. The CIA began to cooperate with Hollywood, permitting filming at Langley and furnishing advice on movie and television scripts (the TV involvement could cut both ways—when Garrett Jones and John Spinelli agreed to interviews for a History Channel program on the CIA in Somalia, the agency demanded the opportunity to vet the material, a unilateral extension of secrecy agreements that cover only written works). Tenet energized the agency's Historical Review Program, which considered some records for declassification, and arranged for the Center for the Study of Intelligence to publish monographs and host conferences that brought together agency officers and scholars.

Morale at Langley rose and remained high until the CIA stumbled into crisis during the second Bush administration. Despite several disasters on his watch—the errors that led to the bombing of the Chinese embassy in Belgrade, for example—when Tenet resigned in 2004 there was grief at the agency. Tenet evoked loyalty, maintained alliances, and accomplished a great deal. Many of the disasters that did occur, including errors on Indian and Pakistani nuclear testing (1998), the 9/11 attacks (2001), intelligence on alleged Iraqi weapons of mass destruction (2002), continued spy scandals, and the failure to conduct vigorous offensive covert operations against terrorist groups, are stories for another day. The vision of George Tenet here may therefore seem more positive than a fuller treatment would indicate. It is nevertheless remarkable that, knowing the picture in a way outsiders cannot, CIA officers held Tenet in such high esteem. Leadership is the obvious explanation.

Director Tenet's handling of the DO is illustrative. At hearings for his nomination as John Deutch's deputy, Tenet had reflected his boss's position that the Directorate for Operations was flawed and in need of reform. Two years later at his own confirmation the nominee put those problems in the past and spoke of actionable intelligence and risk taking. Shortly after taking the helm, Tenet encouraged David Cohen to request reassignment. He then asked Jack Downing to return from retirement and take over the directorate. For associate DDO Tenet chose James L. Pavitt, at the time chief of the "fusion" Counterproliferation Center. Two years later he promoted Pavitt to the top DO position. Director Tenet thus favored expertise from within, cultivating the directorate.

In 1998 the CIA chieftain began ramping up the directorate. Tenet included strengthening the DO in his strategic plan for U.S. intelligence, a management innovation. He adopted a seven-year program to increase the ranks of field officers by a third. Some of the reported $1.5 billion supplementary appropriation that Tenet won went to the directorate (much of the rest went for spy satellites). The director also created a DO "reserve," but this never caught on and just a few dozen former CIA officers signed up.

Tenet permitted the DO to advertise directly for employees in addition to recruits from the agency's career program. Outreach concentrated on a limited number of colleges (sixty-six) where the CIA had had earlier success. He invested in the agency's specialized spy school at Harvey Point, North Carolina. The ultimate aim—increasing DO field officers, then said to number considerably fewer than a thousand—was achieved. In 2000 reports put the number back at a thousand. In 2003 the CIA graduated the largest class ever from its Camp Peary spy school. By 2004 case officers reportedly had reached twelve hundred, among five thousand in the DO as a whole.

Tenet also spoke frequently of the need for more spies and "human intelligence," and mentioned the subject before Congress. He had allies in his quest, including Representative Porter J. Goss, Republican of Florida and chairman of the House Permanent Select Committee on Intelligence, who had been a CIA case officer himself in the 1960s. Goss had also helped engineer the torpedoing of the "whistleblower" provision that failed to become law.

Director Tenet created a high-level assistant for targeting human intelligence. He also rebuilt the agency's Special Activities Division, invigorating CIA paramilitary capabilities. The agency expanded its fleet of secretly owned aircraft. Knuckle-draggers would be critical to the success of later Bush administration invasions into Afghanistan and Iraq. James Pavitt commissioned a review of the DO project-approval system, found too much authority concentrated at the top, and revised procedures to permit more decisions to be made lower down. If the DO remained "risk-averse," that was due to factors other than resources. When the agency's inspector general surveyed capabilities against "hard targets" in 1999, Britt Snider found a persistent impression of rigidity at senior command levels.

Officers like Melissa Mahle—she makes this point in relation to the Pavitt management initiatives only—saw these measures as treating the symptom rather than the disease. Until senior leadership went on the offensive, changing the climate of caution, the fact that the Directorate for Operations existed for the purpose of taking risks would be meaningless. Mahle and others describe a DCI who packaged his covert operations proposals and put forward only those he knew to be within Bill Clinton's comfort zone. The 9/11 Commission quite thoroughly documented a series of covert operations projects aimed at the terrorist Osama bin Laden in Afghanistan in which, in almost every case, Tenet recommended against action at the moment of decision. Similarly Tenet is known to have opposed attempts to overthrow Saddam Hussein in Iraq after the 1995 debacle.

George Tenet insisted that he supported operations with a chance of success and properly opposed those without. In Afghanistan the secret warrior's stance did not differ appreciably from that of the chairman of the Joint Chiefs of Staff, Gen. Hugh Shelton—the first U.S. military chief to rise directly from the ranks of the special operations community—and for many of the same reasons. The CIA director reportedly supported a project against Serbian president Slobodan Milosevic which President Clinton approved in 1998. Tenet did back the inception of a new Afghan secret war, but for intelligence-gathering purposes, sending expeditions of CIA officers to leaders opposing the fundamentalist rulers of Kabul. Before that paramilitary effort progressed beyond initial cash subsidies it was subsumed in the larger enterprise of the Bush administration's war on terrorism.

As for Iraq, little reason existed to believe the exiles and the Kurds any more capable than they had been at the times of previous failures. Ironically, today, after George Tenet's CIA spearheaded the Bush attack on Iraq, the president of that nation is the Kurd Jalal Talabani, the president of the Kurdish federation is Masud Barzani, and Ahmad Chalabi is a key figure in the majority Shiite religious-political alliance. Perhaps nothing succeeds like failure.

"Risk-averse" or not, real risk existed and could frame both political embarrassment and death. Tenet was pulled into unavoidable controversy in 2000 when the Peruvian air force, as part of a joint operation with the CIA in the drug war, shot down a plane filled with U.S. missionaries. Americans died. Investigations by the Intelligence Oversight Board and by Congress followed. That CIA spotters understood the mistake and tried to warn the Peruvians off did not matter. Further embarrassment followed when the Peruvian spy chief with whom the CIA had worked closely proved to be highly corrupt. The net result was that CIA activity in Peru ground to a halt.

Support for military operations continued. In 1988 the Senate intelligence committee found that this CIA function remained imperfect. In particular the SSCI criticized the continued inability of agency and military communications systems to link for the transmission of key intelligence, such as satellite photos, to military users. The issue became more than theoretical a year later when the United States fought a brief war with the Serb Republic over Kosovo. Tenet made progress on that front, but much of it was wiped away by the intelligence snafu in bombing the Chinese embassy in Belgrade. The National Intelligence Support Teams in fact did quite well.

An Israeli-Palestinian peace settlement, a goal close to Clinton's heart, found George Tenet wading in with both feet. President Clinton employed Tenet personally as arbitrator, an intermediary trusted by both sides. Palestine became an overt-covert operation when Tenet launched a project to have the CIA help the parties meet the provisions of several Israeli-Palestinian agreements by training, equipping, and organizing Palestinian security forces. In Israel the CIA station chief advised both sides. Later, as agreements broke down amid Israeli refusals to implement provisions, plus waves of Palestinian violence, the station chief began periodic meetings of the security bosses on both sides. Director Tenet had meetings of his own plus innumerable phone conversations with one side or the other, and attended every major negotiation held during this period.

Beginning in 1998 Tenet traveled to Israel five times to treat the issues personally. The importance of CIA involvement became such that George W. Bush, who announced the end of the Tenet initiative in 2001, was obliged to send him back the following year. Working both sides, Tenet cobbled together confidence-building measures called the Tenet Security Work Program, which might have brought the adversaries to where they could cooperate. The program broke down amid continued violence.

Following the contested presidential election of 2000, George Bush, the son of the forty-first president, took office. His choice for director of central intelligence was George Tenet. Some lobbied for Porter Goss for the job, but Goss took himself out of the running and asked that Bush retain Tenet.

With George Tenet still on the job, the 9/11 attacks led Bush to order the invasion of Afghanistan. A CIA field mission to the northern part of the country led the way under Gary C. Schroen. The station-chief-designate for Kabul when that embassy closed in the late 1980s, and one of the key secret warriors during the final phase of the Reagan-era covert operations, Schroen made the initial contacts and set up intelligence channels, then presided as the agency established two field teams with the anti-Taliban Afghans. "Alpha" worked the northwest with the warlord General Dostum, in his latest incarnation. "Jawbreaker" supported the Afghans in the breakthrough to Kabul. Both were supplemented by Special Forces detachments. Under Gary Berntsen, who replaced Schroen, Jawbreaker would be the CIA element at the battle of Tora Bora, where Osama bin Laden escaped—in Berntsen's view due to insufficient U.S. military forces, but also partly a result of CIA's Afghan allies reluctance to engage. Numbers of Taliban troops got away also. The new Afghan War has continued ever since.

For Iraq the CIA spent a reported tens of millions to prepare an Iraqi covert unit called the "Scorpions," who were to be a resistance front during the 2003 U.S. invasion. The agents never served in their intended role and instead became actors—guards or translators—in the sordid story of U.S. treatment of detainees. Indeed, CIA teams played a significant role in the abuses that rocked American and international public opinion when they became public. Again the risks came home to roost.

Iraq led to George Tenet's demise. The CIA's flawed claims that Saddam possessed weapons of mass destruction, manipulated by the Bush administration to build political basis for war, became so controversial that the agency ultimately stopped defending them. Tenet left in July 2004, citing personal reasons. Porter J. Goss succeeded him but resigned himself in the spring of 2006. His main claim to achievement, refilling the ranks of the clandestine service, is really something that George Tenet began. Goss spoke of a new climate of risk-taking, but his haphazard methods were a disaster. Langley leaked talent as senior CIA officers departed or retired, impelled by the Top Floor's animosity. Goss reopened stations, and defenders bragged of graduating the largest class of DO operators—again—in 2005.

But the fledgling spooks have entered a world where experienced leaders are fewer than ever and much CIA capability is tied down in ongoing wars.

Meanwhile a congressional-presidential commission that reviewed all aspects of the 9/11 attacks produced recommendations including the creation of a new post, director of national intelligence (DNI), to take over the community leadership role previously exercised by the CIA director. This became law in the Intelligence Reform Act of 2004. Porter Goss and his successors will now manage only the CIA. For the nation's first DNI President Bush chose John D. Negroponte, U.S. ambassador to the UN and an NSC official in the first Bush administration. Negroponte's chief experience with intelligence, as seen here, had been in the Nicaraguan secret war.

Finally, political action has become a growth industry, but it evolves in new ways. Langley provided money, political experts, and propagandists to assist moderate politicians in the 2000 Serbian elections. Agency officers trained party activists in Bulgaria—and George Tenet made an unprecedented visit there to secure agreement of officials—but the political muscle was provided by semi-private groups like the National Endowment for Democracy, the National Democratic Institute, and similar entities sponsored by both political parties in the United States. That model also served in the 2005 elections in Iraq, where charges of a covert U.S. role have been made. The Venezuelan government has leveled similar charges concerning an election that took place in that country. This kind of activity harkens back to the CIA and the National Student Association, a recycling of the covert past.

The new model for political action is disturbing from the standpoint of intelligence oversight. Ostensibly private political units have more flexibility than the CIA, as do private security services, which feature prominently in Iraq today. Both kinds of entities offer channels to bypass any legislative controls on covert action. As in Iran-Contra, the possibility of a White House–directed extra-legal covert operation arises.

Political action has been a tool for secret warriors since the inception of the Central Intelligence Agency. It probably enjoyed its greatest sway in East Asia, where the United States essentially determined events in the Philippines for a decade during the 1950s and 1960s, and in Japan where CIA helped make the Liberal Democratic Party unassailable. Political action failed in Indonesia. In South Vietnam the agency innovated the "less is more" tactic of furnishing only cash plus general advice, and singling out a limited number of candidates in key districts; but the Saigon regime's determination to retain power no matter what robbed these tactics of legitimacy, negating the purpose of CIA action. In Australia the CIA proved successful in at least one electoral intervention. At this writing, agency activities in South Korea, Singapore, and elsewhere remain shrouded in secrecy.

Next in terms of the level of Langley's involvement is probably Latin America in the 1960s, where this record shows the CIA determinate in Bolivia and successful in the 1964 Chilean election. Vietnam-style tactics succeeded in Chilean congressional elections but failed in the vote that Salvador Allende won. Agency activities in Ecuador, Paraguay, and Brazil during this period might comprise another detailed volume: suffice it to say that Washington involved itself in those places as well. In Guyana the CIA successfully turned the Jagan-Burnham election in the direction it desired.

The most familiar CIA political actions are those in France and Italy during the agency's first decade. Enthusiasts would insist these were vital missions, that America's Cold War agency was the one to conduct them, and that U.S. interests could have been served in no other way. The counterfactuals are unanswerable, however. It is impossible to demonstrate whether, given the Western European tradition of parliamentary democracy, the French socialist or Communist parties, or the Italian Communist Party, if in power, would actually have led their nations into Moscow's camp. When the socialists came to power in France in the 1980s they proved quite ready to continue their country's alignment with the United States, but that was so late in the Cold War that no conclusion can be drawn. The CIA political actions were successful within their immediate parameters.

After the question of how one judges success, a second drawback to political action is that it represents a wild card. That is, operators purchase victory for national leaders who may not be the people Washington thinks they are. The case of Guyana illustrates this point well. Having backed Forbes Burnham, the CIA found him unresponsive, and Johnson administration officials were reduced to begging the Guyanese leader to act responsibly. Burnham ignored Washington's entreaties for almost four decades, periodically punctuated by elections in which he made liberal use of the manipulative techniques the CIA had taught.

Political action is also a wild card in the sense that activities begun for stipulated purposes may catalyze quite unanticipated events. This occurred in both East Germany in 1953 and Hungary in 1956, when general programs for undermining Russian control of Eastern Europe became national upheavals, leaving the United States vulnerable to charges of instigation and intervention in the internal affairs of other states.

Failed political action contains an inherent temptation to escalate, as tragically shown in Chile. In crisis situations, presidents can choose to intervene or resist doing so. But in a failed political action the intervention threshold has already passed, at a clandestine and relatively cheap level that obscures the gravity of the decision. When failure occurs it becomes easy to see the United States already "in" the situation rather than to accept the humiliation of defeat. Thus political action should not be viewed as the simple act of seeking political influence that is often portrayed. If considered at all, political action should be placed in a perspective that frames the decision in terms of the suitability of action at successive levels of involvement, not merely at the entry point.

A related issue is that these kinds of actions exist within a shifting local and global environment. Political action is conceived for a specific purpose at a moment in time. Yet changing conditions and evolving problems lead to corresponding countermeasures, making political action much different than anticipated and more difficult to halt. Both Italy from 1948 to 1968, and Chile from 1962 to 1973 illustrate this difficulty.

Political action is also irretrievable. Presidents who approve a commando mission or a paramilitary operation may decide to recall the operators before the point of contact, with no one the wiser. With political action, the first bag of cash handed to a foreign national, the first article planted in a newspaper, the first act in other words, bears the seeds of compromise. Even if the action is called off, the evidence of U.S. intervention remains—immersed in a foreign society and not subject to retraction. Since successful action requires sustained association with a broad range of foreign institutions, the evidence multiplies in a way that increases the likelihood of eventual revelation. And the pattern of dispersed knowledge makes it highly likely that the revelation of one piece of evidence, with attendant controversy, will lead to more exposures. Chile again illustrates this problem.

Political action is frequently an element in paramilitary projects, a side activity intended to contribute to attainment of project objectives. This kind of activity is more bounded and more logically related to concrete goals. The appropriate question should be whether the project as a whole is necessary, and beyond that, whether political action and propaganda measures suitably contribute to it.

In seeking influence the United States possesses a whole array of resources other than clandestine services. The Voice of America, State Department information activities, public diplomacy campaigns organized by the White House, student exchange programs, foreign aid—all contribute to American influence abroad. An entire range of public-private and private-sector entities now exist that furnish the kind of electoral assistance that was formerly the province of the secret warriors. A legitimate question is whether covert political action programs are either necessary or appropriate in this context, especially in a post–Cold War world. Nonintervention has real value as a principle in international affairs, and political action makes America herself vulnerable to similar ventures. To understand the sensitivity of these issues, one need go no further than the furor in the United States that resulted from reports that China had intervened in the 1996 election in this country, using exactly the same techniques as the CIA in Chile in 1964. It was Judge Webster, not any crank, who argued that covert action must be consistent with law, American values, and public mores.

Political action is a first resort, not a last one, on any secret warrior's scale of escalation. Intentions can be morally "just" only by means of excruciatingly devious manipulations of principle, and these operations by definition are not proportional, regardless of indigenous political tactics, because they involve CIA foreign intervention. Control is almost always vitiated since CIA tactics respond to a developing political situation, not to a menu of options. Finally, in almost all cases the probability of success is indeterminate at the moment of decision. By far the better course is not to become enmeshed in these moral ambiguities in the first place.

America's most valuable resource is the image and texture of its democracy, its example to the world. The worst aspect of covert political action is that the tool is a clear contradiction of democratic values. Manipulation of peoples anywhere runs directly counter to these professed values. Today, when the Bush administration has made an explicit goal of encouraging a democratic revolution in the Islamic countries, types of activity that subvert democratic values threaten to damage U.S. national interests. Political action should be avoided.

Writing after the controversy over the mining of Nicaraguan harbors, McGeorge Bundy noted that "the dismal historical record of covert military and paramilitary operations over the last 25 years is entirely clear." As the NSC adviser to Presidents Kennedy and Johnson and chairman of their Special Groups, Bundy had some basis for his observation.

The truth is that the record of covert action is not without its successes. Notable among these are the partisan projects during the Vietnam War and Hmong efforts in Laos. A necessary qualification is that the programs were successful in mobilizing paramilitary forces but were not strategically decisive: neither in Laos nor in North Vietnam were adversary forces significantly hampered by the existence or effectiveness of U.S. paramilitary allies. It is also illuminating that in both cases the operations were wartime programs that could count on ample resources, including the expertise of military special warfare forces.

The CIA programs most often cited as successes are Afghanistan, Project Ajax in Iran, and Project Success in Guatemala. Yet these victories produced only short-term benefits. The effort in Afghanistan, like the one in Tibet, had the characteristics of a Cold War spoiling operation. It lurched to success courtesy of policy entrepreneurs' demands for escalation, and with the United States ignoring attempts at political solution. Had the operation not happened, there is a fair argument that the rise of Islamic fundamentalism could have been slowed, at least sufficiently to come to grips with the problem before the travesty of the 9/11 attacks. Washington lost a second opportunity to change the equation when it failed to act more openly in Bosnia in the early 1990s, when the United States could have earned credit with the Muslim world that would have further slowed the rise of terrorism, at a time when it seemed the Israeli-Palestinian problem might actually be moving toward a solution.

Afghan covert action also had other costs for the United States. Those at CIA, State Department intelligence, and elsewhere who worried that Stinger missiles given to the *mujahedeen* would show up in the wrong hands proved exactly correct. Continuing inability to recover all these weapons led to efforts to negotiate international agreements pertaining to handheld surface-to-air missiles as well as consideration of a multibillion-dollar initiative to arm commercial passenger aircraft with anti-missile devices. Ironically, Washington has had to beg the U.S.-installed government of Nicaragua to perfect its own procedures for safeguarding such weapons.

Action in Iran in the 1950s sowed the seeds for virulent anti-Americanism among the successors to the shah. Worse, the 1979–1980 hostage crisis ignited another open-ended subterranean conflict similar to the U.S. vendetta against Castro, except that it would be fought out on the field of terrorism, where Washington was far less equipped to deal with it. Iran became the equivalent of electing to fight on ground of the enemy's choosing. The CIA operations of the 1980s, and the ham-handed tactics of the Reagan administration in Iran-Contra that reinforced Iranian perceptions of the United States as a perfidious adversary, further exacerbated a basically unstable situation. Washington missed a critical opportunity *before* the shah's fall, when a chance existed to gain credit in supporting the creation of a moderate Islamic democracy. In Guatemala the overthrow of Arbenz turned the country away from democracy, the averred aim of the covert action. Neither victory materially affected the balance in the Cold War while, disturbingly, failure would have triggered shifts by forcing those nations into the arms of the Soviet Union. In all cases the benefits were short term, the costs long haul.

A paradigm case for this sort of failure has been Cuba. The vendettas conducted by Eisenhower and Kennedy radicalized Fidel Castro, necessitated Cuban reliance on the Soviets, and converted a traditional U.S. friend into a foe. The covert action also backfired by leading the Cubans and Soviets into nuclear missile deployments, creating a direct military threat to the United States and a crisis that brought this country to the edge of nuclear war. The Cuban-American hostility became entrenched, with further rounds of proxy or direct sparring in lands as distant as Bolivia, the Congo, Angola, Grenada, and Nicaragua.

Operations against the "denied areas" uniformly resulted in failures and have long since been abandoned. Had these been successful, the Soviets would have confronted the need for a response not confined to paramilitary conflict. The People's Republic of China was one denied area where operations redounded to the detriment of the United States. Adventures with Muslim warlords and Li Mi served to identify the United States with Jiang Jieshi and the corrupt Kuomintang. The Chinese Communists were handed a propaganda tool, a "foreign devil" to use as a symbol in solidifying Mao Zedong's control of the nation. The later operation in Tibet, a spoiling effort by definition, was merely incapable of a successful conclusion.

Indonesia was not a denied area, but there the CIA obtained similar results. Sukarno used the apparent American threat as justification for eliminating vestiges of opposition to his own role. This disaster has escaped more intense examination because the military coup of 1965, with apparent CIA connections, turned Indonesia back toward the U.S. orbit. As with political action in Guyana, the coup installed a dictator who then governed without regard to democratic values or the interests of the Indonesian people as a whole.

Most of the other paramilitary operations surveyed have been unalloyed failures, perhaps excepting the Congo, where the outcome is still disputed among former CIA officers. The ledger of failure includes Albania, Angola, and the Kurds in addition to efforts in the denied areas. Track II in Chile failed, mitigated by the success of economic pressures and political action that undermined the Allende government. The Chile case also illustrates what did work—manipulation of foreign aid and international cash flows. It should be quite clear that a paramilitary capability is not essential to that technique. The American action proved fundamentally anti-democratic, installing yet another dictator who reigned for decades. Pious theories about the worth of authoritarian dictators aside, the practical effect of American action ran directly counter to professed ideals of making the world safe for democracy.

Support for military operations has involved a learning curve. At the time of Korea the military wanted to keep CIA out of its business. By 1960, when a joint study group under Lyman Kirkpatrick surveyed U.S. intelligence, the CIA exclusion seemed well established. The reversion of activity to the Pentagon that John Kennedy ordered supposedly closed the matter. But Vietnam drove the military and the CIA back into each other's arms, and the Iran hostage crisis demonstrated the need for CIA support to military operations. Both Somalia and Bosnia illustrate the continuing demands. Robert Gates became the first director to have an associate DDO specifically for support to the military. Bill Clinton issued a presidential directive on the subject. George W. Bush has the CIA supporting his wars in Iraq and Afghanistan.

All the contingency military operations involve differing and diverse arrays of local, tribal, religious, and ethnic factors. Tactical intelligence is the easy part, and there the community has made great progress. Mastering the other aspects is much more difficult, as the current war in Iraq demonstrates anew. There will be more of these adventures. The director of national intelligence and his subordinates would do well to build capability for them.

In all these CIA operations there is a lesson for prospective local allies. Being a superpower, the United States acts in its own interests, which are those of the Great Power. There is little true identity of purpose between the restive minority and the Great Power, but substantial danger for the local minority in accepting paramilitary aid that may later evaporate. Sophisticated partisans will avoid playing the U.S. game, preventing the CIA from exercising true control, again vitiating the objectives (from Washington's perspective) of paramilitary action. The perfect example of successful maneuvering in the face of Washington's interests has been the Iraqis and Kurds, who rolled with the punches through several iterations of covert and conventional operations to emerge as leaders in their country. Others have fared less well.

The United States itself has not emerged unscathed. The term "blowback" has been coined to refer to the potential for actions to recoil and hurt the initiator. Beyond possible international and diplomatic consequences, covert operations have had an impact on U.S. domestic politics. The controversy over funding the National Student Association forced Lyndon Johnson into official acknowledgment and investigation, as the Bay of Pigs did for John Kennedy. Revelation of meddling in Chile significantly increased Richard Nixon's political difficulties. The linkage of the Iran operation with the hostage crisis and the failed U.S. rescue mission contributed to Jimmy Carter's defeat in the 1980 election. The Iran-Contra affair effectively drained the political capital of his successor, Ronald Reagan, who came close to impeachment. Political opponents used the Bosnia arms issue, in this case the mere *allegation* of a covert operation, to inflict a political hit on Bill

Clinton. These were real costs, not to be pretended away. Blowback in turn has forced secret warriors to terminate operations to the peril of their assets.

American national interest suffers each time a paramilitary operation fails. The record shows successes to be few, failures far more numerous, and wartime actions to have been the most useful. War popularized these techniques in the first place. British military historian Michael Howard captured the essence of this development in a lecture he delivered at Oxford University in November 1977:

> The belligerents during the Second World War not only developed weapons of mass destruction: they also developed methods of strategem, subversion and psychological warfare which afterwards remained in their arsenals and became, as it were, institutionalized. In the ideological confrontation that developed after the war and with which we still have to live, honorable men of great ability served their countries by engaging in activities of a kind unjustifiable by any criteria other than the most brutal kind of raison d'état, and by the argument that their adversaries were doing the same.

After building a capability expressly to fight the Russians, secret warriors abandoned action in the denied areas in favor of interventions in the Third World. It took roughly until 1954 for the CIA to generate its global paramilitary capability; then no further paramilitary operations were attempted against the Soviet Union. With the exception of Afghanistan, this is especially true of the twenty-five-year period from 1960 to 1985 of which McGeorge Bundy writes, but it has remained true since. Covert operations have been and are a weapon against the *weak*.

Former intelligence officers almost uniformly support a continued capability for, and reliance on, covert action. This continued to be true even after the excesses in Nicaragua, in statements from such figures as William E. Colby and Ray Cline. Apparent success in Afghanistan fueled further enthusiasm. Robert Gates would say in the 1990s that but for victory in the mountains of Allah he would not believe in covert operations. Retired CIA officers like B. Hugh Tovar and Theodore Shackley even advanced theories of covert action to supply intellectual foundations for secret warfare. Shackley considered covert action a "third option" between doing nothing and going to war. Frank Wisner would have approved.

Visions of covert action are based on a wish and a hope. The theories have been preoccupied with tactical considerations, with menus of measures and conditions for success. Neither the visionaries nor the theories have made much effort to assess the net impact of covert action on American foreign policy. Rather, the argument runs, these techniques have sometimes been useful and therefore should be maintained in perpetuity, regardless of other effects.

In terms of contributions to United States relations with the Third World, paramilitary action has had minimal positive results. The United States committed itself to long-term aid to Iran, Guatemala, Chile, Afghanistan, and Iraq that dwarfed the dollar costs of CIA projects. The numerous failures contributed nothing. Moreover it can be argued that the effort as a whole helped fuel the rise of the "nonaligned" movement—neutralism in world affairs—and the frustrations that led to suicide terrorism, the success of which comes at the expense of Washington's strategy. There appears to be much evidence to buttress McGeorge Bundy's assessment.

An overarching point, clearer than ever after five decades of the CIA experience, is that if relationships with target nations and peoples do improve, that will happen despite and not because of CIA covert action. Some inkling of this phenomenon is evident in the fact that even its proponents now concede that CIA intervention is not a substitute for a foreign policy.

Shifting the focus to paramilitary operations on their own terms, a number of specific weaknesses are visible in the method. These are inherent in the technique, including, to some extent, the complementary methods of political action and psychological warfare.

Langley has been an avid sponsor of "third force" political movements. Third-force movements have been non-Communist, preferably anti-Communist, but also not fascist; today they would be nonfundamentalist as well. During the Cold War an anti-Communist fixation blinded the CIA to other issues. Until very recently no distinction was made for fundamentalist religious movements, which led to the sad fact that CIA cash—passed through Pakistani hands—helped create the fervor of fundamentalism. This was no aberration; the CIA had directly funded similar groups in political action in Indonesia in the 1950s. Other third forces were politically moderate, what in several European countries would be called Christian democratic. In Third World nations, however, these movements tended to be associated with established oligarchies in Latin America, or tribes in Africa and Asia—usually the advantaged minorities rather than the majority ethnic or social groupings. Using such allies often does little to satisfy societal aspirations, and frequently leads only to further upheaval plus additional demands for U.S. support.

Sometimes there is no third force. The typical response then is to use political action to create one. The types of groupings that are put together have limited popular appeal and are locally perceived as agents of U.S. power. This was the case in Laos, Albania, and the Congo. While the assumption in third-force tactics is that they will have wide support, artificial movements sow few grass roots—because they know the United States cannot back away short of abandoning its covert action aims. Artificial movements are correspondingly fragile.

Where arrays of organized political movements exist, the choice is frequently limited. In Indonesia, Allen Dulles's CIA chose to align with separatist military officers and political malcontents. More recently in Nicaragua, the CIA favored former National Guardsmen. Too often the United States lands on the wrong side of these choices. Langley appears to prefer alleged military expertise over political strength, and there have been too many cases where the CIA's side, with its supposed expertise, runs away from the fray.

One special problem of working through local proxies is exposure to political liability as a remit of acts by the local allies. The Indonesian colonels with their smuggling again come to mind, but there is also the drug trafficking by Li Mi's Chinese, Vang Pao's Hmong, and the Afghan *muj*. Allegations of similar activity were laid at the feet of both sides in the Nicaraguan conflict. Afghanistan today is the largest supplier of heroin in the world. Ironically, under the fundamentalist Taliban government, drug production had been eradicated.

Another kind of problem arises from the utilization of local minorities in defense of the nation, as in counterinsurgency in Indochina, which mobilized the montagnards in Vietnam and the Hmong in Laos. In the classical technique, the loyalty of minority peoples is gained through "nation-building," measures designed to give a people a stake in the conflict. The problem resides in the contradiction inherent between building nationhood among a minority as against the existing sovereignty of the national government, itself the object being supported by CIA covert action. The competition usually can end in only one way. A similar sort of calculation lies behind the decision by Nixon and Kissinger and the shah to betray the Kurds.

Paramilitary action is also subject to serious operational difficulties. Freelance raids by the CIA's allies or others can disrupt carefully planned scenarios, as in the episode where the Johnson administration worried over the uncontrolled activities of anti-Castro Cuban exiles. There is also the problem of the CIA officer out of control, the "cowboy" exceeding his instructions. The Central Intelligence Agency is a disciplined organization, but there is more than one instance of an officer pulling the agency out on a limb. The record shows that officers violated orders against direct involvement in the operations against China, Guatemala, Cuba, Angola, and Nicaragua as well as during the campaign in Laos. During the Guatemala action a CIA officer took the instructions of a local ally to bomb a neutral freighter. In Laos a CIA officer assigned to Phoumi Nosavan almost unilaterally changed U.S. policy. In Nicaragua a CIA contract officer concocted a guerrilla warfare manual that broke regulations designed to avoid involvement in assassinations. Another participated in direct attacks on Nicaraguan ports. It is no wonder that Langley paramilitary staffs worry about "cowboys" in the field.

A slightly different problem is the officer who adopts the values and goals of the people CIA is attempting to mobilize. This can lead as surely to insubordination, since Langley's goals are rarely identical to those of the proxies. The agency and the special warfare forces had difficulties of this sort with Tibetans, montagnards, and the Hmong as well as the Cubans.

John Horton, a CIA officer who has worked both sides of the street, as analyst and operator, has reflected on the issues and proposes something of a code of conduct for secret warriors. His first stricture is that the officer remember his oath to protect and defend the Constitution, a defense against cowboy-ism or becoming a loose cannon. Second, Horton notes the obligation to keep promises, easier to say than do as projects are terminated or transformed by higher authority. Third is to accomplish the objective "with the least damage to the persons or institutions involved." These are reasonable guideposts amid the murk of shadowy operations and should be kept in mind by practitioners.

In Tibet, Afghanistan, and the Indochinese war a portion of CIA assistance was soaked up by its own allies while still in the pipeline. These kinds of problems not only reduce effectiveness but are unavoidable, given the requirement for local allies. Yet the phenomenon has become characteristic of secret wars. In large part the CIA conducts its operations today in concert with other nations' security services; some estimates place the proportion at up to 90 percent. Moreover Langley's role has become that of banker, handing out cash to local movements the CIA recruits, then hopes will stay bought. Since the Afghan War this has become the standard pattern. In the early days the CIA used to seek out foreign citizens—third-country "nationals"—to hide its hand. Now the agency seeks third-country intelligence services for the same purpose. This is why the first Bush administration's fight with Congress over findings covering third-country operations was so important.

Control of covert action would seem to imply discipline in the costs of these activities. But available spending data indicate that *no* major operation of this kind ended within its allotted budget. Project Ajax in Iran was estimated as low as $100,000 or $200,000, but cost $10 million. Secret warriors wanted $3.3 million for Project Success; Eisenhower expanded that to $10 million and before the last insurance indemnities were paid off possibly spent twice as much. The Bay of Pigs planners projected costs of $2.6 million, ballooned that to $13 million or $15 million, and before it ended spent something over $46 million. There were additional costs later to ransom prisoners, recompense Cuban exile veterans, and recruit Cubans to the U.S. military. Mongoose added something like $100 million. Laos, Vietnam, and Afghanistan carried price tags in the billions, Angola and Nicaragua in the hundreds of millions. Once the secret warriors accept a covert operation, budget controls tend to be thrown away. In no case does the record show that presidents deciding on covert operations considered the final cost of those initiatives; rather, decisions were based solely on the proximate estimates that were guaranteed to be wrong.

An especially significant point is that for the most part there have been only two types of CIA paramilitary endeavors—those that fail and those that come close to failure. Put differently, the history of the CIA secret wars reveals that every operation accounted a success experienced at least one moment when it stood on the brink of failure. This is true of Afghanistan (where estimates held the *muj* could not win and were running out of steam), Iran (where the shah seized up in fear), and Guatemala (where the Castillo-Armas troops ran away from their first battle). In South Vietnam the American proxy Diem was nearly overthrown in a 1955 coup; in Laos the Hmong were driven from their villages by an enemy offensive before the airfield system was created. In each case either significant escalations or extraordinary political measures were required to rectify the deteriorating situations. Beyond those lie the failures.

Finally, even where a covert operation ends successfully it can become an embarrassment owing to changing patterns of international relations. Good illustrations are the actions against China and in Tibet. The People's Republic was an enemy then, but the Nixon administration later undertook a rapprochement, redefining China as a counterweight to the Soviet Union. The covert actions were suddenly better forgotten. That China actually cooperated with the CIA on actions in Angola (to an extent), Afghanistan, and Cambodia shows the changing distribution of interests in global politics.

When I first addressed these issues in the 1980s, I argued that the legal status of paramilitary action could be clarified if the role of the CIA were to be ended altogether and the function placed squarely within the purview of military special warfare forces. (This would seem to ensure the maintenance of the capability for wartime, when it has been most effective, reduce the propensity to use the technique against the Third World, and focus the CIA on its classic functions. The secret warriors themselves would theoretically be subject to strict military discipline and regulations independent of any move toward intelligence charters.)

Defenders of the CIA like to argue that those who advocate assignment of the covert paramilitary role to the military are somehow uninformed, or perhaps mindlessly critical. But the opposite is in fact true. In the 1980s the evidence showed that Kennedy had actually *ordered* that assignment, that the CIA and the military had only partially implemented it, and that the Church Committee in 1976 had endorsed a similar transfer. Richard Bissell himself told a Council on Foreign Relations study group in 1968 that the decision to take large-scale operations away from the CIA had been a wise one.

The passage of time and more declassified records now show a much widened field of support for this course. At the time of the Nicaragua mining, CIA great Harry Rositzke wrote that an operation that big belonged with the military. Former CIA deputy director Ray Cline—an enthusiast for covert action in his last incarnation as State Department intelligence chief—in his memoir also endorsed handing the function to the military, as did CIA chieftain Robert Gates in his. Declassified records disclose that Allen Dulles took that position after the Bay of Pigs, and that the Kennedy PFIAB did so also. The commission investigating the 9/11 attacks came to the same conclusion. These are not crass critics. It is probably fair to say that military primacy has become the dominant view.

Agency officers like William J. Daugherty make practical objections: the U.S. Special Operations Command does not have legal authority to carry out the kinds of missions that would be covered by a finding; using the CIA more easily disguises the U.S. hand—and the agency already has a presence in many areas of the world where the military does not, plus experts in all the covert action disciplines. Except for the legal argument, which can be solved, the other objections are a wash. The military has attachés everywhere (just like the CIA station chiefs), growing covert capabilities, and employs third-country civilians just like the CIA. Legality has posed no obstacle to Secretary of Defense Donald Rumsfeld, who has expanded the military's ongoing encroachment in covert action roles.

But intervening events also now call military primacy into question. The military's performance in Somalia, Afghanistan, and Iraq, specifically with special forces, affords little confidence in their execution of covert operations in a clandestine, efficient way. To Desert One must be added The Dish, Tora Bora, and Abu

Ghraib. Each of those failures had discreet causes but featured many of the same kinds of lapses with local allies, methods, or politics that figure in the CIA operational record. Special operations successes in Grenada and Panama took place as spearheads of huge invasion forces. The military seems unable to apply a light touch.

While there are good arguments for moving paramilitary responsibility to the military, there is evidence the military does no better at this activity than the CIA, and legal obstacles exist on both sides. The scandals over behavior in Iraq, plus the wholesale failure to exact accountability from military higher commanders, negate the old observations about superior regulation. Excesses in the war on terrorism have sullied the military's standing.

This is not a simple matter. At present the better solution seems to be to maintain the CIA's paramilitary capability and revive it from the atrophied status of an arm that does little more than rent armies, for the day when a deft hand is truly necessary, while striving to rebuild proper regulation for the military. Given circumstances, the issue should be under continuous review.

Other areas that require attention are the activities of private citizens and of the president's own staff. The shenanigans of Secord and company during Iran-Contra, on the one hand, or Edwin Wilson on the other, vividly demonstrate the dangers of total lack of constraint. Private participation in covert operations should be proscribed. Direct action on covert operations by staff of the National Security Council is also a thorny problem. This involves the definition of "operations" since the NSC also conducts sensitive private diplomatic missions and may have a legitimate purpose doing so. But the line must be drawn before covert operations, for the NSC staff has few resources for paramilitary implementation. At the same time this is so critically placed that it is far too easy for a "cowboy" operator to pull the nation in behind him. As the case of Oliver North showed, America cannot afford five-star lieutenant colonels. Although difficult, these problems can be solved.

The Central Intelligence Agency exists to serve the president. There would be no paramilitary actions except for presidential desires. Presidents since Harry Truman have been more or less avid users of the technique, and all have used it at least once. We have explored presidents' control over the CIA in some detail.

Truman concerned himself with creating capabilities. Control he left mostly to subordinates on the 10/2 and 10/5 panels. It was President Eisenhower, with his extensive experience in utilizing staff organizations, who placed intelligence control on a more formal basis, giving explicit coordination and follow-up tasks to the 5412 Group. Through eight years in the White House, however, Ike proved unable to get this group to do everything he wanted it to, and in this regard he left the Oval Office frustrated. President Kennedy did not appreciate the control arrangements and dismantled them. The Bay of Pigs fiasco quickly showed him the error of his action, following which the Special Group was reconstituted. President Johnson continued to use this mechanism with no change except the name.

The Nixon administration left the Special Group in place, retitling it the 40 Committee and with extra presidential watchdogs added. But Nixon allowed the group to atrophy. Decisions on especially sensitive operations were absorbed by the White House and NSC staff dealing directly with agencies, as with Track II in Chile. This reduced the ability of the mechanism to monitor implementation—an activity the president specifically ordered emphasized—and robbed Nixon of the advice of some of his best-informed officials.

Conditions improved somewhat during the presidencies of Ford and Carter but deteriorated greatly during the Reagan era. With the president himself chairing the National Security Planning Group, the potential for honest denial of U.S. approval of covert action evaporated. The very quality of "covertness" disappeared as the administration used the fact of the paramilitary action as a diplomatic instrument and to score political points. The "overt covert operation" furthered the negative impact. Prevented from using CIA in one of its operations, the Reagan administration sought to continue directly through the NSC staff. Executive management units like PFIAB and the Intelligence Oversight Board encouraged covert ventures rather than riding herd on them. The administration's entire posture was never conducive to close scrutiny of covert action proposals. Paramilitary actions of doubtful legality were approved and monitored by a Special Group with its own limitations. The demands for action made it difficult to give proposals requisite attention. Moreover the CIA exhibited a proclivity toward holding on to implementation decisions once initial approvals were secured. Follow-up reviews were to occur only once a year (under a 1988 compromise the congressional committees finally earned the right to study the follow-up reviews), but there is no record that review in fact became established or was continued under successors.

The first President Bush, former CIA director that he was, strenuously resisted broadening of congressional oversight while weakening the PFIAB, in effect maximizing executive freedom of action on covert operations. In a sense it was an accident of history that Bush made greater use of military force than covert action, largely confined to existing programs. Presiding in the wake of Iran-Contra, however, Bush held office as controls on covert action multiplied *inside* the CIA, a push that reached its apogee during the Clinton era. The second President Bush has moved to expand the envelope of covert action as quickly as possible.

Covert action has never been under complete presidential control, even as presidents have total authority to order it. The continuing problem with this authority is that its legal basis rests entirely upon the "such other functions" clause of the 1947 National Security Act. But the legislative history of the act shows that Congress never intended to sanction covert action with that language, and there are several occasions when the CIA's general counsel concluded that paramilitary action was not within its scope. If presidents instead rely on their authority as commander-in-chief of the armed forces, the problem is that the CIA is not an "armed force." If it were, the president would then have to comply with the 1973 War Powers Act for a covert operation. Moreover, if the CIA is to be considered an unofficial armed force, the Constitution (Article I, Section 8) expressly reserves to

Congress, *not* the president, the right to give letters of marque, the eighteenth-century equivalent of grants of combatant status—in other words, presidential findings. Legislation that regulates findings cannot supersede the Constitution.

This legal conundrum would be eliminated if there were a detailed charter specifying missions and methods for the intelligence agencies, but initiatives for charter reform were defeated by the Carter administration in 1978 and 1980. Presidents as politically diverse as Eisenhower and Carter have consistently opposed this intelligence reform. The device of issuing executive orders on intelligence is precisely aimed at avoiding charter law. Nothing in the last two decades has altered this constitutional issue. It is time to end the presidential free ride on covert action.

The congressional oversight committees have had very limited impact on control of intelligence, and their writ is diminishing under the assault of the imperial president. Without a charter, the committees play catch-up with Langley as the administration arbitrarily advances expansive interpretations of sketchy law. This is the underlying meaning of the continuing struggle between the executive branch and Congress over presidential findings and requirements for "full and current" reporting. Demands for written memoranda of notification and for specificity in various areas are helpful—and at least foreclose the travesty of "retrospective" findings or "mental" ones. But the entire process is a thin reed. In particular the exclusion of third-country operations, for which the first President Bush fought hard, remains especially important since these now shield the bulk of CIA activity. The second President Bush, with his haughty assertion of authority to unilaterally circumvent law on warrants for wiretaps—which he conducted covertly—suggests the dangers in leaving the existing system alone. (Bush's program, while not a covert operation, is an indication of presidential attitude toward legal constraints.)

To doubtful legality and haphazard control must be added the conclusions that paramilitary operations pose problems of effectiveness, that they have contributed little to American national security, and that many have been detrimental to the U.S. commitment to support democracy. The issues were sharpened further after the Iran-Contra affair, which showed a way to evade legal strictures by privatizing covert operations. The dilemma is exacerbated by the weakness of the War Powers Act, which excluded the CIA on grounds that it would be covered in omnibus charter legislation that never materialized. On all these counts the law requires revision.

The real danger inherent in the current framework for covert action is the imperial presidency. America learned about rogue presidents in the Watergate scandal. In an era in which irresponsible presidential action may lead to global revulsion for the United States, mass casualty attacks by frustrated individuals, or old-style wars, it is not reasonable to allow so much freedom of action. America tried that after 9/11, only to become bogged down in an entirely avoidable quagmire. Meanwhile presidents' efforts to avoid accountability continue. The people of Puerto Cabezas, Nicaragua, know the true dangers of paramilitary action: hosts to the Bay of Pigs invaders, a quarter-century later they were attacked by CIA raiders.

25

Safe for Democracy

A GREAT PRESIDENT and visionary, Woodrow Wilson advanced concepts that are still central to American policy almost a century later. The notion of making the world safe for democracy and the belief that peoples have the right to determine their form of government both flowed from Wilson's fertile mind. Internationalism—the idea that the United States should play an active role in world affairs—combined with the other elements to comprise Wilsonianism. In playing this international role America would advance the causes of democracy and self-determination. By 1918 President Wilson had put all those things on the table. In one sense the story of America since then has been the history of the waning and waxing of Wilson's ideas.

An atavistic attempt at isolationism became the backlash to Wilson's approach, but the American frontier had advanced to and past the nation's continental land mass while economic and technological developments also required foreign entanglements. Sometime in the 1930s the growth and increasing sophistication of a world economy made isolationism impractical, indeed dangerous to the national interest. During that same decade the rise of fascism and totalitarianism squarely posed the question of democracy versus dictatorship in ways that could not be ignored by American leaders. By presenting these issues in stark fashion, the Spanish Civil War (1936–1939) made it necessary for Americans—both leaders and the public—to stake out a position on the Wilsonian principles. Every American president since Franklin D. Roosevelt, the man in office at that time, has chosen to try to craft a world safe for democracy.

Roosevelt made the United States the "arsenal of democracy" in World War II. The Atlantic Charter that FDR agreed on with British prime minister Winston Churchill in 1941 embraced the democratic idea in at least two of its eight principles: self-determination and protection against forced territorial change. Roosevelt reaffirmed those principles, linking them explicitly to the advance of democracy, as did his successor Harry Truman. The Marshall Plan and Truman Doctrine were Cold War measures, but they were also Truman supporting the European democracies, and he spoke of a democracy based on the conviction that man has the inalienable right to govern himself. As a young cadet at West Point, Dwight Eisenhower marched past Wilson at his first inaugural. As president, Ike insisted the United States would never impose American-style political institutions on others, and he explicitly rejected isolationism.

At his American University speech in April 1963, John F. Kennedy spoke of men and nations growing and building a better life. Lyndon Johnson told the world he did not wish to be a president who built empires, sought grandeur, or extended American dominion. Richard Nixon and Gerald Ford extolled the virtues of democratic principle. Jimmy Carter enshrined human rights as an additional element in the equation. Ronald Reagan declared it would be cultural condescension or worse to say that any people preferred dictatorship to democracy. George Herbert Walker Bush insisted that "abandonment of the worldwide democratic revolution could be disastrous for American security." Bill Clinton saw the enlargement of democracy as a global trend and spoke of his dream of "a world of thriving democracies." And President George W. Bush has declared his specific goal of bringing democracy to the Islamic nations of Africa and the Middle East. Making the world safe for democracy has undeniably been both an aspiration and a goal of U.S. foreign policy, both historical and current.

Ends are clearly not at issue; the real struggle is over means. How many paths to democracy are there? What are the proper tools? Former CIA director John Deutch has propounded an argument that specifically relates intervention to the proclivities of American political parties. Deutch writes:

> It is one matter to adopt a foreign policy that encourages democratic values; it is quite another to believe it just or practical to achieve such results on the ground with military forces. . . . But the notion of intervening in foreign countries to build a society of our preference is not just a Republican or conservative failing. The corresponding Democratic or liberal failing is the view that America has a duty to intervene in foreign countries that egregiously violate human rights and a responsibility to oppose and, where possible, remove totalitarian heads of state.

The party identifications are fuzzy here—after all, it was Ronald Reagan who called Sandinista leader Daniel Ortega a totalitarian in sunglasses—but means are the point.

Essentially there are five sets of tools in America's international relations box. The first is example and behavior, which add texture to the popular image of democracy and contribute to the desirability of that form of government in the eyes of peoples around the globe. The second tool is diplomacy in the time-honored tradition. Encouragement and persuasion, including U.S. information programs, along with promises of aid and trade, have always been important means of encouraging progress. Nothing objectionable there, except perhaps the danger of boosters crossing the boundary into outright propaganda and psychological warfare, smudging the American Dream with nightmarish political coercion.

In the months after the 9/11 attacks it looked for a moment like this tragedy had actually accrued to America's advantage. Peoples throughout the world showed their sympathy for the United States. Opinions of this country elsewhere rose to new highs. But the coin of the Wilsonian vision has become tarnished, and that is the worst imaginable development for American national security. The draconian security measures and abridgements of public freedoms imposed by the second Bush administration have blackened the image of American democracy. Treatment of prisoners by U.S. expeditionary forces in Iraq and Afghanistan, and suspicion of visitors and immigrants to our shores has only confirmed growing negative opinions. When global opinion polls show images of America fallen to distressing lows even among the citizens of traditional allies, that betokens the growing problem. Opinions as measured by the Global Attitudes Project of the Pew Trust recovered somewhat from 2004 to 2005, but the fact remains that fewer than half the respondents expressed a favorable opinion of the United States among every major U.S. ally (Japan did not participate) save Britain, and there favorable ratings dropped. For Australians the United States does not even make the "Top 10" list of their favorite nations. In almost every country, not just allies, favorable opinion in 2005 is lower than in 2000, usually by about a third. In some places the drop is a half or even two-thirds. The main exceptions are Russia, beset by crime and corruption, where America's image has grown brighter, and Pakistan, where it has recovered to turn-of-the-millennium rates.

The Bush administration response, rather than burnishing the image of America by shoring up freedom, has been to go on the offensive, dedicating itself to engineering democratic revolution in the Islamic world. For that it began an anemic information program, which has yet to acquire any real momentum, and relied upon military force and the security services.

The third tool in the international relations kit is economic sanctions. Debates have been and continue to be strenuous as to whether sanctions are worth anything at all. The latest data on the subject pertain to Iraq, where sanctions seem to have strengthened Saddam Hussein's regime; and Libya, where sanctions clearly drove Muammar Gadhafi to seek rapprochement, albeit over an interval of a decade and a half. Not too many governments have that much patience, certainly not this one.

The fourth tool is military force. Iraq demonstrates both the capabilities and limitations of force. One would have to conclude that the military is an exceedingly blunt instrument. Worse, the use of force has contributed to the decline in America's image in the world's eyes. By the summer of 2003, several months after the U.S. conquest of Iraq, peoples in many countries rated the *United States* as the main threat to their security. Huge majorities held that view in half a dozen lands, among them Russia and Pakistan. Places where a majority viewed America as a threat included Kuwait and Jordan, which U.S. security policy had labored to shield. In Turkey the United States continues to be seen as the main enemy, an impression that is universally attributed to the Bush administration's use of force against Iraq. Moreover that view exists in the face of terrorist attacks on that country. The military tool has not added much to America's luster despite the acknowledged potency of U.S. forces. As the Bush administration warily eyes Iran and North Korea, the military instrument has diminished America's image around the globe.

Despite problems of declining image, the United States continues to have an interest in local and regional stability that has carried over from the Cold War. Indeed a debate exists in interested circles over whether Washington is acquiring an empire or should seek to do so. There is considerable basis in both liberal and conservative political beliefs to oppose such a course. There is also the fact that, as a massive debtor nation in a globalized economy, the United States today possesses a narrower base from which to build an empire than any of its predecessors on the road to imperial adventure. Nevertheless the current administration is conducting a global war against terrorist groups that continually throws up temptations to intervene, actions that lead to deeper commitments. One morning Americans may realize that the basket of commitments has reached the level of imperial enterprise.

The frequent official response is to maintain that commitments are tightly controlled, limited, and will be quickly phased out. The time has come to understand such arguments as pretense. George W. Bush positively insisted he would not pursue nation-building in Iraq or Afghanistan. Bill Clinton planned to send troops to Bosnia-Herzegovina, and later to Kosovo, for a short time to enforce cease-fires and separate the combatants. American forces remain in all those places. Haiti was to be a quick in-and-out mission; a UN force has replaced the American one and remains on the island. George H. W. Bush sent U.S. troops to Somalia for a few weeks; getting out took several years. The 1990s introduced the term "mission creep" to denote how initial intentions mushroom with unintended consequences. Today's danger is that the mushrooming will lead to stumbling empire.

There is no lack of fracture lines in the international system which may seem to require Washington's action. Several kinds of potential problems are immediately apparent. One flows directly from the enshrined principle of self-determination. The centrifugal forces that have led to the breakup of nation-states remain strong. The possibility that economic crises may demand intervention is high. And—for this administration at least, with the future yet to be seen—there are self-selected enemies.

Cultural and ethnic problems are rife in many countries. Here we examined the breakup of the former Yugoslavia in a certain amount of (insufficient but suggestive) detail, but the same forces were at work elsewhere. The 1990s brought secessionist movements in several of the successor states to the Soviet Union and similar ethnic cleansing in Rwanda. The possibility for disintegrative crises continues in the Russian states and in Somalia, the Serb Republic, the Sudan, Nigeria, and Israel. Secessionist wars continue in some of those places, in Sri Lanka, and elsewhere. The Kashmir problem remains to be solved between India and Pakistan. Self-determination would dictate standing aside from disintegrative crises and permitting the participants to solve their problems. The principle of nonintervention in the internal affairs of states reinforces that stance. Woodrow Wilson understood the logic: nationalism and ethnic identity can lead to tumult. Within months of enunciating his support for self-determination, Wilson objected that the principle could not be applied everywhere at once without chaos. He was right, but that immediately raises the question of who decides, when and where. Today the consensus on the 1990s is that intervening in Bosnia was the right thing and failure to do so in Rwanda a mistake. Intervention is on the table. There will be many more opportunities.

Another line of fracture exists for economic reasons. Differences persist between the First World and the Third. In a globalized trade environment with large multinational corporations able to exploit national differences in labor practices, raw materials costs, and terms of trade, traditional advantages of an international division of labor are diminishing and may disappear. Global environmental concerns will further exacerbate both internal and international trends. Sharpening economic problems within countries can magnify the effects of other disintegrative processes. People turn to groups or movements which offer them a step up or build a sense of identity, whether these be Islamic terrorist groups, Japanese cults, Liberian gangs, or Rwandan tribes. The temptation is to lash out. These phenomena again open the door for intervention.

Self-selected enemies may or may not be threats, but the whole point of singling them out is to take action. When George W. Bush christened the "Axis of Evil" he added to U.S. national security commitments. The Bush administration has not enhanced America's military capabilities except at the margin, and has committed the largest part of its resources in Iraq and Afghanistan. Meanwhile relations with Iran, not bright to start with, have deteriorated further, while North Korea, previously constrained by a Clinton-era agreement, has begun a crash program to produce nuclear weapons. Few American forces are available to cope with problems in these areas. U.S. troops have in fact been withdrawn from Korea for dispatch to Iraq. Worse, the specific capabilities of the Axis of Evil countries that seem to threaten America's leaders are those least amenable to conventional military means. Diplomacy would be a useful tool, but the present administration essentially tore up an existing agreement and seems committed to negotiated surrender as the solution. While this may seem attractive in the halls of the West Wing, agreements on such a basis are not likely and, if achieved, not likely to hold.

Nuclear facilities in mountain caves in North Korea, or widely dispersed and built underground in Iran, will not be easily neutralized by U.S. aircraft, no matter how many smart bombs they loose. There remains a question as to how much of a threat Korean and Iranian developments actually represent—with shadows of doubt injected by the Bush administration's own hyping of the danger supposedly posed by Saddam's Iraq. If Teheran's bomb is seven to ten years away, or North Korea's has no means of delivery, the problem takes on a different complexion. If the threat is real, however, the alternatives seem to be invasion versus special operations or covert action.

All of which brings us to covert operations, the final tool in Washington's international relations kit. The notion that a lightning strike on cave facilities by Delta Force or U.S. Rangers, a paramilitary raid on the sources of materials for the Iranian plants, or sabotage by the secret warriors might eliminate the problem is a seductive one. The current international system features a great many and a wide variety of actors, including both nations and smaller groups or units; a complex array of security concerns; a continuing demand for purposeful foreign action; an ebbing of resources to mitigate local and regional problems through judicious foreign aid; and continuing obstacles to open military intervention. This logic too indicates continued, perhaps even greater demand for covert operations, including paramilitary ones. A number of arguments may be made in favor of covert action under present circumstances. They are based on expediency.

Unfortunately, far from being a trump card, covert operations continue to suffer from the deficiencies demonstrated here. The covert operation is not a substitute for policy; it has only short-run impact if successful but long-term negative consequences if a failure. The dangers of blowback are both international and political. Yet the seductiveness persists. A list of significant covert actions over the past decades would include Iraq, Afghanistan, Iran, Panama, Africa, actions in concert with China, Pakistan, Saudi Arabia, and others—in essence the list of major U.S. foreign policy concerns. North Korea and modern Iran may be missing from the list only because activities so far remain unknown. Underlying this list is a view of covert action as an automatic component of overt policy. Such a course is fraught with peril for the United States, particularly where the problems of effectiveness and control of covert operations, and the relationship between covert action and war powers, remain unsolved.

The variety of pitfalls in covert action have been shown here in detail. Political actions have indeterminate prospects at the point of decision and are wild cards in execution. They undercut open government information programs and are irretrievable once initiated. Such actions also blur the threshold of intervention, inserting the United States into a situation containing escalatory potential without the president having considered his options and made his intervention decision.

Special problems afflict presidents who put covert action at the top of their options menu. Dwight Eisenhower is the best illustration, and he well shows the linkage in the modern presidential mind between covert operations and the quest for democracy. Eisenhower funded a political action in Indonesia that sought to shift Sukarno's democracy, then escalated to paramilitary action once he failed on the political front. The linkage became explicit when Ike's approval of the paramilitary project directly followed a Sukarno speech that Western-style democracy had failed in his country. Most revealingly, in two instances Eisenhower, who had put democratic values at the core of his psychological warfare projects against Russia, stepped back from the brink when crises erupted in East Germany (1953) and Hungary (1956) with those values at their heart. Even successful political actions, perhaps especially those, may result in demands for greater U.S. support.

On the paramilitary side, engaging in secret wars remains a Faustian bargain. Local allies receive training, skills, and resources that may later be used in ways the U.S. might oppose, or, in the worst case, be turned against the United States itself. In many instances the CIA recruits turn out to be brittle and have little real capability. Washington also incurs the political liability of the faults of its CIA minions. Certain issues of tactics—like the resort to assassinations—remain controversial. In places where the agency secures local allies through emoluments, the problem (well illustrated by the Kurds in Iraq) is whether they will stay bought. Where the project mobilizes a minority group, the question of its interests versus those of the state sharpens in proportion to its success. All these factors stand apart from the basic operational difficulties that arise. The history of U.S. covert action shows conclusively that virtually every project has encountered a moment of near-failure, that the record consists of failures plus those ventures that teetered at the edge before they broke through to success.

Military covert action should be singled out for comment. Past efforts have not been especially efficient or cost-effective, and have been most successful as elements of large conventional operations. Giving the military a major role in covert action today may be creating a fresh boondoggle. The Pentagon already controls the lion's share of the intelligence budget, and Congress, in creating his position, blocked the possibility that the new director of national intelligence might gain effective scrutiny over those funds.

More so than CIA proprietaries in an earlier age, the employment of private individuals and companies in covert action is subject to control and regulation difficulties that have not been recognized. Another category of alliances—with third countries and their security services—remains problematical and yet has assumed much greater weight in CIA covert operations, in each case injecting an entire new set of policy and power concerns over which the United States may have no sway. Presidents have held out for freedom of action in recruiting third countries without pausing to reflect that a measure of regulation in such relationships might actually help impose discipline on the process, or, alternatively, encourage a conjunction of goals and methods between the United States and its allies in these involvements.

Developing trends emphasize the need for proper control over clandestine activity. But little that has happened, including the post-9/11 reforms, suggests reason for optimism. The director of national intelligence is so far an unknown quantity. Whether the DNI will have the span of attention necessary to manage implementation in addition to marshaling the approvals for operations remains an open question, particularly since the legislation establishing the position specifically restricts him from the operational arena in several areas. Among the restricted areas is the Pentagon's intelligence domain, which is expanding at an accelerating rate.

If anything, this history shows that review efforts tend to be cursory or ignored after a time, while many actions take place at such a low level that they never rise to the threshold of executive attention. The Central Intelligence Agency and its cohorts move under their own steam in the absence of such review. Thus presidents have complete authority over covert operations while still lacking full control of them.

Finally, aside from the problem of presidential control, that of executive-legislative relationships in regard to authority for intelligence operations persists. The system of congressional oversight of intelligence has become well established on the surface. But both the president and the CIA (and other agencies) continue to resist full and frank reporting, the very reforms supposedly initiated in the wake of Iran-Contra.

There is no alternative to vigorous oversight by Congress. Instead the process has more closely resembled a dance: the overseers are the gentlemen trying to get close to the lady, being agreeable and going along to win her favors. Americans cannot afford intelligence oversight that becomes just one more part of the problem. Calls are still heard—most recently from the 9/11 Commission—for merging the Senate and House intelligence committees. That notion should be rejected. If two congressional committees can scarcely cover the intelligence terrain, cutting back to one is a recipe for disaster.

The creation of the post of director of national intelligence has not vitiated these problems. After all these years the authority for covert action still rests on a short, ambiguous phrase in the National Security Act of 1947. And the law does not provide for the military role in covert operations that has become increasingly important. The issue of authority for ordering paramilitary operations, most especially, and the related question of the constitutional locus of war powers have yet to be solved.

In making the world safe for democracy, the resort to covert means almost immediately calls into question the disinterestedness and sincerity of American purpose. The United States has never felt itself able to take issues involved in a secret war to the United Nations. In those cases where matters went to the UN in the face of U.S. inaction—Burma, Tibet, Cuba—Washington actively discouraged public debate or even vetoed resolutions in the Security Council. The secret war in Nicaragua led Washington—for the first time in history and in violation of its own international undertakings—to reject the jurisdiction of the International Court of Justice. That same event led to the casting of a veto at the UN Security Council, again the first time in history that the veto was employed to protect a covert operation. None of this advanced the cause of democracy. In all the secret wars from 1947 to the present, no covert operation ever led to a vibrant democracy, and quite a few resulted in dictatorships. Many political actions had the effect of inhibiting the free expression of democratic beliefs.

Yet there is a great temptation to think that things can be accomplished on an unattributable or quasi-covert basis when open intervention seems undesirable. Despite assertions from the public and the repeated, considered conclusions of classified studies by the secret-war managers, proponents continue in the mistaken belief that these actions can be taken in the dark with no one the wiser. That has almost never been the case. The record shows secret wars, like military action, to be a blunt instrument.

Presidents labor under contradictory impulses as they conduct business for the American people. On the one hand is the desire to act, to move a situation in a direction favorable to their perception of U.S. interests. This tendency has led to many, if not all, of the covert operations in our modern history. On the other hand, presidents want to affirm their dedication to principles, among the most powerful of which are democratic values. Hence the constant references in presidential discourse to democracy and the global democratic revolution, of which George W. Bush's democratic venture is only the latest example. The crunch comes when presidents' impulses conflict. Covert operations have impeded far more than they have enhanced the evolution of the democratic tradition. Covert operations should be reserved for the scenarios—more limited in scope and goals—where they can be truly useful. To rely upon them without solving the problems of authority, control, and technique that have been identified here is to open Pandora's box.

Americans at large also harbor aspirations and hopes that impel them in different directions. The people believe in democracy, to be sure. Americans also have sympathy for the downtrodden, certainly supporting the quest of many peoples for self-determination. But Americans are doubtful of the propriety or effectiveness of intervention, and, schooled by the tragedies of Vietnam—and now Iraq—are suspicious of motive. Claims to act in support of democracy have cloaked a host of dubious schemes, and covert action has been a major avenue for the execution of such intrigues. A conflict remains between ends and means, with covert action an especially sensitive technique when employed in the quest for democracy. Opinion can turn with the revelation of an incident, an inept tactic, a blatant failure, most especially from the changing public consensus. Even success can turn sour. What Americans accepted yesterday they may not today, or tomorrow, and those shifts in opinion reverberate in the lives of presidents and secret warriors. In the democratic revolution, covert action is best left in the toolbox.

Notes

1: THE GAMUT OF SECRET OPERATIONS

page

3 "We misunderstood the whole struggle": Tim Weiner, "A Kennedy-C.I.A. Plot Returns to Haunt Clinton," *New York Times*, October 30, 1994, quoted p. 10.

3 "Jagan himself is not an acknowledged Communist" et seq.: Special National Intelligence Estimate (SNIE) 87.2–61, "Prospects for British Guiana," March 21, 1961. Reprinted in Department of State, *Foreign Relations of the United States, 1961–1963, v. 12: American Republics* (Washington, D.C., Government Printing Office, 1996), quoted pp. 514, 516. Hereafter the official documents series *Foreign Relations* shall be cited as FRUS with dates and volume identifications.

5 "We are not inclined to give people such as Jagan": State Cable, Deptel to London 708, August 11, 1961, ibid., p, 520.

5 "We should keep in mind [the] possibility": State Cable, Deptel to London 1165, September 5, 1961, ibid., p. 530.

6 "evasive on all ideological and doctrinal issues": State Department, Memorandum of Conversation, October 25, 1961, ibid., p. 537.

6 "an impression of either wooliness or fellow-travelling": Arthur M. Schlesinger, Jr., *A Thousand Days: John F. Kennedy in the White House* (New York, Fawcett Books, 1967), p. 710.

7 "I must tell you now that I have reached the conclusion" et seq.: State Cable, Deptel to London 4426, February 19, 1962, FRUS, 1961–1963, pp. 544–545.

7 "the damaging effect of such disclosure": Letter, Stevenson to Rusk, February 26, 1962, ibid., pp. 545–546.

7 "You say that it is not possible": Letter, Lord Home to Secretary Rusk, February 26, 1962. ibid., p. 547.

8 "For [the] present I do not believe covert action": State Cable, Rusk Cable (Secto) 28, March 13, 1962, ibid., p. 553. This was sent "EYES ONLY" for acting secretary George Ball.

8 "a program designed to bring about the removal of Cheddi Jagan" et seq.: State Department Paper, "Possible Courses of Action in British Guiana," March 15, 1962, ibid., pp. 555–558, quoted 557–558.

8 "We do not intend to be taken in twice" et seq.: Department of State, Memorandum of Conversation, March 17, 1962, ibid., pp. 558–564, quoted p. 563.

9 "an independent British Guiana under Burnham": Memorandum, Arthur Schlesinger to President Kennedy, June 21, 1962, ibid., p. 572.

11 "Man for Cuba": Richard Helms with William Hood, *A Look Over My Shoulder: A Life in the Central Intelligence Agency* (New York, Random House, 2003), pp. 196, 205, quoted p. 196.

12 "an advocate of extremist measures" et seq.: CIA, SNIE 87.2–62, "The Situation and Prospects in British Guiana," April 11, 1962. CIA, Freedom of Information Act Release (hereafter cited as FOIA), Case EO1994-00324 (declassified October 10, 1997). Note that there are substantial differences between this release and the earlier rendition of this document the CIA provided for compilers of the FRUS volume on Guiana. Among the material deleted from the FRUS version were items regarding Jagan's political position and the observation that Burnham "has a reputation for opportunism and

venality. His racist point of view, so evident in the past, forbodes instability and conflict during any administration under his leadership." Also missing: Burnham's "recklessness and impulsiveness are notorious and could at any time overrule his judgment."

12 " I agree that the evidence shows": Schlesinger June 21 memo, op. cit. But in this paper the White House aide actually says, "Burnham is so impressed by his own importance and self-analysis of popularity" that he was unlikely to make common cause with the United Force Party, while in *A Thousand Days* he writes that Burnham "appeared an intelligent, self-possessed, reasonable man, insisting quite firmly on his 'socialism' and 'neutralism' but stoutly anti-communist," who "seemed well aware that British Guiana had no future at all unless its political leaders tried to temper the racial animosities and unless he in particular gave his party, now predominantly African, a bi-racial flavor" (p. 713). The latter statement implies some willingness on the part of Burnham to work with the UF which, not being African, would accomplish exactly what Schlesinger wanted.

12 "In particular, I think it is unproven that CIA knows how to manipulate": Memo, Bundy to Kennedy, July 13, 1962, FRUS 1961–1963, v. 12, p. 577.

12 "Does CIA think they can carry out a really *covert* operation": Memo, Schlesinger to Kennedy, July 19, 1962, ibid., p. 578.

12 "would provide opportunity for": State Cable (not sent), drafted August 1, 1962, ibid., p. 579.

13 "I think you know about the most interesting development here": NSC, Memo, Kaysen to Bundy, October 5, 1962, John F. Kennedy Library, John F. Kennedy Papers (hereafter abbreviated JFKL:JFKP): National Security File (hereafter abbreviated NSF): Meetings and Memoranda Series, box 320, folder: "Staff Memoranda, Kaysen, 8/62–12/62."

14 "It moves, moderately": McGeorge Bundy, "Weekend Reading, January 26–27, 1963." JFKL: NSF: Meetings and Memoranda Series, box 317, folder: "Index of Weekend Papers, 1/63–3/63."

15 "It was clear that the President regards British Guiana": CIA Memorandum, "White House Meeting on British Guiana," June 21, 1963, FRUS 1961–1963, v. 12, p. 604.

15 "a country with a communist government in control": State Department Cable, Deptel 6918 (London), ibid., p. 606.

15 "would create irresistible pressures in the United States to strike militarily": State Department, Memorandum of Conversation, June 30, 1964, ibid., pp. 607–609, quoted p. 608.

16 "actually testing support for the eventual formation": CIA, Memorandum to McGeorge Bundy, "British Guiana," March 17, 1964, Lyndon Baines Johnson Library: Lyndon Baines Johnson Papers (hereafter LBJL:LBJP): NSF: Intelligence File, box 5, folder: "British Guiana Special File."

17 "No matter what I try to do" et seq.: Delmar Carlson, Memorandum of Conversation, May 25, 1964, FRUS 1964–1968, quoted p. 864.

17 "You don't know Burnham": Department of State, Cable (CIA Channel), June 28, 1964 (declassified February 4, 2005), LBJL:LBJP: NSF: Intelligence File, box 5, folder: "British Guiana, Special Folder."

17 "a dialogue with Jagan might conceivably cool down the . . . security problem": NSC, Memorandum for the Record, British Guiana Meeting, June 30, 1964," July 2, 1964, LBJL:LBJP: NSF: ibid.

17 "I'd stonewall for now": McGeorge Bundy Marginal Note on NSC Memorandum, Chase to Bundy, "British Guiana," July 31, 1964, LBJL:LBJP: NSF: ibid.

18 "secured international assistance" et seq.: Untitled, Undated Paper (between August 17 and 24 according to other evidence), LBJL:LBJP: NSF: ibid. See CIA, Memorandum, Karamessines to Bundy, "British Guiana," August 28, 1964, which appears to comment on this paper. Ibid. A Jagan government official passing through Washington from Canada in early September saw U.S. officials and mentioned a specific report that the government had evidence the United States had been helping Burnham's party as of October 1963. The official's trip to Canada suggests that Jagan indeed did take action on the policy recommendations in the anonymous paper cited above.

18 "it is tough to do so" et seq.: Department of State, Cable, September 11, 1964, ibid.

18 "in a deniable and discreet way": NSC, Gordon Chase–McGeorge Bundy Memorandum, October 17, 1964, FRUS 1964–1968, v. 34, p. 884.

18 "a new victory for the station British Guiana": Philip Agee, *Inside the Company: CIA Diary* (New York: Bantam Books, 1976), p. 418.

19 "We misunderstood the whole struggle": Quoted in Weiner, "A Kennedy–C.I.A. Plot Returns to Haunt Clinton."

20 "Great White Case Officer": G. J. A. O'Toole, *The Encyclopedia of American Intelligence and Espionage* (New York: Facts on File, 1988), p. 171.

23 "Studio Six Productions": Antonio J. Mendez with Malcolm McConnell, *The Master of Disguise: My Secret Life in the CIA* (New York: William Morrow, 1999), pp. 279–282.

2: THE COLD WAR CRUCIBLE

34 "personal snooper": Letter, Harry S Truman to Sidney Souers and William D. Leahy, reprinted in Margaret Truman, *Harry S. Truman* (New York, Pocket Books, 1974), pp. 362–363.

35 "additional services of common concern" et seq.: National Security Act of 1947, Section 102. This law has been widely reprinted. See, for example, William M. Leary, ed., *The Central Intelligence Agency: History and Documents* (Tuscaloosa, University of Alabama Press, 1984), pp. 128–130.

35 "I reviewed this sentence carefully": Clark Clifford with Richard Holbrooke, *Counsel to the President: A Memoir* (New York, Random House, 1991), p. 169.

36 "I'm tired of babying the Soviets": Letter, Harry Truman to James Byrnes, reprinted in Harry S. Truman, *Memoirs: Year of Decisions* (New York, New American Library, 1965), pp. 604–606.

36 "From Stettin in the Baltic to Trieste in the Adriatic": Winston S. Churchill Speech at Westminster College, 1946, in Robert J. Donovan, *Conflict and Crisis* (New York, W. W. Norton, 1977), quoted p. 191.

37 "may come with dramatic suddenness": Walter Millis, ed., *The Forrestal Diaries* (New York, Viking Press, 1951), quoted p. 387.

38 "huge quantities" and "we believe this would be an unauthorized use of the funds" et seq.: CIA, Memorandum, Houston to Hillenkoetter, September 25, 1947. Declassified document in author's possession.

39 "if the President, with his Constitutional responsibilities": Lawrence R. Houston, Letter to the Editor, *New York Times*, July 26, 1982. In connection with this disclaimer by the former CIA general counsel, the reader should be aware that the views Houston expressed to successive directors of central intelligence—which will be shown later in this narrative—differ markedly from his argument in 1982, after retirement. In fact, in both 1962 and 1969 the general counsel rendered legal opinions identical to this one in 1947.

40 "this political warfare thing": CIA, Memo, Hillenkoetter to Aide, June 1948, in Michael Warner, ed. *The CIA Under Harry Truman* (Washington, D.C., CIA, Center for the Study of Intelligence, 1994), p. 203.

40–1 "the overt foreign activities of the US government must be supplemented by covert operations" et seq.: National Security Council, NSC 10/2, "National Security Council Directive on Office of Special Projects, June 18, 1948, reprinted in Leary, *Central Intelligence Agency*, pp. 131–133.

3: THE SECRET WARRIORS

45 "preventive direct action": Peter Grose, *Operation Rollback* (Boston, Houghton Mifflin, 2000), quoted, p. 124.

45 "Wiz," "Ozzard of Wiz" et seq.: David A. Phillips, *The Night Watch: Twenty-five Years of Peculiar Service* (New York, Atheneum, 1977), pp. 25–33.

47 "the Bold Easterners": Stewart Alsop, *The Center: People and Power in Political Washington* (New York, Harper and Row, 1968).

52 "Reality methodically and pitilessly destroyed": K. V. Tauras, *Guerrilla Warfare on the Amber Coast* (New York, Voyages Press, 1962), p. 93.

54 "secret operations, particularly through support of resistance groups": CIA, "The Central Intelligence Agency and National Organization for Intelligence" (Dulles–Jackson–Correa Report), January 1, 1949 (declassified June 3, 1976), p. 131. Document in author's possession.

56 "I feel I've spent three days chewing cotton": Tom Bower, *The Red Web: MI6 and the KGB Master Coup* (London, Mandarin Books, 1993), quoted p. 172.

57 "the correct channels in Europe": William E. Colby and Peter Forbath, *Honorable Men: My Life in the CIA* (New York, Simon and Schuster, 1978), p. 91.

4: "THE KIND OF EXPERIENCE WE NEED"

59 "a clinical experiment to see whether larger rollback operations would be feasible": Anthony Verrier, *Through the Looking Glass* (New York, W. W. Norton, 1983), quoted p. 76.

59 "whenever we want to subvert any place": Kim Philby, *My Silent War* (London, Granada Books, 1969), quoted p. 142.

60 "an exploratory action": Michael Burke, *Outrageous Good Fortune* (Boston, Little Brown, 1984), p. 140.

61 "more a rallying point than a valid basis for a political revolution": Ibid., p. 42.

61 "He was like Talleyrand": Nicolas Bethell, *Betrayed* (New York, Times Books, 1984), quoted p. 59.

61 "My friends state that they would prefer not to approach the visa division": Ralph Blumenthal, "Axis Supporters Enlisted by U.S. in Postwar Role," *New York Times*, June 20, 1982, quoted p. 22.

62 "a purely internal Albanian uprising at this time is not indicated" et seq.: CIA, "Strengths and Weaknesses of the Hoxha Regime in Albania," September 12, 1949 (declassified January 31, 1978), Harry S Truman Library (hereafter HSTL): Truman Papers: President's Secretary's File (hereafter PSF), box 249, folder "Central Intelligence Memos 1949."

62 "place the maximum strain" et seq.: National Security Council (hereafter NSC): "United States Policy Toward the Soviet Satellite States in Eastern Europe," NSC-58, September 14, 1949, paragraphs 37, 42, reprinted in Thomas H. Etzold and John Lewis Gaddis, eds. *Containment* (New York, Columbia University Press, 1978), pp. 211–223.

63 "Are there any kings around": Ralph Blumenthal, "Axis Supporters Enlisted."

63 "the settlement of differences": CIA, "Current Situation in Albania," ORE 71-49, December 15, 1949 (declassified July 5, 1980), HSTL: Truman Papers: PSF: Intelligence File, box 256, folder "ORE Reports 1949 (60–74)."

64 "We'll get it right next time": Verrier, *Through the Looking Glass*, quoted p. 77.

64 "We were used as an experiment": Bethel, *Betrayed*, quoted p. 160.

64 "in the end it was not possible to do without overt air and military support": Blumenthal, "Axis Supporters Enlisted."

64 "welcomed": E. Howard Hunt, *Undercover* (New York: Berkeley Books, 1974), p. 95.

64 "it's all over?" et seq.: ibid.

65 "washerwomen gossiping over their laundry": Evan Thomas, *The Very Best Men* (New York, Simon and Schuster/Touchstone, 1996), quoted p. 42.

67 "like a tame act at a circus": Paul Borel interview, Washington, D.C.

68 "OPC and OSO personnel": Joseph Burkholder Smith, *Portrait of a Cold Warrior* (New York, Ballantine Books, 1981), p. 63.

68 "my dish of tea": Kermit Roosevelt, *Countercoup: The Struggle for the Control of Iran* (New York, McGraw-Hill, 1979), quoted p. 4.

69 "the man who kept the secrets": Thomas Powers, *The Man Who Kept the Secrets* (New York, Knopf, 1979).

69 "I was reminded of how much": Helms and Hood, *A Look Over My Shoulder*, p. 116.

69 "single chain of command": CIA, DCI Directive, "Organization of CIA Clandestine Services," July 15, 1952, in Warner, *The CIA Under Harry Truman*, pp. 460–462.

71–2 "The Ukrainian people have destroyed": *Pravda*, January 25, 1948.

72 "flare ups" and "sometimes amounted to war" et seq.: Nikita Khrushchev, *Khrushchev Remembers: The Last Testament* (New York, Bantam Books, 1976), p. 198.

72 "Ukraine is fighting for its freedom": Telegram, Lachowitz to Truman, August 31, 1947. HSTL: Truman Papers: White House Central Files (hereafter WHCFWHCF): Official File, box NA, folder "1029—Ukraine."

73 "wholesale lying": Philby, *My Silent War*, p. 145; cf. pp. 144–146, 140.

74 "a large disparate body of Americans": Burke, *Outrageous Good Fortune*, p. 155.

77 "At least we're getting the kind of experience we need": Harry Rositzke, *The CIA's Secret Operations* (New York, Reader's Digest Press, 1977), quoted p. 37.

77 "What did we offer these people?": John C. Campbell Interview, HSTL Oral History no. 284, p. 206.

5: THE COVERT LEGIONS

78 "The president is serious": Gordon Gray interview, HSTL Oral History no. 167, pp. 51–52.

83 "it could not think strategically": Edward P. Lilly, "The Psychological Strategy Board and Its Predecessors: Foreign Policy Coordination, 1938–1953," in Gaetano L. Vincitorio, ed., *Studies in Modern History* (New York, St. John's University Press, 1968), p. 365.

83–4 "psychological offensive" et seq.: Department of State, "Emergency Plan for Psychological Offensive (USSR)," April 11, 1951 (declassified October 20, 1976), pp. 1, 2, 3, 4, 7. HSTL: Truman Papers: PSF: Subject File, box 188, folder "Russia, State Department Plan."

84 Various PSB Plan Titles: HSTL: PSF: Psychological Strategy Board series, passim.

85 "Look, you just forget about policy": Gordon Gray interview, HSTL Oral History no. 167, pp. 51–52.

86 "we are actually participating in Europe": Alfred H. Paddock, Jr., *U.S. Army Special Warfare* (Washington, D.C., National Defense University Press, 1982), quoted pp. 60–61.

87 "You're a marked man now": Robert Burns, "CIA–Air Force Unit Kept Secrecy," Associated Press Dispatch, August 29, 1998, 11:09 A.M. EDT, http://pages.progidy.com/military/cia_af.atm

88 "Besides psychological warfare": "Peking Says Flyers Admitted Espionage," Associated Press, *New York Herald Tribune (European Edition)*, November 27, 1954, quoted p. 1.

90 "Fizzland": Anthony Carew, "The Origins of CIA Financing of AFL Programs," *CovertAction Quarterly* 67 (Spring–Summer 1999), p. 56.

93 "particularly effective for democratically-run membership organizations": CIA Study, quoted in Church Committee Final Report, Bk. I, p. 183.

95 "I had to sign off on all these projects": Jonathan Kwitney, "The CIA's Secret Armies in Europe," *Nation*, April 6, 1992, quoted p. 445.

96 "Now we'll finish off the goddamned Commie bastards!": Smith, *Portrait of a Cold Warrior*, quoted p. 102.

6: BITTER FRUITS

100 "what they had in mind": Roosevelt, *Countercoup*, p. 107.

101 "it would be unfair to the American taxpayers": Cable, Dwight D. Eisenhower to Mohammed Mosadegh, June 29, 1953, in Dwight D. Eisenhower, *Mandate for Change: White House Years, 1953–1956* (Garden City, N.Y., Doubleday, 1963), quoted p. 162.

101 "appropriately enthusiastic": Roosevelt, *Countercoup*, quoted p. 10.

102 "quasi-legal overthrow": CIA, "Clandestine Service History: Overthrow of Premier Mossadeq of Iran, November 1952–August 1953" (Wilbur Report), October 1969. This document was leaked to the *New York Times*, which published it in part on April 16, 2000. The history appeared in substantially complete form in *Foreign Policy Bulletin*, v. 11, no. 3, May/June 2000, pp. 90–104.

102 "Factors Involved in the Overthrow of Mossadegh": CIA Intelligence Report, April 16, 1953, ibid., p. 90.

104–5 Shah at Ramsar: Manucher Farmanfarmaian and Roxane Farmanfarmaian, *Blood and Oil: Memoirs of a Persian Prince* (New York, Random House, 1997), pp. 290–292.

105 "The pool was no solace": Roosevelt, *Countercoup*, p. 171.

107 "If we, the CIA, are ever going to try something like this again": Roosevelt, *Countercoup*, quoted p. 210.

109 "the task headed by the CIA": CIA, Memorandum for the Record, "Guatemala," September 11, 1953, in FRUS 1952–1954, p. 105. Note that where many scholars refer to the FRUS series by item numbers in their notes, the references here are to pages.

111 "If you think you can run this operation without United Fruit": Stephen Schlesinger and Stephen Kinzer, *Bitter Fruit* (New York, Doubleday, 1982), quoted p. 110.

112 "Preliminary Conditioning" et seq.: CIA, PB/Success Plan, November 12, 1953, FRUS 1952–1954, p. 137.

112 is a top priority operation": CIA, "Contact Report," November 16, 1953, FRUS, 1952–1954: Guatemala, quoted p. 140.

113 "public opinion" et seq.: *Time*, January 11, 1954, quoted p. 27.

114 "But Arbenz became president in a free election": Phillips, *Night Watch*, quoted p. 34.

114 "supported and partially controlled by CIA": CIA, "Proposed PP Program, Stage Two, FRUS PBSUCCESS," January 25, 1954 (Declassified CIA Historical Review Program, 2003).

114 "in line so they would allow this revolutionary activity": Schlesinger and Kinzer, *Bitter Fruit*, quoted p. 140.

115 "would be projected": CIA, Cable 45998, April 10, 1954, FRUS, 1952–1954: Guatemala, p. 231.

115 "ridiculous": *Time*, January 11, 1954, p. 27.

116 "for disposal by [the] Junta Group": CIA, "Selection of Individuals for Disposal by Junta Group," March 31, 1954 (declassified CIA/CSI July 11, 1995).

116 "Continue the good work": CIA, Memo, "Director's Visit," March 31, 1954 (declassified CIA/HRP, 2003).

116 "the $64-question": CIA, Memorandum, "Disadvantages and Damage Resulting from a Decision to Discontinue or *Substantially* Modify PBSUCCESS," April 15, 1954 (declassified CIA/HRP, 2003). A marginal note on this document indicates it was presented by DDO Frank Wisner to Assistant Secretary

of State Henry F. Holland. The money reference is to an early predecessor of a television quiz show of that era, "The 64,000 Dollar Question."

117 "We have the full green light": CIA, "Contact Report," April 28, 1954, FRUS 1952–1954: Guatemala, quoted p. 262.

117 "Headquarters had never received" et seq.: ibid., p. 263.

118 "reign of terror": Eisenhower, *Mandate for Change*, p. 425.

118 "agents of international communism": ibid., p. 424.

119 "outpost" of the "communist dictatorship": *Public Papers of the Presidents: Dwight D. Eisenhower, 1954* (Washington, D.C.: Government Printing Office, 1960), p. 493.

119 "I think the State Department made a bad mistake": Robert H. Ferrell, ed., *The Diary of James C. Hagerty* (Bloomington, Indiana University Press, 1983), p. 68. Hagerty referred to the principle of innocent passage, without foreign search or seizure, in the international law of the sea.

120 "What do you think Castillo-Armas's chances would be" et seq.: Eisenhower, *Mandate for Change*, quoted p. 425–426.

121 "If you use my airfields": Schlesinger and Kinzer, *Bitter Fruit*, quoted p. 193.

121 "went beyond the established limits of policy": Tom Wicker, et al., "A Plot Scuttled," *New York Times*, April 28, 1966, quoted p. 28. In a September 1979 interview with Schlesinger and Kinzer, however, Bissell qualified his admission somewhat: "You can't take an operation of this scope, draw narrow boundaries of policy around them, and be absolutely sure those boundaries will never be overstepped" (*Bitter Fruit*, quoted p. 194).

122 ""In Iran a Mossadegh, and in Guatemala an Arbenz": Allen W. Dulles, *The Craft of Intelligence* (New York, New American Library, 1965), pp. 207–208.

7: ADVENTURES IN ASIA

131 "covert activity within China": Joint Chiefs of Staff, Joint Staff, "Military Support to Anti-Communist Groups in China," JSPC 958/15, February 16, 1952 (declassified April 19, 1976), Section L, Paragraph 1, Declassified Documents Reference Service.

132 "Yeah, and I'm going to be commandant": Frank Holober, *Raiders of the China Coast: CIA Covert Operations During the Korean War* (Annapolis, Naval Institute Press, 1999), quoted p. 142. Much of the discussion of the offshore island campaign draws from this CIA memoir.

135 "this adventure has cost us heavily": State Department Cable, [August 15, 1951] FRUS 1951, v. 6, p. 288.

136 "Mr. Ambassador, I have it cold" et seq.: David Wise and Thomas B. Ross, *The Invisible Government* (New York, Vintage Books, 1964), quoted p. 131.

137 "What could be more ridiculous": Chester Bowles, *Ambassador's Report* (New York, Harper and Row, 1954), quoted p. 233.

137 "nothing but difficulty" et seq.: White House Office of the Staff Secretary, "Synopsis of State and Intelligence Material Reported to the President," May 29, 1959 (declassified October 31, 1985), Dwight D. Eisenhower Library: Dwight D. Eisenhower Papers (hereafter DDEL:DDEP): White House Office (hereafter WHO): Office of the Staff Secretary (hereafter OSS): Subject Series, Alphabetical Subseries, box 14, folder "Intelligence Briefing Notes, v. I (7)."

141 "we are already making [a] contribution": State Department Cable, Heath to Dulles, February 15, 1954, FRUS 1952–1954, v. 13, p. 1048.

142 "that would tend to keep our participation in the background": Eisenhower, *Mandate for Change*, quoted p. 364.

143 "such a unit will always be useful as a ready striking force" et seq.: Assistant to the Secretary of Defense (Special Operations), "Outline Plan for the Activation of an International Volunteer Air Group," April 26, 1954 (declassified February 18, 1986). DDEL:DDEP: WHO: Office of the Special Assistant for National Security Affairs (hereafter OSANSA): Special Assistant series, Name subseries, box 3, folder "I-General."

8: "ACCEPTABLE NORMS OF HUMAN CONDUCT DO NOT APPLY"

147 "Alternative C" et seq.: Solarium Study, July 1953, FRUS 1952–1954, v. 2, Pt. 1, pp. 416, 419, 418.

147 "a departure from our traditional concepts": Eisenhower quoted in *Washington Post*, December 7, 1984.

147 "who gets it and who gets hurt": Minutes of the NSC Meeting of July 30, 1953, FRUS 1952–1954, v. 2, Pt. 1, p. 439.

148 "equate the costs of the overall efforts to the results achieved": Letter, Dwight D. Eisenhower to James H. Doolittle, July 26, 1954, DDEL:DDEP: Ann Whitman File (hereafter AWF): Administration series, box 14, folder "Dulles, Allen W. (4)."

149 "As long as it remains national policy" et seq.: White House, "Report of the Special Study Group on the Covert Activities of the Central Intelligence Agency" (Doolittle Report), September 30, 1954 (declassified April 1, 1976), pp. 1, 2, Declassified Documents Reference Service, Fiche 78-139(c).

149 "like topsy" et seq.: Eisenhower-Doolittle Meeting, October 19, 1954, Ann Whitman Notes, October 19, 1954. DDEL:DDEP: AWF: Administration series, box 14, folder" Dulles, Allen W. (4)."

150 "I'm not going to be able to change Allen": Leary, *Central Intelligence Agency*, quoted p. 74. Leary reprints the excellent study of the history of the intelligence community written by Church Committee staff analyst Anne Karalekas, from which this is drawn.

150 "shall be the normal channel for giving policy approval" et seq.: NSC, "National Security Council Directive on Covert Operations," NSC5412/1, March 12, 1955 (declassified March 6, 1977), p. 3, DDEL:DDEP: WHO: OSANSA: Special Assistant Series, Presidential subseries, box 2, folder "President's Papers 1955 (7)."

150–1 "The NSC has determined" et seq.: NSC 5412/2, December 28, 1955, reprinted in Leary, *Cental Intelligence Agency*, pp. 146–147.

152 "Well, I guess I'll have to fudge the truth a little" et seq.: Tom Braden, "What's Wrong with the CIA," *Saturday Review*, April 5, 1975, quoted p. 24.

152 "It's not a question of reluctance": Harry Howe Ransom, *The Intelligence Establishment* (Cambridge, Mass., Harvard University Press, 1970), quoted p. 169.

153 "Fellows, tell me this": quoted in a talk by former NSC staffer Karl G. Harr, transcript in Kenneth W. Thompson, ed., *The Eisenhower Presidency* (Lanham, Md., University Press of America, 1984), p. 108.

153 Eisenhower Policy Papers: NSC-143 series; NSC-158, "U.S. Objectives and Actions to Exploit Unrest in Eastern Europe;" NSC-5505/1, "Exploitation of Soviet and European Satellite Vulnerabilities," February 1955; NSC 5505/1, Progress Report, December 14, 1955; NSC-5608/1, "U.S. Policy Toward the Soviet Satellites in Eastern Europe, July 18, 1956. All are available in DDEL:DDEP: WHO: OSANSA: NSC Series, Policy Papers subseries.

154 "I have always regarded it as one of the major coups of my tour": Dulles, *The Craft of Intelligence*, p. 80.

154 "Wisner says you think we ought to release" et seq.: Ray Cline, *Secrets, Spies and Scholars* (Washington, D.C., Acropolis Books, 1976), p. 164.

154 "pending a decision as to what": Letter, Allen Dulles to Dillon Anderson, May 31, 1956 (declassified September 10, 1984), DDEL:DDEP: WHO: OSANSA: Special Assistant Series, Subject series, box 10, folder "USSR (1)." In his *Craft of Intelligence*, Allen Dulles says no more than that the speech was printed by the State Department. Eisenhower's memoir is entirely silent on the matter.

155 "All hell has broken loose in Budapest": Cord Meyer, *Facing Reality: From World Federalism to the CIA* (New York, Harper and Row, 1980), quoted p. 127.

156 "no RFE broadcast": CIA Memorandum, "Radio Free Europe," November 20, 1956 (declassified March 15, 1982), DDEL:DDEP: WHO: OSS, Subject Series, Alpha subseries, box7, folder "CIA v. I (4)."

156 "fairly clearly implies" et seq.: Jane Perlez, "Archives Confirm False Hope Fed Hungary Revolt," *New York Times*, September 28, 1996, quoted p. 2. British journalist Noel Barber, who covered the rising and would be wounded in Hungary, considers RFE to have been highly damaging to Imre Nagy's cause. Barber cites a constant stream of criticisms of Nagy's efforts to forestall Soviet intervention, quoting an RFE military expert who declared the cease-fire accommodation a "Trojan Horse" gambit, as well as other broadcasts advocating rejection of Nagy's cabinet, rejecting the leadership of the defense and foreign ministries (which were loyal to Nagy, not to the Soviets), and instructing listeners on how to make Molotov cocktails at a time when Nagy was trying to calm the situation. Noel Barber, *Seven Days to Freedom: The Hungarian Rising of 1956* (New York, Stein and Day, 1974), pp. 62, 128–30. Of the ninety RFE personnel involved in the Hungarian broadcasts, only the individual responsible for the Molotov cocktail episode is known to have been dismissed.

156 "Where are the Americans?": Jeffrey Blyth, Letter to the Editor, *New York Times*, October 3, 1996, p. A22.

156 "In the Western capitals": Perlez, "Archives Confirm."

156 "an excess of exhuberance": Sig Mickelson, *America's Other Voice: The Story of Radio Free Europe and Radio Liberty* (New York, Praeger Publishers, 1983), pp. 91–104.

156–7 "Radio Free Europe was regularly sending guidances": Frances S. Saunders, *The Cultural Cold War: The CIA and the World of Art and Letters* (New York: New York Press, 1999), quoted p. 303.

157 "as inaccessible to us as Tibet": Dwight D. Eisenhower, *Waging Peace: White House Years, 1956–1960* (Garden City, N.Y., Doubleday, 1965), p. 95.

158 "exactly the end for which the agency's paramilitary capability was designed" et seq.: Colby and Forbath, *Honorable Men*, p. 134–135.

158 "it was clear that the steady barrage": Rositzke, *CIA's Secret Operations*, p. 158.

158 "I am satisfied that RFE did not plan": Meyer, *Facing Reality*, p. 125.

158 "a few of the scripts reviewed do indicate": Letter, Allen Dulles to Andrew Goodpaster, attaching CIA memorandum, "Radio Free Europe," November 20, 1956 (declassified March 15, 1982), paragraph 4, pp. 3–4, DDEL:DDEP: WHO: OSS: Subject series, Alphabetical subseries, box 7, folder" CIA, v. I (4)."

159 "whatever doubt may have existed in the Agency": Colby, *Honorable Men*, p. 135.

159–60 "brutal" and "was in truth a saturation effort": Lyman D. Kirkpatrick, *The Real CIA* (New York: Macmillan, 1968), pp. 147–148.

160 "buccaneers" and "informality": Thomas, *The Very Best Men*, quoted p. 149. Also see Arthur M. Schlesinger, Jr., *Robert Kennedy and His Times* (New York, Ballantine Books, 1979), pp. 490–492.

160 "as far as we have been able to determine": Memorandum, James R. Killian to Dwight D. Eisenhower, December 20, 1956 (declassified October 30, 1996), DDEL:DDEP: WHO: OSANSA: NSC Series, Subject subseries, box 7, folder "PBCFIA First Report (1)."

160–1 "increasingly concerned about the security" et seq.: NSC Memorandum, "Discussion at the Special Meeting in the President's Office on Thursday, January 17, 1957," January 18, 1957 (declassified August 11, 1997), DDEL: DDEP folder "PBCFIA First Report (2)."

161 "The President replied facetiously": NSC, "Memorandum of Discussion at the 352nd Meeting of the NSC, January 22, 1958," January 23, 1958 (declassified July 18, 1989), p. 4, DDEL:DDEP: WHO: OSANSA: NSC Series, box 9, folder "352nd Meeting of the NSC."

39: ARCHIPELAGO

162 "that plans to undertake a coup": Wilbur Crane Eveland, *Ropes of Sand* (New York, W. W. Norton, 1980), p. 180.

165 "Mossadegh example": Douglas Little, "Mission Impossible: The CIA and the Cult of Covert Action in the Middle East," *Diplomatic History* 28, no. 5 (November 2004), quoted p. 694.

165 "We came to power on a CIA train": Said K. Aburish, *Saddam Hussein: The Politics of Revenge* (New York, Bloomsbury, 2000), quoted p. 59.

165 "I spent most of my time": Miles Copeland, *The Game Player* (London: Aurum Press, 1989), p. 168.

167 "I think it's time we held Sukarno's feet to the fire": Smith, *Portrait of a Cold Warrior*, quoted p. 205.

168 "if some plan for doing this were not forthcoming": ibid.

168 "I think it's fair to say": Richard M. Bissell interview, Eisenhower Oral History no. 382, p. 16.

169 "the breakup of Indonesia": Brian Toohey and William Pinwill, *Oyster: The Story of the Australian Secret Intelligence Service* (Melbourne, Mandarin Australia, 1990), quoted p. 70.

169 "Then you got the green light" et seq.: Allen Dulles to Foster Dulles Telephone Notes, September 16, 1957, 4:11 P.M. DDEL: John Foster Dulles Papers (hereafter JFDP): Telephone Series (hereafter TS): box 7, folder "September–October 1957 (3)."

169 "continue the present pattern of our formal relations": NSC, Agenda Note, September 21, 1957 (declassified August 6, 1982), paragraph 6 (c). DDEL:DDEP: WHO: OSANSA: Special Assistant series, Chronological subseries, box 5, folder "September 1957 (2)."

170 "We'll drive Lebanon off the front page": Smith, *Portrait of a Cold Warrior*, quoted p. 240.

170 "extremely significant" et seq.: Foster Dulles to Allen Dulles Telephone Notes, November 29, 1957, 10:58 A.M. DDEL: JFDP: TS, box 7, folder "November–December 1957 (2)." Although Ambassador Allison strove to contain Washington adventurism, he relented in this cable cited by Foster. Allison apparently refers to the same cable in this passage of his memoirs: "We told the State Department it would be necessary to give these people active encouragement if their efforts were to bear fruit. We did not believe, as Washington seemed to, that it would be sufficient to indicate that if a satisfactory new regime was formed, the United States would promptly open negotiations on aid programs. . . . I said we believed it was essential to determine in advance what we were prepared to do for such a government and if this was known, it would give those working for a change added leverage to bring it about." John M. Allison, *Ambassador from the Prairie* (Boston, Houghton Mifflin, 1973), p. 336.

170 "Probably the failure to do so would look suspicious": Foster Dulles to Allen Dulles Telephone Notes, December 1, 1957, 12:51 P.M., DDEL: JFDP: TS, box 7, folder "November–December 1957 (2)."

170 "If this thing goes on the way it is": Allen Dulles to Foster Dulles Telephone Notes, December 8, 1957, 10:10 A.M., ibid.

171 "what he would like" et seq.: Foster Dulles to Christian Herter Telephone Notes, December 8, 1957, 10:16 A.M., ibid.

171 "will get the British with us": Foster Dulles to Hugh Cumming Telephone Notes, December 12, 1957, 10:46 A.M., ibid.

171 "having some amphibious equipment": John Foster Dulles, Telephone Memo, December 7, 1957, 5:57 PM. A.M., DDEL: JFD Papers, Telephone series, box 7, folder "November–December 1957 (1)."

171 "Everything is going all right": Foster Dulles to Allen Dulles Telephone Notes, January 8, 1958, 5:26 P.M., DDEL: JFDP: TS, box 8, folder "Memoranda of Telephone Conversations—General, February 1, 1958–March 31, 1958 (4)."

171 "Padang Group" et seq.: CIA, "Probable Developments in Indonesia," TS-141712-d, January 31, 1958 (declassified October 1985), pp. 1, 3, 4, 10, DDEL:DDEP: WHO: OSANSA: ANSC Series, Briefing Notes subseries, box 11, folder "U.S. Policy Toward Indonesia."

172 "During the stalling period": Foster Dulles to Allen Dulles Telephone Notes, February 4, 1958, 9:58 A.M. JFDT : TS, folder "January–March 1958 (3)."

172 "the subject of Archipelago came up": Allen Dulles to Foster Dulles Telephone Notes, February 5, 1958, ibid.

173 "disgusted" and "you should know" et seq.: Allison, *Ambassador from the Prairie*, p. 336.

173 "The great problem confronting us": Editorial Note on February 27, 1958, NSC Meeting, Department of State, FRUS 1958–1960, v. xvii, Indonesia, p. 49.

173–4 "The Secretary said he does not know": Foster Dulles to Allen Dulles Telephone Notes, February 27, 1958, 4:20 P.M. JFDP: TS, folder "January–March 1958 (2)." I have substituted the name "Allen" for "A" in these notes, as well as the word "Secretary" for the abbreviation "Sec" where they appear in this quotation.

174 "without intrusion from without": *New York Times*, February 21, 1958.

175 "the Boss' deep interest" et seq.: John Foster Dulles, Telephone Memo, April 15, 1958, 2:40 P.M. FRUS 1958–1960, v. xvii, pp. 108–109.

176 "has happened with far greater efficiency and speed": Foster Dulles to Allen Dulles Telephone Notes, April 17, 1958, 12:31 P.M. JFDP: TS, box 8, folder "April–May 1958 (3)."

177 "the East is boiling": Foster Dulles to Allen Dulles Telephone Notes, April 28, 1958, ibid., folder "April–May 1958 (2)."

177 "almost too effective in certain instances": Editorial Note on May 1, 1958, NSC Meeting. FRUS 1958–1960, v. xvii, p. 130.

178 "every rebellion I have ever heard of had its soldiers of fortune": *New York Times*, May 1, 1958.

178 "a lot of confidence in the man": Foster Dulles to Gen. Charles Cabell Telephone Notes, May 19, 1958, 3:02 P.M. JFDP: TS, folder "April–May 1958 (1)."

178 "We're pulling the plug": Kenneth Conboy and James Morrison, *Feet to the Fire* (Annapolis, Naval Institute Press, 1999), quoted p. 143.

179 "anywhere this struggle is being fought": CIA, Memorandum, Allen Dulles to Secretary Dulles et al., May 21, 1958 (declassified July 23, 2001), DDEL: JFD Papers, White House Memoranda Series, box 8, folder "Conversations with Dulles, Allen (1)."

179 "we must disengage": Smith, *Portrait of a Cold Warrior*, quoted p. 247.

179 "The American intervention was a gift to Sukarno": Brian May, *The Indonesian Tragedy* (London, Routledge and Kegan Paul, 1978), p. 80.

180 "this unfortunate situation": PBCFIA Memorandum, Gen. John E. Hull to Dwight D. Eisenhower, October 30, 1958 (declassified April 9, 1997), DDEL, box 7, folder "PBCFIA Third Report (3)."

181 "We used to say": Thompson, *The Eisenhower Presidency*, p. 107.

182 "to obviate any tendency for congressional groups . . . to get into these activities": Memorandum, Andrew Goodpaster to Bryce Harlow, January 2, 1959. DDEL:DDEP: WHO: OSS: Subject series, Alphabetic subseries, box 7, folder "CIA, v. II (2)."

182 "the criteria with respect to what matters shall come before the Group" et seq.: Memorandum, Gordon Gray to Dwight D. Eisenhower, January 18, 1959 (declassified June 8, 1979). DDEL:DDEP: WHO: OSANSA: Subject series, Alphabetic subseries, box 15, folder "Intelligence Matters (8)."

182 "the President . . . referred to one particular activity": NSC, Gordon Gray, "Memorandum of Meeting with the President," June 26, 1959 (declassified October 28, 1981), DDEL:DDEP: WHO: OSANSA: Special Assistant series, box 4, folder "Meetings with the President, 1959 (1)."

10: THE WAR FOR THE ROOF OF THE WORLD

186 "nest of spies" et seq.: Neville Maxwell, *India's China War* (New York, Doubleday, 1972), p. 100.

186 Meeting with American: George N. Patterson, *Tibet in Revolt* (London, Faber and Faber, 1960), pp. 120–122.

187 "buried in the lore of the CIA": L. Fletcher Prouty, *The Secret Team* (Englewood Cliffs, N.J., Prentice-Hall, 1973), p. 351.

191 "I saw the weapons, guns and rifles, come in by night": Han Suyin, *Lhasa: The Open City* (London, Triad Panther Books, 1979), quoted p. 70.

193 "I felt I was standing between two volcanos": Richard Avedon, *In Exile from the Land of Snows* (New York, Knopf, 1984), quoted p. 116.

193 "one of the strangest and most ill-understood coups": Michel Peissel, *The Secret War in Tibet* (Boston, Little, Brown, 1972), p. 116.

194 "if, as a result of the new social experiment": NSC, Memorandum, Gordon Gray to James S. Lay, November 1, 1958, DDEL:DDEP: WHO: OSANSA: Special Assistant series, Subject subseries, box 11, folder "Basic National Security Policy."

194 "if the Tibetans are able to maintain their resistance movement" et seq.: Department of State, "Uprisings in Communist China," undated (declassified July 31, 1985), p. 4, DDEL:DDEP: WHO: OSANSA: NSC: Series, Briefing Notes subseries, box 5, folder "Communist China."

194 "the Tibetan uprisings apparently have resulted": White House, Office of the Staff Secretary, "Synopsis of Intelligence," March 23, 1959 (declassified June 8, 1982), DDEL:DDEP: WHO: OSS: Subject series, Alphabetical subseries, box 14, folder "Intelligence Briefing Notes v. I (5)."

194–5 "command center" and "What is the Home Ministry doing?" et seq.: Chanakya Sen, *Tibet Disappears* (New York, Asia Publishing House, 1960), quoted p. 176.

195 "We have informed embassy New Delhi" et seq.: White House, Office of the Staff Secretary, "Synopsis of Intelligence," April 1, 1959 (declassified December 9, 1983), OSS: Subject series, folder "Intelligence Briefing Notes v. I (6)."

196 "You must help us as soon as possible": Message received April 2, 1959 (declassified July 9, 1981), pp. 2–3. DDEL:DDEP: WHO: OSANSA: Special Assistant series, Alphabetical subseries, box 15, folder "Intelligence Matters (9)."

196 "affirmative and positive action": JCS Paper, FRUS, 1958–1960, v. xix, China, p. 769.

198 "a resolution recognizing [Tibet's] independence or sovereignty" et seq.: Christian Herter to Henry Cabot Lodge, Telephone Notes, October 6, 1959, 1:05 P.M. (declassified January 23, 1986), DDEL: Christian Herter Papers, box 12, folder "CAH Phone Calls 5/4/59–12/31/59."

198 "We Tibetans have determined to fight to the last": Letter, Gompo Tashi to Dwight D. Eisenhower, December 9, 1959, DDEL:DDEP: WHO: OSS: International Series, box 13, folder "Tibet (2)."

198 "channels considered by the embassy": Department of State, Memorandum, Thomas McElhiney to Andrew Goodpaster, December 15, 1959, ibid. State regarded the Tibetan gifts as a miscellaneous protocol matter left over from the president's trip to India. The White House raised no objection.

199 "As a result of the discussion the DCI said he would reorient his thinking": NSC, Gordon Gray, "Memorandum of Meeting with the President," September 15, 1960 (declassified December 11, 1981), DDEL:DDEP: WHO: OSANSA: Special Assistant series, Presidential subseries, box 5, folder "1960 Meetings with the President, v. II (6)."

200 "Mr. Dulles reported to the President on certain consultations he had had": NSC, Gordon Gray, "Memorandum of Meeting with the President," November 28, 1960, ibid., folder "1960 Meetings with the President v. II (3)."

200 "spooky activities" and "deeply unhygienic tribesmen" et seq.: John Kenneth Galbraith, *A Life in Our Times* (Boston, Houghton Mifflin, 1981), p. 395.

201 "I was especially disturbed by this particularly insane enterprise": ibid.

201 "Bulletin of Activities": Avedon, *In Exile* (p. 124), places this incident in 1966, but the release of the Chinese political journals was reported in the press at the time. Multiple sources confirm that notice. The documents were even given extensive analysis in an academic paper by J. Chester Cheng, "Problems of Chinese Leadership as Seen in the Secret Military Papers," *Asian Survey*, June 1964, pp. 861–872.

201 "resulted in a bonanza": Cline, *Secrets, Spies, and Scholars*, p. 181.

203 "a certain operational hubris" et seq.: Kenneth Knaus, *Orphans of the Cold War* (New York, Public Affairs Press, 1999), quoted p. 323.

11: "ANOTHER BLACK HOLE OF CALCUTTA"

204 "In Cuba the rebel drive": White House, Office of the Staff Secretary, "Synopsis of Intelligence and State Material Reported to the President," December 29, 1958 (declassified April 5, 1982), DDEL:DDEP: WHO: OSS: Subject Series, Alphabetic subseries, box 14, folder "Intelligence Briefing Notes v. I (3)."

206 "I am the Che" et seq.: Marvin D. Resnick, *The Black Beret* (New York, Ballantine Books, 1969), quoted pp. 141–142.

206 "far from stable" et seq.: CIA, "Memorandum to Director," February 4, 1959 (declassified July 15, 1981), pp. 1, 3, DDEL:DDEP: AWF: Dulles-Herter series, box 8, folder "Dulles, February 1959."

206 "He is either incredibly naïve" et seq.: Richard Nixon, *RN: The Memoirs of Richard Nixon* (New York: Warner Books, 1979), v. I, p. 250.

207 "With regard to his position on communism" and "We will check back in a year": Department of State, Memorandum, Christian Herter to Dwight D. Eisenhower, with attachment, "Unofficial Visit of Prime Minister Castro," April 23, 1959 (declassified December 22, 1976), DDEL:DDEP: Dulles-Herter series, box 9, folder 'Herter, April 1959 (2).'

208 "anti-communists have an interest in rumors": James M. Keagle, "Toward an Understanding of U.S. Latin American Policy," Princeton University, Ph.D. dissertation, 1982, quoted p. 90.

208 "In view of the special sensitivity": Department of State, Memorandum, Christian Herter to Dwight D. Eisenhower, November 5, 1959 (declassified February 3, 1981), DDEL:DDEP: WHO: OSS: International series, box 4, folder "Cuba (1) [1959]."

208 "He hoped that any refusal" et seq.: Cable, Ambassador Sir Harold Caccia to Foreign Minister Selwyn Lloyd, November 24, 1959, United Kingdom: Public Record Office, reprinted, *New York Times*, March 25, 2001, p. WK7.

209 "'far left' dictatorship" et seq.: CIA, Memorandum, J. C. King to Allen W. Dulles, "Cuban Problems," December 11, 1959, reprinted in Jack B. Pfeiffer, *Official History of the Bay of Pigs Operation: v. III: Evolution of CIA's Anti-Castro Policies, 1959–January 1961*, TS-795052 (DCI-8), CIA History Staff, December 1979 (declassified Historical Review Program, 1998), Appendix A (hereafter cited as Pfeiffer, *CIA History*). The document is held at NARA in the records of the Kennedy Assassination Records Commission. The author is indebted to historians David M. Barrett and Peter Kornbluh for his copy. Excerpts of this document have appeared in the Church Committee staff study *Alleged Assassination Plots* and elsewhere.

209 "removal from Cuba": Dulles's marginalia on King's memorandum is reported in the CIA's official history of the Cuba project, ibid.

209 "over the long run": Church Committee, *Alleged Assassination Plots*, quoted p. 93.

210 "Allen, this is fine" et seq.: Gordon Gray interview, Eisenhower Oral History no. 352, quoted p. 27–28.

210 "stick their necks out further" et seq.: CIA, "Memorandum for the Record," March 9, 1960 (declassified May 7, 1976), Case Files, *Borosage v. CIA et al.* (USDCDDC 75-0944).

211 "any plan for removal of Cuban leaders" et seq.: Church Committee, *Alleged Assassination Plots*, pp. 93, 114–116. Pfeiffer, *CIA History*, v. 3, pp. 64–65. Admiral Burke, when asked about his comment during the Church Committee investigation, insisted he had referred only to general plans that led to the Bay of Pigs, not to any specific notion of attempting assassinations. Note that as of this date the CIA covert action plan for Cuba had yet to be presented, though the draft proposal had been completed the previous day.

211 Black Hole of Calcutta: ibid.

211–2 "A Program of Action Against the Castro Regime" et seq.: The CIA project proposal memorandum appears in full in Pfeiffer, *CIA History*, v. 3, Appendix B. It also appears in the papers of the CIA Inspector General Study of the Cuba operation (Kirkpatrick Report), the Taylor Board Report, the Kennedy Assassination records, and the Eisenhower papers.

213 "the current thinking as to the timetable": NSC, Gordon Gray, "Memorandum of Meeting with the President," July 6, 1960 (declassified October 25, 1977), DDEL:DDEP: WHO: OSANSA: Special Assistant series, Presidential subseries, box 4, folder "1960 Meetings with the President, v. I (1)."

214 "There would be no conceivable hazard involved" et seq.: Gordon Gray, "Memorandum of Conference with the President," August 22, 1960 (declassified April 9, 1998), DDEL:DDEP: WHO: OSS: Subject series, Alphabetic subseries, box 15, folder "Intelligence Matters (17)."

214–5 "It is needed to supply and train" et seq.: Thompson, *Eisenhower Presidency*, p. 219. Stans quotes Dulles and Eisenhower.

216 "I had no desire to become personally involved" et seq.: Bissell, et al., Richard M. Bissell, Jr., with Jonathan E. Lewis and Francis T. Pudlo, *Reflections of a Cold Warrior: From Yalta to the Bay of Pigs* (New Haven: Yale University Press, 1996), p. 157.

216 "It is appropriate to conjecture": CIA, Inspector General, "Memorandum for the Record: Report on Plots to Assassinate Fidel Castro," May 23, 1967 (declassified HRP, 1993), p. 18, NARA, records of the Kennedy Assassination Records Commission.

219 "The CIA men wanted to put in our hands" et. seq.: Thomas J. Watson Institute for International Studies, Brown University, and the National Security Archive (ed. James G. Blight), *Conference Proceedings: The Bay of Pigs: New Evidence from Documents and Testimony of the Kennedy Administration, Brigade 2506 and the Anti-Castro Resistance, 31 May–2 June 1996* (hereafter cited as 1996 Bay of Pigs Conference), pp. 25–27. A book based upon these proceedings was published subsequently: James G. Blight and Peter Kornbluh, eds., *The Politics of Illusion: The Bay of Pigs Invasion Reconsidered* (Boulder, Colo.: Lynne Reiner Publishers, 1997). These proceedings should not be confused with those of the 2001 conference sponsored by the same groups in Havana (referred to several times in the text), which featured the participation of Fidel Castro and other senior Cuban participants. No formal record of the latter conference is available at this writing.

220 "lively appreciation" et seq.: Richard Bissell, *Reflections of a Cold Warrior*, p. 152–153.

221 "In the preparations for and conduct of": Richard M. Bissell, Jr., Oral History, November 9, 1976, DDEL, p. 27.

221 "get the hang of secret operations" et seq.: Helms, *A Look Over My Shoulder*, pp. 176–177.

221 "verbal diarrhea": Pfeiffer, *CIA History*, v. 3, 187–188.

224 "knocked off": 1996 Bay of Pigs Conference, ms., p. 59.

224 "I would talk it to Esterline": CIA, Richard Bissell Interview with Jack Pfeiffer, October 17, 1975 (declassified), p. 31.

224 "By late fall 1960": Bissell, *Reflections of a Cold Warrior*, p. 157.

225 "assault force" et seq.: CIA Cable, Director 09972, October 31, 1960 (declassified March 1985), JFKL: JFKP: NSF: Country File, box 61-b, folder "Cuba: Subjects—Paramilitary Study Group, Part III, Annex 4."

225 "there would occur a point in time": CIA, "Minutes of Special Group Meeting," November 3, 1960 (declassified June 18, 1996), GRFL: GRFP: Rockefeller Commission Parallel File, box 5, folder "Assassination Materials (2) A-I (j)."

228 "discretion for operational action": CIA, Kirkpatrick Report, quoted pp. 62–63.

229 "Drop the rice and beans": Phillips, *Night Watch*, quoted p. 98.

229 "Old Rice and Beans": ibid.

232 "in the position of turning over the government": NSC, Gordon Gray, "Memorandum of Meeting with the President," December 5, 1960 (declassified May 23, 1983), DDEL:DDEP: WHO: OSANSA: Special Assistant series, Presidential subseries, box 5, folder "1960 Meetings with the President v. II (2)."

233 "to the utmost": Clifford, *Counsel to the President*, quoted, p. 344.

235 "Now boys, if you don't intend to go through with this": Gordon Gray interview, Eisenhower Oral History no. 352, DDEL, quoted p. 37.

12: THE BAY OF PIGS: FAILURE AT PLAYA GIRÓN

237 "some problems in Guatemala" et seq.: Victor Andres Triay, ed. *Bay of Pigs: An Oral History of Brigade 2506* (Gainesville: University Press of Florida, 2001), pp. 47, 52, 54. Hunt's account of the visit of *frente* political leaders is in Howard Hunt, *Give Us This Day* (New Rochelle, N.Y., Arlington House, 1973).

238 "quite well": Allen W. Dulles, Oral History, December 5, 1964, JFKL, p. 1.

239 "I did not brief candidates": Peter Grose, *Gentleman Spy: The Life of Allen Dulles* (Boston, Houghton Mifflin, 1994), quoted p. 507.

239 "A search of CIA records": John L. Helgerson, *Getting to Know the President: CIA Briefings of Presidential Candidates* (CIA, Center for the Study of Intelligence, 1996), p. 55.

240 "fighters for freedom" et seq.: Schlesinger, *A Thousand Days*, quoted p. 212. For Nixon's account see his *Six Crises* (New York, Pyramid Books, 1968), pp. 380–381 and 381 n.

240 "an honest misunderstanding": CIA, "Excerpts: Allen Dulles–Eric Severeid Interview," April 26, 1962, p. 6, JFKL: JFKP: National Security File (hereafter JFKL:JFKP: NSF): Agency File, box 271, folder "CIA 3/62–4/62."

241 "I blame Nixon": CIA History Staff, Jacob Esterline CIA interview with Jack Pfeiffer, p. 49. Cf pp. 11–12, 38.

241 "The plan, as we outlined it to him": Richard Bissell Oral History, April 25, 1967, p. 3.

241 "qualified go ahead": Hunt, *Give Us This Day.*

242 "just didn't know beans": Robert Amory, Jr., JFKL Oral History, February 9, 1966, p. 24.

243 "a great increase . . . in popular opposition": National Security Council, Memorandum of Discussion on Cuba, January 28, 1961 (declassified March 22, 2000), JFKL: JFKP: NSF: Country File: Cuba, box 61A, folder "Paramilitary Study Group."

243 "It was very ethereal": President's Review Board (Taylor Committee), Memorandum for the Record, Meeting at 1350 Hours, April 24, 1961, p. 8 (declassified March 22, 2000), ibid.

244 "Military Evaluation of CIA Paramilitary Plan" et seq.: This and the other documents noted subsequently are contained in the Taylor report among its exhibits, JFKL.

244 "Very little plotting goes on": Sarah Booth Conway, "A Peek at Privilege: Inside the Alibi Club," *Washington Post*, June 22, 1992, quoted p. B9.

244 "I'm your man-eating shark": Peter Wyden, *Bay of Pigs: The Untold Story* (New York, Simon and Schuster, 1979), quoted p. 95.

245 "Am I likely to be involved in a bail-out operation" et seq.: Robert L. Dennison interview, U.S. Navy Oral History. *U.S. Naval Institute Proceedings*, October 1979, p. 111.

245 "just about a year ago": David M. Barrett, *The CIA and Congress* (Lawrence, University Press of Kansas, 2005), pp. 440–445, quoted p. 441.

246 "I stood right here at Ike's desk": Theodore Sorensen, *Kennedy* (New York, Bantam Books, 1966), quoted p. 332.

246 "Don't forget": Schlesinger, *A Thousand Days*, quoted p. 227.

246 "If I ever made a suggestion like that": Esterline CIA interview, quoted p. 51.

247 "I say, 'let 'er rip!'": Wyden, *Bay of Pigs*, quoted p. 147.

249 "Have any of you" et seq.: Phillips, *Night Watch*, quoted p. 104.

249–50 "MY OBSERVATIONS": Manuel Artime, et al., "We Who Tried," *Life*, May 10, 1963, quoted p. 34. The original of the cable appears in the Taylor and Kirkpatrick reports and is widely cited elsewhere.

251 "I am forced": Kornbluh, *Bay of Pigs Declassified*, p. 264.

251 "The specific plan for paramilitary support": Memo, McGeorge Bundy to Rusk/McNamara/Dulles, April 15, 1961 (declassified April 29, 1994), JFKL:JFKP: NSF: Country File, box 35, folder "Cuba: General, 1/61–4/61."

252 "like a falling bomb": Charles Pearre Cabell, *Man of Intelligence: Memoirs of War, Peace, and the CIA* (Colorado Springs, Colo., Impavide Publications, 1997), p. 366.

252–3 "I don't think there's any point" et seq.: Bissell, *Reflections of a Cold Warrior*, quoted p. 184. Cabell, *Man of Intelligence*, p. 374.

253 "There's been a little change": Phillips, *Night Watch*, quoted p. 107.

253 "Goddamn it" et seq.: Bissell, *Reflections of a Cold Warrior*, quoted p. 185.

253 "The feeling among the people in the brigade": 1996 Bay of Pigs Conference, ms., p. 69.

256 "almost a Caribbean branch": et seq.: Grayston L. Lynch, *Decision for Disaster: Betrayal at the Bay of Pigs* (Washington, D.C., Brassey's, 1998), p. 15. For the Helms quote, see Helms, *A Look Over My Shoulder*, p. 177. The KGB was the Soviet Union's primary intelligence service, the GRU its military service.

256 "twenty-one Communist homes": Kornbluh, *Bay of Pigs Declassified*, p. 172.

258 "the danger of invasion": Sergei M. Kudryavtsev Diary, Record of Conversation from April 14, 1961, no. 136, released at conference, "The Bay of Pigs: 40 Years After," Havana, March 22, 2001, translation by Svetlana Savranskaya, National Security Archive.

262 "You're missing the party": Tim Weiner, "Bay of Pigs Enemies Finally Sit Down Together," *New York Times*, March 23, 2001, quoted p. A3.

262 "a hell of a barrage": Note, Fidel Castro to Jose Ramon Fernandez, April 17, 1961, 7 P.M. (declassified by the Cuban government, March 3, 2001).

262 "by neutrally painted U.S. planes": Memo, McGeorge Bundy to John F. Kennedy, April 18, 1961 (declassified December 14, 1982), JFKL:JFKP: NSF: Country File, box 35, folder "Cuba: General, 1/61–4/61."

263 "We're already in it up to here": Wyden, *The Bay of Pigs*, quoted p. 271.

264 "I certainly would" et seq.: Nixon, *RN*, I, quoted 287–288, 289.

264 "The chief apparent causes of failure": Eisenhower Diary, April 22, 1961, in Robert H. Ferrell, ed., *The Eisenhower Diaries* (New York: W. W. Norton, 1981), p. 386.

264 "proper legal cover": Nixon, *RN*, I, p. 289.

264 "anything that had as its objective": Eisenhower Diary, April 22, 1961, in Ferrell, *Eisenhower Diaries*.

264 "This story could be called": Eisenhower Diary, June 7, 1961, ibid., p. 390.
266 "a marginal character . . . which increased" et seq.: Taylor Report, June 7, 1961, reprinted in *Operation Zapata: The "Ultrasensitive" Report and Testiony of the Board of Inquiry on the Bay of Pigs* (Frederick, Md., University Press of America, 1981), p. 41.
266 "very fair" et seq.: Bissell CIA interview, p. 43.
266 "We do not feel that any failure of intelligence" et seq.: Taylor Report, *Operation Zapata*, p. 42.
267 "constantly in touch with" et seq.: PFIAB, "Excerpts from Minutes of President's Foreign Intelligence Advisory Board with Respect to Covert Actions Matters," 1961–1963 (declassified September 24, 1998), NARA: Kennedy Assassination Records, box 11, folder "Covert Operation (bulk), March 29, 1971, Staff Paper to Chairman, Tab B."
267 "covert operations dog is wagging the intelligence tail": ibid.
268 "the then Inspector General": Richard Bissell Oral History, p. 48.
269 "probably correct" et seq.: Bissell, *Reflections of a Cold Warrior*, pp. 193–194.
269 "Dulles is a legendary figure": Schlesinger, *A Thousand Days*, quoted p. 258.
272 "splinter . . . into a thousand pieces": Taylor Branch and George Crile, "The Kennedy Vendetta," *Harper's*, August 1975, quoted p. 50.

13: COLD WAR AND COUNTERREVOLUTION

275 "classic communist effort takeover": Madeleine G. Kalb, *The Congo Cables* (New York, Macmillan, 1982), quoted p. 53.
275 "in high quarters" CIA Cable, August 26, 1960, Church Committee, *Alleged Assassination Plots*, p. 28.
276 "third country national": ibid., quoted, p. 29.
277 "ARMS, SUPPLIES": ibid., quoted p. 18, n. 1.
277 "harrowing" and "bought": Richard D. Mahoney, *JFK: Ordeal in Africa* (New York, Oxford University Press, 1983), quoted p. 38.
278 "several sources": Church Committee, *Alleged Assassination Plots*, p. 51.
278 "THANKS FOR PATRICE": Ibid.
283 "I think the answers are so plain": Joint Chiefs of Staff, "CIA Study on Peripheral Wars," September 25, 1955, National Archives: Modern Military Branch; Records Group 218: Radford, 1953–1957, box 48, folder "381 Net Evaluation 1955."
283 "operational" questions: Allen Dulles to Foster Dulles Telephone Notes, March 21, 1958, DDEL:JFDP: TS: box 8, folder "January–March 1958 (1)."
283 "flexible response": Maxwell D. Taylor, *The Uncertain Trumpet* (New York, Harper and Brothers, 1959), passim.
285 "I took advantage of Walt's imminent departure": Memo, Robert Komer to McGeorge Bundy, December 12, 1961, JFKL:JFKP: NSF: Aides' Files, Robert W. Komer, box 414, folder "Special Group (CI): White House Memos, 7/61–5/63."
285–6 "A general problem in threatened underdeveloped countries" et seq.: Enclosure to Memo, John A. Bross to Walt W. Rostow, November 21, 1961 (declassified May 17, 1997), quoted pp. 27–28, 29, 42–43, 41, JFKL:JFKP: NSF: M&M: box 319A, folder "Rostow: Guerrilla and Unconventional Warfare, 10/61–11/61."
286 "Because of its responsibilities in directly related fields": Report of the Counter-Guerrilla Warfare Task Force, "Elements of US Strategy to Deal with 'Wars of National Liberation,'" December 8, 1961 (declassified April 1998), p. ii, JFKL:JFKP: NSF: Aides' Files: Robert Komer, box 414, folder "Special Group (CI): Report of Counter-Guerrilla Warfare Task Force, 12/61."
287 Special Forces Teams: Designations for the various types of teams carried an "F" prefix during the 1950s. The nomenclature used in the text has applied since then.
288 "Guerrilla warfare is not a form of military and psychological magic" et seq.: Walt Rostow, "Guerrilla Warfare," Department of the Army, Office of the Chief of Information, Special Warfare (Washington, D.C., Department of the Army, n.d. [1962]), pp. 25, 23.
288 "a symbol of excellence": John F. Kennedy Letter, April 11, 1962, ibid., p. 3.
288–9 "For the first time in United States history": Tom Compere, ed. *The Army Blue Book* (New York, Military Publishing Institute, 1960), p. 80.
291 "there is no statutory authorization to any agency" et seq.: CIA, Memorandum, Lawrence Houston to John A. McCone, OGC 62-0083, January 15, 1962.

292 "In 1961 I listened with a beginner's credulity": McGeorge Bundy Op-Ed in *New York Times*, June 10, 1985.

293 "just the director the agency needed": Archie Roosevelt, *For Lust of Knowing* (Boston, Little Brown, 1988), p. 465.

294 "very damaging" et seq.: CIA, John McCone, "Memorandum of Conversation with the President," March 25, 1963 (declassified October 14, 1999), JFKL:JFKP: NSF: M&M, box 317A, folder "Meetings with the President, General, 3/63."

294 "light touches" et seq.: Cord Meyer statements to PFIAB, April 23, 1963, "Kennedy Board Considerations of Covert Action Matters by President Kennedy's Foreign Intelligence Advisory Board," no date (declassified September 3, 1998), p. 17, NARA: Records of the Kennedy Assassination Records Commission, box 11, folder "Covert Operations (bulk), March 29, 1971 Paper."

14: THE SECRET WAR AGAINST CASTRO

299 "the only effective way" et seq.: Memo, Richard N. Goodwin to John F. Kennedy, November 1, 1961 (declassified August 30, 1995), National Security Archive release at Bay of Pigs 40th Anniversary Conference.

299–300 "Castro thought that" et seq.: Tad Szulc, "Notes on TS Conversation with JFK," November 9, 1961 (declassified June 23, 1994), NARA: Records Group 223, Records of House Select Committee on Assassinations.

300 "look over the situation": President's Commission on CIA Activities (Rockefeller Commission), Edward Lansdale Deposition, May 16, 1975, pp. 5–6. GRFL:GRFP: Rockefeller Commission Parallel File, box 5, folder "Assassination Materials: Lansdale Deposition."

300 "I am most grateful": Memorandum, Gen. Edward Lansdale to Robert S. McNamara, November 25, 1961 (declassified June 11, 1990), National Security Archive: Edward Lansdale Papers, box 1, folder "1961."

300–1 "use our available assets": John F. Kennedy directive for Mongoose, November 30, 1961. National Security Archive: Cuba Collection.

301 "I decided to lay it right on the line": Note, Gen. Edward Lansdale to Robert F. Kennedy, December 7, 1961, JFKL: Robert F. Kennedy Papers, Attorney General Confidential Files, box 34, folder "The White House (Misc.) 33-0."

301 "The final chapter on Cuba": CIA, Memorandum, Richard Helms to John McCone, January 19, 1962 (declassification date NA), NARA: Kennedy Assassination Records Commission.

302 "It is a fallacy": Memorandum, Arthur Schlesinger to Richard N. Goodwin, "Cuban Covert Plan," July 8, 1961 (declassified April 19, 1996), JFKL: Arthur M. Schlesinger Papers: Classified Subject Files, box WH 31-48, folder "Cuba (3 of 5)."

304–5 "what was wanted" et seq.: Thomas A. Parrott, Memorandum for the Record, October 5, 1961 (declassified April 19, 1996), JFKL:JFKP: NSF: Country File, box 35, folder "Cuba, General 6/61–12/61."

305 "My review does not include the sensitive work": Note, Edward G. Lansdale to Robert F. Kennedy, January 18, 1962, JFKL: Robert F. Kennedy Papers: AG Confidential File, box 34, folder "The White House (Misc.) 33-0."

307 "huge": Lynch, *Decision for Disaster*, p. 170.

309 "What in the hell does a bunch of quacks": Dino A. Brugioni, *Eyeball to Eyeball: The Inside Story of the Cuban Missile Crisis* (New York, Random House, 1990), quoted p. 68.

309 "splitting the regime": Lansdale Memo of August 13, 1962, and William K. Harvey Memo of August 14, 1962, quoted in *Alleged Assassination Plots*, p. 162. cf. pp. 161–169.

310 "I just don't recall at all" et seq.: Lansdale deposition, pp. 11–14.

310 "it might be a possibility:" *Alleged Assassination Plots*, quoted p. 167.

310 "urged and insisted upon action" et seq.: CIA, "Memorandum of Mongoose Meeting," October 4, 1962 (declassified May 7, 1976).

310 "Elimination by Illumination": *Alleged Assassination Plots*, p. 142n. Lansdale's reaction is in Currey, *Edward Lansdale: The Unquiet American* (Boston: Houghton Mifflin, 1988), p. 244. The memorandum proposal is in the papers of the Special Group (Augmented).

311–2 "BELIEVE FLUCTUATIONS IN GO AND STOP ORDERS" et seq.: CIA, Memorandum, [Deleted] to Edward Lansdale, October 29, 1962 (declassified May 7, 1998), JFKL:JFKP: NSF: M&M, box 319, folder "Special Group (Augmented) 10/62–12/62."

313 "Can you imagine" et seq.: Brock Brower, "Why People Like You Joined the CIA," *Washington Monthly*, November 1976, quoted p. 59.

314 "the basic decision must be made": Office of the Vice-President, Memorandum, Howard Burris to Lyndon Johnson, January 25, 1963 (declassified April 28, 1978), Lyndon Baines Johnson Library (hereafter LBJL): Lyndon B. Johnson Papers (hereafter LBJP): Vice-Presidential Security File, box 6, folder "Memos from Burris, July 1962–April 1963."

314 "Keystone Kop capers": Joseph A Califano, Jr., *Inside: A Public and Private Life* (New York, Public Affairs Press, 2004), p. 117.

315 "I am concerned that hit-and-run raids by Cuban exiles": Department of State, Dean Rusk Draft Letter, March 28, 1963 (declassified June 17, 1977), LBJL:LBJP: Vice-Presidential Security File, box 4, folder "NSC (I)."

315 "The intensity I had admired": Califano, *Inside*, p. 121.

316 "we must not, under any circumstance" et seq.: CIA, John McCone Paper, "Memorandum on Cuban Policy," April 25, 1963 (declassified October 22, 1996), p. 6, JFKL:JFKP: NSF: Country File, box 51, folder "Cuba: Subjects—Intelligence Material 4/63."

316 footnote "speaks in circumlocution": Note, McGeorge Bundy, Standing Group Members, April 29, 1963, JFKL:JFKP: NSF: Country File, box 38, folder "Cuba: General, Standing Committee, 4/63."

318 "Even the connoisseurs in Miami": Memorandum, Gordon Chase to McGeorge Bundy, August 28, 1963 (declassified October 18, 1996), JFKL:JFKP: NSF: Country File, box 48, folder "Cuba-Subjects-Exiles, 7/63–9/63."

322 "He was deadly serious": Ray Cline, LBJ Oral History, II, p. 4.

322 "on-again, off-again orders we began getting" et seq: Ted Shackley with Richard A. Finney, *Spymaster: My Life in the CIA* (Washington, D.C., Potomac Books, 2005), p. 76. Note Shackley's use here of the same wording contained in his Cuban Missile Crisis cable.

323 "See all of that": CIA, Jacob Esterline interview with Jack Pfeiffer, November 10–11, 1975, p. 58.

324 "regional dissidence and violence": CIA, SNIE [Deleted] "Short-Term Prospects for the Tshombe Government of the Congo" (declassified February 15, 1990), LBJL:LBJP: NSF: LBJL:LBJP:NSF: Intelligence File: NIE Series, box 8/9, folder "65, Congo."

325 "At a certain point": Victor Dreke, *From the Escambray to the Congo* (ed. Mary-Alice Waters) (New York: Pathfinder Books, 2002), p. 144.

329 "two conflicting establishments" et seq.: Letter, Kwame Nkrumah to Lyndon B. Johnson, February 26, 1964, reprinted in David Rooney, *Kwame Nkrumah: The Political Kingdom in the Third World* (New York, St. Martin's Press, 1988), pp. 243–245, quoted p. 244.

330 "no patience for management": Dewey Clarridge, *A Spy for All Seasons* (New York, Scribner's, 1997), p. 79.

330 "the coup in Ghana": NSC, Memo, Robert Komer to Lyndon Johnson, March 12, 1966 (declassified May 15, 1987), LBJL:LBJP: NSF: Memos to the President, box 6, folder "Komer v. 21, March 1–31, 1966."

330 "We did not throw a match": Rooney, *Kwame Nkrumah*, quoted p. 254.

332 "I would say we reached": U. Alexis Johnson with Jef O. McAllister, *The Right Hand of Power* (Englewood Cliffs, N.J., Prentice-Hall, 1984), p. 349.

333 "Troops have scored their first victories": CIA, "President's Daily Brief," April 25, 1967 (declassified December 10, 2004), Federation of American Scientists, Project on Government Secrecy archives.

334 "as the intelligence community": NSC, Note, Walt W. Rostow to Lyndon B. Johnson, May 11, 1967 (declassified January 7, 1993), National Security Archive: Electronic Briefing Book no. 5, "The Death of Che Guevara," item no. 3.

334 "Ernesto "Che" Guevara [deleted]": CIA, Memorandum, "Cuban-Inspired Guerrilla Activity in Bolivia," June 14, 1967 (declassified January 6, 1993), LBJL:LBJP: NSF, Intelligence File, box 2, folder "Guerrilla Problem in Latin America."

335 "It marks the passing": NSC, Memo, Walt Rostow to Lyndon B. Johnson, October 11, 1967 (declassified January 31, 1997), National Security Archive briefing book, item no. 7.

15: WAR IN SOUTHEAST ASIA

337 "demotic" strategy: Lansdale's own account is *In the Midst of Wars* (New York, Harper & Row, 1972). He articulated the demotic strategy in reports for the Eisenhower administration during the late 1950s.

338 "intense psychological attack" et seq.: Lansdale Report, January 17, 1961, Department of Defense, *United States–Vietnam Relations 1945–1967* (hereafter US-GVN Rel) (Washington, D.C., Government Printing Office, n.d. [1971]), v. 2, book IV.A.5, pp. 66–77.

338 "This is the worst one we've got": Walt W. Rostow, *The Diffusion of Power* (New York, Macmillan, 1972), quoted p. 265.

338 "somehow I found him": U.S. Congress: Senate (98/2): Foreign Relations Committee, *Report: The U.S. Government and the Vietnam War: Executive and Legislative Roles and Relationships* (hereafter cited as USG & VN War) (Washington, D.C., Government Printing Office, 1984), part 2, quoted p. 13.

338 "none of us . . . who were charged with the responsibility": ibid., quoted p. 36.

338 "expand present operations in the field of intelligence": Gilpatric Report, May 6, 1961. US-GVN Rel, v. 11, p. 84.

339 "increased covert offensive operations in the North": Taylor-Rostow Report, November 3, 1961, *The Pentagon Papers: The Senator Gravell Edition: The Defense Department History of United States Decisionmaking in Vietnam* (Boston, Beacon Press, n.d. [1971]), v. 2, p. 653.

342 "I think we should never have done it": Lansdale quoted in USG & VN War, part 2, p. 203.

347 "nothing about Asia and nothing about Laos": Roger Hilsman, *To Move a Nation* (Garden City, N.Y., Doubleday, 1967), quoted p. 125.

347 "We must not allow Laos to fall": White House Office of the Staff Secretary, Andrew Goodpaster, "Memorandum of Conference with the President," December 31, 1960 (declassified May 23, 1983), DDEL:DDEP: WHO: OSS: International Series, box 9, folder "Laos (2)."

351 "a most reluctant militarist": William H. Sullivan, *Obbligato, 1939–1979* (New York: W. W. Norton, 1974), p. 210, 213.

351 "wasn't a bag of rice dropped that he didn't know about": Charles A. Stevenson, *The End of Nowhere* (Boston, Beacon Press, 1972), p. 217.

353 "The agency . . . was flat out in its effort": Richard Helms interview, Lyndon B. Johnson Oral History, II, pp. 18–29.

353 "the war we won": Helms, *A Look Over My Shoulder*, p. 250.

353 "when I found those orders were willfully disobeyed": Sullivan, *Obbligato*, p. 211.

354 "Air America did a magnificent job": William E. Colby interview, Lyndon Johnson Oral History Project, I, p. 54.

355 James Lilley with Jeffrey Lilley, *China Hands* (New York, Public Affairs Press, 2004), p. 128.

357 "It is time the American people were told more": Stevenson, *The End of Nowhere*, quoted p. 209. See *New York Times*, October 29, 1969, and January 23, 1970.

357 "no combatants as such" and "I know of no definition": CIA, Memorandum, Lawrence Houston to Richard Helms, October 30, 1969.

357 "When Senator Symington got up and starting talking about a secret war": Helms interview, Johnson Oral History Project, II, p. 6.

358 "I'm not sure your people ought to be getting involved": Helms interview, II, quoted p. 21.

359 "as a matter of policy": Church Committee, *Final Report*, Book I, pp. 227–230.

359 "IGs, hoping for plum assignments": Floyd L. Paseman, *A Spy's Journey* (St. Paul, Minn., Zenith Press, 2004), p. 80. The change referred to took place in the mid-nineties.

360 "We were caught" et seq.: Henry A. Kissinger, *White House Years 1969–1973* (Boston, Little Brown, 1979), p. 451.

361 "As we discussed" et seq.: Arnold R. Isaacs, *Without Honor* (Baltimore, Johns Hopkins University Press, 1983), quoted pp. 178–179.

361 "undoubted moral obligation: Douglas S. Blaufarb, *The Countrinsurgency Era* (New York, The Free Press, 1977), pp. 166–168.

16: GLOBAL REACH

367 "My job is to hold an umbrella:" Phillips, *Night Watch*, quoted p. 201.

368 "I thought he had the personality of a dead mackerel": "The Cool Pro Who Runs the CIA," *Newsweek*, November 30, 1971, quoted p. 30.

370 "I had all sorts of dirty tricks": Thomas, *Very Best Men*, quoted p. 330.

370 "one of my darkest days": Helms, *A Look Over My Shoulder*, p. 343.

371 "Well, aren't you the lucky one" et seq.: Douglass Cater, "What Did LBJ Know and When Did He Know It?" *Washington Post*, July 19, 1987, quoted p. C7.

371 "start to finish": Helms, *A Look Over My Shoulder*, p. 345.

372 "no useful purpose": Report of the President's Committee Relative to Covert CIA Aid, March 20, 1967, reprinted, U.S. Congress: House Foreign Affairs Committee (90/1), *Hearings: Encouraging Private Participation in International Activities* (Washington, D.C., Government Printing Office, 1967), Pt. 1, p. 5.

372 "Secrecy has a self-destructive potential": Cater, "What Did LBJ Know."

373 "imbalance" et seq.: CIA, "Suggested Press Statement," October 25, 1963, JFLK:JFKP: POF: Staff Memoranda Series, box 62A, folder "Bundy, McGeorge 7/63–11/63." The note from McGeorge Bundy to President Kennedy covering this and the following item make clear Meyer's drafting, with some help from Ambassador Llewelyn Thompson, and that JFK was speaking by agreement with John McCone.

373 "Capitalizing on Communist Dissension," et seq.: CIA, "Suggested Remarks for President Kennedy at the White House Luncheon for the RFE Fund on October 25, 1963," ibid.

373 "Please take steps to make sure": Note, Lyndon Johnson to Richard Helms, December 20, 1966, LBJL:LBJP: WHCF: Confidential File, box 17, folder "FG 11-2, CIA."

374 "I won't fund those radios" et seq.: Helms, *A Look Over My Shoulder*, quoted p. 372.

374 "CIA Orphans" and "could have been more aggressive": Johnson, *Right Hand of Power*, pp. 525, 350.

376 "we plan to use as appropriate": NSC, Memorandum, McGeorge Bundy to Lyndon B. Johnson, October 13, 1965, LBJL:LBJP: National Security File (hereafter NSF): Aides' Files, box 5, folder "Bundy Memos, v. 15 (Sept. 23–Oct. 15, 1965)."

376 "Because they leak": Marginal Note on Memorandum, Walt W. Rostow to Lyndon B. Johnson, June 1, 1966 (declassified September 25, 1979), LBJL:LBJP: NSF: Agency File, box 9, folder "CIA, v. 2."

377 "Don't waffle, don't ramble": Powers, *Man Who Kept the Secrets*, quoted p. 221.

377 the group believes that" et seq.: "Intelligence Activities and Foreign Policy," no date (under cover note of December 5, 1968), LBJL: Clark Clifford Papers, box 15, folder "PFIAB."

377–8 "I look back with chagrin" et seq.: Dean Rusk and Richard Rusk (edited by Daniel S. Papp), *As I Saw It* (New York: W. W. Norton, 1990), pp. 554–555.

378 "The policy arbiters": Quoted from a CIA original document in U.S. Congress, Senate (94/2), Select Committee to Study Governmental Operations with Respect to Intelligence Activities, *Report: Book I: Foreign and Military Intelligence* (hereafter cited as Church Committee Report, v. 1) (Washington, D.C., Government Printing Office, 1976), quoted p. 56.

380 "had not been overcome": NSC, "Minutes of the Meeting of the 303 Committee," December 15, 1967 (declassified March 3, 2003), LBJL:LBJP: NSF: Intelligence Series, box 2, folder "303 Committee."

383 "the character of such secret intervention" et seq.: Lindsay Study Group, "Memorandum for the President-Elect: Covert Operations of the United States Government," December 1, 1968, p. 10, JFKL: Adam Yarmolinsky Papers, Subject File, box 59, folder "Lindsay Group 1967–1968."

383 "designed to discredit": CIA, "Report to the DCI on the Organization of CIA and the Intelligence Community," January 20, 1969 (declassified July 8, 2004), p. 7, NARA: CIA CREST Collection.

383 "did not shake my longstanding impression": Helms, *A Look Over My Shoulder*, p. 377.

384 "I look upon this organization": *Public Papers of the Presidents: Richard Nixon, 1969* (Washington, D.C., Government Printing Office, 1971), p. 203.

384 "the American people need to understand": ibid.

385–6 "I have determined": NSDM-40 "Responsibility for the Conduct, Supervision, and Coordination of Covert Action Operations," February 17, 1970 (declassified 1976).

386 "It is true that": Johnson, *Right Hand of Power*, p. 347.

389 "On Cambodia, did he emphasize": Memorandum, Henry A. Kissinger to Richard M. Nixon, "Your Meeting with Foreign Intelligence Advisory Board Members—Saturday, July 18," no date (declassified December 7, 1994), National Archives: Nixon Library Project: White House Special Files: President's Office File: Memos to the President, box 81, folder "Beginning July 12, 1970."

390 "We believe the Board": Murphy Commission Report, I, p. 99.

391 "the mountain tribes": CIA, "The Kurdish Minority Problem," ORE 71-49, December 8, 1948 (declassified July 5, 1978), p. 1, HSTL:HSTP: PSF Intelligence File, box 258, folder "ORE Reports 1948 (67–78)."

393–4 "Our people's fate in unprecedented danger" et seq.: CIA Kurdish cables: William Safire, *Safire's Washington* (New York, Times Books, 1980), pp. 83–84, 85–86. Versions of these documents appeared in the Pike Committee report, but Safire uses more complete quotations.

394 "Covert action should not be confused with missionary work": ibid.

394 "another of those episodes" et seq.: Henry A. Kissinger, *Years of Renewal* (New York, Simon and Schuster, 1999), quoted pp. 576, 584.

17: THE SOUTHERN CONE

397 "unequivocal support to democracy" et seq.: Schlesinger, *A Thousand Days*, quoted pp. 184, 699.

400 "printed by citizens without political affiliation": Church Committee, *Staff Report: Covert Action in Chile, 1963–1973* (Washington, D.C., Government Printing Office, December 18, 1975), quoted p. 15.

401 "It's the atmosphere" et seq.: Department of State, Memorandum, Deputy Director for Coordination (INR)–Director for Intelligence and Research, "ARA-Agency Meeting, September 30, 1964, FRUS 1964–1968, v. 31, South and Central America, Mexico, Item no. 272.

401 "outside forces": *New York Times*, November 15, 1965, cited in Church Committee, *Covert Action in Chile*, p. 57.

403 "forces for change": Victor Marchetti and John D. Marks, *The CIA and the Cult of Intelligence*, pb 3rd ed., (New York: Dell, 1984), p. 14.

403 "as is so often the case": ibid., p. 15.

404 "could not bring itself to face" and "a great college term paper": Kissinger, *White House Years* , pp. 663, 664.

404 "I am not interested in": Kissinger quoted by Armando Uribe, *The Black Book of American Intervention in Chile* (Boston, Beacon Press, 1974), p. 33.

405 "I don't see why the United States should stand by and let Chile go communist": Seymour Hersh, *The Pursuit of Power* (New York, Summit Books, 1983), quoted p. 265.

405 "grand sum" and "Had I believed": Kissinger, *White House Years*, pp. 666, 669.

405 "I don't think anybody understood": Seymour M. Hersh, "The Price of Power: Kissinger, Nixon and Chile," *Atlantic Monthly*, December 1982, quoted p. 39.

407 "enabled the Station": Church Committee: *Covert Action in Chile*, p. 22.

407 "High-level concern in the Nixon Administration": Central Intelligence Agency, "CIA Activities in Chile," September 18, 2000 (Hinckey Report), p. 7.

407 "all our systems and our foreign policy": H. R. Haldeman, *The Haldeman Diaries: Inside the Nixon White House* (New York: G. P. Putnam's Sons, 1994), for August 6, 1969.

407 "Kissinger problem": *Haldeman Diaries*, August 18, 1970, p. 190; cf. 189 for the weekend's events.

408 "probe all possible aspects" et seq.: NSC, Memorandum for the Record, "Minutes of the Meeting of the 40 Committee, September 8, 1970 (declassified July 22, 1998), Gerald R. Ford Library, Gerald R. Ford Papers (hereafter GRFL:GRFP), Philip Buchen Files, National Security series, box 26, folder "Chronological File (4)."

408 "grouchy": Helms, *A Look Over My Shoulder*, p. 403.

409 "Make the economy scream," and "If I ever": Church Committee Report, *Alleged Assassination Plots*, quoted p. 227–228; "my heart sank": p. 233.

409 "It was my opinion": "Excerpts from Nixon's Responses to the Senate Select Committee," *New York Times*, March 12, 1976, p. 14, Interrogatory 39.

410 "bleak": Helms, *A Look Over My Shoulder*, p. 406.

410 "We were surprised": Meyer, *Facing Reality*, p. 185.

411 "The odds [were] unacceptable": Church Committee, *Alleged Assassination Plots*, quoted p. 233.

411 "Problem is, Helms has marching orders": Phillips, *Night Watch*, p. 221.

411 "There was just no question": Church Committee, *Alleged Assassination Plots*, quoted p. 233.

412 "WE ACCEPT AS HYPOTHESIS": CIA Cable, September 27, 1970 (declassified July 2000), reprinted in Peter Kornbluh, ed., *The Pinochet File* (New York, New Press, 2004), p. 50.

412 "additional help aimed at inducing economic collapse": Cable, E. J. Gerrity to H. S. Geneen, September 29, 1970, reprinted, NACLA, *Latin America & Empire Report*, v. 6, no. 4, April 1972, p. 11. Interviewed by *Business Week* magazine later, John McCone acknowledged these ITT documents were authentic (*Washington Post*, March 31, 1972).

413 "a fertile atmosphere": CIA Paper, "The Coup That Failed: The Effects on Allende and His Political Posture, with Special Emphasis on his Stance Before U.S. Positions, Moderate or Tough," October 15, 1970 (declassified July 2000), reprinted in Kornbluh, *Pinochet File*, p. 61.

413 "every Allende weak spot": CIA, "Memorandum of Conversation," October 15, 1970 (declassified November 1994), reprinted, ibid., p. 63.

413 "IT IS FIRM AND CONTINUING POLICY": CIA Cable, Headquarters–Santiago no. 802, October 16, 1970 (declassified July 2000), ibid., p. 64.

413 "I saw Karamessines today" et seq.: Kissinger, *White House Years*, p. 676.

414 "As far as I was concerned . . . what we were told to do was continue our efforts": Thomas Karamessines testimony to Church Committee, in *Alleged Assassination Plots*, p. 254.

414 "establishment by the Allende government" et seq.: NSC, National Security Study Memorandum 97, "Options Paper on Chile," November 3, 1970 (declassified December 1, 1995), National Security Archive: NSC Directives collection.

414 "The election of Allende as President": NSC, Memorandum, Henry Kissinger to Richard Nixon, "NSC Meeting, November 6—Chile," November 5, 1970 (declassified April 16, 2002), National Security Archive FOIA.

414–5 "immobilism" et seq.: CIA, DCI Briefing for the National Security Council, November 6, 1970 (declassified May 18, 1988). GRFL:GRFP: Presidential Handwriting File: National Security Series, box 32, folder "Intelligence (17)."

415 "We have to do everything we can to bring him down" et seq.: NSC, Memorandum of Conversation, "NSC Meeting—Chile (NSSM-97)," November 6, 1970 (declassified August 16, 2000), Kornbluh, *Pinochet File*, p. 117.

415 "correct but cool" et seq.: NSC, National Security Decision Memorandum 97, "Policy Towards Chile," November 9, 1970 (declassified November 25, 1985), ibid., p. 129.

415 "What our opponents called destabilization": Kissinger, *Years of Renewal*, p. 751.

415 "a number of political actions": William Broe at 40 Committee, November 19, 1970, in Kornbluh, *Pinochet File*, p. 134.

416 "excessive overtures": NIE quoted in Church Committee, *Covert Action in Chile*, p. 46.

417 "He holds a great many secrets" et seq.: Memorandum, Haig to Kissinger, March 10, 1971 (declassified NARA), NARA: NLP: NSC Files: Alexander Haig Files, box 971, folder "Haig Chronological, March 10–20, 1971."

418 "highly charged discussion" et seq.: Nathaniel Davis, *The Last Two Years of Salvador Allende* (Ithaca, Cornell University Press, 1985), p. 315.

420 "Merry Christmas": Phillips, *Night Watch*, quoted p. 247.

421 "Our hand doesn't show" et seq.: Neil Lewis, "Delight Over Coup Is Evident in Transcripts," *New York Times*, May 28, 2004, quoted p. A17.

421 "it is incorrect to say" et seq.: White House, "SFRC Executive Session, Nomination Hearings, September 17, 1973: Chile" (declassified February 7, 1994), pp. 5, 4, GRFL:GRFP: White House Operations File: Robert K. Wolthius Files, box 2, folder "Intelligence Investigations—Chile."

423 "Now that Allende was dead": Kornbluh, *Pinochet File*, p. 217.

424 "Allende's ouster and death" et seq.: CIA, "Prospects for Chile," NIE 94-1-75, June 6, 1975 (declassified March 2, 2001), p. 11, GRFL:GRFP: Kissinger-Scowcroft Parallel File, folder "Chile: Political-Military, General (1): 6/30/75–10/17/75."

428 "The [CIA] effort was made" et seq.: *Public Papers of the Presidents of the United States: Gerald R. Ford, v. I* (Washington, D.C., Government Printing Office, 1975), pp. 150–151.

428 "the ultimate target": Department of State, Action Memorandum, Lawrence Eagleburger and Robert J. McCloskey, "The CIA in Chile," September 24, 1974 (declassified January 22, 1997), GRFL:GRFP: Kissinger-Scowcroft Parallel File: Presidential Country Files, box A5, folder "Chile (1) 8/9/74–3/31/75."

428 "Hill interests who want a series of hearings": Eagleburger and McCloskey, "CIA in Chile," ibid.

429 "There is reason to believe" et seq.: CIA, Memorandum for the Inspector General, "Agency File Review: The ITT-CIA-Chile Question," September 5, 1974 (declassified October 15, 1997), GRFL:GRFP: White House Operations Series, Robert K. Wolthius Files, Subject Series, box 2, folder "Intelligence Investigations—Chile."

18: FROM "ROGUE ELEPHANT" TO RESURRECTION

431 "HUGE CIA OPERATION REPORTED": *New York Times*, December 22, 1974.

431 "press and political firestorm": Colby, *Honorable Men*, pp. 388, 391.

433 "Well Bill, when Hersh's story first came out": ibid., quoted p. 395.

433 "If they come out blood will flow" et seq.: NSC, Memorandum of Conversation, January 4, 1975 (declassified April 20, 2000), GRFL:GRFP: National Security Adviser's Files, Memcon series, box 8, folder "January 4, 1975–Ford, Kissinger."

433 "a lot of dead cats are going to come out" et seq.: NSC, Memorandum of Conversation, January 4, 1975 (declassified May 5, 1999), GRFL:GRFP: National Security Adviser's Files, Memcon series, box 8, folder "January 4, 1975–Ford, Former CIA Director Richard Helms."

434 "everything in the files": Gerald R. Ford, *A Time to Heal* (New York, Berkley Books, 1978), pp. xxiv, 258; cf p. 223–224.

435 "handled the grilling with aplomb" et seq.: Richard L. Holm, *The American Agent: My Life in the CIA* (London, St. Ermin's Press, 2003), pp. 270, 273.

435 "I was proud to be": E. Henry Knocke, "Covert Action and the CIA: An Inside Perspective," May 15, 1989, transcript, p. 13, University of Washington Extension course "American Covert Operations."

435 "He betrayed his own": Clarridge, *A Spy for All Seasons*, p. 159.

436 "fondling files": CIA Memorandum, March 25, 1975, GRFL:GRFP: Richard Cheney Files, Intelligence Series, box 6, folder "Congressional Investigations (1)."

437 "stick it to Kissinger": Ford, *A Time to Heal*, p. 344.

438 "This is an election year": Daniel Schorr, *Clearing the Air* (New York, Berkley Books, 1978), quoted p. 196.

439 "rogue elephant": Ford, *A Time to Heal*, quoted p. xxiv.

439 "a regiment of cloak and dagger men" et seq.: Church Committee, *Final Report: Foreign and Military Intelligence*, I, p. 564.

440 "none of this changed the basic challenge" et seq.: Kissinger, *Years of Renewal*, p. 798.

442 "late and hesitant" William G. Hyland, *Mortal Rivals* (New York: Random House, 1987), p. 137.

442 "probable disclosure" et seq.: Davis memorandum of May 1, 1975, quoted in Nathaniel Davis, "The Angola Decision of 1975: A Personal Memoir," *Foreign Affairs*, Fall 1978, p. 111.

442 "at the direction of National Security Council aides": Pike Report: "The Report the President Doesn't Want You to Read," *Village Voice*, February 16, 1976, p. 85. Substantial portions of the full document appear in this article at pp. 69–94. No official print of the report was ever released. A compilation was published in England by Spokesman Books.

442–3 "important but not vital" et seq.: NSC, Henry Kissinger Memorandum, "Meeting of the National Security Council," June 27, 1975 (declassified July 11, 2000), GRFL:GRFP: National Security Adviser's Files: Kissinger–Scowcroft Files, NSC Meetings Series, box 2, folder "NSC Meeting, 6/27/75."

443 "remains a tinderbox": CIA, "DCI Briefing for 27 June NSC Meeting," June 27, 1975 (declassified July 11, 2000), ibid.

443 "Soviet arms shipments have reversed": NSC, "Minutes, National Security Council Meeting," June 27, 1975 (declassified March 28, 2001), ibid.

444 "massive problems within": Kissinger, *Years of Renewal*, quoted p. 808.

445 "the CIA recommended the operation": U.S. Congress (94/2): House: Government Operations Committee. *Hearings: Oversight of U.S. Government Intelligence Functions* (Washington, D.C., Government Printing Office, 1976), p. 440.

445–6 "sense of tactical feasibility" et seq.: Kissinger, *Years of Renewal*, pp. 812–813.

446 "Gentlemen, we've been given a job": John Stockwell, *In Search of Enemies* (New York, W. W. Norton, 1978), quoted p. 95.

450 "heavy" et seq.: Kissinger, *Years of Renewal*, pp. 814–815.

451 "He read it. Then he grunted and walked out": Stockwell, *In Search of Enemies*, quoted p. 22.

453 "with victory for the Cuban": Kissinger, *Years of Renewal*, p. 851.

454 "compulsive interventionist": Loch Johnson, *A Season of Inquiry* (Lexington: University Press of Kentucky, 1985), quoted p. 170.

455 "What happened in Angola": American Broadcasting Corporation, transcript, "Issues and Answers," September 19, 1976.

457 "There were a lot of people in the DO": Bob Woodward and Walter Pincus, "At CIA, A Rebuilder 'Goes with the Flow,'" *Washington Post*, October 8, 1988, quoted p. A8.

459 "I never presented a finding": Knocke, "Covert Action and the CIA," p. 28.

461 "Our collection capability": Paseman, *A Spy's Journey*, p. 77.

461 "Turner's decision to make the cuts": Tom Gilligan, *CIA Life: 10,000 Days with the Agency* (Guilford, Conn., Foreign Intelligence Press, 1991), p. 188.

461 "nominal 'chief spy'": Clarridge, *A Spy for All Seasons*, p. 165.

462 "Being confident": Stansfield Turner, *Secrecy and Democracy* (Boston, Houghton Mifflin, 1985), p. 194.

462 "perhaps [be] put into statute": NSC, "Report on Presidential Review Memorandum/NSC-11: Intelligence Structure and Mission," February 22, 1977 (declassified October 14, 1997), p. 53, National Security Archive: Electronic Briefing Book no. 144, item 13.

462 "The most frequent criticism of CIA": Robert M. Gates, *From the Shadows: The Ultimate Insider's Story of Five Presidents and How They Fought the Cold War* (New York: Simon and Schuster, 1996), p. 142.

465 "The talent necessary for covert action": Turner, *Secrecy and Democracy*, p. 177.

19: THE MOUNTAINS OF ALLAH

467 "The CIA is a family": Alan D. Fiers, Jr., Testimony in the Nomination of Robert M. Gates for Director of Central Intelligence, September 19, 1991, U.S. Congress (102/1), Senate, Select Committee on Intelligence, *Hearings: Nomination of Robert M. Gates to be Director of Central Intelligence* (Washington, D.C., Government Printing Office, 1992), v. I, p. 680.

467 "to a world which yearned for peace": Jimmy Carter, *Keeping Faith* (New York, Bantam Books, 1982), p. 471.

472 "going to war": Jimmy Carter, quoted in *Washintgon Post*, October 7, 1982.

472 "to make sure that the Soviets paid some price": Zbigniew Brzezinski, *Power and Principle* (New York, Farrar, Straus & Giroux, 1983), p. 434.

474 "father": Bob Woodward, *Veil: The Secret Wars of the CIA, 1981–1987* (New York, Pocket Books, 1988), p. 359.

475 "distorted": Charles G. Cogan, "Partners in Time," *World Policy Journal*, v. 10, no. 2 (Summer 1993), pp. 79–80.

475 "any prolonged occupation": CIA, Special National Intelligence Estimate 11/32-81, "The Soviet Threat to Pakistan," August 12, 1981 (declassified January 7, 1994), National Security Archive: Microfiche Collection "The Soviet Estimate," no. 548.

479 "the withdrawal of Soviet forces": Elie Krakowski interview, CNN: Cold War Series, Soldiers of God, August 1997, part 2, p. 1.

480 "to keep the pot boiling": Gates, *From the Shadows*, quoted p. 252.

481 "Casey would *say*": Diego Cordovez and Selig S. Harrison, *Out of Afghanistan: The Inside Story of the Soviet Withdrawal* (New York, Oxford University Press, 1995), quoted, p. 103.

483 "This is the kind of thing": Joseph E. Persico, *Casey: From the OSS to the CIA* (New York, Viking, 1990), p. 225.

484 "Hmmm, World War III": Steve Coll, *Ghost Wars* (New York, Penguin Books, 2004), quoted p. 128.

486 "We cannot rule out a more serious deterioration" et seq.: CIA, "The Soviet Invasion of Afghanistan: Five Years Later," DI/NESA 85-10084, May 1985 (declassified Historical Review Program), pp. 19, 20.

489 "gratitude in the Afghan's dictionary": Frank Anderson interview, CNN: Cold War Series, Soldiers of God, August 1997, part 2, p. 5.

20: THE REAGAN REVOLUTION

494 "there is no basis for concluding that Mr. Casey is unfit to serve": *New York Times*, July 30, 1981. The conclusion would be reiterated in a Senate Intelligence Committee press release on December 1, 1981.

495 "Just as there is a classic formula": William J. Casey, "The Status of U.S. Intelligence," Speech Text, John Ashbrook Center for Public Affairs, Ashland College, Ashland, Ohio, October 27, 1986, reprinted in Herbert E. Meyer, ed., *Scouting the Future: The Public Speeches of William J. Casey* (Washington, D.C., Regnery Gateway, 1989), p. 36.

496 "special activities": Executive Order 12333 is widely reprinted. See *New York Times*, December 5, 1981. Also U.S. Congress (103/2): Senate: Select Committee on Intelligence. *Report: Legislative Oversight of Intelligence Activities: The U.S. Experience* (Washington, D.C., Government Printing Office, 1994), pp. 87–100.

499 "extremely schizoid" et seq.: Mansur Rafizadeh, *Witness: From the Shah to the Secret Arms Deal, An Insider's Account* (New York, William Morrow, 1987), p. 347.

500 "groping through a maze": quoted in *Washington Post*, December 19, 1986.

501 "Improvement of ties to the United States is not currently an option": White House, *Report of the President's Special Review Board* (Tower Commission) (Washington, D.C., Government Printing Office, 1987), cited p. B-6.

503 "We want Savimbi to know": Woodward, *Veil*, quoted p. 490.

21: BILL CASEY'S WAR

508 "In virtually every covert action": Gates, *From the Shadows*, p. 244.

509 "My plan was simple": Clarridge, *A Spy for All Seasons*, p. 197.

511 "Cuban presence" and "support structure": NSC, "Presidential Finding on Covert Operations in Nicaragua," December 1, 1981 (declassified November 18, 2001), document printed in Peter Korn-

bluh and Malcolm Byrne, eds., *The Iran-Contra Scandal: The Declassified History* (New York, New Press, 1993), p. 11. The presidential finding was originally reported in *Washington Post*, April 3, 1983.

513 "We were all hugging": quoted in *New York Times*, March 18, 1985.

515 Hector Frances: On Frances, see *Miami Herald*, December 1, 1982; *Washington Post*, December 2, 1982; and *New York Times*, December 19, 1982. A transcript of his videotaped statement appeared in the Managua FSLN newspaper *Barricada* on December 2, 1982. An English translation appears in *The Black Scholar*, March/April 1983, pp. 2–16. Journalist Christopher Dickey of the *Washington Post* reported that Frances may not have been a true defector and his statement may have been extracted (*With the Contras* [New York, Simon and Schuster, 1985], p. 154). This is not likely.

516 "We want to give democracy a chance": quoted in *New York Times*, December 2, 1982.

517 "special project": State Department (CIA) Cable, John Negroponte–Thomas Enders et al., May 21, 1983 (declassified June 1, 1998), National Security Archive: Electronic Briefing Book (hereafter cited as EBB) 151/1, item 110.

518 "I HAVE MY DOUBTS ABOUT": State Department (Roger Channel), Cable Managua 2249, May 26, 1983 (declassified June 2, 1998), National Security Archive: EBB 151/1, item 148.

518 "Lau was still the last person to talk to Bermudez": Edgar Chamorro, "Conferssions of a Contra," *New Republic*, August 5, 1985, quoted p. 22.

521 "Pastora glared at the tall man": Arturo Cruz, Jr. *Memoirs of a Counterrevolutionary* (New York, Doubleday, 1989), p. 160.

521 "This was not true": Claridge, *A Spy for All Seasons*, p. 225.

524 "the Sandinistas and Cubans": CIA, Memorandum of Notification, September 19, 1983 (declassified January 15, 1988), reprinted in Kornbluh and Byrne, *Iran-Contra Scandal*, pp. 11–17, quoted p. 12.

525 "The new finding": Gates, *From the Shadows*, quoted p. 301.

525 "Can't we get more pressure": Claridge, *A Spy for All Seasons*, quoted p. 261.

527 "'to sink ships'": Deposition of Edgar Chamorro before the International Court of Justice, September 5, 1985, in Peter Rosset and John Vandermeer, eds., *Nicaragua: Unfinished Revolution, The New Nicaragua Reader* (New York, Grove Press, 1986), quoted p. 242.

527 "Given the limited activity": Claridge, *A Spy for All Seasons*, p. 264.

528 "not one of the happiest episodes": Robert McFarlane testimony before Joint Congressional Committee investigating Iran-Contra, May 13, 1987.

529 "it hit me": Claridge, *A Spy for All Seasons*, p. 269.

530 "as we were supposed to" et seq.: Claridge, *A Spy for All Seasons*, p. 274.

531 "We are": Senate Select Committee on Intelligence, *Report: January 1, 1983, to December 31, 1984* (Washington, D.C., Government Printing Office, 1985), pp. 7–10.

532 "The CIA was directly involved" et seq.: Barry M. Goldwater with Jack Casserly, *Goldwater* (New York, Doubleday, 1988), pp. 301–313, quoted pp. 304, 306. The "run a railroad" text is reprinted in the SSCI report, p. 8.

532 "can only be described as a domestic disinformation campaign:" Robert Simmons as quoted by Senator Daniel Patrick Moynihan, *Congressional Record*, August 12, 1994, s11834.

533 "just another operation" et seq.: Claridge, *A Spy for All Seasons*, p. 274.

534 "The mining episode": George Shultz, *Turmoil and Triumph* (New York, Charles Scribner's Sons, 1993), p. 406.

536 "I am in full agreement": CIA Memorandum, William J. Casey–Robert McFarlane, March 27, 1984 (declassified in the Iran-Contra investigation), reprinted in Kornbluh and Byrne, *Iran-Contra Scandal*, p. 66.

536 All NSPG quotes: Memcon, National Security Planning Group Meeting, June 25, 1984, ibid., pp. 69–82.

537 "Because, he said, that was where the action was": Gilligan, *CIA Life*, p. 229.

22: PROJECT DEMOCRACY

539 "Dictatorships and Double Standards": Jeanne J. Kirkpatrick, "Dictatorships and Double Standards," *Commentary*, November 1979.

540 "I am confident we will pull through this crisis": quoted in *New York Times*, June 1, 1984.

541 "the occasional peacock among the roosters": Mona Charen, "What White House Women Think About White House Men," *Washingtonian*, September 1986, p. 188.

541 "We can do an Admiral Yamamoto": quoted in *Washington Post*, November 30, 1986.

543 "a cat being thrown into a clothes dryer": U.S. Congress (102/1): Senate, Select Committee on Intelligence, *Hearings: Nomination of Robert M. Gates to be Director of Central Intelligence* (Washington, D.C., Government Printing Office, 1992), v. I, p. 678.

543 "Ollie, Alan tells me you are operating": Senate Intelligence Committee, Gates Nomination Hearings, v. I, quoted pp. 655–656.

544-5 "it is time to talk absolutely straight": CIA, Memorandum Robert M. Gates–William J. Casey, December 14, 1984 (declassified), reprinted, Senate Intelligence Committee, *Hearings: Nomination of Robert M. Gates*, v. I, pp. 731–735; quoted pp. 731, 734.

545 "the most sophisticated disinformation and active measures campaign": quoted in *Washington Post*, December 21, 1986.

545 "brothers" et seq.: quotations from Reagan speeches: *New York Times*, March 2, 1985; April 1, 1985; June 6, 1985.

547 "FIELD STATIONS ARE TO CEASE AND DESIST WITH ACTIONS THAT CAN BE CONSTRUED": CIA Cable, c. October 1, 1985. Scott Armstrong, et al., *The Chronology: The Documented Day-by-Day Account of the Secret Military Assistance to Iran and the Contras* (New York, Warner Books, 1987), reprinted p. 66.

549 "would be driven from the field and defeated in detail": Richard Secord testimony, Iran-Contra Hearings, May 5, 1987.

550 "deep personal conviction": NSC, Letter, Robert McFarlane–Lee Hamilton, August 20, 1985, quoted in Armstrong, *Chronology*, p. 147.

550 "my actions, and those of my staff": NSC, Letter, Robert McFarlane–Michael Barnes, September 12, 1985, reprinted in Byrne and Kornbluh, *Iran-Contra Scandal*, pp. 201–204.

552 "What about the airfield?": Elliott Abrams testimony, Iran-Contra Hearings, June 2, 1987.

552 "Give me an account number and I'll fly anything anywhere": Owens testimony, Iran-Contra Hearings, May 19, 1987.

554 "the Wilson gang back in business": Felix Rodriguez testimony, Iran-Contra Hearings, May 27, 1987.

554 "We want every bit of support we can get": Secord testimony Iran-Contra, Hearings, op. cit.

555 "Nicaragua: Prospects for the Insurgency": CIA NIE of March 1986 identified in Select Committee on Intelligence, *Hearings: Nomination of Robert M. Gates*, pt. 3, p. 25.

556 "This is asinine—no black ops ever use this procedure": Richard Secord KL-43 Message, quoted in *Washington Post*, June 14, 1987.

556 "MY OBJECTIVE IS CREATION OF A 2,500 MAN FORCE": KL-43 Message, Joe Fernandez–Oliver North, April 12, 1986, quoted in Tower Board Report, Appendix C, p. 8.

557-8 "Freedom, Regional Security" et seq.: Message to Congress, reprinted in *New York Times*, March 15, 1986, p. 4.

558 "We are only at the beginning" et seq.: Meyer, *Scouting the Future*, p. 27.

559 "monitor Ollie": Abrams testimony Iran-Contra, Hearings, June 2, 9, 1987.

561 "We have to lift some of this on to the CIA": email, North to Poindexter, May 16, 1986, quoted in Armstrong, *Chronology*, p. 369.

561-2 "Max is the only problem" et seq.: Rodriguez testimony, Iran-Contra Hearings.

564 "You went on that mission, didn't you": Robert C. Dutton testimony, Iran-Contra Hearings, May 27, 1987.

566 "wildly speculative false stories" et seq.: Ronald Reagan Speech Text, *New York Times*, November 14, 1986.

567 "public pouting" et seq.: Shultz, *Turmoil and Triumph*, quoted pp. 837–838.

569 "This is the most fucked-up thing": Glenn Garvin, *Everybody Had His Own Gringo: The CIA and the Contras* (Washington, D.C., Brassey's, 1992), quoted p. 203.

23: FULL CIRCLE

573 "I would go over those points in my mind": Gates, *From the Shadows*, p. 417.

574 "He did not lead the troops": Melissa Boyle Mahle, *Denial and Deception: An Insider's View of the CIA from Iran-Contra to 9/11* (New York, Nation Books, 2004), pp. 51–52, quoted p. 52.

574 "did a terrific job": Paseman, *A Spy's Journey*, p. 236.

574 "didn't have the stomach for bold moves": Clarridge, *A Spy for All Seasons*, p. 359.

574 "godsend" and "hill of beans": Gates, *From the Shadows*, p. 419.

576 "somewhat timid operationally": Clarridge, *A Spy for All Seasons*, p. 167.

578 "the American government, including CIA": Gates, *From the Shadows*, p. 449.

582 "it is unclear exactly what sort of discussions" et seq.: President George H. W. Bush, Memorandum of Disapproval, November 30, 1990, U.S. Congress (104/2), Senate Select Committee on Intelligence, Report: *U.S. Actions Regarding Iranian and Other Arms Transfers to the Bosnian Army, 1994–1995* (Washington, D.C., Committee Xerox), quoted p. 23.

582 "The lowest point in my life": Gates, *From the Shadows*, p. 542.

583 "something fairly dramatic": ibid., p. 549.

584 "Pay attention" and "We were not listening": Mahle, *Denial and Deception*, pp. 84, 79.

587 "99.9 FM Mogadishu": Kenneth L. Cain, "The Legacy of Black Hawk Down," *New York Times*, October 3, 2003, quoted p. A27.

588 "Look, do not take on Aideed": Thomas W. Lippman and Barton Gellman, "A Humanitarian Gesture Turns Deadly," *Washington Post*, October 11, 1993, quoted p. A44.

589 Garrett Jones article: "Working with the CIA," *Parameters*, v. 31, no. 4 (Winter 2001–2002).

589 "CNN House": Vernon Loeb, "Confessions of a Hero," *Washington Post*, April 29, 2001, p. F4.

590 "THINGS ARE BAD": Vernon Loeb, "After-Action Report," *Washington Post Magazine*, February 27, 2000, quoted p. 23.

591 "Why don't you go talk": Cain, "Legacy of Black Hawk Down."

591 "the battle of Mogadishu haunted me": Bill Clinton, *My Life* (New York, Knopf, 2004), p. 552.

591 "The Somalia tragedy shocked Clinton": Nancy Soderberg, *The Superpower Myth* (New York, John Wiley, 2005), p. 40.

591 "Mogadishu was a strategic setback": Anthony Lake, *6 Nightmares: Real Threats in a Dangerous World and How America Can Meet Them* (Boston, Little, Brown, 2000), p. 129.

594 "more robust views on national security": Clinton, *My Life*, p. 456.

595 "a textbook case of the politicization of intelligence": Nancy Soderberg, *The Superpower Myth*, p. 45.

596 "Whitewash Wednesday": Douglas Waller, "Wrong Spy for the Job," *Time*, January 9, 1995, quoted p. 36.

597 "Hope to see the madman": "Bush Says He Erred in Assuming Hussein Would Fall After War," *New York Times*, January 15, 1996, p. A4.

598 "The wars with Iran": CIA/DI, "Iraq: Implications of Insurrection and Prospects for Saddam's Survival" (NESA 91-20010), March 16, 1991 (declassified January 23, 2001), p. 7, CIA Electronic Reading Room.

598 "I don't like this": Evan Thomas, Christopher Dickey, and Gregory L. Vistica, "Bay of Pigs Redux," *Newsweek*, March 23, 1998, quoted p. 37.

599 "They needed a lot of help": James Bamford, "The Man Who Sold the War," *Rolling Stone*, November 18, 2005, quoted p. 7 of 10.

600 "a major objective" et seq.: Don Oberdorfer, "U.S. Had Covert Plan to Oust Iraq's Saddam, Bush Adviser Asserts," *Washington Post*, January 20, 1993, quoted p. A4.

600 "The program was too fat": R. Jeffrey Smith and David B. Ottaway, "Anti-Saddam Operation Cost CIA $100 Million," *Washington Post*, September 15, 1996, quoted, p. A28.

600 "does not have the political or military clout": CIA, "Prospects for Iraq: Saddam and Beyond," NIE 93-42, December 1993 (declassified April 2005), p. 24. National Security Archive, "Saddam's Iron Grip," EBB 167, document no. 12.

601 "We lost our way": Jim Hoagland, "How CIA's Secret War on Saddam Collapsed," *Washington Post*, June 26, 1997, quoted p. A28.

602 "THE ACTION YOU HAVE PLANNED": Robert Baer, *See No Evil: The True Story of a Ground Soldier in the CIA's War on Terrorism* (New York, Crown Publishers, 2002), quoted p. 173.

604 "Twenty million dollars": Tim Weiner, "Call in the CIA and Cross Your Fingers," *New York Times*, September 15, 1996, quoted p. E3.

24: THE STRUGGLE FOR CONTROL

608 "The Bosnian people": Tim Weiner, "Permitting Iran to Arm Bosnia Was Vital, U.S. Envoy Testifies," *New York Times*, May 31, 1996, quoted p. A3.

608 "that we allow covert arms supply": Richard C. Holbrooke, *To End a War* (New York, Modern Library, 1999), quoted p. 52, italics in original.

609 "Your instructions are to say": David Halberstam, *War in a Time of Peace* (New York, Scribner's, 2001), quoted p. 334.

611 "much greater than the gross domestic products": William J. Daugherty, *Executive Secrets* (Lexington: University Press of Kentucky, 2004), p. 67.

614 "The field became irrelevant": Mahle, *Denial and Deception*, p. 170.

615 "I fired a lot of people": R. Jeffrey Smith, "Having Lifted CIA's Veil, Deutch Sums Up: I Told You So," *Washington Post*, December 26, 1996, quoted p. A25.

616 "hated": Clinton, *My Life*, p. 737.

619 "My experience with Tony Lake": Tim Weiner, "Nominations Have Made CIA Chief Odd Man Out," *New York Times*, December 12, 1996, quoted p. B7.

619 "He was worn down" et seq,: Clinton, *My Life*, p. 749.

619 "political circus": Letter, Anthony Lake to William J. Clinton, March 17, 1997, reprinted in *New York Times*, March 18, 1997, p. A21.

629 "the dismal historical record of covert military and paramilitary operations": McGeorge Bundy Op-Ed, *New York Times*, June 10, 1985.

632 "The belligerents during the Second World War": Michael Howard, *The Causes of Wars* (Cambridge, Mass., Harvard University Press, 1983), p. 30.

634 "with the least damage": John Horton, "Reflections on Covert Operations and Its Anxieties," *International Journal of Intelligence and Counterintelligence*, v. 4, no. 1 (Spring 1990), p. 82.

25: SAFE FOR DEMOCRACY

641 Bush (1) and Clinton quoted from Betty M. Unterberger, "Self-Determination," in Alexander De-Conde et al., eds., *Encyclopedia of American Foreign Policy* (New York, Charles Scribner's Sons, 2002), v. 3, p. 470.

641 "It is one matter to adopt": John Deutch, "Time to Pull Out. And Not Just From Iraq," *New York Times*, July 15, 2005, p. A27.

A Note on Sources

The following documents are essential sources for the information in this book. Additional listings of official histories, books, and articles may be found at www.ivanrdee.com/safefordemocracy/bibliography.

a. National Archives and Records Administration (NARA): Records of the Kennedy Assassination Records Commission; CIA CREST Database; Records Group 1 : CIA.

b. Harry S Truman Library (NARA) collections: President's Secretary's File (PSF): Intelligence File; PSF: Korean War File; PSF: NSC Meetings File; PSF: Subject File; White House Central File (WHCF): Confidential File; WHCF: Official File Records of the Psychological Strategy Board; Dean Acheson Papers; Clark Clifford Papers; Oral Histories.

c. Dwight D. Eisenhower Library (NARA) collections: Eisenhower Papers (EP): Ann Whitman File (AWF): Administration Series; AWF: DDE Diaries; AWF: Dulles-Herter Series; White House Office (WHO): Office of the Special Assistant for National Security Affairs (OSANSA): Special Assistant Series: Alphabetical Subseries; WHO: OSANSA: Special Assistant Series: NSC Subseries; WHO: OSANSA: Special Assistant Series: Presidential Subseries; WHO: OSANSA: Special Assistant Series: Subject Subseries; WHO: Office of the Staff Secretary (OSS): International Series; WHO: OSS: Subject Series; WHCF: Administration File; John Foster Dulles Papers: Telephone Series; Oral Histories.

d. Lyndon B. Johnson Library (NARA) collections: Lyndon B. Johnson Papers: Declassified and Sanitized Documents: Unboxed Folders; National Security File (NSF): Memos to the President; NSF: Agency File; NSF: Aides' Files; NSF: Intelligence File; NSF: Country File: Laos; NSF: Country File: Vietnam; NSF: Files of Special Committee of NSC; NSF: Subject File; Official File; White House Central File; Official File: Harry McPherson File; Vice-Presidential Security File; Oral Histories; John McCone Papers; Clark Clifford Papers; Paul Warnke Papers; Morton H. Halperin Papers.

e. Richard Nixon Library Project (NARA) collections: Nixon Tapes; Presidential Handwriting File; President's Office File; National Security Adviser's Files; Aides Files: Al Haig, Anthony Lake; White House Central File; H. R. Haldeman Papers.

f. Gerald R. Ford Library (NARA): Presidential Handwriting File; Kissinger-Scowcroft File: Subject Series, NSC Meeting Series, Memcon Series; National Security Adviser's Series: Name Series, Backchannel Message Series; Rockefeller Commission Files; Donald Rumsfeld Files; Richard Cheney Files; Phillip C. Buchen Files; Robert K. Wolthius Files; James E. Connor Files; Ron Nessen Files.

g. Ronald Reagan Library (NARA): White House Operations Files: NSC Executive Secretariat Series; NSC Crisis Management Center Series; Aides' Files: Alton Keel Files; Donald R.

Fortier Files; Howard Teicher Files; Oliver North Files; Craig Coy Files; Geoffrey Kemp Files; James Stark Files.

h. National Security Archive: This private, nongovernment clearing house and repository for documents declassified under the Freedom of Information Act and Mandatory Declassification Review also holds collections of personal papers. Housed at George Washington University, the Archive has several categories of relevant records, including its microfiche document collection publications; electronic briefing books, which are smaller selections of material posted to its website; and the physical documents and papers. Materials used from the Archive include, but are not limited to, Edward G. Lansdale Papers; microfiche collections for U.S. Intelligence Policy, Afghanistan, and Nicaragua; and electronic briefing books on CIA and Former Nazis; a 40th Anniversary Conference on the Bay of Pigs; the Director of National Intelligence; John Negroponte (2 parts); Luis Posada Carriles; and the Cuban Missile Crisis.

i. Freedom of Information Act: These are documents cited with only the name of an agency and a declassification date, which were released under official declassification regulations.

j. Unclassified Executive Documents: This refers to a variety of White House, State Department, and Department of Defense memorandums, reports, and releases that are not secret but form portions of the public record.

k. Congressional Documents: (all such documents are cited by the Congress and session numbers (e.g., 98/1), the originating committee, and the title.

Senate

Foreign Relations (98/2). *Report: The US. Government and the Vietnam War. Executive and Legislative Relationships (4 parts)*. Washington, D.C., Government Printing Office (GPO), 1984.

Government Operations (93/2). *Hearings: Legislative Proposals to Strengthen Congressional Oversight of the Nation's Intelligence Agencies*. Washington, D.C., GPO, 1974.

(100/2). *Hearings: Drugs, Law Enforcement and Foreign Policy* (4 parts). Washington, D.C., GPO, 1988.

(100/2). *Report: Drugs, Law Enforcement and Foreign Policy*. Washington, D.C., GPO, 1988.

Government Operations (94/2) *Hearings: Oversight of U.S. Government Intelligence Functions*. Washington, D.C.; GPO, 1978.

Rules and Administration (94/2). *Hearings: Proposed Standing Committee on Intelligence Activities*. Washington, D.C., GPO, 1978.

Select Committee to Study Governmental Operations with Respect to Intelligence (Church Committee) 94/1. *Interim Report Alleged Assassination Plots Involving Foreign Leaders*. Washington, D.C., GPO, 1975.

(94/1) *Staff Study: Covert Operations in Chile, 1963‑1973*. Washington, D.C., GPO, 1975.

(94/2) *Final Report (in 8 parts with accompanying volumes of bearings), especially books I, IV, VI*. Washington, D.C., GPO, 1978.

Committee on Rules and Administration (94/2). *Hearings: Proposed Standing Committee on Intelligence Activities*. Washington, D.C., GPO, 1976.

Select Committee on Intelligence (94/2). *Hearing: Nomination of E. Henry Knoche*. Washington, D.C., GPO, 1978.

(95/1) *Annual Report*, May 1977. Washington, D.C., GPO, 1977.

(95/2) *Hearings: National Intelligence Reorganizations and Reform Act of 1978*. Washington, D.C., GPO, 1978.

(98/2) *Report, January 1, 1983, to December 31, 1984*. Washington, D.C., GPO, 1985.

(102/1) *Hearings: Nomination of Robert M. Gates to Be Director of Central Intelligence*. (3 parts). Washington, D.C., GPO, 1991.

(102/1) *Report: Nomination of Robert M. Gates to Be Director of Central Intelligence.* Washington, D.C., GPO, 1991.

(104/2) *Report: Legislative Oversight of Intelligence Activities: The U.S. Experience.* Washington, D.C., GPO, October 1994.

(104/2) *Report: U.S. Actions Regarding Iranian and Other Arms Transfers to the Bosnian Army, 1994–1995.* Washington, D.C., Committee Xerox, November 1996.

(105/1) *Special Report: Committee Activities, January 4, 1995, to October 3, 1996.* Washington, D.C., GPO, 1997.

House

Foreign Affairs Committee (Historical Volume, 94/1) *Hearings: The United States and Chile During the Allende Years, 1970–1973.* Washington, D.C., GPO, 1975.

International Relations Committee (104/2). *Final Report of the Select Subcommittee to Investigate the United States Role in Iranian Arms Transfers to Croatia and Bosnia (The "Iranian Green Light" Subcommittee).* Washington, D.C., GPO, 1997.

Permanent Select Committee on Intelligence (95/2). *Hearings: Disclosure of Funds for Intelligence Activities.* Washington, D.C., GPO, 1977.

Permanent Select Committee on Intelligence (97/2). *Staff Report: U.S. Intelligence Performance on Central America: Achievements and Selected Areas of Concern.* Washington, D.C., GPO, 1982.

Select Committee on Intelligence (Pike Committee) 94/1. *Hearings* (various titles, five parts). Washington, D.C., GPO, 1975–1976.

Joint

(100/1) Senate Select Committee on Secret Military Assistance to Iran and the Nicaraguan Opposition / House Select Committee to Investigate Covert Arms Transactions with Iran. *Report of the Congressional Committees Investigating the Iran-Contra Affair*, November 1987. Washington, D.C., GPO, 1987. (Also the Hearings, published Documentary Exhibits, and Depositions of these committees.)

l. Leaked Documents: A number of authentic government documents have entered the public record by means of unauthorized disclosure. These range from Reagan administration decisional documents on Central America (*New York Times*, April 7,1983) to large portions of the Pike Report (*Village Voice*, February 18, 1978). Among the most significant of leaked documents—really a full-scale collection in its own right—is the secret decision-making study assembled for the Department of Defense to explain United States involvement in the Vietnam War. This has been published in several complementary editions. See Neal Sheehan et. al., eds, *The Pentagon Papers* (New York, Bantam Books, 1971). Department of Defense, *United States–Vietnam Relations, 1945–1967* (12 parts) (Washington, D.C., GPO, 1971), also *The Pentagon Papers: The Senator Gravel Edition: The Defense Department History of United States Decisionmaking in Vietnam*, 4 vols. (Boston, Little Brown, n.d. [1972]) four volumes.

m. Central Intelligence Agency Documents:

i) Declassified and Published CIA Official Histories: A series of official histories exists of the tenure of each CIA director and of certain other special subjects. Among the most important of these is Ludwell Lee Montague, *General Walter Bedell Smith as Director of Central Intelligence, October 1950–February 1953.* University Park, Pa., Penn State Press, 1992.

ii) Other CIA monographs:

Internal Histories:

Nicolas Cullather, *Operation PBSUCCESS: The United States and Guatemala, 1952–1954.* CIA History Staff, 1994 (declassified Historical Review Program, 1997).

Donald N. Wilber, *Clandestine Service History: Overthrow of Premier Mossadeq of Iran, November 1952–August 1953*, CS Historical Paper No. 208, March 1954, published October 1969 (declassified Historical Review Program, 2000).
Center for the Study of Intelligence Studies:
Constantine, G. Ted. *Intelligence Support to Humanitarian-Disaster Relief Operations: An Intelligence Monograph.* CSI 95-005, December 1995.
Garthoff, Douglas F. *Directors of Central Intelligence as Leaders of the U.S. Intelligence Community, 1946–2005.* Center for the Study of Intelligence, 2005.
John L. Helgerson, *CIA Briefings of Presidential Candidates, 1952–1992.* Center for the Study of Intelligence, 1996.
Douglas J. MacEachin, *Predicting the Soviet Invasion of Afghanistan: The Intelligence Community's Record.* Center for the Study of Intelligence, April 2002.
Directorate of Intelligence, *Research Study: Indonesia—1965: The Coup That Backfired*, (Unclassified), October 1968.
    iii) Official Statements:
John Deutch, "Statement on Guatemala," September 29, 1995. CIA Text.

Office of the President
President's Special Review Board (Tower Commission). *Report.* Washington, D.C., GPO, 1987.
Intelligence Oversight Board (Harrington Board). *Report on Guatemala Review.* White House Xerox, June 28, 1996.

Office of the Independent Counsel for Iran-Contra Matters
Lawrence E. Walsh, Independent Counsel, *Final Report of the Independent Counsel for Iran/Contra Matters* (3 vols.). Washington, D.C., United States Court of Appeals for the District of Columbia Circuit, Division for the Purpose of Appointing Independent Counsel, Division No. 86-6, August 4, 1993.

Department of State
Foreign Relations of the United States series (cited with period, volume number and subject, and various publication dates).

Index

A NOTE ON THE AUTHOR

John Prados was born in New York City and studied history and international relations at Columbia University, where he received a Ph.D. Since the 1970s he has been a leading historian of national security affairs, intelligence operations, and international security concerns. He has written more than a dozen books in the field, many of them prizewinners. He lives in Silver Spring, Maryland.